MyManagementLab™: Improve Student Engagement Before, During, and After Class

Prep and Engagement

- **Video exercises** – engaging videos that bring business concepts to life and explore business topics related to the theory students are learning in class. Quizzes then assess students' comprehension of the concepts covered in each video.

- **Learning Catalytics** – a "bring your own device" student engagement, assessment, and classroom intelligence system helps instructors analyze students' critical-thinking skills during lecture.

- **Dynamic Study Modules (DSMs)** – through adaptive learning, students get personalized guidance where and when they need it most, creating greater engagement, improving knowledge retention, and supporting subject-matter mastery. Also available on mobile devices.

- **Business Today** – bring current events alive in your classroom with videos, discussion questions, and author blogs. Be sure to check back often, this section changes daily.

- **Decision-making simulations** – place your students in the role of a key decision-maker. The simulation will change and branch based on the decisions students make, providing a variation of scenario paths. Upon completion of each simulation, students receive a grade, as well as a detailed report of the choices they made during the simulation and the associated consequences of those decisions.

Decision Making

Critical Thinking

- **Writing Space** – better writers make great learners—who perform better in their courses. Providing a single location to develop and assess concept mastery and critical thinking, the Writing Space offers automatic graded, assisted graded, and create your own writing assignments, allowing you to exchange personalized feedback with students quickly and easily.

  Writing Space can also check students' work for improper citation or plagiarism by comparing it against the world's most accurate text comparison database available from **Turnitin**.

- **Additional Features** – included with the MyLab are a powerful homework and test manager, robust gradebook tracking, comprehensive online course content, and easily scalable and shareable content.

http://www.pearsonmylabandmastering.com

PEARSON

DEVELOPING MANAGEMENT SKILLS

NINTH EDITION

David A. Whetten
BRIGHAM YOUNG UNIVERSITY

Kim S. Cameron
UNIVERSITY OF MICHIGAN

PEARSON

Boston   Columbus   Indianapolis   New York   San Francisco   Amsterdam
Cape Town   Dubai   London   Madrid   Milan   Munich   Paris   Montréal   Toronto
Delhi   Mexico City   São Paulo   Sydney   Hong Kong   Seoul   Singapore   Taipei   Tokyo

Vice President, Business Publishing: Donna Battista
Editor-in-Chief: Stephanie Wall
Acquisitions Editor: Kris Ellis-Levy
Program Manager Team Lead: Ashley Santora
Program Manager: Sarah Holle
Editorial Assistant: Bernard Ollila
Vice President, Product Marketing: Maggie Moylan
Director of Marketing, Digital Services and Products: Jeanette Koskinas
Executive Product Marketing Manager: Anne Fahlgren
Field Marketing Manager: Lenny Ann Raper
Senior Strategic Marketing Manager: Erin Gardner
Project Manager Team Lead: Judy Leale
Project Manager: Becca Groves
Operations Specialist: Diane Peirano
Creative Director: Blair Brown
Senior Art Director: Janet Slowik

Interior and Cover Designer: Integra Software Services Pvt. Ltd.
Cover Image: Jim Colao/Luxtone Media
Vice President, Director of Digital Strategy & Assessment: Paul Gentile
Manager of Learning Applications: Paul Deluca
Digital Editor: Brian Surette
Digital Studio Manager: Diane Lombardo
Digital Studio Project Manager: Robin Lazrus
Digital Studio Project Manager: Alana Coles
Digital Studio Project Manager: Monique Lawrence
Digital Studio Project Manager: Regina DaSilva
Full-Service Project Management and Composition: Integra Software Services Pvt. Ltd.
Printer/Binder: LSC Communications
Cover Printer: LSC Communications
Text Font: 10/12 Weidemann-Book

Library of Congress Cataloging-in-Publication Data

Whetten, David A. (David Allred),
　　Developing management skills/David A. Whetten, Kim S. Cameron.—9e [edition].
　　　pages cm
　　ISBN 978-0-13-312747-8 (student edition)
　　1. Management—Study and teaching.　2. Management—Problems, exercises, etc.　I. Cameron, Kim S.　II. Title.
HD30.4.W46 2016
658.40071'173—dc23

2014024024

PEARSON

ISBN 10:　　0-13-312747-8
ISBN 13: 978-0-13-312747-8

BRIEF TABLE OF CONTENTS

Preface   xix

Introduction   1

PART I   PERSONAL SKILLS   35

1   Developing Self-Awareness   37
2   Managing Stress and Well-Being   85
3   Solving Problems Analytically and Creatively   133

PART II   INTERPERSONAL SKILLS   187

4   Building Relationships by Communicating Supportively   189
5   Gaining Power and Influence   227
6   Motivating Others   263
7   Managing Conflict   305

PART III   GROUP SKILLS   363

8   Empowering and Engaging Others   365
9   Building Effective Teams and Teamwork   401
10   Leading Positive Change   443

PART IV   SPECIFIC COMMUNICATION SKILLS   487

Module A   Making Oral and Written Presentations   489
Module B   Conducting Interviews   517
Module C   Conducting Meetings   551
Appendix I Glossary   571
Appendix II References   581
Index   609

CONTENTS

Preface   xix

INTRODUCTION   1

THE CRITICAL ROLE OF MANAGEMENT SKILLS   3
The Importance of Competent Managers   4
The Skills of Effective Managers   5
What Are Management Skills?   6
Improving Management Skills   7
An Approach to Skill Development   7
Leadership and Management   9
Contents of the Book   11
Organization of the Book   12
Diversity and Individual Differences   13
Summary   14

SUPPLEMENTARY MATERIAL   15
Diagnostic Survey and Exercises   15
   Personal Assessment of Management Skills (PAMS)   15
   What Does It Take to Be an Effective Manager?   19
   SSS Software In-Basket Exercise   21

SCORING KEY AND COMPARISON DATA   32
Personal Assessment of Management Skills   32
   Scoring Key   32
   Comparison Data   33
What Does It Take to Be an Effective Manager?   33
SSS Software In-Basket Exercise   33

PART I   PERSONAL SKILLS   35

1   DEVELOPING SELF-AWARENESS   37

SKILL ASSESSMENT   38
Diagnostic Surveys for Developing Self-Awareness   38
Developing Self-Awareness   38
   The Defining Issues Test   38

Cognitive Style Indicator   42
Tolerance of Ambiguity Scale   42
Core Self-Evaluation Scale (CSES)   43

SKILL LEARNING   44
Key Dimensions of Self-Awareness   44
The Enigma of Self-Awareness   45
    The Sensitive Line   45
Understanding and Appreciating Individual Differences   47
Important Areas of Self-Awareness   47
    Emotional Intelligence   49
    Values   51
    Ethical Decision Making   57
    Cognitive Style   59
    Attitudes Toward Change   61
    Core Self-Evaluation   63

SUMMARY   65

SKILL ANALYSIS   67
Cases Involving Self-Awareness   67
    Communist Prison Camp   67
    Computerized Exam   69
    Decision Dilemmas   70

SKILL PRACTICE   72
Exercises for Improving Self-Awareness Through Self-Disclosure   72
    Through the Looking Glass   72
    Diagnosing Managerial Characteristics   73
    An Exercise for Identifying Aspects of Personal Culture: A Learning Plan and Autobiography   75

SKILL APPLICATION   77
Activities for Developing Self-Awareness   77
    Suggested Assignments   77
    Application Plan and Evaluation   78

SCORING KEYS AND COMPARISON DATA   79
The Defining Issues Test   79
    Escaped Prisoner   79
    The Doctor's Dilemma   79
    The Newspaper   80
Cognitive Style Indicator   80
    Scoring Key   80
    Comparison Data   81
Tolerance of Ambiguity Scale   81
    Scoring Key   81
    Comparison Data   82
Core Self-Evaluation Scale   82
    Scoring Key   82
    Comparison Data   83

2 MANAGING STRESS AND WELL-BEING   85

SKILL ASSESSMENT   86
Diagnostic Surveys for Managing Stress and Well-Being   86
Managing Stress and Well-Being   86
    Social Readjustment Rating Scale   86
    Social Readjustment Rating Scale   88
    Sources of Personal Stress   89
    Flourishing Scale   90

SKILL LEARNING   90
Managing Stress and Fostering Well-Being   90
Major Elements of Stress   91
    Coping with Stress   92
Managing Stressors   94
Eliminating Stressors   95
    Eliminating Time Stressors Through Time Management   95
    Eliminating Encounter Stressors Through Community, Contribution, and Emotional Intelligence   100
    Eliminating Situational Stressors Through Work Redesign   103
    Eliminating Anticipatory Stressors Through Prioritizing, Goal Setting, and Small Wins   104
Developing Resiliency and Well-Being   106
    Life Balance   106
    Psychological Resiliency   107
Temporary Stress-Reduction Techniques   112

SUMMARY   113

SKILL ANALYSIS   114
Cases Involving Stress Management   114
    The Turn of the Tide   114
    The Case of the Missing Time   117

SKILL PRACTICE   121
Exercises for Long-Term and Short-Run Stress Management and Well-Being   121
    The Small-Wins Strategy   121
    Life-Balance Analysis   123
    Deep Relaxation   125
    Monitoring and Managing Time   126
    Generalized Reciprocity   127

SKILL APPLICATION   128
Activities for Managing Stress   128
    Suggested Assignments   128
    Application Plan and Evaluation   129

SCORING KEYS AND COMPARISON DATA   130
Social Readjustment Rating Scale   130
    Comparison Data   130
Sources of Personal Stress   131
Flourishing Scale   131
    Comparison Data   131

3 SOLVING PROBLEMS ANALYTICALLY AND CREATIVELY   133

SKILL ASSESSMENT   134
Diagnostic Surveys for Creative Problem Solving   134
    Problem Solving, Creativity, and Innovation   134
Solving Problems Analytically and Creatively   134
    How Creative Are You?©   *134*
    Innovative Attitude Scale   136
    Creative Style Assessment   137

SKILL LEARNING   139
Problem Solving, Creativity, and Innovation   139
Steps in Analytical Problem Solving   139
    Defining the Problem   140
    Generating Alternatives   141
    Evaluating Alternatives   141
    Implementing the Solution   142
Limitations of the Analytical Problem-Solving Model   142
Impediments to Creative Problem Solving   143
Multiple Approaches to Creativity   143
Conceptual Blocks   148
    Percy Spencer's Magnetron   148
    Spence Silver's Glue   149
    The Four Types of Conceptual Blocks   149
Review of Conceptual Blocks   157
Conceptual Blockbusting   157
    Stages in Creative Thought   157
    Methods for Improving Problem Definition   158
    Ways to Generate More Alternatives   162
International Caveats   165
Hints for Applying Problem-Solving Techniques   166
Fostering Creativity in Others   166
    Management Principles   166

SUMMARY   170

SKILL ANALYSIS   172
Cases Involving Problem Solving   172
    Coke versus Pepsi   172
    Creativity at Apple   173

SKILL PRACTICE   175
Exercises for Applying Conceptual Blockbusting   175
    Individual Assignment—Analytical Problem Solving (10 minutes)   175
    Team Assignment—Creative Problem Solving (20 minutes)   176
    Moving Up in the Rankings   177
    Keith Dunn and McGuffey's Restaurant   178
    Creative Problem-Solving Practice   182

SKILL APPLICATION   182
Activities for Solving Problems Creatively   182
    Suggested Assignments   182
    Application Plan and Evaluation   183

SCORING KEYS AND COMPARISON DATA   184
How Creative Are You?©   184
    Scoring Key   184
    Comparison Data   185
Innovative Attitude Scale   185
    Comparison Data   185
Creative Style Assessment   186
    Scoring Key   186
    Comparison Data   186

PART II   INTERPERSONAL SKILLS   187

4 BUILDING RELATIONSHIPS BY COMMUNICATING SUPPORTIVELY   189

SKILL ASSESSMENT   190
Diagnostic Surveys for Supportive Communication   190

SKILL LEARNING   190
Building Positive Interpersonal Relationships   190
The Importance of Effective Communication   191
    The Focus on Accuracy   192
What is Supportive Communication?   193
Coaching and Counseling   195
    Coaching and Counseling Issues   195
    Defensiveness and Disconfirmation   197
Principles of Supportive Communication   197
    Supportive Communication Is Based on Congruence, Not Incongruence   197
    Supportive Communication Is Descriptive, Not Evaluative   198
    Supportive Communication Is Problem-Oriented, Not Person-Oriented   201
    Supportive Communication Validates Rather Than Invalidates Individuals   202
    Supportive Communication Is Specific (Useful), Not Global (Nonuseful)   204
    Supportive Communication is Conjunctive, Not Disjunctive   205
    Supportive Communication Is Owned, Not Disowned   205
    Supportive Communication Requires Supportive Listening, Not One-Way Message Delivery   206
The Personal Management Interview   211
International Caveats   214

SUMMARY   214

SKILL ANALYSIS   216
Cases Involving Building Positive Relationships   216
    Find Somebody Else   216
    Rejected Plans   217

SKILL PRACTICE   219
Exercises for Diagnosing Communication Problems and Fostering Understanding   219
    United Chemical Company   219
    Byron vs. Thomas   221
    Active Listening Exercise   223

SKILL APPLICATION   224
Activities For Communicating Supportively   224
   Suggested Assignments   224
   Application Plan and Evaluation   225

SCORING KEYS AND COMPARISON DATA   226

5   GAINING POWER AND INFLUENCE   227

SKILL ASSESSMENT   228

SKILL LEARNING   228
Building a Strong Power Base and Using Influence Wisely   228
Is Power A Four-Letter Word?   229
Abuse of Power   230
   Strategies for Gaining Organizational Power   232
   Sources of Personal Power   232
   Sources of Positional Power   237
   Transforming Power into Influence   241
Influence Strategies: The Three Rs   241
The Pros and Cons of Each Strategy   244
Acting Assertively: Neutralizing Influence Attempts   247

SKILL ANALYSIS   253
Case Involving Power and Influence   253
   Dynica Software Solutions   253

SKILL PRACTICE   254
Exercise for Gaining Power   254
   Repairing Power Failures in Management Circuits   254
Exercise for Using Influence Effectively   255
   Ann Lyman's Proposal   256
Exercises for Neutralizing Unwanted Influence Attempts   256
   Cindy's Fast Foods   257
   9:00 to 7:30   258

SKILL APPLICATION   259
Activities for Gaining Power and Influence   259
   Suggested Assignments   259
   Application Plan and Evaluation   260

SCORING KEYS AND COMPARISON DATA   261

6   MOTIVATING OTHERS   263

SKILL ASSESSMENT   264

SKILL LEARNING   264
Increasing Motivation and Performance   264
Diagnosing Work Performance Problems   265
Enhancing Individuals' Abilities   266
Fostering a Motivating Work Environment   268

Elements of an Effective Motivation Program   269
    Establish Clear Performance Expectations   270
    Remove Obstacles to Performance   272
    Reinforce Performance-Enhancing Behavior   273
    Provide Salient Rewards   281
    Be Fair and Equitable   284
    Provide Timely Rewards and Accurate Feedback   284

SUMMARY   286

SKILL ANALYSIS   289
Case Involving Motivation Problems   289
    Electro Logic   289

SKILL PRACTICE   295
Exercises for Diagnosing Work Performance Problems   295
    Joe Chaney   298
    Work Performance Assessment   298
Exercise for Reshaping Unacceptable Behaviors   299
    Shaheen Matombo   299
    Andre Tate, Manager   299
    Shaheen Matombo, Staff Member   300

SKILL APPLICATION   301
Activities for Motivating Others   301
    Suggested Assignments   301
    Application Plan and Evaluation   302
SKILL PRACTICE Exercise for Reshaping Unacceptable Behaviors   303

SCORING KEYS AND COMPARISON DATA   304

7   MANAGING CONFLICT   305

SKILL ASSESSMENT   306

SKILL LEARNING   306
Interpersonal Conflict Management   306
    Mixed Feelings about Conflict   307
Diagnosing the Type of Interpersonal Conflict   308
    Conflict Focus   309
    Conflict Source   310
Selecting the Appropriate Conflict Management Approach   312
    Choosing Among the Five Strategies   315
    Personal Preferences   316
    Situational Factors   317
Resolving Interpersonal Confrontations Using the Collaborative Approach   319
    A General Framework for Collaborative Problem Solving   319
    The Four Phases of Collaborative Problem Solving   320

SUMMARY   329

SKILL ANALYSIS   332
Case Involving Interpersonal Conflict   332
    Educational Pension Investments   332

SKILL PRACTICE   336

Exercise for Diagnosing Sources of Conflict   336
    SSS Software Management Problems   *336*
Exercises for Selecting an Appropriate Conflict Management Strategy   345
    Bradley's Barn   *345*
    Avocado Computers   *346*
    Phelps, Inc.   *346*
Exercises for Resolving Interpersonal Disputes   347
    Alisa Moffatt   *347*
    Can Larry Fit In?   *351*
    Meeting at Hartford Manufacturing Company   *352*

SKILL APPLICATION   358

Activities for Improving Managing Conflict Skills   358
    Suggested Assignments   *358*
    Application Plan and Evaluation   *360*
SKILL PRACTICE Exercises for Resolving Interpersonal Disputes   361

SCORING KEYS AND COMPARISON DATA   362

PART III   GROUP SKILLS   363

8 EMPOWERING AND ENGAGING OTHERS   365

SKILL ASSESSMENT   366

SKILL LEARNING   366

Empowering and Engaging Others   366
The Meaning of Empowerment   367
Dimensions of Empowerment   368
    Self-Efficacy   *368*
    Self-Determination   *369*
    Personal Consequence   *370*
    Meaning   *370*
    Trust   *371*
    Review of Empowerment Dimensions   *371*
How to Develop Empowerment   372
    A Clear Goal   *372*
    Fostering Personal Mastery Experiences   *373*
    Modeling   *374*
    Providing Support   *374*
    Emotional Arousal   *374*
    Providing Information   *375*
    Providing Resources   *376*
    Connecting to Outcomes   *376*
    Creating Confidence   *377*
    Review of Empowerment Principles   *378*
Inhibitors to Empowerment   380
    Attitudes about Subordinates   *380*
    Personal Insecurities   *380*
    Need For Control   *380*
    Overcoming Inhibitors   *381*

Fostering Engagement   381
    Deciding When to Engage Others   382
    Deciding Whom to Engage   383
    Deciding How to Engage Others   384
    Review Of Engagement Principles   386
International Caveats   386

SUMMARY   388

SKILL ANALYSIS   389
Cases Involving Empowerment and Engagement   389
    Minding the Store   389
    Changing the Portfolio   390

SKILL PRACTICE   391
Exercises for Empowerment   391
    Executive Development Associates   391
    Empowering Ourselves   395
    Deciding to Engage Others   396

SKILL APPLICATION   397
Activities for Empowerment and Engagement   397
    Suggested Assignments   397
    Application Plan and Evaluation   398

SCORING KEYS AND COMPARISON DATA   399

9 BUILDING EFFECTIVE TEAMS AND TEAMWORK   401

SKILL ASSESSMENT   402
Diagnostic Surveys for Building Effective Teams   402
    Team Development Behaviors   402
Building Effective Teams and Teamwork   402
    Diagnosing The Need For Team Building   402

SKILL LEARNING   403
The Advantages of Teams   403
    An Example of an Effective Team   407
Team Development   408
    The Forming Stage   408
    The Norming Stage   409
    The Storming Stage   411
    The Performing Stage   414
Leading Teams   417
    Developing Credibility   417
    Establish SMART Goals and Everest Goals   419
    International Caveats   421
Team Membership   422
    Advantageous Roles   422
    Unproductive Roles   425
    Providing Feedback   426
    International Caveats   427

SUMMARY   427

SKILL ANALYSIS   428
Cases Involving Building Effective Teams   428
   The Tallahassee Democrat's ELITE *Team*   428
   The Cash Register Incident   431

SKILL PRACTICE   432
Exercises in Building Effective Teams   432
   Leadership Roles in Teams   432
   Team Diagnosis and Team Development Exercise   433
   Winning the War on Talent   435
   Team Performance Exercise   437

SKILL APPLICATION   439
Activities for Building Effective Teams   439
   Suggested Assignments   439
   Application Plan and Evaluation   440

SCORING KEYS AND COMPARISON DATA   440
Diagnosing the Need for Team Building   441
   Comparison Data   441
Leadership Roles in Teams (Examples of Correct Answers)   441

10 LEADING POSITIVE CHANGE   443

SKILL ASSESSMENT   444
Diagnostic Surveys for Leading Positive Change   444
Leading Positive Change   444
   Reflected Best-Self Feedback   444

SKILL LEARNING   446
Ubiquitous and Escalating Change   447
The Need for Frameworks   447
A Framework for Leading Positive Change   449
   Establishing A Climate of Positivity   452
   Creating Readiness for Change   457
   Articulating a Vision of Abundance   460
   Generating Commitment to the Vision   463
   Fostering Sustainability   466

SUMMARY   469

SKILL ANALYSIS   471
Cases Involving Leading Positive Change   471
   Corporate Vision Statements   471
   Jim Mallozzi: Implementing Positive Change in Prudential Real Estate and Relocation   477

SKILL PRACTICE   481
Exercises in Leading Positive Change   481
   Reflected Best-Self Portrait   481
   Positive Organizational Diagnosis Exercise   482
   A Positive Change Agenda   483

SKILL APPLICATION   483
Activities for Leading Positive Change   483
    Suggested Assignments   483
    Application Plan and Evaluation   484

SCORING KEYS AND COMPARISON DATA   485
Reflected Best-Self Feedback™ Exercise   485

PART IV   SPECIFIC COMMUNICATION SKILLS   487

Module A   MAKING ORAL AND WRITTEN PRESENTATIONS   489

SKILL LEARNING   490
Making Oral and Written Presentations   490
Essential Elements of Effective Presentations   491
    Formulate a Specific Strategy   491
    Develop a Clear Structure   493
    Support Your Points   495
    Use an Enhancing Style   497
    Style in Oral Communication   498
    Style in Written Communication   501
    Supplement your Presentation by Responding to Questions and Challenges   503

SKILL PRACTICE   507
Exercises for Making Effective Oral and Written Presentations   507
    Speaking as a Leader   507
    Quality Circles at Battle Creek Foods   508
Observer's Feedback form   515

Module B   CONDUCTING INTERVIEWS   517

SKILL LEARNING   518
Planning and Conducting Interviews   518
    Planning the Interview   519
    Conducting the Interview   523
Specific Types of Organizational Interviews   527
    Information-Gathering Interviews   527
    Employment-Selection Interviews   527
    Performance-Appraisal Interviews   528

SKILL PRACTICE   532
Exercises for Conducting Special-Purpose Interviews   532
    Evaluating the New Employee-Orientation Program   532
    Performance-Appraisal Interview with Chris Jakobsen   535
    Employment-Selection Interview at Smith Farley Insurance   542
Observer's Feedback form   549

Module C CONDUCTING MEETINGS 551

SKILL LEARNING 552
Conducting Effective Meetings: A Short Guide for Meeting Managers and Meeting Participants 552
The Five *P*s of Effective Meetings 552
Suggestions for Group Members 557

SKILL PRACTICE 560
Exercises for Conducting Meetings 560
  Preparing and Conducting a Team Meeting at SSS Software 560
  Role Diagnosis 560
  Meeting Evaluation Worksheet 561
SSS Software In-Basket Memos, E-Mails, Faxes, and Voice Mails 562

APPENDIX I GLOSSARY 571

APPENDIX II REFERENCES 581

INDEX 609

New in This Edition

- New to every Chapter Personal Inventory Assessments (P.I.A)
- Chapter 2 now includes a major focus not only on managing stress but also on how to enhance and encourage well-being.
- Chapter 8 replaces the discussion on "delegation" with a focus on "engagement."
- Research continues to appear on factors that predict managerial effectiveness and skillful performance. Therefore, we have updated references, studies, and examples to enhance each chapter's currency.
- In an environment filled with instantaneous technology, sound bites of data, and short attention spans, we have been motivated to shorten each of the book's chapters substantially. With these reductions, however, we have maintained the empirical evidence and the foundational models and frameworks.
- In each chapter, references to video examples found in **Pearson's MyManagementLab**™ are noted.

Why Focus on Management Skill Development?

Given that a "skill development" course requires more time and effort than a course using the traditional lecture/discussion format, we are sometimes asked this question by students, especially those who have relatively little work experience.

Reason #1: It focuses attention on what effective managers actually "do."

In an influential article, Henry Mintzberg (1975) argued that management education had almost nothing to say about what managers actually do from day to day. He further faulted management textbooks for introducing students to the leading theories about management while ignoring what is known about effective management practice. Sympathetic to Mintzberg's critique, we set out to identify the defining competencies of effective managers.

Although no two management positions are exactly the same, the research summarized in the Introduction highlights ten personal, interpersonal, and group skills that form the core of effective management practice. Each chapter addresses one of these skills.

Personal Skills

1. Developing Self-Awareness
2. Managing Personal Stress and Well-Being
3. Solving Problems Analytically and Creatively

Interpersonal Skills

4. Building Relationships by Communicating Supportively
5. Gaining Power and Influence
6. Motivating Others
7. Managing Conflict

Group Skills

8. Empowering and Engaging Others
9. Building Effective Teams and Teamwork
10. Leading Positive Change

Consistent with our focus on promoting effective management practice, the material in these chapters provides guidance for a variety of contemporary management challenges, including: "How can I help others accept new goals, new ideas, new approaches?" "How can I invigorate those who feel outdated and left behind?" "How do I help the 'survivors' of a downsizing pick up the pieces and move on?" "How do I help people with very different agendas and philosophies work together, especially during periods of high stress and uncertainty?"

Anyone tempted to dismissively argue that the answers to these questions are "common sense" would do well to recall Will Rogers' pithy observation: "Common sense ain't common." In addition, the research reported in the Introduction suggests that, in many cases, managers' "common sense" isn't "good sense."

The premise of this book and associated course is that the key to effective management practice is practicing what effective managers—those with "good sense"—do consistently.

Reason #2: It is consistent with proven principles of effective teaching and learning.

A seasoned university professor advised a young colleague, "If your students aren't learning, you're not teaching—you're just talking!" Here's what some authorities on higher education have to say about how effective teachers foster learning:

"All genuine learning is active, not passive. It is a process of discovery in which the student is the main agent, not the teacher." (Adler, 1982)

"Learning is not a spectator sport. Students do not learn much just by sitting in a class listening to teachers, memorizing pre-packaged assignments, and spilling out answers. They must talk about what they are learning, write about it, relate it to past experiences, apply it to their daily lives. They must make what they learn part of themselves." (Chickering & Gamson, 1987)

In their classic book, Bonwell and Elson (1991) list seven defining characteristics of active learning:

1. Students are involved in more than passive listening.
2. Students are engaged in activities (e.g., reading, discussing, writing).
3. There is less emphasis placed on information transmission and greater emphasis placed on developing student skills.
4. There is greater emphasis placed on the exploration of attitudes and values.
5. Student motivation is increased, especially in adult learners.
6. Students receive immediate feedback from their instructor and peers.
7. Students are involved in higher order thinking (analysis, synthesis, evaluation).

Our goals in writing this book were to bridge the academic realm of theory and research and the organizational realm of effective practice and to help students consistently translate proven principles from both realms into personal practice. To accomplish these goals, we formulated a five-step "active" learning model, described in the Introduction. Based on the positive feedback we've received from teachers and students, we can state with confidence that the form of active learning pioneered in this book is a proven pedagogy for management skill mastery.

MYMANAGEMENTLAB SUGGESTED ACTIVITIES

For the 9th edition we the authors are excited that Pearson's MyManagementLab has been integrated fully into the text. These new features are outlined below. Making assessment activities available on line for students to complete before coming to class will allow you the professor more discussion time during the class to review areas that students are having difficulty in comprehending.

Watch It

Recommends a video clip that can be assigned to students for outside classroom viewing or that can be watched in the classroom. The video corresponds to the chapter material and is accompanied by multiple choice questions that re-enforce student's comprehension of the chapter content.

Personal Inventory Assessments (PIA)

Students learn better when they can connect what they are learning to their personal experience. PIA (Personal Inventory Assessments) is a collection of online exercises designed to promote self-reflection and engagement in students, enhancing their ability to connect with concepts taught in principles of management, organizational behavior, and human resource management classes. Assessments are assignable by instructors who can then track students' completions. Student results include a written explanation along with a graphic display that shows how their results compare to the class as a whole. Instructors will also have access to this graphic representation of results to promote classroom discussion.

DETAILED CHAPTER BY CHAPTER CHANGES

Based on suggestions from reviewers, instructors, and students, we have made a number of changes in the ninth edition of Developing Management Skills.

- Chapter 2 now includes a major focus not only on managing stress—usually observed to be a negative influence on individuals—but it focuses on how to enhance and encourage well-being. Stress can be turned to good outcomes if managed effectively, and this 9th edition adopts this positive approach. It highlights ways to flourish and enhance well-being even in the presence of stressful circumstances.

- Chapter 8 replaces the discussion on "delegation" with a focus on "engagement." The theme of employee engagement has become a very important topic in modern organizations as they attempt to enhance their performance and help their employees flourish. That is, employee engagement has become a very hot topic. This chapter provides a framework that helps you engage employees effectively.

- In an environment filled with instantaneous technology, sound bites of data, and short attention spans, we have been motivated to shorten each of the book's chapters substantially. With these reductions, however, we have maintained the empirical evidence and the foundational models and frameworks that distinguish this book from others on the market. We have maintained the scientific and scholarly basis for the prescriptions in each of the chapters because, to be effective managers, students need more substance than found in traditional airport bookstore advice.

- Research continues to appear on factors that predict managerial effectiveness and skillful performance. Therefore, we have updated references, studies, and examples to enhance each chapter's currency. Whereas many of the classic studies and foundational investigations remain in the text, you will find many up-dated studies and examples through the book. This is also the case with exercises, cases, and assessment instruments.

- In each chapter, references to video examples found in Pearson's MyManagementLab are noted. You will want to use these video supplements to illustrate certain concepts and practices discussed in the chapters. They provide real examples of management skill practices in the workplace.

Tips for Getting the Most Out of This Course

Whether you are an undergraduate or MBA student, or an experienced manager, based on our years of teaching management skills, here are some suggestions for making this course a personally meaningful learning experience:

- Read the Introduction carefully. Although this is not a typical management textbook, it is important that you understand its distinctive learner-focused features, especially the five-step learning model: Skill Assessment, Skill Learning, Skill Analysis, Skill Practice, and Skill Application. You'll also find informative research on how much managers' actions impact individual and organizational performance and the characteristics of effective managers.

- Thoughtfully complete the Skill Assessment surveys for each chapter. These diagnostic tools are designed to help you identify which specific aspects of each skill topic most warrant your personal attention.

- Carefully study the Behavioral Guidelines and the summary model at the conclusion of the Skill Learning section of each chapter before reading that section. These written and graphical summaries are designed to bridge the research-informed description of each topic with the skill development activities that follow. To help you internalize research-informed "good sense," be sure to use the Behavioral Guidelines as your frame of reference when reading and discussing Skill Analysis cases and participating in Skill Practice and Skill Application exercises.

- Be sure to complete the Skill Application exercises in each chapter. Management skill mastery requires out-of-class skill practice. How to do this is pretty straightforward if you are currently working in an organization, regardless of whether you are an experienced manager or a new, part-time employee. Whether or not you are currently employed, we encourage you to seek out skill practice opportunities in all aspects of your life, including working in assigned teams in this and other courses, planning social events for a campus or community organization, counseling a troubled sibling or friend, managing end-of-semester deadlines, or handling a difficult issue with a boy/girlfriend or spouse. The sooner you begin—and the more you persist in—practicing what you learn in this course, the more you'll be able to count on these skills as "automatic responses" when you need them as a manager.

INSTRUCTOR RESOURCES

At the Instructor Resource Center, www.pearsonhighered.com/irc, instructors can easily register to gain access to a variety of instructor resources available with this text in downloadable format. If assistance is needed, our dedicated technical support team is ready to help with the media supplements that accompany this text. Visit http://247.pearsoned.com for answers to frequently asked questions and toll-free user support phone numbers.

The following supplements are available with this text:

- Instructor's Resource Manual
- Test Bank
- TestGen® Computerized Test Bank
- PowerPoint Presentation

2015 QUALITATIVE BUSINESS VIDEO LIBRARY

Additional videos illustrating the most important subject topics are available in MyManagementLab, under the Instructor Resources: Business Today.

COURSESMART TEXTBOOKS ONLINE

CourseSmart eTextbooks were developed for students looking to save money on required or recommended textbooks. Students simply select their eText by title or author and purchase immediate access to the content for the duration of the course using any major credit card. With a CourseSmart eText, students can search for specific keywords or page numbers, take notes online, print out reading assignments that incorporate lecture notes, and bookmark important passages for later review. For more information or to purchase a CourseSmart eTextbook, visit www.coursesmart.com.

Acknowledgments

In addition to the informal feedback we have received from colleagues around the world, we would especially like to thank the following people who have formally reviewed material and provided valuable feedback, vital to the revision of this and previous editions:

Richard Allan, University of Tennessee–Chattanooga

Joseph S Anderson, Northern Arizona University

Forrest F. Aven, University of Houston

Lloyd Baird, Boston University

Bud Baker, Wright State University

John D. Bigelow, Boise State University

Ralph R. Braithwaite, University of Hartford

Julia Britt, California State University

Tim Bothell, Brigham Young University

David Cherrington, Brigham Young University

John Collins, Syracuse University

Kerri Crowne, Temple University

Joseph V. DePalma, Farleigh Dickerson University

Todd Dewett, Wright State University

Andrew J. Dubrin, Rochester Institute of Technology

Steven Edelson, Temple University

Crissie M. Frye, Eastern Michigan University

Norma Givens, Fort Valley State University

Barbara A. Gorski, St. Thomas University

Sara Grant, New York University

David Hampton, San Diego State University

Jason Harris-Boundy. San Francisco State University

Stanley Harris, Auburn University

Richard E. Hunt, Rockhurst College
Daniel F. Jennings, Baylor University
Avis L. Johnson, University of Akron
Jay T. Knippen, University of South
　　Florida
Roland Kushner, Lafayette College
Roy J. Lewicki, Ohio State University
Michael Lombardo, Center for Creative
　　Leadership
Charles C. Manz, University of
　　Massachusetts–Amherst
Ralph F. Mullin, Central Missouri State
　　University
Thomas J. Naughton, Wayne State
　　University

J. Randolph New, University of
　　Richmond
Jon L. Pierce, University of Minnesota–
　　Duluth
Lyman Porter, University of California–
　　Irvine
Lyle F. Schoenfeldt, Appalachian State
　　University
Jacop P. Siegel, University of Toronto
Charles Smith, Hofstra University
Noel M. Tichy, University of Michigan
Wanda V. Trenner, Ferris State
　　University
Ulya Tsolmon, Brigham Young University
Kenneth M. York, Oakland University

We especially thank our collaborators who adapted the book for the European and Australian markets as well as those who translated *Developing Management Skills* into Spanish, Russian, Chinese, and Dutch.

We are grateful for the assistance of many dedicated associates who have helped us continually upgrade and enhance *Developing Management Skills*. We wish to acknowledge our colleague, Jeffrey Thompson, Director of the Romney Institute of Public Management, Brigham Young University. Jeff has been a valuable collaborator on our recent revisions and has become a major part of the authoring team.

We would also like to thank Kris Ellis-Levy, Sarah Holle, Rebecca Groves, Meghan DeMaio, and Judy Leale of Pearson Education. In addition, we'd like to express our gratitude to Kristin Jobe of Integra-Chicago for her expert assistance with this edition, as well as Erikson Daniel Conkling, Ivy Tech Community College/Northeast and Linda Hoffman, Ivy Tech Community College/Fort Wayne for their contributions to the MyLab assessment content.

Finally, and most importantly, we express appreciation to our families for their ongoing patience and support, which is reflected in their willingness to share their time with this competing "labor of love"—and to forgive our own gaps between common sense and common practice.

David A. Whetten
Kim S. Cameron

MANAGEMENT CONCEPTS

- The Critical Role of Management Skills
- The Importance of Competent Managers
- The Skills of Effective Managers
- What Are Management Skills?
- Improving Management Skills
- An Approach to Skill Development
- Leadership and Management
- Contents of the Book
- Organization of the Book
- Diversity and Individual Differences
- Summary

SUPPLEMENTARY *MATERIAL*

- Personal Assessment of Management Skills (PAMS)
- What Does It Take to Be an Effective Manager?
- SSS Software In-Basket Exercise

SCORING KEY AND *COMPARISON DATA*

INTRODUCTION

The Critical Role of Management Skills

LEARNING OBJECTIVES

1. INTRODUCE THE IMPORTANCE OF MANAGEMENT SKILLS

2. IDENTIFY ESSENTIAL MANAGEMENT SKILLS

3. EXPLAIN A LEARNING MODEL FOR DEVELOPING MANAGEMENT SKILLS

4. REVIEW THE CONTENTS OF THE BOOK

Introduction

The Critical Role of Management Skills

No one doubts that the twenty-first century will continue to be characterized by chaotic, transformational, rapid-fire change. In fact, almost no sane person is willing to predict what the world will be like 50, 20, or even 10 years from now. Change is just too rapid and ubiquitous. Three quarters of the content on the web was not available three years ago. The development of "nanobombs" has caused some people to predict that personal computers and desktop monitors will land on the scrap heap of obsolescence within 20 years. The new computers will be a product of etchings on molecules leading to personalized data processors injected into the bloodstream, implanted in eyeglasses, or included in wristwatches.

Warren Bennis, a colleague of ours, half-jokingly predicted that the factory of the future would have only two employees, a person and a dog. The person would be there to feed the dog. The dog would be there to keep the person from touching the equipment! Almost no one would argue with the claim that "permanent white water" best characterizes our current environment. Almost everything is in flux, from our technology and methods of transacting business to the nature of education and the definition of the family.

Despite all this change in our environment, there is something that has remained relatively constant. With minor variations and stylistic differences, what have not changed in several thousand years are the basic skills that lie at the heart of effective, satisfying, growth-producing human relationships. Freedom, dignity, trust, love, and respect in relationships have always been among the goals of human beings, and the same principles that brought about those outcomes in the second or seventeenth centuries still bring them about in the twenty-first century. Despite our circumstances, in other words, and despite the technological resources we have available to us, the same basic human skills still lie at the heart of effective human interaction.

This book is built on the presumption that developing management skills—that is, the skills needed to manage one's own life as well as relationships with others—is a ceaseless endeavor. These skills were largely the same a century ago as they are today. The basic behavioral principles that lie at the foundation of these skills are timeless. This is one reason why the shelves of bookstores, blogs, and on-line newsletters are filled with prescriptions of how one more executive or one more company struck it rich or beat out the competition. Thousands of books trumpet prescriptions for how to be successful in business, or in life. Many of these books have made it to the best-seller lists and have enjoyed lengthy stays.

Our intention in this book is not to try to duplicate the popular appeal of the best-selling books nor to utilize the common formula of recounting anecdotal incidents of successful organizations or well-known managers. We have produced a book that remains true to, and is based on, social science and business research. We want to share with you what is known and what is not known about how to develop management skills and how to foster productive, healthy, satisfying, and growth-producing relationships with others in your work setting. *Developing Management Skills* is designed to help you actually improve your personal management competencies—to change your behavior.

This book, therefore, serves more as a practicum or a guide to effective managerial behavior than a description of what someone else has done to successfully manage an organization. It will surely help you think, and it will provide examples of success, but it will have failed if it also does not help you *behave* more competently in your own life.

Whereas the skills focused on in this book are called "management skills," their relevance is not limited just to an organization or work setting. This book could be retitled "life skills," or even "leadership skills." We focus mainly on work settings here because our primary goal is to help you prepare for and improve your own competency in a managerial role. You will discover, however, that these skills are applicable in most areas of your life—with families, friends, volunteer organizations, and your community.

In the next section, we review some of the scientific evidence that demonstrates how management skills are associated with personal and organizational success, and we review several studies of the key management skills that seem to be the most important in our modern-day environment. It is those key skills that this book has targeted. We then describe a model and a methodology for helping you to develop management skills.

A large number of fads abound proclaiming a new way to be a leader, get rich, or both, but our intent is to rely on a proven methodology that has grounding in the scientific literature. We present what has been shown to be a superior process for improving management skills, and we base our claims on scholarly evidence. This Introduction concludes with a brief description of the organization of the rest of the book and the importance of keeping in mind individual differences among people.

The Importance of Competent Managers

In the last couple of decades, an abundance of evidence has been produced demonstrating that skillful management is the single most powerful determinant of organizational success. These studies have been conducted across numerous industry sectors, international settings, and organization types. The research findings now make it almost unquestionable that if organizations want to succeed, they must have competent, skillful managers.

For example, in one study of 968 firms, representing all major industries in the United States, organizations whose managers effectively managed their people—that is, they implemented effective people management strategies and demonstrated personal competency in management skills—had, on the average, a decrease in turnover of more than 7 percent, increased profits of $3,814 per employee, $27,044 more in sales per employee, and $18,641 more in stock market value per employee, compared to firms that had less effective people management (Huselid, 1995; Pfeffer & Veiga, 1999). In a follow-up study of 702 firms, shareholder wealth was an amazing $41,000 per employee higher in companies demonstrating strong people management skills than in firms that had a lower emphasis on people management (Huselid & Becker, 1997).

A study of German firms in 10 industrial sectors produced similar results: "Companies that place workers at the core of their strategies produce higher long-term returns...than their industry peers" (Blimes, Wetzker, & Xhonneux, 1997). A study of five-year survivability in 136 nonfinancial companies that issued IPOs in the late 1980s found that the effective management of people was the most significant factor in predicting longevity, even when accounting for industry type, size, and profits. Firms that did a good job of managing people tended to survive; others did not (Welbourne & Andrews, 1996).

A study by Hanson (1986) investigated the factors that best accounted for financial success over a five-year span in 40 major manufacturing firms. The five most powerful predictors were identified and assessed. They included market share (assuming that the higher the market share of a firm, the higher its profitability); firm capital intensity (assuming that the more a firm is automated and up-to-date in technology and equipment, the more profitable it is); size of the firm in assets (assuming that economies of scale and efficiency can be used in large firms to increase profitability); industry average return on sales (assuming that firms would reflect the performance of a highly profitable industry); and the ability of managers to effectively manage their people (assuming that an emphasis on good people management helps produce profitability in firms). The results revealed that one factor—the ability to manage people effectively—was three times more powerful than all other factors combined in accounting for firm financial success over a five-year period! We repeat, good management was more important than all other factors taken together in predicting profitability.

This is just a small sampling of studies that indicate overwhelmingly that good management fosters financial success, whereas less effective management fosters financial distress. Successful organizations have managers with well-developed management skills. Moreover, the data are clear that management skills are more important in accounting for success than industry, environment, competition, and economic factors combined.

The Skills of Effective Managers

What, then, differentiates effective managers from less effective managers? If developing management skills is so crucial for organizational success, what skills ought to be the focus of our attention? The management literature is filled with lists of attributes, behaviors, orientations, and strategies for enhancing successful performance. In writing this book, we wanted to identify the skills and competencies that separate extraordinarily effective performers from the rest of us. So, in addition to reviewing the managerial and leadership literatures, we also identified 402 individuals who were rated as highly effective managers in their own organizations in the fields of business, health care, education, and state government by asking senior officers to name the most effective managers in their organizations. We then interviewed those people to determine what attributes were associated with managerial effectiveness. We asked questions such as:

❏ How have you become so successful in this organization?

❏ Who fails and who succeeds in this organization and why?

❏ If you had to train someone to take your place, what knowledge and what skills would you make certain that person possessed in order to perform successfully as your successor?

❏ If you could design an ideal curriculum or training program to teach you to be a better manager, what would it contain?

❏ Think of other effective managers you know. What skills do they demonstrate that explain their success?

Table 1	Skills of Effective Managers—One Study

1. Verbal communication (including listening)
2. Managing time and stress
3. Rational and creative decision making
4. Recognizing, defining, and solving problems
5. Motivating and influencing others
6. Delegating and engaging others
7. Setting goals and articulating a vision
8. Self-awareness
9. Team building
10. Managing conflict

Our analysis of the interviews produced about 60 characteristics of effective managers. The 10 identified most often are listed in Table 1. Not surprisingly, these 10 characteristics are all behavioral skills. They are not personality attributes or styles, nor are they generalizations such as "luck," "charisma," or "timing." They also are common across industries, levels, and job responsibilities. The characteristics of effective managers are not a secret.

What Are Management Skills?

There are several defining characteristics of management skills that differentiate them from other kinds of characteristics and practices. First, management skills are *behavioral*. They are not personality attributes or stylistic tendencies. Management skills consist of actions that lead to positive outcomes. Skills can be observed by others, unlike attributes that are purely mental, stylistic, or are embedded in personality.

Second, management skills are *controllable*. The performance of these behaviors is under your own control. Skills may involve other people and require cognitive work, but they are behaviors that you can govern yourself.

Third, management skills are *developable*. Performance can improve. Unlike IQ or certain personality or temperament attributes that remain relatively constant throughout life, you can improve your competency in skill performance through practice and feedback. You can progress from less competence to more competence in management skills, and that outcome is the primary objective of this book.

Fourth, management skills are *interrelated* and *overlapping*. It is difficult to demonstrate just one skill in isolation from others. Skills are not simplistic, repetitive behaviors, but they are integrated sets of complex responses. Fifth, management skills are sometimes *contradictory* or *paradoxical*. For example, the core management skills are neither all soft and humanistic in orientation nor all hard-driving and directive. They are oriented neither toward teamwork and interpersonal relations exclusively nor toward individualism and technical entrepreneurship exclusively. A variety of skills are typical of the most effective managers, and some of them appear incompatible.

To illustrate, Cameron and Tschirhart (1988) assessed the skill performance of more than 500 midlevel and upper-middle managers in about 150 organizations. The most frequently mentioned 25 management skills taken from about a dozen studies in the academic literature (such as those in Table 2) were measured. Statistical analyses revealed that the skills fell into four main groups or clusters. One group of skills focused on participative and human relations skills (for example, supportive communication and team building), while another group focused on just the opposite, that is, competitiveness and control (for example, assertiveness, power, and influence skills). A third group focused on innovativeness and individual entrepreneurship (for example, creative problem solving), while a fourth group emphasized the opposite type of skills, namely, maintaining order and rationality (for example, managing time and rational decision making). One conclusion from that study was that effective managers are required to demonstrate paradoxical skills. That is, the most effective managers are both participative and hard-driving, both nurturing and competitive. They were able to be flexible and creative while also being controlled, stable, and rational (see Cameron, Quinn, DeGraff, & Thakor, 2014). Our objective in this book is to help you develop that kind of behavioral competency and complexity.

Improving Management Skills

It is a bit unnerving that while average IQ scores have increased in the population over the last half-century, social and emotional intelligence scores have actually declined. In the population in general, people are less skilled at managing themselves and managing others than they were 50 years ago (Goleman, 1998). While average IQ scores have jumped approximately 25 points, emotional intelligence scores (EQ) have fallen. In a recent survey of 110 *Fortune* 500 CEOs, 87 percent were satisfied with the level of competence and analytic skills of business school graduates, 68 percent were satisfied with conceptual skills of graduates, but only 43 percent of the CEOs were satisfied with graduates' management skills, and only 28 percent were satisfied with their interpersonal skills and EQ!

The good news is that improvement in developing management skills has been found in both students and managers who have been exposed to in the learning model presented in *Developing Management Skills*. For example, MBA students showed improvement of from 50 to 300 percent on social skills over two years by enrolling in courses based on the approach to developing management skills presented here. A greater amount of improvement occurred among students who applied these skills to aspects of their lives outside the classroom. In addition, a cohort of 45- to 55-year-old executives produced the same results as the MBA students. They also improved dramatically in their management skills even though most were already experienced in senior managerial positions (Boyatzis, 1996, 2000, 2005; Boyatzis, Cowen, & Kolb, 1995; Boyatzis, Leonard, Rhee, & Wheeler, 1996; Leonard, 1996; Rhee, 1997; Wheeler, 1999).

An Approach to Skill Development

The method that has been found to be most successful in helping individuals develop management skills is based on social learning theory (Bandura, 1977; Boyatzis et al., 1995; Davis & Luthans, 1980). This approach marries rigorous conceptual knowledge with opportunities to practice and apply observable behaviors. It relies on cognitive work as well as behavioral work. This learning model, as originally formulated, consisted of four steps: (1) the presentation of behavioral principles or action guidelines, generally using traditional instruction methods such as lecture and discussion; (2) demonstration of the principles by means of cases, films, scripts, or incidents; (3) opportunities to practice the principles through role plays or exercises; and (4) feedback on performance from peers, instructors, or experts.

Our own experience in teaching complex management skills, as well as research on management skills development among MBA students (e.g., Boyatzis et al., 1995; Vance, 1993) has demonstrated that three important modifications are necessary in order for this model to be most effective. First, the behavioral principles must be grounded in social science theory and in reliable research results. To ensure the validity of the behavioral guidelines being prescribed, the learning approach must include scientifically based knowledge about the effects of the management principles being presented.

Second, you must be aware of your current level of skill competency and be motivated to improve upon that level. Most of us receive very little feedback about our current level of skill competency. Most organizations provide some kind of annual or semiannual evaluation (for example, course grades in school or performance appraisal interviews in firms), but these evaluations are usually infrequent and narrow in scope, and they fail to assess performance in most critical skill areas. To help you understand what skills to improve and why, an assessment activity must be part of the model.

In addition, most people find change uncomfortable and therefore avoid taking the risk to develop new behavior patterns. An assessment activity in the learning model helps encourage you to change by illuminating your strengths and weaknesses. This makes it possible to target your improvement efforts more specifically. Assessment activities generally take the form of self-evaluation instruments, case studies, or problems that help highlight personal strengths and weaknesses in a particular skill area.

Third, an application component is needed in the learning model. Most management skill training takes place in a classroom setting where feedback is immediate, and it is relatively safe to try out new behaviors and make mistakes. Therefore, transferring learning to an actual job setting is often problematic. Application exercises help to apply classroom learning to examples from the real world of management. Application exercises often take the form of an outside-of-class intervention, a consulting assignment, self-analysis through journal writing, or a problem-centered intervention, which you can analyze to determine its degree of success or failure.

In summary, evidence suggests that a five-step learning model is most effective for helping you develop management skills (see Cameron & Whetten, 1984; Kolb, 1984; Vance, 1993; Whetten & Cameron, 1983). Table 2 outlines such a model. Step 1 involves the *assessment* of current levels of skill competency and knowledge of the behavioral

Table 2	A Model for Developing Management Skills	
COMPONENTS	**CONTENTS**	**OBJECTIVES**
1. Skill assessment	Survey instruments Role plays	Assess current level of skill competence and knowledge; create readiness to change.
2. Skill learning	Written text Behavioral guidelines	Teach correct principles and present a rationale for behavioral guidelines.
3. Skill analysis	Cases	Provide examples of appropriate and inappropriate skill performance. Analyze behavioral principles and reasons they work.
4. Skill practice	Exercises Simulations Role plays	Practice behavioral guidelines. Adapt principles to personal style. Receive feedback and assistance.
5. Skill application	Assignments (behavioral and written)	Transfer classroom learning to real-life situations. Foster ongoing personal development.

principles. Step 2 consists of the presentation of validated, scientifically based *principles and guidelines* for effective skill performance. Step 3 is an *analysis* step in which models or cases are presented in order to analyze behavioral principles in real organizational settings. This step also helps demonstrate how the behavioral guidelines can be adapted to different personal styles and circumstances. Step 4 consists of *practice* exercises in which experimentation can occur and immediate feedback can be received in a relatively safe environment. Step 5 is the *application* of the skill to a real-life setting outside the classroom with follow-up analysis of the relative success of that application.

Research on the effectiveness of training programs using this general learning model has shown that it produces results superior to those based on more traditional lecture-discussion-case method approaches (Boyatzis et al., 1995; Burnaska, 1976; Kolb, 1984; Latham & Saari, 1979; Moses & Ritchie, 1976; Porras & Anderson, 1981; Smith, 1976; Vance, 1993).

To assist you in improving your own management skills, this book emphasizes practicing management skills rather than just reading about them. We have organized the book with this specific approach in mind.

Leadership and Management

Before outlining the organization of this book, we want to discuss briefly the place of leadership in this volume. Some writers have differentiated between the concepts of "leadership" and "management" (Bass, 1990; Katzenbach, 1995; Nair, 1994; Quinn, 2000; Tichy, 1999). Some have wondered why we concentrate on "management" skills instead of "leadership" skills in this book. We have also been asked by professors, business executives, and students why we have not either changed the title of the book to *Developing Leadership Skills*, or at least included one chapter on leadership in this volume. These queries and suggestions are important and have motivated us to clarify at the outset of the book what we mean by management, and why our approach lies at the heart of leadership as typically defined.

One of the most popular models of leadership is based on the "Competing Values Framework," an organizing framework for leadership and managerial skills. It was developed by examining the criteria used to evaluate organizational performance (Cameron et al., 2014; Quinn & Rohrbaugh, 1983). Extensive research has been conducted on this framework over the past three decades, and a brief explanation will help clarify the relationship between management and leadership skills. This research has shown that both leadership and management skills fall into four clusters or categories as illustrated in Figure 1.

In order to be an effective leader and manager, the research suggests that you must be competent in: (1) people skills, collaboration, teamwork, and interpersonal communication. These are referred to in the academic literature as *clan skills*. (2) creativity, innovativeness, entrepreneurship, and fashioning a vision for the future. These are referred to in the academic literature as *adhocracy skills*; (3) producing results, making fast decisions, competing aggressively, and being comfortable taking charge. These are referred to in the academic literature as *market skills*; and (4) maintaining stability and predictability, increasing quality, being efficient, and maintaining control. These are referred to in the academic literature as *hierarchy skills*.

Clan skills include those required to build effective interpersonal relationships and develop others (e.g., building teamwork, communicating supportively). Adhocracy skills include those required to manage the future, innovate, and promote change (e.g., solving problems creatively, articulating an energizing vision). Market skills include those required to compete effectively and manage external relationships (e.g., motivating others, using power and influence). Hierarchy skills include those required to maintain control

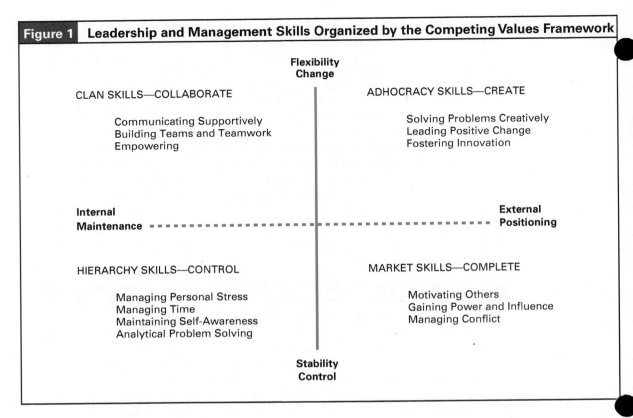

Figure 1 Leadership and Management Skills Organized by the Competing Values Framework

Flexibility
Change

CLAN SKILLS—COLLABORATE

Communicating Supportively
Building Teams and Teamwork
Empowering

ADHOCRACY SKILLS—CREATE

Solving Problems Creatively
Leading Positive Change
Fostering Innovation

Internal
Maintenance

External
Positioning

HIERARCHY SKILLS—CONTROL

Managing Personal Stress
Managing Time
Maintaining Self-Awareness
Analytical Problem Solving

MARKET SKILLS—COMPLETE

Motivating Others
Gaining Power and Influence
Managing Conflict

Stability
Control

and stability (e.g., managing personal stress and time, solving problems rationally) (see Cameron & Quinn, 2006).

In Figure 1, the two top quadrants in the Competing Values Framework—clan and adhocracy—are usually associated with leadership. The two bottom quadrants—market and hierarchy—are usually associated with management. Traditionally, leadership has been used to describe what individuals do under conditions of change. When organizations are dynamic and undergoing transformation, people at the top are expected to exhibit leadership (i.e., pay attention to clan and adhocracy issues). Management, on the other hand, has traditionally been used to describe what executives do under conditions of stability. Thus, management has been linked with the status quo (i.e., pay attention to market and hierarchy issues).

In addition, leadership has sometimes been defined as "doing the right things," whereas management has been defined as "doing things right." Leaders have been said to focus on setting the direction, articulating a vision, transforming individuals and organizations, and creating something new. Managers have been described as focusing on monitoring, directing, and refining current performance. Leadership has been equated with dynamism, vibrancy, and charisma; management with hierarchy, equilibrium, and control.

However, the recent research is clear that such distinctions between leadership and management are neither accurate nor useful (Cameron, Quinn, DeGraff, & Thakor, 2014; Quinn, 2000; Tichy, 1993, 1999). Managers cannot be successful without being good leaders, and leaders cannot be successful without being good managers. No longer do organizations and individuals have the luxury of holding on to the status quo; worrying about doing things right but failing to do the right things; keeping the system stable instead of leading change and improvement; monitoring current performance instead of formulating a vision of the future; concentrating on equilibrium and control instead of vibrancy and charisma. Effective management and leadership are inseparable. The skills required to do one are also required of the other.

No organization in a postindustrial, hyper-turbulent, twenty-first-century environment will survive without executives capable of providing both management and leadership. Leading change and managing stability, establishing vision and accomplishing objectives, breaking the rules and monitoring conformance, although paradoxical, all are required to be successful.

All of us, in other words, need to develop competencies that will enhance our ability to be both leaders and managers. The specific skills in this book represent all four quadrants in the Competing Values Framework of leadership. They serve as the foundation for effective management and for effective leadership. *The skills contained in this book cover both management skills and leadership skills.* We have chosen to use the label "management skills" to subsume the skills associated with leadership as well as with management. When you are promoted, you will be given a managerial role, and your success in that role will depend on the extent to which you have mastered specific skills. You can act as a leader in any context or role, so this book is designed to prepare you to be an effective manager as well as an effective leader.

Contents of the Book

Again, this book focuses on the skills that research has identified as critically important for successful management and leadership. Part I contains three chapters on *personal skills*: Developing Self-Awareness, Managing Stress and Well-Being, and Solving Problems Analytically and Creatively. These skills focus on issues that may not involve other people but instead relate to the management of the self—hence they are called personal skills. Each chapter, however, really includes a cluster of related behaviors, not just one single, simple skill. These clusters of interrelated behaviors comprise the overall management skill indicated in the chapter's title. Figure 2 also points out that each skill cluster is related to and overlaps with other personal management skills, so each relies at least partially on the others to be performed successfully.

Part II focuses on *interpersonal skills*: Building Relationships by Communicating Supportively, Gaining Power and Influence, Motivating Others, and Managing Conflict. These skills focus primarily on issues that arise in your interactions with other people. Overlap exists among these skills, of course, so that you must rely on parts of many skill areas in order to perform any one skill effectively.

Part III includes three chapters on *group skills*: Empowering and Engaging Others, Building Effective Teams and Teamwork, and Leading Positive Change. These skills focus on key issues that arise when you are involved with groups of people either as a leader or as a member of the group. As with all the skills in the book, overlap occurs among the group skills as well as with the personal and interpersonal skills. In other words, as you progress from personal to interpersonal to group skills, the core competencies developed in the previous skill area help support successful performance of the new skill area.

In addition to the ten core management skills in Parts I, II, and III, the supplemental Part IV chapters contain three additional communications skills: Making Oral and Written Presentations, Conducting Interviews, and Conducting Meetings. These supplements cover specialized communication skills that are especially relevant for students who have had little managerial experience or skill training such as writing reports, giving class presentations, interviewing others, or conducting group meetings.

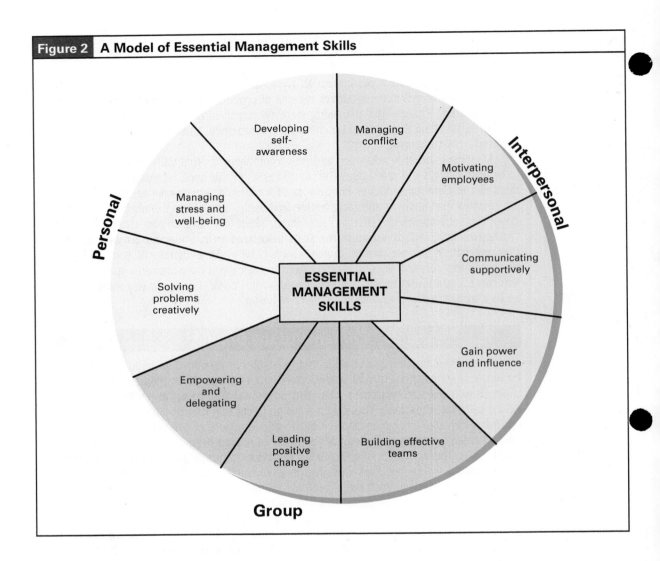

Figure 2 | A Model of Essential Management Skills

ESSENTIAL MANAGEMENT SKILLS

Personal
- Developing self-awareness
- Managing stress and well-being
- Solving problems creatively

Interpersonal
- Managing conflict
- Motivating employees
- Communicating supportively
- Gain power and influence

Group
- Empowering and delegating
- Leading positive change
- Building effective teams

Appendix I contains a glossary of key terms in the text; and Appendix II lists references for excerpted material in the book.

Organization of the Book

Each chapter is organized on the basis of the learning model summarized in Table 3. Specifically, each chapter begins with *Skill Assessment* instruments, followed by the largest section of the chapter, an explanation of the key behavioral guidelines along with evidence from research that the principles identified are effective in practice. This is the *Skill Learning* section. The third section is labeled *Skill Analysis*, and it provides brief case histories that illustrate both effective and ineffective applications of the behavioral principles.

The *Skill Practice* section provides exercises, problems, and role-play assignments in order for you to practice the behavioral guidelines in a safe, simulated managerial situation and to receive feedback from peers and instructors. The last section of each chapter is *Skill Application*. It contains a form to help you generate your own improvement agenda, as well as assignments and ideas for applying the skill in an out-of-class situation.

Table 3	The Organization of Each Chapter
SECTION	**CONTENTS**
Skill Assessment	Instruments designed to identify your current level of skill competency, your styles, and/or key dimensions of the skill. These instruments can be used to identify individual differences, issues surrounding diversity, and areas for personal improvement plans.
Skill Learning	Behavioral guidelines and key principles associated with the skill are explained. Scientific research is used as the basis for prescribed skill performance. Clarifying how to successfully develop and perform the skill is the purpose of this section.
Skill Analysis	Cases and examples are presented in order to provide examples of successful and unsuccessful skill performance. Analytic problem solving is facilitated as recommendations are made for what the key issues are, how performance might be modified, and why success was achieved.
Skill Practice	Exercises and role plays make it possible for individuals to actually practice the skill. Feedback from peers and the instructor will facilitate improvement of the skill in a setting where failure is not costly.
Skill Application	Suggested assignments are provided so that the skill can be applied in a real-life setting. A feedback mechanism is also suggested so that individuals analyze their own success in applying the skill outside the classroom. Improvement plans should always be associated with the application exercises.

Diversity and Individual Differences

One reason developing management skills is difficult is because all of us possess our own unique styles, personalities, and inclinations. We all know that everyone doesn't react in the same way to similar circumstances. It is impossible, therefore, to manage each relationship in exactly the same way, or even to behave the same way from one encounter to the next. Sensitivity to individual differences is an important part of an effective manager's repertoire.

A great deal of research has been conducted on cultural differences, gender differences, ethnic differences, and age differences in organizations (e.g., Cox, 1994; Cox & Beal, 1997). While we will not summarize that extensive research, we do want to highlight the importance of being sensitive to individuality. Two kinds of sensitivities are necessary: one to the uniqueness displayed by each person, and the other to distinctive but general patterns of behavior that characterize groups of people. For example, it is essential that you not only become aware of, but also value and capitalize on the differences that characterize people with whom you associate. The general tendency of us all is to fear or oppose those who are different from us, so we provide a framework to help us all better understand and appreciate differences. We don't emphasize so much *managing diversity* as we do *diagnosing individual differences* so they can be valued, understood, and appreciated.

In Chapter 1, Developing Self-Awareness, we explain a model developed by Frans Trompenaars which relies on seven dimensions found to differ across national and cultural boundaries. These dimensions have been found to be very helpful in assisting people to understand key differences in others. They are: *universalism versus particularism, individualism versus communitarianism, specificity versus diffuseness, neutral versus affective, achievement versus ascription oriented, internal versus external, and past versus present versus future time emphasis*. These dimensions will help you adjust your behaviors when you interact with others from a different culture or nationality. Whereas the behavioral principles upon which the management skills are based are applicable across cultures, genders, ethnic groups, and age cohorts, important nuances may be required of you as you practice among people characterized by these differences. Women may not behave the same as men. Japanese colleagues may not respond the same as German colleagues. Individuals in their sixties may not see the world the same as someone in their twenties. So being sensitive to and valuing individual differences is key.

Summary

In sum, *Developing Management Skills* is not intended just for individuals who plan to enter managerial positions or who currently manage organizations. It is meant to help you better manage many aspects of your life and relationships. It is intended to help you actually change your behavior, to improve your competence, and to become more savvy in your relationships with different kinds of people. It is intended to improve your social and emotional intelligence. John Holt (1964) succinctly summarized our intention by equating management skill to intelligence:

> When we talk about intelligence, we do not mean the ability to get a good score on a certain kind of test or even the ability to do well in school; these are at best only indicators of something larger, deeper, and far more important. By intelligence we mean a style of life, a way of behaving in various situations. The true test of intelligence is not how much we know how to do, but how we behave when we don't know what to do. (p. 165)

Fostering the development of such intelligence is the goal of *Developing Management Skills*.

SUPPLEMENTARY MATERIAL

Diagnostic Survey and Exercises

Personal Assessment of Management Skills (PAMS)

Step 1: To get an overall profile of your level of skill competence, respond to the following statements using the rating scale below. Please rate your behavior as it is, not as you would like it to be. If you have not engaged in a specific activity, answer according to how you think you would behave based on your experience in similar activities. Be realistic; this instrument is designed to help you tailor your learning to your specific needs. After you have completed the survey, the scoring key at the end of the chapter will help you generate an overall profile of your management skill strengths and weaknesses.

Step 2: Get copies of the Associates' version of this instrument from your instructor. An alternate version has been provided in the Instructor's Manual that uses "he" or "she" instead of "I" in the questions. Give copies to at least three other people who know you well or who have observed you in a situation in which you have had to lead or manage others. Those people should complete the instrument by rating your behavior. Bring the completed surveys back to class and compare: (1) your own ratings to your associates' ratings, (2) your associates' ratings to the ratings received by others in the class, and (3) the ratings you received to those of a national norm group.

Subsections of this instrument appear in each chapter throughout the book.

Rating Scale

1 Strongly disagree
2 Disagree
3 Slightly disagree
4 Slightly agree
5 Agree
6 Strongly agree

In regard to my level of self-knowledge:

_____ 1. I seek information about my strengths and weaknesses from others as a basis for self-improvement.

_____ 2. In order to improve, I am willing to be self-disclosing to others (that is, to share my beliefs and feelings).

_____ 3. I am very much aware of my preferred style in gathering information and making decisions.

_____ 4. I have a good sense of how I cope with situations that are ambiguous and uncertain.

_____ 5. I have a well-developed set of personal standards and principles that guide my behavior.

When faced with stressful or time-pressured situations:

_____ 6. I use effective time-management methods such as keeping track of my time, making to-do lists, and prioritizing tasks.

_____ 7. I frequently affirm my priorities so that less important things don't drive out more important things.

_____ 8. I maintain a program of regular exercise for fitness.

_____ 9. I maintain an open, trusting relationship with someone with whom I can share my frustrations.

_____ 10. I know and practice several temporary relaxation techniques such as deep breathing and muscle relaxation.

_____ 11. I maintain balance in my life by pursuing a variety of interests outside of work.

When I approach a typical, routine problem:

_____ 12. I state clearly and explicitly what the problem is. I avoid trying to solve it until I have defined it.

_____ 13. I always generate more than one alternative solution to the problem, instead of identifying only one obvious solution.

_____ 14. I keep steps in the problem-solving process distinct; that is, I define the problem before proposing alternative solutions, and I generate alternatives before selecting a single solution.

When faced with a complex or difficult problem that does not have an easy solution:

_____ 15. I try out several definitions of the problem. I don't limit myself to just one way to define it.

_____ 16. I try to unfreeze my thinking by asking lots of questions about the nature of the problem before considering ways to solve it.

_____ 17. I try to think about the problem from both the left (logical) side of my brain and the right (intuitive) side of my brain.

_____ 18. I do not evaluate the merits of an alternative solution to the problem before I have generated a list of alternatives. That is, I avoid deciding on a solution until I have developed many possible solutions.

_____ 19. I have some specific techniques that I use to help develop creative and innovative solutions to problems.

When trying to foster more creativity and innovation among those with whom I work:

_____ 20. I make sure there are divergent points of view represented or expressed in every complex problem-solving situation.

_____ 21. I try to acquire information from individuals outside the problem-solving group who will be affected by the decision, mainly to determine their preferences and expectations.

_____ 22. I try to provide recognition not only to those who come up with creative ideas (the idea champions) but also to those who support others' ideas (supporters) and who provide resources to implement them (orchestrators).

_____ 23. I encourage informed rule-breaking in pursuit of creative solutions.

In situations where I have to provide negative feedback or offer corrective advice:

_____ 24. I am able to help others recognize and define their own problems when I counsel them.

_____ 25. I am clear about when I should coach someone and when I should provide counseling instead.

_____ 26. When I give feedback to others, I avoid referring to personal characteristics and focus on problems or solutions instead.

_____ 27. When I try to correct someone's behavior, our relationship is almost always strengthened.

_____ 28. I am descriptive in giving negative feedback to others. That is, I objectively describe events, their consequences, and my feelings about them.

_____ 29. I take responsibility for my statements and point of view by using, for example, "I have decided" instead of "They have decided."

_____ 30. I strive to identify some area of agreement in a discussion with someone who has a different point of view.

_____ 31. I don't talk down to those who have less power or less information than I.

_____ 32. When discussing someone's problem, I usually respond with a reply that indicates understanding rather than advice.

In a situation where it is important to obtain more power:

_____ 33. I always put forth more effort and take more initiative than expected in my work.

_____ 34. I am continually upgrading my skills and knowledge.

_____ 35. I strongly support organizational ceremonial events and activities.

_____ 36. I form a broad network of relationships with people throughout the organization at all levels.

_____ 37. In my work I consistently strive to generate new ideas, initiate new activities, and minimize routine tasks.

_____ 38. I consistently send personal notes to others when they accomplish something significant or when I pass along important information to them.

_____ 39. I refuse to bargain with individuals who use high-pressure negotiation tactics.

_____ 40. I always avoid using threats or demands to impose my will on others.

When another person needs to be motivated:

_____ 41. I always determine if the person has the necessary resources and support to succeed in a task.

_____ 42. I use a variety of rewards to reinforce exceptional performances.

_____ 43. I design task assignments to make them interesting and challenging.

_____ 44. I make sure the person gets timely feedback from those affected by task performance.

_____ 45. I always help the person establish performance goals that are challenging, specific, and time bound.

_____ 46. Only as a last resort do I attempt to reassign or release a poorly performing individual.

_____ 47. I consistently discipline when effort is below expectations and capabilities.

_____ 48. I make sure that people feel fairly and equitably treated.

_____ 49. I provide immediate compliments and other forms of recognition for meaningful accomplishments.

When I see someone doing something that needs correcting:

_____ 50. I avoid making personal accusations and attributing self-serving motives to the other person.

_____ 51. I encourage two-way interaction by inviting the respondent to express his or her perspective and to ask questions.

_____ 52. I make a specific request, detailing a more acceptable option.

When someone complains about something I've done:

_____ 53. I show genuine concern and interest, even when I disagree.

_____ 54. I seek additional information by asking questions that provide specific and descriptive information.

_____ 55. I ask the other person to suggest more acceptable behaviors.

When two people are in conflict and I am the mediator:

_____ 56. I do not take sides but remain neutral.

_____ 57. I help the parties generate multiple alternatives.

_____ 58. I help the parties find areas on which they agree.

In situations where I have an opportunity to engage people in accomplishing work:

_____ 59. I help people feel competent in their work by recognizing and celebrating their small successes.

_____ 60. I provide regular feedback and needed support.

_____ 61. I try to provide all the information that people need to accomplish their tasks.

_____ 62. I highlight the important impact that a person's work will have.

When engaging others in work:

_____ 63. I specify clearly the results I desire.

_____ 64. I specify clearly the level of initiative I want others to take (for example, wait for directions, do part of the task and then report, do the whole task and then report, and so forth).

_____ 65. I allow participation by those accepting assignments regarding when and how work will be done.

_____ 66. I avoid upward delegation by asking people to recommend solutions, rather than merely asking for advice or answers, when a problem is encountered.

_____ 67. I follow up and maintain accountability for delegated tasks on a regular basis.

When I am in the role of leader in a team:

_____ 68. I know how to establish credibility and influence among team members.

_____ 69. I am clear and consistent about what I want to achieve.

_____ 70. I build a common base of agreement in the team before moving forward with task accomplishment.

_____ 71. I articulate a clear, motivating vision of what the team can achieve along with specific short-term goals.

When I am in the role of team member:

_____ 72. I know a variety of ways to facilitate task accomplishment in the team.

_____ 73. I know a variety of ways to help build strong relationships and cohesion among team members.

When I desire to make my team perform well, regardless of whether I am a leader or member:

_____ 74. I am knowledgeable about the different stages of team development experienced by most teams.

_____ 75. I help the team avoid groupthink by making sure that sufficient diversity of opinions is expressed in the team.

_____ 76. I can diagnose and capitalize on my team's core competencies, or unique strengths.

_____ 77. I encourage the team to achieve dramatic breakthrough innovations as well as small continuous improvements.

When I am in a position to lead change:

_____ 78. I create positive energy in others when I interact with them.

_____ 79. I emphasize a higher purpose or meaning associated with the change I am leading.

_____ 80. I express gratitude frequently and conspicuously, even for small acts.

_____ 81. I emphasize building on strengths, not just overcoming weaknesses.

_____ 82. I use a lot more positive comments than negative comments.

_____ 83. When I communicate a vision, I capture people's hearts as well as their heads.

_____ 84. I know how to get people to commit to my vision of positive change.

What Does It Take to Be an Effective Manager?

The purpose of this exercise is to help you get a firsthand picture of the role of a manager and the skills required to perform that job successfully.

Your assignment is to interview at least three managers who are employed full-time. You should use the questions below in your interviews, plus use others that you think might help you identify effective management skills. The purpose of these interviews is to give you a chance to learn about critical managerial skills from those who have to use them.

Please treat the interviews as confidential. The names of the individuals do not matter—only their opinions, perceptions, and behaviors. Assure the managers that no one will be able to identify them from their responses. Keep written notes of your interviews. These notes should be as detailed as possible so you can reconstruct the interviews later. Be sure to keep a record of each person's job title and a brief description of his or her organization.

1. Please describe a typical day at work. What do you do all day?

2. What are the most critical problems you face as a manager?

3. What are the most critical skills needed to be a successful manager in your line of work?

4. What are the major reasons managers fail in positions like yours?

5. What are the outstanding skills or abilities of other effective managers you have known?

6. If you had to train someone to replace you in your current job, what key abilities would you focus on?

7. On a scale of 1 (very rarely) to 5 (constantly), can you rate the extent to which you use the following skills or behaviors during your workday?

_____ Managing personal time and stress	_____ Fostering continuous improvement and quality
_____ Facilitating group decision making	_____ Making analytical decisions
_____ Creative problem solving	_____ Using interpersonal communication skills
_____ Articulating an energizing vision	_____ Motivating others
_____ Managing conflict	_____ Capitalizing on your self-awareness
_____ Gaining and using power	_____ Facilitating organizational change
_____ Delegating	_____ Setting specific goals and targets
_____ Active listening	_____ Empowering others
_____ Holding interviews	_____ Giving speeches or presentations
_____ Building teams and teamwork	_____ Defining and/or solving complex problems
_____ Conducting meetings	_____ Negotiating

SSS Software In-Basket Exercise

NOTE: *The SSS Software exercise is used with permission. Copyright © 1995 by Susan Schor, Joseph Seltzer, and James Smither. All rights reserved.*

One way to assess your own strengths and weaknesses in management skills is to engage in an actual managerial work experience. The following exercise gives you a realistic glimpse of the tasks faced regularly by practicing managers. Complete the exercise, and then compare your own decisions and actions with those of classmates.

SSS Software designs and develops customized software for businesses. It also integrates this software with the customer's existing systems and provides system maintenance. SSS Software has customers in the following industries: airlines, automotive, finance/banking, health/hospital, consumer products, electronics, and government. The company has also begun to generate important international clients. These include the European Airbus consortium and a consortium of banks and financial firms based in Kenya.

SSS Software has grown rapidly since its inception eight years ago. Its revenue, net income, and earnings per share have all been above the industry average for the past several years. However, competition in this technologically sophisticated field has grown very rapidly. Recently, it has become more difficult to compete for major contracts. Moreover, although SSS Software's revenue and net income continue to grow, the rate of growth declined during the last fiscal year.

SSS Software's 250 employees are divided into several operating divisions with employees at four levels: Nonmanagement, Technical/Professional, Managerial, and Executive. Nonmanagement employees take care of the clerical and facilities support functions. The Technical/Professional staff performs the core technical work for the firm. Most Managerial employees are group managers who supervise a team of Technical/Professional employees working on a project for a particular customer. Staff who work in specialized areas such as finance, accounting, human resources, nursing, and law are also considered Managerial employees. The Executive level includes the 12 highest-ranking employees at SSS Software. An organization chart in Figure 3 illustrates SSS Software's structure. There is also an Employee Classification Report that lists the number of employees at each level of the organization.

In this exercise, you will play the role of Chris Perillo, Vice President of Operations for Health and Financial Services. You learned last Wednesday, October 13, that your predecessor, Michael Grant, had resigned and gone to Universal Business Solutions, Inc. You were offered his former job, and you accepted it. Previously, you were the Group Manager for a team of 15 software developers assigned to work on the Airbus consortium project in the Airline Services Division. You spent all of Thursday, Friday, and most of the weekend finishing up parts of the project, briefing your successor, and preparing for an interim report you will deliver in Paris on October 21.

It is now 7:00 A.M. Monday and you are in your new office. You have arrived at work early so you can spend the next two hours reviewing material in your in-basket (including some memos and messages to Michael Grant), as well as your voicemail and e-mail. Your daily planning book indicates that you have no appointments today or tomorrow but will have to catch a plane for Paris early Wednesday morning. You have a full schedule for the remainder of the week and all of next week.

Assignment

During the next two hours, review all the material in your in-basket, as well as your voicemail and e-mail. Take only two hours. Using the response form below as a model, indicate how you want to respond to each item (that is, via letter/memo, e-mail, phone/voicemail,

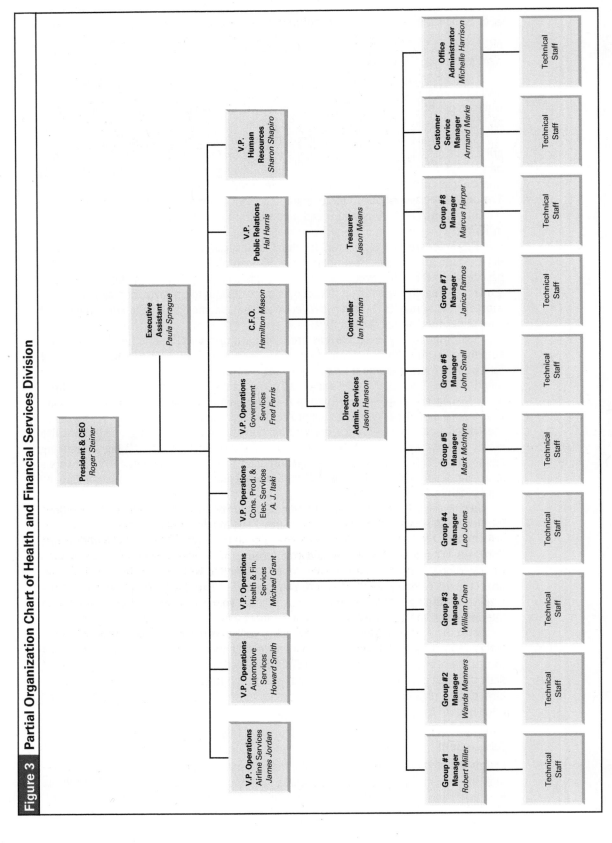

Figure 3 Partial Organization Chart of Health and Financial Services Division

or personal meeting). If you decide not to respond to an item, check "no response" on the response form. All your responses must be written on the response forms. Write your precise, detailed response (do not merely jot down a few notes). For example, you might draft a memo or write out a message that you will deliver via phone/voicemail. You may also decide to meet with an individual (or individuals) during the limited time available on your calendar today or tomorrow. If so, prepare an agenda for a personal meeting and list your goals for the meeting. As you read through the items, you may occasionally observe some information that you think is relevant and want to remember (or attend to in the future) but that you decide not to include in any of your responses to employees. Write down such information on a sheet of paper titled "note to self."

Sample Response Form

Relates to:

Memo # _____   E-mail # _____   Voicemail # _____

Response form:

_____ Letter/Memo   _____ Meet with person (when, where)

_____ E-mail   _____ Note to self

_____ Phone call/Voicemail   _____ No response

ITEM 1 – E-MAIL

TO: All Employees
FROM: Roger Steiner, Chief Executive Officer
DATE: October 15

I am pleased to announce that Chris Perillo has been appointed as Vice President of Operations for Health and Financial Services. Chris will immediately assume responsibility for all operations previously managed by Michael Grant. Chris will have end-to-end responsibility for the design, development, integration, and maintenance of custom software for the health and finance/banking industries. This responsibility includes all technical, financial, and staffing issues. Chris will also manage our program of software support and integration for the recently announced merger of three large health maintenance organizations (HMOs). Chris will be responsible for our recently announced project with a consortium of banks and financial firms operating in Tanzania. This project represents an exciting opportunity for us, and Chris's background seems ideally suited to the task.

Chris comes to this position with an undergraduate degree in Computer Science from the California Institute of Technology and an M.B.A. from the University of Virginia. Chris began as a member of our technical/professional staff six years ago and has most recently served for three years as a Group Manager supporting domestic and international projects for our airlines industry group, including our recent work for the European Airbus consortium.

I am sure you all join me in offering congratulations to Chris for this promotion.

ITEM 2 – E-MAIL

TO: All Managers
FROM: Hal Harris, Vice President, Community and Public Relations
DATE: October 15

For your information, the following article appeared on the front page of the business section of Thursday's *Los Angeles Times*.

In a move that may create problems for SSS Software, Michael Grant and Janice Ramos have left SSS Software and moved to Universal Business Solutions Inc. Industry analysts see the move as another victory for Universal Business Solutions Inc. in their battle with SSS Software for share of the growing software development and integration business. Both Grant and Ramos had been with SSS Software for over seven years. Grant was most recently Vice President of Operations for all SSS Software's work in two industries: health and hospitals, and finance and banking. Ramos brings to Universal Business Solutions Inc. her special expertise in the growing area of international software development and integration.

Hillary Collins, an industry analyst with Merrill Lynch, said "the loss of key staff to a competitor can often create serious problems for a firm such as SSS Software. Grant and Ramos have an insider's understanding of SSS Software's strategic and technical limitations. It will be interesting to see if they can exploit this knowledge to the advantage of Universal Business Solutions Inc."

ITEM 3 – E-MAIL

TO: Chris Perillo
FROM: Paula Sprague, Executive Assistant to Roger Steiner
DATE: October 15

Chris, I know that in your former position as a Group Manager in the Airline Services Division, you probably have met most of the group managers in the Health and Financial Services Division, but I thought you might like some more personal information about them. These people will be your direct reports on the management team.

Group #1: Bob Miller, 55-year-old white male, married (Anna) with two children and three grandchildren. Active in local Republican politics. Well regarded as a "hands-off" manager heading a high-performing team. Plays golf regularly with Mark McIntyre, John Small, and a couple of V.P.s from other divisions.

Group #2: Wanda Manners, 38-year-old white female, single with one school-age child. A fitness "nut" has run in several marathons. Some experience in Germany and Japan. Considered a hard-driving manager with a constant focus on the task at hand. Will be the first person to show up every morning.

Group #3: William Chen, 31-year-old male of Chinese descent, married (Harriet), two young children from his first marriage. Enjoys tennis and is quite good at it. A rising star in the company, he is highly respected by his peers as a "man of action" and a good friend.

Group #4: Leo Jones, 36-year-old white male, married (Janet) with an infant daughter. Recently returned from paternity leave. Has traveled extensively on projects, since he speaks three languages. Has liked hockey ever since the time he spent in Montreal. Considered a strong manager who gets the most out of his people.

Group #5: Mark McIntyre, 45-year-old white male, married (Mary Theresa) to an executive in the banking industry. No children. A lot of experience in Germany and Eastern Europe. Has been writing a mystery novel. Has always been a good "team player," but several members of his technical staff are not well respected and he hasn't addressed the problem.

Group #6: John Small, 38-year-old white male, recently divorced. Three children living with his wife. A gregarious individual who likes sports. He spent a lot of time in Mexico and Central America before he came to SSS Software. Recently has been doing mostly contract work with the federal government. An average manager, has had some trouble keeping his people on schedule.

Group #7: This position vacant since Janice Ramos left. Roger thinks we ought to fill this position quickly. Get in touch with me if you want information on any in-house candidates for any position.

Group #8: Marcus Harper, 42-year-old black African American, married (Tamara) with two teenage children. Recently won an award in a local photography contest. Considered a strong manager who gets along with peers and works long hours.

Customer Services: Armad Marke, 38-year-old male, divorced. A basketball fan. Originally from Armenia. Previously a Group Manager. Worked hard to establish the Technical Services Phone Line, but now has pretty much left it alone.

Office Administrator: Michelle Harrison, 41-year-old white female, single. Grew up on a ranch and still rides horses whenever she can. A strict administrator.

There are a number of good folks here, but they don't function well as a management team. I think Michael played favorites, especially with Janice and Leo. There are a few cliques in this group and I'm not sure how effectively Michael dealt with them. I expect you will find it a challenge to build a cohesive team.

ITEM 4 – E-MAIL

TO: Chris Perillo
FROM: Wanda Manners, Group 2 Manager
DATE: October 15

CONFIDENTIAL AND RESTRICTED

Although I know you are new to your job, I feel it is important that I let you know about some information I just obtained concerning the development work we recently completed for First National Investment. Our project involved the development of asset management software for managing their international funds. This was a very complex project due to the volatile exchange rates and the forecasting tools we needed to develop.

As part of this project, we had to integrate the software and reports with all their existing systems and reporting mechanisms. To do this, we were given access to all of their existing software (much of which was developed by Universal Business Solutions Inc.). Of course, we signed an agreement acknowledging that the software to which we were given access was proprietary and that our access was solely for the purpose of our system integration work associated with the project.

Unfortunately, I have learned that some parts of the software we developed actually "borrow" heavily from complex application programs developed for First National Investment by Universal Business Solutions Inc. It seems obvious to me that one or more of the software developers from Group 5 (that is, Mark McIntyre's group) inappropriately "borrowed" algorithms developed by Universal Business Solutions Inc. I am sure that doing so saved us significant development time on some aspects of the project. It seems very unlikely that First National Investment or Universal Business Solutions Inc. will ever become aware of this issue.

Finally, First National Investment is successfully using the software we developed and is thrilled with the work we did. We brought the project in on time and under budget. You probably know that they have invited us to bid on several other substantial projects.

I'm sorry to bring this delicate matter to your attention, but I thought you should know about it.

ITEM 5A – E-MAIL

TO: Chris Perillo
FROM: Paula Sprague, Executive Assistant to Roger Steiner
DATE: October 15

RE: Letter from C.A.R.E. Services (copies attached)

Roger asked me to work on this C.A.R.E. project and obviously wants some fast action. A lot of the staff are already booked solid for the next couple of weeks. I knew that Elise Soto and Chu Hung Woo have the expertise to do this system and when I checked with them, they were relatively free. I had them pencil in the next two weeks and wanted to let you know. Hopefully, it will take a "hot potato" out of your hands.

ITEM 5B – COPY OF FAX

C.A.R.E.
Child and Adolescent Rehabilitative and Educational Services
A United Way Member Agency
200 Main Street
Los Angeles, California 90230

DATE: October 11
Roger Steiner, CEO
SSS Software
13 Miller Way
Los Angeles, California 90224

Dear Roger,

This letter is a follow-up to our conversation after last night's board meeting. I appreciated your comments during the board meeting about the need for sophisticated computer systems in nonprofit organizations and I especially appreciate your generous offer of assistance to have SSS Software provide assistance to deal with the immediate problem with our accounting system. Since the board voted to fire the computer consultant, I am very worried about getting our reports done in time to meet the state funding cycle.

Thanks again for your offer of help during this crisis.

Sincerely yours,

Janice Polocizwic

Janice Polocizwic
Executive Director

ITEM 5C – COPY OF A LETTER

SSS SOFTWARE
13 Miller Way
Los Angeles, CA 90224

DATE: October 12

Janice Polocizwic
Executive Director, C.A.R.E. Services
200 Main Street
Los Angeles, California 90230

Dear Janice,

I received your fax of October 11. I have asked Paula Sprague, my executive assistant, to line up people to work on your accounting system as soon as possible. You can expect to hear from her shortly.

Sincerely,

Roger Steiner

Roger Steiner
cc: Paula Sprague, Executive Assistant

ITEM 6 – E-MAIL

TO: Michael Grant
FROM: Harry Withers, Group 6 Technical Staff
DATE: October 12

PERSONAL AND CONFIDENTIAL

Our team is having difficulty meeting the submission deadline of November 5 for the Halstrom project. Kim, Fred, Peter, Kyoto, Susan, Mala, and I have been working on the project for several weeks, but we are experiencing some problems and may need additional time. I hesitate to write this letter, but the main problem is that our group manager, John Small, is involved in a relationship with Mala. Mala gets John's support for her ideas and brings them to the team as required components of the project. Needless to say, this has posed some problems for the group. Mala's background is especially valuable for this project, but Kim and Fred, who have both worked very hard on the project, do not want to work with her. In addition, one member of the team has been unavailable recently because of child-care needs. Commitment to the project and team morale have plummeted. However, we'll do our best to get the project finished as soon as possible. Mala will be on vacation the next two weeks, so I'm expecting that some of us can complete it in her absence.

ITEM 7 – VOICEMAIL MESSAGE

Hello, Michael. This is Jim Bishop of United Hospitals. I wanted to talk with you about the quality assurance project that you are working on for us. When Jose Martinez first started talking with us, I was impressed with his friendliness and expertise. But recently, he doesn't seem to be getting much accomplished and has seemed distant and on-edge in conversations. Today, I asked him about the schedule and he seemed very defensive and not entirely in control of his emotions. I am quite concerned about our project. Please give me a call.

ITEM 8 – VOICEMAIL MESSAGE

Hi, Michael. This is Armand. I wanted to talk with you about some issues with the Technical Services Phone Line. I've recently received some complaint letters from Phone Line customers whose complaints have included long delays while waiting for a technician to answer the phone, technicians who are not knowledgeable enough to solve problems, and, on occasion, rude service. Needless to say, I'm quite concerned about these complaints.

I believe that the overall quality of the Phone Line staff is very good, but we continue to be understaffed, even with the recent hires. The new technicians look strong, but are working on the help-line before being fully trained. Antolina, our best tech, often brings her child to work, which is adding to the craziness around here.

I think you should know that we're feeling a lot of stress here. I'll talk with you soon.

ITEM 9 – VOICEMAIL MESSAGE

Hi, Chris, it's Pat. Congratulations on your promotion. They definitely picked the right person. It's great news—for me, too. You've been a terrific mentor so far, so I'm expecting to learn a lot from you in your new position. How about lunch next week?

ITEM 10 – VOICEMAIL MESSAGE

Chris, this is Bob Miller. Just thought you'd like to know that John's joke during our planning meeting has disturbed a few of the women in my group. Frankly, I think the thing's being blown out of proportion, especially since we all know this is a good place for both men and women to work. Give me a call if you want to chat about this.

ITEM 11 – VOICEMAIL MESSAGE

Hello. This is Lorraine Adams from Westside Hospital. I read in today's *Los Angeles Times* that you will be taking over from Michael Grant. We haven't met yet, but your division has recently finished two large million-dollar projects for Westside. Michael Grant and I had some discussion about a small conversion of a piece of existing software to be compatible with the new systems. The original vendor had said that they would do the work, but they have been stalling, and I need to move quickly. Can you see if Harris Wilson, Chu Hung Woo, and Elise Soto are available to do this work as soon as possible? They were on the original project and work well with our people.

Um…(long pause) I guess I should tell you that I got a call from Michael offering to do this work. But I think I should stick with SSS Software. Give me a call.

ITEM 12 – VOICEMAIL MESSAGE

Hi, Chris, this is Roosevelt Moore calling. I'm a member of your technical/professional staff. I used to report to Janice Ramos, but since she left the firm, I thought I'd bring my concerns directly to you. I'd like to arrange some time to talk with you about my experiences since returning from six weeks of paternity leave. Some of my major responsibilities have been turned over to others. I seem to be out of the loop and wonder if my career is at risk. Also, I am afraid that I won't be supported or seriously considered for the opening created by Janice's departure. Frankly, I feel like I'm being screwed for taking my leave. I'd like to talk with you this week.

ITEM 13 – E-MAIL

TO: Michael Grant
FROM: Jose Martinez, Group 1 Technical Staff
DATE: October 12

I would like to set up a meeting with you as soon as possible. I suspect that you will get a call from Jim Bishop of United Hospitals and want to be sure that you hear my side of the story first. I have been working on a customized system design for quality assurance for them using a variation of the J-3 product we developed several years ago. They had a number of special requirements and some quirks in their accounting systems, so I have had to put in especially long hours. I've worked hard to meet their demands, but they keep changing the ground rules. I keep thinking, this is just another J-3 I'm working on, but they have been interfering with an elegant design I have developed. It seems I'm not getting anywhere on this project. Earlier today, I had a difficult discussion with their Controller. He asked for another major change. I've been fighting their deadline and think I am just stretched too thin on this project. Then Jim Bishop asked me if the system was running yet. I was worn out from dealing with the Controller, and I made a sarcastic comment to Jim Bishop. He gave me a funny look and just walked out of the room.

I would like to talk with you about this situation at your earliest convenience.

ITEM 14 – E-MAIL

TO: Chris Perillo
FROM: John Small, Group 6 Manager
DATE: October 15

Welcome aboard, Chris. I look forward to meeting with you. I just wanted to put a bug in your ear about finding a replacement for Janice Ramos. One of my technical staff, Mala Abendano, has the ability and drive to make an excellent group manager. I have encouraged her to apply for the position. I'd be happy to talk with you further about this, at your convenience.

ITEM 15 – E-MAIL

TO: Chris Perillo
FROM: Paula Sprague, Executive Assistant to Roger Steiner
DATE: October 15

Roger asked me to let you know about the large contract we have gotten in Tanzania. It means that a team of four managers will be making a short trip to determine current needs. They will assign their technical staff the tasks of developing a system and software here over the next six months, and then the managers and possibly some team members will be spending about 10 months on site in Tanzania to handle the implementation. Roger thought you might want to hold an initial meeting with some of your managers to check on their interest and willingness to take this sort of assignment. Roger would appreciate an e-mail of your thoughts about the issues to be discussed at this meeting, additional considerations about sending people to Tanzania, and about how you will put together an effective team to work on this project. The October 15 memo I sent to you will provide you with some information you'll need to start making these decisions.

ITEM 16 – E-MAIL

TO: Chris Perillo
FROM: Sharon Shapiro, V.P. of Human Resources
DATE: October 15

RE: Upcoming meeting

I want to update you on the rippling effect of John Small's sexual joke at last week's planning meeting. Quite a few women have been very upset and have met informally to talk about it. They have decided to call a meeting of all people concerned about this kind of behavior throughout the firm. I plan to attend, so I'll keep you posted.

ITEM 17 – E-MAIL

TO: All SSS Software Managers
FROM: Sharon Shapiro, V.P. of Human Resources
DATE: October 15

RE: Promotions and External Hires

Year-to-Date (January through September) Promotions and External Hires

| | Race | | | | | Sex | | |
Level	White	African American	Asian	Hispanic	Native American	M	F	Total
Hires into Executive Level	0 (0%)	0 (0%)	0 (0%)	0 (0%)	0 (0%)	0 (0%)	0 (0%)	0
Promotions to Executive Level	0 (0%)	0 (0%)	0 (0%)	0 (0%)	0 (0%)	0 (0%)	0 (0%)	0

| | Race | | | | | Sex | | |
Level	White	African American	Asian	Hispanic	Native American	M	F	Total
Hires into Management Level	2 (67%)	1 (33%)	0 (0%)	0 (0%)	0 (0%)	2 (67%)	1 (33%)	3
Promotions to Management Level	7 (88%)	0 (0%)	1 (12%)	0 (0%)	0 (0%)	7 (88%)	1 (12%)	8
Hires into Technical/ Professional Level	10 (36%)	6 (21%)	10 (36%)	2 (7%)	0 (0%)	14 (50%)	14 (50%)	28
Promotions to Technical/ Professional Level	0 (0%)	0 (0%)	0 (0%)	0 (0%)	0 (0%)	0 (0%)	0 (0%)	0
Hires into Non-Management Level	4 (20%)	10 (50%)	2 (10%)	4 (20%)	0 (0%)	6 (30%)	14 (70%)	20
Promotions to Non-Management Level	NA	NA	NA	NA	NA	NA	NA	NA

SSS Software Employee (EEO) Classification Report as of June 30

| | Race | | | | | Sex | | |
Level	White	African American	Asian	Hispanic	Native American	M	F	Total
Executive Level	11 (92%)	0 (0%)	1 (8%)	0 (0%)	0 (0%)	11 (92%)	1 (8%)	12
Management Level	43 (90%)	2 (4%)	2 (4%)	1 (2%)	0 (0%)	38 (79%)	10 (21%)	48
Technical/ Professional Level	58 (45%)	20 (15%)	37 (28%)	14 (11%)	1 (1%)	80 (62%)	50 (38%)	130
Non-Management Level	29 (48%)	22 (37%)	4 (7%)	4 (7%)	1 (2%)	12 (20%)	48 (80%)	60
Total	141 (56%)	44 (18%)	44 (18%)	19 (8%)	2 (1%)	141 (56%)	109 (44%)	250

If your instructor is utilizing **MyManagementLab**, log onto mymanagementlab.com and select the Personal Inventory Assessment (PIA) section to complete the following instrument Personal Assessment of Management Skills (PAMS).

SCORING KEY AND COMPARISON DATA

✪ Scoring Keys for the following instruments, along with comparison data, are contained in PIA in MyManagementLab.com; Personal Assessment of Management Skills (PAMS).

Personal Assessment of Management Skills

Scoring Key

SKILL AREA	ITEMS	ASSESSMENT	
		PERSONAL	ASSOCIATES
Developing Self-Awareness	**1–5**		
Self-disclosure and openness	1–2		
Awareness of self	3–5		
Managing Stress	**6–11**		
Eliminating stressors	6–7		
Developing resiliency	8–9		
Short-term coping	10–11		
Solving Problems Creatively	**12–23**		
Rational problem solving	12–14		
Creative problem solving	15–19		
Fostering innovation and creativity	20–23		
Communicating Supportively	**24–32**		
Coaching and counseling	24–25		
Effective negative feedback	26–28		
Communicating supportively	29–32		
Gaining Power and Influence	**33–40**		
Gaining power	33–37		
Exercising influence	38–40		
Motivating Others	**41–49**		
Managing Conflict	**50–58**		
Initiating	50–52		
Responding	53–55		
Mediating	56–58		
Empowering and Engaging	**59–67**		
Empowering	59–62		
Delegating	63–67		

SKILL AREA	ITEMS	ASSESSMENT	
		PERSONAL	ASSOCIATES
Building Effective Teams and Teamwork	**68–77**		
Leading teams	68–71		
Team membership	72–73		
Teamwork	74–77		
Leading Positive Change	**78–84**		
Foster positive deviance	78–80		
Lead positive change	81–82		
Mobilize others	83–84		

Comparison Data (N = 5,000 students)

Compare your scores with at least four referents: (1) If you asked others to rate you using the Associates' version, compare how you rated yourself with how your associates rated you. (2) Compare the ratings you received to those received by other students in the class. (3) Compare the ratings you received to a norm group of approximately 5,000 business school students (see the information below). (4) Compare your score against the maximum possible (510).

For the survey as a whole, if you scored

394.35	=	mean
422 or above	=	you are in the top quartile.
395–421	=	you are in the second quartile.
369–394	=	you are in the third quartile.
368 or below	=	you are in the bottom quartile.

What Does It Take to Be an Effective Manager?

This exercise does not have a solution or scoring data. Answers will vary among students.

SSS Software In-Basket Exercise

This exercise does not have a solution or scoring data. Answers will vary among students.

Part I

Personal Skills

CHAPTERS

1 **DEVELOPING SELF-AWARENESS**
Assessing emotional intelligence
Determining values and moral maturity
Identifying cognitive style
Assessing attitude toward change
Understanding core self-evaluation

2 **MANAGING PERSONAL STRESS**
Coping with stressors
Managing time
Developing resiliency

3 **SOLVING PROBLEMS ANALYTICALLY AND CREATIVELY**
Using the rational approach
Using the creative approach
Fostering innovation in others

SKILL *ASSESSMENT*

- Self-Awareness Assessment
- Emotional Intelligence Assessment
- The Defining Issues Test
- Cognitive Style Indicator
- Locus of Control Scale
- Tolerance of Ambiguity Scale
- Core Self-Evaluation Scale (CSES)

SKILL *LEARNING*

- Key Dimensions of Self-Awareness
- The Enigma of Self-Awareness
- Understanding and Appreciating Individual Differences
- Important Areas of Self-Awareness
- Summary
- Behavioral Guidelines

SKILL *ANALYSIS*

- Communist Prison Camp
- Computerized Exam
- Decision Dilemmas

SKILL *PRACTICE*

- Through the Looking Glass
- Diagnosing Managerial Characteristics
- An Exercise for Identifying Aspects of Personal Culture:
  A Learning Plan and Autobiography

SKILL *APPLICATION*

- Suggested Assignments
- Application Plan and Evaluation

SCORING KEYS AND *COMPARISON DATA*

MyManagementLab™

✪ When you see this icon, visit www.mymanagementlab.com
for self-assessments, video activities, and more.

1

Developing Self-Awareness

LEARNING OBJECTIVES

Increase personal awareness
of your:

1. SENSITIVE LINE
2. EMOTIONAL INTELLIGENCE
3. PERSONAL VALUES AND MORAL MATURITY
4. COGNITIVE STYLE
5. ORIENTATION TOWARD CHANGE
6. CORE SELF-EVALUATION

SKILL *ASSESSMENT* (?)

DIAGNOSTIC SURVEYS FOR DEVELOPING SELF-AWARENESS

✪ If your instructor is utilizing **MyManagementLab**, log onto mymanagementlab. com and select the Personal Inventory Assessment (PIA) section and complete the instruments associated with this chapter.

The assessment instruments in this chapter are briefly described below. The assessments appear either in your text or in PIA. The assessments marked with (blue star) are available only in PIA.

All assessments should be completed before reading the chapter material.

After completing the first assessment save your response to your hard drive. When you have finished reading the chapter, re-take the assessment and compare your responses to see what you have learned.

✪ ❏ The *Self-Awareness Assessment Instrument* measures the extent to which you are self-aware and effectively engage in self-awareness practices.
✪ ❏ The *Emotional Intelligence Assessment* measures your emotional style and intelligence.
❏ The *Defining Issues Test* assesses your moral and values maturity based on your responses to controversial social issues.
❏ The *Cognitive Style Indicator* assesses the way you gather and evaluate information and make decisions.
✪ ❏ The *Locus of Control Scale* measures your opinion about the causes and influences of certain events in your life.
❏ The *Tolerance of Ambiguity Scale* assesses the extent to which you are comfortable in situations where ambiguity and uncertainty are present.
❏ The *Core Self-Evaluation Scale* measures core personality attributes that predict human behavior.

DEVELOPING SELF-AWARENESS

Assessment Section

THE DEFINING ISSUES TEST

This instrument assesses your opinions about controversial social issues. Different people make decisions about these issues in different ways. You should answer the questions for yourself without discussing them with others.

You are presented with three stories. Following each story you are asked to choose between three decisions. Next, you will rate the importance of 12 questions about the story in influencing your decision. After you have completed your ratings, select the four most important questions and rank them from one to four in the spaces provided.

Some statements will raise important issues, but you should ask yourself whether your decision should rest on that issue. Some statements sound high and lofty but are largely gibberish. If you cannot make sense of a statement, or if you don't understand its meaning, mark it 5—"Of no importance." Use the following scale for rating the importance of the statements.

Rating Scale

1	Of great importance	This statement or question makes a crucial difference in making a decision about the problem.
2	Of much importance	This statement or question is something that would be a major factor (though not always a crucial one) in making a decision.
3	Of some importance	This statement or question involves something you care about, but it is not of great importance in reaching a decision.
4	Of little importance	This statement or question is not very important to consider in this case.
5	Of no importance	This statement or question is completely unimportant in making a decision. You would waste your time thinking about it.

The Escaped Prisoner

A man had been sentenced to prison for 10 years. After one year, however, he escaped from prison, moved to a new area of the country, and took on the name of Thompson. For eight years he worked hard, and gradually he saved enough money to buy his own business. He was fair to his customers, gave his employees top wages, and gave most of his own profits to charity. Then one day, Ms. Jones, an old neighbor, recognized him as the man who had escaped from prison eight years before and for whom the police had been looking.

What should Ms. Jones do? (Check one.)

_____ Report him—send him back to prison
_____ Can't decide
_____ Not report him

Importance

_____ 1. Hasn't Mr. Thompson been good enough for such a long time to prove he isn't a bad person?

_____ 2. Every time someone escapes punishment for a crime, doesn't that just encourage more crime?

_____ 3. Wouldn't we be better off without prisons and the oppression of our legal system?

_____ 4. Has Mr. Thompson really paid his debt to society?

_____ 5. Would society be failing what Mr. Thompson should fairly expect?

_____ 6. What benefit would prison be apart from society, especially for a charitable man?

_____ 7. How could anyone be so cruel and heartless as to send Mr. Thompson to prison?

_____ 8. Would it be fair to prisoners who have to serve out their full sentences if Mr. Thompson is let off?

_____ 9. Was Ms. Jones a good friend of Mr. Thompson?

_____ 10. Wouldn't it be a citizen's duty to report an escaped criminal, regardless of the circumstances?

_____ 11. How would the will of the people and the public good best be served?

_____ 12. Would going to prison do any good for Mr. Thompson or protect anybody?

From the list of questions above, select the four most important:

_____ Most important
_____ Second most important
_____ Third most important
_____ Fourth most important

The Doctor's Dilemma

A woman was dying of incurable cancer and had only about six months to live. She was in terrible pain, but was so weak that a large dose of a pain killer such as morphine would probably kill her. She was delirious with pain, and in her calm periods, she would ask her doctor to give her enough morphine to kill her. She said she couldn't stand the pain and that she was going to die in a few months anyway.

What should the doctor do? (Check one.)

_____ Give the woman an overdose that will make her die
_____ Can't decide
_____ Don't give her the overdose

Importance

_____ 1. Is the woman's family in favor of giving her the overdose?

_____ 2. Is the doctor obligated by the same laws as everybody else?

_____ 3. Would people be better off without society regimenting their lives and even their deaths?

_____ 4. Should the doctor make the woman's death from a drug overdose appear to be an accident?

_____ 5. Does the state have the right to force continued existence on those who don't want to live?

_____ 6. What is the value of death prior to society's perspective on personal values?

_____ 7. Should the doctor have sympathy for the woman's suffering, or should he care more about what society might think?

_____ 8. Is helping to end another's life ever a responsible act of cooperation?

_____ 9. Can only God decide when a person's life should end?

_____ 10. What values has the doctor set for himself in his own personal code of behavior?

_____ 11. Can society afford to let anybody end his or her life whenever he or she desires?

_____ 12. Can society allow suicide or mercy killing and still protect the lives of individuals who want to live?

From the list of questions above, select the four most important:

_____ Most important
_____ Second most important
_____ Third most important
_____ Fourth most important

The Newspaper

Rami, a senior in high school, wanted to publish a mimeographed newspaper for students so that he could express his opinions. He wanted to speak out against military build-up and some of the school's rules, such as the rule forbidding boys to wear long hair.

When Rami started his newspaper, he asked his principal for permission. The principal said it would be all right if before every publication Rami would turn in all his articles for the principal's approval. Rami agreed and turned in several articles for approval. The principal approved all of them and he published two issues of the paper in the next two weeks.

But, the principal had not expected that Rami's newspaper would receive so much attention. Students were so excited by the paper that they began to organize protests against the government, hair regulation, and other school rules. Angry parents objected to Rami's opinions. They phoned the principal telling him that the newspaper was unpatriotic and should not be published. As a result of the rising excitement, the principal wondered if he should order Rami to stop publishing on the grounds that the controversial newspaper articles were disrupting the operation of the school.

What should the principal do? (Check one.)

_____ Stop Rami's newspaper
_____ Can't decide
_____ Don't stop it

Importance

____ 1. Is the principal more responsible to the students or to the parents?
____ 2. Did the principal give his word that the newspaper could be published for a long time, or did he just promise to approve the newspaper one issue at a time?
____ 3. Would the students start protesting even more if the principal stopped the newspaper?
____ 4. When the welfare of the school is threatened, does the principal have the right to give orders to students?
____ 5. Does the principal have the freedom of speech to say no in this case?
____ 6. If the principal stopped the newspaper, would he be preventing full discussion of important problems?
____ 7. Would the principal's stop order make Rami lose faith in him?
____ 8. Is Rami really loyal to his school and patriotic to his country?
____ 9. What effect would stopping the paper have on the students' education in critical thinking and judgment?
____ 10. Is Rami in any way violating the rights of others in publishing his own opinions?
____ 11. Should the principal be influenced by some angry parents when it is the principal who knows best what is going on in the school?
____ 12. Is Rami using the newspaper to stir up hatred and discontent?

From the list of questions above, select the four most important:

_____ Most important
_____ Second most important
_____ Third most important
_____ Fourth most important

SOURCE: *Adapted from* Rest, Narvaez, Thoma, & Bebeau, 1999.

COGNITIVE STYLE INDICATOR

This instrument assesses the way you gather and evaluate information and make decisions. There are no right or wrong answers, and the accuracy of your results will depend on the extent to which you honestly answer each question. Please use the following scale in responding to each item.

Rating Scale

1 Totally disagree
2 Disagree
3 Neither agree nor disagree
4 Agree
5 Totally agree

_____ 1. Developing a clear plan is very important to me.

_____ 2. I like to contribute to innovative solutions.

_____ 3. I always want to know what should be done when.

_____ 4. I prefer to look at creative solutions.

_____ 5. I want to have a full understanding of a problem.

_____ 6. I like detailed action plans.

_____ 7. I am motivated by ongoing innovation.

_____ 8. I like to analyze problems.

_____ 9. I prefer a clear structure to do my job.

_____ 10. I like a lot of variety in my life.

_____ 11. I engage in detailed analyses.

_____ 12. I prefer well-planned meetings with a clear agenda.

_____ 13. New ideas attract me more than existing solutions.

_____ 14. I study each problem until I understand the underlying logic.

_____ 15. I make definite appointments and follow-up meticulously.

_____ 16. I like to extend the boundaries.

_____ 17. A good task is a well-prepared task.

_____ 18. I try to avoid routine.

SOURCE: _Cognitive Style Indicator, Cools, E. and H. Van den Broeck. (2007) "Development and Validation of the Cognitive Style Indicator."_ Journal of Psychology, _14: 359–387._

TOLERANCE OF AMBIGUITY SCALE

This assessment helps you better understand how comfortable you are with situations that are inherently ambiguous. Inasmuch as this is a self-diagnostic tool, candid, realistic responses are essential.

Please respond to the following statements by indicating the extent to which you agree or disagree with them. Fill in the blanks with the number from the rating scale that best represents your evaluation of the item.

Rating Scale

1 Strongly disagree
2 Moderately disagree
3 Slightly disagree
4 Neither agree nor disagree
5 Slightly agree
6 Moderately agree
7 Strongly agree

_____ 1. An expert who doesn't come up with a definite answer probably doesn't know too much.

_____ 2. I would like to live in a foreign country for a while.

_____ 3. There is really no such thing as a problem that can't be solved.

_____ 4. People who fit their lives to a schedule probably miss most of the joy of living.

_____ 5. A good job is one where what is to be done and how it is to be done are always clear.

_____ 6. It is more fun to tackle a complicated problem than to solve a simple one.

_____ 7. In the long run it is possible to get more done by tackling small, simple problems rather than large and complicated ones.

_____ 8. Often the most interesting and stimulating people are those who don't mind being different and original.

_____ 9. What we are used to is always preferable to what is unfamiliar.

_____ 10. People who insist upon a yes or no answer just don't know how complicated things really are.

_____ 11. A person who leads an even, regular life in which few surprises or unexpected happenings arise really has a lot to be grateful for.

_____ 12. Many of our most important decisions are based upon insufficient information.

_____ 13. I like parties where I know most of the people more than ones where all or most of the people are complete strangers.

_____ 14. Teachers or supervisors who hand out vague assignments give one a chance to show initiative and originality.

_____ 15. The sooner we all acquire similar values and ideals the better.

_____ 16. A good teacher is one who makes you wonder about your way of looking at things.

SOURCE: *S. Budner (1962), "Intolerance of Ambiguity as a Personality Variable," from* Journal of Personality, *30: 29–50. Reprinted with the permission of Blackwell Publishing, Ltd.*

CORE SELF-EVALUATION SCALE (CSES)

Research has identified four core elements of self-evaluations. This instrument will help you identify the component parts of your overall self-evaluation. Inasmuch as this is a diagnostic tool, candid, realistic responses are essential.

Below are several statements with which you may agree or disagree. Using the response scale below, indicate your level of agreement or disagreement with each statement.

Rating Scale

1 Strongly disagree
2 Disagree
3 Neutral
4 Agree
5 Strongly agree

_____   1. I am confident I get the success I deserve in life.

_____   2. Sometimes I feel depressed.

_____   3. When I try, I generally succeed.

_____   4. Sometimes when I fail I feel worthless.

_____   5. I complete tasks successfully.

_____   6. Sometimes, I do not feel in control of my work.

_____   7. Overall, I am satisfied with myself.

_____   8. I am filled with doubts about my competence.

_____   9. I determine what will happen in my life.

_____   10. I do not feel in control of my success in my career.

_____   11. I am capable of coping with most of my problems.

_____   12. There are times when things look pretty bleak and hopeless to me.

SOURCE: _T. Judge, A. Erez, J. Bono, and C. Thoreson. The core self-evaluation scale: Development of a measure,_ Personnel Psychology, _2003: 303–331._

SKILL *LEARNING*

Key Dimensions of Self-Awareness

For more than 2000 years, knowledge of the self has been considered at the very core of human behavior. The ancient dictum "Know thyself" has been variously attributed to Plato, Pythagoras, Thales, and Socrates. Plutarch noted that this inscription was carved on the Delphic Oracle, that mystical sanctuary where kings and generals sought advice on matters of greatest importance to them. Probably the most oft-quoted passage on the self is Polonius' advice in Hamlet: "To thine own self be true, and it must follow as the night the day, thou canst not then be false to any man."

Philip Massinger reminded us: "He that would govern others must first master himself." Lao Tsu famously stated: "Knowing others is intelligence. Knowing oneself is true wisdom. Mastering others is strength; mastering yourself is true power." Because **self-awareness** lies at the heart of the ability to master oneself and therefore to lead and manage others

effectively, this chapter serves as the foundation for managing oneself and others. Of course, a host of techniques and methods for achieving self-knowledge have long been available—including group methods, meditation and contemplation techniques, altered consciousness procedures, aromatherapy, assorted massages, physical exercise regimens, and biofeedback. More than 195,000 self-help books are currently available on Amazon.com, and it is estimated that Americans spend between $30 billion and $50 billion on self-help therapies.

In this chapter, we do not summarize these various approaches to enhanced self-awareness, nor do we espouse any one procedure in particular. Instead, our objective is to help you understand the importance of self-awareness as a foundation for improving your ability to be a successful manager and a successful person. We provide you with some powerful self-assessment instruments that are predictive of managerial success. By completing these instruments, you will develop an understanding of several key aspects of your own strengths, inclinations, and styles. Our emphasis in this chapter, and throughout the book, is on scientifically validated information linking self-awareness to successful management. We try to avoid generalizations and prescriptions that have not been tested in research.

The Enigma of Self-Awareness

Erich Fromm (1939) was one of the first behavioral scientists to observe the close connection between self-concept and our feelings about others: "Hatred against oneself is inseparable from hatred against others." Carl Rogers (1961) later proposed that self-awareness and self-acceptance are prerequisites for psychological health, personal growth, and the ability to know and accept others. In fact, Rogers suggested that the basic human need is for self-regard, which he found to be more powerful in his clinical cases than physiological needs. In addition, Brouwer (1964, p. 156) asserted that all personal change is preceded by self-awareness:

> The function of self-examination is to lay the groundwork for insight, without which no growth can occur. Insight is the "Oh, I see now" feeling which must consciously or unconsciously precede change in behavior. Insights—real, genuine glimpses of ourselves as we really are—are reached only with difficulty and sometimes with real psychic pain. But they are the building blocks of growth. Thus, self-examination is a preparation for insight, a groundbreaking for the seeds of self-understanding which gradually bloom into changed behavior.

The knowledge we possess about ourselves, which produces our self-concept, is central to improving our management skills. We cannot improve ourselves or develop new capabilities unless we know what level of capability we possess. Considerable empirical evidence suggests that individuals who are self-aware are healthier, perform better in managerial and leadership roles, and are more productive at work (Boyatzis, 2008; Cervone, 1997; Duval, Silva, Lalwani, 2001; Spencer & Spencer, 2008).

On the other hand, self-knowledge may inhibit personal improvement rather than facilitate it because individuals frequently avoid personal growth and new self-knowledge. They resist acquiring additional information in order to protect their self-esteem or

self-respect. If they acquire new knowledge about themselves, it's possible that it will be negative or lead to feelings of inferiority, weakness, incompetence, or shame. So, they avoid new self-knowledge. As Maslow (1962, p. 57) notes:

> We tend to be afraid of any knowledge that would cause us to despise ourselves or to make us feel inferior, weak, worthless, evil, shameful. We protect ourselves and our ideal image of ourselves by repression and similar defenses, which are essentially techniques by which we avoid becoming conscious of unpleasantness or dangerous truths.

We avoid personal growth, then, because we fear finding out that we are not all we would like to be. If there is a better way to be, then our current state must be inadequate or inferior. The realization that we are not totally adequate or knowledgeable is difficult for most of us to accept.

This resistance is the "denying of our best side, of our talents, of our finest impulses, of our highest potentialities, of our creativeness. In brief, this is the struggle against our own greatness" (Maslow, 1962, p. 58). Freud (1956) asserted that to be completely honest with oneself is the best effort an individual can make because complete honesty requires a continual search for more information about the self and a desire for self-improvement. The results of that search are usually uncomfortable.

Seeking knowledge of one's self, therefore, seems to be an enigma: It is a prerequisite for and motivator of growth and improvement, but it may also inhibit growth and improvement. It may lead to progress and advancement or to stagnation and defensiveness because of fear of knowing more. How, then, can improvement be accomplished? How can management skills be developed if the self-knowledge necessary for the development of those skills is resisted?

THE SENSITIVE LINE

One answer relies on the concept of the **sensitive line**. This concept refers to the point at which individuals become defensive or protective when encountering information about themselves that is inconsistent with their self-concept or when encountering pressure to alter their behavior.

Most people regularly experience information about themselves that doesn't quite fit or that is marginally inconsistent. For example, a friend might say, "You look tired today. Are you feeling okay?" If you are feeling fine, the information is inconsistent with your self-awareness. But because the discrepancy is relatively minor and does not confront your fundamental self-image, it would not likely offend you or evoke a strong defensive reaction. It would probably not require that you reexamine and change your self-concept.

On the other hand, the more discrepant the information or the more serious its implications for your self-concept, the closer it would approach your sensitive line—and you would feel a need to defend yourself against it. For example, having a coworker judge you as incompetent may cross your sensitive line if you think of yourself as an effective and productive employee. This would be especially true if the coworker was an influential person. Your response would probably be to defend yourself against the information in order to protect the image you hold of yourself.

This response is known as the **threat-rigidity response** (Staw, Sandelands, & Dutton, 1981; Weick, 1993; Barnett & Pratt, 2000). When individuals are threatened, when they encounter uncomfortable information, or when uncertainty is created, they tend to become rigid. They hunker down, protect themselves, and become risk averse. Consider what happens when you are startled or suddenly shocked by something unexpected. Physically, your body tends to become rigid in order to protect itself. It tightens up to safeguard stability. Similarly, individuals also become rigid—psychologically and emotionally—when they encounter information that threatens their self-concept. They tend to redouble their efforts to protect what is comfortable and familiar (Cameron, 1994; Cameron, Kim, & Whetten, 1987; Weick & Sutcliffe, 2000). They rely on first-learned or most reinforced behavior patterns and emotions. Crossing the sensitive line creates rigidity and self-preservation.

In light of this defensiveness, then, how can increased self-knowledge and personal change ever occur? There are at least two answers. One is that information that is verifiable, predictable, and controllable is less likely to cross the sensitive line than information without those characteristics. That is, if an individual can test the validity of the discrepant information (for example, if some objective standard exists for evaluating the accuracy of the information), if the information is not unexpected or "out-of-the-blue" (for example, if it is received at regular intervals), and if there is some control over what, when, and how much information

is received (for example, if it is requested), the feedback is more likely to be heard and accepted.

The information you receive about yourself in this chapter possesses those three characteristics. You have already completed several self-assessment instruments that have been used extensively in research. Their reliability and validity have been established, and they have been associated with managerial success. Therefore, as you analyze your scores and seek honestly to understand more about your underlying attributes, you can gain important insight that will prove very useful.

A second answer to the problem of overcoming resistance to self-examination lies in the role other people can play in helping us gain self-understanding. It is almost impossible to increase self-awareness unless we interact with and disclose ourselves to others. Unless we are willing to open up to others, to discuss aspects of ourselves that seem ambiguous or unknown, little growth can ever occur. **Self-disclosure**, therefore, is a key to improvement in self-awareness. Harris (1981) points out:

> *In order to know oneself, no amount of introspection or self-examination will suffice. You can analyze yourself for weeks, or meditate for months, and you will not get an inch further— any more than you can smell your own breath or laugh when you tickle yourself.*
>
> *You must first be open to the other person before you catch a glimmering of yourself. Our self-reflection in a mirror does not tell us what we are like; only our reflection in other people. We are essentially social creatures, and our self-understanding resides in association, not in isolation.*

As you engage in the practice exercises in this chapter, therefore, you are encouraged to discuss your insights with someone else. These interactions should be sincere, honest, and motivated by self-understanding and self-improvement. Never should the information you share or receive be used to judge or wound another person. Maintaining a trusting relationship with someone with whom you can share is a critical prerequisite to self-understanding.

Several studies have shown that low self-disclosers are less healthy and more self-alienated than high self-disclosers. College students give the highest ratings for **interpersonal competence** to high self-disclosers. Individuals who are high self-disclosers are liked best, and excessive or insufficient self-disclosure results in less liking and acceptance by others (see, for example, Covey, 1989; Goleman, 1998b). The enigma of self-awareness can be managed, then, by exercising some control over when and what kind of information you receive about yourself and by involving others in your pursuit of self-understanding. The support and feedback individuals receive from others during the **process** of self-disclosure—besides helping to increase feedback and self-awareness—helps information contribute to greater self-awareness without crossing the sensitive line.

Understanding and Appreciating Individual Differences

Another important reason for focusing on self-awareness is to help you develop the ability to diagnose important differences among others with whom you interact. Considerable evidence shows that an individual's effectiveness as a manager is closely related to his or her ability to recognize, appreciate, and capitalize on fundamental differences among others. This topic is commonly discussed in the management literature under the subject of "managing diversity."

Whereas it is difficult to understand all the ramifications of "managing diversity," it is not difficult to be sensitive to certain important differences that affect the way you manage others. This chapter, therefore, has two objectives: (1) to help you better understand your own uniqueness as an individual—to become better equipped to manage yourself—and (2) to help you diagnose, value, and utilize the differences you find in other people.

Self-knowledge will help you understand your own taken-for-granted assumptions, trigger points, sensitive line, comfort zone, strengths and weaknesses, and inclinations. Most importantly, it will help you recognize your own special gifts and strengths and capitalize on your talents. It will help you contribute value in the situations in which you find yourself.

Similarly, being aware of differences in others is an important part of being an effective manager. People often have a tendency to interact with individuals who are like themselves, choose similar people to work with, and exclude others who seem to be different (Berscheid & Walster, 1978). The history of human warfare and conflict illustrates the fact that differences are often interpreted as threatening or menacing. However, research confirms the fact that diversity also enhances creativity, complex problem solving, and success in conditions that are changing or ambiguous. Organizational failure has been shown to occur frequently because of a lack of diversity in the composition of key decision-making bodies (Cameron, Kim, & Whetten, 1987).

One suggestion for successfully managing, valuing, and capitalizing individual differences is to focus on *differences*—not *distinctions*. Recognizing differences is not the same as evaluating distinctions. One is helpful. The other is hurtful. We observe differences. We create distinctions. Recognizing differences allows us to take advantage of others' unique contributions. Creating distinctions creates social barriers between people for the express purpose of reinforcing advantages and disadvantages.

To repeat, self-awareness and understanding differences cannot occur without self-disclosure, sharing, and trusting conversations. Self-knowledge requires an understanding and valuing of differences—not the creation of distinctions. We encourage you, therefore, to use the information you discover about yourself and others to build, grow, and improve your managerial skills.

Important Areas of Self-Awareness

Of course, a large number of dimensions are available to explore in order to develop in-depth self-awareness. For example, numerous aspects of cognitive style have been measured; authors have identified more than a dozen "intelligences" (ranging from social and practical to cognitive and creative); hundreds of personality factors have been investigated in the psychological literature; the mapping of the human chromosome has raised the possibility that thousands of physiological differences may be crucial in understanding behavior; and gender, age, cultural, ethnic, and experience differences all develop individually over time. It is impossible, of course, to accurately select the best or most central aspects of self-awareness because the alternatives are just too numerous.

On the other hand, we selected five of the most critical areas of self-awareness that have been found in research to be key in producing successful management. They are: *emotional intelligence, personal values, cognitive style, orientation toward change*, and *core self-evaluation*. These areas have been found to be among the most important predictors of effective personal and managerial performance—including achieving life success, performing effectively in teams, competent decision making, life-long learning and development, creativity, communication competency, job satisfaction, and job performance (Atwater & Yammarino, 1992; Church & Waclawski, 1999; Cools & Van den Broeck, 2007; Goleman, 1998b; Grant, 2013; Judge et al., 2003; Parker & Kram, 1993; Sosik & Megerian, 1999).

Research on **emotional intelligence**—the ability to correctly diagnose and manage one's own emotions and relationships with others—has been identified as among the most important factors in accounting for success in leaders and managers (Boyatzis, Goleman, & Rhee, 2000; Goleman, 1998a; Oginska-Bulik, N., 2005). Self-awareness has been identified as a crucial aspect of emotional intelligence, and it is more powerful than IQ in predicting success in life (Goleman, 1995).

One study, for example, tried to identify differences between star performers and average managers in 40 companies. Emotional intelligence competencies, including self-awareness, were *twice* as important in contributing to excellence as cognitive intelligence (IQ) and technical expertise (Goleman, 1998a). In a study of a multinational consulting firm, superior performing partners were compared to average performing partners. Superior performers—who had significantly higher emotional intelligence and self-awareness scores—contributed more than twice the revenues to the firm and were four times more likely to be promoted than those with low self-awareness and emotional intelligence (Boyatzis, 1998).

Personal values are included here because they are "the core of the dynamics of behavior, and play so large a part in unifying personality" (Allport, Gordon, & Vernon, 1931, p. 2). That is, all other attitudes, orientations, and behaviors arise out of an individual's values (Hemingway, 2005). Two major types of values are considered in this chapter: *instrumental* and *terminal* (Rokeach, 1973). We present research findings that connect personal development in these two types of values to successful managerial performance. The values assessment instrument is discussed along with information concerning the scores of other groups of people. You will want to compare your scores with those who are close to you as well as with successful managers. Some comparison data is provided for that purpose. Because this discussion of values development is connected to ethical decision making, the implications of managerial ethics are also discussed in this section.

A third area of self-awareness is **cognitive style**, which refers to the manner in which you gather and process information. Researchers have found that individual differences in cognitive style influence perception, learning, problem solving, decision making, communication, and creativity (Cools & Van den Broeck, 2007; Hayes & Allinson, 1994; Kirton, 2003). A large number of dimensions of cognitive style have been identified, but we have selected an instrument in this chapter that captures the most frequently studied dimensions (Cools & Van den Broeck, 2007) and one that links cognitive style to successful managerial behavior.

Fourth, a discussion of **orientation toward change** focuses on methods people use to cope with change in their environment. In the twenty-first century, we are faced with increasingly fragmented, rapidly changing, tumultuous conditions; knowing your orientation toward coping with such change is an important aspect of self-awareness. Two dimensions—*locus of control* and *intolerance of ambiguity*—are measured by two instruments, and research connecting these two dimensions to effective management is discussed in the sections that follow.

Finally, **core self-evaluation** is a construct that captures the essential aspects of core personality (Judge et al., 2003). More than 50,000 studies have been conducted on what has been referred to as "the Big Five" personality dimensions—neuroticism, extroversion, conscientiousness, agreeableness, and openness—but an underlying factor has been found to account for the effects of these personality dimensions: core self-evaluation. By analyzing your scores on the assessment instrument, you not only learn about your underlying personality dimensions, but you also will learn how they are associated with outcomes such as motivation, problem solving, creativity, life satisfaction, and work performance (Johnson, Rosen, & Levy, 2008; Judge, et al., 2005).

These five areas of self-awareness—emotional intelligence, personal values, **learning style,** orientation toward change, and core self-evaluation—constitute important aspects of the self-concept. Figure 1.1 summarizes these five aspects of self-awareness, along with their functions in defining the self-concept.

Again, many other aspects of self-awareness could be considered, but what we value, how we feel about ourselves, how we behave toward others, what we want to achieve, and what we are attracted to all are strongly influenced by our emotional intelligence, values, cognitive style, orientation toward change, and core self-evaluation. These are among the most important building blocks on which other aspects of the self emerge.

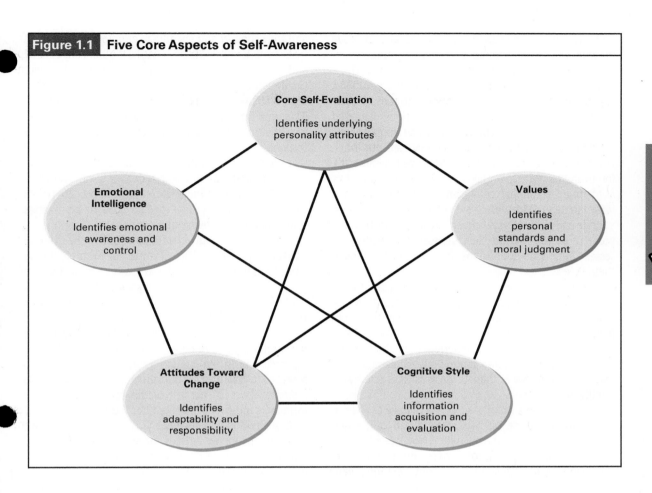

Figure 1.1   Five Core Aspects of Self-Awareness

Core Self-Evaluation

Identifies underlying
personality attributes

**Emotional
Intelligence**

Identifies emotional
awareness and
control

Values

Identifies
personal
standards and
moral judgment

**Attitudes Toward
Change**

Identifies
adaptability and
responsibility

Cognitive Style

Identifies
information
acquisition and
evaluation

EMOTIONAL INTELLIGENCE

Emotional intelligence has become a very popular topic that suffers from the problem that almost all trendy concepts encounter: Its meaning and measurement have become confusing and ambiguous. Emotional intelligence has come to encompass almost everything that is not IQ. Since the publication of Daniel Goleman's book *Emotional Intelligence* in 1995, interest in the concept of emotional intelligence has mushroomed (even though the concept was introduced in 1990 by Salovey and Mayer). Almost 20,000 books have been published on the topic, and scores of consulting companies and executive coaches now advertise themselves as experts in helping others develop emotional intelligence. The number of instruments available to assess emotional intelligence is voluminous (more than 100), although only three or four have been scientifically validated and used in any systematic investigations.

A scan of the scientific and popular writing on emotional intelligence confirms that almost everything is defined as an aspect of emotional intelligence. Multiple definitions abound and are frequently incompatible and contradictory. One way to clarify this problem of multiple definitions is to differentiate between *emotional intelligence* and *emotional competence*. Emotional intelligence refers to the ability to diagnose, understand, and manage emotional cues. Emotional competence refers to the noncognitive capabilities and skills—including social skills—that affect human functioning.

The first definition is the one we have adopted in this chapter. This is because emotional competencies are covered by the topics discussed in the remainder of this text. Whereas emotional competencies are critical for predicting success, in this chapter we adopt a more precise and refined definition of emotional intelligence. Emotional intelligence is, in fact, a prerequisite for developing emotional competence, and we will assist you in other chapters to develop and improve on what is often referred to as emotional competence.

Emotional intelligence refers specifically to: (1) the ability to diagnose and recognize your own emotions, (2) the ability to control your own emotions, (3) the ability to recognize and diagnose emotions displayed by others, and (4) the ability to respond appropriately to those emotional cues. These abilities are not inherent but can be developed and improved. Unlike IQ, for example, which remains relatively constant over a lifetime, emotional intelligence can be enhanced with practice. With concerted effort, you can change your level of emotional intelligence. The instrument you completed in the Skill Assessment section assesses these four dimensions, and we briefly explain them below.

Emotionally intelligent people are able to accurately recognize and label the emotions they are experiencing as well as to *regulate* and control them (Grant, 2013). They are less likely to blow up and lose control, less likely to experience debilitating depression and anxiety, and more likely to manage their own emotional states than those with less emotional intelligence.

Think, for example, of how you behave at a sporting event when the officials make a bad call; when someone gets angry at you; when you are criticized for something you did; or when you receive special accolades and recognition. Emotionally intelligent people remain in control of their emotions, whereas less emotionally intelligent people tend to lose control. This ability does not mean being bland or even-tempered all the time. Emotionally intelligent people may display a wide range of emotions and intensity. Instead, it means that a person is aware of his or her emotions and can control them so that they are not unrestrained.

Emotionally intelligent people are also able to accurately diagnose and empathize with the feelings of others. Empathy refers to the ability to understand and connect with others' feelings. It does not mean sympathizing or adopting others' feelings, and it is not based on a memory of having experienced the same emotions. If someone has experienced a tragedy or loss, for example, emotionally intelligent people can share in and understand those feelings even if they have never experienced something similar. They need not be depressed themselves, for example, in order to understand the depression of others.

Emotionally intelligent people also *respond* appropriately to the emotions of others. Their responses match the intensity of the emotions other people feel,

and they support and encourage emotional expressions (Salovey & Grewal, 2005). That is, if others are excited and happy, they do not remain aloof and withdrawn. On the other hand, they are not merely manipulated in their feelings and responses by the emotions of others. They don't respond merely on the basis of others' feelings. Rather, they remain in personal control of their responses.

One reason emotional intelligence is so important is that it has deteriorated over time. Whereas average IQ points have increased almost 25 points over the last 100 years—people tend to be smarter now than 100 years ago—emotional intelligence scores have actually declined (Goleman, 1998a; Slaski & Cartwright, 2003). Think, for example, of the amount of litigation, conflict, disrespect, bullying, and divorce that characterizes our society. Less emphasis is placed on emotional intelligence development now than in the past.

This is a problem because emotional intelligence has strong predictive power regarding success in management and in life—much stronger, in fact, than IQ scores. For example, it is estimated that IQ accounts for only about 10 percent of the variance in job performance and in life success (Sternberg, 1996), but by adding emotional intelligence (EQ) to the equation, we can account for four times more variance. Emotional intelligence is four times more important than IQ in accounting for success.

For example, in a study of 450 boys who grew up in a small town in Massachusetts, two-thirds lived in welfare families and one-third had IQ scores below 90. They were followed over 40 years, and it was found that IQ had almost nothing to do with life success. Emotional intelligence, on the other hand, was the most predictive factor (Snarey & Vaillant, 1985).

Another study of 80 PhDs in science who attended the University of California at Berkeley in the 1950s found that what accounted for life success 40 years after graduation was mainly emotional intelligence scores. Emotional intelligence was four times more important than IQ in determining who had achieved in their careers, who were evaluated by experts as being highly successful, and who were listed in sources such as *Who's Who* and *American Men and Women of Science* (Feist & Barron, 1996).

In another study of business school undergraduate students, higher emotional intelligence scores were typical of those involved in clubs, Greek organizations, sports teams, and activities in which social interaction was frequent. Higher emotional intelligence was also associated with higher GPAs in both business classes and university classes (Rozell, E. J., Pettijohn, C. E., & Parker, R. S. 2002). Emotional intelligence has been found to be an important predictor of managerial success. In a study of managers on three continents, for example, 74 percent of successful managers had emotional intelligence as their most salient characteristic, whereas this was the case in only 24 percent of the failures. A study at PepsiCo found that company units headed by managers with well-developed emotional intelligence skills outperformed yearly revenue targets by 15 to 20 percent. Those with underdeveloped skills underperformed their targets by about the same amount (Goleman, Boyatzis, & McKee, 2002).

A McBer study comparing outstanding managers with average managers found that 90 percent of the difference was accounted for by emotional intelligence. In a worldwide study of what companies were looking for in hiring new employees, 67 percent of the most desired attributes were emotional intelligence competencies (Goleman et al., 2002). The point of these studies should be clear: Effective managers have developed high levels of competency in emotional intelligence.

The Emotional Intelligence Assessment instrument you completed in the Skill Assessment section provides an evaluation of your competency in the four general areas of emotional intelligence—emotional awareness, emotional control or balance, emotional diagnosis or empathy, and emotional response. A comprehensive and fully valid measure of these factors would require an instrument many times longer than the one included here, so this assessment merely provides a reasonably accurate summary of your emotional intelligence capability. Your scores will help you identify areas of strength as well as aspects of emotional intelligence that you can pursue to become more capable. Becoming aware of your own emotional intelligence is an important aspect of becoming a more effective manager.

VALUES

Values are among the most stable and enduring characteristics of individuals. They are the foundation on which attitudes and personal preferences are formed. They help define our morality and our conceptions of what is "good." Much of what we are is a product of the basic values we have developed throughout our lives.

The trouble with values, unfortunately, is that they are taken for granted, and people are often unaware of them. Unless a person's values are challenged, they remain largely undetected. People especially are not aware that they hold some values as being more important than others. This unawareness leads to actions or behaviors that are sometimes contrary to values. Until people encounter a contradiction or a threat to their basic values, they seldom articulate their values or seek to clarify them.

The values held by each of us are affected by a variety of factors, and a number of ways have been used to measure and describe values. We point out several ways in this chapter—each of which has been widely used in research and in management circles.

One factor is the general value orientations that characterize large groups such as nationalities, ethnic groups, industries, or organizations. Much research has been done, for example, on identifying the differences in values that arise across cultural groups. The point of this research is to identify ways in which nationalities differ from one another, since almost all managers now face the need to manage across national boundaries. In your own life, it is likely that you will interact with individuals who do not share your birth country, and knowing something about their value orientations will help your interactions be more effective. Some values differ systematically across national cultures, and at least some of our values are affected significantly by the country and culture in which we are raised.

Cultural Values

Trompenaars (1996; Trompenaars & Hampden-Turner, 1998, 2004) identified seven value dimensions on which significant differences exist among national cultures. Certain cultures emphasize some values more than others do. Table 1.1 identifies Trompenaars' seven dimensions, and we provide examples of countries that represent each of the value dimensions. No national culture emphasizes one of these dimensions to the exclusion of another, but there are clear differences in the amount of emphasis placed on each dimension.

The first five dimensions of the model refer to how individuals relate to other people. For example, some countries (e.g., the United States, Norway, Sweden, and Switzerland) emphasize a value of **universalism**, in which other people's behavior is governed by universal standards and rules—e.g., do not lie, do not cheat, do not run a red light, even if no one is coming the other way. General societal rules govern behavior.

Table 1.1 Cultural Values Dimensions

VALUE DIMENSIONS	EXPLANATION	EXAMPLE OF COUNTRIES WITH DOMINANCE
Universalism	Societal rules and norms are valued.	United States, Switzerland, Norway, Sweden
Particularism	Individual relationships are valued.	Korea, Venezuela, China, Indonesia
Individualism	Individual contributions are valued.	United States, Nigeria, Denmark, Austria
Collectivism	Team contributions are valued.	Mexico, Indonesia, Japan, Philippines
Affective	Showing emotions is valued.	Iran, Spain, France, Switzerland
Neutral	Unemotional responses are valued.	Korea, Ethiopia, China, Japan
Specific	Segregating life's roles is valued.	Holland, Sweden, Denmark, United Kingdom
Diffuse	Integrating life's role is valued.	China, Nigeria, Singapore, Korea
Achievement	Personal accomplishment is valued.	United States, Norway, Canada, Austria
Ascription	Inherent attributes are valued.	Egypt, Indonesia, Korea, Czech Republic
Past and Present	Past is tightly connected to future.	France, Japan, United Kingdom
Future	Future is disconnected but valued.	United States, Holland
Internal	Individual control is valued.	United States, Canada, Austria, United Kingdom
External	Control comes from outside forces.	Czech Republic, Japan, Egypt, China

SOURCE: F. Trompenaars and C. Hampden-Turner, (2011). Riding the Waves of Culture. *Reprinted with the permission of the McGraw-Hill Companies.*

Other countries (e.g., Korea, China, Indonesia, and Singapore) hold a value of **particularism**, in which the relationship with an individual governs behavior—e.g., is the other person a friend, a family member, a relative?

To illustrate the differences, consider your answer to this question: *You are driving in a car with a close friend who hits a pedestrian while going 40 miles an hour in a 25-mile-an-hour zone. There are no witnesses, and your friend's lawyer says that if you'll testify that he was only traveling 25 miles an hour, he'll get off. Will you lie for him?* People in universalistic cultures are more likely to refuse than people in particularistic cultures. For example, 97 percent of the Swiss and 93 percent of North Americans (Canada and the United States) would refuse to testify, whereas 32 percent of Venezuelans and 37 percent of South Koreans would refuse.

A second value dimension differentiates cultures that value **individualism**—an emphasis on the self, on independence, and on uniqueness—versus **collectivism**—an emphasis on the group, the combined unit, and on joining with others. Individualistic values hold the contributions of individuals to be most valued, whereas collectivism values team contributions.

For example, consider your answer to this question: *What kind of job is found most frequently in your organization, one where everyone works together and you do not get individual credit, or one where everyone is allowed to work individually and you receive individual recognition?* Eastern Europeans (e.g, Russia, Czech Republic, Hungary, Poland) average above 80 percent in agreeing that individual credit is received, whereas Asians (e.g., Japan, India, Nepal) average below 45 percent. (The United States score is 72 percent.)

A third value dimension refers to the display of feelings in public. It identifies an **affective** versus **neutral** orientation. Cultures with high affective values tend to show emotions openly and to deal with problems in emotional ways. Loud laughter, anger, and intense passion may all be displayed in the course of a business negotiation, for example. Cultures with neutral values are more rational and stoic in their approach to problem solving. Instrumental, goal-directed behaviors rather than emotions dominate interactions.

For example, *if you became very upset at work or in class—say you feel slighted, offended, or angry—how likely would you be to display your feelings openly in public?* Managers in Japan, Ethiopia, and Hong

Kong, for example, average 64 percent, 74 percent, and 81 percent respectively in refusing to show emotions publicly. On the other hand, 15 percent of Kuwait managers, 18 percent of Egyptian managers, and 19 percent of Spanish managers would refuse. (The United States score is 43 percent.)

A fourth dimension—**specificity** versus **diffusion**—describes the difference between cultures that segregate the different roles in life to maintain privacy and personal autonomy compared to cultures that integrate and merge their roles. Cultures with specific values separate work relationships from family relationships, for example, whereas diffuse cultures entangle work and home relationships. People with specific values may seem hard to get to know because they keep a boundary between their personal lives and their work lives. People with diffuse values may seem too forward and too superficial because they seem to share personal information freely.

To illustrate the difference, how would you respond to this question: *Your boss asks you to come to her home to help her paint her house. You don't want to do it since you hate painting. Would you refuse?* More than 90 percent of the Dutch and Swedes would refuse, whereas only 32 percent of the Chinese and 46 percent of Nigerians would refuse. (In the United States, 82 percent would refuse.)

A fifth value dimension differentiates cultures that emphasize an **achievement** orientation versus an **ascription** culture. People tend to acquire high status based on their personal accomplishments in some cultures, whereas in other cultures status and prestige are based more on ascribed characteristics such as age, gender, family heritage, or ethnic background. Who you know (ascription) versus what you can do (achievement) helps identify the difference on this value dimension.

For example, the following statement helps highlight achievement versus ascription value differences: *It is important to act the way you are, to be consistent with your true self, even if you do not accomplish the task at hand.* Only 10 percent of managers from Uruguay, 12 percent from Argentina, and 13 percent from Spain disagree with the statement, whereas 77 percent of Norwegians and 75 percent of managers from the United States disagree.

A sixth value dimension relates to how people interpret and manage time. It distinguishes the emphasis placed on the past, present, or future in various cultures. Some cultures, for example, value past and tradition more than future; other cultures place more value on the future than the past. What you have achieved in the past matters more in some cultures than where you are headed in the future. Time differences also exist regarding short- versus long-time horizons. For example, some people are oriented toward very short time horizons where they think in terms of minutes and hours (a short-time horizon). Other people think in terms of months or years (a long-time horizon).

Complete the following brief exercise, for example, to get a sense of your own time horizon. *Use the following scale and give a number to each of the following statements: My past started _____ ago and ended _____ ago. My present started _____ ago and will end _____ from now. My future will start _____ from now and will end _____ from now. Use this rating scale: 7 = years, 6 = months, 5 = weeks, 4 = days, 3 = hours, 2 = minutes, 1 = seconds.*

By way of comparison, people in the Philippines averaged 3.40 on the scale, Irish managers averaged 3.82, and Brazilians averaged 3.85. On the other hand, managers in Hong Kong averaged 5.71, Portugal averaged 5.62, and Pakistan averaged 5.47. (People in the United States averaged 4.30.)

The seventh and final value dimension focuses on internal and external control. (We will discuss this value dimension in more detail later in the chapter.) It differentiates cultures that presume individuals are in control of their own destinies from those that presume nature or external forces control much of what happens. For example, some countries emphasize the value of individuals inventing or creating things (internal control), whereas other countries emphasize the value of taking what already exists or has been created elsewhere and then refining or improving it (external control).

Two statements that illustrate this difference are: *(1) What happens to me is my own doing. (2) Sometimes I feel that I do not have enough control over the directions my life is taking.* More than 80 percent of managers from Uruguay, Norway, Israel, and the United States agree with the first statement, whereas less than 40 percent of Venezuelans, Chinese, and Nepalese agree.

Because virtually every manager will be faced with the opportunity to interact with and manage individuals born in other cultures, being aware of value differences and being able to diagnose and manage those differences is an important prerequisite for success. Of course, stereotyping people based on their national culture, or overgeneralizing based on trends such as those reported here, can be dangerous and misleading. None of us would like to be pigeonholed

LEARNING

based on a general country profile. These dimensions, as you will see, are most useful for increasing sensitivity and helping with diagnosis rather than to place people in categories.

Like countries, organizations, too, have value systems, referred to as an **organizational culture**. Research has found that employees who hold values congruent with their organization's values are more productive and satisfied (Cable & Judge, 1996; Cameron & Quinn, 2011; Glew, 2009; Nwachukwu & Vitell, 1997; Posner & Kouzes, 1993). Holding values that are inconsistent with company values, on the other hand, is a major source of frustration, conflict, and nonproductivity. Being aware of your own priorities and values, the values of your organization, and the general value priorities of your country, are important if you expect to achieve compatibility at work and in a long-term career (Fisher, Macrosson, & Yusuff, 1996). For an in-depth discussion on organizational culture, see Cameron and Quinn (2011).

Personal Values

In a classic study on human values, Rokeach (1973) argued that the total number of values people possess is relatively small and that all individuals possess the same values, but in different degrees. For example, everyone values peace, but some make it a higher priority than others. Two general types of values were identified by Rokeach, and independent priority ratings have been found to exist for each type (that is, the two sets of values are largely unrelated). One general type of values is labeled *instrumental*, or means-oriented; the other type is *terminal*, or ends-oriented.

Instrumental values prescribe desirable standards of conduct or methods for attaining an end. Two types of instrumental values relate to morality and competence. Violating moral values (for example, behaving wrongly) causes feelings of guilt. Violating competence values (for example, behaving incapably) brings about feelings of shame.

Terminal values prescribe desirable ends or goals for the individual. There are fewer terminal values than instrumental values, and the sum total for all individuals in all societies can be identified. Terminal values are either personal (for example, peace of mind) or social (for example, world peace).

Different groups of people tend to differ in the values they hold. For example, in other studies, business school students and professors tend to rate "ambition,"

"capability," "responsibility," and "freedom" higher than people in general. They tend to place lower importance than people in general on concern and helpfulness to others, aesthetics and cultural values, and overcoming social injustice. Compared to the population in general, managers place substantially more value on "sense of accomplishment," "self-respect," "a comfortable life," and "independence." The instrumental value managers held highest for themselves, in fact, was "ambition"; their highest held terminal value was "sense of accomplishment." In other words, personal values (rather than social values) and those oriented toward achievement predominate among managers (Bilsky & Schwartz, 1994; Cable & Judge, 1996; Cavanaugh, 1980; Clare & Sanford, 1979). No gender differences have been found on the Rokeach instrument (Johnston, 1995).

These value preferences may explain why business students and business executives have been criticized for being too self-centered and impatient for personal achievement and promotion (see Introduction). In research conducted by the authors (Cameron, 2011), managers who pursued more humanistic values (such as compassion, humility, trust, and kindness) tended to succeed more than those who did not.

Several authors have argued that the behavior displayed by individuals (that is, the means used to achieve their valued ends) is a product of their level of **values maturity** (e.g., Kohlberg, 1969; Kohlberg & Ryncarz, 1990). Individuals differ in their level of values development, according to these authors, so different sets of instrumental values are held by individuals at different stages of development. People progress from one level of maturity to another; as they do, their value priorities change. Individuals who have progressed to more mature levels of values development possess a qualitatively different set of instrumental values than those at less mature levels.

This theory of values maturity or moral development has received a great deal of attention from researchers, and research findings have important implications for self-awareness and managerial effectiveness. Therefore, we discuss in some detail this notion of values maturity.

Values Maturity

Kohlberg's model is the best known and most widely researched approach to values maturity. It focuses on the kind of reasoning used to reach a decision about an issue that has value or moral connotations. The model consists of three major levels, each of which

Table 1.2 Classification of Moral Judgment into Stages of Development

LEVEL BASIS OF MORAL JUDGMENT	STAGE OF DEVELOPMENT
A PRECONVENTIONAL LEVEL (SELF-CENTERED) Moral value resides in external factors, and consequences, not persons or relationships.	1. *Punishment and Obedience* What is right is determined by avoiding punishment and not breaking an authority's rules. 2. *Individual Instrumental Purpose and Exchange* What is right is meeting one's own immediate interests and what is fair or equal for others.
B CONVENTIONAL LEVEL (CONFORMITY) Moral value resides in duty, maintaining social contracts, keeping commitments.	3. *Mutual Interpersonal Expectations, Relationships, and Conformity* What is right is being concerned with others' feelings and maintaining trust by keeping expectations and commitments. The Golden Rule is relevant. 4. *Social System and Conscience Maintenance* What is right is doing one's duty to society and upholding the social order.
C POSTCONVENTIONAL (PRINCIPLED) Moral value resides in commitment to freely selected standards, rights, and duties.	5. *Prior Rights and Social Contract or Utility* What is right is upholding the rights, values, and contracts of others in society; moral behavior is freely chosen. 6. *Universal Ethical Principles* What is right is guided by internal, universal ethical principles. When laws violate principles, the laws are ignored.

SOURCE: *Adapted from Kohlberg (1981).*

LEARNING

contains two stages. Table 1.2 summarizes the characteristics of each stage.

In brief, the stages are sequential (for example, a person cannot progress to stage 3 before passing through stage 2), and each stage represents a higher level of maturity. Kohlberg uses the terms *preconventional*, *conventional*, and *postconventional* to describe these three levels.

The first level of maturity, the *preconventional* or ***self-centered level,*** includes the first two stages of values development. Moral reasoning and instrumental values are based on personal needs or wants and on the consequences of an act. For example, something could be judged as right or good if it helps an individual obtain a reward or avoid punishment and if the consequences are not negative for someone else. Stealing $50,000 is worse than stealing $500 in the self-centered level because the consequences (that is, the losses) are more negative for someone else. Most children operate at this level of values maturity.

The second level, the *conventional* or ***conformity level,*** includes stages 3 and 4. Moral reasoning is based on conforming to and upholding the conventions and expectations of society. This level is sometimes referred to as the "law and order" level because the emphasis is on adherence to laws and norms. Right and wrong are judged on the basis of whether or not behaviors conform to the rules of those in authority. Respect from others based on obedience is a prized outcome. Stealing $50,000 and stealing $500 are equally wrong in this level because both violate the law. Most American adults function at this level of values maturity.

Third is the *postconventional* or ***principled level.*** It includes the final two stages of maturity and represents the most advanced level of moral reasoning and the most mature set of instrumental values. Right and wrong are judged on the basis of the internalized principles of the individual. Judgments are made on the basis of a set of core values that take precedence.

In the highest stage of maturity, this set of principles is comprehensive (it covers all contingencies), consistent (it is never violated), and universal (it does not change with the situation or circumstance). Thus, stealing $50,000 and stealing $500 are still judged to be wrong, but the basis for the judgment is not the violation of laws or rules; rather, it is the violation of a set of comprehensive, consistent, universal principles developed by the individual. Few individuals, according to Kohlberg, reach this highest level of maturity on a consistent basis. It may be characterized by individuals we consider to be especially wise and exemplary such as Gandhi, Buddha, or Moses.

In short, self-centered individuals view rules and laws as outside themselves, but they obey because, by doing so, they may obtain rewards or avoid punishment. Conformist individuals view rules and laws as outside themselves, but they obey because they have learned and accepted those rules and laws, and they seek the respect of others. Principled individuals examine the rules and laws and develop a set of internal principles that they believe are morally right. If there is a choice to be made between obeying a law or obeying a principle, they choose the principle. Internalized principles supersede rules and laws in principled individuals.

To understand the different levels of values maturity, consider the following story used by Kohlberg (1969):

> In Europe a woman was near death from a special kind of cancer. There was one drug that the doctors thought might save her. It was a form of radium that a druggist in the same town had recently discovered. The drug was expensive to make, but the druggist was charging ten times what the drug cost to make. He paid $200 for radium and charged $2,000 for a small dose of the drug. The sick woman's husband, Heinz, went to everyone he knew to borrow the money, but he could get together only about $1,000, which was half of what it cost. He told the druggist that his wife was dying and begged him to sell the drug at a lower price or let him pay later. But the druggist said, "No, I discovered the drug and I'm going to make money from it." So Heinz grew desperate and began to think about breaking into the store to steal the drug for his wife.

Now answer the following questions in reaction to the story:

Yes	No	
_____	_____	1. Would it be wrong for Heinz to break into the store?
_____	_____	2. Did the druggist have the right to charge that much for the product?
_____	_____	3. Did Heinz have an obligation to steal the drug for his wife?
_____	_____	4. What if Heinz and his wife did not get along? Should Heinz steal the drug for her?
_____	_____	5. Suppose Heinz's best friend were dying of cancer, rather than Heinz's wife. Should Heinz steal the drug for his friend?
_____	_____	6. Suppose the person dying was not personally close to Heinz but in the neighborhood. Should Heinz steal the drug?
_____	_____	7. Suppose Heinz read in the newspaper about a woman dying of cancer. Should he steal the drug for her?
_____	_____	8. Would you steal the drug to save your own life?
_____	_____	9. Suppose Heinz was caught breaking in and brought before a judge. Should he be sentenced to jail?

For individuals in the self-centered level of maturity, stealing the drug might be justified because Heinz's wife had instrumental value: she could provide companionship, help rear the children, and so on. A stranger, however, would not have the same instrumental value for Heinz, so it would be wrong to steal the drug for a stranger. Individuals in the conformity level would base their judgments on the closeness of the relationship and on law and authority. Heinz has an obligation to steal for family members, according to this reasoning, but not for nonfamily members. A governing principle is whether or not an action is against the law (or society's expectations). Principled individuals base their judgments on a set of universal, comprehensive, and consistent principles.

They may answer any question yes or no, but their reasoning will be based on their own internal principles, not on externally imposed standards or expectations. (For example, they might feel an obligation to steal the drug for anyone because they value human life more than property.)

Research on Kohlberg's model of values development reveals some findings that have relevance to managerial behavior. For example, moral judgment stories were administered to college students who had earlier participated in Milgram's (1963) obedience study. Under the guise of a reinforcement-learning experiment, Milgram's subjects had been directed to give increasingly intense electric shocks to a person who was observed to be in great pain. Of the respondents at the principled level (stages 5 and 6), 75 percent refused to administer the shocks (i.e., to hurt someone), while only 12.5 percent of the respondents at the conformity level refused. Higher levels of values development were associated with more humane behavior toward other people.

It should also be noted that Kohlberg's model has been criticized as containing a male bias (Gilligan, 1979, 1980, 1982, 1988; Gibbs & Schnell, 1985). In her investigations of moral dilemmas among women, Gilligan indicated that women tend to value care, relationships, and commitment more highly than do males. The Kohlberg model, which tends to emphasize justice as the highest moral value, is more typical of males than females, she claimed.

Gilligan's criticisms remain controversial among researchers, but they are less relevant to our discussion here because the highest performing individuals develop internalized principles for guiding behavior. Whether these principles are more typical of males or females is largely beside the point. The comprehensive, consistent, and universal nature of the principles is what counts.

Becoming more mature in values development requires that individuals develop a set of internalized principles by which they can govern their behavior (Jordan, Brown, Treviño, & Finkelstein, 2013). The development of those principles is enhanced and values maturity can be increased as value-based issues are confronted, discussed, and contemplated. The more people discuss moral and values-based issues, and the more they are asked to take a personal stance on these kinds of issues, the more maturity in values and moral development occurs.

To help you determine your own level of values maturity, an instrument developed by James Rest at the University of Minnesota's Moral Research Center is included in the Assessment section. It has been used extensively in research because it is easier to administer than Kohlberg's method for assessing maturity. According to Kohlberg (1976, p. 47), "Rest's approach does give a rough estimate of an individual's moral maturity level." Rather than placing a person on one single level of values maturity, it identifies the stage that the person relies on most. That is, it assumes that individuals use more than one level of maturity (or set of instrumental values), but that one level generally predominates. By completing this instrument, therefore, you will identify your predominant level of values maturity. To determine your maturity level, refer to the self-scoring instructions in MyLab section associated with this chapter. An exercise in the Skill Practice section will help you develop or refine principles at the stage 5 and stage 6 level of maturity.

ETHICAL DECISION MAKING

**⊙ MyManagementLab: WATCH IT
Ethics in the Workplace**
Apply what you have learned about management. If your instructor has assigned MyManagementLab, go to mymanagementlab.com to watch a video case and answer questions.

In addition to its benefits for self-understanding, awareness of your own level of values maturity also has important practical implications for **ethical decision making**. By and large, the American public rates the honesty, integrity, and concern for moral values of American business executives as abysmal. A large majority of the public think managers are dishonest, overly profit-oriented, and willing to step on other people to get what they want (Harris & Sutton, 1995; Lozano, 1996). Although 9 out of 10 companies have a written code of ethics, evidence exists to support public perceptions that these documents are not influential in assuring high moral conduct (Elliott & Schroth, 2002; Mitchell, 2002).

The popular press reports an unethical action by a company or a leading executive in business almost every day. Record levels of fines ranging in the billions, long-term prison sentences, and public embarrassment are common nowadays. From leaders in politics to leaders in business, almost no one has confidence that our leaders are playing it absolutely, totally straight.

A recent list of the most unethical companies includes Walmart, Papa Johns, RCA, General Electric, Barrick Gold Corporation, Exxon, Chevron, Dow Chemical, Union Carbide, Siemens, Philip Morris, Halliburton, and Monsanto. Well-known ethical scandals involving E. F. Hutton, General Dynamics, Rockwell, Martin Marietta, Tyco, Lockheed, Bank of Boston, Dow Corning, Martha Stewart, Enron, Global Crossing, Ford, Firestone, General Motors, Toyota, A.H. Robins, J.P. Morgan, and Bank of America have had their day in the press. One cartoon that seems to summarize these goings-on shows a group of executives sitting at a conference table. The leader remarks, "Of course, honesty is one of the better policies."

Corporate behavior that exemplifies unethical decision making is not our principal concern here. More to the point is a study by the American Management Association that included 3,000 managers in the United States. It reported that most individual managers felt they were under pressure to compromise personal standards to meet company goals (Harris & Sutton, 1995). A more recent study found that at least a quarter of Wall Street executives say they have to be unethical to succeed (Plaue, 2012).

Moreover, most individuals have encountered someone else violating ethical standards, but in a majority of cases, nothing is reported. For example, in a survey of federal employees asked whether they had observed any of the following activities in the last year, more than 50 percent answered yes to seeing: stealing funds, stealing property, accepting bribes, sexual harassment, ineligible people receiving funds, deficient goods or services, use of position for personal benefit, taking unfair advantage of a contractor, and serious violation of the law. More than two-thirds did not report what they saw. A survey of senior executives in major corporations showed similar results (Plaue, 2012).

As an illustration, consider the following true incident (names have been changed). How would you respond? Why?

Steve Visco, a top manufacturing manager at Satellite Telecommunications, walked into the office of Neville Lobo, the head of quality control. Steve was carrying an assembled part that was to be shipped to a customer on the West Coast. Steve handed Neville the part and said, "Look Neville, this part is in perfect shape electronically, but the case has a gouge in it. I've seen engineering and they say that the mark doesn't affect form, fit, or

function. Marketing says the customer won't mind because they are just going to bury the unit anyway. We can't rework it, and it would cost $75,000 to make new cases. We will only do 23 units, and they're already made. The parts are due to be shipped at the end of the week." Neville responded, "Well, what do you want from me?" "Just sign off so we can move forward," said Steve. "Since you're the one who needs to certify acceptable quality, I thought I'd better get this straightened out now rather than waiting until the last minute before shipping."

Would you ship the part or not? Discuss this with your class members why or why not. Generate a recommendation for Neville.

This case exemplifies the major values conflict faced over and over again by managers. It is a conflict between maximizing the economic performance of the organization (as indicated by revenues, costs, and profits) or the social performance of the organization (as indicated by obligations to customers, employees, and suppliers). Most ethical trade-offs are conflicts between these two desirable ends: economic versus social performance (Hosmer, 2003). Making these kinds of decisions effectively is not merely a matter of selecting between right and wrong alternatives or between good and bad choices. Most of these choices are between right and right or between one good and another.

Individuals who effectively manage these kinds of ethical trade-offs are those who have a clear sense of their own values and who have developed a principled level of moral maturity. They have articulated and clarified their own internal set of universal, comprehensive, and consistent principles on which to base their decisions. It is seldom the case, of course, that a manager could choose economic performance goals every time or that he or she could choose social performance goals every time. Trade-offs are inevitable.

It is not a simple matter, on the other hand, to generate a personal set of universal, comprehensive, and consistent principles that can guide decision making. According to Kohlberg's research, most adults have neither constructed, nor do they follow, a well-developed set of principles in making decisions. One reason is that they have no model or example of such principles.

We offer some standards against which to test your own values and principles for making moral or ethical choices. These standards are neither comprehensive nor absolute, nor are they independent of one another. They simply serve as reference against which to test ethical decision making and some principles you may include in your personal values statement.

- *Front page test*: Would I be embarrassed if my decision became a headline in the local newspaper? Would I feel comfortable describing my actions or decision to a customer or stockholder?

- *Golden rule test:* Would I be willing to be treated in the same manner?

- *Dignity and liberty test:* Are the dignity and liberty of others preserved by this decision? Is the basic humanity of the affected parties enhanced? Are their opportunities expanded or curtailed?

- *Equal treatment test:* Are the rights, welfare, and betterment of minorities and lower status people given full consideration? Does this decision benefit those with privilege but without merit?

- *Personal gain test:* Is an opportunity for personal gain clouding my judgment? Would I make the same decision if the outcome did not benefit me in any way?

- *Congruence test:* Is this decision or action consistent with my espoused personal principles? Does it violate the spirit of any organizational policies or laws?

- *Procedural justice test:* Can the procedures used to make this decision stand up to scrutiny by those affected?

- *Cost-benefit test:* Does a benefit for some cause unacceptable harm to others? How critical is the benefit? Can the harmful effects be mitigated?

- *Good night's sleep test:* Whether or not anyone else knows about my action, will it produce a good night's sleep?

- *Virtuousness test*: Does this represent the best of the human condition or the highest aspirations to which human beings aspire?

In the Skill Application section of this chapter, you may want to consider these alternatives when constructing your own set of comprehensive, consistent, and universalistic principles. You should be aware, however, that your set of personal principles will also be influenced by your orientation for acquiring and responding to the information you receive. This orientation is called cognitive style.

COGNITIVE STYLE

Each of us is constantly exposed to an overwhelming amount of information, and only part of it can be given attention and acted on at a time. For example, right now you have information entering your brain relating to the functioning of your physical body, the attributes of the room in which you are sitting, the words on this page, the ideas and memories that spring to mind as you read about self-awareness, long-held beliefs, recollections of recent events, and so on. Of course, not all of this information is conscious; otherwise, your brain would become overloaded and you would become psychotic. Over time, we all develop strategies for suppressing some kinds of information and paying attention to other kinds. These strategies become habitual and ingrained, and they result in a unique cognitive style for each of us.

Cognitive style refers to the inclination each of us has to perceive, interpret, and respond to information in a certain way. Cognitive style is based on two key dimensions: (1) the manner in which you *gather information* and (2) the way in which you *evaluate* and act on *information*. A large number of instruments are available to measure different dimensions of cognitive styles (see Cassidy, 2004; Eckstrom, French, & Harmon, 1979; Myers-Briggs Type Inventory-MBTI; Sternberg & Zhang, 2000;), but here we focus on dimensions that have emerged in the most recent research on cognitive style. These dimensions are the ones that most researchers now identify as lying at the heart of cognitive style.

It is important to note that cognitive styles are not the same as personality types. They are not inherent attributes. Rather, they are inclinations toward information and learning that we have developed over time. Hence, cognitive styles can be altered and changed through practice and conscious development (Vance et al., 2007). No one is predestined to think in a particular way.

Based on an extensive literature review of models of cognitive style, we selected an instrument developed by Cools and Van den Broeck (2007) to assess your cognitive style. You completed this instrument in the Skill Assessment section. This instrument assesses three dimensions of your cognitive style—knowing style, planning style, and creating style. These dimensions are independent in the sense that any person can score high or low on any of the three sections. They are not polar opposites from one another but are just different ways that people process information. Each style emphasizes a different

Table 1.3	Attributes of Three Dimensions of Cognitive Style	
	ATTRIBUTES	**POSSIBLE LIABILITIES**
Knowing	Emphasizes facts, details, and data Seeks clear, objective solutions Focuses on validity, credibility of data Emphasizes accuracy and precision	Slow to make decisions Uncreative Resistant to innovation Intolerant of multiple views
Planning	Emphasizes planning and preparation Seeks agendas and outlines Focuses on methods, processes, and follow-up Emphasizes clear actions and routine	Frustrated by the status quo Intolerant of ambiguity Overwhelmed by chaos Can't handle illogical issues
Creating	Emphasizes creativity, risk-taking, and innovation Seeks novelty and ambiguity Focuses on spontaneity and possibilities Emphasizes interaction and getting many inputs	Resistant to structure Tends to break rules May make many mistakes Tends to ignore data and facts

kind of information seeking and response, and the main attributes are summarized in Table 1.3.

Knowing Style

Individuals who score high on the knowing style tend to emphasize facts, details, and data. They seek clear and objective solutions to problems. They are careful, so decisions are usually not made quickly. They do things in the correct way and tend to be critical of unexpected or aberrant behavior. They excel at problems that have one correct answer. Multiple-choice exams are preferred over essay exams.

Research has suggested that these individuals are inclined toward careers in technology, engineering, and law. In college, students with a knowing style tend to major in the physical sciences, engineering, law, and computers. In business, they tend to select careers in areas where numbers and data predominate (e.g., auditing, finance), and they prefer jobs that have a technical problem-solving emphasis (Kolb, Boyatzis, & Mainemelis, 2000; Cool & Van den Broeck, 2007).

Planning Style

Individuals who score high on the planning style are inclined toward preparation and planning. They produce agendas and well-developed outlines for handling information. Having a systematic methodology for gathering and responding to information is important, so these people are well prepared

People with a planning style are best at processing a wide range of information and thinking through problems to reach a solution. Research has shown that people with a planning style are inclined toward

information and science careers, and they prefer lectures, readings, analytical models, and thinking time as their learning activities. In college, these people tend to major in economics, accounting, operations, mathematics, engineering, and medicine. They tend to select careers in the information sciences and in research fields (e.g., educational research, information, and theology), and they prefer jobs in which information gathering predominates (e.g., research and analysis) (Kolb, Boyatzis, & Mainemelis, 2000; Cool & Van den Broeck, 2007).

Creating Style

Individuals who score high on the creating style tend to prefer experimentation and creativity. They seek uniqueness and novelty, and they are comfortable with ambiguity. They tend to search for information broadly and from many sources, so they are usually more social and extroverted (Cools & Van den Broeck, 2007; Furnham, Crump, Batey, & Chamorro-Premuzic, 2009) than other styles. Rules and procedures are often viewed as obstacles and constraints, so they may appear disorganized.

Research shows that these people tend to be imaginative and emotional and prefer working in groups in order to hear a variety of different opinions. In college, people with a creating style tend to major in the arts, history, political science, English, and psychology. They tend to select careers in social services (e.g., psychology, nursing, and public policy) and in arts and communication (e.g., theater, literature, and journalism), and they prefer jobs in which personal interactions predominate (Kolb, Boyatzis, & Mainemelis,

2000; Cool & Van den Broeck, 2007). In business schools, students in sales and marketing and in human resources tend to have higher scores in this style.

Research on these cognitive dimensions has found that no matter what type of problem they face, most people use their preferred cognitive style to approach it. They prefer, and even seek, decision situations and problem types consistent with their own style.

In one study, for example, managers who had a planning style implemented more computer-based systems and rational procedures for decision making than did creating-style managers. Managers in another study defined identical problems differently depending on their different cognitive styles (e.g., some thought the problem required more data, whereas others thought it required brainstorming new ideas). Other studies found that differences in cognitive style led to significantly different decision-making processes in managers (see Henderson & Nutt, 1980; Chenhall & Morris, 1991; Ruble & Cosier, 1990; Kirton, 2003).

It is important to point out that very little relationship has been found between cognitive style and academic performance among college students (Armstrong, 2000; Cool & Van den Broeck, 2007). Cognitive style does not indicate intelligence or capability. Smart people may score high or low on any of the cognitive styles.

Knowing your cognitive style, however, can prove advantageous in several ways, such as when selecting career options, choosing compatible business environments, identifying the best work assignments, selecting compatible teammates, and improving your decision making. It can also help you determine which academic courses or study methods will be most compatible with your cognitive style—for example, a knowing style may feel more comfortable in accounting, a planning style may feel more comfortable in operations, and a creating style may feel more comfortable in advertising. No single course represents only one cognitive style, of course, but the way in which you process information is often more compatible with one kind of course more than others.

People can modify their cognitive styles, of course, as they engage in different kinds of activities, interact with different kinds of people, or manage in different kinds of work environments. Most people tend to adapt to their circumstances. However, substantial evidence shows that people tend to select an occupation that reinforces and is consistent with their dominant cognitive style (Agor, 1985; Chan, 1966; Jones, & Wright, 2010). When they do, they tend to be more successful.

The Cognitive Style Instrument you completed in the Skill Assessment section of this chapter helps you identify the tendencies you have toward gathering, evaluating, and responding to information. Comparing your scores against three different comparison groups will help you gauge your own tendencies and inclinations toward processing information. To fully capitalize on this information, you will also want to consider your own orientation toward change in the next section.

ATTITUDES TOWARD CHANGE

In order to capitalize fully on the strengths of your own cognitive style, you also should be aware of your orientation toward change. This is important because, as the environment in which managers operate continues to become more chaotic, more temporary, more complex, and more overloaded with information, your ability to process information is at least partly constrained by your fundamental attitude about change.

Almost no one disagrees with the prediction that change will increase in the future, both in pace and scope. The challenge of students and managers in the twenty-first century is to prepare for a world that cannot be predicted by the experiences of the past.

No manager at the beginning of the twenty-first century would boast of being stable, constant, or maintaining the status quo. Even now, stability is interpreted more as stagnation than steadiness, and organizations not in the business of major transformation and revolution are generally viewed as recalcitrant. All this is to say that the environment of the twenty-first century is characterized by turbulence, gigantic change, rapid-fire decisions, and chaos. No one will have time to read and analyze a case study. E-business has changed the rules of the game. No one can predict the competitive environment anymore. Customers are no longer geographically constrained, and the standards for servicing them have changed completely.

In this chaotic pace of change—what some refer to as "permanent white water"—being aware of your own orientation toward change is an important prerequisite for successfully coping with it. Two dimensions of change orientation particularly relevant for managers are discussed on the following pages.

Tolerance of Ambiguity

The first important dimension is **tolerance of ambiguity**, which refers to the extent to which individuals are threatened by or have difficulty coping with situations that are ambiguous, where change occurs rapidly or unpredictably, where information is inadequate or unclear, or where complexity exists. People vary in their aptitude for operating successfully in stimulus-rich and information-overloaded environments or in the extent to which they can cope with ambiguous, incomplete, unstructured, dynamic situations. Individuals who have a high tolerance of ambiguity also tend to be more cognitively complex. They tend to pay attention to more information, interpret more cues, and possess more sense-making categories than less complex individuals.

Research has found that people who are more tolerant of ambiguity and cognitively complex are better transmitters of information, more sensitive to internal (nonsuperficial) characteristics of others when evaluating their performance at work, and more behaviorally adaptive and flexible under ambiguous and overloaded conditions than less tolerant and less cognitively complex individuals. Managers with higher tolerance-of-ambiguity scores are more likely to be entrepreneurial in their actions, to be open to new information, and to cope more effectively with major organizational change, downsizing, and role stress and conflict (Armstrong-Stassen, 1998; Haase, Lee, & Banks, 1979; Teoh & Foo, 1997; Timothy, Thoresen, Pucik, and Welbourne, 1999).

The downside is that individuals who are more tolerant of ambiguity have more difficulty focusing on a single important element of information, generate one best answer, and concentrate without being distracted by interruptions. However, for the most part, in an information-rich environment, tolerance of ambiguity and cognitive complexity are more adaptive than the opposite characteristics.

In the Assessment section of this chapter, a Tolerance of Ambiguity Scale (Budner, 1962) assesses the extent to which you have a tolerance for these kinds of complex situations. In scoring the Tolerance of Ambiguity Scale, three different subscale scores are assessed. One is the *novelty* score, which indicates the extent to which you are tolerant of new, unfamiliar information or situations. The second subscale is the *complexity* score, which indicates the extent to which you are tolerant of multiple, distinctive, or unrelated information. The third subscale is the *insolubility* score, which indicates the extent to which you are tolerant of problems that are very difficult to solve because, for example, alternative solutions are not evident, information is unavailable, or the problem's components seem unrelated to each other. In general, the more tolerant people are of novelty, complexity, and insolubility, the more likely they are to succeed as managers in

information-rich, ambiguous environments. They are less overwhelmed by ambiguous circumstances.

It is important to note that cognitive complexity and tolerance for ambiguity are not related to cognitive intelligence, and your score on the Tolerance of Ambiguity Scale is not an evaluation of how smart you are. Most important, individuals can learn to tolerate more complexity and more flexibility in their information-processing abilities.

The first step toward increasing tolerance is becoming aware of where you are now by completing the Assessment section. Then the Skill Analysis and Skill Practice sections of this chapter, along with discussions such as the one in the chapters on problem solving and creativity, provide ways to improve your tolerance for ambiguity and your cognitive complexity. It is also important to note that a positive correlation exists between tolerance of ambiguity and the second dimension of orientation toward change discussed here, internal locus of control.

Locus of Control

The second dimension of orientation toward change is labeled **locus of control**. It is one of the most studied and written-about aspects of orientation toward change. Locus of control refers to the attitude people develop regarding the extent to which they are in control of their own destinies. When individuals receive information about the success or failure of their own actions or when something changes in the environment, they differ in how they interpret that information. People receive reinforcements, both positive or negative, as they attempt to make changes around them. If individuals interpret the reinforcement they receive to be contingent on their own actions, it is called an **internal locus of control** (that is, "I was the cause of the success or failure of the change"). If they interpret the reinforcement as being a product of outside forces, it is called an **external locus of control** (that is, "Something or someone else caused the success or failure"). Over time, people develop a "generalized expectancy" about the dominant sources of the reinforcements they receive. Thus, they become largely internally focused or largely externally focused with regard to the source of control they perceive in a changing environment.

More than 10,000 studies have been done using the locus of control scale. In general, the research suggests that managers in North America have a far greater tendency to have an internal locus of control than, say, Middle Eastern and Far East managers (Trompenaars, 1996). Individuals who have an internal locus of control are less alienated from the work environment, more satisfied with their work, have better relationships with their managers, enjoy better health, and experience less job strain and more position mobility (promotions and job changes) than individuals with an external locus of control (Bernardi, 1997, 2011; Coleman, Irving, & Cooper, 1999; Martin, Thomas, Charles, Epitropaki, & McNamara, 2005; Newton & Keenan, 1990; Ng, Sorensen, & Eby, 2006; Seeman, 1982; Valentine, S. R., Godkin, J., & Doughty, G. P. (2008).

A study of leadership and group performance found that internals were more likely to be leaders and that groups led by internals were more effective than those led by externals (Anderson & Schneider, 1978; Blau, 1993). Internals also were found to outperform externals in stressful situations, to engage in more entrepreneurial activity, to be more active in managing their own careers, and to have higher levels of job involvement than externals (Bonnett & Furnham, 1991; Boone & Brabander, 1997; Cromie, Callahan, & Jansen, 1992; Hammer & Vardi, 1981; Krenl, 1992). Firms led by internals performed significantly better than firms led by externals (Boone, Brabander & Witteloostuijn, 1996). In summarizing the results of this massive array of research on locus of control, the conclusion is consistent. In American culture, people are handicapped by an external locus of control.

On the other hand, research also has found that an internal locus of control is not a panacea for all management problems. Internal locus of control is not always a positive attribute. For example, individuals with an external locus of control have been found to be more inclined to initiate structure as leaders (to help clarify roles). Internals are less likely to comply with leader directions and are less accurate in processing feedback about successes and failures than are externals. Internals also have more difficulty arriving at decisions with serious consequences for someone else (Coleman et al., 1999; Wheeler & Davis, 1979).

It is important to note that locus of control can shift over time, particularly as a function of the position held at work, and that external locus of control does not inhibit individuals from attaining positions of power and influence at the top of organizations. Therefore, no matter what your internal–external score, you can be a successful manager in the right setting, or you can alter your locus of control.

The Locus of Control Scale in the Skill Assessment section helps you generate a score showing the extent to which you have an internal or external locus of control. The scoring key identifies your *External Locus of Control* score. Comparing your own score to the mean scores of several other groups can help you determine the extent to which you are internal (below the mean scores) or external (above the mean scores) in your orientation toward change.

In summary, two key attitudes toward change—tolerance of ambiguity and locus of control—have been found to be associated with success in management roles. Knowing your scores on these two factors can help you capitalize on your strengths and enhance your potential for management success. While substantial research exists associating some positive managerial behaviors with internal locus of control and tolerance of ambiguity, possessing these orientations is neither an assurance of success as a manager nor a solution to the problems that managers face. By knowing your scores, however, you will be able to choose situations in which you are more likely to feel comfortable, perform effectively, and understand the point of view of those whose perspectives differ from yours. Self-understanding is a prerequisite to self-improvement and change.

CORE SELF-EVALUATION

Every person has a distinct personality. This concept of *personality* refers to the relatively enduring combination of traits that makes an individual unique and at the same time produces consistencies in his or her thoughts and behaviors. There is much disagreement about how much of our personality is learned as opposed to being biologically or genetically determined. Some explanation for what makes us unique can certainly be attributed to the genetic predispositions we bring with us when we are born. Yet, a sizable portion of our behavioral makeup is learned and can be changed. We focus in this chapter on factors over which we have some control and can change if we determine to do so.

In the field of personality psychology, there has been a gradual convergence around a few major dimensions of personality. A review of the literature in 2001, for example, found that more than 50,000 studies had been conducted on just three attributes of personality—self-esteem, locus of control, and neuroticism or emotional stability (Bono & Judge, 2003). More than 100 studies a month are published on the topic of self-esteem alone!

It has become popular in psychology to refer to the "Big Five" personality attributes as the most important aspects of personality, although there is insufficient scientific evidence that such a conclusion is merited. These Big Five attributes are the most researched, however, and they include *extroversion* (the extent to which people are inclined toward gregariousness and sociability instead of quiet and reserved); *agreeableness* (the extent to which people are friendly and affable as opposed to being disagreeable and aggressive); *conscientiousness* (the extent to which people are careful, task oriented, and orderly as opposed to being disorganized, flexible, and unreliable); *neuroticism* (the extent to which people are emotionally fragile, negative, and fearful as opposed to being optimistic, positive, and emotionally stable); and *openness* (the extent to which people are curious and open to new ideas as opposed to being rigid or dogmatic). Individuals tend to differ on these five attributes, and scores on these five factors have been used to predict a wide variety of outcomes including behavioral performance, life success, job satisfaction, interpersonal attraction, and intellectual achievement.

Tim Judge and his colleagues have found, however, that differences in the Big Five personality attributes can be explained by a more foundational personality factor. It is referred to as core self-evaluation, or the fundamental evaluation each person has developed about himself or herself. According to Judge and colleagues (2003), core evaluations influence people's appraisals of themselves subconsciously. For the most part, people are not aware of their own core self-evaluations. Yet, when people respond to certain cues—including personality surveys, behavioral signals, or mental stimuli—their responses are determined to a nontrivial extent by this deeper and more fundamental self-appraisal. The assessment instrument Skill Assessment section will be very useful in helping you identify your own core self-evaluation.

Core self-evaluation is sometimes referred to as overall positive self-regard—or the extent to which people value themselves and feel proficient as individuals. It is comprised of four components: (1) *self-esteem*, or the extent to which people see themselves as capable, successful, and worthy (Harter, 1990); (2) *generalized self-efficacy*, or the sense of one's ability to perform capably across a variety of circumstances (Locke, McClear, & Knight, 1996); (3) *neuroticism*, which is reversed-scored, or the tendency to have a negative outlook and pessimistic approach to life (Watson, 2000); and (4) *locus of control*, which has been discussed earlier, referring to a person's beliefs about the extent to which he or she can control his or her own experiences (Rotter, 1966).

Whereas these four personality traits have been studied separately in psychology, it has been discovered that there is a great deal of overlap; and, in combination, they create a single, powerful factor that lies at the core of personality (Judge et al., 2002, 2003, 2005). The commonalties among the four factors that make up core self-evaluation are not difficult to understand. That is, when people view themselves in a positive way, or when they possess high self-esteem, they also tend to feel capable of performing effectively across a variety of situations (generalized self-efficacy), they feel in control of their circumstances (locus of control), and they feel emotionally stable (the opposite of neuroticism). Each of these factors has a slightly different meaning, of course, but the overlap and shared meaning among them is the thing being measured by the Core Self-Evaluation Survey you completed in the Skill Assessment section.

Of course, we have all met people who are self-centered, braggarts, or narcissistic. They seem to possess an abundance of positive self-regard, and we might be tempted to think of them as having very high scores in core self-evaluation. However, these people also are likely to be insensitive to their abrasive impact on others. When threatened, they emphasize winning or getting their way. They tend to look in the mirror more often than others, spend more time thinking about themselves and the impressions they convey, and work to make themselves look good or be in the spotlight. They tend to be manipulative in their relationships with others.

They are, in a word, selfish people. This is not the same as having a positive core self-evaluation. Rather, a positive core self-evaluation includes sensitivity to others and to the environment so that relationships with others are strengthened rather than weakened, developed rather than destroyed. As summarized in Figure 1.2, strong, confident people are better able to lead, manage, and form supportive relationships with others.

Evidence for this fact comes from the studies of the relationships between core self-evaluation and the effectiveness of individuals at work. Individuals with high core self-evaluations tend to be more satisfied with their jobs. They tend to select more challenging jobs, and they tend to find the work in which they are engaged to be more intrinsically fulfilling. They make their work more rewarding and more stimulating to themselves.

In addition to job satisfaction, core self-evaluation is also strongly related to job performance. That is, people who score higher in core self-evaluation tend to perform more successfully at work as employees and as managers (Judge & Bono, 2001). They tend to earn higher salary levels and have less career plateauing than others as well.

Figure 1.2 **The Effects of Core Self-Evaluation**

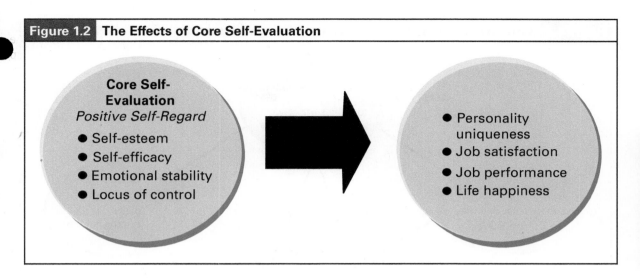

In summary, core self-evaluation scores tend to be a very important predictor of personality differences, job satisfaction, job performance, and life happiness. When people have developed a positive self-regard—when they feel valuable, capable, stable, and in control—they tend to function better at work, in relationships, and in life. Developing management skills and acquiring the competency to perform effectively in work settings is one way to enhance feelings of positive self-regard.

Summary

Corporate America increasingly has begun to discover the power of developing self-awareness among its managers. Each year, millions of executives complete instruments designed to increase self-awareness in a large number of name-brand private and public-sector organizations. An awareness of how individuals differ in their emotional maturity, values priorities and values maturity, cognitive style, orientation toward change, and personality (core self-evaluation) has helped many companies cope better with interpersonal conflicts, botched communications, breakdowns in trust, and misunderstandings. For example, after requiring his top 100 managers to undergo self-awareness training, the president of the computer reservations company of Hilton Hotels and Budget Rent-a-Car stated:

We had some real morale problems. I realized I had a mixed bag of people reporting to me and that this training could help us better understand each other and also understand how we make decisions. We wouldn't have made it through [a recent company crisis] without self-awareness training (Moore, 1987).

Not only does self-awareness training assist you in your ability to understand and manage yourself, but it also is important in helping you develop understanding of the differences in others. You will regularly encounter individuals who possess different styles, different sets of values, and different perspectives than you do. Most work forces are becoming more, not less, diverse. Self-awareness, therefore, can be a valuable tool in helping you develop empathy and understanding for other people as well as more successfully managing yourself. The relationship between the five critical areas of self-awareness and these management outcomes is summarized in Figure 1.3.

Most of the following chapters in this book intend to help you develop and improve your skills in interpersonal or group interaction. But, an important paradox exists in developing management skills. *We can know others only by knowing ourselves, but we can know ourselves only by knowing others.* Our knowledge of others, and therefore our ability to manage or interact successfully with them, comes from connecting what we see in them to our own experience. If we are not self-aware, we have no foundation for knowing certain things about others. Self-recognition leads to recognition and understanding of others. As Harris (1981) puts it:

Nothing is really personal that is not first interpersonal, beginning with the infant's shock of separation from the umbilical cord. What we know about ourselves comes only from the outside, and it is interpreted by the kind of experiences we have had. What we know about others comes only from analogy with our own network of feelings.

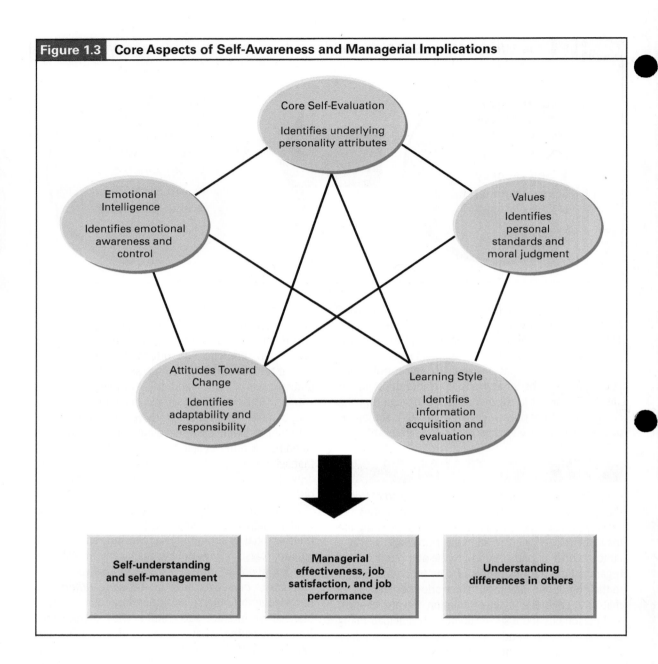

Figure 1.3   Core Aspects of Self-Awareness and Managerial Implications

Core Self-Evaluation

Identifies underlying personality attributes

Emotional Intelligence

Identifies emotional awareness and control

Values

Identifies personal standards and moral judgment

Attitudes Toward Change

Identifies adaptability and responsibility

Learning Style

Identifies information acquisition and evaluation

Self-understanding and self-management

Managerial effectiveness, job satisfaction, and job performance

Understanding differences in others

Behavioral Guidelines

Following are the behavioral guidelines relating to the improvement of self-awareness. These guidelines will be helpful to you as you engage in analysis, practice, and application activities designed to improve your self-awareness.

A. Identify your sensitive line. Determine what information about yourself you are most likely to defend against.

B. Use the seven dimensions of national culture to diagnose differences between your own values orientation and that of individuals from other cultures, age categories, or ethnic groups.

C. Identify a comprehensive, consistent, and universal set of principles on which you will base your behavior. Identify the most important terminal and instrumental values that guide your decisions.

D. Expand your cognitive style, your tolerance of ambiguity, and your internal locus of control by increasing your exposure to new information and engaging in activities with which you are unfamiliar and that will stretch you. Seek ways to expand and broaden yourself.

E. Enhance your emotional intelligence by consciously monitoring your own emotional responses, working to enhance self-control, and by practicing the diagnosis of others' emotional cues.

F. Develop a healthy core self-evaluation and positive self-regard by consciously capitalizing on your personal strengths and by highlighting and building on your successful accomplishments.

G. Engage in honest self-disclosure with someone who is close to you and accepting of you. Check out aspects of yourself about which you are uncertain.

H. Keep a journal, and make time regularly to engage in self-analysis. Balance life's activities with some time for self-renewal and self-awareness development.

 SKILL *ANALYSIS*

CASES INVOLVING SELF-AWARENESS

Communist Prison Camp

To understand the development of increased self-awareness, it is helpful to consider the opposite process, that is, the destruction of self-awareness. Understanding the growth process is often enhanced by understanding the deterioration process. Hence, in the case below, a process of psychological self-destruction is described as it occurred among prisoners of war during the Korean War. Consider how these processes that destroy self-awareness can be reversed to create greater self-awareness. The setting is a prisoner-of-war camp managed by the Communist Chinese.

In such prisons, the total regimen, consisting of physical privation, prolonged interrogation, total isolation from former relationships and sources of information, detailed regimentation of all daily activities, and deliberate humiliation and degradation, was geared to producing a confession of alleged crimes, the assumption of a penitent role, and the adoption of a Communist frame of reference. The prisoner was not informed what his crimes were, nor was he permitted to evade the issue by making up a false confession. Instead, what the prisoner learned he must do was reevaluate his past from the point of view of the Communists and recognize that most of his former attitudes and behavior were actually criminal from this point of view. For example, a priest who had dispensed food to needy peasants in his mission church had to "recognize" that he was actually a tool of imperialism and was using his missionary activities as cover for exploitation of the peasants. Even worse, he had used food as blackmail to accomplish his aims.

The key technique used by the Communists to produce social alienation to a degree sufficient to allow such redefinition and reevaluation to occur was to put the prisoner into a cell with four or more other prisoners who were somewhat more advanced in their "thought reform" than he. Such a cell usually had one leader who was responsible to the prison authorities, and the progress of the whole cell was made contingent on the progress of the least "reformed" member. This condition meant, in practice, that four or more cell members devoted all their energies to getting their least "reformed" member to recognize "the truth" about himself and to confess. To accomplish this they typically swore at, harangued, beat, denounced, humiliated, reviled, and brutalized their victim 24 hours a day, sometimes for weeks or months on end. If the authorities felt that the prisoner was basically uncooperative, they manacled his hands behind his back and chained his ankles, which made him completely dependent on his cellmates for the fulfillment of his basic needs. It was this reduction to an animal-like existence in front of other humans that constituted the ultimate humiliation and led most reliably to the destruction of the prisoner's image of himself. Even in his own eyes, he became something that was not worthy of the regard of his fellow man.

If, to avoid complete physical and personal destruction, the prisoner began to confess in the manner desired of him, he was usually forced to prove his sincerity by making irrevocable behavioral commitments, such as denouncing and implicating his friends and relatives in his own newly recognized crimes. Once he had done this, he became further alienated from his former self, even in his own eyes, and could seek security only in a new identity and new social relationships. Aiding this process of confessing was the fact that the crimes gave the prisoner something concrete to which to attach the free-floating guilt that the accusing environment and his own humiliation usually stimulated.

A good example was the plight of the sick and wounded prisoners of war who, because of their physical confinement, were unable to escape from continual conflict with their interrogator or instructor, and who therefore often ended up forming a close relationship with him. Chinese Communist instructors often encouraged prisoners to take long walks or have informal talks with them and offered as incentives cigarettes, tea, and other rewards. If the prisoner was willing to cooperate and become a "progressive," he could join with other "progressives" in an active group life.

Within the political prison, the group cell not only provided the forces toward alienation but also offered the road to a "new self." Not only were there available among the fellow prisoners individuals with whom the prisoner could identify because of their shared plight, but once he showed any tendency to seek a new identity by truly trying to reevaluate his past, he received again a whole range of rewards, of which perhaps the most important was the interpersonal information that he was again a person worthy of respect and regard.

SOURCE: *Schein, 1960.*

Discussion Questions

1.1. What specific techniques were used to bring about the destruction of self-awareness among the prisoners?

1.2. What processes could be used to create the reverse process, that is, to strengthen of the self-concept?

1.3. Assume you are charged with the orientation of a cohort of new managers in your organization. How would you help them understand their own strengths and inclinations, and how they could best contribute to the firm?

1.4. What mechanisms could the prisoners of war have used to resist a change in their self-concepts?

1.5. What could be done to reform or rebuild the self-awareness of these prisoners? What can be done to help individuals without self-awareness improve that skill?

Computerized Exam

Graduate business school students were all required to take a one-credit-hour current events course. Like other courses in the business school, the final exam was administered on a computer. From a memory bank containing 350 questions, the computer was programmed to select 40 questions for each student, flashing them on the screen one at a time. Students could take the exam any time after the course began in January, whenever they felt ready.

Unfortunately, problems arose. When the test was computerized, a "skip feature" was added to the computer program. This feature was designed so that students could pass over a question they didn't want to answer immediately. The question, theoretically, would return to the screen at a later time, simulating the way in which students skip over and then return to questions on a written exam. However, the skip feature didn't work correctly. Instead of recycling skipped questions back to the student, the computer simply threw them out. Thus, the skip feature became a way for students to avoid any questions they couldn't answer.

Another snafu in the program was that when a certain number of questions were skipped during the exam—apparently between six and ten—the computer automatically ended the test. Scores were immediately flashed to the student and recorded in the computer memory. Scores were calculated on a percentage basis, only counting the questions that the student answered. Skipped questions were not counted as correct or incorrect. Therefore, a student who answered ten questions, nine of them correctly, and skipped enough other questions to trigger the automatic computer shutoff, received a score of 90 percent.

Knowledge of the skip command apparently was widely distributed well before the end of the term. One person estimated that at least half the students knew about it. Upon review, 77 out of 139 members of the graduating class answered fewer than the required 40 questions when they took the exam. When questioned, some students said they didn't realize a programming error had occurred and didn't keep track of how many questions were asked in total. Others argued that "it is like filling out an income tax form. People hire accountants all the time to find loopholes that they can use. That is not illegal, even if the government doesn't advertise the loopholes. The computer program allowed for this loophole, and we did what we did."

1.6. *If you were one of the students in the class:*

a. Would you tell the instructor about the programming error before the end of the term?

b. Report the names of the other students you knew who cheated?

c. Admit that you cheated?

1.7. *If you were the instructor for the course, which of the following would you do?*
   a. Flunk the 77 students who did not complete 40 questions.
   b. Require the 77 students to retake the exam, but let them graduate.
   c. Require all 139 students to retake the course since no student reported the problem, a violation of the student ethical code.
   d. Change the computer program, but do nothing to the students.
   e. Select another alternative.
1.8. *What is your rationale for the decisions you made in questions 1 and 2 above? Discuss your rationale with your colleagues.*
1.9. *What level of values maturity is displayed by each alternative? What ethical principles are demonstrated?*

Decision Dilemmas

For each of the five scenarios below, select the choice you would make if you were in the situation.

1. A young manager in a high-technology firm was offered a position by the firm's chief competitor for almost double her salary. Her firm sought to prevent her from changing jobs, arguing that her knowledge of certain specialized manufacturing processes would give the competitor unfair advantage. Since she had acquired that knowledge through special training and unique opportunities in her current position, the firm argued that it was unethical for her to accept the competitor's offer. What should the young manager do?

   _____ Accept the offer

   _____ Reject the offer

2. A consumer advocate organization conducted a survey to determine whether Wendy's hamburgers were really any more "hot and juicy" than other hamburgers. After testing a Big Mac, a Whopper, a Carl's, Jr. burger, and a Wendy's Hot and Juicy, each hamburger brand received approximately the same number of votes for being the juiciest. The consumer group advocated that Wendy's not advertise its hamburgers to be the juiciest. The company indicated that its own tests showed different results and that the image of the burger was the important thing, not the test results. Should the advertisements cease or not?

   _____ Cease to advertise

   _____ Continue to advertise

3. After several profitable years, the Bob Cummings Organic Vitamin Company was made available for sale. Bob's movie and TV appearances precluded him from being closely involved in the management of such a large company. It became apparent that, if present trends continued, the company would either have to expand substantially or lose a large share of the market. Several firms were interested in purchasing the company for the asking price, but one firm was particularly aggressive. It sponsored several parties and receptions in Bob's honor; a 35-foot yacht was made available for his use during the summer; and several gifts for family members arrived during the holidays. Bob's wife questioned the propriety of these activities. Was it appropriate for Bob to accept the gifts? Should he sell to that firm?

_____ Proper to accept

_____ Not proper

_____ Should not sell

_____ Should sell

4. John Waller was hired to coach football. After two seasons, he was so successful that he was named coach of the year by UPI, _Sporting News_, and ESPN.
He was also very vocal about the need to clean up cheating in college athletics,
especially among competitor schools in his own conference. He heard rumors
about inappropriate alumni gifts to some of his own athletes, but after confronting those involved, he received assurances that the rumors weren't true. At the
beginning of the next season, however, he received conclusive evidence that
seven of the starters on his team, including an All-American player, had received
financial benefits from a wealthy booster. What should Waller do?

_____ Kick them off the team

_____ Suspend them for several games

_____ Warn them but do nothing

_____ Do something else

5. Roger's company had been battered by competition from Asian firms. Not only
were Asian products selling for less money, but their quality was substantially
higher. By investing in some high-technology equipment and fostering better
union–management relations, Roger was relatively certain that the quality gap
could be overcome. But his overhead rate was more than 40 percent above that of
the competitor firms. He reasoned that the most efficient way to lower costs would
be to close one of his older plants, lay off the employees, and increase production
in the newer plants. He knew just which plant would be the one to close. The
trouble was, the community was dependent on that plant as its major employer
and had recently invested a great deal of money for highway repair and streetlight
construction around the plant. Most of the workforce were older people who
had lived in the area most of their lives. It was improbable that they could obtain
alternative employment in the same area. Should Roger close the plant or not?

_____ Close the plant

_____ Do not close

Discussion Questions

Form a small group and discuss the following questions regarding these five scenarios:

1.10. Why did you make the choices you did in each case? Justify each answer.
1.11. What principles or basic values for decision making did you use in each case?
1.12. What additional information would you need in order to be certain about your
choices?
1.13. What circumstances might arise to make you change your mind about your decision? Could there be a different answer to each case in a different circumstance?
1.14. What do your answers tell you about your own emotional intelligence, values,
cognitive style, attitude toward change, and core self-evaluation?

EXERCISES FOR IMPROVING
SELF-AWARENESS THROUGH
SELF-DISCLOSURE

Through the Looking Glass

In the nineteenth century, the concept of "looking-glass self" was developed to describe the process used by people to develop self-awareness. It means that other people serve as a looking glass for each of us. They mirror back our actions and behaviors. In turn, we form our opinions of ourselves as a result of observing and interpreting this mirroring. The best way to form accurate self-perceptions, therefore, is to become vulnerable to others. This usually involves sharing your thoughts, attitudes, feelings, actions, or plans with others. This exercise helps you do that by asking you to analyze your own styles and inclinations and then share and discuss them with others. This sharing exercise will provide insights that you haven't recognized before.

Assignment

In a group of three or four, share your scores on the Skill Assessment instruments. Determine what similarities and differences exist among you as a group. Do systematic ethnic or gender differences exist? Now read aloud the 10 statements listed below. Each person should respond to each statement, but take turns going first. The purpose of your completing the statements aloud is to help you articulate aspects of your self-awareness and to receive reactions to them from others.

1. In taking the assessment instruments, I was surprised by...

2. Some of my dominant characteristics captured by the instruments are...

3. Among my greatest strengths are...

4. Among my greatest areas needing development are...

5. The time I felt most successful was...

6. The time I felt least competent was...

7. My three highest priorities in life are...

8. The way in which I differ most from other people is...

9. I get along best with people who...

10. From what the others in this group have shared, here is an impression I have formed about each of you:

Diagnosing Managerial Characteristics

This exercise is designed to give you practice in diagnosing differences in others' styles and inclinations. Being aware of the styles, values, and attitudes of others will help you manage them more effectively. Below are brief descriptions of four successful managers. They differ in values, learning styles, orientations toward change, and interpersonal orientation. After reading the scenarios, form small groups to discuss the questions that follow.

Michael Dell

Michael Dell is the kind of guy people either love or hate. He is worth more than $13 billion, loves to go to work each day, and is as likely to tear a computer apart and put it back together again as to read a financial report. Several decades after he started assembling computers in his dorm room, Michael is still fascinated with the hardware. Despite his billionaire status, "if anyone believes that he is not the chief technologist in this company, they are naive," says Robert McFarland, former vice president of Dell's federal sales group. Although Dell Computer is the quintessential lean-and-mean company, Michael does not play the part of the whipcracker. After recently receiving an award from the Austin, Texas, Chamber of Commerce, for example, Michael and his wife stayed long after the program was over to chat with everyone who wanted to meet him. He has been described as shy and quiet and not inclined toward public hyperbole. "Michael has a genuine shyness...he is a genuinely mild-mannered, low-key person who was very focused on reaching his objectives," says Brian Fawkes, a former Dell employee. Admittedly, Dell has experienced several missteps and losses, but Michael has been unafraid to learn from missteps. "Michael makes mistakes. He just never makes the same mistake twice," says Mark Tebbe, former president of a firm that Dell acquired.

SOURCE: *Adapted from Darrow, 1998.*

Patrick M. Byrne

As president and chairman of Overstock.com in Salt Lake City, Utah, Byrne was a Marshall Scholar who received his PhD in philosophy from Stanford University. His management style, personality, and core values are illustrated in his interview with *Fast Company*: "Learning philosophy has been useful in teaching me how to get to the heart of things—to be able to deconstruct what the real issues are. People think we're endless debaters, but what we're really doing is refining concepts in order to reach agreement. With negotiations, instead of trying to fight someone on every one of the issues, most of the time it turns out he cares about a whole bunch of things that you don't care about. Make those trade-offs, and he'll think you're being too generous when in fact you're just giving him the sleeves off your vest. Ultimately, philosophy is about values, and that definitely has its place in business. I consider myself a far outsider to Wall Street. There's a whole lot of obfuscation involved. In August, I spoke out on how the Wall Street system was corrupt and how the financial press was co-opted. Because of it I got called a buffoon and wacky; then a lot of lies came out about my being gay, taking cocaine, and hiring a stripper. That's sort of the fifth-grade level we're operating on. It doesn't bother me. When you decide to stand for things, you have to be prepared to face criticism, mockery, and derision."

SOURCE: *Adapted from* **Fast Company**, *2005.*

Maurice Blanks

When Maurice started architecture school, one of the professors said that only 25 percent of the students would make it. Sure enough, Maurice dropped out in his forties after operating his own office in Chicago. He moved to Minneapolis to devote himself full time to Blu Dot, a company he helped create. His discussion about architecture reveals a great deal about his personal attributes. "Architecture is about keeping track of thousands of pieces of information and making sure they're all covered in the design. The implications of failure are pretty high if you don't—people could get hurt. Therefore, you learn that you must be very efficient with information and organization, which naturally translates to running the day-to-day operations of a company. It's funny how the word 'sell' is never used in architecture school, but to me the critiques were kind of informal lessons in sales. For exams, you'd present your work to a jury—professors, peers, local architects, and so on. Their job was to shell you; your job was to defend yourself. It's pretty brutal. Tears are not uncommon. But it taught me how to communicate ideas quickly and tailor information to an audience."

SOURCE: *Adapted from* **Fast Company**, *2005.*

Gordon Bethune

Gordon Bethune has been described as the *other* earthy, exuberant, hard-drinking Texas CEO who turned around an airline that became famous for good service, happy employees, and admirable profitability. Herb Kelleher at Southwest Airlines was the best known, but Gordon Bethune at Continental Airlines was equally successful. A high school dropout mechanic who spent years in the Navy, Gordon took over a twice-bankrupt airline and led it from a $960 million loss to more than $600 million profit in five years. Even from his early years as a Navy mechanic, Gordon was known as superb motivator of people and a network builder. "He had a web of relationships that enabled him to get whatever he needed," said a former commanding officer. At Continental, Gordon turned around a culture where morale was in the pits, on-time performance was abysmal, and everything from the planes to the meals were a mess. Part of the turnaround was due to Gordon's personal attention to employees—for example, he attended the graduation ceremonies of every new class of flight attendants, handed out candy canes to employees during the Christmas season, showed up regularly at employee birthday parties, and held a monthly open house in his office to encourage employee communication. "Anybody who worked here longer than two months could recognize Gordon," said a baggage handler in Newark. When he walked through an airport, employees waved and called out his name. Whereas Gordon was known as an irreverent and wild guy, he demanded precision and standardized levels of service in every place in the company. When he discovered slightly larger white coffee cups in a Houston airport lounge, for example, he was told that they were needed to fit the new coffee maker. He demanded that the coffee maker be changed so that the standard blue cups could be used. No exceptions."

SOURCE: *Adapted from O'Reilly, 1999.*

Discussion Questions

1.15. Rank these individuals from highest to lowest in terms of:
   - ❏ Emotional intelligence
   - ❏ Values maturity
   - ❏ Tolerance of ambiguity
   - ❏ Core self-evaluation

   Justify your evaluations in a discussion with your colleagues and compare your scores.

1.16. What is your prediction about the dominant cognitive styles of each of these individuals? What data do you use as evidence?

1.17. If you were assigned to hire a senior manager for your organization and this was your candidate pool, what questions would you ask to identify:
   - ❏ Cognitive styles
   - ❏ Values orientations
   - ❏ Orientation toward change
   - ❏ Core self-evaluation

   Which one of these people would you hire if you wanted a CEO for your company? Why?

1.18. Assume each of these individuals were members of your team. What would be the greatest strengths and weaknesses of your team? What kinds of attributes would you want to add to your team to ensure that it was optimally heterogeneous?

An Exercise for Identifying Aspects of Personal Culture: A Learning Plan and Autobiography

The purpose of this exercise is to assist you in articulating your key goals and aspirations as well as identifying a personal learning plan to facilitate your success. Because continuous learning is so important for you to succeed throughout your life, we want to help you identify some specific ambitions and to develop a set of procedures to help you reach your potential.

This exercise is accomplished in three steps:

Step 1: (Aspirations): Write an autobiographical story that might appear in *Fortune Magazine, Fast Company*, or the *Wall Street Journal* on this date 15 years from now. This story should identify your notable accomplishments and your newsworthy successes. What will you have achieved that will fulfill your dreams? What outcomes would make you ecstatically happy? What legacy do you want to be known for?

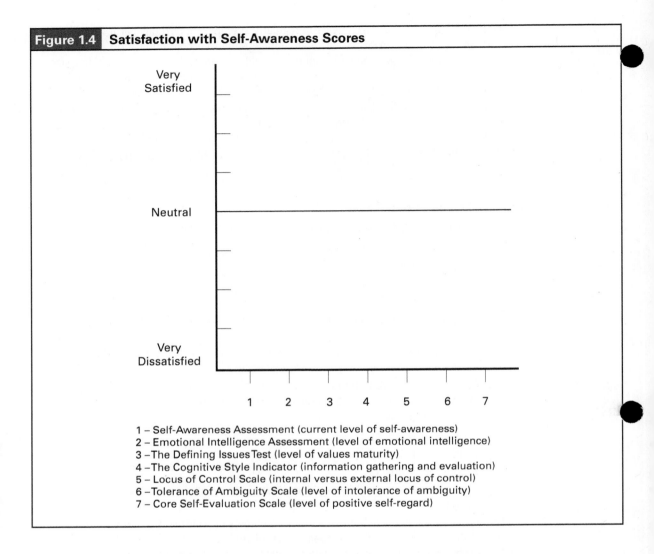

Figure 1.4 Satisfaction with Self-Awareness Scores

Very Satisfied

Neutral

Very Dissatisfied

1 2 3 4 5 6 7

1 – Self-Awareness Assessment (current level of self-awareness)
2 – Emotional Intelligence Assessment (level of emotional intelligence)
3 – The Defining Issues Test (level of values maturity)
4 – The Cognitive Style Indicator (information gathering and evaluation)
5 – Locus of Control Scale (internal versus external locus of control)
6 – Tolerance of Ambiguity Scale (level of intolerance of ambiguity)
7 – Core Self-Evaluation Scale (level of positive self-regard)

Step 2: (Characteristics): Review your scores on the skill assessment instruments. Using Figure 1.4, identify the extent to which you are satisfied with your scores on these various instruments. The vertical axis in the figure ranges from Very Satisfied to Very Dissatisfied. The horizontal axis identifies the five areas of self-awareness being assessed in this chapter. For each of the seven instruments, plot your satisfaction level with how you scored. By joining those points together, you will have created a *Self-Awareness Satisfaction Profile*. This will help you highlight areas in which you will want to improve.

Based on that plot, identify your distinctive competencies, your strengths, and your unique attributes. What are the values, styles, and attitudes that will assist you in achieving the aspirations you have identified in Step 1? In what areas do you want to focus improvement efforts?

Step 3: (Feedback): Interview a member of your family or someone who knows you very well. Ask that person to describe what they see as your unique strengths and capabilities. What does he or she predict for you in your future? Include the following questions in your interview:

❏ Who do you admire a great deal because of their success in life? What capabilities and attributes do they possess?

❑ Who do you know that has failed to achieve their potential? What do you see as the most significant causes of their failure?

❑ What do you see as the distinctive and notable capabilities that I possess?

❑ In what areas do you think I should focus my improvement and development efforts?

❑ What do you see me doing in 15 years?

Step 4: (Planning): Now identify the developmental activities in which you will engage if you are to achieve your aspirations. With the insight you have gained from steps 2 and 3, identify the things you must do to help you achieve what you hope to accomplish. Consider the following activities.

❑ What courses will you take?

❑ What people will you get to know?

❑ In what extracurricular or life-balance activities will you engage?

❑ What will you read?

❑ What spiritual activities will be most meaningful?

This written product should be handed in to your instructor, or it should be given to a family member for safekeeping. Open and reread this document in five years to determine the extent to which you are on track.

ACTIVITIES FOR DEVELOPING SELF-AWARENESS

Suggested Assignments

1.19. Keep a journal for at least the remainder of this course. Record significant discoveries, insights, learnings, and personal recollections—not daily activities. Write in your journal at least twice a week. Give yourself some feedback.

1.20. Ask someone you know well to complete the assessment instruments wherein that person rates you on each item. Compare your own scores and those of this other person. Discuss differences, strengths, and areas of confusion. The goal is to help you increase your self-awareness by getting a picture of yourself from the standpoint of someone else.

1.21. Write down the comprehensive, consistent, and universal principles that guide your behavior under all circumstances. What core principles will you rarely violate? Share the list with someone with whom you have a close relationship.

1.22. After completing the personal assessment instruments and discussing their implications with someone else, write an essay responding to the following four questions: (1) Who am I? (2) What are my main strengths and weaknesses? (3) What do I want to achieve in my life? (4) What legacy do I want to leave?

1.23. Spend an evening with a close friend or relative discussing your emotional intelligence, values, cognitive style, attitude toward change, and core self-evaluation. You may want to have that person complete the instruments, giving his or her impressions of you, so you can compare and contrast your scores. Discuss implications for your future and for your relationship.

1.24. Teach someone else the value of self-awareness in managerial success and explain the relevance of emotional intelligence, values maturity, cognitive style, attitudes toward change, and core self-evaluation. Describe the experience in your journal.

Application Plan and Evaluation

The intent of this exercise is to help you apply this cluster of skills in a real-life, out-of-class setting. Now that you have become familiar with the behavioral guidelines that form the basis of effective skill performance, you will improve most by trying out those guidelines in an everyday context. Unlike a classroom activity, in which feedback is immediate and others can assist you with their evaluations, this skill application activity is one you must accomplish and evaluate on your own. There are two parts to this activity. Part 1 helps prepare you to apply the skill. Part 2 helps you evaluate and improve on your experience. Be sure to write down answers to each item. Don't short-circuit the process by skipping steps.

Part 1. Planning

1. Write down the two or three aspects of this skill of self-awareness that are most important to you. These may be areas of weakness, areas you most want to improve, or areas that are most salient to a problem you face right now. Identify the specific aspects of this skill that you want to apply.

2. Now identify the setting or the situation in which you will apply this skill of self-awareness. Establish a plan for performance by actually writing down a description of the situation. Who else will be involved? When will you do it? Where will it be done?
   Circumstances:
   Who else?
   When?
   Where?

3. Identify the specific behaviors in which you will engage to apply this skill. Operationalize your skill performance.

4. What are the indicators of successful performance? How will you know you have been effective? What will indicate you have performed competently?

Part 2. Evaluation

5. After you have completed your implementation, record the results. What happened? How successful were you? What was the effect on others?

6. How can you improve? What modifications can you make next time? What will you do differently in a similar situation in the future?

7. Looking back on your whole skill practice and application experience, what have you learned? What has been surprising? In what ways might this experience help you in the long term?

✪ Scoring Keys for the following instruments, along with comparison data, are contained in PIA in MyManagementLab.com;

Self Awareness Assessment
Emotional Intelligence Assessment
Locus of Control Scale

The Defining Issues Test

The possibility of misusing and misinterpreting this instrument is high enough that its author, James Rest, maintains control over the scoring procedure associated with its use. Some people may interpret the results of this instrument to be an indication of inherent morality, honesty, or personal worth, none of which the instrument is intended to assess. A scoring manual may be obtained from James Rest, Minnesota Moral Research Center, Burton Hall, University of Minnesota, Minneapolis, MN 55455.

The most difficult moral decisions are experienced as dilemmas. Our purpose is to help you become aware of the moral standards you apply when facing these difficult choices. These standards have been codified by scholars as "stages" of moral development. The stage of the 12 questions you rated for each of the three stories is shown below. Looking for patterns across the three sets of four statements you selected as most important will help you better understand the stage of moral development you most often use.

Escaped Prisoner

1. Hasn't Mr. Thompson been good enough for such a long time to prove he isn't a bad person? (Stage 3)
2. Every time someone escapes punishment for a crime, doesn't that just encourage more crime? (Stage 4)
3. Wouldn't we be better off without prisons and the oppression of our legal system? (Indicates antiauthoritarian attitudes.)
4. Has Mr. Thompson really paid his debt to society? (Stage 4)
5. Would society be failing what Mr. Thompson should fairly expect? (Stage 6)
6. What benefits would prison be apart from society, especially for a charitable man? (Nonsense alternative, designed to identify people picking high-sounding alternatives.)
7. How could anyone be so cruel and heartless as to send Mr. Thompson to prison? (Stage 3)
8. Would it be fair to all the prisoners who had to serve out their full sentences if Mr. Thompson was let off? (Stage 4)
9. Was Ms. Jones a good friend of Mr. Thompson? (Stage 3)
10. Wouldn't it be a citizen's duty to report an escaped criminal, regardless of circumstances? (Stage 4)
11. How would the will of the people and the public good best be served? (Stage 5)
12. Would going to prison do any good for Mr. Thompson or protect anybody? (Stage 5)

The Doctor's Dilemma

1. Whether the woman's family is in favor of giving her an overdose or not. (Stage 3)
2. Is the doctor obligated by the same laws as everybody else if giving her an overdose would be the same as killing her? (Stage 4)

3. Whether people would be much better off without society regimenting their lives and even their deaths. (Indicates antiauthoritarian attitudes.)
4. Whether the doctor could make it appear like an accident. (Stage 2)
5. Does the state have the right to force continued existence on those who don't want to live? (Stage 5)
6. What is the value of death prior to society's perspective on personal values? (Nonsense alternative, designed to identify people picking high-sounding alternatives.)
7. Whether the doctor has sympathy for the woman's suffering or cares more about what society might think. (Stage 3)
8. Is helping to end another's life ever a responsible act of cooperation? (Stage 6)
9. Whether only God should decide when a person's life should end. (Stage 4)
10. What values the doctor has set for himself in his own personal code of behavior. (Stage 5)
11. Can society afford to let everybody end their lives when they want to? (Stage 4)
12. Can society allow suicides or mercy killing and still protect the lives of individuals who want to live? (Stage 5)

The Newspaper

1. Is the principal more responsible to students or to the parents? (Stage 4)
2. Did the principal give his word that the newspaper could be published for a long time, or did he promise to approve the newspaper one issue at a time? (Stage 4)
3. Would the students start protesting even more if the principal stopped the newspaper? (Stage 2)
4. When the welfare of the school is threatened, does the principal have the right to give orders to students? (Stage 4)
5. Does the principal have the freedom of speech to say "no" in this case? (Nonsense alternative, designed to identify people picking high-sounding alternatives.)
6. If the principal stopped the newspaper, would he be preventing full discussion of important problems? (Stage 5)
7. Whether the principal's order would make Rami lose faith in the principal. (Stage 3)
8. Whether Rami was loyal to his school and patriotic to his country. (Stage 3)
9. What effect would stopping the paper have on the students' education in critical thinking and judgment? (Stage 5)
10. Whether Rami was in any way violating the rights of others in publishing his own opinions. (Stage 5)
11. Whether the principal should be influenced by some angry parents when it is the principal who knows best what is going on in the school. (Stage 4)
12. Whether Rami was using the newspaper to stir up hatred and discontent. (Stage 3)

Cognitive Style Indicator

Scoring Key

DIMENSIONS	ITEMS	AVERAGE SCORES
Knowing Style	5, 8, 11, 14	Add scores and divide by 4: _____
Planning Style	1, 3, 6, 9, 12, 15, 17	Add scores and divide by 7: _____
Creating Style	2, 4, 7, 10, 13, 16, 18	Add scores and divide by 7: _____

Comparison Data (N = 11,000 students)

DIMENSION SCORES (AVERAGES)	MEAN	BOTTOM QUARTILE	SECOND QUARTILE	THIRD QUARTILE	TOP QUARTILE
Knowing Style	4.14	3.75 or below	3.76–4.25	4.26–4.5	4.51 or above
Planning Style	4.20	3.86 or below	3.87–4.28	4.29–4.71	4.72 or above
Creating Style	3.92	3.57 or below	3.58–3.99	4.0–4.29	4.30 or above

Tolerance of Ambiguity Scale

Scoring Key

High scores indicate an intolerance of ambiguity. Having high intolerance means that you tend to perceive situations as threatening rather than promising and lack of information or uncertainty would tend to make you uncomfortable. Ambiguity arises from three primary sources: novelty, complexity, and insolubility.

In scoring the instrument, the *even-numbered* items must be reversed. That is, 7 becomes 1, 6 becomes 2, 5 becomes 3, 3 becomes 5, 2 becomes 6, and 1 becomes 7.

1. _____ An expert who doesn't come up with a definite answer probably doesn't know too much.
2. _____ I would like to live in a foreign country for a while. **(reverse)**
3. _____ There is really no such thing as a problem that can't be solved.
4. _____ People who fit their lives to a schedule probably miss most of the joy of living. **(reverse)**
5. _____ A good job is one where what is to be done and how it is to be done are always clear.
6. _____ It is more fun to tackle a complicated problem than to solve a simple one. **(reverse)**
7. _____ In the long run it is possible to get more done by tackling small, simple problems rather than large and complicated ones.
8. _____ Often the most interesting and stimulating people are those who don't mind being different and original. **(reverse)**
9. _____ What we are used to is always preferable to what is unfamiliar.
10. _____ People who insist upon a yes or no answer just don't know how complicated things really are. **(reverse)**
11. _____ A person who leads an even, regular life in which few surprises or unexpected happenings arise really has a lot to be grateful for.
12. _____ Many of our most important decisions are based upon insufficient information. **(reverse)**
13. _____ I like parties where I know most of the people more than ones where all or most of the people are complete strangers.
14. _____ Teachers or supervisors who hand out vague assignments give one a chance to show initiative and originality. **(reverse)**
15. _____ The sooner we all acquire similar values and ideals the better.
16. _____ A good teacher is one who makes you wonder about your way of looking at things. **(reverse)**

Total of odd-numbered items: _____

Total of reversed-scored even-numbered items: _____

Total: _____

After reversing the even-numbered items, compute your score for three dimensions, or kinds, of ambiguous situations.

N = Novelty score (2, 9, 11, 13): _____

C = Complexity score (4, 5, 6, 7, 8, 10, 14, 15, 16): _____

I = Insolubility score (1, 3, 12): _____

Comparison Data (N = 5,000 students)

SCORES	MEAN	FIRST QUARTILE	SECOND QUARTILE	THIRD QUARTILE	FOURTH QUARTILE
Total Dimensions	56.47	49 or below	50–56	57–62	63 or above
Novelty	XX.X	Total or Dim			
Complexity	XX.X				
Insolubility	XX.X				

Core Self-Evaluation Scale

Scoring Key

Reverse your scores for items 2, 4, 6, 8, 10, 12. That is, for these items, 1 becomes 5, 2 becomes 4, 4 becomes 2, and 5 becomes 1. Divide the sum by 12 to produce an average CSES score.

1. _____ I am confident I get the success I deserve in life.
2. _____ Sometimes I feel depressed. **(reverse)**
3. _____ When I try, I generally succeed.
4. _____ Sometimes when I fail, I feel worthless. **(reverse)**
5. _____ I complete tasks successfully.
6. _____ Sometimes, I do not feel in control of my work. **(reverse)**
7. _____ Overall, I am satisfied with myself.
8. _____ I am filled with doubts about my competence. **(reverse)**
9. _____ I determine what will happen in my life.
10. _____ I do not feel in control of my success in my career. **(reverse)**
11. _____ I am capable of coping with most of my problems.
12. _____ There are times when things look pretty bleak and hopeless to me. **(reverse)**
    _____ **Total Score**
÷12 _____ **Average Score**

Next, compute your average score for each dimension, or component, of self-evaluations, by dividing your total for each by 3.

DIMENSIONS	ITEMS	AVERAGE SCORE
Self-esteem	1–3 ÷ 3	_____
Self-efficacy	4–6 ÷ 3	_____
Emotional stability	7–9 ÷ 3	_____
Locus of control	10–12 ÷ 3	_____

Comparison Data (N = 5,000 students)

SCORES (AVERAGES)	MEAN	FIRST QUARTILE	SECOND QUARTILE	THIRD QUARTILE	FOURTH QUARTILE
Total Dimensions	3.73	3.3 or below	3.4–3.8	3.9–4.2	4.3 or above
Self-esteem	X.XX	Total or Ave?			
Self-efficacy	X.XX	Instruct	To compute Ave		
Emotional stability	X.XX				
Locus of control	X.XX				

SKILL *ASSESSMENT*

- Stress Management Assessment
- Time Management Assessment
- Social Readjustment Rating Scale
- Sources of Personal Stress
- Flourishing Scale

SKILL *LEARNING*

- Improving the Management of Stress and Time
- Major Elements of Stress
- Managing Stress
- Eliminating Stressors
- Developing Resiliency and Well-Being
- Temporary Stress-Reduction Techniques
- Summary
- Behavioral Guidelines

SKILL *ANALYSIS*

- The Turn of the Tide
- The Case of the Missing Time

SKILL *PRACTICE*

- The Small-Wins Strategy
- Life-Balance Analysis
- Deep Relaxation
- Monitoring and Managing Time
- Reciprocity Exercise

SKILL *APPLICATION*

- Suggested Assignments
- Application Plan and Evaluation

SCORING KEYS AND *COMPARISON DATA*

MyManagementLab™

✪ When you see this icon, visit www.mymanagementlab.com for self-assessments, video activities, and more.

2

Managing Stress and Well-Being

LEARNING OBJECTIVES

1. ELIMINATE STRESSORS
2. DEVELOP RESILIENCY
3. COPE WITH STRESS IN THE SHORT TERM
4. ENHANCE PERSONAL WELL-BEING

DIAGNOSTIC SURVEYS FOR MANAGING STRESS AND WELL-BEING

PERSONAL INVENTORY ASSESSMENT

✪ If your instructor is utilizing **MyManagementLab**, log onto mymanagementlab.com and select the Personal Inventory Assessment (PIA) section and complete the instruments associated with this chapter.

The assessment instruments in this chapter are briefly described below. The assessments appear either in your text or in PIA. The assessments marked with (blue star) are available only in PIA.

All assessments should be completed before reading the chapter material.

After completing the first assessment save your response to your hard drive. When you have finished reading the chapter, re-take the assessment and compare your responses to see what you have learned.

✪ ❏ The *Stress Management Assessment* measures the extent to which you effectively manage the various sources of stress in your life and the degree to which you have developed stress management skills.

✪ ❏ The *Time Management Assessment* evaluates the degree to which you effectively manage your time and the extent to which you implement effective time management principles.

❏ The *Social Readjustment Rating Scale* identifies the relative importance of events in your life that have occurred in your life in the last year. The weightings associated with these events help identify the impact of stress.

❏ The *Sources of Personal Stress* instrument personalizes your ratings on the *Social Readjustment Rating Scale* by identifying unique stressors occurring in your life right now.

❏ The *Flourishing Scale* measures the extent to which you are experiencing well-being in your life at the present time.

MANAGING STRESS AND WELL-BEING

Assessment Section

SOCIAL READJUSTMENT RATING SCALE

The SRRS self-assessment helps you identify stressful experiences in our life and to understand the level of stress associated with each event, according to research conducted by the authors of the scale.

Rating Scale

Circle any of the following you have experienced in the past year. Using the weightings at the left, total up your score.

Mean Value	Life Event
87	1. Death of spouse/mate
79	2. Death of a close family member
78	3. Major injury/illness to self

Mean Value	Life Event
76	4. Detention in jail or other institution
72	5. Major injury/illness to a close family member
71	6. Foreclosure on loan/mortgage
71	7. Divorce
70	8. Being a victim of crime
69	9. Being a victim of police brutality
69	10. Infidelity
69	11. Experiencing domestic violence/sexual abuse
66	12. Separation or reconciliation with spouse/mate
64	13. Being fired/laid-off/unemployed
62	14. Experiencing financial problems/difficulties
61	15. Death of a close friend
59	16. Surviving a disaster
59	17. Becoming a single parent
56	18. Assuming responsibility for sick or elderly loved one
56	19. Loss of or major reduction in health insurance/benefits
56	20. Self/close family member being arrested for violating the law
53	21. Major disagreement over child support/custody/visitation
53	22. Experiencing/involved in an auto accident
53	23. Being disciplined at work/demoted
51	24. Dealing with unwanted pregnancy
50	25. Adult child moving in with parent/parent moving in with adult child
49	26. Child develops behavior or learning problem
48	27. Experienced employment discrimination/sexual harassment
47	28. Attempting to modify addictive behavior of self
46	29. Discovering/attempting to modify addictive behavior of close family member
45	30. Employer reorganization/downsizing
44	31. Dealing with infertility/miscarriage
43	32. Getting married/remarried
43	33. Changing employers/careers
42	34. Failure to obtain/qualify for a mortgage
41	35. Pregnancy of self/spouse/mate
39	36. Experiencing discrimination/harassment outside the workplace
39	37. Release from jail
38	38. Spouse/mate begins/ceases work outside the home
37	39. Major disagreement with boss/coworker
35	40. Change in residence
34	41. Finding appropriate child care/day care
33	42. Experiencing a large unexpected monetary gain
33	43. Changing positions (transfer, promotion)
33	44. Gaining a new family member

Mean Value	Life Event
32	45. Changing work responsibilities
30	46. Child leaving home
30	47. Obtaining a home mortgage
30	48. Obtaining a major loan other than home mortgage
28	49. Retirement
26	50. Beginning/ceasing formal education
22	51. Receiving a ticket for violating the law
_____	Total score for circled items

SOURCE: *Social Readjustment Rating Scale, Hobson, Charles Jo, Joseph Kaen, Jane Szotek, Carol M. Nethercutt, James W. Tiedmann and Susan Wojnarowicz (1998), "Stressful Life Events: A Revision and Update of the Social Readjustment Rating Scale,"* International Journal of Stress Management, *5: 1–23.*

SOCIAL READJUSTMENT RATING SCALE

College students might find the events listed in this version of SRRS more relevant.

Mean Value	Life Event	
1	100	Death of parent
2	100	Unplanned pregnancy/abortion
3	95	Getting married
4	90	Divorce of parents
5	80	Acquiring a visible deformity
6	70	Fathering a child
7	70	Jail sentence of parent for over one year
8	69	Marital separation of parents
9	68	Death of a brother or sister
10	67	Change in acceptance by peers
11	64	Unplanned pregnancy of sister
12	63	Discovery of being an adopted child
13	63	Marriage of parent to stepparent
14	63	Death of a close friend
15	62	Having a visible congenital deformity
16	58	Serious illness requiring hospitalization
17	56	Failure of a grade in school
18	55	Not making an extracurricular activity
19	55	Hospitalization of a parent
20	53	Jail sentence of parent for over 30 days
21	53	Breaking up with boyfriend or girlfriend
22	51	Beginning to date
23	50	Suspension from school

Mean Value	Life Event	
24	50	Becoming involved with drugs or alcohol
25	50	Birth of a brother or sister
26	47	Increase in arguments between parents
27	46	Loss of job by parent
28	46	Outstanding personal achievement
29	45	Change in parent's financial status
30	43	Accepted at college of choice
31	42	Being a senior in high school
32	41	Hospitalization of a sibling
33	38	Increased absence of parent from home
34	37	Brother or sister leaving home
35	34	Addition of third adult to family
36	31	Becoming a full-fledged member of a church
37	27	Decrease in arguments between parents
38	26	Decrease in arguments with parents
39	26	Mother or father beginning work
_____		Total score for circled items _____

SOURCE: *Pastorino, E. & Doyle-Portillo, S. (2009):* What is Psychology?.
2nd Ed. Belmont, CA: Thompson Higher Education.

SOURCES OF PERSONAL STRESS

This stress-assessment is designed to complement the Social Readjustment Rating Scale (SRRS). Please complete that instrument before beginning this one. Adding the stressors you are experiencing at this time to those identified in SRRS provides a more comprehensive assessment of your current stress level. Together with your SRRS score, refer to the stressors below as you discuss and practice the stress management principles presented in this chapter.

1   Identify the factors that produce the most stress for you right now. What is it that creates feelings of stress in your life?
2   Now give each of these entries a "stress rating," from 1 to 100, indicating the level of stress it is producing. Refer to the weightings used in SRRS as a guide. A rating of 100, for example, might be associated with the death of a spouse or child, while a rating of 10 might be associated with an annoying "backseat driver" in your car pool.

Source of Stress   Rating

_____   _____

_____   _____

_____   _____

_____   _____

_____   _____

_____   _____

_____   _____

FLOURISHING SCALE

Several benefits from living a life characterized as "flourishing" (psychological well-being) have been identified by researchers. Through this self-assessment you will better understand the extent to which the following eight attributes of "flourishing" characterize your current life experience. Inasmuch as this is a self-diagnostic assessment, it is important to respond candidly.

Rating Scale

Below are eight statements with which you may agree or disagree. Using a 1 (strongly disagree) to 7 (strongly agree) scale below, indicate your agreement with each item.

7 Strongly agree
6 Agree
5 Slightly agree
4 Neither agree nor disagree or mixed
3 Slightly disagree
2 Disagree
1 Strongly disagree

_____ 1. I lead a purposeful and meaningful life.

_____ 2. My social relationships are supportive and rewarding.

_____ 3. I am engaged and interested in my daily activities.

_____ 4. I active contribute to the happiness and well-being of others.

_____ 5. I am competent and capable in the activities that are important to me.

_____ 6. I am a good person and live a good life.

_____ 7. I am optimistic about my future.

_____ 8. People respect me.

_____ **Total**

SOURCE: © *Used with permission of Ed Diener and Robert Biswas-Diener. In Diener, E., Wirtz, D., Tov, W., Kim-Prieto, C., Choi. D., Oishi, S., & Biswas-Diener, R. (2009). New measures of well-being: Flourishing and positive and negative feelings.* Social Indicators Research, 39, 247–266.

SKILL *LEARNING*

Our goal in this chapter is to help you manage two personal challenges—one is a major inhibitor of effective management, and one is a key facilitator of effective management. The first part of the chapter highlights a common and serious problem for us all—experiencing negative stress. It is difficult to flourish in our activities when we are facing major stressors in our lives such as overload, anxiety, conflict, tension in relationships, uncertainty, failure, and regret—all sources of stress. We highlight ways in which stress can be minimized or eliminated; in the process, we highlight ways in which personal well-being can be fostered. We provide some guidelines for achieving extraordinary personal effectiveness by focusing on well-being enhancements.

Managing Stress and Fostering Well-Being

Managing negative stress is a crucial management skill in a competent manager's repertoire. Here is why: The American Psychological Association (2009) estimates that the problem of stress on the job siphons off more than $500 billion from the nation's economy. More than 50 percent of workers admit to being less productive at work because of stress, and the median number of days missed at work due to stress is 25—significantly above the six days missed due to illness or accident. Between 75 and 90 percent of all visits to primary care physicians are for stress-related complaints or disorders. And, things are getting worse. The percentage of workers feeling "highly stressed" has more than quadrupled in the last two decades.

Name any other single factor that has produced such a devastating and costly effect on workers, managers, and organizations. When we experience stress, it is difficult to pay attention to almost anything else.

Research on the physiological effects of stress shows widespread and devastating effects, including negative impact on the cardiovascular system, the respiratory system, the endocrine system, the gastrointestinal tract, the female reproductive system, reproductive hormones, male reproductive functioning, immunodepression, neurological disorders, addictions, malignancy immune functions with HIV-1, dental pathology, pain, and anxiety disorders (Hubbard & Workman, 2002). Almost no part of life or health is immune from the effects of stress.

As an illustration of the effects of job-related stress, consider the following true story reported in Baltimore, Maryland:

> The job was getting to the ambulance attendant. He felt disturbed by the recurring tragedy, isolated by the long shifts. His marriage was in trouble. He was drinking too much.
>
> One night it all blew up.
>
> He rode in back that night. His partner drove. Their first call was for a man whose leg had been cut off by a train. His screaming and agony were horrifying, but the second call was worse. It was a child-beating. As the attendant treated the youngster's bruised body and snapped bones, he thought of his own child. His fury grew.
>
> Immediately after leaving the child at the hospital, the attendants were sent out to help a heart attack victim seen lying in a street. When they arrived, however, they found not a cardiac patient but a drunk—a wino passed out. As they lifted the man into the ambulance, their frustration and anger came to a head. They decided to give the wino a ride he would remember.
>
> The ambulance vaulted over railroad tracks at high speed. The driver took the corners as fast as he could, flinging the wino from side to side in the back. To the attendants, it was a joke.
>
> Suddenly, the wino began having a real heart attack. The attendant in back leaned over the wino and started shouting. "Die, you sucker!" he yelled. "Die!"
>
> He watched as the wino shuddered. He watched as the wino died. By the time they reached the hospital, they had their stories straight. Dead on arrival, they said. Nothing they could do.
>
> The attendant, who must remain anonymous, talked about that night at a recent counseling session on "professional burnout"—a growing problem in high-stress jobs.

As this story graphically illustrates, when we face substantial stress in our lives, normal behavior and normal decision making are frequently set aside, and we suffer debilitating effects (Auerbach, 1998; Contrada & Baum, 2011; Staw, Sandelands, & Dutton, 1981; Weick, 1993b). Consequently, we spend the first part of this chapter highlighting the major types of negative stress that we all encounter, and then we show ways to both cope with and minimize negative stress as well as highlight ways in which personal well-being and resiliency can be enhanced.

We begin our discussion by presenting a framework for understanding stress and identifying the strategies to cope with it. This model explains the major types of stressors, the primary reactions to stress, and the reasons some people experience more negative reactions than others. Then we provide specific examples and behavioral guidelines for eliminating and reducing the negative effects of stress and enhancing psychological and social well-being and resilience.

Major Elements of Stress

One way to understand stress is to think of it as the product of a "force field" (Lewin, 1951). Kurt Lewin suggested that all individuals and organizations exist in an environment filled with reinforcing or opposing forces. These forces act to stimulate or inhibit the performance desired by the individual. As illustrated in Figure 2.1, a person's level of performance in an organization results from factors that may either complement or contradict one another. Certain forces drive or motivate changes in behavior, while other forces restrain or block those changes.

According to Lewin's theory, the forces affecting individuals are normally balanced in the force field.

LEARNING

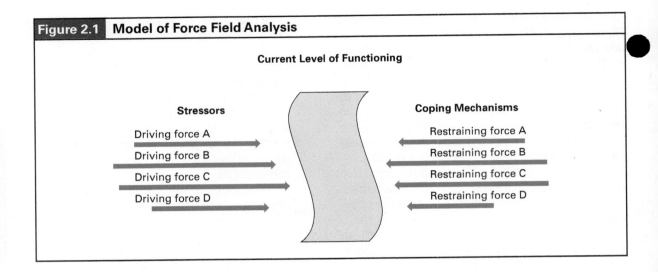

Figure 2.1   Model of Force Field Analysis

Current Level of Functioning

Stressors

Driving force A

Driving force B

Driving force C

Driving force D

Coping Mechanisms

Restraining force A

Restraining force B

Restraining force C

Restraining force D

The strength of the driving forces is exactly matched by the strength of the restraining forces. (In the figure, longer arrows indicate stronger forces.) Performance changes when the forces become imbalanced. That is, if the driving forces become stronger than the restraining forces, or more numerous or enduring, change occurs. Conversely, if restraining forces become stronger or more numerous than driving forces, change occurs in the opposite direction, or people become more and more resistant to change.

Think of stress as represented as driving forces in the model. That is, they exert pressure on the individual to change present levels of performance physiologically, psychologically, and interpersonally. Unrestrained, those forces can lead to pathological results (e.g., anxiety, heart disease, and mental breakdown).

However, most people have developed a certain amount of resiliency—represented by the restraining forces—to counter stressors and inhibit pathological results. These restraining forces include behavior patterns, psychological characteristics, and supportive social relationships. Strong restraining forces lead to low heart rates, good interpersonal relationships, emotional stability, and effective stress management. An absence of restraining forces leads to burnout.

Of course, stress produces positive as well as negative effects. In the absence of any stress, people feel completely bored and lack any inclination to act. Stress is needed to motivate action. However, we are discussing only negative, unproductive stressors in this chapter. Even when high levels of stress are experienced, equilibrium can be restored quickly if there is sufficient resiliency. In the case of the ambulance driver, for example, multiple stressors

overpowered the available restraining forces and burnout occurred.

Figure 2.2 identifies the major categories of **stressors** (driving forces) that managers experience as well as the major attributes of resiliency (restraining forces) that inhibit the negative effects of stress. Each of these forces is discussed in this chapter so that it will become clear how to identify stressors, how to eliminate them, how to develop more resiliency, and how to cope with stress on a temporary basis.

COPING WITH STRESS

In managing stress, using a hierarchy of approaches has been found most effective (Eliot, 2010; Kahn & Byosiere, 1992; Lehrer, 1996). First, the best way to manage stress is to eliminate or minimize stressors with **enactive strategies**. These create, or enact, a new environment for the individual that does not contain the stressors. The second most effective approach is for individuals to enhance their overall capacity to handle stress by increasing their personal resiliency. These are called **proactive strategies** and are designed to initiate action that resists the negative effects of stress. Finally, developing short-term techniques for coping with stressors is necessary when an immediate response is required. These are **reactive strategies**, they are applied as on-the-spot remedies to reduce temporarily the effects of stress.

Individuals are better off if they can eliminate harmful stressors and the potentially negative effects of frequent, potent stress reactions. However, because most individuals do not have complete control over their environments or their circumstances, they can

Figure 2.2 **A General Model of Stress**

EXPERIENCING STRESS

Stressors
• Anticipatory
• Encounter
• Time
• Situational

Reactions
• Physiological
• Psychological

Resiliency
• Psychological
• Social
• Wellbeing

MANAGING STRESS

	Enactive Strategies	Proactive Strategies	Reactive Strategies
Purpose	Eliminate stressors	Develop resiliency strategies	Learn temporary coping mechanisms
Effects	Permanent	Long term	Short term
Approach	Enactive	Proactive	Reactive
Time Required	Long time	Moderate time	Immediate

seldom eliminate all harmful stressors. Their next-best alternative, therefore, is to develop a greater capacity to withstand the negative effects of stress and to mobilize the energy generated by stressors. This is done by enhancing personal resiliency and well-being. Finally, on a temporary basis, individuals can respond to a negatively stressed state by using constructive strategies such as temporary relaxation techniques and contemplative practices. These reactive strategies can also foster resiliency and enhance well-being if used properly.

Unfortunately, most people reverse the order of these three coping strategies. They rely first on temporary reactive methods to cope with stress because these actions can be implemented immediately. But reactive strategies have to be repeated whenever stressors are encountered because their effects are short-lived. Moreover, some common reactive strategies, such as drinking, taking sleeping pills, or letting off steam through anger can become habit-forming and harmful in themselves. Without more long-term

strategies, relying on repetitive reactive strategies can create a vicious or addictive cycle.

It takes more effort to develop proactive resiliency strategies and the effects are more long lasting. But, resiliency strategies can take time to implement, so the payoff is usually not immediate. The best and most permanent strategies are those that eliminate negative stressors altogether. They require the longest time to implement, but because stress is abolished, the payoff is enduring (Stranks, 2013).

○ **MyManagementLab: WATCH IT**
East Haven Fire Department:
Emotions and Moods
Apply what you have learned about management. If your instructor has assigned MyManagementLab, go to mymanagementlab.com to watch a video case and answer questions.

Managing Stressors

Table 2.1 lists the four main types of stressors illustrated in the story of the ambulance driver. The first, **time stressors**, generally result from having too much to do in too little time. These are the most common and most pervasive sources of stress faced by managers in corporations (Eliot, 2010; Kahn & Byosiere, 1992; Stalk & Hout, 1990; Vinton, 1992). As might be expected, significant relationships exist between the presence of time stressors and job dissatisfaction, tension, perceived threat, heart rate, cholesterol levels, skin resistance, and other factors (Contrada & Baum, 2011).

As mentioned in the first chapter on self-awareness, time stressors are experienced differently in different national cultures (Trompenaars, 1996; Trompenaars & Hampden-Turner, 1998), so some cultures such as those in the Philippines, the United States, Ireland, Brazil, India, and Australia experience more time stress because of their emphasis on a short time horizon. In cultures with a longer time horizon (e.g., Hong Kong, Czech Republic, Austria, Sweden, and Portugal), the immediacy of time demands is less prevalent.

Encounter stressors are those that result from interpersonal interactions. Most people have experienced the debilitating effects of a quarrel with a friend, roommate, or spouse; of trying to work with an employee or supervisor with whom there has been an interpersonal conflict; or of trying to accomplish a task in a group divided by lack of trust.

Each of these stressors results from some kind of conflictual interpersonal encounter. Our own research has revealed that encounter stressors in organizations have significant negative effects on productivity and satisfaction (Cameron, 1994; Cameron, Whetten, & Kim, 1987), and encounter stressors have been found by other researchers to be at the very heart of most organizational dysfunction (Likert, 1967; Peters, 1988; Pfeffer, 1998; Thoits, 1995). Differences have also been discovered among national cultures with regard to encounter stressors (Trompenaars & Hampden-Turner, 2004) in that *egalitarian* cultures that emphasize interpersonal relationships as a way to accomplish work (e.g., the United States, Norway, Ireland, and Finland) and country cultures emphasizing *affectivity*, or the public display of emotions (e.g., Iran and Mexico rather than China and Japan), have more encounter stress in the workplace.

The third category of stressors, **situational stressors**, arises from the environment in which a person lives or from an individual's circumstances. One of the most common forms of situational stress is unfavorable working conditions. For the ambulance drivers, these included continual crises, long hours, and isolation from colleagues.

One of the well-researched links between situational stressors and negative consequences involves rapid change, particularly the effects of changes in life events (Hobson et al., 1998; Holmes & Rahe, 1970; Wolff, Wolf, & Hare, 1950). The Social Readjustment Rating Scale (SRRS) tracks the number of changes individuals have experienced over the past 12 months. Since changes in some events are more stressful than others, a scaling method is used to assign weights to each life event. Hobson and colleagues (1998) revised the SRRS so that the weightings of individual items have been updated to match the modern environment, and we included the revised instrument in the Assessment section of this chapter. More than 3,500 studies have been published just since 1995 among a variety of cultures, age groups, and occupations using this SRRS instrument (Goldberger & Breznitz, 2010). (You will note that two different versions of the SRRS are reproduced in the Assessment section—one for adults, and one for nonadults. You should have completed the appropriate version(s) of the instrument in the Assessment section.)

Statistical relationships between the amount of life-event change and physical illness and injury have been found consistently among a wide variety of individuals. For example, in the general population,

Table 2.1 Four Key Sources of Stress

Time Stressors
- Work overload
- Lack of control

Encounter Stressors
- Role conflicts
- Issue conflicts
- Action conflicts

Situational Stressors
- Unfavorable working conditions
- Rapid change

Anticipatory Stressors
- Unpleasant expectations
- Fear

scores of 150 points or below results in a probability of less than 37 percent that a serious illness or injury will occur in the next year, but the probability increases to about 50 percent with scores of 150–300. Those who score over 300 on the SRRS have an 80 percent chance of serious illness or injury (Holmes & Rahe, 1967; Kobasa, 1979; Miller & Rasmussen, 2010). High scores are strongly associated with illness and/or injury, whereas low scores are much less likely to experience illness or injury.

Several studies have been conducted using college and high school athletes to determine if life-event change is related to injury as well as to illness. One study found that college athletes with the lowest scores on the SRRS had a rate of injury (they missed three or more practices) of 35 percent. Those with medium scores had an injury rate of 44 percent, and those with high scores were injured at the rate of 72 percent. Another study showed an athlete injury rate five times as great for high scorers on the SRRS as for low scorers. Still another study found a significant increase in minor physiological symptoms such as headache, nausea, fever, backache, eyestrain, and so forth among high scorers on the SRRS (Andersen & Williams, 1999; Bramwell, Masuda, Wagner, & Holmes, 1975; Coddington & Troxell, 1980; Cordes and Dougherty, 1993).

We must caution, of course, that scoring high on the SRRS does not necessarily guarantee that a person is going to become ill or be injured. A variety of coping skills and personal characteristics may counteract those tendencies. The point is that situational stressors are important factors to consider in learning to manage stress skillfully.

Anticipatory stressors, the fourth category, include potentially disagreeable events that threaten to occur—unpleasant things that have not yet happened, but might happen. Stress results from the anticipation or fear of the event. In the case of the ambulance drivers, the constant threat of anticipating having to witness one more incident of human suffering or death served as an anticipatory stressor. Anticipatory stressors need not be highly unpleasant or severe to produce stress. Investigators have induced high levels of stress by telling individuals that they would experience a loud noise or a mild shock or that someone else might become uncomfortable because of their actions (Milgram, 1963). Fear of failure or fear of embarrassment in front of peers is a common anticipatory stressor. Anxieties about losing a job or not being accepted or liked by colleagues have been identified as common stress producers as well.

Table 2.2	Management Strategies for Eliminating Stressors
TYPE OF STRESSOR	**ELIMINATION STRATEGY**
Time	Effective time management
	Efficient time management
Encounter	Building community
	Contributing
	Emotional and social intelligence
Situational	Work redesign
Anticipatory	Goal setting
	Small wins

Eliminating Stressors

Because eliminating **stressors** is a permanent stress reduction strategy, it is by far the most desirable. Although it is impossible, and even undesirable, for individuals to eliminate all the stressors they encounter, they can effectively eliminate those that are harmful. Table 2.2 outlines several ways to eliminate each of the four types of stressors.

ELIMINATING TIME STRESSORS THROUGH TIME MANAGEMENT

As pointed out earlier, time is usually the greatest source of stress for managers. With a literal explosion of time management books, organizers, consultants, efficiency enhancers, and technological time savers, you'd expect most of us to be pretty good at managing our time. We certainly have all the gadgets and advice we can use. The trouble is, most of us are getting worse. Just look around you. Whom do you know who is a terrific time manager, who isn't overloaded, or who doesn't complain about being stressed because of time?

It's no surprise that time stress is escalating because of the rapidity of change and the overwhelming amounts of information that people encounter in the twenty-first century. In one study, two-thirds of the respondents indicated a desire to put more emphasis on "having free time" (Davidson, 1995). Time stress is an almost universal complaint of practicing managers who face between 237 and 1,073 separate incidents a day.

Two sets of skills are important for effectively managing time and for eliminating time stressors. One set focuses on *efficiently* using time each day. The other set focuses on *effectively* using time over the long term. Because the effectiveness approach to time management serves as the foundation for the efficiency approach, we explain it first. Then we review some techniques for achieving efficiency in time use.

Effective Time Management

Almost everyone suffers now and then from a pervasive feeling of time stress. Somehow, no matter how much time is available, it seems to get filled up and squeezed out. Currently, the most commonly prescribed solutions for attacking problems of time stress are to use calendars and planners, generate to-do lists, and learn to say "no." Almost all of us have tried such tactics but continue to experience enormous time stress. This is not to say that calendars, lists, and saying "no" are never useful. They are, however, examples of an efficiency approach to time management rather than an effectiveness approach. In eliminating time stressors, efficiency without effectiveness is fruitless.

Managing time with an effectiveness approach means that (1) we spend our time on important matters, not just urgent matters; (2) we are able to distinguish clearly between what is important versus what is merely urgent; (3) results rather than methods are

the objectives; and (4) we have a reason not to feel guilty when we must say "no."

A number of time management experts have pointed out the usefulness of a "time management matrix" in which activities are categorized in terms of their relative importance and urgency (Covey, 1989; Lakein, 1989). *Important* activities are those that produce a desired result. They accomplish a valued end, or they achieve a meaningful purpose. *Urgent* activities are those that demand immediate attention. They are associated with a need expressed by someone else, or they relate to an uncomfortable problem or situation that requires a solution as soon as possible. Figure 2.3 outlines this matrix and provides examples of types of activities that fit in each quadrant.

Activities such as handling employee crises or customer complaints are both urgent and important (Cell 1). A ringing telephone, the arrival of emails, texts, or unscheduled interruptions might be examples of urgent but potentially unimportant activities (Cell 2). Important but nonurgent activities include developmental opportunities, innovating, planning, and so on (Cell 3). Unimportant and nonurgent activities are escapes and routines that people may pursue but which produce little valuable payoff: for example, small talk, daydreaming, shuffling paper, or arguing (Cell 4).

Activities in the Important/Urgent quadrant (Cell 1) usually dominate our lives. The trouble is, these activities require us to merely react. They are

---

Figure 2.3   Types of Activities That Determine Time Use

		URGENCY	
		High	**Low**
IMPORTANCE	**High**	1 Crises Customer complaints	3 Developmental opportunities Innovating Planning
	Low	2 Email or texts Ringing telephone Unscheduled interruptions	4 Escapes Routines Arguments

---

usually controlled by someone else, and they may or may not lead to a result we want to achieve.

The problem is even worse in the Unimportant/Urgent quadrant (Cell 2). Demands by others that may meet their needs but serve only as deflections or interruptions to our agenda only escalate a sense of time stress. Because they may not achieve results that are meaningful, purposeful, and important feelings of overload and loss of control can be guaranteed. When these time stressors are experienced over an extended period of time, we often try to escape into Nonimportant/Nonurgent activities (Cell 4) to relieve the stress. We escape, put everything on hold, and, in so doing, often exacerbate our time stress.

A more effective alternative is to focus on activities in the Important/Nonurgent quadrant (Cell 3). Activities that are Important/Nonurgent might be labeled opportunities instead of problems. They are oriented toward accomplishing high-priority results. They prevent problems from occurring rather than just reacting to them. Preparation, preventive maintenance, planning, personal development, and organizing are all "non-have-to" activities that are crucial for long-term success. Because they are not urgent, however, they often get driven out of our schedules. Important/Nonurgent activities should be the top priority on the time management agenda. By ensuring that these kinds of activities get priority, the urgent problems encountered can be reduced. Time stressors can be eliminated.

One of the most difficult, yet crucially important decisions you must make in managing time effectively is determining what is important to you and what is urgent. There are no rules for dividing all activities, demands, or opportunities into those neat categories. Problems don't come with an "Important/Nonurgent" tag attached. In fact, every problem or time demand is important to someone. But if you let others determine what is and is not important, you will never effectively manage your time.

Barry Sullivan, former CEO at First Chicago, for example, reorganized the way he manages his time. Instead of leaving his appointments calendar in the control of his secretary, he now decides what activities he wants to accomplish, then he allocates specific blocks of time to work on those activities. Only then does he make his calendar available to his secretary to schedule other appointments.

Jan Timmer, former CEO of Philips Electronics, assigned an auditor to keep track of the way he used his time. He reported quarterly to the entire company the percent of his time he spent on key company objectives, ensuring that important priorities got the greatest amount of his time.

Priorities and Core Values

The question still remains, however: How can we make certain that we focus on activities that are important, not just urgent? To help you clarify your important priorities, consider the following questions:

❏ What do I stand for? What am I willing to die (or live) for?

❏ What do I care passionately about?

❏ What legacy would I like to leave? What do I want to be remembered for?

❏ What do I want to have accomplished 20 years from now?

❏ If I could persuade everyone to follow a few basic principles, what would they be?

Answering these questions can help you create a personal principles statement. This is an articulation of the criteria you use for evaluating what is important in your life. Other people generally help determine what is urgent. But judging importance must be done in relation to a set of personal principles and values. Table 2.3 presents two different types of personal principles statements. They are provided as examples of the kinds of principles statements you can write for yourself.

Basing time management on core principles that serve to judge the importance of activities is also the key to being able to say "no" without feeling guilty. When you have decided what it is that you care about passionately, what it is you most want to accomplish, and what legacy you want to leave, you can more easily say "no" to activities that aren't congruent with those principles. Effectiveness in time management, then, means that you accomplish what you *want* to accomplish with your time. How you achieve those accomplishments relates to efficiency of time use, to which we now turn.

Efficient Time Management

In addition to approaching time management from the point of view of effectiveness (i.e., aligning time use with core personal principles), it is also important to adopt an efficiency point of view (i.e., accomplishing more by reducing wasted time). Many techniques are available to help managers utilize more efficiently the time they have each day.

Table 2.3	Examples of Personal Principles Statements

FROM MAHATMA GANDHI

Let then our first act every morning be to make the following resolve for the day:

- I shall not fear anyone on earth.
- I shall fear only God.
- I shall not bear ill will toward anyone.
- I shall not submit to injustice from anyone.
- I shall conquer untruth by truth.
- And in resisting untruth I shall put up with all suffering.

FROM WILLIAM ROLFE KERR

Prime Personal and Professional Principles:

- Succeed at home first.
- Seek and merit Divine help.
- Never compromise with honesty.
- Remember the people involved.
- Plan tomorrow today.
- Develop one new proficiency a year.
- Attain visibility by productivity.
- Hustle while I wait.
- Facilitate the success of my colleagues.
- Pursue excellence in all my endeavors.
- Be sincere and gentle yet decisive.
- Be a creative and innovative person.
- Don't fear mistakes.
- Concentrate all abilities on the task at hand.
- Obtain the counsel of others.
- Defend those who are absent.
- Listen twice as much as I speak.
- Be orderly in work and person.
- Maintain a positive attitude and sense of humor.

One way to enhance efficient time use is to be alert to your own tendencies to use time inefficiently. The list of propositions in Table 2.4 shows general patterns of behavior for most individuals in their use of time. In many situations, these tendencies may represent appropriate responses. In others, however, they can get in the way of efficient time management and increase time stressors unless individuals are aware of them and their possible consequences.

To help you identify your own time management practices and to help you determine the efficiency with which you use your time, we included in the Assessment section an instrument to help you diagnose your time management competency: The Time Management Survey. The principles in the survey have all been derived from research on time management, and the scoring information will show you how well you manage your time compared to others. The rules set forth below correspond to the item numbers in the assessment survey.

Of course, no individual can or should implement all of these time management techniques at once. It would be overwhelming. Therefore, it is best to select just a few of these techniques that will lead to the most improvement in your use of time. Saving just 10 percent more time or using an extra 30 minutes a day more wisely can produce astounding results over months and years, in addition to reducing your time stress.

Rule 1 Read selectively. Most reading should be done the way you read a newspaper, that is, skim most of it, but stop to read what seems most important. If you underline or highlight what you find important, you can review it quickly when you need to.

Rule 2 Make a list of things to accomplish today. Focus on what you want to achieve, not just on what you want to do.

Rule 3 Have a place for everything, and keep everything in its place. Letting things get out of place robs you of time in two ways: you need more time to find something when you need it, and you are tempted to interrupt the task you are doing to do something else.

Rule 4 Prioritize your tasks. Each day you should focus first on important tasks, and then deal with urgent tasks.

Rule 5 Do one important thing at a time but several trivial things simultaneously. You can accomplish a lot by doing more than one thing at a time when tasks are routine, trivial, or require little thought.

Rule 6 Make a list of some 5- or 10-minute discretionary tasks. This helps use the small bits of time almost everyone has during his or her day (waiting for something to begin, between meetings or events, talking on the telephone, etc.).

Table 2.4	Typical Patterns of Time Use

- We do what we like to do before we do what we don't like to do.
- We do the things we know how to do faster than the things we do not know how to do.
- We do the things that are easiest before things that are difficult.
- We do things that require a little time before things that require a lot of time.
- We do things for which the resources are available.
- We do things that are scheduled (e.g., meetings) before nonscheduled things.
- We sometimes do things that are planned before things that are unplanned.
- We respond to demands from others before demands from ourselves.
- We do things that are urgent before things that are important.
- We readily respond to crises and to emergencies.
- We do interesting things before uninteresting things.
- We do things that advance our personal objectives or that are politically expedient.
- We wait until a deadline before we really get moving.
- We do things that provide the most immediate closure.
- We respond on the basis of who wants it.
- We respond on the basis of the consequences to us of doing or not doing something.
- We tackle small jobs before large jobs.
- We work on things in the order of arrival.
- We work on the basis of the squeaky-wheel principle (the squeaky wheel gets the grease).
- We work on the basis of consequences to the group.

Rule 7   Divide up large projects. This helps you avoid feeling overwhelmed by large, important, urgent tasks.

Rule 8   Determine the critical 20 percent of your tasks. Pareto's law states that only 20 percent of the work produces 80 percent of the results.

Rule 9   Save your best time for important matters. Do routine work when your energy level is low, your mind is not sharp, or you aren't on top of things. Reserve your high-energy time for accomplishing the most important and urgent tasks.

Rule 10   Reserve some time during the day when others don't have access to you. Use this time to accomplish Important/Nonurgent tasks, or spend it just thinking.

Rule 11   Don't procrastinate. If you do certain tasks promptly, they will require less time and effort than if you put them off.

Rule 12   Keep track of your time. This is one of the best time management strategies. Write down how you use your time each hour over a sustained period.

Rule 13   Set deadlines. Work always expands to fill the time available, so if you don't specify a termination time, tasks tend to continue longer than they need to.

Rule 14   Do something productive while waiting. Try reading, planning, preparing, rehearsing, reviewing, outlining, or memorizing.

Rule 15   Do busy work at only one set time during the day. Reserve your best time for nontrivial tasks.

Rule 16   Reach closure on at least one thing every day. Finishing a task, even a small one, produces a sense of relief and releases stress.

Rule 17   Schedule some personal time. You need some time when no interruptions will occur, when you can get off the "fast track" for a while and be alone.

Rule 18   Allow yourself to worry only at a specified time and avoid dwelling on a worrisome issue at other times.

Rule 19 Write down long-term objectives. You can be efficient and organized but still accomplish nothing unless you have a clear direction in mind.

Rule 20 Be on the alert for ways to improve your management of time. Read a list of time management hints periodically.

Efficient Time Management for Managers

The second list of rules applies to managers at work. The first nine rules deal with conducting meetings, since managers report that approximately 70 percent of their time is spent in meetings (Cooper & Davidson, 1982; Mintzberg, 1973; Panko, 1992).

Rule 1 Hold routine meetings at the end of the day. Energy and creativity levels are highest early in the day and shouldn't be wasted on trivial matters. Furthermore, an automatic deadline—quitting time—will set a time limit on the meeting.

Rule 2 Hold short meetings standing up. This guarantees that meetings will be kept short.

Rule 3 Set a time limit. Identify when the meeting will end at the beginning of every meeting and appointment.

Rule 4 Cancel meetings once in a while. Meetings should be held only if they can achieve a specific objective.

Rules 5, 6, and 7 Have agendas, stick to them, and keep track of time. Keep track of assignments so that they are not forgotten, that follow-up and accountability occur, and that everyone is clear about expectations.

Rule 8 Start meetings on time. Starting on time rewards people who are prompt rather than waiting for laggards.

Rule 9 Prepare minutes of the meeting and follow up. Commitments and expectations made public through minutes are more likely to be fulfilled.

Rule 10 Insist that subordinates suggest solutions to problems. This eliminates the tendency toward upward delegation, or for subordinates to pass along their problems to you and it allows you to choose among subordinates' alternatives rather than generate your own.

Rule 11 Meet visitors in the doorway. It is easier to keep a meeting short if you are standing in the doorway rather than sitting in your office.

Rule 12 Go to subordinates' offices for brief meetings if it is practical. This helps you control the length of a meeting by being free to leave when you choose.

Rule 13 Don't overschedule the day. You should stay in control of at least some of your time each workday.

Rule 14 Have someone else answer telephone calls and scan email, or set your computer filters so that you do not receive irrelevant messages.

Rule 15 Have a place to work uninterrupted. This helps guarantee that when a deadline is near, you can concentrate on your task and concentrate uninterrupted.

Rule 16 Do something definite with every piece of paperwork handled. Sometimes this means throwing it away.

Rule 17 Keep the workplace clean. This minimizes distractions and reduces the time it takes to find things.

Rules 18, 19, and 20 Delegate work, identify the amount of initiative recipients should take with the tasks they are assigned, and give others credit for their success. These rules all relate to effective delegation, a key time management technique. These last three rules are also discussed in the Empowering and Engaging chapter.

Remember that these techniques for managing time are a means to an end, not the end itself. If trying to implement techniques creates more rather than less stress, they should not be applied. However, research has indicated that managers who use these kinds of techniques have better control of their time, accomplish more, have better relations with subordinates, and eliminate many of the time stressors most managers ordinarily encounter (Davidson, 1995; Lehrer, 1996; Turkington, 1998). Saving just 30 minutes a day amounts to one full year of free time during your working lifetime. That's 8,760 hours of free time! You will find that as you select a few of these hints to apply in your own life, the efficiency of your time use will improve and your time stress will decrease.

ELIMINATING ENCOUNTER STRESSORS THROUGH COMMUNITY, CONTRIBUTION, AND EMOTIONAL INTELLIGENCE

Dissatisfying relationships with others, particularly with a direct manager or supervisor, are prime causes of job stress among workers. (This topic is discussed in more depth in Chapter 4.) Encounter stressors result directly from abrasive, conflictual, nonfulfilling relationships.

Even though work is going smoothly, when encounter stress is present, everything else seems wrong. It is difficult to maintain positive energy when you are at odds with someone, when you feel offended, or when feelings of acceptance and amiability aren't typical of your important relationships at work.

Community

One important factor that helps eliminate encounter stress is a closely-knit group or community. When people feel a part of a group, or accepted by someone else, stress is relieved. For example, it was discovered 35 years ago by Dr. Stewart Wolf that in the town of Roseto, Pennsylvania, residents were completely free from heart disease and other stress-related illnesses. He suspected that their protection sprang from the town's uncommon social cohesion and stability. The town's population consisted entirely of descendants of Italians who had moved there 100 years ago from Roseto, Italy. Few married outside the community, the firstborn was always named after a grandparent, conspicuous consumption and displays of superiority were avoided, and social support among community members was a way of life.

Wolf predicted that residents would begin to display the same level of stress-related illnesses as the rest of the country if the modern world intruded. It did, and they did. Residents in Roseto purchased Cadillacs, ranch-style homes, produced mixed marriages, new names, competition with one another, and a rate of coronary disease the same as any other town's (Farnham, 1991). They had ceased to be a cohesive, collaborative clan and instead had become a community of selfishness and exclusivity. Self-centeredness, it was discovered, was dangerous to health.

A similar discovery resulting from the Vietnam and the Persian Gulf wars related to the strength associated with small, primary work teams. In Vietnam, unlike the Persian Gulf, teams of soldiers did not stay together and did not form the strong bonds. The constant injection of new personnel into squadrons and the constant transfer of soldiers from one location to another made soldiers feel isolated, without loyalty, and vulnerable to stress-related illnesses. In the Persian Gulf War, by contrast, soldiers were kept in the same unit throughout the campaign, brought home together, and given lots of time to debrief together after the battle. Using a closely knit group to provide interpretation of, and social support for, behavior was found to be the most powerful deterrent to post-battle trauma. David Marlowe, chief of psychiatry at Walter Reed Army Institute of Research, indicated that "Squad members are encouraged to use travel time en route home from a war zone to talk about their battlefield experience. It helps them detoxify. That's why we brought them back in groups from Desert Storm. Epistemologically, we know it works" (Farnham, 1991).

Developing close relationships with others is a powerful deterrent to encounter stress. One way of developing this kind of relationship is by applying a concept described by Stephen Covey (1989)—an emotional bank account. Covey used this metaphor to describe the trust or feeling of security that one person develops for another. The more "deposits" made in an emotional bank account, the stronger and more resilient the relationship becomes. Conversely, too many "withdrawals" from the account weaken relationships by destroying trust, security, and confidence.

"Deposits" are made through treating people with kindness, courtesy, honesty, and consistency. The emotional bank account grows when people feel they are receiving love, respect, and caring. "Withdrawals" are made by not keeping promises, not listening, not clarifying expectations, showing irritation, or not allowing choice. Because disrespect and autocratic rule devalue people and destroy a sense of self-worth, relationships are ruined because the bank account becomes overdrawn.

The more people interact, the more deposits must be made in the emotional bank account. When you see an old friend after years of absence, you can often pick up right where you left off, because the emotional bank account has not been touched. But when you interact with someone frequently, the relationship is constantly fed or depleted. Cues from everyday interactions are interpreted as either deposits or withdrawals. When the emotional account is well stocked, mistakes, disappointments, and minor abrasions are easily forgiven and ignored. But when no reserve exists, those incidents may become creators of distrust, contention, and stress.

One of the most important ways to make deposits into the emotional bank account is by making contributions to the well-being of others. This principle can be illustrated by studies conducted at the University of Michigan.

Contribution

In one study, Crocker and Park (2004) followed entering freshmen at the university for a year. At the beginning of the first semester, students were asked to identify their goals for the year. Students identified goals that could be categorized into two types.

Most people possess both kinds of goals, but one or the other type tends to predominate. One type of goal is called achievement goals. This is an emphasis on achieving desired outcomes, obtaining rewards, accomplishing something that brings self-satisfaction, enhancing self-esteem, or creating a positive self-image in the eyes of others (e.g., good grades, making the team, and being popular).

The other type of goal focused on providing a benefit to others or on making a contribution. This type of goal centers on what individuals can give compared to what they can get (assisting others, helping to make something better, fostering improvement in something). Contribution goals are motivated more by benevolence than by a desire for acquisition. The researchers found that goals focused on contributing to others produced a growth orientation in individuals over time, whereas self-interest goals produced a proving orientation over time (Crocker, et al., 2006).

These students were monitored for one academic year in terms of how well they got along with roommates, how many times they missed class, how many minor physiological symptoms occurred (e.g., headache, nausea, cramps), how many leadership positions they attained, their grade point averages, and so forth. On every outcome, contribution goals led to higher performance than achievement goals. The study found that contribution goals led to significantly more learning and development, higher levels of interpersonal trust, more supportive relationships, and less stress, depression, and loneliness than did achievement or self-interest goals (Crocker et al., 2006).

These findings are reinforced by a study by Brown and colleagues (2003, 2006) of patients on being treated with kidney dialysis machines. The study focused on two different factors. One was the extent to which the patients were receiving love, support, and encouragement from others (such as family members). The other was the extent to which the patients were providing love, support, and encouragement to others. Even though they were immobile and could not physically respond, patients enjoyed better health when they felt they were contributing to the well-being of others through support, love, and encouragement compared to when they were receiving these things. Contribution-focused goals produced significantly more mental, emotional, and physiological benefits than achievement-focused goals.

In studies of the language that people use to describe their work experiences, Pennebaker (2002) found that a predominance of the word "we" was associated with less stress, more meaningful relationships, and higher levels of satisfaction in work than the predominance of the word "I." Overcoming encounter stress, in other words, can occur by shifting our focus from achievement to contribution. We make deposits in the emotional back account of relationships when we focus on offering contributions to others well-being rather than focusing mainly on getting what we want.

Social and Emotional Intelligence

As we mentioned in Chapter 1, emotional intelligence has become the catch-all phrase that incorporates multiple intelligences—for example, practical intelligence, abstract intelligence, moral intelligence, interpersonal intelligence, spiritual intelligence, mechanical intelligence, and social intelligence (Gardner, 1993; Mayer, Roberts, & Barsade, 2008; Sternberg, 1997). Emotional intelligence consists of a recognition and control of one's own emotions (personal) and the recognition and appropriate response to the behaviors and responses of others (social). Not surprisingly, emotional and social intelligence represent important skills in helping people manage the stresses that arise from interpersonal encounters (Cantor & Kihlstrom, 1987; Goleman, 1998; Halberstadt, Denham, & Dunsmore, 2001; Saarni, 1997).

The social aspect of emotional intelligence refers to the ability to effectively manage relationships with other people. It consists of four main dimensions:

1. An accurate perception of others' emotional and behavioral responses.
2. The ability to cognitively and emotionally understand and relate to others' responses.
3. Social knowledge, or an awareness of what is appropriate social behavior.
4. Social problem solving or the ability to manage interpersonal difficulties.

The most common form of intelligence with which most people are familiar is IQ, or cognitive intelligence. By and large, cognitive intelligence is beyond our control, especially after the first few years of life. It is a product of the gifts with which we were born or our genetic code. Above a certain threshold level, the correlation between IQ and success in life (e.g., achieving high occupational positions, accumulated wealth, luminary awards, satisfaction with life, performance ratings by peers and superiors) is essentially zero. Very smart people have no greater likelihood of achieving success in life or of achieving personal happiness than people with low IQ scores (Goleman, 1998; Spencer & Spencer, 1993; Sternberg, 1997). On the other hand, social and emotional intelligence have strong positive relationships to success in life and to reduced encounter stress.

For example, in a study at Stanford University, four-year-old children were involved in activities that tested aspects of their emotional intelligence. In one study, a marshmallow was placed in front of them, and they were given two choices: eat it now, or wait until the adult supervisor returned from running an errand, then the child would get two marshmallows. A follow-up study with these same children 14 years later, upon graduation from high school, found that students who demonstrated more emotional intelligence (i.e., controlled their own desires and postponed gratification in the marshmallow task) were less likely to fall apart under stress, became less irritated and less stressed by interpersonally abrasive people, were more likely to accomplish their goals, and scored an average of 210 points higher on the SAT college entrance exam (Shoda, Mischel, & Peake, 1990). The IQ scores of the students did not differ significantly, but the emotional intelligence scores were considerably different. Consistent with other studies, emotional and social intelligence predicted success in life as well as the ability to handle encounter stress for these students.

In another study, when managers were able to accurately identify others' emotions and respond to them, they were found to be more successful in their personal lives as well as in their work lives (Lusch & Serpkenci, 1990; Rosenthal, 1977), and were evaluated as the most desired and competent managers (Pilling & Eroglu, 1994).

If social and emotional intelligence are so important, how does one develop them? The answer is neither simple nor simplistic. Each of the chapters in this book contains some suggested answers to this question. The skills we hope to help you develop are among the most important competencies that comprise social and emotional intelligence. In other words, by improving your abilities in the management skills covered in this book—e.g., self-awareness, problem solving, supportive communication, motivating self and others, managing conflict, empowering others, teambuilding, and so on—your social and emotional competence scores will increase.

This is important because a national survey of workers found that employees who rated their manager as supportive and interpersonally competent had lower rates of burnout, lower stress levels, lower incidence of stress-related illnesses, higher productivity, more loyalty to their organizations, and more efficiency in work than employees with nonsupportive and interpersonally incompetent managers (NNL, 1992).

Socially and emotionally intelligent managers affect the success of their employees as much as they affect their own success and encounter stressor will diminish.

ELIMINATING SITUATIONAL STRESSORS THROUGH WORK REDESIGN

For decades, researchers in the area of occupational health have examined the relationship between job strain and stress-related behavioral, psychological, and physiological outcomes.

A review of this research suggests that the single most important contributor to stress that arises from the job is lack of freedom (Adler, 1989; French & Caplan, 1972; Greenberger & Stasser, 1991). In a study of administrators, engineers, and scientists at the Goddard Space Flight Center, researchers found that individuals provided with more discretion in making decisions about assigned tasks experienced fewer time stressors (e.g., role overload), situational stressors (e.g., role ambiguity), encounter stressors (e.g., interpersonal conflict), and anticipatory stressors (e.g., job-related threats). Individuals without discretion and participation experienced significantly more stress.

In response to these dynamics, Hackman, Oldham, Janson, and Purdy (1975) proposed a model of job redesign that has proved effective in reducing stress and in increasing satisfaction and productivity. A detailed discussion of this job redesign model is provided in Chapter 5. The model identifies ways to design work so that people flourish and avoid situational stress. It consists of five factors—**skill variety** (the opportunity to use multiple skills in performing work), **task identity** (the opportunity to complete a whole task), **task significance** (the opportunity to see the impact of the work being performed), **autonomy** (the opportunity to choose how and when the work will be done), and **feedback** (the opportunity to receive information on the success of task accomplishment). That is, to eliminate situational stressors at work, foster these five factors in these ways:

Combine Tasks When individuals are able to work on a whole project and perform a variety of related tasks (e.g., programming all components of a computer software package), rather than being restricted to working on a single repetitive task or subcomponent of a larger task, they are more satisfied and committed.

Form Identifiable Work Units Building on the first step, when teams of individuals performing related tasks are formed and can decide how to complete the work, stress decreases dramatically (for example, assembling an entire component from start to finish, rather than doing separate tasks as on an assembly line). Workers learn one another's jobs, rotate assignments, and experience a sense of completion in their work.

Establish Customer Relationships   One of the most enjoyable parts of a job is seeing the consequences of one's labor. In most organizations, people who do the work are not given a chance to interact with customers or end users, but they perform much better if they do so (Oldham, 2012).

Increase Decision-Making Authority   Being able to influence the what, when, and how of work increases an individual's feelings of control. Cameron, Freeman, and Mishra (1991) found a significant decrease in experienced stress in firms that were downsizing when workers were given authority to make decisions about how and when they did the extra work required of them.

Open Feedback Channels   A major source of stress is not knowing what is expected and how task performance is being evaluated. As managers communicate their expectations more clearly and give timely and accurate feedback, subordinates' satisfaction and performance improve and stress decreases. Providing more information to people on how they are doing always reduces stress.

Evidence that these practices are effective has been reported in several studies that found productivity increases, less absenteeism, fewer errors, and lower levels of stresses experienced by managers as a result of job redesign (Hackman & Oldham, 1980; Oldham, 2012; Singh 1998).

ELIMINATING ANTICIPATORY STRESSORS THROUGH PRIORITIZING, GOAL SETTING, AND SMALL WINS

Anticipatory stressors are experienced by almost everyone. We have all been worried about a presentation, an upcoming exam, an important interview, or what the future will bring. This kind of stress can be good for us by increasing our alertness and preparation. But sometimes it can be almost paralyzing. How can we eliminate or minimize the negative effects of anticipatory stress? Two simple practices can help.

Goal Setting   Establishing a short-term goal can help eliminate or minimize anticipatory stressors by focusing attention on an immediate action or accomplishment instead of on a fearful future. To be effective, certain action steps are needed if short-term goals are to lead to achievement and the elimination of stress (Locke & Latham, 1990). Figure 2.4 outlines the four-step process associated with successful short-term goal setting.

Figure 2.4   **A Model for Short-Term Planning and Goal Setting**

1. Establish a goal
2. Specify actions and behavioral requirements
3. Generate accountability and reporting mechanisms
4. Identify criteria of success and a reward

The first step is easy: just specify a desired goal or objective. The best goals are characterized by five well-known attributes summarized by the acronym SMART:

S = specific (not general)
M = measurable (not subjective)
A = aligned (not deflecting)
R = realistic (not fantasy)
T = time bound (not open-ended)

Unfortunately, this first step alone is not likely to lead to goal achievement or stress elimination. Most of us identify New Year's resolutions, for example, but never follow through. Step 2, therefore, is to identify, as specifically as possible, the activities and behaviors that will lead toward accomplishing the goal. The principle is: The more difficult the goal is to accomplish, the more rigorous, numerous, and specific should be these behaviors and activities.

Several years ago, prior to bariatric surgery, a friend approached us with a problem. She was a wonderfully sensitive, caring, competent single woman in her late 20s who was experiencing a high degree of anticipatory stress because of her size. She had weighed well over 350 pounds for more than 10 years. She was afraid of both the health consequences and the social consequences of not being able to lose weight. With the monitoring of a physician, she set a goal to lose 100 pounds in the next 12 months (Step 1). Because it was to be such a difficult goal to reach, however, she asked us for help in achieving her ambitious objective.

We first identified a dozen or so specific actions and guidelines that would facilitate the attainment of the goal (Step 2). These action steps included, for example, never shopping alone or without a menu, never carrying more than 50 cents in her purse (in order to avoid the temptation to buy a doughnut), exercising with friends each day at 5:30 P.M., forgoing TV at night to reduce the temptation to snack, keeping a food log, and going to bed by 10:30 P.M. The behaviors were rigid, but the goal was so difficult that they were necessary to ensure progress.

Step 3 involves establishing accountability. If no one else will know if the goal was achieved, chances are it will not be. The key principle is: "Make it more difficult to stay the same than to change." This is done by involving others in ensuring accountability for adherence to the plan, establishing a social support network to obtain encouragement from others, and instituting penalties for nonconformance.

In addition to announcing to coworkers, friends, and a church group that she would lose the 100 pounds, our friend renegotiated her work contract so that she would take a cut in salary if she did not achieve her goal. Her doctor registered her for a hospital stay at the end of the 12-month period, so that if she did not achieve the goal on her own, she was to go on an intravenous feeding schedule in the hospital to lose the weight, at a cost of over $250 per day. She made it more difficult and more costly to fail than to succeed.

Step 4 involves establishing an evaluation and reward system. This means identifying the evidence that the goal has been accomplished and the benefits that will be produced with success. This step is crucial because many desirable goals—such as being a better leader, a more empathetic friend, a more patient parent—are not achieved without specific indicators of success. How do I know I have achieved the goal? Identify objective indicators of success.

The purpose of this short-term planning model is to eliminate anticipatory stress by establishing a focus and direction for activity. The anxiety associated with uncertainty and potentially negative events is dissipated when mental and physical energy are concentrated on purposeful activity. (By the way, the last time we saw our friend, her weight was below 200 pounds.)

Small Wins Another principle related to eliminating anticipatory stressors is the small-wins strategy (Weick, 1984). By "small win," we mean a tiny but definite change made in a desired direction. Begin by changing something that is easy to change. Then, change a second thing that is easy to change, and so on. Although each individual success may be relatively modest when considered alone, the multiple small gains eventually mount up, generating a sense of momentum that creates movement toward a desired goal.

When we focus on a small, concrete outcome—giving us a chance to enjoy visible success—we develop heightened confidence and optimism which motivates the pursuit of another small win. By itself, a small win may seem unimportant. A series of wins at seemingly insignificant tasks, however, reveals a pattern that tends to attract allies, deter opponents, and lower resistance to further action. The fear associated with anticipatory change is eliminated as we build self-confidence through small wins. We also gain the support of others as they see progress being made.

In the case of our overweight friend, one key was to begin changing what she could change, a little at a time. Tackling the loss of 100 pounds all at once would have been too overwhelming a task. But she could change the time she shopped, the time she went to bed, and the menu she ate for breakfast. Each successful change generated more and more momentum that, when combined, led to the larger change that she desired. Her ultimate success was a product of multiple small wins.

In summary, the rules for instituting small wins are simple: (1) identify a small, easy-to-change activity that is under your control; (2) change it in a way that leads toward your desired goal; (3) find another small thing to change, and change it; (4) keep track of the changes you are making; and (5) maintain the small gains you have made. Anticipatory stressors are eliminated because the fearful unknown is replaced by a focus on immediate successes.

Developing Resiliency and Well-Being

Now that we have examined various causes of stress and outlined a series of preventive measures, we turn our attention to a second major strategy for managing negative stress as shown in Figure 2.2, the development of **resiliency** to handle the stress that cannot be eliminated. This means not only developing the capacity to effectively manage the negative effects of stress, to bounce back from adversity, and to endure difficult situations (Wright, Masten, & Narayan, 2013), but it also means finding ways to thrive and flourish even in difficult circumstances—that is, the enhance well-being (Diener, Porath, et al., 2011; Spreitzer, et al., 2005;). The Flourishing Scale in the Assessment section of this chapter measures the level of your personal well-being or the extent to which you are flourishing in life. Flourishing provides the resilience you need to cope effectively with stress.

The first studies of resiliency emerged from investigations of children in abusive, alcoholic, poverty, or mentally ill parent circumstances. Some of these children surprised researchers by rising above their circumstances and developing into healthy, well-functioning adolescents and adults. They were referred to as highly resilient individuals (Masten & Reed, 2002).

We all differ widely in our ability to cope with stress. Some individuals seem to crumble under pressure, while others appear to thrive. A major predictor of which individuals cope well with stress and which experience well-being is the amount of resiliency that they have developed. In this section, we highlight several key factors that help individuals develop and enhance personal resiliency and find ways to thrive in the presence of stressful situations.

LIFE BALANCE

The wheel in Figure 2.5 represents the key activities that characterize most people's lives. Each segment in the figure identifies an important aspect of life that must be developed in order to achieve resiliency and well-being. The most resilient individuals are those who have achieved a certain degree of **life balance**. They actively engage in activities in each segment of the circle so that they achieve a degree of balance in their lives.

For example, assume the center of the figure represents the zero point of involvement and the outside edge of the figure represents maximum involvement. Shading in a portion of the area in each of the seven segments would represent the amount of attention paid to each area. (This exercise is included in the Skill Practice section.) Individuals who are best able to cope with stress would shade in a substantial portion of each segment, indicating they have spent time developing a variety of dimensions of their lives. Overemphasizing one or two areas to the exclusion of others often creates more stress than it eliminates. Life balance is key (Hill, Hawkins, Ferris, & Weitzman, 2001; Lehrer, 1996; Murphy, 1996; Rostad & Long, 1996; White, Hill, McGovern, Mills, & Smeaton, 2003).

This prescription, of course, seems counterintuitive. Generally, when we are feeling stress in one area of life, such as an overloaded work schedule, we respond by devoting more time and attention to it. While this is a natural reaction, it is counterproductive for several reasons. First, the more we concentrate exclusively on work, the more restricted and less creative we become. We lose perspective, cease to take fresh points of view, and become overwhelmed more easily. That is why several major corporations send senior managers on high-adventure wilderness retreats, foster volunteer community service, or encourage engagement in completely unrelated activities outside of work.

Second, refreshed and relaxed minds think better. A bank executive commented recently during an executive development workshop that he gradually has become convinced of the merits of taking the

Figure 2.5 | **Balancing Life Activities**

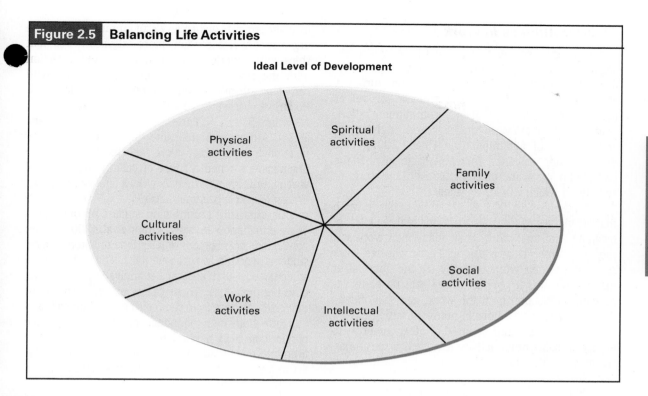

Ideal Level of Development

weekend off from work. He finds that he gets twice as much accomplished on Monday as his colleagues who have been in their offices all weekend.

Third, the cost of stress-related illness decreases markedly when employees participate in well-rounded wellness programs. A study by the Association for Fitness in Business concluded that companies receive an average return of $3 to $4 on each dollar invested in health and wellness promotion. AT&T, for example, expects to save $72 million in the next 10 years as a result of investment in wellness programs for employees.

Well-developed individuals, who give time and attention to cultural, physical, spiritual, family, social, and intellectual activities in addition to work, are more productive and less stressed than those who are workaholics (Adler & Hillhouse, 1996; Hepburn, McLoughlin, & Barling, 1997; White, Hill, McGovern, Mills, & Smeaton, 2003). A great deal of literature is available on physical fitness, spiritual development, strengthening families, and so forth, so in this section, we concentrate on just two common areas of well-being: the development psychological resiliency and social resiliency. These are not competencies that can be accomplished by lunchtime or by the weekend. Rather, achieving life balance and resiliency requires ongoing commitment and continuous effort.

PSYCHOLOGICAL RESILIENCY

Psychological resiliency refers to the ability of a person to return to the original condition after experiencing trauma, challenge, or threat. It is the ability to bounce-back or withstand negative stressors. In materials science this capacity is referred to as "tensility." Psychological resiliency also includes the idea of flourishing in the presence of negative stress. This is similar to as "post-traumatic growth," or excelling as a result of facing negative or difficult conditions. Psychological resiliency has been the focus of a great deal of research (for example, see Reich, Zautra & Hall 2010; Sutcliffe & Vogus, 2003; Wadey, Evans, Hanton, & Neil, 2012), and the prescriptions for developing psychological resiliency are relatively consistent across studies and populations (Ungar, 2008). They include access to supportive, loving relationships; development of self-awareness, self-confidence, and self-efficacy; involvement in spiritual or religious activities; and the establishment of personal goals (Bandura, 2012; Maddi, 2013; Masten & Obradovic, 2006).

These topics are all addressed earlier and in other chapters in this book, but here we highlight three practices that have been found to produce resiliency as well as flourishing in the presence of stress. They include meaningfulness in work, reciprocity, and gratitude.

Meaningfulness in Work

A well-established relationship exists between engaging in meaningful work and positive outcomes including reductions in stress, depression, turnover, absenteeism, dissatisfaction, and cynicism, as well as increases in well-being, resiliency, commitment, effort, engagement, empowerment, happiness, satisfaction, and a sense of fulfillment (see Chen, 2007). One way to foster resiliency, therefore, is to identify the profound purpose and meaningfulness of the work (or activity) in which you are engaged.

Wrzesniewski (2003, 2012) found in her research that individuals typically associate one of three kinds of meaning with their work. They define their work as a *job*, as a *career*, or as a *calling*. Those who see work as a *job* do their work primarily for the financial or material rewards it provides. They gain no particular personal satisfaction from the work, and they pursue their interests and passions in nonwork settings. Work is a means for obtaining financial or other resources to engage in some other activity (e.g., "Give me the assignment, and I'll do it. This job helps me make my car payments").

Other individuals have a *career* orientation. They are motivated by accomplishment and success. They work to achieve the prestige, power, recognition, and advancement that come from performing their work well. They desire to be distinguished members of their organizations, and they use work to acquire promotion, notoriety, title, or advancement. Work is a means for achieving personal growth, recognition, and capability development (e.g., "I want to reach a senior leadership position in this organization; I want to improve my skills").

The third orientation, the sense of work as a *calling*, characterizes individuals who are driven by the meaning associated with the work itself. The actual tasks involved in their work provide intrinsic motivation and profound purpose. They consider their work inherently fulfilling, and they seek for a greater good, regardless of the material rewards offered by the work. Their work possesses a sense of meaning that reaches beyond personal benefit or the acquisition of reward (e.g., "I care deeply about what I am doing at work").

High levels of meaningfulness in work not only relieve stress but are associated with positive outcomes and extraordinary individual and organizational performance (Grant, 2008). For example, workers with a calling orientation reported fewer negative effects of stress, higher levels of trust and confidence in management, higher levels of commitment to the organization, less conflict, more satisfactory relationships with coworkers, and higher levels of satisfaction with the tasks themselves compared to those with career or job orientations (Wrzesniewski, McCauley, Rozin, & Schwartz, 1997; Cook & Wall, 1980; Mowday, Steers, & Porter, 1979; Taylor & Bowers, 1972). Moreover, significantly higher levels of organizational performance were detected in health-care organizations when a sense of calling predominated among employees (Wrzesniewski & Dutton, in press; Wrzesniewski & Landman, 2000).

In especially enlightening studies of the effects of meaningfulness in work, Grant et al. (2007, 2008) conducted investigations of telephone solicitors (mostly students working in part-time jobs). The task of these students was to place calls to university alumni requesting donations. These callers experienced almost universal rejection from the recipients of their calls and had little motivation to produce inasmuch as they were required to read a standardized script and received little information about the impact of their work. The voluntary turnover rate among the callers was approximately 350 percent.

In the study, half of the callers were exposed for just five minutes to a scholarship student who benefited from the solicitations. This student simply thanked the callers for their efforts and explained that he or she would not have been able to attend the university had these solicitors not raised the money that provided the scholarship funds. The fact that they were raising money for scholarships had made a profound difference in his or her life. The other half of the callers were not exposed to a scholarship student and received no such message.

The results of the studies were startling (Grant, 2007; 2008; Grant et al., 2007). Student callers exposed to a scholarship student increased their productivity (number of calls made) and effectiveness (amount of money raised) by a factor of three compared to callers who received no information about meaningfulness. The results not only were seen immediately after the intervention (a week later), but the consequences could be seen more than a month later. As illustrated in Figure 2.6, even in a negative, stressful, boring job, identifying the meaningfulness associated with the work produced dramatically higher performance.

It is important to remember that a sense of calling is not dependent on the type of work performed. Rather, it is associated with the positive

Figure 2.6 | Productivity of Workers One Month Later

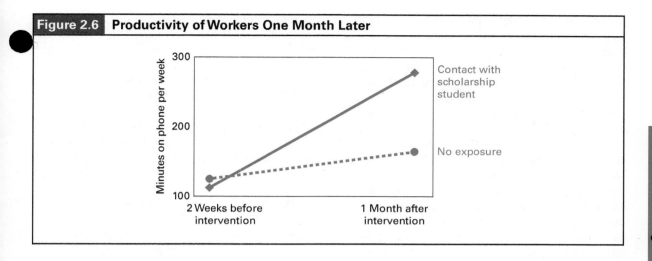

meaning inherent in the work (Bellah et al., 1985; Wrzesniewski, 2003). Any kind of work—even that typically thought of as physically, socially, or morally tainted—can be **reframed** in a positive light (Ashforth & Kreiner, 1999). Put another way, exactly the same task may be viewed as a job or as a calling depending on the perspective of the individual. Even the most noxious and unpleasant of tasks can be reinterpreted as a calling that has a profound purpose (Pratt & Ashforth, 2003).

Work is associated with meaningfulness when it possesses one or more of four key attributes summarized in Table 2.5:

(1) *The work has an important positive impact on the well-being of human beings* (Brown et al., 2003; Grant, 2008; Grant et al., 2007). Individuals who can see the effects of their work on others—who were aware of the contributions they made to the welfare of people—have a significantly higher sense of meaningfulness, experience higher well-being, and produce significantly higher performance and engagement in the organization.

Some companies, for example, Medtronic, regularly invite patients whose lives have been transformed by the medical devices they manufacture to give speeches at employee gatherings. Google posts comments from customers, some of them indicating the life-changing benefits of using Google, on its company website. Huffy manufacturing employees visit customers to observe how people use their products and how these products affect their lifestyles.

(2) *The work is associated with an important virtue or a personal value* (Bright, Cameron, & Caza, 2006; Weber, 1992). Certain values tend to be universal, for example, caring, helpfulness, frugality, compassion, and assisting the disadvantaged. Attaching the work to such values tends to enhance its meaningfulness for individuals.

For example, Jeff Schwartz, CEO at Timberland, decided to substantially increase the percentage of organically grown cotton in the clothes the company manufactures in order to reduce exposure to carcinogens by migrant workers who pick corporately grown cotton. Even in the absence of any customer demand or regulatory encouragement, and at a substantial expense to the company's bottom line, Schwartz's intention was to provide a benefit to a disadvantaged group of individuals who would likely never be customers but whose lives could be made better by Timberland's change in policy (Schwartz, 2001).

(3) *The work has an impact that extends beyond the immediate time frame or creates a ripple effect* (Cameron & Lavine, 2006; Crocker, Nuer, Olivier, & Cohen, 2006). A number of authors such

Table 2.5 | Enablers of Meaningfulness in Work

1. The work has an important positive impact on the well-being of human beings.

2. The work is associated with an important virtue or a personal value.

3. The work has an impact that extends beyond the immediate time frame or creates a ripple effect.

4. The work builds supportive relationships and fosters generalized reciprocity.

as Lawrence and Nohria (2002) and Covey (2004) suggested that a basic human need is to create a legacy and to extend influence beyond the immediate time frame. Rather than to seek for immediate personal benefit or self-aggrandizement, these authors highlighted the benefits of having an effect on long-term consequences, including flourishing in stressful circumstances.

Cameron and Lavine (2006) documented this effect in studying the cleanup of the Rocky Flats Nuclear Arsenal—60 years ahead of schedule, $30 billion under budget, and 13 times cleaner than required by federal standards. Union members had to be willing to work themselves out of a job as quickly as possible—a stance completely contradictory to the fundamental purposes of unions—while maintaining high levels of morale and safety among remaining workers. This remarkable performance occurred because employees found profound meaningfulness in what they believed to be a multigenerational impact of their efforts. The fact that a dangerous location would be removed but also that it would become a wildlife refuge—the only such site on the eastern slope of the Rocky Mountains, and a safe environment for a thousand years to come—was a driving force in motivating the sacrifices that were required to succeed.

Creating a ripple effect means that some behaviors create a repetitive action. When, for example, a person displays a virtuous behavior—assisting someone in need, expressing thanks, displaying kindness, showing courage—the tendency is for other people to follow suit. They tend to repeat the virtuous actions themselves, so kindness begets kindness, love fosters love, gratitude leads to thankfulness, and so forth.

(4) *The work builds supportive relationships and fosters generalized reciprocity* (Baker, 2012, 2013; Polodny, Khurana, & Hill-Popper, 2005). In almost every aspect of life, social support makes things easier. Physically people are healthier, live longer, handle stress better, perform at higher levels, and function better cognitively when they experience supportive relationships with others (Cameron, 2013; Dutton, 2003; Heaphy & Dutton, 2006). A recent meta-analytic review of 148 scientific studies representing more than 300,000 individuals concluded that interpersonal relationships are a better predictor of mortality rates, cardio vascular disease, cancer, and various infections than was smoking, excessive alcohol consumption, obesity, and lack of physical exercise (Holt-Lunstad, Smith, & Layton, 2010).

Poignant testimony to the value of social support systems during periods of high stress comes from the experiences of soldiers captured during World War II and the Korean and Vietnam wars. When it was possible for prisoners to form permanent, interacting groups, they maintained better health and morale and were able to resist their captors more effectively than when they were isolated or when groups were unstable. Indeed, the well-documented technique used by the Chinese during the Korean War for breaking down soldiers' resistance to their indoctrination efforts involved weakening group solidarity through planting seeds of mistrust and doubt about members' loyalty.

Developing strong interpersonal relationships is the topic of Chapter 4, but in addition, this chapter describes an important technique for building supportive relationships in connection with stress reduction and fostering well-being. The technique centers on *generalized reciprocity.*

Generalized reciprocity occurs when a person contributes something to another person that is not directly connected to receiving something in return that is personally beneficial. The contribution occurs because it will be good for someone else. This principle is illustrated by former Prudential CEO Jim Mallozzi as a way to foster more resiliency in his firm.

During Mallozzi's first meeting as CEO of his firm with 2,500 sales personnel in a large auditorium, he asked participants to take out their iPhones and Blackberries and turn them on instead of turning them off. He requested that each person text or email one great idea for how to get a new client, how to close a sale, or how to keep a customer for life. The objective was to help someone else in the company be more successful. More than 2,200 ideas were shared, and Mallozzi reported that these ideas were still being actively used 15 months later.

One practice for fostering generalized reciprocity is contained in the Skill Practice section of this chapter. It was introduced by Wayne Baker at the University of Michigan and helps identify new ideas and previously unrecognized resources among individuals (see www.humaxnetworks.com). A reciprocity network is created when each individual in a group makes a request. These can be personal requests ("I need a person to feed my dog while I'm out of town") or they can be work-related requests ("I would like to know how to motivate my sales team"). Other individuals in the group then respond to these requests with resources, knowledge, or connections that may provide value. A network is created when people with requests are linked up to people with resources or assistance.

As it turns out, human beings have an inherent tendency toward reciprocity. If I give someone something and he or she does not reciprocate, or at least say "thank you," we label that person selfish, insensitive, and inappropriate. All economic and exchange systems are based on the principle of reciprocity. Taking something from a store without giving something in return is called stealing. Not only have we all been taught that our social order is based on reciprocity.

"Generalized reciprocity" occurs when the tendency to give back or to contribute is not directly connected to the direct receipt of something beneficial. Contribution occurs because it will be good for someone or something else. It is important to note that we tend to rate others as more effective leaders, more desirable friends, and higher performers at work when they contribute to others unselfishly (Putnam, 2013).

Gratitude

Another seemingly simple but powerful tool for building resiliency and personal well-being is the practice of gratitude. Feelings and expressions of gratitude have dramatic effects on individuals and groups. For example, Emmons (2003) induced feelings of gratitude in students by assigning them to keep journals as part of a semester-long experiment. Some of the students were required to keep "gratitude journals" on a daily or weekly basis. They wrote down events or incidents that happened during the day (or week) for which they were grateful. Other students were assigned to write down events or incidents that were frustrating, and still other students were assigned to write down events or incidents that were merely neutral.

The students who kept gratitude journals, compared to frustrated students and neutral students, had higher levels of well-being; experienced fewer physical symptoms such as headaches and colds; felt better about their lives as a whole; were more optimistic about the coming week; had higher states of alertness, attentiveness, determination, and energy; reported fewer hassles and less stress in their lives; engaged in more helping behavior toward other people; experienced better sleep quality; and had a sense of being more connected to others. In addition, they were absent and tardy less often and had higher grade point averages. Feelings of gratitude had significant impact on student classroom performance as well as on their personal lives (Emmons, 2008).

Figure 2.7 illustrates one reason such positive results occur. Individuals experiencing gratitude demonstrate a more consistent and healthy heart rhythm than individuals experiencing frustration. Physiological health, cognitive functioning, and performance at work are substantially higher when gratitude is fostered, at least partly because of the harmonious pattern adopted by the body. Emmons (2008) also found that expressions of gratitude by one person tended to motivate others to express gratitude, so a self-perpetuating, virtuous cycle occurred when gratitude was expressed. Gratitude elicited positive behavior on the part of other people (e.g., they were more likely to loan money or provide compassionate support) as well as reciprocal behavior. For example, a handwritten "thank you" on a restaurant bill by the server elicited about 11 percent higher tips, and visits by case workers and social workers were 80 percent higher if they were thanked for coming (McCullough, Emmons, & Tsang, 2002).

Engaging in gratitude visits (e.g., simply visiting another person in order to express gratitude), writing gratitude letters (e.g., sharing feelings of thanks with another person), keeping gratitude journals (e.g., writing down three things daily for which you are grateful), and distributing daily gratitude cards (e.g., handing out some written expressions of appreciation to coworkers each day) all have been shown in empirical investigations to

Figure 2.7 | **Heart Rhythms in Gratitude and Frustration Conditions**

SOURCE: *McCraty & Childre, 2004*

produce important impacts on individuals and organizations (see Seligman, Steen, Park, & Peterson, 2005). Despite being easy to implement, their effects are powerful and significant in fostering resiliency and helping to enhance well-being.

Temporary Stress-Reduction Techniques

Thus far, we have emphasized eliminating sources of stress and developing resiliency to stress. These are the most desirable stress-management strategies because they have a permanent or long-term effect on your well-being. However, the occurrence of stressors is sometimes beyond your control so it may be impossible to eliminate them. Moreover, developing resiliency often takes time, so on occasion we must use temporary reactive mechanisms in order to maintain equilibrium. Although increased resilience can buffer the harmful effects of stress, we must sometimes take immediate action in the short term to cope with the stress we encounter.

Implementing short-term strategies reduces stress temporarily so that longer-term stress-elimination or resiliency strategies can be implemented. Short-term strategies are largely reactive and must be repeated whenever stressors are encountered because, unlike other strategies, their effects are only temporary. On the other hand, they are especially useful for immediately calming feelings of anxiety or apprehension. You can use them when you are asked a question you can't answer, when you become embarrassed by an unexpected event, when you are faced with a presentation or an important meeting, or almost any time you are suddenly stressed and must respond in a short period of time. Although more than 150,000 books are available from on temporary stress-reduction techniques since 1990, we review only four of the best-known and easiest to learn techniques here. The first two are physiological; the last two are psychological.

Muscle relaxation involves easing the tension in successive muscle groups. Each muscle group is tightened for five or ten seconds and then completely relaxed. Starting with the feet and progressing to the calves, thighs, stomach, and on to the neck and face, one can relieve tension throughout the entire body. All parts of the body can be included in the exercise. One variation is to roll the head around on the neck several times, shrug the shoulders, or stretch the arms up toward the ceiling for five to ten seconds, then release the position and relax the muscles. The result is a state of temporary relaxation that helps eliminate tension and refocus energy.

A variation of muscle relaxation involves **deep breathing**. This is done by taking several successive slow, deep breaths, holding them for five seconds, and exhaling completely. You should focus on the act of breathing itself, so that your mind becomes cleared for a brief time while your body relaxes. After each deep breath, muscles in the body should consciously be relaxed.

A third technique uses **imagery and fantasy** to eliminate stress temporarily by changing the focus of your thoughts. Imagery involves visualizing an event, using "mind pictures." An increasingly common practice for athletes is to visualize successful performance or to imagine themselves achieving their goal. Research has confirmed both the stress-reduction advantages of this technique as well as the performance enhancement benefits (e.g., Andersen & Williams, 1999; Deepak, 1995).

In addition to visualization, imagery also can include recollections of sounds, smells, and textures. Your mind focuses on pleasant experiences from the past (e.g., a fishing trip, family vacation, visit with relatives, or day at the beach) that can be recalled vividly. Fantasies, on the other hand, are not past memories but make-believe events or images. It is especially well known, for example, that children often construct imaginary friends, make-believe occurrences, or special wishes that are comforting to them when they encounter stress. Adults also use daydreams or other fantasy experiences to get them through stressful situations. The purpose of this technique is to relieve anxiety or pressure temporarily by focusing on something pleasant so that other, more productive stress-reducing strategies can be developed for the longer term.

This is similar to various forms of meditative practices including, for example, loving kindness meditation. Loving kindness meditation is a well-developed contemplative practice that focuses on self-generated feelings of love, compassion, and good will toward oneself and others. Essentially, people focus on their feelings of positive regard for people close to them. Similar practices include writing and contemplating gratitude journal entries, engaging in personal prayer, and pondering spiritual inspiration. These practices, essentially, put people in a reflective and peaceful condition.

The results of recent research on these kinds of practices are compelling. Studies show that engaging in contemplative practices diminishes stress-related cortisol, insomnia, symptoms of autoimmune illnesses, PMS, asthma, falling back into depression, general emotional distress, anxiety, and panic. It helps control blood sugar in type 2 diabetes, detachment from negative reactions, self-understanding, and general well-being. Links have also been uncovered with heart rate, oxytocin, vagal nerve tone, blood pressure, obesity, incidence of cancer, heart disease, various infections, and, surprisingly, the actual cortical thickness of the brain (Fredrickson, et al., 2008; Hozel, et al., 2010; Kok, et al., 2014).

The fourth technique is called **rehearsal**. Using this technique, people work themselves through potentially stressful situations, trying out different scenarios and alternative reactions. Appropriate reactions are rehearsed, either in a safe environment before stress occurs, or "off-line," in private, in the middle of a stressful situation. Removing oneself temporarily from a stressful circumstance and working through dialogue or reactions, as though rehearsing for a play, can help one regain control and reduce the immediacy of the stressor.

Summary

We began this chapter by explaining stress in terms of a relatively simple model. Four kinds of stressors—time, encounter, situational, and anticipatory—cause negative physiological, psychological, and social reactions in individuals. These reactions are moderated by the resiliency that individuals have developed for coping with stress. The best way to manage stress is to eliminate it through effective and efficient time management, fostering community and making contributions, enhancing emotional and social intelligence, work redesign, prioritizing, goal setting, and small wins. This strategy has permanent consequences, but it often takes an extended period of time to implement.

The next most effective stress management strategy is improving one's resiliency. Physiological resiliency is strengthened through increased cardiovascular conditioning and improved diet. Psychological resiliency, hardiness, and personal well-being are improved by focusing on meaningfulness in work, reciprocity, and gratitude. These strategies produce long-term benefits, but they often cannot be implemented on the spot. They are medium-term strategies that enhance hardiness over time.

When circumstances make it impossible to apply longer-term strategies for reducing stress, short-term relaxation techniques can temporarily alleviate the symptoms of stress. These strategies have short-term consequences, but they can be applied immediately and repeated over and over again.

Behavioral Guidelines

Following are specific behavioral guidelines for improving your stress management skills and fostering personal well-being.

1. Address stress by first trying to eliminate the stressors, then focus on developing resiliency and personal well-being to create hardiness in stressful situations, and finally learn temporary stress coping methods to reduce stress in the short-term.

2. Use proven time management practices. Make sure to use time effectively as well as efficiently by generating your own personal mission statement. Make sure that low-priority tasks do not drive out time to work on high-priority activities. Make better use of your time by using the guidelines in the Time Management Survey in the Assessment Section. Give important activities priority over urgent ones.

3. Build collaborative relationships with individuals based on mutual trust, respect, honesty, and kindness. Make "deposits" into the "emotional bank accounts" of other people. Form close, stable relationships among those with whom you work.

4. Consciously work to improve your emotional intelligence by learning and practicing the principles discussed in other chapters of this book.

5. Reaffirm priorities and short-term goals that provide direction and focus to activities. Make your goals SMART.

6. Increase your psychological resiliency through life balance, especially by consciously engaging in physical, intellectual, cultural, social, family, and spiritual activities.

7. Increase your resilience by implementing a small-wins strategy. Identify and celebrate the small successes that you and others achieve.

8. Learn at least one relaxation technique and practice it regularly.
9. Increase social resiliency by forming an open, trusting, sharing relationship with at least one other person. Facilitate a mentoring relationship with someone who can affirm your worth as a person and provide support during periods of stress.
10. Identify the meaningfulness of your work that is more important than your own personal reward.
11. Establish some contributions goals that make a difference to those around you, and give contribution goals at least as high priority as achievement goals.
12. Implement at least one gratitude practice such as a gratitude journal, gratitude visits, or gratitude cards.

SKILL *ANALYSIS*

CASES INVOLVING STRESS MANAGEMENT

The Turn of the Tide

Not long ago I came to one of those bleak periods that many of us encounter from time to time, a sudden drastic dip in the graph of living when everything goes stale and flat, energy wanes, enthusiasm dies. The effect on my work was frightening. Every morning I would clench my teeth and mutter: "Today life will take on some of its old meaning. You've got to break through this thing. You've got to!"

But the barren days went by, and the paralysis grew worse. The time came when I knew I had to have help. The man I turned to was a doctor. Not a psychiatrist, just a doctor. He was older than I, and under his surface gruffness lay great wisdom and compassion. "I don't know what's wrong," I told him miserably, "but I just seem to have come to a dead end. Can you help me?"

"I don't know," he said slowly. He made a tent of his fingers and gazed at me thoughtfully for a long while. Then, abruptly, he asked, "Where were you happiest as a child?"

"As a child?" I echoed. "Why, at the beach, I suppose. We had a summer cottage there. We all loved it."

He looked out the window and watched the October leaves sifting down. "Are you capable of following instructions for a single day?"

"I think so," I said, ready to try anything.

"All right. Here's what I want you to do."

He told me to drive to the beach alone the following morning, arriving not later than nine o'clock. I could take some lunch; but I was not to read, write, listen to the radio, or talk to anyone. "In addition," he said, "I'll give you a prescription to be taken every three hours."

He then tore off four prescription blanks, wrote a few words on each, folded them, numbered them, and handed them to me. "Take these at nine, twelve, three, and six."

"Are you serious?" I asked.

He gave a short bark of laughter. "You won't think I'm joking when you get my bill!"

The next morning, with little faith, I drove to the beach. It was lonely, all right. A northeaster was blowing; the sea looked gray and angry. I sat in the car, the whole day stretching emptily before me. Then I took out the first of the folded slips of paper. On it was written: LISTEN CAREFULLY.

I stared at the two words. "Why," I thought, "the man must be mad." He had ruled out music and newscasts and human conversation. What else was there? I raised my head and I did listen. There were no sounds but the steady roar of the sea, the creaking cry of a gull, the drone of some aircraft high overhead. All these sounds were familiar. I got out of the car. A gust of wind slammed the door with a sudden clap of sound. "Am I supposed to listen carefully to things like that?" I asked myself.

I climbed a dune and looked out over the deserted beach. Here the sea bellowed so loudly that all other sounds were lost. And yet, I thought suddenly, there must be sounds beneath sounds—the soft rasp of drifting sand, the tiny wind-whisperings in the dune grasses—if the listener got close enough to hear them.

On an impulse I ducked down and, feeling fairly ridiculous, thrust my head into a clump of sea-oats. Here I made a discovery: If you listen intently, there is a fractional moment in which everything seems to pause, wait. In that instant of stillness, the racing thoughts halt. For a moment, when you truly listen for something outside yourself, you have to silence the clamorous voices within. The mind rests.

I went back to the car and slid behind the wheel. LISTEN CAREFULLY. As I listened again to the deep growl of the sea, I found myself thinking about the white-fanged fury of its storms.

I thought of the lessons it had taught us as children. A certain amount of patience: You can't hurry the tides. A great deal of respect: The sea does not suffer fools gladly. An awareness of the vast and mysterious interdependence of things: Wind and tide and current, calm and squall and hurricane, all combine to determine the paths of the birds above and the fish below. And the cleanness of it all, with every beach swept twice a day by the great broom of the sea.

Sitting there, I realized I was thinking of things bigger than myself—and there was relief in that.

Even so, the morning passed slowly. The habit of hurling myself at a problem was so strong that I felt lost without it. Once, when I was wistfully eyeing the car radio, a phrase from Carlyle jumped into my head: "Silence is the element in which great things fashion themselves."

By noon, the wind had polished the clouds out of the sky, and the sea had merry sparkle. I unfolded the second "prescription." And again I sat there, half amused and half exasperated. Three words this time: TRY REACHING BACK.

Back to what? To the past, obviously. But why, when all my worries concerned the present or the future?

I left the car and started tramping reflectively along the dunes. The doctor had sent me to the beach because it was a place of happy memories. Maybe that was what I was supposed to reach for: the wealth of happiness that lay half-forgotten behind me.

I decided to experiment: to work on these vague impressions as a painter would, retouching the colors, strengthening the outlines. I would choose specific incidents and recapture as many details as possible. I would visualize people complete with dress and gestures. I would listen (carefully) for the exact sound of their voices, the echo of their laughter.

The tide was going out now, but there was still thunder in the surf. So I chose to go back 20 years to the last fishing trip I made with my younger brother. (He died in the Pacific during World War II and was buried in the Philippines.) I found that if I closed my eyes and really tried, I could see him with amazing vividness, even the humor and eagerness in his eyes that far-off morning.

ANALYSIS

In fact, I could see it all: the ivory scimitar of beach where we were fishing; the eastern sky smeared with sunrise; the great rollers creaming in, stately and slow. I could feel the backwash swirl warm around my knees, see the sudden arc of my brother's rod as he struck a fish, hear his exultant yell. Piece by piece I rebuilt it, clear and unchanged under the transparent varnish of time. Then it was gone.

I sat up slowly. TRY REACHING BACK. Happy people were usually assured, confident people. If, then, you deliberately reached back and touched happiness, might there not be released little flashes of power, tiny sources of strength?

This second period of the day went more quickly. As the sun began its long slant down the sky, my mind ranged eagerly through the past, reliving some episodes, uncovering others that had been completely forgotten. For example, when I was around 13 and my brother 10, Father had promised to take us to the circus. But at lunch there was a phone call: Some urgent business required his attention downtown. We braced ourselves for disappointment. Then we heard him say, "No, I won't be down. It'll have to wait."

When he came back to the table, Mother smiled. "The circus keeps coming back, you know."

"I know," said Father. "But childhood doesn't."

Across all the years I remembered this and knew from the sudden glow of warmth that no kindness is ever wasted or ever completely lost.

By three o'clock the tide was out and the sound of the waves was only a rhythmic whisper, like a giant breathing. I stayed in my sandy nest, feeling relaxed and content— and a little complacent. The doctor's prescriptions, I thought, were easy to take.

But I was not prepared for the next one. This time the three words were not a gentle suggestion. They sounded more like a command. REEXAMINE YOUR MOTIVES.

My first reaction was purely defensive. "There's nothing wrong with my motives," I said to myself. "I want to be successful—who doesn't? I want to have a certain amount of recognition—but so does everybody. I want more security than I've got—and why not?"

"Maybe," said a small voice somewhere inside my head, "those motives aren't good enough. Maybe that's the reason the wheels have stopped going around."

I picked up a handful of sand and let it stream between my fingers. In the past, whenever my work went well, there had always been something spontaneous about it, something uncontrived, something free. Lately it had been calculated, competent—and dead. Why? Because I had been looking past the job itself to the rewards I hoped it would bring. The work had ceased to be an end in itself, it had been merely a means to make money, pay bills. The sense of giving something, of helping people, of making a contribution, had been lost in a frantic clutch at security.

In a flash of certainty, I saw that if one's motives are wrong, nothing can be right. It makes no difference whether you are a mailman, a hairdresser, an insurance salesman, a housewife—whatever. As long as you feel you are serving others, you do the job well. When you are concerned only with helping yourself, you do it less well. This is a law as inexorable as gravity.

For a long time I sat there. Far out on the bar I heard the murmur of the surf change to a hollow roar as the tide turned. Behind me the spears of light were almost horizontal. My time at the beach had almost run out, and I felt a grudging admiration for the doctor and the "prescriptions" he had so casually and cunningly devised. I saw, now, that in them was a therapeutic progression that might well be of value to anyone facing any difficulty.

LISTEN CAREFULLY: To calm a frantic mind, slow it down, shift the focus from inner problems to outer things.

TRY REACHING BACK: Since the human mind can hold but one idea at a time, you blot out present worry when you touch the happiness of the past.

REEXAMINE YOUR MOTIVES: This was the hard core of the "treatment," this challenge to reappraise, to bring one's motives into alignment with one's capabilities and conscience. But the mind must be clear and receptive to do this—hence the six hours of quiet that went before.

The western sky was a blaze of crimson as I took out the last slip of paper. Six words this time. I walked slowly out on the beach. A few yards below the high water mark I stopped and read the words again: WRITE YOUR TROUBLES ON THE SAND.

I let the paper blow away, reached down and picked up a fragment of shell. Kneeling there under the vault of the sky, I wrote several words on the sand, one above the other. Then I walked away, and I did not look back. I had written my troubles on the sand. And the tide was coming in.

SOURCE: *"The Day at the Beach" Copyright by Arthur Gordon, 1959.*

Discussion Questions

2.1. What is effective about these strategies for coping with stress, and why did they work?

2.2. What troubles, challenges, or stressors do you face right now to which these prescriptions might apply?

2.3. Are these prescriptions effective coping strategies or merely escapes?

2.4. What other prescriptions could the author take besides the four mentioned here? Generate your own list based on your own experiences with stress.

The Case of the Missing Time

At approximately 7:30 A.M. on Tuesday, June 23, 1959, Chet Craig, manager of the Norris Company's Central Plant, swung his car out of the driveway of his suburban home and headed toward the plant located some six miles away, just inside the Midvale city limits. It was a beautiful day. The sun was shining brightly and a cool, fresh breeze was blowing. The trip to the plant took about 20 minutes and sometimes gave Chet an opportunity to think about plant problems without interruption.

The Norris Company owned and operated three printing plants. Norris enjoyed a nationwide commercial business, specializing in quality color work. It was a closely held company with some 350 employees, nearly half of whom were employed at the Central Plant, the largest of the three Norris production operations. The company's main offices were also located in the Central Plant building.

Chet had started with the Norris Company as an expediter in its Eastern Plant, just after he graduated from Ohio State. After three years Chet was promoted to production supervisor, and two years later he was made assistant to the manager of the Eastern Plant. He was transferred to the Central Plant as assistant to the plant manager and one month later was promoted to plant manager when the former manager retired (see Figure 2.8).

Chet was in fine spirits as he relaxed behind the wheel. As his car picked up speed, the hum of the tires on the newly paved highway faded into the background. Various thoughts occurred to him, and he said to himself, "This is going to be the day to really get things done."

He began to run through the day's work, first one project, then another, trying to establish priorities. After a few minutes he decided that the open-end unit scheduling was probably the most important, certainly the most urgent. He frowned for a moment as he recalled that on Friday the vice president and general manager had

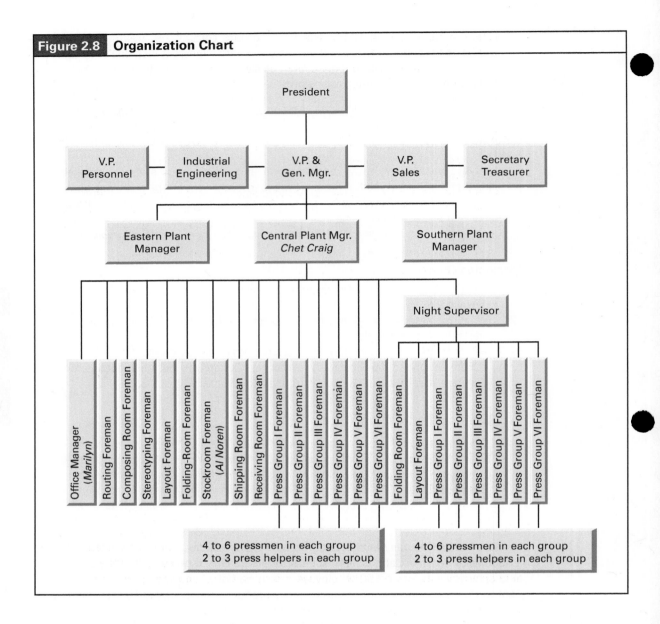

Figure 2.8 Organization Chart

casually asked him if he had given the project any further thought. Chet realized that he had not been giving it much thought lately. He had been meaning to get to work on this idea for over three months, but something else always seemed to crop up. "I haven't had much time to sit down and really work it out," he said to himself. "I'd better get going and hit this one today for sure." With that he began to break down the objectives, procedures, and installation steps of the project. He grinned as he reviewed the principles involved and calculated roughly the anticipated savings. "It's about time," he told himself. "This idea should have been followed up long ago." Chet remembered that he had first conceived of the open-end unit scheduling idea nearly a year and a half ago, just prior to his leaving Norris's Eastern Plant. He had spoken to his boss, Jim Quince, manager of the Eastern Plant, about it then, and both agreed that it was worth looking into. The idea was temporarily shelved when he was transferred to the Central Plant a month later.

A blast from a passing horn startled him, but his thoughts quickly returned to other plant projects he was determined to get underway. He started to think through a procedure for simpler transport of dies to and from the Eastern Plant. Visualizing the notes on his desk, he thought about the inventory analysis he needed to identify and eliminate some of the slow-moving stock items, the packing controls that needed revision, and the need to design a new special-order form. He also decided that this was the day to settle on a job printer to do the simple outside printing of office forms. There were a few other projects he couldn't recall offhand, but he could tend to them after lunch, if not before. "Yes, sir," he said to himself, "this is the day to really get rolling."

Chet's thoughts were interrupted as he pulled into the company parking lot. When he entered the plant Chet knew something was wrong as he met Al Noren, the stockroom foreman, who appeared troubled. "A great morning, Al," Chet greeted him cheerfully.

"Not so good, Chet; my new man isn't in this morning," Noren growled.

"Have you heard from him?" asked Chet.

"No, I haven't," replied Al.

Chet frowned as he commented, "These stock handlers assume you take it for granted that if they're not here, they're not here, and they don't have to call in and verify it. Better ask Human Resources to call him."

Al hesitated for a moment before replying, "Okay, Chet, but can you find me a man? I have two cars to unload today."

As Chet turned to leave he said, "I'll call you in half an hour, Al, and let you know."

Making a mental note of the situation, Chet headed for his office. He greeted the group of workers huddled around Marilyn, the office manager, who was discussing the day's work schedule with them. As the meeting broke up, Marilyn picked up a few samples from the clasper, showed them to Chet, and asked if they should be shipped that way or if it would be necessary to inspect them. Before he could answer, Marilyn went on to ask if he could suggest another clerical operator for the sealing machine to replace the regular operator, who was home ill. She also told him that Gene, the industrial engineer, had called and was waiting to hear from Chet.

After telling Marilyn to go ahead and ship the samples, he made a note of the need for a sealer operator for the office and then called Gene. He agreed to stop by Gene's office before lunch and started on his routine morning tour of the plant. He asked each foreman the types and volumes of orders they were running, the number of people present, how the schedules were coming along, and the orders to be run next; helped the folding-room foreman find temporary storage space for consolidating a carload shipment; discussed quality control with a pressman who had been running poor work; arranged to transfer four people temporarily to different departments, including two for Al in the stockroom; and talked to the shipping foreman about pickups and special orders to be delivered that day. As he continued through the plant, he saw to it that reserve stock was moved out of the forward stock area, talked to another pressman about his requested change of vacation schedule, had a "heart-to-heart" talk with a press helper who seemed to need frequent reassurance, and approved two type and one color-order okays for different pressmen.

Returning to his office, Chet reviewed the production reports on the larger orders against his initial productions and found that the plant was running behind schedule. He called in the folding-room foreman and together they went over the lineup of machines and made several necessary changes.

During this discussion, the composing-room foreman stopped in to cover several type changes, and the routing foreman telephoned for approval of a revised printing schedule. The stockroom foreman called twice, first to inform him that two standard,

ANALYSIS

fast-moving stock items were dangerously low, later to advise him that the paper stock for the urgent Dillion job had finally arrived. Chet made the necessary subsequent calls to inform those concerned.

He then began to put delivery dates on important and difficult inquiries received from customers and salesmen. (The routine inquiries were handled by Marilyn.) While he was doing this he was interrupted twice, once by a sales correspondent calling from the West Coast to ask for a better delivery date than originally scheduled, once by the personnel vice president asking him to set a time when he could hold an initial training and induction interview with a new employee.

After dating the customer and salesmen inquiries, Chet headed for his morning conference in the executive offices. At this meeting he answered the sales vice president's questions in connection with "hot" orders, complaints, and the status of large-volume orders and potential new orders. He then met with the general manager to discuss a few ticklish policy matters and to answer "the old man's" questions on several specific production and personnel problems. Before leaving the executive offices, he stopped at the office of the secretary-treasurer to inquire about delivery of cartons, paper, and boxes and to place a new order for paper.

On the way back to his own office, Chet conferred with Gene about two current engineering projects concerning which he had called earlier. When he reached his desk, he looked at his watch. It was 10 minutes before lunch, just time enough to make a few notes of the details he needed to check in order to answer the knotty questions raised by the sales manager that morning.

After lunch Chet started again. He began by checking the previous day's production reports, did some rescheduling to get out urgent orders, placed appropriate delivery dates on new orders and inquiries received that morning, and consulted with a foreman on a personal problem. He spent some 20 minutes at the TWX going over mutual problems with the Eastern Plant.

By midafternoon Chet had made another tour of the plant, after which he met with the personnel director to review with him a touchy personal problem raised by one of the clerical employees, the vacation schedules submitted by his foremen, and the pending job-evaluation program. Following this conference, Chet hurried back to his office to complete the special statistical report for Universal Waxing Corporation, one of Norris' best customers. As he finished the report, he discovered that it was 10 minutes after six and he was the only one left in the office. Chet was tired. He put on his coat and headed through the plant toward the parking lot; on the way he was stopped by both the night supervisor and night layout foremen for approval of type and layout changes.

With both eyes on the traffic, Chet reviewed the day he had just completed. "Busy?" he asked himself. "Too much so—but did I accomplish anything?" His mind raced over the day's activities. "Yes and no" seemed to be the answer. "There was the usual routine, the same as any other day. The plant kept going and I think it must have been a good production day. Any creative or special-project work done?" Chet grimaced as he reluctantly answered, "No."

With a feeling of guilt, he probed further. "Am I an executive? I'm paid like one, respected like one, and have a responsible assignment with the necessary authority to carry it out. Yet one of the greatest values a company derives from an executive is his creative thinking and accomplishments. What have I done about it? An executive needs some time for thinking. Today was a typical day, just like most other days, and I did little, if any, creative work. The projects that I so enthusiastically planned to work on this morning are exactly as they were yesterday. What's more, I have no guarantee that tomorrow night or the next night will bring me any closer to their completion. This is the real problem and there must be an answer."

Chet continued, "Night work? Yes, occasionally. This is understood. But I've been doing too much of this lately. I owe my wife and family some of my time. When you come down to it, they are the people for whom I'm really working. If I am forced to spend much more time away from them, I'm not meeting my own personal objectives. What about church work? Should I eliminate that? I spend a lot of time on this, but I feel I owe God some time, too. Besides, I believe I'm making a worthwhile contribution in this work. Perhaps I can squeeze a little time from my fraternal activities. But where does recreation fit in?"

Chet groped for the solution. "Maybe I'm just rationalizing because I schedule my own work poorly. But I don't think so. I've studied my work habits carefully and I think I plan intelligently and delegate authority. Do I need an assistant? Possibly, but that's a long-term project and I don't believe I could justify the additional overhead expenditure. Anyway, I doubt whether it would solve the problem."

By this time Chet had turned off the highway onto the side street leading to his home—the problem still uppermost in his mind. "I guess I really don't know the answer," he told himself as he pulled into his driveway. "This morning everything seemed so simple, but now…" His thoughts were interrupted as he saw his son running toward the car calling out, "Mommy, Daddy's home."

SOURCE: *Based on Prod. #: KEL071-PDF-ENG, Kellogg School of Management, 1973.*

Discussion Questions

2.5. What principles of time and stress management are violated in this case?

2.6. What are the organizational problems in the case?

2.7. Which of Chet's personal characteristics inhibit his effective management of time?

2.8. If you were hired as a consultant to Chet, what would you advise him?

SKILL *PRACTICE*

EXERCISES FOR LONG-TERM AND SHORT-RUN STRESS MANAGEMENT AND WELL-BEING

In this section, we provide five exercises to help you practice good stress management. We strongly urge you to complete the exercises with a partner who can give you feedback and who will monitor your progress in improving your skill. Because managing stress is a personal skill, most of your practice will be done in private. But having a partner who is aware of your commitment will help foster substantial improvement. The reciprocity exercise requires that you perform it in a group.

The Small-Wins Strategy

An ancient Chinese proverb states that long journeys are always made up of small steps. In Japan, the feeling of obligation to make small, incremental improvements in one's work is known as kaizen. In this chapter the notion of small wins was explained as a way to break apart large problems and identify small successes in coping with them. Each of these approaches represents the same basic philosophy—to recognize incremental successes—and each helps an individual build up psychological resiliency to stress.

Assignment

Answer the following questions. An example is given to help clarify each question, but your response need not relate to the example.

1. What major stressor do you currently face? What creates anxiety or discomfort for you? (For example, "I have too much to do.")

2. What are the major attributes or components of the situation? Divide the major problem into smaller parts or subproblems. (For example, "I have said 'yes' to too many things. I have deadlines approaching. I don't have all the resources I need to complete all my commitments right now.")

3. What are the subcomponents of each of those subproblems? Divide them into yet smaller parts. (For example, "I have the following deadlines approaching: a report due, a large amount of reading to do, a family obligation, an important presentation, a need to spend some personal time with someone I care about, a committee meeting that requires preparation.")

Attribute 1:

Attribute 2:

Attribute 3:

And so on:

4. What actions can I take that will affect any of these subcomponents? (For example, "I can engage the person I care about in helping me prepare for the presentation.

I can write a shorter report than I originally intended. I can carry the reading material with me wherever I go.")

5. What actions have I taken in the past that have helped me cope successfully with similar stressful circumstances? (For example, "I have found someone else to share some of my tasks. I have gotten some reading done while waiting, riding, and eating. I have prepared only key elements for the committee meeting.")

6. What small thing should I feel good about as I think about how I have coped or will cope with this major stressor? (For example, "I have accomplished a lot when the pressure has been on in the past. I have been able to use what I had time to prepare to its best advantage.")

Repeat this process when you face major stressors. The six specific questions may not be as important to you as (1) breaking the problem down into incremental parts and then breaking those parts down again, and (2) identifying actions that can be done that will be successful in coping with components of the stressor.

Life-Balance Analysis

The prescription to maintain a balanced life seems both intuitive and counterintuitive. On the one hand, it makes sense that life should have variety and that each of us should develop multiple aspects of ourselves. Narrowness and rigidity are not highly valued by anyone. On the other hand, the demands of work, school, or family, for example, can be so overwhelming that we don't have time to do much except respond to those demands. Work could take all of our time. So could school. So could family. The temptation for most of us, then, is to focus on only a few areas of our lives that demand our attention and leave the other areas undeveloped. This exercise helps you discover which areas those might be and which areas need more attention.

Assignment

Use Figure 2.9 below to complete this exercise. In responding to the four items in the exercise, think of the amount of time you spend in each area, the amount of experience and development you have had in the past in each area, and the extent to which development in each area is important to you.

1. In Figure 2.9, shade in the portion of each section that represents the extent to which that aspect of your life has been well developed. In other words, rate how satisfied you are that each aspect is adequately cultivated.

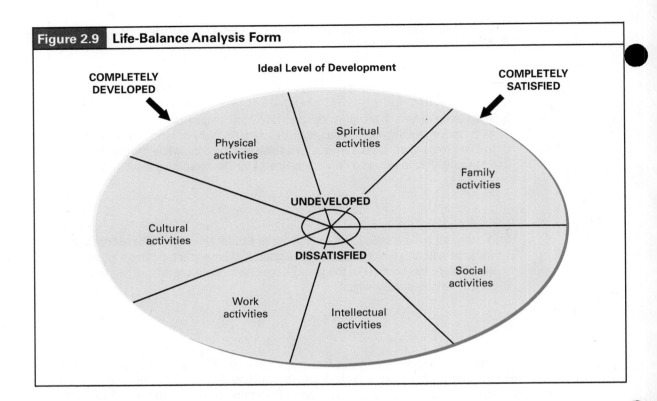

Figure 2.9   Life-Balance Analysis Form

Ideal Level of Development

COMPLETELY
DEVELOPED

COMPLETELY
SATISFIED

Spiritual
activities

Physical
activities

Family
activities

UNDEVELOPED

Cultural
activities

DISSATISFIED

Social
activities

Work
activities

Intellectual
activities

2. Now write down at least one thing you can start doing to improve your development in the areas that need it. For example, you might do more outside reading to develop culturally, invite a foreign visitor to your home to develop socially, engage in regular prayer or meditation to develop spiritually, begin a regular exercise program to develop physically, and so on.

3. Because the intent of this exercise is not to add more pressure and stress to your life but to increase your resiliency through life balance, identify the things you will *stop* doing in various areas that will make it possible to achieve better life balance.

4. To make this a practice exercise and not just a planning exercise, do something today that you have on your list for items 2 and 3 above. Write down specifically what you'll do and when. Don't let the rest of the week go by without implementing something you've written.

Deep Relaxation

To engage in deep relaxation, you need to reserve time that can be spent concentrating on relaxation. Cognitive control and physiological control are involved. By focusing your mind, you can positively affect both your mental and physical states (Davis, Eshelman, & McKay, 1980). This exercise describes one technique that is easily learned and practiced.

The deep-relaxation technique presented below combines key elements of several well-known formulas. It is recommended that this technique be practiced for 20 minutes a day, three times a week. Reserve at least 30 minutes to engage in this exercise for the first time.

Find a quiet spot with a partner. You may want to do this in the classroom itself the first time. Have that person read the instructions below. Do not rush through the instructions. Allow time between each step to complete it unrushed. When you have finished, switch roles. (Since you will be practicing this exercise later in a different setting, you may want to make a tape recording of these instructions. Alternatively, agree to do the exercise regularly with a friend or a spouse.)

Assignment

Step 1: Assume a comfortable position. You may lie down. Loosen any tight clothing. Close your eyes and be quiet. Slow down and let go.

Step 2: Focus on your body and on relaxing specific muscles. Tune out all other thoughts. Assume a passive attitude.

Step 3: Now tense and relax each of your muscle groups for five to ten seconds each. Do it in the following order:

Forehead. Wrinkle your forehead. Try to make your eyebrows touch your hairline for five seconds, then relax.

Eyes and nose. Close your eyes as tightly as you can for five seconds, then relax.

Lips, cheeks, and jaw. Draw the corners of your mouth back and grimace for five seconds, then relax.

Hands. Extend your arms in front of you. Clench your fists tightly for five seconds, then relax.

Forearms. Extend your arms out against an invisible wall and push forward for five seconds, then relax.

Upper arms. Bend your elbows and tense your biceps for five seconds, then relax.

Shoulders. Shrug your shoulders up to your ears for five seconds, then relax.

Back. Arch your back off the floor for five seconds, then relax.

Stomach. Tighten your stomach muscles by lifting your legs off the ground about two inches for five seconds, then relax.

Hips and buttocks. Tighten your hip and buttock muscles for five seconds, then relax.

Thighs. Tighten your thigh muscles by pressing your legs together as tightly as you can for five seconds, then relax.

Feet. Bend your ankles toward your body as far as you can for five seconds, then point your toes for five seconds, then relax.

Toes. Curl your toes as tightly as you can for five seconds, then relax.

Step 4: Focus on any muscles that are still tense. Repeat the exercise for that muscle group three or four times until it relaxes.

Step 5: Now focus on your breathing. Do not alter it artificially, but focus on taking long, slow, deep breaths. Breathe through your nose and exhale through your mouth. Concentrate exclusively on the rhythm of your breathing until you have taken at least 45 breaths.

Step 6: Now focus on the heaviness and warmth of your body. Let all the energy in your body seep away. Let go of your normal tendency to control your body and mobilize it toward activity.

Step 7: With your body completely relaxed, relax your mind. Picture a person for whom you have loving feelings, feelings of gratitude, or feelings of reverence. Concentrate fully on the person and on your feelings for him or her for at least three minutes without letting any other thoughts enter your mind. Begin now.

Step 8: Now open your eyes, slowly get up, and return to your hectic, stressful, anxiety-ridden, Type-A environment better prepared to cope with it effectively.

Monitoring and Managing Time

Time management is the most often identified problem faced by managers and business school students. Most people feel overwhelmed at least part of the time with having too much to accomplish in too little time. It is interesting, however, that even though people may be extremely busy, if they feel that their time is *discretionary*—that is, it can be used in any way that they choose, such as in recreation, playing with friends or family, or by themselves—they feel less stress. Increasing discretionary time, therefore, is a key to effective time management.

This exercise helps you identify and better manage your discretionary time. It takes one full week to complete. It requires that you record how you spend your time for the next seven days. Virtually every executive who is a good time manager has completed this exercise and, in fact, regularly repeats this exercise.

Assignment

Complete the following five steps, then use a partner to get feedback and ideas for improving and refining your plans.

Step 1: Beginning today, keep a time log for one full week. Record how you spend each 30-minute block in the next seven 24-hour periods. Using the following format, record the log in your own notebook, diary, or journal. Simply write down what you did during the 30-minute period. If you did multiple things, record them one above the other.

TIME	ACTIVITY	REQUIRED/ DISCRETIONARY	PRODUCTIVE/ UNPRODUCTIVE
12:00–1:00			
1:00–1:30			
1:30–2:00			
2:00–3:00			
.			
.			
.			
23:00–23:30			
23:30–24:00			

Step 2: Beneath the heading "Required/Discretionary," write whether the time spent in each 30-minute block was required by someone or something else (R) or was discretionary (D). That is, to what extent did you have a choice about whether or not you would engage in this activity? You don't have a choice about a certain amount of sleep, for example, or attending class. But you do have a choice about watching TV or spending time socializing.

Step 3: Beneath the heading "Productive/Unproductive," rate the extent to which each activity was productive. That is, identify the extent to which the activity achieved what it was intended to achieve. To what extent did the activity accomplish your own goals or lead to improvements of some kind? Use the following scale for your rating:

4 Time was used productively

3 Time was used somewhat productively

2 Time was used somewhat unproductively

1 Time was used unproductively

Step 4: Draw up a plan for increasing the amount of discretionary time you have during the week. Refer to the Time Management Survey in the Assessment Section for suggestions. Write down the things you will *stop* doing and *start* doing.

Step 5: Identify ways in which you can use your discretionary time more productively, especially any blocks of time you rated 1 or 2 in step 3. What will you do to make sure the time you control is used for more long-term benefit? What will you stop doing that impedes your effective use of time?

Generalized Reciprocity

Creating a reciprocity network requires that you form a group or that are a member of a participating organization. The network is formed among members of this group. The purpose of the exercise is to enhance relationships, provide a way for you to contribute to one another, and build a network of resources, relationships, and good will (see Baker, 2012).

Reciprocity networks are created among individuals in a group by having members identify needs or requests and then having others in the group respond to those needs or requests with resources or contacts. Building a reciprocity network occurs in four steps:

Step 1: Write down the names of each of the people in the group in a row at the top of a board. This could be done across the top of a white board or on flip chart pages. Post the pages containing the names on a wall.

Step 2: Each individual in the group writes down a specific request, a need, or an issue with which he or she needs help. These issues may be personal or work-related. The requests must have characteristics described as SMART, which are:

S – *Specific*: A resource or resolution to the request must be available.

M – *Meaningful*: It is not trivial or irrelevant but refers to something important.

A – *Action-oriented*: There must be action that can be taken in response to the request.

R – *Real need*: The request must be tied to a genuine need.

T – *Time bound*: A time frame is given for when the request is needed.

Examples of work-related requests might be: "I need to find an expert that can assist me with some Excel spreadsheets;" "I need a new IT software system to streamline our inventory control;" "I need to become more recognized as a potential leader in my organization;" "I need to determine how to downsize my unit by 15 percent."

Examples of personal requests might be: "I need tickets to the game in two weeks;" "I need to get in better physical shape;" "I need to find a great gift for my spouse;" "I need help with my statistics class."

Step 3: The individual stands up and publicly describes the request to his or her colleagues and posts it below his or her name. An easy way to do this is to write the request on a Post-it Note.

Step 4: Colleagues listen to each person's verbalized request. Each colleague writes down a resource, a contact, or some assistance that might address these requests. Again, this can easily be done on a Post-it Note. Be sure that each person writes his or her name on the Post-it Note so that follow-up connections can be reached. Group members will not be able to respond to every request, but the more responses each person can make the better. Two kinds of contributions may be made. One kind of contribution is that you have the resource, such as knowledge, information, expertise, budget, product, emotional support, and so forth. Another kind of contribution is that you have contacts, such as someone you know who has the resource. You can provide a referral so that the requestor can connect to this person.

Step 5: After taking time to write contributions on separate notes, each person takes time to publicly explain his or her contribution to the requests for which he or she can add value. Each response is posted below the note containing the request. Sharing aloud these contributions tends to stimulate the thinking of others who may also realize some additional resource or contribution.

Step 6: After each person has had a chance to explain aloud his or her contributions to the requests with which he or she can help, provide time for each person to connect with each resource provider associated with his or her request. The network is formed when requesters and resource providers connect and exchange valuable information.

An important outcome of this practice is to uncover new ideas and new resources that were previously unknown or unrecognized. Baker (2012) found that individuals who offer the most contributions tend to be rated as more competent leaders, more interpersonally effective, and higher performers in their organizations than others. That is, people who are willing to demonstrate generalized reciprocity—to contribute without expecting a personal benefit in return—are more successful leaders.

SKILL *APPLICATION*

ACTIVITIES FOR MANAGING STRESS

Suggested Assignments

2.9. Do a systematic analysis of the stressors you face in your job, family, school, and social life. List the types of stressors you face, and identify strategies to eliminate or sharply reduce them. Record this analysis in your journal.

2.10. Find someone you know well who is experiencing a great deal of stress. Teach him or her how to manage that stress better by applying the concepts, principles, techniques, and exercises in this chapter. Describe what you taught and record the results in your journal.

2.11. Implement at least three of the time management techniques suggested in the Time Management Survey or elsewhere that you are not currently using but think you might find helpful. In your time log, keep track of the amount of time these techniques save you over a one-month period. Be sure to use that extra time productively.

2.12. With a coworker or colleague, identify ways in which your work at school, job, or home can be redesigned to reduce stress and increase productivity. Use the hints provided in the chapter to guide your redesign.

2.13. Write a personal principles statement. Specify precisely your core principles; those things you consider to be central to your life and your sense of self-worth; and the legacy you want to leave. Identify at least one thing that you want to accomplish in your life that you would like to be known for. Begin working on it today.

2.14. Establish a SMART, short-term goal or plan that you wish to accomplish this year. Make it compatible with the top priorities in your life. Specify the behavioral action steps, the reporting and accounting mechanisms, and the criteria of success and rewards. Share this plan with others you know so that you have an incentive to pursue it even after you finish this class.

2.15. Identify at least one or two contribution goals that are equally important to your achievement goals. Make sure they are meaningful, and use the goal setting framework to actually make progress.

2.16. Pick at least one relaxation technique. Learn it and practice it on a regular basis. Record your progress in your journal.

2.17. Start keeping a gratitude journal.

2.18. Identify the profound purpose or meaningfulness associated with your work or your major activities in life. That is, identify your calling.

Application Plan and Evaluation

The intent of this exercise is to help you apply this cluster of skills in a real-life, out-of-class setting. Now that you have become familiar with the behavioral guidelines that form the basis of effective skill performance, you will improve most by trying out those guidelines in an everyday context. Unlike a classroom activity, in which feedback is immediate and others can assist you with their evaluations, this skill application activity is one you must accomplish and evaluate on your own. There are two parts to this activity: Part 1 helps prepare you to apply the skill, and Part 2 helps you evaluate and improve on your experience. Be sure to write down answers to each item. Don't short-circuit the process by skipping steps.

Part 1: Planning

2.19. Write down the two or three aspects of this skill that are most important to you. These may be areas of weakness, areas you most want to improve, or areas that are most salient to a problem you face right now. Identify the specific aspects of this skill that you want to apply.

2.20. Now identify the setting or the situation in which you will apply this skill. Establish a plan for performance by actually writing down a description of the situation. Who else will be involved? When will you do it? Where will it be done?

Circumstances:
Who else?
When?
Where?

2.21. Identify the specific behaviors in which you will engage to apply this skill. Operationalize your skill performance.

2.22. What are the indicators of successful performance? How will you know you have been effective? What will indicate you have performed competently?

Part 2: Evaluation

2.23. After you have completed your implementation, record the results. What happened? How successful were you? What was the effect on others?

2.24. How can you improve? What modifications can you make next time? What will you do differently in a similar situation in the future?

2.25. Looking back on your whole skill practice and application experience, what have you learned? What has been surprising? In what ways might this experience help you in the long term?

SCORING KEYS AND COMPARISON DATA

✪ Scoring Keys for the following instruments, along with comparison data, are contained in PIA in MyManagementLab.com;

Stress Management, Time Management Assessment.

Social Readjustment Rating Scale

Comparison Data (N = 5,000 students)

TOTAL SCORE	MEAN	BOTTOM QUARTILE	SECOND QUARTILE	THIRD QUARTILE	TOP QUARTILE
	257.76	122 or below	123–221	222–346	347 or above

According to the authors of these instruments, scores of 150 points or below resulted in a probability of less than 37 percent that a serious illness would occur in the next year, but the probability increased to about 50 percent with scores of 150–300. Those who scored over 300 on the SRRS had an 80 percent chance of serious illness. Research results also show an injury rate among athletes five times as great for high scorers on the SRRS as for low scorers.

Sources of Personal Stress

This exercise does not have a solution or scoring data. However, in as much as this instrument was designed to complement SRRS, the explanations of scores for that assessment are relevant.

Flourishing Scale

Comparison Data

The range of scores for this instrument is between 8 and 56. Below are the percentiles associated with each score, as reported by the authors of the instrument.

SCORE	PERCENTILE	SCORE	PERCENTILE
25	1	45	44
29	3	46	53
32	5	47	60
34	7	48	70
36	10	49	77
37	13	50	83
38	15	51	87
39	18	52	90
40	21	53	93
41	24	54	96
42	28	55	90
43	33	56	100
44	39		

SKILL ASSESSMENT

- Problem Solving, Creativity, and Innovation
- How Creative Are You?
- Innovative Attitude Scale
- Creative Style Assessment

SKILL LEARNING

- Problem Solving, Creativity, and Innovation
- Steps in Analytical Problem Solving
- Limitations of the Analytical Problem-Solving Model
- Impediments to Creative Problem Solving
- Multiple Approaches to Creativity
- Conceptual Blocks
- Conceptual Blockbusting
- International Caveats
- Hints for Applying Problem-Solving Techniques
- Fostering Creativity in Others
- Summary
- Behavioral Guidelines

SKILL ANALYSIS

- Coke versus Pepsi
- Creativity at Apple

SKILL PRACTICE

- Individual Assignment—Analytical Problem Solving
- Team Assignment—Creative Problem Solving
- Moving Up in the Rankings
- Keith Dunn and McGuffey's Restaurant
- Creative Problem-Solving Practice

SKILL APPLICATION

- Suggested Assignments
- Application Plan and Evaluation

SCORING KEYS AND COMPARISON DATA

MyManagementLab™

When you see this icon, visit www.mymanagementlab.com for self-assessments, video activities, and more.

3

Solving Problems Analytically and Creatively

LEARNING OBJECTIVES

1. INCREASE PROFICIENCY IN ANALYTICAL PROBLEM SOLVING
2. RECOGNIZE PERSONAL CONCEPTUAL BLOCKS
3. ENHANCE CREATIVITY BY OVERCOMING CONCEPTUAL BLOCKS
4. FOSTER INNOVATION AMONG OTHERS

DIAGNOSTIC SURVEYS FOR CREATIVE PROBLEM SOLVING

PROBLEM SOLVING, CREATIVITY, AND INNOVATION

PERSONAL INVENTORY ASSESSMENT

✪ If your instructor is utilizing **MyManagementLab**, log onto mymanagementlab.com and select the Personal Inventory Assessment (PIA) section and complete the instruments associated with this chapter.

The assessment instruments in this chapter are briefly described below. The assessments appear either in your text or in PIA. The assessments marked with (blue star) are available only in PIA.

All assessments should be completed before reading the chapter material.

After completing the first assessment save your response to your hard drive. When you have finished reading the chapter, re-take the assessment and compare your responses to see what you have learned.

✪ ❏ The *Problem Solving, Creativity, and Innovation Assessment* measures the extent to which you effectively solve analytic problems and creative problems and the degree to which you have developed a competency for creativity and innovation.

❏ The *How Creative Are You? Assessment* evaluates the degree to which you are characterized by the attitudes, values, and motivations associated with creativity.

❏ The *Innovative Attitude Scale* identifies the extent to which you practice innovation in your daily activities.

❏ The *Creative Style Assessment* measures your personal style as it relates to creativity.

SOLVING PROBLEMS ANALYTICALLY AND CREATIVELY

Assessment Section

HOW CREATIVE ARE YOU?©

How creative are you? The following test helps you determine if you have the personality traits, attitudes, values, motivations, and interests that characterize creativity. It is based on several years' study of attributes possessed by men and women in a variety of fields and occupations who think and act creatively.

Be as frank as possible. Try not to second-guess how a creative person might respond. Turn to the end of the chapter to find the answer key and an interpretation of your scores.

Rating Scale

For each statement, write in the appropriate letter:

A Agree
B Undecided or Don't Know
C Disagree

_____ 1. I always work with a great deal of certainty that I am following the correct procedure for solving a particular problem.

_____ 2. It would be a waste of time for me to ask questions if I had no hope of obtaining answers.

_____ 3. I concentrate harder on whatever interests me than do most people.

_____ 4. I feel that a logical step-by-step method is best for solving problems.

_____ 5. In groups, I occasionally voice opinions that seem to turn some people off.

_____ 6. I spend a great deal of time thinking about what others think of me.

_____ 7. It is more important for me to do what I believe to be right than to try to win the approval of others.

_____ 8. People who seem uncertain about things lose my respect.

_____ 9. More than other people, I need to have things interesting and exciting.

_____ 10. I know how to keep my inner impulses in check.

_____ 11. I am able to stick with difficult problems over extended periods of time.

_____ 12. On occasion, I get overly enthusiastic.

_____ 13. I often get my best ideas when doing nothing in particular.

_____ 14. I rely on intuitive hunches and the feeling of "rightness" or "wrongness" when moving toward the solution of a problem.

_____ 15. When problem solving, I work faster when analyzing the problem and slower when synthesizing the information I have gathered.

_____ 16. I sometimes get a kick out of breaking the rules and doing things I am not supposed to do.

_____ 17. I like hobbies that involve collecting things.

_____ 18. Daydreaming has provided the impetus for many of my more important projects.

_____ 19. I like people who are objective and rational.

_____ 20. If I had to choose from two occupations other than the one I now have, I would rather be a physician than an explorer.

_____ 21. I can get along more easily with people if they belong to about the same social and business class as myself.

_____ 22. I have a high degree of aesthetic sensitivity.

_____ 23. I am driven to achieve high status and power in life.

_____ 24. I like people who are sure of their conclusions.

_____ 25. Inspiration has nothing to do with the successful solution of problems.

_____ 26. When I am in an argument, my greatest pleasure would be for the person who disagrees with me to become a friend, even at the price of sacrificing my point of view.

_____ 27. I am much more interested in coming up with new ideas than in trying to sell them to others.

_____ 28. I would enjoy spending an entire day alone, just "chewing the mental cud."

_____ 29. I tend to avoid situations in which I might feel inferior.

_____ 30. In evaluating information, the source is more important to me than the content.

_____ 31. I resent things being uncertain and unpredictable.

_____ 32. I like people who follow the rule "business before pleasure."

_____ 33. Self-respect is much more important than the respect of others.

_____ 34. I feel that people who strive for perfection are unwise.

_____ 35. I prefer to work with others in a team effort rather than solo.

_____ 36. I like work in which I must influence others.

_____ 37. Many problems that I encounter in life cannot be resolved in terms of right or wrong solutions.

_____ 38. It is important for me to have a place for everything and everything in its place.

_____ 39. Writers who use strange and unusual words merely want to show off.

_____ 40. Below is a list of terms that describe people. Choose 10 words that best characterize you.

energetic	persuasive	observant
fashionable	self-confident	persevering
original	cautious	habit-bound
resourceful	egotistical	independent
stern	predictable	formal
informal	dedicated	forward-looking
factual	open-minded	tactful
inhibited	enthusiastic	innovative
poised	acquisitive	practical
alert	curious	organized
unemotional	clear-thinking	understanding
dynamic	self-demanding	polished
courageous	efficient	helpful
perceptive	quick	good-natured
thorough	impulsive	determined
realistic	modest	involved
absent-minded	flexible	sociable
well-liked	restless	retiring

SOURCE: *Excerpted from* How Creative Are You? *By Eugene Raudsepp. Copyright ©1981 by Eugene Raudsepp. Used by permission. Published by Perigee Books/G.P. Putnam's Sons, Inc.*

INNOVATIVE ATTITUDE SCALE

This self-assessment helps you compare yourself with a set of attitudes that have been shown to foster innovation. While there are many factors that influence innovative behavior, relevant attitudes are good predictors. In as much as this is a diagnostic tool, candid, realistic responses are essential.

Indicate the extent to which each of the following statements is true of either your actual behavior or your intentions at work. That is, describe the way you are or the way you intend to be on the job. Use the scale for your responses.

Rating Scale
5 Almost always true
4 Often true
3 Not applicable
2 Seldom true
1 Almost never true

_____ 1. I am always trying to do things in different ways.

_____ 2. I love to dissect problems into pieces in order to see the whole picture.

_____ 3. I have an open-door policy at work; anyone can come talk to me about anything.

_____ 4. I am always the one people turn to for a creative way to look at old problems.

_____ 5. I am more willing to take risks than my coworkers or fellow students.

_____ 6. I provide a unique perspective in group work.

_____ 7. I believe in not judging others' ideas until we have considered multiple alternatives.

_____ 8. I am willing to ask questions to gain as many different perspectives as possible.

_____ 9. I always try to carve out time in my schedule to develop new ideas and work on projects that may only be of interest to me.

_____ 10. I hardly ever make it through a meeting or class without making a comment.

_____ **Total**

SOURCE: _Innovative Attitude Scale,_ John E. Ettlie & Robert D. O'Keefe (1982), _"Innovative Attitudes, Values, and Intentions in Organizations,"_ Journal of Management Studies, _19: 163–182._

CREATIVE STYLE ASSESSMENT

Research has identified four creativity styles. These can be thought of as forms of, or approaches to, creativity. This self-assessment helps you identify your preferred style. In as much as this is a diagnostic tool, candid, realistic responses are essential.

Rating Scale

Four alternatives exist in each of the items below. You should divide 100 points among each of the four alternatives, depending on which alternative is most similar to you. Rate yourself as you are right now, not as you would like to be or as you think you should be. No correct answers exist, so be as accurate as you can. For example, in question 1, if you think alternative "A" is very similar to you, "B" is somewhat similar, and "C" and "D" are hardly similar at all, you might give 50 points to A, 30 points to B, and 10 points each to C and D. Any combination of numbers is acceptable, including 100, 0, 0, 0, or 25, 25, 25, 25. **Just be sure that for each question, the total points add up to 100.**

1. I usually approach difficult problems by:
   _____ a. Brainstorming solutions
   _____ b. Carefully evaluating alternatives
   _____ c. Engaging other people
   _____ d. Responding quickly

   100

2. My friends and colleagues usually think of me as:
   _____ a. Creative
   _____ b. Systematic
   _____ c. Collaborative
   _____ d. Competitive

   100

3. I am good at:
   _____ a. Experimenting
   _____ b. Administering
   _____ c. Empowering people
   _____ d. Meeting challenges

   100

4. When I complete a project or an assignment, I am likely to:
   _____ a. Come up with a new project
   _____ b. Review the results to see how I might be able to improve them
   _____ c. Share what I have learned with others
   _____ d. Determine the grade or the evaluation of the results

   100

5. I would describe myself as:
   _____ a. Flexible
   _____ b. Organized
   _____ c. Supportive
   _____ d. Driven

   100

6. I like to work on projects that:

_____ a. Let me invent something new

_____ b. Create practical improvements

_____ c. Get other people involved

_____ d. Can be completed quickly

100

7. When solving a problem, I:

_____ a. Enjoy exploring a lot of options

_____ b. Collect a lot of data

_____ c. Communicate a lot with others

_____ d. Emphasize getting the job done

100

SOURCE: *Adapted from "Creative Style Assessment," J. DeGraff and K.A. Lawerence, (2002). Creativity at Work. San Francisco: Jossey-Bass, pp. 46–49. © by John Wiley and Sons.*

SKILL *LEARNING*

Problem Solving, Creativity, and Innovation

Problem solving is a skill required of every person in almost every aspect of life. Seldom does an hour go by without the need to solve some kind of problem. The manager's job, in particular, is inherently a problem-solving job. If there were no problems in organizations, there would be no need for managers. Therefore, it is hard to conceive of an incompetent problem solver succeeding as a manager.

In this chapter, we offer specific guidelines and techniques for improving problem-solving skills. Two kinds of problem solving—analytical and creative—are addressed. Effective managers are able to solve problems both analytically and creatively, even though different skills are required for each type of problem.

First, we discuss analytical problem solving—the kind of problem solving managers use many times each day. Then we turn to creative problem solving, a kind of problem solving that occurs less frequently, yet this creative problem-solving ability often separates career successes from career failures, heroes from goats, and achievers from derailed executives. It can also produce a dramatic impact on organizational effectiveness. A great deal of research has highlighted the positive relationship between creative problem solving and successful organizations (Csikszentmihalyi, 2013; Sternberg, 1999). This chapter provides guidelines for how you can become a more effective problem solver, both analytical and creative, and concludes with a brief discussion of how managers can foster creative problem solving and **innovation** among the people with whom they work.

Steps in Analytical Problem Solving

Most people, including managers, don't particularly like problems. Problems are time consuming, they create stress, and they never seem to go away.

Malcolm Gladwell, in his intriguing book, *Blink* (2005), argued that people are able to make decisions and reach conclusions on very little data—thin slices of behavior—because of their intuitive sense. In one or two seconds, people can reach a conclusion as valid as the one made after studying a problem for a long time. First impressions count, he argued, and are valid a lot of the time. These first impressions and instantaneous judgments are valid, however, mainly when problems are not complex, when people have experience with the issue they are judging, and when they have developed an attunement to their own internal cues (that is, they have developed adequate self-awareness and emotional intelligence) (Gigerenzer & Gaissmaier, 2011).

Most of the time, the problems we face are complicated, multifaceted, and ambiguous. In such instances, effective problem-solving techniques are required, and they rely on a systematic and logical approach. This approach involves at least four steps.

DEFINING THE PROBLEM

The most widely accepted model of analytical problem solving is summarized in Table 3.1. This method is well known and widely utilized in almost all firms.

Many large organizations (e.g., Ford Motor Company, General Electric, Hewlett-Packard, Microsoft, and Apple) spend millions of dollars to teach their managers this type of problem solving as part of their productivity and improvement process. Variations on this four-step approach have been implemented in various firms (e.g., Ford uses an eight-step approach), but all the steps are merely derivations of the standard model we discuss here.

The first step is to *define* a problem. This involves diagnosing a situation so that the focus is on the real problem, not just its symptoms. For example, suppose you must deal with an employee who consistently fails to get work done on time. Slow work might be the problem, or it might be only a symptom of another underlying problem such as bad health, low morale,

Table 3.1	A Model of Problem Solving
STEP	**CHARACTERISTICS**
1. Define the problem.	• Differentiate fact from opinion. • Specify underlying causes. • Tap everyone involved for information. • State the problem explicitly. • Identify what standard is violated. • Determine whose problem it is. • Avoid stating the problem as a disguised solution.
2. Generate alternative solutions.	• Postpone evaluating alternatives. • Be sure all involved individuals generate alternatives. • Specify alternatives that are consistent with goals. • Specify both short-term and long-term alternatives. • Build on others' ideas. • Specify alternatives that solve the problem.
3. Evaluate and select an alternative.	• Evaluate relative to an optimal standard. • Evaluate systematically. • Evaluate relative to goals. • Evaluate main effects and side effects. • State the selected alternative explicitly.
4. Implement and follow up on the solution.	• Implement at the proper time and in the right sequence. • Provide opportunities for feedback. • Engender acceptance of those who are affected. • Establish an ongoing monitoring system. • Evaluate based on problem solution.

lack of training, or inadequate rewards. Defining the problem, therefore, requires a wide search for information. The more relevant information that is acquired, the more likely it is that the problem will be defined accurately. As Charles Kettering put it, "It ain't the things you don't know that'll get you in trouble, but the things you know for sure that ain't so."

Following are some attributes of good problem definition:

1. Factual information is differentiated from opinion or speculation. Objective data are separated from perceptions and suppositions.
2. All individuals involved are tapped as information sources. Broad participation is encouraged in order to capture as much information as possible.
3. The problem is stated explicitly. This often helps point out ambiguities in the definition.
4. The problem definition clearly identifies what standard or expectation has been violated. Problems, by their very nature, involve the violation of some standard or expectation.
5. The problem definition must address the question "Whose problem is this?" No problems are completely independent of people. Identify for whom this is a problem.
6. The definition is not simply a disguised solution. Saying "The problem is that we need to motivate slow employees" is inappropriate because the problem is stated as a solution. The problem should be described, not resolved.

Managers often propose a solution before an adequate definition of a problem has been given. This may lead to solving the wrong problem or to reaching conclusions that are misleading or inadequate. Effectively identifying the problem is usually the single most important step in problem solving.

GENERATING ALTERNATIVES

The second step is to generate alternative solutions. This requires postponing the selection of any one solution until several alternatives have been proposed. Much research on problem solving (e.g., March, 1999, 2006) supports the prescription that the quality of solutions can be significantly enhanced by considering multiple alternatives.

The problem with evaluating and selecting an alternative too early is that we may rule out some good ideas by just not getting around to thinking about them. We hit on an idea that sounds good and we go with it, thereby never even thinking of alternatives that may be better in the long run.

Some rules of thumb for good alternative generation are:

1. The evaluation of each proposed alternative is postponed. As many relevant alternatives as possible should be proposed before evaluation is allowed.
2. Alternatives are proposed by all individuals involved in the problem. Broad participation in proposing alternatives improves solution quality and group acceptance.
3. The alternative solutions being proposed are consistent with the organization's or the group's goals or desired outcomes.
4. Alternatives take into consideration both short- and long-term consequences.
5. Alternatives build on one another. Bad ideas may become good ones if they are combined with or modified by other ideas.
6. Alternatives solve the problem that has been defined. Another problem may also be important, but it should be ignored if it does not directly affect the problem being considered.

EVALUATING ALTERNATIVES

The third problem-solving step is to evaluate and select an alternative. This step involves carefully weighing the advantages and disadvantages of the proposed alternatives before making a final selection. In selecting the best alternative, skilled problem solvers make sure that alternatives are judged in terms of the extent to which they will solve the problem without causing other unanticipated problems; the extent to which all individuals involved will accept the alternative; the extent to which implementation of the alternative is likely; and the extent to which the alternative fits within organizational constraints (e.g., is consistent with policies, norms, and budget limitations).

The classic description of the difficulty with problem solving—made almost 50 years ago—still remains as a core principle in problem solving (March & Simon, 1958):

Most human decision making, whether individual or organizational, is concerned with the discovery and selection of satisfactory alternatives; only in exceptional cases is it concerned with the discovery and selection of optimal alternatives. To optimize requires processes several orders of magnitude more complex than those required to satisfy. An example is the difference between searching a haystack to find the sharpest needle in it and searching the haystack to find a needle sharp enough to sew with.

Some attributes of good evaluation are:

1. Alternatives are evaluated relative to an optimal, rather than a satisfactory, standard. Determine what is best rather than just what will work.
2. Adequate time for evaluation and consideration is allowed so that each alternative is given due consideration.
3. Alternatives are evaluated in terms of the goals of the organization and the needs and expectations of the individuals involved. Organizational goals should be met, but individual preferences should also be considered.
4. Alternatives are evaluated in terms of their probable effects. Both side-effects and direct-effects on the problem are considered as well as long- and short-term effects.
5. The selected alternative is stated explicitly. This ensures that everyone involved understands and agrees with the same solution and avoids disagreements later.

IMPLEMENTING THE SOLUTION

The final step is to implement and follow up on the solution. A surprising amount of the time, people faced with a problem will try to jump to step 4 before having gone through steps 1 through 3. That is, they react to a problem by trying to implement a solution before they have defined it, analyzed it, or evaluated alternative solutions. It is important to remember, therefore, that "getting rid of the problem" by solving it will not occur successfully without the first three steps in the process.

Chapter 10 in this book discusses rules of thumb for successfully implementing solutions including overcoming resistance, generating commitment from others, and ensuring that the solution is sustainable.

An important reminder is exemplified by Calvin Coolidge's well-known quotation:

Nothing in the world can take the place of perseverance. Talent will not; nothing is more common than unsuccessful people with talent. Genius will not; unrewarded genius is almost a proverb. Education will not; the world is full of educated derelicts. Persistence and determination alone are omnipotent.

Of course, any implementation requires follow-up to prevent negative side effects and ensure solution of the problem. Follow-up not only helps ensure effective implementation, but it also serves a feedback function by providing information that can be used to improve future problem solving.

Some attributes of effective implementation and follow-up are:

1. Implementation occurs at the right time and in the proper sequence. It does not ignore constraining factors, and it does not come before steps 1, 2, and 3 in the problem-solving process.
2. Implementation occurs using a "small-wins" strategy—one small action at a time—in order to discourage resistance and engender support.
3. The implementation process includes opportunities for feedback. How well the solution works is communicated, and recurring information exchange occurs.
4. Participation by individuals affected by the problem solution is fostered in order to create support and commitment.
5. An ongoing measurement and monitoring system is set up, long-term as well as short-term effects are assessed.
6. Evaluation of success is based on problem solution, not on side benefits. Although the solution may provide some positive outcomes, it is unsuccessful unless it solves the problem being considered.

Limitations of the Analytical Problem-Solving Model

Most experienced problem solvers are familiar with the preceding steps in analytical problem solving, which are based on empirical research results and sound rationale (March, 1994; Miller, Hickson, & Wilson, 1996; Mitroff, 1998; Williams, 2001; Zeitz, 1999). Unfortunately, most of us do not always practice these steps. The demands of our lives often pressure us into circumventing some steps, and problem solving suffers as a result. When these four steps are followed, however, effective problem solving is markedly enhanced.

On the other hand, simply learning about and practicing these four steps does not guarantee that an individual will effectively solve all types of problems. These problem-solving steps are most effective mainly when the problems faced are straightforward, when alternatives are readily definable, when relevant information is available, and when a clear standard exists against which to judge the correctness of a solution.

The main tasks are to agree upon a single definition, gather the accessible information, generate alternatives, and make an informed choice. But many managerial problems are not of this type. Definitions, information, alternatives, and standards are often ambiguous or not readily available. In a complex, fast-paced, digital world, these conditions appear less and less frequently. Hence, knowing the steps in problem solving and being able to implement them are not necessarily the same thing.

It may not be clear how much information is needed, what the complete set of alternatives is, or how one knows if the information being obtained is accurate. Analytical problem solving may help, but something more is needed to address these problems successfully. Tom Peters said, in characterizing the modern world faced by managers: "If you're not confused, you're not paying attention."

Table 3.2 summarizes some reasons why analytical problem solving is not always effective in day-to-day managerial situations. Some problems are simply not amenable to systematic or rational analysis. Sufficient and accurate information is not always available. Outcomes may not be predictable. Means-ends connections may not be evident. In order to solve such problems, a new way of thinking may be required, and we refer to this as creative problem solving.

Impediments to Creative Problem Solving

As mentioned in the beginning of the chapter, analytical problem solving is focused on getting rid of problems. Creative problem solving is focused on generating something new (DeGraff & Lawrence, 2002). The trouble is, most people have trouble solving problems creatively. There are two reasons why.

First, most of us misinterpret creativity as being one-dimensional—that is, creativity is limited to generating new ideas. We are often not aware of the multiple strategies available for being creative, so our repertoire is restricted. Second, all of us have developed certain conceptual blocks in our problem-solving activities, of which we are mostly not aware. These blocks inhibit us from solving certain problems effectively. These blocks are largely personal, as opposed to interpersonal or organizational, so skill development is required to overcome them.

In this chapter, we focus primarily on the skills involved in helping you become a better creative problem solver. A large literature exists on how managers and leaders can foster creativity in organizations, but this is not our focus (Mumford, 2011; Zhou & Shalley, 2008). Rather, we are interested in helping you strengthen and develop your personal skills and expand your repertoire of creative problem-solving alternatives.

Multiple Approaches to Creativity

One of the most sophisticated approaches to creativity identifies four distinct methods for achieving it. This approach is based on the Competing Values Framework (Cameron, Quinn, DeGraff, & Thakor, 2014), which identifies competing or conflicting dimensions that describe people's attitudes, values, and behaviors. Figure 3.1 describes the four different types of creativity and their relationships. These four types have been developed by our colleague Jeff DeGraff (DeGraff & Lawrence, 2002).

For example, achieving creativity through **imagination** refers to the *creation* of new ideas, breakthroughs, and radical approaches to problem solving. People who pursue creativity in this way tend to be experimenters, speculators, and entrepreneurs, and they define creativity as exploration, new product innovation, or developing unique possibilities. When facing difficult problems in need of problem solving, their approach is focused on coming up with untested possibilities and unique solutions.

Well-known examples include Steve Jobs at Apple, the developer of the iPhone and the Macintosh computer, and Walt Disney, the creator of animated movies and theme parks. Both of these people approached problem solving by generating radically new ideas and products that created entirely new industries.

Table 3.2	Some Constraints on the Analytical Problem-Solving Model
STEP	**CONSTRAINTS**
1. Define the problem.	• There is seldom consensus as to the definition of the problem. • There is often uncertainty as to whose definition will be accepted. • Problems are usually defined in terms of the solutions already possessed. • Symptoms get confused with the real problem. • Confusing information inhibits problem identification.
2. Generate alternative solutions.	• Solution alternatives are usually evaluated one at a time as they are proposed. • Few of the possible alternatives are usually known. • The first acceptable solution is usually accepted. • Alternatives are based on what was successful in the past.
3. Evaluate and select an alternative.	• Limited information about each alternative is usually available. • Search for information occurs close to home—in easily accessible places. • The type of information available is constrained by factors such as primacy versus recency, extremity versus centrality, expected versus surprising, and correlation versus causation. • Gathering information on each alternative is costly. • Preferences of which is the best alternative are not always known. • Satisfactory solutions, not optimal ones, are usually accepted. • Solutions are often selected by oversight or default. • Solutions often are implemented before the problem is defined.
4. Implement and follow up on the solution.	• Acceptance by others of the solution is not always forthcoming. • Resistance to change is a universal phenomenon. • It is not always clear what part of the solution should be monitored or measured in follow-up. • Political and organizational processes must be managed in any implementation effort. • It may take a long time to implement a solution.

People may also achieve creativity, however, through opposite means—that is, by developing incrementally better alternatives, *improving* on what already exists, or clarifying the ambiguity that is associated with the problem. Rather than being revolutionaries and risk takers, they are systematic, careful, and thorough. Creativity comes by finding ways to improve processes or functions.

An example is Ray Kroc, the magician behind McDonald's remarkable success. As a salesman in the 1950s, Kroc bought out a restaurant in San Bernardino,

California, from the McDonald brothers and, by creatively changing the way hamburgers were made and served, he created the largest food service company in the world. He didn't invent fast food—White Castle and Dairy Queen had long been established—but he changed the processes. Creating a limited, standardized menu, uniform cooking procedures, consistent service quality, cleanliness of facilities, and inexpensive food—no matter where in the world you eat—demonstrated a very different approach to creativity. Instead of breakthrough ideas, Kroc's secret was incremental

Figure 3.1   Four Types of Creativity

Flexibility

Incubation
Be sustainable

capitalize on teamwork,
involvement,
coordination and
cohesion, empowering
people, building trust

Imagination
Be new

experimentation,
exploration, risk taking,
transformational ideas,
revolutionary thinking,
unique visions

Internal ──────────────────────── **External**

Improvement
Be better

incremental
improvements, process
control, systematic
approaches, careful
methods, clarifying
problems

Investment
Be first

rapid goal achievement,
faster responses than
others, competitive
approaches, attack
problems directly

Control

LEARNING

SOURCE: *Adapted from DeGraff & Lawrence, 2002.*

improvements on existing ideas. This type of creativity is referred to as **improvement**.

A third type of creativity is called **investment**, or the pursuit of rapid goal achievement and *competitiveness*. People who approach creativity in this way meet challenges head on, adopt a competitive posture, and focus on achieving results faster than others. People achieve creativity by working harder than the competition, exploiting others' weaknesses, and being first to offer a product, service, or idea, even if it not their own. The advantages of being a "first mover" company are well-known.

This kind of creativity can be illustrated by Honda President Kawashima in the "Honda-Yamaha Motorcycle War." Honda became the industry leader in motorcycles in Japan in the 1960s but decided to enter the automobile market in the 1970s. Yamaha saw this as an opportunity to overtake Honda in motorcycle market share in Japan. In public speeches at the beginning of the 1980s, Yamaha's President Koike promised that

Yamaha would soon overtake Honda in motorcycle production because of Honda's new focus on automobiles. At the beginning of the year, Honda's president replied: "As long as I am president of this company, we will surrender our number one spot to no one... *Yamaha wo tubusu*!"—meaning, we will smash, break, annihilate, destroy Yamaha. In the next year, Honda introduced 81 new models of motorcycles and discontinued 32 models for a total of 113 changes to its product line. In the following year, Honda introduced 39 additional models and added 18 changes to the 50cc line. Yamaha's sales plummeted 50 percent and the firm endured a loss of 24 billion yen for the year. Yamaha's president conceded: "I would like to end the Honda-Yamaha war... From now on we will move cautiously and ensure Yamaha's relative position as second to Honda." Approaching creativity through investment—rapid response, competitive maneuvering, and being the first mover—characterized Honda president Kawashima's approach to creativity.

The fourth type of creativity is **incubation**. This refers to an approach to creative activity through teamwork, involvement, and coordination among individuals. Creativity occurs by unlocking the potential that exists in interactions among networks of people. Individuals who approach creativity through incubation encourage people to work together, foster trust and cohesion, and empower others. Creativity arises from a collective mindset and sharing ideas.

For example, Mahatma Gandhi was probably the only person in modern history who has single-handedly stopped a war. Lone individuals have started wars, but Gandhi was creative enough to stop one. He did so by mobilizing networks of people to pursue a clear vision and set of values. Gandhi would probably have been completely noncreative and ineffective had he not been adept at capitalizing on incubation dynamics. By mobilizing people to march to the sea to make salt, or to burn passes that demarcated ethnic group status, Gandhi was able to engender creative outcomes that had not been considered possible. He was a master at incubation by connecting, involving, and coordinating people.

The same could be said for Bill Wilson, the founder of Alcoholics Anonymous, whose 12-step program is the foundation for almost all addiction treatment organizations around the world—gambling addiction, drug addiction, eating disorders, and so on. To cure his own alcoholism, Wilson began meeting with others with the same problem and, over time, developed a very creative way to help himself as well as other people overcome their dependencies. The genius behind Alcoholics Anonymous is the creativity that emerges when human interactions are facilitated and encouraged.

Figure 3.2 helps place these four types of creativity into perspective. You will note that imagination

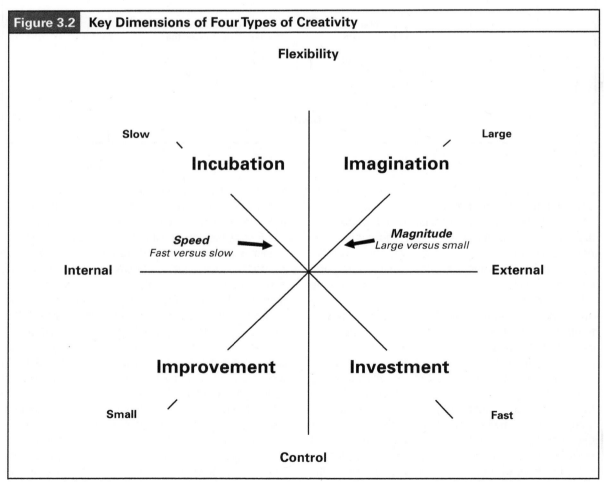

Figure 3.2 **Key Dimensions of Four Types of Creativity**

SOURCE: *Adapted from DeGraff & Lawrence, 2002.*

and improvement emphasize opposite approaches to creativity. They differ in the *magnitude* of the creative ideas being pursued. Imagination focuses on new, revolutionary solutions to problems. Improvement focuses on small, incremental solutions. Investment and incubation are also contradictory and opposing in their approach to creativity. They differ in *speed* of response. Investment focuses on fast, competitive responses to problems, whereas incubation emphasizes more developmental and deliberate responses.

It is important to point out that no one approach to creativity is best. Different circumstances call for different approaches. For example, Ray Kroc and McDonald's would not have been successful with an imagination strategy (revolutionary change), and Walt Disney would not have been effective with an incubation strategy (group consensus). Kawashima at Honda could not afford to wait for an incubation strategy (slow, developmental change), whereas it would have made no sense for Gandhi to approach creativity using investment (a competitive approach). Circumstances in which each of these

four approaches to creativity is most effective are listed in Figure 3.3.

This figure shows that imagination is the most appropriate approach to creativity when breakthroughs are needed and when original ideas are necessary—*being new*. The improvement approach is most appropriate when incremental changes or tightening up processes are necessary—*being better*. The investment approach is most appropriate when quick responses and goal achievement takes priority—*being first*. And, the incubation approach is most appropriate when collective effort and involvement of others is important—*being sustainable*.

The Creativity Assessment survey that you completed in the Assessment section helps identify your own preferences regarding these different approaches to creativity. You were able to create a profile showing the extent to which you are inclined toward imagination, improvement, investment, or incubation as you approach problems calling for creativity. Your profile will help you determine which kinds of problems you are inclined to solve when creativity is required. Of course, having a preference is not the same as having

---

Figure 3.3 | **Examples of Situations in Which Each Approach Is Effective**

Incubation *Be sustainable*	**Imagination** *Be new*
Existence of a diverse community with strong values; need for collective effort and consensus; empowered workforce	Need for brand-new, breakthrough products or services; emerging markets; resources needed for experimentation
Internal	**External**
Improvement *Be better*	**Investment** *Be first*
Requirement for quality, safety, and reliability; high technical specialization; effective standardized processes	Fast results are a necessity; highly competitive environments; emphasis on bottom-line outcomes

SOURCE: *Adapted from DeGraff & Lawrence, 2002.*

ability or possessing competence in a certain approach, so the remainder of this chapter will help with your creative competence development.

Conceptual Blocks

The trouble is, each of these different approaches to creativity can be inhibited. That is, in addition to being unaware of the multiple ways in which we can be creative, most of us have difficulty in solving problems creatively because of the presence of **conceptual blocks**. Conceptual blocks are mental obstacles that constrain the way problems are defined, and they can inhibit us from being effective in any of the four types of creativity. Conceptual blocks limit the number of alternative solutions that people think about (Adams, 2001; Tan & Parnell, 2013). Every individual has conceptual blocks, but some people have more numerous and more intense ones than others. These blocks are largely unrecognized or unconscious, so the only way individuals can be made aware of them is to be confronted with problems that are unsolvable because of them. Conceptual blocks result largely from the thinking processes that problem solvers use when facing problems. Everyone develops some conceptual blocks over time. In fact, we need some of them to cope with everyday life. Here's why.

At every moment, each of us is bombarded with far more information than we can possibly absorb. For example, you are probably not conscious right now of the temperature of the room, the color of your skin, the level of illumination overhead, or how your toes feel in your shoes. All of this information is available to you and is being processed by your brain, but you have tuned out some things and focused on others. Over time, you must develop the habit of mentally filtering out some of the information to which you are exposed; otherwise, information overload would drive you crazy. These filtering habits eventually become conceptual habits or blocks. Though you are

not conscious of them, they inhibit you from registering some kinds of information and, therefore, from solving certain kinds of problems.

In this section, we focus on problems that require creative rather than analytical solutions. We introduce some tools and techniques that help overcome conceptual blocks and unlock problem-solving creativity. First consider these two examples that illustrate creative problem solving and breaking through conceptual blocks.

PERCY SPENCER'S MAGNETRON

During World War II, the British developed one of the best-kept military secrets of the war, a special radar detector based on a device called the magnetron. This radar was credited with turning the tide of battle in the war between Britain and Germany and helping the British withstand Hitler's Blitzkrieg. In 1940, Raytheon was one of several U.S. firms invited to produce magnetrons for the war effort.

The workings of magnetrons were not well understood, even by sophisticated physicists. Even among the firms that made magnetrons, few understood what made them work. A magnetron was tested, in those early days, by holding a neon tube next to it. If the neon tube got bright enough, the magnetron tube passed the test. In the process of conducting the test, the hands of the scientist holding the neon tube got warm. It was this phenomenon that led to a major creative breakthrough that eventually transformed lifestyles throughout the world.

At the end of the war, the market for radar essentially dried up, and most firms stopped producing magnetrons. At Raytheon, however, a scientist named Percy Spencer had been fooling around with magnetrons, trying to think of alternative uses for the devices. He was convinced that magnetrons could be used to cook food by using the heat produced in the neon tube. But Raytheon was in the defense business. Next to its two prize products—the Hawk and Sparrow missiles—cooking devices seemed odd and out of place. Percy Spencer was convinced that Raytheon should continue to produce magnetrons, even though production costs were prohibitively high. But Raytheon had lost money on the devices, and now there was no available market for magnetrons. The consumer product Spencer had in mind did not fit within the bounds of Raytheon's business.

As it turned out, Percy Spencer's solution to Raytheon's problem produced the microwave oven and a revolution in cooking methods throughout the world. Later, we will analyze several problem-solving techniques illustrated by Spencer's creative triumph.

SPENCE SILVER'S GLUE

A second example of creative problem solving began with Spence Silver's assignment to work on a temporary project team within the 3M company. The team was searching for new adhesives, so Silver obtained some material from AMD, Inc., which had potential for a new polymer-based adhesive. He described one of his experiments in this way: "In the course of this exploration, I tried an experiment with one of the monomers in which I wanted to see what would happen if I put a lot of it into the reaction mixture. Before, we had used amounts that would correspond to conventional wisdom" (Nayak & Ketteringham, 1986).

The result was a substance that failed all the conventional 3M tests for adhesives. It didn't stick. It preferred its own molecules to the molecules of any other substance. It was more cohesive than adhesive. It sort of "hung around without making a commitment." It was a "now-it-works, now-it-doesn't" kind of glue.

For five years, Silver went from department to department within the company trying to find someone interested in using his newly found substance in a product. Silver had found a solution; he just couldn't find a problem to solve with it. Predictably, 3M showed little interest. The company's mission was to make adhesives that adhered ever more tightly. The ultimate adhesive was one that formed an unbreakable bond, not one that formed a temporary bond.

After four years the task force was disbanded, and team members were assigned to other projects. But Silver was still convinced that his substance was good for something. He just didn't know what. As it turned out, Silver's solution spawned a multibillion-dollar business for 3M—in a unique product called Post-it Notes.

These two examples are positive illustrations of how solving a problem in a unique way can lead to phenomenal business success. To understand how to solve problems creatively, however, we must first consider the blocks that inhibit creativity.

THE FOUR TYPES OF CONCEPTUAL BLOCKS

Table 3.3 summarizes four types of conceptual blocks that inhibit creative problem solving. Each is discussed and illustrated with problems or exercises. We encourage you to complete the exercises and solve the problems as you read the chapter, because doing so

Table 3.3	Conceptual Blocks That Inhibit Creative Problem Solving
1. *Constancy*	
• Vertical thinking	Defining a problem in only one way without considering alternative views
• One thinking language	Not using more than one language to define and assess the problem
2. *Commitment*	
• Stereotyping based on past experience	Present problems are seen only as the variations of past problems
• Ignoring commonalities	Failing to perceive commonalities among elements that initially appear to be different
3. *Compression*	
• Distinguishing figure from ground	Not filtering out irrelevant information or finding needed information
• Artificial constraints	Defining the boundaries of a problem too narrowly
4. *Complacency*	
• Noninquisitiveness	Not asking questions
• Nonthinking	A bias toward activity in place of mental work

will help you become aware of your own conceptual blocks. Later, we shall discuss in more detail how you can overcome those blocks.

Constancy

One type of conceptual block occurs because individuals become wedded to one way of looking at a problem or using one approach to define, describe, or solve it. It is easy to see why **constancy** is common in problem solving. Being constant, or consistent, is a highly valued attribute for most of us. We like to appear at least moderately consistent in our approach to life, and constancy is often associated with maturity, honesty, and even intelligence. We judge lack of constancy as untrustworthy, peculiar, or airheaded.

Some prominent psychologists theorize, in fact, that a need for constancy is the primary motivator of human behavior (Festinger, 1957; Heider, 1946; Newcomb, 1954). Many psychological studies have shown that once individuals take a stand or employ a particular approach to a problem, they are highly likely to pursue that same course without deviation in the future (see Cialdini, 2001, for multiple examples).

On the other hand, constancy can inhibit the solution of some kinds of problems. Consistency sometimes drives out creativity. Two illustrations of the constancy block are vertical thinking and using only one thinking language.

Vertical Thinking The term **vertical thinking** was coined by Edward de Bono (1968, 2000). It refers to defining a problem in a single way and then pursuing that definition without deviation until a solution is reached. No alternative definitions are considered. All information gathered and all alternatives generated are consistent with the original definition. De Bono contrasted lateral thinking (de Bono, 2013) to vertical thinking in the following ways: vertical thinking focuses on continuity, lateral thinking focuses on discontinuity; vertical thinking chooses, lateral thinking changes; vertical thinking is concerned with stability, lateral thinking is concerned with instability; vertical thinking searches for what is right, lateral thinking searches for what is different; vertical thinking is analytical, lateral thinking is provocative; vertical thinking is concerned with where an idea came from, lateral thinking is concerned with where the idea is going; vertical thinking moves in the most likely directions, lateral thinking moves in the least likely directions; vertical thinking develops an idea, lateral thinking discovers the idea.

Plenty of examples exist of creative solutions that occurred because an individual refused to get stuck with a single problem definition. Alexander Graham Bell was trying to devise a hearing aid when he shifted definitions and invented the telephone. Harland Sanders was trying to sell his recipe to restaurants when he shifted definitions and developed his Kentucky Fried Chicken business. Karl Jansky was studying telephone static when he shifted definitions, discovered radio waves from the Milky Way galaxy, and developed the science of radio astronomy.

In developing the microwave industry, Percy Spencer shifted the definition of the problem from "How can we save our military radar business at the end of the war?" to "What other applications can be made for the magnetron?" Other problem definitions followed, such as: "How can we make magnetrons cheaper?" "How can we mass-produce magnetrons?" "How can we convince someone besides the military to buy magnetrons?" "How can we enter a consumer products market?" "How can we make microwave ovens practical and safe?" And so on. Each new problem definition led to new ways of thinking about the problem, new alternative approaches, and, eventually, to a new microwave oven industry.

Spence Silver at 3M began with "How can I get an adhesive that has a stronger bond?" but switched to "How can I find an application for an adhesive that doesn't stick firmly?" Eventually, other problem definitions followed: "How can we get this new glue to stick to one surface but not another (e.g., to notepaper but not normal paper)?" "How can we replace staples, thumbtacks, and paper clips in the workplace?" "How can we manufacture and package a product that uses nonadhesive glue?" "How can we get anyone to pay $1.00 a pad for scratch paper?" And so on.

Shifting definitions is not easy, of course, because it is not natural. It requires you to deflect your tendency toward constancy. Later, we will discuss some hints and tools that can help you overcome the constancy block while avoiding the negative consequences of inconsistency.

A Single Thinking Language A second manifestation of the constancy block is the use of only one **thinking language**. Most people think in words—that is, they think about a problem and its solution in terms of verbal language. **Analytical problem solving** reinforces this approach. Some writers, in fact, have argued that thinking cannot even occur without words (Feldman, 1999; Vygotsky, Hanfmann, & Vakar, 1962). Other thought languages are available, however, such as nonverbal or symbolic languages (e.g., mathematics), sensory imagery (e.g., smelling or tactile sensation), feelings and emotions (e.g., happiness, fear, or anger), and visual imagery (e.g., mental pictures). The more languages available to problem solvers, the better and more creative will be their solutions.

Percy Spencer at Raytheon is a prime example of a visual thinker:

> *One day, while Spencer was lunching with Dr. Ivan Getting and several other Raytheon scientists, a mathematical question arose. Several men, in a familiar reflex, pulled out their slide rules, but before any could complete the equation, Spencer gave the answer. Dr. Getting was astonished. "How did you do that?" he asked. "The root," said Spencer shortly. "I learned cube roots and squares by using blocks as a boy. Since then, all I have to do is visualize them placed together." (Scott, 1974, p. 287)*

The microwave oven depended on Spencer's command of multiple thinking languages. Furthermore, the new oven would never have gotten off the ground without a critical incident that illustrates the power of visual thinking.

By 1965, Raytheon was just about to give up on any consumer application of the magnetron when a meeting was held with George Foerstner, president of the recently acquired Amana Refrigeration Company. In the meeting, costs, applications, manufacturing obstacles, and production issues were discussed. Foerstner galvanized the entire microwave oven effort with the following statement, as reported by a Raytheon vice president.

> *George says, "It's no problem. It's about the same size as an air conditioner. It weighs about the same. It should sell for the same. So we'll price it at $499." Now you think that's silly, but you stop and think about it. Here's a man who really didn't understand the technologies. But there is about the same amount of copper involved, the same amount of steel as an air conditioner. And these are basic raw materials. It didn't make a lot of difference how you fit them together to make them work. They're both boxes; they're both made out of sheet metal; and they both require some sort of trim. (Nayak & Ketteringham, 1986, p. 181)*

In several short sentences, Foerstner had taken one of the most complicated military secrets of World War II and translated it into something no more complex than a room air conditioner. He had painted a picture of an application that no one else had been able to capture by describing a magnetron visually, as a familiar object, not as a set of calculations, formulas, or blueprints.

A similar occurrence in the Post-it Note chronology also led to a breakthrough. Spence Silver had been trying for years to get someone in 3M to adopt his unsticky glue. Art Fry, another scientist with 3M, had heard Silver's presentations before. One day while singing in North Presbyterian Church in St. Paul, Minnesota, Fry was fumbling around with the slips of paper that marked the various hymns in his book. Suddenly, a visual image popped into his mind.

> *I thought, "Gee, if I had a little adhesive on these bookmarks, that would be just the ticket." So I decided to check into that idea the next week at work. What I had in mind was Silver's adhesive.... I knew I had a much bigger discovery than that. I also now realized that the primary application for Silver's adhesive was not to put it on a fixed surface like bulletin boards. That was a secondary application. The primary application concerned paper to paper. I realized that immediately." (Nayak & Ketteringham, 1986, pp. 63–64)*

Years of verbal descriptions had not led to any applications for Silver's glue. Tactile thinking (handling the glue) also had not produced many ideas. However, thinking about the product in visual terms, as applied to what Fry initially called "a better bookmark," led to the breakthrough that was needed.

To illustrate the differences among thinking languages, consider the following simple problem:

> *Figure 3.4 shows seven matchsticks. By moving only one matchstick, make the figure into a true equality (i.e., the value on one side equals the value on the other side). Before looking up the answers in www.mymanagementlab.com, try defining the problem by using different thinking languages. What thinking language is most effective?*

Figure 3.4 The Matchstick Configuration

Commitment

Commitment can also serve as a conceptual block to creative problem solving. Once individuals become committed to a particular point of view, definition, or solution, it is likely that they will follow through on that commitment. Cialdini (2001) reported a study, for example, in which investigators asked Californians to put a large, poorly lettered sign on their front lawns saying DRIVE CAREFULLY. Only 17 percent agreed to do so. However, after signing a petition favoring "keep California beautiful," the people were again asked to put the DRIVE CAREFULLY sign on their lawns, and 76 percent agreed to do so. Once they had committed to being active and involved citizens (i.e., to keeping California beautiful), it was consistent for these people to agree to the large unsightly sign as visible evidence of their commitment. Most people have the same inclination toward being consistent and maintaining commitments.

Two forms of commitment that produce conceptual blocks are stereotyping based on past experiences and **ignoring commonalities**.

Stereotyping Based on Past Experiences

March (1999) pointed out that a major obstacle to innovative problem solving is that individuals tend to define present problems in terms of problems they have faced in the past. Current problems are usually seen as variations on some past situation, so the alternatives proposed to solve the current problem are ones that have proven successful in the past. Both problem definitions and proposed solutions are therefore restricted by past experience. This restriction is referred to as **perceptual stereotyping** (Adams, 2001).

When individuals receive an initial cue regarding the definition of a problem, all subsequent problems are frequently framed in terms of the initial cue. Of course, this is not all bad, because perceptual stereotyping helps organize problems on the basis of a limited amount of data, and the need to consciously analyze every problem encountered is eliminated. On the other hand, perceptual stereotyping prevents individuals from viewing a problem in novel ways.

The creation of Post-it Notes provides an example of overcoming stereotyping based on past experiences. Spence Silver at 3M described his invention in terms of breaking stereotypes based on past experience.

> *The key to the Post-It adhesive was doing the experiment. If I had sat down and factored it out beforehand, and thought about it, I wouldn't have done the experiment. If I had really seriously cracked the books and gone through the literature, I would have stopped. The literature was full of examples that said you can't do this. (Nayak & Ketteringham, 1986, p. 57)*

This is not to say that one should avoid learning from past experience or that failing to learn the mistakes of history does not doom us to repeat them. Rather, it is to say that commitment to a course of action based on past experience can sometimes inhibit viewing problems in new ways, and can even prevent us from solving some problems at all. Consider the following problem as an example.

Assume there are four volumes of Shakespeare on the shelf (see Figure 3.5), and the pages of each volume are exactly two inches thick and the covers of each volume are each one-sixth of an inch thick. Assume that a bookworm began eating at page 1 of Volume 1, and it ate straight through to the last page of Volume IV. What distance did the worm cover? Solving this problem is relatively simple, but it requires that you overcome a stereotyping block to get the correct answer. (Why is 5 inches the correct answer?)

Ignoring Commonalities
A second manifestation of the commitment block is failure to identify similarities

Figure 3.5 Shakespeare Riddle

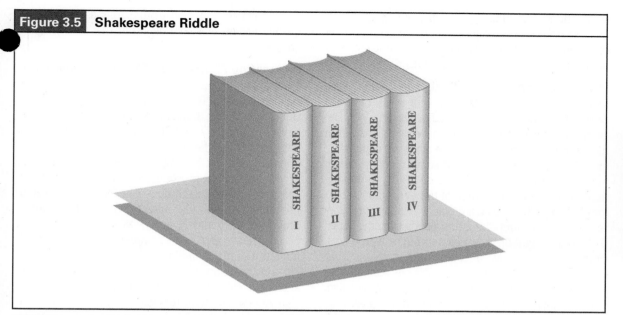

SOURCE: *"Shakespeare Riddle" from* Creative Growth Games *by Eugene Raudsepp and George P. Haugh, Copyright ©1977 by Eugene Raudsepp & George P. Haugh, Jr. Used with permission of Berkley Publishing Group, a division of Penguin Group (USA) Inc.*

among seemingly disparate pieces of data. This is among the most commonly identified blocks to creativity. It means that a person becomes committed to a particular point of view, to the fact that elements are different, and, consequently, becomes unable to make connections, identify themes, or perceive commonalities.

The ability to find one definition or solution for two seemingly dissimilar problems is a characteristic of creative individuals (see Sternberg, 1999). The inability to do this can overload a problem solver by requiring that every problem encountered be solved individually.

The discovery of penicillin by Sir Alexander Fleming resulted from his seeing a common theme among seemingly unrelated events. Fleming was working with some cultures of staphylococci that had accidentally become contaminated. The contamination, a growth of fungi, and isolated clusters of dead staphylococci led Fleming to see a relationship no one else had ever seen previously and thus to discover a wonder drug.

The famous chemist Friedrich Kekule saw a relationship between his dream of a snake swallowing its own tail and the chemical structure of organic compounds. This creative insight led him to the discovery that organic compounds such as benzene have closed rings rather than open structures (Koestler, 1964).

For Percy Spencer at Raytheon, seeing a connection between the heat of a neon tube and the heat required to cook food was the creative connection that led to his breakthrough in the microwave industry. One of Spencer's colleagues recalled: "In the process of testing a bulb [with a magnetron], your hands got hot. I don't know when Percy really came up with the thought of microwave ovens, but he knew at that time—and that was 1942. He [remarked] frequently that this would be a good device for cooking food." Another colleague described Spencer this way: "The way Percy Spencer's mind worked is an interesting thing. He had a mind that allowed him to hold an extraordinary array of associations on phenomena and relate them to one another" (Nayak & Ketteringham, 1986, pp. 184, 205). Similarly, the connection Art Fry made between a glue that wouldn't stick tightly and marking hymns in a choir book was the final breakthrough that led to the development of the revolutionary Post-it Note business.

To test your own ability to see commonalities, try the following activity: What are some common terms that apply to both the substance water and the field of finance? (For example, "financial float.") (Some of the answers are in www.mymanagementlab.com.)

Compression

Conceptual blocks also occur as a result of **compression** of ideas. Looking too narrowly at a problem, screening out too much relevant data, and making assumptions that inhibit problem solution are common examples. Two especially cogent examples of compression are artificially constraining problems and not distinguishing figure from ground.

Artificial Constraints Sometimes people place boundaries around problems, or constrain their approach to them, in such a way that the problems become impossible to solve. Such constraints arise from hidden assumptions people make about problems they encounter. People assume that some problem definitions or alternative solutions are off limits, so they ignore them. For an illustration of this conceptual block, look at Figure 3.6. This is a problem you have probably seen before. Without lifting your pencil from the paper, draw four straight lines that pass through all nine dots. Complete the task before reading further.

By thinking of the figure as more constrained than it actually is, the problem becomes impossible to solve. It is easy if you break out of your own limiting assumptions on the problem. Now that you have been cued, can you do the same task with only three lines? What limiting constraints are you placing on yourself?

If you are successful, now try to do the task with only one line. Can you determine how to put a single straight line through all nine dots without lifting your pencil from the paper? Both the three-line solution and some one-line solutions are provided in www.mymanagementlab.com.

Artificially constraining problems means that the problem definition and the possible alternatives are limited more than the problem requires. Creative problem solving requires that individuals become adept at

recognizing their hidden assumptions and expanding the alternatives they consider—whether they imagine, improve, invest, or incubate.

Separating Figure from Ground Another illustration of the compression block is the reverse of artificial constraints. It is the inability to constrain problems sufficiently so that they can be solved. Problems almost never come clearly specified, so problem solvers must determine what the real problem is. They must filter out inaccurate, misleading, or irrelevant information in order to define the problem correctly and generate appropriate alternative solutions. The inability to separate the important from the unimportant, and to compress problems appropriately, serves as a conceptual block because it exaggerates the complexity of a problem and inhibits a simple definition.

How well do you filter out irrelevant information and focus on the truly important part of a problem? Can you ask questions that get to the heart of the matter? Consider Figure 3.7. For each pair, find the pattern on the left that is embedded in the more complex

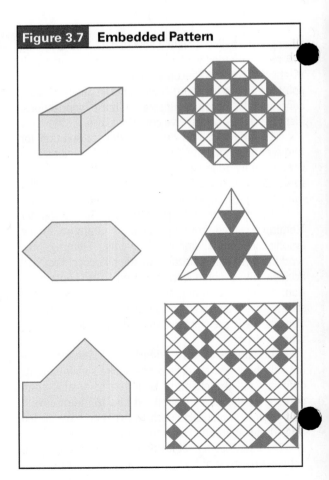

Figure 3.7 Embedded Pattern

Figure 3.6 The Nine-Dot Problem

pattern on the right. On the complex pattern, outline the embedded pattern. Now try to find at least two figures in each pattern. (See www.mymanagementlab.com for some solutions.)

Overcoming this compression block—separating figure from ground and artificially constraining problems—was an important explanation for the microwave oven and Post-it Note breakthroughs. George Foerstner's contribution to the development and manufacture of the microwave oven was to compress the problem, that is, to separate out all the irrelevant complexity that constrained others. Whereas the magnetron was a device so complicated that few people understood it, Foerstner focused on its basic raw materials, its size, and its functionality. By comparing it to an air conditioner, he eliminated much of the complexity and mystery, and, as described by two analysts, "He had seen what all the researchers had failed to see, and they knew he was right" (Nayak & Ketteringham, 1986, p. 181).

On the other hand, Spence Silver had to add complexity, to overcome compression, in order to find an application for his product. Because the glue had failed every traditional 3M test for adhesives, it was categorized as a useless configuration of chemicals. The potential for the product was artificially constrained by traditional assumptions about adhesives—more stickiness, stronger bonding is best—until Art Fry visualized some unconventional applications—a better bookmark, a bulletin board, scratch paper, and, paradoxically, a replacement for 3M's main product, tape.

Complacency

Some conceptual blocks occur not because of poor thinking habits or inappropriate assumptions but because of fear, ignorance, insecurity, or just plain mental laziness. Two especially prevalent examples of the **complacency** block are a lack of questioning and a bias against thinking.

Noninquisitiveness Sometimes the inability to solve problems results from an unwillingness to ask questions, obtain information, or search for data. Individuals may think they will appear naive or ignorant if they question something or attempt to redefine a problem. Asking questions puts them at risk of exposing their ignorance. It also may be threatening to others because it implies that what they accept may not be correct. This may create resistance, conflict, or even ridicule by others.

Creative problem solving is inherently risky because it potentially involves interpersonal conflict. It is risky also because it is fraught with mistakes. As Linus Pauling, the Nobel laureate, said, "If you want to have a good idea, have a lot of them, because most of them will be bad ones." Years of nonsupportive socialization, however, block the adventuresome and inquisitive stance in most people. Most of us are not rewarded for bad ideas. To illustrate, answer the following questions for yourself:

1. When would it be easier to learn a new language, when you were five years old or now? Why?
2. How many times in the last month have you tried something for which the probability of success was less than 50 percent?
3. When was the last time you asked three "why" questions in a row?

To illustrate the extent of our lack of inquisitiveness, how many of the following commonly experienced questions can you answer?

❑ Why are people immune to their own body odor?

❑ What happens to the tread that wears off tires?

❑ Why doesn't sugar spoil or get moldy?

❑ Why doesn't a two-by-four measure two inches by four inches?

❑ Why is a telephone keypad arranged differently from that of a calculator?

❑ Why do hot dogs come 10 in a package while buns come 8 in a package?

❑ How do military cadets find their caps after throwing them in the air at football games and graduation?

❑ Why is Jack the nickname for John?

Most of us adopt a habit of being a bit complacent in asking such questions, let alone finding out the answers. We often stop being inquisitive as we get older because we learn that it is good to be intelligent, and being intelligent is interpreted as already knowing the answers, instead of asking good questions. Consequently, we learn less well at 25 than at 5, take fewer risks, avoid asking why, and function in the world without really trying to understand it. Creative problem solvers, on the other hand, are frequently engaged in inquisitive and experimental behavior.

Spence Silver at 3M described his attitude about the complacency block this way:

> People like myself get excited about looking for new properties in materials. I find that very satisfying, to perturb the structure slightly and just see what happens. I have a hard time talking people into doing that—people who are more highly trained. It's been my experience that people are reluctant just to try, to experiment—just to see what will happen. (Nayak & Ketteringham, 1986, p. 58)

Bias Against Thinking A second manifestation of the complacency block is in an inclination to avoid doing mental work. This block, like most of the others, is partly a cultural bias as well as a personal one. For example, assume that you passed by your roommate's or colleague's office one day and noticed him leaning back in his chair, staring out the window. A half-hour later, as you passed by again, he had his feet up on the desk, still staring out the window. And 20 minutes later, you noticed that his demeanor hadn't changed much. What would be your conclusion? Most of us would assume that the fellow was not doing any work. We would assume that unless we saw action, he wasn't being productive.

When was the last time you heard someone say, "I'm sorry. I can't go to the ball game (or concert, dance, party, or movie) because I have to think?" Or, "I'll do the dishes tonight. I know you need to catch up on your thinking"? That these statements sound silly illustrates the bias most people develop toward action rather than thought, or against putting their feet up, rocking back in their chair, looking off into space, and engaging in solitary cognitive activity. This does not mean daydreaming or fantasizing, just thinking.

A particular conceptual block exists in Western cultures against the kind of thinking that uses the right hemisphere of the brain. **Left-hemisphere thinking**, for most people, is concerned with logical, analytical, linear, or sequential tasks. Thinking using the left hemisphere is apt to be organized, planned, and precise. Language and mathematics are left-hemisphere activities. **Right-hemisphere thinking**, on the other hand, is concerned with intuition, synthesis, playfulness, and qualitative judgment. It tends to be more spontaneous, imaginative, and emotional than left-hemisphere thinking. The emphasis in most formal education is toward left-hemisphere thought development even more in Eastern cultures than in Western cultures. Problem solving on the basis of reason, logic, and utility is generally rewarded, while problem solving based on sentiment, intuition, or pleasure is frequently considered tenuous and inferior.

A number of researchers have found that the most creative problem solvers are **ambidextrous** in their thinking. That is, they use both left- and right-hemisphere thinking and easily switch from one to the other (Hermann, 1981; Hudspith, 1985; Martindale, 1999). Creative ideas arise most frequently in the right hemisphere but must be processed and interpreted by the left, so creative problem solvers use both hemispheres equally well.

Try the exercise in Table 3.4. It illustrates this ambidextrous principle. There are two lists of words. Take about two minutes to memorize the first list. Then, on a piece of paper, write down as many words as you can remember. Now take about two minutes and memorize the words in the second list. Repeat the process of writing down as many words as you can remember.

Most people remember more words from the first list than from the second. This is because the first list contains words that relate to visual perceptions. They connect with right-brain activity as well as left-brain activity. People can draw mental pictures or fantasize about them. The same is true for creative ideas. The more both sides of the brain are used, the more creative the ideas.

Table 3.4	Exercise to Test Ambidextrous Thinking	
List 1	**List 2**
sunset	decline
perfume	very
brick	ambiguous
monkey	resources
castle	term
guitar	conceptual
pencil	about
computer	appendix
umbrella	determine
radar	forget
blister	quantity
chessboard	survey

Review of Conceptual Blocks

So far, we have suggested that certain conceptual blocks prevent individuals from solving problems creatively and from engaging in the four different types of creativity. These blocks narrow the scope of problem definition, limit the consideration of alternative solutions, and constrain the selection of an optimal solution. Unfortunately, many of these conceptual blocks are unconscious, and it is only by being confronted with problems that are unsolvable because of conceptual blocks that individuals become aware that they exist.

We have attempted to make you aware of your own conceptual blocks by asking you to solve some simple problems that require you to overcome these mental barriers. These conceptual blocks are not all bad, of course; not all problems should be addressed by creative problem solving. But research has shown that individuals who have developed creative problem-solving skills are far more effective with complex problems that require a search for alternative solutions than others who are conceptually blocked (Basadur, 1979; Collins & Amabile, 1999; Sternberg, 1999; Williams & Yang, 1999).

In the next section, we provide some techniques and tools that help overcome these blocks and improve creative problem-solving skills.

Conceptual Blockbusting

Conceptual blocks cannot be overcome all at once because most blocks are a product of years of habit-forming thought processes. Overcoming them requires practice in thinking in different ways over a long period of time. You will not become a skilled creative problem solver just by reading this chapter. On the other hand, by becoming aware of your conceptual blocks and practicing the following techniques, research has demonstrated that you can enhance your **creative problem solving** skills.

STAGES IN CREATIVE THOUGHT

A first step in overcoming conceptual blocks is recognizing that creative problem solving is a skill that can be developed. Being a creative problem solver is not an inherent ability that some people naturally have and others do not have. Jacob Rainbow, an employee of the U.S. Patent Office who has more than 200 patents by himself, described the creative process as follows:

> *So you need three things to be an original thinker. First, you have to have a tremendous amount of information—a big data base if you like to be fancy. Then you have to be willing to pull the ideas, because you're interested. Now, some people could do it, but they don't bother. They're interested in doing something else. It's fun to come up with an idea, and if nobody wants it, I don't give a damn. It's just fun to come up with something strange and different. And then you must have the ability to get rid of the trash which you think of. You cannot only think of good ideas. And by the way, if you're not well-trained, but you've got good ideas, and you don't know if they're good or bad, then you send them to the Bureau of Standards, National Institute of Standards, where I work, and we evaluate them. And we throw them out. (Csikszentmihalyi, 1996, p. 48)*

In other words, gather a lot of information, use it to generate a lot of ideas, and sift through your ideas and get rid of the bad ones. Researchers generally agree that creative problem solving involves four stages: *preparation, incubation, illumination*, and *verification* (see Albert & Runco, 1999; Nickerson, 1999; Poincare, 1921; Ribot, 1906; Wallas, 1926).

The **preparation stage** includes gathering data, defining the problem, generating alternatives, and consciously examining all available information. The primary difference between skillful creative problem solving and analytical problem solving is in how this first step is approached. Creative problem solvers are more flexible and fluent in data gathering, problem definition, alternative generation, and examination of options. In fact, it is in this stage that training in creative problem solving can significantly improve effectiveness because the other three steps are not amenable to conscious mental work (Adams, 2001; Ward, Smith, & Finke, 1999). The following discussion, therefore, is limited primarily to improving functioning in this first stage.

The **incubation stage** involves mostly unconscious mental activity in which the mind combines unrelated thoughts in pursuit of a solution. Conscious effort is not involved. **Illumination**, the third stage, occurs when an insight is recognized and a creative solution is articulated. **Verification** is the final stage, which involves evaluating the creative solution relative to some standard of acceptability.

In the preparation stage, two types of techniques are available for improving creative problem-solving abilities. One technique helps individuals think about and *define problems more creatively*; the other helps individuals gather information and *generate more alternative solutions* to problems.

One major difference between creative problem solvers and other people is that creative problem solvers are less constrained. They allow themselves to be more flexible in the definitions they impose on problems and the number of solutions they identify. They develop a large repertoire of approaches to problem solving. In short, they engage in what Csikszentmihalyi (1996) described as "playfulness and childishness." They try more things and worry less about their false starts or failures. As Interaction Associates (1971, p. 15) explained:

> *Flexibility in thinking is critical to good problem solving. A problem solver should be able to conceptually dance around the problem like a good boxer, jabbing and poking, without getting caught in one place or "fixated." At any given moment, a good problem solver should be able to apply a large number of strategies [for generating alternative definitions and solutions]. Moreover, a good problem solver is a person who has developed, through his understanding of strategies and experiences in problem solving, a sense of appropriateness of what is likely to be the most useful strategy at any particular time.*

We now present a few tools and hints that we have found to be especially effective and relatively simple to help unfreeze you from your normal skeptical, analytical approach to problems and increase your playfulness. They relate to (1) defining problems and (2) generating alternative solutions.

METHODS FOR IMPROVING PROBLEM DEFINITION

Problem definition is probably the most critical step in creative problem solving. Once a problem is defined, solving it is often relatively simple. However, as explained in Table 3.2, individuals tend to define problems in terms with which they are familiar. Even well-trained scientists suffer from this problem: "Good scientists study the most important problems

they think they can solve" (Medawar, 1967). When a problem is faced that is new or complex or does not appear to have an easily identified solution, the problem either remains undefined or is redefined in terms of something familiar.

Unfortunately, new problems may not be the same as old problems, so relying on past definitions may impede the process of solving current problems, or lead to solving the wrong problem. Applying techniques for creative problem definition can help individuals see problems in alternative ways so their definitions are less narrowly constrained. Three such techniques for improving and expanding the definition process are discussed below.

Make the Strange Familiar and the Familiar Strange

One well-known, well-tested technique for improving creative problem solving is called **synectics** (Gordon, 1961; Roukes, 1988). The goal of synectics is to help you put something you don't know in terms of something you do know, then reverse the process back again. The point is, by analyzing what you know and applying it to what you don't know, you can develop new insights and perspectives. The process of synectics relies on the use of analogies and metaphors, and it works this way.

First, you form a definition of a problem (make the strange familiar). Then you try to transform that definition so it is made similar to something completely different that you know more about (make the familiar strange). That is, you use analogies and metaphors (synectics) to create this distortion. Postpone the original definition of the problem while you examine the analogy or the metaphor. Then impose this same analysis on the original problem to see what new insights you can uncover.

For example, suppose you have defined a problem as low morale among members of your team. You may form an analogy or metaphor by answering questions such as the following about the problem:

- ❏ What does this remind me of?
- ❏ What does this make me feel like?
- ❏ What is this similar to?
- ❏ What is this opposite of?

Your answers, for example, might be: This problem reminds me of trying to get warm on a cold day (I need more activity). It makes me feel like I do when visiting a hospital ward (I need to smile and go out of my way to empathize with people). It is similar to the loser's locker room after an athletic contest (I need to find an alternative purpose or goal). This isn't like a well-tuned automobile (I need to do a careful diagnosis). And so on. Metaphors and analogies should connect what you are less sure about (the original problem) to what you are more sure about (the metaphor). By analyzing the metaphor or analogy, you may identify attributes of the problem that were not evident before. New insights can occur and new ideas can come to mind.

Many creative solutions have been generated by such a technique. For example, William Harvey was the first to apply the "pump" analogy to the heart, which led to the discovery of the body's circulatory system. Niels Bohr compared the atom to the solar system and supplanted Rutherford's prevailing "raisin pudding" model of matter's building blocks. Consultant Roger von Oech (1986) helped turn around a struggling computer company by applying a restaurant analogy to the company's operations. The real problems emerged when the restaurant, rather than the company, was analyzed.

Major contributions in the field of organizational behavior have occurred by applying analogies to other types of organization, such as machines, cybernetic or open systems, force fields, clans, and so on. Probably the most effective analogies (called parables) were used by Jesus to teach principles that otherwise were difficult for individuals to grasp (for example, the prodigal son, the good Samaritan, a shepherd and his flock).

Some hints to keep in mind when constructing analogies include:

- ❏ Include action or motion in the analogy (e.g., driving a car, cooking a meal, attending a funeral).
- ❏ Include things that can be visualized or pictured in the analogy (e.g., circuses, football games, crowded shopping malls).

- ❏ Pick familiar events or situations (e.g., families, kissing, bedtime).
- ❏ Try to relate things that are not obviously similar (e.g., saying an organization is like a big group is not nearly as rich a simile as saying that an organization is like, say, a psychic prison or a poker game).

Four types of analogies are recommended as part of synectics: **personal analogies**, in which individuals try to identify themselves as the problem ("If I were the problem, how would I feel, what would I like, what could satisfy me?"); **direct analogies**, in which individuals apply facts, technology, and common experience to the problem (e.g., Brunel solved the problem of underwater construction by watching a shipworm tunneling into a tube); **symbolic analogies**, in which symbols or images are imposed on the problem (e.g., modeling the problem mathematically or diagramming the process flow); and **fantasy analogies**, in which individuals ask the question "In my wildest dreams, how would I wish the problem to be resolved?" (e.g., "I wish all employees would work with no supervision.").

Elaborate on the Definition

There are a variety of ways to enlarge, alter, or replace a problem definition once it has been specified. One way is to force yourself to generate at least two alternative hypotheses for every problem definition. That is, specify at least two plausible definitions of the problem in addition to the one originally accepted. Think in plural rather than singular terms. Instead of asking, "What is the problem?" "What is the meaning of this?" "What will be the result?" ask instead questions such as: "What are the problems?" "What are the meanings of this?" "What will be the results?"

As an example, look at Figure 3.8. Select the figure that is different from all the others.

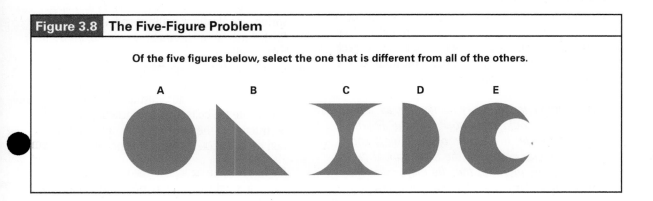

| Figure 3.8 | The Five-Figure Problem |

Of the five figures below, select the one that is different from all of the others.

A   B   C   D   E

A majority of people select B first. If you did, you're right. It is the only figure that has all straight lines. On the other hand, quite a few people pick A. If you are one of them, you're also right. It is the only figure with a continuous line and no points of discontinuity. Alternatively, C can also be right, with the rationale that it is the only figure with two straight and two curved lines. Similarly, D is the only one with one curved and one straight line, and E is the only figure that is nonsymmetrical or partial. The point is, there can often be more than one problem definition, more than one right answer, and more than one perspective from which to view a problem.

Another way to elaborate definitions is to use a question checklist. This is a series of questions designed to help you think of alternatives to your accepted definitions. Several creative managers have shared with us some of their most fruitful questions, such as:

❏ Is there anything else?
❏ Is the reverse true?
❏ Is this a symptom of a more general problem?
❏ Who sees it differently?

Nickerson (1999) reported an oft-used acronym—SCAMPER—designed to bring to mind questions having to do with **S**ubstitution, **C**ombination, **A**daptation, **M**odification (Magnification–Minimization), **P**utting to other uses, **E**limination, and **R**earrangement.

As an exercise, take a minute now to think of a problem you are currently experiencing. Write it down so it is formally defined. Now manipulate that definition by answering the four questions in the checklist. If you can't think of a problem, try the exercise with this one. "I am not as attractive/intelligent/creative as I would like to be." How would you answer the four questions?

Reverse the Definition

A third tool for improving and expanding problem definition is to reverse the definition of the problem. That is, turn the problem upside down, inside out, or back to front. Reverse the way in which you think of the problem. For example, consider the following problem:

A tradition in Sandusky, Ohio, for as long as anyone could remember was the Fourth of July parade. It was one of the largest and most popular events on the city's annual calendar. Now, in 1988, the city mayor was hit with some startling and potentially disastrous news. The state of Ohio was mandating that liability insurance be carried on every attraction—floats, bands, majorettes—that participated in the parade. To protect against the possibility of injury or accident of any parade participant, each had to be covered by liability insurance.

The trouble, of course, was that taking out a liability insurance policy for all parade participants would require far more expense than the city could afford. The amount of insurance required for that large a number of participants and equipment made it impossible for the city to carry the cost. On the one hand, the mayor hated to cancel an important tradition that everyone in town looked forward to. On the other hand, to hold the event would break the city budget. If you were a consultant to the mayor, what would you suggest?

Commonly suggested alternatives in this problem include the following:

1. Try to negotiate with an insurance company for a lower rate. (However, the risk is merely being transferred to the insurance company.)
2. Hold fund-raising events to generate enough money to purchase the insurance policy, or find a wealthy donor to sponsor the parade. (However, this may deflect potential donations away from, or may compete with, other community service agencies such as United Way, Red Cross, or local churches that also sponsor fund-raisers and require donations.)
3. Charge a "participation fee" to parade participants to cover the insurance expense. (However, this would likely eliminate most high school, middle school, and elementary school bands and floats. It would also reduce the amount of money float builders and sponsoring organizations could spend on the actual float. Such a requirement would likely be a parade killer.)
4. Charge a fee to spectators of the parade. (However, this would require restricted access to the parade, an administrative structure to coordinate fee collection and ticketing, and the destruction of the sense of community participation that characterized this traditional event.)

Each of these suggestions is good, but each maintains a single definition of the problem. Each assumes that the solution to the problem is associated with solving the financial problem associated with the liability insurance requirement. Each suggestion, therefore, brings with it some danger of damaging the traditional nature of the parade or eliminating it altogether. If the problem is reversed, other answers normally not considered become evident. That is, the need for liability insurance at all could be addressed.

Here is an excerpt from a newspaper report of how the problem was addressed:

Sandusky, Ohio (AP) The Fourth of July parade here wasn't canceled, but it was immobilized by liability insurance worries. The band marched in place to the beat of a drum, and a country fair queen waved to her subjects from a float moored to the curb.

The Reverse Community parade began at 10:00 A.M. Friday along Washington Row at the north end of the city and stayed there until dusk. "Very honestly, it was the issue of liability," said Gene Kleindienst, superintendent of city schools and one of the celebration's organizers. "By not having a mobile parade, we significantly reduced the issue of liability," he said.

The immobile parade included about 20 floats and displays made by community groups. Games, displays, and food booths were in an adjacent park. Parade chairman Judee Hill said some folks didn't understand, however. "Someone asked me if she was too late for the parade, and she had a hard time understanding the parade is here all day," she said.

Those who weren't puzzled seemed to appreciate the parade for its stationary qualities. "I like this. I can see more," said 67-year-old William A. Sibley. "I'm 80 percent blind. Now I know there's something there," he said pointing to a float.

Spectator Emmy Platte preferred the immobile parade because it didn't go on for "what seemed like miles," exhausting participants. "You don't have those little drum majorettes passing out on the street," she commented.

Baton twirler Tammy Ross said her performance was better standing still. "You can throw better. You don't have to worry about dropping it as much," she explained.

Mr. Kleindienst said community responses were favorable. "I think we've started a new tradition," he said.

By reversing the definition, Sandusky not only eliminated the problem without damaging the tradition and without shifting the risk to insurance companies or other community groups, it added a new dimension that allowed at least some people to enjoy the event more than ever.

This reversal is similar to what Rothenberg (1979, 1991) referred to as **Janusian thinking**. Janus was the Roman god with two faces that looked in opposite directions. Janusian thinking means thinking contradictory thoughts at the same time: that is, conceiving two opposing ideas to be true concurrently. Rothenberg claimed, after studying 54 highly creative artists and scientists (e.g., Nobel Prize winners), that most major scientific breakthroughs and artistic masterpieces are products of Janusian thinking. Creative people who actively formulate antithetical ideas and then resolve them produce the most valuable contributions to the scientific and artistic worlds. Quantum leaps in knowledge often occur.

An example is Einstein's account (1919, p. 1) of having "the happiest thought of my life." He developed the concept that, "for an observer in free fall from the roof of a house, there exists, during his fall, no gravitational field... in his immediate vicinity. If the observer releases any objects, they will remain, relative to him, in a state of rest. The [falling] observer is therefore justified in considering his state as one of rest." Einstein concluded, in other words, that two seemingly contradictory states could be present simultaneously: motion and rest. This realization led to the development of his revolutionary general theory of relativity.

In another study of creative potential, Rothenberg and Hausman (2000) found that when individuals were presented with a stimulus word and asked to respond with the word that first came to mind, highly creative students, Nobel scientists, and prize-winning artists responded with antonyms significantly more often than did individuals with average creativity. Rothenberg argued, based on these results, that creative people think in terms of opposites more often than do other people (also see research by Blasko & Mokwa, 1986).

For our purposes, the whole point is to reverse or contradict the currently accepted definition in order to expand the number of perspectives considered. For instance, a problem might be that morale is too

Table 3.5	Techniques for Improving Problem Definition
1.	**Make the strange familiar and the familiar strange** (for example, analogies and metaphors).
2.	**Elaborate on the definition** (for example, question checklists and SCAMPER).
3.	**Reverse the definition** (for example, Janusian thinking and opposition).

Table 3.6	Techniques for Generating More Alternatives
1.	**Defer judgment** (for example, brainstorming).
2.	**Expand current alternatives** (for example, subdivision).
3.	**Combine unrelated attributes** (for example, morphological synthesis and relational algorithm).

high instead of (or in addition to) too low in our team (we may need more discipline), or maybe employees need less motivation (more direction) instead of more motivation to increase productivity. Opposites and backward looks often enhance creativity.

These three techniques for improving creative problem definition are summarized in Table 3.5. Their purpose is not to help you generate alternative definitions just for the sake of alternatives but to broaden your perspectives, to help you overcome conceptual blocks, and to produce more elegant (i.e., high-quality and parsimonious) solutions. They are tools or techniques that you can easily use when you are faced with the need to solve problems creatively.

WAYS TO GENERATE MORE ALTERNATIVES

Because a common tendency is to define problems in terms of available solutions (i.e., the problem is defined as already possessing a certain set of possible solutions, e.g., March & Simon, 1958; March 1999), most of us consider a minimal number and a narrow range of alternatives in problem solving. Most experts agree, however, that the primary characteristics of effective creative problem solvers are their **fluency** and their **flexibility of thought** (Sternberg, 1999).

Fluency refers to the number of ideas or concepts produced in a given length of time. Flexibility refers to the diversity of ideas or concepts generated. While most problem solvers consider a few homogeneous alternatives, creative problem solvers consider many heterogeneous alternatives.

The following techniques are designed to help you improve your ability to generate a large number and a wide variety of alternatives when faced with problems, whether they be imagination, improvement, investment, or incubation. They are summarized in Table 3.6.

Defer Judgment

Probably the most common method of generating alternatives is the technique of **brainstorming** developed by Osborn (1953). This tool is powerful because most people make quick judgments about each piece of information or each alternative solution they encounter. Brainstorming is designed to help people generate alternatives for problem solving without prematurely evaluating, and hence discarding, them. It is practiced by having a group of people get together and simply begin sharing ideas about a problem—one at a time, with someone recording the ideas that are suggested. Four main rules govern brainstorming:

1. No evaluation of any kind is permitted as alternatives are being generated. Individual energy is spent on generating ideas, not on defending them.
2. The wildest and most divergent ideas are encouraged. It is easier to tighten alternatives than to loosen them up.
3. The quantity of ideas takes precedence over the quality. Emphasizing quality engenders judgment and evaluation.
4. Participants should build on or modify the ideas of others. Poor ideas that are added to or altered often become good ideas.

The idea of brainstorming is to use it in a group setting so individuals can stimulate ideas in one another. Often, after a rush of alternatives is produced at the outset of a brainstorming session, the quantity of ideas often rapidly subsides. But to stop at that point is an ineffective use of brainstorming. When easily identifiable solutions have been exhausted, that's when the truly creative alternatives are often produced in brainstorming groups. So keep working. Apply some of the tools described in this chapter for expanding definitions and alternatives. Brainstorming often begins with a flurry of ideas that then diminish.

If brainstorming continues and members are encouraged to think past that point, breakthrough ideas often emerge as less common or less familiar alternatives are suggested. After that phase has unfolded in brainstorming, it is usually best to terminate the process and begin refining and consolidating ideas.

Recent research has found that brainstorming in a group may be less efficient and more time consuming than alternative forms of brainstorming due to free riders, unwitting evaluations, production blocking, and so on. One widely used alternative brainstorming technique is to have individual group members generate ideas on their own then submit them to the group for exploration and evaluation (Finke, Ward, & Smith, 1992). Alternatively, electronic brainstorming in which individuals use chat rooms or their own computer to generate ideas has shown positive results as well (Siau, 1995). What is clear from the research is that generating alternatives in the presence of others produces more and better ideas than can be produced alone.

The best way to get a feel for the power of brainstorming groups is to participate in one. Try the following exercise based on an actual problem faced by a group of students and university professors. Spend at least 10 minutes in a small group, brainstorming your ideas.

> *The business school faculty has become increasingly concerned about the ethics associated with modern business practice. The general reputation of business executives is in the tank. They are seen as greedy, dishonest, and untrustworthy. What could the faculty or the school do to affect this problem?*

How do you define the problem? What ideas can you come up with? Generate as many ideas as you can following the rules of brainstorming. After at least 10 minutes, assess the fluency (the number) and flexibility (the variety) of the ideas you generated as a team.

Expand Current Alternatives

Sometimes, brainstorming in a group is not possible or is too costly in terms of the number of people involved and hours required. Managers facing a fast-paced twenty-first-century environment may find brainstorming to be too inefficient. Moreover, people sometimes need an external stimulus or way to break through conceptual blocks to help them generate new ideas. One useful and readily available technique for expanding alternatives is **subdivision**, or dividing a problem into smaller parts. This is a well-used and proven technique for enlarging the alternative set.

For example, March and Simon (1958, p. 193) suggested that subdivision improves problem solving by increasing the speed with which alternatives can be generated and selected.

> *The mode of subdivision has an influence on the extent to which planning can proceed simultaneously on the several aspects of the problem. The more detailed the factorization of the problem, the more simultaneous activity is possible, hence, the greater the speed of problem solving.*

To see how subdivision helps develop more alternatives and speeds the process of problem solving, consider the problem, common in the creativity literature, of listing alternative uses for a familiar object. For example, in one minute, how many uses can you list for a Ping-Pong ball? Ready...go.

The more uses you identify, the greater is your fluency in thinking. The more variety in your list, the greater is your flexibility in thinking. You may have included the following in your list: bob for a fishing line, Christmas ornament, toy for a cat, gearshift knob, model for a molecular structure, wind gauge when hung from a string, head for a finger puppet, miniature basketball. Your list will be much longer.

Now that you have produced your list, apply the technique of subdivision by identifying the specific characteristics of a Ping-Pong ball. That is, divide it into its component attributes. For example, weight, color, texture, shape, porosity, strength, hardness, chemical properties, and conduction potential are all attributes of Ping-Pong balls that help expand the uses you might think of. By dividing an object mentally into more specific attributes, you can arrive at many more alternative uses (e.g., reflector, holder when cut in half, bug bed, ball for lottery drawing, inhibitor of an electrical current, and so on).

One exercise we have used with students and executives to illustrate this technique is to have them write down as many of their leadership or managerial strengths as they can think of. Most people list 10 or 12 attributes relatively easily. Then we analyze the various aspects of the manager's role, the activities in which managers engage, the challenges that most managers face from inside and outside the organization, and so on. We then ask these same people to write down another list of their strengths as managers.

The list is almost always more than twice as long as the first list. By identifying the subcomponents of any problem, far more alternatives can be generated than by considering the problem as a whole.

Try this by yourself. Divide your life into the multiple roles you play—student, friend, neighbor, leader, brother or sister, and so on. If you list your strengths associated with each role, your list will be much longer than if you just create a general list of personal strengths.

Combine Unrelated Attributes

A third technique focuses on helping problem solvers expand alternatives by forcing the integration of seemingly unrelated elements. Research in creative problem solving has shown that an ability to see common relationships among disparate factors is a major factor differentiating creative from noncreative individuals (Feldman, 1999). Two ways to do this are through morphological synthesis (Koberg & Bagnall, 2003) and the relational algorithm (Crovitz, 1970). (For literature reviews, see Finke, Ward, & Smith, 1992; and Starko, 2001.)

With **morphological synthesis**, a four-step procedure is involved. First, the problem is written down. Second, attributes of the problem are listed. Third, alternatives to each attribute are listed. Fourth, different alternatives from the attributes list are combined together.

This seems a bit complicated so let us illustrate the procedure. Suppose you are faced with the problem of an employee who takes an extended lunch break almost every day despite your reminders to be on time. Think of alternative ways to solve this problem. The first solution that comes to mind for most people is to sit down and have a talk with (or threaten) the employee. If that doesn't work, most of us would reduce the person's pay, demote or transfer him or her, or just fire the person. However, look at what other alternatives can be generated by using morphological synthesis (see Table 3.7).

You can see how many more alternatives come to mind when you force together attributes that aren't obviously connected. The matrix of attributes can create a very long list of possible solutions. In more complicated problems—for example, how to improve quality, how to better serve customers, how to improve the reward system, how to land a great job—the potential number of alternatives is even greater, and, hence, more creativity is required to analyze them.

The second technique for combining unrelated attributes in problem solving, the **relational algorithm**, involves applying connecting words that force a relationship between two elements in a problem.

Table 3.7	Morphological Synthesis

Step 1. Problem statement: The employee takes extended lunch breaks every day with friends in the cafeteria.

Step 2. Major attributes of the problem:

AMOUNT OF TIME	START TIME	PLACE	WITH WHOM	FREQUENCY
More than 1 hour	12 noon	Cafeteria	Friends	Daily

Step 3. Alternative attributes:

AMOUNT OF TIME	START TIME	PLACE	WITH WHOM	FREQUENCY
30 minutes	11:00	Office	Coworkers	Weekly
90 minutes	11:30	Conference Room	Boss	Twice a Week
45 minutes	12:30	Restaurant	Management Team	Alternate Days

Step 4. Combining attributes:

1. A 30-minute lunch beginning at 12:30 in the conference room with the boss once a week.

2. A 90-minute lunch beginning at 11:30 in the conference room with coworkers twice a week.

3. A 45-minute lunch beginning at 11:00 in the cafeteria with the management team every other day.

4. A 30-minute lunch beginning at 12:00 alone in the office on alternate days.

For example, the following is a list of some words that connect other words together. They are called "relational" words.

about	across	after
against	opposite	or
out	among	and
as	at	over
round	still	because
before	between	but
so	then	though
by	down	for
from	through	till
to	if	in
near	not	under
up	when	now
of	off	on
where	while	with

To illustrate the use of this technique, suppose you are faced with the following problem: *Our customers are dissatisfied with our service.* The two major subjects in this problem are *customers* and *service.* They are connected by the phrase *are dissatisfied with*. With the relational algorithm technique, the relational words in the problem statement are removed and replaced with other relational words to see if new ideas for alternative solutions can be identified. For example, consider the following connections where new relational words are used:

- ❏ Customers *among* service (e.g., customers interact with service personnel)

- ❏ Customers *as* service (e.g., customers deliver service to other customers)

- ❏ Customers *and* service (e.g., customers and service personnel work collaboratively together)

- ❏ Customers *for* service (e.g., customer focus groups can help improve service)

- ❏ Service *near* customers (e.g., change the location of the service to be nearer customers)

- ❏ Service *before* customers (e.g., prepare personalized service before the customer arrives)

- ❏ Service *through* customers (e.g., use customers to provide additional service)

- ❏ Service *when* customers (e.g., provide timely service when customers want it)

By connecting the two elements of the problem in different ways, new possibilities for problem solution can be formulated.

International Caveats

The perspective taken in this chapter has a clear bias toward Western culture. It focuses on analytical and creative problem solving as methods for addressing specific issues. Enhancing creativity has a specific purpose: to solve certain kinds of problems better. Creativity in Eastern cultures, on the other hand, is often defined differently. Creativity is focused less on creating solutions than on uncovering enlightenment, one's true self, or the achievement of wholeness or self-actualization (Chu, 1970; Kuo, 1996). It is aimed at getting in touch with the unconscious (Maduro, 1976). In both the East and the West, however, creativity is viewed positively. Gods of creativity are worshipped in West African cultures (Olokun) and among Hindus (Vishvakarma), for example (Ben-Amos, 1986; Wonder & Blake, 1992), and creativity is often viewed in mystical or religious terms rather than managerial or practical terms.

In fostering creative problem solving in international settings or with individuals from different countries, Trompenaars and Hampden-Turner's (1987, 2004) model is useful for understanding the caveats that must be kept in mind. Countries differ, for example, in their orientation toward *internal control* (Canada, United States, United Kingdom) versus *external control* (Japan, China, Czech Republic). In internal cultures, the environment is assumed to be changeable, so creativity focuses on attacking problems directly. In external cultures, because individuals assume less control of the environment, creativity focuses less on problem resolution and more on achieving insight or oneness with nature. Changing the environment is not the usual objective.

Similarly, cultures emphasizing a **specific orientation** (Sweden, Denmark, United Kingdom, and France) are more likely to challenge the status quo and seek new ways to address problems than cultures emphasizing a *diffuse culture* (China, Nigeria, India, and Singapore) in which loyalty, wholeness, and long-term relationships are more likely to inhibit individual creative effort.

This is similar to the differences that are likely in countries emphasizing *universalism* (Korea, Venezuela, China, and India) as opposed to *particularism* (Switzerland, United States, Sweden, United Kingdom, and Germany). Cultures emphasizing universalism tend to focus on generalizable outcomes and consistent rules or procedures. Particularistic cultures are more inclined to search for unique aberrations from the norm, thus having more of a tendency toward creative solution finding. Managers encouraging conceptual blockbusting and creative problem solving, in other words, will find some individuals more inclined toward the rule-oriented procedures of analytical problem solving and less inclined toward the playfulness and experimentation associated with creative problem solving than others.

Hints for Applying Problem-Solving Techniques

Not every problem is amenable to these techniques and tools for conceptual blockbusting, of course, nor is every individual equally inclined or skilled. Our intent in presenting these six suggestions is to help you expand the number of options available to you for defining problems and generating additional alternatives. They are most useful with problems that are not straightforward, are complex or ambiguous, or are imprecise in their definitions. All of us have enormous creative potential, but the stresses and pressures of daily life, coupled with the inertia of conceptual habits, tend to submerge that potential. These hints are ways to help unlock it again.

Reading about techniques or having a desire to be creative is not, alone, enough to make you a skillful creative problem solver, of course. Although research has confirmed the effectiveness of these techniques for improving creative problem solving, they depend on application and practice as well as an environment that is conducive to creativity. Here are six practical hints that will help facilitate your own ability to apply these techniques effectively and improve your creative problem solving ability.

1. *Give yourself some relaxation time.* The more intense your work, the more your need for complete breaks. Break out of your routine sometimes. This frees up your mind and gives room for new thoughts.
2. *Find a place (physical space) where you can think.* It should be a place where interruptions are eliminated, at least for a time. Reserve your best time for thinking.
3. *Talk to other people about ideas.* Isolation produces far fewer ideas than does conversation. Make a list of people who stimulate you to think. Spend some time with them.
4. *Ask other people for their suggestions about your problems.* Find out what others think about them. Don't be embarrassed to share your problems, but don't become dependent on others to solve them for you.

5. *Read a lot.* Read at least one thing regularly that is outside your field of expertise. Keep track of new thoughts from your reading.
6. *Protect yourself from idea-killers.* Don't spend time with "black holes"—that is, people who absorb all of your energy and light but give nothing in return. Don't let yourself or others negatively evaluate your ideas too soon.

You'll find these hints useful not only for enhancing creative problem solving but for analytical problem solving as well. Figure 3.9 summarizes the two problem-solving processes—analytical and creative—and the factors you should consider when determining how to approach each type of problem. In brief, when you encounter a problem that is straightforward—outcomes are predictable, sufficient information is available, and means-ends connections are clear—analytical problem-solving techniques are most appropriate. You should apply the four distinct, sequential steps. On the other hand, when the problem is not straightforward—that is, information is ambiguous or unavailable and alternative solutions are not apparent—you should apply creative problem-solving techniques in order to improve problem definition and alternative generation.

Fostering Creativity in Others

Unlocking your own creative potential is important but insufficient, of course, to make you a successful manager. A major challenge is to help unlock it in other people as well. Fostering creativity among those with whom you work is at least as great a challenge as increasing your own creativity. In this last section of the chapter, we briefly discuss some principles that will help you better accomplish the task of fostering creativity.

MANAGEMENT PRINCIPLES

Neither Percy Spencer nor Spence Silver could have succeeded in his creative ideas had there not been a support system present that fostered creative problem solving. In each case, certain characteristics were present in their organizations, fostered by managers around them, which made their innovations possible. In this section, focus on activities in which individual managers can engage that foster creativity. Table 3.8 summarizes three management principles that help engender creative problem solving among others.

Figure 3.9 | A Model of Analytical and Creative Problem Solving

Problem Assessment
- Outcomes predictable?
- Sufficient information present?

Yes → **Constraints**
- Definitional problems
- Solution-generation problems
- Evaluation and selection problems
- Implementation and follow-up problems

Analytical Problem Solving
- Define the problem
- Generate alternative solutions
- Evaluate and select alternatives
- Implement and follow up on the solution

No → **Conceptual Blocks**
- Constancy
- Commitment
- Compression
- Complacency

Four Approaches to Creativity
- Imagination
- Improvement
- Investment
- Incubation

Creative Problem-Solving Tools
- To improve problem definition:
  - Make the familiar strange and the strange familiar
  - Elaborate definitions
  - Reverse the definition
- To improve the generation of alternatives:
  - Defer judgment
  - Expand current alternatives
  - Combine unrelated attributes

LEARNING

Pull People Apart; Put People Together

Percy Spencer's magnetron project involved a consumer product closeted away from Raytheon's mainline business of missiles and other defense contract work. Spence Silver's new glue resulted when a polymer adhesive task force was separated from 3M's normal activities. The Macintosh computer was developed by a task force taken outside the company and given space and time to work on an innovative computer. Many new ideas come from individuals being given time and resources and allowed to work apart from the normal activities of the organization. Establishing bullpens, practice fields, or sandlots is as good a way to develop new skills in business as it has proven to be in athletics. Because most businesses are designed to produce the 10,000th part correctly or to service the 10,000th customer efficiently, they do not function well at producing the first part. That

Table 3.8	Three Principles for Fostering Creativity	
PRINCIPLE	**EXAMPLES**
1. Pull people apart; put people together.	• Let individuals work alone as well as with teams and task forces. • Encourage minority reports and legitimize "devil's advocate" roles. • Encourage heterogeneous membership in teams. • Separate competing groups or subgroups.
2. Monitor and prod.	• Talk to customers. • Identify customer expectations both in advance and after the sale. • Hold people accountable. • Use "sharp-pointed" prods.
3. Reward multiple roles.	• Idea champion • Sponsor and mentor • Orchestrator and facilitator • Rule breaker

is why pulling people apart is often necessary to foster innovation and creativity. This principle is the same as providing autonomy and discretion for other people to pursue their own ideas.

On the other hand, forming teams (putting people together) is almost always more productive than having people work by themselves. Such teams should be characterized by certain attributes, though. For example, Nemeth (1986) found that creativity increased markedly when minority influences were present in the team, for example, when "devil's advocate" roles were legitimized, when a formal minority report was always included in final recommendations, and when individuals assigned to work on a team had divergent backgrounds or views. "Those exposed to minority views are stimulated to attend to more aspects of the situation, they think in more divergent ways, and they are more likely to detect novel solutions or come to new decisions" (Nemeth, 1986, p. 25). Nemeth found that those positive benefits occur in groups even when the divergent or minority views are wrong.

Similarly, Janis (1971) found that narrow-mindedness in groups (dubbed **groupthink**) was best overcome by establishing competing groups working on the same problem, participation in groups by outsiders, assigning a role of critical evaluator in the group, and having groups made up of cross-functional participants. The most productive groups are those characterized by fluid roles, lots of interaction among members, and flat power structures. On the other hand, too much diversity, too much disagreement, and too much fluidity can sidetrack groups, so devil's advocates must be aware of when to line up and support the decision of the group. Their role is to help groups rethink quick decisions or solutions that have not been considered carefully enough, not to avoid making group decisions or solving problems.

You can help foster creativity among people you manage, therefore, by pulling people apart (e.g., giving them a bullpen, providing them with autonomy, encouraging individual initiative) as well as putting people together (e.g., putting them in teams, enabling minority influence, and fostering heterogeneity).

Monitor and Prod

Neither Percy Spencer nor Spence Silver was allowed to work on their projects without accountability. Both men eventually had to report on the results they accomplished with their experimentation and imagination. At 3M, for example, people are expected to allocate 15 percent of their time away from company business to work on new, creative ideas. They can even appropriate company materials and resources to work on them. However, individuals are always held accountable for their decisions. They need to show results for their "play time."

Holding people accountable for outcomes, in fact, is an important motivator for improved performance. Two innovators in the entertainment industry captured this principle with these remarks:

"The ultimate inspiration is the deadline. That's when you have to do what needs to be done. The fact that twice a year the creative talent of this country is working until midnight to get something ready for a trade show is very good for the economy. Without this kind of pressure, things would turn to mashed potatoes" (von Oech, 1986, p. 119).

One way Woody Morcott, former CEO at Dana Corporation, held people accountable for creativity was to require that each person in the company submit at least two suggestions for improvement each month. At least 70 percent of the new ideas had to be implemented. Woody admitted that he stole the idea during a visit to a Japanese company where he noticed workers huddled around a table scribbling notes on how some ideas for improvement might work. At Dana, this requirement is part of every person's job assignment. Rewards are associated with such ideas as well. A plant in Chihuahua, Mexico, for example, rewards employees with $1.89 for every idea submitted and another $1.89 if the idea is used. "We drill into people that they are responsible for keeping the plant competitive through innovation," Morcott said (personal communication).

In addition to accountability, creativity is stimulated by what Gene Goodson, formerly at Johnson Controls, called "sharp-pointed prods." After taking over the automotive group at that company, Goodson found that he could stimulate creative problem solving by issuing certain mandates that demanded new approaches to old tasks. One such mandate was, "There will be no more forklift trucks allowed in any of our plants." At first hearing, that mandate sounded absolutely outrageous. Think about it. You have a plant with tens of thousands of square feet of floor space. The loading docks are on one side of the building, and many tons of heavy raw materials are unloaded weekly and moved from the loading docks to work stations throughout the entire facility. The only way it can be done is with forklifts. Eliminating forklift trucks would ruin the plant, right?

Wrong. This sharp-pointed prod demanded that individuals working in the plant find ways to move the work stations closer to the raw materials, to move the unloading of the raw materials closer to the work stations, or to change the size and amounts of material being unloaded. The innovations that resulted from eliminating forklifts saved the company millions of dollars in materials handling and wasted time; dramatically improved quality, productivity, and efficiency; and made it possible for Johnson Controls to capture some business from their Japanese competitors.

One of the best methods for generating useful prods is to regularly monitor customer preferences, expectations, and evaluations. Many of the most creative ideas have come from customers, the recipients of goods and services. Identifying their preferences in advance and monitoring their evaluations of products or services later are good ways to get creative ideas and to foster imagination, improvement, investment, and incubation. All employees should be in regular contact with their own customers, asking questions and monitoring performance.

In summary, you can foster creativity by holding people accountable for new ideas and by stimulating them with periodic prods. The most useful prods generally come from customers.

Reward Multiple Roles

The success of Post-it Notes at 3M is more than a story of the creativity of Spence Silver. It also illustrates the necessity of people playing multiple roles in enabling creativity and the importance of recognizing and rewarding those who play such roles. Without a number of people playing multiple roles, Spence Silver's glue would probably still be on a shelf somewhere.

Four crucial roles for enabling creativity in others include the **idea champion** (the person who comes up with creative problem solutions), the **sponsor** or mentor (the person who helps provide the resources, environment, and encouragement for the idea champion to work on his idea), the **orchestrator** or facilitator (the person who brings together cross-functional groups and necessary political support to facilitate implementation of creative ideas), and the **rule breaker** (the person who goes beyond organizational boundaries and barriers to ensure success of the creative solution). Each of these roles is present in most important innovations in organizations, and all are illustrated by the Post-it Note example.

This story has four major parts.

1. Spence Silver, while fooling around with chemical configurations that the academic literature indicated wouldn't work, invented a glue that wouldn't stick. Silver spent years giving presentations to any audience at 3M that would listen, trying to pawn off his glue

on some division that could find a practical application for it. But nobody was interested.

2. Henry Courtney and Roger Merrill developed a coating substance that allowed the glue to stick to one surface but not to others. This made it possible to produce a permanently temporary glue, that is, one that would peel off easily when pulled but would otherwise hang on forever.

3. Art Fry found a problem that fit Spence Silver's solution. He found an application for the glue as a "better bookmark" and as a note pad. No equipment existed at 3M to coat only a part of a piece of paper with the glue. Fry therefore carried 3M equipment and tools home to his own basement, where he designed and made his own machine to manufacture the forerunner of Post-it Notes. Because the working machine became too large to get out of his basement, he blasted a hole in the wall to get the equipment back to 3M. He then brought together engineers, designers, production managers, and machinists to demonstrate the prototype machine and generate enthusiasm for manufacturing the product.

4. Geoffrey Nicholson and Joseph Ramsey began marketing the product inside 3M. They also submitted the product to the standard 3M market tests. The product failed miserably. No one wanted to pay $1.00 for a pad of scratch paper. But when Nicholson and Ramsey broke 3M rules by personally visiting test market sites and giving away free samples, the consuming public became addicted to the product.

In this scenario, Spence Silver was both a rule breaker and an idea champion. Art Fry was also an idea champion, but more importantly, he orchestrated the coming together of the various groups needed to get the innovation off the ground. Henry Courtney and Roger Merrill helped sponsor Silver's innovation by providing him with the coating substance that would allow his idea to work. Geoff Nicholson and Joe Ramsey were both rule breakers and sponsors in their bid to get the product accepted by the public. In each case, not only did all these people play unique roles, but they did so with tremendous enthusiasm and zeal. They were confident of their ideas and willing to put their time and resources on the line as advocates. They fostered support among a variety of constituencies, both within their own areas of expertise as well as among outside groups. Most organizations are inclined to give in to those who are sure of themselves, persistent in their efforts, and savvy enough to make converts of others.

Not everyone can be an idea champion. But when managers reward and recognize those who sponsor and orchestrate the ideas of others, creativity increases in organizations. Teams form, supporters replace competitors, and innovation thrives. Facilitating multiple role development is the job of the managers who want to foster creativity. Figure 3.10 summarizes this process.

Summary

In the twenty-first century, almost no manager or organization can afford to stand still, to rely on past practices, and to avoid innovation. In a fast-paced environment in which the half-life of knowledge is about three years and the half-life of almost any technology is counted in weeks and months instead of years, creative problem solving is increasingly a prerequisite for success. The digital revolution makes the rapid production

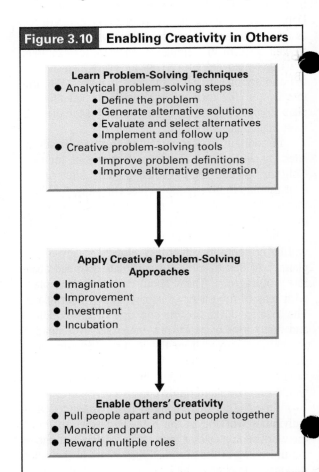

Figure 3.10 Enabling Creativity in Others

Learn Problem-Solving Techniques
- Analytical problem-solving steps
  - Define the problem
  - Generate alternative solutions
  - Evaluate and select alternatives
  - Implement and follow up
- Creative problem-solving tools
  - Improve problem definitions
  - Improve alternative generation

Apply Creative Problem-Solving Approaches
- Imagination
- Improvement
- Investment
- Incubation

Enable Others' Creativity
- Pull people apart and put people together
- Monitor and prod
- Reward multiple roles

of new ideas almost mandatory. This is not to negate the importance of analytical problem solving, of course. The quality revolution of the 1980s and 1990s taught us important lessons about carefully proscribed, sequential, and analytic problem-solving processes. Error rates, response times, and missed deadlines dropped dramatically when analytical problem solving was institutionalized in manufacturing and service companies.

In this chapter, we have discussed a well-developed model for solving problems. It consists of four separate and sequential stages: defining a problem, generating alternative solutions, evaluating and selecting the best solution, and implementing the chosen solution. This model, however, is mainly useful for solving straight-forward problems. Many problems faced by managers are not of this type, and frequently managers are called on to exercise creative problem-solving skills. That is, they must broaden their perspective of the problem and develop alternative solutions that are not immediately obvious.

We have discussed four different types of creativity and encouraged you to consider all four when faced with the need to be creative. However, we have also illustrated eight major conceptual blocks that inhibit most people's creative problem-solving abilities. Conceptual blocks are mental obstacles that artificially constrain problem definition and solution and that keep most people from being effective creative problem solvers.

Overcoming these conceptual blocks is a matter of skill development and practice in thinking, not a matter of innate ability. Everyone can become a skilled creative problem solver with practice. Becoming aware of these thinking inhibitors helps individuals overcome them. We also discussed three major techniques for improving creative problem definition and three major techniques for improving the creative generation of alternative solutions. Specific suggestions were offered that can help implement these six techniques.

We concluded by offering some hints about how to foster creativity among other people. Becoming an effective problem solver yourself is important, but effective managers can also enhance this activity among those with whom they work.

Behavioral Guidelines

Below are specific behavioral action guidelines to help guide your skill practice in analytical and creative problem solving.

A. Follow the four-step procedure outlined in Table 3.1 when solving straightforward problems. Keep the steps separate, and do not take shortcuts—define the problem, generate alternative solutions, evaluate the alternatives, select and implement the optimal solution.

B. When approaching a difficult or complex problem, remember that creative solutions need not be a product of revolutionary and brand-new ideas. Four different types of creativity are available to you—imagination, improvement, investment, and incubation.

C. Try to overcome your conceptual blocks by consciously doing the following:
   ❏ Use lateral thinking in addition to vertical thinking.
   ❏ Use several thought languages instead of just one.
   ❏ Challenge stereotypes based on past experiences.
   ❏ Identify underlying themes and commonalities in seemingly unrelated factors.
   ❏ Delete superfluous information and fill in important missing information when studying the problem.
   ❏ Avoid artificially constraining problem boundaries.
   ❏ Overcome any unwillingness to be inquisitive.
   ❏ Use both right- and left-brain thinking.

D. To enhance creativity, use techniques that elaborate problem definition such as:
   ❏ Make the strange familiar and the familiar strange by using metaphors and analogies.
   ❏ Develop alternative (opposite) definitions and apply a question checklist.
   ❏ Reverse the definition.

E. To enhance creativity, use techniques that elaborate possible alternative solutions such as:
- ❏ Defer judgment.
- ❏ Subdivide the problem into its attributes.
- ❏ Combine unrelated problem attributes.

F. Foster creativity among those with whom you work by doing the following:
- ❏ Provide autonomy, allowing individuals to experiment and try out ideas.
- ❏ Put people together who hold different perspectives into teams to work on problems.
- ❏ Hold people accountable for innovation.
- ❏ Use sharp-pointed prods to stimulate new thinking.
- ❏ Recognize, reward, and encourage multiple roles, including idea champions, sponsors, orchestrators, and rule breakers.

SKILL *ANALYSIS*

CASES INVOLVING PROBLEM SOLVING

Coke versus Pepsi

Back in the 1980s, the Coca-Cola Company became very concerned about its future. Coke held a dominant position in market share around the world with 18 percent compared to Pepsi-Cola's 4 percent. However, Coke's market share began to erode versus Pepsi until by the end of the decade, Coke had slipped to 12 percent market share while Pepsi had increased to 11 percent. More importantly, Pepsi began advertising the "Pepsi Challenge" in which consumers were asked to choose between Coke and Pepsi in blind taste tests. Pepsi claimed that its product won these tests time and time again. Even exclusive Coke drinkers, Pepsi claimed, chose the taste of Pepsi above the taste of Coke.

Coca-Cola's management claimed that these tests were rigged or were merely a marketing ploy. However, Coke secretly conducted its own tests in which cola drinkers were given two drinks—one marked M and one marked Q. They were given a drink and asked to identify the taste they preferred. To their shagrin, Coke's executives found the same result. Cola drinkers preferred the taste of Pepsi 57 percent to 43 percent for Coke. The sweeter, smoother taste of Pepsi seemed to be preferred by a wide margin. In a very competitive marketplace where a tenth of a percentage point is worth millions in revenues, this gap was enormous.

One alternative for Coke was to defend its share of the marketplace by continuing to advertise and market its product, and to ensure that Coke product placement was more widespread and better positioned that Pepsi's. That is, one option was to ensure that consumers were simply more aware of Coke and had easier access to it than Pepsi.

Another alternative was to engage in a massive R&D effort and find a new product that would match or exceed Pepsi's taste among cola drinkers. Coke selected this latter strategy. The R&D lab spent multiple-millions to produce a new product labelled *New Coke*. In blind taste tests, New Coke beat Pepsi by 6 to 8 percentage points among cola drinkers, so Coke was confident that it had a hit product on its hands. The company's CEO, Roberto C. Goizueta, announced that this was "the surest move the company has ever made."

With a great deal of fanfare, Coke announced the release of the New Coke, assuming that it would be a major market success and blunt Pepsi's rise in market share. Instead, New Coke was a sales disaster. Sales of New Coke were abysmal and declined from the outset. Coca-Cola executives scrambled to respond to consumers demand that the original Coke be brought back. With a declining new product on the market and the abandonment of the traditional Coke, senior executives were under tremedous pressure to respond quickly. The result, as we all know, was the re-introduction of Coke Classic (a supposed inferior-tasting product) several months later in an attempt to save the company.

Discussion Questions

3.1. What conceptual blocks were experienced by Coke executives?

3.2. What is the difference between a blind taste test and taking a six-pack home and consuming the entire amount? What do you suppose were the results of that test?

3.3. How do explain the success of Coke versus Pepsi over the last 20 years? What would you now advise Pepsi to do?

3.4. How do problem-solving and decision-making processes change under time pressures or crises?

3.5. Knowing what you know about problem solving, what kinds of conceptual blockbusters could be useful to Pepsi executives, or to Coke executives? What rules of thumb seem relevant in these kinds of situations?

3.6. What do you learn from this case that would help you advise other organizations, such as Microsoft in protecting its market from Google, Barnes & Noble.com in displacing Amazon.com, or American Greetings in becoming the dominant player in the greeting-card business? What practical hints do you derive from this classic case of competitive marketplace dynamics?

Creativity at Apple

In his annual speech in Paris in 2003, Steven Jobs, the lionized CEO of Apple Computer, Inc., proudly described Apple in these terms: "Innovate. That's what we do." And innovate they have. Jobs and his colleagues, Steve Wozniak and Mike Markkula, invented the personal computer market in 1977 with the introduction of the Apple II. In 1980, Apple was the number one vendor of personal computers in the world. Apple's success, in fact, helped spawn what became known as Silicon Valley in California, the mother lode of high technology invention and production for the next three decades.

Fortune magazine named Apple the most admired company in the United States in 2008, and in the world from 2008 to 2012. On September 30, 2013, Apple surpassed Coca-Cola to become the world's most valuable brand in the Omnicom Group's "Best Global Brands" report. As of May 2013, Apple maintains 408 retail stores in 14 countries as well as the online Apple Store and iTunes Store, the latter of which is the world's largest music retailer. Apple is the largest publicly traded corporation in the world by market capitalization, with an estimated market capitalization of $446 billion in January 2014. As of Q1 2014, Apple's five-year growth average is 39 percent for top line growth and 45 percent for bottom line growth. Apple is the most successful startup company of all time, by market capitalization, revenue, and growth, and astoundingly, in July 2011, due to the American debt-ceiling crisis, Apple's financial reserves were briefly larger than those of the U.S. government.

This success has occurred as a result of Apple's incredible inventiveness and creativity in developing new products, On the other hand, the market is questioning whether Apple can keep up this pace and remain a world-class innovation factory.

The success of the company, of course, rests on the fact that Apple created the personal computer market, first with Apple II and then with Macintosh computers and the OS operating system. It created the first computer network with its Macintosh machines since Windows-based PC's did not network until the mid-1990s. Apple introduced the first handheld, pen-based computing device known as the Newton and followed that up with a wireless mouse, ambient-lit keyboards for working in the dark, and the fastest computer on the market in 2003. In 2003, Apple also introduced the first legal, digital music store for downloading songs—iTunes—along with its compatible technology, iPods. This was followed by iPhones, iPod touch, iPads, iTV, Apple Stores, and iCloud. Progress is now being made in iCars. In other words, Apple has been at the forefront of product and technological innovation for almost 40 years. Apple has been, hands down, the most innovative company in its industry and one of the most innovative companies on the planet.

If one takes seriously the messages being declared loudly and prominently in the business press and in the broader global society today, innovation and creativity are the keys to success. "Change or die." "Innovate or get passed over." "Be creative to be successful." A key tenet on which progressive, market-based, capitalistic societies are based is the idea of creative destruction. That is, without creativity and innovation, individuals and organizations become casualties of the second law of thermodynamics—they disintegrate, wither, disorganize, and die. New products are needed to keep consumers happy. Obsolescence is ubiquitous. Innovation and creativity, consequently, are touted as being at the very heart of success. For more evidence, just skim over the more than 300,000 book titles when you log onto Amazon and search using the key word "innovation."

On the other hand, consider some of the most innovative companies in recent American history. Xerox Corporation's famed Palo Alto Research Center gave the world laser printing, the Ethernet, Windows-type software, graphical user interfacing, and the mouse, yet it is notorious for not having made any money at all. Polaroid introduced the idea of instant images, yet it filed for bankruptcy in 2001. The Internet boom in the late 1990s was an explosion of what is now considered to be worthless innovation. And, Enron may have been the most innovative financial company ever.

Similarly, Amazon, Southwest Airlines, eBay, Wal-Mart, and Dell are examples of incredibly successful companies, but these firms did not invent any new products or technologies. They are acknowledged as innovative and creative companies, but they don't hold a candle to Apple. Instead of new products, they have invented new processes, new ways to deliver products, new distribution channels, new marketing approaches. It is well known that Henry Ford didn't invent the automobile. He simply invented a new way to assemble a car at a cost affordable to his own workers. The guy who invented the automobile hardly made a dime.

The trouble is, creativity as applied to business processes—manufacturing methods, sales and marketing, employee incentive systems, or leadership development—are usually seen as humdrum, nitty gritty, uncool, plodding, unimaginative, and boring. Creative people and creative companies that capture headlines are usually those that come up with great new product ideas or splashy features. Scan the list of *Fortune* 500 companies and judge how many are product champions versus process champions. Decide for yourself which is the driver of economic growth: good innovation or good management.

Discussion Questions

3.7. Consider the four approaches to creativity. What approach(es) has Apple relied on? What alternatives have other firms in the industry pursued? What other alternatives could Apple implement?

3.8. Assume you were a consultant to the CEO at Apple. What advice would you give on how Apple could capitalize on its creativity? How can Apple make money based on its own inclination to pursue creativity in certain ways?

3.9. What are the major obstacles and conceptual blocks that face Apple right now? What do employees need to watch out for?

3.10. What tools for fostering creative problem solving are applicable to Apple, and which would not be workable? Which ones do you think are used the most there?

EXERCISES FOR APPLYING CONCEPTUAL BLOCKBUSTING

The purpose of this exercise is to have you practice problem solving—both analytical and creative. Two actual scenarios are provided below. Both present real problems faced by real managers. They are very likely the same kinds of problems faced by your own business school and by many of your local businesses. Your assignment in each case is to identify a solution to the problem. You will approach the problem in two ways: first using analytical problem solving techniques; second, using creative problem-solving techniques. The first approach—analytical problem solving—you should accomplish by yourself. The second approach—creative problem solving—you should accomplish in a team. Your task is to apply the principles of problem solving to come up with realistic, cost-efficient, and effective solutions to these problems. Consider each scenario separately. You should take no more than 10 minutes to complete the analytical problem-solving assignment. Then take 20 minutes to complete the creative problem-solving assignment.

Individual Assignment—Analytical Problem Solving (10 minutes)

1. After reading the first case, write down a specific problem definition. What precisely worded problem are you going to solve? Complete the sentence: The problem I am going to solve is...

2. Now identify at least four or five alternative solutions. What ideas do you have for resolving this problem? Complete this sentence: Possible ways to resolve this problem are...

3. Next, evaluate the alternatives you have proposed. Make sure you don't evaluate each alternative before proposing your complete set. Evaluate your set of alternatives on the basis of these criteria: Will this alternative solve the problem you have defined? Is this alternative realistic in terms of being cost-effective? Can this solution be implemented in a short time frame?

4. Now write down your proposed solution to the problem. Be specific about what should be done and when. Be prepared to share that solution with other team members.

Team Assignment—Creative Problem Solving (20 minutes)

1. Now form a team of four or five people. Each team member should share his or her own definition of the problem. It is unlikely that they will all be the same, so make sure you keep track of them. Now add at least three more plausible definitions of the problem. In doing so, use at least two techniques for expanding problem definition discussed in the text. Each problem definition should differ from the others in what the problem is, not just a statement of different causes of the problem.

2. Now examine each of the definitions you have proposed. Select one that the entire team can agree upon. Since it is unlikely that you can solve multiple problems at once, select just one problem definition that you will work on.

3. Share the four or five proposed solutions that you generated on your own, even if they don't relate to the specific problem your team has defined. Keep track of all the different alternatives proposed by team members. After all team members have shared their alternatives, generate at least five additional alternative

solutions to the problem you have agreed upon. Use at least two of the techniques for expanding alternatives discussed in the text.

4. Of all the alternatives your team proposed, select the five that you consider to be the most creative and having the highest probability of success.

5. Select one team member from each team to serve as a judging panel. This panel is charged with selecting the team with the most creative and potentially successful alternatives to the problem. Team members cannot vote for their own team.

6. Each team now shares their five alternatives with the class. The judging panel selects the winner.

Moving Up in the Rankings

Business schools seem to have lost the ability to evaluate their own quality and effectiveness. With the emergence of rankings of business schools in the popular press, the role of judging quality seems to have been captured by publications such as *Business Week, U.S. News and World Report*, and the *Financial Times*. The accreditation association for business schools, AACSB, mainly assesses the extent to which a school is accreditable or not, a 0–1 distinction, so a wide range in quality exists among accredited business schools. More refined distinctions have been made in the popular press by identifying the highest rated 50, the first, second, or third tiers, or the top 20. Each publication relies on slightly different criteria in their rankings, but a substantial portion of each ranking rests on name recognition, visibility, or public acclaim. In some of the polls, more than 50 percent of the weighting is placed on the reputation or notoriety of the school. This is problematic, of course, because reputation can be deceiving. One recent poll rated the Harvard and Stanford undergraduate business programs among the top three in the country, even though neither school has an undergraduate business program. Princeton's law school has been rated in the top five in several polls, even though, you guessed it, no such law school exists.

Other criteria sometimes considered in various ranking services include student selectivity, percent of students placed in jobs, starting salaries of graduates, tuition costs compared to graduates' earnings, publications of the faculty, student satisfaction, recruiter satisfaction, and so on. By and large, however, name recognition is the single most crucial factor. It helps predict the number of student applicants, the ability to hire prominent faculty members, fund-raising opportunities, corporate partnerships, and so on.

Many business schools have responded to this pressure to become better known by creating advertising campaigns, circulating internal publications to other business schools and media outlets, and hiring additional staff to market the school. Most business school deans receive an average of 20 publications a week from other business schools, for

PRACTICE

example, and an editor at *Business Week* reported receiving more than 100 per week. Some deans begrudge the fact that these resources are being spent on activities other than improving the educational experience for students and faculty. Given constrained resources and tuition increases that outstrip the consumer price index every year, spending money on one activity precludes it from being spent on others. On the other hand, most deans acknowledge that this is the way the game must be played.

As part of a strategy to increase visibility, one business school hired world-renowned architect Frank O. Gehry to design a new business school building. Photographs of models of the building are reproduced below. It is a $70 million building that houses all the educational activities of the school. Currently this particular school does not appear in the top 20 on the major rankings lists. However, like about 75 other business schools in the world, it would very much like to reach that level. That is, the school would like to displace another school currently listed in the top 20. One problem with this new landmark building is that it is so unusual, so avant-garde, that it is not even recognized as a building. Upon seeing a photograph for the first time, some people don't even know what they're looking at. On the other hand, it presents an opportunity to leapfrog other schools listed higher in the rankings if the institution is creative in its approach. The challenge, of course, is that no one is sure exactly how to make this happen.

Keith Dunn and McGuffey's Restaurant

Keith Dunn knew exactly what to expect. He knew how his employees felt about him. That's why he had sent them the questionnaire in the first place. He needed a shot of confidence, a feeling that his employees were behind him as he struggled to build McGuffey's Restaurants, Inc., beyond two restaurants and $4 million in annual sales.

Gathering up the anonymous questionnaires, Dunn returned to his tiny corporate office in Asheville, North Carolina. With one of his partners by his side, he ripped open the first envelope as eagerly as a Broadway producer checking the reviews on opening night. His eyes zoomed directly to the question where employees were asked to rate the three owners' performance on a scale of 1 to 10.

A zero. The employee had scrawled in a big, fat zero. "Find out whose handwriting this is," he told his partner, Richard Laibson.

He ripped open another: zero again. And another. A two. "We'll fire these people," Dunn said to Laibson coldly. Another zero.

A one.

"Oh, go work for somebody else, you jerk!" Dunn shouted.

Soon he had moved to fire 10 of his 230 employees. "Plenty of people seemed to hate my guts," he says.

Over the next day, though, Dunn's anger subsided. "You think, I've done all this for these people and they think I'm a total jerk who doesn't care about them," he says. "Finally, you have to look in the mirror and think, 'Maybe they're right.'"

For Dunn, that realization was absolutely shattering. He had started the company three years earlier out of frustration over all the abuse he had suffered while working at big restaurant chains. If Dunn had one overriding mission at McGuffey's, it was to prove that restaurants didn't have to mistreat their employees.

He thought he had succeeded. Until he opened those surveys, he had believed that McGuffey's was a place where employees felt valued, involved, and appreciated. "I had no idea we were treating people so badly," he says. Somewhere along the way, in the day-to-day running of the business, he had lost his connection with them and left behind the employee-oriented company he thought he was running.

Dunn's 13-year odyssey through some big restaurant chains left him feeling as limp as a cheeseburger after a day under the heat lamps. Ponderosa in Georgia. Bennigan's in Florida and Tennessee. TGI Friday's in Texas, Tennessee, and Indiana. Within one six-month period at Friday's, he got two promotions, two bonuses, and two raises; then his boss left, and he got fired. That did it. Dunn was fed up with big chains.

At the age of 29, he returned to Atlanta, where he had attended Emory University as an undergraduate and where he began waiting tables at a local restaurant.

There he met David Lynn, the general manager of the restaurant, a similarly jaded 29-year-old who, by his own admission, had "begun to lose faith." Lynn and Dunn started hatching plans to open their own place, where employees would enjoy working as much as customers enjoyed eating. They planned to target the smaller markets that the chains ignored. With financing from a friend, they opened McGuffey's.

True to their people-oriented goals, the partners tried to make employees feel more appreciated than they themselves had felt at the chains. They gave them a free drink and a meal at the end of every shift, let them give away appetizers and desserts, and provided them a week of paid vacation each year.

A special camaraderie developed among the employees. After all, they worked in an industry in which a turnover rate of 250 percent was something to aspire to. The night before McGuffey's opened, some 75 employees encircled the ficus tree next to the bar, joined hands, and prayed silently for two minutes. "The tree had a special energy," says Dunn.

Maybe so. By the third night of operation, the 230-seat McGuffey's had a waiting list. The dining room was so crowded that after three months the owners decided to add a 58-seat patio. Then they had to rearrange the kitchen to handle the volume. In its first three and a half months, McGuffey's racked up sales of about $415,000, ending the year just over $110,000 in the red, mostly because the partners paid back the bulk of their $162,000 debt right away.

Word of the restaurant's success reached Hendersonville, North Carolina, a town of 30,000 about 20 miles away. The managing agent of a mall there—*the* mall there— even stopped by to recruit the partners. They made some audacious requests, asking him to spend $300,000 on renovations, including the addition of a patio and upgraded equipment. The agent agreed. With almost no market research, they opened the second McGuffey's 18 months later. The first, in Asheville, was still roaring, having broken the $2 million mark in sales its first year, with a marginal loss of just over $16,000.

By midsummer, the 200-seat Hendersonville restaurant was hauling in $35,000 a week. "Gee, you guys must be getting rich," the partners heard all around town. "When are you going to buy your own jets?" "Everyone was telling us we could do no wrong," says Dunn. The Asheville restaurant, though, was developing some problems. Right after the Hendersonville McGuffey's opened, sales at Asheville fell 15 percent. But the partners shrugged it off; some Asheville customers lived closer to Hendersonville, so one restaurant was probably pulling some of the other's customers. Either way, the customers were still there. "We're just spreading our market a little thinner," Dunn told his partners. When Asheville had lost another 10 percent and Hendersonville 5 percent, Dunn blamed the fact that the drinking age had been raised to 21 in Asheville, cutting into liquor sales.

By the end of that year, the company recorded nearly $3.5 million in sales, with nominal losses of about $95,000. But the adulation and the expectation of big money and fancy cars were beginning to cloud the real reason they had started the business. "McGuffey's was born purely out of frustration," says Dunn. Now, the frustration was gone. "You get pulled in so many directions that you just lose touch," says Laibson. "There are things that you simply forget."

What the partners forgot, in the warm flush of success, were their roots.

"Success breeds ego," says Dunn, "and ego breeds contempt." He would come back from trade shows or real-estate meetings all pumped up. "Isn't this exciting?" he'd ask an employee. "We're going to open a new restaurant next year." When the employee stared back blankly, Dunn felt resentful. "I didn't understand why they weren't thrilled," he says. He didn't see that while his world was constantly growing and expanding, his employees' world was sliding downhill. They were still busing tables or cooking burgers and thinking, "Forget the new restaurant; you haven't said hello to me in months; and by the way, why don't you fix the tea machine?"

"I just got too good, and too busy, to do orientation," he says. So he decided to tape orientation sessions for new employees, to make a film just like the one he had been subjected to when he worked at Bennigan's. On tape, Dunn told new employees one of his favorite stories, the one about the customer who walks into a chain restaurant and finds himself asking questions of a hostess sign because he can't find a human. The moral: "McGuffey's will never be so impersonal as to make people talk to a sign." A film maybe, but never a sign.

Since Dunn wasn't around the restaurants all that much, he didn't notice that employees were leaving in droves. Even the departure of Tom Valdez, the kitchen manager in Asheville, wasn't enough to take the shine off his "glowing ego," as he calls it.

Valdez had worked as Dunn's kitchen manager at TGI Friday's. When the Hendersonville McGuffey's was opening up, Dunn recruited him as kitchen manager. A few months later, Valdez marched into Dunn's office and announced that he was heading back to Indianapolis. "There's too much b.s. around here," he blurted out. "You don't care about your people." Dunn was shocked. "As soon as we get this next restaurant opened, we'll make things the way they used to be," he replied. But Valdez wouldn't budge. "Keith," he said bitterly, "you are turning out to be like all the other companies." Dunn shrugged. "We're a big company, and we've got to do big-company things," he replied.

Valdez walked out, slamming the door. Dunn still didn't understand that he had begun imitating the very companies that he had so loathed. He stopped wanting to rebel against them; under the intense pressure of growing a company, he just wanted to master their tried-and-true methods. "I was allowing the company to become like the companies we hated because I thought it was inevitable," he says.

Three months later, McGuffey's two top managers announced that they were moving to the West Coast to start their own company. Dunn beamed, "Our employees learn so much," he would boast, "that they are ready to start their own restaurants."

Before they left, Dunn sat down with them in the classroom at Hendersonville. "So," he asked casually, "how do you think we could run the place better?" Three hours later, he was still listening. "The McGuffey's we fell in love with just doesn't exist anymore," one of them concluded sadly.

Dunn was outraged. How could his employees be so ungrateful? Couldn't they see how everybody was sharing the success? Who had given them health insurance as soon as the partners could afford it? Who had given them dental insurance this year? And who—not that anyone would appreciate it—planned to set up profit sharing next year?

Sales at both restaurants were still dwindling. This time, there were no changes in the liquor laws or new restaurants to blame. With employees feeling ignored, resentful, and abandoned, the rest rooms didn't get scrubbed as thoroughly, the food didn't arrive quite as piping hot, the servers didn't smile so often. But the owners, wrapped up in themselves, couldn't see it. They were mystified. "It began to seem like what made our company great had somehow gotten lost," says Laibson.

Shaken by all the recent defections, Dunn needed a boost of confidence. So he sent out the one-page survey, which asked employees to rate the owners' performance. He was crushed by the results. Out of curiosity, Dunn later turned to an assistant and asked a favor. Can you calculate our turnover rate? Came the reply: "220 percent, sir."

Keith Dunn figured he would consult the management gurus through their books, tapes, and speeches. "You want people-oriented management?" he thought. "Fine. I'll give it to you."

Dunn and Laibson had spent a few months visiting 23 of the best restaurants in the Southeast. Driving for hours, they'd listen to tapes on management, stop them at key points, and ask, "Why don't we do something like this?" At night, they read management books, underlining significant passages, looking for answers.

"They were all saying that people is where it's at," says Dunn. "We've got to start thinking of our people as an asset," they decided. "And we've got to increase the value of that asset." Dunn was excited by the prospect of forming McGuffey's into the shape of a reverse pyramid, with employees on top. Keeping employees, he now knew, meant keeping employees involved.

He heard one consultant suggest that smart companies keep managers involved by tying their compensation to their performance. McGuffey's had been handing managers goals every quarter; if they hit half the goals, they pocketed half their bonus. Sound reasonable? No, preached the consultant, you can't reward managers for a halfhearted job. It has to be all or nothing. "From now on," Dunn told his managers firmly, "there's no halfway."

Dunn also launched a contest for employees. Competition, he had read, was a good way of keeping employees motivated.

So the CUDA (Customer Undeniably Deserves Attention) contest was born. At Hendersonville and Asheville, he divided the employees into six teams. The winning team would win $1,000, based on talking to customers, keeping the restaurant clean, and collecting special tokens for extra work beyond the call of duty.

Employees came in every morning, donned their colors, and dug in for battle. Within a few weeks, two teams pulled out in front. Managers also seemed revitalized. To Dunn, it seemed like they would do anything, anything, to keep their food costs down, their sales up, their profit margins in line. This was just what all the high-priced consultants had promised.

But after about six months, only one store's managers seemed capable of winning those all-or-nothing bonuses. At managers' meetings and reviews, Dunn started hearing grumblings. "How come your labor costs are so out of whack?" he'd ask. "Heck, I can't win the bonus anyway," a manager would answer, "so why try?" "Look, Keith," another would say, "I haven't seen a bonus in so long, I've forgotten what they look like." Some managers wanted the bonus so badly that they worked understaffed, didn't fix equipment, and ran short on supplies.

The CUDA contest deteriorated into jealousy and malaise. Three teams lagged far behind after the first month or so. Within those teams people were bickering and complaining all the time: "We can't win, so what's the use?" The contest, Dunn couldn't help but notice, seemed to be having a reverse effect than the one he had intended. "Some people were really killing themselves," he says. About 12, to be exact. The other 100-plus were utterly demoralized.

Dunn was angry. These were the same employees who, after all, had claimed he wasn't doing enough for them. But OK, he wanted to hear what they had to say. "Get feedback," the management gurus preached; "find out what your employees think." Dunn announced that the owners would hold informal rap sessions once a month.

"This is your time to talk," Dunn told the employees who showed up—all three of them. That's how it was most times, with three to five employees in attendance, and the owners dragging others away from their jobs in the kitchen. Nothing was sinking in, and Dunn knew it. He now was clear about what didn't work. He just needed to become clear about what would work.

SOURCE: *Inc: The Magazine for Growing Companies by J. Hyatt. Copyright 1989 by Mansueto Ventures LLC. Reproduced with permission of Mansueto Ventures LLC in the format CD-ROM via Copyright Clearance Center.*

PRACTICE

Creative Problem-Solving Practice

In a team of colleagues, apply as many of the creative problem-solving tools as you can in developing alternative solutions to any of the following problems. Different teams may take different problems and then report their solutions to the entire class. You may substitute a current pressing issue you are facing instead of one of these problems if you choose. Try consciously to break through your conceptual blocks and apply the hints that can help you expand your problem definition and the alternatives you consider to be relevant. Keep in mind the four different approaches to creativity.

Problem 1: Consumers now have access to hundreds of television channels and thousands of shows on demand. The average person is lost. Without major advertising dollars, many networks, not to mention many programs, simply get ignored. How could you address this problem?

Problem 2: At least 20 different rankings of schools appear periodically in the modern press. Students are attracted to schools that receive high rankings, and resources tend to flow to the top schools more than to the bottom schools. What could be done to affect the rankings of your own school?

Problem 3: In the last five years, Virgin Atlantic Airlines has been growing at double digit rates while most U.S.-based airlines have struggled to make any money at all. What could the U.S. airline industry do to turn itself around?

Problem 4: The newspaper industry has been slowly declining over the past several decades. People rely less and less on newspapers to obtain the news. What could be done to reverse this trend?

Have a team of observers watch the analytical and creative problem-solving process as it unfolds. Use the Observers' forms at the end of the chapter to provide feedback to the individuals and the teams on the basis of how well they applied the analytical and creative problem-solving techniques.

SKILL **APPLICATION**

ACTIVITIES FOR SOLVING PROBLEMS CREATIVELY

Suggested Assignments

3.11. Teach someone else how to solve problems creatively. Explain the guidelines and give examples from your own experience. Record everything in your journal.

3.12. Think of a problem that is important to you right now for which there is not an obvious solution. It may relate to your family, your classroom experiences, your work situation, or some interpersonal relationship. Use the principles and techniques discussed in the chapter to work out a creative solution to that problem. Spend the time it takes to do a good job, even if several days are required. Describe the experience in your journal.

3.13. Help direct a group (your family, roommates, social club, church, etc.) in a carefully crafted analytical problem-solving process—or a creative problem-solving exercise—using techniques discussed in the chapter. Record your experience in your journal.

3.14. Write a letter to your dean or a CEO of a firm identifying solutions to some perplexing problem facing his or her organization right now. Write about an issue that you care about. Be sure to offer suggested solutions. This will require that you apply in advance the principles of problem solving discussed in the chapter.

Application Plan and Evaluation

The intent of this exercise is to help you apply this cluster of skills in a real-life, out-of-class setting. Now that you have become familiar with the behavioral guidelines that form the basis of effective skill performance, you will improve most by trying out those guidelines in an everyday context. Unlike a classroom activity, in which feedback is immediate and others can assist you with their evaluations, this skill application activity is one you must accomplish and evaluate on your own. There are two parts to this activity: Part 1 helps prepare you to apply the skill, and Part 2 helps you evaluate and improve on your experience. Be sure to write down answers to each item. Don't short-circuit the process by skipping steps.

Part 1: Planning

3.15. Write down the two or three aspects of this skill that are most important to you. These may be areas of weakness, areas you most want to improve, or areas that are most salient to a problem you face right now. Identify the specific aspects of this skill that you want to apply.

3.16. Now identify the setting or the situation in which you will apply this skill. Establish a plan for performance by actually writing down a description of the situation. Who else will be involved? When will you do it? Where will it be done?

> Circumstances:
> Who else?
> When?
> Where?

3.17. Identify the specific behaviors in which you will engage to apply this skill. Operationalize your skill performance.

3.18. What are the indicators of successful performance? How will you know you have been effective? What will indicate you have performed competently?

Part 2: Evaluation

3.19. After you have completed your implementation, record the results. What happened? How successful were you? What was the effect on others?

3.20. How can you improve? What modifications can you make next time? What will you do differently in a similar situation in the future?

3.21. Looking back on your whole skill practice and application experience, what have you learned? What has been surprising? In what ways might this experience help you in the long term?

SCORING KEYS AND COMPARISON DATA

✪ Scoring Keys for the following instrument, along with comparison data, are contained in PIA in MyManagementLab.com;

Problem Solving, Creativity, & Innovation

How Creative Are You?©

Scoring Key

Circle and add up the values assigned to each item below.

ITEM	A. AGREE	B. UNDECIDED/ DON'T KNOW	C. DISAGREE
1	0	1	2
2	0	1	2
3	4	1	0
4	−2	0	3
5	2	1	0
6	−1	0	3
7	3	0	−1
8	0	1	2
9	3	0	−1
10	1	0	3
11	4	1	0
12	3	0	−1
13	2	1	0
14	4	0	−2
15	−1	0	2
16	2	1	0
17	0	1	2
18	3	0	−1
19	0	1	2
20	0	1	2
21	0	1	2
22	3	0	−1

Item	A. Agree	B. Undecided/ Don't Know	C. Disagree
23	0	1	2
24	−1	0	2
25	0	1	3
26	−1	0	2
27	2	1	0
28	2	0	−1
29	0	1	2
30	−2	0	3
31	0	1	2
32	0	1	2
33	3	0	−1
34	−1	0	2
35	0	1	2
36	1	2	3
37	2	1	0
38	0	1	2
39	−1	0	2

40. These words have values of 2:

energetic	perceptive
resourceful	innovative
original	self-demanding
enthusiastic	persevering
dynamic	dedicated
flexible	courageous
observant	curious
independent	involved

These words have values of 1:

self-confident	informal
thorough	alert
restless	forward-looking
	open-minded

The remaining words have a value of 0.

Total Score _____

Comparison Data (N = 5,000 students)

Total Score	Mean	Bottom Quartile	Second Quartile	Third Quartile	Top Quartile
	55.99	47 or below	48–55	56–65	66 or above

Innovative Attitude Scale

Comparison Data (N = 5,000 students)

Total Score	Mean	Bottom Quartile	Second Quartile	Third Quartile	Top Quartile
	36	32 or below	33–35	36–38	39 or above

Creative Style Assessment

Scoring Key

Add up the points you gave to all of the "A" alternatives, the "B" alternatives, the "C" alternatives, and the "D" alternatives. Then divide by 7 to get an average score for each of the alternatives. Plot your score on the profile below, connecting the lines so that you produce some kind of kite-like shape.

Total of As: _____/7   Average score for A: _____ Imagine
Total of Bs: _____/7   Average score for B: _____ Incubate
Total of Cs: _____/7   Average score for C: _____ Invest
Total of Ds: _____/7   Average score for D: _____ Improve

Comparison Data (N = 5,000 students)

DIMENSION SCORES (AVERAGES)	MEAN	FIRST QUARTILE	SECOND QUARTILE	THIRD QUARTILE	FOURTH QUARTILE
Imagination	24.70	20 or below	20.01–24.29	24.30–29.29	29.30 or above
Incubation	25.92	21.43 or below	21.44–25.71	25.72–29.99	30 or above
Investment	25.47	20.71 or below	20.72–25.71	25.72–29.99	30 or above
Improvement	24.04	18.57 or below	18.58–23.99	23.30–28.57	28.58 or above

Part II

Interpersonal Skills

CHAPTERS

4   **BUILDING RELATIONSHIPS BY COMMUNICATING SUPPORTIVELY**
Coaching
Counseling
Listening

5   **GAINING POWER AND INFLUENCE**
Gaining power
Exercising influence
Increasing authority

6   **MOTIVATING OTHERS**
Diagnosing poor performance
Creating a motivating environment
Rewarding accomplishments

7   **MANAGING CONFLICT**
Identifying sources
Selecting strategies
Resolving confrontations

SKILL ASSESSMENT

- Communicating Supportively
- Communication Styles

SKILL LEARNING

- Building Positive Interpersonal Relationships
- The Importance of Effective Communication
- What Is Supportive Communication?
- Coaching and Counseling
- Principles of Supportive Communication
- The Personal Management Interview
- International Caveats
- Summary
- Behavioral Guidelines

SKILL ANALYSIS

- Find Somebody Else
- Rejected Plans

SKILL PRACTICE

- United Chemical Company
- Byron vs. Thomas
- Active Listening Exercise

SKILL APPLICATION

- Suggested Assignments
- Application Plan and Evaluation

SCORING KEYS AND COMPARISON DATA

MyManagementLab™

When you see this icon, visit www.mymanagementlab.com for self-assessments, video activities, and more.

4

Building Relationships by Communicating Supportively

LEARNING OBJECTIVES

1. BUILD SUPPORTIVE RELATIONSHIPS EVEN WHEN DELIVERING NEGATIVE FEEDBACK

2. AVOID DEFENSIVENESS AND DISCONFIRMATION IN INTERPERSONAL COMMUNICATION

3. IMPROVE ABILITY TO APPLY PRINCIPLES OF SUPPORTIVE COMMUNICATION

4. IMPROVE RELATIONSHIPS BY USING PERSONAL MANAGEMENT INTERVIEWS

189

DIAGNOSTIC SURVEYS FOR SUPPORTIVE COMMUNICATION

⭐ If your instructor is utilizing **MyManagementLab**, log onto mymanagementlab.com and select the Personal Inventory Assessment (PIA) section and complete the instruments associated with this chapter.

P I A
PERSONAL INVENTORY ASSESSMENT

The assessment instruments in this chapter are briefly described below. The assessments appear either in your text or in PIA. The assessments marked with (blue star) are available only in PIA.

All assessments should be completed before reading the chapter material.

After completing the first assessment save your response to your hard drive. When you have finished reading the chapter, re-take the assessment and compare your responses to see what you have learned.

⭐ ❏ The *Communicating Supportively Assessment* measures the extent to which you demonstrate supportive communication, especially when providing negative or corrective feedback.

⭐ ❏ The *Communication Styles Assessment* helps identify your dominant style of communicating when faced with problems or the need to provide assistance.

Building Positive Interpersonal Relationships

A great deal of research supports the idea that **positive interpersonal relationships** are a key to creating positive energy in people's lives (Baker, 2000; Dutton, 2003). When people experience positive interactions—even if they are just temporary encounters—they are elevated, revitalized, and enlivened. Positive relationships create positive energy. All of us have experienced people who give us energy—they are pleasant to be around, they lift us, and they help us flourish. We also have encountered people who have the reverse effect—we feel depleted, less alive, and emotionally exhausted when we interact with them. Such encounters are personally de-energizing.

The effects of positive relationships are much stronger and more long-lasting than just making people feel happy or uplifted, however. When individuals are able to build relationships that are positive and that create energy, important physiological, emotional, intellectual, and social consequences result. For example, people's physical well-being is significantly affected by their interpersonal relationships. Individuals in positive relationships recover from surgery twice as fast as those in conflicting or negative relationships. They have fewer incidences of cancer and fewer heart attacks, and they recover faster if they experience them. They contract fewer minor illnesses such as colds, flu, or headaches; they cope better with stress; and they actually have fewer accidents (i.e., being in the wrong place at the wrong time). As might be expected, they also have a longer life expectancy. These benefits occur because positive relationships actually strengthen the immune system, the cardiovascular system, and the hormonal system (Dutton, 2003; Heaphy & Dutton, 2008; Reis & Gable, 2003).

Positive relationships also help people perform better in tasks and at work, and learn more effectively. That is, positive relationships help people feel safe and secure, so individuals are more able to concentrate on the tasks at hand (Carmeli, Brueller, & Dutton, 2009). They are less distracted by feelings of anxiety, frustration, or uncertainty that accompany almost all relationships that are nonpositive. People are more inclined to seek information and resources from people who are positively energizing, and they are less likely to obtain what they need to succeed if it means interacting with energy-depleting people. The amount of information exchange, participation, and commitment with other people is significantly higher when relationships are positive, so productivity and success at work are also markedly higher (see Dutton, 2003; Dutton & Ragins, 2007), for a review of studies).

Positive emotions—such as joy, excitement, and interest—are a product of positive relationships, and these emotions actually expand people's mental capacities. Feelings of joy and excitement, for example, create a desire to act, to learn, and to contribute to others. Moreover, the amount of information people pay attention to, the breadth of data they can process, and the quality of the decisions and judgments they make are all enhanced in conditions in which positive relationships are present. People's intellectual capacities are actually broadened (mental acuity expands), they learn more and more efficiently, and they make fewer mental errors when experiencing positive relationships (Fredrickson, 2001, 2009).

Not surprisingly, the performance of organizations is also enhanced by the presence of positive relationships among employees. Positive relationships foster cooperation among people, so the things that get in the way of highly successful performance—such as conflict, disagreements, confusion and ambiguity, unproductive competition, anger, or personal offense—are minimized (Cameron, Mora, Leutscher, & Calarco, 2011). Employees are more loyal and committed to their work and to the organization when positive relationships exist, and information exchange, dialogue, and knowledge transfer are significantly enhanced. Creativity and innovation, as well as the ability of the system to adapt to change, are substantially higher when positive relationships characterize the workforce (Gittell, 2003; Gittell, Cameron, & Lim, 2006).

It is hard to find a reason why people would *not* want to build and enhance positive relationships with other human beings. Many advantages and very few liabilities are associated with positive interpersonal relationships. Creating such relationships sounds like a simple prescription, of course, but it is much easier said than done. It is not difficult to build positive relationships with people who are like us, to whom we are attracted, or who behave according to our expectations. But when we encounter people who are abrasive, who are not easy to like, or who make a lot of errors or blunders, building relationships is more difficult. In other words, building positive relationships in negative circumstances or with negative people requires special skill.

Arguably the most important skill in building and strengthening positive relationships is the ability to communicate with people in a way that enhances feelings of trust, openness, and support. In this chapter we focus on helping you develop and improve this skill.

Of course, all of us communicate constantly, and we all feel that we do a reasonably good job of it. We haven't gotten this far in life without being able to communicate effectively. On the other hand, in study after study, communication problems are identified as the single biggest impediment to positive relationships and positive performance in organizations (Carrell & Willmington, 1996; Thorton, 1966). We focus in this chapter on this most important skill that effective managers must possess: the ability to communicate supportively.

The Importance of Effective Communication

In an age of electronic communication, the most frequently used means of passing messages to other people is via electronic technology. Messages containing 140 or fewer characters dominate interpersonal interactions. Yet, surveys have consistently shown that the ability to effectively communicate face to face is the characteristic judged by managers to be most critical in determining promotability (see surveys reported by Brownell, 1986, 1990; Furnham, 2008; Goleman, 1998; Hargie, 1997; Randle, 1956; Steil, Barker, & Watson, 1983). In fact, the increasing reliance on electronic forms of communication (e.g., texting, Twitter) has been found to diminish competency in interpersonal communication (Nie, 2001).

Not surprisingly, the quality of communication between managers and their employees is also fairly low (Madlock, 2008; Schnake, Dumler, Cochran, & Barnett, 1990; Yrle, Hartman, & Galle, 2002), yet it is face-to-face, one-on-one communication that dominates all the other types in predicting managerial success. In a study of 88 organizations, both profit and nonprofit, Crocker (1978) found that, of 31 skills assessed, interpersonal communication skills, including listening, were rated as the most important.

At least 80 percent of a manager's waking hours are spent in verbal communication, so it is not surprising that serious attention has been given to a plethora of procedures to improve interpersonal communication. Scholars have written extensively on communicology, semantics, rhetoric, linguistics, cybernetics, syntactics, pragmatics, proxemics, and canalization; and thousands of books have been produced on the physics of the communication process—encoding, decoding, transmission, media, perception, reception, and noise. Similarly, volumes are available on effective public-speaking techniques, making formal presentations, and the processes of organizational communication. Most colleges and universities have academic departments dedicated to the field of speech communication; most business schools provide a business communication curriculum; and many organizations have public communication departments and intraorganizational communication specialists such as newsletter editors and speech writers.

Even with all this available information about the communication process and the dedicated resources in many organizations for fostering better communication, most managers still indicate that poor communication is their biggest problem (McNaughtan, 2012; Schnake et al., 1990). In a study of major manufacturing organizations undergoing large-scale changes, we asked two key questions: (1) What is your major problem in trying to get organizational changes implemented? and (2) What is the key factor that explains your past success in effectively managing organizational change? To both questions, a large majority of managers gave the same answer: communication.

Ironically, however, most individuals feel they are effective communicators. They tend to think that communication problems are a product of others' weaknesses, not their own, so motivation to improve is frequently low (Brownell, 1990; Carrell & Willmington, 1996; Cupach, & Spitzberg, 2007; Golen, 1990).

THE FOCUS ON ACCURACY

Much of the writing on interpersonal communication focuses on the *accuracy* of the information communicated. The emphasis is generally on making certain that messages are transmitted and received with little alteration or variation from original intent. In the English language, in particular, we face the danger of miscommunicating with one another merely because of the nature of our language. For example, Table 4.1 lists 22 examples of the same word whose meaning and pronunciation are completely different, depending on the circumstances. No wonder individuals from other cultures and languages have trouble communicating accurately in the United States.

This doesn't account, of course, for the large number of variations in English-language meaning throughout the world. For example, because in England a billion is a million million, whereas in the United States and Canada a billion is a thousand million, it is easy to see how misunderstanding can occur regarding financial performance. Similarly, in an American meeting, if you "table" a subject, you postpone its discussion. In a British meeting, to "table" a topic means to discuss it now.

Fortunately, much progress has been made recently in improving the transmission of accurate messages—that is, in improving their clarity and precision. Primarily through the development of a sophisticated information-based technology, major strides have been taken to enhance communication speed and accuracy in organizations. Computer networks with multimedia capabilities now enable members

Table 4.1	Inconsistent Pronunciations in the English Language

- We polish Polish furniture.
- He could lead if he would get the lead out.
- A farm can produce produce.
- The dump was so full it had to refuse refuse.
- The Iraqi soldiers decided to desert in the desert.
- The present is a good time to present the present.
- In the college band, a bass was painted on the head of a bass drum.
- The dove dove into the bushes.
- I did not object to that object.
- The insurance for the invalid was invalid.
- The bandage was wound around the wound.
- There was a row among the oarsmen about how to row.
- They were too close to the door to close it.
- The buck does funny things when the does are present.
- They sent a sewer down to stitch the tear in the sewer line.
- She shed a tear because of the tear in her skirt.
- To help with planting, the farmer taught his sow to sow.
- The wind was too strong to be able to wind the sail.
- After a number of Novocaine injections, my jaw got number.
- I had to subject the subject to a series of tests.
- How can I intimate this to my most intimate friend?
- I spent last evening evening out a pile of dirt.

of an organization to reliably transmit messages, documents, video images, and sound almost instantaneously anywhere in the world.

However, comparable progress has not occurred in the interpersonal aspects of communication. People still become offended at one another, make insulting statements, and communicate clumsily. Individuals still communicate in abrasive, insensitive, and unproductive ways. Rather than building and enhancing positive relationships, they damage relationships. More often than not, it is the interpersonal aspect of communication that stands in the way of effective message delivery rather than the inability to deliver accurate information (Cupach, & Spitzberg, 2007; Golen, 1990).

Ineffective communication may lead individuals to dislike each other, be offended by each other, lose confidence in each other, refuse to listen to each other, and disagree with each other, as well as cause a host of other interpersonal problems. These interpersonal problems, in turn, generally lead to restricted communication flow, inaccurate messages, and misinterpretations of meanings. Figure 4.1 summarizes this process.

To illustrate, consider the following situation. Latisha is introducing a new goal-setting program to the organization as a way to overcome some productivity problems. After Latisha's carefully prepared presentation in the management council meeting, Jose raises his hand. "In my opinion, this is a naive approach to solving our productivity issues. The considerations are much more complex than Latisha seems to realize. I don't think we should waste our time by pursuing this plan any further."

Jose's opinion may be justified, but the manner in which he delivers the message will probably eliminate any hope of its being dealt with objectively. Instead, Latisha will probably hear a message such as, "You're naive," "You're stupid," or "You're incompetent." Therefore, we wouldn't be surprised if Latisha's

response is defensive or even hostile. Any good feelings between the two have probably been jeopardized, and their communication will probably be reduced to self-image protection. The merits of the proposal will be smothered by personal defensiveness. Future communication between the two will probably be minimal and superficial.

What is Supportive Communication?

In this chapter, we focus on a kind of interpersonal communication that helps you communicate accurately and honestly, especially in difficult circumstances, without jeopardizing interpersonal relationships. It is not hard to communicate supportively—to express confidence, trust, and openness—when things are going well and when people are doing what you like. But when you have to correct someone else's behavior, when you have to deliver negative feedback, or when you have to point out shortcomings of another person, communicating in a way that builds and strengthens the relationship is more difficult.

This type of communication is called **supportive communication**. Supportive communication seeks to preserve or enhance a positive relationship between you and another person while still addressing a problem, giving negative feedback, or tackling a difficult issue. It allows you to communicate information to others that is not complimentary, or to resolve an uncomfortable issue with another person but, in the process, strengthen your relationship.

Supportive communication has eight attributes, which are summarized in Table 4.2. Later in the chapter, we expand on each attribute. When supportive communication is used, not only is a message delivered accurately, but the relationship between the two communicating parties is strengthened and enhanced by the interchange. Positive feelings and mutual respect

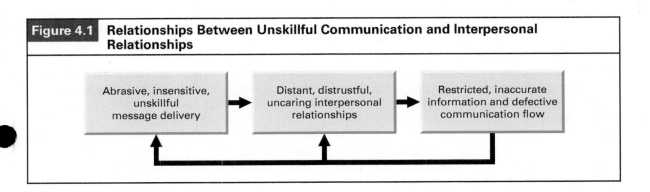

Figure 4.1 | **Relationships Between Unskillful Communication and Interpersonal Relationships**

Abrasive, insensitive, unskillful message delivery → Distant, distrustful, uncaring interpersonal relationships → Restricted, inaccurate information and defective communication flow

Table 4.2	The Eight Attributes of Supportive Communication		
• Congruent, Not Incongruent			
A focus on honest messages where verbal statements match thoughts and feelings			
Example: "Your behavior really upset me."		*Not*	*"Do I seem upset? No, everything's fine."*
• Descriptive, Not Evaluative			
A focus on describing an objective occurrence, describing your reaction to it, and offering a suggested alternative			
Example: "Here is what happened; here is my reaction; here." is a suggestion that would be more acceptable."		*Not*	*"You are wrong for doing what you did"*
• Problem-Oriented, Not Person-Oriented			
A focus on problems and issues that can be changed rather than people and their characteristics			
Example: "How can we solve this problem?"		*Not*	*"Because of you a problem exists."*
• Validating, Not Invalidating			
A focus on statements that communicate respect, flexibility, collaboration, and areas of agreement			
Example: "I have some ideas, but do you have any suggestions?"		*Not*	*"You wouldn't understand, so we'll do it my way."*
• Specific, Not Global			
A focus on specific events or behaviors and avoid general, extreme, or either-or statements			
Example: "You interrupted me three times during the meeting."		*Not*	*"You're always trying to get attention."*
• Conjunctive, Not Disjunctive			
A focus on statements that flow from what has been said previously and facilitate interaction			
Example: "Relating to what you just said, I'd like to raise another point."		*Not*	*"I want to say something (regardless of what you just said)."*
• Owned, Not Disowned			
A focus on taking responsibility for your own statements by using personal ("I") words			
Example: "I have decided to turn down your request because..."		*Not*	*"You have a pretty good idea, but it wouldn't get approved."*
• Supportive Listening, Not One-Way Listening			
A focus on using a variety of appropriate responses, with a bias toward reflective responses			
Example: "What do you think are the obstacles standing in the way of improvement?		*NOT*	*"As I said before, you make too many mistakes. You're just not performing."*

result. People feel energized and uplifted, even when the information being communicated is negative.

The goal of supportive communication is not merely to be liked by other people or to be judged to be a nice person, nor is it used to produce social acceptance. As pointed out previously, positive interpersonal relationships have practical, instrumental value in organizations. Researchers have found that organizations fostering supportive interpersonal relationships enjoy higher productivity, faster problem solving, higher-quality outputs, and fewer conflicts and subversive activities than groups and organizations in which relationships are less positive (Huselid, 1995; Stephens, Heaphy, & Dutton, 2012).

Moreover, delivering outstanding customer service is almost impossible without supportive communication. Customer complaints and misunderstandings frequently require supportive communication skills to resolve. Not only must managers be competent in using this kind of communication, but they must also help their subordinates develop this competency.

Hansen & Wernerfelt (1989) found, for example, that the presence of good interpersonal relationships between managers and subordinates was three times more powerful in predicting profitability in 40 major corporations over a five-year period than the four next most powerful variables—market share, capital intensity, firm size, and sales growth rate—combined. Supportive communication, therefore, isn't just a "nice-person technique," but a proven competitive advantage for both managers and organizations.

Coaching and Counseling

One of the ways to illustrate the principles of supportive communication is to discuss two common roles performed by managers, parents, friends, and coworkers: coaching and counseling others. In coaching, managers pass along advice and information, or they set standards to help others improve their skills and behaviors. In counseling, managers help others recognize and address problems involving their level of understanding, emotions, or perspectives. Thus, coaching focuses on abilities, counseling on attitudes.

The skills of coaching and counseling also apply to a broad array of activities, of course, such as motivating others, handling customer complaints, passing critical or negative information upward, handling conflicts between people, negotiating for a certain position, and so on. Because most of us are involved in coaching and counseling at some time, we will show you how they relate to supportive communication and strengthening interpersonal relationships.

Skillful coaching and counseling are especially important in (1) rewarding positive performance and (2) correcting problem behaviors or attitudes. Both of these activities are discussed in more detail in Chapter 6 on Motivating Others. In that chapter, we discuss the

content of rewarding and correcting behavior (i.e., *what* to do). Here, we focus on the *processes* of rewarding and correcting behavior (i.e., *how* to do it).

What makes coaching and counseling so challenging is the risk of offending or alienating other people when their attitudes or behaviors are inappropriate, disruptive, or harmful. That risk is so high that many managers ignore completely the feelings and reactions of others by taking a directive, hard-nosed, "shape up or ship out" approach. "You are wrong, and you will change or else." Alternatively, they soft-pedal, avoid confrontations, or merely drop hints for fear of hurting feelings and destroying relationships—the "don't worry, be happy" approach. "Well, it's not so bad." The principles we describe in this chapter not only facilitate accurate message delivery in sensitive situations, but their effective use can produce higher levels of motivation, increased productivity, and better interpersonal relationships.

COACHING AND COUNSELING ISSUES

Coaching situations are not the same as counseling situations, and the differences between the two are crucial for building strong, supportive relationships. To introduce the differences between coaching and counseling situations, consider the following two scenarios:

Jagdip Ahwal is the manager of the division sales force in your firm, which makes and sells components for the aerospace industry. He reports directly to you. Jagdip's division consistently misses its sales projections, its revenues per salesperson are below the firm average, and Jagdip's monthly reports are almost always late. You make another appointment to visit with Jagdip after getting the latest sales figures, but he isn't in his office when you arrive. His secretary tells you that one of Jagdip's sales managers dropped by a few minutes ago to complain that some employees are coming in late for work in the morning and taking extra-long coffee breaks. Jagdip had immediately gone with the manager to his sales department to give the salespeople a "pep talk" and to remind them of performance expectations. You wait for 15 minutes until he returns.

Betsy Christensen has an MBA from a prestigious Big Ten school and has recently joined your firm in the financial planning group. She came with great recommendations and credentials. However, she seems to be trying to enhance her own reputation at the expense of others in her group. You have heard increasing complaints lately that Betsy acts arrogantly, is self-promotional, and is openly critical of other group members' work. In your first conversation with her about her performance in the group, she denied that there is a problem. She said that, if anything, she was having a positive impact on the group by raising its standards. You schedule another meeting with Betsy after this latest set of complaints from her coworkers.

What are the basic problems in these two cases? Which one is primarily a coaching problem and which is primarily a counseling problem? How would you approach them so that the problems get solved and, at the same time, your relationships with Jagdip and Betsy are strengthened? What would you say, and how would you say it, so that the best possible outcomes result? This chapter can help you improve your skill in handling such situations effectively.

Although no situation is completely one thing versus the other, in the case with Jagdip Ahwal, the basic need is primarily for **coaching**. Coaching situations are those in which managers must pass along advice and information or set standards for others. People are advised on how to do their jobs better and to be coached to better performance. Coaching problems are usually caused by lack of ability, insufficient information and understanding, or incompetence on the part of individuals. In these cases, the accuracy of the information passed along by managers is important. The other person must understand clearly what the problem is and how to overcome it. Athletic coaches are prime examples.

In the Jagdip Ahwal case, Jagdip was accepting upward delegation from his subordinates, and he was not allowing them to solve their own problems. In Chapter 2 on Managing Stress and Well-Being, we learned that upward delegation is one of the major causes of ineffective time management. By not insisting that his subordinates bring recommendations for solutions to him instead of problems and by intervening directly in the problems of his subordinate's subordinates, Jagdip became overloaded himself. He didn't allow his subordinates to do their jobs. Productivity almost always suffers in cases in

which one person is trying to resolve all the problems and run the whole show. Jagdip needs to be coached regarding how to avoid upward delegation and how to delegate responsibility as well as authority effectively. Chapters 6 on Motivating Employees and Chapter 8 on Empowerment and Engagement provide guidelines for diagnosing the reasons for poor performance and for delegating effectively.

The Betsy Christensen case illustrates primarily a **counseling** problem. Managers need to counsel others instead of coach them when the problem stems from attitudes, personality, defensiveness, or other factors tied to emotions. Betsy's competency or skill is not a problem, but her unwillingness to recognize that a problem exists or that a change is needed requires counseling by the manager. Betsy is highly qualified for her position, so coaching or giving advice would not be a useful approach. Instead, an important goal of counseling is to help Betsy understand that a problem exists, that her attitude is of critical importance, and alternatives exist to address the problem.

Coaching applies to ability problems, and the manager's approach is, "I can help you do this better." Counseling applies to attitude problems, and the manager's approach is, "I can help you recognize that a problem exists."

Although many problems involve both coaching and counseling, it is important to recognize the difference between these two types of problems because a mismatch of problem with communication approach can aggravate, rather than resolve, a problem. Giving direction or advice (coaching) in a counseling situation often increases defensiveness or resistance to change.

For example, advising Betsy Christensen about how to do her job or focusing on the behaviors she should not be doing (such as criticizing others' work) will probably only magnify her defensiveness because she doesn't perceive that she has a problem. Similarly, counseling in a situation that calls for coaching simply side-steps the problem and doesn't resolve it. Jagdip Ahwal knows that a problem exists, for example, but he doesn't know how to resolve it. Coaching, not problem recognition, is needed.

The question that remains is, "How do I effectively coach or counsel another person? What behavioral guidelines help me perform effectively in these situations?" Both coaching and counseling rely on the same set of key supportive communication principles summarized in Table 4.1, which we'll now examine more closely.

Table 4.3	Two Major Obstacles to Effective Interpersonal Communication

Supportive communication engenders feelings of support, understanding, and helpfulness. It helps overcome the two main obstacles resulting from poor interpersonal communication:

Defensiveness

- One individual feels threatened or attacked as a result of the communication.
- Self-protection becomes paramount.
- Energy is spent on constructing a defense rather than on listening.
- Aggression, anger, competitiveness, and avoidance are common reactions.

Disconfirmation

- One individual feels incompetent, unworthy, or insignificant as a result of the communication.
- Attempts to reestablish self-worth take precedence.
- Energy is spent trying to portray self-importance rather than on listening.
- Showing off, self-centered behavior, withdrawal, and loss of motivation are common reactions.

DEFENSIVENESS AND DISCONFIRMATION

If principles of supportive communication are not followed when coaching or counseling subordinates, two major obstacles result that lead to a variety of negative outcomes (Brownell, 1986; Burleson, 2009; Cupach & Spitzberg, 2007; Czech & Forward, 2010; Gibb, 1961). These two obstacles are defensiveness and disconfirmation (see Table 4.3).

Defensiveness is an emotional and physical state in which a person is agitated, estranged, confused, and inclined to strike out (Gordon, 1988). Defensiveness arises when a person feels threatened or punished by the communication. If I feel that you are attacking me, I will defend myself. That is, self-protection becomes more important than listening, so defensiveness blocks both the message and the interpersonal relationship. Energy is spent on constructing a defense rather than on listening. Aggression, anger, competitiveness, or avoidance are common reactions.

The second obstacle, **disconfirmation**, occurs when people feel put down, ineffectual, or insignificant because of the communication. They feel that their self-worth is in question, so they feel unworthy or insignificant. They focus more on establishing self-worth and self-importance rather than listening. Reactions are often self-aggrandizing or show-off behaviors, loss of motivation, withdrawal, and loss of respect for the offending communicator.

The eight attributes of supportive communication, which we explain and illustrate in the following pages, serve as behavioral guidelines for overcoming defensiveness and disconfirmation in coaching and counseling. They are also guidelines for how to deliver negative feedback and critical messages in ways that build and strengthen relationships.

Principles of Supportive Communication

1. SUPPORTIVE COMMUNICATION IS BASED ON CONGRUENCE, NOT INCONGRUENCE

Most researchers and observers agree that the best interpersonal communications, and the best relationships, are based on **congruence**. That is, what is communicated, verbally and nonverbally, matches exactly what you are thinking and feeling (Dyer, 1972; Hyman, 1989; Knapp & Vangelisti, 1996; Rogers, 1961; Schnake et al., 1990). Congruence simply means being honest and authentic. It means communicating what you intend.

Two kinds of **incongruence** are possible: One is a mismatch between what you are experiencing and what you are aware of. For example, you may not even be aware that you are experiencing anger or hostility toward another person, even though the anger or hostility is really present. In severe cases, therapists are required to help individuals reach greater congruence between experience and awareness. People repress their deep seeded anger, sadness, or fear.

A second kind of incongruence, and the one more closely related to supportive communication, is a mismatch between what you think or feel and what you communicate. For example, you may be aware of feeling angry but be unwilling to admit that the feeling exists. People sometimes feel guilty about their thoughts or feelings, thinking them to be inappropriate or wrong.

When building interpersonal relationships, and when coaching and counseling others, genuine, honest, authentic statements are always better than artificial or dishonest statements. People who hold back their authentic feelings or opinions, or who don't express what's really on their minds, create the impression that a hidden agenda exists. Other people sense that there is something else not being said, or that an opinion or thought is not being expressed. Therefore, they trust the communicator less and focus on trying to figure out what the hidden message is, not on listening or trying to improve the relationship. The connection between the two communicators stays superficial and distrusting. So, unless communication is genuine, open, and respectful, and unless it is also *perceived* to be genuine, open, and respectful, false impressions and miscommunication result. Congruence is a prerequisite of trust, and trust lies at the heart of positive relationships.

Carl Rogers (1961) suggested that congruence in communication lies at the heart of "a general law of interpersonal relationships." After 40 years of clinical treatment of psychological problems in patients, Rogers concluded that this one law was the fundamental key to all positive relationships. Specifically, when people are congruent in their communication with their experience and awareness, the interpersonal relationship tends to be characterized by more trust, greater understanding, better psychological adjustment, and higher levels of satisfaction with the relationship. When incongruence is present, however, communication accuracy and satisfaction deteriorate, misunderstanding occurs more frequently, the relationship becomes unsatisfying, and psychological adjustment is low.

Congruence also relates to matching the content of the words spoken to the communicator's manner and tone of voice. "What a nice day" can mean the opposite if muttered sarcastically, or "I'm just trying to help" can mean something very different if said without sincerity.

Striving for congruence, being honest and open, or demonstrating authenticity does not mean, of course, that we should blow off steam immediately upon getting upset, nor does it mean that we cannot repress certain inappropriate feelings (e.g., keeping anger, disappointment, or aggression under wraps). Other principles of supportive communication must also be practiced, and achieving congruence at the expense of all other consideration is not productive.

On the other hand, in problematic interactions, when reactive feedback must be given, or when correcting someone else's behavior, we are more likely to express too little congruence than too much. This is because we are afraid to respond in a completely honest way, or we are not sure how to communicate congruently without being offensive. It is often a matter of not knowing *how* to be congruent. Saying exactly what we feel, of course, can sometimes offend the other person.

Consider the problem of a person who is not performing up to expectations and displays a nonchalant attitude even after having been given hints that your team's rating is being negatively affected. What could you say that will strengthen the relationship with this person and still resolve the problem? How can you express honest feelings and opinions and still remain nonjudgmental? How can you ever be completely honest without offending other people?

This is even more difficult when you consider how to respond supportively to someone who constantly has bad breath or displays poor manners while eating. The more personal or delicate the feedback, the more difficult it is to be completely congruent. This is why you must implement more than one principle of supportive communication.

2. SUPPORTIVE COMMUNICATION IS DESCRIPTIVE, NOT EVALUATIVE

Being congruent is very challenging in isolation—that is, without using other principles of supportive communication, you will probably not be effective. If your friend asks you, "How did I do?" and he or she didn't do so well, it is difficult to know how to respond honestly without being offensive. We worry about hurting other people's feelings, so the key is to separate descriptive from evaluative communication (Czech & Forward, 2013; Harvey & Harris, 2010).

Evaluative communication makes a judgment or places a label on other individuals or on their behavior: "You are doing it wrong." "You are incompetent." "You messed up." Such evaluation generally makes other people feel attacked or denigrated, and, consequently, to respond defensively. They see the communicator as judgmental. Examples of their responses might be: "I am *not* doing it wrong." "I am more capable than *you* are." "I might as well give up." Arguments, bad feelings, or emotional withdrawal lead to a deterioration in the interpersonal relationship.

The tendency to evaluate others is strongest when the issue is emotionally charged or when a person feels personally attacked. For example, it is more threatening to provide negative messages when others may be emotionally wounded, as when commenting on a sensitive or personally important issue. Sometimes people try to resolve their own bad feelings or anxieties by placing a label on others: "You are dumb" implies "Therefore, I am smart, so I feel better." Or, they may have such strong feelings that they want to punish the other person for violating their expectations or standards: "What you have done deserves to be punished. You have it coming." Most often, evaluations occur merely because people don't have any other alternatives in mind. They don't know how to be congruent without being judgmental or evaluating the other person.

The problem with evaluative communication is that it is likely to be self-perpetuating. Placing a label on someone else generally leads that person to place a label on you, which makes you defensive in return. When you are defensive and the other person is defensive, it's not hard to see why effective communication does not occur. Both the accuracy of the communication and quality of the relationship weaken. Arguments and accusations ensue.

An alternative to evaluation is **descriptive communication**. It is difficult to avoid evaluating other people without having an alternative strategy, so descriptive communication is designed to reduce the tendency to evaluate and to perpetuate a defensive interaction. It allows a person to be congruent and authentic as well as being helpful. Descriptive communication involves three steps, summarized in Table 4.4.

First, *describe objectively your observation of the event that occurred or the behavior that you think needs to be modified.* As objectively and dispassionately as possible, talk about *what* happened instead of about the person involved. Identify elements of the behavior that can be confirmed by someone else. Behavior should be compared to accepted standards rather than to personal opinions or preferences. Subjective impressions or attributions about the motives of another person should be avoided. The description, "You have finished fewer projects this month than anyone else in the division" or "I noticed that you made several comments in opposition to JR's proposal" can be confirmed by an objective record. They relate to the observed behaviors or to an objective standard, not to the motives or personal

---

Table 4.4	Descriptive Communication

Step 1: Describe objectively the event, behavior, or circumstance.

- Avoid accusations.
- Present data or evidence.

Example: Three clients have complained to me this month that you have not responded to their requests.

Step 2: Focus on the behavior and your reaction, not on the other person's attributes.

- Describe your reactions and feelings.
- Describe the objective consequences that have resulted or will result.

Example: I'm worried because each client has threatened to go elsewhere if we aren't more responsive.

Step 3: Focus on solutions.

- Avoid discussing who's right or wrong.
- Suggest an acceptable alternative.
- Be open to other alternatives.

Example: We need both to win back their confidence and to show them you are responsive. I suggest you offer to do a free analysis of their systems.

characteristics of the person. There is less likelihood of the other person feeling unfairly treated, since no evaluative label is placed on the behavior or the person. Describing a behavior, as opposed to evaluating a behavior, is relatively neutral.

Second, *describe your (or others') reactions to the behavior, or describe the consequences of the behavior.* Rather than projecting onto another person the cause of the problem, focus on the reactions or consequences the behavior has produced. This requires that you are aware of your own feelings and reactions and are able to describe them. Using one-word descriptions for feelings is often an effective method: "I'm concerned about our productivity." "Your level of accomplishment frustrates me." "I was very uncomfortable." Similarly, the consequences of the behavior can be pointed out: "Profits are off this month." "Department quality ratings are down." "Your comments resulted in other participants shutting down."

Describing feelings or consequences lessens the likelihood of defensiveness since the problem is framed in the context of your feelings or objective consequences, not the attributes of the other person. If those feelings or consequences are described in a nonaccusing way, then the focus can be on problem solving rather than on defending against evaluations. That is, if *I* am concerned, *you* have less of a reason to feel defensive.

Third, *suggest a more acceptable alternative.* This focuses the discussion on the suggested alternative, not on the person. It also helps the other person save face and avoid feeling personally criticized or denigrated. The individual is separated from the behavior. Self-esteem is preserved because it is the behavior—something controllable—not the person, that can be modified.

Of course, care should be taken not to give the message, "I don't like the way things are, so what are *you* going to do about it?" The change need not be the responsibility of only one of the communicating parties. Instead, the emphasis should be on finding a solution that is acceptable to both people, not on deciding who is right and who is wrong or who should change and who shouldn't. For example, "I suggest that you identify what it would take to complete six more projects than you did last month," "I would like to help you identify the things that are standing in the way of higher performance." "You might want to ask some questions to gather more information before making a final judgment."

One concern that is sometimes expressed regarding descriptive communication is that these steps may not work unless the other person knows the rules too. We have heard people say that if both people know about supportive communication, it works; otherwise, the person who doesn't want to be supportive can subvert any positive result.

For example, the other person might say, "I don't care how you feel," or "I have an excuse for what happened, so it's not my fault," or "It's too bad if this annoys you. I'm not going to change." How might you respond to these responses? Do you abandon principles of descriptive communication and become evaluative and defensive in return? Do you engage in the "Yes, you are." "No, I'm not." "Yes, you are." "No, I'm not." kind of argument?

An alternative exists. This display of lack of concern, or a defensive reaction, now becomes the priority problem. The problem of low performance, for example, will be very difficult to address as long as the more important interpersonal problem between you and the other person is blocking progress. In effect, the focus must shift from coaching to counseling, from focusing on ability to focusing on attitude. If two people cannot work on the problem together, no amount of communication about the consequences of poor performance will be productive. Instead, the focus of the communication should be shifted to the lack of concern in the relationship, or the obstacles that inhibit working together to improve performance. Staying focused on the problem, remaining congruent, and using descriptive language become critical.

So, you do not abandon the three steps. You simply switch the focus. You might respond, "I'm surprised to hear you say that you don't care how I feel about this problem (step 1). Your response is very disconcerting, and I think it might have important implications for the productivity of our team (step 2). I suggest we spend some time trying to identify the obstacles you feel are inhibiting our ability to work together on this problem (step 3)." "Or, I suggest that we ask a third party to help us resolve our differences in perspective."

It has been our experience that few individuals are completely recalcitrant regarding the desire to improve. Few are completely unwilling to work on problem solving when they believe that you have their interests at heart. Most people want to perform successfully, to be a part of a productive and satisfying team, and to be contributors. When you use supportive communication principles, not as manipulative devices but as genuine techniques to foster development and improvement, we have seldom found that people will not accept these genuine, authentic, congruent expressions. This applies to cultures all over the globe.

It is important to keep in mind that the steps of descriptive communication do not imply that one person should do all the changing. Frequently, a middle ground must be reached on which both individuals are satisfied (e.g., one person becomes more tolerant of deliberate work, and the other person becomes more conscious of trying to work faster). It is important to follow up these kinds of interaction sessions with discussions to monitor and clarify what was heard, what the reactions were, and whether progress is being made. A person's performance problems, for example, may stem from poor work habits developed over time. Such habits are not likely to change abruptly even if a coaching session goes especially well. Moreover, it is important to ensure that misinterpretation of the message or its intent did not occur after the fact. Reinforcing a sense of caring and genuine concern is an important follow-up step.

Sometimes, of course, it is necessary to make evaluative statements. When this is the case, the evaluations should be made in terms of an established criteria or standards (e.g., "Your behavior does not meet the prescribed standard"), some probable outcomes (e.g., "Continuation of your behavior will lead to worse consequences"), or some past successes by the same individual (e.g., "This behavior is not as good as your past behavior"). The important point is to avoid disconfirming the other person or arousing defensiveness.

3. SUPPORTIVE COMMUNICATION IS PROBLEM-ORIENTED, NOT PERSON-ORIENTED

Problem-oriented communication focuses on problems and solutions rather than on personal traits. Person-oriented communication focuses on the characteristics of the individual, not the event. "This is the problem" rather than "You are the problem" illustrates the difference between problem and person orientation. Problem-oriented communication is useful even when personal appraisals are called for because it focuses on behaviors and events. Person-oriented communication, on the other hand, often focuses on personal attributes that rarely can be changed or controlled, and it can send the message that the individual is inadequate.

Statements such as "You are dictatorial" and "You are insensitive" describe the person, while "I was left out of the decision making" and "Two people complained to me about the tone of the meeting" describe problems. Imputing motives is person-oriented ("It's because you want to control other people"), whereas describing overt behaviors is problem-oriented ("You made several sarcastic comments in the meeting today").

One problem with person-oriented communication is that, while most people can change their behavior, few can change their personalities. Because nothing can generally be done to accommodate person-oriented communication, it leads to a deterioration in the relationship rather than to problem solving.

Person-oriented messages often try to persuade the other individual that "this is how you should feel" or "this is what kind of person you are" (e.g., "You are an incompetent manager, a lazy worker, or an insensitive office mate"). But since most individuals accept themselves pretty much as they are, their common reaction to person-oriented communication is to defend themselves against it or reject it outright. Even when communication is positive (e.g., "You are a wonderful person"), it may not be viewed as trustworthy if it is not tied to a behavior or an accomplishment (e.g., "I think you are terrific because of the extra-mile service you rendered to our organization"). The absence of a meaningful referent is the key weakness in person-oriented communication.

In building positive, supportive relationships, problem-oriented communication should also be linked to accepted standards or expectations rather than to personal opinions. Personal opinions are more likely to be interpreted as person-oriented and arouse defensiveness than statements in which the behavior is compared to an accepted standard or performance. For example, the statement, "I don't like the way you dress" is an expression of a personal opinion and will probably create resistance, especially if the listener does not feel that your opinions are any more legitimate than his or her own. On the other hand, "Your dress is not in keeping with the company dress code," or "In this firm, everyone is expected to wear a tie to work," are comparisons to external standards that have some legitimacy. Feelings of defensiveness are less likely to arise since the problem, not the person, is being addressed. In addition, other people are more likely to support a statement based on a commonly accepted standard.

Supportive communicators need not avoid expressing personal opinions or feelings about the behavior or attitudes of others. When doing so, however, they should keep in mind the following additional principles.

4. SUPPORTIVE COMMUNICATION VALIDATES RATHER THAN INVALIDATES INDIVIDUALS

Validating communication helps people feel recognized, understood, accepted, and valued. Communication that is **invalidating** arouses negative feelings about self-worth, identity, and relationships to others. It denies the presence, uniqueness, or importance of other individuals (Ellis, 2004; Waller, Corstorphine, & Mountford, 2007). Barnlund's (1968) observation more than a quarter century ago is even more true today:

> People often do not take time, do not listen, do not try to understand, but interrupt, anticipate, criticize, or disregard what is said; in their own remarks they are frequently vague, inconsistent, verbose, insincere, or dogmatic. As a result, people often conclude conversations feeling more inadequate, more misunderstood, and more alienated than when they started. (p. 618)

Communication is invalidating when it denies the other person an opportunity to establish a mutually satisfying connection or when contributions cannot be made by both parties. When you don't allow the other to finish a sentence, adopt a competitive win-or-lose stance, send confusing messages, or disqualify the other person from making a contribution, communication is invalidating. You can invalidate people in four main ways: superiority, rigidity, indifference, and imperviousness (Brownell, 1986; Cupach & Spitzberg, 1994; Sieburg, 1978; Steil et al., 1983).

Communication that is superiority oriented gives the impression that you are informed while others are ignorant, adequate while others are inadequate, competent while others are incompetent, or powerful while others are impotent. It creates a barrier between you and the person to whom the message is sent. **Superiority-oriented communication** can take the form of put-downs, in which others are made to look bad so that you look good. Or it can take the form of "one-upmanship," in which you try to elevate yourself in the esteem of others. One form of one-upmanship is withholding information, either boastfully ("If you knew what I knew, you would feel differently") or coyly to trip people up ("If you had asked me, I could have told you how to avoid this mistake"). Boasting almost always makes others uncomfortable, mainly because it is designed to convey superiority.

Another common form of superiority-oriented communication is the use of jargon, acronyms, or words in such a way as to exclude others or to create barriers in a relationship. Doctors, lawyers, government employees, and many professionals are well known for their use of jargon or acronyms, designed to exclude others or to elevate themselves rather than to clarify a message. Speaking a foreign language in the presence of individuals who don't understand it may also be done to create the impression of exclusiveness or superiority. In most circumstances, using words or language that a listener can't understand is bad manners because it invalidates the other person.

Rigidity in communication is a second major type of invalidation: The communication is portrayed as absolute, unequivocal, or unquestionable. No other opinion or point of view could possibly be considered. Individuals who communicate in dogmatic, "know-it-all" ways often do so in order to minimize others' contributions or to invalidate others' perspectives.

It is possible to communicate rigidity, however, in ways other than just being dogmatic. Rigidity is also communicated by:

- ❏ Reinterpreting other viewpoints to conform to one's own
- ❏ Never saying, "I don't know," but having an answer for everything
- ❏ Appearing unwilling to tolerate criticisms or alternative points of view
- ❏ Reducing complex issues to overly-simplistic definitions or generalizations
- ❏ Placing exclamation points after statements so the impression is created that the statement is final, complete, or unqualified
- ❏ Resistance to receiving personal feedback

Indifference is communicated when the other person's existence or importance is not acknowledged. A person may do this by using silence, by making no verbal response to the other's statements, by avoiding eye contact or any facial expression, by interrupting the other person frequently, by using impersonal words ("people should not" instead of "you should not"), or by engaging in unrelated activity during a conversation. You appear not to care about the other person and give the impression of being impervious to the other person's feelings or perspectives. To be indifferent is to exclude others, to treat them as if they are not even present.

Imperviousness means that the communicator does not acknowledge the feelings or opinions of the other person. They are either labeled illegitimate—"You shouldn't feel that way" or "Your opinion is incorrect"—or they are labeled as ignorant—"You don't understand," "You've been misinformed," or (worse yet) "Your thinking is naive." Being impervious means to ignore or make unimportant the personal feelings or thoughts of another. It serves to exclude the other person's contribution to the conversation or the relationship, and it makes the other person feel illegitimate or unimportant.

Invalidation is even more destructive in interpersonal relationships than criticism or disagreement because criticism and disagreement do, in fact, validate the other person by recognizing that what was said or done is worthy of correction, response, or notice. As William James (1965) stated, "No more fiendish punishment could be devised, even were such a thing physically possible, than that one could be turned loose in a society and remain absolutely unnoticed by all the members thereof."

Validating communication, on the other hand, helps people feel recognized, understood, accepted, and valued. It has four attributes: It is *egalitarian, flexible, two-way*, and *based on agreement*.

Respectful, egalitarian communication (the opposite of superiority-oriented communication) is especially important when a person with a higher status interacts with a person of a lower status. When a hierarchical distinction exists between individuals, for example, it is easy for subordinates to feel invalidated since they have access to less power and information than their managers. Supportive communicators, however, help subordinates feel that they have a stake in identifying problems and resolving them by communicating an egalitarian stance. They treat others as worthwhile, competent, and insightful and emphasize joint problem solving rather than projecting a superior position. They can do this merely by asking for opinions, suggestions, and ideas. Even without hierarchical differences, however, communicating respectfully and in an egalitarian way is important. When people of different nationalities, ethnic groups, or genders are communicating, for example, some people are almost always vulnerable to feeling excluded or inferior. In those circumstances, egalitarian and inclusive statements are especially important in order to foster supportive relationships.

Flexibility in communication refers to your willingness to communicate that the other person may possess additional data and other alternatives that may make a contribution to the problem solution or to the relationship. It simply implies being receptive to other people. It means communicating genuine humility—not self-abasement or weakness—and a willingness to learn and to be open to new experience. It means remaining open to new insights. As Benjamin Disraeli noted, "To be conscious that you are ignorant is a first great step toward knowledge."

Perceptions and opinions are not presented as facts in flexible communication but are stated provisionally. No claim is made for the absolute truthfulness of opinions or assumptions. "I may be wrong, but..." is flexible. "I am right," is inflexible. Flexible communication conveys a willingness to enter into joint problem solving rather than to control the other person or to assume a master–teacher role. However, being flexible is not synonymous with being wishy-washy. "Gee, I can't make up my mind" is wishy-washy, whereas "I have my own opinions, but what do you think?" suggests flexibility.

Two-way communication is an implied result of respectfulness and flexibility. Individuals feel validated when they are asked questions, given "air time" to express their opinions, and encouraged to participate actively in the interpersonal interaction. Two-way interchange communicates the message that the other person is valued, which is a prerequisite for building collaboration and teamwork (see Chapter 9 on Building Effective Teams and Teamwork).

Your communication also validates another when it *identifies areas of agreement* and joint commitment. One way to express validation based on agreement is to identify positive behaviors, positive attitudes, and positive consequences. Almost all models of negotiation, teambuilding, and conflict resolution prescribe that you find areas of agreement upon which everyone can concur. Agreement makes progress possible. Similarly, highlighting positive factors also provides positive energy and a willingness to invest in the conversation.

Some examples of ways to positively validate others include pointing out important points made by the other person before pointing out trivial ones, areas of agreement before areas of disagreement, advantages of the other person's statements before disadvantages, compliments before criticisms, and positive next steps before past mistakes. The point is, validating other people helps create feelings of self-worth and self-confidence that can translate into self-motivation and improved performance. Positive relationships result. Invalidation, on the other hand, seldom produces such positive outcomes, yet it is a common form of response when people encounter something that they feel a need to criticize or correct.

LEARNING

5. SUPPORTIVE COMMUNICATION IS SPECIFIC (USEFUL), NOT GLOBAL (NONUSEFUL)

Specific statements are supportive because they identify something that can be easily understood and acted upon. In general, the more specific a statement is, the more effective it is in motivating improvement. For example, the statement "You have trouble managing your time" is too general to be useful, whereas "You spent an hour scheduling meetings today when that could have been done by your assistant" provides specific information that can serve as a basis for behavioral change. "Your communication needs to improve" is not nearly as useful as a more specific "In this role play exercise, you used evaluative statements 60 percent of the time and descriptive statements 10 percent of the time."

Specific statements avoid extremes and absolutes. The following are extreme or global (and nonuseful) statements that lead to defensiveness or disconfirmation:

A: "You never ask for my advice."
B: "Yes, I do. I always consult you before making a decision."

A: "You have no consideration for others' feelings."
B: "I do so. I am always considerate."

A: "This job stinks."
B: "You're wrong. It's a great job."

Another common type of global communication is the either–or statement, such as "You either do what I say or I'll fire you," "Life is either a daring adventure or nothing," (Helen Keller), and "If America doesn't reduce its national debt, our children will never achieve the standard of living we enjoy today."

The problem with extreme and either–or statements is that they deny any alternatives. The possible responses of the recipient of the communication are severely constrained. To contradict or deny the statement generally leads to defensiveness and arguments. A statement by Adolf Hitler in 1933 illustrates the point: "Everyone in Germany is a National Socialist; the few outside the party are either lunatics or idiots."

A friend of ours was asked to serve as a consultant to a labor and management committee in a company. As he entered the room and was introduced as a professor, the union president declared: "Either he goes or I go." What would you do in this situation? How would you use supportive communication when the union president has made a global statement that either excludes you or cancels the negotiations? Our friend's reply was, "I hope there are more alternatives than that. Why don't we explore them?" This response provided a way for communication to continue and for the possibility of a supportive relationship to be formed.

Specific statements are more useful in interpersonal relationships because they focus on behavioral events and indicate gradations in positions. More useful forms of the examples above are the following:

A: "You made that decision yesterday without asking for my advice."
B: "Yes, I did. While I generally like to get your opinion, I didn't think it was necessary in this case."

A: "By using sarcasm in your response to my request, you gave me the impression you don't care about my feelings."
B: "You are right. I know I am often sarcastic without thinking how it affects others."

A: "The pressure to meet deadlines often affects the quality of my work."
B: "Since deadlines are part of our work, let's discuss ways to manage the pressure."

Specific statements may not be useful if they focus on things over which another person has no control. "I hate it when it rains," for example, may relieve some personal frustration, but nothing can be done to change the weather. Similarly, communicating the message (even implicitly) "The sound of your voice (or your personality, your weight, your tastes, your ethnicity, etc.) bothers me" only proves frustrating for the interacting individuals. Such a statement is usually interpreted as a personal attack. The reaction is likely to be, "What can I do about that?" or "I don't even understand what you mean." Specific communication is useful to the extent that it focuses on an identifiable problem or behavior about which something can be done (e.g., "It bothers me when you talk so loudly in the library that it disturbs others' concentration").

Even when offering compliments to another person, being specific is better than being global or general. For example, providing positive feedback to someone by saying "You are a nice person" is not nearly as helpful as describing an incident or a behavior that created that impression; for example, "You seem to always smile when I see you, and you express interest in my work." Whereas both statements are pleasant to hear, the specific comment is much more helpful than the general comment.

6. SUPPORTIVE COMMUNICATION IS CONJUNCTIVE, NOT DISJUNCTIVE

Conjunctive communication is connected to previous messages in some way. It flows smoothly. **Disjunctive communication** is disconnected from what was stated before.

Communication can become disjunctive in at least three ways. First, there can be a lack of equal opportunity to speak. When you interrupt another, when you dominate by controlling "air time," or when two or more people try to speak at the same time, the communication is disjunctive. A smooth transition does not occur between one statement and the next.

Second, extended pauses are disjunctive. When you pause for long periods in the middle of your statements or when there are long pauses before responses, the communication is disjunctive. Pauses need not be total silence; the space may be filled with "umm," "aaah," or a repetition of something stated earlier, but the communication does not progress.

Third, topic control can be disjointed. When you decide unilaterally what the next topic of conversation will be (as opposed to having it decided bilaterally), the communication is disjunctive. You may switch topics, for example, with no reference to what was just said, or you may control the other person's communication topic by directing what should be responded to. Sieburg (1969) found that more than 25 percent of the statements made in small-group discussions failed to refer to or even acknowledge prior speakers or their statements.

These three factors—taking turns speaking, management of timing, and topic control—contribute to something called "interaction management." In an empirical study of perceived communication competence, Wiemann (1977, p. 104) found that "the smoother the management of the interaction, the more competent the communicator was perceived to be." People who took turns, who did not dominate with pauses or excessive air time, and who connected what they said to what others had said in the past were judged as competent communicators. In fact, interaction management was concluded to be the most powerful determinant of perceived communication

competence in his experimental study. Individuals who used conjunctive communication were rated as being significantly more competent in interpersonal communication than were those whose communication was disjunctive.

You can be conjunctive by asking questions based directly on a previous statement, by waiting for a sentence to be completed before beginning a response (e.g., not finishing a sentence for someone else), and by saying only three or four sentences at a time before pausing to give the other person a chance to add input. All of us have been in interactions in which one person goes on and on and on without allowing others to comment or contribute. Interaction, exchange, and give-and-take are necessary for supportive communication to occur. Figure 4.2 illustrates the continuum of conjunctive and disjunctive statements.

7. SUPPORTIVE COMMUNICATION IS OWNED, NOT DISOWNED

Taking responsibility for your statements and acknowledging that the source of the ideas is yourself and not another person or group is called **owned communication**. Using first-person words, such as "I," "me," "mine," indicates owned communication. **Disowned communication** is suggested when you use third-person or first-person-plural words: "We think," "They said," or "One might say." Disowned communication is attributed to an unknown person, group, or to some external source (e.g., "Lots of people think"). You avoid taking responsibility for the message and therefore avoid investing in the interaction. This may convey the message that you are aloof or uncaring about the other person or are not confident enough in your ideas to take responsibility for them. Having a trusting relationship is highly dependent on owned communication.

Glasser (1965, 2000) based his approach to mental health—reality therapy—on the concept of taking responsibility for, or owning, communication and behavior. According to Glasser, healthy people accept responsibility for their statements and behaviors. Unhealthy people attribute what they feel or say to someone or something else (e.g., "My being cranky isn't my fault because my roommate stayed up all night playing loud music"). One result of disowned communication is that the listener is never sure whose point of view the message represents: "How can I respond if I don't know to whom I am responding?" "If

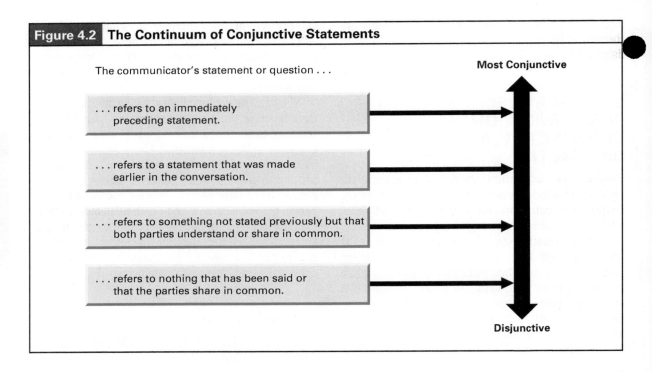

Figure 4.2 **The Continuum of Conjunctive Statements**

The communicator's statement or question . . .

. . . refers to an immediately preceding statement.

. . . refers to a statement that was made earlier in the conversation.

. . . refers to something not stated previously but that both parties understand or share in common.

. . . refers to nothing that has been said or that the parties share in common.

Most Conjunctive

Disjunctive

I don't understand the message, whom can I ask since the message represents someone else's point of view?"

Moreover, an implicit message associated with disowned communication is, "I want to keep distance between you and me." You communicate as a representative rather than as a person, as a message-conveyer rather than an interested individual. Owned communication, on the other hand, indicates a willingness to invest yourself in a relationship and to act as a colleague or helper.

This last point suggests that when you act as a coach or a counselor, you should encourage others to own their own statements. This can be done by example but also by asking the other person to restate disowning statements, as in this exchange:

> *SUBORDINATE: Everyone else says my work is fine.*
> *MANAGER: So no one besides me has ever expressed dissatisfaction with your work or suggested how to improve it?*
> *SUBORDINATE: Well...Mark complained that I took shortcuts and left him to clean up after me.*
> *MANAGER: Was his complaint fair?*
> *SUBORDINATE: Yeah, I guess so.*
> *MANAGER: What led you to take shortcuts?*
> *SUBORDINATE: My work was piling up, and*

> *I felt I had too much to do.*
> *MANAGER: Does this happen often, that your work builds up and you look for shortcuts?*
> *SUBORDINATE: More than I'd like.*

Here the manager has used conjunctive questions to guide the subordinate away from disowning responsibility toward acknowledging a behavior that may be affecting others' performance.

8. SUPPORTIVE COMMUNICATION REQUIRES SUPPORTIVE LISTENING, NOT ONE-WAY MESSAGE DELIVERY

The previous seven attributes of supportive communication all focus on message delivery, where you are the initiator of the communication. But another aspect of supportive communication—*listening and responding* effectively to someone else's statements—is at least as important as delivering supportive messages (Bodie, St. Cyr, Pence, Rold, & Honeycutt, 2012; Imhof & Janusik, 2006; Johnston, Reed, & Lawrence, 2011). As Maier, Solem, and Maier (1973, p. 311) stated: "In any conversation, the person who talks the most is the one who learns the least about the other person. The good supervisor therefore must become a good listener."

Nichols (2009) found that the older people get, the less effective they are at listening. In a study of listening effectiveness, 90 percent of first and second graders were found to be effective listeners, 44 percent in junior high school, and just 28 percent of high schoolers. Yet, Kramer (1997) found that good listening skills accounted for 40 percent of the variance in effective leadership. In a survey of personnel directors in 300 businesses and industries conducted to determine what skills are most important in becoming a manager, Crocker (1978) reported that effective listening was ranked highest. Similarly, people who are judged to be the most "wise," or to possess the attribute of wisdom—and, therefore, are the most sought-after people with whom to interact—were rated as the best listeners (Kramer, 2000; Sternberg, 1990).

Despite its importance in managerial success, however, and despite the fact that most people spend at least 45 percent of their communication time listening, most people have underdeveloped listening skills. Tests have shown, for example, that individuals are usually about 25 percent effective in listening; that is, they listen to and understand only about a fourth of what is being communicated (Bostrom, 1997; Huseman, Lahiff, & Hatfield, 1976). Geddie (1999) reported that in a survey across 15 countries, listening was found to be the poorest communication skill.

When individuals are preoccupied with meeting their own needs (e.g., saving face, persuading someone else, winning a point, avoiding getting involved), when they have already made a prior judgment, or when they hold negative attitudes toward the communicator or the message, they don't listen effectively. Because

a person listens at the rate of 500 words a minute but speaks at a normal rate of only 125 to 250 words a minute, the listener's mind can dwell on other things half the time. Therefore, being a good listener is neither easy nor automatic. It requires developing the ability to hear and understand the message sent by another person, while at the same time helping to strengthen the relationship between the interacting parties.

Responding

People do not know they are being listened to unless you make some type of response. This can be simple eye contact and nonverbal responsiveness such as smiles, nods, and eye contact. However, when you coach or counsel someone, you also must select carefully from a repertoire of verbal response alternatives which clarify the communication as well as strengthen the interpersonal relationship. The mark of a supportive listener is the ability to appropriately respond to others' statements (Bostrom, 1997).

The appropriateness of a response depends to some degree on whether the focus of the interaction is primarily coaching or counseling. Of course, seldom can these two activities be separated from one another completely—effective coaching often involves counseling and effective counseling sometimes involves coaching—and attentive listening involves the use of a variety of responses. Some responses, however, are more appropriate under certain circumstances than others.

Figure 4.3 lists four major response types and arranges them on a continuum from most directive

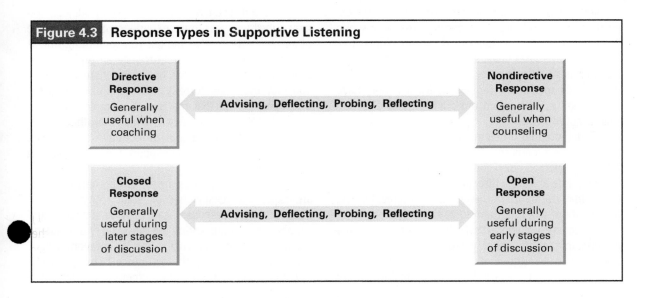

Figure 4.3   Response Types in Supportive Listening

| **Directive Response** Generally useful when coaching | ← Advising, Deflecting, Probing, Reflecting → | **Nondirective Response** Generally useful when counseling |

| **Closed Response** Generally useful during later stages of discussion | ← Advising, Deflecting, Probing, Reflecting → | **Open Response** Generally useful during early stages of discussion |

and closed to most nondirective and open. Closed responses eliminate discussion and provide direction to individuals. They represent methods by which the listener can control the topic of conversation. Open responses, on the other hand, allow the communicator, not the listener, to control the topic of conversation. Each of these response types has certain advantages and disadvantages, and none is appropriate all the time under all circumstances.

Most people get in the habit of relying heavily on one or two response types, and they use them regardless of the circumstances. On the average, about 80 percent of most people's responses have been found to be evaluative (Bostrom, 1997; Rogers, 1961). Supportive listening, however, avoids evaluation and judgment as a first response, and instead relies on flexibility in response types and the appropriate match of responses to circumstances. The four major types of responses are discussed below.

Advising

Assume that someone comes to you and says: "I am having a real problem with my friend, and I'm not sure how to handle it." An **advising response** provides direction, evaluation, personal opinion, or instructions. Such a response imposes on the other person your point of view, and it allows you to control the topic of conversation.

The advantages of an advising response are that it helps the other person understand something that may have been unclear before, it helps identify a problem solution, and it can provide clarity about how the other person should act or interpret the problem. It is most appropriate when you have expertise that the other person doesn't possess or when the other person is in need of direction. Supportive listening sometimes means that you do the talking, but this is usually appropriate only when advice or direction is specifically requested. Most people have a tendency to offer much more advice and direction than is appropriate.

Four potential problems are created by an advising response. One is that it can produce dependence. The other person may get used to having someone else generate answers, directions, or clarifications. He or she may not figure out issues and solutions for him or herself but delegate them to you.

A second problem is that advising may create the impression that the other person is not understood. Rogers (1961) found that most people, even when they seem to be asking for advice, mainly desire

understanding and acceptance, not advice. They want you to just understand and empathize, not take control. The problem with advising is that it removes the opportunity for the other person to stay focused on the issue. Advice shifts the control of the conversation away from the communicator.

A third problem with advising is that you tend to concentrate more on the legitimacy of your advice or your solutions than on simply listening attentively. When you are expected to generate advice and direction, you tend to focus more on your own experience than on the communicator's experience. It is difficult to simultaneously be a good listener and a good adviser.

A fourth potential problem with advising is that you can imply that the communicator doesn't have the necessary understanding, expertise, insight, or maturity to solve his or her own problem. You may give the impression that you think he or she needs help because of their incompetence.

Therefore, when advice is asked for or is an appropriate response, it should be communicated as your own opinion or experienced, but other alternatives may be available. Ask the other person for his or her perspective or for his or her reaction. This permits the person to accept or reject the advice without feeling an obligation that the advice has to be accepted, or that he or she is rejecting you.

Deflecting

A **deflecting response** switches the focus from the communicator's problem to one you select. You deflect attention away from the original problem or the original statement. You essentially changes the subject. You may substitute your own experience for that of the other person (e.g., "Let me tell you something similar that happened to me") or introduce an entirely new topic (e.g., "That reminds me of the time that...”). You may think the current problem is unclear to the other person and that the use of examples or analogies will help. Or, you may feel that the other person needs to be reassured that others have experienced the same problem and that support and understanding are available.

Deflecting responses are most appropriate when an expanded perspective or some reassurance is needed. These responses can provide empathy and support by communicating the message: "I understand because of what happened to me (or someone else)." They can also convey the assurance "Things will be fine. Others have also had this experience." Deflection is also often used to avoid embarrassing you or the other person. Changing the subject or answering a question other than the one asked are common occurrences when the problem discussed is uncomfortable or embarrassing.

The disadvantages of deflecting responses are that they can imply that the other person's problem is not important or that your experience is more significant than that of the other person. They may produce competitiveness or feelings that you are trying to one-up the other person. Deflection can be interpreted as, "My experience is more worthy of discussion than yours." Or it may simply change the subject from something that is important and central to the other person to a topic that is not as important. ("I want to talk about something important to me, but you changed the subject to your own experience.")

Deflecting responses are most effective when they are conjunctive—that is, when they are clearly connected to what the other person just said, when your response leads directly back to the other person's concerns, and when the reason for the deflection is made clear. That is, deflecting can produce desirable outcomes if the other person feels supported and understood, not invalidated, by the change in topic focus.

Probing

A **probing response** asks a question about what the other person just said or about the problem he or she has shared. The intent of a probe is to acquire additional information, to help the other person say more about the topic, to help you become more empathetic with more insight, or to help you develop more appropriate responses. For example, an effective way to avoid being evaluative and judgmental is to continue to ask questions. Questioning helps you adopt the other person's frame of reference so that in coaching situations suggestions can be specific (not global) and in counseling situations statements can be descriptive (not evaluative). Questions tend to be more neutral in tone than direct statements.

A study of top management team communication, for example, found that high-performing teams had a balance between inquiry (asking questions or probing) and advocacy (declaring or advocating a perspective). Questions and probes received equal time and emphasis in the team members' interactions. Low-performing teams were heavily oriented toward advocacy (i.e., telling, advising) and away from inquiry and probing (i.e., asking) (Losada & Heaphy, 2004).

Questioning, however, can sometimes have the unwelcome effect of switching the focus of attention from the other person's statement to the reasons behind it. The questions "Why do you think that way?" or "Why is this a problem for you?" for example, might pressure the other person to justify a feeling or a perception rather than just report it. Similarly, probing responses can serve to deflect attention away from the actual problem and toward a topic you want to discuss (e.g., "Instead of discussing your feelings about your job, tell me why you didn't respond to my memo"). Probing responses can also allow the other person to lose control of the conversation, especially when difficult subjects need to be addressed (e.g., "Why aren't you performing up to your potential?" allows all kinds of other issues to be raised that may or may not be apropos.)

Two important hints should be kept in mind to make probing responses more effective. One is that "why" questions are seldom as effective as "what" questions. "Why" questions lead to topic changes, escapes, and speculations more often than to valid information. For example, the question "Why do you feel that way?" can lead to off-the-wall statements such as "Because I am a redhead," or "Because my father was an alcoholic and my mother beat me," or "Because Dr. Phil said so." These are silly examples, but they illustrate how ineffective "why" questions can be. "What do you mean by that?" is likely to be more fruitful.

A second hint is to tailor the probes to fit the situation. You can use at least four types of probing responses. When the other person's statement does not contain enough information, or part of the message is not understood, an **elaboration probe** should be used (e.g., "Can you tell me more about that?"). When the message is not clear or is ambiguous, a **clarification probe** is best (e.g., "What do you mean by that?"). A **repetition probe** works best when the communicator is avoiding a topic, hasn't answered a previous question, or a previous statement is unclear (e.g., "Once again, what do you think about this?"). A **reflection probe** is most effective when the communicator is encouraged to keep pursuing the same topic in greater depth (e.g., "So, you are saying that you feel discouraged?"). Table 4.5 summarizes these four kinds of questions or probes.

Probing responses are especially effective in turning hostile or conflictive conversations into supportive conversations. Asking questions can often turn attacks into consensus, evaluations into descriptions, general statements into specific statements, disowned statements into owned statements, or person-focused

LEARNING

Table 4.5	**Four Types of Probing Responses**
TYPE OF PROBE	**EXPLANATION**
Elaboration	Use when more information is needed. ("Can you tell me more about that?")
Clarification	Use when the message is unclear or ambiguous. ("What do you mean by that?")
Repetition	Use when topic drift occurs or statements are unclear. ("Once again, what do you think about this?")
Reflection	Use to encourage more in-depth pursuit of the same topic. ("So, you are saying that you are having difficulty?")

declarations into problem-focused declarations. In other words, probes can often be used to help others use supportive communication when they have not been trained in advance to do so.

Reflecting

The primary purpose of the **reflecting response** is to mirror back to the communicator the message you heard and to communicate understanding and acceptance of the person. Reflecting the message *in different words* allows the speaker to feel listened to, understood, and free to explore the topic in more depth. Reflective responding involves paraphrasing and clarifying the message. Instead of simply mimicking the communication, you contribute meaning, understanding, and acceptance to the conversation while still allowing the other person to pursue topics of his or her choosing.

Athos and Gabarro (1978); Brownell (1986); Steil, Barker, and Watson (1983); Wolvin and Coakley (1988); and others argue that this response should be the most frequently used and is most typical in supportive communication. It should dominate especially in coaching and counseling situations. It leads to the clearest communication, the most two-way exchanges, and the most supportive relationships. For example:

SUPERVISOR: Jerry, I'd like to hear about any problems you've been having with your job over the last several weeks.
SUBORDINATE: Don't you think they ought to do something about the air conditioning in the office? It gets to be like an oven in here every afternoon! They said they were going to fix the system weeks ago!
SUPERVISOR: It sounds like the delay is really beginning to make you angry.

SUBORDINATE: It sure is! It's just terrible the way maintenance seems to being goofing off instead of being responsive.
SUPERVISOR: So it's frustrating... and discouraging.
SUBORDINATE: Amen. And by the way, there's something else I want to mention....

A potential disadvantage of reflective responses is that the other person may get the feeling that you do not understand, are not listening carefully, or are just mimicking what was just stated. If he or she keeps hearing reflections of what was just said, a response might be, "I just said that. Aren't you listening to me?" Reflective responses, in other words, can be perceived as an artificial "technique" or as a superficial response to a message.

Therefore, you should keep the following rules in mind when using reflective responses.

1. Avoid repeating the same response over and over, such as "So, you feel that...," "Are you saying that...?" or "What I heard you say was...."
2. Avoid mimicking the communicator's words. Instead, restate what you just heard in a way that helps ensure that you understand the message and the communicator knows that you understand.
3. Avoid an exchange in which you do not contribute equally to the conversation, but serve only as a mimic. (You can use understanding or reflective responses while still taking equal responsibility for the depth and meaning of the communication.)
4. Respond to the personal rather than the impersonal. Responding to individuals is always

more important than responding to circumstances or facts.

5. Respond to expressed feelings before responding to content. When a person expresses feelings, they are the most important part of the message. They may stand in the way of the ability to communicate clearly unless acknowledged.

6. Respond with empathy and acceptance. Avoid the extremes of complete objectivity, detachment, or distance on the one hand, or overidentification (accepting the feelings as your own) on the other.

7. Avoid expressing agreement or disagreement with the statements. Use listening responses to help the other person explore and analyze the problem. Later you can draw on this information to help fashion a solution.

The Personal Management Interview

Not only are the eight attributes of supportive communication effective in normal discourse and problem-solving situations, but they can be most effectively applied when specific interactions with subordinates are planned and conducted frequently. One important difference between effective and ineffective managers is the extent to which they provide their subordinates with opportunities to receive regular feedback, to feel supported and bolstered, and to be coached and counseled. Providing these opportunities is difficult, however, because of the tremendous time demands most managers face. Many managers want to coach, counsel, train, and develop subordinates, but they simply never find the time. Therefore, one important mechanism for applying supportive communication and for providing subordinates with development and feedback opportunities is to implement a **personal management interview (PMI) program**.

This program is probably the most frequently adopted tool that managers employ in the executive education programs we teach when they commit themselves to improving relationships with their subordinates and team members. We have received more feedback about the success of the PMI program than almost any other management improvement technique we have shared. It is a very simple and straightforward technique for implementing supportive communication and building positive relationships

in organizations as well as in family settings, community groups, church service, or athletic teams.

A PMI program is a regularly scheduled, one-on-one meeting between a manager and those for whom he or she is responsible. In a study of the performance of working departments and intact teams in a variety of organizations, Boss (1983) found that effectiveness increased significantly when managers conducted regular, private meetings with members on a biweekly or monthly basis. In a study of health care organizations holding these regular personal management interviews compared to those that did not, significant differences were found in organizational performance, employee performance and satisfaction, and personal stress management scores. The organizations that had instituted a PMI program were significantly higher performers on all the personal and organizational performance dimensions. Figure 4.4 compares the performance effectiveness of teams and departments that implemented the program versus those that did not.

Our own personal experience is also consistent with the empirical findings. We have conducted personal management interviews with individuals for whom we have responsibility in a variety of professional, community, and church organization settings. We also have conducted these sessions with our individual family members. Rather than being an imposition and an artificial means of communication, these sessions—held one-on-one with each child or each member of the unit—have been incredibly productive. Close bonds have resulted, open sharing of information and feelings has emerged, and the meetings themselves are eagerly anticipated by both us and those with whom we have conducted the PMI.

Instituting a PMI program consists of two steps. First, a *role-negotiation session* is held in which expectations, responsibilities, standards of evaluation, reporting relationships, and so on, are clarified. If possible, this meeting is held at the outset of the relationship or when you decide to begin a PMI process. Unless such a meeting is held, most individuals do not have a crystal clear idea of exactly what is expected of them or on what basis they will be evaluated. Most people have a clear idea of their job responsibilities from formal job descriptions, but the informal expectations, the interpersonal relationships, the values and culture, and the evaluation processes are usually not very clear. In a role-negotiation session, this uncertainty is addressed.

The manager and subordinate negotiate all job-related issues that are not prescribed by policy or by mandate. A written record is made of the agreements

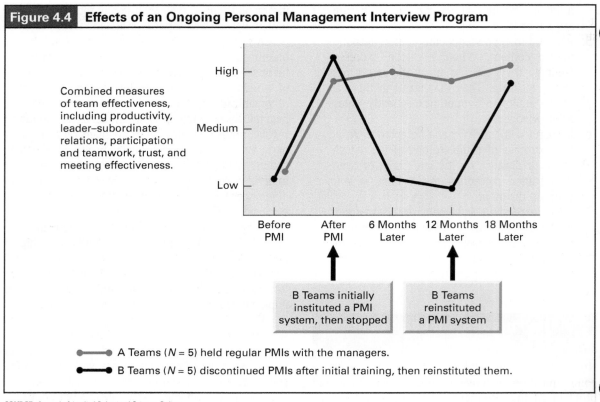

Figure 4.4 | **Effects of an Ongoing Personal Management Interview Program**

Combined measures of team effectiveness, including productivity, leader–subordinate relations, participation and teamwork, trust, and meeting effectiveness.

High
Medium
Low

Before PMI | After PMI | 6 Months Later | 12 Months Later | 18 Months Later

B Teams initially instituted a PMI system, then stopped

B Teams reinstituted a PMI system

A Teams (*N* = 5) held regular PMIs with the managers.

B Teams (*N* = 5) discontinued PMIs after initial training, then reinstituted them.

SOURCE: *Journal of Applied Behavioral Science*, Online.

and responsibilities that result from the meeting which can serve as an informal contract between the manager and the subordinate. The goal of a role-negotiation session is to obtain clarity regarding what each person expects from the other, what the goals and standards are, and what the ground rules for the relationship will be. Because this role negotiation is not adversarial but rather focuses on supportiveness and building a positive relationship, the eight supportive communication principles should always characterize the interaction.

When we hold PMIs in our families, these agreements often center on household chores, planned vacations, father–daughter or father–son activities, family rules, values, and so on. This role-negotiation session, to repeat, is simply a meeting to establish ground rules, spell out expectations, and clarify standards. It provides a foundation upon which the relationship can be built and helps foster better performance on the part of the manager as well as the subordinate.

The second, and most important, step in a PMI program is a set of ongoing, one-on-one meetings between the manager and each subordinate. These meetings are regular (not just when a mistake is made or a crisis arises) and private (not overheard by others). It is not a department staff meeting, a family gathering, or an end-of-the-day check-up. The meeting occurs one-on-one. We have never seen this program work when these meetings have been held less frequently than once per month—both in organizations and in families. Many times managers choose to hold them more frequently depending on the percent of their work and the time pressures they face.

This meeting provides each person with a chance to communicate freely, openly, and collaboratively. It also provides managers with the opportunity to coach and counsel subordinates and to help them improve their own skills or job performance. Therefore, each meeting lasts from 45 to 60 minutes and focuses on items such as the following: (1) managerial and organizational problems, (2) information sharing, (3) interpersonal issues, (4) obstacles to improvement, (5) training in management skills, (6) individual needs, (7) feedback on job performance and personal capabilities, and (8) personal concerns or problems.

This meeting is not just a time to sit and chat. It has two overarching, crucial objectives: (1) to foster improvement and (2) to strengthen relationships. If improvement does not occur as a result of the meeting, it is not being held correctly. If relationships are not strengthened over time, something is not working as it should. The meeting always leads toward action items to be accomplished before the next meeting, some by the subordinate and others by the manager. Those action items are reviewed at the end of the meeting and reviewed again at the beginning of the next meeting. Accountability is maintained for improvement.

This is not a meeting just to hold a meeting. Without agreements as to specific actions that will be taken, and the accountability that will be maintained, it can be a waste of both people's time. This means both parties prepare for the meeting, and both bring agenda items to be discussed. It is not a formal appraisal session called by the manager, but a development and improvement session in which both the manager and subordinate have a stake. It does not replace formal performance appraisal sessions, but it supplements them. The purposes of PMIs are not to conduct evaluation or performance appraisals. Rather, they provide a chance for subordinates to have personal time with the manager to work out issues, report information, receive coaching and counseling, and improve performance.

Consequently, these PMI sessions help eliminate unscheduled interruptions and long, inefficient group meetings. At each subsequent meeting, action items are reviewed from previous meetings, so that continuous improvement is encouraged. The PMIs, in other words, become an institutionalized continuous improvement activity. They are also a key to building the collaboration and teamwork needed in organizations. Table 4.6 summarizes the characteristics of the personal management interview program.

The major objection to holding these PMI sessions, of course, is lack of time. Most people think that they simply cannot impose on their schedules a group of one-on-one meetings with each of their team members, subordinates, or children. Boss' research (1983) found, however, that a variety of benefits resulted in teams that instituted this program. It not only increased their effectiveness, but it improved individual accountability, department meeting efficiency, and communication flows. Managers actually

Table 4.6	**Characteristics of a Personal Management Interview Program**

- The interview is regular and private.
- The major intent of the meeting is continuous improvement in personal, interpersonal, and organizational performance, so the meeting is action oriented.
- Both the manager and the subordinate prepare agenda items for the meeting. It is a meeting for improving both of them, not just for the manager's appraisal.
- Sufficient time is allowed for the interaction, usually about an hour.
- Supportive communication is used so that joint problem solving and continuous improvement result (in both task accomplishment and interpersonal relationships).
- The first agenda item is a follow-up on the action items generated by the previous meeting.
- Major agenda items for the meeting might include:
  - Managerial and organizational problems
  - Organizational values and vision
  - Information sharing
  - Interpersonal issues
  - Obstacles to improvement
  - Training in management skills
  - Individual needs
  - Feedback on job performance
  - Personal concerns and problems
- Praise and encouragement are intermingled with problem solving but are more frequently communicated.
- A review of action items generated by the meeting occurs at the end of the interview.

found that more discretionary time became available because the program reduced interruptions, unscheduled meetings, mistakes, and problem-solving time. Furthermore, participants defined it as a success experience in itself. When correction or negative feedback had to be communicated, and when coaching or counseling was called for (which is typical of almost every manager–subordinate relationship at some point), supportive communication helped strengthen the interpersonal relationship at the same time that problems were solved and performance improved. In summary, setting aside time for formal, structured interaction between managers and their subordinates in which supportive communication played a part produced markedly improved bottom-line results in those organizations that implemented the program.

International Caveats

We point out in other chapters that it is important to keep in mind that cultural differences sometimes call for a modification of the skills discussed in this book. For example, Asian managers are often less inclined to be open in initial stages of a conversation, and they consider managers from the United States or Latin America to be a bit brash and aggressive because they may be too personal too soon. Similarly, certain types of response patterns may differ among cultures—for example, deflecting responses are more typical of Eastern cultures than Western cultures. The language patterns and language structures across cultures can be dramatically different, and considerable evidence exists that individuals are most effective interpersonally, and they display the greatest amount of emotional intelligence, when they recognize, appreciate, and capitalize on these differences among others.

On the other hand, whereas stylistic differences may exist among individuals and among various cultures, certain core principles of effective communication are universally associated with effective communication. The research on interpersonal communication among various cultures and nationalities confirms that the eight attributes of supportive communication are effective in all cultures and nationalities (Gudykunst, Ting-Toomey, & Nishida, 1996; Triandis, 1994). These eight factors have almost universal applicability in solving interpersonal problems.

We have used Trompenaars' (1996, 1998) model of cultural diversity to identify key differences among people raised in different cultural contexts. (Chapter 1 in this book provides a more detailed explanation of these value dimensions.) Differences exist, for example, on an *affectivity orientation* versus a *neutral orientation*. Affective cultures (e.g., the Middle East, Southern Europe, and South Pacific) are more inclined to be expressive and personal in their responses than neutral cultures (e.g., East Asia, and Scandinavia). Sharing personal data and engaging quickly in sensitive topics may be comfortable for people in some cultures but very uncomfortable in others. The timing and pace of communication will vary, therefore, among different cultures.

Similarly, *particularistic* cultures (e.g., Korea, China, and Indonesia) are more likely to allow individuals to work out issues in their own way compared to *universalistic* cultures (e.g., Norway, Sweden, and the United States) where a common pattern or approach is preferred. This implies that reflective responses may be more common in particularistic cultures and advising responses more typical of universalistic cultures. When individuals are assumed to have a great deal of individual autonomy, coaching responses (directing, advising, and correcting) are less common than counseling responses (empathizing, probing, and reflecting) in interpersonal problem solving.

Trompenaars (1996), Gudykunst and Ting-Toomey (1988), and others' research clearly points out, however, that the differences among cultures are not great enough to negate or dramatically modify the principles outlined in this chapter. Regardless of the differences in cultural background of those with whom you interact, being problem centered, congruent, descriptive, validating, specific, conjunctive, owned, and supportive in listening are all judged to indicate managerial competence and serve to build strong interpersonal relationships. Sensitivity to individual differences and styles is an important prerequisite to effective communication.

Summary

The most important barriers to effective communication in organizations are interpersonal. Much technological progress has been made in the last two decades in improving the accuracy of message delivery in organizations, but communication problems still persist among people, regardless of their relationships or roles. A major reason for these problems is that a great deal of communication does not support a positive interpersonal relationship. Instead, it frequently engenders distrust, hostility, defensiveness, and feelings of incompetence and low self-esteem. Ask any manager about the major problems being faced in their organizations, and communication problems will most assuredly appear near the top of the list.

Dysfunctional communication is seldom associated with situations in which compliments are given, congratulations are made, a bonus is awarded, or other positive interactions occur. Most people have little trouble communicating effectively in positive or complimentary situations. The most difficult, and potentially harmful, communication patterns are most likely to emerge when you are giving feedback on poor performance, saying "no" to a proposal or request, resolving a difference of opinion between two people, correcting problem behaviors, receiving criticism from others, providing feedback that could hurt another person's feelings, or encountering other negative interactions. Handling these situations in a way that fosters interpersonal growth and engenders stronger positive relationships is one mark of an effective manager. Rather than harming a relationship, using supportive communication builds and strengthens the relationship even when delivering negative news.

In this chapter, we pointed out that effective managers adhere to the principles of supportive communication. Thus, they ensure greater clarity and understanding of messages while making other persons feel accepted, valued, and supported. Of course, it is possible to become overly concerned with applying a technique or following a rule in trying to incorporate these principles and thereby to defeat the goal of being supportive. You can become artificial, inauthentic, or incongruent by focusing on technique alone, rather than on honest, caring communication. But if the principles are practiced and consciously implemented in everyday interactions, they can be important tools for improving your communication competence.

Behavioral Guidelines

The following behavioral guidelines will help you practice supportive communication:

A. Differentiate between coaching situations—which require giving advice and direction to help foster behavior change—and counseling situations, in which understanding and problem recognition are the desired outcomes.

B. Communicate congruently by acknowledging your authentic feelings and thoughts. Make certain your statements match your feelings and thoughts and you communicate genuinely.

C. In communicating congruently, avoid creating defensiveness or disconfirmation by using the eight rules of supportive communication.

D. Use descriptive, not evaluative, statements. Describe objectively what occurred, describe your reactions to events and their objective consequences, and suggest acceptable alternatives.

E. Use problem-oriented statements rather than person-oriented statements. That is, focus on behavioral referents or characteristics of events, not attributes of the person.

F. Use validating statements that acknowledge the other person's importance and uniqueness. Communicate your investment in the relationship by demonstrating your respect for the other person and your flexibility and humility in being open to new ideas or new data. Foster two-way interchanges rather than dominating or interrupting the other person. Identify areas of agreement or positive characteristics of the other person before pointing out areas of disagreement or negative characteristics.

G. Use specific rather than global (either–or, black-or-white) statements, and, when trying to correct behavior, focus on things that are under the control of the other person rather than factors that cannot be changed.

H. Use conjunctive statements that refer to what was said previously. Ensure equal speaking opportunities for others participating in the interaction. Do not cause long pauses that dominate the time. Be careful not to completely control the topic being discussed. Acknowledge what was said before by others.

I. Own your statements, and encourage the other person to do likewise. Use personal words ("I") rather than impersonal words ("they").

J. Demonstrate supportive listening. Make eye contact and be responsive nonverbally. Use a variety of responses to others' statements, depending on whether you are coaching or counseling someone else. Have a bias toward the use of reflective responses.

K. Implement a personal management interview program with people for whom you have responsibility, and use supportive communication to coach, counsel, foster personal development, and build strong positive relationships.

CASES INVOLVING BUILDING POSITIVE RELATIONSHIPS

Find Somebody Else

Ron Davis, the relatively new general manager of the machine tooling group at Parker Manufacturing, was visiting one of the plants. He scheduled a meeting with Mike Leonard, a plant manager who reported to him.

RON: Mike, I've scheduled this meeting with you because I've been reviewing performance data, and I wanted to give you some feedback. I know we haven't talked face-to-face before, but I think it's time we review how you're doing. I'm afraid that some of the things I have to say are not very favorable.

MIKE: Well, since you're the new boss, I guess I'll have to listen. I've had meetings like this before with new people who come in my plant and think they know what's going on.

RON: Look, Mike, I want this to be a two-way interchange. I'm not here to read a verdict to you, and I'm not here to tell you how to do your job. There are just some areas for improvement I want to review.

MIKE: OK, sure, I've heard that before. But you called the meeting. Go ahead and lower the boom.

RON: Well, Mike, I don't think this is lowering the boom. But there are several things you need to hear. One is what I noticed during the plant tour. I think you're too chummy with some of your female personnel. You know, one of them might take offense and level a sexual harassment suit against you.

MIKE: Oh, come on. You haven't been around this plant before, and you don't know the informal, friendly relationships we have. The office staff and the women on the floor are flattered by a little attention now and then.

RON: That may be so, but you need to be more careful. You may not be sensitive to what's really going on with them. But that raises another thing I noticed—the appearance of your shop. You know how important it is in Parker to have a neat and clean shop. As I walked through this morning, I noticed that it wasn't as orderly and neat as I would like to see it. Having things in disarray reflects poorly on you, Mike.

MIKE: I'll stack my plant up against any in Parker for neatness. You may have seen a few tools out of place because someone was just using them, but we take a lot of pride in our neatness. I don't see how you can say that things are in disarray. You've got no experience around here, so who are you to judge?

RON: Well, I'm glad you're sensitive to the neatness issue. I just think you need to pay attention to it, that's all. But regarding neatness, I notice that you don't dress like a plant manager. I think you're creating a substandard impression by not wearing a tie, for example. Casualness in dress can be used as an excuse for workers to come to work in really grubby attire. That may not be safe.

MIKE: Look, I don't agree with making a big separation between the managers and the employees. By dressing like people out on the shop floor, I think we eliminate a lot of barriers. Besides, I don't have the money to buy clothes that might get oil on them every day. That seems pretty picky to me.

RON: I don't want to seem picky, Mike. But I do feel strongly about the issues I've mentioned. There are some other things, though, that need to get corrected. One is the appearance of the reports you send into division headquarters. There are often mistakes, misspellings, and, I suspect, some wrong numbers. I wonder if you are paying attention to these reports. You seem to be reviewing them superficially.

MIKE: If there is one thing we have too much of, it's reports. I could spend three-quarters of my time filling out report forms and generating data for some bean counter in headquarters. We have reports coming out our ears. Why don't you give us a chance to get our work done and eliminate all this paperwork?

RON: You know as well as I do, Mike, that we need to carefully monitor our productivity, quality, and costs. You just need to get more serious about taking care of that part of your responsibility.

MIKE: OK. I'm not going to fight about that. It's a losing battle for me. No one at headquarters will ever decrease their demand for reports. But, listen, Ron, I also have one question for you.

RON: OK. What's that?

MIKE: Why don't you go find somebody else to pick on? I need to get back to work.

Discussion Questions

4.1. What principles of supportive communication and supportive listening are violated in this case?

4.2. If you were to change this interaction to make it more productive, what would you change?

4.3. Categorize each of the statements by naming the rule of supportive communication that is either illustrated or violated.

4.4. Conduct a role play. Handle the key issues that exist between Ron and Mike. Identify the principles you used to make this a productive conversation. If you were Ron, what would you do in your follow-up meeting with Mike?

Rejected Plans

The following dialogue occurred between two employees in a large firm. The conversation illustrates several characteristics of supportive communication.

SUSETTE: How did your meeting go with Mr. Schmidt yesterday?

LEONARDO: Well, uh, it went...aaah...it was no big deal.

SUSETTE: It looks as if you're pretty upset about it.

LEONARDO: Yeah, I am. It was a totally frustrating experience. I, uh, well, let's just say I would like to forget the whole thing.

SUSETTE: Things must not have gone as well as you had hoped they would.

LEONARDO: I'll say! That guy was impossible. I thought the plans I submitted were very clear and well thought out. Then he rejected the entire package.

SUSETTE: You mean he didn't accept any of them?

LEONARDO: You got it.

SUSETTE: I've seen your work before, Leonardo. You've always done a first-rate job. It's hard for me to figure out why your plans were rejected by Schmidt. What did he say about them?

LEONARDO: He said they were unrealistic and too difficult to implement, and...

SUSETTE: Really?

LEONARDO: Yeah, and when he said that I felt he was attacking me personally. But, on the other hand, I was also angry because I thought my plans were very good, and, you know, I paid close attention to every detail in those plans.

SUSETTE: I'm certain that you did.

LEONARDO: It just really ticks me off.

SUSETTE: I'll bet it does. I would be upset, too.

LEONARDO: Schmidt has something against me.

SUSETTE: After all the effort you put into those plans, you still couldn't figure out whether Schmidt was rejecting you or your plans, right?

LEONARDO: Yeah. Right. How could you tell?

SUSETTE: I can really understand your confusion and uncertainty when you felt Schmidt's actions were unreasonable.

LEONARDO: I just don't understand why he did what he did.

SUSETTE: Sure. If he said your plans were unrealistic, what does that mean? I mean, how can you deal with a rationale like that? It's just too general—meaningless, even. Did he mention anything specific? Did you ask him to point out some problems or explain the reasons for his rejection more clearly?

LEONARDO: Good point, but, uh, you know...I was so disappointed at the rejection that I was kinda like in outer space. You know what I mean?

SUSETTE: Yeah. It's an incapacitating experience. You have so much invested personally that you try to divest as fast as you can to save what little self-respect is left.

LEONARDO: That's it all right. I just wanted to get out of there before I said something I would be sorry for.

SUSETTE: Yet, in the back of your mind, you probably figured that Schmidt wouldn't risk the company's future just because he didn't like you personally. But then, well...the plans were good! It's hard to deal with that contradiction on the spot, isn't it?

LEONARDO: Exactly. I knew I should have pushed him for more information, but, uh, I just stood there like a dummy. But what can you do about it now? It's spilled milk.

SUSETTE: I don't think it's a total loss, Leonardo. I mean, from what you have told me—what he said and what you said—I don't think that a conclusion can be reached. Maybe he doesn't understand the plans, or maybe it was just his off day. Who knows? It could be a lot of things. What would you think about pinning Schmidt down by asking for his objections, point by point? Do you think it would help to talk to him again?

LEONARDO: Well, I would sure know a lot more than I know now. As it is, I wouldn't know where to begin revising or modifying the plans. And you're right,

I really don't know what Schmidt thinks about me or my work. Sometimes I just react and interpret with little or no evidence.

SUSETTE: Maybe, uh...maybe another meeting would be a good thing, then.

LEONARDO: Well, I guess I should get off my duff and schedule an appointment with him for next week. I am curious to find out what the problem is, with the plans, or me. (Pause) Thanks, Susette, for helping me work through this thing.

Discussion Questions

4.5. Categorize each statement in the case according to the supportive communication characteristic or type of response it represents. For example, the first statement by Leonardo obviously is not very congruent, but the second one is much more so.

4.6. Which statements in the conversation were most helpful? Which were least helpful, or could have produced defensiveness or closed off the conversation?

4.7. If you were the coach of Susette, how would you assist her in being more competent as a supportive communicator? How would you coach Leonardo to be more supportive even though it is he who faces the problem?

SKILL *PRACTICE*

EXERCISES FOR DIAGNOSING COMMUNICATION PROBLEMS AND FOSTERING UNDERSTANDING

United Chemical Company

The role of manager encompasses not only one-on-one coaching and counseling with an employee but also frequently entails helping other people understand coaching and counseling principles for themselves. Sometimes it means refereeing interactions and, by example, helping other people learn about correct principles of supportive communication. This is part of the task in this exercise. In a group setting, coaching and counseling become more difficult because multiple messages, driven by multiple motives, interact. Skilled supportive communicators, however, help each group member feel supported and understood in the interaction, even though the solution to an issue may not always be the one he or she would have preferred.

Assignment

In this exercise, you should apply the principles of supportive communication you have read about in the chapter. First, you will need to form groups of four people each. Next, read the case and assign the following roles in your group: Max, Marquita, Keeshaun, and an observer. Assume that a meeting is being held with Max, Marquita, and Keeshaun immediately after the end of the incidents in the following case. Play the roles you have been assigned and try to resolve the problems. The observer should provide feedback to the three players at the end of the exercise. An Observer's Feedback Form can be found at the end of the chapter.

The Case

The United Chemical Company is a large producer and distributor of commodity chemicals, with five production plants in the United States. The main plant in Baytown, Texas, is not only a production plant but also the company's research and engineering center.

The process design group consists of eight male engineers and their supervisor, Max Kane. The group has worked together steadily for a number of years, and good relationships have developed among all the members. When the workload began to increase, Max hired a new design engineer, Marquita Davis, a recent master's degree graduate from one of the foremost engineering schools in the country. Marquita was assigned to a project that would expand the capacity of one of the existing plant facilities. Three other design engineers were assigned to the project along with Marquita: Keeshaun Keller (age 38, 15 years with the company), Sam Sims (age 40, 10 years with the company), and Lance Madison (age 32, 8 years with the company).

As a new employee, Marquita was very enthusiastic about the opportunity to work at United. She liked her work very much because it was challenging and it offered her a chance to apply much of the knowledge she had gained in her university studies. On the job, Marquita kept mostly to herself and her design work. Her relations with her fellow project members were friendly, but she did not go out of her way to have informal conversations with them during or after working hours.

Marquita was a diligent employee who took her work seriously. On occasions when a difficult problem arose, she would stay after hours in order to come up with a solution. Because of her persistence, coupled with her more current education, Marquita usually completed her portion of the various project stages several days ahead of her colleagues. This was somewhat irritating to her because on these occasions she had to go to Max to ask for additional work to keep her busy until her coworkers caught up to her. Initially, she had offered to help Keeshaun, Sam, and Lance with their assignments, but each time she was abruptly turned down.

About five months after Marquita had joined the design group, Keeshaun asked to see Max about a problem the group was having. The conversation between Max and Keeshaun went as follows:

MAX: Keeshaun, I understand you want to discuss a problem with me.

KEESHAUN: Yes, Max, I don't want to waste your time, but some of the other design engineers want me to discuss Marquita with you. She is irritating everyone with her know-it-all, pompous attitude. She's just not the kind of person we want to work with.

MAX: I can't understand that, Keeshaun. She's an excellent worker, and her design work is always well done and usually flawless. She's doing everything the company wants her to do.

KEESHAUN: The company never asked her to disrupt the morale of the group or to tell us how to do our work. The animosity in our group could eventually result in lower-quality work for the whole unit.

MAX: I'll tell you what I'll do. Marquita has a meeting with me next week to discuss her six-month performance. I'll keep your thoughts in mind, but I can't promise an improvement in what you and the others believe is a pompous attitude.

KEESHAUN: Immediate improvement in her behavior is not the problem; it's her coaching others when she has no right to. She publicly shows others what to do. You'd think she was lecturing an advance class in design with all her high-powered, useless equations and formulas. She'd better back off soon, or some of us will quit or transfer.

During the next week, Max thought carefully about his meeting with Keeshaun. He knew that Keeshaun was the informal leader of the design engineers and generally spoke for the other group members. On Thursday of the following week, Max called Marquita into his office for her mid-year review. One portion of the conversation went as follows:

MAX: There is one other aspect I'd like to discuss with you about your performance. As I just related to you, your technical performance has been excellent; however, there are some questions about your relationships with the other workers.

MARQUITA: I don't understand. What questions are you talking about?

MAX: Well, to be specific, certain members of the design group have complained about your apparent "know-it-all attitude" and the manner in which you try to tell them how to do their job. You're going to have to be patient with them and not publicly call them out about their performance. This is a good group of engineers, and their work over the years has been more than acceptable. I don't want any problems that will cause the group to produce less effectively.

MARQUITA: Let me make a few comments. First of all, I have never publicly criticized their performance to them or to you. Initially, when I finished ahead of them, I offered to help them with their work but was bluntly told to mind my own business. I took the hint and concentrated only on my part of the work. What you don't understand is that after five months of working in this group I have come to the conclusion that what is going on is a rip-off of the company. The other engineers are goldbricking; they're setting a work pace much slower than they're capable of. They're more interested in the music from Sam's radio, the local football team, and the bar they're going to go to for TGIF. I'm sorry, but this is just not the way I was raised or trained. And finally, they've never looked on me as a qualified engineer, but as a woman who has broken their professional barrier.

SOURCE: *Based on United Chemical Company. Szilagyi, A. D. and M. J. Wallace,* Organizational Behavior and Performance, Third Edition, *pp. 204–205. © 1983. Glenview, IL: Scott Foresman*

Byron vs. Thomas

Effective one-on-one coaching and counseling are skills required in many settings in life, not just in management. It is hard to imagine a parent, roommate, Little League coach, room mother, or good friend who would not benefit from training in supportive communication. Because there are so many aspects of supportive communication, however, it is sometimes difficult to remember all of them. That is why practice, with observation and feedback, is so important. These attributes of supportive communication can become a natural part of your interaction approach as you conscientiously practice and receive feedback from a colleague.

Assignment

In the following exercise, one individual should take the role of Hal Byron, and another should take the role of Judy Thomas. To make the role-play realistic, do not read each other's role descriptions. When you have finished reading, hold a meeting between Hal Byron and Judy Thomas. A third person should serve as the observer. An Observer's Feedback Form to assist in providing feedback is at the end of the chapter.

Hal Byron, Department Head

You are Hal Byron, head of the operations group—the "back room"—in a large bank corporation. This is your second year on the job, and you have moved up rather quickly in the bank. You enjoy working for this firm, which has a reputation for being one of the finest in the region. One reason is that outside opportunities for management development and training are funded by the bank. In addition, each employee is given an opportunity for a personal management interview each month, and these sessions are usually both productive and developmental.

One of the department members, Judy Thomas, has been in this department for 19 years, 15 of them in the same job. She is reasonably good at what she does, and she is always punctual and efficient. She tends to get to work earlier than most employees in order to peruse the *American Banker* and *USA Today*. You can almost set your watch by the time Judy visits the restroom during the day and by the time she makes her phone call to her daughter every afternoon.

Your feeling about Judy is that although she is a good worker, she lacks imagination and initiative. This has been indicated by her lack of merit increases over the last five years and by the fact that she has had the same job for 15 years. She's content to do just what is assigned, nothing more. Your predecessor must have given hints to Judy that she might be in line for a promotion, however, because Judy has raised this with you more than once. Because she has been in her job so long, she is at the top of her pay range, and without a promotion, she cannot receive a salary adjustment above the basic cost-of-living increase.

The one thing Judy does beyond the basic minimum job requirements is to help train young people who come into the department. She is very patient and methodical with them, and she seems to take pride in helping them learn the ropes. She has not been hesitant to point out this contribution to you. Unfortunately, this activity does not qualify Judy for a promotion, nor could she be transferred into the training and development department. Once you suggested that she take a few courses at the local college, paid for by the bank, but she matter-of-factly stated that she was too old to go to school. You surmise that she might be intimidated because she doesn't have a college degree.

As much as you would like to promote Judy, there just doesn't seem to be any way to do that in good conscience. You have tried putting additional work under her control, but she seems to be slowing down in her productivity rather than speeding up. The work needs to get done, and expanding her role just puts you behind schedule.

This interview coming up is probably the time to level with Judy about her performance and her potential. You certainly don't want to lose her as an employee, but there is not going to be a change in job assignment for a long time unless she changes her performance dramatically.

Judy Thomas, Department Member

You are a member of the operations group in a large bank corporation. You have been with the bank now for 19 years, 15 of them in the same job. You enjoy the company because of its friendly climate and because of its prestigious image in the region. It's nice to be known as an employee of this firm. However, lately you have become more dissatisfied as you've seen person after person come into the bank and get promoted ahead of you. Your own boss, Hal Byron, is almost 20 years your junior. Another woman who joined the bank the same time you did is now a senior vice president. You can't understand why you've been neglected. You are efficient and accurate in your work, you have a near-perfect attendance record, and you consider yourself to be a good employee. You have gone out of your way on many occasions to help train and orient young people who are just joining the bank. Several of them have written letters later telling you how important your help was in getting them promoted. A lot of good that does you!

The only thing you can figure out is that there is a bias against you because you haven't graduated from college. On the other hand, others have moved up without a diploma. You haven't taken advantage of any college courses paid for by the bank, but after a long day at work, you're not inclined to go to class for another three hours. Besides, you only see your family in the evenings, and you don't want to take time away from them. It doesn't take a college degree to do your job, anyway.

Your monthly personal management interview is coming up with your department head, Hal Byron, and you've decided the time has come to get a few answers. Several things need explaining. Not only haven't you been promoted, but you haven't even received a merit increase for five years. You're not getting any credit for the extra contributions you make with new employees, nor for your steady, reliable work. Could anyone blame you for being a little bitter?

Active Listening Exercise

Form a trio of colleagues who hold differing opinions about any of the following topics. Hold a 10- or 15-minute conversation about any of the topics. Take a position on the issue. Make a case for your point of view. Convince your partners that you are right. When you are finished, complete the short questionnaire below, and discuss the results together. Offer any helpful feedback to your colleagues that you think may be appropriate.

1. Should the United States have invaded Iraq in 2014?
2. Should late-term abortions be performed?
3. Is global warming a critical issue?
4. Should the United States prosecute and deport illegal aliens?
5. Should English become the national language in the United States?
6. Does the international media have a liberal bias, and does it matter either way?
7. Are business school rankings helpful or harmful?
8. Who is the world's most dangerous person?
9. Should professional athletes be allowed to compete in the Olympics?
10. Should the United Nations exist?

Rate your two colleagues on the following items using this response scale:

1 = *Strongly disagree*
2 = *Disagree*
3 = *Neither*
4 = *Agree*
5 = *Strongly agree*

ITEM	COLLEAGUE 1	COLLEAGUE 2
My colleague...		
1. Maintained eye contact and interest	1 2 3 4 5	1 2 3 4 5
2. Used inquiry more than advocacy	1 2 3 4 5	1 2 3 4 5
3. Interrupted	1 2 3 4 5	1 2 3 4 5
4. Displayed appropriate emotional engagement	1 2 3 4 5	1 2 3 4 5
5. Used a variety of response types	1 2 3 4 5	1 2 3 4 5
6. Used reflective responses	1 2 3 4 5	1 2 3 4 5

Reverse the scoring for item 3, and add up the scores for each colleague. Provide those scores to one another and discuss the results. Provide helpful feedback to one another.

PRACTICE

ACTIVITIES FOR COMMUNICATING SUPPORTIVELY

Suggested Assignments

4.8. Tape record an interview with someone such as a coworker, friend, or spouse. Focus on an issue or challenge faced right now by that person. Diagnose the situation to determine if you should be a coach or a counselor. (Our bet is that it will be the latter.) Conduct a conversation in which you apply the principles of supportive communication discussed in the chapter. (The Rejected Plans case provides an example of such an interview.) Use the tape to determine how you could improve your own supportive communication skill.

4.9. Teach someone you know the concepts of supportive communication and supportive listening. Provide your own explanations and illustrations so the person understands what you are talking about. Describe your experience in your journal.

4.10. Identify a person with whom you have had a disagreement, some difficulty in the past, or some discomfort in your relationship. This could be a roommate, parent, friend, or instructor. Approach that person and ask to hold a conversation in which you discuss the interpersonal problem. To be successful, you'll discover how crucial supportive communication is in the conversation. When you have finished, write up the experience in as much detail as possible. What did you say and what did the other person say? What was especially effective and what didn't work so well? Identify areas in which you need to improve.

4.11. Write two mini–case studies. One should recount an effective coaching or counseling situation. The other should recount an ineffective coaching or counseling situation. The cases should be based on a real event, either from your own personal experience or from the experience of someone you know well. Use principles of supportive communication and listening in your cases.

Application Plan and Evaluation

The intent of this exercise is to help you apply this cluster of skills in a real-life, out-of-class setting. Now that you have become familiar with the behavioral guidelines that form the basis of effective skill performance, you will improve most by trying out those guidelines in an everyday context. Unlike a classroom activity, in which feedback is immediate and others can assist you with their evaluations, this skill application activity is one you must accomplish and evaluate on your own. There are two parts to this activity: Part 1 helps prepare you to apply the skill, and Part 2 helps you evaluate and improve on your experience. Be sure to write down answers to each item. Don't short-circuit the process by skipping steps.

Part 1: Planning

4.12. Write down the two or three aspects of this skill that are most important to you. These may be areas of weakness, areas you most want to improve, or areas that are most salient to a problem you face right now. Identify the specific aspects of this skill that you want to apply.

4.13. Now identify the setting or the situation in which you will apply this skill. Establish a plan for performance by actually writing down a description of the situation. Who else will be involved? When will you do it? Where will it be done?

      Circumstances:
      Who else?
      When?
      Where?

4.14. Identify the specific behaviors in which you will engage to apply this skill. Operationalize your skill performance.

4.15. What are the indicators of successful performance? How will you know you have been effective? What will indicate you have performed competently?

Part 2: Evaluation

4.16. After you have completed your implementation, record the results. What happened? How successful were you? What was the effect on others?

4.17. How can you improve? What modifications can you make next time? What will you do differently in a similar situation in the future?

4.18. Looking back on your whole skill practice and application experience, what have you learned? What has been surprising? In what ways might this experience help you in the long term?

SCORING KEYS AND COMPARISON DATA

✪ Scoring Keys for the following instruments, along with comparison data, are contained in PIA in MyManagementLab.com;

Communicating Supportively
Communication Styles

SKILL ASSESSMENT

- Gaining Power and Influence
- Using Influence Strategies

SKILL LEARNING

- Building a Strong Power Base and Using Influence Wisely
- Is Power A Four-Letter Word?
- Abuse of Power
- Influence Strategies: The Three Rs
- The Pros and Cons of Each Strategy
- Acting Assertively: Neutralizing Influence Attempts

SKILL ANALYSIS

- Dynica Software Solutions

SKILL PRACTICE

- Repairing Power Failures in Management Circuits
- Ann Lyman's Proposal
- Cindy's Fast Foods
- 9:00 to 7:30

SKILL APPLICATION

- Suggested Assignments
- Application Plan and Evaluation

SCORING KEYS AND COMPARISON DATA

5

Gaining Power and Influence

LEARNING OBJECTIVES

1. ENHANCE PERSONAL AND POSITIONAL POWER

2. USE INFLUENCE APPROPRIATELY TO ACCOMPLISH EXCEPTIONAL WORK

3. NEUTRALIZE INAPPROPRIATE INFLUENCE ATTEMPTS

MyManagementLab™

⊘ When you see this icon, visit www.mymanagementlab.com for self-assessments, video activities, and more.

SKILL *ASSESSMENT* (?)

✪ If your instructor is utilizing **MyManagementLab**, log onto mymanagementlab.com and select the Personal Inventory Assessment (PIA) section and complete the instruments associated with this chapter.

The assessment instruments in this chapter are briefly described below. The assessments appear either in your text or in PIA. The assessments marked with (blue star) are available only in PIA.

All assessments should be completed before reading the chapter material.

After completing the first assessment save your response to your hard drive. When you have finished reading the chapter, re-take the assessment and compare your responses to see what you have learned.

✪ ❑ The *Gaining Power and Influence* Assessment measures the extent to which you exhibit competency in gaining power and influence in a work context.

✪ ❑ The *Using Influence Strategies* Assessment measures your preferences for three different influence strategies that will be discussed in the chapter.

SKILL *LEARNING* ▽

Building a Strong Power Base and Using Influence Wisely

"The difference between someone who can get an idea off the ground and accepted in an organization and someone who can't isn't a question of who has the better idea. It's a question of who has political competence. Political competence isn't something you're born with, but a skill you learn. It's an out-in-the-open process of methodically mapping the political terrain, building coalitions, and leading them to get your idea adopted." So says Samuel Bacharach, a Cornell University professor who has spent his career negotiating the halls of powerful New York businesses and labor unions (Bacharach, 2005, p. 93).

The skill of political competence is particularly relevant for today's workforce, where young managers are taking positions traditionally reserved for battle-tested pros who understand from experience the ins and outs of gaining power and influence. The challenge might be particularly difficult for the Millennial generation (those currently in their 20s and early 30s), who are coming into the work place with very different views about how power should work. Millennials, according to researcher and consultant Dan Shawbel, fundamentally reject the idea of strict hierarchies at work and believe they should have as much of a voice as senior people in their organizations (Shawbel,

2012). This may be why some young, inexperienced managers report difficulties managing "up"—getting their bosses to respect them—as well as managing "down"—getting their older subordinates to respect their position (Leger, 2000).

> ✪ **MyManagementLab: WATCH IT**
> **Power and Political Behavior**
> Apply what you have learned about management. If your instructor has assigned MyManagementLab, go to mymanagementlab.com to watch a video case and answer questions.

Nothing is more demoralizing than feeling you have a creative new idea or a unique insight into a significant organizational problem and then coming face-to-face with your organizational impotence. This is often the experience of young college graduates who enter the workplace feeling energetic, optimistic, and supremely confident that their "awesome" ability, state-of-the-art training, and indefatigable energy will rocket them up the corporate ladder. However, many soon become discouraged and embittered. They blame "the old guard" for protecting their turf and not being open to new ideas. One young manager stated dejectedly, "Hell is knowing you have a better solution than someone else but not being able to get the votes."

Despite Millennials' disdain for hierarchies, most organizations still rely on status to determine how things get done. Consequently, young managers cannot simply hope that their ideas will speak for themselves. They need to develop skills to influence others if they want to make a difference. Kerry Patterson and his colleagues, authors of *Influencer*, tell a story about a group of employees who had received valuable training and were attempting to transfer it to their workplace. Many were unsuccessful in doing so. But the ones who were able to implement new ideas exhibited a set of skills that allowed them to be influential. They "...skillfully challenged their supervisor. They were candid with peers who weren't carrying their weight. And finally, they were capable of talking to senior management—the same senior managers more cynical peers avoided—about policies or practices that they believed impeded improvements" (Patterson, et al., 39). Developing the confidence and skills to speak up effectively made all the difference for these employees.

Is Power A Four-Letter Word?

John Gardner has observed, "In this country—and in most democracies—power has such a bad name that many people persuade themselves they want nothing to do with it" (1990). For these people, power is a "four-letter word," conjuring up images of vindictive, domineering bosses and manipulative, cunning subordinates. It is associated with dirty office politics engaged in by ruthless individuals who use as their handbooks for corporate guerrilla warfare books such as *Winning Through Intimidation*, and who subscribe to the philosophy of Heinrich von Treitschke: "Your neighbor, even though he may look upon you as a natural ally against another power which is feared by you both, is always ready, at the first opportunity, as soon as it can be done with safety, to better himself at your expense.... Whoever fails to increase his power, must decrease it, if others increase theirs" (Mulgan, 1998, p. 68).

Those with a distaste for power argue that teaching managers and prospective managers how to increase their power is tantamount to sanctioning the use of primitive forms of domination. They support this argument by pointing to the devastating tragedies of corporate power abuse in recent decades, such as Jeff Skilling's arrogant deceptions that led to the downfall of Enron and Bernie Madoff's exploitation of

trusting friends as he perpetrated the most egregious Ponzi scheme in history.

This negative view of "personal power" is especially common in cultures that place a high value on ascription, rather than achievement, and on collectivism, rather than individualism (Triandis, 1994; Trompenaars, 1996). People who value ascription believe power resides in stable, personal characteristics such as age, gender, level of education, ethnic background, or social class. Hence, focusing on "getting ahead," "taking charge," and "making things happen" seems contrary to the natural social order. Those who place a high value on collectivism may worry that placing too much emphasis on increasing a single individual's power might not be in the best interests of the larger group. For these reasons, some might find this chapter's focus on developing individual power overly "American" in its cultural orientation. We acknowledge that the principles we discuss tend to lean toward an achievement orientation and individualistic values. For those who feel uncomfortable modeling their own behavior after the principles and guidelines in this chapter, we suggest you think of this as a useful "translation guide" for helping you understand how American business managers view power and how American corporations treat power. In addition, we hope readers will understand that they are likely to interact with individuals from different cultures who will probably believe some of these strategies are ineffective and/or inappropriate.

Many American business leaders and scholars make a persuasive case that power is not inherently negative but is in fact critical for succeeding in management. Robert Dilenschneider, president and chief executive officer (CEO) of a leading public relations firm, states: "The use of influence is itself not negative. It can often lead to a great good. Like any powerful force—from potent medicine to nuclear power—it is the morality with which influence is used that makes all the difference" (Dilenschneider, 1990, p. xviii; see also Dilenschneider, 2007). Power need not be associated with aggression, brute force, craftiness, or deceit. Power can also be viewed as a sign of personal efficacy. It is the ability to mobilize resources to accomplish productive work. People with power shape their environment, whereas the powerless are molded by theirs.

Management guru Warren Bennis, seeking the quintessential ingredients of effective leaders, interviewed 90 individuals who had been nominated by peers as the most influential leaders in all walks of

Table 5.1	Indicators of a Manager's Upward and Outward Power

Powerful managers can:

- Intercede favorably on behalf of someone in trouble.
- Get a desirable placement for a talented subordinate.
- Get approval for expenditures beyond the budget.
- Get items on and off the agenda at policy meetings.
- Get fast access to top decision makers.
- Maintain regular, frequent contact with top decision makers.
- Acquire early information about decisions and policy shifts.

SOURCE: *Reprinted by permission of* Harvard Business Review. *Indicators of a Manager's Upward and Outward Power. From "Power Failures in Management Circuits" by R. Kanter, 57. Copyright © 1979 by the Harvard Business School Publishing Corporation; all rights reserved.*

our society. Bennis found these individuals shared one significant characteristic: They made *others* feel powerful. They were influential because they used their power to help peers and subordinates accomplish exceptional tasks (Bennis & Nanus, 2003).

One of the classic scholars of organizational power, Rosabeth Kanter, pointed out that powerful managers not only can accomplish more personally, but they can also pass on more information and make more resources available to subordinates. For this reason, people tend to prefer bosses with "clout." Subordinates tend to feel they have higher status in an organization and their morale is higher when they perceive that their boss has considerable upward influence. In contrast, Kanter argues, powerlessness tends to foster bossiness, rather than true leadership. "In large organizations, at least," she notes, "it is powerlessness that often creates ineffective, desultory management and petty, dictatorial, rules-minded managerial styles" (1979, p. 65).

Kanter (1979) has identified several indicators of a manager's upward and outward power in an organization. These are shown in Table 5.1. In some respects, these serve as a set of behavioral objectives for our discussion of power and influence.

Abuse of Power

But what about Lord Acton's well-known dictum, "Power corrupts, and absolute power corrupts absolutely"? Hardly a week goes by that new evidence of

this seemingly ageless observation isn't reflected in news headlines. Doesn't that suggest effective managers should avoid power because "abuse of office," with a likely fall from power, will inevitably follow?

In the Greek plays of Sophocles, for instance, the viewer is confronted with the image of great and powerful rulers transformed by their prior success so that they are filled with a sense of their own worth and importance—hubris—which causes them to be impatient of the advice of others and unwilling to listen to opinions different from their own. Yet in the end, they are destroyed by events that they discover they cannot control. Oedipus is destroyed soon after the crowds say (and he believes) "he is almost like a God"; King Creon, at the zenith of his political and military power, is brought down as a result of his belief in the infallibility of his judgments.

Headlines of business trade periodicals regularly trumpet claims of modern-day hubris among business elites (Bunker, Kram, & Ting, 2002). One recent example is Aubrey McClendon, the CEO of Chesapeake Energy, who was near the top of the list of "Worst CEOs of 2012" according to *BusinessWeek* (Lavelle, 2012). McClendon took a notoriously cavalier attitude toward the company's finances, using the company jet and employee time for his personal purposes and striking a corporate sponsorship deal for a professional sports team he happened to own. He also borrowed more than $1 billion over a three-year period in undisclosed loans against his stake in the company.

Sophocles warns us never to be envious of the powerful until we see the nature of their endings. Support for the modern-day relevance of this timeless warning is reflected in the results of studies of both successful and failed corporate executives (McCall & Lombardo, 1983; Shipper & Dillard, 2000). In the first study of its kind, scholars at the Center for Creative Leadership identified approximately 20 executives who had risen to the top of their firms and matched them with a similar group of 20 executives who had failed to reach their career aspirations. Earlier, both groups had entered their respective organizations with equal promise. There were no noticeable differences in their preparation, expertise, education, and so forth. However, over time, the second group's careers had become "derailed" by the personal inadequacies shown in Table 5.2.

It is sobering to note how many of these problems relate to the ineffective use of power in interpersonal

Table 5.2	Characteristics That Derail Managers' Careers

- Lack of sensitivity to others; abrasive and intimidating
- Acting cold, aloof, and arrogant
- Untrustworthiness
- Being overly ambitious; playing politics and always trying to move up
- Inability to delegate to others or to build a team
- Over-dependency on others (e.g., a mentor)

SOURCE: *Based on* Psychology Today, *Copyright © 2006 www.psychologytoday.com.*

relationships. In general, this group tends to support Lord Acton's dictum as well as the warnings of Sophocles. They were given a little authority, and they failed to be good stewards of it.

This observation is consistent with the research findings of David McClelland, who has spent many years studying what he considers to be one of the fundamental human needs, the "need for power" (McClelland & Burnham, 2003). According to McClelland, whether leaders maintain their power in the long-term or not depends on the motives behind their use of power. Managers who use their power to advance the goals of the organization develop sustainable influence, whereas those who use their power for personal gain tend to succumb to the tragic legacy of the power abuser. Recent laboratory research has begun to paint a fascinating picture of how motives affect people's use of power. Serena Chen and her colleagues have shown that when people who are fundamentally self-interested assume a position of power, they tend to make others do more work. In contrast, people with a strong sense of social responsibility actually take more work upon themselves when they assume a position of power (Chen, Lee-Chai & Bargh, 2001). These and other studies suggest that power doesn't so much shape us, as *reveal* our true motives. Power has the capacity to bring out both the best and the worst in groups and organization, depending on the motives for its use (Bunderson & Reagans, 2011).

Figure 5.1 depicts the relationship between power and personal effectiveness as we have described it. Both a lack of power and the abuse of power are debilitating and counterproductive. In contrast, empowerment results from sufficient amounts of personal

Figure 5.1	Personal Power: Stepping Stone or Stumbling Block

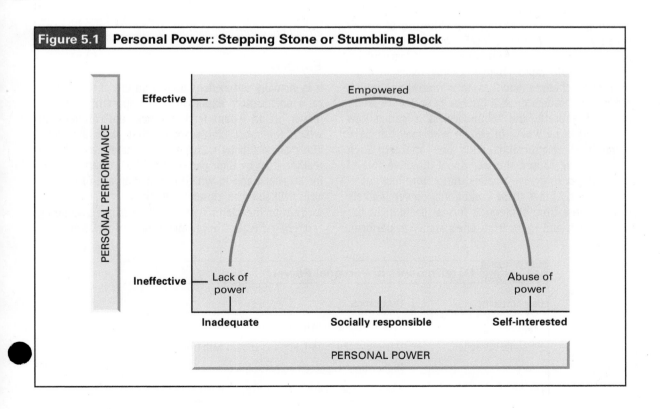

power motivated by social responsibility (or in other words, an orientation toward benefitting others).

The purpose of this chapter is to help managers "stay on top of the power curve," as represented by the indicators of organizational power reported by Kanter in Table 5.1. This is accomplished with the aid of two specific management skills:

❏ Gaining power (overcoming feelings of powerlessness); and

❏ Converting power effectively into interpersonal influence in ways that avoid the abuse of power.

We define power as the potential to influence other people's behavior. This is an important departure from traditional definitions that focus on authority-based control, as in "powerful" bosses having authority over their subordinates or "powerful" parents having control over their children. Along with other scholars in the field, we urge a shift in the definition of power from "controlling others" to "being able to get things done."

STRATEGIES FOR GAINING ORGANIZATIONAL POWER

Our discussion to this point should be viewed as an argument that we need not avoid the use of power because of its inherent dangers, but rather that we need to learn how to use it wisely. This is particularly true given the rapid changes taking place in organizations—changes such as telecommuting, which means that leaders must influence people who aren't physically present, and "boundaryless" organizations composed of networks of people who may not have hierarchical relationships with one another. Such changes have caused the traditional directive role of the manager to evolve to something more like coach and mentor. Under these conditions, power is likely to come less from someone's formal position in the organization and more from one's ability to perform.

These conditions make the notion of empowerment particularly important for your effectiveness in today's organizations.

Two basic factors determine a person's power in an organization: personal attributes and position characteristics. Naturally, the importance of each factor varies depending on the organizational context. For example, position title is extremely important in a strong hierarchical system, such as the military or civil service, and personal power may be more important in nonhierarchical settings. Nevertheless, experts tend to agree that developing both positional and personal power is vital for managerial success. Burt (1977), for instance, argued that managers with high position power are in a better position to capitalize on their personal power because their connections allow them to leverage their personal knowledge and abilities. Meanwhile, low-status individuals can increase their personal power by drawing on whatever position power they hold (Sauer, 2011). Hence, it makes sense for managers seeking to increase their influence in an organization to increase both sources of power.

SOURCES OF PERSONAL POWER

Four personal characteristics are important sources of power. As Table 5.3 shows, these are *expertise, personal attraction, effort,* and *legitimacy.*

Expertise

It is virtually self-evident that in an era of technological sophistication, expertise is an important source of power. In an e-commerce business environment, in which the most highly sought-after skills are more likely possessed by teenagers who have never had a real job than by their parents who have been working for 20 years, and in which the median age of millionaires will soon be closer to 30 than to 60, it is hard to dispute the claim that expertise is the ascending "coin of the realm" in business. Increasingly, what you

Table 5.3	Determinants of Personal Power
CHARACTERISTIC	**DESCRIPTION**
Expertise	Task-relevant knowledge or experience
Personal attraction	Desirable characteristics associated with friendship
Effort	Higher-than-expected commitment of time
Legitimacy	Behavior consistent with key organizational values

know is more important than who you know in getting a job, and what you can do technically is the key to what you can become organizationally. **Expertise**, or work-related knowledge, is the great organizational equalizer because it can come from formal education, self-directed learning, or on-the-job experience.

Because most management positions are not in small "dot.com" companies, but in larger, more diversified businesses, our focus will be on expertise as a source of personal power in large organizational settings. Expertise is especially important in established business organizations because of their preference for a highly rationalized decision-making process (Bunderson, 2003; Pfeffer, 1977). In an environment in which decisions are supposed to be made by objectively considering information supporting each alternative, people who have knowledge can quickly accrue power because they come to be seen as reliable experts. At the same time, expertise among junior employees can be problematic. When subordinates clearly have superior expertise, their bosses might become jealous or feel threatened. The skillful subordinate, therefore, makes knowledge available in a manner that does not threaten the boss's credibility and right to make the final decision.

Expertise is an important way for someone with low position power to gain influence. People with less formal status in the organization may not be very visible compared to top managers; their jobs are often routine; and their tasks, by themselves, are generally not linked to the most central objectives and concerns of the firm. However, staff members can compensate for weak position-power by developing expertise in a particular aspect of organizational life. This might involve a new accounting system, tax loopholes, safety and pollution regulations, or recent legal precedents in acquisitions.

There is, however, a catch-22 associated with expert power. Becoming an expert on a subject typically requires considerable time and effort, and in organizations using rapidly changing technologies, individuals must continually upgrade their expertise to avoid the "sell-by date" of their knowledge (Grove, 1983). Given the investment required to stay up to date in a particular area of specialization, it is easy to become typecast as a specialist. In fact, becoming an expert can cause you to become "cognitively entrenched," meaning that you become less flexible in problem solving and generating new ideas (Dane, 2010). If you are interested in moving into general management positions, this can be a hindrance. Given the dynamic environment facing today's organizations, overspecialization may be a recipe for obsolescence.

Aspiring young managers must be careful not to limit advancement opportunities by focusing their attention on very narrow aspects of a business's activities. This is tempting for individuals who are overly anxious to establish a power base. There are always small niches in an organization to which power-hungry novices can quickly lay claim. Only when they have fallen into the specialist trap do they recognize the value of building a broad base of knowledge about a wide variety of organizational activities to enhance their long-term attractiveness for promotion.

Attraction

We will consider three ways in which interpersonal **attraction** is a source of personal power: charisma, agreeable behavior, and physical characteristics.

First, charismatic leadership has been the subject of extensive scholarly study (Yukl, 2002). The word "charisma" had Greek origins, meaning favor or grace from God. The idea that charismatic leaders are favored by God stems from the observation that some people have an uncommon ability to engender devotion and enthusiasm—a seemingly mystical quality that cannot be acquired in a skill development workshop. This quality is reflected in comments like the following: "When she makes a presentation in a management meeting, her presence is so powerful any message sounds good"; "His magnetic personality enables him to attract the most qualified and dedicated people to his department—everyone wants to work for him." These anecdotal comments are consistent with research showing that a leader's charisma is associated with higher positivity among followers (Erez et al., 2008).

How do we explain which qualities make someone charismatic? Research on this topic (Conger & Kanungo, 1998) has found that leaders are more likely to be considered charismatic if they (1) express a vision that is inspiring; (2) incur personal sacrifice and even risk their personal well-being in pursuing their vision; (3) recommend the use of unconventional, nontraditional approaches to achieving shared goals; (4) have a seemingly uncanny feel for what is possible, including an acute sense of timing; and (5) demonstrate sensitivity to members' needs and concerns. It has also been shown that people tend to attribute charisma to leaders of high-performing organizations (Agle et al., 2006) and to people who are central in their organization's communication network (Balkundi et al., 2011). This research implies that it is a mistake to treat charisma as an inborn, inimitable

Table 5.4	Characteristics of Likable People

We like people when we have reason to believe they will:

- Support an open, honest, and loyal relationship.
- Foster intimacy by being emotionally accessible.
- Provide unconditional, positive regard and acceptance.
- Endure some sacrifices if the relationship should demand them.
- Provide social reinforcement in the form of sympathy or empathy.
- Engage in the social exchanges necessary to sustain a relationship.

SOURCE: *Adapted from Canfield and LaGaipa, 1970.*

trait. The behaviors and characteristics associated with charismatic leadership are far from mystical.

A related source of interpersonal attraction is much more mundane, but equally powerful. Social psychologists who have done research on interpersonal attraction have isolated several critical behaviors that determine what they call *agreeable behavior.* These behaviors are the kinds one would normally associate with friendship. Studies of this type have identified several major factors that foster interpersonal attraction. Some of these are shown in Table 5.4 (Anderson, John, Keltner, & Kring, 2001; Canfield & LaGaipa, 1970; Furman, 2001).

How can we relate this information on friendship to the supposedly hard-nosed world of management? Must you become good friends with your coworkers, subordinates, or boss? Not necessarily. It is often inappropriate to establish a close friendship with someone in your office. But people who display agreeable behaviors to their coworkers will likely help others feel empowered (Hogg, 2001; Mechanic, 1962).

An impressive amount of evidence supports this idea. For example, research shows that people are more effective persuaders if their audience finds them likable. Likable individuals are viewed as more trustworthy and impartial than disliked individuals. Subordinates who are liked by their supervisor also tend to be given the benefit of the doubt in performance appraisals. Research also shows that bosses use rewards rather than coercion to influence subordinates they like (Allinson, Armstrong, & Hayes, 2001; Tedeschi, 1974). In fact, one study showed that likability completely overwhelms competence when people choose work partners; we would generally

rather work with an agreeable person than someone who is good at what they do (Casciaro & Lobo, 2008).

We don't want to overemphasize this point, nor do we mean to suggest "good guys" always win, but there is an impressive amount of evidence that individuals with agreeable personalities become more influential than those with disagreeable personalities. Their arguments are given more credence, their influence attempts are less likely to evoke resistance, and coworkers seem less threatened if they are promoted.

The third basis for interpersonal attraction, *physical appearance,* operates independently of personality or even behavior (Hosoda, Stone-Romero, & Coats, 2003; Langlois et al., 2000). Studies have shown that we tend to associate socially desirable personality traits with people we judge to have attractive appearances. We tend to assume they lead highly successful lives, hold prestigious jobs, and are successful marriage partners and parents. In addition, attractive individuals are judged to be masters of their own fate—pursuing their own goals, imbued with a sense of mission—rather than being buffeted by environmental forces. In general, people tend to assume that attractive individuals are also virtuous and efficacious.

There is considerable evidence that these are not merely fanciful attributions. In some respects, attractive people *are* more successful. Research has found that, on average, physically attractive people are paid more than their counterparts in organizations (Judge, Hurst & Simon, 2009). Reflective of a societal double standard, women who make the highest salaries have a below-average body weight, whereas men are paid the most when their body weight is greater than average (Judge & Cable, 2011). In a work setting, the written work of attractive people is more likely to be judged of high quality, and attractive people are more likely to receive high performance appraisals from their supervisors than are other people (Hosoda et al., 2003; Langlois et al., 2000).

Findings on personal attraction are somewhat difficult to transform into concrete suggestions for personal development. There is not much one can do as an adult to radically transform one's basic appearance. However, this information is still highly relevant for managers for two reasons. First, in many experimental studies, scholars simply used dress and grooming to distinguish "attractive" research confederates from "unattractive" ones (Thompson, 2001, p. 141). Hence, it appears unnecessary for most people to resort to plastic surgery and other artificial forms of physical enhancement to boost their self-confidence. Personal grooming matters a great deal. Second, people can usually improve the impressions they make on others regardless of their physical features. Conveying a confident, friendly air increases your perceived attractiveness.

Effort

A high level of personal **effort** is one of the most highly prized characteristics of employees because it means they are dependable, reliable human resources. If individuals can be counted on to stay late to get out a delivery following a technological breakdown, to catch an early-morning flight to visit a promising new customer, or to take a night class to learn a new software program, they earn the trust of their coworkers and their supervisors. Being known as a person who will do "whatever it takes" to get the job done is a valuable personal asset, especially in today's highly uncertain and rapidly changing business climate. As one classic article argues, employees who expend effort at work tend to make their overburdened supervisors look good, thus creating a sense of indebtedness from those higher in the hierarchy (Mechanic, 1962).

In addition to creating indebtedness, high levels of effort enhance other personal characteristics. For example, individuals who work hard at a task tend to increase their knowledge of the subject, and thus their expertise. Therefore, they are more likely to be sought out for advice and to gather information that is relevant to other members of the organization.

The efficacy of personal effort is borne out in the career of George Bodenheimer, who was the longest-tenured president in the 30-year history of ESPN. Unlike most network executives, who are hired away from other networks, Bodenheimer is a homegrown product of ESPN. As a young man, he was fascinated by the cable television industry and decided he wanted to work for the fledgling sports network. However, the only position he could land was mailroom clerk. Still, he applied himself with great gusto and quickly gained the attention of others in the organization. Over the years, Bodenheimer worked through some 15 different positions, including marketing, accounts, and sales. His stellar work ethic ultimately led him to executive functions. Under his tenure, ESPN expanded to many new creative outlets, and Bodenheimer has become known as a pioneer in the cable and media industries.

Before leaving this topic, we want to make a distinction between extraordinary effort and extraordinary image. Some people put forth a lot of effort simply to make a show and impress others. Just putting in face

Table 5.5	**Managing the Relationship with Your Boss**

Make sure you understand your boss, including:

- Your boss's goals and objectives
- The pressures on him or her
- Your boss's strengths, weaknesses, blind spots
- His or her preferred work style

Assess yourself, including:

- Your own strengths and weaknesses
- Your personal style
- Your predisposition toward dependence on authority figures

Develop and maintain a relationship that:

- Fits the needs and styles of you both
- Is characterized by mutual expectations
- Keeps your boss informed
- Is based on dependability and honesty
- Selectively uses your boss's time and resources

SOURCE: *Adapted and reprinted by permission of* Harvard Business Review. *From J. J. Gabarro & J. P. Kotter, "Managing the Relationship with Your Boss," May–June 1993. Copyright 1993 by the Harvard Business School Publishing Corporation; all rights reserved.*

time or drawing inordinate attention to your own effort can backfire, especially if you aren't producing real value for your organization. Based on their intensive examination of effective boss–subordinate relationships in major corporations, Jack Gabarro and John Kotter (Gabarro & Kotter, 2007) suggest several highly relevant guidelines for directing your efforts to the benefit of your boss. As shown in Table 5.5, these include understanding your boss's pressures and priorities as well as assessing your own needs and strengths. This knowledge helps you improve your performance by targeting your efforts to maximize their impact.

Legitimacy

Another important source of personal power is **legitimacy**, which you achieve when your actions are congruent with the prevailing value system of the organization. Legitimacy increases one's acceptance in the organization, and acceptance is a key to personal influence. Bingham and his colleagues (Bingham, et al; 2014) have shown, for instance, that employees who contribute to their organization's ideological goals become more influential than employees who simply focus on getting ahead socially.

Organizational leaders tend to be vigilant in defending core organizational values, and they work hard to socialize newcomers to the "proper" modes of thinking and acting. Often, new members or outsiders fail to understand the importance of an organization's unique culture. They might find the organization's way of doing things peculiar or overly conventional. But it is vital for new employees to appreciate how important the organization's values and culture are to their own success.

Organizational values are important both historically and strategically. Here's why: Good leaders understand that a precondition for their organization becoming a market leader is to be perceived as a unique player in the market (e.g., not just another computer company). They strive to create distinctiveness that merits attention from the financial community, potential employees, and customers. This may involve placing a premium on quality, economy, value, service, loyalty to employees, civic involvement, or some other core value. This uniqueness is the basis for internal organizational pride and external projections of excellence.

The leader (often the founder) articulates this vision and institutionalizes it as part of the organization's culture (Deal & Kennedy, 1982; Peters, 1978; Schein, 1999). Leaders use culture to expresses the "hows" and "whys" of doing business the "right" way. For example, Harold Geneen at ITT consistently stressed, "Search for the unshakable facts"; Tom Jones at Northrop emphasized, "Everybody at Northrop is in marketing"; John DeButts at AT&T drummed into employees, "The system is the solution"; and Ed Rust at State Farm frequently asked colleagues, "How would a good neighbor handle this?"

New members of an organization are taught what is acceptable behavior through stories (for example, the engineer who worked for 72 hours straight to save a project), rites (graduation or promotion ceremonies), and symbols (uniforms, or no private offices for managers). The savvy newcomer looks beyond formal position statements, probing for answers to questions such as: "What are the organization's 'sacred cows'?" "What is the source of organizational pride?" "Who are the corporate heroes?" "What are the revered traditions?"

Many organizational practices make sense only when viewed as symbolic support for fundamental values. For example, a large insurance firm stipulates that no one can be promoted above a certain level in any department unless he or she has completed the requirements for insurance industry professional certification. Young employees in data processing, accounting, or personnel might chafe under the edict to take classes on the details of the insurance business, but they miss the symbolic meaning of this requirement. The founders of the firm felt that the organization's key to success was a workforce deeply committed to the overarching goal of providing excellent services and products in the insurance business at large, rather than becoming too entrenched in their department's interests. In this organization, taking insurance courses has become synonymous with commitment to the organization's mission, and organizational commitment is a litmus test for organizational advancement.

This does not mean a nonconformist can't get ahead in the corporate world. It simply suggests he or she will be held to a higher standard in terms of other sources of personal power such as expertise and effort. A conversation during a promotion review meeting in a major corporation reflects this attitude: "Sometimes I don't know where he's coming from, but he is so blasted smart and he works so darn hard, we have no choice but to promote him."

Before leaving the subject of organizational culture and personal legitimacy, it is important to raise an ethical question. We have described how conforming to the organization's culture helps you accrue power, but that doesn't mean strict conformity is morally right or that it is necessarily in the best long-term interests of the firm. In fact, evidence suggests that successful organizations have members who are capable of both gaining power by fitting in and using that power to challenge the prevailing belief where necessary (Pascale, 1985). Unchallenged organizational beliefs often interfere with a company's necessary adaptation to changing competitive and regulatory conditions. However, challenges are most successful when mounted by members whose commitment to the organization has been the most loyal. "Paying your dues" creates legitimacy, and legitimacy is a prerequisite for effective criticism.

In summary, we have highlighted four sources of personal power, which are all rooted in the individual's characteristics rather than in the positions or titles they hold. These personal characteristics have one thing in common—they are the ingredients of trust (Dirks & Ferrin, 2001; Hosmer, 1995). One meaning of the term *trustworthy* is "being above suspicion." Hence, individuals who are deemed trustworthy by their peers are likely candidates for positions of power and influence in organizations because organizational

Table 5.6 The Relationship Between the Sources of Personal Power and Personal Trustworthiness

SOURCES OF PERSONAL POWER	RELATED PERSONAL CHARACTERISTIC	REQUIREMENTS FOR PERSONAL TRUSTWORTHINESS
Expertise	Reliable	Ability: *Can* they make good on their commitments?
Effort	Dependable	
Attraction	Likable	Motivation: *Will* they make good on their commitments?
Legitimacy	Acceptable	

authority in their hands is less threatening. As shown in Table 5.6, a direct relationship exists among the four bases of personal power we have discussed and the requirements for personal trust. Basically, the trustworthiness of an individual's claims, promises, or commitments is a function of two factors: (1) How likely is it that the person *can* do what he or she says? and (2) How likely is it the person *will* do what he or she says? In other words, questions of trust involve assessment of probable performance informed by judgments about the individual's ability and motivation. This is why organizations place a great deal of emphasis on only putting proven performers in positions of high trust (or, in other words, positions of power).

SOURCES OF POSITIONAL POWER

Not all power stems from personal characteristics. In addition, the nature of one's position and task assignments play an important role. Four important characteristics of a position account for its power potential in an organization: *centrality, flexibility, visibility,* and *relevance* (Fiol, O'Connor, & Aguinis, 2001; Kanter, 1979; Pfeffer, 1994). These are shown in Table 5.7.

Centrality

Based on extensive data collection over more than a dozen years, one consulting firm reports that, "Failure to build strong relationships and teamwork with peers and subordinates is the chief culprit in 61% of new hires and promotions that don't work out" (Fisher, 2005). As suggested by this study, one of the most important ways of gaining power in an organization is by occupying a position of **centrality** in a broad network of relationships. Networks are critical to effective performance for one compelling reason: No one has all the necessary information and resources to accomplish what's expected of him or her. Indeed, one study of effective management concluded that a key factor in distinguishing high and low performers was their ability to establish informal relationships via networks. "Lone wolves" in informal networks were unable to gather the information, resource commitments, and personal support necessary to accomplish unusual, important tasks (Kaplan & Mazique, 1983; Sparrowe, Liden, & Kraimer, 2001). On the other hand, those who have extensive and diverse social networks earn higher salaries and are more successful than those with a narrower set of contacts (Pfeffer & Konrad, 1991; Sparrowe et al., 2001).

Increasing one's power by becoming more central in a communication or work-flow network represents

Table 5.7 Determinants of Position-Power

CHARACTERISTIC	DESCRIPTION
Centrality	Access to information in a communication network
Flexibility	Amount of discretion vested in a position
Visibility	Degree to which task performance is seen by influential people in the organization
Relevance	Alignment of assigned tasks and organizational priorities

a very different approach from conventional strategies of power building. Typically, young aspiring employees think only in terms of increasing their power by moving up the organizational career ladder. They mistakenly assume that power is the exclusive right of hierarchical position. If they are not promoted as quickly as they would like, they assume they have limited power to make change or accomplish extraordinary things. Inexperienced, ineffective organizational members grumble about not having enough formal power to get work done, and they covet the influence wielded on higher levels.

In contrast, savvy organizational members realize that informal network power is available to individuals at all levels. In fact, simply being able to "read" the social network is associated with power. In a classic study, Krackhardt (1990) found that people who could more accurately describe the advice network in their organization (i.e., they knew who sought advice from whom) were rated by others as more powerful. Numerous studies show that being central in one's organizational network increases not only perceived status, but also salary and long-term career success. It is critical, then, for new organization members to understand that informal personal power generally precedes, rather than follows from, formal organizational power. A promotion is simply a formal recognition by senior management that an individual has demonstrated the ability to get work done using informal networks.

One of the more interesting research findings about network centrality is that the *type* of network one builds matters a lot. Most people develop networks with people who share similar backgrounds and experience as themselves. Their social contacts tend to know their other social contacts, so the network becomes very dense and interconnected. Ron Burt (1992) and others have argued that the most effective networks, in contrast, are networks that have many **structural holes**. A structural hole exists when two people in your network are not connected to each other. In such cases, you become a bridge between two different sources of information. Your value increases because you can monitor the flow of information between parties and provide unique value to each of the two people to whom you are connected.

Building a network rich in structural holes does not come naturally for most people. It means branching out to interact with people who may come from a very different background than oneself. In fact, one study showed that being an "organizational misfit" with an atypical career path can actually *strengthen* your influence; an unusual background affords one

opportunities to bring unique information to the organization and to broker relationships across structural holes, thus giving more opportunities for influence (Kleinbaum, 2012). Considerable evidence shows that having a diverse network increases your ability to develop organizational power, regardless of your position. Recent research shows that a diverse network also increases creativity (Sosa, 2011).

A striking example of the merits of building a diverse network is Adam Rifkin. In the early 1990s, Rifkin was a doctoral student in computer engineering and a fan of the band Green Day. He created a fan website for the band, one of the first of its kind. In 1994, he received a complaint email about his site from someone who disagreed with his labeling Green Day a "punk band." Rifkin decided to take the feedback to heart. He reached out to the complainer and ultimately decided to change his description of the band. Based on the experience, he created a separate website to direct his followers to other punk bands. The author of the email was impressed with Rifkin's response. Five years later, Rifkin was working on some social media start-up ideas. Struggling for direction and resources, he started looking through his old emails to see who might be able to help him. He came across the old email complaining about the Green Day site, and reached out to its author, Graham Spencer. Spencer had since founded Excite, a pioneering search engine. He had sold it the year before for $6.7 billion. Spencer remembered Rifkin and offered help. With Spencer's assistance, Rifkin created some of the earliest successful social media ventures. He was the founder of Renkoo, which developed Facebook and MySpace applications used by 36 million people. Rifkin is now the CEO of PandaWhale, a successful social networking website (Grant, 2013).

This example illustrates the merits of using unpredictable circumstances to establish a broad network of contacts. One of the biggest mistakes individuals make at the outset of their management careers is to become isolated. Some people assume that getting ahead in their department is sufficient for getting ahead in the organization. As a result, they concentrate all their attention on accomplishing their narrow work responsibilities or on building strong relations only with their immediate coworkers. If you look at organizations only in terms of vertical structures, you will see how isolated a communication network in a single department can become. In contrast, it is important to become a central actor in the organization's broad communication network, not just the department's. This can be done by going to lunch with people in other departments, reading the annual reports of all the divisions, volunteering for interdepartmental task forces, and seeking out boundary-spanning positions that require you to work with other departments.

It is important that managers seeking to form wide-reaching social networks understand that social relations look very different in different cultural settings. Specifically, research has shown that members of different cultures differ in terms of how many and what types of friendships they are likely to form at work, the extent to which they mix socioemotional and instrumental social ties, and the strength and longevity of their social relations (Morris, Podolny, & Ariel, 2000). For example, American business relationships are characterized by the norms of the marketplace (they must be profitable). In contrast, Chinese business relationships are characterized by a familial orientation (doing whatever is good for the organization), German relationships are characterized by a legal-bureaucratic orientation (play by the rules), and Spanish relationships are characterized by an affiliative orientation (sociability and friendship) (Morris et al., 2000).

Flexibility

A critical requirement for building a power base is **flexibility**, or discretion—that is, freedom to exercise one's judgment. A person who has little latitude to improvise, innovate, or demonstrate initiative will find it extremely difficult to become powerful. A flexible position has few rules or established routines governing how work should be done. In addition, flexibility means that a manager need not seek a supervisor's approval to make nonroutine decisions. People in flexible positions perform tasks that allow considerable judgment.

Flexibility is correlated with the life cycle of a position. New tasks are less likely to be routinized than old ones. Similarly, the number of rules governing a position tends to be positively related to the number of individuals who have previously occupied it. The same logic applies to the life cycle of a decision-making process. The longer a group has been meeting to discuss an issue, the more difficult it is to have any significant amount of influence over its deliberations. The critical decisions about how discussions will be conducted, what evidence should be examined, and which alternatives are germane are all made early in a group's history. To make a difference, therefore, it is preferable to be a participant from the beginning, or to take on new roles or new tasks.

One indication of the amount of flexibility inherent in a position is the reward system governing it. If an organization rewards people for being reliable and predictable, that suggests the organization will penalize people who use discretion. On the other hand, if organizations reward people for unusual performance and innovation, discretion is encouraged. For example, a company may teach salespeople how to close a deal but at the same time encourage them to figure out better ways to do the task. Individuals with a high need for power should avoid a job that is governed by the reliable performance criterion—no matter how attractive it might appear in other aspects—because it will strip them of a necessary prerequisite of power.

Some managers in low discretion positions might feel like they are completely stymied in using flexibility as a power source. However, recent research suggests that people with a **proactive personality** can often create their own sense of flexibility. Proactive personality has been defined as a tendency to effect change in one's environment (Bateman & Crant, 1993). Proactive people focus on finding new opportunities, taking initiative, and persisting in the process of making positive changes happen. Scholars have provided strong evidence that proactive people are promoted more quickly and make higher salaries (Seibert et al., 1999). They also tend to receive higher performance evaluations from supervisors, but only if they are adept at building their network so that their initiatives have support from others (Thompson, 2005). Achieving flexibility at work may have as much to do with the employee's own behavior as it does with the characteristics of the role. Striving for flexibility by taking personal initiative to add value and solve problems is one technique for increasing one's power in roles that don't naturally afford a lot of discretion.

Visibility

A sage corporate executive once counseled a young, aspiring MBA, "The key formula for promotion is excellent performance multiplied by visibility." Obviously, highly visible but poor performance will not lead to promotion, but the real message of this advice is that an excellent, but obscure, performance won't either. Of course, no one likes the person who is always showing off and demanding the spotlight. But developing power does require you to achieve **visibility** in your organization, so that people recognize you and see you making contributions.

LEARNING
i

One way to increase your visibility is to foster frequent contact with senior officials, decision makers, and informal leaders. If your normal work activities don't bring you into contact with important people, you may be able to heighten your visibility through participation in company or outside programs, meetings, and conferences. Many a young career has been advanced by a strong presentation at a trade association convention or board meeting. Volunteering to make presentations, and thus to act as the "face" of your department, is an excellent route to increasing visibility.

Recognizing this point, an enterprising junior executive in a large Chicago conglomerate seized on a chance occurrence to impress the chairman of the board. By a strange set of circumstances, the young executive was asked to fill in for the secretary of the board of directors and take notes at a stockholders' meeting. Making sure he arrived early, he greeted every person who entered the boardroom and then introduced that person to every other member in the room. The fact that this young man was able to put everyone at ease (not to mention remember the names of a large number of strangers) so impressed the chairman, he subsequently provided several opportunities for him to advance rapidly in the organization.

The importance of face-to-face contact in establishing visibility cannot be overemphasized. Inexperienced managers, for instance, often assume they will get credit for writing an excellent report. Unfortunately, this is not always the case. If another member of the team gives a very good presentation of the report to an executive committee, the presenter will likely receive a disproportionately large share of the credit for the work. Busy executives tend to be more impressed by what they see in a meeting than by what they read in their offices, particularly if they observe their fellow executives giving approving nods and smiles during the presentation. The benefits of the positive reaction tend to go to the person who is in front of them at the time.

Another important opportunity for gaining visibility is participation in problem-solving task forces. Being asked to serve in this capacity conveys to others that you have valuable expertise. More importantly, if the task force's report is received well by senior officials, your name will be associated with the group responsible for the "breakthrough," particularly if it comes during a time of uncertainty or change. For example, heads of government whose accomplishments stand out dramatically in a historical perspective are those who proposed remedies during major crises. Consider that Winston Churchill is credited with helping Britain survive World War II. On the smaller scale of a business firm, this truism is equally reliable. The power a person gains is directly proportional to his or her visibility in successfully handling change or crisis.

An additional source of visibility is name recognition. Elected officials recognize the value of keeping their names before the electorate, so they place signs at state and city boundaries and entrances to public transportation terminals welcoming travelers. In organizations, there are analogous opportunities for enhancing your visibility. For example, if your office regularly sends information to the public or other departments, try enclosing a signed cover note. If you are new to an organization, introduce yourself to other members. If you have a good idea, formally communicate it to the appropriate parties in person as well as in a follow-up memo. If someone has recently accomplished something significant, send a note expressing congratulations and appreciation.

Relevance

This leads us to the fourth critical characteristic of powerful positions, **relevance**, which means being associated with activities directly related to central objectives and issues in an organization. As one manager put it, "My peers are responsive to me because the functions that I manage are the lifeblood of the organization…my presence in their office implies that there's a vital concern of one sort or another that needs to be dealt with" (Kaplan & Mazique, 1983, p. 10).

Paul Lawrence and Jay Lorsch (1986) argued for the importance of identifying a company's "dominant competitive issue," which is the organizational activity that most accounts for the firm's competitiveness in its industry. An organization's dominant competitive issue depends on the industry in which it operates. For instance, companies that use a flow-process form of technology, such as oil refineries and chemical plants, are most dependent on effective marketing because of their sizable capital investment and small range of product alternatives. In contrast, companies using a standard mass-production (assembly-line) form of technology, with a stable line of products and established customers, are most dependent on the efficiency of their production processes. Finally, high-tech firms, or companies producing custom-designed products, are most successful when they had strong research and development departments. Employees that attach themselves to their particular organization's dominant competitive issue are more likely to develop power based on relevance.

Thinking about relevance may be particularly important for employees who work in departments that aren't directly connected to the organization's dominant competitive issue. For instance, Tony Rucci, former chief administrative officer at Cardinal Health, argues that in today's lean corporate environment, human resource departments have to demonstrate to management how they contribute to the bottom line. As the *Wall Street Journal* argued, "strong HR departments are now focusing on boosting productivity by helping employees better understand what's expected of them and by showing managers how to be more effective" (Rendon, 2010).

These trends have significant implications for relevance. An individual who seeks influential positions must be sensitive to the relevance of his or her department's activities for the company. For example, a design engineer who works for an oil company is less likely to become influential than one who works for an electronics firm, and operations researchers will have more influence in companies with established product lines and an assembly-line production process. Computer scientists are more likely to feel empowered in a software development firm than if they are working for an insurance company or a public utility. In the latter organization, computer programming is viewed as a support function, with only an indirect effect on profitability.

Of course, it isn't usually easy to change functions just to increase one's relevance. But there are often other ways to increase relevance in one's current position; for instance, assuming an outreach role can connect one to relevant functions or projects. Employees can act as a representative to, or an advocate for, projects and causes that are important to the organization. Another key role is that of evaluator. Positions that serve as checkpoints become powerful by virtue of the fact that they create dependence. The role of trainer or mentor to new members of a work unit is another powerful position. It places you in a critical position to reduce uncertainty for newcomers and substantially enhance their performance. Newcomers are generally apprehensive, and they will appreciate your showing them the ropes. Also, successful performance in this developmental role earns you the respect and admiration of those colleagues who stand to benefit from your effective training.

To summarize, we have discussed four aspects of organizational positions that are critical to the achievement of power. As Table 5.7 shows, centrality and relevance encourage the gaining of power through horizontal relationships. In other words, power stemming from centrality and relevance is based on relationships

to other lateral positions and activities in the organization. However, visibility and flexibility are linked to hierarchical power. Flexibility reflects the amount of discretion vested in a position by superiors. A highly visible position has close ties with higher levels of authority, so a noteworthy performance in a visible position receives more recognition, which is an important prerequisite for an individual's upward mobility in an organization.

TRANSFORMING POWER INTO INFLUENCE

Having discussed the skill of gaining power, we now turn our attention to converting power into influence. This concept requires an understanding of the difference between power and influence. As we stated at the beginning of this chapter, many popular books on this subject suggest power is an end in itself. Our goal here is not to help people gain power for its own sake. When the weak seek power simply because they are tired of being pushed around, tyranny generally follows their ascension. Our interest, instead, is in helping people accomplish the exceptional in organizations, recognizing that this generally requires political clout. The well-meaning but politically naive seldom make major contributions to organizations. Consequently, our focus is on how you can become influential as well as powerful.

Influential people have power, but not all powerful people have influence. Influence entails actually securing the consent of others to work with you in accomplishing an objective. Many powerful people cannot do that, as evidenced by the chronic inability of American presidents to convince Congress to pass what the president considers to be essential legislation. The skill of transforming power into influence hinges on engendering support and commitment from others, rather than resistance and resentment.

Influence Strategies: The Three Rs

Power becomes influence when others willingly consent to behave according to the desires of the power holder. The strategies used by managers to influence others fall into three broad categories: *retribution, reciprocity,* and *reason* (Allen, Madison, Porter, Renwick, & Mayer, 1979; Kipnis, 1987; Kipnis, Schmidt, & Wilkinson, 1980). Table 5.8 lists these strategies and the corresponding direct and indirect approaches. Specific examples of these strategies are shown in Table 5.9 (Cialdini, 2001; Marwell & Schmitt, 1967).

Table 5.8 | Influence Strategies

STRATEGIES	DIRECT APPROACH	INDIRECT APPROACH
Retribution: Force others to do what you say	1. Coercion (threaten)	2. Intimidation (pressure)
Reciprocity: Help others want to do what you say	3. Bargaining (exchange)	4. Ingratiation (obligate)
Reason: Show others that it makes sense to do what you say (or goals)	5. Present facts (or needs)	6. Appeal to personal values

Table 5.9 | Examples of Influence Strategies

RETRIBUTION (COERCION AND INTIMIDATION)

General form:	"If you don't do X, you will regret it!"
Threat:	"If you do not comply, I will punish you."
Social pressure:	"Others in your group have agreed; what's your decision?"
Had enough?:	"I will stop nagging you if you comply."
Perceived scarcity and time pressure:	"If you don't act now, you'll lose this opportunity/cause problems for others."
Avoid causing pain to others:	"If you don't agree, others will be hurt/disadvantaged."

RECIPROCITY (EXCHANGE AND INGRATIATION)

General form:	"If you do X, you'll receive Y."
Promise:	"If you comply, I will reward you."
Esteem:	"People you value will think better (worse) of you if you do (do not) comply."
Pregiving:	"I will do something you like for you; then will you do this for me?"
Obligation:	"You owe me compliance because of past favors." (Even though I implied there would be no future obligation.)
Reciprocal compromise:	"I have lowered my initial offer/price, and now I expect you to reciprocate" (no matter how unreasonable my initial position was).
Escalation of commitment:	"I'm only interested in a small commitment." (But I'll be back later for more.)

REASON (PERSUASION BASED ON FACTS, NEEDS, OR PERSONAL VALUES)

General form:	"I want you to do X, because it's consistent with/good for/necessary to…"
Evidence:	"These facts/experts' opinions demonstrate the merits of my position/request."
Need:	"This is what I need; will you help me out?"
Goal attainment:	"Compliance will enable you to reach a personally important objective."
Value congruence:	"This action is consistent with your commitment to X."
Ability:	"This endeavor would be enhanced if we could count on your ability/experience."
Loyalty:	"Because we are friends/minorities, will you do this?"
Altruism:	"The group needs your support, so do it for the good of us all."

You may have mixed reactions to these lists. Some strategies will probably strike you as particularly effective; others may seem inappropriate or even manipulative or dishonest. Our purpose in listing these is not to imply that all of these strategies ought to be used. Rather, we present the full arsenal of influence strategies so that you can informatively choose those with which you feel most comfortable and so that you can be aware when others are attempting to influence you.

These three influence strategies rely on different mechanisms for obtaining compliance. **Retribution** is based on personal threat, which typically stems from formal authority. The direct form of this approach, *coercion*, involves an explicit threat to impose sanctions if the manager's will is not obeyed. Recognizing their vulnerability to the boss' sanctions, subordinates generally comply, reluctantly.

Intimidation is an indirect form of retribution because the threat is only implied. The manager's intimidating interpersonal style suggests the possibility of organizationally based sanctions for noncompliance, even if he or she does not make an overt threat. Intimidation can take many forms: for instance, a manager publicly criticizing a subordinate's report, systematically ignoring a subordinate during meetings, or handing out impossible tasks to junior executives.

Acts of intimidation are generally accompanied by emphasis on the power holder's authority. Intimidators tend to give assignments in their own office, in a highly formal manner, and while highlighting the vulnerability of the target (e.g., mentioning his junior grade or short tenure with the organization). This sets the stage for an implicit threat (e.g., "If people aren't willing to work overtime on this project, corporate headquarters is going to pull the plug on our budget and a number of younger employees will get hurt").

Intimidation can also occur through peer pressure. Managers who know that a majority of their subordinates support a controversial action can use group dynamics to secure the compliance of the minority. This is done by telling the majority that a decision must be unanimous and it's their responsibility to demonstrate leadership by securing the commitment of all members. Or, the manager can apply pressure directly to the holdout members of the group by stressing the need for harmony, mutual support, and working for the common good.

The second strategy extracts compliance from others by invoking the norm of **reciprocity**. Reciprocity operates on the principle of satisfying the self-interest of both parties. Reciprocity commonly involves straightforward *bargaining* in which each party gains something from the exchange. In bargaining, both parties are aware of the costs and benefits associated with striking a deal, and their negotiations focus on reaching an agreement that is satisfactory to both. *Ingratiation*, however, is more subtle. It involves using friendliness and favors to incur social obligations. When compliance is required or support is needed, previous benefactors are then reminded of their debts. A recent study shows that ingratiation is most effective when it is subtle rather than overt (Stern & Westphal, 2010). Other research shows that ingratiation has some negative side effects; recipients of ingratiation tend to exhibit overconfidence and an unwillingness to make needed changes (Park, et al., 2011).

Managers use reciprocity in many ways. These include striking deals with influential opinion leaders to support a new program, asking subordinates to work overtime in exchange for an extended weekend, doing small favors for the boss so one can occasionally take longer lunch hours, and formally negotiating with staff members to get them to accept undesirable assignments.

Comparing the strategies of retribution and reciprocity, it should be clear that the former is more ethically suspect than the latter. Retribution strategies ignore the rights of others and the norm of fairness, whereas reciprocity strategy honors both. An emphasis on retribution leads to ignoring the quality of the ongoing relationship between the parties, while reciprocity recognizes the value of strengthening interdependence between people.

The third influence approach is based on the manager's persuasive ability. Instead of seeking compliance by using one's position of authority, this approach appeals to **reason**. The manager uses the inherent merits of the request to convince the influence target to choose compliance themselves. Here, the focus is on helping others to see why your ideas make sense. Direct forms of persuasion rely on articulating compelling *facts or needs* describing why the request is critical for the organization. For example, "If your shift doesn't work overtime tonight, we will lose $5,000 worth of product. Will you pitch in and help us solve this problem?" In the indirect form of reason, the manager appeals to the other person's *personal values or goals*. These might include focusing on the other person's desire to be altruistic, a loyal team member, or respected as an expert.

Because persuasion is sometimes confused with manipulation, it is important here to distinguish between the two. A persuasive appeal is explicit and direct, while a manipulative act is implicit and deceptive. The persuader respects the autonomy of decision makers and trusts their ability to judge evidence effectively. In contrast, a manipulator has low regard for the abilities of decision makers and doesn't trust them to make good decisions. Manipulators have the same objectives as authoritarian leaders—they simply use more subtle tactics. Manipulative managers, therefore, often appear to the casual observer to be using a democratic leadership style. In fact, they are actually "illusory democrats" because, while their actions may appear democratic, they have no inclination to share power. They use a democratic style only because it makes others less defensive and therefore more vulnerable to their power initiatives (Dyer, 1972).

The Pros and Cons of Each Strategy

As Table 5.10 notes, each approach has advantages and limitations (Cuming, 1984; Mulder, Koppelaar, de Jong, & Verhage, 1986). The retribution strategy produces immediate action and work that conforms to the manager's specifications. But the retribution strategy comes with high costs. Of the three strategies, it is the most likely to engender resistance. Most people do not like to be forced to do something. Effective managers use this approach sparingly, generally reserving it for crises or as a last resort when the other strategies have failed. It is best suited to situations in which the goals of the parties are competing or independent. This approach is effective only when the target person perceives that the manager has both the power and the will to follow through on his or her threat. Otherwise, the person being influenced may be tempted to call the manager's bluff. Also, the threatened sanctions must be sufficiently severe that disobedience is unthinkable.

When used repeatedly, the retribution approach produces resentment and alienation, which frequently generates overt or covert opposition. Because these conditions tend to stifle initiative and innovative behavior—even when the individual complies—organizational performance may suffer.

The reciprocity strategy allows the manager to obtain compliance without causing resentment, since both parties benefit from the agreement. It is most appropriate when each party controls some outcomes valued by the other party and there are established rules to govern the transaction, including provisions for adjudication of grievances.

Even under these conditions, however, reciprocity requires some degree of trust. If individuals have reneged on past agreements, their credibility as negotiating partners becomes suspect. Reciprocity is also best suited to situations in which the power holder needs the target person to perform specific unambiguous assignments.

The chief disadvantage of this approach, when used frequently, is that it engenders a highly instrumental view of work. The other person begins to expect that every request is open for negotiation and that every completed assignment will result in a reward of equal value. Consequently, relying solely on reciprocity might undercut employees' commitment levels; they may start to view their work only calculatively and downplay the value of working hard to achieve organizational goals, other than for personal gain.

The assets and liabilities of the third approach—reason—are more complicated. The objective of the rational strategy is a higher form of compliance, that is, internalized commitment. In other words, the goal is for the employee to voluntarily choose to comply. Commitment relies on teaching correct principles and explaining legitimate needs and then trusting the good intent and sound judgment of subordinates to act appropriately. In its ideal form, commitment decreases the need for surveillance and enhances the subordinate's initiative, commitment, and creativity.

The principal disadvantage of the rational, or reason, approach is the amount of time required to build the trust and mutual understanding required to make it operate effectively. The required time increases as the number of involved people expands. Also, because the success of this strategy depends on shared goals and values, persuasion through reason is difficult to implement when the parties have dissimilar backgrounds, subscribe to competing philosophies, or are assigned conflicting responsibilities, such as maintaining quality versus meeting deadlines.

In their classic studies on influence strategies, Schmidt and Kipnis (1987; Kipnis & Schmidt, 1988) provided compelling evidence supporting the superior benefits of the approach based on reason. Individuals who rely primarily on reason and logic to influence others are rated as highly effective by their bosses, and they report low levels of job-related stress and high levels of job satisfaction. In contrast, individuals who persistently use any other approach to get their way tend to receive lower performance ratings and experience higher levels of personal stress and job dissatisfaction.

Table 5.10 Comparisons Among Influence Strategies

INFLUENCE STRATEGY	WHEN TO USE IT	POSSIBLE ADVANTAGES	POSSIBLE DISADVANTAGES	POSSIBLE COMPLAINTS
Retribution	• Unequal power, in influencer's favor • Commitment and quality not important • Tight time constraints • Serious violation • Issue not important to target • If issue is important, retribution not likely • Specific, unambiguous request • Resistance to request is likely	• Quick, direct action	• Stifles commitment, creativity • Insecurity of boss • Engenders resentment • Must increase seriousness of threats to maintain pressure	• Violation of rights • Ethical violations
Reciprocity	• Parties mutually dependent • Each party has resources valued by other • Adequate time for negotiating • Established exchange norms exist • Parties viewed as trustworthy • Commitment to broad goals and values not critical • Needs are specific and short-term	• Low incidence of resentment • Justification for request not required	• Engenders instrumental view of work (expectation of specific rewards for specific actions) • Encourages people to feel that the terms of assignments are open for negotiation	• Unfairness, dashed expectations, manipulation
Reason	• Adequate time for extensive discussion • Common goals/values • Parties share mutual respect/credibility • Parties share ongoing relationship	• Need for surveillance reduced	• Considerable time required to build trust (time increases as number of people increases) • Requires common goals and values	• Difference of opinions, conflicting perceptions of priorities

Overall, it appears that higher-numbered strategies in Table 5.8 are more effective than lower-numbered strategies. This ordering reflects the overall value system portrayed here: direct is better than indirect; open is better than closed; exchange is better than intimidation; and sincere requests are better than guile.

One justification for this conclusion is that the higher-numbered strategies are more likely to be perceived as fair and just, in part because they usually involve an explanation. Research on organizational change has consistently shown that people are more willing to change when they understand why. For example, in a study of 187 employees in seven business firms that had just been relocated, they rated the process as fair, even though they felt the move was unfavorable, when they understood the reasons behind the action (Daly, 1995).

It is important to point out how cultural preferences need to be factored into your choice of influence strategy. First, your influence strategy needs to be congruent with your personal cultural values. Second, it needs to be congruent with the cultural values of the influence "target." Third, it needs to be congruent with the general context in which your relationship is embedded. As an extreme case of these three situational factors, one can imagine a Japanese manager trying to influence an African employee in an auto plant in Germany. Granted, our claims about the merits and liabilities of these various influence attempts are clearly rooted in traditional American cultural norms (which include egalitarian relations, direct communication, and individualism). In contrast, members of cultures that place a high value on social obligation may prefer reciprocity influence strategies. In addition, cultures that emphasize indirect communication methods, such as storytelling and inference making, would likely prefer the indirect over the direct strategies. Similarly, individuals who place particular importance on hierarchical relationships may feel more comfortable with the forcing strategies (Thompson, 2001).

Exercising Upward Influence— A Special Case of the Reason Strategy

One particular form of influence warrants special attention. Our discussion of the "Three Rs" has largely focused on influencing others either "downward" (e.g., subordinates) or laterally (e.g., peers). The role that is obviously missing from this set of influence targets is "the boss." Given Kanter's (1979) notion discussed earlier in this chapter that organizational power can be measured in terms of one's control over making "exceptions to the rule," it is important that we examine strategies for getting exceptional requests granted by exerting upward influence. As you recall, Table 5.1 listed a number of exceptions that subordinates believed were the result of having a "boss with clout." For instance, bosses with clout might be able to intercede on behalf of someone in trouble, get a desirable placement for a talented subordinate, or get approval for expenditures beyond the budget.

Given the stress we've placed on using power to have a positive, constructive influence in an organization, it is important to underscore the merits of managers using their power to benefit their subordinates by exerting upward and outward influence. If subordinates perceive that their unit leader's clout will shield them from outside, disruptive pressures and help them break down artificial organizational barriers to getting the job done right, then they are naturally inclined to strengthen their boss's power base.

One approach to upward influence that has received a great deal of attention is called **issue selling** (Dutton & Ashford, 1993). Issue selling is the process of drawing leaders' attention to those issues or problems that concern you most, notwithstanding the numerous other issues that compete for their attention. Busy leaders tend to devote attention to those issues that they perceive are most consequential. Effectively influencing upward, therefore, means that you need to convince your boss that a particular issue you espouse is so important that it demands his or her timely attention. Table 5.11 contains a summary of the key strategies for exercising upward influence through effective issue selling (Dutton & Ashford, 1993; Dutton & Duncan, 1987).

Michael Useem, Director of the Center for Leadership and Change Management, provides additional perspective on influencing upward. In an interview regarding his book, *Leading Up: How to Lead Your Boss So You Both Win*, Useem says, bluntly, "If people are afraid to help their leaders lead, their leaders will fail" (Breen, 2001). He offers several tips for what he calls "trickle-up leadership." First, you've got to speak up to lead up. He notes that even in the Marine Corps officers are expected to speak up if their superior issues a flawed order. Second, before you lead up, you've got to team up. When the implications of your message will require a major change of course, it is particularly important to work with allies, especially those who add credibility to your argument. Third, lead up, don't argue up. When offering a contrary perspective, disagree without being disagreeable. By modeling open-mindedness, support, and trustworthiness, your example of how you disagree may be your most important message, especially during times of high stress and conflict. Fourth, don't try to be all things to everyone, or else you'll end up being nothing to anybody. Superiors are more willing to hear bad news from subordinates whose judgment they can trust and whose loyalty is unquestioned; simply trying to keep everyone happy will lead others to question your loyalty.

Table 5.11 Ways to Sell Issues Upward

PRINCIPLE	EXPLANATION
Congruence	The issue must be congruent with your position and role. A person in the marketing department trying to sell an issue relating to computers would be less effective than would an information specialist.
Credibility	Maintain credibility by being honest, open, non-self-serving, and straightforward. Demonstrate that your interest in the issue is not mere personal gain. Issues that seem self-serving are more difficult to sell.
Communication	Gain or maintain access to a broad communication network. Use multiple communication channels, including face-to-face conversations, written memos, email, conferences, news clippings, and so on.
Compatibility	Select issues that are compatible and in harmony with the organization. Avoid issues that contradict the company culture.
Solvability	The issue must be solvable. Make it clear that the issue can be solved. Show that solution alternatives are available. Unresolvable issues don't capture attention.
Payoff	Clearly point out the long-term payoff, for the organization or the manager, of addressing the issue. The higher the potential payoff appears to be, the more likely the issue will receive attention.
Expertise	Identify the expertise needed to solve the problem. Issues are more likely to capture attention if it is clear that the expertise necessary to resolve them resides in the organization, or better still, under the purview of the top manager or boss.
Responsibility	Point out the responsibility that top managers have to address the issue. Emphasize the negative consequences associated with ignoring the issue or leaving it unresolved.
Presentation	Ensure that the issue is presented succinctly, in emotionally positive terms, with supporting data and novel information. Complex and convoluted information does not capture attention, so the issue must be explained in precise, simple terms.
Bundling	Bundle similar issues together with other important issues that interest top managers. Point out the relationship between your issue and other issues already being addressed.
Coalitions	The issue must be sponsored by other people who will help see the issue. Building coalitions of supporters makes the issue hard to ignore.
Visibility	Present and sell the issue in a public forum rather than in a private meeting. The more individuals who hear about the issue, the more likely it is to reach the boss's agenda.

SOURCE: *Adapted from Dutton and Ashford, 1993.*

Acting Assertively: Neutralizing Influence Attempts

In general, managers are more effective when they assume that others are reasonable, well meaning, and motivated. Unfortunately, in some cases, these assumptions are proven false. When this happens, it is important to be prepared to protect ourselves from unwanted, inappropriate efforts by others to influence our actions. Recalling Figure 5.1, lack of power is just as harmful to our personal performance as excessive use of power. Therefore, it is just as important to be skillful at resisting unwanted influence attempts as it is to influence the behavior of others. Tables 5.8 and 5.9

contain an impressive arsenal of influence strategies. Is it possible to neutralize the impact of such a highly developed, well-conceived set of tools? Many people succumb to these influence attempts, either because they are unaware of the social dynamics affecting their decisions or because they feel compelled to give in without offering any resistance. The importance of avoiding relationships in which individuals in power positions attempt to foster dependency in others has been the subject of research on the "toxic effects of tyranny in organizations" (Bies & Tripp, 1998). A summary of the characteristics of abusive bosses, from this study, is shown in Table 5.12. As you examine the following strategies for neutralizing inappropriate

Table 5.12	Characteristics of Abusive Bosses

- Micromanager—obsessed with details and perfection

- Inexplicit direction with decisive delivery—treats everything as a priority, requiring immediate, careful attention

- Mercurial mood swings—responses are very unpredictable

- Obsession with loyalty and obedience—believes "You are either for me or against me"

- Status derogation—criticizes subordinates in public, to the point of ridicule

- Capricious actions—known for arbitrariness and hypocrisy

- Exercises raw power for personal gain—feels entitled to the "spoils of victory"

SOURCE: *Adapted from Bies and Tripp, 1988.*

influence attempts, you might find it useful to use these characteristics of abusive relationships as a frame of reference.

Neutralizing Retribution Strategies Used by Others

Coercive and intimidating actions are intended to create a power imbalance based on dependence. This is the most detrimental form of influence, and therefore it should be resisted most vigorously and directly. You can use several approaches. The following can be thought of as a hierarchy of preferred responses (begin with the first and progress to the next responses, if necessary).

A. **Use countervailing power to shift dependence to interdependence.** The primary reason individuals (particularly bosses) rely heavily on the threat of retribution is to take advantage of a perceived inequality in power. Obviously, the boss has the final say, but the larger the perceived discrepancy in power, the greater the temptation for the boss to exploit the powerless. To resist retribution, focus your boss's attention on your mutual dependence, that is, your interdependence. Explain the negative consequences of failing to respect your rights and acting cooperatively. As part of this discussion, it may be appropriate to discuss more acceptable means of satisfying the boss's demands.

B. **Confront the exploiting individual directly.** All individuals, no matter what their job or organizational status, must protect their personal rights. One of those rights is to be treated as an intelligent, mature, responsible adult. To initiate a complaint effectively, key elements include describing the problem in terms of behaviors, consequences, and feelings, persisting until understood, and making specific suggestions. These techniques can be used to stress the seriousness of your concerns. If necessary, you should specify actions you are willing to take to stop coercive behavior. For example, whistle-blowing involves registering a complaint with an external governing body.

C. **Actively resist.** As a last resort, you should consider "fighting fire with fire." A work slow-down, deliberate disobedience to orders, or reporting the problem to a senior manager might be necessary. Again, this step should be pursued only after all other efforts to counter unwanted threats and demands have failed.

Neutralizing Reciprocity Strategies by Others

Many of the persuasion strategies used in sales and advertising fall into this category. In the marketplace, your concern is to avoid being duped. In the workplace, your concern is to avoid being manipulated. The following hierarchically arranged actions should be helpful in either situation. Once again, begin with the first response and follow with others if necessary.

A. **Examine the intent of any gift or favor-giving activity.** When a favor or gift is offered, you should consider the motives of the person, the appropriateness of their behavior, and the probable consequences of accepting. You should ask yourself questions such as "Is the giver likely to profit from this?" "Is this transaction inappropriate, unethical, or illegal?" "Is there a stated or implied expectation of reciprocation, and would I feel good about complying if the gift or favor were not offered?" In brief, when in doubt about a benefactor's motives, ask questions or decline the gift.

B. **Confront individuals who are using manipulative bargaining tactics.** Common ploys used in these situations are escalating commitments ("I'm only interested in a small commitment [now]") and reciprocal compromises ("I've lowered my [extreme] initial position; now I expect you [in the spirit of fair play] to also offer a compromise"). Simply drawing attention to these attempts at manipulation will enhance your power in the relationship. State that you do not approve of the manipulative strategy; then propose an alternative exchange, with emphasis on the merits of the case or the true value of the product rather than on the craftiness of the negotiators. You will thus be able to reshape the exchange process and avoid being manipulated.

C. **Refuse to bargain with individuals who use high-pressure tactics.** If steps 1 and 2 have failed, refuse to continue the discussion unless high-pressure tactics, such as imposing unrealistic time constraints or emphasizing the limited supply of the commodity or service, are dropped. If you suspect the dynamics of the negotiation process may be clouding your judgment about the value of the object or the importance of the issue, ask yourself, "Would I be interested in this item if there were an unlimited supply and no decision-making deadline?" If the answer is negative, either disengage from the negotiation process or focus your attention on its inequality. By shifting attention from content to process, you neutralize the advantage of a more experienced or powerful bargainer. By refusing to continue unless artificial constraints of time and supply are removed, you can establish fairer terms of trade.

Neutralizing Reason Strategies by Others

Although strategies based on reason are the most egalitarian of influence attempts, they can still create or exacerbate conditions of inequity. The following ordered guidelines should help you avoid these situations:

A. **Explain the adverse effects of compliance on performance.** Often, others' pressing priorities are your incidentals. The fact that someone can present a legitimate, convincing case does not mean you should comply with the request. For example, a request may be reasonable, but its timing bad; compliance would mean your having to miss important personal deadlines or neglect your customers. You should discuss these concerns with the influencer. By acknowledging the other person's

need, explaining your concerns about personal compliance, and then, helping to find alternatives, you avoid becoming overcommitted without giving offense.

B. **Defend your personal rights.** If you have used step 1 and your petitioner persists, focus the discussion on your personal rights. If individuals frequently come to you for help because they mismanage their time or resources, appeal to their sense of fairness. Ask if it is right to ask you to get behind in your own work in order to bail them out of their predicaments. Coworkers have the right to request your help in a pinch, but you also have the right to say no when even reasonable requests place you at a serious disadvantage or when they stem from the negligence or overdependence of others.

C. **Firmly refuse to comply with the request.** If your efforts to explain why you are unable to comply have not worked, you should firmly restate your refusal and terminate the discussion. Some people believe that their case is so compelling that they have difficulty believing others won't comply. If your coworker still "won't take no for an answer," it's probably because your "no" was not firm enough. As a last resort, you may have to seek the support of a higher authority.

Summary

In Figure 5.2, we highlight the two skills discussed in this chapter: gaining power and translating power into influence. We began by discussing sources of power such as personal attributes and position characteristics. One must develop both of these to maximize one's potential as a power holder. A strong person in a weak position and a weak person in a strong position are both at a disadvantage. Ideally, one should become a strong person in a strong position.

A manager must establish a power base in order to get work accomplished and obtain commitments to important objectives. But power without influence is not sufficient. Consequently, we discussed how to translate power into influence by selecting an appropriate influence strategy and implementing it in a way that minimizes resistance. In general, the higher-numbered strategies in Table 5.8 are the most effective. Persuasion tends to build trust and encourage internalized commitment, while coercion and intimidation erode trust, produce only superficial compliance, and encourage servility.

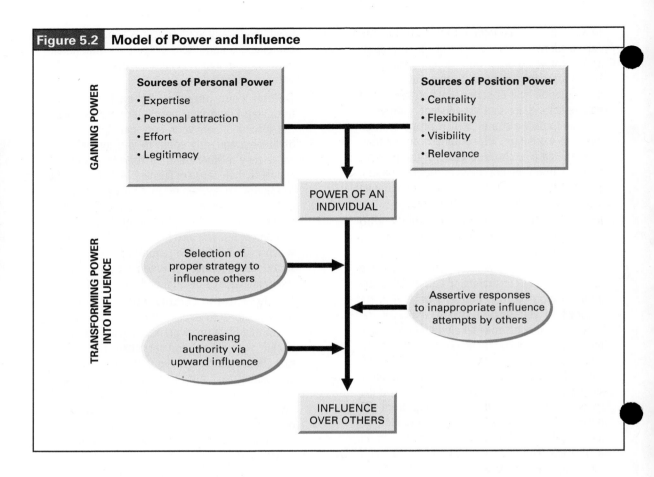

Figure 5.2 Model of Power and Influence

GAINING POWER

Sources of Personal Power
- Expertise
- Personal attraction
- Effort
- Legitimacy

Sources of Position Power
- Centrality
- Flexibility
- Visibility
- Relevance

POWER OF AN INDIVIDUAL

TRANSFORMING POWER INTO INFLUENCE

Selection of proper strategy to influence others

Assertive responses to inappropriate influence attempts by others

Increasing authority via upward influence

INFLUENCE OVER OTHERS

The unbridled use of power tends to increase resistance among subordinates, which in turn erodes the manager's power base. It also transforms the nature of the manager's stewardship over subordinates. The more a manager dominates subordinates, the more dependent they become on management's initiatives. As a result, managers tend to overvalue their contribution to their workers' job-performance activities ("Without me, they would be lost"). This inflated sense of self-importance encourages abuse of power that weakens the manager's influence and may even lead others to demand the manager's resignation. Thus, the abuse of power is both organizationally and personally destructive.

Power need not be abused, however. Managers who wield power effectively work within acknowledged constraints, but they figure out ways to do things right. They take full responsibility for their subordinates' performance, as well as for their commitment to their work and their membership in the organization.

Translating power into influence should not only be directed downward (i.e., toward organizational subordinates) but also upward (i.e., toward organizational superiors). Incompetent attempts to influence upward can quickly derail a manager's career, while competent upward influence can markedly enhance it. By helping to set the agenda of senior managers (issue selling) and by working for senior management's success (benefiting the boss), a manager's influence can increase significantly. When applying these two principles, however, managers should be motivated not by a thirst for mere self-aggrandizement, but by an honest desire to benefit their companies and strengthen their bosses' position.

The counsel of the late A. Bartlett Giamatti, former president of Yale University and commissioner of Major League Baseball, serves as a particularly fitting conclusion to this discussion: "Far better to conceive of power as consisting in part of the knowledge of when not to use all the power you have...Whoever knows how to restrain and effectively release power finds...that power flows back to him" (1981, p. 169).

Behavioral Guidelines

Effective management within an organization includes both gaining power and exercising influence wisely. Key guidelines for gaining power include:

1. Enhance your personal power in the organization by:
   - ❑ Developing your knowledge and skills to the point of becoming an acknowledged expert.
   - ❑ Enhancing your attractiveness to others, for example, by fostering the attributes of friendship (genuineness, intimacy, acceptance, validation of self-worth, tolerance, and social exchange) and by attending to professional appearance.
   - ❑ Being extremely dependable and, when appropriate, putting forth more effort than expected.
   - ❑ Increase your legitimacy by aligning your behaviors and decisions with core organizational values.

2. Increase the centrality of your position by:
   - ❑ Expanding your network of communication contacts.
   - ❑ Staying abreast of relevant information.
   - ❑ Serving as the source of information for others.

3. Increase the latitude and flexibility of your job by:
   - ❑ Reducing the percentage of routine activities.
   - ❑ Expanding task variety and novelty.
   - ❑ Initiating new ideas.
   - ❑ Getting involved in new projects.
   - ❑ Participating in the early stages of decision-making processes.
   - ❑ Seeking unusual and design-oriented jobs, rather than those that are repetitive and maintenance oriented.

4. Increase the visibility of your job performance by:
   - ❑ Expanding the number of contacts you have with senior people.
   - ❑ Making oral presentations of written work.
   - ❑ Participating in problem-solving task forces.
   - ❑ Inviting senior managers to help you recognize important accomplishments within your work group.
   - ❑ Sending personal notes of congratulations or cover notes accompanying reports or useful information.

5. Increase the relevance of your tasks to the organization by:
   - ❑ Becoming an internal coordinator or external representative.
   - ❑ Providing services and information to other units.
   - ❑ Monitoring and evaluating activities within your own unit.
   - ❑ Expanding the domain of your work activities.
   - ❑ Becoming involved in activities central to the organization's top priorities.
   - ❑ Becoming a trainer or mentor for new members.

   The general guidelines for influencing others effectively involve matching your influence strategy to specific situations, acting assertively when others attempt to influence you inappropriately, and empowering others. In general, use reason strategies more often than reciprocity strategies, and reciprocity more than threats of retribution. Use open, direct approaches in preference to indirect, manipulative approaches.

6. Use reason strategies when:
   - ❑ There are few time constraints.
   - ❑ Initiative and innovation are vital.
   - ❑ Interpersonal trust is high.

LEARNING

- ❏ The relationship is long term.
- ❏ Interpersonal conflict is not high.
- ❏ Personal goals are congruent and/or respected by both parties.
- ❏ It is important for the other person to understand why the request is being made.

7. Use reciprocity strategies when:
- ❏ The parties are mutually dependent.
- ❏ There are clearly specified rules governing interpersonal transactions.
- ❏ Long-term commitment to common goals and values is not important.
- ❏ There is sufficient time to reach satisfactory agreements.

8. Use retribution strategies when:
- ❏ There is a substantial imbalance of power between the parties.
- ❏ The ongoing commitment of the other person is not critical.
- ❏ Quality and innovation are not important.
- ❏ Opposition is acceptable (e.g., when personnel replacement is possible, if necessary).
- ❏ Extensive surveillance is possible.
- ❏ No other alternatives exist.

9. To neutralize reason influence strategies of others:
- ❏ Explain the negative consequences of compliance.
- ❏ Defend your rights.
- ❏ Firmly refuse to comply with request.

10. To neutralize reciprocity, influence strategies of others:
- ❏ Examine the context of any gift- or favor-giving activity.
- ❏ Confront individuals using escalating or compromising tactics.
- ❏ Refuse to bargain with individuals using high-pressure tactics.

11. To neutralize retribution influence strategies of others:
- ❏ Use countervailing power to shift dependence to interdependence.
- ❏ Confront the exploitative individual directly.
- ❏ Actively resist.

12. To sell issues to your superiors:
- ❏ Select issues that are congruent with your position or role.
- ❏ Present the issue honestly and without being self-serving.
- ❏ Communicate the issue broadly.
- ❏ Select an issue that is compatible with the culture.
- ❏ Select a solvable issue.
- ❏ Clarify the payoff to be achieved.
- ❏ Identify the needed expertise.
- ❏ Point out senior managers' responsibility for the issue.
- ❏ Be succinct, use emotional imagery, and provide supporting data and novel information.
- ❏ Bundle the issue with other similar important issues.
- ❏ Find like-minded supporters.
- ❏ Use public forums.

CASE INVOLVING POWER AND INFLUENCE

Dynica Software Solutions

Dynica Technologies recently announced plans to construct a new production facility in River Woods. The new facility would replace the company's original production facility, which is adjacent to the company headquarters in Edgemont. In announcing the new facility, the company stated that, to the extent possible, it would be staffed by Edgemont plant personnel and that the excess personnel would be transferred to other Dynica plants in neighboring states.

Dynica management views the River Woods facility as the plant of the future, featuring lower processing costs and manpower requirements, as well as state-of-the-art environmental standards. In a recent press release, the Dynica CEO noted they were replacing one of the least environmentally friendly plants in the industry with a facility that will be "greener" than any of their competitors' production plants.

Dynica is also using the River Woods plant to pilot a new decentralized management structure. In the past, the firm's marketing activities were directed from the home office by a vice president. Manufacturing operations and certain other departments were under the control of the company's senior vice president. In this centralized, functional arrangement none of the company's four production facilities had a general manager. Instead, each department in a plant reported on a line basis to its functional counterpart at the home office (e.g., director of production, director of engineering). In contrast, the new River Woods plant manager will be responsible for the management of all functions and personnel, except marketing and sales.

There is general consensus among the top management team that the long-term viability of the firm depends on the success of this initiative. However, some have expressed concerns about the difficulty of the task facing the River Woods general manager. They point to the shift from functional lines of communication and accountability to a plant-level focus, as well as the challenges of upgrading the skills of the Edgemont plant personnel, working out the bugs in new applications of advanced manufacturing processes to design and production, and dealing with the inevitable complaints from employees in a small company town who are not satisfied with their new assignments and who might serve as the catalyst for unionizing the facility.

Discussion Questions

5.1. If you were part of the selection committee for the River Woods plant manager position, based on what you've learned about the sources of personal power in this chapter, describe what you'd consider to be the ideal candidate's qualifications.

5.2. If you were offered the new River Woods plant manager position, based on what you've learned about the sources of position power, what actions would you take to ensure that as the company's first general manager you had the necessary clout to accomplish your assigned duties?

5.3. Using the information on influence strategies in the second half of this chapter as your guide, strategize how you would address the challenges you are likely to encounter if you accepted the position of River Woods plant manager.

EXERCISE FOR GAINING POWER

Repairing Power Failures in Management Circuits

Rosabeth Kanter (1979) argues that much of what is labeled "poor management" in organizations is simply individuals protecting their diminished power bases. Instead of criticizing these managers as incompetent, she proposes we bolster their feelings of personal power. If we solve the real problem of perceived lack of power, the undesirable symptoms of poor leadership often evaporate. This point of view is consistent with the principles discussed in this chapter.

Assignment

In this exercise, you are asked to give advice to individuals who feel powerless. For each of the situations below, form groups to explore opportunities for enhancing the power base of these three individuals. Prepare to report your recommendations.

Situation 1: Department Store Manager

Six months ago, Kate Shalene was promoted from her sales associate position to become a manager of the accessories department at an upscale department store. She was proud of her new promotion, but surprised to discover she felt increasingly powerless. Instead of being a stepping stone, this position was feeling more and more like a dead end. Managers above her were about her age and the hoped-for company expansion was beginning to appear unlikely. She was not a central part of the organization, and she felt no one ever noticed her unless she messed up. She was expected to be supportive of her subordinates, but they never returned the favor. She was expected to absorb their flak without support from above. In general, she felt as though she was constantly "getting it from both ends." Her job was extremely rule-bound, so she had little discretion in what she did or how she did it. She had only modest control over the pay or benefits of her subordinates because their union agreement left very little flexibility. So she felt powerless to reward them or punish them in ways that really mattered.

As a result, she found she was more and more apt to impose rules to get subordinates to do what she wanted. She became increasingly jealous of any successes and recognition achieved by her subordinates, so she tended to isolate them from people higher up in the organization and from complete information. She lost her penchant for informality and became increasingly rigid in following standard operating procedures. Predictably, her subordinates were becoming more resentful and less productive.

Situation 2: Human Resource Professional

Shawn Quinn came to his organization a year ago as a senior human resources professional. He believed the position might be a way for him to achieve considerable visibility with the top brass, but instead he felt isolated and forgotten. As a staff officer, he had almost no decision-making authority except in his narrow area of expertise. Most of what went on in the organization occurred without his involvement. Innovation and entrepreneurial activity were completely out of his realm. While some of the finance and marketing officers were given opportunities for professional development, no one seemed to care about his becoming more experienced and capable. They saw him only as a specialist. Because his job didn't necessarily require that he interact with people outside of his division, he had little opportunity to cultivate relationships that might lead to contacts with someone near the top.

What hurt was that a consultant had been hired a few times to work on projects that were part of his area. If consultants could be brought in to do his work, he thought, he must not be very important to the organization.

Shawn found himself being more and more turf conscious. He didn't want others encroaching on his area of expertise. He tried to demonstrate his competence to others, but the more he did so, the more he became defined as a specialist, outside the mainstream of the organization. Overall, he felt he was losing ground in his career.

Situation 3: Chief Financial Officer

May Phelps has been her company's CFO for three years. When she obtained the position, she felt that her ultimate career goal had been achieved. Now she was not so sure. Surprisingly, she discovered myriad constraints limiting her discretion and initiative. For example, the job had so many demands and details associated with it that she never had time to engage in any long-term planning. There always seemed to be one more crisis that demanded her attention. Unfortunately, most of the constraints were from sources she couldn't control, such as government regulations, demands for greater accountability made by the board of directors and by stockholders, union relationships, equal opportunity statutes, and so on. She had built her reputation as a successful manager by being entrepreneurial, creative, and innovative, but none of those qualities seemed appropriate for the demands of her current work. Furthermore, because she was so mired in managing financial reporting, she had become more and more out of touch with the information flow in the organization. Some things had to remain confidential with her, but her secrecy made others unwilling to share information with her. She had assistants who were supposed to be monitoring the organization and providing her with information, but she often felt they only told her what she wanted to hear.

May had begun to hear rumors that certain special-interest groups were demanding her removal from the top job. She responded by becoming more dictatorial and defensive, with the result that the organization was becoming more control-oriented and conservative. She felt that she was on a downward spiral, but she couldn't find a way to reverse the trend. "I always thought the saying 'It's lonely at the top' was just a metaphor," she mused.

EXERCISE FOR USING INFLUENCE EFFECTIVELY

Managers are given formal power in an organization by virtue of their position of authority. However, they often find this authority does not readily translate into actual influence. Particularly when they are working with peers, they find it necessary to develop informal relationships through making deals, persuasive arguments, and so forth. These relationships form the basis of real influence in an organization.

Assignment

After reading the following case, assume the roles of staff members for Ann Lyman, a recently hired marketing executive. Divide into small groups and conduct an informal staff discussion in which you design a plan for influencing Ann's colleagues and superiors to support her proposal. First, decide which general influence strategy (or combination of strategies) is most appropriate for this situation. Second, using Table 5.7, recommend specific actions for implementing your general strategy. Prepare to present your suggestions, including justifications.

Ann Lyman's Proposal

Ann Lyman was recently hired by the Challenge Products Corporation (CPC) as a senior marketing executive for the electronic housewares division. Her previous experience at Pearces, a major competitor, had earned her a reputation for being a creative and hard-working manager. Her department at Pearces had increased its sales at least 15 percent per year over the past five years, and she had been featured in a lead article in *Contemporary Management.* This combination of competence and visibility was what attracted the attention of John Dilworth, the CEO of Challenge. John was troubled about the two-quarter decline in electronic sales. This was the core of CPC's business, and he could not risk losing market share.

In the past, CPC's products had dominated such a large market share that, ironically, marketing wasn't considered very important. Production touted its high quality and low costs, purchasing emphasized its contribution to keeping costs low, and engineering stressed the durability of its designs. CPC products, it was argued by many, "sold themselves."

But that was before the cheaper, "look-alike" products from Asia flooded the discount stores. No longer could CPC expect high customer loyalty simply because it was the oldest, best-known, most reliable name brand on the shelf. Ann was convinced that in order for CPC to stay competitive, the company needed to expand its product line, offering more options at different price levels. She felt it also needed to branch out into "trend designs" that appealed to the contemporary lifestyles of young adults.

These changes had far-reaching ramifications for other departments at CPC. For one thing, they meant engineering would have to shorten its design cycle, provide support for a broader range of products, and emphasize customer-oriented, rather than functional, features. These changes would obviously not sit well with the production department, which jealously protected its long production runs based on standard orders and relatively few model changes. It also stressed ease of fabrication and assembly. In addition, purchasing would be required to find new sourcing alternatives for nonstandard parts, which would make it more difficult to get volume discounts and ensure quality.

After three months on the job, Ann felt she was ready to make her proposal to John. She pushed her staff hard to add the finishing touches before John left on his two-week vacation to Lake Tahoe. She wasn't disappointed—he thought it was a winner. He was excited and ready to "sign on." But he was also realistic about the difficulty they faced convincing others that these changes were necessary. Ann's counterparts in production, purchasing, and engineering would certainly object. "It'll be a hard sell, but I think you have some good ideas," he concluded. "While I'm away, I'd like you to design a plan for getting the cooperation of the other departments. You can count on me for general support, but the culture in this organization isn't consistent with sending out an edict. You'll have to figure out how to get their support some other way."

EXERCISES FOR NEUTRALIZING UNWANTED INFLUENCE ATTEMPTS

An important aspect of becoming empowered and influential is reducing inappropriate dependence. Obviously, interdependence in both social circles and work circles is essential to healthy organizational life. Most forms of interdependence are natural and healthy. However, sometimes individuals attempt to turn interdependence into dependence by exercising inappropriate influence. Their objective is to increase their power over others by creating a significant imbalance of power.

Assignment

In each of the following role plays, assume the role of the person who needs to resist unwanted influence (Betty or Pat). Prior to the beginning of the role play, review the relevant behavioral guidelines (guidelines 9 through 11 pages 209–210), determine which combination is most appropriate, and plan your strategy for dealing with this problem. Do not read the other role descriptions (Bill or Lynn). Following the role play, an assigned observer will give you feedback using the Observer's Feedback Form (found at the end of the chapter) as a guide.

Cindy's Fast Foods

Betty, Assistant Manager

You are the assistant manager of Cindy's, a fast-food franchise in a college town. You are one of the few student employees who has stayed on after graduation. You weren't ready to move away after graduation because of family obligations, and there weren't many other job opportunities locally. The spring before graduation, the owner offered you the job of assistant manager. The timing was perfect because the offer would relieve the pressure on you to pursue teaching jobs in which you really weren't interested. Your work at Cindy's had sparked your interest in business, and your student-teaching experience had not been very successful. Even though your parents weren't too pleased about paying four years' tuition at an expensive private liberal arts college to have you end up "cooking hamburgers" for a career, their feelings mellowed when you explained the opportunities you would have to advance and possibly purchase a franchise. "Besides," you told them, "I'll only be in this position for three years, and then I can decide whether I want to apply for a manager's position or try again for a teaching job."

It's hard to believe it's been two years since graduation. Your manager, Bill, has done a conscientious job helping you learn the ropes as a manager. He has worked you hard, but trained you well. You feel indebted to him for his help. You have become quite close friends, although his occasional dirty jokes and sexist comments with the guys on break in the back room make you feel uncomfortable.

One night after the rest of the crew has gone home, you are finishing your work for the day. These late nights are the one really bad feature of your job. Just as you are about to turn out the lights, Bill comes in. It is not unusual for him to stop by at closing. He is single, likes to bowl after work, and sometimes drops by later on his way home. You are just putting on your coat when he asks you to come into his office. He shuts the door, and pulls up a chair next to you. "Betty, I've been watching your performance very closely. You're a hard worker. The employees enjoy your management style. And I've taken a liking to you as well. I think I have a good shot at transferring to a much larger store in Cincinnati. I'll be glad to get out of this one-horse town and gain more visibility closer to corporate headquarters."

You start getting a little nervous as he moves his chair closer to yours. "I think you would be a really good replacement for me, but you haven't completed your full term as assistant. So I'll need to ask for a special exception to the corporate policy. And I'll have to put in a good word for you with the owner. However, there's some risk involved for me, because the regional manager is a real stickler on rules, and I've asked him to recommend me for the Cincinnati job. But I'd be willing to take that risk under certain conditions." As he waits for a response, you know very well where this conversation is headed.

Bill, Manager

You have been attracted to Betty for some time. You find her very attractive, and you enjoy her company. You have several times manufactured excuses to have personal chats with her or to be alone with her. You think Betty finds you attractive, also. It seems that she has been extra friendly lately. You figure she's either bucking for your job or sending you signals that she'd like to expand your relationship beyond strictly business—or both.

Besides, you feel she owes you something. You have worked extra hard to train her, and you've been dropping hints to the owner that you think Betty might be ready to move up.

9:00 to 7:30

Pat Simpson, Loan Officer

You are a member of a small consumer loan company. The staff consists of you, another loan officer, and a secretary. Last month, a larger financial institution acquired your firm and made some personnel changes. The other loan officer, with whom you had worked for four years, was replaced by Lynn Johnson. Having entered the company at about the same time, you and Lynn have known each other for years. In fact, you worked in the Ann Arbor office together for a year. During that time, you were both single, and together you enjoyed the night life of Detroit. You learn Lynn is still single and "living it up." In contrast, you have been married for about three years. You looked forward to working with Lynn again but wondered if your lack of interest in the local night scene would affect your relationship. Lynn has the reputation of being capable but lazy. She's known for taking in lots of loan applications and then striking bargains with or cajoling coworkers into helping out with the dreaded credit-checking process. You wonder if this practice has anything to do with the fact that her uncle was a founding partner in the bank.

After Lynn arrives, you are shocked at the difference in your work attitudes and lifestyles. "Boy, what a difference three years makes!" you think to yourself. You and your previous office mate, Jim, were both married, and both of you favored a vigorous working tempo from 9:00 to 5:15, taking lunch when convenient. You and Jim had a great working relationship, and the loan volume in your office increased steadily. There was even some discussion of expanding the size of the staff. In contrast, Lynn prefers leisurely mornings that begin around 10:30, luncheons as long as Mexican siestas, and a flurry of activity between 4:00 and 7:30 P.M.

You and your spouse are experiencing some marital turbulence, and you feel it is very important to be home in the evenings. Your spouse has begun attending night classes and leaves for school at 8:00 P.M. The educational program is an extremely intense three-year ordeal. Unfortunately, the stress level already seems unbearable. When you stay at the office late, you not only miss dinner together but you don't even see each other until after class, when you are both so tired there is no opportunity for quality time. It seems as though most weekends are devoted to homework.

Because the office staff is so small, the difference in workday rhythms is creating a serious hardship on you. Lynn doesn't function very well in the morning and has begun expressing irritation when you rush out the door at closing time. Lately, your relationship has become strained. You handle most of the walk-in business early in the morning, eat lunch at your desk, and have your paperwork done by 5:30 at the latest. In contrast, Lynn is just getting into high gear about 4:00. Because company rules require checking each other's loan approvals, Lynn becomes testy when you say you can't stay after 5:30 to check her work. Some evenings you have relented and stayed until 7:00 or 8:00, but your spouse got very upset. When you don't stay late, you are greeted by a stack of paperwork on your desk in the morning, which makes it difficult for you to meet with new customers. Several times Lynn has tried to get you to do the credit checks on her loan applications, saying that the press of new business was too great.

Something has got to change! You decide to go to lunch with Lynn today and tell her how you feel.

Lynn Johnson, Loan Officer

You have worked for this firm for 10 years, and you are very good at your work. During that time, you have passed up offers from larger financial institutions because you like the flexibility of working in a small office. Besides, your family is financially well off, so you aren't concerned about making a lot of money.

In every other office, your coworkers have been willing to accommodate your work style. They recognize you are one of the top loan officers in the company—and having the right last name doesn't hurt any—so they make allowances for your quirks.

But your new office mate (and, you thought, old friend) is an exception. Since you arrived, the relationship has been testy because of your different schedules. You don't understand why there can't be more tolerance for your work style. After all, you get the job done, and that's what counts. Besides, your requests for assistance are not that unreasonable; other coworkers have always been willing to comply.

Thinking about the impending discussion, you realize how important it is for you to get Pat to change her work habits to conform with yours. You certainly hope you can convince Pat to pitch in and help you when you get behind. "I mean, that's what coworkers (and old friends) are for, right?" you muse on the way to work. During the discussion, you plan to stress the reasonableness of your requests. Others have never objected strenuously; why should Pat? If that doesn't work, you plan to try and work out a bargain. Maybe you could put in a good word for Pat with your uncle, a founder of the company. Pat's career hasn't exactly skyrocketed, and she is probably itching to move to a larger office in a metropolitan city. Possibly, her title could be upgraded to Senior Loan Officer.

SKILL *APPLICATION*

ACTIVITIES FOR GAINING POWER AND INFLUENCE

Suggested Assignments

5.4. Select a friend or associate who has complained to you about feeling powerless in an organizational position. This might be a person who holds a relatively insignificant leadership position in a campus organization or a low-level position in a work organization. Perhaps the individual feels his or her personal abilities do not command respect in that position. Sit down with this person and teach him or her the guidelines for gaining power in an organization. (You might use the Assessment Survey at the beginning of this chapter as a diagnostic instrument.) As part of this conversation, design a specific plan of action for increasing both the position and personal bases of power. Discuss the outcomes of this plan with your friend and report on his or her success.

5.5. Using the guidelines for gaining power, develop a plan for increasing your power in an organizational setting. Describe the setting, including the factors you feel account for your feelings of powerlessness. Use your score on the Assessment Survey as a diagnostic aid. Formulate a detailed strategy for increasing your positional and personal power. Report on your results and describe the benefits of becoming more empowered.

APPLICATION

5.6. Over time, analyze your efforts to influence other people. Use the "Three Rs" model to catalog your strategies. Consider why you used each strategy. Did you repeatedly rely on one or two strategies, or did you vary your approach according to circumstances? Keep track of the outcome of each attempt. Did you seem to have more success with one of the strategies? Next, select a person you have attempted to influence, one with whom you have a close, ongoing relationship. Discuss the alternative influence strategies with that person and ask him or her what effect the frequent use of each approach might have on your relationship.

5.7. Watch at least two realistic dramas (movies, plays, TV). Observe the influence strategies used by various characters. Which form of influence did they use most frequently, and why? Did certain people demonstrate a preference for a particular strategy? If so, was this based on personality traits, gender roles, authority relationships, or other situational factors? How successful were these influence attempts, and what impact did they have on ongoing relationships?

5.8. Identify a specific relationship in which you are regularly asked to do things that you feel are inappropriate. Using the relevant guidelines for resisting unwanted influence, formulate a strategy for assertively responding to the next attempt. Role-play this approach with a friend or coworker and incorporate his or her suggestions. After you implement your plan, report on the outcome. What was the reaction? Were you successful in communicating your position? Was an understanding reached regarding future interactions that is more fair? Based on this experience, examine other relationships for which this approach might be appropriate.

Application Plan and Evaluation

The intent of this exercise is to help you apply this cluster of skills in a real-life, out-of-class setting. Now that you have become familiar with the behavioral guidelines that form the basis of effective skill performance, you will improve most by trying out those guidelines in an everyday context. Unlike a classroom activity, in which feedback is immediate and others can assist you with their evaluations, this skill application activity is one you must accomplish and evaluate on your own. There are two parts to this activity. Part 1 helps prepare you to apply the skill, and Part 2 helps you evaluate and improve on your experience. Be sure to write down answers to each item. Don't short-circuit the process by skipping steps.

Part 1: Planning

5.9. Write down the two or three aspects of this skill that are most important to you. These may be areas of weakness, areas you most want to improve, or areas that are most salient to a problem you face right now. Identify the specific aspects of this skill that you want to apply.

5.10. Now identify the setting or the situation in which you will apply this skill. Establish a plan for performance by actually writing down a description of the situation. Who else will be involved? When will you do it? Where will it be done?

Circumstances:
Who else?
When?
Where?

5.11. Identify the specific behaviors you will engage in to apply this skill. Operationalize your skill performance.

5.12. What are the indicators of successful performance? How will you know you have been effective? What will indicate you have performed competently?

Part 2: Evaluation

5.13. After you have completed your implementation, record the results. What happened? How successful were you? What was the effect on others?

5.14. How can you improve? What modifications can you make next time? What will you do differently in a similar situation in the future?

5.15. Looking back on your whole skill practice and application experience, what have you learned? What has been surprising? In what ways might this experience help you in the long term?

SCORING KEYS AND COMPARISON DATA

✪ Scoring Keys for the following instruments, along with comparison data, are contained in PIA in MyManagementLab.com;

Gaining Power and Influence
Using Influence Strategies

SKILL ASSESSMENT

- Diagnosing Poor Performance and Enhancing Motivation
- Work Performance Assessment

SKILL LEARNING

- Increasing Motivation and Performance
- Diagnosing Work Performance Problems
- Enhancing Individuals' Abilities
- Fostering a Motivating Work Environment
- Elements of an Effective Motivation Program
- Summary
- Behavioral Guidelines

SKILL ANALYSIS

- Electro Logic

SKILL PRACTICE

- Joe Chaney
- Work Performance Assessment
- Shaheen Matombo

SKILL APPLICATION

- Suggested Assignments
- Application Plan and Evaluation

SCORING KEYS AND COMPARISON DATA

6

Motivating Others

LEARNING OBJECTIVES

The readings and activities in this chapter are designed to help you:

1. DIAGNOSE WORK PERFORMANCE PROBLEMS

2. ENHANCE THE WORK-RELATED ABILITIES OF OTHERS

3. FOSTER A MOTIVATING WORK ENVIRONMENT

MyManagementLab™

✪ When you see this icon, visit www.mymanagementlab.com for self-assessments, video activities, and more.

PERSONAL INVENTORY ASSESSMENT

⭐ If your instructor is utilizing **MyManagementLab**, log onto mymanagementlab. com and select the Personal Inventory Assessment (PIA) section and complete the instruments associated with this chapter.

The assessment instruments in this chapter are briefly described below. The assessments appear either in your text or in PIA. The assessments marked with (blue star) are available only in PIA.

All assessments should be completed before reading the chapter material.

After completing the first assessment save your response to your hard drive. When you have finished reading the chapter, re-take the assessment and compare your responses to see what you have learned.

⭐ ❑ The *Diagnosing Poor Performance and Enhancing Motivation* assessment measures the extent to which you exhibit competency in motivating others so that you can tailor your learning to your specific needs.

⭐ ❑ The *Work Performance Assessment* evaluates your own motivation and performance in a current (or recent) work setting.

SKILL *LEARNING* ▽ⓘ

Increasing Motivation and Performance

Focus groups at Intermountain Healthcare, a Utah-based health care organization with more than 23,000 employees, revealed that a majority of front-line workers would not leave their jobs unless another employer offered them a 20 percent increase in pay and a 30 percent increase in benefits. Such commitment is an extremely valued commodity in our current economy. Most organizations struggle to retain their best employees and to motivate them to high performance. Comments from three front-line workers at Intermountain Healthcare reveal that a motivating work environment and the organization's clear values are what foster their strong sense of commitment (Interview with Alison Mackey).

"I have never worked at a place where people have been so concerned about their employees. And because of that we can turn around and give the same to our customers."

"I think [Intermountain Healthcare] is a system that's concerned about its employees, and as a result it can attract employees with strong technical and people-based knowledge and experience."

"The values that [Intermountain Healthcare] stands for make me never want to leave" (Intermountain Healthcare Employee Opinion Survey Database).

The efforts Intermountain Healthcare has taken to create such a motivating work environment have improved its clinical care and its bottom line. The Gallup Organization has honored Intermountain Healthcare for three consecutive years as one of its "Great Workplaces" in the United States, an honor that only 32 companies received in 2013. *Modern Healthcare* consistently lists the organization near the top of its Top 100 Integrated Health Systems (number 3 in 2013).

Organizations like Intermountain Healthcare, that have highly motivated and committed employees, are well equipped to compete in any market, be it health care or heavy industry. But like any distinctive competence, employee commitment is difficult to achieve; if it were otherwise it would have no competitive value.

After winning an unprecedented seventh NBA title as a coach, Phil Jackson was asked what his method was for motivating professional basketball players. He responded, "I don't motivate my players. You cannot motivate someone; all you can do is provide a motivating environment and the players will motivate themselves" (Jackson, 2000). We believe the imagery of "manager-as-coach" and "motivation-as-facilitation," as suggested by one of the most successful coaches of our time, provides the appropriate backdrop for our discussion. Whether managers are working with a group of steel workers, computer programmers, artists, or basketball players, their common challenge is to create a work environment where employees are most likely to motivate themselves.

The core of this chapter outlines a six-step process for accomplishing this goal. But first, to set the stage for this discussion, we begin with one of the most nettlesome problems facing managers—how to diagnose the causes of a specific employee's poor performance. Managers who don't get this step right will have little success at helping their employees because they likely will be trying to solve the wrong problem.

Diagnosing Work Performance Problems

There is a tendency for supervisors to assume that poor performance is always a matter of low motivation (Bitter & Gardner, 1995). That is, when employees fail to meet performance expectations, supervisors tend to blame the employee for putting forth insufficient commitment and effort. The tendency to make snap judgments about why things happen is what psychologists call an attribution (Ross, 1977; Choi, Nisbett, & Norenzayan, 1999). Supervisors generally believe that if they work harder they will perform better. Consequently, they assume the same is true of their employees, regardless of their work environment or resources. The problem with this attribution is that it lends itself to simplistic solutions, reminiscent of the Chinese proverb, "For every hundred men hacking away at the leaves of a diseased tree, only one man stoops to inspect the roots."

Let's consider some work conditions that illustrate the need to "stoop and inspect the roots" of poor worker performance: It is estimated that one-third of American employees have irregular work schedules (often involving night work), commonly known as shift work. In a recent article on the challenges facing shift workers, a story told of a supervisor who sought permission from the human resources department to fire a worker because he didn't "stay on task;" he often walked around talking to others and occasionally fell asleep on the job. The supervisor concluded that the employee lacked the motivation for the job. However, research on shift workers challenges the simplistic idea that "poor performance equals low motivation and commitment." For example, shift workers sleep two to three hours less per night than day workers. They are four to five times more likely to experience digestive disorders due to eating the wrong foods at the wrong times. Chronic fatigue affects 80

percent of shift workers, while 75 percent report feeling isolated on the job. Drug and alcohol abuse are three times greater among permanent shift workers than among those with traditional work hours (Perry, 2000). Clearly, there is much more to the story here than poor motivation.

To avoid simplistic, ill-informed diagnoses of work performance problems, managers need a model to guide their thinking. Several scholars (e.g., Gerhart, 2003; Steers, Porter, & Bigley, 1996; Vroom, 1964) have summarized the determinants of task performance as follows:

$$Performance = Ability \times Motivation\ (Effort)$$

where

$$Ability = Aptitude \times Training \times Resources$$

$$Motivation = Desire \times Commitment$$

According to these formulas, **performance** is the product of ability multiplied by motivation, **ability** is the product of aptitude multiplied by training and resources, and **motivation** is the product of desire and commitment. The multiplicative function in these formulas suggests that all elements are essential. For example, workers who have 100 percent of the motivation and 75 percent of the ability required to perform a task can perform at an above-average rate. However, if these individuals have only 10 percent of the ability required, no amount of motivation is likely enable them to perform satisfactorily.

Aptitude refers to the native skills and abilities a person brings to a job. These involve physical and mental capabilities; but for many people-oriented jobs, they also include personality characteristics. Most of our inherent abilities can be enhanced by education and *training*. Indeed, much of what we call native ability in adults can be traced to previous skill-enhancement experiences, such as modeling the social skills of parents or older siblings. Nevertheless, it is useful to consider training as a separate component of ability, since it represents an important mechanism for improving employee performance. Ability should be assessed during the job-matching process by screening applicants against the skill requirements of the job. If an applicant has minor deficiencies in skill aptitude but many other desirable characteristics, an intensive training program can be used to increase the applicant's qualifications to perform the job.

The third component of our definition of ability is adequate *resources*. Frequently, highly capable and well-trained individuals are placed in situations that inhibit job performance. Specifically, they aren't given the resources (technical, personnel, and political) to perform assigned tasks effectively.

Motivation represents an employee's *desire* and *commitment* to perform. The result of motivation is job-related effort. Some people want to complete a task (high desire) but are easily distracted or discouraged (low commitment). Others plod along persistently (high commitment), but their work is half-hearted (low desire).

The first diagnostic question that supervisors must ask themselves when dealing with a poor performer is: "Is this an ability or motivation problem?" The answer to that question has far-reaching ramifications for manager-subordinate relations. Research has shown that when managers perceive that employees lack motivation, they tend to apply more pressure on them. They may justify their use of a forceful influence strategy on the grounds that the subordinate has a "poor attitude," is "hostile to authority," or "lacks dedication." Unfortunately, if the manager's assessment is incorrect and poor performance is really related to ability rather than motivation, their forceful response actually worsens the problem. When poor performers feel that management is insensitive to their problems—such as a lack of resources, inadequate training, or unrealistic time schedules—they tend to lose what motivation they had. Their desire and commitment decreases in response to management's insensitive, "iron-fisted" actions. Seeing this response, management will feel that their original diagnosis is confirmed, and they will use even stronger forms of influence to force compliance. The resulting vicious cycle is extremely difficult to break and underscores the high stakes involved in accurately diagnosing poor performance problems.

In this chapter, we will examine the two components of performance in more detail, beginning with ability. We'll discuss manifestations of low ability and poor motivation, their causes, and some proposed remedies. We'll devote more attention to motivation, since motivation is more central to day-to-day manager-subordinate interactions. While ability tends to remain stable over long periods of time, motivation fluctuates; therefore, it requires closer monitoring and frequent recharging.

Enhancing Individuals' Abilities

A person's lack of ability might inhibit good performance for several reasons. Ability may have been assessed improperly during the screening process prior to employment, the technical requirements of a job may have been radically upgraded, or a person who performed very well in one position may have been promoted into a higher-level position that is too demanding. (The Peter Principle states that people are typically promoted one position above their level of competence.) In addition, human and material resource support may have been reduced because of organizational budget cutbacks.

As noted by Quick (1977, 1991), managers should be alert for individuals who show signs of ability deterioration. Following are three danger signals for management positions:

A. **Taking refuge in a specialty.** Managers show signs of insufficient ability when instead of managing they retreat to their technical specialty. This often occurs when managers feel insecure about problems outside their area of expertise and experience. Anthony Jay, in *Management and Machiavelli* (1967), dubs this type of manager "George I," after the King of England who, after assuming the throne, continued to be preoccupied with the affairs of Hanover, Germany, whence he had come.

B. **Focusing on past performance.** Another danger sign is measuring one's value to the organization in terms of past performance or on the basis of former standards. Some cavalry commanders in World War I relied on their outmoded knowledge of how to conduct successful military campaigns and, as a result, failed miserably in mechanized combat. This form of obsolescence is common in organizations that fail to shift their mission in response to changing market conditions.

C. **Exaggerating aspects of the leadership role.** Managers who have lost confidence in their ability tend to be very defensive. This often leads them to exaggerate one aspect of their managerial role. Such managers might delegate most of their responsibilities because they no longer feel competent to perform them well. Or they might become nuts-and-bolts administrators who scrutinize every detail to an extent far beyond its practical value. Still others become "devil's advocates," but rather than stimulating creativity, their negativism thwarts efforts to change the familiar.

There are five principal tools available for overcoming poor performance problems due to lack of ability: *resupply, retrain, refit, reassign,* and *release.* We will discuss these in the order in which a manager should consider them.

The **resupply** option focuses on whether the employee has been provided the resources necessary to do the job, including personnel, budget, and political clout. Asking "Do you have what you need to perform this job satisfactorily?" allows the subordinate to express his or her frustration related to inadequate support. Given the natural tendency for individuals to blame external causes for their mistakes, managers should explore their subordinates' complaints about lack of support in detail to determine their validity. Even if employees exaggerate their claims, starting your discussion of poor performance in this manner signals your willingness to help them solve the problem from their perspective rather than to find fault from your perspective.

The next least threatening option is to **retrain**. According to the American Society for Training and Development, American companies spent over $156 billion on employee learning and development in 2011. About 30 percent of that amount (close to $50 billion) was spent on external trainers and other resources outside the company (Miller, 2012). This is a sizeable expenditure for American corporations, but the reasons for these expenditures are clear. First of all, technology is changing so quickly that employees' skills can soon become obsolete. It has been estimated that 50 percent of employees' skills become outdated within three to five years (Moe & Blodget, 2000). Second, employees will typically fill a number of different positions throughout their careers, each demanding different proficiencies. Finally, demographic changes in our society will lead to an increasingly older workforce. In order for companies to remain competitive, more and more of them must retrain their older employees.

Training programs can take a variety of forms. For example, many firms are using interactive technical instruction and business games that simulate problems managers are likely to experience. More traditional forms of training include subsidized university courses and in-house technical or management seminars. Some companies have experimented with company sabbaticals to release managers or senior technical specialists from the pressures of work so they can concentrate on retooling. The most rapidly increasing form of training is internet-based "distance learning." The American Society for Training and Development reports that technology-based teaching methods now represent 41.7 percent of all formal learning among *Fortune* 500 firms (Miller, 2012).

In many cases, however, resupplying and retraining are insufficient remedies for poor performance. When this happens, the next step should be to explore **refitting** poor performers to their task assignments. While the subordinates remain on the job, the components of their work are analyzed, and different combinations of tasks and abilities that accomplish organizational objectives and provide meaningful and rewarding work are explored. For example, an assistant may be brought in to handle many of the technical details of a first-line supervisor's position, freeing up more time for the supervisor to focus on people development or to develop a long-term plan to present to upper management.

If a revised job description is unworkable or inadequate, the fourth alternative is to **reassign** the poor performer, either to a position of less responsibility or to one requiring less technical knowledge or interpersonal skills. For example, a medical specialist in a hospital who finds it increasingly difficult to keep abreast of new medical procedures but has demonstrated management skills might be shifted to a full-time administrative position.

The last option is to **release**. If retraining and creative redefinition of task assignments have not worked and if there are no opportunities for reassignment in the organization, the manager should consider releasing the employee from the organization. This option is generally constrained by union agreements, company policies, seniority considerations, and government regulations. Frequently, however, chronic poor performers who could be released are not because management chooses to sidestep a potentially unpleasant task. Instead, the decision is made to set these individuals "on the shelf," out of the mainstream of activities, where they can't cause any problems. Even when this action is motivated by humanitarian concerns ("I don't think he could cope with being terminated"), it often produces the opposite effect. Actions taken to protect an unproductive employee from the embarrassment of termination just substitute the humiliation of being ignored. Obviously, termination is a drastic action that should not be taken lightly. However, the consequences for the unproductive individuals and their coworkers of allowing them to remain after the previous four actions have proven unsuccessful should be weighed carefully in considering this option.

This approach to managing ability problems is reflected in the philosophy of Wendell Parsons, CEO of Stamp-Rite. He argues that one of the most challenging aspects of management is helping employees recognize that job enhancements and advancements are not always possible. Therefore, he says, "If a long-term employee slows down, I try to turn him around by saying how much I value his knowledge and experience, but pointing out that his production has slipped too much. If boredom has set in and I can't offer the employee a change, I encourage him to face the fact and consider doing something else with his life." (Nelton, 1988).

Fostering a Motivating Work Environment

The second component of employee performance is motivation. While it is important to see to the training and support needs of subordinates and to be actively involved in the hiring and job-matching processes to ensure adequate aptitude, the influence of a manager's actions on the day-to-day motivation of subordinates is equally vital. In fact, recent research shows that simply enhancing someone's skills does not improve motivation nearly as much as activities specifically designed to enhance motivation (Kaifeng, et al., 2012). Effective managers devote considerable time to gauging and strengthening their subordinates' motivation.

In one of the seminal contributions to management thought, Douglas McGregor (1960) introduced the term *Theory X* to refer to a management style characterized by close supervision. The basic assumption of this theory is that people really do not want to work hard or assume responsibility. Therefore, in order to get the job done, managers must coerce, intimidate, manipulate, and closely supervise their employees. In contrast, McGregor espouses a *Theory Y* view of workers. He argues that workers basically want to do a good job and assume more responsibility; therefore, management's role is to assist workers to reach their potential by productively channeling their inherent motivation to succeed. Unfortunately, McGregor believed that most managers subscribe to *Theory X* assumptions about workers' motives.

The alleged prevalence of the *Theory X* view brings up an interesting series of questions about motivation. What is the purpose of teaching motivation skills to managers? Should managers learn these skills so they can help employees reach their potential? Or are we teaching these skills to managers so they can more effectively manipulate their employees' behavior? Do managers even have the time and cognitive capacity to attend simultaneously to employee morale and the organization's "bottom line?"

Contemporary research, as well as the success of acclaimed organizational motivation programs (Harter, Schmidt, & Hayes, 2002), supports the position that morale and performance are actually linked. As Figure 6.1 shows, effective motivational efforts not only can but *must* focus on increasing both satisfaction and productivity. Managers who emphasize satisfaction to the exclusion of performance will be seen as nice people, but their **indulging** management style undermines organizational performance.

A strong emphasis on performance to the exclusion of satisfaction is equally ineffective. This time, instead of indulging, the manager is **imposing**. In this situation, managers have little concern for how employees feel about their jobs. The boss issues orders, and the employees must follow them. Exploited employees are unhappy employees, and unhappy employees may seek employment with the competition. Thus, while imposing may increase productivity in the short run, its long-term effects generally decrease productivity through increased absenteeism, employee turnover, and in some cases, even sabotage and violence.

When managers emphasize neither satisfaction nor performance, they are **ignoring** their responsibilities

Figure 6.1	Relationship Between Satisfaction and Performance

EMPHASIS ON PERFORMANCE

		Low	High
EMPHASIS ON SATISFACTION	High	Indulging	Integrating
	Low	Ignoring	Imposing

and the realities of their organization. The resulting neglect reflects a *lack* of management. Paralyzed between what they consider to be mutually exclusive options of emphasizing performance or satisfaction, managers choose neither. The resulting neglect, if allowed to continue, may ultimately lead to the failure of the work unit.

The **integrating** motivation strategy emphasizes performance and satisfaction equally. Effective managers are able to combine what appear to be competing forces; they capitalize on the apparent tensions between productivity and employee satisfaction to forge creative new approaches to motivation. However, this does not mean that both objectives can be fully satisfied in every specific case. Some trade-offs occur naturally in ongoing work situations. However, in the long run, both objectives should be given equal consideration.

The integrative view of motivation proposes that while managers should not downplay the importance of employees' feeling good about what they are doing and how they are being treated, managers' concern for keeping employees satisfied should not overshadow their responsibility to hold people accountable for results. Managers should avoid the twin traps of working to engender high employee morale for its own sake or pushing for short-term results at the expense of long-term commitment. The best managers have productive people who are also satisfied with their work environment (Kotter, 1996).

Elements of an Effective Motivation Program

We now turn to the core of this discussion: a step-by-step program for creating an integrative, synergistic motivational program grounded in the belief that employees can simultaneously be high performers and personally satisfied. The key assumptions underlying our framework are summarized in Table 6.1.

It is useful to note that the prevailing wisdom among organizational scholars regarding the relationships between motivation, satisfaction, and performance has changed dramatically over the past several decades. When the authors took their first academic courses on this subject, they were taught the following model:

Satisfaction → Motivation → Performance

However, over the course of our careers we have observed the following criticisms of this "contented cows give more milk" view of employee performance.

Table 6.1	Key Assumptions Underlying Our Framework

1. Employees typically start out motivated. Therefore, a lack of motivation is a learned response, often fostered by misunderstood or unrealistic expectations.

2. The role of management is to create a supportive, problem-solving work environment in which facilitation, not control, is the prevailing value.

3. Rewards should encourage high personal performance consistent with management objectives.

4. Motivation works best when it is based on self-governance.

5. Individuals should be treated fairly.

6. Individuals deserve timely, honest feedback on work performance.

First, as researchers began collecting longitudinal data on the predictors of performance, they discovered that the satisfaction → motivation → performance causal logic was wrong. For reasons we will discuss later in this chapter, it is now believed that:

Motivation → Performance → Satisfaction

Second, the correlations among these three variables was very low, suggesting that a large number of additional factors needed to be added to this basic model. For example, we now know that performance leads to satisfaction when it is clear to the employee that rewards are based on performance, as compared with seniority or membership. The addition of fair rewards (more generally referred to as outcomes) into this formula has so dramatically improved our understanding of motivation that it has been incorporated into a revised model:

Motivation → Performance → Outcomes → Satisfaction

The remainder of this chapter is basically an account of the improvements that have been made over the past few decades in this basic "four factors" model of work motivation. We will also introduce several additional factors that we now know must be included in a comprehensive motivation program. For example, earlier in this chapter we introduced the notion that people's performance is a function of *both* their motivation and their ability. This suggests we need to add ability to the basic model as a second factor (besides motivation) contributing to performance. Each of the following sections of this chapter introduce additional variables that, like ability, need to be added to the basic, four-factor model. Table 6.2 shows the key building blocks of the complete model, in the form of six diagnostic questions, organized with reference to the "four-factor" model of motivation. A model encapsulating these questions will be used to summarize our presentation at the end of the chapter (Figure 6.5), and a diagnostic tool based on these questions will be described in the Skill Practice section (Figure 6.7).

ESTABLISH CLEAR PERFORMANCE EXPECTATIONS

As shown in Table 6.2, the first two elements of our comprehensive motivational program focus on the motivation → performance link. We begin by focusing on the manager's role in establishing clear expectations and then shift to the manager's role in enabling members of a work group to satisfy those expectations.

Based on data collected since 1993, Right Management Consultants reported that one-third of all managers who change jobs fail in their new positions within 18 months (Fisher, 2005). According to this study, the primary tip for getting off to a good start is asking your boss exactly what's expected of you and how soon you're supposed to deliver it. Ironically, however, people in managerial positions are less likely to receive a clear job description or detailed performance expectations then people who do entry-level work. Too often, the organization's attitude seems to be: "We pay people to know without being told."

Discussions of goal setting often make reference to an insightful conversation between Alice in Wonderland and the Cheshire Cat. When confronted with a choice among crossing routes, Alice asked the Cat which one she should choose. In response, the Cat asked Alice where she was heading. Discovering Alice had no real destination in mind, the Cat appropriately advised her any choice would do. It is surprising how often supervisors violate the common sense notion that they need to make sure individuals under their charge not only understand which road they should take, but what constitutes an acceptable pace for the journey.

Table 6.2	Six Elements of an Integrative Motivation Program

MOTIVATION → PERFORMANCE

1. Establish moderately difficult goals that are understood and accepted.

   Ask: "Do subordinates understand and accept my performance expectations?"

2. Remove personal and organizational obstacles to performance.

   Ask: "Do subordinates feel it is possible to achieve this goal or expectation?"

PERFORMANCE → OUTCOMES

3. Use rewards and discipline appropriately to extinguish unacceptable behavior and encourage exceptional performance.

   Ask: "Do subordinates feel that being a high performer is more rewarding than being a low or average performer?"

OUTCOMES → SATISFACTION

4. Provide salient internal and external incentives.

   Ask: "Do subordinates feel the rewards used to encourage high performance are worth the effort?"

5. Distribute rewards equitably.

   Ask: "Do subordinates feel that work-related benefits are distributed fairly?"

6. Provide timely rewards and specific, accurate, and honest feedback on performance.

   Ask: "Are we getting the most out of our rewards by administering them on a timely basis as part of the feedback process?"

   Ask: "Do subordinates know where they stand in terms of current performance and long-term opportunities?"

With this parable in mind, managers should begin assessing the motivational climate of their work environment by asking, "Do people here understand and accept performance expectations?" The foundation of an effective motivation program is proper **goal setting** (Locke & Latham, 2002). Perhaps no other concept in the field of organizational behavior has received more empirical support than that good goal-setting increases individual effort. Goals appear to be particularly effective in increasing performance for people high in conscientiousness (Colbert & Witt, 2009). Numerous studies also show that groups with goals significantly outperform groups without goals. Goal-setting theory argues that goals enhance performance because they mobilize our efforts, direct our attention, and encourage both persistence and strategy development (Sue-Chan & Ong, 2002). Not all goals work this well, however. Goals have to incorporate particular traits in order to make a difference in our effort and performance. Effective goal setting includes three critical components: a good goal-setting *process*, the right goal *characteristics*, and consistent implementation of *feedback*.

The first requirement for effective goals is adopting a good **goal-setting process**. Research has shown that people are more likely to "buy into" goals if they get to be part of the goal-setting process. Work groups perform better when they choose their goals rather than have them assigned (Sue-Chan & Ong, 2002).

Sometimes, however, it is difficult to allow for extensive participation in the establishment of work goals. For example, a computer programming unit may not have any say about which application programs are assigned to the group or what priority is assigned each incoming task. Still, the manager can involve unit members in deciding how much time to allocate to each assignment ("What is a realistic goal for completing this task?") or who should receive which job assignment ("Which type of programs would you find challenging?").

Shifting from process to content, research has shown that **goal characteristics** significantly affect the likelihood of goal achievement (Locke & Latham, 2002). Effective goals are *specific, consistent*, and *appropriately challenging*.

Goals that are **specific** are measurable, unambiguous, and behavioral. Specific goals reduce misunderstanding about what behaviors will be rewarded. Admonitions such as "be dependable," "work hard," "take initiative," or "do your best" are too general and too difficult to measure and are therefore of limited motivational value. In contrast, when a new

vice president of operations was appointed at a major midwestern steel factory, he targeted three goals: Reduce finished product rejection by 15 percent (quality); reduce average shipment period by two days (customer satisfaction); and respond to all employee suggestions within 48 hours (employee involvement). These easily measurable goals resulted in performance increases.

Goals should also be **consistent**. An already hardworking assistant vice president in a large metropolitan bank complains she cannot increase both the number of reports she writes in a week and the amount of time she spends "on the floor," visiting with employees and customers. Goals that are inconsistent—in the sense that they are logically impossible to accomplish simultaneously—create frustration and alienation. A recent study showed that organizations that set many weakly correlated goals leads to a "performance freeze," where employees are essential paralyzed with confusion about what behavior is most important (Ethiraj & Levinthal, 2009). When subordinates complain that goals are incompatible or inconsistent, managers should be flexible enough to reconsider their expectations.

One of the most important characteristics of goals is that they are **appropriately challenging** (Knight, Durham, & Locke, 2001). Simply stated, "stretch" goals are more motivating than easy goals. One explanation for this is called "achievement motivation" (Atkinson, 1992; Weiner, 2000). According to this perspective, motivated workers size up new tasks in terms of both their chances for success and the significance of the anticipated accomplishment. To complete a goal anyone can reach is not rewarding enough for highly motivated individuals. In order for them to feel successful, they must believe an accomplishment represents a meaningful achievement. Given their desire for success and achievement, it is clear these workers will be most motivated by challenging, but reachable, goals.

Although no single standard of difficulty fits all people, it is important to keep in mind that high expectations generally foster high performance and low expectations decrease performance (Davidson & Eden, 2000). As one experienced manager said, "We get about what we expect." Warren Bennis, author of *The Unconscious Conspiracy: Why Leaders Can't Lead*, agrees. "In a study of schoolteachers, it turned out that when they held high expectations of their students, that alone was enough to cause an increase of 25 points in the students' IQ scores" (Bennis, 1984, 2003).

In addition to selecting the right type of goal, an effective goal program must also include **feedback**. Feedback provides opportunities for clarifying expectations, adjusting goal difficulty, and gaining recognition. Therefore, it is important to provide benchmark opportunities for individuals to determine how they are doing. These along-the-way progress reports are particularly critical when the time required to complete an assignment or reach a goal is very long. For example, feedback is very useful for projects such as writing a large computer program or raising a million dollars for a local charity. In these cases, feedback should be linked to accomplishing intermediate stages or completing specific components.

REMOVE OBSTACLES TO PERFORMANCE

One of the key ingredients of an effective goal program is a supportive work environment. After setting goals, managers should shift their focus to facilitating successful accomplishment by focusing on the ability part of the performance formula. They can start by asking "Do subordinates feel it is possible to achieve this goal?" Help from management must come in many forms, including making sure the worker has the aptitude required for the job, providing the necessary training, securing needed resources, and encouraging cooperation and support from other work units. It is

the manager's job to make the paths leading toward the targeted goals easier for the subordinate to travel.

Helping clear employees' paths toward their goals is the essence of the **"path goal" theory of leadership** (House & Mitchell, 1974; see also, Schriesheim & Neider, 1996; Shamir, House, & Arthur, 1993), which is depicted in Figure 6.2. This theory answers the question, "How much help should I give?" The model proposes that the level of a manager's involvement should vary according to what subordinates need, how much they expect, and how much support is available to them from other organizational sources.

The theory begins its answer to these questions by focusing on two *traits of the employee's task*: structure and difficulty. A task that is highly structured (i.e., that has a lot of built-in order and direction and is easy to complete) does not require extensive management direction. If managers offer too much advice, they will come across as controlling, bossy, or nagging because it is already clear to the subordinates what they should do. On the other hand, for an unstructured (i.e., ambiguous) and complex task, management's direction and strong involvement in problem-solving activities will be seen as constructive and satisfying.

The second factor that influences how much involvement management should provide is the *expectations of the subordinates*. One characteristic that shapes employee expectations about management involvement is desire for autonomy. Individuals who

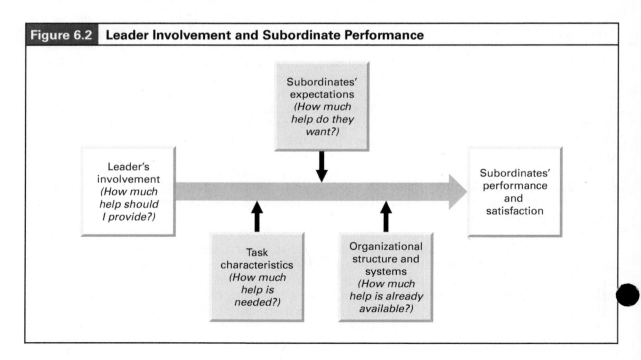

Figure 6.2 **Leader Involvement and Subordinate Performance**

prize autonomy and independence prefer managers with a highly participative leadership style because it gives them more latitude for controlling what they do. In contrast, people who prefer the assistance of others in making decisions, establishing priorities, and solving problems prefer greater management involvement.

Another characteristic that impacts employee expectations is their own ability and experience levels. Capable and experienced employees feel they need less assistance from their managers because they are adequately trained, know how to obtain the necessary resources, and can handle political entanglements with their counterparts in other units. On the other hand, it is frustrating for relatively new employees, or those with marginal skills, to feel that their manager has neither the time nor interest to listen to basic questions.

The third component that path-goal theory argues is important for deciding how involved managers should be is *the availability of organizational support.* Management involvement should complement, rather than duplicate, organizational sources of support. Specifically, managers should become more involved when performance standards are not clear, organizational rewards are insufficient, and organizational controls governing performance are inadequate.

In short, the path-goal model encourages managers to tailor their style to employee conditions, as shown in Table 6.3. Managers' direct involvement should be calibrated to the nature of the work and the availability of organizational support as well as the ability and experience of the individuals. If managers are insensitive to these contingencies, some employees may see them as interfering, while others will feel lost.

REINFORCE PERFORMANCE-ENHANCING BEHAVIOR

Referring back to the basic "four-factor" model of motivation, we now shift our focus from the antecedents of work performance (the motivation → performance link) to its consequences (the performance → outcomes link). Once managers have helped establish clear goals and cleared the paths to goal completion, the next step in an effective motivational program is to encourage goal accomplishment by linking performance to extrinsic outcomes (rewards and discipline) and fostering intrinsic outcomes.

The key diagnostic question here is: "Do employees feel that being a high performer is more rewarding than being a low or average performer?" To create an environment where the answer to this question is "yes," managers should consider two related principles: (1) in general, managers should link rewards to performance, rather than seniority or membership; and (2) managers should use discipline to extinguish counterproductive behaviors and use rewards to reinforce productive behaviors.

Use Rewards as Reinforcers

When managers link rewards to desired behaviors, they reinforce that behavior (Luthans & Stajkovic, 1999; Stajkovic & Luthans, 2001). These rewards also signal to the rest of the organization what is most valued. Ed Lawler, one of the foremost authorities on reward systems, underscored this point when he said, "Often the early reward systems of an organization are particularly important in shaping its culture. They reinforce certain behavior patterns and signal how

Table 6.3	Factors Influencing Management Involvement		
Contingencies		**Conditions Appropriate for High Management Involvement**	**Conditions Appropriate for Low Management Involvement**
Task structure		Low	High
Task mastery		Low	High
Subordinate's desire for autonomy		Low	High
Subordinate's experience		Low	High
Subordinate's ability		Low	High
Strength of group norms		Low	High
Effectiveness of organization's controls and rewards		Low	High

highly valued different individuals are by the organization. They also attract a certain type of employee and in a host of little ways indicate what the organization stands for and values" (Lawler, 2000a, p. 39).

Some modern management practices seem to challenge the principle that rewards should be linked to performance. Many companies are minimizing distinctions between workers by providing attractive universal benefits like recreational facilities, library services, day care, and attractive stock option programs for all employees. One aeronautics firm in France tried to help employees foster a stronger personal connection to the company by allowing them to use company tools and time to create personal artifacts (Anteby, 2008). Cognex Corporation provides incentives such as free films and refreshments at the local movie theater or the use of a limo for five hours. The company's CEO, Dr. Robert J. Shillman says, "Give people $500, they put it in the bank and they won't remember it. We like to do memorable things that get a bang for the buck" (Lublin, 2006).

Although there are obvious motivational benefits from employees receiving life-enhancing "perks," when universal benefits are the center of a motivation program, then the organization runs the risk of undermining the motivation of high performers. Although there is evidence that some companies decrease turnover by employing creative incentives, focusing exclusively on incentives that everyone receives may come with a cost. Overlooking the vital link between performance and rewards may make it difficult for organizations to attract and retain the strongest performers (Pfeffer, 1995).

This discussion of the appropriate use of rewards reminds us of the need to take into consideration cultural values and expectations. For example, individuals from collectivist cultures tend to favor rewards delivered at the group level (Graham & Trevor, 2000; Parker, 2001; Triandis, 1994). So, in addition to all of the factors managers must consider in developing incentives, they must also take into consideration the employees' culturally based assumptions about what is the appropriate unit of analysis (group or individual) for measuring and rewarding performance. If a manager is planning a bonus system for a work unit consisting of a mixture of individuals holding collectivist and individualist value perspectives, the manager should look for ways to factor these conflicting perspectives into the design of the bonus program.

It is also important to point out that nonfinancial rewards (such as awards) can be a valuable part of an effective performance-reinforcing program. Lawler argues that firms will get the greatest motivational impact from awards programs if they follow these guidelines: (1) give the awards publicly, (2) use awards infrequently, (3) embed them in a credible reward process, (4) use the awards presentation to acknowledge past recipients, and (5) make sure the award is meaningful within the organization's culture (Lawler, 2000a, p. 72–73).

The Role of Managers' Actions as Reinforcers

An effective motivational program goes beyond the design of the formal organizational reward system, including such things as pay, promotions, and the like. Managers must also recognize that their daily interactions with subordinates constitute an important source of motivation. It is difficult for even highly sensitive and aware managers to understand fully the impact of their actions on the behavior and attitudes of subordinates. Unfortunately, some managers don't even try to monitor these effects. When managers are unaware of their impact on employee motivation, they sometimes actually reinforce *undesirable* behaviors. This has been called "the folly of rewarding A while hoping for B" (Kerr, 1995). Take the example of a vice president of research and development who has a low tolerance for conflict. She might genuinely want her work teams to generate creative breakthroughs. But if she consistently rewards only the teams that avoid disagreement, then her employees might think twice before bringing up new and challenging ideas. In a way, rewarding only unity and harmony means that she is unintentionally *punishing* work groups that are trying to push beyond the status quo. In other words, she has "hoped for B" (creativity) but "rewarded A" (conformity).

Table 6.4 provides some dos and don'ts for encouraging subordinates to assume more initiative. This list demonstrates the power that managers' actions have in shaping behavior. Actions and reactions that might appear insignificant to the boss often have strong reinforcing or extinguishing effects on subordinates. Hence the truism, "Managers get what they reinforce, not what they want," and its companion, "People do what is inspected, not what is expected." Indeed, the reinforcing potential of managers' reactions to subordinates' behaviors is so strong that it has been argued, "The best way to change an individual's behavior in a work setting is to change his or her manager's behavior" (Thompson, 1978, p. 52). Given the considerable leverage managers have over

Table 6.4 | Guidelines for Fostering Subordinate Initiative

Do	Don't
Ask "How are we going to do this? What can I contribute to this effort? How will we use this result?" thus implying your joint stake in the work and results.	Imply that the task is the employee's total responsibility, that they hang alone if they fail. Individual failure means organizational failure.
Use an interested, exploring manner, asking questions designed to bring out factual information.	Play the part of an interrogator, firing questions as rapidly as they can be answered. Also, avoid asking questions that require only "yes" or "no" replies.
Keep the analysis and evaluation as much in the employees' hands as possible by asking for their best judgment on various issues.	React to their presentations on an emotional basis.
Present facts about organization needs, commitments, strategy, and so on, which permit them to improve, and interest them in improving what they propose to do.	Demand a change or improvement in a preemptory tone of voice or on what appears to be an arbitrary basis.
Ask them to investigate or analyze further if you feel that they have overlooked some points or overemphasized others.	Take their planning papers and cross out, change dates, or mark "no good" next to certain activities.
Ask them to return with their plans after factoring these items in.	Redo their plans for them unless their repeated efforts show no improvement.

SOURCE: *Reprinted with the permission of Simon & Schuster Adult Publishing Group, from* Putting Management Theories to Work *by Marion S. Kellogg, revised by Irving Burstiner. Copyright © 1979 by Prentice Hall. All rights reserved.*

their subordinates' motivation to reach optimal performance, it is important that they learn how to use rewards and punishments effectively to produce positive, intended results consistently.

Use Rewards and Discipline Appropriately

Psychologists use the term "operant conditioning" to describe the process of shaping others' behavior through linking rewards and punishments with behaviors (Komaki, Coombs, & Schepman, 1996). This approach uses a wide variety of motivational strategies that involve the presentation or withdrawal of positive or negative reinforcers. Although there are important theoretical and experimental differences in these strategies, such as between negative reinforcement and punishment, for the purposes of our discussion we will focus on three types of management responses to employee behavior: no response (ignoring), negative response (disciplining), and positive response (rewarding).

Psychologists have shown that providing no response to a behavior leads to an elimination (or "extinction") of that behavior. However, it's tricky to transfer the extinction strategy from the psychologist's laboratory to the manager's work environment. In most managerial situations, people interpret a nonresponse to their behavior as a positive sign ("I guess nobody has any objections to what I'm doing"). If your assistant sheepishly slips a delinquent report on your desk, and you ignore his behavior because you are busy with other business, he may be so relieved at not being reprimanded for his tardiness that he actually feels reinforced.

This simple example underscores an important point: any behavior repeatedly exhibited in front of a supervisor is being rewarded somehow, regardless of the boss's intention. Thus, if an employee is chronically late or continually submits sloppy work, the manager must ask where the reinforcement for this behavior is coming from. While extinction plays an important role in the learning process when conducted in strictly controlled laboratory conditions, it is a less useful technique in organizational settings because the interpretation of a supposedly neutral response is impossible to control.

Ironically, managers sometimes unwittingly use extinction in precisely the wrong way. One fascinating study exhibited how failing to give recognition eroded people's persistence. Student subjects in the study were asked to complete mindless paperwork for minimal financial rewards, and were told they could stop participating whenever they wished. Each time the subjects finished a page of work, they handed it to the experimenter, who either acknowledged the sheet (looked at it and nodded before placing it in a pile), ignored it (didn't look at it before placing it on the pile) or shredded it (immediately put it in a shredder without even looking at it). As you might expect, subjects whose work was shredded were the quickest to withdraw from the experiment. But more surprisingly, subjects whose work was ignored quit the experiment almost as quickly (Ariely, Kamenica & Prelec, 2008). Failing to recognize an employee's good behaviors might extinguish them almost as quickly as if you destroyed his or her work.

Since extinction as a management tool is problematic, the primary focus of our discussion will be on the proper use of disciplining and rewarding strategies, as shown in Figure 6.3.

The **disciplining** approach involves responding negatively to an employee's behavior in order to discourage future occurrences. For example, if an employee is consistently late, a supervisor may reprimand him with the hope of decreasing the employee's tardiness. Nagging subordinates for their failure to obey safety regulations is another example.

The **rewarding** approach consists of linking desired behaviors with employee-valued outcomes. When a management trainee completes a report in a timely manner, the supervisor should praise his promptness. If a senior executive takes the initiative to solve a thorny, time-consuming problem on her own, she could be given some extra time to enjoy a scenic location at the conclusion of a business trip. Unfortunately, even simple rewards like these appear to be the exception, not the rule. Dr. Noelle Nelson, the author of a book on the power of appreciation in the workplace (2005), points out that according to U.S. Department of Labor data, the number one reason people leave their job is that they do not feel appreciated. She also points to a Gallup poll report that 65 percent of workers said they didn't receive a single word of praise or recognition during the past year. Elaborating on these data, Nelson argues even the most energetic and effective employees get worn down when they are rarely acknowledged for their good work and only singled out when they make mistakes.

Disciplining and rewarding are both viable and useful techniques, and each has its place in the effective manager's motivational repertoire. However, as Figure 6.3 shows, each technique is associated with different behavior-shaping goals. Discipline should be used to extinguish unacceptable behaviors. However, once an individual's behavior has reached an acceptable level, negative responses will not push the behavior up to the exceptional level. It is difficult to encourage employees to perform exceptional behaviors through nagging, threatening, or related forms of discipline. The left-hand side of Figure 6.3 shows that subordinates work to remove an aversive response rather than to gain a desired reward. Only through positive reinforcement do employees have control over achieving what they want and, therefore, the incentive to reach a level of exceptional performance.

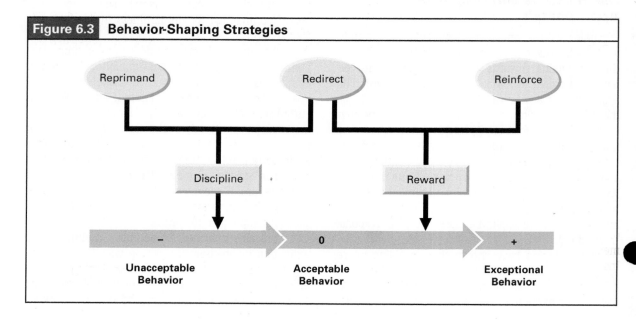

Figure 6.3   Behavior-Shaping Strategies

The emphasis in Figure 6.3 on matching discipline and rewards with unacceptable and acceptable behaviors, respectively, highlights two common misapplications of reinforcement principles. First, top performers frequently get upset because they feel "management is too soft on those guys who are always screwing things up." Thinking it is good management practice always to be upbeat and optimistic and to discourage negative interactions, some managers try to downplay the seriousness of mistakes by ignoring them, by personally fixing errors, or by encouraging the high performers to be more tolerant and patient. Sometimes managers feel so uncomfortable with confronting personal performance problems they are willing to overlook all but the most egregious mistakes. Although there is a lot to be said for managers having a positive attitude and giving poor performers the benefit of the doubt, their failure to reprimand and redirect inappropriate behaviors leads to two undesirable outcomes: The work unit's morale is seriously threatened, and the poor performers' behaviors are not improved.

Just as some managers find it unpleasant to issue reprimands for poor performance, other managers have difficulty praising exceptional performance. As a result, subordinates complain, "Nothing ever satisfies him." This second misapplication of the negative-response behavior-shaping strategy is just as dysfunctional as the indiscriminate use of praise. These managers mistakenly believe the best way to motivate people is by always keeping expectations a little higher than their subordinates' best performance and then reminding them of their imperfection. In the process, they run the risk of burning out their staff or inadvertently encouraging lower performance ("We'll get chewed out anyway, so why try so hard?"). Furthermore, the irony is that this method creates a competitive, self-defeating situation in which subordinates look forward to the boss's making mistakes—the bigger, the better!

Unfortunately, many managers genuinely believe this is the best way to manage in all situations. They define their role as that of a "sheepdog," circling the perimeter of the group, nipping at the heels of those who begin to stray. They establish a fairly broad range of acceptable behaviors and then limit their interactions with employees to barking at those who exceed the boundaries. This negative, desultory style of management creates a demoralizing work environment and does not foster exceptional performance. Instead, workers are motivated to stay out of the boss's way and to avoid doing anything unusual or untried. Innovation and involvement are extinguished, and

mundane performance becomes not only acceptable but desirable.

Having looked at the consequences of misapplying rewards and discipline, we will now turn our attention to the proper use of behavior-shaping techniques. The mark of exceptional managers is their ability to foster exceptional behavior in their subordinates. This can be accomplished by using a nine-step behavior-shaping process, applicable to the full range of subordinates' behaviors. Managers can use these steps either to correct unacceptable behaviors or to transform acceptable behaviors into exceptional ones. They are designed to avoid the harmful effects typically associated with the improper use of discipline discussed in the previous section (Wood & Bandura, 1989). They also ensure the appropriate use of rewards.

Strategies for Shaping Behavior

Table 6.5 shows the nine steps for improving behaviors. These are organized into three broad initiatives: *reprimand, redirect*, and *reinforce*. As shown in Figure 6.3, steps 1 through 6 (reprimand and redirect) are used to extinguish unacceptable behaviors and replace them with acceptable ones. Steps 4 through 9 (redirect and reinforce) are used to transform acceptable behaviors into exceptional behaviors.

An important principle to keep in mind when issuing a **reprimand** is that discipline should immediately follow the offensive behavior and focus exclusively on the specific problem. A reprimand is not an appropriate time to dredge up old concerns or make general, unsubstantiated accusations. The focus of the discussion should be on eliminating a problem behavior, not on making the subordinate feel bad. Focusing on a specific behavior decreases the likelihood that the employee will view the reprimand as a generalized and hostile attack.

After reprimanding, it is important to **redirect** inappropriate behaviors into appropriate channels. The process of redirection helps people understand how they can receive rewards in the future. Redirection clarifies to workers exactly how they can improve. Keep in mind that the ultimate goal of any negative feedback should be to transform inappropriate behaviors into appropriate ones, *not* simply to punish someone.

Finally, the negative effects of a reprimand quickly subside if the manager begins using rewards to **reinforce** desirable behaviors shortly thereafter. But this is only possible if workers know how to achieve positive outcomes and see the rewards as personally salient (a subject we'll discuss in detail shortly).

Table 6.5	Guidelines for Improving Behaviors

Reprimand

1. Identify the specific inappropriate behavior. Give examples. Indicate that the action must stop.

2. Point out the impact of the problem on the performance of others, on the unit's mission, and so forth.

3. Ask questions about causes and explore remedies.

Redirect

4. Describe the behaviors or standards you expect. Make sure the individual understands and agrees that these are reasonable.

5. Ask if the individual will comply.

6. Be appropriately supportive. For example, praise other aspects of their work, identify personal and group benefits of compliance; make sure there are no work-related problems standing in the way of meeting your expectations.

Reinforce

7. Identify rewards that are salient to the individual.

8. Link the attainment of desirable outcomes with incremental, continuous improvement.

9. Reward (including using praise) all improvements in performance in a timely and honest manner.

Foster Intrinsic Outcomes

So far, our discussion of the performance → outcomes link has focused on **extrinsic outcomes**. These are things like pay and promotions and praise that are controlled by someone other than the individual performer. In addition, the motivating potential of a task is affected by **intrinsic outcomes**, which the individual experiences personally as a result of successful task performance. They include a sense of purpose, feelings of accomplishment, self-esteem, and the development of new skills.

Effective managers understand that intrinsic rewards are critical for work performance. No matter how many externally controlled rewards managers use, if individuals find their jobs uninteresting and unfulfilling, performance will suffer. Some people have stronger needs for intrinsic rewards than others. For example, researchers have discovered that for highly intelligent people, job satisfaction is closely linked to the degree of difficulty they encounter in performing their work (Ganzach, 1998). Younger workers, too, seem to place a greater emphasis on intrinsic rewards and meaningfulness. The Millennial generation (people born between the early 1980s and 2000s) has often been described as generally idealistic and focused on doing work that serves a cause. Adam Grant, the author of *Give and Take*, argues that people perform best at work when they are focused on helping and giving to others. His research showed, for instance,

that students who worked at a university telefund (as cold callers asking for alumni donations) increased their fundraising effectiveness by 400 percent after listening to one scholarship recipient describe how much the alumni donations meant to her personally. The impact of that single conversation was still impacting employee performance three months later (Grant, 2011). Researchers are also finding that many workers long for a sense of "calling" at work—a belief that they are doing work they were meant to do and that serves an important cause. One example is a study of zookeepers, whose sense of calling propelled them to devote tremendous effort and sacrifice for their animals at work, even with very limited extrinsic rewards (Bunderson & Thompson, 2009). For employees that seek intrinsic rewards through their work, motivation may be less a matter of offering the right rewards and more about fine-tuning the fit between the job and the person occupying it.

Motivating Workers by Redesigning Work

Work design is the process of matching job characteristics to workers' skills and interests. One classic work-design model proposes that there are particular job characteristics that explain the motivating potential of the job. Figure 6.4 shows the relationship between the core job characteristics, the psychological states they produce in employees, and the resulting

Figure 6.4   Designing Highly Motivating Jobs

Figure 6.4   Designing Highly Motivating Jobs

personal and work outcomes (Hackman & Oldham, 1980). A variety of empirical research has found that these five core job dimensions—skill variety, task identity, task significance, autonomy, and feedback—are positively related to job satisfaction.

The greater a variety of skills one uses at work, the more one perceives the work as meaningful or worthwhile. Similarly, the more an individual can perform a complete job from beginning to end (task identity) and the more the work has a direct effect on the work or lives of other people (task significance), the more the employee will view the job as meaningful. On the other hand, when the work requires few skills, only part of a task is performed, or there seems to be little effect on others, experienced meaningfulness is low.

In addition, the more autonomy one has at work (i.e., freedom to choose how and when to do particular jobs), the more responsibility one feels for successes and failures. Increased responsibility results in increased commitment to one's work. Managers can increase employee autonomy by such things as instituting flexible work schedules, decentralizing decision making, or removing formalized controls, such as punching a time clock. Autonomy appears to be

particularly important for employees doing knowledge-intensive work (Haas, 2010).

Finally, the more feedback individuals receive about how well they are doing their jobs, the more knowledge they have about how to improve. Recent research shows that employees invest more time in tasks that provide more and better feedback (Northcraft, Schmidt & Ashford, 2011). Manager might provide feedback directly to employees, or create opportunities for them to gain feedback through direct contact with clients.

By enhancing these five core job dimensions, manager can enhance the potential for employees to feel motivated. Employees who have well-designed jobs enjoy doing them because they are intrinsically satisfying.

This discussion of work design suggests five managerial action guidelines that can help increase desirable personal and work outcomes. These are summarized in Table 6.6. The first one is to *combine tasks*. A combination of tasks is by definition a more challenging and complex work assignment. It requires workers to use a wider variety of skills, which makes the work seem more challenging and meaningful. A related managerial principle is to *form identifiable work units* so task

Table 6.6	Strategies for Increasing the Motivational Potential of Assigned Work	
Combine tasks	→	Increase skill variety and task significance
Form identifiable work units	→	Increase task identity and significance
Establish client relationships	→	Increase autonomy, task identity, and feedback
Increase authority	→	Increase autonomy, task significance, and task identity
Open feedback channels	→	Increase autonomy and feedback

identity and task significance can be increased. For example, clerical work in a large insurance firm was handled by 80 employees organized by functional task. To create higher levels of task identity and task significance, the firm reorganized the clerical staff into eight self-contained groups. Each group handled all business associated with specific clients. As a result, they felt a greater sense of meaningfulness because they were using a greater variety of skills, were engaged in completing an entire task, and could see their contributions more clearly.

The third guideline for enhancing jobs is to *establish client relationships*. A client relationship involves an ongoing personal relationship between an employee (the producer) and the client (the consumer). The establishment of this relationship can increase autonomy, task identity, and feedback. Interacting with the beneficiaries of one's work can have a surprisingly positive impact on employee effort and effectiveness (like it did for the telefund employees we mentioned in the previous section). One example of a company taking this principle seriously is Caterpillar, Inc., which assigns members of each division's R&D group to make regular contacts with their major clients.

The fourth suggestion, *increase authority*, refers to granting more authority for making job-related decisions to workers. As supervisors delegate more authority and responsibility, their subordinates' perceived autonomy, task significance, and task identity increase. Historically, workers on auto assembly lines have had little decision-making authority. However, in conjunction with increased emphasis on quality, many plants now allow workers to adjust their equipment, reject faulty materials, and even shut down the line if a major problem is evident.

The final managerial suggestion is to *open feedback channels*. Workers need to know how well or how poorly they are performing their jobs if any kind of improvement is expected. Younger workers, in particular expect frequent feedback. One study showed that 85 percent of "Generation Y" workers want "frequent and candid performance feedback," while only half of Baby Boomer employees do. This trend has led some organizations to seek creative mechanisms for providing employees more feedback. Ernst & Young, for instance, has developed a system called the "feedback zone," which allows employees to request or submit feedback at any time (Hite, 2008). Open feedback systems give employees ample opportunity to understand how they are doing, and increases their potential motivation to strive to do better.

The overall record of job redesign interventions is impressive. Historically, firms that carefully redesign jobs typically report a substantial increase in productivity, work quality, and worker satisfaction (reflected in lower rates of absenteeism). For example, early results of the job redesign movement included the following: The Social Security Administration increased productivity 23.5 percent among a group of 50 employees; General Electric realized a 50 percent increase in product quality as a result of a job redesign program; and the absenteeism rate among data-processing operators at Travelers Insurance decreased 24 percent (Kopelman, 1985).

In summary, managers should recognize that both intrinsic and extrinsic outcomes are necessary ingredients of effective motivational programs. Because most people value interesting and challenging work activities more than material rewards, good wages and job security will do little to overcome the negative effects of individuals' feeling that their abilities are underutilized. In addition, because people vary so much in their preferences and values, managers should not assume that a narrow-gauged, outcomes-contingent, performance-reinforcing motivation program will satisfy the needs and interests of a broad group of individuals. This brings us to the subject of reward salience.

PROVIDE SALIENT REWARDS

Having established a link between performance and outcomes (rewards and discipline) as part of an integrative motivational program, we now move to the final link in the four-factor model of motivation: Outcomes → Satisfaction. In the following sections we will discuss the three remaining elements of our motivational program, as shown in Table 6.2. Each of these elements has been shown to affect how satisfied individuals are with their work-related outcomes. The likelihood that a reward will actually reinforce a specific performance-enhancing behavior depends on the extent to which the reward recipient: (1) actually values the outcome, (2) believes that the reward allocation process was handled fairly, and (3) receives the reward in a timely manner.

We begin this discussion, with diagnostic question 4: "Do subordinates feel the rewards used to encourage high performance are worth the effort?" One of the biggest mistakes managers make in implementing a reward program is misunderstanding their subordinates' preferences. For example, managers often assume that most people prefer cash incentives. But according to a 2004 study conducted by the University of Chicago, performance improves much faster when it is linked *noncash* rewards (14.6 percent increase for cash vs. 38.6 percent increase for noncash) (Cook, 2005, p. 6). Managers need to develop a sound understanding of their employees' personal needs and motivations before adopting a particular incentive.

Personal Needs and Personal Motivation

One of the most enduring theories of motivation is based on our scientific understanding of human needs. The **hierarchical needs model** argues that people are motivated to satisfy their most basic unfulfilled need. That is, until a lower-level need has been satisfied, a higher-level need won't become activated. Probably the best-known example of a hierarchical needs model was proposed by Abraham Maslow (1970). He posited five levels of needs, beginning with *physiological*, followed by *safety, belongingness, esteem*, and *self-actualization*. Clay Alderfer proposed a more parsimonious hierarchical model (1977) that contained only three levels, or categories: *existence, relatedness*, and *growth*. Like Maslow, Alderfer proposed that satisfied needs become dormant unless a dramatic shift in circumstances increases their salience. For example, a middle-level executive who is fired during a hostile takeover may suddenly find her interest in personal growth is overwhelmed by a pressing need for security.

Table 6.7	Comparison of Hierarchical Needs Theories	
Maslow		**Alderfer**
Self-actualization		Growth
Esteem		
Belongingness		Relatedness
Safety		
Physiological		Existence

While hierarchical needs theories help us understand general developmental processes, from child to adult, they aren't very useful for understanding the day-to-day motivation levels of adult employees. A comparison of these hierarchical needs models is shown in Table 6.7.

> ⊗ **MyManagementLab: WATCH IT**
> **Joie de Vivre Hospitality: Employee Motivation**
> Apply what you have learned about management. If your instructor has assigned MyManagementLab, go to mymanagementlab.com to watch a video case and answer questions.

An alternative perspective can be found in Murray's **manifest needs model** (McClelland, 1971, p. 13). Murray proposes that individuals can be classified according to the strengths of their various needs. In contrast to hierarchical models, in which needs are categorized based on their inherent strength (hunger is a stronger need than self-actualization), Murray argues that people have divergent and often conflicting needs. He listed about two dozen needs, but later studies have suggested only three or four of them are relevant to the workplace, including the needs for *achievement, affiliation*, and *power*.

Need for achievement is defined as an individual's personal "competition with a standard of excellence" (McClelland, Arkinson, Clark, & Lowell, 1953, p. 111). Individuals with a high need for achievement exhibit: (1) a tendency to set moderately difficult goals, (2) a strong desire to assume personal responsibility for work activities, (3) a single-minded focus on accomplishing a task, and (4) a strong desire for detailed feedback on task performance. Need for achievement has been shown to be a good predictor of job performance. In addition, it is highly correlated with a person's preference for an enriched job with greater responsibility and autonomy.

The second of Murray's needs, **need for affiliation**, involves relying on other individuals in order to feel reassured and acceptable (Birch & Veroff, 1966, p. 65). People with a high need for affiliation tend to exhibit: (1) a sincere interest in the feelings of others; (2) a tendency to conform to the expectations of others, especially those whose affiliation they value; and (3) a strong desire for reassurance and approval from others. In contrast to the need for achievement, the need for affiliation does not seem to be strongly correlated with job performance.

Rounding out Murray's model is the **need for power**, which represents a desire to influence others and to control one's environment. Individuals with a high need for power seek leadership positions and tend to influence others in a fairly open, direct manner. McClelland and Burnham (2003) suggest two manifestations of the need for power. Individuals with a high need for *personal power* tend to seek power and influence for its own sake. To them, control and dominance and conquest are important indicators of personal efficacy. These leaders inspire their subordinates to perform heroic feats, but for the sake of the leader, not the organization. In contrast, individuals with high *institutional power* needs are more oriented toward using their influence to advance the goals of the group or organization. According to McClelland, these people: (1) are organization minded, feeling personally responsible for advancing the purposes of the organization; (2) enjoy work and accomplishing tasks in an orderly fashion; (3) are often willing to sacrifice their own self-interests for the good of the organization; (4) have a strong sense of justice and equity; and (5) seek expert advice and are not defensive when their ideas are criticized.

Using Need Theory to Identify Personally Salient Outcomes

Understanding need theory helps managers anticipate whether particular rewards will be effective reinforcers for specific individuals. In practice, this means managers need to understand what motivates each of their subordinates. Table 6.8 demonstrates the difficulty of this task. These research results highlight differences in what various types of organizational members tend to see as highly motivating aspects of their work. For example, while on average the employees in this study placed the highest value on "interesting work" and the lowest value on "sympathetic

help with personal problems," we see significant differences in the ratings for these two outcomes across gender, age, and income categories. It is easy to spot equally disparate outcome preferences expressed by different groups of workers for many of the other benefits and rewards, in the left-hand column, commonly used by business firms to attract, retain, and motivate employees.

In the abstract, it is not surprising to learn that individuals with different demographic and economic profiles have different needs and, thus, bring different expectations to the workplace. But at least one research study suggests that managers are not particularly good at predicting how their subordinates would rank the outcomes shown in Table 6.8 (LeDue, 1980). More particularly, this research suggests that managers tend to base their answers to the question, "What motivates your subordinates?" on two faulty assumptions. First, they assume the outcome preferences among their subordinates are fairly homogenous, and second, they assume their personal outcome preferences are similar to those held by their subordinates. Knowing this, the data shown in Table 6.8 illustrates how easy it is for managers with a certain gender, age, and income profile to systematically misread the salient needs of subordinates representing a different profile. Furthermore, it is not difficult to imagine individual circumstances that would result in a person's preferences being significantly different from those of others with a similar demographic and economic profile. In summary, this data underscores the importance of managers getting to know their subordinates well enough that they can effectively match individual and group performance expectations with personally salient outcomes.

The importance of gaining this person-specific information is illustrated in the case of a stockbroker who was promoted to office manager because upper management in the home office felt he was "the most qualified and most deserving." Unfortunately, they failed to ask him if he wanted to be promoted. They assumed that because they had worked hard to qualify for their management positions, all hard workers were similarly motivated. Two weeks after receiving his "reward" for outstanding performance, the supersalesman-turned-manager was in the hospital with a stress-related illness.

Effective managers gain information about active needs and personal values through frequent, supportive, and generally informal discussions with their subordinates about expectations, responsibilities, challenges, and opportunities. When engaging in discussions such as these, it is important to keep in mind that there are always trade-offs between the rewards employees might value. In the abstract, everyone values everything. In reality, we have to make tough choices about which reinforcers to use, and those choices reflect our underlying needs and values. Thus, it might be particularly instructive to see how an employee responds to a discussion about how a colleague's new job provides opportunities for more pay, but at the expense of being away from home three nights a week. Similarly, the opportunity to be involved with the design of a new product line also might mean longer hours at work, higher levels of personal stress, and the possibility that the failure to meet high expectations may reflect negatively on the team members.

The data reported in Table 6.8 is also relevant for individuals in a position to shape the pay and benefits package for an entire organization. Scanning these results, it is easy to pick out differences between the ratings of blue-collar vs. white-collar, unskilled and skilled, lower and higher level employees. Recognizing the wide diversity in outcome preferences within the employee ranks of most large businesses, many firms, ranging from investment banks, like Morgan Stanley, to manufacturing firms, like American Can, have experimented with "cafeteria-style" incentive systems (Abbott, 1997; Lawler, 1987). This approach takes much of the guesswork out of linking an individual's organizational membership and work performance with personally salient outcomes, by allowing employees some say in the matching process. Using this approach, employees receive a certain number of work credits based on performance, seniority, or task difficulty, and they are allowed to trade those in for a variety of benefits, including upgraded insurance packages, financial planning services, disability income plans, extended vacation benefits, tuition reimbursement for educational programs, and so forth.

Table 6.8 — What Workers Want, Ranked by Subgroups*

	All Employees	Men	Women	Under 30	31-40	41-50	Over 50	Under $25,000	$25,001-$40,000	$40,001-$50,000	Over $50,000	Blue-Collar Unskilled	Blue-Collar Skilled	White-Collar Unskilled	White-Collar Skilled	Lower Nonsupervisory	Middle Nonsupervisory	Higher Nonsupervisory
Interesting work	1	1	2	4	2	3	1	5	2	1	1	2	1	1	2	3	1	1
Full appreciation of work done	2	2	1	5	3	2	2	4	3	3	2	1	6	3	1	4	2	2
Feeling of being in on things	3	3	3	6	4	1	3	6	1	2	4	5	2	5	4	5	3	3
Job security	4	5	4	2	1	4	7	2	4	4	3	4	3	7	5	2	4	6
Good wages	5	4	5	1	5	5	8	1	5	6	8	3	4	6	6	1	6	8
Promotion and growth in organization	6	6	6	3	6	8	9	3	6	5	7	6	5	4	3	6	5	5
Good working conditions	7	7	10	7	7	7	4	8	7	7	6	9	7	2	7	7	7	4
Personal loyalty to employees	8	8	8	9	9	6	5	7	8	8	5	8	9	9	8	8	8	7
Tactful discipline	9	9	9	8	10	9	10	10	9	9	10	7	10	10	9	9	9	10
Sympathetic help with personal problems	10	10	7	10	8	10	6	9	10	10	9	10	8	8	10	10	10	9

*Ranked from 1 (highest) to 10 (lowest).

SOURCE: *Courtesy of George Mason University. Results are from a study of 1,000 employees conducted in 1995.*

BE FAIR AND EQUITABLE

Once appropriate rewards have been determined for each employee, managers must then consider how to distribute those rewards (Cropanzano & Folger, 1996). This brings us to concerns about equity. Any positive benefits of salient rewards will be negated if workers feel they are not receiving their fair share. The relevant diagnostic question here is, "Do subordinates feel that work-related benefits are distributed fairly?" (As in the previous section, we will focus here only on rewards. However, the same principles also apply to the equitable use of discipline.)

Equity refers to workers' perceptions of the fairness of rewards. Evaluations of equity are based on a social comparison process in which workers individually compare what they are getting out of the work relationship (outcomes) to what they are putting into the work relationship (inputs). Outcomes include such items as pay, fringe benefits, increased responsibility, and prestige while inputs may include hours worked and work quality as well as education and experience. Employees compare the ratio of their outcomes to inputs with the corresponding ratios of other individuals, judged to be an appropriate comparison group. The outcome of this comparison is the basis for beliefs about fairness.

If workers perceive inequity when they compare their outcome/input ratio with that of similar others, they will be motivated to restore equity in some way. One way they can seek to restore equity is through behavioral changes. For instance, they might request a pay raise (seek to increase their outcomes) or they can decrease their effort at work or find excuses not to do difficult assignments (decrease their inputs). Employees might also restore equity through cognitive adjustments. For instance, they may rationalize that their inputs are not as valuable as they thought (i.e., that their talents or training lag behind that of their peers) or that their coworkers are actually working harder (or more effectively) than they thought they were.

The strength of people's yearning for fairness underscores the need for managers to closely monitor subordinates' perceptions of equity (Janssen, 2001). In some cases, a manager might learn through conversations with employees that their comparison processes are faulty. For example, employees might misunderstand the value placed on certain inputs, such as experience versus expertise or quantity versus quality; or they might have unrealistic views of their own or others' performance. Since most people tend to believe that their leadership skills are better than average, these discrepancies are common.

However, just as often these discussions uncover real inequities. For example, the hourly rate of a worker may not be keeping up with recent skill upgrades or increased job responsibilities. The act of identifying and correcting legitimate inequities generates commitment and loyalty among employees. For example, a manager in the computer industry felt he had been unfairly passed over for promotion by a dishonest rival. Utilizing the company's open-door policy, he took his case to a higher level in the firm. After a thorough investigation, the decision was reversed and the rival reprimanded. The individual's response was, "After they went to bat for me, I could never leave the company."

The important thing to keep in mind about equity and fairness is that we are dealing with perceptions. Consequently, whether the employees' beliefs are accurate or distorted, legitimate or ill-founded, to the employees themselves, they are both accurate and legitimate until proven otherwise. A basic principle of social psychology states: "That which is perceived as being real is real in its consequences." Therefore, effective managers should constantly perform "reality checks" on their subordinates' perceptions of equity using questions such as: "What criteria for promotions, pay raises, and so on do you feel management should be placing more/less emphasis on?" "Relative to others similar to you in this organization, do you feel your job assignments, promotions, and so on are appropriate?" "Why do you think Alice was recently promoted over Jack?"

PROVIDE TIMELY REWARDS AND ACCURATE FEEDBACK

Up to this point, we have emphasized that employees need to understand and accept performance standards; they should feel that management is working hard to help them reach their performance goals; they should feel that available internal and external rewards are personally attractive; they should believe rewards and reprimands are distributed fairly; and they should feel these outcomes are administered primarily on the basis of performance.

All these elements are necessary for an effective motivational program, but they are not sufficient. As we noted earlier, a common mistake is to assume all rewards are reinforcers. In fact, the reinforcing potential of a "reward" depends on its being linked in the mind of the reward recipient to the specific behaviors the reward giver desires to strengthen. ("When I did behavior X, I received outcome Y. And, because I value Y, I am going to repeat X.") The ability of reward recipients to make this reinforcing (X behavior–Y outcome) mental connection is related to two specific aspects of how the reward is administered: (1) the length of time between the occurrence of the desirable behavior and the receipt of the reward and (2) the specificity of the explanation for the reward. These are the two final components of our motivational program. Hence, the sixth and final diagnostic question contains two parts. The first is, "Are we getting the most out of our rewards by administering them on a timely basis as part of the feedback process?"

As a general rule, the longer the delay in the administration of rewards, the less reinforcement value they have. Ironically, in a worst-case situation, the mistiming of a reward may actually reinforce undesirable behaviors. For instance, if a manager gives an employee a long-overdue raise only when she complains about the unfairness of the reward system, the manager may actually be reinforcing complaining rather than good work performance. Moreover, failure to give a reward immediately after a desired behavior makes it difficult for employees to sustain desirable behaviors in the future, since they may lose confidence that rewards will follow their sustained efforts.

Unfortunately, although timing is a critical contributor to the reinforcement potential of a reward, it is frequently ignored in everyday management practice. The formal administrative apparatus of many organizations often delays for months the feedback on the consequences of employee performance. It is customary practice to restrict in-depth discussions of job performance to formally designated appraisal interviews, which generally take place every 6 or 12 months. ("I'll have to review this matter officially later, so why do it twice?") The problem with this common practice is the resulting delay between performance and outcomes dilutes the effectiveness of any rewards or discipline dispensed as a result of the evaluation process.

In contrast, effective managers understand the importance of immediate, spontaneous rewards. They use the formal performance evaluation process to discuss long-term trends in performance, solve problems inhibiting performance, and set performance goals. But they don't expect these infrequent general discussions to significantly alter an employee's motivation.

For this, they rely on brief, frequent, highly visible performance feedback.

Peters and Waterman, in their classic book *In Search of Excellence* (1988), stress the importance of immediacy by relating the following amusing anecdote:

> At Foxboro, a technical advance was desperately needed for survival in the company's early days. Late one evening, a scientist rushed into the president's office with a working prototype. Dumbfounded at the elegance of the solution and bemused about how to reward it, the president bent forward in his chair, rummaged through most of the drawers in his desk, found something, leaned over the desk to the scientist, and said, "Here!" In his hand was a banana, the only reward he could immediately put his hands on. From that point on, the small "gold banana" pin has been the highest accolade for scientific achievement at Foxboro. (pp. 70–71)

The implication for effective management is clear: Effective rewards are spontaneous rewards. Reward programs that become highly routinized, especially those linked to formal performance appraisal systems, lose their immediacy.

There is a second critical aspect of reinforcement timing: the consistency of reward administration. Administering a reward every time a behavior occurs is called continuous reinforcement. Administering rewards on an intermittent basis (the same reward is always used but is not given every time it is warranted) is referred to as partial, or intermittent, reinforcement. Neither approach is clearly superior; both approaches have trade-offs. Continuous reinforcement represents the fastest way to establish new behavior. For example, if a boss consistently praises a subordinate for writing reports using the manager's preferred format, the subordinate will readily adopt that style in order to receive more and more contingent rewards. However, if the boss suddenly takes an extended leave of absence, the learned behavior will be highly vulnerable to extinction because the reinforcement pattern is broken. In contrast, while partial reinforcement results in very slow learning, it is very resistant to extinction. The persistence associated with gambling behavior illustrates the addictive nature of a partial reinforcement schedule. Not knowing when the next payoff may come preserves the myth that the jackpot is only one more try away.

LEARNING

It is important to realize that continuous reinforcement systems are very rare in organizations unless they are mechanically built into the job, as in the case of the piece-rate pay plan. Seldom are individuals rewarded every time they make a good presentation or effectively handle a customer's complaint. When we recognize that most nonassembly-line work in an organization is typically governed by a partial reinforcement schedule, we gain new insights into some of the more frustrating aspects of a manager's role. For example, it helps explain why new employees seem to take forever to catch on to how the boss wants things done. It also suggests why it is so difficult to extinguish outdated behaviors, particularly in older employees.

This brings us to the second half of the sixth diagnostic question, related to the accuracy of feedback, "Do subordinates have a realistic view of where they stand in terms of their performance and potential?" In addition to the timing of feedback, the content of feedback significantly affects its reinforcement potential. As a rule of thumb, to increase the motivational potential of performance feedback, be very specific—including examples whenever possible. Keep in mind that feedback, whether positive or negative, is itself an outcome. The main purpose for giving people feedback on their performance is to reinforce productive behaviors and extinguish counterproductive behaviors. But this can only occur if the feedback focuses on specific behaviors. To illustrate this point, compare the reinforcement value of the following, equally positive, messages: "You are a great member of this team—we couldn't get along without you." "You are a great member of this team. In particular, you are willing to do whatever is required to meet a deadline."

It is especially important for managers to provide accurate and honest feedback when a person's performance is marginal or substandard. There are many reasons why managers are reluctant to "tell it like it is" when dealing with poor performers. It is unpleasant to deliver bad news of any kind. Therefore, it is easy to justify sugarcoating negative information, especially when it is unexpected, on the basis that you are doing the recipient a favor. In practice, it is rarely the case that a poor performer is better off not receiving detailed, honest, accurate feedback. If the feedback is very general, or if it contains mixed signals, improvement is frustratingly difficult. And if a person truly is not well suited for a particular job, then no one benefits from delaying encouragement to seek other work opportunities.

When managers are reluctant to share unflattering or unhopeful feedback, it is often because they are unwilling to spend sufficient time with individuals receiving negative feedback to help them thoroughly understand their shortcomings, put them in perspective, consider options, and explore possible remedies. It is sometimes easier to pass on an employee with a poor performance record or unrealistic expectations to the next supervisor than it is to confront the problem directly, provide honest and constructive feedback, and help the individual respond appropriately. This is why the skill of supportively communicating negative performance information is one of the most difficult to master—and therefore one that is highly prized. If you are particularly interested in polishing this skill, we recommend you review the specific techniques described under the heading "Use Rewards and Discipline Appropriately."

Summary

Our discussion of enhancing work performance has focused on specific analytical and behavioral management skills. We first introduced the fundamental distinction between ability and motivation. Then we discussed several diagnostic questions for determining whether inadequate performance was due to insufficient ability. A five-step process for handling ability problems (resupply, retrain, refit, reassign, and release) was outlined. We introduced the topic of motivation by stressing the need for placing equal emphasis on concerns for satisfaction and performance. The remainder of this chapter focused on the second skill by presenting six elements of an integrative approach to motivation.

The summary model shown in Figure 6.5 (and its "diagnostic" version discussed in the Skill Practice section as Figure 6.7) highlights our discussion of an expanded version of the basic "four factors" model of motivation. The resulting comprehensive model underscores the necessary role of, as well as the interdependence among, the various components. Skilled managers incorporate all components of this model into their motivational efforts rather than concentrating only on a favorite subset. There are no shortcuts to effective management. All elements of the motivation process must be included in a total, integrated program for improving performance and satisfaction.

The fact that the flowchart begins with motivation is important because it makes explicit our assumption that individuals are inherently motivated to work hard and do a good job. Recall that motivation is manifested as work effort and effort consists of desire and commitment. This means that motivated employees have the desire to initiate a task and the commitment to do their best. Whether their motivation is sustained over time

Figure 6.5 | Integrative Model of Motivation Enhancement

1–6: Key to six diagnostic questions in Table 2.

Note: 1–6: Key to six diagnostic questions in Table 6.2.

depends on the remaining elements of the model, which are actually amplifications of the motivation → performance link, the performance → outcomes link, and the outcomes → satisfaction link. These crucial links in the motivational process can best be summarized as questions pondered by individuals who are asked to work harder, change their work routine, or strive for a higher level of quality: First, "If I put forth more effort, am I likely to be able to perform up to performance expectations?" Second, "Will my level of performance matter in this organization?" Third, "Will the experience of being a high performer likely be personally rewarding?"

Beginning on the left side of the model, we see that the combination of goals and ability determines the extent to which effort is successfully transformed into performance. In the path-goal theory of leadership, the importance of fitting the right job to the right person and providing necessary resources and training is emphasized. These factors must be combined with effective goal setting (understanding and accepting moderately difficult goals) if increased effort is to result in increased performance.

The next section of the model focuses on reinforcing good performance, in terms of both increasing the frequency of performance-enhancing behaviors and linking outcomes to successful goal accomplishment. It is important to keep in mind that people are, in general, motivated by both extrinsic and intrinsic outcomes. In addition, the effective manager is adept at using the full range of behavior-shaping tools, spanning the spectrum from discipline to rewards. Although our discussion focused more on rewards than discipline, when faced with the challenge of providing constructive but negative performance feedback, and developing an accompanying plan for remediation, Table 6.5 provides a useful set of guidelines.

Proceeding to the outcomes → satisfaction segment of the model, the importance of perceived equity and reward salience stands out. Individuals must believe the rewards offered are appropriate, not only for their personal performance level but also in comparison to the rewards achieved by "similar" others. The subjective value that individuals attach to incentives for performance reflects their personal relevance, or salience. Rewards with little personal value have low motivational potential. These subjective factors combine with the timeliness and accuracy of feedback to determine the overall motivational potential of rewards.

Based on their perceptions of outcomes, workers will experience varying degrees of satisfaction or dissatisfaction. Satisfaction creates a positive feedback loop, increasing the individual's motivation, as manifested by increased effort. Dissatisfaction, on the other hand, results in decreased effort and, therefore, lower performance and rewards. If uncorrected, this pattern may ultimately result in absenteeism or turnover.

Behavioral Guidelines

This discussion is organized around key diagnostic models and questions that serve as the basis for enhancing the following skills: (1) properly diagnosing performance problems, (2) initiating actions to enhance individuals' abilities, and (3) strengthening the motivational aspects of the work environment.

Table 6.2 summarizes the process for properly diagnosing the causes of poor work performance in the form of six diagnostic questions. (A "decision tree" version of these questions is included in the Skill Practice section as Figure 6.7.)

The key guidelines for creating a highly motivating work environment are:

A. Clearly define an acceptable level of overall performance or specific behavioral objective.
   ❑ Make sure the individual understands what is necessary to satisfy expectations.
   ❑ Formulate goals and expectations collaboratively, if possible.
   ❑ Make goals as challenging and specific as possible.

B. Help remove all obstacles to reaching performance objectives.
   ❑ Make sure the individual has adequate technical information, financial resources, personnel, and political support.
   ❑ If a lack of ability appears to be hindering performance, use the resupply, retrain, refit, reassign, or release series of remedies.
   ❑ Gear your level of involvement as a leader to how much help a person expects, needs, and how much help is otherwise available.

C. Make rewards and discipline contingent on high performance or drawing nearer to the performance objective.
   ❑ Carefully examine the behavioral consequences of your nonresponses. (Ignoring a behavior is rarely interpreted as a neutral response.)
   ❑ Use discipline to extinguish counterproductive behavior and rewards to reinforce productive behaviors.

D. When discipline is required, treat it as a learning experience for the individual.
   ❑ Specifically identify the problem and explain how it should be corrected.
   ❑ Use the reprimand and redirect guidelines in Table 6.5.

E. Transform acceptable into exceptional behaviors.
   ❑ Reward each level of improvement.
   ❑ Use the redirect and reward guidelines in Table 6.5.

F. Use reinforcing rewards that appeal to the individual.
   ❑ Allow flexibility in individual selection of rewards.
   ❑ Provide salient external rewards as well as satisfying and rewarding work (intrinsic satisfaction).
   ❑ To maintain salience, do not overuse rewards.

G. Periodically check subordinates' perceptions regarding the equity of reward allocations.
   ❑ Correct misperceptions related to equity comparisons.

H. Provide timely rewards and accurate feedback.
   ❏ Minimize the time lag between behaviors and feedback on performance, in-
      cluding the administration of rewards or reprimands. (Spontaneous feedback
      shapes behavior best.)
   ❏ Provide specific, honest, and accurate assessments of current performance and
      long-range opportunities.

CASE INVOLVING MOTIVATION PROBLEMS

Electro Logic

Electro Logic (EL) is a small R&D firm located in a midwestern college town adjacent to a major university. Its primary mission is to perform basic research on, and development of, a new technology called "Very Fast, Very Accurate" (VFVA). Founded four years ago by Steve Morgan, an electrical engineering professor and inventor of the technology, EL is primarily funded by government contracts, although it plans to market VFVA technology and devices to nongovernmental organizations within the year.

The government is very interested in VFVA, as it will enhance radar technology, robotics, and a number of other important defense applications. EL recently received the largest small-business contract ever awarded by the government to research and develop this or any other technology. Phase I of the contract has just been completed, and the government has agreed to Phase II contracting as well.

The organizational chart of EL is shown in Figure 6.6. Current membership is 75, with roughly 88 percent in engineering. The hierarchy of engineering titles and requirements for each are listed in Table 6.9. Heads of staff are supposedly appointed based on their knowledge of VFVA technology and their ability to manage people. In practice, the president of EL hand-picks these people based on what some might call arbitrary guidelines: most of the staff leaders were or are the president's graduate students. There is no predetermined time frame for advancement up the hierarchy. Raises are, however, directly related to performance appraisal evaluations.

Working directly with the engineers are the technicians. These people generally have a high school degree, although some also have college degrees. They are trained on the job, although some have gone through a local community college's program on microtechnology fabrication. The technicians perform the mundane tasks of the engineering department: running tests, building circuit boards, manufacturing VFVA chips, and so on. Most are full-time, hourly employees.

The administrative staff is composed of the staff head (with an MBA from a major university), accountants, personnel director, graphic artists, purchasing agent, project controller, technical writers/editors, and secretaries. Most of the people in the administrative staff are women. All are hourly employees except the staff head, personnel director, and project controller. The graphic artists and technical writer/editor are part-time employees.

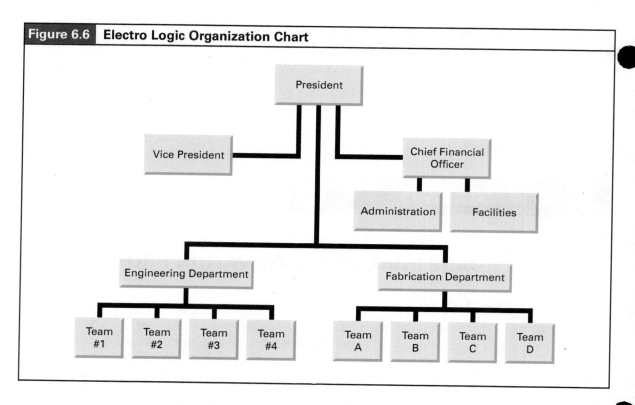

Figure 6.6 Electro Logic Organization Chart

The facilities staff is composed of the staff head and maintenance personnel. EL is housed in three different buildings, and the primary responsibility of the facilities staff is to ensure that the facilities of each building are in good working order. Additionally, the facilities staff is often called on to remodel parts of the buildings as the staff continues to grow.

EL anticipates a major recruiting campaign to enhance the overall staff. In particular, it is looking for more technicians and engineers. Prior to this recruiting campaign, however, the president of EL hired an outside consultant to assess employee needs as well as the morale and overall effectiveness of the firm. The consultant has been observing EL for about three weeks and has written up some notes of her impressions and observations of the company.

Table 6.9 Engineering Titles and Requirements

TITLE	REQUIREMENT
Member of Technical Staff	BSEE, MSEE
Senior Member of Technical Staff	PhD, MSEE with 2 years of industrial experience; BSEE with 5 years of industrial experience
Research Engineer	PhD with 2 years of industrial experience
	BSEE or MSEE with 7 years of industrial experience
Research Scientist	PhD with appropriate experience in research
Senior Research Scientist	PhD with appropriate industrial and research experience

Consultant's Notes from Observations of Electro Logic

Facilities: Electro Logic (EL) is housed in three different buildings. Two are converted houses, and one is an old school building. Senior managers and engineers are in the school, and others are scattered between the houses.

Meetings: Weekly staff meetings are held in the main building to discuss objectives and to formulate and review milestone charts.

Social interaction: A core group of employees interact frequently on a social basis; for example, sports teams, parties. The administrative staff celebrates birthdays at work. The president occasionally attends.

Work allocation: Engineers request various tasks from the support staff, which consists of technicians and administrative unit personnel. There is obviously some discretion used by the staff in assigning priorities to the work requests, based on rapport and desirability of the work.

Turnover: The highest turnover is among administrative personnel and technicians. Exit interviews with engineers indicate they leave because of the company's crisis-management style, better opportunities for career advancement and security in larger organizations, and overall frustration with EL's "pecking order." Engineers with the most responsibility and authority tend to leave.

Salary and benefits: In general, wages at EL are marginal by national and local standards. A small group of scientists and engineers do make substantial salaries and have a very attractive benefits package, including stock options. Salaries and benefits for new engineers tend to be linked to the perceived level of their expertise.

Offices and facilities: Only EL's president, vice president, and chief financial officer have their own offices. Engineers are grouped together in "pods" by project assignment. There is very little privacy in these work areas, and the noise from the shared printer is distracting. The head of administration shares a pod with the personnel director, facilities head, and the project controller. One to three secretaries per building are located in or near the reception areas. The large building has an employee lounge with three vending machines. There is also a coffee-and-tea station. The smaller buildings have only a soft-drink vending machine in the reception area.

Consultant's Interviews with Employees

After making these observations, the consultant requested interviews with a cross-section of the staff for the purpose of developing a survey to be taken of all employees. Presented below are excerpts from those interviews.

Pat Klausen, Senior Member of the Technical Staff

CONSULTANT: What is it about Electro Logic (EL) that gives you the most satisfaction?

PAT: I really enjoy the work. I mean, I've always liked to do research, and working on VFVA is an incredible opportunity. Just getting to work with Steve (EL's president and VFVA's inventor) again is exciting. I was his graduate student about six years ago, you know. He really likes to work closely with his people—perhaps sometimes too closely. There have been times when I could have done with a little less supervision.

CONSULTANT: What's the least satisfying aspect of your work?

PAT: Probably the fact that I'm never quite sure we'll be funded next month, given the defense budget problems and the tentativeness of our research. I've got a family to consider, and this place isn't the most stable in terms of its financial situation. Maybe it'll change once we get more into commercial production. Who knows?

CONSULTANT: You've offered some general positives and negatives about EL. Can you be more specific about day-to-day dealings? What's good and bad about working here on a daily basis?

PAT: You're sure this isn't going to get back to anyone? Okay. Well, in general I'm not satisfied with the fact that too often we end up changing horses in the middle of the stream, if you know what I mean. In the past seven months, three of my engineers and four of my techs have been pulled off my project onto projects whose deadlines were nearer than mine. Now I'm faced with a deadline, and I'm supposed to be getting more staff. But I'll have to spend so much time briefing them that it might make more sense for me to just finish the project myself. On the other hand, Steve keeps telling me that we have to be concerned with EL's overall goals, not just our individual concerns—you know, we have to be "team players," "good members of the family." It's kind of hard to deal with that, though, when deadlines are bearing down and you know your butt's on the line, team player or not. But if you go along with this kind of stuff and don't complain, the higher-ups treat you well. Still, it seems to me there's got to be a better way to manage these projects.

CONSULTANT: What are the positive aspects of your daily work?

PAT: Well, the people here are all great to work with. They know their stuff or can learn quickly. I tend to be a social person and I really like socializing with these people. We play softball and basketball together and do happy hours and stuff. I like that. I've got some good friends here, which helps get my work orders filled quickly, if you know what I mean.

Bob Christensen, Member of the Technical Staff

CONSULTANT: You said earlier that Steve was your adviser for your M.S. So you've known him a long time.

BOB: Yes, that's right. I've known Professor Morgan—Steve—for about eight years. I had him for a few undergraduate classes; then, of course, he was my adviser for my two-year master's program, and now I've worked at Electro Logic (EL) for two years.

CONSULTANT: It seems as if you enjoy working with Steve.

BOB: Oh, yeah. But I really don't get to work directly with him anymore. I'll see him at meetings and such, but that's about it.

CONSULTANT: So he's not your immediate supervisor?

BOB: No, but for the amount of time I spend with my supervisor, Steve might as well be. My boss and I meet maybe once every three weeks for about an hour to see if all is well. And that's it. The rest of the time, I'm on my own. I used to talk to Steve when I had questions, but he's gotten so busy now that it's hard to see him—you need to make an appointment a few days in advance.

CONSULTANT: Do you think your supervisor treats all his staff this way?

BOB: To be honest, I have heard some complaints. In fact, about six months ago, the situation was so bad, some other people and I had a meeting with him. He promised that he would be more available to us and was, for about a month. Then we got involved in a new proposal, so he made himself scarce again. So nothing's really changed. We're coming up on finalizing the proposal now, and it's important that I see him, ask him questions. The last few drafts I've submitted to him, he's returned, rewritten in his own way, and with no explanation of the changes. Sometimes I think he treats me like somebody who doesn't know anything, as if I had no training whatsoever. I realize his neck is on the line with this project, but sometimes it seems that he uses being busy to avoid talking to me.

Chris Chen, Research Scientist

CONSULTANT: What kind of characteristics should a person have if he/she wants to work as a research scientist at Electro Logic (EL)?

CHRIS: Well, certainly technical knowledge is important. When I've interviewed recent college grads for entry-level positions, I am always concerned with their GPA. I like to see straight-A averages, if possible. But for experienced research scientists, technical knowledge shows up in their publication records, mostly. So I'll read their papers. I also think a research scientist has to be highly self-motivated, not look to others for praise and such. Particularly here. If you want someone to tell you you've done a good job, you'll be waiting a long time. It's not clear to me that research scientists really get the support we need from the rest of the staff here. Work orders are often lost or put off for one reason or another. Senior members seem to get more techs than scientists do, and they certainly get more attention from Steve. The rumor is that these guys also get higher raises than the scientists; allegedly, this is to keep pay at an equitable rate—you know, they're supposedly more valuable to the company. Of course, everybody knows that most of the senior members are Steve's old graduate students, and so he takes care of them really well. One of the things that really galls me is that I need to keep up my publication record to maintain my career options. But publishing is frowned on because it takes time away from your work. I've even been told that my work can't be published because of proprietary rights or that the defense department considers the information classified. However, if somebody important is working with me and needs the publication, then it's full steam ahead.

CONSULTANT: You sound pretty disgruntled with your work.

CHRIS: It's not my work so much. I'm really very happy doing this work—it's cutting-edge, after all. The problem is I'm never quite sure where the work is going. I do my part of a project, and unless I go out of my way to talk to other people, I never find out the final results of the total project. That's just something you learn to live with around here—being part of a system that's not particularly open.

Meg Conroy, Assistant to the Head of Administration

CONSULTANT: You've only been here a short time, is that correct?

MEG: That's right—just a little over a year.

CONSULTANT: Why did you take the job?

MEG: Well, I was in my last semester of college and was looking for a job, like most college seniors. My fiancé at the time—now he's my husband—was already working for Electro Logic (EL) and found out that there was an opening. So I applied.

CONSULTANT: So you were a business major in school?

MEG: Oh, no. I was a history major.

CONSULTANT: Do you like your job?

MEG: It has a lot to offer. I get paid pretty well for what I'm doing. And I'm learning a lot. I just wish the company would let me take some classes in administration, like accounting. The auditors ask some pretty tough questions. Steve says we should hire that expertise, but I'd still be responsible for supervising the people.

CONSULTANT: Is there any particular aspect about your job that you really find satisfying?

MEG: Well, let me think. I guess I like the fact that I get to do a lot of different tasks so that things don't get so boring. I would hate to have to do the same thing, day in and day out. A lot of times, I go to the library to do research on different things, and that's nice because it gets me out of the office.

CONSULTANT: What don't you like about your job?

MEG: Well, I often get the feeling that administration isn't taken seriously. You know, the engineers could get along without us quite nicely, or so they seem to think. The whole structure of the department shows that we're the catch-all department: if you don't fit anywhere else, they put you in here. Perhaps some of that is because our department is primarily women—in fact, I've been told that 95 percent of all the female employees are in administration. Sometimes it's hard to work with the engineers because they treat you like you don't know anything, and they always want things to be done their way. Clearly, the engineers get the money and consideration and yet, well, we do contribute quite a lot to the whole team, as Steve would say. But words of praise just aren't as impressive as actions. Sure, we get our birthday parties, but that still seems to be a little patronizing. We rarely get to see what's going on in the research area. I've asked a number of engineers specific questions, and they just kind of look at me with a blank stare and give me some really simplified answer. It seems to me if you want to build a family, like the president says, you can't treat administration like a bad relation.

P. J. Ginelli, Technician

CONSULTANT: I gather you've just been through your semiannual performance appraisal. How did it go?

P. J.: Like I expected. No surprises.

CONSULTANT: Do you find these appraisals useful?

P. J.: Sure. I get to find out what he thinks of my work.

CONSULTANT: Is that all?

P. J.: Well, I suppose it's a nice opportunity to understand what my supervisor wants. Sometimes he's not so clear during the rest of the year. I suppose he's been given specific goals from higher-ups before he talks with me, so he's clear and then I'm clear.

CONSULTANT: Do you like what you're doing?

P. J.: Oh yeah. The best part is that I'm not at the main building and so I don't have to put up with the "important" people, you know? I've heard from other techs that those guys can be a real pain—trying to be nice and all, but really just being a bother. I mean, how can you get your stuff done when the president's looking over your shoulder all the time? On the other hand, if the president knows your name, I suppose that's a good thing when it comes to raises and promotions. But my boss sticks up for his techs; we get a fair deal from him.

CONSULTANT: Do you think you'll be able to get ahead at Electro Logic (EL)?

P. J.: Get ahead? You mean become an engineer or something? No, and I really don't want to do that. Everyone around here keeps pushing me to move up. I'm afraid to tell people how I really feel for fear they'll decide I don't fit into this high-tech environment. I don't want to be the "black sheep of the family." I like where I am, and if the raises keep coming, I'll keep liking it. One of my kids is starting college next year, and I need the money to help her out. I get a lot of overtime, particularly when contract deadlines are near. I suppose the rush toward the end of contracts gives some people big headaches, but for me, I don't mind. The work is pretty slow otherwise, and so at least I'm working all the time and then some. But my family wishes my schedule was more predictable.

CONSULTANT: Do you think you'll continue working for EL?

P. J.: I'm not sure I want to answer that. Let's just say that my ratings on the performance appraisal were good, and I expect to see an improvement in my pay. I'll stay for that.

Chalida Montgomery, Technician

CONSULTANT: In general, what are your feelings about the work you do for Electro Logic (EL)?

CHALIDA: Well, I feel my work is quite good, but I also feel that I perform rather boring, tedious tasks. From what my supervisor says, the kinds of things I do are what electrical engineering students do in their last year of classes. I gather their final project is to make a circuit board, and that's what I do, day in and day out.

CONSULTANT: What is it that you would like to do?

CHALIDA: Well, it would be nice to be able to offer some input into some of the designs of these boards. I know I don't have a PhD or anything, but I do have lots of experience. But because I'm a tech, the engineers don't really feel I've got much to offer—even though I build the boards and can tell from the design which one will do what the designer wants it to do. I also would like to maybe supervise other technicians in my department. You know, some kind of advancement would be nice. As it is, lots of techs ask me how to do things, and of course I help, but then they get the credit. Around here, you have to have a piece of paper that says you're educated before they let you officially help other people.

Discussion Questions

6.1. Using the behavioral guidelines and Figure 6.5 as diagnostic aids, what are the strengths and weaknesses of Electro Logic (EL) from a motivational perspective?

6.2. What are the high-priority action items you would include in a consulting report to Steve Morgan, president of EL? Focus on specific actions that he could initiate that would better use the abilities of the staff and foster a more motivating work environment.

SKILL PRACTICE

EXERCISES FOR DIAGNOSING WORK PERFORMANCE PROBLEMS

Proper diagnosis is a critical aspect of effective motivation management. Often, managers become frustrated because they don't understand the causes of observed performance problems. They might experiment with various "cures," but the inefficiency of this trial-and-error process often only increases their frustration level. In addition, the accompanying misunderstanding adds extra strain to the manager-subordinate relationship. This generally makes the performance problem even more pronounced, which in turn prompts the manager to resort to more drastic responses, and a vicious downward spiral ensues.

The performance diagnosis model in Figure 6.7 offers a systematic way for managers and subordinates to pinpoint collaboratively the causes of dissatisfaction and performance problems. It assumes that employees will work hard and be good performers if the work environment encourages these actions. Consequently, rather than jumping to conclusions about poor performance stemming from deficiencies in personality traits or a bad attitude, this diagnostic process helps managers focus their attention on improving the selection, job design, performance evaluation, and reward-allocation systems. In this

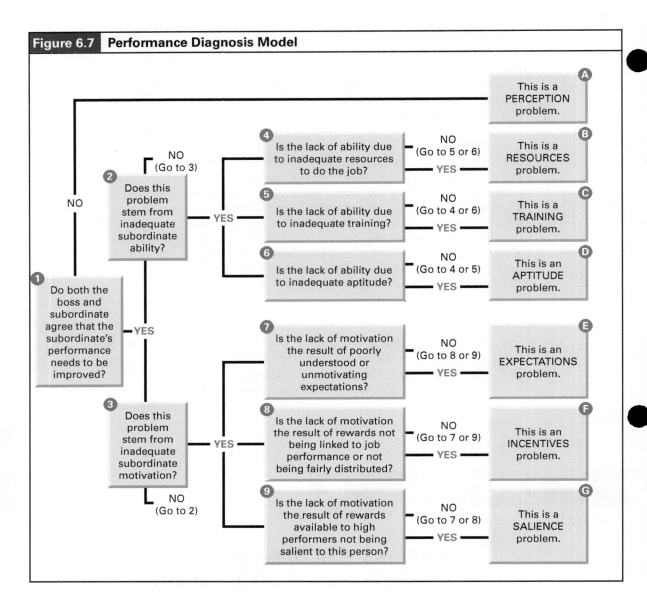

Figure 6.7   Performance Diagnosis Model

① Do both the boss and subordinate agree that the subordinate's performance needs to be improved?

— NO → Ⓐ This is a PERCEPTION problem.

— YES →

② Does this problem stem from inadequate subordinate ability?

NO (Go to 3)

YES →

④ Is the lack of ability due to inadequate resources to do the job?
  — NO (Go to 5 or 6)
  — YES → Ⓑ This is a RESOURCES problem.

⑤ Is the lack of ability due to inadequate training?
  — NO (Go to 4 or 6)
  — YES → Ⓒ This is a TRAINING problem.

⑥ Is the lack of ability due to inadequate aptitude?
  — NO (Go to 4 or 5)
  — YES → Ⓓ This is an APTITUDE problem.

③ Does this problem stem from inadequate subordinate motivation?

YES →

NO (Go to 2)

⑦ Is the lack of motivation the result of poorly understood or unmotivating expectations?
  — NO (Go to 8 or 9)
  — YES → Ⓔ This is an EXPECTATIONS problem.

⑧ Is the lack of motivation the result of rewards not being linked to job performance or not being fairly distributed?
  — NO (Go to 7 or 9)
  — YES → Ⓕ This is an INCENTIVES problem.

⑨ Is the lack of motivation the result of rewards available to high performers not being salient to this person?
  — NO (Go to 7 or 8)
  — YES → Ⓖ This is a SALIENCE problem.

manner, the specific steps necessary to accomplish work goals and management's expectations are examined to pinpoint why a worker's performance is falling short.

The manager and low-performing subordinate should follow the logical discovery process in the model, step by step. They should begin by examining the current perceptions of performance, as well as the understanding of performance expectations, and then proceed through the model until the performance problems have been identified. The model focuses on seven of these problems.

❑ **Perception Problem:** "Do you agree your performance is below expectations?" A perception problem suggests that the manager and subordinate have different views of the subordinate's current performance level. Unless this disagreement is resolved, it is futile to continue the diagnostic process. The entire problem-solving process is based on the premise that both parties recognize the existence of a problem and are interested in solving it. If agreement does not exist, the manager should focus on resolving the discrepancy in perceptions, including clarifying current expectations (Problem 5).

- **Resources Problem**: "Do you have the resources necessary to do the job well?" Ability has three components, and these should be explored in the order shown in the model. This order reduces a subordinate's defensive reactions. Poor performance may stem from a lack of resource support. Resources include material and personnel support as well as cooperation from interdependent work groups.

- **Training Problem**: "Is a lack of training interfering with your job performance?" Individuals may be asked to perform tasks that exceed their current skill or knowledge level. Typically, this problem can be overcome through additional training or education.

- **Aptitude Problem**: "Do you feel this is the right job/blend of work assignments for you?" This is the most difficult of the three ability problems to resolve because it is the most basic. If the resupply (providing additional resources) and retraining solutions have been explored without success, then more drastic measures may be required. These include refitting the person's current job requirements, reassigning him or her to another position, or, finally, releasing him or her from the organization.

- **Expectations Problem**: "What are your performance expectations for this position? What do you think my expectations are?" This problem results from poor communication regarding job goals or job requirements. In some cases, the stated goals may be different from the desired goals. In other words, the employee is working toward one goal while the supervisor desires another. This often occurs when subordinates are not sufficiently involved in the goal- or standard-setting process. When this results in unrealistic, imposed expectations, motivation suffers.

- **Incentives Problem**: "Do you believe rewards are linked to your performance in this position?" Either the individual does not believe that "performance makes a difference" or insufficient performance feedback and reinforcement have been given. The manager should also ask, "Do you feel rewards are being distributed equitably?" This provides an opportunity to discuss subordinates' criteria for judging fairness. Often, unrealistic standards are used.

- **Salience Problem**: "Are the performance incentives attractive to you?" Salience refers to the importance an individual attaches to available rewards. Often, the incentives offered to encourage high performance are not highly valued by a particular individual. Managers need to be creative in generating a broad range of rewards and flexible in allowing subordinates to choose among rewards.

Assignment

Option 1:

Read the case, "Joe Chaney," and privately use the diagnostic model (see Figure 6.7) to pinpoint plausible performance problems. Next, discuss in small groups your individual assessments and list specific questions you should ask Joe to accurately identify, from his point of view, the obstacles to his high performance. Finally, brainstorm ideas for plausible solutions. Prepare to represent your group in role-playing a problem-solving interview with Joe.

Option 2:

Administer the Work Performance Assessment survey to several employees. Using the scoring key at the end of this chapter, categorize the obstacles to high performance and satisfaction reported by the respondents. Then get together in small groups, with each group assuming the role of a management task force charged with the responsibility to analyze this employee survey data. Discuss the patterns in the data as well as possible remedies for these problems, using the behavioral guidelines and motivational models in the chapter as guides. Prepare a report on your analysis and recommendations for specific changes.

Joe Chaney

Joe Chaney joined your architectural firm two years ago as a draftsman. He is 35 years old and has been a draftsman since graduating from a two-year technical school right after high school. He is married and has four children. He has worked for four architectural firms in 12 years.

Joe came with mediocre recommendations from his previous employer, but you hired him anyway because you needed help desperately. Your firm's workload has been extremely high due to a local construction boom. The result is that a lot of the practices that contribute to a supportive, well-managed work environment have been overlooked. For instance, you can't remember the last time you conducted a formal performance review or did any career counseling. Furthermore, the tradition of closing the office early on Friday for a social hour was dropped long ago. Unfortunately, the tension in the office runs pretty high some days due to unbearable time pressures and the lack of adequate staff. Night and weekend work have become the norm rather than the exception.

Overall, you have been pleasantly surprised by Joe's performance. Until recently, he worked hard and consistently produced high-quality work. Furthermore, he frequently volunteered for special projects, made lots of suggestions for improving the work environment, and has demonstrated an in-depth practical knowledge of architecture and the construction business. However, during the past few months, he has definitely slacked off. He doesn't seem as excited about his work, and several times you have found him daydreaming at his desk. In addition, he has gotten into several heated arguments with architects about the specifications and proper design procedures for recent projects.

After one of these disagreements, you overheard Joe complaining to his officemate, "No one around here respects my opinion. I'm just a lowly draftsman. I know as much as these hotshot architects, but because I don't have the degree, they ignore my input, and I'm stuck doing the grunt work. Adding insult to injury, my wife has had to get a job to help support our family. I must be the lowest-paid person in this firm." In response to a question from a coworker regarding why he didn't pursue a college degree in architecture, Joe responded, "Do you have any idea how hard it is to put bread on the table, pay a Seattle mortgage, work overtime, be a reasonably good father and husband, plus go to night school? Come on, be realistic!"

Work Performance Assessment

Respond to the following statements, based on your current work situation.

Rating Scale

1 Strongly disagree

2 Disagree

3 Neutral

4 Agree

5 Strongly agree

_____ 1. My supervisor and I agree on the quality of my performance.

_____ 2. I feel I have adequate training to perform my current job assignments.

_____ 3. I believe that my native skills and abilities are matched very well with my job responsibilities.

_____ 4. I believe that I have adequate resources and supplies to do my job well.

_____ 5. I understand my boss's expectations and generally feel they are realistic.

_____ 6. I believe that rewards are distributed fairly, on the basis of performance.

_____ 7. The rewards and opportunities available to me if I perform well are attractive to me personally.

_____ 8. My supervisor indicates that I am not performing as well as I should, but I disagree.

_____ 9. I could do a much better job if I had more training.

_____ 10. I believe that my job is too difficult for my ability level.

_____ 11. I believe that my job performance is hindered by a lack of supplies and resources.

_____ 12. I believe my boss's expectations are unclear and unrealistic.

_____ 13. I believe my boss plays favorites in allocating rewards.

_____ 14. I do not find the rewards and opportunities available to high performers very appealing.

EXERCISE FOR RESHAPING UNACCEPTABLE BEHAVIORS

Shaheen Matombo

One of the most challenging aspects of management is transforming inappropriate behaviors into appropriate behaviors. Managers commonly take insufficient action to transform negative actions into positive ones. Some of these insufficient responses include assuming that ignoring an employee's shortcomings will make them go away; praising positive aspects of an individual's performance in hopes that this will encourage him or her to rechannel unproductive energies; discussing problems in vague, general terms in a group meeting, in hopes that the unproductive person will "take a hint" and change; and getting upset with an individual and demanding that he or she "shape up."

Assignment

Assume the role of Andre Tate in the following case. After reading the case, review the applicable behavioral guidelines shown on the Observer's Feedback Form at the end of the chapter. In small groups, discuss how you would resolve this problem. Prepare to role-play your discussion with Shaheen Matombo. After the discussion, assigned observers will provide feedback on your performance, using the Observer's Feedback Form as a guide. Unless you are assigned to play her role, do not read the role instructions for Shaheen prior to the interview.

Andre Tate, Manager

Shaheen has been a member of your staff for only three months. You don't know much about her other than that she is a single parent who has recently entered the workforce after a difficult divorce. She is often 10 to 20 minutes late for work in the morning. You are the manager of a very hectic customer relations office for a utility company. The phones start ringing promptly at 8:00. When she is late for work, you have to answer her phone, and this interrupts your work schedule. This morning, you are particularly annoyed. She is 25 minutes late, and the phones are ringing like crazy. Because you have been forced to answer them, it will be difficult for you to complete an important assignment by the noon deadline. You are getting more upset by the minute.

While you are in the middle of a particularly unpleasant phone conversation with an irate customer, you look out your window and see Shaheen bounding up the steps to the

PRACTICE

building. You think to yourself, "This is ridiculous, I've got to put a stop to her tardiness. Maybe I should just threaten to fire her unless she shapes up." Upon further reflection, you realize that would be impractical, especially during this period of retrenchment after the rate hike was turned down. Given the rumors about a possible hiring freeze, you know it may be difficult to refill any vacancies.

Also, Shaheen is actually a pretty good worker when she is there. She is conscientious and has a real knack with cranky callers. Unfortunately, it has taken her much longer than expected to learn the computer program for retrieving information on customer accounts. She frequently has to put callers on hold while she asks for help. These interruptions have tended to increase an already tense relationship with the rest of the office staff. She has had some difficulty fitting in socially; the others are much younger and have worked together for several years. Shaheen is the first new hire in a long time, so the others aren't used to breaking someone in. Three of your staff have complained to you about Shaheen's constant interruptions. They feel their productivity is going down as a result. Besides, she seems to expect them to drop whatever they are doing every time she has a question. They had expected their workload to be lighter when a new person was hired, but now they are having second thoughts. (In the past, you have had enough time to train new hires, but your boss has had you tied up on a major project for almost a year.)

Shaheen enters the office obviously flustered and disheveled. She has "I'm sorry" written all over her face. You motion for her to pick up the blinking phone line and then scribble a note on a tablet while you complete your call: "See me in my office at 12:00 sharp!" It's time you got to the bottom of Shaheen's disruptive influence on an otherwise smooth-flowing operation.

Shaheen Matombo, Staff Member

Boy, what a morning! Your babysitter's father died during the night, and she called you from the airport at 6:30 A.M. saying she would be out of town for three or four days. You tried three usually available backups before you finally found someone who could take Keen, your 3-year-old. Then Shayla, your seventh-grader, went through five outfits before she was satisfied that she had just the right look for her first yearbook picture. It's a miracle that Buddy, your oldest, was able to pull himself out of bed after getting only five hours of sleep. On top of football and drama, he's now joined the chess team, and they had their first tournament last night. Why did it have to fall on the night before his final in physics? This morning you wished you had his knack for juggling so many activities. By the time you got the kids delivered, you were already 10 minutes behind schedule. Then there was this incredible accident on the expressway that slowed traffic to a crawl.

As you finally pull off the downtown exit ramp, you notice you're almost 20 minutes late for work. As you desperately scan the side streets for a parking space, you begin to panic. "How am I going to explain this to Andre? He'll be furious. I'm sure he's upset about my chronic lateness. On top of that, he's obviously disappointed with my lack of computer skills, and I'm sure the others complain to him about having to train a newcomer." You're sure that one of the reasons you got the job was that you had completed a computer class at the local community college. Unfortunately, there hadn't been much carryover to the incredibly complex computer program you use at work. (It seems to defy every convention of logic.)

"What am I going to tell him about my being late for work so often?" Unfortunately there isn't an easy answer. "Maybe it will get better as the kids and I get used to this new routine. It's just very difficult to get the kids to the bus stop and the sitter, commute 20 minutes, and arrive precisely at 8:00. I wonder if he would allow me to come in at 8:30

and only take a half-hour lunch. Staying late wouldn't work because they close down the computers at 5:00, unless there was some paperwork I could do for half an hour."

Then what about the problems with the computer and the other staff members? "Sooner or later, he's going to get on my case about those things. Is it my fault I don't think like a computer? Some people might be able to sit down and figure this program out in a couple of hours, but not me. So is that my fault or should someone be giving me more training? I wish the others weren't so cliquish and unwilling to help me out. I wonder why that's the case. It's like they're afraid I'll become as good as they are if they share their experience with me. I wish Andre had more time to help me learn the ropes, but he seems to always be in meetings."

"Well, I'm probably going to catch it this morning. I've never been this late. Maybe I'll be back home full time sooner than I expected."

ACTIVITIES FOR MOTIVATING OTHERS

Suggested Assignments

6.3. Identify a situation in which you have some responsibility for another person whose performance is significantly below your expectation. Using the Work Performance Assessment Survey included in the Skill Practice section, collect information on the individual's perceptions of the situation. Using the diagnostic model (decision tree) in that section, specifically identify the perceived performance problems. Compare these results with your own views of the situation. Conduct an interview with the individual and discuss the results, highlighting areas of disagreement. Based on this discussion, formulate a plan of action that both parties accept. If inadequate ability is a problem, follow the resupply, retrain, refill, reassign, and release remedial steps. If insufficient effort is a problem, use the steps for reprimanding, redirecting, and rewarding discussed in this chapter as a resource for this discussion. Implement this plan for a period of time and then report on the results.

6.4. Focus on some aspect of your own work in which you feel performance is below your (or others') expectations. Using the Work Performance Assessment survey (Skill Assessment), identify the specific obstacles to improved performance. Then formulate a plan for overcoming these obstacles, including getting commitments from others. Discuss your plan with individuals affected by it and arrive at a set of actions all parties accept. Implement the plan for a period of time and report on your results. How successful were you in making the changes? Did your performance improve as expected? Based on this experience, identify other aspects of your work that you could improve on in a similar fashion.

6.5. Identify four or five situations in which you are typically provoked to exhibit punishing behavior. These might involve friends, family members, or work associates. Examine these situations and identify one in which punishment (discipline) is not working. Using the guidelines for reprimanding, redirecting, and rewarding, design a specific plan for shaping the other person's behaviors so you can begin rewarding positive actions. Report on your results. Based on this experience, consider how you might be able to use this strategy in other similar situations.

6.6. Using the six-step model for creating a motivational work environment (see Table 6.2), design a specific plan for managing a new relationship (e.g., a new subordinate) or a new phase in an old relationship (e.g., friend, family member, or subordinate about to begin work on a new project). Write down specific directions for yourself for implementing each of the six steps. Discuss your plan with this individual and ask for suggestions for improvement. Make sure your perceptions of the key aspects of the plan are consistent with his or hers. Implement your plan for a period of time and then report on the consequences. Based on this experience, identify changes that would be appropriate in similar situations.

SOURCE: *J. Richard Hackman & Greg R. Oldham*, Work Redesign, *1st © 1980. Electronically reproduced by permission of Pearson Education, Inc., Upper Saddle River, New Jersey.*

Application Plan and Evaluation

The intent of this exercise is to help you apply this cluster of skills in a real-life, out-of-class setting. Now that you have become familiar with the behavioral guidelines that form the basis of effective skill performance, you will improve most by trying out those guidelines in an everyday context. Unlike a classroom activity, in which feedback is immediate and others can assist you with their evaluations, this skill application activity is one you must accomplish and evaluate on your own. There are two parts to this activity. Part 1 helps prepare you to apply the skill, and Part 2 helps you evaluate and improve on your experience. Be sure to write down answers to each item. Don't short-circuit the process by skipping steps.

Part 1: Planning

6.7. Write down the two or three aspects of this skill that are most important to you. These may be areas of weakness, areas you most want to improve, or areas that are most salient to a problem you face right now. Identify the specific aspects of this skill that you want to apply.

6.8. Now identify the setting or the situation in which you will apply this skill. Establish a plan for performance by actually writing down a description of the situation. Who else will be involved? When will you do it? Where will it be done?

    Circumstances:
    Who else?
    When?
    Where?

6.9. Identify the specific behaviors you will engage in to apply this skill. Operationalize your skill performance.

6.10. What are the indicators of successful performance? How will you know you have been effective? What will indicate you have performed competently?

Part 2: Evaluation

6.11. After you have completed your implementation, record the results. What happened? How successful were you? What was the effect on others?

6.12. How can you improve? What modifications can you make next time? What will you do differently in a similar situation in the future?

6.13. Looking back on your whole skill practice and application experience, what have you learned? What has been surprising? In what ways might this experience help you in the long term?

SKILL PRACTICE
Exercise for Reshaping Unacceptable Behaviors

Observer's Feedback Form

RATING

1 = Low
5 = High

Reprimand

_____ 1. Identified the specific inappropriate behavior. Gave examples. Indicated that the action must stop

_____ 2. Pointed out the impact of the problem on the performance of others, the unit's mission, and so forth

_____ 3. Asked questions about causes and explored remedies

Redirect

_____ 4. Described the behaviors or standards expected; made sure the individual understood and agreed that these are reasonable

_____ 5. Asked if the individual would comply

_____ 6. Was appropriately supportive; for example, praised other aspects of the person's work, identified personal and group benefits of compliance, and made sure there were no legitimate obstacles in the way of meeting stated expectations

Reinforce

_____ 7. Identified rewards that were salient to the individual

_____ 8. Linked the attainment of desirable outcomes with incremental, continuous improvement

_____ 9. Rewarded (including using praise) all improvements in performance in a timely and honest manner

Comments:

_____
_____
_____
_____
_____

SCORING KEYS AND COMPARISON DATA

✪ Scoring Keys for the following instruments, along with comparison data, are contained in PIA in MyManagementLab.com;

Diagnosing Poor Performance and Enhancing Motivation
Work Performance Assessment

SKILL **ASSESSMENT**

- Managing Interpersonal Conflict
- Strategies for Handling Conflict

SKILL **LEARNING**

- Interpersonal Conflict Management
- Diagnosing the Type of Interpersonal Conflict
- Selecting the Appropriate Conflict Management Approach
- Resolving Interpersonal Confrontations Using the Collaborative Approach
- Summary
- Behavioral Guidelines

SKILL **ANALYSIS**

- Educational Pension Investments

SKILL **PRACTICE**

- SSS Software Management Problems
- Bradley's Barn
- Avocado Computers
- Phelps, Inc.
- Alisa Moffatt
- Can Larry Fit In?
- Meeting at Hartford Manufacturing Company

SKILL **APPLICATION**

- Suggested Assignments
- Application Plan and Evaluation

SCORING KEYS AND *COMPARISON DATA*

7

Managing Conflict

LEARNING OBJECTIVES

1. DIAGNOSE THE FOCUS AND SOURCE OF CONFLICTS

2. UTILIZE APPROPRIATE CONFLICT MANAGEMENT STRATEGIES

3. RESOLVE INTERPERSONAL CONFRONTATIONS THROUGH COLLABORATION

MyManagementLab™

When you see this icon, visit www.mymanagementlab.com for self-assessments, video activities, and more.

⭐ If your instructor is utilizing **MyManagementLab**, log onto mymanagementlab.com and select the Personal Inventory Assessment (PIA) section and complete the instruments associated with this chapter.

The assessment instruments in this chapter are briefly described below. The assessments appear either in your text or in PIA. The assessments marked with (blue star) are available only in PIA.

All assessments should be completed before reading the chapter material.

After completing the first assessment save your response to your hard drive. When you have finished reading the chapter, re-take the assessment and compare your responses to see what you have learned.

⭐ ❏ The *Managing Interpersonal Conflict* assessment measures the extent to which you exhibit competency in managing conflict in a work context.

⭐ ❏ The *Strategies for Handling Conflict* assessment measures your preferences for five different conflict management strategies that will be discussed in the chapter.

SKILL *LEARNING* ▽

Interpersonal Conflict Management

A conflict over issues is not only likely within top-management teams, but also valuable. Such conflict provides executives with a more inclusive range of information, a deeper understanding of the issues, and a richer set of possible solutions. [In our ten-year study] we found that the alternative to conflict is usually not agreement but apathy and disengagement. In fast paced markets, successful strategic decisions are most likely to be made by teams that promote active and broad conflict over issues without sacrificing speed. The key to doing so is to mitigate interpersonal conflict. (Eisenhardt, Kahwajy, & Bourgeois, 1997, pp. 84–85)

One of the leading causes of business failure among major corporations is too much agreement among top management. The lack of tension between competing perspectives can foster a climate of complacency. This problem is compounded when boards of directors fail to play an aggressive oversight role. They avoid conflict with the internal management team who appear unified on key issues and very confident of their positions. Although managers often view a lack of conflict as a sign of good leadership, in reality it is a leading indicator of being out of touch with significant changes in the marketplace (Argenti, 1976).

Conflict is an essential, ubiquitous part of organizational life. In fact, given the current business trends toward workforce diversity, globalization, and joint ventures, how managers from different organizations and cultures deal with conflict is an increasingly important predictor of organizational success (Seybolt, Derr, & Nielson, 1996; Tjosvold, 1991; Memeth, 2004). Conflict is the lifeblood of vibrant, progressive, stimulating organizations. It sparks creativity, stimulates innovation, and encourages personal improvement (Blackard & Gibson, 2002; Farh, Lee & Farh, 2010; Pascale, 1990; Wanous & Youtz, 1986).

> ⚙ **MyManagementLab: WATCH IT**
> **CH2MHill: Conflict and Negotiation**
> Apply what you have learned about management. If your instructor has assigned MyManagementLab, go to mymanagementlab.com to watch a video case and answer questions.

Andrew Grove, former president of Intel, echoed these themes: "Many managers seem to think it is impossible to tackle anything or anyone head-on, even

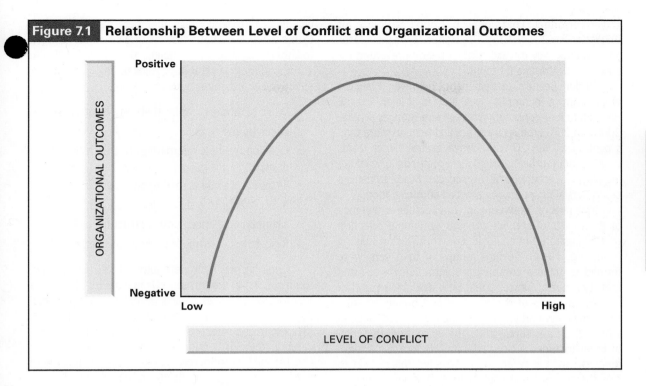

Figure 7.1 Relationship Between Level of Conflict and Organizational Outcomes

ORGANIZATIONAL OUTCOMES

Positive

Negative

Low   High

LEVEL OF CONFLICT

in business. By contrast, we at Intel believe that it is the essence of corporate health to bring a problem out into the open as soon as possible, even if this entails a confrontation. Dealing with conflicts lies at the heart of managing any business. As a result, confrontation—facing issues about which there is disagreement—can be avoided only at the manager's peril. Workplace politicking grows quietly in the dark, like mushrooms; neither can stand the light of day" (Grove, 1984).

However, we all have ample evidence that conflict often produces harmful results. Interpersonal conflict can sap people's energy and demoralize their spirit. Also, some types of conflicts, regardless of frequency, generally produce dysfunctional outcomes. These include personality conflicts and arguments over things that can't be changed.

As Figure 7.1 shows, scholars generally agree that some conflict is both inevitable and beneficial in effective organizations (Brown, 1983). As illustrated in this figure, a moderate level of the right kind of conflict appears to be healthy for most organizations.

MIXED FEELINGS ABOUT CONFLICT

The well-known American psychologist, Abraham Maslow (1965), observed that people generally have a high degree of ambivalence regarding the value of

conflict. On the one hand, managers *intellectually* appreciate the value of conflict and competition. They agree it is a necessary ingredient of the free-enterprise system. On the other hand, their actions often demonstrate conflict avoidance whenever possible. This ambivalence about conflict is a recurring theme in *Moneyball,* a book, and subsequently a feature film, about the Oakland A's baseball team and their general manager Billy Beane, based on the book by Michael Lewis.

Beane believed that baseball scouts and managers had become hidebound by tradition in relying on faulty assumptions about which statistics mattered in predicting a player's future success. For instance, he believed that statistics like batting averages and stolen bases were relics of a past century, and no longer good indicators of a player's potential in the modern game. As manager of the A's, Beane advocated the use of a new statistical method to evaluate players. *Moneyball* depicts the frequent, heated battles that Beane had with his scouting staff and the team's coach as he challenged their assumptions. Beane was a constant source of conflict, in part because of his revolutionary ideas, and in part because of his dogged determination to force change upon the organization. At one point, he reportedly put his staff members in their place by saying, "We're going to run the organization from the top down. We're controlling player personnel. That's our job. I don't apologize for that" (Lewis, 2014: 138). Resistance to Beane's ideas and his tendency toward conflict nearly prevented his ideas from gaining a foothold.

Under Beane's management, however, Oakland went from a perennial weakling in Major League Baseball to four consecutive playoff appearances (2000–2003). In 2002, the A's were the first team in more than a century to win 20 consecutive games. Other teams quickly adopted Beane's statistical methods for evaluating players. Despite all of this success, Beane remains a controversial figure among baseball administration.

The tension between our intellectual acceptance of the merits of conflict and our emotional rejection of it is illustrated in a classic study of decision making (Boulding, 1964). Several groups of managers were formed to solve a complex problem. They were told that their performance would be judged by a panel of experts in terms of the quantity and quality of solutions they generated. The groups were identical in size and composition, with the exception that half of them included a "confederate." Before the experiment began, the researcher instructed this person to play the role of "devil's advocate." This person was to challenge the group's conclusions, forcing the others to examine critically their assumptions and the logic of their arguments. At the end of the problem-solving period, the recommendations made by both sets of groups were compared. The groups with the devil's advocates had performed significantly better on the task. They had generated more alternatives, and their proposals were judged as superior. After a short break, the groups were reassembled and told that they would be performing a similar task during the next session. However, before they began discussing the next problem, they were given permission to eliminate one member. In every group containing a confederate, he or she was the one asked to leave. The fact that every high-performance group expelled their unique competitive advantage because that member made others feel uncomfortable demonstrates a widely shared reaction to conflict: "I know it has positive outcomes for the performance of the organization, as a whole, but I don't like how it makes me feel, personally."

We believe that much of the ambivalence toward conflict stems from a lack of confidence in one's personal knowledge and skills about how to constructively manage tense, emotionally charged confrontations. A 10-year study conducted by Kathy Eisenhardt and her colleagues at Stanford University (Eisenhardt et al., 1997) provides important guidance. In their *Harvard Business Review* article, they report, "The

challenge is to encourage members of management teams to argue without destroying their ability to work together" (p. 78). What makes this possible? These authors identify several key "rules of engagement" for effective conflict management:

- ❏ Work with more, rather than less, information.
- ❏ Focus on the facts.
- ❏ Develop multiple alternatives to enrich the level of debate.
- ❏ Share commonly agreed-upon goals.
- ❏ Inject humor into the decision process.
- ❏ Maintain a balanced power structure.
- ❏ Resolve issues without forcing consensus.

Thus far, we have determined that: (1) interpersonal conflict in organizations is inevitable; (2) conflict that focuses on issues or facts (rather than on personality differences) can actually enhance decision making; (3) despite the intellectual acceptance of the value of conflict, there is a widespread tendency to avoid it; and (4) the key to increasing one's comfort level with conflict is to become proficient in particular skills.

Consistent with this book's skill-development orientation, the remainder of this chapter focuses on increasing your competence-based confidence. We focus on three essential conflict-related skills that a large body of research identifies as essential for managers. First, they must be able to accurately diagnose the types of conflict, including their causes. For example, managers need to understand how cultural differences and other forms of demographic diversity can spark conflicts in organizations. Second, having identified the sources of conflict, managers must be able to select an appropriate conflict management strategy. Third, skillful managers must develop the skills to resolve interpersonal disputes effectively while maintaining working relationships between disputants. We now turn our attention to these three broad management proficiencies.

Diagnosing the Type of Interpersonal Conflict

Because interpersonal conflicts come in many varieties, our first skill-building task involves the art of diagnosis. In any type of clinical setting, from medicine to management, it is common knowledge that effective intervention is predicated upon accurate diagnosis. Figure 7.2 presents a categorizing device for diagnosing the *type of conflict*, based on two critical identifying characteristics: focus and source.

Figure 7.2	Categorizing Different Types of Conflict

By understanding the *focus of the conflict*, we gain an appreciation for the substance of the dispute (what is fueling the conflict), and by learning more about the origins, or *source of the conflict*, we better understand how it got started (the igniting spark).

CONFLICT FOCUS

We can categorize conflicts as primarily focused on either *people* or *issues* (Eisenhardt et al., 1997; Jehn & Mannix, 2001). In other words, conflicts can be about relationships between people (e.g., tensions over personality or value differences, hard feelings over past events, taking offense at something another person said), or they can be about competing ideas, proposals, interests, or resources. The distinction between people-focused and issue-focused conflicts helps us understand why some managers believe that conflict is the lifeblood of their organization while others believe that each and every conflict episode sucks life from their organization. Research has shown that people-focused conflicts threaten effectiveness whereas issue-based conflicts actually enhance performance as long as people feel psychologically safe at work (Bradley, et al., 2012) and have the skills to manage it effectively and openly (Bradley, et al., 2013; de Dreu & Weingart, 2002; Jehn, 1997). So, when people talk about the benefits of "productive conflict," they are virtually always referring to issue-focused conflict.

Of course, all interpersonal conflicts involve people, but **people-focused conflict** refers to the "in your face" kind of confrontations in which emotions run high and people feel moral indignation. Accusations of harm, demands for justice, and feelings of resentment are the common markers of personal disputes. Personal disputes are extremely difficult to resolve, and the long-term effects of the dispute on interpersonal relations can be devastating. The longer this type of dispute goes on, the larger the gulf between the parties becomes.

Person-oriented conflicts consume a tremendous amount of an organization's time. One survey reports that managers estimate that 18 percent of their working time is occupied by dealing with personal conflict. That amounts to approximately nine weeks of management time each year spent in this nonproductive activity (Messmer, 1996).

In contrast to emotionally fraught people-focused conflicts, **issue-focused conflicts** are more like rational negotiations, which can be thought of as "an interpersonal decision-making process by which two or more people agree how to allocate scarce resources" (Thompson, 2001, p. 2). In issue-based conflicts, manager-negotiators are typically acting as agents, representing the interests of their department, function, or project. Although negotiators may have conflicting priorities for how the scarce resources should be utilized, most negotiators recognize the need to find an amicable settlement that appears fair to all parties. This is because in organizational life there usually is no such thing as one-time-only negotiations. One veteran manager observed that he uses a simple creed to govern his dealings with others, "It's a small world and a long life"— meaning there is no long-term personal advantage to short-term gains won through unfair means.

Although our discussion of conflict management draws liberally on the negotiations literature, our objective is to prepare readers for highly charged emotional confrontations in which untrained initiators attempt to transfer their frustration to someone else. Being on the receiving end of a "surprise personal attack" is threatening, and so the unskilled respondent is likely to fight back, escalating the conflict with counteraccusations or defensive retorts. That's why experienced mediators agree that when a disagreement "gets personal," it often becomes intractable.

CONFLICT SOURCE

We now shift our diagnostic lens from understanding the focus, or content, of a conflict ("What's this about?") to the source, or origin, of the conflict ("How did it get started?"). Managers, especially those who feel uncomfortable with conflict, often behave as though interpersonal conflict is the result of personality defects. They label people who are frequently involved in conflicts "troublemakers" or "bad apples" and attempt to transfer or dismiss them as a way of resolving disagreements. While some individuals seem to have a propensity for making trouble and appear to be disagreeable under even the best of circumstances, "sour dispositions" actually account for only a small percentage of organizational conflicts (Hines, 1980; Schmidt & Tannenbaum, 1965).

This proposition is supported by research on performance appraisals (Latham & Wexley, 1994). It has been shown that managers generally attribute poor performance to personal deficiencies in workers, such as laziness, lack of skill, or lack of motivation. However, when workers are asked the causes of their poor performance, they generally explain it in terms of problems in their environment, such as insufficient supplies or uncooperative coworkers. While some face-saving is obviously involved here, this line of research suggests that managers need to guard against the reflexive tendency to assume that bad behaviors imply bad people. In fact, people who express aggressive or harsh behaviors often have good intentions but are simply unskilled in handling intense, emotional experiences.

Table 7.1	Sources of Conflict
Personal differences	Perceptions and expectations
Informational deficiencies	Misinformation and misrepresentation
Role incompatibility	Goals and responsibilities
Environmental stress	Resource scarcity and uncertainty

In contrast to the personality-defect theory of conflict, we propose four sources of interpersonal conflict in Table 7.1. These are *personal differences, informational deficiencies, role incompatibility,* and *environmental stress.* **Personal differences** are a common source of conflict because individuals bring different backgrounds to their roles in organizations. Their values and needs have been shaped by different socialization processes, depending on their cultural and family traditions, level of education, breadth of experience, and so forth. As a result, their interpretations of events and their expectations about relationships with others in the organization vary considerably. Conflicts stemming from incompatible personal values and needs are some of the most difficult to resolve. They often become highly emotional and take on moral overtones. Under these conditions, a disagreement about what is *factually correct* easily turns into a bitter argument over *who is morally right.*

At first glance, it might appear that personal differences and people-focused conflict are the same thing. They are not. It might help to think of personal differences as a set of lenses that each member of an organization uses to make sense of daily experiences and to make value judgments, in terms of what is good and bad, appropriate and inappropriate. When someone has used a particular lens or perspective for a long time, it becomes a strongly held belief that the individual may never question. It is easy to see how challenges to these strongly held interpretations of the world could spark interpersonal conflicts. However, that does not necessarily mean that the conflict will become personal. Even when one's deeply held beliefs are challenged, one still has choices regarding what path their dispute will take. Will they focus on the issues (e.g., the fact that you and I have differing views or values) or the people (e.g., I question your competence, intent, acceptance, understanding, etc.)?

This question is particularly relevant for managers working in an organizational environment characterized by demographic and value diversity. On the one hand, a diverse workforce can be a strategic organizational asset (Cox, 1994), but on the other, very different people have the potential to experience intense conflicts—which can become an organizational liability (Lombardo & Eichinger, 1996; Pelled, Eisenhardt, & Xin, 1999). From various studies of diversity in organizations (Cox & Blake, 1991; Morrison, 1996), some of the consistently cited benefits of an effectively managed, diverse workforce include:

❑ Cost savings from reducing turnover rates among minority employees

❑ Improved creativity and problem-solving capabilities due to the broader range of perspectives and cultural mindsets

❑ Perceptions of fairness and equity in the workplace

❑ Increased flexibility that positively affects motivation and minimizes conflict between work and nonwork demands (e.g., family, personal interests, leisure)

Research suggests that diverse groups might have less confidence in their performance than homogenous groups, but they actually perform better (Phillips, Liljenquist, & Neale, 2009). The benefits of diversity don't come without challenges, however. Consider the old saying: "To create a spark, strike two unlike substances together." The spark of creativity in groups might also require some collisions between diverse perspectives and ideas. For example, imagine a team that includes one member who is extremely laid back and casual by nature, and who enjoys generating imaginative ideas. In contrast, another member of the team is highly formal, anxious, and detail-oriented. There are obvious ways in which these two members could develop person-based conflict stemming from annoyance around differing styles. On the other hand, if these two team members can learn to manage their differences with each other, they could experience great synergy; the detail-oriented teammate may be exactly the right demeanor to help the creative teammate see her ideas through to execution.

Interpersonal collisions can also happen because people from different ethnic and cultural groups often have very different views about the value of, and justifications for, interpersonal disputes (Adler, 2002; Trompenaars, 1994, 1996). In other words our cultural background shapes our views of what is worth "fighting for" and what constitutes "a fair fight" (Sillars & Weisberg, 1987; Weldon & Jehn, 1995; Wilmot & Hocker, 2001). The potential for harmful conflict is even greater when confrontations involve members of majority and minority groups within an organization. This is where "diversity-sensitive" managers can help out by considering questions like: Are both participants from the majority culture of the organization? If one is from a minority culture, to what extent is diversity valued in the organization? To what extent do members of these minority and majority cultures understand and value the benefits of a diverse workforce for our organization? Has this particular minority group or individual had a history of conflict within the organization? If so, are there broader issues regarding the appreciation of personal differences that need to be addressed?

The second source or cause of conflict among members of an organization is **informational deficiencies**. An important message may not be received, a boss's instructions may be misinterpreted, or decision makers may arrive at different conclusions because they use different databases. Conflicts based on misinformation or misunderstanding tend to be factual; hence, clarifying previous messages or obtaining additional information generally resolves the dispute. This might entail rewording the boss's instructions, reconciling contradictory sources of data, or redistributing copies of misplaced messages. This type of conflict is common in organizations, but it is also easy to resolve. Because these confrontations do not necessarily challenge value systems, they tend to be less emotional. Once the breakdown in the information system is repaired, disputants are generally able to resolve their disagreement with minimal resentment. For example, one employee felt deeply hurt when a project she expected to supervise was entrusted with another coworker. Assuming that her manager was somehow unhappy with her, she kept her distance and began interpreting everything her boss did as evidence of his dissatisfaction with her. Only later did she discover that her boss had withheld the project because he knew she was in line for a promotion that would prevent her from seeing the project through. Her resentment evaporated, of course, and she apologized to her supervisor for contributing to a conflict based on incomplete information.

A third source of conflict is **role incompatibility**, which is inherent in complex organizations where members' tasks are highly interdependent. This type of conflict is exemplified by the classic goal conflicts between line and staff, production and sales, and marketing and research and development (R&D). Each unit has different responsibilities in the organization, and as a result each places different priorities on organizational goals (e.g., customer satisfaction, product quality, production efficiency, compliance with government regulations). It is also typical of firms whose multiple product lines compete for scarce resources.

During the early days at Apple, the Apple II division accounted for a large part of the company's revenue. It viewed the newly created Macintosh division as an unwise speculative venture. The natural rivalry was made worse when a champion of the Macintosh referred to the Apple II team as "the dull and boring product division." Because this type of conflict stems from the fundamental incompatibility of the job responsibilities of the disputants, it can often be resolved only through the mediation of a common superior.

Another major source of conflict is **environmentally induced stress**. When an organization is forced to operate on an austere budget, its members are more likely to become embroiled in disputes over domain claims and resource requests. Scarcity tends to lower trust, increase ethnocentrism, and reduce participation in decision making. These are ideal conditions for incubating interpersonal conflict (Cameron, Kim, & Whetten, 1987).

When a large eastern bank announced a major downsizing, the threat to employees' security was so severe that it disrupted long-time, close working relationships. Even friendships were not immune to the effects of the scarcity-induced stress. Long-standing golf foursomes and car pools were disbanded because tension among members was so high.

Another environmental condition that fosters conflict is uncertainty. When individuals are unsure about their status in an organization, they become very anxious and prone to conflict. This type of "frustration conflict" often stems from rapid, repeated change. If task assignments, management philosophy, accounting procedures, and lines of authority are changed frequently, members find it difficult to cope with the resulting stress, and sharp, bitter conflicts can easily erupt over seemingly trivial problems. This type of conflict is generally intense, but it dissipates quickly once a change becomes routinized and individuals' stress levels are lowered.

When a major pet food manufacturing facility announced that one-third of its managers would have to support a new third shift, the feared disruption of personal and family routines prompted many managers to think about sending out their résumés. In addition, the uncertainty of who was going to be required to work at night was so great that even routine management work was disrupted by posturing and infighting.

Before we conclude our discussion of the sources of interpersonal conflict, it is useful to point out that people from particular cultural backgrounds might tend to be drawn into particular types of conflict. For example, one of the primary dimensions of cultural values emerging from Geert Hofstede's (1980) seminal research was tolerance for uncertainty. Some cultures, such as Japan's, have a high uncertainty avoidance, whereas other cultures, like the United States, are much more uncertainty tolerant. Extrapolating from these findings, if an American firm and a Japanese firm have created a joint venture in an industry known for highly volatile sales (e.g., short-term memory chips), one would expect that the Japanese managers would experience a higher level of uncertainty-induced conflict than their American counterparts. In contrast, because American culture places an extremely high value on individualism (another of Hofstede's key dimensions of cultural values), one would expect that the U.S. managers in this joint venture would experience a higher level of conflict stemming from their role interdependence with their Japanese counterparts.

Selecting the Appropriate Conflict Management Approach

Now that we have examined different types of conflict in terms of their focus and sources, we shift our attention to strategies for managing conflict of any type. As revealed in the Pre-Assessment survey, people's responses to interpersonal confrontations tend to fall into five categories: *forcing, accommodating, avoiding, compromising*, and *collaborating* (Volkema & Bergmann, 2001). These responses can be organized along two dimensions, as shown in Figure 7.3 (Ruble & Thomas, 1976). These five approaches to conflict reflect different degrees of cooperativeness and assertiveness. A cooperative response is intended to satisfy the needs of the interacting person whereas an assertive response focuses on the needs of the focal person. The cooperativeness dimension reflects the importance of the relationship whereas the assertiveness dimension reflects the importance of the issue. As you will see in the following discussion, cooperativeness and assertiveness are not mutually exclusive.

The **forcing response** (assertive, uncooperative) is an attempt to satisfy one's own needs at the expense

Figure 7.3 Two-Dimensional Model of Conflict Behavior

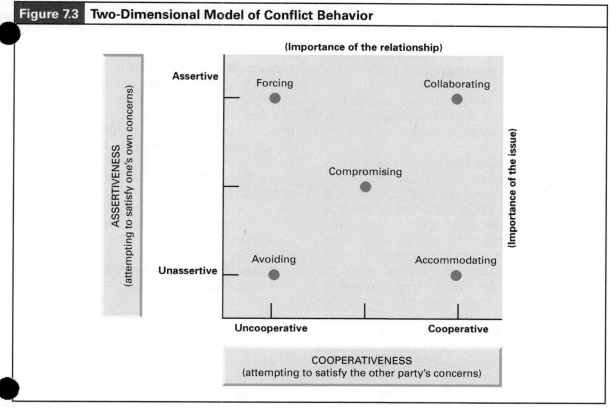

SOURCE: *Adapted from Ruble & Thomas, 1976.*

of the needs of the other individual. This can be done by using formal authority, physical threats, manipulation ploys, or by ignoring the claims of the other party. The blatant use of the authority of one's office ("I'm the boss, so we'll do it my way") or other forms of intimidation reflect an egoistic leadership style that may actually reflect a lack of self-confidence on the leader's part. Managers who rely on forcing strategies may simply ignore proposals that threaten their personal interests and may use manipulative tactics to get their way, even while striving to appear democratic in their leadership style.

The problem with the repeated use of this conflict management approach is that it breeds hostility and resentment. While observers may intellectually admire authoritarian or manipulative leaders because they appear to accomplish a great deal, their management styles generally produce a backlash in the long run as people become increasingly unwilling to absorb the emotional costs. Often, followers will actively work to undermine the power base of the authoritarian leader.

The **accommodating approach** (cooperative, unassertive) satisfies the other party's concerns while neglecting one's own. Unfortunately, some boards of directors take an accommodating approach in their interactions with management of failing firms, and thus neglect their vital oversight responsibilities. The difficulty with the habitual use of the accommodating approach is that it emphasizes preserving a friendly relationship at the expense of critically appraising issues and protecting personal rights. This may result in others taking advantage of you, which lowers your self-esteem as you observe yourself being used by others to accomplish their objectives while you fail to make any progress toward your own.

The **avoiding response** (uncooperative, unassertive) neglects the interests of both parties by sidestepping the conflict or postponing a solution. Avoiding is a lose-lose alternative because it ensures that neither parties' true interests are met. This strategy is often the response of managers who are emotionally ill-prepared to cope with the stress associated with confrontations, or it might reflect recognition that a relationship is not strong enough to absorb the fallout of an intense conflict. The repeated use of this approach causes considerable frustration for others because issues never seem to get resolved and the really tough problems are consistently avoided. When mangers adopt avoiding as their default conflict management strategy, people often rush in to fill the leadership void, creating considerable confusion and animosity in the process.

The **compromising response** occupies the intermediate space between high and low levels of both assertiveness and cooperativeness. A compromise is an attempt to obtain partial satisfaction for both parties, in the sense that both receive the proverbial "half loaf." To accomplish this, both parties are asked to make sacrifices to obtain a common gain. While this approach has considerable practical appeal to managers, its indiscriminate use is counterproductive. If subordinates are continually told to "split the difference," they may conclude that their managers are more interested in resolving disputes than solving problems. This creates a climate of expediency that encourages game playing, such as asking for twice as much as you need.

A common mistake made in mergers is placing undue emphasis on "being fair to both sides" by compromising on competing corporate policies and practices. When decisions are made on the basis of "spreading the pain evenly" or "using half of your procedures and half of ours," rather than on the basis of merit, then harmony takes priority over value. Ironically, actions taken in the name of "keeping peace in the merged families" often end up being so illogical and impractical that the emerging union is doomed to operate under a pall of constant internal turmoil and conflict.

The **collaborating approach** (cooperative, assertive) is an attempt to address fully the concerns of both parties. It is often referred to as the "problem-solving" mode. In this mode, the intent is to find solutions that are satisfactory to both parties rather than to find fault or assign blame. In this way, both parties can feel that they have "won." This is the only win-win strategy among the five. Although the collaborative approach is not appropriate for all situations, when used appropriately, it has the most beneficial effect on the involved parties. It encourages norms of collaboration and trust while acknowledging the value of assertiveness. It encourages individuals to focus their disputes on problems and issues rather than on personalities. Finally, it cultivates the skills necessary for self-governance, so that effective problem solvers feel empowered. The collaborative approach to problem solving and conflict resolution works best in an environment supporting openness, directness, and equality. In an interview with Steven Jobs after he began NeXT, the editors of *Inc.* magazine posed to him the following question regarding the perils of being a celebrity boss: "It must help you in attracting the best minds to your new computer firm, but once they're there, aren't they intimidated, working for a legend?" Job's response was:

> It all depends on the culture. The culture at NeXT definitely rewards independent thought, and we often have constructive disagreements—at all levels. It doesn't take a new person long to see that people feel fine about openly disagreeing with me. That doesn't mean I can't disagree with them, but it does mean that the best ideas win. Our attitude is that we want the best. Don't get hung up on who owns the idea. Pick the best one, and let's go. (Gendron & Burlingham, 1989)

Table 7.2 shows a comparison of the five conflict management approaches. In this table, the fundamentals of each approach are laid out, including its objective, how that objective is reflected in terms of an expressed point of view, and a supporting rationale. In addition, the likely outcomes of each approach are summarized.

One important area of organizational research provides additional insights into the five conflict management approaches we have just described. Scholars of **negotiation strategies** have shown that people generally adopt one of two general approaches to their negotiations: *distributive* or *integrative*. Negotiators who adopt a **distributive bargaining** perspective tend to assume that resources are scarce and limited, so their negotiations focus on dividing up a "fixed pie." People who negotiate with an **integrative perspective**, in contrast, search for collaborative ways of "expanding the pie" by avoiding fixed, incompatible positions (Bazerman & Neale, 1992; Murnighan, 1992, 1993; Thompson, 2001). Because of the assumption of scarce resources, distributive negotiators tend to assume an adversarial, competitive posture. They believe that one of the parties can improve

Table 7.2 A Comparison of Five Conflict Management Approaches

APPROACH	OBJECTIVE	POINT OF VIEW	SUPPORTING RATIONALE	LIKELY OUTCOME
1. Forcing	Get your way.	"I know what's right. Don't question my judgment or authority."	It is better to risk causing a few hard feelings than to abandon an issue you are committed to.	You feel vindicated but other party feels defeated and possibly humiliated.
2. Avoiding	Avoid having to deal with conflict.	"I'm neutral on that issue." "Let me think about it." "That's someone else's problem."	Disagreements are inherently bad because they create tension.	Interpersonal problems don't get resolved, causing long-term frustration manifested in a variety of ways.
3. Compromising	Reach an agreement quickly.	"Let's search for a solution we can both live with so we can get on with our work."	Prolonged conflicts distract people from their work and engender bitter feelings.	Participants become conditioned to seek expedient, rather than effective, solutions.
4. Accommodating	Don't upset the other person.	"How can I help you feel good about this encounter?" "My position isn't so important that it is worth risking bad feelings between us."	Maintaining harmonious relationships should be our top priority.	The other person is likely to take advantage of you.
5. Collaborating	Solve the problem together.	"This is my position. What is yours?" "I'm committed to finding the best possible solution." "What do the facts suggest?"	The positions of both parties are equally important (though not necessarily equally valid). Equal emphasis should be placed on the quality of the outcome and the fairness of the decision-making process.	The problem is most likely to be resolved. Also, both parties are committed to the solution and satisfied that they have been treated fairly.

only at the other party's expense. Consequently, they often overlook opportunities to pursue collaborating as a conflict management strategy. At best, they tend to gravitate toward compromise, which means that they may miss creative solutions that generate a "win-win."

In contrast, integrative bargainers approach negotiations with a predisposition to look for "win-win" outcomes. They adopt problem-solving techniques instead of adversarial ones. They express interest in finding the best solution for both parties, rather than picking between the parties' preferred solutions (de Dreu, Koole, & Steinel, 2000; Fisher & Brown, 1988). Of course, in "win-win" solutions are not always possible, but integrative negotiators are far more likely to discover them than those who adopt a distribute approach to negotiating. As Table 7.3 shows, collaborating is the only management strategy that is integrative in nature.

Table 7.3 Comparison Between Negotiation and Conflict Management Strategies

Negotiation Strategies	Distributive	Integrative
Conflict Management	Compromising	Collaborating
Strategies	Forcing	
	Accommodating	
	Avoiding	

CHOOSING AMONG THE FIVE STRATEGIES

Although collaborating is the only conflict management strategy that seeks to produce "win-win" outcomes, it's not always the best strategy to use. In fact, each of the five strategies has their place. So the question for good conflict managers is not "Which strategy is the best one?" but rather "Which strategy should I use in *this* situation?" The appropriateness of a management strategy depends on its congruence with both personal preferences and situational factors.

PERSONAL PREFERENCES

As reflected in the "Strategies for Handling Conflict" survey in the Skill Assessment section of this chapter, it is important that we understand our personal preferences for managing conflict. If we don't feel comfortable with a particular approach, we are not likely to use it, no matter how convinced we are that it is the best available tool for a particular conflict situation. Although there are numerous factors that affect our personal preferences for how we manage conflict, including basic personality differences, two are worth particular note: ethnic culture and gender.

Research suggests that *ethnic culture* strongly affects individual preferences for the five conflict management strategies (Seybolt et al., 1996; Weldon & Jehn, 1995). For example, individuals from Asian cultures tend to prefer the nonconfrontational styles of accommodating and avoiding (Rahim & Blum, 1994; Ting-Toomey et al., 1991; Xie, Song, & Stringfellow, 1998), whereas, by comparison, Americans and South Africans prefer the forcing approach (Rahim & Blum, 1994; Seybolt et al., 1996; Xie et al., 1998). In general, compromise is the most commonly preferred approach across cultures (Seybolt et al., 1996), possibly because compromising may be viewed as the least costly alternative and the approach that most quickly reaches acceptable levels of fairness to both parties.

The research on the relationship between preferred conflict management style and *gender* is less clear-cut. Some studies report that males are more likely to use the forcing response, whereas females tend to select the compromising approach (Kilmann & Thomas, 1977; Ruble & Schneer, 1994). In contrast, other studies found gender to have little influence on an individual's preferred responses to conflict (Korabik, Baril, & Watson, 1993). Overall, it appears that gender is probably not a strong predictor of one's preference for conflict management styles, but that people still cling to sex-role expectations about conflict management preferences (Keashly, 1994).

Even though people have preferences for particular conflict management strategies, it is important to point out that those preferences are just general tendencies. Most people are able to draw upon more than just one conflict management style. This is important

because, given the variety of causes or forms of conflict, effective conflict management requires the use of a variety of strategies.

The research on this matter is illuminating. In a classic study on conflict management strategies, 25 executives were asked to describe two conflict situations—one with bad results and one with good (Phillips & Cheston, 1979). These incidents were then categorized in terms of the conflict management approach used. As Figure 7.4 shows, there were 23 incidents of forcing, 12 incidents of problem solving, 5 incidents of compromise, and 12 incidents of avoidance. Admittedly, this was a very small sample of managers, but the results are striking nonetheless. For instance, forcing was by far the most commonly used strategy (twice as many incidents as problem solving and nearly five times as many as compromising). This is a bit surprising since the study also showed that forcing was as likely to produce bad results as good. In contrast, collaborative problem solving was always linked with positive outcomes. Avoidance generally led to negative results.

If forcing is clearly not the superior conflict management strategy, why do senior executives have such a propensity for it? A likely answer is expediency. Some evidence for this answer comes from a study of the preferred influence strategies of more than 300 managers in three countries (Kipnis & Schmidt, 1983). This study showed that when subordinates are reluctant to comply with a request, managers tend to become directive, falling back on their organizational power to insist on compliance. So pervasive was this pattern that the authors of this study proposed an "Iron Law of Power: The greater the discrepancy in power between influence and target, the greater the probability that more directive influence strategies will be used" (p. 7).

A second prominent finding in Figure 7.4 is that some conflict management approaches were never used for certain types of issues. In particular, managers did not report a single case of problem solving or compromising when personal problems were the source of the conflict. These strategies were used primarily for managing conflicts involving incompatible goals and conflicting reward systems between departments.

We can draw two conclusions from the research on the use of different conflict management approaches. First, no one approach is most effective for managing every type of conflict. Second, managers are more effective in dealing with conflicts if they feel comfortable using a variety of approaches (Savage et al., 1989). These conclusions point out the need to

Figure 7.4 | Outcomes of Conflict Resolution by Conflict Type and Method of Resolution

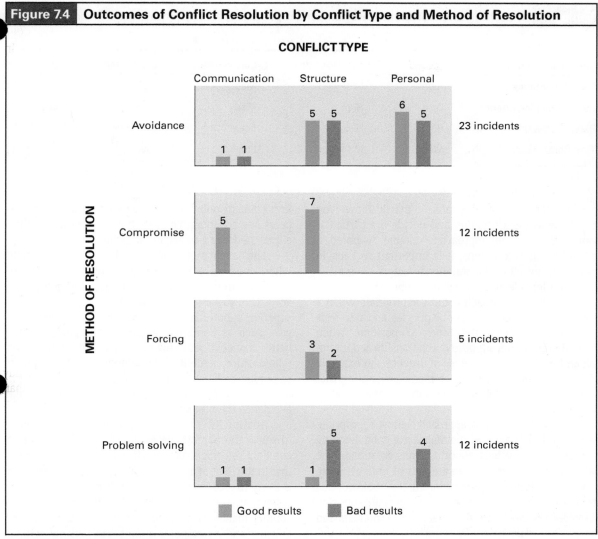

SOURCE: *Based on The Regents of the University of California. Reprinted from the* California Management Review. *Vol. 21, No. 4.*

understand the conditions under which each conflict management technique is most effective. The situational circumstances that support the use of each strategy are summarized in Table 7.4.

SITUATIONAL FACTORS

Table 7.4 identifies four important incident-specific circumstances that can be used to select the appropriate conflict management approach.

A. How important is the disputed issue? (In the table, "High" signifies extremely important; "Low" signifies not very important)

B. How important is the relationship? ("High" signifies a critical, ongoing, one-of-a-kind, partnership; "Low" signifies a one-time transaction, for which there are readily available alternatives)

C. What is the relative level of power, or authority, between the disputants? ("High" signifies that the actor has higher status than the conflict partner; "Equal" signifies that the two parties are peers; "Low" signifies that the actor has a lower status than the conflict partner)

D. To what extent is time a significant constraint in resolving the dispute? ("High" signifies that the dispute must be resolved quickly; "Low" signifies that time is not a salient factor)

Table 7.4	Matching the Conflict Management Approach with the Situation				
	CONFLICT MANAGEMENT APPROACH				
SITUATIONAL FACTORS	**FORCING**	**ACCOMMODATING**	**COMPROMISING**	**COLLABORATING**	**AVOIDING**
Issue Importance	High	Low	Med	High	Low
Relationship Importance	Low	High	Med	High	Low
Relative Power	High	Low	Equal	Low-High	Equal
Time Constraints	Med-High	Med-High	Low	Low	Med-High

The advantage of this table is that it allows you to quickly assess a situation and decide if a particular conflict management approach is suitable. As noted in the following descriptions, it is important to keep in mind that not all of the situational factors are equally important for selecting a particular approach.

The forcing approach is most appropriate when a conflict involves core values or policies and one feels compelled to defend the "correct" position; when maintaining a close, supportive relationship is not critical; and when there is a sense of urgency. An example of such a situation might be a manager insisting that a summer intern follow important company safety regulations.

The accommodating approach is most appropriate when the importance of maintaining a good working relationship outweighs all other considerations. The nature of the issues and the amount of time available play a secondary role in determining the choice of this strategy. Accommodation becomes especially appropriate when the issues are not vital to your interests and the problem must be resolved quickly.

Trying to reach a compromise is most appropriate when the issues are complex and moderately important, there are no simple solutions, and both parties have a strong interest in different facets of the problem. The other essential situational requirement is adequate time for negotiation. The classic case is a bargaining session between representatives of management and labor to avert a scheduled strike. Experience has shown that negotiations work best between parties with equal power who are committed to maintaining a good long-term relationship.

The collaborating approach is most appropriate when the issues are critical, maintaining an ongoing supportive relationship between peers is important, and time constraints are not pressing. Although collaboration can also be an effective approach for resolving conflicts between a superior and subordinate, it is

important to point out that when a conflict involves peers, the collaborative mode is more appropriate than either the forcing or accommodating approach.

The avoidance approach is most appropriate when one's stake in an issue is not high and there is not a strong interpersonal reason for getting involved, regardless of whether the conflict involves a superior, subordinate, or peer. Although other strategies, such as compromise and collaboration, have a better chance of resolving problems without damaging relationships, sometimes the amount of time required to pursue these strategies is too great to justify using them. Occasionally, extreme time pressures make avoidance the best strategy.

Admittedly, this is a very rational view of how to select the appropriate approach(es) for resolving a conflict. You might wonder if it is realistic to believe that in the heat of an emotional confrontation a person is likely to step back and make this type of deliberate, systematic assessment of the situation. But the best conflict managers learn to conduct this analysis very quickly, and to respond almost instinctively with a strategy that is well-suited to the occasion.

Although we are encouraging you to take a thoughtful, analytical approach to resolving disputes, that doesn't mean you can count on the other parties to the dispute adopting the same strategy. For example, when conflicts involve individuals from very different cultural traditions, it is not uncommon for them to disagree about how to resolve their differences, or even about whether the conflict should be resolved at all. If parties to a conflict hold very different views regarding time, power, ambiguity, the rule of norms, or the importance of relationships, one can expect they will have difficulty agreeing on the appropriate course of action for resolving their dispute (Trompenaars, 1994). Put simply: if you don't agree on *how* you are going to reach an agreement, it doesn't do you much good to discuss *what* that agreement might look like.

Consequently, good conflict managers must strive to clarify assumptions, interpretations, and expectations early in the conflict management process.

To summarize this section, regardless of your personal preferences for conflict management styles, it is important to stretch your "comfort zone" and become proficient in the application of the full range of choices. It is also important to match your choice of conflict management strategy with the salient situational factors, including issue and relationship importance, relative power, and time constraints. Finally, it is important for parties of a dispute to discuss their assumptions regarding the appropriate process for resolving their differences, especially when they come from very different backgrounds.

Resolving Interpersonal Confrontations Using the Collaborative Approach

We now shift our attention from when to use each of the strategies to how one can best implement the collaborative approach when circumstances support it. We have chosen to focus on this approach for two reasons. First, as noted throughout our discussion, collaboration is the best overall approach. Effective managers treat it as their "default option"—unless there is a compelling reason to try something else. Second, it is also the hardest approach to implement effectively. In the study by Kipnis and Schmidt (1983), discussed earlier, most managers expressed general support for the collaborative approach, but when it appeared that things were not going their way, they reverted back to a directive approach. By comparison, it is fairly simple for managers to either give in or impose their will, but resolving differences in a truly collaborative manner is a complicated and taxing process. As a result, unskilled managers often opt for less challenging approaches. To help you gain proficiency in using the collaborative approach, the remainder of this chapter describes behavioral guidelines for effectively resolving interpersonal confrontations in a collaborative manner.

A GENERAL FRAMEWORK FOR COLLABORATIVE PROBLEM SOLVING

The addition of "problem solving" to this title warrants a brief explanation. When two disputants agree to work toward a collaborative solution, they are basically agreeing to share an attitude or value. They are, in a sense, agreeing not to force the other party to accept a one-sided solution. But skill development requires more than an attitude adjustment—we need to understand the actual competencies required for effective conflict resolution. We describe a problem-solving process that involves an orderly, deliberate, reasoned approach to dispute resolution and that enables disputants to make good on their commitment to work together. This structured approach is particularly useful when applied to people-focused conflicts. In these situations, it is helpful to have a framework to organize your thoughts and to discipline your emotions.

We will begin our discussion of the collaborative problem-solving process by introducing a general, six-step framework adapted from the integrative bargaining literature discussed earlier (Stroh, Northcraft, & Neale, 2002). We will then use this broad outline to develop a more detailed set of problem-solving guidelines.

A. **Establish overarching goals.** In order to foster a climate of collaboration, both parties to a dispute need to focus on what they share in common. For instance, the parties might agree that the shared goal is increased productivity, lower costs, reduced design time, or improved relations between departments, for example. Starting with shared goals sensitizes the parties to the mutual benefits of resolving their differences. The step is characterized by the general question, "What common goals support these discussions?"

B. **Separate the people from the problem.** After clarifying the mutual benefits behind the discussion, participants should next focus their attention on the real issue: solving the problem (as opposed to "fixing" another person). Interpersonal confrontations are more likely to result in mutual satisfaction if the parties depersonalize their disagreement and suppress their desires for revenge or one-upmanship. In other words, each participant should view the other party as the advocate of a point of view, not as a rival. The problem solver would say, "That is an unreasonable position" rather than, "You are an unreasonable person."

C. **Focus on interests, not positions.** Positions are demands or assertions; interests constitute the reasons behind the demands. Experience shows that it is easier to establish agreement on interests, given that they tend to be broader and multifaceted. This step involves redefining and broadening problems to make them more tractable. It involves asking "why" questions to get to the heart of the other person's needs. A characteristic collaborative statement is, "Help me understand why you advocate that position."

D. **Invent options for mutual gains.** This step focuses on generating creative solutions. By focusing both parties' attention on brainstorming novel, mutually agreeable solutions, the interpersonal dynamics naturally shift from competitive to collaborative. In addition, the more options and combinations there are to explore, the greater the probability of finding common ground. This step can be summarized as, "Now that we better understand each other's underlying concerns and objectives, let's brainstorm ways of satisfying both our needs."

E. **Use objective criteria for evaluating alternatives.** No matter how collaborative both parties may be, there are bound to be some incompatible interests. Rather than seizing on these as opportunities for testing wills, it is far more productive to determine what is fair. This requires both parties to examine how fairness should be judged. A shift in thinking from "getting what I want" to "deciding what makes most sense" fosters an open, reasonable attitude. It encourages parties to avoid overconfidence or overcommitment to their initial position. This approach is characterized by asking, "What is a fair way to evaluate the merits of our arguments?"

F. **Define success in terms of real gains, not imaginary losses.** If a manager seeks a 10 percent raise and receives only 6 percent, that outcome can be viewed as either a 6 percent improvement or a 40 percent shortfall. The first interpretation focuses on gains, the second on losses (in this case, unrealized expectations). The outcome is the same, but the manager's satisfaction with it varies substantially. It is important to recognize that our satisfaction with an outcome is affected by the standards we use to judge it. Recognizing this, the collaborative problem solver facilitates resolution by judging the value of proposed solutions against reasonable standards. This perspective is reflected in the question, "Does this outcome constitute a meaningful improvement over current conditions?"

THE FOUR PHASES OF COLLABORATIVE PROBLEM SOLVING

Notice how the problem-solving approach encourages collaboration by keeping the process focused on *shared problems* and *sharing solutions*. These are important themes to remember, especially when you utilize the collaborative approach to resolve a people-focused conflict. Because of the degree of difficulty inherent in this undertaking, we will continue using the people-focused conflict context in our remaining discussion. For information on how to manage issue-focused conflicts using various negotiation strategies, see Murnighan (1992, 1993) and Thompson (2001).

We have organized our detailed discussion of behavioral guidelines around the four phases of the **problem-solving process**: (1) *problem identification*, (2) *solution generation*, (3) *action plan formulation and agreement*, and (4) *implementation and follow-up*. In the midst of a heated exchange, the first two phases are the most critical steps, as well as the most difficult to implement effectively. If you are able to achieve agreement on what the problem is and how you intend to resolve it, the details of the agreement, including a follow-up plan, should follow naturally. In other words, we are placing our skill-building emphasis where skillful implementation is most critical.

We have also organized our guidelines around specific roles in a dispute. Confrontations typically involve at least two actors: an **initiator** and a **responder**. A dyadic conflict sometimes represents a greater challenge for responders because they have responsibility for transforming a complaint into a problem-solving discussion. This requires considerable patience and self-confidence because unskilled initiators will generally begin the discussion by blaming the responder for the problem. In this situation, an unskilled responder will likely become defensive and look for an opportunity to "even the score."

If these lose-lose dynamics persist, a **mediator** is generally required to cool down the dispute, reestablish constructive communication, and help the parties reconcile their differences. The presence of a mediator removes some pressure from the responder because an impartial referee provides assistance in moving the confrontation through the problem-solving phases.

The following guidelines provide a model for acting out the initiator, responder, and mediator roles in such a way that problem solving can occur. In our discussion of each role, we will assume that other participants in the conflict are not behaving according to their prescribed guidelines.

Initiator-Problem Identification

A. Maintain Personal Ownership of the Problem

It is important to recognize that when you are upset and frustrated, this is your problem, not the other person's. You may feel that your boss or coworker is the source of your problem, but the first step in addressing your concern is acknowledging accountability for your feelings. Suppose someone enters your office with a smelly cigar without asking if it is all right to smoke. The fact that your office is going to stink for the rest of the day may infuriate you, but the odor does not present a problem for your smoking guest. One way to determine ownership of a problem is to identify whose needs are not being met. In this case, your need for a clean working environment is not being met, so the smelly office is your problem.

The advantage of taking ownership of a problem when registering a complaint is that it reduces defensiveness (Adler, Rosenfeld, & Proctor, 2001; Alder & Rodman, 2003). In order for you to get a problem solved, the respondent must not feel threatened by your initial statement of that problem. By beginning the conversation with a request that the responder help solve your problem, you immediately establish a problem-solving atmosphere. For example, you might say, "Bill, do you have a few minutes? I have a problem I need to discuss with you."

B. Succinctly Describe Your Problem in Terms of Behaviors, Consequences, and Feelings

A useful model for remembering how to state your problem effectively has been prescribed by Gordon (2000): "I have a problem. When you do X, Y results, and I feel Z." Although we don't advocate the memorization of set formulas for improving communication skills, keeping this model in mind will help you implement three critical elements in your "problem statement."

First, describe the specific behaviors (X) that present a problem for you. This will help you avoid the reflexive tendency when you are upset to give feedback that is evaluative and not specific. One way to do this is to specify the expectations or standards that have been violated. For example, a subordinate may have missed a deadline for completing an assigned task, your boss may gradually be taking over tasks previously delegated to you, or a colleague in the accounting department may have repeatedly failed to provide you with data required for an important presentation.

Second, outline the specific, observable consequences (Y) of these behaviors. Simply telling others that their actions are causing you problems is often sufficient stimulus for change. In fast-paced work environments, people generally become insensitive to the impact of their actions. They don't intend to cause offense, but they become so busy meeting deadlines associated with "getting the product out the door" that they tune out subtle negative feedback from others. When this occurs, bringing to the attention of others the consequences of their behaviors will often prompt them to change.

Unfortunately, not all problems can be resolved this simply. At times, offenders are aware of the negative consequences of their behaviors, yet they persist in them. In such cases, this approach is still useful in stimulating a problem-solving discussion because it presents concerns in a nonthreatening manner. Possibly, the responders' behaviors are constrained by the expectations of their boss or by the fact that the department is currently understaffed. Responders may not be able to change these constraints, but this approach will encourage them to discuss them with you so you can work on the problem together.

Third, describe the feelings (Z) you experience as a result of the problem. It is important that the responder understand that the behavior is not just inconvenient. You need to explain how it is affecting you personally by engendering feelings of frustration, anger, or insecurity. Explain how these feelings are interfering with your work. They may make it more difficult for you to concentrate, to be congenial with customers, to be supportive of your boss, or to be willing to make needed personal sacrifices to meet deadlines.

We recommend using this three-step model as a general guide. The order of the components may vary, and you should obviously not use the same words every time. Observe how the key elements in the "XYZ" model are used in different ways in Table 7.5.

C. Avoid Drawing Evaluative Conclusions and Attributing Motives to the Respondent

When exchanges between two disputing parties become vengeful, each side often has a different perspective about the justification of the other's actions. Typically, each party believes that he or she is the victim of the other's aggression. In international conflicts, opposing nations often believe they are acting defensively

Table 7.5   Examples of the "XYZ" Approach to Stating a Problem

Model:

"I have a problem. When you do X (behavior), Y results (consequences), and I feel Z."

Examples:

I have to tell you that I get upset [feelings] when you make jokes about my bad memory in front of other people [behavior]. In fact, I get so angry so that I find myself bringing up your faults to get even [consequences].

I have a problem. When you say you'll be here for our date at six and don't show up until after seven [behavior], the dinner gets ruined, we're late for the show we planned to see [consequences], and I feel hurt because it seems as though I'm just not that important to you [feelings].

The employees want to let management know that we've been having a hard time lately with the short notice you've been giving when you need us to work overtime [behavior]. That probably explains some of the grumbling and lack of cooperation you've mentioned [consequences]. Anyhow, we wanted to make it clear that this policy has really got a lot of the workers feeling pretty resentful [feeling].

SOURCE: *Adapted from Adler, 1977.*

rather than offensively. Similarly, in smaller-scale conflicts, each side may have distorted views of its own hurt and the motives of the "offender" (Kim & Smith, 1993). Therefore, in presenting your problem, avoid the pitfalls of making accusations, drawing inferences about motivations or intentions, or attributing the responder's undesirable behavior to personal inadequacies. Statements such as, "You are always interrupting me," "You haven't been fair to me since the day I disagreed with you in the board meeting," and "You never have time to listen to our problems and suggestions because you manage your time so poorly" are ineffective for initiating a problem-solving process.

Another key to reducing defensiveness is to delay proposing a solution until both parties agree on the nature of the problem. When you become so upset with someone's behavior that you feel it is necessary to initiate a complaint, it is often because the person has seriously violated your expectations. For example, you might feel that your manager should have been less dogmatic and listened more during a goal-setting interview. Consequently, you might be tempted to offer immediate prescriptions for a more democratic or sensitive style.

Besides creating defensiveness, the principal disadvantage to initiating problem solving with a suggested remedy is that it hinders the problem-solving process. Before completing the problem-articulation phase, you have immediately jumped to the solution-generation phase, based on the assumption that you know all the reasons for, and constraints on, the other person's behavior. You will jointly produce better, more acceptable, solutions if you present your statement of the problem and discuss it thoroughly before proposing potential solutions.

D. Persist Until Understood There are times when the respondent will not clearly receive or acknowledge even the most effectively expressed message. Suppose, for instance, that you share the following problem with a coworker:

Something has been bothering me, and I need to share my concerns with you. Frankly, I'm uncomfortable [feeling] with your heavy use of profanity [behavior]. I don't mind an occasional "damn" or "hell," but the other words bother me a lot. Lately I've been avoiding you [consequences], and that's not good because it interferes with our working relationship, so I wanted to let you know how I feel.

When you share your feelings in this nonevaluative way, it's likely that the other person will understand your position and possibly try to change behavior to suit your needs. On the other hand, there are a number of less satisfying responses that could be made to your comment:

Listen, these days everyone talks that way. And besides, you've got your faults, too, you know! [Your coworker becomes defensive, rationalizing and counterattacking.]

Yeah, I suppose I do swear a lot. I'll have to work on that someday. [Gets the general drift of your message but fails to comprehend how serious the problem is to you.]

Listen, if you're still angry about my forgetting to tell you about that meeting the other day, you can be sure that I'm really sorry. I won't do it again. [Totally misunderstands.]

Speaking of avoiding, have you seen Chris lately? I wonder if anything is wrong with him. [Is discomfited by your frustration and changes the subject.]

In each case, the coworker does not understand or does not wish to acknowledge the problem. In these situations, you must reiterate your concern until the other party acknowledges it as a problem to be solved. Otherwise, the problem-solving process will terminate at this point and nothing will change. Repeated assertions can take the form of restating the same phrase several times or reiterating your concern with different words or examples that you feel may improve comprehension. To avoid introducing new concerns or shifting from a descriptive to an evaluative mode, keep in mind the "XYZ" formula for feedback.

E. Encourage Two-Way Discussion You can establish a better problem-solving climate by inviting the respondent to express opinions and ask questions. There may be a reasonable explanation for another's disturbing behavior. Or the person may have a radically different view of the problem. The sooner this information is introduced into the conversation, the more likely you can resolve the issue.

As a rule of thumb, an initiator should keep his or her opening statement brief. The longer the opening statement of the problem, the more likely it is to encourage a defensive reaction. The longer we talk, the more worked up we get, and the more likely we are to violate principles of supportive communication. As a result, the other party begins to feel threatened, starts mentally outlining a rebuttal or counterattack, and stops listening empathetically to our concerns. Once these dynamics enter the discussion, the collaborative approach is usually discarded in favor of the accommodating or forcing strategies, depending on the circumstances. When this occurs, it is unlikely that the actors will be able to reach a mutually satisfactory solution to their problem without third-party intervention.

F. Manage the Agenda: Approach Multiple or Complex Problems Incrementally One way to shorten your opening statement is to approach complex problems incrementally. Rather than raising a series of issues all at once, focus initially on a simple or rudimentary problem. Then, as you gain greater appreciation for the other party's perspective and share some problem-solving success, you can discuss more challenging issues. This is especially important when trying to resolve a problem with a person who is important to your work performance but who does not have a long-standing relationship with you. The less familiar you are with the other's opinions and personality, as well as the situational constraints influencing his or her behaviors, the more you should approach a problem-solving discussion as a fact-finding and rapport-building mission. This is best done by focusing your introductory statement on a specific manifestation of a problem and then opening the conversation to the responder. For example, "Bill, we had difficulty getting that work order processed on time yesterday. What seemed to be the problem?"

Initiator-Solution Generation

G. Focus on Commonalities as the Basis for Requesting a Change Once both parties clearly understand the problem, the discussion should shift to the solution-generation phase. Most disputants share at least some personal and organizational goals, believe in many of the same fundamental principles of management, and operate under similar constraints. These commonalities can serve as a useful starting point for generating solutions. The most straightforward approach to changing another's offensive behavior is to make a request. The legitimacy of a request will be enhanced if it is linked to common interests. These might include shared values, such as treating coworkers fairly and following through on commitments, or shared constraints, such as getting reports in on time and operating within budgetary restrictions. Pointing out how a change in the respondent's behavior would positively affect your shared fate will reduce defensiveness: "Jane, one of the things we have all worked hard to build in this audit team is mutual support. We are all pushed to the limit getting this job completed by the third-quarter deadline next week. Will you reconsider your position on not working overtime, at least until we can all get through this crisis together?"

Responder-Problem Identification

Now we shift our attention to the **responder role**—the person who is supposedly the source of the problem. In a work setting, you could find yourself as the responder if one of your employees tells you that you are making unrealistic demands, a supervisor claims you are not following proper procedures, or if a coworker accuses you of claiming credit for ideas she generated. The following guidelines show how to respond to the initiator's behavior so you can have a productive problem-solving experience.

LEARNING

A. Establish a Climate for Joint Problem Solving by Showing Genuine Interest and Concern
When a person complains to you, do not treat that complaint lightly. While this may seem self-evident, managers often make the mistake of trying to quickly brush a concern under the rug because they are so busy with other demands. Consequently, unless the other person's emotional condition necessitates dealing with the problem immediately, it is sometimes better to set up a time for another meeting if your current time pressures will make it difficult to give the complaint the attention it deserves.

In most cases, the initiator will be expecting you to set the tone for the meeting. You will quickly undermine collaboration if you overreact or become defensive. Even if you disagree with the complaint and feel it has no foundation, you need to respond empathetically to the initiator's statement of the problem. This is done by conveying an attitude of interest and receptivity through your posture, tone of voice, and facial expressions.

One of the most difficult aspects of establishing the proper climate for your discussion is responding appropriately to the initiator's emotions. Sometimes you may need to let a person blow off steam before trying to address the substance of a specific complaint. In some cases, the therapeutic effect of being able to express negative emotions to the boss will be enough to satisfy a subordinate. This occurs frequently in high-pressure jobs in which tempers flare easily as a result of the intense stress.

However, an emotional outburst can be very detrimental to problem solving. If an employee begins verbally attacking you or someone else, and it is apparent that the individual is more interested in getting even than in solving an interpersonal problem, you may need to interrupt and interject some ground rules for collaborative problem solving. By explaining calmly to the other person that you are willing to discuss a genuine problem but that you will not tolerate personal attacks or scapegoating, you can quickly determine the initiator's true intentions. In most instances, he or she will apologize, emulate your emotional tone, and begin formulating a useful statement of the problem.

B. Seek Additional, Clarifying Information About the Problem by Asking Questions
As shown in Figure 7.5, untrained initiators typically present complaints that are so general and evaluative that they aren't useful problem statements. It is difficult to understand how you should respond to a general, vague comment like "You never listen to me during our meetings," followed by an evaluative, critical comment like "You obviously aren't interested in what I have to say." If you and the initiator are going to transform a personal complaint into a joint problem, you must redirect the conversation from general and evaluative accusations to descriptions of specific behaviors.

The problem is that when you are getting steamed up over what you believe are unfair and unjustified accusations, it is difficult to avoid fighting back. ("Oh yeah, well I haven't wanted to say this about you before, but since you've brought up the subject...") The single best way to keep your mind focused on transforming a personal attack into a jointly identified problem is to limit your responses to questions. As the authors of the book *Crucial Conversations* put it, "at the very moment when most people become furious, we need to become curious" (Patterson, et al., 2012, p. 157). If you stick with asking clarifying questions you are going to get better-quality information and you are going to demonstrate your commitment to joint problem solving.

As shown in Figure 7.5, one of the best ways of doing this is to ask for examples ("Can you give me an example of what I did during a staff meeting that led you to believe I wasn't listening to what you had to say?"). Building on our discussion of the "XYZ" model in the initiator's guidelines, you might find it useful to ask for examples of your offending actions and their harmful consequences, including damaged feelings ("Can you give me a specific example of my behavior that concerns you?" "When I did that, what were the specific consequences for your work?" "How did you feel when that happened?").

C. Agree with Some Aspect of the Complaint
This is an important point that is difficult for some people to accept because they wonder how it is possible to agree with something they don't believe is true. They may also be worried about reinforcing complaining behavior. In practice, this step is probably the best test of whether a responder is committed to using the collaborative approach to conflict management rather than the avoiding, forcing, or accommodating approach. People who use the forcing mode will grit their teeth while listening to the initiator, just waiting to find a flaw they can use to launch a counterattack. Or they will simply respond, "I'm sorry, but that's just the way I am. You'll simply have to get used to it." Accommodators will apologize profusely and ask for forgiveness. People who avoid conflicts will acknowledge and agree with the initiator's concerns, but only

Figure 7.5   Respondents' Effective Use of Clarifying Questions

Transform Complaints . . .

From   *To*

General   ➡   Specific

Evaluative   ➡   Descriptive

Motives and   ➡   Actions and
Reasons   Consequences

Using Clarifying Questions:

"Can you give me an example?"
"What do you mean by that label/term?"
"Can you help me understand what your conclusion is based on?"
"When did this first become a problem for you?"
"How often has this occurred?"
"What specific actions have led you to believe that I'm taking sides in this issue?"
"What were some of the harmful consequences of my decision?"

in a superficial manner because their only concern is how to terminate the awkward conversation quickly.

In contrast, collaborators will demonstrate their concerns for both cooperation and assertiveness by looking for points in the initiator's presentation with which they can genuinely agree. It is usually possible to validate the other person's viewpoint without conceding your own position. Even in the most blatantly malicious and hostile verbal assault (which may be more a reflection of the initiator's insecurity than evidence of your inadequacies), there is generally a grain of truth. For example, a few years ago, a junior faculty member in a business school who was being reviewed for promotion received a very unfair appraisal from one of his senior colleagues. Since the junior member knew that the critic was going through a personal crisis, he could have dismissed the criticism as irrelevant and tendentious. However, one particular phrase— "You are stuck on a narrow line of research"—kept coming back to his mind. There was something there that couldn't be ignored. Rather than taking the feedback as simply a vindictive reproach, he considered whether it had some validity. Ultimately, the junior faculty member took this small idea (which had been buried amidst the senior faculty's unfair ranting) and made a major career decision that produced very positive outcomes. Furthermore, by publicly giving the senior colleague credit for the suggestion, he substantially strengthened the interpersonal relationship.

There are a number of ways you can agree with a message without accepting all of its ramifications (Adler et al., 2001). You can find an element of truth, as in the incident related above. Or you can agree in principle with the argument: "I agree that managers should set a good example" or "I agree that it is important for salesclerks to be at the store when it opens." If you can't find anything substantive with which to agree, you can always agree with the initiator's perception of the situation: "Well, I can see how you would think that. I have known people who deliberately shirked their responsibilities." Or you can agree with the person's feelings: "It is obvious that our earlier discussion greatly upset you."

In none of these cases are you necessarily agreeing with the initiator's conclusions or evaluations, nor are you conceding your position. You are trying to understand, to foster a problem-solving, rather than argumentative, discussion. Generally, initiators prepare for a complaint session by mentally cataloguing all the evidence supporting their point of view. Once the discussion begins, they introduce as much evidence as necessary to make their argument convincing; that is, they commit themselves to keep arguing until you agree. Consequently, establishing a basis of agreement early on is the key to moving toward the problem-solving stage.

Responder-Solution Generation

D. Ask for Suggestions of Acceptable Alternatives Once you are certain you fully understand the initiator's complaint, move on to the solution-generation phase by asking the initiator for recommended solutions. This triggers an important transition in the discussion by shifting attention from the negative to the positive and from the past to the future. It also communicates your regard for the initiator's opinions. Some managers listen patiently to a subordinate's complaint, say they will rectify the problem, and then terminate the discussion. This leaves the initiator guessing about the outcome of the meeting. Will you take the complaint seriously? Will you really change? If so, will the change resolve the problem? It is important to eliminate this ambiguity by agreeing on a plan of action. If the problem is particularly serious or complex, it is useful to write down specific agreements, including assignments and deadlines, as well as providing for a follow-up meeting to check progress.

In addition to initiators and responders, there is one more role to consider in the problem-solving process. Frequently, it is necessary for managers (and others) to adopt the role of mediator in a dispute between two other parties (Karambayya & Brett, 1989; Kressel & Pruitt, 1989; Stroh et al., 2002). The following guidelines are intended to help mediators avoid the common pitfalls associated with this role, which are shown in Table 7.6.

Mediator-Problem Identification

A. Acknowledge That a Conflict Exists and Propose a Problem-Solving Approach for Resolving It
When a mediator is called in, it means the disputants have failed as problem solvers.

Therefore, the first step for an effective mediator is to establish a problem-solving framework. To do this, the mediator must first take seriously the problems between conflicting parties, and not belittle them. Remarks such as, "I'm surprised that two intelligent people like you have not been able to work out your disagreement. We have more important things to do here than get all worked up over such petty issues" will make both parties defensive and interfere with any serious problem-solving efforts. While you might wish that your subordinates could have worked out their disagreement without bothering you, this is not the time to lecture them on self-reliance. Seldom is this conducive to problem solving.

One early decision a mediator has to make is whether to convene a joint problem-solving session or meet separately with the parties first. The diagnostic criteria shown in Table 7.7 should help you weigh the trade-offs. First, what is the current position of the disputants? Are both aware that a problem exists? Are they equally motivated to work on solving the problem? The more similar the awareness and motivation of the parties, the more likely it is that a joint session will be productive. If there is a serious discrepancy in awareness and motivation, the mediator should work to reduce that discrepancy through one-on-one meetings before bringing the disputants together.

Second, what is the current relationship between the disputants? Does their work require them to interact frequently? Is a good working relationship critical

Table 7.6	**Ten Ways to Fail as a Mediator**

1. After you have listened to the argument for a short time, begin to nonverbally communicate your discomfort with the discussion (e.g., sit back, begin to fidget).

2. Communicate your agreement with one of the parties (e.g., through facial expressions, posture, chair position, reinforcing comments).

3. Say that you shouldn't be talking about this kind of thing at work or where others can hear you.

4. Discourage the expression of emotion. Suggest that the discussion would better be held later after both parties have cooled off.

5. Suggest that both parties are wrong. Point out the problems with both points of view.

6. Suggest partway through the discussion that possibly you aren't the person who should be helping solve this problem.

7. See if you can get both parties to attack you.

8. Minimize the seriousness of the problem.

9. Change the subject (e.g., ask for advice to help you solve one of your problems).

10. Express displeasure that the two parties are experiencing conflict (e.g., imply that it might undermine the solidarity of the work group).

SOURCE: *Adapted from Morris & Sashkin, 1976.*

Table 7.7	Choosing a Format for Mediating Conflicts		
FACTORS		**HOLD JOINT MEETINGS**	**HOLD SEPARATE MEETINGS FIRST**
Awareness and Motivation			
• Both parties are aware of the problem.		Yes	No
• They are equally motivated to resolve the problem.		Yes	No
• They accept your legitimacy as a mediator.		Yes	No
Nature of the Relationship			
• The parties hold equal status.		Yes	No
• They work together regularly.		Yes	No
• They have an overall good relationship.		Yes	No
Nature of the Problem			
• This is an isolated (not a recurring) problem.		Yes	No
• The complaint is substantive in nature and easily verified.		Yes	No
• The parties agree on the root causes of the problem.		Yes	No
• The parties share common values and work priorities.		Yes	No

for their individual job performance? What has their relationship been in the past? What is the difference in their formal status in the organization? As we discussed earlier, joint problem-solving sessions are most productive between individuals of equal status who are required to work together regularly. This does not mean that joint meetings should not be held between a supervisor and subordinate, only that greater care needs to be taken in preparing for such a meeting. Specifically, if a department head becomes involved in a dispute between a worker and a supervisor, the department head should make sure that the worker does not feel this meeting will serve as an excuse for two managers to gang up on an hourly employee.

Separate fact-finding meetings with the disputants prior to a joint meeting are particularly useful when the parties have a history of recurring disputes, especially if these disputes should have been resolved without a mediator. Such a history often suggests a lack of conflict management or problem-solving skills on the part of the disputants, or it might stem from a broader set of issues that are beyond their control. In these situations, individual coaching sessions prior to a joint meeting will increase your understanding of the root causes and improve the individuals' abilities to resolve their differences. Following up these private meetings with a joint problem-solving session in which the mediator coaches the disputants through the process

for resolving their conflicts can be a positive learning experience.

Third, what is the nature of the problem? Is the complaint substantive in nature and easily verifiable? If the problem stems from conflicting role responsibilities and the actions of both parties in question are common knowledge, then a joint problem-solving session may be preferable. However, if the complaint stems from differences in managerial style, values, personality characteristics, and so forth, bringing the parties together immediately following a complaint may seriously undermine the problem-solving process because it may pose threats to the participants' self-image. To avoid individuals feeling as though they are being ambushed in a meeting, you should discuss serious personal complaints with them ahead of time, in private.

B. While Seeking Out the Perspective of Both Parties, Maintain a Neutral Posture Regarding the Disputants—If Not the Issues

Effective mediation requires impartiality. If a mediator shows strong personal bias in favor of one party in a joint problem-solving session, the other party may simply walk out. However, such personal bias is more likely to emerge in private conversations with the disputants. Statements such as, "I can't believe he really did that!" and "Everyone seems to be having trouble working with Charlie these days" imply that the mediator is taking sides, and any attempt to appear impartial in a joint meeting will seem like mere window dressing to appease the other party. No matter how well-intentioned or justified these comments might be, they destroy the credibility of the mediator in the long run. In contrast, effective mediators respect both parties' points of view and make sure that both perspectives are expressed adequately.

Occasionally, it is not possible to be impartial on issues. One person may have violated company policy, engaged in unethical competition with a colleague, or broken a personal agreement. In these cases, the challenge of the mediator is to separate the offense from the offender. If a person is clearly in the wrong, the inappropriate behavior needs to be corrected, but in such a way that the individual doesn't feel his or her image and working relationships have been permanently marred. This can be done most effectively when correction occurs in private.

C. Serve as a Facilitator, Not as a Judge

When parties must work closely together and have a history of chronic interpersonal problems, it is often more important to teach problem-solving skills than to resolve a specific dispute. This is done best when the mediator adopts the posture of facilitator. It is important that the mediator avoid being seduced into "rendering a verdict" by comments from the disputants such as, "Well, you're the boss; tell us which one is right." The problem with a mediator's assuming the role of judge is that it sets in motion processes antithetical to effective interpersonal problem solving. The parties focus on persuading the mediator of their innocence and the other party's guilt rather than striving to improve their working relationship with the assistance of the mediator. The disputants work to establish facts about what happened in the past rather than to reach an agreement about what ought to happen in the future. Consequently, a key aspect of effective mediation is helping disputants explore multiple alternatives in a nonjudgmental manner.

D. Manage the Discussion to Ensure Fairness—Keep the Discussion Issue Oriented, Not Personality Oriented

It is important that the mediator maintain a problem-solving atmosphere throughout the discussion. This is not to say that strong emotional statements don't have their place. People often associate effective problem solving with a calm, highly rational discussion of the issues. However, placid, cerebral discussions may not solve all problems, and impassioned statements don't have to be insulting. The critical point about process is that it should be centered on the issues and the consequences of continued conflict on performance. Good mediators focus the discussion on specific behaviors, not on "personality quirks." Attributions of motives or overgeneralizing about each other's proclivities distract participants from the problem-solving process. It is important that the mediator establish and maintain these ground rules.

It is also important for a mediator to ensure that neither party dominates the discussion. A relatively even balance in the level of inputs improves the quality of the final outcome. It also increases the likelihood that both parties will accept the final decision because there is a high correlation between feelings about the problem-solving process and attitudes about the final solution. If one party tends to dominate a discussion, the mediator can help balance the exchange by asking the less talkative individual direct questions: "Now that we have heard Bill's view of that incident, how do you see it?" "That's an important point, Brad, so let's make sure Brian agrees. How do you feel, Brian?"

Mediator-Solution Generation

E. Explore Options by Focusing on Interests, Not Positions

As noted earlier in this section, positions are demands, whereas interests are the underlying needs, values, goals, or concerns behind the demands. Focusing only on positions may cause disputants to feel that they have irreconcilable differences. Mediators can help by examining the interests behind the positions.

The mediator's job is to help disputants surface their unspoken interests and to discover where they intersect and where they conflict. In order to flesh out each party's interests, ask "why" questions: "Why have they taken this position?" "Why does this matter to them?" Understand that there is probably no single, simple answer to these questions. Each side may represent a number of constituents, each with special interests.

After each side has articulated its underlying interests, help the parties identify areas of agreement and reconcilability. It is common for participants in an intense conflict to feel that they are on opposite sides of all issues—that they have little in common. Helping them recognize that there are areas of agreement and reconcilability often represents a major turning point in resolving long-standing feuds.

F. Make Sure All Parties Fully Understand and Support the Solution Agreed Upon, and Establish Follow-Up Procedures

The last two phases of the problem-solving process are (1) agreement on an action plan and (2) follow-up. We will discuss these within the context of the mediator's role, but they are equally relevant to the other roles.

A common mistake of ineffective mediators is terminating discussions prematurely, on the supposition that once a problem has been solved in principle, the disputants can be left to work out the details on their own. Or a mediator may assume that because one party has recommended a solution that appears reasonable and workable, the second disputant will be willing to implement it.

To avoid these mistakes, it is important to stay engaged in the mediation process until both parties have agreed on a detailed plan of action. You might consider using the familiar planning template—who, what, how, when, and where—as a checklist for making sure the plan is complete. Carefully explore any hesitancy on the part of either disputant ("Tom, I sense that you are somewhat less enthusiastic than Sue about this plan. Is there something that bothers you?").

When you are confident that both parties support the plan, check to make sure they are aware of their respective responsibilities and then propose a mechanism for monitoring progress. For example, you might schedule another formal meeting, or you might stop by both individuals' offices to get a progress report. As you go forward, be open to needed "good faith" modifications of the proposal to accommodate unforeseen implementation issues. Consider using a follow-up meeting to celebrate the successful resolution of the dispute and to discuss "lessons learned" for future applications.

Summary

Conflict is a difficult and controversial topic. In most cultures, it has negative connotations because it runs counter to the notion that we should get along with people by being kind and friendly. Although many people intellectually understand the value of conflict, they feel uncomfortable confronting it. Their discomfort may result from a lack of understanding of the conflict process as well as from a lack of training in how to handle interpersonal confrontations effectively. In this chapter, we have addressed these issues by introducing both analytical and behavioral skills.

A summary model of conflict management, shown in Figure 7.6, contains four elements: (1) diagnosing the sources of conflict; (2) selecting an appropriate conflict management strategy; (3) effectively implementing the strategy, using a collaborative problem-solving process when possible, which should lead to (4) a successful resolution of the dispute. Note that the final outcome of our model is successful dispute resolution. Given our introductory claim that conflict plays an important role in organizations, our concluding observation is that the objective of effective conflict management is the successful resolution of disputes, not the elimination of conflict altogether.

The diagnostic element of our summary model contains two important components. First, assessing the source or type of conflict provides insights into the "whys" behind a confrontation. We have considered four common causes of conflict: personal differences, discrepancies in information, role incompatibilities, and environmentally induced stress. These "types" of conflict differ in both frequency and intensity. For example, information-based conflicts occur frequently, but they are easily resolved because disputants have low personal stakes in the outcome. In contrast, conflicts grounded in differences of perceptions and expectations are generally intense and difficult to defuse.

The second important component of the diagnostic process is assessing the relevant situational factors, so as to determine the feasible set of responses. Important contextual factors that we considered included the importance of the issue, the importance of the relationship, the relative power of the disputants, and the degree to which time was a limiting factor.

The purpose of the diagnostic phase of the model is to choose wisely between the five conflict management approaches: avoiding, compromising, collaborating, forcing, and accommodating. These reflect different degrees of assertiveness and cooperativeness, or the priority given to satisfying one's own concerns versus the concerns of the other party, respectively.

As shown in Figure 7.6, personal preferences, reflecting a person's ethnic culture, gender, and personality, play a key role in our conflict management strategies. If we feel comfortable with an approach, we are likely to use it effectively. However, because effective problem solvers use a variety of tools, one shouldn't pass over an appropriate tool because we feel discomfort about it. For this reason, it is important for conflict managers to stretch their natural "comfort zone" through skill development activities.

Figure 7.6 Summary Model of Conflict Management

Diagnosis   Selection   Implementation   Outcome

Type (Source) of conflict

Situational considerations

Personal preferences

Conflict management approach

Collaborative problem-solving process

Dispute resolution

That is why, as shown in the figure, we elected to focus on the implementation of one conflict management approach that is generally the most effective but also often the most challenging—collaborative problem solving. The behaviors guidelines we provide below reflect our emphasis on collaborative problem solving as the preferred conflict management strategy when circumstances permit it.

Behavioral Guidelines

Effective conflict management involves both good analysis and skillful behaviors. The analytic process involves diagnosing the causes of a conflict and understanding the situational factors that help you select the appropriate conflict management strategy. The behavior element involves implementing the chosen strategy effectively to reach a successful resolution of the dispute.

Behavioral guidelines for the diagnostic aspect of conflict management include the following:

A. Collect information on the sources of conflict. Identify the source by examining the focus of the dispute. The four sources or types of conflict are: personal differences (perception and expectations), information deficiency (misinformation and misinterpretation), role incompatibility (goals and responsibilities), and environmental stress (resource scarcity and uncertainty).

B. Examine relevant situational factors, including the importance of the issue, the importance of the relationship, the relative power of the disputants, and the degree to which time is a factor.

C. Take into consideration your personal preferences for using the various conflict management approaches. These preferences tend to reflect important elements of your personal identity, including ethnic culture, gender, and personality.

D. Utilize the collaborative approach for managing conflict unless specific conditions dictate the use of an alternative approach.

Behavioral guidelines for the collaborative (problem-solving) strategy for conflict management are summarized below. These are organized according to three roles. Guidelines for the problem-identification and solution-generation phases of the problem-solving process are specified for each role. Guidelines for the action plan and follow-up phases are the same for all three roles.

INITIATOR
Problem Identification

A. Maintain personal ownership of the problem.
- ❑ Succinctly describe your problem in terms of behaviors, consequences, and feelings. ("When you do X, Y happens, and I feel Z.")
- ❑ Stick to the facts (e.g., use a specific incident to illustrate the expectations or standards violated).
- ❑ Avoid drawing evaluative conclusions and attributing motives to the respondent.

B. Persist until understood; encourage two-way discussion.
- ❑ Restate your concerns or give additional examples.
- ❑ Avoid introducing additional issues or letting frustration sour your emotional tone.
- ❑ Invite the respondent to ask questions and express another perspective.

C. Manage the agenda carefully.
- ❑ Approach multiple problems incrementally, proceeding from simple to complex, easy to difficult, concrete to abstract.
- ❑ Don't become fixated on a single issue. If you reach an impasse, expand the discussion to increase the likelihood of an integrative outcome.

Solution Generation

A. Make a request.
- ❑ Focus on those things you share in common (principles, goals, constraints) as the basis for recommending preferred alternatives.

RESPONDER
Problem Identification

A. Establish a climate for joint problem solving.
- ❑ Show genuine concern and interest. Respond empathetically, even if you disagree with the complaint.
- ❑ Respond appropriately to the initiator's emotions. If necessary, let the person "blow off steam" before addressing the complaint.

B. Seek additional information about the problem.
- ❑ Ask questions that channel the initiator's statements from general to specific and from evaluative to descriptive.

C. Agree with some aspect of the complaint.
- ❑ Signal your willingness to consider making changes by agreeing with facts, perceptions, feelings, or principles.

Solution Generation

A. Ask for suggestions and recommendations.
- ❑ To avoid debating the merits of a single suggestion, brainstorm multiple alternatives.

MEDIATOR
Problem Identification

A. Acknowledge that a conflict exists.
- ❏ Select the most appropriate setting (one-on-one conference versus group meeting) for coaching and fact-finding.
- ❏ Propose a problem-solving approach for resolving the dispute.

B. Maintain a neutral posture.
- ❏ Assume the role of facilitator, not judge. Do not belittle the problem or berate the disputants for their inability to resolve their differences.
- ❏ Be impartial toward disputants and issues (provided policy has not been violated).
- ❏ If correction is necessary, do it in private.

C. Manage the discussion to ensure fairness.
- ❏ Focus discussion on the conflict's impact on performance and the detrimental effect of continued conflict.
- ❏ Keep the discussion issue oriented, not personality oriented.
- ❏ Do not allow one party to dominate the discussion. Ask directed questions to maintain balance.

Solution Generation

A. Explore options by focusing on the interests behind stated positions.
- ❏ Explore the "whys" behind disputants' arguments or demands.
- ❏ Help disputants see commonalities among their goals, values, and principles.
- ❏ Use commonalities to generate multiple alternatives.
- ❏ Maintain a nonjudgmental manner.

ALL ROLES
Action Plan and Follow-Up

A. Ensure that all parties support the agreed-upon plan.
- ❏ Make sure the plan is adequately detailed (Who, What, How, When, and Where).
- ❏ Verify understanding of, and commitment to, each specific action.

B. Establish a mechanism for follow-up.
- ❏ Create benchmarks for measuring progress and ensuring accountability.
- ❏ Encourage flexibility in adjusting the plan to meet emerging circumstances.

CASE INVOLVING INTERPERSONAL CONFLICT

Educational Pension Investments

Educational Pension Investments (EPI), located in New York, invests pension funds for educational institutions. It employs approximately 75 people, 25 of whom are responsible for actual investment activities. The company manages about $5 billion of assets and derived an income of about $10 million.

The firm was incorporated almost 30 years ago by a group of academic professionals who wanted to control the destiny of their retirement years by pursuing investments that would be consistent and safe. The firm has weathered rapid technological change and economic volatility. Leadership has consistently resisted opportunities to "make it big" and instead stayed with less profitable but relatively secure investments.

Dan Richardson has an MBA from Wharton and is one of the founders of EPI. He started out working in the research department and has worked in every department since then. The other partners, comfortable with Dan's conservative yet flexible nature, elected him to the position of CEO 13 years ago. After that, Dan became known as "the great equalizer." He works hard to make sure that all the partners are included in decisions. Over the years, he has become the confidant of the other seniors and the mentor of the next generation. EPI's employees look to Dan for leadership and direction. Dan's management philosophy is built on the concept of loyalty. As he is fond of saying, "My dad was a small town banker. He told me, 'Look out for the other guys and they'll look out for you.' Sounds corny, I know, but I firmly believe in this philosophy."

Given Dan's practice of consistent and safe investing, EPI's growth has not kept pace with other investment opportunities. As a result, Dan has reluctantly begun to consider the merits of a more aggressive investment approach. Part of Dan's reconsideration is that several of the younger analysts are beginning to refer to EPI as "stodgy." Some are leaving EPI for positions in more aggressive firms.

One evening, Dan talked about his concern with his racquetball partner and longtime friend, Mike Roth. Mike also happened to be an investment broker in another firm. An MBA graduate from the University of Illinois, Mike's accomplishments in research had brought him widespread recognition. Everyone respected him for his knowledge, his work ethic, and his uncanny ability to predict trends.

When Mike heard Dan's concerns about EPI's image and need for an aggressive approach, he suggested to his friend that what EPI needed was some fresh blood, someone who could infuse enthusiasm into the organization—someone like him. He told Dan, "I can help you get things moving. In fact, I've been developing some concepts that would be perfect for EPI."

Dan brought up the idea of hiring Mike at the next staff meeting, but the idea was met with caution and skepticism. "Sure, he's had a brilliant career on paper," said one senior partner. "But he's never stayed in one place long enough to really validate his success. Look at his résumé. During the past seven years, he's been with four different firms, in four different positions."

"That's true," said Dan, "but his references all check out. In fact, he's been described as a rising star, aggressive, productive. He's just what we need to help us explore new opportunities."

Another partner responded, "A friend of mine worked with Mike a while back and said that while he is definitely good, he's a real maverick—in terms of both investment philosophy and lifestyle. Is that what we really want at EPI?"

Throughout the discussion, Dan defended Mike's work record. He repeatedly pointed out Mike's impressive performance. He deflected concerns about Mike's reputation by saying that he was a loyal and trusted friend. Largely on Dan's recommendation, the other partners agreed, although somewhat reluctantly, to hire Mike. When Dan offered Mike the job, he promised Mike the freedom and flexibility to operate a segment of the fund as he desired.

Mike took the job and performed his responsibilities at EPI in a superior manner. Indeed, he was largely responsible for increasing the managed assets of the company by 150 percent. However, this increase came at a price. From the day Mike moved in, junior analysts enjoyed working with him very much. They liked his fresh, new approach, and were encouraged by the spectacular results. This caused jealousy among the other partners, who thought Mike was pushing too hard to change the tried-and-true traditions of the firm. It was not uncommon for sharp disagreements to erupt in staff meetings, with one or another partner coming close to storming out of the room. Throughout this time, Dan tried to soothe ruffled feathers and maintain an atmosphere of trust and loyalty.

Mike seemed oblivious to all the turmoil he was causing. He was optimistic about potential growth opportunities. He believed that voice-activated technology, 3-D printing, and cloud databases were the "waves of the future." Because of this belief, he wanted to direct the focus of his portfolio toward these emerging technologies. "Investments in small firm stocks in these industries, coupled with an aggressive market timing strategy, should yield a 50 percent increase in performance." He rallied support for this idea not only among the younger members of EPI, but also with the pension fund managers who invested with EPI. Mike championed his position and openly questioned the traditional philosophy. "We should compromise on conservatism and achieve some real growth while we can," Mike argued. "If we don't, we'll lose the investors' confidence and ultimately lose them."

Most of the senior partners disagreed with Mike, stating that the majority of their investors emphasized security above all else. They also disagreed with the projected profits, stating that "We could go from 8 to 12 percent return on investment (ROI); then again, we could drop to 4 percent. A lot depends on whose data you use." They reminded Mike, "The fundamental approach of the corporation is to provide safe and moderate-income mutual funds for academic pension funds to invest in. That's the philosophy we used to solicit the investments originally, and that's the approach we are obligated to maintain."

Months passed, and dissension among the managers grew. Mike began to criticize his detractors openly as he talked with younger EPI employees. In addition, he assigned research department employees to focus on high-tech investments, distracting them from investigating more traditional investments. This disrupted the operations of other EPI managers because their funds relied on timely input from the researchers and other support staff. Amidst a rapidly spreading undercurrent of tension, one of the founding partners, Tom Watson, approached Dan one day. Conservative in his ways, Watson was the partner who walks the office and always has time to stop and chat. He began the conversation.

"Dan, I speak for most of the senior staff when I say that we are very troubled by Mike's approach. We've expressed ourselves well enough for Mike to understand, but his actions defy everything we've said. He's a catastrophe just waiting to happen."

"I can understand your concern, Tom," replied Dan. "I'm troubled, too. We have an opportunity to attract new business with some of Mike's new ideas. And the younger staff love working on his projects. But he has stirred up a lot of turmoil."

Tom agreed. "The real issue is that EPI is no longer presenting a unified image. Mike is willfully defying the stated objectives of our organization. And some of our oldest clients don't like that."

"That's true, Tom. On the other hand, some of our newer clients are really encouraged by Mike's approach—and his track record is extremely impressive."

"Come on, Dan. You and I both know that many experts feel the market is overheating. Mike's paper profits could quickly be incinerated if the budget and trade deficits don't turn around. We can't stake the reputation of the firm on a few high-flying technology stocks. Dan, the other senior partners agree. Mike must either conform to the philosophy and management practices of this organization or else resign."

Reflecting on the situation, Dan realized he faced the most difficult challenge of his career. He felt a strong personal investment in helping Mike succeed. Not only had he hired Mike over the objections of several colleagues; he had personally helped him "learn the ropes" at EPI. Beyond that, Dan was haunted by his promise to Mike that he would have the freedom and flexibility to perform the requirements of the position as he pleased. However, this flexibility had clearly caused problems within EPI.

Finally, bowing to the pressure of his peers, Dan called Mike in for a meeting, hoping to find some basis for compromise. Their conversation proceeded as follows:

DAN: I gather you know the kinds of concerns the senior partners have expressed regarding your approach.

MIKE: I guess you've talked with Tom. Well, we did have a small disagreement earlier this week.

DAN: The way Tom tells it, you're willfully defying corporate objectives and being insubordinate.

MIKE: Well, it's just like Watson to see progressive change as an attempt to take away his power.

DAN: It's not quite that simple, Mike. When we founded EPI, we all agreed that a conservative stance was best. And right now, with the economic indicators looking soft, many experts agree that it may still be the best alternative.

MIKE: Dan, what are you going to rely on—predictions or performance? These concerns are just smokescreens to deflect attention away from the sub-par records of other portfolio managers. Old views need to be challenged and ultimately discarded. How else are we going to progress and keep up with our competitors?

DAN: I agree we need to change, Mike—but gradually. You have great ideas and terrific instincts, but you can't change a 30-year-old firm overnight. You can help me promote change, but you're pushing so fast, others are digging in their heels. The rate of change is just as important as the direction.

MIKE: You're telling me. And at this rate, it doesn't make much difference which direction we're headed in.

DAN: Come on, Mike. Don't be so cynical. If you'd just stop rubbing people's noses in your performance record and try to see things from their perspective, we could calm things down around here. Then maybe we could start building consensus. (*Mike's emotions betray his impatience with the pace of the organization; he becomes agitated.*)

MIKE: I've always admired your judgment, and I value your friendship, but I honestly think you're kidding yourself. You seem to think you can get this firm to look like it's progressive—shrugging off its stodgy image—without taking any risks or ruffling any feathers. Are you interested in appearance or substance? If you want appearance, then hire a good PR person. If you want substance, then back me up and we'll rewrite the record book. Get off the fence, Dan, before your butt's full of slivers.

DAN: Mike, it simply isn't that easy. I'm not EPI, I'm simply its caretaker. You know we make decisions around here by consensus; that's the backbone of this organization. To move ahead, the confidence of the others has to be won, especially the confidence of the seniors. Frankly, your reputation as a maverick makes it hard to foster confidence in, and loyalty to, your plans.

MIKE: You knew my style when you hired me. Remember how you made it a point to promise me flexibility and autonomy? I'm not getting that any more, Dan. All I'm getting is grief, even though I'm running circles around your conservative cronies.

DAN: Well, that may be true. But your flamboyance...

ANALYSIS

MIKE: Oh, yeah. The sports car, the singles lifestyle, the messy office. But, again, that's appearance, Dan, not substance. Performance is what counts. That's what got me this far, and that's my ticket out. You know I could walk into any firm in town and write my own plan.

DAN: Well, there's no reason to be hasty.

MIKE: Do you honestly believe this can be salvaged? I think not. Maybe it's time for me to be moving on. Isn't that why you called me in here anyway? (*Dan, feeling uncomfortable, breaks eye contact and shifts his gaze to the New York skyline. After a long pause, he continues, still gazing out of the window.*)

DAN: I don't know, Mike. I feel I've failed. My grand experiment in change has polarized the office; we've got two armies at war out there. On the other hand, you really have done a good job here. EPI will no doubt lose a good part of its customer base if you leave. You have a loyal following, with both customers and staff. If you go, so do they—along with our shot at changing our image.

MIKE: It's just like you, Dan, to take this problem personally. Blast it, you take everything personally. Even when I beat you at racquetball. Your heart's in the right place—you just can't ever seem to make the cutthroat hit. You know and I know that EPI needs a change in image. But it doesn't appear to be ready for it yet. And I'm certainly not willing to move slowly.

DAN: Yeah. Maybe. It's just hard to give up... [long pause]. Well, why don't we talk more about this after the reception tonight? Come on over and see Joanie and the kids. Besides, I'm dying to show off my new boat.

MIKE: What you see in sailing is beyond me. It's a waste of time, lazily drifting on gentle breezes.

DAN: Save it for later, "Speed King." I've got to get ready for tonight.

Discussion Questions

7.1. What are the sources of conflict in this case?

7.2. What approaches to conflict management are used by the actors in this situation? How effective was each?

7.3. Based on the behavioral guidelines for the collaborative approach, how could Dan have managed this conflict more effectively?

EXERCISE FOR DIAGNOSING SOURCES OF CONFLICT

SSS Software Management Problems

In order to manage conflict between others effectively, it is important to be aware of early warning signs. It is also important to understand the underlying causes of disagreements. Conflict that is unmanaged, or managed ineffectively, interferes with work-group performance. A key to managing conflict effectively is recognizing it in its early stages and understanding its roots.

Assignment

Read the memos, faxes, voice mail, and email messages that follow. As you examine each of these documents, look for evidence of organizational conflicts. Identify the two conflicts that you think are most significant for you to address in your role as Chris Perillo. Begin your analysis of these conflicts by identifying their likely sources or causes. Use Figure 7.2 as a diagnostic tool for identifying the type of conflict, based on its source and focus. Prepare to present your analysis, along with supporting evidence from the memos. Also, share your ideas regarding how this analysis of the causes of conflict would influence your approach to resolving the conflict.

SSS Software In-Basket Memos, E-mails, Faxes, and Voice Mails

ITEM 1 – EMAIL

TO: All Employees
FROM: Roger Steiner, Chief Executive Officer
DATE: October 15

I am pleased to announce that Chris Perillo has been appointed as Vice President of Operations for Health and Financial Services. Chris will immediately assume responsibility for all operations previously managed by Michael Grant. Chris will have end-to-end responsibility for the design, development, integration, and maintenance of custom software for the health and finance/banking industries. This responsibility includes all technical, financial, and staffing issues. Chris will also manage our program of software support and integration for the recently announced merger of three large health maintenance organizations (HMOs). Chris will be responsible for our recently announced project with a consortium of banks and financial firms operating in Tanzania. This project represents an exciting opportunity for us, and Chris's background seems ideally suited to the task.

Chris comes to this position with an undergraduate degree in Computer Science from the California Institute of Technology and an MBA from the University of Virginia. Chris began as a member of our technical/professional staff six years ago and has most recently served for three years as a group manager supporting domestic and international projects for our airlines industry group, including our recent work for the European Airbus consortium.

I am sure you all join me in offering congratulations to Chris for this promotion.

ITEM 2 – EMAIL

TO: All Managers
FROM: Hal Harris, Vice President, Community and Public Relations
DATE: October 15

For your information, the following article appeared on the front page of the business section of Thursday's *Los Angeles Times*.

In a move that may create problems for SSS Software, Michael Grant and Janice Ramos have left SSS Software and moved to Universal Business Solutions Inc. Industry analysts see the move as another victory for Universal Business Solutions Inc. in their battle with SSS Software for share of the growing software development and integration business. Both Grant and Ramos had been with SSS Software for over seven years.

Grant was most recently Vice President of Operations for all SSS Software's work in two industries: health and hospitals, and finance and banking. Ramos brings to Universal Business Solutions Inc. her special expertise in the growing area of international software development and integration.

Hillary Collins, an industry analyst with Merrill Lynch, said "the loss of key staff to a competitor can often create serious problems for a firm such as SSS Software. Grant and Ramos have an insider's understanding of SSS Software's strategic and technical limitations. It will be interesting to see if they can exploit this knowledge to the advantage of Universal Business Solutions Inc."

ITEM 3 – EMAIL

TO: Chris Perillo
FROM: Paula Sprague, Executive Assistant to Roger Steiner
DATE: October 15

Chris, I know that in your former position as a group manager in the Airline Services Division, you probably have met most of the group managers in the Health and Financial Services Division, but I thought you might like some more personal information about them. These people will be your direct reports on the management team.

Group #1: Bob Miller, 55-year-old white male, married (Anna) with two children and three grandchildren. Active in local Republican politics. Well regarded as a "hands-off" manager heading a high-performing team. Plays golf regularly with Mark McIntyre, John Small, and a couple of VPs from other divisions.

Group #2: Wanda Manners, 38-year-old white female, single with one school-age child. A fitness "nut" and has run in several marathons. Some experience in Germany and Japan. Considered a hard-driving manager with a constant focus on the task at hand. Will be the first person to show up every morning.

Group #3: William Chen, 31-year-old male of Chinese descent, married (Harriet), two young children from his first marriage. Enjoys tennis and is quite good at it. A rising star in the company, he is highly respected by his peers as a "man of action" and a good friend.

Group #4: Leo Jones, 36-year-old white male, married (Janet) with an infant daughter. Recently returned from paternity leave. Has traveled extensively on projects since he speaks three languages. Has liked hockey ever since the time he spent in Montreal. Considered a strong manager who gets the most out of his people.

Group #5: Mark McIntyre, 45-year-old white male, married (Mary Theresa) to an executive in the banking industry. No children. A lot of experience in Germany and Eastern Europe. Has been writing a mystery novel. Has always been a good "team player," but several members of his technical staff are not well respected and he hasn't addressed the problem.

Group #6: John Small, 38-year-old white male, recently divorced. Three children living with his wife. A gregarious individual who likes sports. He spent a lot of time in Mexico and Central America before he came to SSS Software. Recently has been doing mostly contract work with the federal government. An average manager, has had some trouble keeping his people on schedule.

Group #7: This position vacant since Janice Ramos left. Roger thinks we ought to fill this position quickly. Get in touch with me if you want information on any in-house candidates for any position.

Group #8: Marcus Harper, 42-year-old African American male, married (Tamara) with two teenage children. Recently won an award in a local photography contest. Considered a strong manager who gets along with peers and works long hours.

Customer Services: Armand Marke, 38-year-old male, divorced. A basketball fan. Originally from Armenia. Previously a group manager. Worked hard to establish the Technical Services Phone Line, but now has pretty much left it alone.

Office Administrator: Michelle Harrison, 41-year-old white female, single. Grew up on a ranch and still rides horses whenever she can. A strict administrator.

There are a number of good folks here, but they don't function well as a management team. I think Michael played favorites, especially with Janice and Leo. There are a few cliques in this group, and I'm not sure how effectively Michael dealt with them. I expect you will find it a challenge to build a cohesive team.

ITEM 4 – EMAIL

TO: Chris Perillo
FROM: Wanda Manners, Group 2 Manager
DATE: October 15

CONFIDENTIAL AND RESTRICTED

Although I know you are new to your job, I feel it is important that I let you know about some information I just obtained concerning the development work we recently completed for First National Investment. Our project involved the development of asset management software for managing their international funds. This was a very complex project due to the volatile exchange rates and the forecasting tools we needed to develop.

As part of this project, we had to integrate the software and reports with all their existing systems and reporting mechanisms. To do this, we were given access to all of their existing software (much of which was developed by Universal Business Solutions Inc.). Of course, we signed an agreement acknowledging that the software to which we were given access was proprietary and that our access was solely for the purpose of our system integration work associated with the project.

Unfortunately, I have learned that some parts of the software we developed actually "borrow" heavily from complex application programs developed for First National Investment by Universal Business Solutions Inc. It seems obvious to me that one or more of the software developers from Group 5 (that is, Mark McIntyre's group) inappropriately "borrowed" algorithms developed by Universal Business Solutions Inc. I am sure that doing so saved us significant development time on some aspects of the project. It seems very unlikely that First National Investment or Universal Business Solutions Inc. will ever become aware of this issue.

Finally, First National Investment is successfully using the software we developed and is thrilled with the work we did. We brought the project in on time and under budget. You probably know that they have invited us to bid on several other substantial projects.

I'm sorry to bring this delicate matter to your attention, but I thought you should know about it.

ITEM 5A – EMAIL

TO: Chris Perillo
FROM: Paula Sprague, Executive Assistant to Roger Steiner
DATE: October 15
RE: Letter from C.A.R.E. Services (copies attached)

Roger asked me to work on this C.A.R.E. project and obviously wants some fast action. A lot of the staff are already booked solid for the next couple of weeks. I knew that Elise Soto and Chu Hung Woo have the expertise to do this system and when I checked with them, they were relatively free. I had them pencil in the next two weeks and wanted to let you know. Hopefully, it will take a "hot potato" out of your hands.

ITEM 5B – COPY OF FAX

C.A.R.E.
Child and Adolescent Rehabilitative and Educational Services
A United Way Member Agency
200 Main Street
Los Angeles, California 90230

DATE: October 11
Roger Steiner, CEO
SSS Software
13 Miller Way
Los Angeles, California 90224

Dear Roger,

This letter is a follow-up to our conversation after last night's board meeting. I appreciated your comments during the board meeting about the need for sophisticated computer systems in nonprofit organizations and I especially appreciate your generous offer of help to have SSS Software provide assistance to deal with the immediate problem with our accounting system. Since the board voted to fire the computer consultant, I am very worried about getting our reports done in time to meet the state funding cycle.

Thanks again for your offer of help during this crisis.

Sincerely yours,

Janice Polocizwic

Janice Polocizwic
Executive Director

ITEM 5C – COPY OF A LETTER

SSS SOFTWARE
13 Miller Way
Los Angeles, CA 90224

DATE: October 12

Janice Polocizwic
Executive Director, C.A.R.E. Services
200 Main Street
Los Angeles, California 90230

Dear Janice,

I received your fax of October 11. I have asked Paula Sprague, my executive assistant, to line up people to work on your accounting system as soon as possible. You can expect to hear from her shortly.

Sincerely,

Roger Steiner

Roger Steiner
cc: Paula Sprague, Executive Assistant

ITEM 6 – E-MAIL

TO: Michael Grant
FROM: Harry Withers, Group 6 Technical Staff
DATE: October 12

PERSONAL AND CONFIDENTIAL

Our team is having difficulty meeting the submission deadline of November 5 for the Halstrom project. Kim, Fred, Peter, Kyoto, Susan, Mala, and I have been working on the project for several weeks, but we are experiencing some problems and may need additional time. I hesitate to write this letter, but the main problem is that our group manager, John Small, is involved in a relationship with Mala. Mala gets John's support for her ideas and brings them to the team as required components of the project. Needless to say, this has posed some problems for the group. Mala's background is especially valuable for this project, but Kim and Fred, who have both worked very hard on the project, do not want to work with her. In addition, one member of the team has been unavailable recently because of child-care needs. Commitment to the project and team morale have plummeted. However, we'll do our best to get the project finished as soon as possible. Mala will be on vacation the next two weeks, so I'm expecting that some of us can complete it in her absence.

ITEM 7 – VOICE MAIL MESSAGE

Hello, Michael. This is Jim Bishop of United Hospitals. I wanted to talk with you about the quality assurance project that you are working on for us. When Jose Martinez first started talking with us, I was impressed with his friendliness and expertise. But recently, he doesn't seem to be getting much accomplished and has seemed distant and on-edge in conversations. Today, I asked him about the schedule and he seemed very defensive and not entirely in control of his emotions. I am quite concerned about our project. Please give me a call.

ITEM 8 – VOICE MAIL MESSAGE

Hi, Michael. This is Armand. I wanted to talk with you about some issues with the Technical Services Phone Line. I've recently received some complaint letters from Phone Line customers whose complaints have included long delays while waiting for a technician to answer the phone, technicians who are not knowledgeable enough to solve problems, and, on occasion, rude service. Needless to say, I'm quite concerned about these complaints.

I believe that the overall quality of the Phone Line staff is very good, but we continue to be understaffed, even with the recent hires. The new technicians look strong, but are working on the help-line before being fully trained. Antolina, our best tech, often brings her child to work, which is adding to the craziness around here.

I think you should know that we're feeling a lot of stress here. I'll talk with you soon.

ITEM 9 – VOICE MAIL MESSAGE

Hi, Chris, it's Pat. Congratulations on your promotion. They definitely picked the right person. It's great news—for me, too. You've been a terrific mentor so far, so I'm expecting to learn a lot from you in your new position. How about lunch next week?

ITEM 10 – VOICE MAIL MESSAGE

Chris, this is Bob Miller. Just thought you'd like to know that John's joke during our planning meeting has disturbed a few of the women in my group. Frankly, I think the thing's being blown out of proportion, especially since we all know this is a good place for both men and women to work. Give me a call if you want to chat about this.

ITEM 11 – VOICE MAIL MESSAGE

Hello. This is Lorraine Adams from Westside Hospital. I read in today's *Los Angeles Times* that you will be taking over from Michael Grant. We haven't met yet, but your division has recently finished two large million-dollar projects for Westside. Michael Grant and I had some discussion about a small conversion of a piece of existing software to be compatible with the new systems. The original vendor had said that they would do the work, but they have been stalling, and I need to move quickly. Can you see if Harris Wilson, Chu Hung Woo, and Elise Soto are available to do this work as soon as possible? They were on the original project and work well with our people.

Um...(long pause) I guess I should tell you that I got a call from Michael offering to do this work. But I think I should stick with SSS Software. Give me a call.

ITEM 12 – VOICE MAIL MESSAGE

Hi, Chris, this is Roosevelt Moore calling. I'm a member of your technical/professional staff. I used to report to Janice Ramos, but since she left the firm, I thought I'd bring my concerns directly to you. I'd like to arrange some time to talk with you about my experiences since returning from six weeks of paternity leave. Some of my major responsibilities have been turned over to others. I seem to be out of the loop and wonder if my career is at risk. Also, I am afraid that I won't be supported or seriously considered for the opening created by Janice's departure. Frankly, I feel like I'm being screwed for taking my leave. I'd like to talk with you this week.

ITEM 13 – EMAIL

TO: Michael Grant
FROM: Jose Martinez, Group 1 Technical Staff
DATE: October 12

I would like to set up a meeting with you as soon as possible. I suspect that you will get a call from Jim Bishop of United Hospitals and want to be sure that you hear my side of the story first. I have been working on a customized system design for quality assurance for them using a variation of the J-3 product we developed several years ago. They had a number of special requirements and some quirks in their accounting systems, so I have had to put in especially long hours. I've worked hard to meet their demands, but they keep changing the ground rules. I keep thinking, this is just another J-3 I'm working on, but they have been interfering with an elegant design I have developed. It seems I'm not getting anywhere on this project. Earlier today, I had a difficult discussion with their Controller. He asked for another major change. I've been fighting their deadline and think I am just stretched too thin on this project. Then Jim Bishop asked me if the system was running yet. I was worn out from dealing with the Controller, and I made a sarcastic comment to Jim Bishop. He gave me a funny look and just walked out of the room.

I would like to talk with you about this situation at your earliest convenience.

ITEM 14 – EMAIL

TO: Chris Perillo
FROM: John Small, Group 6 Manager
DATE: October 15

Welcome aboard, Chris. I look forward to meeting with you. I just wanted to put a bug in your ear about finding a replacement for Janice Ramos. One of my technical staff, Mala Abendano, has the ability and drive to make an excellent group manager. I have encouraged her to apply for the position. I'd be happy to talk with you further about this, at your convenience.

ITEM 15 – EMAIL

TO: Chris Perillo
FROM: Paula Sprague, Executive Assistant to Roger Steiner
DATE: October 15

Roger asked me to let you know about the large contract we have gotten in Tanzania. It means that a team of four managers will be making a short trip to determine current needs. They will assign their technical staff the tasks of developing a system and software here over the next six months, and then the managers and possibly some team members will be spending about 10 months on site in Tanzania to handle the implementation. Roger thought you might want to hold an initial meeting with some of your managers to check on their interest and willingness to take this sort of assignment. Roger would appreciate an e-mail of your thoughts about the issues to be discussed at this meeting, additional considerations about sending people to Tanzania, and about how you will put together an effective team to work on this project. The October 15 memo I sent to you will provide you with some information you'll need to start making these decisions.

ITEM 16 – EMAIL

TO: Chris Perillo
FROM: Sharon Shapiro, VP of Human Resources
DATE: October 15

RE: Upcoming meeting

I want to update you on the rippling effect of John Small's sexual joke at last week's planning meeting. Quite a few women have been very upset and have met informally to talk about it. They have decided to call a meeting of all people concerned about this kind of behavior throughout the firm. I plan to attend, so I'll keep you posted.

ITEM 17 – EMAIL

TO: All SSS Software Managers
FROM: Sharon Shapiro, VP of Human Resources
DATE: October 15
RE: Promotions and External Hires

Year-to-Date (January through September) Promotions and External Hires

Level	White	African American	Asian	Hispanic	Native American	M	F	Total
			Race				Sex	
Hires into Executive Level	0 (0%)	0 (0%)	0 (0%)	0 (0%)	0 (0%)	0 (0%)	0 (0%)	0
Promotions to Executive Level	0 (0%)	0 (0%)	0 (0%)	0 . (0%)	0 (0%)	0 (0%)	0 (0%)	0
Hires into Management Level	2 (67%)	1 (33%)	0 (0%)	0 (0%)	0 (0%)	2 (67%)	1 (33%)	3
Promotions to Management Level	7 (88%)	0 (0%)	1 (12%)	0 (0%)	0 (0%)	7 (88%)	1 (12%)	8
Hires into Technical/ Professional Level	10 (36%)	6 (21%)	10 (36%)	2 (7%)	0 (0%)	14 (50%)	14 (50%)	28
Promotions to Technical/ Professional Level	0 (0%)	0 (0%)	0 (0%)	0 (0%)	0 (0%)	0 (0%)	0 (0%)	0
Hires into Non-management Level	4 (20%)	10 (50%)	2 (10%)	4 (20%)	0 (0%)	6 (30%)	14 (70%)	20
Promotions to Non-management Level	NA	NA	NA	NA	NA	NA	NA	NA

SSS Software Employee (EEO) Classification Report as of June 30

Level	White	African American	Asian	Hispanic	Native American	M	F	Total
			Race				*Sex*	
Executive Level	11 (92%)	0 (0%)	1 (8%)	0 (0%)	0 (0%)	11 (92%)	1 (8%)	12
Management Level	43 (90%)	2 (4%)	2 (4%)	1 (2%)	0 (0%)	38 (79%)	10 (21%)	48
Technical/ Professional Level	58 (45%)	20 (15%)	37 (28%)	14 (11%)	1 (1%)	80 (62%)	50 (38%)	130
Non-management Level	29 (48%)	22 (37%)	4 (7%)	4 (7%)	1 (2%)	12 (20%)	48 (80%)	60
Total	141 (56%)	44 (18%)	44 (18%)	19 (8%)	2 (1%)	141 (56%)	109 (44%)	250

NOTE: The SSS Software exercise is used with permission. Copyright © 1995 by Susan Schor, Joseph Seltzer, and James Smither. All rights reserved.

EXERCISES FOR SELECTING AN APPROPRIATE CONFLICT MANAGEMENT STRATEGY

Not all conflicts are alike; therefore, they cannot all be managed in exactly the same way. Effective managers are able to assess accurately the true causes of conflict and to match each type of conflict with an appropriate management strategy.

Assignment

For each of the following brief scenarios, select the most appropriate conflict management strategy. Refer to Table 4 for assistance in matching situational factors with strategies.

Bradley's Barn

You have decided to take your family out to the local steakhouse, Bradley's Barn, to celebrate your son's birthday. You are a single parent, so getting home from work in time to prepare a nice dinner is very difficult. On entering the restaurant, you ask the hostess to seat you in the nonsmoking section because your daughter, Shauna, is allergic to tobacco smoke. On your way to your seat, you notice that the restaurant seems crowded for a Monday night.

After you and your children are seated and have placed your orders, your conversation turns to family plans for the approaching holiday. Interspersed in the general conversation is a light banter with your son about whether or not he is too old to wear "the crown" during dinner—a family tradition on birthdays.

Suddenly, you become aware that your daughter is sneezing and her eyes are beginning to water. You look around and notice a lively group of businesspeople seated at the table behind you; they are all smoking. Your impression is that they are celebrating some type of special occasion. Looking back at Shauna, you realize that something has to be done quickly. You ask your son to escort Shauna outside while you rush to the front of the restaurant and find the hostess.

Discussion Questions

7.4. What are the salient situational factors?

7.5. What is the most appropriate conflict management strategy?

Avocado Computers

When the head of Avocado Computers ran into operational problems at his production facility, he hired you away from a competitor. It meant a significant increase in pay and the opportunity to manage a state-of-the-art production facility. What's more, there were very few other female production managers in Silicon Valley. Now you've been on the job a year, and it's been exciting to see your staff start working together as a team to solve problems, improve quality, and finally get the plant up to capacity. In general, Bill, the owner, has also been a plus. He is energetic, fair, and a proven industry leader. You feel fortunate to be in a coveted position, in a "star" firm, in a growth industry.

However, there is one distraction that bugs you. Bill is a real stickler about cleanliness, order, and appearance. He wants the robots all painted the same color, the components within the computer laid out perfectly on a grid, the workers wearing clean smocks, and the floor "clean enough to eat off." You are troubled by this compulsion. "Sure," you think, "it might impress potential corporate clients when they tour the production facility, but is it really that important? After all, who's ever going to look for symmetrical design inside their computer? Why should customers care about the color of the robot that built their computers? And who, for Pete's sake, would ever want to have a picnic in a factory?"

Today is your first yearly performance appraisal interview with Bill. In preparation for the meeting, he has sent you a memo outlining "Areas of Strength" and "Areas of Concern." You look with pride at the number of items listed in the first column. It's obvious that Bill likes your work. But you are a bit miffed at the single item of concern: "Needs to maintain a cleaner facility, including employee appearance." You mull over this "demerit" in your mind, wrestling with how to respond in your interview.

Discussion Questions

7.6. What are the salient situational factors?

7.7. What is the most appropriate conflict management strategy?

Phelps, Inc.

You are Philip Manual, the head of sales for an office products firm, Phelps, Inc. Your personnel sell primarily to small businesses in the Los Angeles metropolitan area. Phelps is doing about average for this rapidly growing market. The firm's new president, Jose Ortega, is putting a lot of pressure on you to increase sales. You feel that a major obstacle is the firm's policy on extending credit. Celeste, the head of the credit office, insists that all new customers fill out an extensive credit application. Credit risks must be low; credit terms and collection procedures are tough. You can appreciate her point of view, but you feel it is unrealistic. Your competitors are much more lenient in their credit examinations; they extend credit to higher risks; their credit terms are more favorable; and they are more lenient in collecting overdue payments. Your sales personnel frequently complain that they aren't "playing on a level field" with their competition. When you brought this concern to Jose, he said he wanted you and Celeste to work things out. His instructions didn't give many clues to his priorities on this matter. "Sure, we need to increase sales, but the small business failure in this area is the highest in the country, so we have to be careful we don't make bad credit decisions."

You decide it's time to have a serious discussion with Celeste. A lot is at stake.

Discussion Questions

7.8. What are the salient situational factors?

7.9. What is the most appropriate conflict management strategy?

EXERCISES FOR RESOLVING INTERPERSONAL DISPUTES

The heart of conflict management is resolving intense, emotionally charged confrontations. We have discussed guidelines for utilizing the collaborative (problem-solving) approach to conflict management in these situations. Assuming that the collaborative approach is appropriate for a particular situation, we have provided general guidelines for the roles of initiator, responder, and mediator.

Assignment

Following are three situations involving interpersonal conflict and disagreement. After you have finished reading the assigned roles, review the appropriate behavioral guidelines. Do not read any of the role descriptions except those assigned to you.

In the first exercise (Alisa Moffatt), students assigned to play Alisa will practice applying the guidelines for the initiator's role. In the second exercise (Can Larry Fit In?), students assigned to play the role of Larry's boss, Melissa, will practice the guidelines for the respondent's role. In the third exercise (Meeting at Hartford Manufacturing Company), students assigned to play the role of Lynn Smith will practice the guidelines for resolving conflicts among subordinates. For each exercise, an observer will be assigned to give students playing the roles of Alisa, Melissa, or Lynn feedback on their performance, using the Observer's Feedback Form at the end of the chapter as their guide.

Alisa Moffatt

Alisa Moffatt, Production Manager, Sunburst Solutions

Alisa Moffatt was born the fourth of 7 children in a low-income family in the deep South. When Alisa was 14, her parents moved the family to rural Wisconsin, hoping for better educational opportunities for their children. The Moffatts chose a neighborhood where the vast majority of the students in the schools were Caucasian. They wanted their children to feel proud of their African American heritage, but they also wanted them to learn to excel in an environment where they were an ethnic minority. Alisa's parents struggled to care for the family while they both filled multiple jobs. They doggedly emphasized the importance of education and insisted on outstanding schoolwork.

PRACTICE

Alisa flourished at her high school, earning one of the top GPAs in her class. She also found a group of supportive friends who were like-minded in their commitment to go to college. Even though she was the only African American in her class, she felt accepted by her peers. But Alisa often sensed that her teachers and school administrators treated her differently. She felt that some of them talked down to her, while others treated her with superficial kindness – as if they had to handle her delicately. In one instance, a school counselor advised Alisa to think about going to a technical college rather than applying for a four-year university because, as he said, "You might find that you fit in better in that sort of environment." The comment infuriated Alisa, because she felt the counselor was judging her by her race. But her parents advised her to let it slide off her back and prove her abilities through her work.

After graduation, Alisa was accepted to several top universities, but decided to stay close to home and attend the University of Wisconsin, majoring in mathematics. Toward the end of her first year of school, and after much personal angst, she decided to openly declare her homosexuality. Alisa's parents initially responded with shock and disappointment, which caused her great emotional turmoil. She was surprised and hurt that some of her new friends seemed no longer to want to associate with her. The following semester, Alisa's grades plummeted, and she found that she had lost interest in her studies. She spent one semester on academic probation, and then changed her major two times. She considered dropping out of school altogether. However, she remembered her parents' commitment to education, and all the sacrifices that they had made for her. Even though they were struggling with her sexual orientation, she wanted to honor her parents' values and pursue her education to forge a better life than her parents had.

With a renewed resolve, Alisa turned her attention back to her studies. She discovered a passion for business and changed her major (yet again) to management. Over time, Alisa's parents became more understanding and supportive. After 5 years of college, Alisa graduated with a 3.4 GPA, a far cry from her original goals, but an accomplishment that she was proud of, considering the adversity she had faced.

After graduating, Alisa considered several job offers, including a fast-track management development program for a major corporation in Chicago. She couldn't stop thinking about her parents, though, and decided that the most important thing she could do was to rebuild her relationship with them. She rejected her lucrative job offers and instead moved back to her hometown and found work in Human Resources at a small production facility there. It was a healing time with her family, but frustrating professionally. Working in a unionized environment, Alisa struggled to gain the respect of the blue-collar workforce. She suspected that both her gender and her skin color had something to do with the fact that employees referred to her as "uppity" and "over her head." And although she kept her sexual orientation to herself in this rather conservative town, she wondered if the occasional snicker meant that people suspected she was gay.

After four years of professional frustration, and at the urging of her parents, Alisa decided to get an MBA. After acing the GMAT, Alisa was accepted into the MBA program at Northwestern University in Chicago. She was invigorated by the intellectual environment of the program, and felt a sense of direction that she had been lacking for years. That first year, Alisa met Jocelyn Walker, an African American doctoral student in chemistry at Northwestern. They became close confidantes, and within a year they had moved in together and entered into a long-term committed relationship. The two graduated together, and Jocelyn received an offer to teach at a college in the Phoenix area. Alisa was thrilled when she was able to land a position at Sunburst Solutions, a high-growth technology firm in Phoenix. She was hired as the manager of one of several production departments, with direct supervision over eight entry-level technicians.

Alisa was surprised to learn that she was the first African American to assume a managerial position in the young firm. She was also the only member of the LGBT community in the management ranks. She found herself being very guarded at work about her sexual orientation, and rarely mentioned Jocelyn to others. Over time, she learned that there was a handful of junior-level technicians who were gay. Two of them told her that it was best not to bring up sexual orientation at Sunburst, however, because of thinly-veiled prejudice. This made Alisa all the more cautious about discussing her personal life at work, and she naturally found herself gravitating toward her gay colleagues on a social level. After six months in the office, however, the director of Alisa's division, Kyle Huang, began making subtle comments to Alisa that suggested he thought she wasn't blending well with her managerial-level colleagues. For instance, one day he said in passing, "So, I guess you'll be having lunch with all your blue-collar friends again today?"

Alisa's relationship with Kyle, who was her direct supervisor, was strained from the very beginning. Kyle was a hard-driven 37-year old "corporate climber" type. He was also openly proud of his conservative social views, and relished political debate. Kyle had the ear of Sunburst's president, who viewed Kyle as a protégé. Alisa felt that Kyle communicated differently with her than he did with the other office managers in his division. He was quicker to correct her, and seemed to second-guess her decisions – sometimes challenging her plans in front of her own employees. Alisa felt that, yet again, she had to go beyond usual standards in order to prove herself.

Alisa's best sounding board about her frustrations was Jocelyn. "I'm so tired of always being second-guessed," Alisa said to Jocelyn one evening. "I feel like I've spent my entire life trying to overcome stereotypes. It's exhausting. I can't just be myself at work. And Kyle treats me like I'm incompetent even though my results are as good as any other manager in the company. His prejudice is so obvious. Today, he announced that he's asking Dale Westlund to be the liaison with a big new client from Texas. Dale was hired at Sunburst the same time as I was, but he has less experience than me. He manages another production department, but my department's product is far more important to the client than his is. And, get this: most of the new client's management team is black. I would have been the obvious choice to represent the company, so it's a slap in the face that he didn't choose me. I have to believe that he's uncomfortable having someone who is gay represent the firm."

"I know what you are talking about," said Jocelyn. "I don't think people always mean to be disrespectful, but they can be pretty transparent about their rejection. Just the other day, I mentioned to one of my senior colleagues that I'm living with my girlfriend. He got this shocked look on his face and then said, 'I wish you hadn't told me that.' I don't think he meant to belittle me, but it felt really hurtful."

"I had something hurtful happen yesterday too," said Alisa pensively. "I was having coffee in the breakroom and I heard one of my fellow managers talking to someone out in the hall. She was complaining that she had just gotten a bad haircut and was saying her hair was now 'as bad as Alisa's—all edgy and butch.' Then she said, 'Maybe she should just have a sex change and get it over with.' I sat there in the break room trying not to cry and wondering if I was back in junior high school. She has no idea I heard her, but still, I'm not sure I'm going to be able to look her in the face now."

"I'm not sure it would do much good to confront her about it anyway," Jocelyn sympathized. "I figure that all I can do is to stay above the fray... treat others with the respect I think we all deserve, and hope that people come to respect me for it. I don't have time to be a successful scholar *and* crusade against every piece of prejudice I see."

Alisa seemed dubious, "But Kyle's biases are holding me back. If I don't confront him about the way he talks down to me, how will other people see me as credible? And it really feels like discrimination to me that he chose Dale over me for the client assignment. I mean, he's using my sexuality as a factor in my career opportunities. At what point do I have to speak up to defend myself?"

PRACTICE

Kyle Huang, Director of Production, Sunburst Solutions

Kyle Huang is a 37-year-old lifelong Arizonan who is the director over several production departments at Sunburst Solutions in Phoenix. He supervises the manager of each department, who in turn supervises anywhere from 8 to 12 entry-level technicians. Kyle has worked at Sunburst for nearly a decade, and has thrived there. The president of the company is a friend of his father, and has treated Kyle as a promising protégé. Kyle expects a promotion to vice president level in the next year or two. One of the objectives he is pursuing to improve his chances for promotion is to increase the diversity of the production division's staff. Sunburst has received complaints from some of its clients, as well as several employees, that the culture of Sunburst is too homogenous. Although Kyle, as a staunch political conservative, chose Sunburst in part because so many people there share his values, he also feels convinced that the company needs to embrace more diverse perspectives to maintain its creativity and competitive edge.

Hiring Alisa Moffatt out of Northwestern University's MBA program was a coup. She is the first African-American hired into the management level at Sunburst, and only the second woman. It wasn't until a couple of months into her employment that Kyle realized Alisa is gay, and living with a same-sex partner – another first in the management ranks. Kyle's conservative upbringing hasn't necessarily equipped him to appreciate Alisa's lifestyle. He feels a little uncomfortable around her and worries about what he will do if she becomes vocal about gay rights in Sunburst's conservative environment. So far, Alisa has never brought this issue up, and he has decided that Alisa's personal life should be a non-issue in the workplace as long as she does her job and doesn't make waves.

Alisa's introduction to Sunburst has been rocky, however. Kyle has noticed that Alisa seems timid and withdrawn in meetings with her fellow managers. Rather than socialize with management, she prefers to spend time with a handful of technicians, some of whom he believes are also gay. Kyle's concern is that Alisa is missing opportunities to network with her colleagues, which means that she hasn't built the level of trust with them that is so important for interdepartmental collaboration.

Kyle has also found that Alisa is difficult to coach. When he gives her constructive advice, she invariably averts her eyes, which makes Kyle wonder if she is rejecting his advice, or not understanding it. He feels like he has to repeat his suggestions to her several times just to make sure it's registering. A couple of times, he has actually lost his cool and expressed impatience toward her in public. He has felt bad about that, but Alisa has never brought it up to him.

Kyle was having a conversation with the Vice President of Production, Howard Graham, when the "Alisa Problem" came up (as it often does). "Look Howard, I still would hire Alisa in a second. I know she's one of the smartest managers we have. She wasn't just a token hire. The problem is that she seems to have come with a chip on her shoulder, and I have no idea how to knock it off."

Howard responded, "I agree. There is untapped potential there. We really need her to be a success story to show that we have a welcoming culture. Are you sure there's nothing more you could be doing to get her out of her shell? Frankly, I was a little surprised that you didn't ask her to be the contact point for our new client in Texas. That might have been a turning point for her if we showed her that sort of trust."

"You know, Howard," Kyle said after some reflection, "I thought long and hard about that one. Alisa does manage a product that matters a lot to the client, so it would have made sense in some ways to assign her. But the reason I asked Dale to do it instead is that I know he can put people at their ease. Dale is probably not as bright as Alisa, and he certainly has less supervisory experience, but he does a great job of building relationships across departments. And then there is the fact that Alisa is gay. Our Texas client is a privately-owned firm that wears its conservative values on its sleeve. I just don't think Alisa will be able to connect with them."

"I get that, Kyle," Howard responds. "But we are possibly setting a precedent here. This assignment could mean that Dale will advance more quickly than Alisa in the organization. If Alisa feels that she is more qualified – and in some ways she is – then she could interpret this decision as discriminatory because of her race... or maybe even her sexual preference."

"That isn't the case at all. I'm making a business decision here." Kyle said adamantly. "I have other plans to help Alisa advance. In fact, I have a special project in mind for her. It will just take me a couple of months before I am ready to go public with it. In the meantime, I need a diplomat for the Texas client. That's why I'm choosing Dale. If Alisa turns this into a race issue – or sexual orientation issue – then she is way off base."

Can Larry Fit In?

Melissa, Office Manager

You are the manager of an auditing team sent to Bangkok, Thailand, to represent a major international accounting firm headquartered in New York. You and Larry, one of your auditors, were sent to Bangkok to set up an auditing operation. Larry is about seven years older than you and has five more years of seniority in the firm. Your relationship has become very strained since you were recently designated as the office manager. You feel you were given the promotion because you have established an excellent working relationship with the Thai staff as well as a broad range of international clients. In contrast, Larry has told other members of the staff that your promotion simply reflects the firm's heavy emphasis on affirmative action. He has tried to isolate you from the all-male accounting staff by focusing discussions on sports, local night spots, and so forth.

You are sitting in your office reading some complicated new reporting procedures that have just arrived from the home office. Your concentration is suddenly interrupted by a loud knock on your door. Without waiting for an invitation to enter, Larry bursts into your office. He is obviously very upset, and it is not difficult for you to surmise why he is in such a nasty mood.

You recently posted the audit assignments for the coming month, and you scheduled Larry for a job you knew he wouldn't like. Larry is one of your senior auditors, and the company norm is that they get the choice assignments. This particular job will require him to spend two weeks away from Bangkok in a remote town, working with a company whose records are notoriously messy.

Unfortunately, you have had to assign several of these less desirable audits to Larry recently because you are short of personnel. But that's not the only reason. You have received several complaints from the junior staff (all Thais) recently that Larry treats them in a condescending manner. They feel he is always looking for an opportunity to boss them around, as if he were their supervisor instead of an experienced, supportive mentor. As a result, your whole operation works more smoothly when you can send Larry out of town on a solo project for several days. It keeps him from coming into your office and telling you how to do your job, and the morale of the rest of the auditing staff is significantly higher.

Larry slams the door and proceeds to express his anger over this assignment.

Larry, Senior Auditor

You are really ticked off! Melissa is deliberately trying to undermine your status in the office. She knows that the company norm is that senior auditors get the better jobs. You've paid your dues, and now you expect to be treated with respect. And this isn't the first time this has happened. Since she was made the office manager, she has tried to keep you out of the office as much as possible. It's as if she doesn't want her rival for leadership of the office around. When you were asked to go to Bangkok, you assumed that you would be made the office manager because of your seniority in the firm. You are certain that the decision to pick Melissa is yet another indication of reverse discrimination against white males.

In staff meetings, Melissa has talked about the need to be sensitive to the feelings of the office staff as well as the clients in this multicultural setting. "Where does she come off preaching about sensitivity! What about my feelings, for heaven's sake?" you wonder. This is nothing more than a straightforward power play. She is probably feeling insecure about being the only female accountant in the office and being promoted over someone with more experience. "Sending me out of town," you decide, "is a clear case of 'out of sight, out of mind.'"

Well, it's not going to happen that easily. You are not going to roll over and let her treat you unfairly. It's time for a showdown. If she doesn't agree to change this assignment and apologize for the way she's been treating you, you're going to register a formal complaint with her boss in the New York office. You are prepared to submit your resignation if the situation doesn't improve.

Meeting at Hartford Manufacturing Company

Hartford Manufacturing Company is the largest subsidiary of Connecticut Industries. Since the end of World War I, when it was formed, Hartford Manufacturing has become an industrial leader in the Northeast. Its sales currently average approximately $25 million a year, with an annual growth of approximately six percent. There are more than 850 employees in production, sales and marketing, accounting, engineering, and management.

Lynn Smith is general manager. He has held his position for a little over two years and is well respected by his subordinates. He has the reputation of being firm but fair. Lynn's training in college was in engineering, so he is technically minded, and he frequently likes to walk around the production area to see for himself how things are going. He has also been known to roll up his sleeves and help work on a problem on the shop floor. He is not opposed to rubbing shoulders with even the lowest-level employees. On the other hand, he tries to run a tight company, and employees pretty well stick to their assigned tasks. He holds high expectations for performance, especially from individuals in management positions.

Richard Hooton is the director of production at Hartford Manufacturing. He has been with the company since he was 19 years old, when he worked on the dock. He has worked himself up through the ranks and now, at age 54, is the oldest of the management personnel. Hooton has his own ideas of how things should be run in production, and he is reluctant to tolerate any intervention from anyone, even Lynn Smith. Because he has been with the company so long, he feels he knows it better than anyone else, and he believes he has had a hand in making it the success that it is. His main goal is to keep production running smoothly and efficiently.

Barbara Price is the director of sales and marketing. She joined the company about 18 months ago, after completing her MBA at Dartmouth. Before going back to school for a graduate degree, she held the position of assistant manager of marketing at Connecticut Industries. Price is a very conscientious employee and is anxious to make a name for herself. Her major objective, which she has never hesitated to make public, is to be a general manager some day. Sales at Hartford Manufacturing have increased in the past year to near-record levels under her guidance.

Chuck Kasper is the regional sales director for the New York region. He reports directly to Barbara Price. The New York region represents the largest market for Hartford

Manufacturing, and Chuck is considered the most competent salesperson in the company. He has built personal relationships with several major clients in his region, and it appears that some sales occur as much because of Chuck Kasper as because of the products of Hartford Manufacturing. Chuck has been with the company for 12 years, all of them in sales.

This is Friday afternoon, and tomorrow Lynn Smith leaves for Copenhagen at noon to attend an important meeting with potential overseas investors. He will be gone for two weeks. Before he leaves, there are several items in his in-basket that must receive attention. He calls a meeting with Richard Hooton and Barbara Price in his office. Just before the meeting begins, Chuck Kasper calls and asks if he may join the meeting for a few minutes, since he is in town and has something important to discuss that involves both Lynn Smith and Richard Hooton. Smith gives permission for him to join the meeting, since there may not be another chance to meet with Kasper before the trip. The meeting convenes, therefore, with Smith, Hooton, Price, and Kasper all in the room.

Assignment

Groups of four individuals should be formed. Each person should take the role of one of the characters in the management staff of Hartford Manufacturing Company. A fifth person should be assigned to serve as an observer to provide feedback at the end of the meeting, using the Observer's Feedback Form at the end of the chapter as a guide. The letters described in the case that were received by Lynn Smith are shown in Figures 7.7, 7.8, and 7.9. Only the person playing the role of Lynn Smith should read the letters, and no one should read the instructions for another staff member's role. (The letters will be introduced by Lynn Smith during the meeting.)

Lynn Smith, General Manager

Three letters arrived today, and you judge them to be sufficiently important to require your attention before you leave on your trip. Each letter represents a problem that requires immediate action, and you need commitments from key staff members to resolve these problems. You are concerned about this meeting because these individuals don't work as well together as you'd like.

For example, Richard Hooton is very difficult to pin down. He always seems suspicious of the motives of others and has a reputation for not making tough decisions. You sometimes wonder how a person could become the head of production in a major manufacturing firm by avoiding controversial issues and blaming others for the results.

In contrast, Barbara Price is very straightforward. You always know exactly where she stands. The problem is that sometimes she doesn't take enough time to study a problem before making a decision. She tends to be impulsive and anxious to make a decision, whether it's the right one or not. Her general approach to resolving disagreements between departments is to seek expedient compromises. You are particularly disturbed by her approach to the sales incentive problem. You felt strongly that something needed to be done to increase sales during the winter months. You reluctantly agreed to the incentive program because you didn't want to dampen her initiative. But you aren't convinced this is the right answer, because, frankly, you're not yet sure what the real problem is.

Chuck Kasper is your typical, aggressive, "take no prisoners" sales manager. He is hard-charging and uncompromising. He is great in the field because he gets the job done, but he sometimes ruffles the feathers of the corporate staff with his uncompromising, "black-and-white" style. He is also fiercely loyal to his sales staff, so you're sure he'll take the complaint about Sam St. Clair hard.

Figure 7.7

T. J. Koppel, Inc.
General Accountants
8381 Spring Street
Hartford, Connecticut 06127

February 10, 2001

Mr. Lynn Smith
General Manager
Hartford Manufacturing Company
7450 Central Avenue
Hartford, CT 06118

Dear Mr. Smith:

As you requested last month, we have now completed our financial audit of Hartford Manufacturing Company. We find accounting procedures and fiscal control to be very satisfactory. A more detailed report of these matters is attached. However, we did discover during our perusal of company records that the production department has consistently incurred cost overruns during the past two quarters. Cost per unit of production is approximately 5 percent over budget. While this is not a serious problem given the financial solvency of your company, we thought it wise to bring it to your attention.

Respectfully,

T. J. Koppel

TJK: srw

In contrast to the styles of these others, you have tried to use an integrating approach to problem solving: focusing on the facts, treating everyone's inputs equally, and keeping conversations about controversial topics problem-focused. One of your goals since taking over this position two years ago is to foster a "team" approach within your staff.

[*Note*: For more information about how you might approach the issues raised by these letters in your staff meeting, review the collaborating approach in Table 7.2 as well as the mediator's behavioral guidelines at the end of the Skill Learning section of this chapter.]

Figure 7.8

ZODIAK INDUSTRIES
6377 Atlantic Avenue
Boston, Massachusetts 02112

February 8, 2001

Mr. Lynn Smith
General Manager
Hartford Manufacturing Company
7450 Central Avenue
Hartford, CT 06118

Dear Mr. Smith:

We have been purchasing your products since 1975, and we have been very satisfied with our relations with your sales personnel. However, we have had a problem of late that requires your attention. Your sales representative for the Boston region, Sam St. Clair, has appeared at our company the last three times looking and smelling like he was under the influence of alcohol. Not only that, but our last order was mistakenly recorded, so we received the wrong quantities of products. I'm sure you don't make it a practice to put your company's reputation in the hands of someone like Sam St. Clair, so I suggest you get someone else to cover this region. We cannot tolerate, and I'm sure other companies in Boston cannot tolerate, this kind of relationship. While we judge your products to be excellent, we will be forced to find other sources if some action is not taken.

Sincerely yours,

Miles Andrew
Chief of Purchasing

:ms

PRACTICE

Richard Hooton, Director of Production

The only times you have had major problems in production were when the young know-it-alls fresh from college have come in and tried to change things. With their progressive management concepts, coupled with fuzzy-headed "interpersonal effectiveness" training, they have more often made a mess of things than helped to improve matters. The best production methods have been practiced for years in the company, and you have yet to see anyone who could improve on your system.

On the other hand, you have respect for Lynn Smith as the general manager. Because he has experience and the right kind of training, and is involved in the production part

Figure 7.9

HARTFORD MANUFACTURING COMPANY
7450 Central Avenue
Hartford, Connecticut 06118

"A subsidiary of CONNECTICUT INDUSTRIES"

Memorandum

TO: Lynn Smith, General Manager
FROM: Barbara Price, General Supervisor, Sales and Marketing
DATE: February 11, 2007

Mr. Smith:

In response to your concerns, we have instituted several incentive programs among our sales force to increase sales during these traditionally slow months. We have set up competition among regions, with the salespeople in the top region being honored in the company newsletter and given engraved plaques. We have instituted a "vacation in Hawaii" award for the top salesperson in the company. And we have instituted cash bonuses for any salesperson who gets a new customer order. However, in the last month these incentives have been in operation, sales have not increased at all. In fact, in two regions they have decreased by an average of 5 percent.

What do you suggest now? We have advertised the incentives as lasting through this quarter, but they seem to be doing no good. Not only that, but we cannot afford to provide the incentives within our current budget, and unless sales increase, we will be in the red.

Regretfully, I recommend dropping the program.

---

of the organization, he often has given you good advice and has shown special interest. He mostly lets you do what you feel is best, however, and he seldom dictates specific methods for doing things.

Your general approach to problems is to avoid controversy. You feel uncomfortable when production is made the scapegoat for problems in the company. Because this is a manufacturing business, it seems as if everyone tries to pin the blame for problems on the production department. You've felt for years that the firm was getting away from what it does best: mass producing a few standard products. Instead, the trend has been for marketing and sales to push for more and more products, shorter lead times, and greater customization capability. These actions have increased costs and caused significant production delays as well as higher rejection rates.

[*Note*: During the upcoming meeting, you should adopt the avoidance approach shown in Table 7.2. Defend your turf, place blame on others, defer taking a stand, and avoid taking responsibility for making a controversial decision.]

Barbara Price, Director of Sales and Marketing

You are anxious to impress Lynn Smith because you have your eye on a position that is opening up at the end of the year in the parent company, Connecticut Industries. It would mean a promotion for you. A positive recommendation from Lynn Smith would carry a lot of weight in the selection process. Given that both Hartford Manufacturing and Connecticut Industries are largely male dominated, you are pleased with your career advancement so far, and you are hoping to keep it up.

One current concern is Lynn Smith's suggestion some time ago that you look into the problem of slow sales during the winter months. You implemented an incentive plan that was highly recommended by an industry analyst at a recent trade conference. It consists of three separate incentive programs: (1) competition among regions in which the salesperson in the top region would have his or her picture in the company newsletter and receive an engraved plaque, (2) a vacation in Hawaii for the top salesperson in the company, and (3) cash bonuses for salespeople who obtained new customer orders. Unfortunately, these incentives haven't worked. Not only have sales not increased for the company as a whole, but sales for two regions are down an average of five percent. You have told the sales force that the incentives will last through this quarter, but if sales don't improve, your budget will be in the red. You haven't budgeted for the prizes, since you expected the increased sales to more than offset the cost of the incentives.

Obviously, this was a bad idea—it isn't working—and it should be dropped immediately. You are a bit embarrassed about this aborted project. But it is better to cut your losses and try something else rather than continue to support an obvious loser.

In general, you are very confident and self-assured. You feel that the best way to get work done is through negotiation and compromise. What's important is making a decision quickly and efficiently. Maybe everyone doesn't get exactly what he or she wants, but at least they can get on with their work. There are no black and whites in this business— only "grays" that can be traded off to keep the management process from bogging down with "paralysis by analysis." You are impatient over delays caused by intensive studies and investigations of detail. You agree with Tom Peters: action is the hallmark of successful managers.

[*Note*: During this meeting, use the compromise approach shown in Table 7.2. Do whatever is necessary to help the group make a quick decision so you can get on with the pressing demands of your work.]

Chuck Kasper, Regional Sales Director

You don't get back to company headquarters often because your customer contacts take up most of your time. You regularly work 50 to 60 hours a week, and you are proud of the job you do. You also feel a special obligation to your customers to provide them with the best product available in the timeliest fashion. This sense of obligation comes not only from your commitment to the company but also from your personal relationships with many of the customers.

Lately, you have been receiving more and more complaints about late deliveries of Hartford Manufacturing's products to your customers. The time between their ordering and delivery is increasing, and some customers have been greatly inconvenienced by the delays. You have made a formal inquiry of production to find out what the problem is. They replied that they are producing as efficiently as possible, and they see nothing wrong with past practices. Richard Hooton's assistant even suggested that this was just another example of the sales force's unrealistic expectations.

Not only will sales be negatively affected if these delays continue, but your reputation with your customers will be damaged. You have promised them that the problem will be quickly solved and that products will begin arriving on time. Since Richard Hooton is so rigid, however, you are almost certain that it will do no good to talk with him. His subordinate probably got his negative attitude from Hooton.

In general, Hooton is a 1980s production worker who is being pulled by the rest of the firm into the new age. Competition is different, technology is different, and management is different, but Richard is reluctant to change. You need shorter lead times, a wider range of products, and the capacity to do more customized work. Sure, this makes production's work harder, but other firms are providing these services with high-tech applications. Hartford Manufacturing is clearly behind the learning curve.

Instead of getting down to the real problems, the home office, in their typical high-handed fashion, announced an incentives plan. This implies that the problem is in the field, not the factory. It made some of your people angry to think they were being pressed to increase their efforts when they weren't receiving the backup support in Hartford to get the job done. Sure, they liked the prizes, but the way the plan was presented made them feel as if they weren't working hard enough. This isn't the first time you have questioned the judgment of Barbara, your boss. She certainly is intelligent and hard-working, but she doesn't seem very interested in what's going on out in the field. Furthermore, she doesn't seem very receptive to "bad news" about sales and customer complaints.

Note: During this meeting, use the forcing approach to conflict management and negotiations shown in Table 7.2. However, don't overplay your part, because you are the senior regional sales manager, and if Barbara continues to move up fast in the organization, you may be in line for her position.

ACTIVITIES FOR IMPROVING MANAGING CONFLICT SKILLS

Suggested Assignments

7.10. Select a specific conflict with which you are very familiar. Using the framework for identifying the sources of conflict discussed in this chapter, analyze this situation carefully. It might be useful to compare your perceptions of the situation with those of informed observers. What type of conflict is this? Why did it occur? Why is it continuing? Next, using the guidelines for selecting an appropriate conflict management strategy, identify the general approach that would be most appropriate for this situation. Consider both the personal preferences of the parties involved and the relevant situational factors. Is this the approach that the parties have been using? If not, attempt to introduce a different perspective into the relationship and explain why you feel it would be more productive. If the parties have been using this approach, discuss with them why it has not been successful thus far. Share information on specific behavioral guidelines or negotiation tactics that might increase the effectiveness of their efforts.

7.11. Select three individuals who are from diverse cultural backgrounds and have work experience outside of their native culture. Discuss with them the sources (especially the personal differences) of previous conflicts they have experienced at work. Ask them about their preferences in dealing with conflict situations. What strategies do they prefer to use? How do they generally attempt to resolve disputes? What relevant situational factors influence the way they manage conflict situations with individuals from other cultures and with individuals of their own cultures? With the help of these three persons, identify specific behavioral guidelines for managing conflict more effectively with other persons from their respective cultures.

7.12. Identify a situation in which another individual is doing something that needs to be corrected. Using the respondent's guidelines for collaborative problem solving, construct a plan for discussing your concerns with this person. Include specific language designed to state your case assertively without causing a defensive reaction. Role-play this interaction with a friend and incorporate any suggestions for improvement. Make your presentation to the individual and report on your results. What was the reaction? Were you successful in balancing assertiveness with support and responsibility? Based on this experience, identify other situations you feel need to be changed and follow a similar procedure.

7.13. Volunteer to serve as a mediator to resolve a conflict between two individuals or groups. Using the guidelines for implementing the collaborative approach to mediation, outline a plan of action prior to your intervention. Be sure to consider carefully whether or not private meetings with the parties prior to your mediation session are appropriate. Report on the situation and your plan. How did you feel? Which specific actions worked well? What was the outcome? What would you do differently? Based on this experience, revise your plan for use in related situations.

7.14. Identify a difficult situation involving negotiations. This might involve transactions at work, at home, or in the community. Review the guidelines for integrative bargaining and identify the specific tactics you plan to use. Write down specific questions and responses to likely initiatives from the other party. In particular, anticipate how you might handle the possibility of the other party's using a distributive negotiation strategy. Schedule a negotiation meeting with the party involved and implement your plan. Following the session, debrief the experience with a coworker or friend. What did you learn? How successful were you? What would you do differently? Based on this experience, modify your plan and prepare to implement it in related situations.

Application Plan and Evaluation

The intent of this exercise is to help you apply this cluster of skills in a real-life, out-of-class setting. Now that you have become familiar with the behavioral guidelines that form the basis of effective skill performance, you will improve most by trying out those guidelines in an everyday context. Unlike a classroom activity, in which feedback is immediate and others can assist you with their evaluations, this skill application activity is one you must accomplish and evaluate on your own. There are two parts to this activity. Part 1 helps prepare you to apply the skill, and Part 2 helps you evaluate and improve on your experience. Be sure to write down answers to each item. Don't short-circuit the process by skipping steps.

Part 1: Planning

7.15. Write down the two or three aspects of this skill that are most important to you. These may be areas of weakness, areas you most want to improve, or areas that are most salient to a problem you face right now. Identify the specific aspects of this skill that you want to apply.

7.16. Now identify the setting or the situation in which you will apply this skill. Establish a plan for performance by actually writing down a description of the situation. Who else will be involved? When will you do it? Where will it be done?

Circumstances:
Who else?
When?
Where?

7.17. Identify the specific behaviors you will engage in to apply this skill. Operationalize your skill performance.

7.18. What are the indicators of successful performance? How will you know you have been effective? What will indicate you have performed competently?

Part 2: Evaluation

7.19. After you have completed your implementation, record the results. What happened? How successful were you? What was the effect on others?

7.20. How can you improve? What modifications can you make next time? What will you do differently in a similar situation in the future?

7.21. Looking back on your whole skill practice and application experience, what have you learned? What has been surprising? In what ways might this experience help you in the long term?

SKILL PRACTICE
Exercises for Resolving Interpersonal Disputes

Observer's Feedback Form

RATING
  1 = Low
  5 = High

Initiator

———————— Maintained personal ownership of the problem, including feelings

———————— Avoided making accusations or attributing motives; stuck to the facts

———————— Succinctly described the problem (behaviors, outcomes, feelings)

———————— Specified expectations or standards violated

———————— Persisted until understood

———————— Encouraged two-way interaction

———————— Approached multiple issues incrementally (proceeded from simple to complex, easy to hard)

———————— Appealed to what the disputants had in common (goals, principles, constraints)

———————— Made a specific request for change

Respondent

———————— Established a climate for joint problem solving

———————— Showed genuine concern and interest

———————— Responded appropriately to the initiator's emotions

———————— Avoided becoming defensive or overreacting

———————— Sought additional information about the problem (shifted general to specific, evaluative to descriptive)

APPLICATION

—————— Focused on one issue at a time, gradually broadened the scope of the discussion, searched for integrative solution

—————— Agreed with some aspect of the complaint (facts, perceptions, feelings, or principles)

—————— Asked for suggestions for making changes

—————— Proposed a specific plan of action

Mediator

—————— Acknowledged that a conflict exists; treated the conflict and disputants seriously

—————— Broke down complex issues, separated the critical from the peripheral; began with a relatively easy problem

—————— Helped disputants avoid entrenched positions by exploring underlying interests

—————— Remained neutral (facilitator, not judge) and impartial toward issues and disputants

—————— Kept the interaction issue oriented (e.g., pointed out the effect of the conflict on performance)

—————— Made sure that neither party dominated conversation, asked questions to maintain balance

—————— Kept conflict in perspective by emphasizing areas of agreement

—————— Helped generate multiple alternatives, drawn from common goals, values, or principles

—————— Made sure that both parties were satisfied and committed to the proposed resolution

Comments:

SCORING KEYS AND COMPARISON DATA

✪ Scoring Keys for the following instruments, along with comparison data, are contained in PIA in MyManagementLab.com;

Managing Interpersonal Conflict
Strategies for Handling Conflict

Part III

Group Skills

CHAPTERS

8 **EMPOWERING AND ENGAGING OTHERS**
Empowering Others
Engaging Others
Sharing Power

9 **BUILDING EFFECTIVE TEAMS AND TEAMWORK**
Diagnosing Team Development
Building Teamwork
Fostering Effective Team Leadership

10 **LEADING POSITIVE CHANGE**
Creating Positive Deviance
Leading Positive Change
Mobilizing the Capabilities of Others

SKILL *ASSESSMENT*

- Effective Empowerment and Engagement
- Personal Empowerment Assessment

SKILL *LEARNING*

- Empowering and Engaging Others
- A Management Dilemma Involving Empowerment
- The Meaning of Empowerment
- Historical Roots of Empowerment
- Dimensions of Empowerment
- How to Develop Empowerment
- Inhibitors to Empowerment
- Fostering Engagement
- International Caveats
- Summary
- Behavioral Guidelines

SKILL *ANALYSIS*

- Minding the Store
- Changing the Portfolio

SKILL *PRACTICE*

- Executive Development Associates
- Empowering Ourselves
- Deciding to Engage Others

SKILL *APPLICATION*

- Suggested Assignments
- Application Plan and Evaluation

SCORING KEYS AND *COMPARISON DATA*

MyManagementLab™

✪ When you see this icon, visit www.mymanagementlab.com for self-assessments, video activities, and more.

8

Empowering and Engaging Others

LEARNING OBJECTIVES

1. EMPOWER OTHERS
2. EMPOWER YOURSELF
3. ENGAGING OTHERS EFFECTIVELY

✪ If your instructor is utilizing **MyManagementLab**, log onto mymanagementlab.com and select the Personal Inventory Assessment (PIA) section and complete the instruments associated with this chapter.

The assessment instruments in this chapter are briefly described below. The assessments appear either in your text or in PIA. The assessments marked with (blue star) are available only in PIA.

All assessments should be completed before reading the chapter material.

After completing the first assessment save your response to your hard drive. When you have finished reading the chapter, re-take the assessment and compare your responses to see what you have learned.

✪ ❑ *Effective Empowerment and Engagement Instrument* assesses your competency in empowering others with whom you work and the extent to which you can effectively engage other people in the work.

✪ ❑ *The Personal Empowerment Assessment* measures the extent to which you experience an empowering environment in your role at work or as a student.

SKILL *LEARNING* ▽ⓘ

Empowering and Engaging Others

Many management books are oriented toward helping managers know how to control others' behavior. They focus on how managers can increase employees' performance, engender conformity, or motivate employees to achieve certain objectives. This book, too, includes skills that will help you motivate people to do what you want them to do (see the chapter on Motivating Others) or achieve power and influence over them (see the Gaining Power and Influence chapter). This chapter, however, focuses on a skill called **empowerment** and effectively engaging others in work.

Empowerment is based on assumptions that are different from those associated with motivating others or influencing others (see Chapters 5 and 6). Empowerment means providing freedom for people to successfully do what *they want* to do, rather than getting them to do what *you want* them to do. Managers who empower people remove controls, constraints, and boundaries for them instead of motivating, directing, or influencing their behavior. Rather than being a "push" strategy, in which managers induce employees to respond in desirable ways through incentives and influence techniques, empowerment is a "pull" strategy. It focuses on ways managers can design a work situation so that it energizes and provides intrinsic

encouragement to employees. In the context of such a strategy, workers accomplish tasks because they are intrinsically attracted by them, not because of an extrinsic reward system or influence technique.

Empowering others, however, can lead to dilemmas. On the one hand, evidence shows that empowered employees are more productive, more satisfied, and more innovative and that they create higher-quality products and services than unempowered employees (Babakus, Yavas, Karatepe, & Avci, 2003; Greenberger & Stasser, 1991; Spreitzer, 1992). Organizations are more effective when an empowered workforce exists (Conger & Kanungo, 1988; Gecas, 1989; Pieterse, Van Knippenberg, Schippers, & Stam, 2010; Seibert, Wang, & Courtright, 2011).

On the other hand, empowerment means giving up control and letting others make decisions, set goals, accomplish results, and receive rewards. It means that other people probably will get credit for success. Managers with high needs for power and control (see McClelland, 1975) face a challenge when they are expected to sacrifice their needs for someone else's gain. They may ask themselves: "Why should others get the credit when I am in charge? Why should I allow others to exercise power, and even facilitate their acquiring more power, when I naturally want to receive rewards and recognition myself?"

The answer is that you don't need to sacrifice desired rewards, recognition, or effectiveness in order to be a skillful empowering manager. On the contrary, through real empowerment, managers actually multiply their own effectiveness. They and their organizations become more successful than they could have been otherwise (Maynard, Gilson, & Mathieu, 2012). Nevertheless, for most managers, empowerment is a skill that must be developed and practiced, because despite the high visibility of the concept of empowerment in popular literature, its actual practice is all too rare in modern management. Survey after survey has reported that a majority of employees do not feel empowered, are not engaged, and do not believe that they make a difference at work (e.g., Asplund & Blacksmith, 2012).

In this chapter, we begin by discussing the core dimensions of empowerment and, in particular, how to effectively empower other people. In the second part of the chapter, we discuss a special situation in which empowerment is essential: engaging other people in work. We conclude with a summary model and a list of behavioral guidelines for successfully empowering and engaging others.

The Meaning of Empowerment

To empower means to enable. It means to help people develop a sense of self-confidence. It means to help people overcome feelings of powerlessness or helplessness. It means to energize people to take action. It means to mobilize intrinsic motivation to accomplish a task. Empowered people not only possess the wherewithal to accomplish something, but they also think of themselves differently than they did before they were empowered. They feel more capable and confident.

It is important to note that empowerment and power are not the same. Creating empowerment is not merely giving power to someone. Both concepts connote the ability to get things done, but Table 8.1 contrasts these concepts and highlights their differences.

For example, you can give someone else power, but people must accept empowerment for themselves. It cannot be bestowed on someone. That is, I cannot empower you; I can only create the circumstances in which you can empower yourself.

As explained in the chapter on gaining power and influence, the acquisition of power is based on several personal and positional factors. In each case, other people need to acknowledge your power, follow your lead, and acquiesce to your influence in order for you to have power. The underlying source of your power is other people.

For example, you may have power because you have more resources or political support than someone else. Thus, you can reward others and have *reward power*. Alternatively, you may have the ability to penalize or sanction others as a result of your strength or support so you have *sanctioning power*. Your title or position may give you power over others, thus giving you *traditional power*. You may possess more knowledge or information than others, giving you *expertise power*. Or, you may be personally attractive or charismatic, thus having *referent power*. French and Raven (1960) identified these five factors as the primary bases of power. Regardless of whether these are the five factors that create power or whether there are others, each can be conveyed to another person. Each depends on others acknowledging it. Each can be bestowed on someone else.

In the case of empowerment, however, people can be empowered even if no one acknowledges their personal attributes or positions. Victor Frankl, Nelson Mandela, and Mahatma Gandhi are examples of individuals who, despite the absence of the attributes of power, maintained complete empowerment in dismal circumstances (i.e., in prison and in bigoted environments). This is because the source of empowerment is internal. Its source is within the individual, not as a result of social acceptance, political support, or title. You accept and create empowerment for yourself.

Table 8.1	The Difference Between Power and Empowerment	
POWER	**EMPOWERMENT**
The capacity to get others to do what you want	The capacity to get others to do what they want
To get more implies taking it away from someone else	To get more does not affect how much others have
Comes from an external source	Comes from an internal source
Ultimately, few people have it	Ultimately, everyone can have it
Leads to competition	Leads to cooperation

LEARNING

In addition, if I become more powerful, that generally means you become less powerful. If I have the power to get someone to do what I want, but that differs from what you want, my power and your power come into conflict. That is why, ultimately, relatively few people have power. Power gets concentrated among a few people in most organizations. Furthermore, power struggles are almost universal in organizations and even small groups. Who has enough power to have his or her way is a common problem, and it almost always leads toward conflict.

On the other hand, every person can be empowered without affecting any other person's position or stature. It merely leads to each of us being enabled to accomplish what we choose. Empowerment, in fact, is more likely to lead to cooperation and collaboration than to conflict.

A key to successfully enable empowerment is to understand its core components. In the next section, we summarize the five key dimensions of empowerment, and provide guidelines for how to foster them. Think of these five dimensions as a formula. A multiplication sign goes between each of the dimensions. That is, if any one dimension is absent or zero, then empowerment is zero. All five must be present for empowerment to be present.

> ✪ MyManagementLab: **WATCH IT**
> **Zappos: Motivating Employees Through Company Culture**
> Apply what you have learned about management. If your instructor has assigned MyManagementLab, go to mymanagementlab.com to watch a video case and answer questions.

Dimensions of Empowerment

In one of the best empirical studies of empowerment, Spreitzer (1992) identified four dimensions of empowerment. We have added one dimension to her model, based on the research of Mishra (1992). Subsequent research has confirmed that in order for you to empower others successfully, you must engender these five qualities in those they intend to empower. Skillful empowerment means producing (1) a sense of *self-efficacy*, (2) a sense of *self-determination*, (3) a sense of *personal consequence*, (4) a sense of *meaning*, and

Table 8.2	Five Core Dimensions of Empowerment
DIMENSION	**EXPLANATION**
Self-efficacy	A sense of personal competence
Self-determination	A sense of personal choice
Personal consequence	A sense of having impact
Meaning	A sense of value in activity
Trust	A sense of security

(5) a sense of *trust* (see Table 8.2). When these five dimensions of empowerment are present, empirical evidence is clear: individuals and organizations perform better than normal (also see Maynard, Gilson, & Mathieu, 2012).

No one can force another to be empowered, of course, but fostering an environment where these five factors are present makes it highly likely that people will accept empowerment for themselves. Empowered people not only are more productive, but they also are more confident, they feel more freedom, they feel more important, and they feel more comfortable in their work and work setting.

After explaining these five dimensions, we provide guidelines for engendering each one.

SELF-EFFICACY

When people are empowered, they have a sense of **self-efficacy,** or the feeling that they possess the capability and competence to perform a task successfully. Empowered people not only feel *competent*, they feel *confident* that they can perform adequately. They are self-assured. They feel a sense of personal mastery and believe they can learn and grow to meet new challenges (see Bandura, 1989; Bennis & Nanus, 1985; Conger & Kanungo, 1988; Gecas, 1989; Zimmerman, 1990). Some writers believe this is the most important element in empowerment because having a sense of self-efficacy determines whether people will try and persist in attempting to accomplish a difficult task (Biron & Bamberger, 2010).

> *The strength of people's conviction in their own effectiveness is likely to affect whether they would even try to cope with given situations....They get involved in activities and behave assuredly when they*

judge themselves capable of handling situations that would otherwise be intimidating....Efficacy expectations determine how much effort people will expend and how long they will persist in the face of obstacles and aversive experiences. (Bandura, 1977, pp. 193–194)

Our colleague Roger Goddard and his associates found that a sense of efficacy among students in a classroom—what he referred to as "collective efficacy"—is a more powerful predictor of success in school than any other single factor (Goddard, Hoy, & Hoy, 2002). That is, when students believe in themselves, when they have confidence that they can succeed, and when they have faith that a successful outcome will occur, their grades are higher, their test scores are higher in math and reading, and their absenteeism and tardiness are lower. Collective efficacy is a more important factor in determining these outcomes than race; gender; socioeconomic status; attending a large or small, inner-city or suburban school; or ethnic makeup of the class! (Also see Caprara, Vecchione, Alessandri, Gerbino, & Barbaranelli, 2011).

A great deal of additional research has been done on the consequences of self-efficacy and its opposite, powerlessness, in relation to physical and psychological health (Bandura, 2012; Xanthopoulou, Bakker, & Fischbach, 2013). For example, self-efficacy has been found to be a significant factor in overcoming phobias and anxieties (Bandura, 1986), alcohol and drug abuse (Seeman & Anderson, 1983), eating disorders (Schneider & Agras, 1985), smoking addiction (DiClemente, 1985), depression (Seligman, 1975), and increasing tolerance for pain (Neufeld & Thomas, 1977). Recovery from illness and injury and coping with job loss or disruptions is more effective and more rapid among people who have developed a strong sense of self-efficacy because they are more physically and psychologically resilient and better able to change negative behaviors (Brouwer, et al., 2010; Gecas, Seff, & Ray, 1988; Schwalbe & Gecas, 1988).

Bandura (1977, 2012) suggested that three conditions are necessary for people to feel a sense of self-efficacy: (1) a belief that they have the ability to perform a task, (2) a belief that they are capable of putting forth the necessary effort, and (3) a belief that no outside obstacles will prevent them from accomplishing the task. In addition to these three prescriptions, we will suggest other ways later to enhance self-efficacy.

SELF-DETERMINATION

Empowered people also have a sense of **self-determination,** meaning that they have a sense of *having choices.* "To be self-determining means to experience a sense of choice in initiating and regulating one's own actions" (Deci, Connell, & Ryan, 1989, p. 580). People feel self-determined when they can voluntarily and intentionally involve themselves in tasks rather than being forced to or prohibited from involvement (Deci & Ryan, 2012). Their actions are a consequence of personal freedom and autonomy.

Empowered individuals have alternatives and a sense of freedom; therefore, they develop a sense of responsibility for and ownership of their activities (Rappoport, Swift, & Hess, 1984; Rose & Black, 1985; Staples, 1990; Zimmerman, 1990). They are able to take initiative on their own accord, make independent decisions, and try out new ideas (Conger & Kanungo, 1988; Thomas & Valthouse, 1990; Vogt & Murrell, 1990). Rather than feeling that their actions are predetermined, externally controlled, or inevitable, they experience an internal locus of control.

Research shows that a strong sense of self-determination is associated with a variety of positive outcomes in the workplace—for example, less alienation in the work environment (Maddux, 2002), more work satisfaction (Organ & Green, 1974), higher levels of work performance (Anderson, Hellreigel, & Slocum, 1977), more entrepreneurial and innovative activity (Hammer & Vardi, 1981), high levels of job involvement (Runyon, 1973), greater work motivation (Gagne & Deci, 2005), and less job strain (Gemmill & Heisler, 1972). In medical research, recovery from severe illness has been found to be associated with having the patient "reject the traditional passive role and insist on being an active participant in his own therapy" (Gecas, 1989, p. 298). People who are helped to feel that they can have personal impact on what happens to them, even with regard to the effects of disease, are more likely to experience positive outcomes than those who lack this feeling (Weinstein & Deci, 2011).

Self-determination is associated most directly with having choices about the *methods* used to accomplish a task, the amount of *effort* to be expended, the *pace* of the work, and the *time frame* in which it is to be accomplished. Empowered individuals have a feeling of ownership for tasks because they can determine how tasks are accomplished, when they are accomplished, and how quickly they are completed. Clearly, having a choice is the critical component of self-determination. Later, we will offer specific suggestions for fostering self-determination.

LEARNING

PERSONAL CONSEQUENCE

Empowered people have a sense that when they act, they can produce a result. Think of an assembly line job where a worker screws a nut on a bolt, but if he makes an error, someone down the line will correct it. Such a person will have little sense that he can have a meaningful effect on the outcome of the product or that he has control over the outcome.

On the other hand, people with a sense of personal consequence believe that expending effort will produce a result. Personal consequence refers to "an individual's beliefs at a given point in time in his or her ability to effect a change in a desired direction" (Greenberger, Stasser, Cummings, & Dunham, 1989, p. 165). It is the conviction that through your own actions, you can influence what happens. You have a sense of control, and you can have *impact*.

Empowered individuals do not believe that obstacles in the external environment control their actions; rather, they believe that those obstacles can be overcome (Thornton, & Tizard, 2010). They have a feeling of *active control*—which allows them to bring their environment into alignment with their wishes—as opposed to *passive control*—in which their wishes are brought into alignment with environmental demands (see Greenberger & Stasser, 1991; Rappoport et al., 1984; Rothbaum, Weisz, & Snyder, 1982; Thomas & Velthouse, 1990; Zimmerman & Rappoport, 1988). Instead of being reactive to what they see around them, people with a sense of personal consequence try to influence what they see. For you to feel empowered, you must not only perceive that what you do produces an effect but that you can produce the effect yourself.

Having a sense of personal consequence is related to internal locus of control discussed in the chapter on Self-Awareness, but it is not the same thing. (You completed the Locus of Control instrument in Chapter 1.) You learned that most people have developed an orientation toward internal or external locus of control which characterizes their general approach to life. Helping people experience empowerment, however, means helping others develop a sense that they can produce a desired result, regardless of their personality dimension. Some ideas for how to foster a sense of consequence are discussed later.

Research suggests that people are intrinsically motivated to seek personal consequence or a feeling of control (Spreitzer, 2008; White, 1959). We all strive to maintain a sense of control of ourselves and our situations. In fact, even small losses of personal control can be harmful physically and emotionally. For example, loss of control has been found to lead to depression, stress, anxiety, low morale, loss of productivity, burnout, learned helplessness, and even increased death rates (see Greenberger & Stasser, 1991; Langer, 1983; Xanthopoulou, Bakker, & Fischbach, 2013). Having a sense of personal control over outcomes or consequences, then, appears necessary for health as well as for empowerment.

On the other hand, even the most empowered people are not able to completely control everything that happens to them. No one can produce all the consequences he or she desires. Nevertheless, empowerment helps people increase the number of personal outcomes that they can impact. Often, this is a matter of clarifying in what areas personal consequence is possible.

MEANING

Empowered people also have a sense of meaning. They value the purpose or outcomes of the activity in which they are engaged. Their own ideals and standards are perceived as consistent with what they are doing. The activity "counts" in their own value system. Not only do they feel that they can produce a result (i.e., personal consequence), but they believe in and care about what they produce (Bennis & Nanus, 1985; Block, 1987; Bunderson & Thompson, 2009; Conger & Kanungo, 1988; Manz & Sims, 1989). Meaningfulness, then, refers to a perception of producing *value*.

Activities infused with meaning create a sense of purpose, passion, or mission for people. They provide a source of energy and enthusiasm, rather than draining energy and enthusiasm from people. Merely getting paid, helping an organization earn money, or just doing a job does not create a sense of meaning for most people. Something more fundamental, more personal, and more value-laden must be linked to the activity. Almost all people want to feel that they are spending their time on something that will produce lasting benefit, that will make the world a better place, or that is associated with a personal value (Bunderson & Thompson, 2009).

Acquiring personal benefit from an activity does not guarantee meaning. For example, service to others may bring no personal reward, yet it may be far more meaningful than work that produces a hefty paycheck. Involvement in activities without meaning, on the other hand, often produces disengagement, boredom, or exhaustion. Other incentives—such as perks or extra pay—are required to get people to invest in the work. Unfortunately, these extra incentives are costly to organizations and represent nonvalue-added expenses that constrain organizational efficiency and effectiveness. It costs companies a lot of money to require work that has little or no meaning to workers.

Research on meaningfulness in work has found that when individuals engage in work that they feel is meaningful, they are more committed to it and more involved in it (Wrzesniewski, 2012). They have a higher concentration of energy and are more persistent in pursuing desired goals than when a sense of meaningfulness is low. People feel more excitement and passion for their work and have a greater sense of personal significance and self-worth because of their association with activities that are meaningful. Individuals empowered with a sense of meaningfulness also are more innovative, upwardly influential, and personally effective than those with low meaningfulness scores (Bramucci, 1977; Deci & Ryan, 1987; Pratt & Ashforth, 2003; Spreitzer, 1992; Vogt & Murrell, 1990; Wrzesniewski, 2003).

TRUST

Finally, empowered people have a sense of trust (Helliwell & Huang, 2011). They are confident that they will be treated fairly and equitably. They maintain an assurance that even if they are in subordinate positions, the ultimate outcome of their actions will be justice and goodness as opposed to harm or damage. Usually, this means they have confidence that those holding authority or power positions will not harm or injure them, and that they will be treated honestly. However, even in circumstances in which individuals holding power positions do not demonstrate integrity and fairness, empowered people can still maintain a sense of *personal security*. Their trust is placed in principles not in persons. Trust also implies that individuals are willing to place themselves in a position of vulnerability (Zand, 1972), and have faith that, ultimately, no harm will come to them as a result of their trust (Barber, 1983; Deutsch, 1973; Luhmann, 1979; Mishra, 1992).

How can a person maintain trust and a sense of security even when caught in a circumstance that seems unfair, inequitable, or even dangerous? In his attempts to gain independence for minorities in South Africa, for example, Gandhi determined that he would burn the passes that the British government required

be carried by all native Indians but not by white South African citizens. Gandhi called a meeting and publicly announced his intent to resist this law by burning the passes of each of his Indian supporters. In a now-famous incident, after Gandhi burned several of the passes, the British police intervened by clubbing him with nightsticks. Despite the beating, Gandhi continued to burn passes.

Where is the trust or sense of security in this case? How can Gandhi be empowered in the process of being beaten by the police? In what did Gandhi have trust? Was Gandhi empowered or not?

The answer is: Gandhi's sense of security and trust came not from the British authorities but from his faith in the principles that he espoused. His sense of security was associated with his belief that doing the right thing always leads, ultimately, to the right consequence.

Research on trust has also found a great deal of positive outcomes (Lau, Lam, & Wen, 2013). For example, individuals with high levels of trust are more apt to replace superficiality and facades with directness and intimacy. They are more apt to be open, honest, and congruent rather than deceptive or shallow. They are more search-oriented and self-determining, and more self-assured and willing to learn. They have a larger capacity for interdependent relationships, and they display a greater degree of cooperation and risk-taking in groups than do those with low trust.

Trusting people are more willing to try to get along with others and to be a contributing part of a team. They are also more self-disclosing, more honest in their own communication, and more able to listen carefully to others. They have less resistance to change and are better able to cope with unexpected traumas than are those with low levels of trust. Individuals who trust others are more likely to be trustworthy themselves and to maintain high personal ethical standards (see Gibb & Gibb, 1969; Golembiewski & McConkie, 1975; Mishra, 1992).Trusting others, in other words, allows people to act in a confident and straightforward manner, without wasting energy on self-protection, trying to uncover hidden agendas, or playing politics (Chan, Taylor, & Markham, 2008). In brief, a sense of trust empowers people by feeling secure.

REVIEW OF EMPOWERMENT DIMENSIONS

The main point of our discussion thus far is to make the point that fostering the five attributes of empowerment in individuals produces positive outcomes.

Research findings associated with each of the five dimensions of empowerment—*self-efficacy* (a sense of competence), *self-determination* (a sense of choice), *personal consequence* (a sense of impact), *meaning* (a sense of value), and *trust* (a sense of security)—strongly support the fact that both personal and organizational advantages result when people feel empowered. Negative consequences occur, on the other hand, when people experience the opposite of empowerment, such as powerlessness, helplessness, and alienation. Helping people feel a certain way about themselves and their work helps them to be more effective in the behaviors they display.

Some cynical students (and a few practicing managers) have argued that empowering people is unnecessary and a waste of time in many situations because there are always "free riders." Some people, they say, are not inclined to want empowerment. They just want to get by on as little as possible. They don't want to get involved in teams or classes. They shy away from taking initiative. They would rather just follow directions.

This occurs, however, when people do not value the outcome that has been assigned (absence of a sense of value), when they believe that someone else will produce the result without their input (absence of a sense of personal consequence), when they don't trust that their contribution will be valued (absence of trust), or when they don't believe that they have anything to contribute (absence of self-efficacy). When the five dimensions of empowerment are present, on the other hand, almost all people will become actively engaged and pursue empowerment.

Research by Hackman and Oldham (1980) found that more than 80 percent of workers have high "growth need strength," or a desire to grow and contribute in their jobs. Helping to foster the five dimensions of empowerment responds to this inherent need for growth and contribution.

The next section of this chapter discusses specific actions managers can take to facilitate empowerment in others.

How to Develop Empowerment

People tend to experience empowerment in environments that help them flourish, when they can produce success, and when they experience satisfaction in their work. They are especially in need of empowerment, however, when they are faced with situations they perceive to be threatening, unclear, overly controlled, coercive, or isolating; when they experience inappropriate feelings of dependency or inadequacy; when they feel stifled in their ability to do what they would like to do; when they are uncertain about how to behave; when they feel that some negative consequence is imminent; and when they feel unrewarded and unappreciated. Empowerment, in other words, matters to almost everyone in almost every circumstance.

Research by a variety of scholars (Bandura, 1986, 2012; Hackman & Oldham, 1980; Quinn & Spreitzer, 1997; Wrzesniewski, 2003, 2012) has produced at least nine specific prescriptions for fostering empowerment. These prescriptions help produce a sense of competence, choice, impact, value, and security. They include: (1) articulating a clear vision and goals, (2) fostering personal mastery experiences, (3) modeling, (4) providing support, (5) creating emotional arousal, (6) providing necessary information, (7) providing necessary resources, (8) connecting to outcomes, and (9) creating confidence. Each of these prescriptions is discussed below. Figure 8.1 illustrates their relationships to the five core dimensions of empowerment.

Some of these prescriptions are similar to the guidelines found in the chapters on Building Relationships by Communicating Supportively, Gaining Power and Influence, and Motivating Others. Because a completely separate and unique set of managerial skills does not exist for communicating with, influencing, and motivating others, some commonality and overlap is inevitable. On the other hand, the context of empowerment sheds a different light on some of the guidelines you have read about before.

A CLEAR GOAL

Creating an environment in which individuals can feel empowered requires that they be guided by a clear goal of what is to be achieved and how they can contribute. A great deal of research confirms that having goals motivates individuals to achieve higher performance than if they have no goals (Rawsthorne & Elliot, 1999; Ryan & Deci, 2000).

It makes sense that if you are assigned a task but are given no targets or standards for performance, you are unlikely to perform as well as if you are clear about the objective and the level of performance expected of you. Goal setting is a common strategy for helping individuals improve their performance. If we want high performance, we almost always establish goals as a way to attain it. Locke and Latham (2006) identified

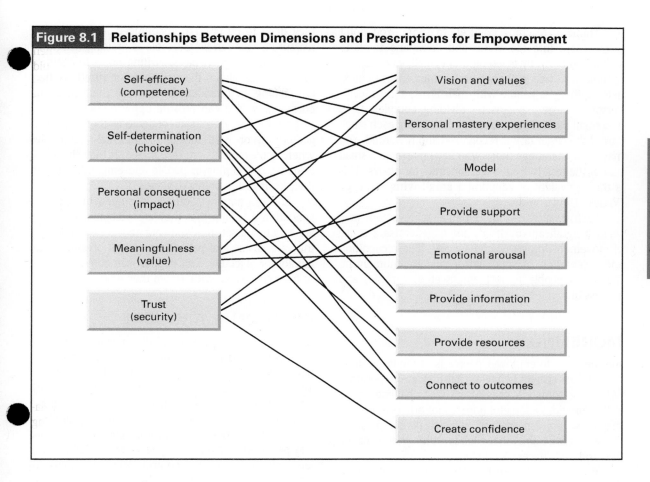

Figure 8.1 Relationships Between Dimensions and Prescriptions for Empowerment

Self-efficacy (competence)	Vision and values
Self-determination (choice)	Personal mastery experiences
Personal consequence (impact)	Model
Meaningfulness (value)	Provide support
Trust (security)	Emotional arousal
	Provide information
	Provide resources
	Connect to outcomes
	Create confidence

the attributes of the most effective goals, and the acronym **SMART goals** best summarizes these attributes.

❑ *S - Specific goals*—goals that are identifiable, behavioral, and observable.

❑ *M - Measurable goals*—goals that can be assessed objectively and where the degree of successful accomplishment can be determined.

❑ *A - Aligned goals*—goals that are congruent with the overall purposes of the organization or that are consistent with the person's values.

❑ *R - Realistic goals*— goals that are capable of being achieved, not mere fantasy, or considered to be nonsense. Realistic does not mean easily achieved, because difficult, stretch goals are better motivators and predict higher levels of accomplishment than do easy goals (Locke & Latham, 2006).

❑ *T - Time-bound goals*—goals where a deadline for accomplishing the goals is specified. Goals that have no ending point are not effective.

The point is that individuals are empowered as they are provided SMART goals that help clarify how they achieve a valued outcome.

FOSTERING PERSONAL MASTERY EXPERIENCES

Bandura (1986) found that the single most important thing you can do to empower other people is to help them experience personal mastery over some challenge or problem. By successfully accomplishing a task, defeating an opponent, or resolving a problem, people develop a sense of mastery. Personal mastery can be fostered by providing people with the opportunity to accomplish successively more difficult tasks that eventually lead to the accomplishment of larger, more desirable goals. The key is to start with easy tasks and then progress by small steps to more difficult tasks until the person experiences a sense of mastery over an entire challenge (also see Paglis, 2010).

Think of teaching children to swim. You don't throw them into the water and command them to swim. You begin by teaching them small, easy tasks—putting their face in the water, teaching them to kick, helping them to paddle with their arms, and so forth. Personal mastery begins by dividing complex tasks into small parts. Then, success in achieving each small part of the larger task is recognized and rewarded. You may even encourage those who have mastered a small part of the task to lead or demonstrate for others. This is the equivalent of adopting a **small-wins strategy** (Weick, 1984).

Each small win or incremental achievement may seem insignificant by itself, but it generates a sense of movement, progress, and success. The recognition and celebration of small wins generate momentum that leads people to feel empowered, capable, and successful.

MODELING

Another way to empower people is to model or demonstrate the correct behavior that they are to perform. Observing someone else succeed at challenging activities provides a forceful impetus for others to believe that they, too, can succeed. It helps people presume that a task is do-able, that a job is within their capabilities, and that success is possible.

Because it may not be possible for you to model desired behaviors personally for every single person you want to empower, you may draw people's attention to other individuals who have been successful in similar circumstances. Or, you might make it possible for them to associate with visible role models who could serve as examples or mentors.

Think of what happens when a barrier is broken. In track and field athletics, for example, once John Thomas broke the seven-foot high jump mark and Roger Bannister broke the four-minute mile record, a host of other athletes quickly exceeded that standard. But before the first person broke those barriers, they were considered insurmountable. It took someone to demonstrate that the standard could be exceeded in order for others to experience the empowerment necessary to replicate the accomplishment themselves.

PROVIDING SUPPORT

A fourth technique for helping others experience empowerment is providing them with social and emotional support. If people are to feel empowered, they need to be praised, encouraged, approved, and reassured. This can be as simple as praising what they do well on a regular basis, writing notes to them or their families about the valuable contributions they are making, or providing feedback to them in a supportive way. You can provide opportunities for them to become part of a team or include them in social gatherings, or hold formal or informal ceremonies where achievements are recognized. It may simply be a matter of listening to people and empathizing with their feelings and points of view.

You can empower others, in other words, by engendering a feeling that they are accepted, that they are a valued asset, that you care about them, and that they are an integral part of the overall organizational mission or objective. This support can come from you or from colleagues with whom they work.

EMOTIONAL AROUSAL

Emotional arousal means replacing negative emotions such as fear, anxiety, or crabbiness with positive emotions such as excitement, passion, or anticipation. To empower people, managers help make the work environment fun and attractive. They ensure that the purpose behind the work is clear. They ensure that people's right brain (the side that controls emotions and passions) is involved in the work as well as their left brain (the side that controls logic and analysis). They provide positive energy to people, and as a result, both empowerment and performance increase (Esmaeili, et ak., 2011).

Bandura (1977) found that the absence of positive emotional arousal makes it difficult, if not impossible, for individuals to feel empowered. However, emotional arousal doesn't simply mean tooting horns, increasing the decibel levels, listening to speeches, or superficially creating excitement. Instead, emotional arousal occurs most likely when what individuals are doing is connected to values they hold dear. To feel a sense of empowerment, workers must see how what they are doing every day is associated with something that is important to them. Employees get more excited, for example, about working for the betterment of humankind, for the improvement of the quality of people's lives, and for personal growth and development, than they do for a 10 percent increase in salary or hitting a profit target. This is not to say that attaining financial goals is unimportant. But emotional arousal is associated more with personal values than with organizational profitability.

Emotional arousal is also associated with the attributes of work people do. This connection is best illustrated by the following truism: *"People are willing to pay for the privilege of working harder than they will work when they are paid."*(Coonradt, 2007). Consider what happens around mid-November in Utah and Colorado when the first major snowfall graces the ski resorts. Work and school absenteeism skyrocket. People sacrifice a day's pay, don their $400 skis, their $300 boots, their $500 ski outfit, buy $100 in gasoline to drive to the nearest ski resort, pay $115 for a lift ticket, eat a $35 hot dog for lunch, and return at the end of the day complete exhausted—paying for the privilege of working harder than they would work when they are paid.

The question is, why? Why will people spend more money to work harder, exhausting themselves, to endure uncomfortable environmental conditions, and to put their bodies at risk than they would possibly tolerate at work? The answer is obvious: "Because it's fun. It's recreation. It provides energy and enjoyment. People feel empowered."

The attributes that create this kind of emotional arousal can be applied to work settings as well. These attributes make activities fun and recreational, and they can be as typical of work as they are of leisure (Duckworth, Peterson, Matthews, & Kelly, 2007). For example, almost all fun, recreational activity has a clear *goal* (e.g., winning, exceeding a personal best). Without a clearly defined objective, we don't get excited. This goal is almost always pitted against a standard that we care about (e.g., winning the NCAA championship, bowling a 300 game). In addition, the *scorekeeping* and *feedback* systems are objective, self-administered, and continuous. In a basketball game, for example, we all know that a free throw always counts one point, that the winner is the team that makes the most baskets, and that there is never a time when we cannot find out the exact score of the game. One reason why we get excited watching athletic events is because we know the score all the time. This is unfortunately rare in most workplaces and classrooms. When we know the score, it increases emotional arousal.

Furthermore, in recreation, the *out-of-bounds* is clearly identified. We know the consequence of kicking a soccer ball over the end line, of hitting a ball to the left side of third base, or of stepping over the end of the takeoff board in the long jump. They are all out-of-bounds, and we are very clear that out-of-bounds behavior stops action.

You can help empower people through emotional arousal, not just by being a cheerleader, delivering charismatic speeches, and keeping the work climate fun, but also by capitalizing on some of the principles of recreation that create excitement: clear goals; objective, self-administered, and continuous scorekeeping and feedback; and clearly defined out-of-bounds behavior.

PROVIDING INFORMATION

Kanter (1983) identified information as one of the most crucial managerial "power tools." When you provide your people with more, rather than less information, those people gain a sense of empowerment and are more likely to work productively, successfully, and in harmony with your wishes. You actually enhance your power base by involving others in the pursuit of desirable outcomes. With more information, people tend to experience more self-determination, personal control, and trust. The resulting sense of empowerment enhances the probability that others will support you and try to assist you. Providing information to people makes them more likely to collaborate with you (Gilbert, Laschinger, & Leiter, 2010).

To be sure, it is possible to overload people with information and to create anxiety and burnout with too much data. But our experience has been that most people suffer from too little information instead of too much. Block (1987) argued:

> *Sharing as much information as possible is the opposite of the military notion that only those who "need to know" should be informed. Our goal is to let people know our plans, ideas, and changes as soon as possible.... If we are trying to create the mindset that everyone is responsible for the success of this business, then our people need complete information. (p. 90)*

Our own research confirms the importance of providing information to enhance empowerment (Cameron, Freeman, & Mishra, 1993). In one study, for example, we interviewed CEOs of large, well-known companies every six months to assess organizational changes and strategies they were using to cope with declining revenues. In one firm, not much progress was being made in improving the financial outlook. The CEO was very careful to share information on financial, productivity, cost, and climate indicators in the company only with his senior management team. No one else in the firm had access to that information. A change of CEO, however, led to a dramatic change in information-sharing policy. The new CEO began to provide information to every single employee in the firm. No data were treated as the sole possession of senior management. The sweepers had the same access as the vice presidents.

The resulting empowerment that employees experienced led to dramatic results. Employee-initiated improvements increased markedly, morale and commitment surged, and the resulting financial turnaround made the CEO look like a genius. He attributed his success to his willingness to empower employees by sharing the information they needed to know to improve.

PROVIDING RESOURCES

In addition to providing information, empowerment is also fostered by providing people with other kinds of resources that help them accomplish their tasks (Zhang & Bartol, 2010). In this sense, you empower others by acting more like a blocking back on a (U.S.) football team than a quarterback. You are less a director and commander than a resource provider (creating time for someone else to throw a pass or make a handoff), and an obstacle eliminator (blocking on-rushing defensive linemen) than the center of attention. When you empower others, your primary mission is to help them accomplish their objectives.

This means ensuring that they receive, for example, adequate training and development experiences, technical and administrative support, needed space, time, people, or equipment, access to communication and interpersonal networks, and discretion to pursue activities in the way they consider best. This does not mean, of course, that empowered people get everything they want. It is unrealistic to assume that unlimited resources are available—including your own time and attention.

On the other hand, the most important resources that you can provide are those that help people achieve control over their own work and lives; that is, to foster a sense of self-efficacy and self-determination. When individuals feel that they have what they need to be successful and that they have the freedom to pursue what they want to accomplish, performance is significantly higher than when these types of resources are not available (Spreitzer, 1992).

Log-on to Zappos.com, or to About Google, and watch a short video or two. You will see companies completely dedicated to empowering their employees to take care of customers, of work, and of one another.

Bill Marriott of the Marriott Corporate has a saying that "Customers Come Second. Employees Come First." He is convinced that empowering his workforce with necessary resources guarantees spectacular customer service.

CONNECTING TO OUTCOMES

One of the important lessons learned by U.S. manufacturing companies as a result of the Japanese entrance into the North American automobile and consumer electronics industries was that workers experience more empowerment when they can see the outcomes of their work. It was often a surprise to U.S. companies, for example, that their Japanese counterparts regularly visited customers in their homes or place of business, regularly observed how the products that the workers produced were used, and regularly received feedback directly from end users. This connection to the ultimate customer helped workers feel more empowered as well as provided a valuable source of improvement ideas (Dorio & Shelley, 2011). People are motivated at work when they can interact with ultimate customers in order to see the effects of their work.

A related idea is to provide employees with the authority to resolve problems on the spot. When employees are given discretion to resolve a problem, respond immediately to a customer's complaint, or fix the error instantly, without having to get approvals and sign-offs, not only is customer satisfaction dramatically increased (an average improvement of 300 percent), but workers feel far more empowered as well.

Another of the highly effective ways to enhance employee motivation and satisfaction is to create **task identity,** that is, the opportunity to accomplish a whole task (Hackman, Oldham, Janson, & Purdy, 1975). Individuals become frustrated and lack a sense of empowerment when they work on only part of a task, never see the end result of their work, and are blocked from observing the impact that their job creates. Having task identity implies that individuals can plan, implement, and evaluate the success of their efforts. The effects of what is accomplished can be assessed as well as the outcome. To feel empowered, in other words, you will want to know whether you successfully completed your assigned job as well as whether that job made any difference to the overall success of your work unit. The more clear that connection is, the more you will feel empowered.

CREATING CONFIDENCE

An additional technique for engendering empowerment is to create a sense of confidence that others have in you as the leader. Rather than being on guard or suspicious, workers are secure in their feeling that you and the organization are honorable and that you have their best interests at heart. This confidence helps drive out uncertainty, insecurity, and ambiguity, and it creates an environment of safety, security, and trust.

There are at least two reasons why individuals feel more empowered as they develop greater confidence in you as their leader or manager. First, the wasteful, unproductive behaviors associated with mistrust and suspicion are avoided. When people distrust one another, they don't listen, they don't communicate clearly, they don't try hard, and they don't collaborate. On the other hand, when trust exists, individuals are free to experiment, to learn, and to contribute without fear of retribution.

Second, individuals who are admirable and honorable always create positive energy for others and make them feel more capable and acceptable. Universities often trumpet the number of Nobel Prize winners on their faculties, the past Heisman trophy winners on their football teams, the number of outstanding faculty members in their business schools, and the notable achievements of their best students. Although other members of the university may have nothing to do with the achievements being publicized, they gain an enhanced self-image and a sense of empowerment because they are affiliated with the same organization. For the same reasons, creating confidence in you as a leader helps employees develop a sense of empowerment in your organization.

In creating such a sense of confidence and trustworthiness, five factors are especially important: (1) *reliability*, (2) *fairness*, (3) *caring*, (4) *openness*, and (5) *competence*. You create confidence, and thereby engender empowerment in others, as you display these five characteristics.

- ❏ *Reliability.* If you want people to have confidence in you, you must be reliable. This means being consistent, dependable, and stable. Your actions must be congruent with your words and attitudes.

- ❏ *Fairness.* You must be equitable and fair and must not take advantage of people. When you make judgments, workers need to be clear about the criteria you use. and the standards by which you judge others. These judgments must be seen as unbiased and fair.

- ❏ *Caring.* You must show a sense of personal concern for others and help each one feel important. You can do this by pointing out strengths and contributions of others and by using supportive communication when correcting mistakes or providing negative feedback.

- ❏ *Openness.* You build confidence as you remain open and accessible. This means that you share information openly and honestly, and you don't keep secrets that could harm others. This does not suggest that you don't keep confidences, because keeping confidences is crucial. Rather, it means that other people should not have to worry about hidden agendas that could negatively affect them.

- ❏ *Competence.* People need to be made aware of your competence. They need to be assured that you have the necessary ability, experience, and knowledge to lead and to solve problems. Without flaunting your expertise, you should inspire a feeling on the part of employees that their confidence in your expertise and proficiency is not misplaced.

The power of creating confidence in others is illustrated by our interviews with several CEOs. The key role of trust and confidence in management is hard to miss (see Cameron et al., 1993; Mishra, 1992).

If they don't believe what I'm telling them, if they think it's all a bunch of bull, they will never go out there and work a little harder. They won't work a little better. They're not going to be receptive to change unless they understand and trust the things that we're talking about are true. I think trust is the biggest single issue.

What's most important in my organization is this: being truthful. Don't b.s. anyone. Tell them what it is. Right or wrong or different. Tell them the truth.

My people are all 150 percent dedicated to helping one another. Because not one of them can do it alone, and they need each other badly. But here comes the openness and trust. You have to talk straight. You have to be open and honest. You have to create trust.

Successful managers create confidence by being authentic, honorable, and trustworthy.

REVIEW OF EMPOWERMENT PRINCIPLES

Table 8.3 summarizes the list of actions that we have discussed on the previous pages in relation to the nine prescriptions for empowerment. It provides a list of things you can do to empower other people. Not all of these suggestions are relevant in every circumstance or with every person, of course, but developing the skill of empowerment at least partly depends on knowing what alternatives are available as well as knowing how to implement them. This list is not comprehensive; other activities may be equally effective in empowering people. But the nine prescriptions and the suggestions associated with each of them represent actions that you will want to practice as you try to improve your competence in the skill of empowerment. The Skill Practice section of this chapter provides an opportunity for you to do this.

Research suggests that empowered individuals are most inclined to empower others. For that reason, we included an Assessment instrument at the beginning of this chapter that measures the extent to which you experience empowerment in your own work. Your scores on the instrument entitled Personal Empowerment Assessment indicate how much your own work is empowering for you in terms of self-efficacy, self-determination, personal control, meaning, and trust. Knowing what provides a sense of empowerment for you can be helpful as you consider ways in which you, in turn, can empower

Table 8.3	Practical Suggestions for Empowering Others
Articulate a Clear Vision and Goals	
• Create a picture of a desired future.	
• Use word pictures and emotional language to describe the vision.	
• Identify specific actions and strategies that will lead to the vision.	
• Establish SMART goals.	
• Associate the vision and goals with personal values.	
Foster Personal Mastery Experiences	
• Break apart large tasks and assign one part at a time.	
• Assign simple tasks before difficult tasks.	
• Highlight and celebrate small wins.	
• Incrementally expand job responsibilities.	
• Give increasingly more responsibility to solve problems.	
Model Successful Behaviors	
• Demonstrate successful task accomplishment.	
• Point out other people who have succeeded.	
• Facilitate interaction with other role models.	
• Find a coach.	
• Establish a mentor relationship.	
Provide Support	
• Praise, encourage, express approval for, and reassure.	
• Send letters or notes of praise to family members or coworkers.	
• Regularly provide feedback.	
• Foster informal social activities to build cohesion.	
• Supervise less closely and provide time-slack.	
• Hold recognition ceremonies.	

Table 8.3	Continued

Arouse Positive Emotions

- Foster activities to encourage friendship formation.
- Periodically send light-hearted messages.
- Use superlatives in giving feedback.
- Highlight compatibility between important personal values and organizational goals.
- Clarify impact on the ultimate customer.
- Foster attributes of recreation in work: clear goals, effective scorekeeping and feedback systems, and out-of-bounds behavior.

Provide Information

- Provide all task-relevant information.
- Continuously provide technical information and objective data.
- Pass along relevant cross-unit and cross-functional information.
- Provide access to information or people with senior responsibility.
- Provide access to information from its source.
- Clarify effects of actions on customers.

Provide Resources

- Provide training and development experiences.
- Provide technical and administrative support.
- Provide needed time, space, or equipment.
- Ensure access to relevant information networks.
- Provide more discretion to commit resources.

Connect to Outcomes

- Provide a chance to interact directly with those receiving the service or output.
- Provide authority to resolve problems on the spot.
- Provide immediate, unfiltered, direct feedback on results.
- Create task identity, or the opportunity to accomplish a complete task.
- Clarify and measure effects as well as direct outcomes.

Create Confidence

- Exhibit reliability and consistency.
- Exhibit fairness and equity.
- Exhibit caring and personal concern.
- Exhibit openness and honesty.
- Exhibit competence and expertise.

others. The other instrument that you completed in the Skill Assessment section (Effective Empowerment and Engagement) identified the extent to which you behave in ways that empower people with whom you work and the extent to which you are effective in engaging other people in work. How much you actually demonstrate the behaviors discussed above is assessed by these assessments.

Inhibitors to Empowerment

If the data are clear that empowering people produces superior results, and if techniques for enhancing empowerment are clear, why then is empowerment in organizations so rare? Why do a majority of people feel that they are alienated from their work, unengaged, and flourishing (Cameron, Dutton, & Quinn, 2003)?

In his book on managerial empowerment, Peter Block (1987) noted that empowerment is very difficult to accomplish:

> *Many managers have tried repeatedly to open the door of participation to their people, only to find them reluctant to walk through it. [In a study of managers who were offered total responsibility for their work areas], about 20 percent of the managers took the responsibility and ran with it, about 50 percent of the managers cautiously tested the sincerity of the offer and then over a period of six months began to make their own decisions. The frustrating part of the effort was that the other 30 percent absolutely refused to take the reins. They clutched tightly to their dependency and continued to complain that top management did not really mean it, they were not given enough people or resources to really do their job, and the unique characteristics of their particular location made efforts at participative management unreasonable. (p. 154)*

Many managers and employees are reluctant to accept empowerment, but they are even more reluctant to offer empowerment. Several surveys have examined the reasons managers have for not being willing to empower their employees (Byham, 1988; Newman & Warren, 1977; Preston & Zimmerer, 1978), and these reasons can be organized into three broad categories.

ATTITUDES ABOUT SUBORDINATES

People who avoid empowering others often believe that they are not competent enough to accomplish the work, aren't interested in taking on more responsibility, are already overloaded and unable to accept more responsibility, would require too much time to train, or shouldn't be involved in tasks or responsibilities typically performed by someone else. They feel that the problem of nonempowerment lies with other people, not with themselves. The rationale is: I'm willing to empower my people, but they just won't accept the responsibility. On the other hand, as pointed out above, these assumptions are far more typical of individuals who use them as an excuse to avoid empowering than they are of people in general. A vast majority of people seek empowerment (Kanter, 2008).

PERSONAL INSECURITIES

Some people fear they will lose the recognition and rewards associated with successful task accomplishment if they empower others. They are unwilling to share their expertise or "trade secrets" for fear of losing power or position. Or, they have an intolerance for ambiguity, which leads them to feel that they personally must know all the details about projects assigned to them. Or, they prefer working on tasks by themselves rather than getting others involved, or they are unwilling to absorb the costs associated with subordinates making mistakes.

The rationale is: I'm willing to empower people, but when I do, they either mess things up or try to grab all the glory. Unfortunately, when people try to be the heroes, obtain all the recognition for themselves, or avoid involving other people, they almost never accomplish what they could have by capitalizing on the expertise and energy of others. The empirical data are abundant showing that empowered teams do better than even the most competent individual (see Chapter 9, Building Effective Teams and Teamwork).

NEED FOR CONTROL

People unwilling to empower others also often have a high need to be in charge and to direct and govern what is going on. They presume that an absence of clear direction and goals will lead to confusion, frustration, and failure on the part of employees. They feel that direction from the top is mandatory. The rationale is: I'm willing to empower people, but they require clear directions and a clear set of guidelines; otherwise, the lack of instructions leads to confusion.

Whereas it is true that clear goals and specific directions enhance performance, self-established goals are always more motivating than those prescribed by someone else. Thus, people will perform better if they are empowered to establish their own goals rather than to have someone else superimpose them as a prerequisite to success.

OVERCOMING INHIBITORS

The rationale associated with each of these inhibitors may be partially true, of course, but they nevertheless inhibit you from achieving the success that is associated with skillful empowerment. Even if you demonstrate the willingness and courage to empower others, success still requires skillful implementation. Incompetent empowerment, in fact, can undermine rather than enhance the effectiveness of an organization and its employees.

For example, giving employees freedom without clear directions or resources has been found to lead to psychological casualties among individuals, as manifested by increased depression (Alloy, Peterson, Abrahamson, & Seligman, 1984), heightened stress (Averill, 1973), decreased performance and job satisfaction (Greenberger et al., 1989), lowered alertness, and even increased mortality (Langer & Rodin, 1976). Of course, these negative consequences are not solely associated with incompetent empowerment, but they have been noted in situations in which attempted empowerment was ineffective and unskillful. The point is, the guidelines provided previously are not just interesting ideas but are necessary for capturing the value that effective empowerment can produce.

Fostering Engagement

The situation in which empowerment is most needed is when other people must become involved in accomplishing work. Obviously, if a person is doing a task alone, knowing how to empower others is largely irrelevant. On the other hand, it is impossible for a manager to perform all the work needed to carry out an organization's mission, so work and the responsibility to carry it out must involve others. All managers, therefore, are required to engage their employees if they are to accomplish the tasks of the organization and create long-term success.

Engagement has become a very popular topic in the last decade or so, but its meaning has become more and more ambiguous instead of clarified. Engagement is sometimes used synonymously with morale, satisfaction, loyalty, commitment, and self-motivated actions. Sometimes authors have equated fostering engagement with "servant leadership," or helping other people flourish in a work context (Greenleaf, 2002).

In this chapter we take a very specific approach to engagement by focusing on how you get other people to become involved in work as well as how to help them achieve success. An empirically validated framework is used to address three questions: *when, with whom,* and *how* should you engage others in getting work done?

The skillful engagement of others has a variety of advantages in addition to merely accomplishing more work. As shown in Table 8.4, it also provides important benefits to those whom you engage.

Specifically, empowered engagement can help develop subordinates' capabilities and knowledge, so that their personal effectiveness is increased. It can be a technique to encourage personal mastery experiences. Engagement can also be used to demonstrate trust and confidence in the person receiving the assignment. Mishra & Mishra (2013) summarized research showing that individuals who felt trusted by their managers were significantly more effective than those who didn't feel that way. Engagement coupled with empowerment can be used to enhance the commitment of individuals receiving work. Research has consistently

Table 8.4	Advantages of Engaging Others
ADVANTAGE	**EXPLANATION**
Time	Increases the discretionary time of the manager
Development	Develops knowledge and capabilities of those being engaged
Trust	Demonstrates trust and confidence in those being engaged
Commitment	Enhances the commitment of those being engaged
Information	Improves decision making with better information
Efficiency	Enhances efficiency and timeliness of decisions
Coordination	Fosters work integration among those being engaged

demonstrated a positive relationship between having an opportunity to participate in work and subsequent satisfaction, productivity, commitment, acceptance of change, and desire for more work (Lorinkova, Pearsall, & Sims, 2013).

Enhancing engagement can also be used to improve the quality of decision making by bringing to bear more information, closer to the source of the problem, than the manager has alone. Engaging those who have direct access to relevant information can enhance efficiency (i.e., require less time and fewer resources) as well as effectiveness (i.e., result in a better decision).

Finally, fostering engagement can increase the coordination and integration of work by ensuring that information and final accountability are shared and not the sole responsibility of one person. Enhancing engagement, in other words, can ensure that no cross-purposes occur and that different tasks are not producing contradictory effects. Competently administered, engagement can produce all five dimensions of empowerment: a sense of competence, choice, impact, value, and security.

We now present some guidelines for deciding *when* to engage others, *whom* you should engage, and, finally, *how* to most effectively engage other people in accomplishing work.

DECIDING WHEN TO ENGAGE OTHERS

Fostering engagement involves deciding, first of all, when to engage others in work and when to perform it yourself. To determine when engagement is most appropriate, you should ask five basic questions (Vroom & Yetton, 1973; Vroom & Jago, 1974). Vroom's research indicates that when you follow the guidelines provided by these questions, successful results are four times more likely than when these questions are not considered. These questions are helpful guidelines to determine whether you should engage a single other person or whether you should engage many others.

1. *Do other people have the necessary (or superior) information or expertise?* In many cases, other people may actually be better qualified than you are to make decisions and perform tasks because they are more familiar with customer preferences, hidden costs, work processes, and so forth. They may be closer to the action than you are.

2. *Is the commitment of other people critical to successful implementation?* Participation in the decision-making process increases commitment to the final decision. When employees have some latitude in performing a task (i.e., what work they do, how they do it, and when they do it), they generally must be involved in the decision-making process to ensure their cooperation. Whereas participation usually will increase the time required to make a decision, it will substantially decrease the time required to implement it.

3. *Will other peoples' capabilities be expanded by this assignment?* Engagement can quickly get a bad name in a work team if it is viewed as a mechanism used by the boss to get rid of his or her undesirable tasks. Therefore, engagement should be consistent, not just when overloads occur. It should reflect an overall management philosophy emphasizing employee development and support. Enhancing the abilities and interests of others should be a central motive in delegating tasks.

4. *Do other people share with you and each other common values and perspectives?* If others do not share a similar point of view with one another and with you, unacceptable solutions, inappropriate means, and outright errors may be perpetuated. This produces a need for closer supervision and frequent monitoring. Articulating a clear mission and objective for people you want to engage is crucial. In particular, you must be clear about why the work is to be done. Coonradt (2007) found that important people are always told why, but less important people are merely told what, how, or when. Telling others why the work is meaningful creates a common perspective.

5. *Is there sufficient time to do an effective job of engaging others?* It takes time to save time. To avoid misunderstanding, you must spend sufficient time explaining the task and discussing acceptable procedures and options. Time must be available for adequate training, for questions and answers, and for opportunities to check on progress.

Enhancing engagement depends on a positive answer to each of the preceding questions. If any of these conditions is not present when engagement is being considered, the probability is greater that it will not be effective. More time will be required, lower quality will result, more frustration will be experienced, and less empowerment will occur. However, a negative answer to any of the preceding questions does not necessarily mean that effective engagement is forever precluded, because you can change situations so that other people get more information, develop common perspectives, have adequate time to receive delegation, and so forth.

DECIDING WHOM TO ENGAGE

If you have decided to engage others in a task, you must now consider whether to involve only a single individual or a team of people. If the decision is made to form a team, it is also important to decide how much authority to give the members of the team. For example, you should determine if the team will only investigate the problem and explore alternatives or if it will make the final decision. You must also outline whether or not you will participate in the team's deliberations. Figure 8.2 presents a model for helping you decide who should be engaged in tasks—individuals or teams—and whether you should be an active participant in a team if it is formed.

Figure 8.2 is constructed as a "tree diagram" that allows you to ask questions and, as a result of the answer to each question, move along a path until a final

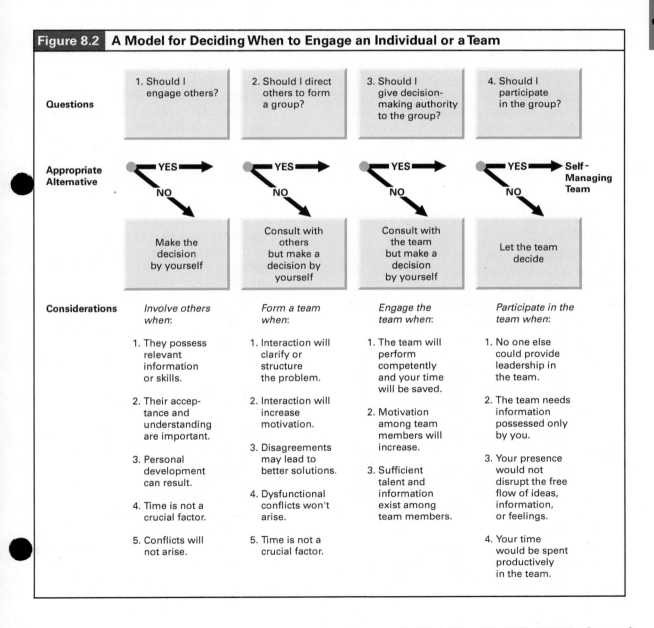

Figure 8.2 **A Model for Deciding When to Engage an Individual or a Team**

alternative is identified (Huber, 1980; Vroom & Jago, 1974). Here is how it works:

If you were a manager determining whether to involve others in accomplishing a task or making a decision, you should look over the considerations below the boxed question, "Should I engage others in the task or the decision?" If you decide that others do not possess relevant information or skills, that their acceptance is not important, that no personal development can occur for members of the team, that time is tight, or that conflicts will arise among the other people, you should answer "no" to this question. The tree then prescribes that you perform the task or make the decision yourself. However, if you answer "yes" to this question, you then move on to the next question: "Should I direct other people to form a team?"

Look over the five considerations below that question and then continue through the model. Any of the considerations below a question can result in a "no" answer. The most participative and empowering alternative is to engage others in a team and then participate as an equal member of the team. The least empowering response, of course, is to do the work yourself.

DECIDING HOW TO ENGAGE OTHERS

When a decision has been made to engage others in a task, and the appropriate people to engage have been identified, engagement has just begun. Positive outcomes of engagement are contingent upon your following 10 proven principles throughout the process.

1. *Begin with the end in mind.* You must articulate clearly the desired results intended from involving others. Be clear about what is to be accomplished, why it is important, and what benefits will result. Unless people know why a task is important and what is to be achieved by performing it, they are unlikely to act at all.
2. *Identify boundaries.* In addition to the desired ends, you must clearly specify the constraints under which the tasks will be performed. Every organization has rules and procedures, resource constraints, or boundaries that limit the kind of action that can be taken. These should be clarified when engaging others. For example, be clear about deadlines, the time frame for reporting back, and to whom the report should be made.

3. *Specify level of initiative.* You must clarify the level of initiative expected. No other oversight causes more confusion than the failure to delineate expectations regarding the level of initiative expected or permitted. At least five levels of initiative are possible, each of which may vary in terms of the amount of empowerment available to others. These initiative levels differ in terms of the amount of control permitted over the timing and content of the work. The five alternatives are:

- *Wait to be told what to do.* Take action only after specific directions are given. This alternative is the least engaging because it permits no initiative on the part of other people. There is no control over timing, that is, when the task is to be accomplished, or content, that is, what is to be done.
- *Ask what to do before acting.* Some discretion is provided to others in that they have some control over the timing of the task, but not its content. Others may formulate their own ideas for approaching the task, but because no action can be taken until you give approval, engagement is constrained.
- *Recommend, then take action.* This alternative is more engaging because others are given some freedom over both the timing and the content of the work. However, at least three different types of recommendations are possible, each with a different level of engagement. One is for others to simply gather information, present it to you, and you decide what needs to be done. Another is for others to determine alternative courses of action for each part of the task, leaving you to choose which course will be followed. Still another possibility is to outline a course of action for accomplishing the entire task and have the whole package approved at once. Progressively more engagement is associated with each of these three recommendation types.
- *Act, then report results immediately.* Others are given the freedom to act on their own initiative, but they are required to report to you immediately upon completion to ensure that their actions are correct and compatible with your objectives. They may be permitted to perform only one part of a task at a time, reporting the results of each individual

step. Or, they may be given the discretion to perform the entire task, reporting only when the final result has been accomplished. The latter alternative, of course, is the most engaging, but it depends on others possessing the necessary ability, information, experience, or maturity.

❑ *Initiate action, and report only routinely.* Others receive complete control over timing and over content of the tasks assigned. Reporting occurs only in a routine fashion to maintain coordination. When others have sufficient ability, information, experience, and maturity, this level of initiative is not only the most engaging but also the likeliest to produce high satisfaction and motivation among others (Hackman & Oldham, 1980).

The important point for you to remember is that you must be very clear about which of these levels of initiative you expect of those involved in the work.

4. *Allow participation.* Other people are more likely to engage willingly, perform tasks competently, and experience empowerment when they help decide what tasks are to be assigned to them and when. Often, you cannot allow complete choice about such matters, but providing opportunities to decide when tasks will be completed, how accountability will be determined, when work will begin, or what methods and resources will be used in task accomplishment increases employees' engagement. You should encourage others to ask questions and seek information regarding delegated assignments, and they should also feel free to express ideas about the parameters of the work in which they are engaged.

5. *Match authority with responsibility.* It is crucial to match the amount of responsibility given with the amount of authority provided. Nothing is more frustrating, and disengaging, that to be given responsibility but not have the authority to accomplish the task. An important part of developing a sense of self-determination and a sense of personal control—both critical dimensions of empowerment—is ensuring a match between responsibility and authority.

Although you cannot delegate *ultimate* accountability, you can delegate *prime* accountability. This means that "the buck stops," eventually, at your desk. Final blame for failure cannot be given away. This is ultimate accountability. On the other hand, you can delegate prime accountability, which means that others can be given responsibility for producing desired results, but you maintain ultimate responsibility for success or failure.

6. *Provide adequate support.* When you engage other people in work, you must provide as much support to them as possible. This involves making other people aware, presenting clearly stated expectations, providing relevant information, and ensuring that adequate resources are available. This support not only aids task accomplishment but also communicates interest and concern on your part.

Another form of support is to publicly bestow credit—but not blame. Even though prime accountability has been delegated, pointing out mistakes or faults in front of others embarrasses workers, creates defensiveness, fosters the impression that you are trying to pass the buck and get rid of final accountability, and guarantees that workers will be less willing to initiate action on their own in the future. Correcting mistakes, critiquing work, and providing negative feedback on task performance should be done in private, where the probability of problem solving and training can be enhanced.

7. *Focus accountability on results.* Once you have engaged others in work, you generally should avoid closely monitoring the way in which they accomplish the work. Excessive supervision of methods destroys the five dimensions of empowerment: self-efficacy, self-determination, personal control, meaningfulness, and trust. Successful accomplishment of a task, after all, rather than use of your preferred procedures, is the primary goal. This assumes, of course, that agreement on acceptable levels of performance has occurred, so you must clearly specify what level of quality or what level of achievement is expected.

8. *Be consistent.* The time for you to engage others is before you have to. If you only involve others when you are overloaded or highly stressed, two problems result. First, a primary reason for engaging others is forgotten—namely helping other people flourish. They feel that they are merely "pressure valves" for relieving your stress rather than valued team members.

Second, there is no time for training, providing needed information, or engaging in two-way discussions. Instead of enhancing engagement, you create resistance or negative feelings in others.

Another key is to delegate both pleasant and unpleasant tasks. Sometimes you are tempted to keep for yourself the tasks you like to perform and pass less-desirable work along to others. It is easy to see the detrimental consequences this has on morale, motivation, and performance. When individuals feel that they are being used only to perform the "dirty work," engagement suffers. Consistency then means that you engage others on an ongoing basis, not just when overworked, and that you involve others in both pleasant and unpleasant tasks.

9. *Avoid upward delegation.* Although it is important to engage others in work for their own development, you must be careful to avoid what is called "upward delegation." This means that other people try to have you solve their problems or accept responsibility for their work. For example, suppose someone you have engaged in a task comes to you and says, "I have a problem. This assignment just isn't turning out very well. What do you suggest I do?" If you reply, "Gee, I'm not sure. Let me think about it, and I'll get back to you," you have just become the owner of the task and promised to report back to the other person. You have accepted upward delegation, and this inhibits the other person from experiencing engagement.

One way to avoid upward delegation is to insist that the people whom you are engaging in work take responsibility for developing their own solutions. A more appropriate response might have been, "What do you recommend?" "What alternatives do you think I should consider?" "What have you done so far?" "What do you think would be a good first step?" Rather than sharing problems and asking for advice, other people will be more engaged if they share proposed solutions or recommendations.

10. *Clarify consequences.* Be clear about the consequences of successful task accomplishment. What are the rewards for success, what opportunities might open up, what is the impact on the organization's mission, what learning and development can occur, what benefits will be provided to others, and so on.

When people become aware that they can make a difference, that they can contribute something meaningful, and that there may be some payoffs for themselves, engagement is significantly more likely. Most importantly, The more you can highlight the meaningfulness of the work, or the value that is being produced, the more engaged people will be in the work.

REVIEW OF ENGAGEMENT PRINCIPLES

We have provided you with 10 principles summarizing *how* to engage others, 5 criteria for determining *when* to engage others, and 4 questions for identifying *to whom* to engage in work. Research results clearly show that when you foster empowered engagement, the following consequences occur:

❑ Other people readily accept the opportunity to be involved.

❑ The work has a high probability of being successfully completed.

❑ Morale and motivation remain high.

❑ Other peoples' problem-solving abilities are increased.

❑ More discretionary time becomes available.

❑ Interpersonal relationships are strengthened.

❑ People have a greater tendency to help one another and to display prosocial behavior.

Figure 8.3 summarizes the relationships among these principles.

International Caveats

Empowerment and engagement are sometimes misinterpreted as a soft approach to management, an abrogation of responsibility by leaders, an invitation for the inmates to run the asylum, and a prescription for chaos. Strong leadership, visionary managers, and take-charge bosses are usually the ones we read about in the newspapers and business magazines. A great deal of attention is given to people who "take command of the situation" and "stay out front of the troops."

With such a definition, empowerment is not a popular alternative in many cultures where, for example, an emphasis on *universalism, individualism,*

Figure 8.3 Relationships Among Principles of Effective Engagement

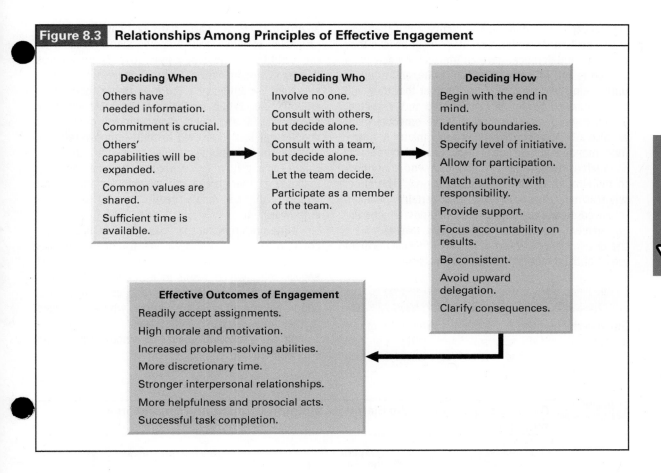

Deciding When

Others have needed information.

Commitment is crucial.

Others' capabilities will be expanded.

Common values are shared.

Sufficient time is available.

Deciding Who

Involve no one.

Consult with others, but decide alone.

Consult with a team, but decide alone.

Let the team decide.

Participate as a member of the team.

Deciding How

Begin with the end in mind.

Identify boundaries.

Specify level of initiative.

Allow for participation.

Match authority with responsibility.

Provide support.

Focus accountability on results.

Be consistent.

Avoid upward delegation.

Clarify consequences.

Effective Outcomes of Engagement

Readily accept assignments.

High morale and motivation.

Increased problem-solving abilities.

More discretionary time.

Stronger interpersonal relationships.

More helpfulness and prosocial acts.

Successful task completion.

---

specificity, and *ascription* are dominant. (Recall from Chapter 1 that the Trompenaars [1996, 1998] model differentiates cultures on the basis of seven dimensions: *universalism* versus *particularism*, *individualism* versus *communitarianism*, *neutrality* versus *affectivity*, *specificity* versus *diffuseness*, *achievement* versus *ascription*, *internal* versus *external* control, and *past*, *present*, or *future* time orientation.) Empowerment is sometimes viewed as contrary to some of these values in that maintaining consistency with rules and procedures (universalism) rather than encouraging experimentation and team innovation may seem to make empowerment less desirable. Focusing on individual performance (individualism) rather than team or collective effort may be viewed as contrary to empowerment. Involving only a limited amount of the self in the work setting or task assignment (specificity) rather than engaging multiple roles and in-depth relationships colleagues also may be interpreted as inconsistent with empowerment and empowered engagement. A focus on ascribed status, title, and traditional position (ascription) rather than a blurring of hierarchical lines

and focusing on merit or contribution also appears to contradict the aims of empowerment. Hence, empowerment may seem to be a concept that is more acceptable in cultures with a strong orientation toward particularism, collectivity, diffuseness, and achievement orientation.

On the other hand, abundant research has found the principles of empowerment and engagement discussed in this chapter to be applicable across almost all cultures. It is a misconception to believe that these principles do not work effectively in Eastern cultures as well as Western cultures, or in Western Europe as well as South America, or in Africa as well as the Polynesian Islands. Principles of empowerment are relevant to old and young, male and female, northern hemisphere or southern hemisphere.

This is because the five principles of empowerment are connected to fundamental human needs that transcend national or ethnic cultures. Virtually everyone has needs for, and performs better when they are exposed to, an environment in which they:

(1) feel capable, confident, and competent; (2) experience freedom, discretion, and choice; (3) believe they can make a difference, have an impact, and achieve a desired result; (4) sense meaning, value, and a higher purpose in their activities; and (5) trust that they will not be harmed or abused but honored and respected. In other words, the keys to effective empowerment are also keys to effective human performance at a very fundamental level. Strong leaders are not lone rangers so much as they are savvy individuals who know how to mobilize those they lead and manage. Therefore, whereas individual differences must certainly be taken into account and the pace at which empowerment and engagement can be fully implemented may vary with the circumstances, these principles of empowerment are essential to effective managerial performance.

Summary

Empowerment means helping to develop in others a sense of self-efficacy, self-determinism, personal control, meaning, and trust. The current business environment is not particularly compatible with the principles of managerial empowerment. Because of the turbulent, complex, competitive circumstances that many organizations face, managers frequently experience a tendency to be less, rather than more, empowering. When managers feel threatened, they become rigid and seek more control over other people, not less. However, without empowered employees, organizations cannot succeed in the long run. Learning how to be a competent empowering manager is therefore a critical skill for individuals who probably will face a predilection not to practice empowerment.

Nine prescriptions that managers can use to empower others were discussed. We also offered a series of principles and criteria for ensuring empowered engagement, which result in a variety of beneficial outcomes—both in terms of task accomplishment and in helping other people flourish who are engaged in the work. Figure 8.4 illustrates the relationships among the various elements of empowerment and engagement.

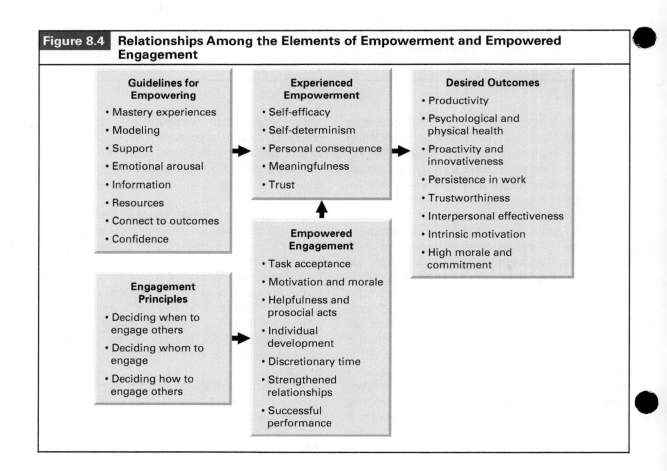

Figure 8.4 Relationships Among the Elements of Empowerment and Empowered Engagement

Guidelines for Empowering
- Mastery experiences
- Modeling
- Support
- Emotional arousal
- Information
- Resources
- Connect to outcomes
- Confidence

Engagement Principles
- Deciding when to engage others
- Deciding whom to engage
- Deciding how to engage others

Experienced Empowerment
- Self-efficacy
- Self-determinism
- Personal consequence
- Meaningfulness
- Trust

Empowered Engagement
- Task acceptance
- Motivation and morale
- Helpfulness and prosocial acts
- Individual development
- Discretionary time
- Strengthened relationships
- Successful performance

Desired Outcomes
- Productivity
- Psychological and physical health
- Proactivity and innovativeness
- Persistence in work
- Trustworthiness
- Interpersonal effectiveness
- Intrinsic motivation
- High morale and commitment

Behavioral Guidelines

As you practice empowering and engaging others, you will want to use the following guidelines as cues. *To ensure empowerment in others, follow these guidelines:*

A. Foster self-efficacy or a sense of competence by fostering personal mastery experiences and pointing out successful role models.

B. Foster self-determination or a sense of personal choice by providing alternatives and information to people.

C. Foster personal consequence or a sense of personal impact by allowing people to see the effects of their work on end users or on those affected by the results.

D. Foster meaningfulness or a sense of value by clarifying vision and values and connecting to something of inherent value.

E. Foster trust or a sense of security by providing support and creating confidence, primarily by being consistent, honest, open, and fair.

F. Engage others in work by applying the guidelines provided in the chapter to determine *when* to engage others, *whom* to engage, and *how* to most effectively engage others.

CASES INVOLVING EMPOWERMENT AND ENGAGEMENT

Minding the Store

> *On January 1, Ruth Cummings was formally named branch manager for the Saks Fifth Avenue store in a suburb of Denver. Her boss, Ken Hoffman, gave her this assignment on her first day: "Ruth, I'm putting you in charge of this store. Your job will be to run it so that it becomes one of the best stores in the system. I have a lot of confidence in you, so don't let me down."*

One of the first things Ruth did was to hire an administrative assistant to handle inventories. Because this was such an important part of the job, she agreed to pay her assistant slightly more than the top retail clerks were making. She felt that having an administrative assistant would free her to handle marketing, sales, and personnel matters—areas she felt were crucial if the store was to be a success.

Within the week, however, she received a call from Hoffman: "Say, Ruth, I heard that you hired an administrative assistant to handle inventories. Don't you think that is a bit risky? Besides, I think paying an assistant more than your top sales clerk is damaging to morale in the store. I wish you had cleared this with me before you made the move. It sets a bad precedent for the other stores, and it makes me look like I don't know what is going on in the branches."

Three weeks later, Ruth appeared on a local noontime talk show to discuss new trends in fashion. She had worked hard to make contact with the hosts of the show, and she felt that public exposure like this would increase the visibility of her store. Although the TV spot lasted only 10 minutes, she was pleased with her performance and with the chance to get public exposure.

Later that night at home, she received another phone call from Hoffman: "Don't you know the policy of Saks? Any TV appearances made on behalf of the store are to be cleared through the main office. Normally, we like to have representatives from the main store appear on these kinds of shows because they can do a better job of plugging our merchandise. It's too bad that you didn't notify someone of your intentions. This could be very embarrassing for me."

Just before Easter, Ruth was approached in the store by one of the sales clerks. A customer had asked to charge approximately $3,000 worth of china as a gift for his wife. He had been a customer of the store for several years and Ruth had seen him on several occasions, but store rules indicated that no charge could be made for more than $1,000 for any reason. She told the customer that she was not authorized to okay a charge of that amount, but that if he would visit the main store in Denver, maybe arrangements could be made.

Later in the day, an irate Hoffman called again: "What in the world are you thinking about, Ruth? Today we had a customer come into the main store and say that you wouldn't make a sale to him because the charge was too much. Do you know how long he has been a customer of ours? Do you know how much he spends in the store every year? I certainly hope we have not lost him as a customer because of your blunder. This makes me very upset. You've just got to learn to use your head."

Ruth thought about the conversation for several days and finally decided that she needed to see Ken Hoffman. She called his secretary to schedule an appointment for the following day.

Discussion Questions

8.1. What guidelines related to empowerment were violated by Ken Hoffman? By Ruth Cummings?

8.2. What guidelines related to engagement were violated by Ken Hoffman? By Ruth Cummings?

8.3. What should Ruth Cummings and Ken Hoffman discuss in their meeting? Identify specific agenda items that should be raised.

8.4. What are the questions that Ruth should ask Ken to help her acquire the necessary elements of empowerment? What questions should Ken ask Ruth to be better able to ensure her success?

8.5. If you were an outside consultant attending the meeting, what advice would you give Ken? What advice would you give Ruth?

Changing the Portfolio

You are head of a staff unit reporting to the vice president of finance. He has asked you to provide a report on the firm's current portfolio, including recommendations for changes in the current selection criteria. Doubts have been raised about the efficiency of the existing system given the current market conditions, and there is considerable dissatisfaction with prevailing rates of return.

You plan to write the report, but at the moment you are perplexed about the approach to take. Your own specialty is the bond market, and it is clear to you that detailed knowledge of the equity market, which you lack, would greatly enhance the value of the report. Fortunately, four members of your staff are specialists in different segments of the equity market. Together, they possess a vast amount of knowledge about the intricacies of investment. However, they seldom agree on the best way to achieve anything when it comes to investment philosophy and strategy.

You have six weeks before the report is due. You have already begun to familiarize yourself with the firm's current portfolio and have been provided by management with a specific set of constraints that any portfolio must satisfy. Your immediate problem is to come up with some alternatives to the firm's present practices and to select the most promising for detailed analysis in your report.

Discussion Questions

8.6. Should this decision be made by you alone? Why or why not?

8.7. If you answered the question, "Should I involve others?" affirmatively, which alternative in Figure 8.2 should be used in making a decision? Justify your choice.

8.8. What are the most important considerations in deciding whom to involve in this task?

8.9. If others are to become involved, how much empowerment should they have? What would you do specifically to achieve the appropriate level of empowerment?

SKILL *PRACTICE*

EXERCISES FOR EMPOWERMENT

Executive Development Associates

Assume you are Mary Ann O'Connell, general manager at Executive Development Associates. Your firm provides outplacement, training and development, career planning, and head-hunting services for a large number of *Fortune* 500 companies. You have been at the corporate board meeting for the last three days in the Rocky Mountains, and you relied on your secretary to screen out all but the most important or urgent messages. You slipped into the office on the way home from the airport Monday evening, just to check your electronic messages and your mail. Aside from a host of phone calls to return, here is the collection of messages retrieved from your email file and mail box.

Assignment

1. For each message, outline specifically the plan you will implement to empower others effectively to solve these problems. Determine who should be involved, what level of initiative should be taken, what actions you can take to ensure empowerment, how accountability should be maintained, and so on.

2. Write out the actions you'd take in response to each item. A worksheet has been provided on the next page to remind you of what you should consider as you record your responses.

3. After you have completed your own responses to each item, form a team of fellow students and share your plans. Provide feedback to one another on what is especially good, what could be improved, and what could be added to each person's action plan. In particular, what principles of empowerment are included, which are omitted, and which are contradicted?

Solving Problems Through Empowerment Worksheet

For each message, write out your plan of action. This plan should include answers to the questions listed below. Not every question is relevant to each message, but most are, and they can guide your action plan. After you have formed your own responses, form a team of fellow students and share these plans in turn. Provide feedback to one another on what is especially good, what could be improved, and what could be added to each action plan.

1. Who should be involved in resolving this issue? Will you form a team?

2. What kinds of personal mastery experiences can be provided for whomever you involve? Can you model successful behavior?

3. What kinds of support, information, and resources can be provided?

4. How will you create emotional arousal and create confidence in others?

5. What are the main considerations in deciding if you should engage others in each task?

6. If you opt for engaging others, what will you do to:

    Begin with the end in mind?
    Identify boundaries?
    Specify level of initiative?
    Allow for participation?
    Match authority with responsibility?
    Provide support?
    Maintain accountability?
    Ensure consistency?
    Avoid upward delegation?
    Clarify consequences?

INTEROFFICE MEMORANDUM

DATA PROCESSING CENTER

DATE: 15 June
TO: Mary Ann O'Connell, General Manager
FROM: Roosevelt Monroe, for the Data Processing Staff

After looking over last quarter's audit, it is clear that the number of complaints our group is receiving from individuals throughout the company is escalating. The problem is an obvious one to us. It is, simply, that several incompatible software systems have evolved over the last several years in various departments, and it is becoming increasingly difficult to coordinate across units. As you know, some data have to be retyped two or three times into different systems because of these incompatibilities.

The trouble is, our own employees, not to mention our customers, are becoming increasingly impatient with our slow turnaround time. They focus squarely on our group as the bottleneck. We think the rising complaint numbers in the quarterly audit are misleading, however, and they divert us from the real cause of the problem.

We're writing this memo to you to collectively urge you to address this issue as soon as possible. At a minimum, it should be discussed at our upcoming staff meeting on Tuesday. So far, the data processing staff is taking the blame for not getting data processed fast enough, yet it is really the fault of the system, not our unit.

We'll look forward to hearing from you on Tuesday.

INTEROFFICE MEMORANDUM

HUMAN RESOURCES DEPARTMENT

DATE: 15 June
TO: Mary Ann
FROM: Lucy

I was excited by your speech at the senior management meeting last week in which you established a new challenge for all senior executives. With the new competitive environment that we face, the vision that you articulated for our future is both exciting and challenging and, I think, an important step forward. It really makes clear the key success factors that should drive our business.

In particular, I think your directive for all senior executives to disseminate the vision throughout the organization to their own subordinates is a good way to get the message delivered. However, you made a statement in your speech that has me troubled. You said, "We used to pay you on the basis of new accounts generated, quarterly earnings, customer satisfaction ratings, and new product designs. Our new barometer is going to be how you're doing in disseminating the vision throughout your own units."

Frankly, I'm perplexed as to how we'll ever measure this directive. As the one who has to administer the appraisal and compensation systems, I'm not sure what criteria we'll look for or what indicators we'll use to determine success. I'm afraid that we'll create dissatisfaction if we don't have something specific outlined. Our people, especially those who may not perform, will think it is purely arbitrary. Do you really mean to have us change the appraisal and compensation systems to include this new criterion? How do you propose we measure effective performance? What would you like me to do to support your statement? Did you mean to make the statement that you did?

This is rather urgent because I have a staff meeting Tuesday afternoon, and I promised to have a response by then. I've already stalled until I had a chance to talk to you.

COPY OF A LETTER

Midwest State University

24 May

Dear Ms. O'Connell:

I am happy to be joining Executive Development Associates after several years at Midwest State University. As you know, leaving Midwest State has been quite traumatic for me, and that is what motivated me to make a request of you. I'm convinced that the reason I didn't receive tenure at Midwest State is because the expectations were never clear about what my responsibilities were and what the criteria were for success.

I know your company is very professional and employees are pretty much on their own, but I'm feeling a need to get some specific performance requirements outlined for me. I'm sure that I can be a good addition to your company, but I want to be clear about what your expectations are.

I have set a meeting with you on Tuesday through your secretary. Would you please outline a specific set of responsibilities and expectations for my job as instructor in the training and development department? If possible, I'd like it in writing to avoid any misunderstanding. Regardless, I'll look forward to talking to you Tuesday.

Thank you for your consideration.

Sincerely,

Lester Frost

INTEROFFICE MEMORANDUM

Training and Development

DATE: Monday, A.M.
TO: Mary Ann
FROM: Pam
RE: Tom Kinnir's Jury Duty

I know you're just getting back, but we've got an emergency on our hands.

I was just notified this morning by Tom that he has been selected for jury duty and that (can you believe it) he is being sequestered! Holy cow, Mary Ann, this couldn't come at a worse time. As our expert on activity-based costing, Tom is the only guy we have who can teach the topic. So what's the trouble, you say? The trouble is that we have over 100 corporate trainers showing up here for a seminar on Friday, and the seminar isn't prepared yet. Tom said that he has some notes and a few transparencies on his desk, but he had planned to spend this entire week designing and preparing it. Not only don't any of us know the topic very well, but we're not even sure what information we need, what data still needs to be gathered, who's got what, and how we go about filling in. Help! We're counting on this seminar to make budget this quarter, and we're feeling a little ticked off at Tom for waiting until the last minute. What do we do next?

By the way, how were the Rocky Mountains???

INTEROFFICE MEMORANDUM

Outplacement Department

DATE: Monday, A.M.
TO: Mary Ann O'Connell
FROM: Aneil Mishra
RE: Pending Plant Closure

You may have missed the news over the weekend. It was announced in the paper that Detroit Manufacturing has filed for Chapter 11 protection and that they're closing their Toledo plant. That means about 4,000 people will be out of work.

If we want the business, we've got to get moving right away. They will be looking at proposals from outplacement firms next week. We've got to get our proposal together, identify staff, determine a budget, and prepare a presentation in the next day or two.

Sounds like a great opportunity. I'll stop by tomorrow when you get back.

Empowering Ourselves

In this exercise, your task is to identify ways in which the empowerment of members of the graduating students this year in your own institution can be enhanced. You should use the principles of empowerment in the chapter to identify specific ways in which the empowerment of this group of people can be increased. What can be done, practically speaking, to effect empowerment?

Make certain that you don't merely identify what others could do, what the administration could implement, or what hypothetically could occur. Rather, identify very practical and realistic factors that could empower this graduating class. What could they do as a group? What could you do? What personal responsibility could they take for their own empowerment?

Do not treat this exercise as hypothetical or fantasy. Actually identify behaviors that you can implement that will enhance empowerment. Use the suggestions in the text as well as others that you add to those lists.

	Things That Can Be Done to Enhance the Empowerment of the Graduating Class
Self-Efficacy (personal competence)	
Self-Determination (personal choice)	
Personal Consequence (personal impact)	
Meaningfulness (personal value)	
Trust (personal security)	

Now form a team with three or four colleagues. Share your ideas with the group. For each dimension of empowerment, identify the most powerful ideas you hear from the team members. Add at least one new idea to your list. Also, identify when and how you'll actually implement your list. Use your team to help specify actual behaviors that you can implement.

Deciding to Engage Others

Engaging others in work is one of the most deceiving management skills because it seems so easy to accomplish. Just tell someone what to do, or ask them to become involved, and they'll do it, right? Unfortunately, this is seldom the case, and this exercise is designed to help you determine when and how to engage others more effectively. To accomplish this exercise you'll need to use the framework in Figure 8.2.

For each of the two scenarios that follow, ask the following questions:

- ❏ *Should I involve others or make the decision by myself?*
- ❏ *If I involve others, should I direct them to form a team, or should I consult them individually and make the decision by myself?*
- ❏ *If I form a team, should I grant decision-making authority to the team, or should I consult with the team but make the decision by myself?*
- ❏ *If I involve the team, should I participate in the team, or should I let the team decide?*

After you have made a decision about how to handle each of these two scenarios, form a group of colleagues. Share your decision and your rationale with the team. Reach a consensus regarding the most appropriate strategy to use in each of these two cases. For comparison purposes, an analysis by experts for the two cases is contained at the end of the chapter. It is provided only to enhance your team discussion.

An Emergency Request

You are a general plant supervisor and seven product lines involving four of your eight foremen must be disrupted to satisfy an emergency request from an important client. You naturally wish to minimize the disruption. No additional personnel are available, and time limits to complete the new project are restrictive. The plant is new and is the only industrial plant in an economically depressed area dominated by farming. You can count on everyone pulling his or her own weight. The wages in the plant are substantially above farm wages, and the workers' jobs depend on the profitability of this plant—the first new industrial development in the area in 15 years. Your subordinates are relatively inexperienced, and you have been supervising them more closely than you might if the plant had been in a well-established industrial area and your subordinates were more experienced. The changes involve only standard procedures and are routine for someone of your experience. Effective supervision poses no problems. Your problem is how to reschedule the work to meet this emergency within the time limit with minimum disruption of the existing product lines. Your experience in such matters should enable you to figure out a way of meeting the request that will minimize the disruption of existing product lines.

Biological Warfare

You are the executive vice president of a small pharmaceutical manufacturer. You have the opportunity to bid on a contract for the Defense Department pertaining to biological warfare. The contract is outside the mainstream of your business; however, it could make economic sense, since you do have unused capacity in one of your plants, and the manufacturing processes are not dissimilar. You have written the document to accompany the bid and now have the problem of determining the dollar value of the quotation you think will win the job for your company. If the bid is too high, you will undoubtedly lose to one of your competitors. If it is too low, you could lose money on the program. There are many factors to consider in making this decision, including the cost of the new raw materials and the additional administrative burden of relationships with a new client, not to speak of factors that are likely to influence the bids of your competitors, such as how much they need this particular contract. You have been busy assembling the necessary data to make this decision, but there remain several unknowns, one of which involves the manager of the plant in which the new products will be manufactured. Of all your subordinates, only he can estimate the costs of adapting the present equipment to its new purpose, and his cooperation and support will be necessary if the specifications of the contract are to be met. However, in an initial discussion with him when you first learned of the possibility of the contract, he seemed adamantly opposed to the idea. His experience has not particularly equipped him to evaluate projects like this one, so you were not overly influenced by his opinions. From the nature of his arguments, you inferred that his opposition was ideological rather than economic. You recall that he was once involved in a local peace organization and was one of the most vocal opponents in the company to the Vietnam and the Persian Gulf Wars.

SKILL APPLICATION

ACTIVITIES FOR EMPOWERMENT AND ENGAGEMENT

Suggested Assignments

8.10. Teach someone else (your spouse, a colleague, your boss) how to empower others and engage others effectively. Include the principles in Table 8.3 in your discussion. Use your own examples and illustrations.

8.11. Interview a manager about his or her empowerment practices. Try to determine what is especially effective, what doesn't work, what comes off as condescending, and what motivates people to perform. Identify the extent to which the manager knows and uses the principles discussed in the Skill Learning section of this chapter.

8.12. Think of a situation you now face with which you would like some help. It may be a task you want to accomplish, a tough decision you need to make, or a team you want to form. Make sure you think of something that requires the involvement

APPLICATION

of other people. Write down specific things you can do to engage other people to help you. How can you help them do what they want to do while simultaneously having them do what you want them to do?

8.13. Schedule a meeting with a manager who is not very good at empowerment. (Finding such a person shouldn't be difficult because most leaders tend to be more authoritarian and bureaucratic than empowering.) As a student who has learned about and practiced empowerment and engagement, share what you have learned and offer suggestions that could help this manager improve.

Application Plan and Evaluation

The intent of this exercise is to help you apply this cluster of skills in a real-life, out-of-class setting. Now that you have become familiar with the behavioral guidelines that form the basis of effective skill performance, you will improve most by trying out those guidelines in an everyday context. Unlike a classroom activity, in which feedback is immediate and others can assist you with their evaluations, this skill application activity is one you must accomplish and evaluate on your own. There are two parts to this activity. Part 1 helps prepare you to apply the skill, and Part 2 helps you evaluate and improve on your experience. Be sure to write down answers to each item. Don't short-circuit the process by skipping steps.

Part 1: Planning

8.14. Write down the two or three aspects of this skill that are most important to you. These may be areas of weakness, areas you most want to improve, or areas that are most salient to a problem you face right now. Identify the specific aspects of this skill that you want to apply.

8.15. Now identify the setting or the situation in which you will apply this skill. Establish a plan for performance by actually writing down a description of the situation. Who else will be involved? When will you do it? Where will it be done?

> Circumstances:
> Who else?
> When?
> Where?

8.16. Identify the specific behaviors in which you will engage to apply this skill. Operationalize your skill performance.

8.17. What are the indicators of successful performance? How will you know you have been effective? What will indicate you have performed competently?

Part 2: Evaluation

8.18. After you have completed your implementation, record the results. What happened? How successful were you? What was the effect on others?

8.19. How can you improve? What modifications can you make next time? What will you do differently in a similar situation in the future?

8.20. Looking back on your whole skill practice and application experience, what have you learned? What has been surprising? In what ways might this experience help you in the long term?

SCORING KEYS AND COMPARISON DATA

✪ Scoring Keys for the following instruments, along with comparison data, are contained in PIA in MyManagementLab.com;

Effective Empowerment and Engagement
Personal Empowerment Assessment

SCORING KEYS AND COMPARISON DATA

SKILL **ASSESSMENT**

- Team Development Behaviors
- Diagnosing the Need for Teambuilding

SKILL **LEARNING**

- The Advantages of Teams
- Team Development
- Leading Teams
- Team Membership
- Summary
- Behavioral Guidelines

SKILL **ANALYSIS**

- The *Tallahassee Democrat's* ELITE Team
- The Cash Register Incident

SKILL **PRACTICE**

- Leadership Roles in Teams
- Team Diagnosis and Team Development Exercise
- Winning the War for Talent
- Team Performance Exercise

SKILL **APPLICATION**

- Suggested Assignments
- Application Plan and Evaluation

SCORING KEYS AND *COMPARISON DATA*

9

Building Effective Teams and Teamwork

LEARNING OBJECTIVES

1. DIAGNOSE AND FACILITATE TEAM DEVELOPMENT
2. BUILD HIGH-PERFORMANCE TEAMS
3. FACILITATE TEAM LEADERSHIP
4. FOSTER EFFECTIVE TEAM MEMBERSHIP

MyManagementLab™

⊙ When you see this icon, visit www.mymanagementlab.com for self-assessments, video activities, and more.

DIAGNOSTIC SURVEYS FOR BUILDING EFFECTIVE TEAMS

TEAM DEVELOPMENT BEHAVIORS

PERSONAL INVENTORY ASSESSMENT

✪ If your instructor is utilizing **MyManagementLab**, log onto mymanagementlab.com and select the Personal Inventory Assessment (PIA) section and complete the instruments associated with this chapter.

The assessment instruments in this chapter are briefly described below. The assessments appear either in your text or in PIA. The assessments marked with (blue star) are available only in PIA.

All assessments should be completed before reading the chapter material.

After completing the first assessment save your response to your hard drive. When you have finished reading the chapter, re-take the assessment and compare your responses to see what you have learned.

✪ ❑ The *Team Development Behaviors Assessment* measures the extent to which you demonstrate effective leadership behaviors when you are the leader of a team as well as the extent to which you are an effective team member.

❑ The *Diagnosing the Need for Teambuilding Assessment* helps you identify the extent to which a team you know well or a team of which you are a member is in need of development and improvement.

BUILDING EFFECTIVE TEAMS AND TEAMWORK

Assessment Section

DIAGNOSING THE NEED FOR TEAM BUILDING

Teamwork has been found to dramatically affect organizational performance. Some managers have credited teams with helping them to achieve incredible results. On the other hand, teams don't work all the time in all organizations. Therefore, managers must decide when teams should be organized. To determine the extent to which teams should be formed in order to accomplish tasks, respond to the items below.

Think of an organization in which you participate (or will participate) that needs to accomplish a task, provide a service, or has the assignment to produce a result. Answer these questions with that organization in mind.

Rating Scale

Write a number from a scale of 1 to 5 in the blank at the left; 1 indicates that there is little evidence; 5 indicates there is a lot of evidence.

_____ 1. Output has declined or is lower than desired.

_____ 2. Complaints, grievances, or low morale are present or are increasing.

_____ 3. Conflicts or hostility between members is present or is increasing.

_____ 4. Some people are confused about assignments, or their relationships with other people are unclear.

_____ 5. Lack of clear goals and lack of commitment to goals exist.

_____ 6. Apathy or lack of interest and involvement by members is in evidence.

_____ 7. Insufficient innovation, risk taking, imagination, or initiative exists.

_____ 8. Ineffective and inefficient meetings are common.

_____ 9. Working relationships across levels and units are unsatisfactory.

_____ 10. Lack of coordination among functions is apparent.

_____ 11. Poor communication exists; people are afraid to speak up; listening isn't occurring; and information isn't being shared.

_____ 12. Lack of trust exists among members and between members and senior leaders.

_____ 13. Decisions are made that some members don't understand, or with which they don't agree.

_____ 14. People feel that good work is not rewarded or that rewards are unfairly administered.

_____ 15. People are not encouraged to work together for the good of the organization.

_____ 16. Customers and suppliers are not part of organizational decision making.

_____ 17. People work too slowly and there is too much redundancy in the work being done.

_____ 18. Issues and challenges that require the input of more than one person are being faced.

_____ 19. People must coordinate their activities in order for the work to be accomplished.

_____ 20. Difficult challenges that no single person can resolve or diagnose are being faced.

_____ **Total**

SOURCE: *Adapted from Diagnosing the Need for Team Building, William G. Dyer. (1987)* Team Building: Issues and Alternatives. *Reading, MA: Addison Wesley. Reprinted with permission of Addison Wesley.*

SKILL *LEARNING*

We have all heard statements describing the importance of teams. From athletics to evolution, from corporations to politics, the value of teamwork and teambuilding has been emphasized. For example:

"Teamwork is the fuel that allows common people to attain uncommon results." (Andrew Carnegie)

"We must all hang together, or most assuredly, we shall all hang separately." (Benjamin Franklin)

"In the long history of humankind (and animal kind, too) those who learned to collaborate and improvise most effectively have prevailed." (Charles Darwin)

"Coming together is a beginning. Keeping together is progress. Working together is success." (Henry Ford)

"Great things in business are never done by one person. They are done by a team of people." (Steven Jobs)

"Talent wins games, but teamwork and intelligence win championships." (Michael Jordan)

"The main ingredient of stardom is the rest of the team." (John Wooden)

"The team! The team! The team!" (Bo Schembechler, former Michigan football coach)

The Advantages of Teams

One important reason for an emphasis on teams is that participation in teams is fun for most people. There is something inherently attractive about engaging in teamwork. Consider, for example, the two advertisements that appeared next to one another in a metropolitan newspaper, both seeking to fill the same type of position. They are reproduced in Figure 9.1. While neither advertisement is negative or inappropriate, they are noticeably different. Which job would you rather take? Which firm would you rather work for? For most of us, the team-focused job seems much more desirable. This chapter focuses on helping you to flourish in these kinds of team settings.

Our Team Needs One Good Multiskilled Maintenance Associate

Our Team is down one good player. Join our group of multiskilled Maintenance Associates who work together to support our assembly teams at American Automotive Manufacturing.

We are looking for a versatile person with skills in one or more of the following: ability to set up and operate various welding machinery, knowledge in electric arc and M.I.G. welding, willingness to work on detailed projects for extended time periods, and general overall knowledge of the automobile manufacturing process. Willingness to learn all maintenance skills a must. You must be a real team player, have excellent interpersonal skills, and be motivated to work in a highly participative environment.

Send qualifications to:

AMM

American Automotive Manufacturing
P.O. Box 616
Ft. Wayne, Indiana 48606
Include phone number. We respond to all applicants.

Maintenance Technician/Welder

Leading automotive manufacturer looking for Maintenance Technician/Welder. Position requires the ability to set up and operate various welding machinery and a general knowledge of the automobile production process. Vocational school graduates or 3–5 years of on-the-job experience required. Competitive salary, full benefits, and tuition reimbursement offered.

Interviews Monday, May 6, at the Holiday Inn South, 3000 Semple Road, 9:00 A.M. to 7:00 P.M. Please bring pay stub as proof of last employment.

NMC

National Motors Corporation
5169 Blane Hill Center
Springfield, Illinois 62707

Whether you are a student, a manager, a subordinate, or a homemaker, it is almost impossible to avoid being a member of a team. Some form of teamwork permeates most people's daily lives. Most of us are members of discussion groups, friendship groups, neighborhood groups, sports teams, or even families in which tasks are accomplished and interpersonal interaction occurs. Teams, in other words, are simply groups of people who are interdependent in the tasks they perform, who affect one another's behavior through interaction, and who see themselves as a unique entity. What we discuss in this chapter is applicable to team activity in most kinds of settings, although we focus mainly on teams and teamwork in employing organizations rather than in homes, classrooms, or in the world of sports. The principles we review related to effective team performance, team leadership, and team participation, however, are virtually the same across all these kinds of teams.

For example, empowered teams, autonomous work groups, semiautonomous teams, self-managing teams, self-determining teams, crews, platoons, cross-functional teams, top management teams, **quality circles,** project teams, task forces, virtual teams, emergency response teams, and committees are all examples of the various manifestations of teams and teamwork that appear in the scholarly literature, and research has been conducted on each of them. Our focus is on helping you develop skills that are relevant in most or all of these kinds of situations, whether as a team leader or a team member.

Developing team skills is important because of the tremendous explosion in the use of teams in work organizations over the last couple of decades. For example, 79 percent of *Fortune* 1000 companies reported that they used self-managing work teams, and 91 percent reported that employee work groups were utilized (Lawler, 1998; Lawler, Mohrman, & Ledford, 1995). More than two-thirds of college students participate in an organized team, and almost no one can graduate from a business school anymore without participating in several team projects or group activities. Teams are ubiquitous in both work life and at school. Possessing the ability to lead and manage teams and teamwork, in other words, has become a commonplace requirement in most organizations. In one survey, the most desired skill of new employees was found to be the ability to work in a team (Wellins, Byham, & Wilson, 1991).

One reason for the escalation in the desirability of teamwork is that increasing amounts of data show improvements in productivity, quality, and morale when teams are utilized. Many companies have attributed improvements in performance directly to the institution of teams in the workplace (Cohen & Bailey, 1997; Guzzo & Dickson, 1996; Hamilton, Nickerson, & Owan, 2003; Katzenbach & Smith, 1993; Senge, 1991). For example, by using teams in their organizations:

❑ Shenandoah Life Insurance Company in Roanoke, Virginia, saved $200,000 annually because of reduced staffing needs, while increasing its volume 33 percent.

❑ Westinghouse Furniture Systems increased productivity 74 percent in three years.

❑ AAL increased productivity by 20 percent, cut personnel by 10 percent, and handled 10 percent more transactions.

❑ Federal Express cut service errors by 13 percent.

❑ Carrier reduced unit turnaround time from two weeks to two days.

❑ Volvo's Kalamar facility reduced defects by 90 percent.

❑ General Electric's Salisbury, North Carolina, plant increased productivity by 250 percent compared to other GE plants producing the same product.

❑ Corning cellular ceramics plant decreased defect rates from 1,800 parts per million to 9 parts per million.

❑ AT&T's Richmond operator service increased service quality by 12 percent.

❑ Dana Corporation's Minneapolis valve plant trimmed customer lead time from six months to six weeks.

❑ General Mills plants became 40 percent more productive than plants operating without teams.

❑ A garment-making plant increased its productivity 14 percent by adopting a team-based production system.

Table 9.1 reports the positive relationships between employee involvement in teams and several dimensions of organizational and worker effectiveness. Lawler, Mohrman, and Ledford (1995) found that among firms that were actively using teams, both organizational and individual effectiveness were above average and improving in virtually all categories of performance. In firms without teams or in which teams were infrequently used, effectiveness was average or low in all categories.

Of course, a variety of factors can affect the performance and usefulness of teams. Teams are not inherently effective just because they exist. A decade ago, for example, a *Sports Illustrated* cover story labeled the Los Angeles Clippers NBA basketball team the worst team in the history of professional sports from its inception to 20 years later (Lidz, 2000)—evidence that just because a group of talented people get together does not mean an effective team can be created. In the last few years, however, the Clippers have become one of the best basketball teams on the West Coast of the United States.

Hackman (1993) identified a set of common inhibitors to effective team performance, including rewarding and recognizing individuals instead of the team, not maintaining stability of membership over time, not providing team members with autonomy, not fostering interdependence among team members, and failing to orient all team members. And Verespei (1990) observed:

> All too often corporate chieftains read the success stories and ordain their companies to adopt work teams—NOW. Work teams don't always work and may even be the wrong solution to the situation in question.

The instrument, entitled "Diagnosing the Need for Teambuilding" in the Skill Assessment section of this chapter, helps identify the extent to which the work teams in which you are involved are performing effectively and the extent to which they need teambuilding. Often, teams can take too long to make decisions; they can drive out effective action by becoming too insular; and they can create confusion, conflict, and frustration for their members. All of us have been irritated by being members of an inefficient team, a team dominated by a single person, a team with slothful members, or a team in which standards are compromised in order to get agreement from everyone. The common adage that "a camel is a horse designed by a team" illustrates one of the many potential liabilities of a team.

On the other hand, a great deal of research has been conducted to identify the factors associated with high performance in teams. Factors such as *team composition* (e.g., heterogeneity of members, size of the team, familiarity among team members), *team motivation* (e.g., team potency, team goals, team rewards, team feedback), *team type* (e.g., virtual teams, cockpit crews, quality circles) and *team structure* (e.g., team member autonomy, team norms, team decision-making processes) have been studied to determine

Table 9.1	Impact of Involvement in Teams on Organizations and Workers
PERFORMANCE CRITERIA	**PERCENT INDICATING IMPROVEMENT**
Changed management style to more participatory	78
Improved organizational processes and procedures	75
Improved management decision making	69
Increased employee trust in management	66
Improved implementation of technology	60
Elimination of layers of management supervision	50
Improved safety and health	48
Improved union-management relations	47
PERFORMANCE CRITERIA	**PERCENT INDICATING POSITIVE IMPACT**
Quality of products and services	70
Customer service	67
Worker satisfaction	66
Employee quality of work life	63
Productivity	61
Competitiveness	50
Profitability	45
Absenteeism	23
Turnover	22

(N = 439 of the *Fortune* 1000 firms)

SOURCE: *Impact of involvement in teams on organizations and workers, Lawler, E. E., Mohman, S. A., & Ledford, G. E. (1992). Creating high performance organizations: Practices and results of employee involvement and total quality in Fortune 1000 companies. Reprinted with permission of John Wiley & Sons, Inc.*

how best to form and lead teams (see comprehensive reviews by Cohen & Bailey, 1997; Guzzo & Dickson, 1996; Hackman, 2003; Shuffler, Burke, Kramer, & Salas, 2012).

Several thousand studies of groups and teams have appeared in just the last decade. Self-managing work teams, problem-solving teams, therapy groups, task forces, interpersonal growth groups, student project teams, and many other kinds of teams have been studied extensively. Studies have ranged from teams meeting for just one session to teams whose longevity extends over several years. Membership in teams has varied widely, ranging from children to aged people, top executives to line workers, students to instructors, volunteers to prison inmates, professional athletes to playground toddlers. The analyses have included a variety of predictors of performance such as team member roles, unconscious cognitive processes, group dynamics, problem-solving strategies, communication patterns, leadership actions, interpersonal needs, decision-making quality, innovativeness, and productivity (e.g., Ancona & Caldwell, 1992; Gladstein, 1984; Senge, 1991; Wellins et al., 1991; Shuffler, Burke, Kramer, & Salas, 2012).

We will not spend time in this chapter reviewing the extensive literature associated with teams, nor the multitude of factors that have been associated with team performance. Instead, we focus on a few key skills that will help you lead and participate effectively in most kinds of teams. We particularly focus here on teams that are faced with a task to accomplish. This may be a work team at your job, a project team composed of fellow students, an ad hoc team discussing an issue, or a self-managing team in a service organization. Regardless of the kind of team in which you participate, you will want to improve your skills in helping the team become a high-performing unit. Team success is a major factor in most people's individual success.

We concentrate first on helping you understand the development of teams and how to diagnose the key issues present in each of four stages of team development. When you lead or become a member of a team, knowing about the developmental phases and predictable issues that arise will give you an advantage and help make you a more effective leader and team member. We focus on helping you improve your capability to lead teams in and through these various stages.

⊘ **MyManagementLab: WATCH IT**
Joie de Vivre Hospitality:
Employee Motivation

Apply what you have learned about teamwork. If your instructor has assigned MyManagementLab, go to mymanagementlab.com to watch a video case and answer questions.

AN EXAMPLE OF AN EFFECTIVE TEAM

To illustrate some of the principles we discuss in this chapter, we briefly describe one of the most effective team efforts we know about. It is the team formed to plan and conduct the logistical support for the United States' engagement in the Persian Gulf War (Desert Storm)—the original conflict motivated by Iraq's threatened invasion of Kuwait. General Gus Pagonis was the designated leader of this team, which was organized as a result of an announcement by the President of the United States that the U.S. would send troops to Saudi Arabia in order to confront the Iraqi aggression into Kuwait.

The tasks Pagonis faced were daunting. He was charged with building a team that could transport more than half a million people and their personal belongings to the other side of the world, on short notice. But transporting the people was only part of the challenge. Supporting them once they arrived, moving them into position, supporting their battle plans, and then getting them and their equipment back home in record time were even greater challenges.

More than 122 million meals had to be planned, moved, and served—approximately the number eaten by all the residents of Wyoming and Vermont

in three months. Fuel (1.3 billion gallons) had to be pumped—about the same amount used in Montana, North Dakota, and Idaho in a year—in order to support soldiers driving 52 million miles. Tanks, planes, ammunition, carpenters, cashiers, morticians, social workers, doctors, and a host of support personnel had to be transported, coordinated, fed, and housed. More than 500 new traffic signs had to be constructed and installed in order to help individuals speaking several different languages navigate the relatively featureless terrain. Five hundred tons of mail had to be sorted and processed each day. More than 70,000 contracts with suppliers had to be negotiated and executed. All green-colored equipment—more than 12,000 tracked vehicles and 117,000 wheeled vehicles—had to be repainted desert brown and then repainted green when shipped home. Soldiers had to be trained to fit in with an unfamiliar culture that was intolerant of typical soldier-relaxation activity. Supplies had to be distributed at a moment's notice to several different locations, some of them behind enemy lines, in the heat of battle. Traffic control was monumental, as evidenced by one key checkpoint near the front where 18 vehicles per minute passed, seven days a week, 24 hours a day, for six weeks. More than 60,000 enemy prisoners of war had to be transported, cared for, and detained.

Because the war ended far sooner than predicted, an even more daunting challenge presented itself—getting all those supplies and personnel back home. Most of the equipment, ammunition, and food had to be brought back home because it had been unpacked but was mostly unused. That required thorough scrubbing to remove microorganisms or pests and re-shrinkwrapping a huge amount of supplies. Since large, bulk containers had been broken up into smaller units during the war, it took twice as long to gather and ship materials out of Saudi Arabia as it did to ship them in. Yet, personnel were eager to return home at the end of the campaign, so the pressure for speed was at least as great as at the outset of the conflict. In short, Pagonis' team faced a set of tasks that had never before been accomplished on that scale, and they were to do it in a time frame that would have been laughable if it weren't factual.

The teambuilding and teamwork skills used to accomplish these tasks were detailed in Pagonis' book, *Moving Mountains*. Pagonis was awarded a third star during Desert Storm as a result of his outstanding leadership in the field of battle. He helped plan and execute the famous "end run" that took the Iraqi army completely by surprise. Most observers now agree that it was the success of the logistics team that really won the Persian Gulf War for the United States and saved tens of thousands, if not hundreds of thousands, of lives. We use excerpts from his description of this team's functioning to illustrate principles of effective teambuilding and team leadership in the sections that follow.

Team Development

Regardless of whether you play the role of team leader or team member, in order to function effectively in a team it is important that you understand that all teams progress through stages of development. These stages cause the dynamics within the team to change, the relationships among team members to shift, and effective leader behaviors to be modified. In this section, we outline the four major stages that teams pass through from early stages of development—when a team is still struggling to become a coherent entity—to a more mature stage of development—when the team has become a highly effective, smoothly functioning unit. The skill we want you to develop is to be able to diagnose the stage of your team's development so that you will know what kinds of behaviors will most effectively enhance your team's performance.

Evidence of predictable patterns of team development has been available since the early part of this century (Dewey, 1933; Freud, 1921). In fact, despite the variety in composition, purpose, and longevity of the teams investigated in a large array of studies, the stages of group and team development have been strikingly similar (Cameron & Whetten, 1984; Hackman, 2003; Quinn & Cameron, 1983). The research shows that teams tend to develop through four separate, sequential stages. These stages were first labeled by Tuckman (1965) as **forming, norming, storming,** and **performing**. Because of their rhyme and parsimony, these labels are still widely used today. (Tuckman's second and third stages are reversed in this chapter based on the research of Greiner, 1972; Cameron & Whetten, 1981; and Bonebright, 2010).

Table 9.2 summarizes the four main stages of team development. In order for teams to be effective and for team members to benefit most from team membership, teams must progress through the first three stages of development to achieve Stage 4. In each separate stage, unique challenges and issues predominate, and it is by successfully diagnosing and managing these issues and challenges that a team matures and becomes more effective. For each of the four stages, we first identify major team member issues and questions, and then we identify the management responses that help the team effectively transcend that stage of development.

THE FORMING STAGE

When team members first come together, they are much like an audience at the outset of a concert. They are not a team but an aggregation of individuals sharing a common setting. Something must happen for them to feel that they are a cohesive unit. When you meet with a group of people for the first time, for example, chances are that you do not feel integrated or

Table 9.2	**Four Stages of Team Development**
STAGE	**EXPLANATION**
Forming	The team is faced with the need to become acquainted with its members, its purpose, and its structure. Relationships must be formed and trust established. Clarity of direction is needed from team leaders.
Norming	The team is faced with creating cohesion and unity, differentiating roles, identifying expectations for members, and enhancing collaboration. Providing supportive feedback and fostering commitment to a vision are needed from team leaders.
Storming	The team is faced with disagreements, counter-dependence, differing points of view, and the need to manage conflict. Challenges include violations of team norms and expectations and overcoming groupthink. Focusing on process improvement, recognizing team achievement, and fostering win/win relationships are needed from team leaders.
Performing	The team is faced with the need for continuous improvement, innovation, speed, and capitalizing on core competencies. Sponsoring team members' new ideas, orchestrating their implementation, and fostering extraordinary performance are needed from the team leaders.

cohesive with the group right away. Several questions are probably on your mind, such as:

- Who are these other people?
- What is expected of me?
- Who is going to lead?
- What is supposed to happen?

The questions uppermost in the minds of participants in a new team have to do with establishing a sense of security and direction, getting oriented, and becoming comfortable with the new situation. Sometimes, new team members can articulate these questions, while at other times they are little more than general feelings of discomfort or disconnectedness. Uncertainty and ambiguity tend to predominate as individuals seek some type of understanding and structure. Because there is no shared history with the team, there is no unity among members. Thus, the typical interpersonal relationships that predominate in this stage are:

- Silence
- Self-consciousness
- Dependence
- Superficiality
- Mild discomfort

Even though some individuals may enter a team situation with great enthusiasm and anticipation, they are usually hesitant to demonstrate their emotions to others until they begin to feel at ease. Moreover, without knowing the rules and boundaries, it feels risky to speak out or to even ask questions. Seldom are new members willing to actively query a leader when a team first meets together, even though uncertainty prevails. When a leader asks questions of team members, rarely does someone jump at the chance to give an answer. When answers are given, they are likely to be brief. Little interaction occurs among team members themselves, most communication is targeted at the team leader or person in charge, and each individual is generally thinking more of himself or herself than of the team. Interactions tend to be formal and guarded. Congruent behaviors are masked in the interest of self-protection.

Individuals cannot begin to feel like a team until they become familiar with the rules and boundaries of their setting. They don't know whom to trust, who will take initiative, what constitutes normal behavior, or what kinds of interactions are appropriate. They are not yet a real team but only a collection of individuals. Therefore, the task of the team in this stage is less

focused on producing an output than on developing the team itself. Helping team members become comfortable with one another takes precedence over task accomplishment. To help a team effectively manage this first stage of development, you should:

- Orient members and answer questions.
- Establish trust.
- Establish relationships among members and with the leader(s).
- Establish clarity of purpose, norms, procedures, and expectations.

This stage may be brief, but it is not a time to rely on free and open discussion and consensus decision making to accomplish an outcome. Direction, clarity, and structure are needed instead. The first task is to ensure that all team members know one another and that their questions are answered. Because relatively little participation may occur during this stage, the temptation may be to rush ahead or to short-circuit introductions and instructions. However, teams tend to flounder later if the challenges of this stage are not adequately managed.

In the case of the Persian Gulf logistics team, the first critical task was to make certain that objectives, rules and regulations, time frames, and resources were clearly laid out. Each member of the team had to become comfortable with his or her team membership:

The team got down to work with a redoubled sense of urgency. They were soon fully familiar with the plan that had been roughed out. We quickly got to a joint understanding of what I took to be our role in the theater. Our session...was very successful, mainly because from the outset we had a well-defined structure for invention. We worked toward several clearly expressed goals, and there was an imposed time limit to keep us on track. And finally, our various experiences were complementary. We needed each other and we knew it. (Pagonis, 1993, pp. 82–83)

THE NORMING STAGE

Once team members have become oriented, achieved clarity about the team's goals, and accepted their place in the team, the main challenge of the team is to create a cohesive unit or a "sense of teamwork." Norms, rules, and expectations are clarified in the first stage, but an underlying team culture and informal relationships among members must also be developed. The need to

LEARNING

move the team from a group of individuals sharing a common goal to a highly cohesive unit is the motivation that leads the team to a new stage of development—the norming stage. The more team members interact with one another, the more they develop common behaviors and perspectives. They experience a certain amount of pressure to conform to the expectations of other team members, so the team begins to develop a character and culture of its own. We all have experienced strong peer pressure, the clearest example of the dynamics in this stage of team development. A new cohesive team culture affects the amount of work done by the team, its style of communicating, approaches to problem solving, and even team member dress.

The major focus of team members, in other words, shifts from overcoming uncertainty in the forming stage to developing the norms of a unified group. Typical questions in team members' minds during this stage include:

❑ What are the norms and values of the team?

❑ How can I best get along with everyone else?

❑ How can I show my support to others?

❑ How can I fit in?

During the, norming stage, team members become contented with team membership and begin to value the team's goals more than their own personal goals. Individual needs are met through the team's accomplishments. The team, rather than the leader or a single person, takes responsibility for solving problems, confronting and correcting mistakes, and ensuring success. Agreement and a willingness to get along characterize the climate of the team. Individuals experience feelings of loyalty to one another, and the interpersonal relationships that most characterize team members include:

❑ Cooperativeness

❑ Conformity to standards and expectations

❑ Heightened interpersonal attraction

❑ Ignoring disagreements

This norming stage is a time when effective teams encourage relationship-building roles. Participation by all team members is encouraged. To effectively manage this second stage of development, you should:

❑ Maintain unity and cohesion.

❑ Facilitate participation and empowerment.

❑ Show support to team members.

❑ Provide feedback on team and team member performance.

A major problem may arise in this stage of development, however, and this is an increasing inability to engender diversity and varied perspectives in the team. Whereas team members may feel extremely satisfied with their tightly bonded unit, the team risks a danger of developing *groupthink* (Janis, 1972). Groupthink occurs when the cohesiveness and inertia developed in a team drives out good decision making and problem solving. The preservation of the team takes precedence over accurate decisions or high-quality task accomplishment. Not enough differentiation and challenge to the team's mind-set occurs.

Groupthink

Irv Janis (1972) conducted research in which he chronicled several high-performing teams that in one instance performed in a stellar fashion but performed disastrously in another instance. His classic example was the cabinet of President John F. Kennedy. This team worked through what is often considered one of the best sets of decisions ever made in handling the Cuban Missile Crisis, in which the former Soviet Union was inhibited from placing warhead missiles in Cuba by means of a high-stakes confrontation by Kennedy and his cabinet. This was also the same team, however, that earlier had made disastrous decisions related to the Bay of Pigs fiasco, in which a planned overthrow of Fidel Castro's government in Cuba became a logistical nightmare, a confluence of indecision, and an embarrassing defeat for the same subsequently high-functioning team.

What was the difference? Why did the same team do so well in one circumstance and so poorly in another? Janis' answer is groupthink. Groupthink typically occurs when the following attributes develop in teams that are stuck in the norming stage.

❑ *Illusion of invulnerability.* Members feel assured that the team's past success will continue. ("Because of our track record, we cannot fail.")

❑ *Shared stereotypes.* Members dismiss disconfirming information by discrediting its source. ("Those people just don't understand these things.")

❑ *Rationalization.* Members rationalize away threats to an emerging consensus. ("We know the wrongheaded reasons they don't agree with us.")

❑ *Illusion of morality.* Members believe that they, as moral individuals, are not likely to make wrong decisions. ("This team would never knowingly make a bad decision or do anything immoral or unethical.")

❑ *Self-censorship.* Members keep silent about misgivings and try to minimize doubts. ("I must be wrong if others don't think the way I do.")

❑ *Direct pressure.* Sanctions are imposed on members who explore deviant viewpoints. ("If you don't agree, why don't you just leave the team?")

❑ *Mind guarding.* Members protect the team from being exposed to disturbing ideas. ("Don't listen to them. We need to keep the rabble rousers at bay.")

❑ *Illusion of unanimity.* Members conclude that the team must have reached a consensus since the most vocal members are in agreement. ("If a few vocal people express agreement, there must be a consensus.")

The problem with groupthink is that it leads teams to commit more errors than normal. For example, consider the following commonly observed scenario.

Not wanting to make a serious judgment error, a leader convenes a meeting of his or her team. In the process of discussing an issue, the leader expresses a preference for one option. Other team members, wanting to appear supportive, present arguments justifying the decision. One or two members tentatively suggest alternatives, but they are strongly overruled by the majority. The decision is carried out with even greater conviction than normal because everyone is in agreement, but the consequences are disastrous. How did this happen?

While the leader brought the team together to avoid making a bad decision, the presence of groupthink actually made a bad decision more likely. Without the social support provided by the team, the leader may have been more cautious in implementing a personally preferred but uncertain decision.

To manage this tendency to develop groupthink, effective teams must move through the norming stage into the storming stage. The team must develop attributes that will foster diversity, heterogeneity, and even productive conflict in the team's processes (Ben-Hur, Kinley, & Jonsen, 2012). In particular, Janis makes the following suggestions for addressing groupthink:

❑ *Critical evaluators.* At least one team member should be assigned to perform the role of critic or evaluator of the team's decisions.

❑ *Open discussion.* The team leader should not express an opinion at the outset of the team meeting but should encourage open discussion of differing perspectives by team members.

❑ *Subgroups.* Multiple subgroups in the team may be formed to develop independent proposals.

❑ *Outside experts.* Invite outside experts to listen to the rationale for the team's decision and critique it.

❑ *Devil's advocate.* Assign at least one team member to play devil's advocate during the discussion if it seems that too much homogeneity exists in the team's discussion.

❑ *Second-chance meetings.* Sleep on the team's decision and revisit it afresh the next day. The expression of team members' second thoughts should be encouraged.

In other words, teams in the norming stage become cohesive and highly integrated entities, and while this is critical to produce cohesion, teamwork, and commitment, it may also create a tendency to preserve high involvement and good feeling at the expense of all else. Having a cohesive family feeling is necessary to pull the separate members together and to create a singular identity, but it can prove disastrous if important information is filtered out, contrary points of view are squelched, or nonconformity in any form is punished. Effective teams must also move on to the next stage, the storming stage of development.

THE STORMING STAGE

Whereas the comfortable climate that team members develop in the norming stage can lead to an excessive amount of agreement and homogeneity, it also can lead to the opposite phenomenon. That is, once team members begin to feel comfortable with the team, they often feel comfortable enough to explore different roles. Some may tend toward task facilitation—focusing on getting work done—for example, while others may tend toward relationship building—focusing on interpersonal dynamics. This differentiation of team members' roles invariably leads the team into a stage of potential conflict and counterdependence—a storming stage.

Playing different roles causes team members to develop different perspectives and to develop ideas that challenge the leadership and direction of the team. Almost every effective team goes through a stage in which team members question the legitimacy of the team's direction, the leader, the roles of other team members, the opinions or decisions of others, and the task objectives. Up to now, the team was largely characterized by harmony and consensus.

Individual differences were suppressed in order to create a sense of team. However, such a condition will not last forever without team members becoming uncomfortable about losing their individual identity, subjugating their feelings, or stifling differing perspectives. The team's long-term success, therefore, will depend on how well it manages the storming stage of development. Typical questions that arise in team members' minds during this stage are:

- How will we handle dissension?
- How can we make decisions amidst disagreement?
- How will we communicate negative information?
- Do I want to maintain my membership in the team?
- How far can I step out of bounds?

An old Middle Eastern proverb states: "All sunshine makes a desert." Similarly, team development implies that some struggles must occur, some discomfort must be experienced, and some obstacles must be overcome for the team to prosper. The team must learn to deal with adversity—especially that produced by its own members. Tendencies toward groupthink must be attacked head-on. If team members are more interested in keeping peace than in solving problems and accomplishing tasks, the team will never become effective. No one wants to remain in a team that will not allow for individuality and uniqueness and that wants to maintain harmony more than it wants to accomplish its goals. Consequently, harmony is sometimes sacrificed as the team attacks problems and accomplishes objectives.

Of course, team members do not cease to care about one another, and they remain committed to the team and its success. But they do begin to take sides on issues, to find that they are more compatible with some team members than others, and to align themselves with certain points of view. This leads to:

- Coalitions or cliques
- Competition among team members
- Disagreement with the leader
- Challenging others' points of view

During Desert Storm, for example, a relatively rigid military command hierarchy—along with the urgency of the mission to be performed—inhibited large deviations from established norms and rules, but small aberrations began to emerge as Pagonis' team developed. Logistics team members painted personal logos on some tanks and trucks, insider code names were given to people and locations as a bit of sarcasm, and challenges to top-brass mandates became more common in briefing rooms. This testing of norms and boundaries is sometimes merely an expression of a need for individuality, while in other instances it is a product of strong feelings that the team can be improved. The main task issues to be addressed by the team in this stage include:

- Managing conflict
- Legitimizing productive expressions of individuality
- Turning counterdependence into interdependence
- Fostering consensus-building among heterogeneous perspectives
- Encouraging helpful expressions of disagreement

Conflict, coalition formation, and counterdependence create conditions that may lead to the norms and values of the team being questioned. Rather than being stifled or resisted, however, effective teams encourage members to turn those challenges into constructive suggestions for improvement. It is important for team members to feel that they can legitimately express their personal uniqueness and idiosyncrasies, so long as they are not destructive to the overall team.

It is clear from research on teams that when they face difficult or complex problems, teams are more effective if membership is heterogeneous than if all team members act, believe, and see things the same way (Campion, Medsker, & Higgs, 1993; Hackman, 2003; Shin, Kim, Lee, & Bian, 2012). Diversity is productive in fostering creativity, individuality, and solutions to difficult problems (Cox, 1994). It has been said that "teams make complex problems simple." The trouble is, "teams also make simple problems complex," so diversity and heterogeneity are not universally appropriate. The first two stages of team development, in fact, are purposeful in minimizing diversity and heterogeneity. In this stage, however, maintaining flexibility in the team implies that tolerance for individuality is acceptable and that changes and improvements are promoted.

General Pagonis' philosophy about the way to manage differences was to encourage their expression:

The key is to be open to different experiences and perspectives. If you can't tolerate different kinds of people, you're not likely to learn from different kinds of perspectives. Effective leaders encourage contrary opinions, an important source of vitality. This is especially true in the military where good ideas come in an incredible variety of packages. (Pagonis, 1993, p. 24)

In the storming stage of development, tensions arise between forces pushing the team toward cohesion and forces pushing it toward differentiation. At the same time strong bonds of team unity have been fostered, individuals begin differentiating themselves from one another and adopting unique roles in the team. They become complementary (Mitchell & Prins, 2004). This complementarity of roles may actually foster team cohesion and productivity rather than conflict if, as a leader in the team, you will:

❏ Identify an external enemy (rather than one another) as a target for competition.

❏ Reinforce team commitment with recognition of team-level performance.

❏ Maintain visibility of vision and superordinate goals.

❏ Turn members into leaders by having team members teach the group's values and vision to others.

Pagonis' logistics team illustrates the value of the first three suggestions above—identifying an external enemy, team-level recognition, and vision.

In the presence of the enemy, our strength was flexibility, both as individuals and as a group. Organizations must be flexible enough to adjust and conform when their environments change. But the flexibility can degenerate into chaos in the absence of well-established goals.... Once everyone in the organization understands the goals of the organization, then each person sets out several objectives by which to attain those goals within his or her own sphere of activity.... When it works, cooperation and collegiality are enhanced, and in-fighting and suboptimization are minimized. (Pagonis, 1993, p. 83)

The fourth suggestion above is illustrated well by a process used effectively by Xerox Corporation to address stiff competition from external competitors. Figure 9.2 illustrates a process implemented by Xerox where members were turned into leaders in order to ensure that a common vision and common processes were implemented throughout the

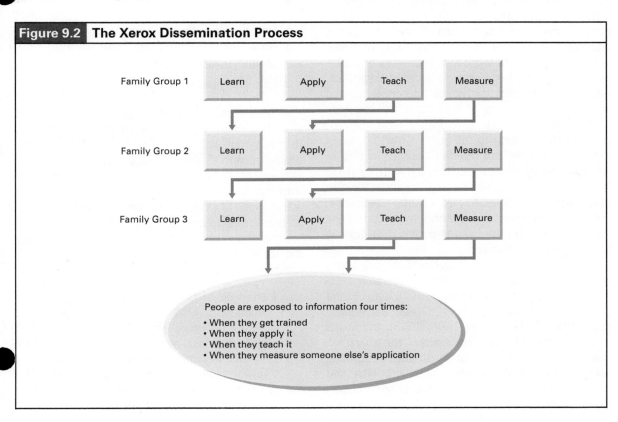

Figure 9.2 **The Xerox Dissemination Process**

Family Group 1: Learn → Apply → Teach → Measure

Family Group 2: Learn → Apply → Teach → Measure

Family Group 3: Learn → Apply → Teach → Measure

People are exposed to information four times:
• When they get trained
• When they apply it
• When they teach it
• When they measure someone else's application

company. To ensure that all units and all managers were working in harmony, the company divided itself into hierarchical family teams. A four-step process was then implemented:

1. *Learn.* Core principles, vision, and values were taught and discussed.
2. *Apply.* Action plans were formed and an improvement agenda was implemented.
3. *Teach.* The principles and successful experiences were taught to the next-lower family team.
4. *Inspect.* The performance and action plans of this lower family team were measured and monitored.

Teams were exposed to the desired information four times: when they learned it, when they applied it, when they taught it, and when they inspected it. More importantly, because team members were engaged in teaching others, their commitment to the team, even in light of differentiated roles, was enhanced.

THE PERFORMING STAGE

The performing stage of development represents highly effective and efficient team functioning. Because the team has worked through the issues embedded in each of the previous stages of development, it is able to work at a high level of performance. The team has overcome issues of skepticism, uncertainty, nonparticipativeness, dependence, and self-centeredness typical of the first, or forming stage of development. It has developed a clear mission, personal commitment to the team, a high degree of loyalty and morale, and has overcome tendencies toward groupthink that can occur in the norming stage. It has fostered differentiation and variety while also overcoming tendencies toward counterdependence, conflict, polarization, and disharmony typical of the storming stage. It now has the potential to develop the attributes of a high-performing team.

A listing of attributes of high-performance teams is provided in Table 9.3, based on research summarized in Cohen and Bailey (1997), Guzzo and Dickson (1996), Hackman (1990; 2003), Katzenbach and Smith (1993), Lawler, (1998, 2003), and Yeatts and Hyten (1998). This summarizes the characteristics that must be present in all high-performing teams, and it provides a good guideline for what you want to strive for when you are leading or participating in a team.

The team in the performing stage is not, of course, free of challenges. The common issues that tend to dominate members of high-performing teams are:

❏ How can we help one another thrive?
❏ How can we foster continuous improvement and creativity?
❏ How can we build on our core competence?
❏ How can we maintain a high level of energy in the team?

Team members' questions in this stage change from being static to being dynamic. They shift in focus from merely accomplishing objectives to fostering change and improvement and achieving extraordinarily positive performance. Continuous improvement replaces accomplishment as an objective. Up to this point, the team has been trying to manage and resolve issues that lead to three key outcomes: (1) accomplishing tasks or objectives, (2) coordinating and integrating team members' roles, and (3) assuring the personal well-being of all team members. It can now turn its attention to achieving a level of performance above the ordinary. The interpersonal relationships of team members are characterized by:

❏ High mutual trust
❏ Unconditional commitment to the team
❏ Mutual training and development
❏ Entrepreneurship

Team members in this stage exhibit a sense of shared responsibility and concern for one another as they carry out their work. Their relationships are not limited merely to accomplishing a task together, but also extend to ensuring that each team member is learning, developing, and flourishing. Coaching and assisting one another is common. In General Pagonis' high-performing team, for example, team members were continuously teaching one another and helping the team and its individual members become more competent.

I arranged to take a day or two away from headquarters with a group of key people from the command [team]. We use this brief respite from our everyday activities to take a long look at what our organization is doing. These sessions...gave us a chance to work as a group, in a focused way.... From Day One, I held large, open classes where we discussed

Table 9.3	Some Attributes of High-Performing Teams

- *Performance outcomes*

  High-performing teams do things. They produce something; they don't just discuss it. Without accomplishment, teams dissolve and become ineffective over time.

- *Specific, shared purpose and vision*

  The more specific the purpose, the more commitment, trust, and coordination can occur. Individuals don't work for themselves; they work for one another in pursuit of the shared purpose. The shared purpose can also be the same as a motivating vision of what the team should achieve.

- *Mutual, internal accountability*

  The sense of internal accountability is far greater than any accountability imposed by a boss or outsider. Self-evaluation and accountability characterize a high-performing team.

- *Blurring of formal distinctions*

  Team members do whatever is needed to contribute to the task, regardless of previous positions or titles. Team membership and team roles are more predominant than outside status.

- *Coordinated, shared work roles*

  Individuals always work in coordination with others on the team. The desired output is a single group product, not a set of individual products.

- *Inefficiency leading to efficiency*

  Because teams allow for lots of participation and sharing, mutual influence about purpose, and blurring of roles, they may initially be inefficient. As the team develops, because they come to know one another so well and can anticipate each other's moves, they become much more efficient than single people working alone.

- *Extraordinarily high quality*

  Teams produce outcomes above and beyond current standards of performance. They surprise and delight their various constituencies with quality levels not expected and never before obtained. An intolerance of mediocrity exists, so standards of performance are very high.

- *Creative continuous improvement*

  Large-scale innovations as well as never-ending small improvements characterize the team's processes and activities. Dissatisfaction with the status quo leads to a constant flow of new ideas, experimentation, and a quest for progress.

- *High credibility and trust*

  Team members trust one another implicitly, defend members who are not present, and form interdependent relationships with one another. Personal integrity and honesty characterize team activities and team member interactions.

- *Clarity of core competence*

  The unique talents and strategic advantages of the team and its members are clear. The ways in which these competencies can be utilized to further the team's objectives are well understood. Extraneous activities and deflections from the team's core mission are given low priority.

scenarios and potential solutions. I would pose a question to the group: "O.K., you have a ship that docked at Ad Dammam this morning. It's ready to be unloaded, and the onboard crane breaks. What's our response?" Collectively, the group would work toward one of several solutions.... These group sessions served several useful purposes at once. Obviously, they brought potential challenges into the open so we could better prepare for them.... Equally important, they promoted collaborative discussion across ranks and disciplines. (Pagonis, 1993, pp. 101, 177)

In addition to multifaceted relationships and unconditional commitment to one another, high-performing team members also take responsibility individually for continuously improving the team and its processes.

Experimentation, trial-and-error learning, freewheeling discussions of new possibilities, and personal responsibility by everyone for upgrading performance is typical. The team adopts a set of behaviors that help to foster and perpetuate this stage of development, including:

❑ Capitalizing on their core competencies

❑ Fostering innovation and continuous improvement

❑ Enhancing flourishing relationships

❑ Encouraging positive deviance

The most effective teams in this stage develop the capacity to perform beyond the norm. They achieve outcomes that are extraordinary. They extend the boundaries of what is possible. They become positively deviant. After having moved through the first three stages of development in the Persian Gulf War, for example, General Pagonis' logistics team moved into a stage characterized by activities that exceeded expected levels of performance. On one occasion, for example, Pagonis directed two team members to generate a solution to the problem of how to provide combat troops with decent meals on the front lines.

> Imagine that you've been at some remote and desolate desert site for weeks, or even months, consuming dehydrated or vacuum-packed military rations. One day, unannounced, an odd-looking vehicle with the word "Wolfmobile" painted on it comes driving into your camp. The side panels open up, and a smiling crew inside offers to cook you a hamburger to order. "Side of fries? How about a Coke?" Morale shot up everywhere the Wolfmobiles pulled in—a little bit of home in the desert. (Pagonis, 1993, p. 129)

This incident illustrates the major opportunity associated in the fourth stage of development—to help team members expand their focus from merely accomplishing their work and maintaining good interpersonal relationships to upgrading and elevating the team's performance. This level of performance unlocks positive energy and makes it impossible to ever return to a lower level of performance again.

An example of the power of high-performing teams and their effects of members is a story told by our friend Bob Quinn (2005) in which an upper-level executive in a major manufacturing organization was expressing frustration with his company. "The trouble with my firm," lamented the executive, "is that they cannot stand excellence." He illustrated his frustration by recounting the following incident.

One day in his plant, a major problem occurred on the assembly line, and the line had to be shut down and repaired. The issue was serious and required personnel from multiple shifts to come to the plant to work on the problem. As a gesture of goodwill on his part, this executive purchased lunch—pizza, hot dogs, and soft drinks—for these employees who were going the extra mile for the company. They completed the task at the highest levels of quality and in record time. Sometime later, a representative from the finance department entered the office of this executive, slapped a piece of paper down on the desk, and exclaimed, "We can't pay this bill for the food. You know that it is against corporate policy to purchase food for employees from your budget. This bill will not be reimbursed."

Of course, no one could fault the finance department representative—he was simply doing his job and reinforcing the rules. Flabbergasted, however, the executive responded: "Look, I cannot do the same things we have always done and expect different results. I have to break rules once in a while in the service of achieving excellence or extraordinary performance. Buying lunch made all the difference to these employees. It's what accounted for our success."

"This incident just proves," stated the executive, "that my firm cannot stand excellence. They cannot tolerate being extraordinary." Our friend Bob offered this executive some advice. He simply proposed that the executive give up and conform to the rules and expectations. Stop trying to achieve extraordinary levels of success. The executive's reply was telling, however, and illustrates the power of high-performing teams in this fourth stage of development. His reply was: "I can't quit trying. Once I have experienced excellence, normal performance is just not good enough anymore. I can't stand still and not strive for extraordinary results."

Teams in this fourth stage of development are not all outstanding, of course, and unfortunately, **positive deviance** is rare. But, once team members experience this kind of excellence, team performance stuck in the first three stages of development will never be satisfactory again. Some of the prescriptions for achieving these levels of extraordinary success are highlighted in the sections below as we discuss skills involved in leading teams and in being an effective member of teams.

One important factor in creating effective teams, of course, is the role of the leader. As pointed out by Hackman (2003), however, it is not the personal *style* of the leader that makes a difference. Multiple leadership styles can be effective, and no one style has particular advantages over others. Rather, it is the skills and capabilities of the leader or the tools and techniques put into practice that account for effective versus ineffective team performance. We highlight two especially critical aspects of team leadership here. Not only are these two aspects of team leadership observable in General Pagonis, but they have emerged in the scholarly literature as critical factors in leading almost any kind of team (Edmonson, 1999; Hackman, 1990). The first is developing credibility and influence among team members. The second is establishing a motivating vision and goals for the team.

DEVELOPING CREDIBILITY

To be an effective team leader, you must have the respect and commitment of team members. That is, you must develop credibility (Kouzes & Posner, 1987, 2011). Establishing credibility and the capacity to influence team members is the first key challenge you will face as a leader of teams. Giving directions, articulating goals, or trying to motivate team members are all wasted efforts if you have not established credibility and respect (Helliwell & Huang, 2011). General Pagonis described this leadership challenge in the following way:

> I have found, time and time again in commands around the world, that my troops are more invested in their work and better motivated when they understand and buy into the ultimate goals of the operation. Reason counts for far more than rank, when it comes to motivation. And motivation is the root of all organizational progress. Over the years I have developed a very distinctive leadership style. Gus Pagonis' command style, like everyone else's, is unique. This meant that I had choices to make. Would I rather have the world's best port operation officer, if he was someone who didn't already know my style? Or would I rather have the world's second best port operation officer who knew my style intimately and was comfortable with it? The answer was obvious; we couldn't waste time

> fighting our own systems. Equally important, we couldn't afford the time that would be wasted as a new person tried to impress me, or get on my good side. We needed an instant body of leaders, strengthened by a united front. We needed to know that we could depend on one another unconditionally. We needed the confidence that the mission, and not personal advancement, would always be paramount in the mind of each participant. (Pagonis, 1993, p. 78, 84)

In earlier chapters, we identified ways to enhance a manager's influence (Chapter 5) and trust (Chapter 8), which are components of credibility. In this chapter, we highlight additional behaviors you can use to help establish leadership credibility in a team.

Team members, of course, will not follow a person whom they don't trust, who is hypocritical or dishonest, or whose motives appear to be personal aggrandizement instead of the welfare of the team. In fact, Kouzes and Posner (2011) identified credibility as the single most important requirement for leadership effectiveness. Once credibility has been established, then goals for the team can be articulated and the team can move toward high performance. The seven behaviors summarized in Table 9.4 are keys to building and maintaining credibility and influence among team members. Whereas they are simple and straightforward, much scholarly evidence exists that support their efficacy (see Cialdini, 1995; Druskat & Wheeler, 2000; Hackman, 2003; Katzenbach & Smith, 1993; Kramer, 1999; Manz & Sims, 1987; Turner, 2000).

1. *Demonstrate integrity.* Chief among the behaviors that create leadership credibility is the demonstration of integrity. Integrity means that you do what you say, you behave congruently with your values, and you are believable in what you espouse. Individuals who appear to say one thing and do another, who are not honest in their feedback, or who do not follow through with promises are perceived to lack integrity and are ineffective as leaders of teams.

2. *Be clear and consistent.* Expressing certainty about what you want and where you are going, without being dogmatic or stubborn, helps produce confidence on the part of others. Being wishy-washy or inconsistent in your viewpoints inhibits credibility. The electorate in most countries throughout the world rates

Table 9.4	Ways to Build Team Leader Credibility

Team leaders build credibility with their team members by:

- Demonstrating integrity, representing authenticity, and displaying congruence (Walk the talk)
- Being clear and consistent about what they want to achieve (Trustworthy and transparent)
- Creating positive energy by being optimistic and complimentary (Help others flourish)
- Using commonality and reciprocity (Build a foundation)
- Managing agreement and disagreement among team members by using one-sided and two-sided arguments appropriately—one-sided in situations when all team members agree, two-sided when consensus is not preexisting (Effective influence techniques)
- Encouraging and coaching team members to help them improve (Mentoring and tutoring)
- Sharing information about the team, providing perspective from external sources, and encouraging participation (Informing and involving)

their politicians very low in credibility because most candidates appear to be inconsistent in their statements, changing perspectives depending on the audience (Cialdini, 1995). Credible people, on the other hand, can be trusted to be consistent and transparent.

3. *Create positive energy.* Stay optimistic and complimentary. Most teams do not perform effectively when there is a climate of criticism, cynicism, or negativity. Criticizing team members, past leaders, others outside the team, or even being critical of the circumstances in which the team finds itself are usually not effective ways to help a team perform well. Individuals and teams perform better when positive energy exists—optimism, compliments, celebrations of success, and recognition of progress. This does not mean being unrealistic or a "Pollyanna." Instead, it means that when you are seen as a source of positive energy and enthusiasm, you have more credibility and influence among team members.

4. *Use commonality and reciprocity.* If you express views that are held in common with team members, they are more likely to agree with your later statements. If you want to foster team change, or move the team toward an outcome that appears to be risky or uncomfortable, begin by expressing views with which other team members agree. It can be as simple as "I know you all have very busy schedules." Or, "We have a lot of diversity of opinion in our team on this issue." These kinds of statements work because of the principle of reciprocity. Team members have a

tendency to agree with you more if they have received something from you in advance, even if it is merely your agreement with their point of view. After you have expressed agreement with them, you can then lead them toward goals or targets that may stretch them or that may be uncomfortable or uncertain.

5. *Manage agreement and disagreement.* When team members initially agree with you, it's more effective if you use a one-sided argument. That is, present only one point of view and support it with evidence. When team members tend to disagree with you at the outset, use two-sided arguments. That is, first present both sides of the case and then show how your own point of view is superior to the contrary perspective. Keep in mind that when team members agree with you, the first statements you make tend to hold more weight and are remembered the longest. When they disagree with you, the last statements made tend to carry the most weight.

6. *Encourage and coach.* Encouragement means to help others develop courage—to tackle uncertainty, to achieve beyond their current performance, to disrupt the status quo. Encouraging team members not only involves compliments and supportive statements, it also involves assistance and resources. Coaching, as pointed out in Chapter 4, means helping to show the way, providing information or advice, and assisting team members with task requirements. Effective encouragement and coaching involves giving positively reinforcing comments as well as helpful advice or direction.

7. *Share information.* Building credibility means coming to understand the perspectives of team members as well as a sense of their talents and resources. Coming to know your team members well is crucial for successful leadership. One way to do this is to use the principle of "frequent checking." This merely involves asking questions and checking with team members regularly to determine levels of agreement, obstacles, dissatisfactions, needs, and interpersonal or team issues. Importantly, credibility grows as knowledge is shared. Being the source from which others can acquire needed information builds credibility and influence, so sharing is crucial (Mesmer-Magnus, & DeChurch, 2009; Srivastava, Bartol, & Locke, 2006).

As stated by General Pagonis:

Keeping [team members] abreast of your actions, as well as the rationale behind those actions, puts everybody on an equal information footing. I believe that information is power, but only if it is shared.... Very early on I had gotten in the habit of sneaking John Carr into these briefing sessions with CINC [General Schwarzkopf and others] by having Carr flip my slides in and out of the overhead projector. That way, he stayed as smart and as current about the CINC's plans as I did. (Pagonis, 1993, p. 88, 131)

ESTABLISH Smart GOALS AND EVEREST GOALS

Once team members have confidence in you as a leader, you can then identify goals and levels of performance to which team members can aspire.

There are two kinds of goals that characterize high-performing teams, and leaders must identify and espouse both kinds. The first are called **SMART goals,** and the second are called **Everest goals**. The purpose for establishing clear goals is so that every person on the team can give a similar answer to the question: What are we trying to achieve? Leaders who clearly articulate the desired outcomes for and with the team are more likely to experience high performance from the team. Goal-directed performance, in fact, always exceeds performance disassociated with goals (Locke, 1990). Figure 9.3 illustrates this point.

It shows that when people are given *no goals* ("Here is your task. Go do it."), their performance tends to be low, even though most people will perform at a minimum level even when they are not certain of the standard that they should achieve. However, being provided with an *easy goal* ("The average is 10 tasks per day, but you can shoot for 4.") leads to even lower performance. People tend to work toward the standard that has been established, and when it is easy, they slack off. Establishing *general goals* ("Do your best.") results in improved performance over easy goals, but identifying *difficult goals* ("The average is 10 tasks per day, but you should shoot for 12.") produces far higher levels of performance. The kinds of goals that produce

---

| Figure 9.3 | **The Effect of Goals on Performance** |

SOURCE: *"Practicing Positive Leadership," Cameron, K. (2013).*

the highest levels of performance, however, are difficult goals that possess five characteristics. The acronym SMART identifies these attributes. SMART goals are:

- ❏ **S**pecific—The goal is clear, and precise targets and standards are identified.
- ❏ **M**easurable—The goal can be assessed and quantified. The extent to which the goal has been achieved is obvious.
- ❏ **A**ligned—The goal is supportive of and consistent with the goals of the broader organization. People are not pursuing their own objectives independent of their team.
- ❏ **R**ealistic—While being difficult and causing performance to stretch, the goal is not foolhardy or a fantasy.
- ❏ **T**ime-bound—An end point is identified or a completion date established so that goal achievement is not open-ended.

Consider the difference between goal statements such as "We will be the best in our industry," compared to a goal statement that is SMART: "We will achieve a 5 percent improvement in the on-time delivery of our products by the end of the quarter." The latter provides a more motivating goal in that it is specific, measurable, aligned with key outcomes, realistic, and time-bound. It gives people something they can easily understand and shoot for.

It is important to keep in mind, however, that articulating motivating goals and identifying the methods to achieve them are different. Goals specify the target. Methods specify the means for achieving the target. Goals are crucial to successful team leadership. Dictating methods is often lethal. Pagonis' team illustrates this well:

> *I never tell a subordinate how to carry out a specific goal. Dictating terms to a subordinate undermines innovation, decreases the subordinate's willingness to take responsibility for his or her actions, increases the potential for suboptimization of resources, and increases the chances that the command will be dysfunctional if circumstances change dramatically. Our first month in the theater only underscored my sense that our [team] would have to be incredibly elastic. (Pagonis, 1993, p. 119)*

The second type of goal that effective team leaders articulate is called an *Everest goal (Cameron, 2013).* An Everest goal goes beyond normal goal setting. It represents an ultimate achievement, an extraordinary accomplishment, or a beyond-the-norm outcome. Achieving it requires everything one can give. Like setting your sights on getting to the summit of Mount Everest, an Everest goal is clear and compelling, serves as a unifying focal point, builds team spirit, engages people, and creates positive energy and excitement. An Everest goal is stimulating because it connects to a profound passion. People get it right away, with little explanation. An Everest goal is visionary, not just tactical or strategic, and it leaves people better for having engaged in its pursuit. It requires extraordinary effort to achieve, and maybe a little luck.

Five attributes characterize an Everest goals:

1. Everest goals represent *positive deviance.* They extend beyond expectations and represent extraordinary achievement.
2. Everest goals represent inherent value and worth. They possess *profound meaning and purpose.* Achieving the outcomes themselves are sufficient and are not a means to obtain another end.
3. Everest goals possess an *affirmative bias.* They do not merely focus on solving problems, reducing obstacles, overcoming challenges, or removing difficulties. Rather, they focus on opportunities, possibilities, and potential.
4. Everest goals represent a *contribution.* They focus on providing benefit to others or making a contribution rather than merely receiving a reward or recognition. Everest goals emphasize what individuals can give compared to what they can get.
5. Everest goals are *inherently energizing.* They do not need another source of motivation to pursue them. People are not exhausted by pursuing Everest goals, but instead they are uplifted, elevated, and energized. Everest goals are not the same as mere stretch goals or difficult goals. They extend beyond the mere difficult.

An excerpt from a climber who finally made it to the top of Mount Everest after three failed attempts illustrates the difference between Everest goals and more traditional stretch or difficult goals:

> *I realized something on that night in the dark on Everest. What I realized was that real winning had nothing to do with beating someone else, or crossing the finish line first,*

or standing on top. Winning wasn't anything external at all. It was an internal satisfaction, a deep inner sense of pride and joy. Success can only be measured within ourselves, by ourselves. It has nothing to do with other people's perception of our achievements. It has everything to do with our own perceptions of our efforts...Success isn't standing on the podium, or hearing the cheers of others, or standing on the summit at all. It's giving it your all....I think that in anything in life, if you give it everything you possibly can, you really do succeed....Our business in life is not to get ahead of others but to get ahead of ourselves, to break our own records, to outstrip our yesterday by our today, to do our work with more force than ever before. We took comfort in the words of Gandhi: 'Full effort is full victory'...

I have come to understand that for me this notion of success is upside down. In fact, a traditional end—the summit, an Olympic gold medal, or wealth—only serves as a navigational tool, a marker to give the process direction. The end for me is a greater depth and breadth of character. I measure this in terms of greater integrity, better business and communication skills, and a higher personal motivation to become stronger. More simply, my aim is to become as internally knowledgeable and as externally aware as possible. The process, the experience, the struggle, the hard-won lessons, these are ends in themselves. (Clarke & Hobson, 2005, pp. 168, 169)

Identifying such a goal, of course, is neither automatic nor easy. Such goals don't just roll off the tips of our tongues. Most people identify few of these in a lifetime. But articulating such a goal as a leader of a team creates automatic passion, commitment, and positive energy. Team members catch fire. They become more innovative, more cohesive, and higher performing than they could be otherwise. The most highly effective teams in history have been guided by Everest goals.

Examples of high performing companies that established Everest goals include Ford Motor Company's goal to democratize the automobile (in the early 1900s); or Boeing's goal to bring the world into the jet-age (in the 1950s); or Sony's goal to change the image of poor quality in Japan (in 1960s); or Apple's goal for one person, one computer (in the 1980s); or the University of Michigan's CK Prahalad goal to help 500,000 Indians will become employable in 10 years (in the 2000s).

In summary, being an effective leader of a team requires at least two key skills that often do not receive adequate attention: (1) developing credibility among team members and (2) articulating SMART and Everest goals for the team. Whereas these are obviously not the only skills that effective team leaders possess, without these two core capabilities, it is unlikely that the teams you lead will achieve high levels of Stage 4 performance.

INTERNATIONAL CAVEATS

We have pointed out throughout the book that individuals in different cultures exhibit differences in values and orientations (Trompenaars, 1996, 1998). Diagnosing, understanding, and capitalizing on individual differences, we repeat, is a crucial skill of competent managers. The seven value orientations identified by Trompenaars provide a useful tool for identifying those individual differences. That is, you can understand differences among people by assessing them on the extent to which they emphasize one value orientation over its opposite: *universalism* versus *particularism*, *individualism* versus *communitarianism*, *neutrality* versus *affectivity*, *specificity* versus *diffuseness*, *achievement* versus *ascription*, *internal* versus *external* control, and *past*, *present*, or *future* time orientation. The first chapter in this book provides a more detailed explanation of these value dimensions.

Individual differences may require that some modification be made in these team leadership behaviors. For example, if you are leading a team with members from cultures that tend to have a *collectivist* (e.g., Mexico, Japan, France, Philippines) as opposed to an *individualist* orientation, team members will expect to be involved in the creation and articulation of the goals. They will be less comfortable with the goals coming from a single leader, regardless of his or her credibility and influence. Consequently, the Everest goal and its accompanying SMART goals should be designed with active participation of team members.

Similarly, team members from countries where a *neutral* (e.g., Korea, China, Japan, New Zealand) as opposed to an *affective* culture predominates, may be less energized by language filled with superlatives and passion. Their orientation toward task accomplishment and factual data may mute their responses to

LEARNING

emotional language. Consequently, being sensitive to the wording of your Everest goal statement will help make it more motivating.

On the other hand, the differences in cultural values among different nationalities are not so great as to negate the overall effectiveness of the two key skills mentioned above—building credibility and articulating goals. The data from thousands of managers worldwide support the effectiveness of these two key skills for team leaders, regardless of national differences (see Trompenaars & Hampden-Turner, 1998). You may need to be sensitive to the potential need to modify your behaviors based on the composition of your team, but team composition will not have as strong an influence on team effectiveness as the leadership skills you display. (For one review of team composition influences, see Guzzo & Dickson, 1996.)

Team Membership

Most of the time, most of us will not serve as the leader of the teams in which we participate. Whereas you will want to prepare for the leadership roles you will play in the future, the vast majority of the time you will be an active member of a team, working for the common good of the group, rather than the person in charge. You will be valuable to your team because of the contributions you make in nonleadership roles. Fortunately, these contributions can have significant impact on your team's performance.

One of the most amazing statements made by General Pagonis as he reviewed the outcomes of Desert Storm related to the performance of his team, even when he was not the active leader:

> I meet with skepticism, even disbelief, when I tell people that I didn't issue a single order during the ground war. This is only slightly a stretch of the truth. Yes, people sought and got guidance. But the people in my command knew exactly what they were supposed to do in almost every conceivable circumstance. They had been trained and encouraged to think on their feet. I felt they could even deal with the inconceivable. (Pagonis, 1993, p. 148)

Team members were not only guided by an overarching goal and a clear understanding of what they were to accomplish, but they had become an extraordinarily high-performing team because of the roles played by team members. Pagonis described it this way:

"Truth be told, we spent less of our time as logisticians, and more of our time as managers, fixers, firefighters, father confessors, and cheerleaders. There was simply nobody else around to play those roles" (p. 87).

In this section, we point out two main skills associated with team membership—playing advantageous roles, and providing helpful feedback to others. Once again, these skills are not complicated, but they have been found to be highly effective in helping team members influence team success (see Parker, 1996).

ADVANTAGEOUS ROLES

Most teams face two main challenges: (1) accomplishing the task that has been assigned and (2) building unity and collaboration among the team members. As a member of a team, you can enhance or inhibit those two challenges almost as much as you can as the team leader. All of us have experienced teams that just seem to click, that are able to get results quickly and effectively, and are fun to be in. Those dynamics don't happen by chance but depend on certain key roles played by team members.

A great deal of research has been done on the power of group pressure and the influence of team members on one another. The classic Solomon Asch experiments (1951) were among the first to highlight the influence of team members on one another. The Asch experiments showed, for example, that when other team members verbally agree with a statement that was obviously false—say, "The federal government controls the stock market"—the person being observed also tended to verbalize agreement with the obviously false statement—even if he or she disagrees with it. Team members' statements and behavior dramatically influence the behaviors of one another.

Most teams don't operate on the basis of blatant pressure tactics, of course, but team performance can be markedly enhanced by having team members play certain roles that facilitate task accomplishment and group cohesion.

Two main types of roles exist that enhance team performance: **task-facilitating roles** and **relationship-building roles** (Schein, 1976). It is difficult for team members to emphasize both types of roles equally, and most people tend to contribute in one area more than the other. That is, some team members tend to be more task-focused whereas others tend to be more relationship-focused. Task-facilitating roles are those that help the team accomplish its outcomes

Table 9.5	Task-Facilitating Roles
ROLE	**EXAMPLES**
Direction giving	"This is the way we were instructed to approach our task."
	"Everyone write down your ideas, then share them."
Information seeking	"What did you mean by that?"
	"Does anyone else have more information about this?"
Information giving	"Here are some relevant data."
	"I want to share some information that may be helpful."
Elaborating	"Building on your idea, here is an additional alternative."
	"An example of what you just said is . . ."
Urging	"We have only 10 minutes left, so we need to move more quickly."
	"We can't quit now. We're close to finalizing our proposal."
Monitoring	"You maintain accountability for the first recommendation, and I'll handle the second."
	"Here are some criteria we can use to judge our success."
Process analyzing	"It seems as if the energy level in the team is beginning to decline."
	"I've noticed that the females are participating less than the males in our team."
Reality testing	"Let's see if this is really practical."
	"Do you think this is workable given our resources?"
Enforcing	"We're beginning to wander in our comments; let's stay on task."
	"Since we agreed not to interrupt one another, I suggest we stick to our pact."
Summarizing	"It seems to me that these are the conclusions we have reached."
	"In summary, you have made three points . . ."

LEARNING

or objectives. Table 9.5 identifies the most common task-facilitating roles. They include:

❑ *Direction giving.* Identifying ways to proceed or alternatives to pursue and clarifying goals and objectives.

❑ *Information seeking.* Asking questions, analyzing knowledge gaps, requesting opinions, beliefs, and perspectives.

❑ *Information giving.* Providing data, offering facts and judgments, and highlighting conclusions.

❑ *Elaborating.* Building on the ideas expressed by others; providing examples and illustrations.

❑ *Urging.* Imploring team members to stay on task and to achieve team goals.

❑ *Monitoring.* Checking on progress, developing measures of success and helping to maintain accountability for results.

❑ *Process analyzing.* Analyzing processes and procedures used by the team in order to improve efficiency and timeliness.

❑ *Reality testing.* Exploring whether ideas presented are practical or workable; grounding comments in reality.

❑ *Enforcing.* Helping to reinforce team rules, reinforcing standards, and maintaining agreed-upon procedures.

❑ *Summarizing.* Combining ideas and summing up points made in the team; helping members understand the conclusions that have been reached.

When you perform task-facilitating roles, you help the team work more efficiently and effectively in achieving its objectives. Without having at least one team member displaying task-facilitating behaviors, teams tend to take longer to achieve their objectives and have difficulty staying focused. Sometimes keeping the team "on task" is the most important thing you can do. These roles are especially important when:

❑ Progress toward goal accomplishment is slow.

❑ The team is being deflected from its task.

❑ Time pressures exist.

❑ The assignment is complex or ambiguous and it is not clear how to proceed.

❑ No one else is helping the team move toward task accomplishment.

You don't have to be a task master to be an effective facilitator of outcomes. In fact, just recognizing that the team is in need of task facilitation is a big part of being an effective team member. In most effective teams, you will find several members performing these task-facilitation roles.

In addition to accomplishing tasks, an overwhelming amount of evidence exists suggesting that high-performing teams pay attention to interpersonal issues. They are cohesive, interdependent, and have positive affect among team members (Cohen & Bailey, 1997; Druskat & Wolff, 1999; Dutton, 2003; Gully, Divine, & Whitney, 1995; Mullen & Copper, 1994; Parker, 1996). Relationship-building roles are those that emphasize the interpersonal aspects of the team. They focus on assisting team members feel good about one another, enjoy the team's work, and maintain a tension-free climate. Table 9.6 identifies the most common relationship-building roles:

❑ *Supporting.* Praising the ideas of others, showing friendliness, and pointing out others' contributions

❑ *Harmonizing.* Mediating differences between others and finding a common ground in disputes and conflicting points of view

Table 9.6	Relationship-Building Roles
ROLE	**EXAMPLES**
Supporting	"Your ideas are terrific!"
	"I really appreciate your honesty and openness. It's refreshing."
Harmonizing	"I hear the two of you saying essentially the same thing."
	"The disagreements being expressed don't seem to be all that crucial."
Tension relieving	"Hey folks, let's lighten up!"
	"This reminds me of the new conference table we bought. It sleeps 12."
Confronting	"How does your comment address the topic we are discussing?"
	"You are not taking as much responsibility as the other team members."
Energizing	"Your insights are terrific!"
	"This team is the most enjoyable group I've been in for a long time."
Developing	"How can I help you?"
	"Let me give you some assistance with that."
Consensus building	"It seems like we're all saying pretty much the same thing."
	"Can we all at least agree on point number 1, even if we disagree on the rest?"
Empathizing	"I know how you feel."
	"This must be a very sensitive topic for you given your personal experience."

- *Tension relieving.* Using jokes and humor to reduce tension and put others at ease
- *Confronting.* Challenging unproductive or disruptive behaviors; helping to ensure proper behavior in the team
- *Energizing.* Motivating others toward greater effort; exuding enthusiasm
- *Developing.* Assisting others to learn, grow, and achieve; orienting and coaching members of the team
- *Consensus building.* Helping build solidarity among team members, encouraging agreement, and helping interactions to be smooth
- *Empathizing.* Reflecting group feelings and expressing empathy and support for team members

All of us have been on a team or in a class when a fellow participant is funny, actively engaging with others, or especially supportive of others. The chemistry of the group just seems to improve under such conditions. It becomes easier to work and more enjoyable to be a team member. A certain amount of magnetism and positive energy exists. People tend to take more responsibility, collaborate more readily, and try harder to find consensual outcomes. These are the results that occur by performing relationship-building roles. They assist the team in working more effectively together.

Without both task-facilitating and relationship-building roles, teams struggle to perform effectively. Some members must ensure that the team accomplishes its tasks, while others must ensure that members remain bonded together interpersonally. These are usually not the same individuals, and at certain points in time, different roles may become more dominant than others. The key is to have a balance between task-oriented roles and relationship-building roles displayed in the team. The downfall of many teams is that they become unidimensional—for example, they emphasize task accomplishment exclusively, or they put too much emphasis on relationships.

UNPRODUCTIVE ROLES

Of course, each role can also have a downside if performed ineffectively or in inappropriate circumstances. For example, the *elaborating* role may be disruptive if the team is trying to reach a quick decision; the *tension relieving* role may be annoying if the team is trying to be serious; the *enforcing* role may create resistance when

the team is already experiencing high levels of pressure; the *consensus building* role may mask real differences of opinion and tension among team members.

However, it is even more likely that team members will display other unproductive roles rather than inappropriately play task or relationship roles. Unproductive roles inhibit the team or its members from achieving what they could have achieved, and they destroy morale and cohesion. They are called **blocking roles**. We point out a few of them here because, as you analyze the teams to which you belong, you may recognize these roles being performed and be able to confront them. Among the common blocking roles are:

- *Dominating.* Excessive talking, interrupting, or cutting others off
- *Overanalyzing.* Splitting hairs and examining every detail excessively
- *Stalling.* Not allowing the group to reach a decision or finalize a task by sidetracking the discussion, being unwilling to agree, repeating old arguments, and wasting time
- *Remaining passive.* Not being willing to engage in the team's task. Staying on the fringe or refusing to interact with other team members; expecting others to do the team's work
- *Overgeneralizing.* Blowing something out of proportion and drawing unfounded conclusions
- *Faultfinding.* Being unwilling to see the merits of others' ideas or criticizing others excessively
- *Premature decision making.* Making decisions before goals are stated, information is shared, alternatives are discussed, or problems are defined
- *Presenting opinions as facts.* Failing to examine the legitimacy of proposals and labeling personal opinions as truth
- *Rejecting.* Rejecting ideas based on the person who stated them rather than on their merits
- *Pulling rank.* Using status, expertise, or title to get ideas accepted rather than discussing and examining their value
- *Resisting.* Blocking all attempts to change, improve, or make progress; being disagreeable and negative about virtually all suggestions from other team members
- *Deflecting.* Not staying focused on the topic of the team's discussion; changing the subject of discussion or making comments that deflect attention away from the main points

Each of these blocking roles has the potential to inhibit a team from efficiently and effectively accomplishing its task by crushing morale, destroying consensus, creating conflict, hampering progress, exhausting or frustrating members, and making ill-informed decisions. When you recognize that blocking roles are displayed, you will want to confront this unproductive behavior honestly and openly, and use supportive communication to suggest more helpful roles. When you are familiar with productive task facilitating and relationship building roles, you will be able to assist others in making the team more effective.

PROVIDING FEEDBACK

When you provide feedback to others—whether corrective feedback in response to unproductive roles or mere suggestions for team improvement—you will want to keep in mind several well-proven rules of thumb. Giving feedback to anyone—team members, family members, colleagues, or even strangers—you should use the following principles of effective feedback summarized in Table 9.7:

❑ *Focus feedback on behavior rather than personal attributes.* Individuals can control and change their behavior. They cannot change their personalities or physical characteristics. For example, "Your comments are not on the topic" is more effective than "You are completely naïve."

❑ *Focus feedback on observations rather than inferences and on descriptions rather than judgments.* Facts and objective evidence are more trustworthy and acceptable than opinions and conjectures. For example, "The data don't

support your point" is more effective than "You just don't get it, do you?"

❑ *Focus feedback on behavior related to a specific situation, preferably to the "here and now," rather than on abstract or past behavior.* It will merely frustrate people if they cannot pinpoint a specific incident or behavior to which you are referring. Similarly, people cannot change something that has already happened. For example, "You have yet to agree with anyone's comments" is more effective than "You have always been a problem in this team."

❑ *Focus feedback on sharing ideas and information rather than giving advice.* Unless requested, avoid giving direct instructions and demands. Instead, help recipients identify changes and improvements themselves. For example, "How do you suggest we can break this logjam and move forward?" is more effective than "This is what we must do now."

❑ *Focus feedback on the amount of information that the recipient can use, rather than on the amount you might like to give.* Information overload causes people to stop listening. Not enough information leads to frustration and misunderstanding. For example, "You seem to have reached a conclusion before all the facts have been presented" is more effective than "Here are some evidence you should consider, and here are some more, and here are some more, and here are some more."

❑ *Focus feedback on the value it may have to the receiver, not on the emotional release it provides for you.* Feedback should be for the good of the

Table 9.7	Rules for Effective Team Feedback	
EFFECTIVE FEEDBACK	**INEFFECTIVE FEEDBACK**
Focus on behaviors	Focus on the person
Focus on observations	Focus on inferences or opinions
Focus on descriptions	Focus on evaluations
Focus on a specific situation or incident	Focus on abstract or general situations
Focus on the present	Focus on the past
Focus on sharing ideas and information	Focus on giving advice
Give feedback that is valuable to the receiver	Give feedback that provides an emotional release
Give feedback at an appropriate time and place	Give feedback when it is convenient for you

recipient, not merely for you to let off steam. For example, "I must say that your excessive talking is very troublesome to me and not helpful to the group" is more effective than "You are being a jerk, and you are making me really upset."

❑ *Focus feedback on time and place so that personal data can be shared at appropriate times.* The more specific feedback is, or the more it can be anchored in a specific context, the more helpful it can be. For example, "During a break, I would like to chat with you about something" is more effective than "You think your title gives you the right to force the rest of us to agree with you, but it's just making us angry."

INTERNATIONAL CAVEATS

These team member skills may require some modification in different international settings or with teams comprised of international members (Trompenaars & Hampen-Turner, 1998). Whereas the team member skills discussed above have been found to be effective in a global context, it is naïve to expect that everyone will react the same way to team member roles.

For example, in cultures that emphasize *affectivity* (e.g., Iran, Spain, France, Italy, and Mexico), personal confrontations and emotional displays are more acceptable than in cultures that are more *neutral* (e.g., Korea, China, Singapore, and Japan), where personal references are more offensive. Humor and displaying enthusiastic behavior is also more acceptable in affective cultures than neutral cultures. Similarly, status differences are likely to play a more dominant role in *ascription*-oriented cultures (e.g., Czech Republic, Egypt, Spain, and Korea), than in *achievement*-oriented cultures (e.g., United States, Norway, Canada, Australia, United Kingdom), in which knowledge and skills tend to be more important. Appealing to data and facts in the latter cultures will carry more weight than in the former cultures.

Some misunderstanding may also arise, for example, in cultures emphasizing different *time frames.* Whereas some cultures emphasize just-in-time, short-term time frames (e.g., United States), others emphasize long-term future time frames (e.g., Japan). The story is told of the Japanese proposal to purchase Yosemite National Park in California. The first thing the Japanese submitted was a 250-year business plan. The reaction of the California authorities was, "Wow, that's 1,000 quarterly reports." The urgency to move a team forward toward task accomplishment, in other words, may be seen differently by different cultural groups. Some cultures (e.g., Japan) are more comfortable spending substantial amounts of time on relationship-building activities before moving toward task accomplishment.

Summary

All of us are members of multiple teams—at work, at home, at school, and in the community. Teams are increasingly prevalent in the workplace and in the classroom because they have been shown to be powerful tools to improve the performance of individuals and organizations. Consequently, it is important to become proficient in leading and participating in teams.

It is obvious that merely putting people together and giving them an assigned task does not make them into an effective team. Students often complain about an excessive amount of teamwork in business schools, but most of it is less real teamwork than a repetitive experience of aggregating people together and assigning them a task. In this chapter, we reviewed three types of team skills: diagnosing and facilitating team development, leading a team, and being an effective team member. Figure 9.4 illustrates the relationship of these three key skills to high-performing team performance. These three skills are ones that you have no doubt engaged in before, but to be a skillful manager, you will need to hone your ability to perform each of these skill activities competently.

Behavioral Guidelines

A. Learn to diagnose the stage in which your team is operating in order to help facilitate team development and perform your role appropriately. Know the key characteristics of the forming, norming, storming, and performing stages of development.

B. Provide structure and clarity in the forming stage, support and encouragement in the norming stage, independence and exploration in the storming stage, and foster innovation and positive deviance in the performing stage.

C. When leading a team, first develop credibility as a prerequisite to having team members follow you.

Figure 9.4 Management Skills for High-Performing Teams

Leading Teams
- Develop credibility
- Articulate a vision

Team Membership
- Play task-facilitation roles
- Play relationship-building roles
- Provide feedback

Team Development
- Diagnose stage development
- Foster team development and high performance

High-Performing Teams
- Desired outcomes
- Shared purpose
- Accountability
- Blurred distinctions
- Coordinated roles
- Efficiency and participation
- High quality
- Creative continuous improvement
- Credibility and trust
- Core competence

D. Based on your established credibility, establish two types of goals for and with your team: SMART goals and Everest goals.
E. As a team member, facilitate task performance in your team by encouraging the performance of different roles listed in Table 9.5.
F. As a team member, facilitate the development of good relationships in your team by encouraging the performance of different roles listed in Table 9.6.
G. When encountering team members who block the team's performance with disruptive behaviors, confront the behavior directly and/or isolate the disruptive member.
H. Provide effective feedback to unhelpful team members that have characteristics listed in Table 9.7.

SKILL *ANALYSIS*

CASES INVOLVING BUILDING EFFECTIVE TEAMS

The *Tallahassee Democrat*'s ELITE Team

Katzenbach and Smith (1993, pp. 67–72), as part of their extensive research on teams, observed the formation of a team at the Tallahassee Democrat, the only major newspaper left in Tallahassee, Florida. Here is their description of how the team, which called itself "ELITE Team," performed over time. All incidents and names are factual. As you read the description, look for evidence of team development stages.

Fred Mott, general manager of the **Democrat**, recognized [the declining profitability and distribution of most major metropolitan newspapers] earlier than many of his counterparts. In part, Mott took his lead from Jim Batten, who made "customer obsession" the central theme of his corporate renewal effort shortly after he became Knight-Ridder's CEO. But the local marketplace also shaped Mott's thinking. The *Democrat* was Tallahassee's only newspaper and made money in spite of its customer service record. Mott believed, however, that further growth could never happen unless the paper learned to serve customers in ways "far superior to anything else in the market-place." The ELITE Team story actually began with the formation of another team made up of Mott and his direct reports. The management group knew they could not hope to build a "customer obsession" across the mile-high barriers isolating production from circulation from advertising without first changing themselves. It had become all too common, they admitted, for them to engage in "power struggles and finger pointing."

Using regularly scheduled Monday morning meetings, Mott's group began to "get to know each other's strengths and weaknesses, bare their souls, and build a level of trust." Most important, they did so by focusing on real work they could do together. For example, early on they agreed to create a budget for the paper as a team instead of singly as function heads.

Over time, the change in behavior at the top began to be noticed. One of the women who later joined the ELITE Team, for example, observed that the sight of senior management holding their "Monday morning come-to-Jesus" meetings really made a difference to her and others. "I saw all this going on and I thought, 'What are they so happy about?'"

Eventually, as the team at the top got stronger and more confident, they forged a higher aspiration: to build customer focus and break down the barriers across the broad base of the paper....

A year after setting up the new [team], however, Mott was both frustrated and impatient. Neither the Advertising Customer Service department, a series of customer surveys, additional resources thrown against the problem in the interim, nor any number of top management exhortations had made any difference. Ad errors persisted, and sales reps still complained of insufficient time with customers. In fact, the new unit had turned into another organizational barrier.

Customer surveys showed that too many advertisers still found the *Democrat* unresponsive to their needs and too concerned with internal procedures and dead-lines. People at the paper also had evidence beyond surveys. In one instance, for example, a sloppily prepared ad arrived through a fax machine looking like a "rat had run across the page." Yet the ad passed through the hands of seven employees and probably would have found its way into print if it had not been literally unread-able! As someone commented, "It was not anyone's job to make sure it was right. If they felt it was simply their job to type or paste it up, they just passed it along." This particular fax, affectionately known as the "rat tracks fax," came to symbolize the essential challenge at the *Democrat*....

At the time, Mott was reading about Motorola's quality programs and the goal of zero defects. He decided to heed Dunlap's advice by creating a special team of workers charged with eliminating all errors in advertisements. Mott now admits he was skeptical that frontline people could become as cohesive a team as he and his direct reports. So he made Dunlap, his trusted confidante, the leader of the team that took on the name ELITE for "ELIminate The Errors."

A year later, Mott was a born-again believer in teams. Under ELITE's leadership, advertising accuracy, never before tracked at the paper, had risen sharply and stayed above 99 percent. Lost revenues from errors, previously as high as $10,000 a month, had dropped to near zero. Ad sales reps had complete confidence in the Advertising

Customer Service department's capacity and desire to treat each ad as though the *Democrat*'s existence were at stake. And surveys showed a huge positive swing in advertiser satisfaction. Mott considered all of this nothing less than a minor miracle.

The impact of ELITE, however, went beyond numbers. It completely redesigned the process by which the *Democrat* sells, creates, produces, and bills for advertisements. More important yet, it stimulated and nurtured the customer obsession and cross-functional cooperation required to make the new process work. In effect, this team of mostly frontline workers transformed an entire organization with respect to customer service.

ELITE had a lot going for it from the beginning. Mott gave the group a clear performance goal (eliminate errors) and a strong mix of skills (12 of the best people from all parts of the paper). He committed himself to follow through by promising, at the first meeting, that "whatever solution you come up with will be implemented." In addition, Jim Batten's customer obsession movement helped energize the task force.

But it took more than a good sendoff and an overarching corporate theme to make ELITE into a high-performance team. In this case, the personal commitments began to grow, unexpectedly, over the early months as the team grappled with its challenge. At first, the group spent more time pointing fingers at one another than coming to grips with advertising errors. Only when one of them produced the famous "rat tracks fax" and told the story behind it did the group start to admit that everyone—not everyone else—was at fault. Then, recalls one member, "We had some pretty hard discussions. And there were tears in those meetings."

The emotional response galvanized the group to the task at hand and to one another. And the closer it got, the more focused it became on the challenge. ELITE decided to look carefully at the entire process by which an ad was sold, created, printed, and billed. When it did, the team discovered patterns in the errors, most of which could be attributed to time pressures, bad communication, and poor attitude....

Commitment to one another drove ELITE to expand its aspirations continually. Having started with the charge to eliminate errors, ELITE moved on to break down functional barriers, then to redesigning the entire advertising process, then to refining new standards and measures for customer service, and, finally, to spreading its own brand of "customer obsession" across the entire *Democrat*....Inspired by ELITE, for example, one production crew started coming to work at 4 a.m. to ease time pressures later in the day....

To this day, the spirit of ELITE lives on at the *Democrat*. "There is no beginning and no end," says Dunlap. "Every day we experience something we learn from." ELITE's spirit made everyone a winner—the customers, the employees, management, and even Knight-Ridder's corporate leaders. CEO Jim Batten was so impressed that he agreed to pay for managers from other Knight-Ridder papers to visit the *Democrat* to learn from ELITE's experience. And, of course, the 12 people who committed themselves to one another and their paper had an impact and an experience none of them will ever forget.

SOURCE: The Tallahassee Democrat's Elite Team Katzenbach, *Jon R. and Douglas K. Smith (1993) The Wisdom of Teams. Harvard Business School Press, 67–72.*

Discussion Questions

9.1. What were the stages of development of the ELITE Team? Identify specific examples of each of the four stages of team development in the case.

9.2. How do you explain the team's reaching a high-performance condition? What were the major predictive factors?

9.3. Why didn't Mott's top management team reach a high level of performance? What was his team lacking? Why was an ELITE team needed?

9.4. Make recommendations about what Mott should do now to capitalize on the ELITE Team experience. If you were to become a consultant to the *Tallahassee Democrat*, what advice would you give Mott about how he can capitalize on teambuilding?

The Cash Register Incident

Read the following scenario by yourself. Then complete a three-step exercise, the first two steps by yourself, and the third step with a team. A time limit is associated with each step.

> *A store owner had just turned off the lights in the store when a man appeared and demanded money. The owner opened a cash register. The contents of the cash register were scooped up, and the man sped away. A member of the police force was notified promptly.*

Step 1: After reading these instructions, close your book. Without looking at the scenario, rewrite it as accurately as you can. Describe the incident as best you can using your own words.

Step 2: Assume you observed the incident described in the paragraph above. Later, a reporter asks you questions about what you read in order to write an article for the local newspaper. Answer the questions from the reporter by yourself. Do not talk with anyone else about your answers. Put a Y, N, or DK in the response column. Since reporters are always pressed for time, take no more than two minutes to complete step 2.

Answer

Y   Yes, or true

N   No, or false

DK   Don't know, or there is no way to tell

Step 3: The reporter wants to interview your entire team together. As a team, discuss the answers to each question and reach a consensus decision—that is, one with which everyone on the team agrees. Do not vote or engage in horse-trading. The reporter wants to know what you all agree on. Complete your team discussion in 10 minutes.

Statements About the Incident

"As a reporter, I am interested in what happened in this incident. Can you tell me what occurred? I'd like you to address the following eleven questions."

Statement

Alone   *Team*

_____ _____   1. Did a man appear after the owner turned off his store lights?

_____ _____   2. Was the robber a man?

_____ _____   3. Is it true that the man did not demand money?

<table>
<tr><td>_____</td><td>_____</td><td>4. The man who opened the cash register was the owner, right?</td></tr>
<tr><td>_____</td><td>_____</td><td>5. Did the store owner scoop up the contents of the cash register?</td></tr>
<tr><td>_____</td><td>_____</td><td>6. OK, so someone opened the cash register, right?</td></tr>
<tr><td>_____</td><td>_____</td><td>7. Let me get this straight, after the man who demanded the money scooped up the contents of the cash register, he ran away?</td></tr>
<tr><td>_____</td><td>_____</td><td>8. The contents of the cash register contained money, but you don't know how much?</td></tr>
<tr><td>_____</td><td>_____</td><td>9. Did the robber demand money of the owner?</td></tr>
<tr><td>_____</td><td>_____</td><td>10. OK, by way of summary, the incident concerns a series of events in which only three persons are involved: the owner of the store, a man who demanded money, and a member of the police force?</td></tr>
<tr><td>_____</td><td>_____</td><td>11. Let me be sure I understand. Is it true that the following events occurred: Someone demanded money, the cash register was opened, its contents were scooped up, and a man dashed out of the store?</td></tr>
</table>

When you have finished your team decision making and mock interview with the reporter, the instructor will provide correct answers. Calculate how many answers you got right as an individual, and then calculate how many right answers your team achieved. Also go back and compare your own description of the incident with the actual wording of the scenario. How did you do? How accurate were you in your description?

Discussion Questions

9.5. How many individuals did better than the team as a whole? (In general, more than 80 percent of people do worse than the team.)

9.6. What changes would be needed in order for your team score to be even better?

9.7. How do you explain the superior performance of most teams over even the best individuals?

9.8. Under what conditions would individuals do better than teams in making decisions?

SKILL *PRACTICE*

EXERCISES IN BUILDING EFFECTIVE TEAMS

Leadership Roles in Teams

Assume you have been appointed as the leader of a team of colleagues. In each of the scenarios below, identify the major issues you need to address and the key actions you should take to ensure the success of the team. *What is your role as a leader?*

9.9. The team has just come together for the first time, and this is its first meeting.

9.10. You join a team that has been together for several meetings and has, unfortunately, had a history of being unproductive, goofing off, and partying with one another a bit too much.

9.11. Your team is experiencing a lot of conflict among members. Strongly held points of view exist that seem not to be compatible. Factions have begun to arise in the team.

9.12. Your team is well-oiled and highly functioning, and you want to make sure that this high level of performance not only continues but improves.

Team Diagnosis and Team Development Exercise

In order to help you develop the ability to diagnose team stage development, consider a team in which you are now a member. If you belong to a team as part of this class, select that one. You may also select a team at your employment, in your church or community, or a team in another class in school. Complete the following three-step exercise:

Step 1: Use the following questions to help you determine the stage of development in which your team is operating. Create a score for your team for each stage of development. Identify the stage in which the team seems to operate the most.

Step 2: Identify what actions or interventions would lead your team to the next higher stage of development. Specify what dynamics need to change, what team members need to do, and/or how the team leader could foster more advanced team development.

Step 3: Share your scores and your suggestions with others in class in a small-group setting, and add at least one good idea from someone else's diagnosis to your own design.

Use the following scale in your rating of your team right now.

Rating Scale

1 Not typical at all of my team
2 Not very typical of my team
3 Somewhat typical of my team
4 Very typical of my team

Stage 1

_____ 1. Not everyone is clear about the objectives and goals of the team.

_____ 2. Not everyone is personally acquainted with everyone else in the team.

_____ 3. Only a few team members actively participate.

_____ 4. Interactions among team members are very safe or somewhat superficial.

_____ 5. Trust among all team members has not yet been established.

_____ 6. Many team members seem to need direction from the leader in order to participate.

Stage 2

_____ 7. All team members know and agree with the objectives and goals of the team.

_____ 8. Team members all know one another.

_____ 9. Team members are very cooperative and actively participate in the activities of the team.

_____ 10. Interactions among team members are friendly, personal, and nonsuperficial.

_____ 11. A comfortable level of trust has been established among team members.

_____ 12. A strong unity exists in the team, and team members feel very much a part of a special group.

Stage 3

_____ 13. Disagreements and differing points of view are openly expressed by team members.

_____ 14. Competition exists among some team members.

_____ 15. Some team members do not follow the rules or the team norms.

_____ 16. Subgroups or coalitions exist within the team.

_____ 17. Some issues create major disagreements when discussed by the team, with some members on one side and others on the other side.

_____ 18. The authority or competence of the team leader is being questioned or challenged.

Stage 4

_____ 19. Team members are committed to the team and actively cooperate to improve the team's performance.

_____ 20. Team members feel free to try out new ideas, experiment, share something crazy, or do novel things.

_____ 21. A high level of energy is displayed by team members and expectations for performance are very high.

_____ 22. Team members do not always agree, but a high level of trust exists and each person is given respect, so disagreements are resolved productively.

_____ 23. Team members are committed to helping one another succeed and improve, so self-aggrandizement is at a minimum.

_____ 24. The team can make fast decisions without sacrificing quality.

Scoring

Add up the scores for the items in each stage of team development. Generally, one stage clearly stands out as having the highest scores. Team stages develop sequentially, so the highest stage in which scores occur is usually the dominant stage of development. Based on these scores, identify ways to move the team to the next level.

Total of Stage 1 items _____

Total of Stage 2 items _____

Total of Stage 3 items _____

Total of Stage 4 items _____

Winning the War on Talent

In this exercise, you will form teams of six members. Your team will have an overall objective to achieve, and each team member will have individual objectives. The exercise is accomplished in seven steps and it should take a total of 50 minutes to complete steps 1 through 6.

Step 1: In your team, read the scenario on the next page about the problem of attracting and retaining talented employees in twenty-first century organizations. Your team objective is to generate two innovative but workable ideas for how to retain good teachers in the public school system. You will have 15 minutes to develop the ideas.

Step 2: When each team has completed the assignment, each is given two minutes to present the two ideas. These ideas will be evaluated, and a winning team will be selected based on the following criteria:

❑ The ideas are workable and affordable.

❑ The ideas are interesting, innovative, and unusual.

❑ The ideas have a good chance of making a difference if they are implemented.

Step 3: In addition to the team assignment, each team member is assigned to play three team member roles during the discussion. A role assignment schedule is listed below. Team members may select the roles they wish to play, or an instructor can assign the roles. One purpose of this individual assignment is to give team members practice in playing either task-facilitation roles or relationship-building roles in a team setting, so you should take these assignments seriously. Remember, however, that you have only 15 minutes. When your team has completed its task, each team member will rate the effectiveness of every other team member in how well they played their roles and how much they helped the team accomplish its task. You will have five minutes to complete the ratings.

TEAM MEMBER NAME	ROLES	PERFORMANCE RATING (1) LOW–(10) HIGH PERFORMANCE FEEDBACK
1	Direction giving	
	Urging	
	Enforcing	
2	Information seeking	
	Information giving	
	Elaborating	

(continued)

TEAM MEMBER NAME	ROLES	PERFORMANCE RATING (1) LOW–(10) HIGH PERFORMANCE FEEDBACK
3	Monitoring Reality testing Summarizing	
4	Process analyzing Supporting Confronting	
5	Harmonizing Tension relieving Energizing	
6	Developing Consensus building Empathizing	

Step 4: Each team member uses the form above to rate the performance of, and provide feedback to, every other member of the team. In completing the form, make sure you focus on how well each person performed his or her assigned roles. Identify at least one thing you noticed about the performance of each team member so that you can provide personal feedback to each one. Remember that the overall purpose of this exercise is to give you practice in playing effective roles in teams and providing feedback to team members. You are given five minutes for this rating task.

Step 5: When each team has completed its task, one representative from each team is selected to form a judging team. This judging team evaluates the quality of the ideas produced by each team. A winning team is announced as a result of their deliberations. (Other class members will want to observe and rate the performance of this judging team and its members as they make their selection.) The judging team will be given 10 minutes to select the winning team.

Step 6: Teams meet again so that personal feedback can be given. Each team member takes a total of three minutes to give feedback to the other members of his or her team based on the evaluation form above. A total of 20 minutes will be required to provide this feedback.

Step 7: Hold a class discussion about what you observed regarding team members' roles. Especially, reflect on your own experience trying to play those roles and what seemed to be most effective in facilitating task accomplishment and in building team cohesion.

The Problem Scenario

Almost to a person, the chief concern expressed by senior executives in most "old economy" firms is how to attract and retain managerial talent. With the economy expected to grow at almost three times the growth of the job market, finding competent employees will be a continuing challenge for the next several years. The allure of dot.com firms, high-growth companies, and high-risk–high-return ventures has created an incredibly difficult environment for organizations whose chief competitive advantage is intellectual capital and human talent. Headhunters, venture capitalists, and even firms' customers are aggressively trying to lure away management talent any way they can. A recent survey of Wall Street investment bankers revealed that more than half had been approached by an Internet company. Armed with venture capital dollars and business plans promising swift public offerings, it is easy to see why many are succeeding in attracting managerial talent away from traditional companies. Compensation packages in the seven figures are not unusual.

In this highly competitive environment where intellectual capital is at a premium, consider the difficulty faced by nonprofit organizations, local or state governments, arts organizations, or educational institutions whose budgets are constrained far below the high-priced world of the "new economy." How will they compete for talent when they cannot come close to the salaries of firms whose market capitalization exceeds the GDP of many African countries?

In particular, the U.S. public education system has suffered tremendously in this environment. The United States spends more per child than any other country, and the costs of education are increasing far faster than the consumer price index. However, it is well known that more than a quarter of public school students drop out before high school graduation, and of those who remain, the percent passing proficiency exams is woefully low—in some school districts, less than 10 percent. The average tenure of public school teachers is less than seven years, and that number is dropping rapidly as these knowledge workers can find positions elsewhere at triple and quadruple their school salaries. Add to that the difficulties escalating in the classroom resulting from students in single-parent homes, marginal economic circumstances, threats of violence, and behavioral disruptions, and it is clear why teaching is a difficult profession, even if monetary compensation were higher.

Numerous alternatives have been proposed, but few have addressed the problem of teacher attraction and retention. Your task as a team is to identify two answers to the question: How can we attract and retain teachers in the public schools of the United States? You may want to consider what is being done in the school systems in other countries or in highly effective school systems in America.

Team Performance Exercise

The purpose of this exercise is to help you practice the dynamics of team formation, development, and effective performance. The most important part of the exercise is having you practice effective team leadership and team membership and accurately diagnosing the stages of team development so you can behave appropriately.

Your instructor will form you into teams of five members each. Your task as a team is to create a five-pointed star in the form that you drew when you were a child (see Figure 9.5). You will do this with a piece of rope that has been tied at the ends to form a circle. Here is how this exercise will occur:

1. You will find a 50-foot piece of rope on the floor. Each member of your team will surround the rope and take hold of it with both hands. Once you have taken hold of the rope, you cannot let go until the exercise has been completed.

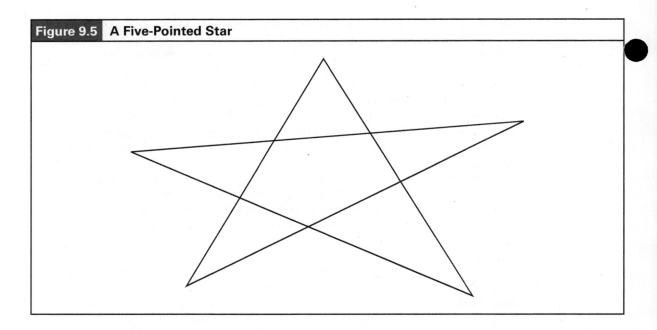

Figure 9.5 | **A Five-Pointed Star**

2. You will be given five minutes to plan how you are going to create the star, with all the appropriate crisscrosses. You may not move at all during this five-minute planning period. You must stay exactly where you are. Practicing is not permitted.

3. Once you have finished the five-minute planning session, you may not talk out loud again. The task must be completed in complete silence. You may not communicate verbally with any other member of your team. Only nonverbal communication is permitted. Remember, once you have taken hold of the rope, you cannot let go with either hand.

4. When the instructor gives the signal, you will start moving in order to create your five-sided star. When you have finished, you will place the rope down on the floor in exactly the position in which you are standing. You may not rearrange or move the rope on the floor. The rope should accurately represent your team members' positions.

5. The quality of your results will be evaluated by the instructor and the winning team announced.

When you have finished the task, discuss the following questions:

9.13. As a team, what was especially effective, and what was especially ineffective in planning for task accomplishment in advance?

9.14. What hints about initial stages of team development were utilized?

9.15. What happened to your team dynamics over the duration of the activity? Did they change from one stage to another? Did you end up as a high-performing team?

9.16. What team leadership and membership roles did each of your team members play? Which were the most effective?

9.17. What were the differences between teams that accomplished the task the most quickly and with the highest quality compared to the others?

9.18. How did you make up for the inability to communicate as a team during the task?

9.19. What do you wish you could do differently to be more efficient and more effective if you were to do another task together?

ACTIVITIES FOR BUILDING
EFFECTIVE TEAMS

Suggested Assignments

9.20. Teach someone else how to determine which stage of development a team is in and what behaviors are most effective in each separate stage.

9.21. Analyze the characteristics of a team in which you are a member. Determine in what ways its functioning could be improved. Based on the attributes of high-performance teams, identify what could be done to improve its performance.

9.22. Conduct a role analysis of a real team meeting in which members are trying to make a decision, solve a problem, or examine an issue. Who performed what roles? Which team members were most helpful? Which team members were least helpful? Provide feedback to the team on what roles you saw being played, what roles were missing, and what improvements could have made the team more effective.

9.23. Write out a formal vision statement for a team you are leading. Make certain that the vision possesses the attributes of effective, energizing vision statements discussed in the chapter. Identify specifically what you can do to get team members to commit to that vision.

9.24. Do an in-depth analysis of an effective team leader you know. Focus specifically on the ways in which he or she has developed credibility and continues to influence team members. Identify what followers say about credibility, not just the leader.

9.25. Teach someone, or coach someone, on how to become an effective leader of a team, and how to become an effective team member. Demonstrate or exemplify the skills you teach that person.

Application Plan and Evaluation

The intent of this exercise is to help you apply this cluster of skills in a real-life, out-of-class setting. Now that you have become familiar with the behavioral guidelines that form the basis of effective skill performance, you will improve most by trying out those guidelines in an everyday context. Unlike a classroom activity, in which feedback is immediate and others can assist you with their evaluations, this skill application activity is one you must accomplish and evaluate on your own. There are two parts to this activity. Part 1 helps prepare you to apply the skill, and Part 2 helps you evaluate and improve on your experience. Be sure to write down answers to each item. Don't short-circuit the process by skipping steps.

Part 1: Planning

9.26. Write down the two or three aspects of this skill that are most important to you. These may be areas of weakness, areas you most want to improve, or areas that are most salient to a problem you face right now. Identify the specific aspects of this skill that you want to apply.

9.27. Now identify the setting or the situation in which you will apply this skill. Establish a plan for performance by actually writing down a description of the situation. Who else will be involved? When will you do it? Where will it be done?

> Circumstances:
> Who else?
> When?
> Where?

9.28. Identify the specific behaviors in which you will engage to apply this skill. Operationalize your skill performance.

9.29. What are the indicators of successful performance? How will you know you have been effective? What will indicate you have performed competently?

Part 2: Evaluation

9.30. After you have completed your implementation, record the results. What happened? How successful were you? What was the effect on others?

9.31. How can you improve? What modifications can you make next time? What will you do differently in a similar situation in the future?

9.32. Looking back on your whole skill practice and application experience, what have you learned? What has been surprising? In what ways might this experience help you in the long term?

SCORING KEYS AND COMPARISON DATA

✪ Scoring Keys for the following instrument, along with comparison data, are contained in PIA in MyManagementLab.com;

Team Development Behaviors

Diagnosing the Need for Team Building

Comparison Data (N = 10,000 students)

TOTAL SCORE	MEAN	BOTTOM QUARTILE	SECOND QUARTILE	THIRD QUARTILE	TOP QUARTILE
	54.22	38 or below	39–52	53–69	70 or above

LEADERSHIP ROLES IN TEAMS
(Examples of Correct Answers)

SCENARIO 1:

1. Explain the goals and objectives of the team.
2. Ensure that people get to know one another.
3. Give members a chance to ask questions. Address uncertainties.
4. Establish a relationship between yourself and each team member.
5. Build trust.

SCENARIO 2:

1. Facilitate participation of all team members.
2. Foster team cohesion so that peer pressure toward conformity is strong.
3. Provide honest feedback in a supportive way.
4. Guard against groupthink by establishing subgroups, devil's advocates, or critical evaluators.
5. Create a sense of team identify and ownership.

SCENARIO 3:

1. Make it legitimate for team members to disagree with one another in helpful ways.
2. Ensure respectful, supportive questioning and listening.
3. Work toward interdependence rather than independence so people work collaboratively.
4. Find areas of common agreement.
5. Reinforce the team's goal and purpose.

SCENARIO 4:

1. Encourage entrepreneurship and innovative ideas.
2. Push for positive deviance and extraordinarily levels of high performance.
3. Capitalize on the most positive energizing team members.
4. Work to maintain high levels of openness and trust among team members.
5. Articulate and reinforce an Everest goal.

SCORING KEYS AND COMPARISON DATA

SKILL **ASSESSMENT**

- Leading Positive Change
- Reflected Best-Self Feedback Exercise
- Positive Practices Survey

SKILL **LEARNING**

- Leading Positive Change
- Ubiquitous and Escalating Change
- The Need for Frameworks
- Tendencies Toward Stability
- A Framework for Leading Positive Change
- Summary
- Behavioral Guidelines

SKILL **ANALYSIS**

- Corporate Vision Statements
- Jim Mallozzi: Implementing Positive Change in Prudential Real Estate and Relocation

SKILL **PRACTICE**

- Reflected Best-Self Portrait
- Positive Organizational Diagnosis Exercise
- A Positive Change Agenda

SKILL **APPLICATION**

- Suggested Assignments
- Application Plan and Evaluation

SCORING KEYS AND *COMPARISON DATA*

10

Leading Positive Change

LEARNING OBJECTIVES

1. LEARN HOW TO CREATE POSITIVE DEVIANCE IN ORGANIZATIONS

2. DEVELOP THE CAPABILITY TO LEAD POSITIVE CHANGE

3. ACQUIRE THE ABILITY TO MOBILIZE THE CAPABILITIES OF OTHERS IN ACHIEVING POSITIVE CHANGE

MyManagementLab™

✪ When you see this icon, visit www.mymanagementlab.com for self-assessments, video activities, and more.

DIAGNOSTIC SURVEYS FOR LEADING POSITIVE CHANGE

⭐ If your instructor is utilizing **MyManagementLab**, log onto mymanagementlab.com and select the Personal Inventory Assessment (PIA) section and complete the instruments associated with this chapter.

The assessment instruments in this chapter are briefly described below. The assessments appear either in your text or in PIA. The assessments marked with (blue star) are available only in PIA.

All assessments should be completed before reading the chapter material.

After completing the first assessment save your response to your hard drive. When you have finished reading the chapter, re-take the assessment and compare your responses to see what you have learned.

⭐ ❑ The *Leading Positive Change Assessment* measures the extent to which you effectively lead the process of change and, especially, the degree to which you have developed skills in leading positive change.

❑ The *Reflected Best-Self Feedback Exercise* provides you with information on your greatest strengths, your behavior when you are at your very best, and the ways in which you make unique contributions.

⭐ ❑ The *Positive Practices Survey* identifies the extent to which the organization you are rating possesses the characteristics of the very highest performing organizations. It shows the degree to which your organization is flourishing and is likely to exceed performance expectations.

LEADING POSITIVE CHANGE

Assessment Section

REFLECTED BEST-SELF FEEDBACK

All of us can recall our own extraordinary moments, those moments when we felt that our best self was brought to light, affirmed by others, and put into practice. These memories are seared into our minds as moments in which we have felt alive, true to our deepest selves, and pursuing our full potential as human beings. Over time, we collect these experiences into a portrait of who we are when we are at our personal best. To help compose a best-self portrait, it is important to draw on the perceptions of significant others who have unique and valuable insights into our strengths and enduring talents. The Reflected Best-Self Feedback Exercise creates an opportunity for us to receive feedback regarding who are when we are at our best. A detailed explanation of this exercise, including the research that supports its effectiveness in helping people become better leaders, can be found at: www.bus.umich.edu/positive. Look under POS teaching tools.

In this exercise, you will gather information about yourself from other people who know you well. In the Skill Practice section of the chapter, you will be asked to develop a best self-portrait based on this feedback. The first step is to gather the information. Here is how you go about it.

Identify 20 people who know you well. These may be colleagues (former or current), friends (old or recent), family members, neighbors, class members, or anyone who has had extended contact with you. Select individuals who will give you an honest opinion. The more diverse the group, the better. Also, realize that due to time constraints, everyone may not be able to respond. You need at least 10 responses to complete this part of assignment, so ask enough people to ensure at least 10 responses, but try for 20.

Compose your feedback request using the sample email included below and send it to the 20 people you select. While this request may seem awkward or difficult for you, people have found this assessment to be a profound learning activity, and other people are quite willing to participate in this exercise. You will find that this actually strengthens your relationships in many cases.

SOURCE: *Roberts, L. M., Spreitzer, G., Dutton, J., Quinn, R., Heaphy, E., Barker, B. (2005). How to play to your strengths,* Harvard Business Review, *83: 75–80*

Sample E-mail Request for Feedback

I am taking a course that requires me to construct a profile of my unique strengths. I have been asked to contact 20 people who know me well. I would like to invite you to help me with this exercise. I am to request that each person provide me with three stories of when I displayed my best strengths.

This will require that you think about your interactions with me and identify times when you saw me add unique value and perform at my best. Please provide examples so I can understand the situation and the characteristics you are describing. I have attached some examples of what these stories could look like. Please use these only as a guide.

Feedback Examples

1. *One of your greatest strengths is: The ability to get people to work together and give all they have to a task.*

For example, I think of the time that: We were doing the Alpha project. We were getting behind and the stress was building. We started to close down and get very focused on just meeting our deadline. You noticed that we were not doing our best work and stopped the group to rethink our approach. You asked whether we wanted to just satisfy the requirements or whether we wanted to really do good and important work. You reminded us of what we were capable of doing and how each of us could contribute to a better outcome. No one else in that room would have thought to do that. As a result, we did meet the deadline and created a result we all feel proud of.

2. *One of your greatest strengths is: Being happy all the time.*

For example, I think of the time that: We had just lost the league championship game, and we were all really down in the dumps. All of us knew we could have played better, and we were really in a funk. You were the one who pumped us up and made us feel better—not in a superficial or silly way, but by expressing genuine pleasure at having a chance to play and being together as friends. I really admire you for being able to see the good in a situation and being such a positive person.

3. **One of your greatest strengths is:** *The capacity to persist in the face of adversity.*
   For example, I think of the time that: *We were past our deadline on a major report. Frank quit and we were left short-handed. Instead of getting discouraged, you became more focused than I have ever seen anyone get. I think you went 48 hours without sleep. I was amazed that you could produce such a quality product under those conditions.*

Your feedback to me: Please provide me with three examples of the strengths you observed by completing the following statements.

1. **One of your greatest strengths is:**
   For example, I think of the time that:

2. **One of your greatest strengths is:**
   For example, I think of the time that:

3. **One of your greatest strengths is:**
   For example, I think of the time that:

Please e-mail your responses to me by [insert a date]. Thank you very much for your cooperation. I will be sure to share with you what I learn.

When you have obtained this feedback, you will be guided in developing a Best-Self Portrait in the Skill Practice section of this chapter.

SOURCE: *Adapted from, "Reflected best-self exercise: Assignment and instructions for participants." Center for Positive Organizational Scholarship, Ross School of Business, University of Michigan, Product #01B, 2003.*

SKILL *LEARNING*

The word **leadership** is often used as a catch-all term to describe almost any desirable behavior by a manager. "Good leadership" is frequently the explanation given for the success of almost any positive organizational performance—from stock price increases to upward national economic trends to happy employees. Magazine covers trumpet the remarkable achievements of leaders, and the person at the top is almost always credited with being the cause of the success or failure. Coaches are fired when players don't perform, CEOs lose their jobs when customers choose a competitor, and presidents are voted out of office when the economy goes south.

Contrarily, leaders are often given hero status when their organizations succeed (e.g., Gandhi, Welch, Jobs, Buffett). The leader as scapegoat, and hero, is an image that is alive and well in modern society. Rationally speaking, however, most of us recognize that there is much more to organizational success than the leader's behavior, but we also recognize that leadership is one of the most important influences in helping organizations perform well (Cameron, 2012; Cameron & Lavine, 2006; Pfeffer, 1998).

Some writers have differentiated between the concepts of leadership and management (Kotter, 1999; Tichy, 1993, 1997). *Leadership* has often been described as what individuals do under conditions of change. When organizations are dynamic and undergoing transformation, people exhibit leadership. *Management*, on the other hand, has traditionally been associated with the status quo. Maintaining stability is the job of the manager. Leaders have been said to focus on setting direction, initiating change, and creating something new. Managers have been said to focus on maintaining steadiness, controlling variation, and refining current performance. Leadership has been equated with dynamism, vibrancy, and charisma; management with predictability, equilibrium, and control. Hence, leadership is often defined as "doing the right things," whereas management is often defined as "doing things right."

Recent research is clear, however, that such distinctions between leadership and management, which may have been appropriate in previous decades, are no longer useful (Cameron & Lavine, 2006; Cameron & Quinn, 1999; Quinn, 2000, 2004). Managers cannot be successful without being good leaders, and leaders cannot be successful without being good managers. No longer do organizations and individuals have the luxury of holding on to the status quo; worrying about doing things right without also doing the right things; keeping the system stable without also leading change and improvement; maintaining current performance without also creating something new; concentrating on equilibrium and control without also concentrating on vibrancy and charisma. Effective management and leadership are largely inseparable. The skills required to do one are also required for the other (Cameron, Quinn, DeGraff, & Thakor, 2014).

No organization in a postindustrial, hyperturbulent, twenty-first-century environment will survive without individuals capable of providing both management and leadership. Leading change and managing stability, establishing vision and accomplishing objectives, breaking the rules and monitoring conformance, although paradoxical, all are required to be successful. Individuals who are effective managers are also effective leaders much of the time. The skills required to be effective as a leader and as a manager are essentially identical.

On the other hand, Quinn (2004) has reminded us that no person is a leader all of the time. Leadership is a *temporary* condition in which certain skills and competencies are displayed.

> *Understanding that leadership is a temporary, dynamic state brings us to a radical redefinition of how we think about, enact, and develop leadership. We come to discover that most of the time, most people, including CEOs, presidents, and prime ministers, are not leaders. We discover that anyone can be a leader. Most of the time, none of us are leaders. (Quinn, 2004)*

In this chapter, we focus on the most common activity that demonstrates leadership—leading change. It is while engaging in this task that the temporary state of leadership is most likely to be revealed. That is, despite the heroic image of leaders, every person can develop the skills needed to lead change. Everyone can, and most everyone does, demonstrate leadership at some point. On the other hand, effectively leading change involves a complex and difficult-to-master set of skills, so assistance is required in order to do it successfully. This is because of the difficulties associated with change.

Ubiquitous and Escalating Change

It is not news that we live in a dynamic, turbulent, and even chaotic world. Almost no one would try to predict with any degree of certainty what the world will be like in 10 years. Things change too fast. We know that the technology currently exists, for example, to put the equivalent of a full-size computer in a wristwatch, or inject the equivalent of a laptop computer into the bloodstream. New computers are beginning to be etched on molecules instead of silicon wafers. The half-life of any technology you can name—from complex computers to nuclear devices to software—is less than six months. Anything can be reproduced in less than a half a year.

The mapping of the human genome is probably the greatest source for change, for not only can we now change a banana into an agent to inoculate people against malaria, but new organ development and physiological regulation promise to dramatically alter population life styles. As of this writing, more than 100 whole animals have been patented. Whereas it took 10 years to produce a generic alternative to a normal pharmaceutical drug in 1965, currently the process takes approximately one day. In 1980, it took a year to assemble 12,000 DNA base pairs; by 1999, it took less than a minute, and now millions of base pairs can be assembled in less than one second. Between the dawn of mankind and 2003, the planet produced one exabyte of data, but we now produce one exabyte of data each day. Who can predict the changes that will result? Hence, not only is change ubiquitous and constant, but almost everyone predicts that it will escalate exponentially.

The Need for Frameworks

Frameworks or theories help provide stability and order in the midst of constant change. To illustrate the importance of frameworks, consider a simple experiment conducted by Nobel laureate Herbert A. Simon. Experimental subjects were shown a chess board as it appeared midgame. Some of these individuals were experienced chess players, some were novices. They were allowed to observe the chess board for 10 seconds, and then the board was wiped clean. The subjects were asked to replace the pieces on the board exactly as they had appeared before the board was cleared. This experiment was conducted on a computer, so wiping the chess board clean was simple, and multiple trials could be generated for each person. Each trial showed a different configuration of a chess game midway through.

The question being investigated was: Which group was best at replacing the chess pieces, the novices or the experienced players? After looking at the board for 10 seconds, which individuals would be most accurate in placing each piece in its previous location? An argument could be made for either group.

On the one hand, the minds of novices would not be cluttered by preconceptions. They would look at the board with a fresh view. It is similar to the answer to the question: When is the best time to teach a person a new language, age 3 or age 30? The fact that 3-year-olds can learn a new language more quickly than 30-year-olds suggests that novices might also be better at this task because of their lack of preconceptions. On the other hand, the contrary argument is that experience ought to count for something, and the familiarity of experienced players with the chess board should allow them to be more successful.

The results of the experiment were dramatic. Novices accurately replaced the pieces less than five percent of the time. Experienced players were accurate more than 80 percent of the time. When experienced chess players looked at the board, they saw familiar patterns or what might be called frameworks. They said things like this: "This looks like the Leningrad

defense, except this bishop is out of place and these two pawns are arranged differently." Experienced players identified the patterns quickly, and then they paid attention to the few exceptions on the board. Novices, on the other hand, needed to pay attention to every single piece as if it were an exception, since no pattern (or framework) was available to guide their decisions.

Frameworks serve the same function for managers. They clarify complex or ambiguous situations. Individuals familiar with frameworks can manage complex situations effectively because they can respond to fewer exceptions. Individuals without frameworks are left to react to every piece of information as a unique event or an exception. The best managers possess the most, and the most useful, frameworks. When they encounter a new situation, they do not become overwhelmed or stressed because they have frameworks that can help simplify and clarify the unfamiliar.

In this chapter, we provide you with a very useful framework for managing change. But, we are interested in having you not only manage change and learn to cope with the chaotic environment that currently exists. Instead, we want you to become skillful at leading *positive change*. Leading positive change and managing change are not the same things.

To illustrate the difference between commonplace change and positive change, consider the continuum in Figure 10.1 (Cameron, 2003a). It shows a line

---

Figure 10.1 | A Continuum of Negative and Positive Deviance

Individual:	Negative Deviance	Normal	Positive Deviance
Physiological *(Medical research)*	Illness	Health	Vitality
Psychological *(Psychological research)*	Illness	Health	Flow

Organizational and Managerial:
(Management and organizational research)

	Negative Deviance	Normal	Positive Deviance
Revenues	Unprofitable	Profitable	Generous
Effectiveness	Ineffective	Effective	Excellent
Efficiency	Inefficient	Efficient	Extraordinary
Quality	Error-prone	Reliable	Flawless
Ethics	Unethical	Ethical	Virtuous
Relationships	Conflictual	Compatible	Caring
Adaptation	Threat-rigidity	Coping	Flourishing

Deficit gaps   *Abundance gaps*

SOURCE: *Cameron, 2003b.*

depicting normal, healthy performance in the middle, with unhealthy, negative performance on the left and unusually positive performance on the right. Most organizations and most managers strive to maintain performance in the middle of the continuum—healthy, effective, efficient, reliable, compatible, and ethical. It is in the middle of the continuum where things are most comfortable.

We usually refer to the left end of the continuum as **negative deviance**. This refers to mistakes, errors, and problems. Most managers spend much of their time trying to get their employees and their units away from the negative deviance end of the continuum and near the more acceptable middle point. A lot of pressure is brought to bear on people who are negatively deviant.

However, the same pressure usually exists for individuals on the right side of the continuum. Think, for example, of people you have encountered who are positively deviant at work—flawless performers, flourishing in everything they do, and constantly extraordinary. They are too perfect. They make people feel uncomfortable. They make others feel guilty. They are ratebusters. We accuse them of showing up other people. A lot of pressure exists to get them back in line or within a normal range of performance. Most of the time, we insist that others stay in the middle range. Being on either the right side or the left side of the continuum is usually interpreted as against the rules. Resistance occurs to both regular change—from negative deviance to normal performance—and to positive change—from normal performance to positive deviance.

For the most part, leaders and managers are charged with the responsibility to ensure that their organizations are operating in the middle range of Figure 10.1. They are consumed with the problems and challenges that threaten their organizations from the left side of the continuum (e.g., unethical behavior, dissatisfied employees or customers, financial losses, and so on.) Most leaders and managers are content if they can get their organizations to that middle state—profitable, effective, and reliable. In fact, almost all research on organizational change has focused on how to ensure that organizations can perform in the normal range (Cameron, 2014).

The right end of the continuum in Figure 10.1 represents organizations that are positively deviant—they strive to be extraordinarily positive. Instead of just being effective, efficient, reliable, they might strive to be benevolent, flourishing, and flawless.

The right side of the continuum represents an **abundance approach** to performance. The left side of the continuum represents a **deficit approach** to performance (Cameron, 2012; Cameron & Lavine, 2006). Much more attention has been paid to solving problems, surmounting obstacles, battling competitors, eliminating errors, making a profit, and closing deficit gaps than to identifying the flourishing and life-giving aspects of organizations. Closing deficit gaps gets a lot more attention than closing abundance gaps (Cameron, 2008). Our colleague Jim Walsh (1999) found, for example, that words such as "win," "beat," and "competition" have dominated the business press over the past two decades, whereas words such as "virtue," "caring," and "compassion" have seldom appeared at all. Less is known, therefore, about managing the right side of the continuum in Figure 10.1, since most research on leadership, management, and organizations focuses on the left and center points of the continuum. Leading change usually means closing deficit gaps. In this chapter, however, we focus on leading change that closes abundance gaps.

A Framework for Leading Positive Change

Leading positive change is a management skill that focuses on unlocking positive human potential. Positive change enables individuals to experience appreciation, positive energy, vitality, and meaningfulness in their work. It focuses on creating abundance and human well-being. It fosters positive deviance. It acknowledges that positive change engages the heart as well as the mind.

A Case Example An example of this kind of change occurred in a New England hospital that faced a crisis of leadership when the popular vice president of operations was forced to resign (Cameron, 2012; Cameron & Caza, 2002). Most employees viewed him as the most innovative and effective administrator in the hospital and as the chief exemplar of positive energy and change. Upon his resignation, the organization was thrown into turmoil. Conflict, backbiting, criticism, and adversarial feelings permeated the system. Eventually, a group of employees appealed to the board of directors to replace the current president and CEO with this ousted vice president. Little confidence was expressed in the current leadership, and the hospital's performance was deteriorating. Their lobbying efforts were eventually successful in that the president and CEO resigned under pressure, and the popular vice president was hired back as president and CEO.

Within six months of his return, however, the decimated financial circumstances at the hospital led to an announced downsizing aimed at reducing the workforce by 10 percent. The hospital faced millions of dollars in losses. This newly hired CEO had to eliminate the jobs of some of the very same people who supported his return. The most likely results of this action were an escalation in the negative effects of downsizing loss of loyalty and morale, perceptions of injustice and duplicity, and blaming and accusations. Based on research on the effects of downsizing, a continuation of the tumultuous, antagonistic climate was almost guaranteed (Cameron, Whetten, & Kim, 1987; Datta, Guthrie, Basuil, & Pandey, 2010).

Instead, the opposite results occurred. Upon his return, the new CEO made a concerted effort to lead positive change in the organization, not merely manage the required change. He focused on closing abundance gaps, not merely deficit gaps. He consciously focused on positive change rather than following normal change formulas. He institutionalized forgiveness, optimism, trust, and integrity. Throughout the organization, stories of compassionate acts of kindness and virtue were almost daily fare.

One typical example involved a nurse who was diagnosed with terminal cancer. Respondents reported that when word spread of the man's illness, doctors and staff members from every area in the hospital donated vacation days and personal leave time so that he would continue to collect a salary even though he could not work. Fortunately, the pool of days expired just before he died, so he was never terminated, and he received a salary right up to his last day.

Employees also reported that the personal and organizational damage done by the announced downsizing—friends losing jobs, budgets being cut—was formally forgiven. Employees released grudges and moved toward an optimistic future. One indication was the language used throughout the organization, which commonly included words such as love, hope, compassion, forgiveness, and humility, especially in reference to the leadership that announced the downsizing actions.

We are in a very competitive health care market, so we have differentiated ourselves through our compassionate and caring culture....I know it sounds trite, but we really do love our patients....People love working here, and their family members love us too....Even when we downsized, [our leader] maintained the highest levels of integrity. He told the truth, and he shared everything. He got the support of everyone by his genuineness and personal concern....It wasn't hard to forgive. (Representative responses from a focus group interview of employees, 2002)

Even the redesigned physical architecture of the hospital reflected its positive approach to change, being designed to foster a more humane climate for patients and to communicate the virtuousness of the organization. For example, the maternity ward installed queen-sized beds (which didn't previously exist) so husbands could sleep with their wives rather than sitting in a chair all night; numerous communal rooms were created for family and friend gatherings; hallways and floors were all carpeted; volunteer pets were brought in to comfort and cheer up patients; original paintings on walls displayed optimistic and inspiring themes; nurses' stations were all within eyesight of patients' beds; Jacuzzis were installed in the maternity ward; special meals were prepared to fit patients' dietary preferences; and so on. Employees indicate that the leadership of positive change—not merely the management of change—was the key to their recovery and thriving. Special language, activities, and processes were important parts of employees' explanations for the organization's renewal. Figure 10.2 illustrates the financial turnaround associated with the hospital's concentrated focus on virtuousness.

Five Skills for Leading Positive Change This chapter reviews the five key management skills and activities required to effectively lead positive change. They include (1) establishing a climate of positivity, (2) creating readiness for change, (3) articulating a vision of abundance, (4) generating commitment to the vision, and (5) creating sustainability of the positive change (Avey, Wernsing, & Luthans, 2008; Cameron & Ulrich, 1986). Figure 10.3 summarizes these steps, and we discuss them below.

○ MyManagementLab: **WATCH IT**
Red Frog Events: Leadership and Managing People
Apply what you have learned about teamwork. If your instructor has assigned MyManagementLab, go to mymanagementlab.com to watch a video case and answer questions.

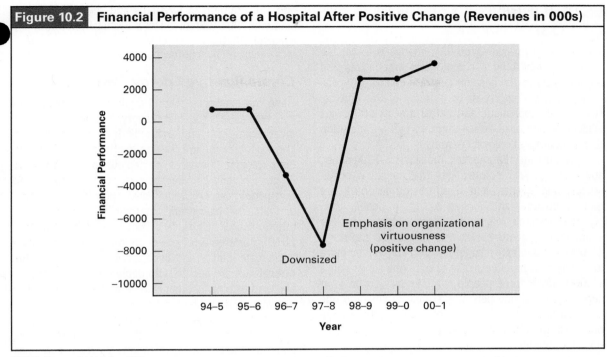

Figure 10.2 Financial Performance of a Hospital After Positive Change (Revenues in 000s)

SOURCE: *Cameron, Bright, & Caza, 2003.*

Leaders of positive change are not all CEOs, of course, nor are they in titled or powerful positions. On the contrary, the most important leadership demonstrated in organizations usually occurs in departments, divisions, and teams and by individuals who take it upon themselves to enter a temporary state of leadership (Meyerson, 2001; Quinn, 2004). These principles apply as much to the first-time manager, in other words, as to the experienced executive.

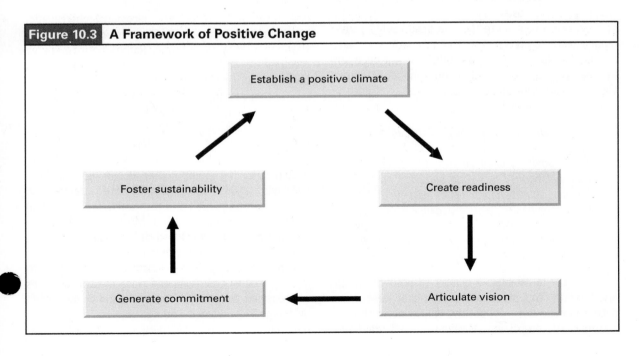

Figure 10.3 A Framework of Positive Change

ESTABLISHING A CLIMATE OF POSITIVITY

The first step in leading positive change is to set the stage by establishing a climate that emphasizes and reinforces positivity. Because constant change is typical of all organizations, most of us most of the time focus on the problematic and native aspects of change. Difficulties and obstacles capture more of our attention than pleasant and enjoyable events.

To illustrate, Baumeister, Bratslavsky, Finkenauer, and Vohs (2001) pointed out that negative occurrences, bad events, and disapproving feedback are more influential and longer lasting in people than positive, encouraging, and upbeat occurrences. For example, if someone breaks into your home and steals $1,000, it will create a larger reaction and will be more long-lasting in its effects than if someone sends you a $1,000 gift. If three people compliment you on your appearance and one person is critical of you, the one criticism will carry more weight than the three compliments. In other words, according to Baumeister's review of the literature, "bad is stronger than good."

People tend to pay more attention to negative than positive phenomena, and for good reason. Ignoring a negative event or a threat could be costly or dangerous. Ignoring a positive, pleasant experience, on the other hand, just means that you missed out on something enjoyable. No major consequence is likely to occur. Therefore, managers and organizations—which are constantly confronted by problems, challenges, and obstacles—have a tendency to focus on negatives much more than on positives. Negative tendencies take precedence. To lead positive change, therefore, is to go against the grain. It is not necessarily a natural thing to do. On the other hand, Mahatma Gandhi's statement illustrates the necessity of positivity, even though it is difficult:

> *Keep your thoughts positive, because your thoughts become your words. Keep your words positive, because your words become your behavior. Keep your behavior positive, because your behavior becomes your habits. Keep your habits positive because your habits become your values. Keep your values positive, because your values become your destiny. (Gold, 2002)*

In order to establish a climate of positivity in an organization, you must help establish at least three necessary conditions: (1) positive energy networks; (2) a climate of compassion, forgiveness, and gratitude; and (3) attention to strengths and the best self (see Cameron, 2013; Fredrickson & Branigan, 2005; Zhang & Bartol, 2010).

Create Positive Energy Networks

Have you ever been around a person who just makes you feel good? You leave every interaction happier, more energized, and uplifted? In contrast, do you know people who are constantly critical, negative, and discouraging? They seem to deplete your own reserve of positive energy? Recent research has discovered that people can be identified as "positive energizers" or "negative energizers" in their relationships with others (Baker, Cross, & Wooten, 2003; Cameron, 2013). **Positive energizers** are those who strengthen and create vitality and liveliness in others. **Negative energizers** are people who deplete the good feelings and enthusiasm in other people and make them feel diminished, devalued, or drained.

Research shows that positive energizers are higher performers, enable others to perform better, and help their own organizations succeed more than negative energizers (Baker et al., 2003; Powley, 2009; Ramlall, 2008). People who drain energy from others tend to be critical, express negative views, fail to engage others, and are more self-centered than positive energizers. Being a positive energizer is associated with being sensitive in interpersonal relationships, trustworthy, supportive of others, actively engaged in social interactions, flexible and tolerant in thinking, and unselfish. They are not necessarily charismatic, giddy, or just Pollyannaish. They are not just enthusiastic and smile all the time. Rather, positive energy creators are optimistic contributors, and others feel better by being around them.

Recent research has discovered that being a positive energizer in an organization is four times more predictive of success than being at the center of an information network (i.e., being the most informed person) or than being the person with the most influence (i.e., having an important title or senior position). Displaying positive energy, in other words, tends to be a very powerful predictor of personal as well as organizational success (Baker, 2001). Most importantly, positive energy can be developed. It is crucial for creating a climate of positivity in preparation for change.

To create a positive climate, you will want to identify positive energizers and place them in positions where others can interact with them and be influenced by them. The research findings are clear that people who interact with positive energizers perform better, as do the positive energizers themselves. One prescription, then, is to make sure that you and others rub shoulders with positive energizers. The performance of the entire team will improve. You can help foster positive energy in other people by (1) exemplifying or role modeling positive energy yourself—that is, focus on helping other people flourish; (2) recognizing and rewarding people who are positive energizers—they seldom receive any recognition or thanks; and (3) providing opportunities for individuals to form friendships at work—which usually are positive energy creators.

Ensure a Climate of Compassion, Forgiveness, and Gratitude

A second aspect of a climate of positivity is the appropriate display of compassion, forgiveness, and gratitude in organizations. These terms may sound a bit saccharine and soft—even out of place in a serious discussion of developing management skills for the competitive world of business. Yet, recent research has found them to be very important predictors of organizational success. Companies with high scores on these attributes performed significantly better than others (Cameron, 2003b). That is, when managers fostered compassionate behavior among employees, forgiveness for missteps and mistakes, and gratitude resulting from positive occurrences, their firms excelled in profitability, productivity, quality, innovation, and customer retention. Managers who reinforced these virtues were more successful in producing bottom-line results (Cameron, Mora, Leutscher, & Calarco, 2011; Rego, Ribeiro, & Cunha, 2010).

Paying attention to these concepts simply acknowledges that employees at work have human concerns—they feel pain, experience difficulty, and encounter injustice in their work and personal lives. Think of people you know, for example, who are currently managing a severe family illness, experiencing a failed relationship, coping with hostile and unpleasant coworkers or associates, or facing overload and burnout. Many organizations don't allow personal problems to get in the way of getting the job done. Human concerns take a backseat to work-related concerns. Regardless of what is happening personally, responsibilities and performance expectations remain the same.

To lead positive change, however, you must build a climate in which human concerns are acknowledged and where healing and restoration can occur. Because change always creates pain, discomfort, and disruption, you will want to be sensitive to the human concerns that can sabotage many change efforts. Without a reserve of goodwill and positive feelings, almost all change fails. Therefore, unlocking people's inherent tendency to feel compassion, to forgive mistakes, and to express gratitude helps build the human capital and reserve needed to successfully lead positive change (Hazen, 2008). How might that occur?

Compassion Kanov and colleagues (2003) found that **compassion** is enhanced in organizations when you foster three things: **collective noticing, collective feeling,** and **collective responding** (also see Boyatzis, Smith, & Blaize, 2006). When people are suffering or experiencing difficulty, the first step is to notice or be attentive to what is occurring. An iron-clad rule exists at Cisco Systems, for example, where CEO John Chambers must be notified within 48 hours of the death or serious illness of any Cisco employee or family member. People are on the lookout for colleagues who need help.

The second step is to enable the expression of collective emotion. Gatherings or events where people can share feelings (grief, support, or love) help build a climate of compassion. For example, a memorial service for a recently deceased executive at which the CEO shed tears was a powerful signal to organization members that responding compassionately to human suffering was important to the organization (Frost, 2003).

The third step is collective responding, meaning that you ensure that an appropriate response is made when healing or restoration is needed. In the aftermath of the September 11, 2001 tragedy, many examples of compassion—and noncompassion—were witnessed in organizations around the country. While some leaders modeled caring and compassion in the responses they fostered, others stifled the healing process (see Dutton, Frost, Worline, Lilius, & Kanov, 2002).

Forgiveness Most managers assume that **forgiveness** has a precarious place in the work setting. Because of high quality standards, the need to eliminate mistakes, and a requirement to "do it right the first time," managers assume they cannot afford to let errors go unpunished. Forgiving mistakes will just encourage people to be careless and unthinking, they assume. However, forgiveness and high standards are not incompatible. This is because forgiveness is not the same as pardoning, condoning, excusing, forgetting, denying, minimizing, or trusting (Enright & Coyle, 1998).

To forgive does not mean relieving the offender of a penalty (i.e., pardoning), or concluding that the offense is acceptable, not really serious, or should be forgotten (i.e., condoned, excused, denied, minimized). The memory of the offense need not be erased for forgiveness to occur. Instead, forgiveness in an organization involves the capacity to abandon justified resentment, bitterness, and blame, and, instead, to adopt positive, forward-looking approaches in response to harm or damage (Bright & Exline, 2012; Caldwell & Dixon, 2010; Cameron & Caza, 2002).

For example, because minor offenses and disagreements occur in almost all human interactions, especially in close relationships, most people are practiced forgivers. Without forgiveness, relationships could not endure and organizations would disintegrate into squabbles, conflicts, and hostilities. One explanation for the successful formation of the European Economic Union, for example, is forgiveness (Glynn, 1994). Collectively speaking, the French, Dutch, and British forgave the Germans for the atrocities of World War II, as did other damaged nations. Likewise, the reciprocal forgiveness demonstrated by the United States and Vietnam after the Vietnam War helps explain the flourishing economic and social interchange that developed in subsequent decades. On the other hand, the lack of peace in certain war-torn areas of the world can be at least partly explained by the refusal of organizations and nations to forgive one another for past trespasses (Helmick & Petersen, 2001).

The importance of forgiveness in organizations, and societies, is illustrated by Nobel laureate Desmond Tutu in his description of postapartheid South Africa:

Ultimately, you discover that without forgiveness, there is no future. We recognize that the past cannot be remade through punishment.... There is no point in exacting vengeance now, knowing that it will be the cause for future vengeance by the offspring of those we punish. Vengeance leads only to revenge. Vengeance destroys those it claims and those who become intoxicated with it...therefore, forgiveness is an absolute necessity for continued human existence. (Tutu, 1998, p. xiii; 1999, p. 155)

Forgiveness is enhanced in organizations when you:

1. Acknowledge the trauma, harm, and injustice that their organization members have experienced, but they define the occurrence of hurtful events as an opportunity to move forward toward a new goal.

2. Associate the outcomes of the organization (e.g., its products and services) with a higher purpose that provides personal meaning for organization members. This higher purpose replaces a focus on self (e.g., retribution, self-pity) with a focus on a higher objective.

3. Maintain high standards and communicate the fact that forgiveness is not synonymous with tolerance for error or lowered expectations. Use forgiveness to facilitate excellence by refusing to focus on the negative and, instead, focus on achieving excellence.

4. Provide support by communicating that human development and human welfare are as important in the organization's priorities as the financial bottom line. This kind of support helps employees catch sight of a way to move past the injury.

5. Pay attention to language, so that terms such as forgiveness, compassion, humility, courage, and love are acceptable; this language provides a humanistic foundation upon which most forgiveness occurs.

Gratitude Observing acts of compassion and forgiveness—not to mention being the recipient of them—creates a sense of **gratitude** in people (Emmons, 2007). Expressions of gratitude by one person tend to motivate others to express gratitude, so a self-perpetuating, virtuous cycle occurs. Gratitude is crucial in organizations because it leads people to return a favor, do good in return for receiving good, behave compassionately and equitably. Simmel referred to gratitude as "the moral memory of mankind...if every grateful action...were suddenly eliminated, society (at least as we know it) would break apart" (1950, p. 388).

Feelings of gratitude have been found to have dramatic effects on individual and organizational performance. For example, Emmons (2003) induced feelings of gratitude in students by assigning them to keep journals as part of a semester-long assignment. Some of the students were required to keep "gratitude journals" on a daily or weekly basis. They wrote down events or incidents that happened during the day (or week) for which they were grateful. Other students were assigned to write down events or incidents that were frustrating. Still other students were assigned to write down events or incidents that were merely neutral. Students keeping gratitude journals, compared to frustrated students and neutral students, experienced fewer physical symptoms such as headaches, nausea, and colds; felt better about their lives as a whole; were more optimistic about the coming week; had higher states of alertness, attentiveness, determination, and energy; reported fewer hassles in their lives; engaged in more helping behavior toward other people; experienced better sleep quality; and had a sense of being more connected to others. In addition, they were absent and tardy less often and had higher grade point averages. Feelings of gratitude had significant impact on student classroom performance as well as people's personal lives.

McCraty and Childre (2004) explained one reason positive effects of gratitude occur in people's lives. They studied heart rhythms of people when they experienced frustrating or stressful work conditions, and compared those heart rhythms to changes that occurred when people were induced into a gratitude condition. Figure 10.4 shows the differences. Each pattern shows 100 seconds of heart rhythms. The change occurred when this particular individual was induced to change from frustration to gratitude. It is easy to see physiologically why performance and health are enhanced by gratitude.

Emmons also found that gratitude elicits positive behaviors on the part of other people (e.g., they are more likely to loan money, provide compassionate support, and behave reciprocally). For example, a handwritten "thank you" on a restaurant bill by the server elicits about 11 percent higher tips, and visits by case workers and social workers are 80 percent higher if they are thanked for coming (McCullough, Emmons, & Tsang, 2002). People respond positively to expressions of gratitude. Thus, not only does gratitude help people *feel* good but *do* good as well.

You can engender gratitude in an organization simply by expressing 'thank you' frequently and conspicuously, even for small acts and small successes. Do you ever thank the custodians, food service works, or maintenance personnel in your building, for example? Expressing gratitude will have a powerful effect on performance

Pay Attention to Strengths and the Best Self

Identifying people's strengths (or what they do right) and then building on them creates more benefit than identifying weaknesses (or what people do wrong) and trying to correct them (Rath, 2001). For example, managers who spend more time with their strongest performers (rather than their weakest performers) achieved double the productivity. In organizations where workers have a chance to "do what they do best every day," productivity is one-and-a-half times greater than in normal organizations. People who are given feedback on their strengths are significantly more likely to feel highly engaged and to be more productive than people who are given feedback on their weaknesses. Students who are given feedback on their talents have fewer days of absenteeism, are tardy less often, and have higher GPAs than students who get no feedback on their talents. The strongest readers make more improvement in a speed-reading class designed to improve reading than the poor readers (Biswas-Diener, Kashdan, T. B. & Minhas, 2011; Clifton & Harter, 2003).

Another example of this principle comes from a study of top management teams engaged in strategic planning for their organizations. Losada and Heaphy (2003) studied 60 teams of senior executives who met to set objectives, refine budgets, and identify plans for the upcoming year. The research focused on investigating why some teams, and their organizations, performed better than others. The teams were categorized into high, medium, or low performing

Figure 10.4 | **Heart Rhythms in Frustration and in Gratitude Conditions**

These are actual heart rhythm patterns resulting from in an induced state of frustration followed by an induced gratitude condition.

SOURCE: *McCraty & Childre, (2004). "The Grateful Heart." In Emmons, R. A. & Mc Cullough, M. E. (Eds.). The Psychology of Gratitude, 230–255. New York: Oxford University Press.*

groups based on three measures of performance: productivity, customer satisfaction, and associates' ratings of leaders' competency. To explain differences among the groups, the communication patterns of the teams were carefully monitored and analyzed. The single most important factor in predicting success—which was four times more powerful in predicting success than any other factor—was the ratio of positive comments to negative comments. Positive comments are those that express appreciation, support, helpfulness, or compliments. Negative comments express criticism, disapproval, or blame. The results of the research were dramatic. In high-performing teams, the ratio of positive to negative comments was 5:1. Five times more positive comments were made than negative comments. In medium-performing teams, the ratio was 1:1. In low-performing teams, the ratio was 0.36:1. In other words, in low-performing teams, there were three negative comments for every positive comment.

Note that the positivity ratio is not 100:1 or 5:0. That is, critical and corrective comments are always needed and cannot be ignored. But negative comments are most effective if they occur in a climate of positivity. The amount of positive communication among team members, compared to negative communication, dramatically predicts the performance of their organizations. This ratio holds in athletics teams, legislative sessions, and family functioning (Cameron, 2012). Therefore, in your own teams and organizations, your ratio of positive to negative communication will have an important impact of the performance of others.

Reflected Best-Self Feedback One technique you can use to foster a positive climate and build on strengths is called the **"reflected best-self feedback"** process (Quinn, Dutton, & Spreitzer, 2003). It is a technique developed at the Ross School of Business at the University of Michigan and has been adopted at a large number of universities and corporations. It is designed to provide people with feedback on their strengths and unique capabilities. This kind of information is not frequently given to people, if ever, but receiving it allows individuals to build on their unique strengths in a positive way. Figure 10.5 illustrates the kind of feedback resulting from this exercise.

Begin at the bottom of the figure. Most of us have a lot of weaknesses—areas that are underdeveloped, areas in which we are uninformed, areas in which we have little skill. Most feedback systems provide information on what those areas are and how we compare to other people's capabilities in the same areas. Those are labeled **weaknesses** in Figure 10.5. We also all have areas in which we perform competently. We do fine—not stellar, but good enough. Those are areas of **competence**. A third category is areas of well-developed skill. We're outstanding performers in some areas. We have special capabilities or talents, and we do better than most people. These are areas of **strength**. Finally, we all have areas that are unique to us. If we don't contribute what we have, or if we don't share our capacities and gifts, no one else has the ability to do so. Our talent or skill is special. We refer to this area as **uniquenesses**. Research indicates

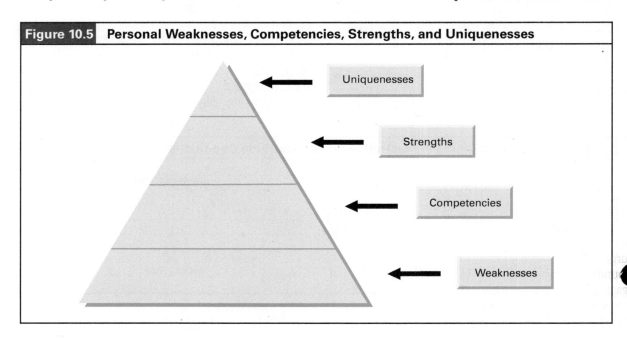

Figure 10.5 | **Personal Weaknesses, Competencies, Strengths, and Uniquenesses**

that capitalizing on our strengths and uniquenesses produces more success than trying to work on and overcome weaknesses—even though weaknesses may be more numerous and more obvious (Clifton & Harter, 2003; Rath, 2001).

If you engaged in the reflected best-self feedback process as part of the Skill Pre-Assessment section of this chapter, you received feedback that identifies your key strengths and unique talents—information that is both rare and extremely valuable. These themes represent your best-self strengths and uniquenesses.

The power of this feedback is that it comes in the form of incidents and stories, not numbers or trend lines, so it is connected directly to your behaviors and skills. These are the strengths and uniquenesses that you can build upon and display more often. This kind of feedback does not even mention weaknesses or shortcomings, so it does not motivate you to overcome areas of deficiency. Rather, it helps you develop strategies to capitalize on your best self.

Of course, completely ignoring weaknesses and inadequacies is not healthy either. Focusing exclusively on the positive and disregarding critical weaknesses is not apt to be productive in the long run. It's just that most individuals, and most organizations, concentrate on the negative and are likely to ignore, or at least short-change, the positive. The reflective best-self feedback technique is a way to counterbalance that tendency.

Summary Few people live or work in a positive organizational climate in which people flourish and experience positive energy. The role of the leader of positive change, therefore, is to facilitate and engender these characteristics by creative a climate of positivity. Table 10.1 summarizes some specific behaviors that you can implement. Creating positive energy networks, fostering compassion, forgiveness, and gratitude, building on others' strengths, and using positive communication all are initial steps to effectively leading positive change.

CREATING READINESS FOR CHANGE

In addition to establishing a climate of positivity, you must help others understand the importance and urgency of the change. A positive climate is a crucial foundation, but leading positive change requires engaging individuals in the actual process of change. The second step in leading positive change, therefore, is to create readiness among those to be involved in the change. Many techniques are available to do this, and we mention just four here.

Benchmark Best Practice and Compare Current Performance to the Highest Standards

One way to create readiness for change is to compare current levels of performance to the highest standards you can find. Identifying who else performs at spectacular levels helps you set a standard toward which people can aspire. It identifies a target of opportunity. This is referred to as **benchmarking**, and it involves finding best practice, studying it in detail, and then planning to exceed that performance. "Shooting ahead of the duck" is the principle. This doesn't mean copying others. It means learning from and exceeding what others do. Planned performance goes beyond the best practice, otherwise benchmarking is merely mimicking.

When you compare your performance to others, you can use several different kinds of standards:

- ❏ **Comparative standards**, or comparing current performance to similar individuals or organizations (e.g., "Here is how we are doing relative to our best competitors.")
- ❏ **Goal standards**, or comparing current performance to your publicly stated goals (e.g., "Here is how we are doing compared to the goals we have established.")
- ❏ **Improvement standards**, or comparing current performance with your past improvements (e.g., "Here is how we are doing compared to our improvement trends of the past year.")
- ❏ **Ideal standards**, or comparing current performance with an idea or perfect standard (e.g., "Here is how we are doing relative to a zero defect standard.")
- ❏ **Stakeholder expectations**, or comparing current performance with the expectations of customers, employees, or other stakeholders (e.g., "Here is how we are doing in meeting customer demands.")

Which standard of comparison you choose will depend, of course, on which standard is the most important to your organization members and which standard is perceived to be reachable. The purpose of these comparisons is to highlight the opportunities available by finding a higher level of performance and showing the possibility of achieving it.

Table 10.1	Establishing a Climate of Positivity

1. Create positive energy networks.

   - Place positive energizers in places where others can interact with them and be influenced by them.
   - Model positive energy yourself.
   - Recognize and reward positive energizers.
   - Provide opportunities for people to form close friendships at work.

2. Ensure a climate of compassion, forgiveness, and gratitude.

   - Be on the lookout to notice human concerns.
   - Find ways to foster the collective expression of emotions.
   - Enable a collective response to difficulty, pain, or distress.
   - Publicly and personally acknowledge trauma and harm.
   - Identify higher purpose outcomes that people will value.
   - Maintain high standards and look toward the future after mistakes.
   - Provide personal support to people who have been harmed.
   - Pay attention to language so that virtuous words are acceptable.
   - Express gratitude frequently and conspicuously, even for small acts.
   - Keep track of things that go right (not just that go wrong).

3. Identify and give people feedback on their strengths and unique competencies.

   - Implement a reflected best-self feedback process.
   - Spend time with your strongest performers.
   - Work to capitalize on strengths rather than focusing on overcoming weaknesses.
   - Use five positive comments for every negative comment in your interactions with others.

Identifying benchmark standards also helps ensure that new information, new ideas, and new perspectives will be imported, and that standards not considered possible before may become realistic. Studying others who may be doing the same job better than you may be accomplished by sponsoring visitors, holding learning events (symposia and colloquia) or conferences, creating study teams, and scheduling visits to other sites. The objective is to unfreeze people from reliance on past practice by learning that there may be a better way.

Institute Symbolic Events

To be successful in leading positive change you must signal the end of the old way of doing things and the beginning of a new way of doing things. One effective way to accomplish this is to use an event to signify a positive change or a new future.

For example, during the 1980s Chrysler was experiencing very dark days. The company was bankrupt, and no one knew for sure if it would survive. Lee Iacocca was hired to be the new CEO. Tens of thousands of cars sat idle in the "sales bank" (Chrysler's term for cars parked in vacant lots) waiting to be sold. In his first closed-door speech to senior executives, Iacocca announced that the sales bank would be abolished. All cars in the sales bank would be sold at "distressed prices." "But," he said, "I want to keep one. You know what people do when they pay off the mortgage; they burn it on the front lawn. I want to burn that last car on the front lawn of headquarters, so the whole world knows it's over!" (Cameron, 1985). A symbolic event was held, in fact, in which the last car in the sales bank was burned at headquarters, symbolizing a new future under Iacocca.

The symbolic imagery was far more powerful than a mere inspirational speech. Symbolic events capture hearts as well as heads of people, and this is required for positive change to occur.

Create a New Language

Another way to create readiness for change is to help organization members begin to use different words to describe old realities. When new language is used, perspectives change. For example, a key goal for the theme park division at Disney Corporation is to provide the best service in the world. The trouble is, most of Disney's theme park employees in the summer months are college students working at temporary jobs and not particularly invested in being a park sweeper or concession stand cashier. Disney addresses this challenge by making sure that all new employees at Disney are taught that they have been hired by central casting, not the personnel department. They are cast members, not employees. They wear costumes, not uniforms. They serve guests and audience members, not tourists. They work in attractions, not rides or arcades. They have roles in the show and play characters (even as groundskeepers), not merely work a job. During working hours, they are onstage and must go offstage to relax, eat, or socialize.

The intent of this alternative language is to change the way these employees think about their work, to place them in a mind-set that they wouldn't have considered otherwise. At Disney, summer employees are in show business—on stage, playing a role, performing for an audience. Changing language helps unfreeze old interpretations and helps create new ones.

Bennis and Nanus (1984) observed that the most successful leaders in education, government, business, the arts, and the military are those who have developed a special language. Most notable is the absence in their vocabularies of the word *failure*. These individuals simply haven't allowed themselves, or others around them, to accept the possibility of failure. Alternative descriptors are used, such as temporary slowdown, false start, miscue, error, blooper, stumble, foul-up, obstacle, disappointment, or nonsuccess. These leaders use an alternative language in order to interpret reality for their organizations, to foster a willingness to try again, and to foster an inclination toward positive change. This language communicates the fact that failure is not an option. Success is just around the corner.

Overcome Resistance

Every change always creates resistance among some people. Because change is always uncomfortable and produces uncertainty about what the future will bring, most people are inclined to resist in some way. The three techniques for creating readiness mentioned above will be helpful, but in addition, you will want to consider these ideas as well. Their intent is to get people who normally would block the change to become supporters and advocates.

- ❏ Identify who are the resistors, who will let the change happen, who will help the change to happen, and who will be champions of the change. Nurture champions and first followers. Give them recognition, and encourage them to energize others.

- ❏ Encourage participation by others in the planning and execution of trhe change. Participation almost always reduces resistance and fosters support.

- ❏ Identify benefits, advantages, and future possibilities associated with the change. Show what negative things will happen if the change is not successful. Identify examples of past success.

- ❏ Preserve the self-esteem of the resistors. Do not force them to comply. Do not denigrate their points of view. Find ways to legitimize their opinions, fears, and rationale, but help them see a way through their obstacles.

- ❏ Find common areas of agreement. The cardinal rule in successful negotiation is to find something upon which both parties can agree and build freom there. In overcoming rsistsance, the same rule applies. Identify something that you all have in common and capitalize on this common core for moving forward.

Summary

Creating readiness is a step designed to mobilize individuals in the organization to actively engage in the positive change process. It involves more than merely unfreezing people. Making people uncomfortable is a frequent prescription for getting people ready for change, and it often works. Making people uncomfortable, however, will usually escalate resistance. Leading positive change, therefore, focuses on creating readiness in ways that unlock positive motivations rather than resistance. It provides optimistic alternatives rather than fear. Benchmarking best practice, positive symbols, and new language are three practical ways to do it, as summarized in Table 10.2.

Establishing a climate of positivity and creating readiness for change does little good, of course, if there

Table 10.2	Creating Readiness in Others to Pursue Positive Change

1. Benchmark best practice, and compare current performance to the highest standards.
   - Use comparable others as standards.
   - Use stated goals as standards.
   - Use past improvement as a standard.
   - Use an ideal as a standard.
   - Use others' expectations as a standard.
2. Institute symbolic events to signal the positive change.
   - Interpret events or activities as indicators of the beginning of a new era.
   - Manage people's interpretations and mental images of incidents so that they reinforce the intended change.
   - Pay as much attention to the meaning of change as the substance of the change.
3. Create a new language that illustrates the positive change.
   - Use words associated with the change that capture people's imagination.
   - Use passionate and inspiring language.
   - Use words that communicate and reinforce a new direction.
4. Overcome resistance
   - Identify resistors, helpers, and champions. Reinforce champions and first followers.
   - Encourage participation.
   - Identify benefits, advantages, and future possibilities.
   - Preserve the self-esteem of resistors.
   - Find common areas of agreement.

is not a clear idea of where the positive change is heading. That is why the third step in the framework refers to articulating a clear, motivating vision of abundance.

ARTICULATING A VISION OF ABUNDANCE

Positive change seldom occurs without a leader articulating a **vision of abundance** (see Figure 10.1). By abundance we mean a vision that focuses on something that makes a profound difference, something that outlasts one's own life, and something that has enduring impact. Visions of abundance are different from visions of goal achievement or effectiveness—such as earning a certain percent profit, becoming number one in the marketplace, or receiving personal recognition. Visions of abundance speak to the heart as well as the head.

For example, the vision of Richard Bogomolny, the CEO of Finast Supermarkets in Cleveland, Ohio,

was to improve the quality of life for residents of blighted areas of Cleveland who would otherwise never have access to a reasonably priced grocery store with competitive prices. He invested in new, state-of-the-art supermarkets in poor urban neighborhoods, stocking shelves with ethnic foods that were not popular in suburban stores, and providing an environment of safety and cleanliness along with offering prices competitive with suburban shopping centers. Finast stores have now become the social gathering places for entire neighborhoods, have provided training and employment for the chronically unemployed, and, at the same time, have become a highly profitable investment for the company (Bollier, 1996). Without the leader's clear statement of a vision of abundance, the overwhelming tendencies toward merely solving problems, addressing obstacles, and making money drive out positive change.

Most organizations have mission statements or goal statements, but a **vision statement**—especially a vision of abundance— is something different. Visions include the universalistic values and principles that will guide behavior. They provide glimpses of possibilities, not just probabilities. They provide optimism and hope, and they evoke deeper meaning than mission statements or goals (Nahrgang, et al, 2013). Visions of abundance possess several important characteristics that are central to the positive change process.

Include Left-Brain and Right-Brain Features

Many years ago, neurosurgeons discovered that the brain consists of two hemispheres that can actually work independently when surgically separated. The left hemisphere controls rational cognitive activities such as sequential thinking, logic, deduction, numeric thought, and so on. Activities such as reading, solving math problems, and rational analysis are dominated by *left-brain thinking*.

The right hemisphere, on the other hand, controls nonrational cognitive activities such as intuition, creativity, fantasy, emotions, pictorial images, and imagination. Composing music, storytelling, and artistic creation are most likely tied to *right-brained thinking*.

Of course, neither hemisphere operates autonomously from the other, and both kinds of mental activity are required in complex tasks. But that is precisely the point. Vision statements of leaders must contain rational targets, goals, and action plans (left-brain components), as well as metaphors, colorful language, and imagination (right-brain components). Unfortunately, most managers and most organizations emphasize the left-brain side in their mission statements--for example, increased market share, becoming number one in the industry, or raising quality standards—but give little attention to exciting language, pictures and images of the future, or the emotions of members.

In the Skill Analysis section of this chapter, several corporate vision statements are provided for you to analyze. Note the differences among them in the relative emphasis on right-brain versus left-brain thinking.

Articulating the *left-brained* side of the vision is facilitated by answering the following questions:

❏ What are our most important strengths as an organization? Where do we have a strategic advantage?

❏ What major problems and obstacles do we face? What stands in the way of significant improvement?

❏ What are the primary resources that we need? What information is required?

❏ Who are our key customers? What must be done to respond to their expectations?

❏ What measurable outcomes will we accomplish? What are the criteria to be monitored?

Articulating the *right-brained* side of the vision is aided by answering the following questions:

❏ What is the best we can achieve? What represents peak performance?

❏ What stories or events can we tell that characterize what we stand for?

❏ What metaphors or analogies can we use that will identify what the future of our organization will look like?

❏ What symbols are appropriate for helping capture people's imaginations?

❏ What colorful and inspirational language can exemplify what we believe in?

The most motivating vision statements—for example, Churchill's "Never Give In" speech, Kennedy's "Ask Not What Your Country Can Do for You" speech, Mandela's "A Dream for Which I Am Prepared to Die" speech, Martin Luther King's "I Have a Dream" speech—all contain both left-brained and right-brained elements. Leaders of positive change pay attention to both in articulating their vision statements.

Make Vision Statements Interesting

Murray Davis (1971) published a now-classic article on what causes some kinds of information to be judged interesting or uninteresting. The truth or veracity of the information has little to do with that judgment, according to Davis. Rather, what's interesting depends on the extent to which the information contradicts weakly held assumptions and challenges the status quo. If new information is consistent with what is already known, people tend to dismiss it as common sense. If new information is obviously contradictory to strongly held assumptions, or if it blatantly challenges the core values of the organization's members, it is labeled ridiculous, silly, or blasphemous. Information that helps create new ways to view the future, that challenges the current state of things (but not core values), is viewed as interesting. New insights are created and people are drawn to the information because it makes them think, or it uncovers a new way to think (see Bartunek, Rynes, & Ireland, 2006).

Inspiring vision statements are interesting. They contain challenges and prods that confront and alter the ways people think about the past and the future. They are not outlandish or cavalier in their message, just provocative. For example, Ralph Peterson, former CEO of CH2MHill (a large environmental and engineering firm) indicated that "corporate immortality" was the ultimate objective of the company, meaning that the firm was in business to create outcomes that would last well beyond the lifetime of the firm. Jeffrey Schwartz, CEO of Timberland, the shoe and clothing company, espoused a vision related to doing good in order to do well—organizational virtuousness is equally important to organizational profitability. Tom Gloucer, former CEO of Reuters, espoused the vision that Reuters would become the fastest company in the world. Steven Jobs, former CEO of Apple, espoused a vision of one person—one computer throughout the entire world.

These examples are not intended to illustrate the best vision statements, of course, nor even vision statements that energize you personally. But, in each case, they carried a strong and motivating message for those in their organizations. They helped paint a mental picture of something that people cared about but which challenged the normal perception of things. The fact that they are interesting statements is what captured attention and the positive energy of others.

Include Passion and Principles

Visions of abundance are grounded in core values that organization members believe in, that have personal relevance, and about which they feel passionate. Such vision statements increase people's desire to affiliate with the leader and with the organization. A vision focused on "increasing productivity" is less energizing and inspiring than a vision based on "changing people's lives." "Achieving profitability" is less magnetic than "helping people flourish."

In addition, elements of the vision are best phrased using superlatives. Notice the difference in how you feel about the following comparisons: "phenomenal performance" versus "successful." Or, "passionately engaged" versus "committed." Or, "explosive growth" versus "good progress." Or, "awesome products" versus "useful items." Visions based on the former phrases engender more enthusiasm and passion than those based on the latter phrases.

Consider as an example of such language the vision statement of John Sculley, former CEO of Apple Computer Company:

> *We are all part of a journey to create an extraordinary corporation. The things we intend to do in the years ahead have never been done before.... One person, one computer is still our dream.... We have a passion for changing the world. We want to make personal computers a way of life in work, education, and the home. Apple people are paradigm shifters.... We want to be the catalyst for discovering new ways for people to do things.... Apple's way starts with a passion to create awesome products with a lot of distinctive value built in.... We have chosen directions for Apple that will lead us to wonderful ideas we haven't as yet dreamed. (Sculley, 1987)*

Finally, the vision statement must be straightforward and simple. A common error of leaders is to be too complicated, too lengthy, or too multifaceted in their vision statement. Most great leaders acknowledge that they have very few major objectives in mind. Their visions help people focus.

Attach the Vision to a Symbol

Effective vision statements are associated with a symbol. This is more than a symbolic event that helps create readiness for change. Rather, people must associate the vision with something tangible they see or hear. This reminds people of the vision on a regular basis. That symbol may be a logo, a phrase from a speech, a flag, a physical structure, or other reminders of where the vision is taking the organization.

The turnaround at Ford Motor Company after William Clay Ford took over was symbolized by the resurrection of the blue Ford oval on the headquarters building. Chrysler returned to the classic Chrysler logo instead of the five-pointed star. Malden Mills reconstructed a plant that had been devastated by fire on the same property to symbolize human commitment and corporate compassion. The replacement structures for the World Trade Center towers are targeted specifically to symbolize a positive and uplifting future after the devastating tragedy. Logos such as the golden arches, Nike Swoosh, or Mickey Mouse are carefully publicized, even protected, because of the symbolic messages that they communicate about the companies they represent.

Table 10.3 summarizes some specific behaviors you can use in articulating a high-impact vision of abundance.

Table 10.3   Articulating a Vision of Abundance

1. Focus on creating positive deviance rather than correcting problems.
   - Focus on possibilities more than probabilities.
   - Focus on extraordinary, spectacular achievement rather than just winning or being seen as successful.
2. Include left-brain images by asking questions such as:
   - What are our most important strengths?
   - What major problems and obstacles do we face?
   - What are the primary resources that we need?
   - What must be done to respond to customers' expectations?
   - What measurable outcomes will we accomplish?
   - What are the criteria to be monitored?
3. Include right-brain images by asking questions such as:
   - What represents peak performance?
   - What symbols, metaphors, or stories can help capture people's imaginations?
   - What colorful and inspirational language can exemplify what we believe in?
4. Make the vision interesting by challenging weakly held assumptions.
   - Associate the vision with core values that have personal meaning.
   - Ensure a straightforward and simple message.
   - Use exciting and energizing language.
5. Attach the vision to a symbol to constantly remind people of the vision.
   - Create visual images such as logos, flags, or signs.
   - Make certain that the visual symbol is closely associated with the vision so it remains a constant reminder.

GENERATING COMMITMENT TO THE VISION

Once this vision of abundance has been articulated, it is necessary for leaders to help organization members commit to that vision, to sign up, to adopt the vision as their own, and to work toward its accomplishment. The whole intent of a vision is to mobilize the energy and human potential of individuals who are to implement and be affected by it. Among the ways to generate commitment to a vision are three discussed below. Others are discussed in depth in the chapters on motivation, empowerment, and teamwork.

Apply Principles of Recreation

An interesting truism was identified by Chuck Coonradt (2007): "*People will pay for the privilege of working harder than they will work when they are paid.*" Think about that for a minute. People are willing to spend more money in order to work harder than they will work when they are receiving remuneration. Under certain circumstances, individuals are more committed to doing work that actually costs them money than they are to doing work for which they receive remuneration wage. How can that be? In what circumstances might that be the case?

Consider the following hypothetical example. Suppose you live in Utah in the winter and, as you arrive at work, you find that the furnace is out of order. As the temperature falls to 65 degrees Fahrenheit you put on a coat. At 60 degrees you complain that it is too cold to work. At 55 degrees you leave, confident that no one could expect you to perform in such adverse conditions. Then you put on your $500 ski outfit, grab your $750 skis and boots, race off to the slopes in order to pay $115 for a lift ticket, $75 for gas, and $30 for a junk-food lunch. You will spend all day long in 10-degree weather working much harder skiing than you would have worked at the firm where you could have been paid.

If this sounds unusual, consider the skyrocketing absenteeism rates in companies and schools when the first big snow falls in ski areas, when the surf is up in cities close to the beach, or the first day of hunting or fishing season. People regularly choose to pay to work harder than they would consider working when they are paid.

Well, you say, that's because it's fun. It's recreation. And you're right. But there is no reason why the work performed in a regular job cannot be typified by the same principles that characterize recreation. In other words, what causes people to *want* to engage in recreational work can also be what causes them to be equally committed to their occupational work. At least five characteristics are typical of **recreational work** (Coonradt, 2007).

1. Goals are clearly defined.
2. Scorekeeping is objective, self-administered, peer-audited, and compared to past performance.
3. Feedback is frequent.
4. Personal choice is present; rules are consistent and don't change until the season is over.
5. A competitive environment is present.

Consider the game of (American) football. Each year the University of Michigan averages about 112,000 fans per game, every one of whom knows exactly what the goal is—to score more points than the opponent. There is no need for a periodic performance appraisal system, because the score changes only when a team crosses the goal line or kicks a field goal. There is no guessing about how to get ahead. Feedback is not only frequent, it is continuous. If the clock goes down, they stop the game. No one would consider playing if the time and the score were not kept continuously.

Within the rules of the game, every participant and fan has personal choice. Players can go full speed or not; fans can cheer or not; the team can run the ball or pass. No one forces people to perform a role that they don't want to perform. Coordination and control occur because everyone knows the rules, and the rules don't change. Off-side is off-side, a first down is a first down, and a touchdown is a touchdown. When a receiver is wide open and makes an easy catch in the end zone, no one could imagine an NCAA committee deliberating about how many points the score is worth. No one would say, "Easy catch; wide open;

worth only 4.5 points." No one would stand for that, and 112,000 people would go crazy. The rules simply don't change in recreation.

Plus, the environment is one of competition—both against an opponent and against personal past performance. The stimulation of competing against something is fun. Playing against someone who is markedly less skilled—beating them 100 to 0, is not much fun.

Despite the inherent motivation and commitment associated with these principles, many leaders behave inconsistently with them. Their vision is not stated clearly and precisely. There is no objective, self-administered evaluation system. The scorekeeping system is controlled hierarchically, by managers one step above, instead of being peer-audited and continuous, as in recreation. Criteria of evaluation are vague and inconsistently administered. Organization feedback often comes only when quarterly earnings statements are tabulated, and then it is often focused on what went wrong. Personal freedom is too often constrained, as evidenced by the elaborate bureaucratic rules and policies that typify most large organizations. It is not unusual to have the criteria of success change in the middle of the game, especially if a new manager takes over. And most employees never see how what they do makes any difference at all in obtaining the ultimate goal, or winning against a competitor.

The point is, one way for leaders to generate commitment to the vision is to identify clear, consistent goals associated with the vision (Nahrgang, et al, 2013). Identify the criteria that will indicate progress toward reaching the vision which each organization member can monitor. Provide mechanisms for frequent feedback to organization members. Give individuals personal choice and the maximum discretion possible. Maintain a consistency and stability of the rules of the game and expectations. Identify a competitive standard against which performance can be evaluated. Like commitment to recreation, commitment to your vision will also become strong and long-lasting by applying principles of recreation. People will be inclined to pursue it eagerly.

Ensure Public Commitments

Another well-documented way to enhance commitment to a vision is to have people state their commitments aloud, in public. Individuals are motivated to behave consistently with their public declarations (Salancik, 1977). The internal need for congruence ensures that public statements will be followed by consistent actions. After making public pronouncements, individuals are more committed and more consistent in their behavior to that which they have espoused (Baker, 2001; Cialdini, 2008).

For example, during World War II, good cuts of meat were in short supply in the United States. Lewin (1951) found that a significant difference existed between the commitment level of shoppers who promised out loud to buy more plentiful but less desirable cuts of meat (e.g., liver, kidneys, brains) compared to those who made the same promise in private.

In another study, students were divided in a college class into two groups. All students set goals for how much they would read and what kinds of scores they would get on exams. Only half the students were allowed to state these goals publicly to the rest of the class. By midsemester, the students who stated their goals publicly averaged 86 percent improvement. The nonpublic goal-setting students averaged 14 percent improvement.

When the Tennessee Valley Authority (TVA) was attempting to build a dam in the late 1940s, it found that local farmers vehemently resisted the efforts because of the land that would be flooded. To overcome this resistance and elicit farmers' commitment to the project, the TVA made local farmers members of the board that would supervise the construction efforts. These local farmers began to make public statements on behalf of the TVA project and, over time, became strongly committed to it (Selznick, 1949).

This point is, you will be more effective in leading positive change if you look for opportunities to have others make public statements in favor of your vision, or to restate the vision themselves. Assigning individuals to explain the vision to outside groups or to other employees, or forming discussion groups so that others can help refine or clarify the vision, are examples of how opportunities for public statements can be fostered in order to enhance commitment.

Institute a Small-Wins Strategy

People become committed to change when they see progress being made or success being achieved. We are all more committed to winners than to losers. Fans attend more games when the team has a good record than when it has a poor record. The number of people claiming to have voted for a winning candidate always exceeds by a large margin the actual number of votes received. In other words, when we see success,

or progress being made, we are more committed to respond positively, to continue that path, and to offer our support.

Leaders of positive change create this kind of support by identifying small wins—a strategy that was discussed in Chapter 2, as well as being mentioned in discussions of problem solving and empowerment. This small-wins strategy is applicable in a variety of skill-building activities, so we repeat part of the discussion here. The key message is that surfacing and publicizing small wins creates commitment and builds momentum for desired change (Weick, 1981). For example, we have observed leaders, when beginning a major change initiative, starting with small changes such as a new coat of paint, abolishing reserved parking spaces, adding a display case for awards, flying a flag, holding regular social events, instituting a suggestion system, and so on. Each of these small changes is designed to create commitment to the visualized change.

A small-wins strategy, in other words, is designed to create a sense of momentum by creating minor, quick changes. As a refresher, the basic rule of thumb for small wins is: *Find something that is easy to change. Change it. Publicize it, or recognize it publicly. Then, find a second thing that's easy to change, and repeat the process.*

Small wins create commitment because: (1) they reduce the importance of any one change ("It is no big deal to make this change."); (2) they reduce demands on any group or individual ("There isn't a lot to do."); (3) they improve the confidence of participants ("At least I can do that."); (4) they help avoid resistance or retaliation ("Even if they disagree, it's only a small loss."); (5) they attract allies and create a bandwagon effect ("I want to be associated with this success."); (6) they create the image of progress ("Things seem to be moving forward."); (7) if they don't work they only create a small flop ("No major harm is done and no long-lasting effects occur."); (8) they provide initiatives in multiple arenas ("Resistance cannot be coordinated or organized in a single area.") (Weick, 1993).

Creating commitment to your vision will be enhanced, in other words, by applying principles of recreational work, providing opportunities for public statements of commitment, and instituting small wins. As summarized in Table 10.4, you can create commitment to that which you *say*, that which you *do*, and that which you *reward*, but, without consistency and frequency, not necessarily to that which you *want*.

Table 10.4	Generating Commitment to the Vision

1. Apply principles of recreation to the work associated with the vision:

   - Clearly define goals.
   - Ensure that scorekeeping is objective, self-administered, peer-audited, and compared to past performance.
   - Ensure frequent (or continuous) feedback.
   - Provide opportunity for personal choice.
   - Ensure that rules are consistent and don't change.
   - Provide a competitive environment.

2. Provide opportunities for people to publicly commit to the vision.

   - Hold events where people can verbalize their commitment.
   - Ask people to teach others about, or recruit others to sign up for, the vision.

3. Institute a strategy of small wins.

   - Find something easy to change.
   - Change it.
   - Publicize it.
   - Repeat the process multiple times.

FOSTERING SUSTAINABILITY

The final step in leading positive change is to ensure that the change is sustained. General officers in the United States Army refer to this step as **"creating irreversible momentum"**, that is, ensuring that the positive change gains such momentum that it cannot be thwarted (U.S. Army, 2003). The objective is to ensure that even if the leader leaves, the positive change will continue because of the sustainable impetus put in place and the irreversible momentum created.

Fostering sustainability doesn't happen quickly, of course, and the four previous steps in positive change—establishing a climate of positivity, creating readiness, articulating a vision, and generating commitment—all must be successfully accomplished first. But, without sustainability the other steps are largely irrelevant because the change will not last. It will be a temporary false-start. So, how do you foster sustainability for a positive change? We provide three suggestions.

Turn Students into Teachers

Most of the time we assume that it is the leader's responsibility to articulate the vision of abundance, and everyone else listens to it and accepts it. Teachers teach what students need to know and students learn it for the exam. The person in charge gives directions and the rest of us follow.

The most effective leaders, however, provide an opportunity for everyone in the organization to articulate the vision, or to teach others about the desired positive change. This process requires that every person develop "a teachable point of view" (Tichy, 1997). Developing your own teachable point of view means that you come to believe in something, and you can clearly explain what it is and why. In other words, you get to the point where you can articulate the vision in your own words. You are given opportunities to teach others what you understand the positive change to be. You are required to develop your own perspective on the positive change in a way that it can be explained and illustrated to someone else. You are transformed from a student into a teachers or visionay.

Researchers at the National Training Laboratories in Bethel, Maine, developed a **"learning stair"** (see Figure 10.6). Their studies found that people remember 5 percent of what they hear in a lecture, 10 percent of what they read, 20 percent of what they view in a video, 30 percent of what they observe being demonstrated, 50 percent of what they discuss in a group, 75 percent of what they apply, and 90 percent of what they teach to others. By teaching someone else about

Figure 10.6 The Learning Stairs (from the NTL Institute)

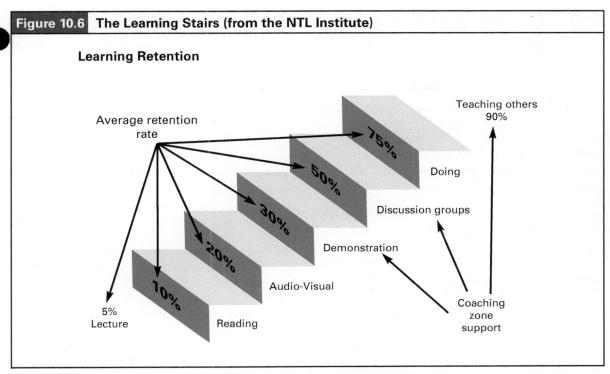

Learning Retention

Average retention rate

Teaching others 90%

75%

Doing

50%

Discussion groups

30%

Demonstration

20%

Audio-Visual

10%

Coaching zone support

5% Lecture

Reading

SOURCE: *The Learning Stairs; NTL Institute for Applied Behavioral Science, 1091 South Bell Street, #300, Arlington VA 22202.*

the vision or the intended positive change, you remember it, become committed to it, and make it a part of your own personal agenda.

One manifestation of this principle was at Xerox under Rex Kern, a remarkable leader who turned that company around in the late 1980s and early 1990s. Kern's focus was on rapidly institutionalizing a positive change process by turning students into teachers. He spent time sharing his vision of positive change with his top leadership team. Then these leaders were required to apply what they heard; that is, to implement personal action agendas and make personal changes.

Then, most importantly, they were required to teach the positive change vision to someone else. Who would they teach? They taught the next level of leaders in the firm. They were also required to assess or monitor the positive change. This was in order to identify measurable indicators, milestones, and hard data to ensure that the positive change was really taking place. It was a way to guard against lip service with no real substance. What did they assess? It was the action agendas and managerial experiments implemented by the leaders they taught. The process continued down through all the organizational levels.

Each person, in other words, was exposed to the vision four times: when they learned it from their leader; when they applied it; when they taught it; and when they assessed it. Within a year, Xerox achieved stunning results. It is widely acknowledged that this process was key in turning Xerox around as a company and in labeling Rex Kern as one of the great corporate leaders of the twentieth century.

Build Human Capital

Human capital refers to the resources inherent in the human beings who are employed by the organization. Like financial capital, human capital can be deployed, wasted, or developed. For positive change to have staying power, for it to last beyond the lifetime of the leader, people throughout the organization must have developed the capability to lead the vision themselves, to institute positive change, and to carry on under their own initiative. In other words, well-developed human capital is always the chief predictor of growth in financial capital.

No company can make money over time without well-developed human capital—meaning capable and skilled employees. Sustaining positive change occurs as individuals throughout the organization develop the capacity to lead positive change themselves. This can happen in many ways, of course, but a good example of the core principle is illustrated by a large Asian company in which we conducted research.

This particular company requires that each time a senior manager is promoted, he or she is required to take a three-month leave of absence. The person must actually leave work for three full months. For one of the months the manager is required to intensively study religion or ethics, and then document it, usually with a written report. For another month the individual is required to study history or a major historical figure, and then document it. The third month must be spent studying business, broadly defined. So, at the end of three months, three documents have been prepared. If, after the three months, the business has run smoothly with no major hitches, then the promotion occurs. That is, the person is promoted at the end of the three-month leave, not before.

Why would a large company implement such a strange promotion system at substantial risk and expense? Why not just send the manager to a week-long executive education program at a university? Why remove a senior leader for three full months?

This is part of the process for creating sustainability. The three-month leave of absence provides a chance for self-development, personal enrichment, and broadening of perspective. Senior managers are required to study religion or ethics because all business decisions are based on some set of values or standards. The firm wants to make certain that these people spend time intelligently thinking through their own value system. To avoid the trap of becoming short-term in orientation, studying history helps broaden viewpoints and helps assure that the mistakes of the past aren't repeated. Studying business principles helps expand the knowledge base and competence of the managers.

Most importantly, however, the leave of absence is essentially a test. The key value in this company is that human capital must be developed if success is to be achieved, so the leave of absence serves as a test of whether the manager has really developed his or her employees. If the organization performs less well when subordinates are in charge, then the manager is not prepared to be promoted. All managers have the responsibility to help develop others to be as competent as they are in leading positive change, and managers are held accountable for that development.

The point is, a key to ensuring that positive change is sustained is to have capable people in place. Providing organization members with developmental opportunities—that is, chances to increase their own skill set—is an investment in the long-term future of the organization and in the continuing success of positive change.

Metrics, Measurement, Milestones

A third aspect of sustainability is the establishment of **metrics** (or specific indicators of success), **measures** (or methods for assessing levels of success), and **milestones** (or benchmarks to determine when detectable progress will have occurred). These three factors help ensure accountability for change, make it clear whether or not progress is being made, and provide visible indicators that the change is successful. The adage "You get what you measure" is an illustration of this principle.

Change becomes institutionalized when it becomes a part of what people are held accountable to achieve. When it is clear what the measures are, people tend to respond to those measures. If you are measured on your test scores in a class but not on the extra reading you do, you will likely spend more effort and time studying for the exams than reading extra materials. It is only when you are measured on different criteria that you shift your focus. Consequently, institutionalizing positive change means that clear metrics are identified, a measurement system is put into place, and a milestone is identified for when the change must have been accomplished.

As an illustration of these points is Jan Carlzon's (1987) approach to institutionalizing his vision in the once-struggling Scandinavian Airlines.

> *Employees at all levels must understand exactly what the target is and how best to achieve it. Once the frontline personnel...have taken on the responsibility of making specific decisions, these employees must have an accurate feedback system for determining whether the decisions they are making are, in fact, the ones that will accomplish the company's overall goals.... The necessity of measuring results is particularly crucial for those employees who affect customer service but don't have face-to-face contact with these customers. Ticket agents get immediate feedback on their job performance hundreds of times a day from the customers they serve. However, other workers such as baggage handlers have no such advantages. In fact, loading and unloading cargo is probably the most thankless job we have at SAS.... The baggage handlers never come into contact with the passenger, and so they never*

get positive or negative feedback from them. Lacking this, they need clear targets and other means of measuring how well they are meeting their goals. (pp. 108–109)

The keys to establishing effective metrics, measures, and milestones for positive change are:

1. Identify two or three metrics or indicators that specify the result that is to be achieved. (A common mistake is to measure too many things. The key is to focus on a few core items.) These should not be metrics associated with effort or methods, but they should focus on results or outcomes. Specifically, they should address the outcomes desired from the vision of abundance. At SAS Airlines, one metric includes the elapsed time between the plane pulling up to the gate and the first bag being delivered on the carousel.
2. Determine a measurement system. Data should be collected at certain time intervals in particular ways. This may be reports, surveys, or face-to-face meetings. At SAS, daily logs are kept of baggage handler performance. These measures do not focus on hours worked or how many bags are handled. They focus on the key outcomes desired, namely, speed and accuracy of delivery.
3. Milestones are specified, meaning that at a certain point in time, a measurable amount of progress will have been achieved. For example, by the end of the month baggage handler timeliness will have improved one percent. By the

end of the year, it will have improved 15 percent. Milestones simply create a time frame for keeping track of real progress.

Fostering sustainability for a vision of abundance and positive change, in sum, depends on making it a part of daily life and the habitual behavior displayed by individuals throughout the organization. No positive change can survive if it depends solely on the leader. Specific behaviors associated with these strategies are summarized in Table 10.5.

Summary

Most approaches to change focus on overcoming challenges, addressing obstacles, and solving problems. This chapter identifies an alternative approach to change in which the goal is to create abundance and extraordinarily positive change. This kind of change unlocks something called the *heliotropic effect* (Cameron, 2013).

To explain the heliotropic effect, let us pose this question: What happens over time when you put a plant in a window? The answer, of course, is that the plant begins to lean toward the light. This illustrates a natural inclination in every living system toward positive energy—toward light—and away from negative energy or from the dark. The reason is that light is life-giving and energy creating, and all living systems are inclined toward that which gives life.

When you are able to foster positive change in organizations, you unleash the heliotropic effect in your people. They tend to exude positive energy and to work towards positive outcomes, not just problem solving or

Table 10.5	**Institutionalizing the Vision and Creating Irreversible Momentum**

1. Turn students into teachers.
   - Provide opportunities for people to develop a teachable point of view.
   - Make certain that others are required to articulate the vision themselves.
2. Build human capital.
   - Ensure training and development opportunities for others so they can be leaders of positive change.
   - Encourage the formation of networks and friendships that provide support.
3. Identify metrics, measures, and milestones.
   - Identify when measurable progress will be achieved.
   - Identify what the specific criteria will be for evaluating success.
   - Determine how successful achievement of the vision will be ascertained.
   - Maintain accountability for the success of the positive change.

getting rid of obstacles. They achieve outcomes that would be improbable otherwise. Fostering virtuousness, positive energy, strengths, aspirational targets, and inspiring language are among the ways to unlock the heliotropic effect. This effect has been demonstrated in a variety of ways within organizations and individuals—physiologically, psychologically, emotionally, visually, and socially (see Cooperrider, 1990; Cameron, 2003b, 2012, 2013; Bright, Cameron, & Caza, 2006). It is also documented in a study by Cameron and Lavine (2006).

In this chapter we provided a simple and easily remembered framework for accomplishing positive change and unleashing the power of the heliotropic effect. Five sets of skills and activities were explained: (1) establishing a climate of positivity, (2) creating readiness for change, (3) articulating a vision of abundance, (4) generating commitment to the vision, and (5) fostering sustainability of the positive change. Specific behavioral guidelines for implementing this approach to change are provided next.

Behavioral Guidelines

Figure 10.7 summarizes the skill set involved in leading positive change. Because change is so pervasive in organizations, every leader must manage change much of the time. However, positive change cuts across the grain and goes against the tendencies of most leaders. Negative, problem-focused concerns consume most leaders and managers.

Figure 10.7 | A Framework for Leading Positive Change

Leading positive change requires a different skill set. The following are the behavioral guidelines for achieving positive change:

A. Establish a climate of positivity by creating positive energy networks; ensure a climate of compassion, forgiveness, and gratitude; and identify and give feedback to people on their strengths and unique competencies.

B. Create readiness in others to pursue positive change by benchmarking best practice, and comparing current performance to the highest standards; institute symbolic events to signal positive change; and create a new language that illustrates the positive change.

C. Articulate a vision of abundance by focusing on creating positive deviance rather than correcting negative deviance; include right-brain as well as left-brain images; and make the vision interesting by challenging weakly held assumptions.

D. Generate commitment to the vision by applying principles of recreational work associated with the vision; provide opportunities for people to publicly commit to the vision; and institute a strategy of small wins.

E. Foster sustainability of the vision, or create irreversible momentum, by turning students into teachers; help people develop teachable points of view and articulating the vision themselves; build human capital among others; and identify metrics, measures, and milestones for success.

CASES INVOLVING LEADING POSITIVE CHANGE

Corporate Vision Statements

Here are examples of four vision statements by well-known leaders of companies in the United States—Google, Toyota, Johnson & Johnson, and Microsoft. Each of these leaders was, at the time, considered to be among the most successful change leaders in the world. Analyze their statements in light of the principles discussed in the Skill Learning section of this chapter.

❏ How effective are each of these vision statements?

❏ What would be your prediction about the success of these firms based on the statements of their leaders?

❏ What are your suggestions for improvement?

Ten Things Google Has Found to Be True

1. Focus on the user and all else will follow.

Since the beginning, we've focused on providing the best user experience possible. Whether we're designing a new Internet browser or a new tweak to the look of the homepage, we take great care to ensure that they will ultimately serve **you** rather than our own internal goal or bottom line. Our homepage interface is clear and simple, and pages load instantly. Placement in search results is never sold to anyone, and advertising is not only clearly marked as such, it offers relevant content and is not distracting. And when we build new tools and applications, we believe they should work so well you don't have to consider how they might have been designed differently.

2. It's best to do one thing really, really well.

We do search. With one of the world's largest research groups focused exclusively on solving search problems, we know what we do well, and how we could do it better. Through continued iteration on difficult problems, we've been able to solve complex issues and provide continuous improvements to a service that already makes finding information a fast and seamless experience for millions of people. Our dedication to improving search helps us apply what we've learned to new products, like Gmail and Google Maps. Our hope is to bring the power of search to previously unexplored areas, and to help people access and use even more of the ever-expanding information in their lives

3. Fast is better than slow.

We know your time is valuable, so when you're seeking an answer on the web you want it right away—and we aim to please. We may be the only people in the world who can say our goal is to have people leave our homepage as quickly as possible. By shaving excess bits and bytes from our pages and increasing the efficiency of our serving environment, we've broken our own speed records many times over, so that the average response time on a search result is a fraction of a second. We keep speed in mind with each new product we release, whether it's a mobile application or Google Chrome, a browser designed to be fast enough for the modern web. And we continue to work on making it all go even faster.

4. Democracy on the web works.

Google search works because it relies on the millions of individuals posting links on websites to help determine which other sites offer content of value. We assess the importance of every web page using more than 200 signals and a variety of techniques, including our patented PageRank™ algorithm, which analyzes which sites have been "voted" to be the best sources of information by other pages across the web. As the web gets bigger, this approach actually improves, as each new site is another point of information and another vote to be counted. In the same vein, we are active in open source software development, where innovation takes place through the collective effort of many programmers.

5. You don't need to be at your desk to need an answer.

The world is increasingly mobile: People want access to information wherever they are, whenever they need it. We're pioneering new technologies and offering new solutions for mobile services that help people all over the globe to do any number of tasks on their phone, from checking email and calendar events to watching videos, not to mention the several different ways to access Google search on a phone. In addition, we're hoping to fuel greater innovation for mobile users everywhere with Android, a free, open source mobile platform. Android brings the openness that shaped the Internet to the mobile world. Not only does Android benefit consumers, who have more choice and innovative new mobile experiences, but it opens up revenue opportunities for carriers, manufacturers and developers.

6. You can make money without doing evil.

Google is a business. The revenue we generate is derived from offering search technology to companies and from the sale of advertising displayed on our site and on other sites across the web. Hundreds of thousands of advertisers worldwide use AdWords to promote their products; hundreds of thousands of publishers take advantage of our AdSense program to deliver ads relevant to their site content. To ensure that we're ultimately serving all our users (whether they are advertisers or not), we have a set of guiding principles for our advertising programs and practices:

- ❑ We don't allow ads to be displayed on our results pages unless they are relevant where they are shown. And we firmly believe that ads can provide useful information if, and only if, they are relevant to what you wish to find—so it's possible that certain searches won't lead to any ads at all.

- ❑ We believe that advertising can be effective without being flashy. We don't accept pop-up advertising, which interferes with your ability to see the content you've requested. We've found that text ads that are relevant to the person reading them draw much higher clickthrough rates than ads appearing randomly. Any advertiser, whether small or large, can take advantage of this highly targeted medium.

- ❑ Advertising on Google is always clearly identified as a "Sponsored Link," so it does not compromise the integrity of our search results. We never manipulate rankings to put our partners higher in our search results and no one can buy better page rank. Our users trust our objectivity and no short-term gain could ever justify breaching that trust.

7. There's always more information out there.

Once we'd indexed more of the HTML pages on the Internet than any other search service, our engineers turned their attention to information that was not as readily accessible. Sometimes it was just a matter of integrating new databases into search, such as adding a phone number and address lookup and a business directory. Other efforts required a bit more creativity, like adding the ability to search news archives, patents, academic journals, billions of images and millions of books. And our researchers continue looking into ways to bring all the world's information to people seeking answers.

8. The need for information crosses all borders.

Our company was founded in California, but our mission is to facilitate access to information for the entire world, and in every language. To that end, we have offices in dozens of countries, maintain more than 150 Internet domains, and serve more than half of our results to people living outside the United States. We offer Google's search interface in more than 110 languages, offer people the ability to restrict results to content written in their own language, and aim to provide the rest of our applications and products in as many languages as possible. Using our translation tools, people can discover content written on the other side of the world in languages they don't speak. With these tools and the help of volunteer translators, we have been able to greatly improve both the variety and quality of services we can offer in even the most far-flung corners of the globe.

9. You can be serious without a suit.

Our founders built Google around the idea that work should be challenging, and the challenge should be fun. We believe that great, creative things are more likely to happen with the right company culture—and that doesn't just mean lava lamps and rubber balls. There is an emphasis on team achievements and pride in individual accomplishments that contribute to our overall success. We put great stock in our employees—energetic, passionate people from diverse backgrounds with creative approaches to work, play, and life. Our atmosphere may be casual, but as new ideas emerge in a café line, at a team meeting or at the gym, they are traded, tested, and put into practice with dizzying speed—and they may be the launch pad for a new project destined for worldwide use.

10. Great just isn't good enough.

We see being great at something as a starting point, not an endpoint. We set ourselves goals we know we can't reach yet, because we know that by stretching to meet them we can get further than we expected. Through innovation and iteration, we aim to take things that work well and improve upon them in unexpected ways. For example, when one of our engineers saw that search worked well for properly spelled words, he wondered about how it handled typos. That led him to create an intuitive and more helpful spell checker.

Even if you don't know exactly what you're looking for, finding an answer on the web is our problem, not yours. We try to anticipate needs not yet articulated by our global audience, and meet them with products and services that set new standards. When we launched Gmail, it had more storage space than any email service available. In retrospect offering that seems obvious—but that's because now we have new standards for email storage. Those are the kinds of changes we seek to make, and we're always looking for new places where we can make a difference. Ultimately, our constant dissatisfaction with the way things are becomes the driving force behind everything we do.

Update: We first wrote these "10 things" several years ago. From time to time we revisit this list to see if it still holds true. We hope it does—and you can hold us to that. (September 2009)

SOURCE: *Used by permission. google.com/corporate/tenthings.html*

Toyota's Mission and Guiding Principles

Established in 1990, revised in 1997. (Translation from original Japanese.)

1. Honor the language and spirit of the law of every nation and undertake open and fair corporate activities to be a good corporate citizen of the world.

2. Respect the culture and customs of every nation and contribute to economic and social development through corporate activities in the communities.

3. Dedicate ourselves to providing clean and safe products and to enhancing the quality of life everywhere through all our activities.

4. Create and develop advanced technologies and provide outstanding products and services that fulfill the needs of customers worldwide.

5. Foster a corporate culture that enhances individual creativity and teamwork value, while honoring mutual trust and respect between labor and management.

6. Pursue growth in harmony with the global community through innovative management.

7. Work with business partners in research and creation to achieve stable, long-term growth and mutual benefits, while keeping ourselves open to new partnerships.

Five Main Principles of Toyota

❑ Always be faithful to your duties, thereby contributing to the company and to the overall good.

❑ Always be studious and creative, striving to stay ahead of the times.

❑ Always be practical and avoid frivolousness.

❑ Always strive to build a homelike atmosphere at work that is warm and friendly.

❑ Always have respect for God, and remember to be grateful at all times.

SOURCE: *Based on English translation of Japanese mission statement from 1990s, www.toyota.com.*

Johnson & Johnson
Our Credo
James Burke, CEO

We believe our first responsibility is to the doctors, nurses and patients,
to mothers and all others who use our products and services.

In meeting their needs everything we do must be of high quality.
We must constantly strive to reduce our costs in order to maintain reasonable prices.
Customers' orders must be serviced promptly and accurately.
Our suppliers and distributors must have an opportunity to make a fair profit.

We are responsible to our employees,
the men and women who work with us throughout the world.
Everyone must be considered as an individual.
We must respect their dignity and recognize their merit.
They must have a sense of security in their jobs.
Compensation must be fair and adequate, and working
conditions clean, orderly and safe.
We must be mindful of ways to help our employees
fulfill their family responsibilities.

Employees must feel free to make suggestions and complaints.
There must be equal opportunity for employment, development
and advancement for those qualified.
We must provide competent management,
and their actions must be just and ethical.

We are responsible to the communities in which we live and work
and to the world community as well.
We must be good citizens—support good works and charities
and bear our fair share of taxes.
We must encourage civic improvements and better health and education.
We must maintain in good order the property we are privileged to use,
protecting the environment and natural resources.

Our final responsibility is to our stockholders.
Business must make a sound profit.
We must experiment with new ideas.
Research must be carried on, innovative programs developed and mistakes paid for.
New equipment must be purchased, new facilities provided
and new products launched.
Reserves must be created to provide for adverse times.
When we operate according to these principles, the stockholders
should realize a fair return.

Johnson & Johnson

SOURCE: *Courtesy of Johnson & Johnson.*

ANALYSIS

Microsoft

Bill Gates

2004 Excerpts

Microsoft was built on innovation, and our future depends on it. We are in an extraordinary position to deliver even greater value to customers through a broad set of technologies, designed to complement each other and many third-party products and services. This is what we mean by *integrated innovation*, which is key to our business strategy.

To drive innovation, Microsoft has a long-term commitment to research and development. Our investment to date has brought about many of the successful products we offer today, and has built an increasingly valuable store of intellectual property. In fiscal 2004, we applied for more than 2,000 patents on some of our recent innovations. During the coming year, we plan to file for another 3,000 patents, which will make us one of the largest patent filers in the world. Our innovations are available for broad use in others' products through our patent licensing programs.

A key focus of our innovation is security. Beyond the advances in Windows XP SP2, we are developing advanced technologies that will help isolate computers from Internet attacks and make them more resilient when they are attacked. We are making it easier for customers to keep their systems updated with our latest, most secure software.

In addition, we are collaborating with other industry leaders to develop more effective community responses to security threats, and working closely with governments around the world to bring cybercriminals to justice. Through this broad, multipronged approach, our goal is to help bring significant improvements in security, and help preserve the benefits of technology for everyone.

Our innovation is also focused on exciting market opportunities across our businesses, which we believe hold great potential for growth over the next several years.

As we innovate in technology, we are equally focused on crisp execution. In particular, we are working to deliver an unparalleled customer and partner experience. Across the company, we have created new listening, feedback, and response systems to help us get closer to customers and respond quickly and appropriately. Using automated error-reporting technologies, we have fixed a large majority of the computer crashes and hangs reported by customers, and our strengthened field response system has favorably resolved most nontechnical issues reported by customers.

Microsoft competes vigorously, and we always will. At the same time, we are committed to maintaining positive relationships within our industry, including with competitors, and to forging strong relationships with governments. We are also committed to helping make technology safer and easier to use. We work to help protect the safety of children online, for example, through our partnership with the International Centre for Missing and Exploited Children. We are deeply engaged in industry efforts to protect peoples' privacy online, counter the problem of identity theft, and curb the spam epidemic.

SOURCE: *2004 Annual Report. Reprinted with permission from Microsoft Corporation.*

Discussion Questions

First answer the following questions by yourself, and then form a team of colleagues and share your answers. Reach consensus regarding a rank ordering.

Step 1: Rank order these four firms based on these famous leaders' statements about their companies (1 = the best, and 4 = the worst).

	Google	Toyota	J&J	Microsoft
1. Which of the vision statements do you think represents the most effective positive leadership?	____	____	____	____
2. Based on these statements, what is your prediction about future success in each firm in the next 10 years, from most to least successful? Ignore the health of the industry itself—e.g., computers, autos, software, pharmaceuticals—and predict how each firm will do in its own industry based on these statements.	____	____	____	____
3. Which statement has the clearest and most inspiring vision for the future?	____	____	____	____
4. Which statement do you believe has been institutionalized the most thoroughly, and the least thoroughly?	____	____	____	____

Step 2: Based on what you now know about leading positive change, what advice would you give each of these leaders if you were to make suggestions about how to more effectively establish a climate of positivity, create readiness for change, articulate a vision of abundance, generate commitment, and foster sustainability.

Jim Mallozzi: Implementing Positive Change in Prudential Real Estate and Relocation

In an extensive interview with Jim Mallozzi, CEO of Prudential Real Estate and Relocation Company, Jim describes the variety of ways in which he has implemented principles related to the positive change framework described in this chapter. Among the positive practices Jim implemented are utilizing positive energy networks to create a "change team," developing a reciprocity network among company employees, articulating Everest goals, fostering positive leadership in the senior team, celebrating strengths, successes, and achievements, implementing reflected best-self feedback, and demonstrating caring and compassion with customers and potential customers. As a consequence of these initiatives, Jim achieved dramatic improvements in financial performance, improved customer satisfaction scores, and markedly enhanced employee engagement. This interview provides examples of how a leader can make a major impact in his organization's performance by creatively applying positive organizational change.

You were then appointed as the CEO of Prudential Real Estate and Relocation. What were the challenges and obstacles you found?
In the summer of 2009, as the financial markets were coming out of one of the worst recessions since the great depression, I was asked to take over Prudential's Real Estate and Relocation business (PRERS). The real estate side sells residential and commercial real estate franchises across North America. The relocation side helps families move throughout the world. It serves both U.S. government employees and large corporations. When I took over in the fall of 2009, we were facing a 70 million dollar loss per year. The company had lost 140 million dollars the year before. I could see that the organization just didn't have confidence in itself.

Morale in our company and among our customers was not high. I called my good friend Kim Cameron and asked him to help me with the change effort. We started by bringing in Kim to work with our senior management team—what we call the "Gang of 30." Some of them were very reticent; others were curious. Fortunately, they were all patient.

What specifically did you do with your senior team? How did you start the process to turn around the company?
We started with a variety of exercises to show them that when you start with the positive, when you ask people to genuinely help you achieve what you're trying to do, fabulous things can happen. One very simple exercise we began with in our senior team was this: Select three people, one at a time, and tell those people three things you value about them. In corporate America, and in most places in life, people usually tell you, "Here are the three things that you need to change." Rarely do they tell you, "Here are the three things that you're fabulous at." When you do that, the energy just goes up. We started with that very simple but powerful exercise, and it got people's attention.

Did this activity translate into the rest of the organization?
About four months later we held our big annual convention. We invited 2500 real estate agents from all over the country. This was my first presentation to this group as the new CEO. In the middle of my keynote address, I asked for the houselights to come up. I asked everybody to take out their Blackberries and their iPhones and turn them *on* as opposed to turn them *off*. I asked them all to text or email one great idea—how to get a new client, how to close a sale, how to keep a customer for life. I said, "Take your very best idea, your absolutely best one, and share it. Let's do it right now." I had somebody bring my Blackberry on stage, and I participated as well. We did that for about four or five minutes, and then I invited them to continue to do it for the next 36 hours—until the end of the convention. Do you know how many ideas we came up with? Over two thousand two hundred. We've been using those ideas for the last fifteen months. We've taken that very simple idea of reciprocity—just ask for help and you never know where help comes from—and we are building it into the culture of our company, and we're now using technology and social networking to keep it alive 24/7. We made remarkable progress in measurable targets such as growing revenues, keeping expenses flat, increasing customer service, and ultimately getting us back on a profitable basis. For us to accomplish any of this, we needed to draw on lots of sources of inspiration.

How is positive change different from the usual approach to change you have seen?
Like most companies, we do client surveys where 5 is outstanding and 1 is negative. We have always obsessed over the scores of 1, 2 and 3 and tried to get rid of those. To implement positive change we tried something different. We decided to look at the scores of 4 and 5 and figure out why were we outstanding. We want to know how to be a 5 company—how to define it, how to measure it, and how to replicate it. I happened to be in France three or four weeks ago. I was talking about positive principles with our French employees, and they were struggling a little bit. I asked, "So how do we get to be 5s?" They kind of looked at me very quizzically. I wondered if it was a language translation problem. Should I have said it in French? They responded: "No, we don't even measure anything north of 3." So I asked: "How do you know when you're outstanding?" It was a completely new idea to them. They said: "We don't." Then I asked them to try something. "Tell me when you have been outstanding. Tell me when you've seen our organization at its best." One person stood up and said, "Well I've seen our employees at our best, and I've seen us be a 5, just today. We have

had people at the Charles De Gaulle Airport 24/7 for the last week greeting relocated employees who are coming back after being forced to evacuate Japan after the earthquake and tsunami." We are a relocation company, so we helped these people move there. She said, "They had to leave all their goods behind them. They have no place to live. They are being forced back into this country. We were there greeting them at the airport, helping them find a place to live, giving them bottled water as they get off the plane, helping them get back into France as quickly as we can. No other company is doing that. We are the only ones out there doing it on behalf of our clients." And I said, "That's it. You're a 5. You're helping people when they're the most vulnerable in their lives. That's to be celebrated. It's positively deviant and so different than everybody else." My job not only in France but throughout the whole firm is just to make sure people have the vision and the tools, and then I get the heck out of the way because they'll do it. It is important to try to create a culture that not only allows but encourages positive deviance.

You dramatically changed your customer satisfaction scores. Can you explain how that happened?

We set a goal to positively "wow" our best clients. For example, about 18 months ago, I was visiting our London operations meeting with a variety of clients. British Petroleum (BP) is one of our clients in Europe. I talked about positive change and how we were trying to change the culture of our company. I said that we wanted to engage them and learn from them. Then, about three or four weeks later, the Deep Water Horizon oil spill occurred with the unfortunate loss of a dozen or so lives and one of the largest environmental spills in history. You could read and see on TV that the folks at BP were being blasted in the U.S. and throughout the global press regarding their reaction times, what they were doing, what they were not doing, and so forth. The folks at BP were feeling pretty bad about all this. So I called up the senior HR person whom I knew, and I said, "Listen, I can see what's going on in the States. I'm sorry that this is happening for you. I understand you're trying to move a lot of people into the Gulf area to deal with this crisis. I would like to offer the services of our company to you, free of charge, for the duration of the crisis." He said, "Why would you make such an offer?" "The very simple answer is that we all have a responsibility for what's going on in the Gulf. We all need to try to help in ways large and small. This is the best way that I can think of to help you. If you'd like to take us up on it, great, if you don't, that's fine. I certainly understand." About two days later I got a call back from the folks at BP. They said, "Well, first off, thank you so much for calling. There have been a number of vendors that we currently do business with throughout the world. Most have asked us to write them a check. You were the only one that offered to help us free of charge. We probably won't take you up on the offer, but we very much appreciate the gesture." I said, "That's fine. If you change your mind, we're happy to do whatever we can to help." Well, sure enough, about six months later they decided to go out for RFP (a request for a proposal) for a new vendor for relocation. We were invited to be one of the participants. Of course, the end of the story is not yet written. We don't know how it will turn out. But, we use this example with our associates to encourage them to be positively outrageous. It's okay to help others and not expect anything in return. When we do that, fabulous things can happen.

How did you roll out positive change to the rest of the organization?

As we started to introduce positive change into our organization, we began with the "Gang of 30." But we knew we needed to get the message out to our 1300 employees in seven countries representing 30 plus cultures. We knew we needed some help. So, we identified a set of positively energizing and positively deviant people. They were not the most senior or experienced people, but they were people who provided a real uplift to the organization. We selected 26 of them from across the world and brought them into headquarters. For some of these folks it was their first trip to the United States. I talked about how we wanted to change the company, and I told them that I needed their help. They were very excited by the challenge. I charged them to introduce positive change principles to 90 percent of our associates worldwide in 60 days, so that at least 1100 people had a working knowledge of what we mean by positive change in 60 days. That meant members of the change team had to understand what positive change is and have the ability to teach it to others. Then I said, "Tell me what you need to accomplish the challenge. I'm going to leave the room, and I'll come back in a couple of hours. Work with Kim. Tell me what you need to accomplish this." I came back a couple of hours later, and they said, "Okay, Jim, we're willing to take on the challenge, but here are four things we need from you. You know what? Within 60 days they had accomplished not only 90 percent, but it was 93 percent. Our employee opinion scores went up in 9 out of 10 categories. They have now created their own self-sustaining effort in continuing to bring the principles of positive change into our organization. It's been fabulous to see.

Did everyone get on-board? Did you get 100 percent agreement to adopt a positive perspective?

My own experience is about 50 to 60 percent of the people, if you're lucky, will get it pretty much out of the box. About 20 to 30 percent of the folks kind of sit on the sideline and say, "Is this just Jim's management thing du jour?" About ten percent of the people will positively reject everything that I talk about. They will just say, "It doesn't make any sense. Sorry, it's not working for me." And that's okay. I don't argue with them. They will be out of alignment with where we're trying to drive the organization, and they should go to a place where they will be in alignment. I quickly encourage them to go there. I've done a lot of recruiting of both senior and middle level executives into our company in the last 18 months, and people want to join a positively oriented company, even if you're asking them to accept the same or less pay. The younger the person is, the truer it is.

Source: *Adapted from Cameron, K.S. and Plews, E. (2012) "Positive leadership in Action."* Organizational Dynamics, *41: 99–105.*

Discussion Questions

10.1. What elements of positive change do you see implemented by Jim Mallozzi?

10.2. In what ways did Jim try to foster positively deviance performance?

10.3. What aspects of positive change did he leave out? What would you advise him to do going forward to foster sustainability?

10.4. What was Jim's vision of abundance?

EXERCISES IN LEADING POSITIVE CHANGE

Reflected Best-Self Portrait

The Skill Assessment section of this chapter suggested that you engage in a powerful assessment process that reveals your best self, or the unique strengths and contributions you display. If you obtained that feedback, you will want to analyze that data to create a best-self portrait. Read all of your feedback and take notes on the key insights. Look for commonalities across the individuals who provided you with feedback. Create themes where you find commonalities, and link the examples to them. You may find it useful to use a table such as the following.

COMMONALITY/THEME	EXAMPLES GIVEN	MY INTERPRETATION
1. Creative	1. Innovative builder of new projects at work. 2. Found new solutions for old problems. 3. Guided the team in transforming itself.	My ideas tend to be interesting and creative. I tend to bring new ideas to people with whom I work. I am innovative in my approach to problem solving.
2.	1. 2. 3.	
3.	1. 2. 3.	

Step 1: Now, create a written portrait of your best self that captures the basic themes in your data. Identify when you are at your very best and what attributes and capabilities you display. Write at least one paragraph describing yourself using your best-self feedback as the data. Here are some reflective questions that you may want to consider as you craft your self-portrait.

- ❏ What have you learned about your own key strengths and uniquenesses?
- ❏ What was surprising to you about your feedback?
- ❏ What circumstances bring out your best?
- ❏ How do you intend to follow up or capitalize on this feedback?
- ❏ What career or life implications does this feedback hold?
- ❏ What has changed, or could change, as a result of obtaining this feedback?

Write up your conclusions and your commitments as a result of reading through the feedback. Writing will have a clarifying and focusing effect, and you are not likely to get

PRACTICE

this kind of data very often in your life. Don't miss the opportunity to craft something meaningful for yourself.

Step 2: Read your best-self portrait with a team of colleagues. Get verbal feedback from them about what you have written. That is, your colleagues will help you clarify and become specific about your best-self attributes.

Source: http://positiveorgs.bus.umich.edu, search term "Reflected Best Self Exercise"

Positive Organizational Diagnosis Exercise

Step 1: Select an organization that you can diagnose. If you are not currently working in one, volunteering in one, or leading one, select your own school or university. Your objective is to identify the strengths, peak experiences, and examples of positive deviance in the organization (rather than the problems and challenges). These kinds of data are seldom gathered in organizations, and people are not often asked to provide this kind of data. However, in every organization, something works well. When cued to do so, people can always identify things that are spectacular about their organization.

Furthermore, the questions we ask and the language we use helps determine our vision of the future. When people have experienced success in the past, they are more willing to pursue a vision of the future, knowing that they have achieved extraordinary success in the past. They are confident that they can do it again.

Here are some examples of questions you should ask in diagnosing the positive aspects of an organization, a group, or even your own family.

- *Best-in-Class*: Put yourself in clients' or customers' shoes. What would they say makes this organization the best there is?
- *Careers*: What do you love about this organization that makes you want to come to work each day?
- *Leadership*: Who are the leaders in your organization you admire the most, and why? What do they do that is extraordinary?
- *Communication*: When did you have an extremely satisfying and productive interchange with someone you care deeply about? What happened?
- *Teamwork*: When have you experienced delight at extraordinary cooperation and teamwork that emerged in this organization? What happened?
- *Culture*: What is especially fun, energizing, revitalizing about your culture? What turns you on?
- *Aspiration*: What are your highest aspirations for this organization? What do you really hope for?
- *Work*: What is the best you have ever seen accomplished in the work here? What was achieved that exceeded everyone's expectations?

When you ask these kinds of questions, you will detect more enthusiasm being displayed by the person responding, and you will note an unleashing of positive energy. This is in contrast to more typical questions used in organizational diagnosis:

- What are your major problems and challenges?
- Where are your deficits?
- What is troublesome to people in this organization?
- What needs fixing?
- In what areas are you missing your targets?
- Who is doing better than you are, and why?

Craft your own interview format for conducting a positive diagnosis of an organization, a group, or a family. Use the positive questions above as a guide. Interview a representative sample of people in that organization (or all the members of your family).

Step 2: Now, write up the equivalent of a best-self portrait for the organization. Address these questions regarding the organization.

❑ What are the strengths and unique qualities of this organization?
❑ In what ways can it capitalize on its competencies?
❑ What is the vision that drives the organization?
❑ What recommendations do you have for positive change?

A Positive Change Agenda

Write out a detailed plan for leading positive change in an organization in which you are participating. You need not be the formal leader of that organization, since most real change is initiated from places within the organization rather than the leader's office. Most great leaders simply capitalize on the ideas and agendas of their people.

In crafting your plan, address the following questions with very specific and actionable ideas. Do not simply say something like: "I'll treat people better." That is not specific enough and does not identify an action. Instead, say, "I will compliment someone every day." That's more doable and measurable.

1. In what ways will you work to create a positive climate? What will you actually do?
2. In what specific ways will you create readiness in others to pursue positive change?
3. What is your specific vision of abundance? How will you communicate it so that it is accepted and energizing to people?
4. How will you generate commitment to that vision among others? Identify specific actions.
5. What will you do to institutionalize and create irreversible momentum for your positive change?

Now, identify the specific things you will need to do personally to exemplify and model your positive change? How will you enhance your own credibility?

SKILL *APPLICATION* 🔧

ACTIVITIES FOR LEADING POSITIVE CHANGE

Suggested Assignments

10.6. Find someone you know well who is working in an organization. Teach him or her the principles of leading positive change. Use the concepts, principles, techniques, and exercises provided in this chapter. Describe what you taught and record the results in your journal.

10.7. Do a systematic analysis of the things that occur in your life for which you are grateful. What is going right, and what makes life worth living? Consider your job, family, school, and social life. Keep a "gratitude journal" for at least a semester (a three-month period). Make an entry in it at least once a week. Note what else changes in your life compared to before you began the journal.

10.8. Identify at least one person in your circle of acquaintances who is positively energizing to you. When you are around this person, you simply feel better. Make certain that you interact with that person on a frequent and consistent basis.

10.9. Identify an example of best practice. That is, find someone or some organization that is unique in being the best there is at something. Try to identify what it is that accounts for that extraordinary performance. What factors could be generalized to others or to other settings?

10.10. Identify a symbol that can serve as a constant reminder of your own—or your organization's—vision of abundance. Select something that is positively energizing and that can remind you every time you see it that you are pursuing a meaningful, uplifting vision.

10.11. Establish a close mentoring relationship with someone with whom you work or go to school. Your mentor may be a professor, a senior manager, or someone who has been around longer than you have. That relationship should build your self-esteem and be energizing to you. Make certain, however, that the relationship is reciprocal, not one-way.

Application Plan and Evaluation

The intent of this exercise is to help you apply this cluster of skills in a real-life, out-of-class setting. Now that you have become familiar with the behavioral guidelines that form the basis of effective skill performance, you will improve most by trying out those guidelines in an everyday context. Unlike a classroom activity, in which feedback is immediate and others can assist you with their evaluations, this skill application activity is one you must accomplish and evaluate on your own. There are two parts to this activity. Part 1 helps prepare you to apply the skill, and Part 2 helps you evaluate and improve on your experience. Be sure to write down answers to each item. Don't short-circuit the process by skipping steps.

Part 1: Planning

10.12. Write down the two or three aspects of this skill that are most important to you. These may be areas of weakness, areas of strength, or areas that are most salient to a situation you face right now. Identify the specific aspects of this skill that you want to apply.

10.13. Now identify the setting or the situation in which you will apply this skill. Establish a plan for performance by actually writing down a description of the situation. Who else will be involved? When will you do it? Where will it be done?

Circumstances:
Who else?
When?
Where?

10.14. Identify the specific behaviors in which you will engage to apply this skill. Operationalize your skill performance.

10.15. What are the indicators of successful performance? How will you know you have been effective? What will indicate you have performed competently?

Part 2: Evaluation

10.16. After you have completed your implementation, record the results. What happened? How successful were you? What was the effect on others?

10.17. How can you improve? What modifications can you make next time? What will you do differently in a similar situation in the future?

10.18. Looking back on your whole skill practice and application experience, what have you learned? What has been surprising? In what ways might this experience help you in the long term?

SCORING KEYS AND COMPARISON DATA

✪ Scoring Keys for the following instruments, along with comparison data, are contained in PIA in MyManagementLab.com;

Leading Positive Change
Positive Practices Survey

Reflected Best-Self Feedback™ Exercise

This exercise does not have a solution or comparison data. Answers will vary among students.

Part IV

Specific Communication Skills

MODULES

A **MAKING ORAL AND WRITTEN PRESENTATIONS**
Formulating strategy and structure utilizing an enhanced style

B **CONDUCTING INTERVIEWS**
Conducting general interviews
Conducting specific purpose interviews

C **CONDUCTING MEETINGS**
Conducting productive meetings

SKILL **LEARNING**

- Making Oral and Written Presentations
- Essential Elements of Effective Presentations
- Summary and Behavioral Guidelines

SKILL **PRACTICE**

- Speaking as a Leader
- Quality Circles at Battle Creek Foods

Making Oral and Written Presentations

SKILL DEVELOPMENT OBJECTIVES

- MAKE IMPACTFUL AND ENGAGING ORAL PRESENTATIONS
- WRITE CLEARLY AND PERSUASIVELY
- RESPOND APPROPRIATELY TO QUESTIONS AND CHALLENGES

Making Oral and Written Presentations

Taylor Billingsley was hired as a sales representative in the Apex Communications Corporation in 1972. With training and hard work, she advanced through the levels of the corporation, finally landing the position of senior vice president in charge of personnel. Although she had anticipated this position would require some adjustments, she was surprised at the kinds of challenges she faced during her first few weeks on the job. Taylor had a lot of ideas about how to make the personnel division work more efficiently, but she realized almost immediately she had to convince others to adopt them. In addition, she had to establish her own credibility—to make her employees and interested outsiders understand and appreciate her personal commitments and management style.

In the first few days on the job, Taylor had several opportunities to communicate her philosophy and expectations during a number of meetings with the departments in her division. Some of these meetings were formal, such as when she first accepted the position; others were more informal, including lunch meetings with the division heads. Immediately following the announcement of her appointment, she also wrote a memo to her division heads and their employees outlining some of her ideas for moving the department forward. In separate memos she addressed the personnel development and financial benefits departments, introducing a new project and encouraging them to move ahead full speed to develop a new policy on research teams.

Then Taylor began a round of visits with people who worked in her division. She talked individually with several workers and responded to the questions posed by informal groups. She was asked to write up her evaluation of morale among workers in her division and forward it to the corporate chief executive officer. The latest financial reports released by the company's controller's office revealed that quarterly figures were down unexpectedly; it seemed certain costs had risen dramatically. Taylor was concerned and adjusted a report she had written for a scheduled meeting with the region's top executives to reflect these new developments. Later, she spoke to an assembled employee group in the cafeteria in an effort to calm their fears about job cuts. At another facility located in a tough urban environment, the task proved more difficult. Workers were outspokenly critical of the company and challenged much of the information she presented. Following these meetings, Taylor was the featured dinner speaker at a regional Chamber of Commerce meeting.

Taylor Billingsley was experiencing the challenges of management in her new position. During her first two weeks, she addressed dozens of groups on a broad range of subjects; she wrote even more reports and memos. In most of this communication, Taylor was not simply presenting facts. Instead, she was conveying support, pointing a new direction, generating enthusiasm, communicating a sense of caring, building goodwill, and underscoring the value of teamwork. Some situations called for polite, ceremonial messages; others were confrontational. Some covered familiar material; others stretched her ability to find the right words to convey her ideas. At the end of her first two weeks, Taylor began to appreciate the importance of communication skills.

Managers have to master the basic elements of public communication and be flexible enough to adapt them to varying situations (Barrett, 1977; Mambert, 1976; Peoples, 1988; Sanford & Yeager, 1963; Wilcox, 1967). Like Taylor Billingsley, you may find yourself addressing many different audiences through speeches and in writing. Like Taylor Billingsley, you will probably discover very quickly your effectiveness as a manager depends in large part upon your ability to communicate with your coworkers and customers. Unfortunately, new managers are often lacking in these skills. According to a survey of major business recruiters, the biggest deficiencies in college graduates were the lack of good oral communication and writing skills (*Endicott Report*, 1992). Researchers have observed elaborate training programs are ineffective if basic skills, such as writing, are not present (Maruca, 1996). Considering that speaking and writing skills are central to good management and many new employees are also relatively weak in these areas, we should turn our attention to how managers can improve these two critical skills. Let's focus first on the core ingredients of good communication and then examine the specific requirements of speaking and writing.

Essential Elements of Effective Presentations

How can one person meet all of the communication demands confronting a good manager? There are five basic steps to making effective presentations—we'll label them the Five *S*'s. These five *S*'s are sequential in the sense that each step builds upon the preceding steps. Good communication depends heavily on adequate forethought and preparation. As shown in Figure A.1, the first three steps involve preparation, the fourth and fifth focus on the spoken or written presentation itself. Adequate preparation is the cornerstone of effective communication (Collins and Devanna, 1990; Gelles-Cole, 1985; Wells, 1989).

1. Formulate a *strategy* for the specific audience and occasion. This is the phase in which you develop your purposes in relationship to the audience and situation.
2. Develop a clear *structure*. This step translates your broad strategy into specific content.
3. *Support* your ideas with examples, illustrations, and other material adapted to your audience. This will reinforce your ideas.
4. Prepare your material to create a presentation *style* that will enhance your ideas. How you present your ideas is often as important as what you present.
5. *Supplement* your presentation with confident, informed responses to questions and challenges. Your performance in a spontaneous, free-flowing discussion or exchange of memos should be as impressive and informative as your prepared presentation.

We have maintained throughout this book that effective personal performance is a function of skill, knowledge, and practice. This is especially the case with communication. The key to gaining confidence in making oral and written presentations is preparation and practice. If you follow the basic five steps, you should be on your way to delivering effective messages. Specific guidelines for implementing these five steps are presented in the following sections.

FORMULATE A SPECIFIC STRATEGY

Identify Your Purpose

Michael Sheehan, a leading communications consultant whose clients include CEOs of major firms and presidential candidates, lists as his number one rule for effective communication: "Know your objective, know your audience. It sounds easy, but it's really the hardest art of communications" (Reingold, 2004). In line with this recommendation, before collecting information or writing notes, you should clarify your general purpose for speaking or writing. Are you trying to motivate, inform, persuade, demonstrate, or teach? Your general purpose is to inform if you are providing information, demonstrating a technique, or delivering a report. When your purpose is to inform, you are concerned with the transmission and retention of ideas and facts. On the other hand, if you are motivating workers for higher production, convincing others to adopt your ideas, or stimulating pride in the company, your general purpose is to persuade. Persuasion requires the use of motivational language, convincing argument, and audience adaptation. Your general purpose may affect how you structure your message and how you supplement your ideas as well as your style of presentation. That is why it is important to identify your general purpose first.

Your specific purpose should be easier to determine once you have identified your general purpose (see Figure A.2). You can discover your specific purpose by asking, "What do I want my listeners to learn?" or "What behaviors or attitudes do I want my listeners to adopt?" You may answer, "I want my listeners or readers to learn the six steps in our new accounting procedure" or "I want them to spend more time with customers."

Figure A.1 | **The Five *S*'s Approach to an Effective Presentation**

| Formulate **strategy** for specific audience. | → | Develop a clear **structure**. | → | **Support** your points with evidence. | → | Combine ideas with an enhancing presentation **style**. | → | **Supplement** with informed responses to questions. |

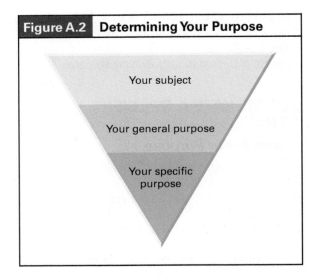

Figure A.2 **Determining Your Purpose**

Your subject

Your general purpose

Your specific purpose

Each of these is a specific purpose. It determines how you will tailor the remainder of your preparation to your audience and the demands of the situation.

Tailor Your Message to Your Specific Audience

The success of your communication is partially dependent on your audience's understanding and receptivity.

The key to developing an audience-appropriate message is to understand their knowledge of the topic, their attitude toward your message, and their expectations of your presentation. If they already know what you are trying to teach them, they'll become bored and possibly hostile. Start with what they already know, then expand on it. If you are teaching a new accounting procedure, begin with the one your listeners currently use, then add the new steps. Remember audiences retain more information if the material is associated with something they already know, rephrased and repeated, reinforced with visual aids, and limited to three to five new ideas. Motivated listeners retain more, so, early in your message, explain how they can use the information.

Your audience's attitudes toward your message are also critical to consider. Hostile receivers don't learn as readily as eager receivers. If your audience is hostile, start by setting realistic goals. If you try to do too much, you might trigger a boomerang effect in which your audience becomes even more hostile. Emphasize common ground by sharing similar values or parallel goals. For example, you might point out that increased profits are good for everyone in the company or everyone has a stake in improving plant conditions.

For hostile or uncommitted listeners it is important to develop a two-sided message (see Table A.1). Present both sides of the issue. Use strong arguments built on logic and extensive evidence (Sprague & Stuart, 1996). Choose neutral language as you develop your ideas. In these situations, it is also important to build your credibility. Show yourself to be calm, fair, reasonable, and well informed. Use humor directed at yourself to ease tension (Sprague & Stuart, 1996).

Meet the Demands of the Situation

Your receivers' expectations of your presentation are also important. The situation frequently determines expectations, such as the level of formality. Some situations

Table A.1	**One-Sided Versus Two-Sided Messages**

You should use a one-sided message when:

• Your audience already favors your position.

• Your audience is not well educated in general or on the topic.

• You require a public commitment from your audience.

You should use a two-sided message when:

• Your audience initially disagrees with your position.

• Your audience is well educated in general or on the topic.

• Your audience will experience counterpersuasion on the topic.

Research suggests the best way to present a two-sided message is to first give the arguments that support your position. Organize those arguments beginning with the weakest and ending with the strongest. Then, present the argument of your opposition. Organize the opposition arguments beginning with the strongest and ending with the weakest. In this way, you take advantage of your listeners' tendency to remember the most recent thing they hear: your strong argument and your opponent's weak argument.

SOURCE: *Adapted from Sproule, 1991.*

clearly demand more formal presentations. If you are expected to address a board meeting, you should prepare carefully. On the other hand, if you are asked for your off-the-cuff comments, a prepared speech is not appropriate or practical. In this case, it is permissible to present more spontaneous remarks. Written communication also involves certain expectations. Invitations to a company picnic can be posted on bulletin boards, but invitations to a board of directors meeting are sent individually. Some situations are tricky. For example, television often appears informal; however, you should carefully think out your comments. Banquets and ceremonies may encourage an informal, friendly atmosphere, but don't be fooled. These aren't the same settings as one-on-one or small-group events.

The settings of business presentations can create a number of constraints you must anticipate. (Remember forethought and preparation are keys to effective communication.) Consider these common occurrences. A meeting schedule runs over so your 20-minute presentation must be condensed to 5 minutes. Be prepared with a short version that highlights information that will serve your strategy. After presenting your committee's proposal for changing customer service procedures, which the committee has studied for three months, an influential nonmember distributes an outline of a competing proposal. Be prepared to answer specific criticisms of your proposal while maintaining a tone of cordial professionalism.

Language is also affected by the situation. More formal language choices and more correct sentence structure are demanded by formal situations. Slang, colloquialisms, contractions, and less rigid grammar can add to the ease of informal settings. Determine your audience's expectations and adapt your language to them. Most experts agree your language should be one step more intense than your audience's.

DEVELOP A CLEAR STRUCTURE
Begin with a Forecast

In general, an effective introduction does three things. First, it catches the listeners' attention and sets a tone for the message. Second, it provides your listeners with a reason for listening or reading. Finally, it gives them a road map or quick sketch of the message.

At a supervisor's meeting, you might start out your talk on a new plan for production changes this way: "Do you realize we have not changed our basic production process in four years? In that time, seven new competitors have entered the market, and we've lost 9 percent of market share. But with three changes, we can get more production, which will generate 3 percent more profits and pay raises in the next fiscal year. First, we reorganize Bay 2; second, we install a track between the parts room and the assembly line; and, third, we set up a phone connection between the parts room and the assembly line. Let me spend a few minutes filling out the details of each change and explaining why these changes will save us money."

This introduction gets your audience's attention because it portrays the immediacy of the problem and shows why your listeners have an important stake in what you have to say. By setting the larger context of increased competition, you intensify their reason for listening and counter possible resistance to change, which is common in organizations.

Choose an Appropriate Organizational Pattern

Organization is critical because it affects comprehension of the message. Learners retain more when messages are organized. Organization also affects your credibility as a speaker or writer. A person who is organized is viewed more positively than one who is not—and organization affects attitude change. Your receivers are more likely to be influenced by your viewpoint if it is organized. Finally, an organized message is more likely to be retained, and thus to influence the listener.

There are many patterns of organization to choose from (see Table A.2). In general, you should order your thoughts using continua such as time, direction, causal process, problem-solving sequence, complexity, space, or familiarity. A related technique is to organize your material as a series of answers to typical questions. Another common technique is called *sandwiching*. This involves three steps. First, you emphasize the advantages of the plan. Second, you realistically assess the risks or concerns associated with it. Third, you reinforce the benefits by showing how they outweigh the costs, demonstrate how risks can be minimized with proposed safeguards, or show how resistance to change can be overcome.

As you plan your message consider your listeners' orientation. The main question to ask is; "What does my audience already know or think?" Start from that point, then move closer to the desired knowledge or point of view.

Written and spoken communication vary in the amount of detailed information that can be conveyed in a single effort. Because a memo or report can be reread, the receiver doesn't have to remember all the information. However, speeches can't be reheard. It's more important to limit the amount of information presented orally. How many points can you make in a speech?

Table A.2	Common Patterns of Organization
STRATEGY	**EXPLANATION**
Chronological	Traces the order of events in a time sequence (such as past, present, and future, or first step, second step, and third step).
Spatial	Arranges major points in terms of physical distance (such as north, central, and south) or direction from each other (such as internal and external).
Causal	Develops ideas from cause (such as diagnosing a disease from its causes) to effect or results to cause (such as from its symptoms to the disease).
Topical	Enumerates aspects of the topic (such as size, color, shape, or texture).
Monroe's Motivated Sequence	Follows a five-step process: 1. Gaining attention 2. Showing a need 3. Presenting a solution 4. Visualizing the results when the solution is implemented 5. Calling for action to implement the solution
Familiarity-acceptance order	Begins with what the listener knows or believes and moves on to new ideas.
Inquiry order	Develops the topic in steps the same way you acquire the information or solve a problem.
Question-answer	Raises and answers a series of listeners' questions.
Problem-solution	First establishes that a problem exists then develops a plan to solve the problem.
Elimination order	Surveys all the available solutions and systematically eliminates each possibility until one remains.

Three main points are preferred by most speakers, but many listeners can remember up to five main points. Seven chunks of information is about the limit of a person's immediate short-term memory at any one time. Since people must remember what you have said if they are to act on it, dividing your speech into no more than five major chunks should make your ideas easier to remember (Miller, 1967). If your presentation is long, consider using visual aids, such as PowerPoint slides or handouts, to reinforce the message.

Use Transitions or Signposts to Signal Your Progress

It is important to give your audience a "road map" at the beginning of your message. Don't stop there. Continue to help them follow you through it. To do this, signal when you're moving from one idea to another by summarizing the first idea, then forecasting the new idea. This is especially important in oral communication, since listeners will only hear your message once; it is critical you provide signposts during your speech. You should indicate major transitions

between ideas, such as: "We've just seen how the two standard types of data storage operate, now let's look at the advantages and disadvantages of each storage system." In written form, you can signal transitions by indenting, numbering, or using bullets to highlight information. You can call your reader's attention to key words with italicized or bold print.

Conclude on a High Note

Two important psychological concepts are at work in communication—primacy and recency. Primacy is the first impression received and recency is the last. People tend to remember the first and last things they read or hear in messages. It's easy to understand why the most important parts of any presentation are the first and last impressions it creates. You establish an initial feeling in your introduction that colors the rest of the presentation, and the impression created during the conclusion influences the audience's overall evaluation of your message. Since these are the most important segments of your presentation, they warrant the most preparation. You should plan your message with the beginning and end in mind, that is, consider your specific purpose statement as you develop your introduction and conclusion. Some people write the conclusion first because this allows them to organize the rest of their material so it naturally flows into the conclusion.

Reach closure at the end of your speech or written message by summarizing your ideas for a final time. Research shows this kind of reinforcement helps listeners retain information. Normally, people remember less than 20 percent of what they hear or read. If you preview the information in your introduction, reinforce it in internal summaries, and then summarize in the conclusion, you will increase the odds that your audience will remember your ideas.

The last statements you make after your summary should create a sense of closure and add to the memorability of your message. These statements can take a variety of forms. You can call for action, reinforce your audience's commitment to action, or establish feelings of goodwill (see Table A.3 for further suggestions). For example, you might emphasize legitimacy by highlighting several authoritative quotes, emphasize the "I'm here to help" theme, predict conditions in the future, underscore the utility of your proposal by emphasizing its impact on the bottom line, or use an emotional appeal to increase commitment and loyalty.

SUPPORT YOUR POINTS

Choose a Variety of Support

There are many reasons to use supporting materials, or evidence, as you develop your message. Most research concludes that supporting material makes a great difference in the impact of ideas. This is true even if you are not well known to your receivers or if they find your credibility moderate to low. What kind of support should you choose? Table A.4 illustrates some of the many kinds of supporting materials available. Messages are strongest when they are built upon a variety of supporting materials. For example, reinforce statistics on profit sharing with a specific instance, such as how those numbers will affect a person on the assembly line.

Consider Your Listeners When Choosing Your Support

The kinds of supporting materials you choose partially depends on your audience. If the evidence is new to them, it will have more impact. Videotapes,

Table A.3	Types of Introductions and Conclusions

When you select an introduction or conclusion, ask yourself if it orients your audience to your purposes and clearly signals the beginning or ending of your speech.

1. Refer to the subject or occasion.
2. Use a personal reference or greeting.
3. Ask a rhetorical question.
4. Make a startling statement.
5. Use a quotation.
6. Tell a humorous story.
7. Use an illustration.
8. Issue a challenge or appeal.
9. Use suspense.
10. Appeal to the listener's self-interest.
11. Employ a visual aid.
12. Refer to a recent incident.
13. Compliment the audience or a member of the audience.
14. Refer to the preceding speaker.
15. Request a specific action.

Table A.4	Types of Supporting Materials
Examples	Specific instances that illustrate the point or clarify the idea: For example, "Our plants in Detroit and Sacramento use Quality Circles."
Statistics	Numbers that express relationships of magnitude, segments, or trends: For example, "Currently, a full 32% of our workforce is involved in Quality Circle decision-making, and that is up 17% over the past two years."
Testimony	The opinions or conclusions of others, particularly experts: For example, "After studying our plants, professor Henry Wilson of the Harvard School of Business observed American workers are not group motivated. He concluded 'American workers cannot be expected to respond well to Quality Circles for that reason.'"

recordings, or photos also have greater impact. People who are highly dogmatic are more affected by evidence than those who are not so dogmatic. People are likely to believe evidence that agrees with their own position more than evidence that does not. So their initial position determines the extent to which they will find evidence believable. If your receivers find the source or types of evidence to be believable or credible, it will be more effective (see Table. A.5).

Use Visual Aids as Support

There are as many reasons to use visual aids as there are types of visual aids (see Table A.6). Visual aids help people process and retain data (Seiler, 1971). In addition to enhancing comprehension and memory, visual aids can heighten the persuasive impact of your ideas if they engage receivers actively in the communicative exchange. Your credibility and your persuasiveness are enhanced by good visual aids. With these functions in mind, remember visual aids should be simple, clear, and professional (see Table A.7). The purpose of a visual aid is to augment your presentation, not replace it or distract from it. Unfortunately, this last point is lost by many professionals who treat presentations as slide shows in which screen displays and even sound effects—not the presenter—become the center of attention.

Table A.5	Using Supporting Materials

There is a great deal of research on the use of supporting materials or evidence in oral presentations. The following patterns seem to emerge:

1. If you have low to moderate credibility, evidence will probably increase your persuasive effectiveness.

2. There seems to be minimal difference between emotional and logical evidence.

3. Using evidence is usually better than not using it.

4. There seems to be little difference between biased sources and objective sources in their final impact on audiences.

5. Good speech delivery may improve the potency of evidence when sources of the evidence are unknown or have low credibility.

6. Evidence can reinforce the long-term effectiveness of persuasion.

7. Evidence is most effective when listeners are not familiar with it.

8. People are more likely to believe evidence that agrees with their own position.

9. Highly dogmatic people are more affected by evidence than are less dogmatic people.

10. Evidence produces more attitude change when the course and source qualifications are provided.

11. Speakers with low credibility are seen as more credible when they cite evidence.

12. Using irrelevant evidence or poorly qualified sources may produce an effect opposite to what the speaker intends.

SOURCE: *From* Persuasion: Reception, and Responsibility *6th edition by Larson.* © *1992. Reprinted with the permission of Wadsworth, a division of Thomson Learning: www.thomsonrights.com. Fax 800 730–2215.*

Table A.6	Functions of Visual Aids

According to research, using effective visual aids in an oral presentation:

- Makes your presentation up to 50% more memorable.
- Significantly clarifies complex or detailed information.
- Portrays you as more professional and better prepared.
- Speeds up group decision making.
- Shortens meeting time by up to 28%.
- Makes your message 43% more persuasive.

SOURCES: *Osborn & Osborn, 1991, and Gronbeck et al., 1992.*

Computer-aided graphics make it easier than ever to supplement your main ideas with visual materials. They also make it easier to create cluttered, excessive visual and sound images that distract the audience from your strategic message. Select and design visual aids to reinforce your strategy and ideas, and to make them clearer. Keep in mind each type of visual aid communicates information in a different way. In general, visual aids such as slides, photographs, and posters can help an audience *feel* the way you do. They enhance the emotional dimension of a presentation. On the other hand, descriptive or written materials help an audience *think* the way you do. Numbers and charts reinforce cognitive processes; photographs reinforce affective processes. Use tables and graphs to highlight relationships and patterns, not to convey comprehensive data. If necessary, use supplemental handouts of comprehensive tables and charts.

USE AN ENHANCING STYLE

Up to this point, the preparation of oral and written messages is very similar. Whether you intend to deliver a speech or write a memo, you need to develop

Table A.7	Checklist for Using Visual Aids

As you prepare your visual aids, ask yourself the following questions:

- ❑ Can I avoid making the visual aid the most important aspect of my speech? Will it be more than just an ornament?
- ❑ Can I translate complex numbers into bar or line graphs for easier comprehension?
- ❑ Am I comfortable with using the visual aid? Have I practiced with it so using it is natural, and it does not break the flow of ideas in my speech?
- ❑ Is it large enough to be seen by everyone without straining?
- ❑ Is all the printing short and neat?
- ❑ Is the visual aid colorful and involving? Studies show color highlights aid recall of information.
- ❑ Are my visual aids professional: neat, attractive, and accurate?
- ❑ Have I made the necessary arrangements for special visual aids in advance?
- ❑ Can I use the visual aid without blocking my audience's view of it? Will I be able to maintain good eye contact with my listeners while using the visual aid?
- ❑ Can I avoid reaching across my body or waving the visual aid in front of my face?
- ❑ Can I avoid distracting my listeners by keeping the visual aid covered or out of sight before and after I use it?
- ❑ What will I do if the visual aid fails to work? Am I prepared for unexpected contingencies such as a burned-out projector bulb or a room that cannot be darkened?
- ❑ Have I planned for assistance or volunteers in advance if they are needed?
- ❑ Will a pointer be needed?
- ❑ Will all charts be secured so I don't have to hunt for them on the floor in the middle of my speech?
- ❑ Am I using a variety of visual aids to increase my listeners' interest?
- ❑ If I'm using handouts, can I adjust to the distraction caused by passing them around? Can I compete with listeners who will read the handout rather than listen to me?
- ❑ Can I speak over the noise of a projector or other machine?

LEARNING

your strategy by identifying your purposes, structuring your message, and supporting your ideas with evidence. The fourth step requires separate treatment of oral and written messages because they are stylistically very different forms of communication. We'll first focus on oral presentations.

STYLE IN ORAL COMMUNICATION

Prepare Your Notes

The mark of effective presenters is the appearance of effortlessness. Some speakers have such command of their material it appears they are ad libbing. Most of us prefer such a conversational style (see Table A.8), but don't be fooled by appearances. Hours of preparation and practice preceded the actual performance. You've already been introduced to the three steps of preparation, but how do you develop the fourth stage of your preparation for oral communication?

After you have carefully considered your strategy, structure, and support, you should prepare your speaking notes. To do this, simply write your key points in a rough outline following the organizational pattern you have chosen. What you do next depends on your method of presentation. Most often, you will speak in a conversational manner that is not memorized or read; this is referred to as extemporaneous speaking. Extemporaneous presentation is desirable because it is natural and flexible; it applies to most situations. To prepare, copy key words on note cards to stimulate your memory; standard pages are often distracting. Write out quotations, statistics, or anything that requires exact wording. Highlight places where you intend to use visual aids, pause for questions, or present an exhibit. To rehearse, go through the speech, phrasing your ideas in language that seems natural. You may find yourself phrasing ideas with different words each time. That is okay. It will increase the conversational quality of your speech because your words will be typical of oral style and natural expression. It will help you develop flexibility, allowing you to adjust to different wording and flow of ideas.

If the occasion is formal and demands precise wording or exquisite prose, you should prepare a word-for-word manuscript to memorize or read. Then you should rehearse with the manuscript, trying to achieve as much natural flow in the dialogue as possible. This form of presentation is rare, but it may be required for discussing legal and financial issues, making announcements to the press, or conducting special ceremonies. Otherwise, avoid using written scripts and memorization for presentations because they disrupt the natural flow of conversational style and break eye contact with your listeners. Because manuscripts are prepared in written form first, they usually take on the style of written language. Unless you are a practiced speechwriter, your manuscript will sound like written rather than oral speech (see Table A.9).

Practice Your Presentation

It is a good idea to rehearse your presentation under simulated conditions—in a similar room, with listeners who can give you suggestions for improvement. Time your presentation so you know if it is necessary to cut or expand your ideas. Research shows practicing a speech for short periods of time over the course of several days is more successful in reducing anxiety and improving memory than concentrated practice. So give the speech to yourself during breakfast, at your morning coffee break, as you walk to a midafternoon meeting, and before bed. Distributed practice is more efficient and yields better results than massed practice.

Table A.8	Differences Between Public Speaking and Conversation

Folk wisdom holds that giving a speech is just like talking to another person. While it is true most people prefer a conversational style of public speaking, there are at least three noteworthy differences between giving speeches and holding conversations:

1. Public speaking is more highly structured. It requires more detailed planning and development. Specific time limits may be imposed, and the speaker does not have the advantage of being able to respond individually to listeners.

2. Public speaking requires more formal language. Slang, jargon, and poor grammar all lower speaker credibility, even in informal speech situations. Listeners usually react negatively to poor language choices. In fact, many studies show some kinds of language, such as obscene language, dramatically lower a speaker's credibility.

3. Public speaking requires a different method of delivery. The speaker's voice must be adjusted in volume and projection, posture is more correct, and distracting mannerisms and verbal habits are avoided.

SOURCE: *Adapted from Lucas, 1989.*

Table A.9	Differences Between Oral and Written Styles

Why do we instantly recognize a memorized speech? Why does a meeting transcript sound funny? The answer to both questions is oral style differs from written style. Memorized speeches from manuscripts reveal their written style, and conversations that are read reveal their oral style. Oral style differs from written style in the following ways:

1. The average sentence length is shorter (about 16 words) in conversations.

2. Vocabulary is more limited in speaking than in writing. "I" and "you" make up almost 8% of the words used in speaking; fewer than 50 words make up almost half of the total vocabulary we use when we speak.

3. Spoken vocabulary consists of more short words.

4. Speakers use more words referring to themselves such as "I," "me," and "we"; listeners rate this as more interesting.

5. More qualifying terms (such as "much," "many," and "a lot") and allness terms (such as "none," "never," and "always") are used in speaking.

6. More phrases and terms indicating hesitation are apparent in speaking, such as "it seems to me," "apparently," "in my opinion," and "maybe."

7. Fewer precise numbers are used in speaking.

8. Speakers use more contractions and colloquial expressions such as "can't," "wouldn't," "wow," and "chill out."

One final note on language: There is some evidence that we use lexical diversity as a cue to a speaker's socioeconomic status, competence, and perceived similarity.

SOURCE: *Copyright 1978 From* Oral and Written Style *by L. Einhorn. Reproduced by permission of Taylor & Francis Group, LLC. www.taylorandfrancis.com.*

Practice Using Your Visual Aids

This will help you get used to managing them and give you some idea of how long your speech will take with the visual aids. Prepare for the totally unexpected. What if the roar of an overhead plane drowns out your voice? What if the microphone goes dead, a window blows open, or the room becomes extremely hot? Compensate for minor disruptions by slowing your rate, raising your volume a little, and continuing. You will encourage listeners to listen to your message rather than be temporarily distracted. For other disruptions, a good rule of thumb is to respond the same way you would if you were in the audience. Take off your jacket if it is too hot, close the window, raise your voice if listeners can't hear you, or pause to allow a complex idea to sink in.

As you practice, think about how you will channel your anxiety. Most speakers report feeling anxious before they speak; it's normal. To manage your anxiety, channel it into positive energy. Prepare well in advance for the speech—develop your ideas, support them, and practice your delivery. Even if you are anxious, you will have something important to say. It may help to visualize the speaking situation. Close your eyes, relax, and think about how it's going to feel and what your audience will look like as they watch you. Expect to feel a little momentary panic as you get up to speak; it will evaporate as you progress into the speech. Remember to think about your ideas rather than how nervous you feel. Focus on your message. Also remember anxiety about speaking never really goes away. Most experienced speakers still get podium panic. The advantage of experience is you learn how to cope by converting your anxiety into energy and enthusiasm. That gives you an extra sparkle as you speak. Above all, don't tell your listeners you are nervous. This will divert their attention from your ideas to your anxiety. Usually, listeners can't tell a speaker is nervous—only speakers know, and they should keep that secret.

Convey Controlled Enthusiasm for Your Subject

When a survey was given to 1,200 people asking them to identify the characteristics of effective presentations (Peoples, 1988), the results contained adjectives such as flexible, cooperative, audience-oriented, pleasant, and interesting. What was striking about these results is that only the last item on the list of 12 outstanding characteristics was specifically related to the content of the presentations. This suggests the preceding discussion of effective format, while necessary, is not sufficient to guarantee your success. Put another way, a rambling, poorly organized presentation will surely produce an overall negative evaluation. On the other hand, a well-organized, highly logical, and easy-to-follow presentation that is poorly delivered will also be viewed negatively. This study suggests style is extremely important in oral communication.

Years of research on student evaluations of classroom teaching performance have consistently shown that enthusiasm is the hallmark of a good teacher. Students will forgive other deficiencies if the teacher obviously loves the subject and is genuinely interested in conveying that appreciation to the students. The same holds true for presenters. Your posture, tone of voice, and facial expressions are all critical indicators of your attitude. Speak standing if you can, move occasionally, and use gestures to convey an attitude of earnestness. Remember, your audience will become infected with your enthusiasm.

Although enthusiasm is important, it must be controlled. Do not confuse enthusiasm with loudness. A good rule is to use vigorous but conversational tones of voice and inflections. Avoid bellowing or preaching at your listeners. Be sure you can be easily heard and your tone is sufficiently emphatic to convey meaning effectively. In general, your speech should resemble an animated or lively conversation.

Use Delivery to Enhance Your Message

Another key to maintaining audience attention is effective delivery. Eye contact is the most important tool for establishing audience involvement. It makes listeners feel as if they are involved in a one-on-one, semiprivate discussion with you. In this culture, we value directness and honesty. One of the expressions of these values is direct eye contact. Effective eye contact means looking directly at members of the audience, one at a time, on a random, rotating basis. Generally, the smaller the group, the longer you can look at each person. Maintaining eye contact is also your primary source of audience feedback as you are presenting. If your audience appears puzzled, you may need to pause and review your key ideas.

It is important to use physical space and body movement to enhance your message. Remember presentations are like movies, not snapshots. Alternate moving and standing still, speaking and listening, doing and thinking. Intersperse your lecture with chalkboard use, demonstration, audience participation, and audiovisual aids so no single activity occupies a large portion of the presentation. Add some spice to your presentation by including personal anecdotes, references to members of the group, unusual facts, vital information, and vibrant images. Whenever appropriate,

arrange the podium area to accommodate physical movement. Physical movement can be used to punctuate important points, signal transitions, build rapport with a person who asks a question, heighten the interest of particular segments of the audience, and help your listeners stay alert by refocusing their attention.

Other aspects of physical space affect the quality of your presentation. If possible, arrange the podium area and seating in the room to remove distractions. In more intimate settings, group participants so there is less space between them. Eliminate unnecessary or distracting materials from the podium, such as unused equipment, signs, and displays. Keep your visual aids covered until they are used and keep the chalkboard clean. Focus your listeners' attention on you and your message.

You can use space to convey intimacy or distance. Position yourself roughly in the middle of your audience from left to right and in a spot where you can comfortably maintain eye contact. With this in mind, you can deliberately alter your presentation style to build rapport with members of the audience. Move closer if you intend to build intimacy or tension; move to a comfortable distance when your ideas are neutral.

Gestures can also add to a presentation. They should appear to be spontaneous and natural in order to enhance, rather than distract from, your message. They should be relaxed, not rigid. Use them to accentuate your normal mode of expression. To some extent, when you concentrate on your message, not your movements, the appropriate gestures will come naturally. Remember your gestures should be smooth, relatively slow, and not too low (below your waist), too high (above your shoulders), or too wide (more than two feet from your body). If you are using a podium, step slightly behind or to the side of the podium so it does not block your listeners' view of your movement. The general rules for gestures change as your audience becomes larger. You must adapt to large groups by making larger, more dramatic gestures.

Avoid any gestures or movements that distract from your message. Irrelevant movement such as jingling change in a pocket, toying with notes, shifting from foot to foot, twisting hair, or adjusting eyeglasses are annoying. In fact, any movement repeated too often creates a distraction. Practice using a variety of body movements to illustrate or describe, enumerate, add emphasis, or direct attention. For variety, some gestures should involve the entire upper body, not just your dominant hand.

STYLE IN WRITTEN COMMUNICATION

Like oral communication, written communication is a skill; it can be learned. Written communication follows the same three preparation steps as oral communication. The writer determines strategies, structure, and support before actually putting pen to paper. As with effective presentations, good writing draws on careful analysis of the audience and situation. In a business setting, "every document is a response to a problem or opportunity requiring that some consensus be achieved or action taken" (Poor, 1992, p. 38).

There are significant differences between oral and written communication style. Although it lacks the interpersonal dimension of immediacy, written communication offers one tremendous advantage over oral communication—it lasts. Written documents can be retained, studied, duplicated, and filed for the future. This means they are essentially capable of conveying much more detailed information. While written communication offers these advantages, it also makes different demands on the communicator; written communication demands precision.

Develop Mechanical Precision in Your Writing

Your professional image is judged by the appearance of your written communication. Cross outs, erasures, typographical errors, or other sloppiness detract from your written message, just as awkward mannerisms can distract from your oral message. Grammatical precision is also required—misspellings, punctuation errors, and poor grammar are marks of uneducated writers. This is certainly not an image you want to convey. You may expect a secretary or clerical worker to catch and correct all these things, and many times that happens. However, when you sign or otherwise endorse the final product, you alone are accountable for any errors it contains. It is essential to develop the habit of proofreading final drafts before you sign them.

Violations of the rules of grammar and punctuation may affect more than just your credibility. They can also disrupt your reader. If the reader is distracted by typos, confusing grammar, or ambiguous pronouns, your ideas may become lost; such errors can cripple the impact of your message. Some recruiters toss out résumés that contain mechanical errors. Their reasoning is if job applicants can't take the time to proofread a short résumé, they may be sloppy on the job, too. Some readers are insulted by poor grammar; others automatically consider themselves superior to the writer. While these

may not be logical reactions, they occur, and more important, they block your effectiveness. You may argue correct grammar and punctuation are not vital. Maybe not, but you take a chance every time you present careless work to another reader. Consider the campaign of Charles Day for a seat on local government. His campaign flyers, delivered house to house, carried the banner, "Vote Charles Day for School Bord." Would you want a man who apparently can't spell make decisions on academic matters for your neighborhood schools? The impression is if you don't have the time or incentive to check your own writing, you won't pay attention to details in the work of others.

Practice Factual Precision in Your Writing

Getting the facts right is important. If you send a memo calling for a meeting but record an incorrect meeting date, you'll suffer the consequences of inconveniencing others. Accuracy is critical, but that's just the beginning. It's up to the writer to create sentences that make the meaning unmistakably clear to the reader. Many times writers know the facts but omit important details in writing. Omission occurs when you have all the facts or circumstances but as you write, you assume the reader knows the facts. Write with your reader in mind. This assumes you have analyzed who your readers are and understand what information they need and expect. What basic information is important for readers to know in order to understand your message? Instead of starting with the central part of the message, provide the background first, such as: "In response to your memo of February 2, requesting corrections to our policy on grievances, we have taken three actions. First..." If you're not sure what to include, ask someone who doesn't know the details of the situation to read what you have written.

Ambiguity is another barrier to clear writing. Many times we write as we speak, throwing in phrases as we would speak them. Unlike speakers, writers can't use nonverbal cues to convey specific meanings or associations. Since readers may not have the advantage of asking questions or getting immediate feedback, they are left to determine associations for themselves. Consider how ambiguity creates a lack of precise factual meaning in this memo:

> *The next meeting of the department is scheduled for next week. Matt Olsen has told Leo Robinson to report on the union elections. His report will follow announcements. We will elect new officers at our upcoming meeting.*

This memo doesn't pass the standard test of clear writing. If the memo was sent on Friday and received on Monday, which week contains the meeting? Who is giving the report? The pronoun "his" causes confusion since it could refer to either Matt Olsen or Leo Robinson. Which "upcoming meeting" will result in the election of officers? Will it be the meeting called by the memo or another "upcoming meeting"? Because it can breed confusion, annoyance, and wasted time, such a sloppy memo can have an adverse effect on the relationship between the writer and recipients that can affect their subsequent communication. Seen in this light, the memos a manager routinely writes are an important factor in managing relationships strategically and productively.

Construct Written Messages with Verbal Precision

Achieving verbal precision is different from mechanical or factual precision. Verbal precision is based on the accuracy of the words chosen to express the ideas. In an ideal world, words would provide the exact meaning you intended, but words can't replicate reality. Rather, words are symbols of objects and ideas. Add to this inexact representation the reader's own subtle shadings of meaning, and you can see why it's difficult to achieve verbal precision. Put another way, a word has two levels of meaning: its denotation, or the meaning agreed upon by most people who use the word, and its connotation, or the personal dimension of meaning brought to the word by the receiver.

Communication depends on a blend of both denotative and connotative meanings. Consider the noun *Greenpeace*. Its denotative reference is to a specific international environmental organization. The connotative meaning varies widely. For many environmentalists, Greenpeace is leading a worthy crusade. However, for some governments and companies, the organization is, at best, a nuisance. These are the connotative references of a single word. Consider the difficulty in creating the right blend of denotative and connotative meaning in entire documents. You need to be aware of both types of meaning of the words you use. Frequently, you may recognize your own connotative meaning but be unaware of how others may react. While connotation is often a personal matter, you can attempt to judge this meaning by thinking from your receivers' viewpoint. What is their most likely reaction?

The key to verbal precision in writing is clarity. The fundamental questions you must ask yourself are: "Does the word or phrase convey my meaning without confusion?" or "Could anyone reading this memo for the first time understand the ideas directly and simply?" A secondary question is whether the written message conveys unintentional meanings stimulated by connotative meanings of words or phrases. The impact of connotations once more underlines the importance of knowing your audience and of being aware of what is appropriate for one audience or another.

Pay Attention to Tone

The tone of your writing is directly related to your diction, or word choices. For example, compare these two statements: "Our company will purchase the product" and "We'll buy it." The second sounds more informal because it uses pronouns and a contraction. In general, longer words and sentences tend to convey a more formal tone.

Using the appropriate level of formality in your writing calls for you to analyze the nature of the writing situation. An invitation to a reception for the company's board of directors calls for formal language. When you are writing to strangers or up the chain of command, it is safer to be formal. When you are communicating across or down the chain, you may often be informal. However, a letter of reprimand to a subordinate should be formal in tone.

Tone in business writing goes beyond its relative formality. It reflects on the nature of the writer as a person and therefore affects how the reader feels about the writer. Its impact can be significant and often unexpected. For example, a terse letter may be interpreted as sarcastic or angry even if the writer did not intend sarcasm or anger. Consider a customer who writes a long letter expressing problems with a product. What would the customer think if this response were mailed back: "Thank you for your letter of January 12. We always enjoy hearing from our customers." Although this response has the trappings of courtesy, it seems insincere and perhaps sarcastic. It hardly seems that the respondent read the customer's letter—there is nothing about its contents—or that the letter was "enjoyed." Although the response shows factual and mechanical precision, the tone is inappropriate and potentially damaging to the relationship with this customer.

In most cases, even disappointing news can be expressed in a positive way. Consider an employer who responds to a job applicant by writing, "In a company as well respected as ours, we rarely have time to consider applications such as yours." Not only is the news bad, the arrogant tone also needlessly humiliates the applicant. A response with a more positive tone might be: "We read your application with interest but currently do not have any openings in your specialties. Best wishes with your continued search." The news is still bad, but the polite tone shows respect for the applicant and promotes a professional image for the company.

Compare the following sentence and its more positive version: "Because of recent heavy demand, we will be unable to ship the items you ordered until July 15," and "Although recent demand has been heavy, we will be able to ship the items you ordered July 15." A slight variation in wording here changes a tone of helplessness to one of helpfulness.

Under most business writing conditions, you should be cordial. You should express tact and friendliness appropriate to your relationship with the reader. This attitude will have a positive effect on your word choices, which in turn will more likely convey an appropriate tone.

One area of modern business writing where failing to pay attention to tone has cost many bad feelings and lost time is e-mail. By its nature, e-mail encourages rapid-fire exchanges, especially when busy workers face an in-box filled with messages, many of which are ill-considered and unclear. E-mail is not a phone conversation in which tone of voice and other cues can clarify your meaning and in which you can read the listener's vocal cues. However, many e-mailers seem to forget the difference. They don't state the context of their message; they don't give needed background information; they don't organize their message; they don't make careful word choices that convey a cordial tone. By not taking the time to consider their message in light of the situation and the receiver, e-mailers can convey inappropriately demanding tones or disapproving tones if their requests aren't met promptly. The antagonism created by the poor tone of e-mail messages can delay solving the business problem at hand and negatively affect the work relationships of the e-mailers.

Use the Proper Format

Like it or not, first impressions count, even in written communication. Sloppiness suggests the writer doesn't take the message seriously; odd or unconventional formats hint the writer is ignorant or unprofessional. You should become acquainted with the physical layout of letters, memos, proposals, and other common forms of written business communication. Others expect you to have this basic knowledge; many handbooks and computer software programs are available to guide you in the development of these formats. Some companies have style guides that precisely prescribe the formats for all documents representing the company.

While there are several acceptable formats for written communication such as business letters, the reader should be able to pick up specific information at a glance. In the business letter, this information includes: the intended recipient of the letter, the sender, the sender's address for return correspondence, any enclosures, and recipients of copies of the letter. All of this information is separate from the body of the letter and should be clearly visible.

Because memos are intended to communicate within an organization, their format is different from that of letters. Instead of business letterhead, memo letterhead is used. Basic information can also be obtained at a glance. The top of the memo should include: To, From, Date, and Subject headings. Usually, salutations and closings are not considered necessary within an organization.

Proposals are much lengthier and require special attention to supporting information such as tables, graphs, and charts. The best ways to represent such data can be found in readily available resources on business writing.

Whatever the final format, there is one objective in all written business communication: Your message should be simple, direct, and clear. Anything that interrupts your reader's movement through your writing limits its effectiveness. Any imprecision—a mechanical blunder, a factual omission, or a strange word—calls attention to itself and, like an odd gesture in spoken communication, diverts attention away from your ideas. As a writer, you must aim at clear, direct transmission of your message.

SUPPLEMENT YOUR PRESENTATION BY RESPONDING TO QUESTIONS AND CHALLENGES

Prepare Thoroughly to Handle Questions

Answering questions and responding to objections is a vital part of the communication process because it allows us to interact directly with our listeners. We can learn about how our listeners are thinking and their responses to our ideas from their questions; it's a two-way street.

The key to formulating effective responses is the same as the key to developing good speeches—careful preparation. Read broadly and talk with experts in your field. Don't read just the material that supports your point of view but also read what the opposition is saying. The best defense can be a good offense, and this is no exception. Ask your colleagues to critique your material, discuss their questions and objections with them, and collect supporting documentation or evidence. You can also practice your responses. Begin by considering what your listeners might ask or find someone opposed to your position who will list questions for you. Then, practice your responses to these questions.

Despite your best efforts, you may get an overwhelmingly hostile response from your listeners. Don't be afraid to take a stand that disagrees with them. People may not agree with you but they will respect your sincerity. If someone throws you a curve, don't apologize or bluff your way through with an inadequate response. Be honest and direct, tell them if you don't have the answer. Invite them to discuss the problem further at a later time and follow up on your invitation. The next time someone asks the same question, you will be prepared.

Respond to Objections in an Orderly Manner

In general, answer questions as succinctly as possible. Rambling answers may make it appear as though you are hedging or unsure. They also suggest an inability to think concisely. You can answer objections in four steps:

1. *Restate the objection.* This gives you time to think, shows your interest, and makes sure everyone understands the question. Restatement recognizes the objection and clarifies it for everyone in the audience.
2. *State your position.* Give a concise, direct statement of what you believe to make it clear where you stand.
3. *Offer support for your position.* This is the critical part of the response. Provide evidence that shows your position is the right one.
4. *Indicate the significance of your rebuttal.* Show the impact of adopting your position. Offer reasons for doing so.

Following the four steps we've outlined, a good response to an objection might take this form:

1. Joe has stated a management-by-objectives system won't work in our factory because supervisors don't want input from the cutting floor (restatement of the objection).

2. I think a management-by-objectives system will work and it will increase worker satisfaction (statement of your position).
3. I'm basing my position on a group of studies done in our Newark plant last year. Output increased 0.5 percent during the first month, and more importantly, workers reported more job satisfaction. They had fewer sick days, too (support for the position).
4. If our plant is similar to the Newark plant—and I think it is—then I believe our supervisors will notice the same gains here. Until Joe can provide us with a reason to stick with the current system, I think we ought to give the new one a try—we stand to get more output and better job satisfaction (significance of rebuttal).

Practice this format until it becomes automatic. It builds up your own case while responding to the objection. Since this format rationally shores up your position, it increases your credibility as well. And, it increases the chances that others will agree with you.

Maintain Control of the Situation

You need to balance being sensitive to feedback and flexible enough to respond to legitimate concerns with avoiding prolonged, unproductive interchanges. Recognizing everyone's right to ask questions or offer alternative positions is important because it grants audience members respect. On the other hand, you also have every right to decide what is relevant for consideration. You shouldn't allow one or two members of your audience to dictate the pace or direction of your presentation. This places you in a position of weakness that undermines your credibility. If you should alter your position, make certain the majority of your listeners view it as a responsible shift rather than an effort to placate a minority voice.

Keep exchanges on an intellectual level. Arguments and rebuttals can degenerate into name-calling in which little is settled. Effective communication is more likely to occur when the calm voice of reason dominates than when you squabble with your listeners.

You'll soon learn people don't always ask questions just because they want information. Some people crave attention; others may sabotage your position if they perceive your ideas as a threat. Planning for these possibilities will give you more options; foresight enables you to respond appropriately. You might answer hostile questions with further questions, drawing out your interrogator and regaining the offensive. Or you might broaden the discussion. Don't get trapped into an argument with one person. Involve others to determine if this is an isolated concern or a legitimate issue. Finally, you might express your willingness to discuss special or detailed issues but defer extensive discussion until the end of your presentation.

Summary and Behavioral Guidelines

A key aspect of management is communication, and formal presentations are an essential communication tool. Therefore, effective managers must be able to create effective informative and persuasive messages. You can enhance your speaking and writing with thorough preparation and repeated practice. This chapter has outlined a number of guidelines based on the Five *S*'s model:

1. Formulate a *strategy* for the specific audience and occasion.
2. Develop a clear *structure*.
3. *Support* your points with evidence adapted to your audience.
4. Practice presenting your material in a *style* that will enhance your ideas.
5. *Supplement* your presentation by effectively responding to questions and challenges.

Strategy

1. Identify your general and specific purposes.
2. Tailor your message to your audience.
   - ❏ Understand their needs, desires, knowledge level, and attitude toward your topic.
   - ❏ Make sure your approach is audience-centered.
   - ❏ Present both sides of the issue if your audience is hostile or uncommitted.
3. Meet the demands of the situation.
   - ❏ More formal situations demand formal language and sentence structure.
   - ❏ Informal situations allow slang and less rigid language use.

Structure

4. Begin with a forecast of your main ideas.
   - ❏ Catch your audience's attention as you begin.
   - ❏ Provide them with a reason for listening or reading.
   - ❏ Give them an outline of the message so they can follow along.
5. Choose your organizational pattern carefully.
   - ❏ Start with what your listeners already know or think.
   - ❏ Use organization to increase your credibility.
   - ❏ Move from familiar to unfamiliar, simple to complex, old to new, or use other continua for organizing your thoughts.
   - ❏ Make no more than three to five main points in oral communication.
6. Use transitions to signal your progress.
7. Conclude on a high note.
   - ❏ Take advantage of greater audience attention at the conclusion of your message.
   - ❏ Reach closure by reinforcing through a summary of your ideas.
   - ❏ Use your last statements to call for action, reinforce the commitment to action, or establish a feeling of goodwill.

Support

8. Choose a variety of support.
   - ❏ The most effective support is not well known to your listeners.
   - ❏ Support increases your credibility.
   - ❏ You may use a wide variety of supporting material.

9. Consider your audience when choosing your support.
   - ❏ New evidence and live videotapes have more impact.
   - ❏ The audience's initial position determines the extent to which they find evidence believable.
   - ❏ Using evidence is better than not using evidence.
10. Use visual aids as support.
    - ❏ Visual aids have a dramatic impact on comprehension and retention.
    - ❏ Visual aids also enhance persuasion.
    - ❏ Keep visual aids simple and effective.

Style in Oral Communication

11. Prepare your notes.
    - ❏ Remember, the crucial effect is conversational style.
    - ❏ Extemporaneous presentation requires limited notes combined with frequent delivery practice.
    - ❏ Formal occasions demand precise wording that requires a manuscript or memorized speech.
12. Practice your presentation.
    - ❏ Use distributed practice rather than massed practice.
    - ❏ Practice using your visual aids and plan for the unexpected.
    - ❏ Plan to channel your speaking anxiety.
13. Convey controlled enthusiasm for your subject.
    - ❏ Effective speakers communicate excitement about their topics.
    - ❏ Your posture, tone of voice, and facial expressions all indicate your attitude.
    - ❏ Your speech should resemble an animated conversation.
14. Engage your audience with effective delivery.
    - ❏ Eye contact is the most critical tool.
    - ❏ Use physical space and body movement to enliven your message.
    - ❏ Use space to convey intimacy or distance.
    - ❏ Use gestures to accentuate your normal mode of expression.
    - ❏ Avoid any movement that distracts from your message.

Style in Written Communication

15. Develop mechanical precision in your writing.
    - ❏ Project a professional image.
    - ❏ Errors may distract your readers and disrupt the impact of your message.
16. Practice factual precision in your writing.
    - ❏ Accuracy ensures your meaning will be communicated clearly.
    - ❏ Ambiguity prevents factual precision.
17. Construct written messages with verbal precision.
    - ❏ Words cannot replicate reality.
    - ❏ Consider denotative and connotative meanings of words as you write them.
    - ❏ The key to verbal precision is clarity.
18. Pay attention to tone.
    - ❏ Tone is directly related to word choice.
    - ❏ Adjust the tone of your message to the formality of the situation.
    - ❏ Tone affects how readers feel about the writer.
    - ❏ Writing should express appropriate cordiality.
    - ❏ Positive phrasing is preferable to negativity.
19. Use the proper format.
    - ❏ You are responsible for creating an impression of professionalism.
    - ❏ Business letters, memos, and proposals all have special formats.

20. Anticipate questions and thoroughly prepare responses.
    - ❏ Rehearse answers to difficult questions.
    - ❏ Handle hostile listeners with honesty and directness.
21. Respond to objections in an orderly fashion.
    - ❏ Restate the objection.
    - ❏ State your position.
    - ❏ Offer support for your position.
    - ❏ Indicate the significance of your rebuttal.
22. Maintain control of the situation.
    - ❏ Balance the demands of specific individuals with the interest of the group.
    - ❏ Keep exchanges on an intellectual level.
    - ❏ Plan for the questioner who has a personal agenda.

EXERCISES FOR MAKING EFFECTIVE ORAL AND WRITTEN PRESENTATIONS

Speaking as a Leader

As illustrated in the opening case about Taylor Billingsley at Apex Communications, one of the major challenges facing leaders is the requirement to deliver a wide range of presentations. Effective communicators must be skilled at both informing and inspiring. They must be able to hold their own with hostile audiences as well as to impress content experts and instill confidence in novices. They must be skilled at building consensus, pointing out new directions, and explaining complex topics. This exercise, adapted from Richard Linowes, provides an opportunity to practice speaking on a variety of leadership topics.

Assignment

To practice playing this important leadership role, prepare a talk and a memo on one of the following topics. Your speech should last from three to five minutes, unless you are otherwise instructed. Your memo should not exceed two pages. Create a context for your communication by assuming a management role in a familiar organization. Before beginning, explain the details of the context to your audience (either orally or in a written summary). Briefly explain your organizational position, the makeup of the audience, and their expectations of your presentation. (For the memo, attach a one-page background statement.) The specific content of your communication is less important than how well it is prepared and how persuasively it is delivered. Prepare to respond to questions and challenges.

In preparing your presentation, review the behavioral guidelines at the end of the Skill Learning section. The checklist in this exercise may also be useful. You will receive feedback based on the criteria shown in the Observer's Feedback Form.

Topics for Leadership Talks

1. **Taking Charge of an Established Group.** The speaker is a manager newly assigned to a group that has worked together under other managers for some time.
2. **Announcing a New Project.** The speaker is announcing a new undertaking to members of his or her department and is calling on all to rally behind the effort.
3. **Calling for Better Customer Service.** The speaker is motivating all employees to be as attentive and responsive as possible to customers.
4. **Calling for Excellence and High-Quality Work.** The speaker is motivating all employees to perform their jobs with a commitment to meeting the highest possible standards.
5. **Announcing the Need for Cost Reductions.** The speaker is requesting everyone look for ways to cut expenditures and immediately begin to slash spending.
6. **Commending a Job Well Done.** The speaker is extolling a group of people who have worked very hard for an extended period to produce outstanding results.
7. **Calming a Frightened Group of People.** The speaker is endeavoring to restore calm and confidence to those who feel panic in the face of distressing business developments.
8. **Addressing a Challenging Opposition.** The speaker is presenting a heartfelt belief to a critical, even hostile, audience.
9. **Mediating Between Opposing Parties.** The speaker is serving as judge or arbiter between two groups who are bitterly opposed on a key issue.
10. **Taking Responsibility for Error.** The speaker is a spokesperson for an institution whose actions have produced an unfortunate result that affects the audience.
11. Reprimanding Unacceptable Behavior. The speaker is rebuffing certain individuals who have failed to perform up to required levels.
12. **Petitioning for Special Allowances.** The speaker is presenting the case for an institution seeking certain rights that must be authorized by some external body.

Checklist for Developing Effective Presentations

1. What are my general and specific objectives?
2. What is the context of my communication? (My audience, the situation, etc.)
3. How will I open and close the communication?
4. How will I organize my information?
5. How will I get and keep the attention of my audience?
6. What supporting materials will I use?
7. What visual aids (graphs, charts, objects, etc.) will I use?
8. How will I tailor the presentation to my audience?
9. What format will I use in my presentation?
10. What questions or responses will likely occur?

Quality Circles at Battle Creek Foods

A management tool made popular in Japan is widely used in U.S. firms. Ironically, Edward Deming, an American, first brought the notion of "statistical quality control," a management tool, to the Japanese in the early post-World War II years. The Japanese combined these ideas with the assumption the person who performs a job is the one who best knows how to identify and correct its problems. As a result, the Japanese, with Deming's help, developed the "quality circle." A quality circle is a group of people (usually about 10) who meet periodically to discuss and develop solutions to problems related to quality, productivity, or product cost.

The purpose of this exercise is to give you an opportunity to make a presentation on this important topic.

Assignment

You are the director of personnel at Battle Creek Foods, a leading manufacturer of breakfast cereal. Productivity has been sagging industrywide, and your organization is starting to see its effect on profitability. In response, you have been asked by the corporate executive committee to make a 20-minute oral presentation (or prepare a five-page memo) on quality circles. The committee has heard that QCs have been initiated at several plants by your leading competitor, and it would like your recommendation as to whether Battle Creek Foods should follow suit. The committee's only previous exposure to QCs is what each member has read in the popular press. Using the following reference material, prepare a presentation on quality circles. Explain the QC structure and process, and the advantages and disadvantages of QCs. The final section of the presentation should include a recommendation regarding their adoption at your plants. Prepare to respond to questions and challenges.

In preparing your presentation, refer to the behavioral guidelines for effective presentations at the end of the Skill Learning section and the checklist in the preceding exercise. You will receive feedback based on the Observer's Feedback Form.

A Look at Some of the Evidence

Quality circles, on balance, appear to be making a positive contribution to product quality, profits, morale, and even improved employee attendance (DuBrin, 1985, pp. 174–185). The widespread attention QCs have received in recent years has led logically to their evaluation by both businesspeople and researchers. Here we will rely on several types of evaluation methods, sampling first the positive evidence, and then the negative.

Favorable Outcomes with QCs

Honeywell, a high-technology electronics firm, has become a pioneer in the application of QCs in North America. Honeywell currently operates several hundred QCs in the United States. Typically, about a half-dozen assembly workers are brought together every two weeks by a first-level supervisor or team leader. "We feel this type of participatory management program not only increases productivity," says Joseph Riordan, director of Honeywell Corporate Productivity Services, "but it also upgrades the quality of work life for employees. Line workers feel they are more a part of the action. As a result, we find the quality of work improves and absenteeism is reduced. With this kind of involvement, we have, in many cases, been able to increase the capacity of a line without the addition of tooling or extra shifts."

Honeywell used the quality circle method to manage the problem of winning a renewable bid for a government contract. "Here was a situation," Riordan relates, "where we already had cut our rejects down, where all of the learning had effectively gone out of the process." The problem was assigned to the quality circle representing that particular work area. "They came up with a suggestion for further automating the process that enabled us to improve our competitive position by about 20 percent and win the contract."

In an attempt to determine the appropriateness of QCs to North American firms, a team of researchers set up a one-year field experiment at a metal fabricating facility of an electronics firm.

Eleven quality circles, averaging nine production employees each, were established. Performance was measured by a computerized monitoring system created from the company's existing employee performance reporting system. Both quantity and quality measurements were taken. Employee attitudes were also assessed, using the Motivating Potential Score (MPS) of the Hackman-Oldham Job Diagnostic Survey.

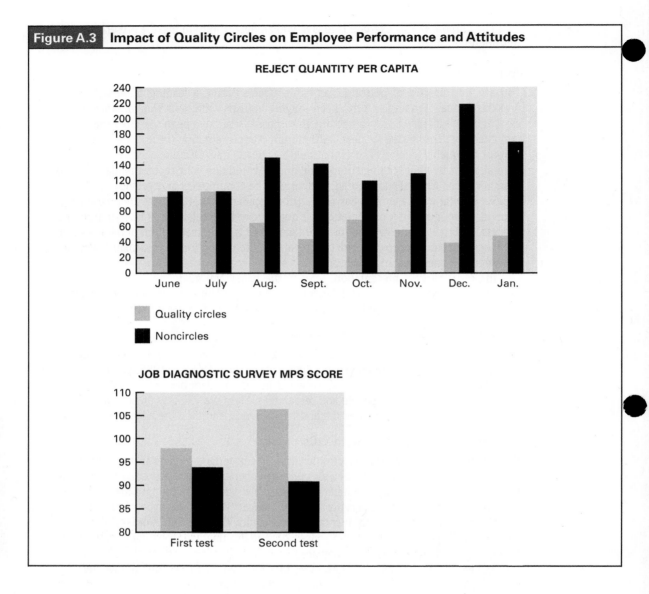

Figure A.3 Impact of Quality Circles on Employee Performance and Attitudes

REJECT QUANTITY PER CAPITA

☐ Quality circles
■ Noncircles

JOB DIAGNOSTIC SURVEY MPS SCORE

The major result of the circle program was its positive impact on reject rate, as shown in the top half of Figure A.3. Reject rates per capita for quality circle participants dropped by one-third to one-half of the former rates by the time the program had run three months. Surprisingly, the reject rates for the control group increased during the same period.

An explanation offered by the researchers for these results is circle members tackled the issues of internal communication as a top priority item. For example, one of the initial projects implemented by the QCs was improving training manuals and procedures, including translating materials into a worker's native language if the worker desired. Careful attention to better training in fundamentals prevented many errors.

Circle members also made fewer errors. In addition, the defective parts the circle members did make tended to be less expensive to scrap or rework into usable parts. The explanation given for these results is circle training instructs employees how to prioritize problems on the basis of dollar impact on the company. The cost savings generated by the lower reject rate represented a 300 percent return on the cost of investment in the program.

The impact of QCs on participants' level of work satisfaction was equally impressive. Results shown in Figure A.3 indicate the Motivating Potential Score (MPS) for the circle participants increased, while the control group showed a decrease. No other changes were present in the work environment that would impact the experimental group differently than the control group. The researchers therefore concluded the improvement in employee job attitudes could be attributed to the circle training program and the problem-solving activity. The job characteristic most influenced by the quality activity was skill variety: the extent to which a job requires a variety of skills.

Negative Outcomes with Quality Circles

Despite the favorable outcomes reported, many negative results have also been reported. A review of the results of the first surge of QC activity in the United States revealed as many as 75 percent of initially successful programs were no longer in operation after a few years. Even Lockheed, one of the American pioneers in this method, had decreased its involvement with quality circles. Robert Cole, a recognized authority on the Japanese workforce, made these pessimistic remarks:

> [The] fact is that the circles do not work very well in many Japanese companies. Even in those plants recognized as having the best operating programs, management knows that perhaps only one-third of the circles are working well, with another third borderline, and one-third simply making no contribution at all. For all of the rhetoric of voluntarism, in a number of companies the workers clearly perceive circle activity as coercive. Japanese companies face a continuing struggle to revitalize circle activity to ensure that it does not degenerate into ritualistic behavior.

A study of quality circles in 29 companies, conducted by Matthew Goodfellow, found only eight of them to be cost-effective in terms of gains in productivity. Management consultant Woodruff Imberman investigated the 21 unsuccessful QC efforts and found four major causes of failure. First, in many firms, the employees intensely disliked management. Their antagonism carried over into the quality circles, which some employees perceived to be a management ploy to reduce overtime and trim the workforce by increasing productivity.

Second, most organizations did a poor job of selling the QCs. Instead of conducting individual discussions with employees, they relied on flip charts, booklets, and formal management presentations. The workers were left wondering, "What's in it for me?"

Third, the supervisors chosen to lead the circles received some training in human relations and group dynamics, but they felt little of this information satisfied the specific needs of their own departments.

Fourth, most of the 21 firms regarded the QC programs merely as a way of improving the efficiency of production techniques. They did not realize QCs cannot succeed unless top management is willing to shift its philosophy toward emphasizing good relations among employees and between management and workforce. This last point hints at the importance of establishing the conditions that allow a quality circle program to succeed.

Key Elements of a Successful Program

Quality circle programs show some variation from company to company, whether these companies are engaged in manufacturing or service. They may differ in how frequently they meet, how much authority is granted to the team leader or supervisor, whether they use a group facilitator in addition to a supervisor, and how much coordination there is with the existing quality-control department. Based on the judgments of several observers, the successful programs have certain elements in common.

PRACTICE

Quality circles work best in firms where good employee-management relations already exist. QCs are not likely to succeed in organizations suffering from acrimonious union-management conflict or high levels of distrust between employees and management.

Top management is committed to the program. Without commitment from top management, the initiation of a QC program is inadvisable. Instead, the director of a circle project should first prepare reports on other companies where QCs have been successful and present them to top management.

Circle leaders use a participative leadership style. Laurie Fitzgerald, a QC consultant, advocates the "leader as a worker for the members" concept. When the circle leader takes on a highly authoritarian role, the members are usually unresponsive.

The right people and the right area are selected. For quality circles to be effective, the program manager has to be enthusiastic, persistent, and hardworking. The facilitator or team leader must be energetic and cooperative. Also, another important step in getting the program off the ground is to select an area of the company where one can expect cooperation and enthusiasm from participants.

Program goals are stated explicitly. Objectives should be made clear in order to avoid confusion or unreasonable expectations from the circle program. Among the goals of QC programs are improving product quality, increasing productivity, improving communications between workers and supervisors, decreasing product costs, improving the quality of work life, and preparing people for future supervisory assignments.

The program is well publicized throughout the firm. Once the program is started, information about it should be disseminated widely throughout the company. Better communication results in less resistance and fewer negative rumors about the program. The content of the communication should be open and positive.

The program starts slowly and grows slowly. A gradual introduction of the program helps expose people to new concepts and helps reduce doubts about its intention and potential merit.

The QC program is customized to meet the needs of the firm. A subtle source of failure in some QC programs is the use of a canned set of procedures that don't fit local circumstances. A QC participant whose work is data processing may have difficulty with the translation of a case from the aerospace industry. A workable compromise is to use standard training as a framework and build on it with the unique problems of the firm in question.

Quality circles are used as a method of employee development. A key purpose of these circles is to foster personal development of the participating workers. If managers intend to install a QC as a tool for their own selfish gain, they would do better not to begin.

Management is willing to grant recognition for ideas originating in the circles. If management attempts to manipulate the circle volunteers or take away from them the credit for improvements, the program will most likely backfire. More will be lost than gained.

Membership is voluntary. As with job enrichment and all forms of participative management, employee preference is an influential factor. Employees who desire to contribute their ideas will generally perform better than employees who are arbitrarily assigned to a QC.

Achievements of quality circles are recognized as results of group, not individual, effort. Recognizing them as such decreases showing off and competitiveness and increases cooperation and interdependence within the group or department. Quality circles, not individual employees, should receive credit for innovations and suggestions for improvement.

Ample training is provided. Program volunteers generally need some training in conference techniques or group dynamics. At a minimum, the circle leader will need skills in group participation methods. Otherwise, he or she will wind up lecturing about topics such as quality improvement and productivity improvement. Leaders and participants will also need training in the use of whatever statistical and problem-solving methods are to be used. Following are eight major problem-solving techniques and their purposes:

1. Brainstorming is used to identify all problems, even those beyond the control of circle members.
2. A check-sheet is used to log problems within the circle's sphere of influence within a certain time frame.
3. A Pareto chart graphically illustrates check-sheet data to identify the most serious problems; that is, the 20 percent of the problems that cause 80 percent of the major mistakes.
4. A cause-and-effect diagram graphically illustrates the cause of a particular problem.
5. Histograms or bar charts are graphed to show the frequency and magnitude of specific problems.
6. Scatter diagrams or "measles charts" identify major defect locations, which show up as dense dot clusters on the pictures of products.
7. Graph-and-control charts monitor a production process and are compared with production samples.
8. Stratification, generally accomplished by inspecting the same products from different production areas, randomizes the sampling process.

Creativity is encouraged. As illustrated above, brainstorming or variations thereof fit naturally into the quality circle method and philosophy. Maintaining an attitude of "anything goes" is particularly important, even if rough ideas must be refined later. If half-processed ideas are shot down by the leader or other members, idea generation will extinguish quickly.

Projects are related to members' actual job responsibilities. Quality circles are not arenas for amateur speculation about other people's work. People make suggestions about improving the quality of work for which they are already responsible. They should, however, be willing to incorporate information from suppliers and customers.

The Arguments For and Against Quality Circles

A major argument for quality circles is they represent a low-cost, efficient vehicle for unleashing the creative potential of employees. In the process, highly desirable ends are achieved, such as improvements in the quality of both products and work life. Quality circles, in fact, are considered part of the quality of work life movement.

Another favorable feature of these circles is they are perceived positively by all—management, workers, unions, and stockholders. A firm contemplating implementing such a program thus runs no risk of either internal or external opposition. (It is conceivable, however, that opposition will be forthcoming if management fails to act on quality circle suggestions.)

Quality circles contribute to organizational effectiveness in another important way. They have emerged as a useful method of developing present and future managers. Recently, a major computing manufacturing firm established a quality circle program. After the program had been operating for two years, the director of training observed the supervisors who were quality circle leaders were significantly more self-confident, knowledgeable, and poised than other supervisors who were attending the regular training program. The director believed the supervisors' involvement in the QC training programs and activities had been the major contributor to this difference.

One major criticism of quality circles is many of them are not cost-effective. Furthermore, even more pessimistic is the criticism that the reported successes of QCs may be attributable to factors other than the actual quality circle program. One explanation is the attention paid to employees by management may be the force behind the gains in productivity and morale (the well-known Hawthorne effect). Another possible explanation of the successes of quality circle programs is the gains are due to improved group dynamics and problem-solving techniques. Therefore, an entire QC program need not be conducted just to achieve these gains.

A discouraging argument has been advanced that quality circles may not be suited to North American workers. Matsushita Electric, a leading user of the quality circle method in Japan, does not use circles in its U.S. plant (located in Chicago) because it does not consider the American worker suited to circle activities. Perhaps Matsushita management believes Americans are too self-oriented to be group oriented.

Quality circles may prove to be breeding grounds for friction and role confusion between the quality-control department and the groups themselves. Unless management carefully defines the relationship of quality circles vis-à-vis the quality-control department, much duplication of effort (and therefore waste of resources) will inevitably result.

Exclusive reliance upon volunteers for the circles may result in the loss of potentially valuable ideas. Many nonassertive people may shy away from participation in the circles despite their having valid ideas for product improvement.

Some employees who volunteer to join quality circles may do so for the wrong reasons. The circle may develop the reputation of being "a good way to get away from the line for a while and enjoy a coffee break and a good bull session." (To counter such an abuse of the quality-circle program, QC group members might monitor the quality of input from their own group members.)

Guidelines for Action

An early strategic step in implementing a quality circle is to clarify relationships between the circle and the formal quality-control department. Otherwise, the quality-control department may perceive the circle as a redundancy or threat. One effective arrangement is for the quality circle to complement the quality-control department; the QC department thus does not become subject to the loss of authority.

Membership in the circle should be voluntary and on a rotating basis. In many instances, a team member will soon run out of fresh ideas for quality improvement. Rotating membership will result in a wider sampling of ideas being generated. Experience suggests that group size should be limited to nine.

Quality circles should be implemented on a pilot basis. As the circle produces results and wins the acceptance of managers and employees alike, it can be expanded as the demand for its output increases.

Do not emphasize quick financial returns or productivity increases from the output of the quality circles. The program should be seen as a long-range project that will raise the quality consciousness of the organization. (Nevertheless, as noted in the report from Honeywell, immediate positive results are often forthcoming.)

Management must make good use of many of the suggestions coming from the quality circle yet still define the limits of the power and authority of the circle. On the one hand, if none of the circle's suggestions are adopted, the circle will lose its effectiveness as an agent for change. Circle members will become discouraged because of their lack of clout. On the other hand, if the circle has too much power and authority, it will be seen as a governing body for technical change. Under the latter circumstances, people may use the circle for political purposes. An individual who wants to get a technical modification authorized may try to influence a member of the quality circle to suggest modification during a circle meeting.

Training in group dynamics and methods of participative management will be particularly helpful. It may also prove helpful at the outset to appoint a group facilitator (an internal or external consultant) who can help the group run more smoothly.

Observer's Feedback Form

RATING
1 = Low
5 = High

Strategy

_____ 1. Identified the general and specific purposes.

_____ 2. Tailored the message to the audience's needs, attitudes, knowledge level, and so forth.

_____ 3. Met the expectations of the audience by using appropriate language and style.

Structure

_____ 4. Began with a forecast of the main ideas and captivated the audience's interest by giving them an important reason to listen.

_____ 5. Chose an appropriate organizational structure; for example, moved from familiar to unfamiliar and simple to complex.

_____ 6. Used transitions, including internal summaries, to signal progress.

_____ 7. Concluded on a high note; reinforced major points; summarized key actions.

Support

_____ 8. Used a variety of supporting information, examples, and so forth, to increase the credibility and understanding of major points.

_____ 9. Used supporting material (both the content and format of evidence and illustrations) appropriate for the audience.

_____ 10. Used effective, simple visual aids to enhance comprehension and retention of the message.

Style in Oral Communication

_____ 11. Used notes to create a conversational style.

_____ 12. Presentation had obviously been well-rehearsed, including the use of visual aids, and so forth.

_____ 13. Conveyed controlled enthusiasm for the subject through the tone of voice, posture, and facial expressions.

_____ 14. Engaged the audience through effective eye contact, physical arrangement of the room, and appropriate gestures.

Style in Written Communication

_____ 15. Document was mechanically precise; that is, it contained no errors that detracted from the message.

_____ 16. Document was factually precise; that is, the content was accurate.

_____ 17. The choice of words communicated the message clearly and unambiguously.

_____ 18. The tone matched the topic and the audience (e.g., formality, emotion, directness).

_____ 19. Used the appropriate format for the type of correspondence.

Supplement: Questions and Answers

_____ 20. Handled questions and challenges thoughtfully, candidly, and assertively.

_____ 21. Responded to objections in an orderly manner; for example, restated the objection, restated your position, offered further support for your position, and explained the significance of your rebuttal.

_____ 22. Maintained control of the meeting by balancing the demands of specific individuals with the interests of the group and keeping the discussion focused on the issues.

- Planning and Conducting Interviews
- Specific Types of Organizational Interviews
- Summary and Behavioral Guidelines

SKILL *PRACTICE* ⓘ

- Evaluating the New Employee-Orientation Program
- Performance Appraisal Interview with Chris Jakobsen
- Employment-Selection Interview at Smith Farley Insurance

B

Conducting Interviews

SKILL DEVELOPMENT OBJECTIVES

- ADOPT GENERAL GUIDELINES FOR EFFECTIVE INTERVIEWS
- APPLY APPROPRIATE GUIDELINES FOR INFORMATION-GATHERING INTERVIEWS
- UTILIZE APPROPRIATE GUIDELINES FOR EMPLOYMENT-SELECTION INTERVIEWS
- IMPLEMENT APPROPRIATE GUIDELINES FOR PERFORMANCE-APPRAISAL INTERVIEWS

SKILL *LEARNING*

Planning and Conducting Interviews

Except for conversations, interviews are perhaps the most frequently occurring form of communication (Sincoff & Goyer, 1984); they certainly occur regularly in organizations. Individuals interview to obtain a position; they interview to gather information to perform their jobs; and managers interview subordinates to review their performance and provide counseling and coaching.

Interviews are so common they are often taken for granted. People view interviews as simply conversations during which information is gathered. While interviews are similar to conversations, there are important differences. An **interview** is a specialized form of communication conducted for a specific task-related purpose (Downs, Smeyak, & Martin, 1980; Lopez, 1975). Indeed, one reason why some managers perform poorly as interviewers is they treat this "purposeful communication" too casually, as though it were merely a conversation. As a result of poor planning and lack of attention to managing the interview process, they fail to accomplish their purpose and often alienate the interviewee in the process.

These outcomes are illustrated in the following counseling interview between Joe Van Orden, director of management services, and Kyle Isenbarger, a management consultant on his staff (DuBrin, 1981).

JOE: Kyle, I have scheduled this meeting with you because I want to talk about certain aspects of your work. My comments are not all favorable.

KYLE: Since you have formal authority over me, I guess I don't have much choice. Go ahead.

JOE: I'm not a judge reading a verdict to you. I want your input.

KYLE: But you called the meeting; go ahead with your complaints. Particularly any with foundation. I remember once when we were having lunch you told me you didn't like the fact I wore a brown suit with a blue shirt. I would put that in the category of unfounded.

JOE: I'm glad you brought up appearance. I think you present a substandard impression to clients. A consultant is supposed to look sharp, particularly at the rates we charge clients. You often present the impression you cannot afford good clothing. Your pants are baggy. Your ties are unstylish and often foodstained.

KYLE: The firm may charge those high rates, but the money I receive does not allow me to purchase fancy clothing. Besides, I have very little interest in trying to dazzle clients with my clothing. I have heard no complaints from them.

JOE: Nevertheless, I think your appearance should be more businesslike. Now, let's talk about another concern. A routine audit of your expense account shows a practice I think is improper. You charged one client for a Thursday night dinner for three consecutive weeks, yet your airline ticket receipt shows you returned home at three in the afternoon each week. That kind of behavior is unprofessional. How do you explain your charges for these phantom dinners?

KYLE: The flight ticket may say 3 P.M., but with our unpredictable weather, the flight could very well be delayed. If I eat at the airport, then my wife won't have to run the risk of preparing a dinner for me that goes to waste. Food is very expensive.

JOE: But how can you eat dinner at 3 P.M. at the airport?

KYLE: I consider any meal after one in the afternoon to be dinner.

JOE: Okay for now. I want to comment on your reports to clients. They are much more careless than they should be. I know you are capable of more meticulous work. I saw an article you prepared for publication that was first-rate and professional. Yet on one report you misspelled the name of the client company. That's unacceptable.

KYLE: A good secretary should have caught that mistake. Besides, I never claimed I was able to write perfect reports. There are only so many hours in the working day to spend on writing up reports.

Effective interviews don't just happen. Like other purposeful communication activities, interviews must be properly planned and executed. To help you become an effective interviewer, this supplement includes a series of guidelines, organized according to the schema shown in Figure B.1. First, we present broad guidelines for planning and conducting interviews in general. These guidelines are divided into two steps: planning the interview and conducting the interview. Following this discussion, we will give more specific guidelines for conducting specialized interviews with limited purposes: gathering information, selecting new employees, and reviewing subordinate performance.

PLANNING THE INTERVIEW
Establish the Purpose and Agenda

As is the case with any kind of planned communication event, you need to define clearly your purpose for holding the interview. In an interview, as in an oral presentation, ask yourself what it is you want to accomplish. Do you want to gather information? Persuade? Counsel? Evaluate? Not only do you need to consider what you want to accomplish in terms of the *content* of the interview, you must also consider the *relationship* you want to develop with the other participant. Consider who your interview partner is and how what you say will affect the already existing relationship. This resembles the process of adapting your message to your audience in an oral presentation

but is somewhat easier since there is only one member in your interview "audience." Also consider the situation in which the interview will occur. Are participants under pressures of deadlines? Can you arrange not to be interrupted?

Once you've determined your purpose, develop an agenda. Consider what kinds of information you need to obtain with respect to your purpose. Based on this, write out a list of topics that need to be covered in the interview. While these topics do not have to be listed in any particular order, you may want to prioritize them.

Create Good Questions That Encourage Information Sharing

Questions arise out of your purpose and agenda and are the fundamental means by which you obtain information in an interview. Any interviewer can ask questions; only well-prepared interviewers ask effective questions—ones that elicit the information they need. Make sure the questions are worded clearly and they ask for the information you want. Adapting to your interviewee is critical. Phrase your questions in language the interviewee can understand and in ways that will enhance your relationship with that person.

Different types of questions can be used for different effects and different types of information-gathering purposes. **Open questions** such as, "How is your work going?" or "How has the new regulation affected department morale?" elicit general information. Use open questions when you want to let the interviewee talk without restriction. They allow interviewees freedom to discuss how they feel, what their priorities are, and how much they know about a topic. Thus, open questions are useful for developing rapport. Remembering the answers to open questions is a problem, particularly if the interviewee talks on and on. Open questions are also time-consuming, and using them too often makes it difficult for the interviewer to control the interview. However, if you are looking for broad, general information, ask open questions.

If, on the other hand, you need specific information, ask closed questions. **Closed questions** such as, "Where were you last employed?" or "Would you rather work on Project A or Project Z?" restrict the possible answers an interviewee can give. They are appropriate when you have limited time or want to clarify a point made in an answer to an open question. Table B.1 suggests when to use open or closed questions.

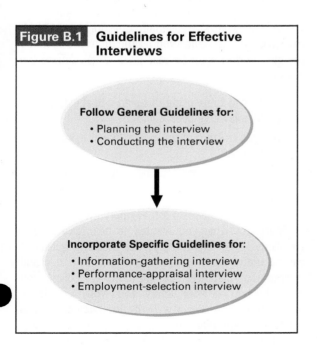

| Figure B.1 | Guidelines for Effective Interviews |

Follow General Guidelines for:
- Planning the interview
- Conducting the interview

Incorporate Specific Guidelines for:
- Information-gathering interview
- Performance-appraisal interview
- Employment-selection interview

Table B.1 When to Use Open and Closed Questions

Use open questions when you want to:

- Discover the interviewee's priorities.
- Discover the interviewee's frame of reference.
- Let the interviewee talk through his or her opinions without constraints.
- Ascertain the depth of the interviewee's knowledge.
- Ascertain how articulate the interviewee is.

Use closed questions when you want to:

- Save time, energy, and money.
- Maintain control over the interview situation.
- Obtain very specific information from the interviewee.
- Encourage the interviewee to reconstruct a specific event.
- Encourage a shy person to talk.
- Avoid extensive explanations on the part of the interviewee.
- Clarify a point made in answer to an open question.

SOURCE: *Adapted from Downs, Smeyak, & Martin, 1980.*

As you plan your questions, pay close attention to how the questions are worded. Often, an unprepared interviewer will ask questions that are difficult to answer or prevent open, honest answers. One example is the **double-barreled question**:

- If there's anything that would make you stay, what would it be?
- If you had no choice but to use this system, how would you use it productively?
- Why should we adopt this insurance plan when none of our competitors has adopted it?

Each of these questions assumes a condition that the interviewee may not agree with but then calls for the interviewee to support or defend the condition. The first question assumes the interviewee is looking for a reason to stay; the second assumes the system can be used productively; the third suggests something is wrong with the plan. Such questions may lead to hypothetical answers that don't reflect the interviewee's honest position.

Another potentially problematic question is the **false bipolar question**. A bipolar question offers the interviewee two choices: "Did you vote yes or no on the union contract?" This can be a legitimate and appropriate question. However, suppose you asked this question: "Do you approve or disapprove of overtime work?" Most people do not totally approve or disapprove of overtime work; yet this question forces interviewees to choose from limited, or false, options, neither of which likely represents their true stand on the issue. Thus, if you use bipolar questions, make sure the options you offer are the only two possible options; otherwise, you will obtain inaccurate information.

A final type of problematic question is the **leading question**, in which you let the interviewee know the answer you want to hear by how you phrase the question:

- Don't you think using this plan will alleviate the problems we've been having?
- Are you in favor of this policy like all your coworkers?
- Of course, you want the best for your family, don't you?

It would not take an astute interviewee very long to figure out what you wanted to hear, and so you are likely to get biased responses. Leading questions can be useful when a biased answer is intended and desired. For instance, the question "Of course you want the best for your family, don't you?" would be useful in a sales interview if the interviewer tries to persuade a potential buyer to buy a set of encyclopedias. However, if you do not realize you have asked a

Table B.2 Rewording Badly Constructed Questions

DOUBLE-BARRELED QUESTION	PROBLEM	BETTER QUESTION
1. If there's anything that would make you stay, what would it be?	The question ignores the reason behind the interviewee's decision and implies it can be changed.	Why do you want to leave our organization? (Let interviewee respond.) Is there anything I can do to change your mind?
2. If you had no choice but to use this system, how would you use it productively?	The question avoids an open analysis of the system and forces the interviewee to defend it.	What do you feel are the benefits of this system? (Let interviewee respond.) What do you feel are the disadvantages of this system?
3. Why should we adopt this insurance plan when none of our competitors has adopted it?	The question raises a suspicion something is wrong with the plan and urges the interviewee to put the suspicion to rest rather than to evaluate the plan.	Do you think we should adopt this insurance? (Let interviewee respond.) Do you think it offers us new benefits? (Let interviewee respond.) Have any of our competitors adopted it?

FALSE BIPOLAR QUESTION	PROBLEM	BETTER QUESTION
1. Do you prefer working with people or working alone?	The question assumes there are only two possible choices.	Do you work well with other people? (Can be followed with appropriate probe.)
2. Do you approve or disapprove of the union contract?	The question assumes there are only two ways to view the issue.	What are your feelings concerning the union contract?

LEADING QUESTION	PROBLEM	BETTER QUESTION
1. Don't you think using this plan will alleviate the problems we've been having?	The question identifies the expected answer, making it difficult for the interviewee to disagree.	Do you think this plan will be useful in alleviating the problems we've been having?
2. Are you in favor of this policy like all your coworkers?	The question places interviewee in the position of siding with the "right" side.	What is your attitude toward this policy?
3. Of course, you want the best for your family, don't you?	The question associates response with a desirable goal (getting the best for the family), making it difficult for the interviewee to say no.	This product offers you some real advantages. Could I take some of your time to tell you about them?

leading question, you will not know whether you are receiving a biased answer, which can create a serious problem. Table B.2 offers ways to reword these three types of badly constructed questions.

Structure the Interview Using Interviewing Aids

After determining the purpose and agenda, and after formulating your questions, the next step in preparing for an interview is to develop a structure. To do this, you need to think about three things: the interview guide, the questioning sequence, and transitions. The interview guide is an outline of the topics and subtopics you want to cover, usually with specific questions

listed under each heading. In other words, it is the finalized version of the agenda. Alternative interview guide formats will be discussed later.

While you are constructing the interview guide, you will also need to be concerned with the sequence of questions; that is, how they will interconnect. The two most common types of question sequences are the **funnel sequence** and the **inverted funnel sequence**.

The funnel sequence begins with general questions and then moves toward increasingly specific questions. The inverted funnel sequence reverses this order, beginning with specific questions and moving toward more open questions toward the end. Table B.3 shows examples of these two sequences. Your choice of which sequence to use depends on what you want

Table B.3	Funnel and Inverted Funnel Question Sequences

Funnel: From General to Specific

How do you feel about the new regulations concerning smoking in the building?

Are these regulations fair?

How are these regulations curtailing smoking among employees?

Inverted Funnel: From Specific to General

How are the new smoking regulations curtailing smoking among employees?

Do you think these regulations are fair?

In general, how do you feel about these new regulations?

Use the funnel sequence when:

• You want to discover the interviewee's frame of reference.

• You want to avoid leading the interviewee.

• You want to maximize your ability to probe issues.

• The interviewee is willing to talk about the issues.

Use the interverted funnel sequence when:

• You want to get at specific facts before general reactions.

• You want to motivate a reluctant interviewee.

• You want to jog the interviewee's memory.

SOURCE: *Adapted from Downs et al., 1980.*

to accomplish in the interview. Table B.3 also summarizes when you should use each of these sequences, depending on your goals.

After establishing the sequence of your questions, you should consider what kinds of transitions you can use to help the interviewee follow along. The transitions in an interview perform the same function as transitions in an oral presentation: They help listeners maintain focus and keep them aware of where the speaker is in terms of the overall organization. Transitions are difficult to prepare ahead in unstructured interviews, yet a good interviewer will keep in mind transitions should be used when a topic change occurs. A simple statement such as, "I see what you're saying about that situation. Do you think you could help me with another issue?" allows you to move from one topic into the next. You may also use a brief summary of the interviewee's responses to wrap up one topic before moving to the next one.

Plan the Setting to Enhance Rapport

The interview location can have a major impact on the interview atmosphere and interview outcome. If you hold the interview in your office or an organizational meeting room, you will create a formal atmosphere. On the other hand, if you conduct the interview in a more neutral area, such as a restaurant, the climate will be more relaxed. The choice of setting depends on your goals for the interview. The most important point to remember about the setting is that, if at all possible, you should try to hold the interview in a setting that will be conducive to encouraging the kind of communication you seek.

Anticipate Problems and Prepare Responses

As you prepare for an interview, you should consider what kinds of problems you might encounter. Imagine how the interviewee might respond to what you have to ask, and prepare for his or her objections and questions. Consider the personality of the interviewee and how you might have to adapt to either draw the person out or to control his or her tendency to dominate. Anticipate how much time you will need to ask your questions and how much time your interviewee has to give you. Each interview will offer unique problems. If you can plan for some of these situations, you will be able to handle

Table B.4 Interview Preparation Checklist

1. Have I determined my general purpose?
2. Have I written out my specific purposes and agenda?
   a. Do I know exactly what I want to accomplish in terms of content?
   b. Do I know exactly what I want to accomplish in terms of the relationship with the interviewee?
3. Do my questions all relate to my purposes and agenda?
4. Are my questions clearly worded in language the interviewee can understand?
5. Are my questions worded in an unbiased manner?
6. Have I chosen an appropriate interview structure for the situation?
7. Have I chosen an appropriate question sequence for the interview situation?
8. Have I developed potential transitions to be used in the interview?
9. Have I chosen a physical setting suited to the topics and the interviewee?
10. Have I planned ways to deal with problems that could develop during the interview?

them better during the actual interview than if you had not considered them at all.

Table B.4 provides a checklist for helping prepare for an interview.

CONDUCTING THE INTERVIEW

Couple thorough preparation with sensitive implementation. Because an interview is an interpersonal communication situation, in this section we will first briefly review the concept of supportive communication as it applies to interviews. Then we will look at the three stages of the interview—the introduction, body, and conclusion—and discuss the functions of each. We will offer suggestions for developing the necessary skills to conduct an interview effectively. Finally, we will discuss ways of recording the interview information.

Establish and Maintain a Supportive Communication Climate

The climate of the interview refers to the tone of the interview and the general atmosphere in which the interview occurs. An interview, like any other interpersonal communication event, should be a supportive interaction, one in which participants feel free to communicate accurately. As the interviewer, you set the climate of the interview in the introduction when you begin to build rapport with the interviewee. In general, you should seek to build a comfortable, open

climate, free of incongruence. Maintaining a supportive and productive climate requires you constantly analyze and adapt to the interaction as it occurs. When you sense the climate is no longer supportive, move away from the content level of the interview and address the relational level. Consider this excerpt from an information-gathering interview:

INTERVIEWER: Thanks for taking the time to speak with me today.

INTERVIEWEE: Oh, it's no problem at all. What can I do for you?

INTERVIEWER: Well, I was wondering if you could tell me a little about the incident that occurred on the shop floor last week. First, do you have any idea how it started?

INTERVIEWEE: No, not really. I was doing my job and then, all of a sudden, the two of them were at it.

INTERVIEWER: I see. You didn't hear them talking before they began to fight?

INTERVIEWEE: No. Like I said, it seemed to start out of the blue.

INTERVIEWER: Weren't you paying attention?

INTERVIEWEE: How was I to know they were going to fight?!

By now, the questions are obviously beginning to irritate the interviewee. The interviewer has continued to probe an issue that the interviewee seems to think has already been covered sufficiently. The interviewer should move away from this one point and attempt to ease the interviewee's discomfort before continuing.

> INTERVIEWER: You're right. You really weren't in a position to anticipate this situation. Perhaps, though, you could describe to me what happened after the fight.

At this point, the interviewee may be hesitant to disclose fully. The interviewer may have to continue to strengthen relational support until the interviewee appears to be comfortable in answering the questions.

A supportive climate is not maintained solely by verbal behaviors. Listening analytically is also essential to maintaining the climate of an interview. If you do not show you are listening and responding to what the interviewee is saying, he or she will not want to continue talking with you. In general, you should listen for *comprehension* of the content of the interview, for *empathy* with the interviewee, and for *evaluation* of information and feelings (Stewart & Cash, 1985).

Introduce the Interview

Supportive communication begins immediately in the introduction, where you establish the tone and set the climate of the interview. You should greet the interviewee in such a way as to build positive rapport. The impressions created in the initial minutes of an interview are crucial to its success (Stewart & Cash, 1985). Therefore, you should try to convey as favorable an impression as possible. After the greeting, you need to motivate the interviewee to participate willingly in the interview. Some common ways of doing this are to ask for the interviewee's help or tell the interviewee why he or she was chosen as a source of information. Finally, the introduction should contain an orientation to the total interview. You should tell an interviewee: (1) the purpose of the interview, (2) how he or she will help meet that purpose, and (3) how the information obtained during the interview will be used. The introduction should end with a transition into the body of the interview. Using a transition statement, such as, "Now then, let me begin by asking..." or "Now that you understand what's going to happen during the next few minutes, let's move on to the questions" tells the interviewee the "real" interview is about to begin.

Conduct the Body of the Interview

Generally, the body of the interview will follow your interview guide, which is a predetermined sequence of questions. There are three types of guides: structured, semistructured, and unstructured. If the interview guide is structured, you will simply read the questions on the guide and record the interviewee's answers. A semistructured guide lists several recommended questions under each topic. The interviewer then selects the most appropriate questions for a specific candidate. A sample interview guide for a semistructured employment interview is shown in Table B.5.

If the interview guide is unstructured, then you will use the guide only as an agenda. For example, an unstructured interview guide for a termination interview might simply list a few general topics for discussion, for example, "What did he or she like and dislike about the work and the company?" "Why is he or she leaving?" "Any suggestions for improvement?" Particularly in an unstructured interview, an interviewee will need encouragement to answer your questions as fully as possible. In order to encourage complete answers, you will need to follow his or her initial responses with probing questions. Probing well depends directly on your ability to listen well and analyze the content and relational information the interviewee offers you. Probing questions are rarely planned ahead because you cannot predict how the interviewee will respond to your questions. You will want to probe when you feel that, for whatever reason, you are receiving an inadequate response to your question.

The kind of probing you do will depend on the responses given by your interviewee and the kind of information you are looking for. If you feel the response is superficial or inadequate due to lack of information, you should use an **elaboration probe**, such as:

- ❏ "Tell me more about that issue."
- ❏ "Why do you suppose it happened that way?"
- ❏ "Was there anything else going on at the time?"

If you need to clarify the information given by the interviewee, use a **clarification probe**, such as:

- ❏ "What does job satisfaction mean to you?"
- ❏ "You said you are unhappy with this policy. Can you tell me specifically what aspects make you feel this way?"
- ❏ "Earlier you mentioned you enjoyed working with people. Can you provide a specific example?"

A **reflective probe** is also used when you want elaboration or clarification. It is nondirective in nature

Table B.5 Sample Interview Questions for an Employment Interview

EDUCATION	WORK EXPERIENCE	SELF-EVALUATION
• What was there about your major that appealed to you?	• How did you obtain your current job?	• What do you know about our industry or company?
• What was your most rewarding experience in college?	• What duties occupy most of your time?	• What interests you about our product or service?
• What subjects were the most difficult for you to master? Why?	• What part of your work do you like the most and the least?	• What is your long-term career objective?
• If you were starting college all over again, what courses would you take?	• What has been your greatest frustration and your greatest joy?	• What are your greatest strengths and weaknesses?
• What difficulties did you experience in getting along with other students and faculty?	• What things about your supervisor did you like and dislike?	• What have you done that has demonstrated initiative and willingness to work hard?
• What did you learn from your extracurricular activities?	• What criticisms of your work have you received?	• What do you think determines a person's progress in a good company?
		• What are your plans for self-improvement during this year?
		• What are the three most important things in your life?

and generally mirrors or repeats some aspect of the answer the interviewee just gave you:

- ❏ "You think, then, this policy will work?"
- ❏ "Are you saying your supervisor doesn't offer the kind of supervision you need?"
- ❏ "Is it correct to assume you would be willing to relocate?"

If the interviewee does not answer your question, you may need to use a **repetition probe**. Simply paraphrase the question or repeat it verbatim. If you want the interviewee to keep on talking freely, use *silence* to encourage him or her to do so. Silence tends to communicate you expect more from the interviewee. Be careful not to wait too long, though; give an interviewee enough time to think but not enough time to become uncomfortable. Responses such as "I see," "Hmmmm," and "Okay, go on" are nondirective and nonevaluative ways of encouraging the interviewee to speak. Table B.6 summarizes these probes and when to use them.

The effective use of probing questions is perhaps the most important skill an interviewer can develop. It is also the most difficult to develop. Too often, an interviewer leaves an interview and thinks about all the things that could have been discussed if only the topic had been followed up with appropriate probes. Or perhaps the interview was ineffective because the interviewer probed into irrelevant topics and thus spent too much time gathering relatively useless information. An effective interviewer needs to learn when to probe and when to stop. If you have planned appropriately, you will be aware of the issues you want to cover and at what depth. Follow your interviewee's cues as well as your agenda in determining when and how much to probe issues.

Conclude the Interview

The third stage of the interview is the conclusion. When you conclude an interview, you should accomplish four purposes. First, be sure you indicate explicitly the interview is about to end. Say something such as, "Well, that's all the questions I have" or "You've been very helpful." This helps the interviewee understand if he or she has any questions, they should be asked now. Second, try to summarize the information you obtained. This serves as a check on the accuracy of the information you have just obtained: the interviewee can correct your impressions if they seem to be in error. Third, let the interviewee know what's going

Table B.6	Types of Probes and When to Use Them

- Use an *elaboration* probe when an answer seems superficial or inadequate in some way:

  INTERVIEWER: How have you been able to adapt to your new job responsibilities?

  INTERVIEWEE: Well, each day I find myself challenged by something new.

  INTERVIEWER: Why don't you tell me more about a specific challenge.

- Use a *clarification* probe when you need to clarify information given by the interviewee:

  INTERVIEWER: How do you feel about working overtime?

  INTERVIEWEE: Well, it's okay some of the time.

  INTERVIEWER: Can you tell me specifically when you would be willing to work overtime?

- Use a *reflective* probe when you want elaboration or clarification but want to obtain it in a nondirective manner:

  INTERVIEWER: So how are you adapting to your new responsibilities?

  INTERVIEWEE: Well, each day I find myself challenged by something new.

  INTERVIEWER: Really? Something new each day?

- Use a *repetition* probe when the interviewee doesn't answer your question:

  INTERVIEWER: What do you believe to be the most difficult aspect of your job?

  INTERVIEWEE: Well, that's not an easy question. My supervisor says I have problems with meeting productivity quotas.

  INTERVIEWER: But what do *you* believe to be the most difficult aspect of your job?

- Use *silence* when you want to encourage the interviewee to continue talking:

  INTERVIEWER: Do you think we should continue our policy concerning absenteeism?

  INTERVIEWEE: Yes, I do.

  INTERVIEWER: (pauses for 10 seconds)

  INTERVIEWEE: Yes, I think it's good policy because...

to happen next: Will you need to meet again? Will you make a report? Finally, make sure you continue to build the relationship by expressing appreciation for his or her time and thoughtful responses.

Record the Information

While you may have planned the interview perfectly and asked all the right questions and probes, if you cannot remember accurately the information obtained, the interview cannot be considered a success. After all, you prepared and conducted the interview to get information, not simply because you wanted to have a conversation with someone. The first point you need to recognize concerning remembering interview information is simple: Memory alone will not work. Relying solely on memory leaves open the possibility of forgetting the information or adjusting it to meet your own needs. Even if you summarize the interview

as soon as it is over, you run the risk of reinterpreting the information in ways the interviewee did not mean. However, if summarizing the interview is your preferred choice, make sure you write your summary immediately after the interview. Additionally, you might want to use your interview guide as a basis for summarizing: Review your questions and write out the interviewee's answers.

A better way to remember information is to take notes during the interview. Make sure you advise the interviewee you will take notes. Take notes as unobtrusively as possible so as not to make the interviewee uncomfortable. Learn how to write notes while still maintaining eye contact with the interviewee. This is a difficult skill to master, but it can be done; journalists use this skill frequently with great success. Develop your own shorthand so you are, in fact, taking notes and not recording the interview verbatim. If you need a verbatim account of the interview, then you should use a tape recorder. First ask the interviewee if he or she minds being tape-recorded. Keep the recorder out of sight if possible so neither you nor the interviewee feels threatened by it. One final way to help you remember the interview information is to have a second interviewer participate in the interview. After the interview, your discussion will function as a check on each other's memory of what occurred.

Specific Types of Organizational Interviews

The information presented in the preceding sections will help you plan and conduct almost any type of interview. However, there are some special types to plan and consider. In this section, we will briefly describe the most common types of organizational interviews and apply the general principles presented earlier to specific issues and circumstances.

INFORMATION-GATHERING INTERVIEWS

The information-gathering interview is the one most frequently held in organizations and is also the one that is most like a conversation. You might conduct this type of interview when you need to gather facts about an issue or to help in a problem-solving situation. If you treat these fact-finding missions as interviews, you will be in a better position to gather accurate, useful information because you will take the time to plan ahead. Clearly, you need to follow the planning steps discussed above: decide on a general purpose and create an agenda; develop questions; develop the structure of the interview; plan the setting; and anticipate problems.

Furthermore, the information-gathering interview is the only interview for which you can choose the expert. In other organizational interviews, such as the selection interview or the performance-appraisal interview, you have little choice of whom you will see. However, when you want to gather information about some topic or problem, you choose the interviewee. This choice is based on two factors: who *can* give you the information you need and who is *willing* to give you this information (Stano & Reinsch, 1982). Too often, interviewers will talk to interviewees who are willing but who do not have the necessary information. For instance, suppose your organization is considering the implementation of a flextime work schedule and you have been assigned to write a feasibility

report. While you may get some interesting opinions from a colleague on the advantages of such a schedule, it would be better if you could find an expert on flextime for your interview. On the other hand, if you wanted to find out how well received such a change would be, then you would talk to colleagues rather than an expert.

The nature of an information-gathering interview is such that the interviewee may not realize he or she is being interviewed. Thus, it may be difficult to keep the interviewee on track and responsive to your questions. More so than in any other interview, you as the interviewer must remain flexible and adaptive to your interviewee. Choose a physical setting that will encourage talk and provide an appropriate climate. The funnel sequence works well in information-gathering interviews because of its ability to immediately elicit general information and the interviewee's feelings on the subject. However, the inverted funnel may be a better choice if you will be interviewing a number of people on the same topic and you need to maintain consistency in evaluating their responses.

EMPLOYMENT-SELECTION INTERVIEWS

The employment interview is used to help current organizational members choose new members. During the selection interview, the interviewer tries to assess whether job candidates will fit into the organization and if they have the appropriate skills for the job. In addition, the interviewer often tries to sell the organization itself to the interviewee. Questions asked during the selection interview address four general topics: prior work experience, education and training, personality characteristics, and related activities and interests. The nature of the job and the interviewee will dictate which topics will be emphasized.

As Table B.7 shows, there are three sources of information you should review when creating questions for a selection interview:

1. Review the *job description* to assess the technical skills and experience needed by the person. Also review the job environment to determine the desirable personal qualities required. Create your questions based on these reviews; avoid asking merely generic questions.

2. Look at the *evaluation form* your company uses to assess prospective employees. Make sure some of your questions deal with the topics on this evaluation form. For instance, if one

Table B.7	Formulating Selection Interview Questions

- Use the *job description* to formulate questions concerning task-related skills and personality characteristics.
- Use the selection interview *evaluation form* to formulate questions that can help you assess the applicant on the basis of your organization's general criteria for employees.
- Use the applicant's *résumé* and *cover letter* to formulate questions concerning the applicant's specific skills and prior work experience.

of the topics on this form is communication skills, create questions that specifically address this subject. In this case, you may want to ask the applicant about his or her writing skills and how he or she has used them in the past.

3. One final piece of information you should use for developing questions for a selection interview is the applicant's *résumé* and *cover letter*. Read these documents carefully. If there are gaps in time between jobs, ask the applicant about them. If the information on the résumé is too general, develop questions to get at the specifics. Remember most people create résumés with a very specific goal in mind: to obtain an interview. Therefore, the information tends to be a summary of all the good aspects of that person's career to date. Additionally, all information tends to be written in glowing language. Be prepared to reach beyond this language to obtain clarifying information. For example, suppose you came across this line in a cover letter: "I've had years of experience in leadership positions." Clearly, you would want to ask this applicant for more specific information: "How many years?" "What kinds of positions were these?" "What were your specific leadership responsibilities?"

In constructing interview questions, be sure to include some that focus on specific experiences. For instance, you might want to ask something such as, "Can you tell me about a time when you successfully met a goal you set?" The interviewee may be reluctant to be specific, but you should probe until the interviewee offers you useful, specific, behavioral information.

Why is behavioral information so important? Many experts believe the best way to assess future job performance is to assess past behavior: Past behavior predicts future performance. If you can find out how the interviewee behaved in real situations in the past that are similar to those he or she is likely to face in your organization, you can determine if his or her style will fit into your organization and work well with other members.

Take care that you ask a balanced series of questions: Ask for negative information as well as positive. This will help you obtain a well-rounded picture of the interviewee and also expose hidden bias. For instance, you might want to follow the positive question with something like: "Well, now tell me about a time when you failed to meet a goal you set." Again, make sure the person gives you specific behavioral information.

In conclusion, remember your primary purpose in a selection interview is to find a person who is qualified for a particular opening in your organization. Table B.8 details a six-step process (using the acronym PEOPLE) used by a major firm to help interviewers accomplish this purpose. It follows the general interviewing model outlined in the first half of this supplement.

PERFORMANCE-APPRAISAL INTERVIEWS

The performance-appraisal interview is usually part of a larger professional appraisal system. The goal of this system is to evaluate a member of an organization and often to provide feedback to a subordinate concerning ways to improve job performance. While every organization differs in the specifics of carrying out the performance-appraisal system, there are some common aspects.

Generally, prior to the performance-appraisal interview, written evaluations are prepared by the subordinate, the superior, or both people. There are any number of types of evaluation forms, including an essay form, on which the manager writes a description of the subordinate's work, with no real set format; *forced-choice ratings*, in which the manager chooses a statement from many which describes the subordinate in one area; or a *graphic rating scale*, in which the manager rates the subordinate on various areas on a 1–7 numerical scale. In most cases, though, you will be asked to back up your assessment of the subordinate with specific and concrete information. For instance, if you are using a graphic rating scale and indicate the employee performed unsatisfactorily, you should write out in objective terms why you have made this assessment. The subordinate has a right to

Table B.8	Selection Interview Format (PEOPLE-Oriented Process)

P = Prepare

  1. Review application, résumé, transcripts, and other background information.

  2. Prepare both general and individual-specific questions.

  3. Prepare suitable physical arrangements.

E = Establish Rapport

  1. Try to make applicant comfortable.

  2. Convey genuine interest.

  3. Communicate supportive attitude with voice and manner.

O = Obtain Information

  1. Ask questions.

  2. Probe.

  3. Listen carefully.

  4. Observe the person (dress, mannerisms, body language).

P = Provide Information

  1. Describe current and future job opportunities.

  2. Sell positive features of firm.

  3. Respond to applicant's questions.

L = Lead to Close

  1. Clarify responses.

  2. Provide opportunity for final applicant input.

  3. Explain what happens next.

E = Evaluate

  1. Assess match between technical qualifications and job requirements.

  2. Judge personal qualities (leadership, maturity, team orientation).

  3. Make a recommendation.

LEARNING

know, and you have the responsibility to back up your decisions with evidence.

It is the responsibility of the interviewer to prepare the structure of the performance-appraisal interview. The interviewer should set a definite time and place for the interview, considering the effects these choices will have on the interview and the interviewee. The interviewer must decide on the general purpose of the interview and the agenda. Common topics that are often brought up in performance-appraisal interviews include job knowledge, job performance, job goals, career goals and opportunities, and interpersonal skills.

The difficult aspect of the performance-appraisal interview is that people tend to shy away from evaluating others or being evaluated in face-to-face situations. Both participants in a performance-appraisal interview may be apprehensive. As the interviewer, you need to reassure the interviewee that you are conducting the performance-appraisal interview as a means of assisting in the interviewee's development. Keep in mind that people do not like to be criticized, and balance your criticisms with reassurances and commendations.

In conducting a performance-appraisal interview, you must decide beforehand on your objectives. The

Table B.9	Types of Performance-Appraisal Interviews
Tell-and-Sell Interview	
Used for purely evaluative purposes. Manager tells the employee the evaluation and then persuades the employee to follow recommendations for improvement.	
Tell-and-Listen Interview	
Used for purely evaluative purposes. Manager tells the employee the evaluation and then listens to the employee's reactions to the evaluation in a nonjudgmental manner.	
Problem-Solving Interview	
Used for employee-development purposes. Manager does not offer evaluation but lets employee decide his or her weak areas and works with employee to develop plan for improvement.	
Mixed-Model Interview	
Used for both evaluative and development purposes. Manager begins interview with problem-solving session and concludes with a more directive tell-and-sell approach.	

objectives should then dictate the form of the interview. In general, three types of appraisal interviews seek to meet specific objectives (Maier, 1958), and a fourth type can be used to meet multiple objectives (Beer, 1987). These interview types are summarized in Table B.9.

The first type of appraisal interview is called the *tell-and-sell* interview. This approach is evaluative in nature. First, you *tell* the subordinate how you have evaluated him or her, and then you *sell* the subordinate on the ways you have chosen to improve his or her performance. This type of interview should be used when you must be very clear about your expectations. This format is also effective with young employees who find it difficult to evaluate themselves, with very loyal employees or those who strongly identify with the organization or the appraiser, and with employees who do not want to have a say in how to develop their job and role in the organization (Downs et al., 1980).

If, however, you want to let the subordinate respond to your evaluation, you would use the *tell-and-listen* appraisal format. In this interview, you first *tell* the employee your evaluation; then you *listen* to his or her reactions without displaying any agreement or disagreement. The objective of this interview is evaluative, but you also want to hear the subordinate's viewpoints and work with the subordinate to help him or her accept your evaluation. Active listening directed at helping the subordinate work through his or her feelings about the evaluation and past performance will help you successfully complete a tell-and-listen appraisal. This type of interview works best with people

who have a high need to participate in their jobs, with interviewees who are relatively close in status to the interviewer, and with subordinates who are highly educated (Downs et al., 1980).

The third general type of performance appraisal is the *problem-solving* interview. In this interview, evaluating the person is no longer the goal. Rather, the appraiser's role is to help the employee develop a plan for improving his or her performance. The performance deficiencies are determined by the subordinate, not the supervisor. Your goal as the interviewer is to avoid judgments and evaluations; rather, you offer suggestions for solutions to the problems defined by the interviewee. You form a partnership with the subordinate to solve the problems he or she brings up.

Finally, if your objectives are to both perform an evaluation and offer developmental coaching, you could choose to use a *mixed-model* interview (Beer, 1987). In this type of appraisal interview, you begin with a problem-solving framework and end the interview with a more directive tell-and-sell approach. In this way, you can both help a subordinate meet the development goals as well as offer your own evaluation and plan for development.

No matter which type of interview you choose, a performance-appraisal interview should contain all the elements of a general interview: build rapport and orient the interviewee to the subject; conduct the body of the interview in a supportive manner; conclude by specifying what is going to happen. Additionally, the performance-appraisal interview generally includes a discussion of a specific plan for improvement or change.

Summary and Behavioral Guidelines

While many people consider interviewing a process that just happens, we have argued that effective interviewing requires planning and thought. The steps shown in Figure B.1 provide a framework for enhancing your interviewing skills. The first step, thorough preparation, is essential for a successful interview. Planning involves deciding on your purposes, questions, structure, setting, and responses to anticipated problems. During the actual interview, work toward establishing and maintaining a supportive and productive climate. Keep in mind every interview should have an introduction, body, and conclusion and you need to develop ways to record the information you obtain during the interview.

There are a variety of organizational interviews, but the most common are the information-gathering interview, the employment-selection interview, and the performance-appraisal interview. Each of these interviews has very different objectives and specific means to reach them. Be flexible in how you conduct these interviews. As in any communication activity, you should adapt to the situation, your personality, and the person with whom you are conversing.

Interviewing is a vital management skill. When done well, an interview can provide you with information not otherwise available. This information can then better inform the decisions you make as you act out your role in the organization.

Following are general behavioral guidelines for planning and conducting interviews. Specific guidelines for specialized interviews are incorporated into the Observer's Feedback Forms in the Skill Practice exercises.

Planning the Interview

1. Specify your purposes and plan an agenda.
   - ❏ Determine your general purpose: to gather information, persuade, discipline, or evaluate.
   - ❏ Compose an agenda, prioritizing all topics.
2. Formulate questions.
   - ❏ Determine the type of questions (closed or open) that are consistent with the objectives.
   - ❏ Write specific questions for each topic on the agenda.
   - ❏ Use appropriate language in your questions.
   - ❏ Avoid biased or leading questions.
3. Develop the interview guide.
   - ❏ Select the appropriate format: structured, semistructured, or unstructured.
   - ❏ Use either the funnel or inverted funnel question sequence.
   - ❏ Formulate transition statements between topics.
4. Select a setting that is consistent with your objectives.
5. Identify potential complications that might occur during the interview and develop contingency plans.

Conducting the Interview

6. Establish and maintain a supportive climate.
   - ❏ Greet interviewee and initiate a brief social conversation.
   - ❏ Foster a positive communications climate by constant analysis of, and adaptation to, the interview process.
   - ❏ Use effective listening skills and nonverbal language (eye contact, posture, and gestures) to foster cooperation.
7. Introduce the interview.
   - ❏ State the purpose of the interview.
   - ❏ Clarify interviewee's and interviewer's roles.

- ❑ Specify the time frame of the interview.
- ❑ Indicate how the information will be used.
- ❑ Use a transition to signal the beginning of the interview.
8. Conduct the interview.
   - ❑ Use the interview guide to manage the flow of the interview.
   - ❑ Use probing questions when elaboration or clarification are required.
   - ❑ Be flexible and adapt to the flow of the interview.
9. Conclude the interview.
   - ❑ Signal the interview is about to end.
   - ❑ Summarize the information you have collected.
   - ❑ Clarify details or technical information.
   - ❑ Review what will happen as a result of the interview.
   - ❑ Strengthen the relationship by expressing appreciation.
10. Record the interview content, using the appropriate format.
    - ❑ Write a summary immediately after the interview.
    - ❑ Take notes during the interview (sustaining eye contact).
    - ❑ Use a tape recorder (with the interviewee's permission).
    - ❑ Use a second interviewer to improve your recall.

EXERCISES FOR CONDUCTING SPECIAL-PURPOSE INTERVIEWS

Evaluating the New Employee-Orientation Program

You work for a high-tech electronics firm that was recently purchased by a large, multibusiness conglomerate. Your company produces components for highly sophisticated communications equipment used by the government. This is an exciting, but somewhat confusing, period in the company's history. The new parent company, BETA Products, is known as a Japanese-like firm. It emphasizes high productivity, along with employee commitment and loyalty.

BETA is sending a human resources management team to inspect your organization in two weeks. In advance, they have sent a list of programs they want to review, including your new employee-orientation program. Your boss, the vice president of human resources, has given you the assignment of preparing a 30-minute briefing on this program to the BETA task force. Specifically, she has asked you to interview representatives of various groups in your organization to determine their perceptions of the program's merits and shortcomings.

Currently, when a new employee enters your organization, he or she goes through an extensive orientation session. During this session, the new employee meets with a member of the Human Resources Department to learn about company policies and procedures and receive the Employee's Handbook. This session can last from two to three hours, depending on the participants. At the end of the session, the new employee is assigned a mentor, a member of the new employees department who has been with the organization for at least one year. The role of the mentor is to help the new employee become familiar with his or her new job and coworkers. The mentor is expected to meet with the new employee on a semiregular basis for at least six months. The relationship can continue if both parties agree. This orientation program has been used for about three years but has never been formally evaluated.

Assignment

To complete this assignment, you have scheduled interviews with several department heads, mentors, and current trainees. Prepare the interview you would conduct with the person from whom you are assigned to gather information about the orientation program. Before beginning this task, review the behavioral guidelines for planning an effective interview at the end of the Skill Learning section. You should also consult Tables B.1 through B.3, and Table B.6. In small groups, compare your questions with others. What did you leave out? What questions need to be reworded? What types of probes may be needed? After this discussion, split up into triads and take turns serving as the interviewer, interviewee, and observer. Do not look at the following role descriptions while planning this exercise. An observer will give feedback using the Observer's Feedback Form as a guide.

Role Descriptions for Interviewees

Trainee

You've just found out you are going to be interviewed on the mentor program with which you've been involved for three months. You've been quite happy with the program and would like to see it continued; in fact, someday, you want to be a mentor to new employees.

Many of your friends have pointed out you have a tendency to talk too fast, talk a lot, and tend to dominate a conversation. You realize when you get nervous or involved in an issue, you do talk a lot. You are certainly nervous about this interview because you are very involved in the program and you've heard through the grapevine the program might be cut. You feel that would be terrible. You really want to let the interviewer know how much you've learned from your mentor and the whole orientation program. What you have to say is important, and you want to make sure the interviewer hears all the good things you have to say about the program.

You are particularly positive about the program because it contrasts with your experience from your former job. In that organization, you were merely given a cursory overview of the company benefits through a videotape presentation. Furthermore, because there was no standardized mentoring program, new employees were left to fend for themselves. They were given no clear picture of what the company expected of them, no encouragement, and no sense of involvement in a group effort. As a result, a great deal of confusion and misunderstanding resulted. Here, in contrast, you have appreciated being able to get answers to your questions from one person. Overall, you feel as though this approach enabled you to become proficient in your job very quickly.

Department Head

You've just found out you are going to be interviewed on the mentor program, and it couldn't have come at a worse time. You've just lost one of your best employees, and you have been scrambling to try to find a replacement. You're really not interested in spending time to think about this interview or participate in it. You'd rather use the time on employment interviews to find a new assistant.

In fact, you tend to be uncomfortable in interviews of any kind. Because you tend to be shy, this kind of one-on-one formal conversation always makes you feel uncomfortable.

You don't mind it so much when you are the interviewer—at least then you have some control over the situation. But you don't feel you've ever been a really good interviewee. The direct questions always make you feel as if you are on trial; as a result, you withdraw and appear to be uncooperative, even defensive.

You think the interviewer should be talking to people more directly involved in the program. You really don't have much to do with it anyway, except for matching up people. The program seems to work okay, but no doubt trainees would learn just as quickly if they sought out their own mentors. You know many of your staff members feel the program is worthwhile, so you'll back it up, albeit reluctantly. However, you would much rather write an evaluation of the program than have to talk about it to a relative stranger.

Mentor

You've just found out you are going to be interviewed on the mentor program, a program with which you've been involved for six months. When you first became a mentor, you were excited about the possibilities. Now, however, experience has shown the program is a waste of time. Too often, the trainees use their mentors as a crutch, both at work and in their social lives. The program inspires a dependency you find counterproductive and time wasting.

You've found yourself in the position of practically taking over trainees' jobs because they got used to relying on your expertise. You've thought this might simply be a result of your own personality—too willing to help, perhaps—but you've also noticed this behavior in other mentors and trainees.

Furthermore, you haven't noticed any significant difference in productivity between people who have gone through the program and people who haven't. In fact, because of the development of social relationships, your feeling is that productivity has probably declined: there is too much gossip and goofing off and not enough concentration on tasks.

You think the company ought to abandon the program. While a brief orientation might be useful to new hires, you no longer can justify the amount of time you put into the program, given the results. Even this evaluation of the program is taking up your valuable time.

Observer's Feedback Form

RATING

1 = Low
5 = High

Introduction

1. Did interviewer

_____   use a friendly greeting?

_____   begin to build rapport?

_____   state purpose?

_____   orient interviewee?

_____   refer to taking notes or recording interview?

Body

2. Did interviewer

_____ use appropriate question sequence?

_____ use a variety of question types?

_____ use internal summaries and transitions?

_____ respond to interviewee with good secondary questions (probes)?

_____ use silence when appropriate?

_____ maintain rapport with interviewee?

_____ handle problematic interviewee well?

Closing

3. Did interviewer

_____ sum up?

_____ maintain/encourage good interpersonal relationship?

_____ indicate what would happen with information?

_____ set up another meeting, if appropriate?

_____ thank interviewee?

Nonverbals

4. Did interviewer

_____ wear appropriate clothing?

_____ maintain eye contact with interviewee?

_____ use purposeful gestures?

_____ use appropriate tone of voice?

_____ maintain good posture?

_____ look enthusiastic and interested in what interviewee had to say?

_____ take notes inconspicuously?

_____ avoid verbal pauses such as uh, uhm, and so forth?

Comments:

Performance-Appraisal Interview with Chris Jakobsen

Background Information for Pat Ginelli

You are vice president of the Commercial Loan Division at Firstbank, a medium-sized, state-licensed bank. You have been with Firstbank for four years and have conducted a number of performance-appraisal interviews. During your tenure, you have increased your division's profits by 45 percent. Your goal is to increase this level by another 15 percent before the end of next year. In order to do so, you need to have aggressive, dynamic, and dedicated loan officers working for you.

Chris Jakobsen has been with Firstbank for three years. This will be your first review of Chris's performance because he was transferred to your department five months ago to fill a loan officer position vacated by Helen Smith, who had worked in the Personal Loan Division. You agreed to the transfer after reviewing Chris's credentials and past performance appraisal forms. Chris appeared to be qualified for the position, and the performance appraisal reports indicated that Chris's work was rated from above average to outstanding.

Unfortunately, you have been extremely disappointed with Chris's performance in your department. For a longtime bank employee, he seems surprisingly unfamiliar with standard procedures and protocol. Last week, he told a customer there shouldn't be any problem getting approval for her loan application. She wanted to open a boutique in a renovated building downtown. However, the review committee turned it down because the building hadn't met code yet.

There are several other deficiencies in Chris's performance. In contrast to Helen, Chris seems inattentive to detail. He has frequently left out important information on loan applications, causing needless delays in processing. Furthermore, he doesn't seem to be able to keep up with the workload. It takes him twice as long as it should to handle routine paperwork, and he seems totally ill at ease with your department's computerized information system. Due to a favorable investment environment and the recent opening of a local industrial park, your group's workload is up 50 percent from a year ago. You simply can't tolerate having to take extra time to make sure Chris is doing things right the first time.

In Chris's favor, he is extremely punctual and his attendance has been perfect. He also keeps a very neat work area and takes pride in his own appearance. Furthermore, as a native of the community and an active civic leader, he has very good contacts in the business community. It is also clear that everyone likes Chris. He is jovial and easygoing. He has a quick wit that livens up even the most routine and dull staff meeting. He loves treating coworkers during happy hour after work. Unfortunately, he sometimes loses perspective and gets carried away. Indeed, you've wondered at times how this free spirit ended up in a bank job. Certainly his attitude runs counter to your more formal and reserved personality, but it's hard to deny he has charm and class.

In general, Chris seems to have plenty of potential, but at best his current work performance is only average (an "expected" rating on your company's form). He just hasn't applied himself to his new position. You wonder if this is the right work for him or if perhaps he hasn't had adequate training. You spent some time orienting Chris to the group and assigned Jim, a veteran of the department, to act as his mentor. But, in retrospect, the local business boom has made it difficult for you and Jim to help Chris learn the ropes. Your days seem to be filled up with meetings with local investors and city planners. Still, it bugs you that he never asks questions. If he needs help with the technical aspects of the job, why doesn't he ever ask for assistance?

You have scheduled the interview with Chris for later in the day in your office. You know your review will make him very unhappy and probably put him on the defensive. He obviously has high aspirations for advancing in the bank and has received pretty positive feedback in the past. You've got to figure out some way to get him to improve. Your department is short-handed as it is, and everyone must contribute his or her share.

As you contemplate the unpleasant task ahead, you reflect, "Boy, I certainly miss Helen. I never had to have this type of conversation with her."

Assignment for Pat Ginelli

In preparation for this interview, complete a draft of the performance evaluation form in Exhibit 1 (the form is located after Chris's assignment). In keeping with standard practice, you have given a blank copy of the form to Chris and asked him to do a self-evaluation. He will bring his completed form to the interview.

After you have completed your draft, identify the type of performance-appraisal interview you feel is most appropriate for this situation (see Table B.9). Also, review the behavioral guidelines at the end of the Skill Learning section. Then formulate a series of questions consistent with your overall strategy. Finally, anticipate questions and objections Chris might initiate and prepare responses. Compare your plans in small groups and make revisions. Use the Interview Checklist in Table B.4 to guide your discussion.

Upon completion of your small-group discussion, prepare to conduct the interview with Chris. Do not look at the background information for Chris's role prior to the interview. An observer will use the Observer's Feedback Form to give you feedback.

Background Information for Chris Jakobsen

You have been with Firstbank, a medium-sized, state-licensed bank, for three years. For most of that time, you worked in the Personal Loan Division as a loan officer. You liked your job, your clients, and the people with whom you worked. You had hoped your first move at Firstbank would be a promotion within the Personal Loan Division. However, five months ago, you were transferred to the Commercial Loan Division to replace a loan officer who had worked in that position for 10 years. You did not really want to transfer, but you realized the move would, in fact, put you in a better position for the next upward move. Your former supervisor indicated you would not have to stay in this position very long if you kept receiving good ratings on your performance appraisal forms, and you have always received outstanding or above-average ratings. He argued you really needed to gain exposure to other departments in the bank as well as to other managers. Your new boss, Pat Ginelli, is a real rising star in the bank.

You expect your new supervisor, Pat, is going to be pretty tough on you. You feel frustrated and upset because you don't think there has been any change in your effort or commitment. Since you have been in the department, Pat's attitude toward you has seemed very distant and formal. You know Pat thinks the person you replaced was an excellent worker who contributed greatly to Pat's goal of achieving a 15 percent increase in profits this year. But certainly she doesn't expect you to immediately pick up where a 10-year veteran left off.

Then there's the problem of training. She promised to give you a thorough orientation when you arrived, but instead you were shunted off to Jim. He seemed sincere and interested in helping out, and he told you to come and ask questions whenever you needed help. However, when you asked about the department's loan-application procedure, he made you feel like an idiot for asking such a basic question, and you've never gone back. Furthermore, Pat always seems to be in meetings. You realize she is bringing in important business for the bank, so you feel it would be inappropriate to distract her with your basic questions.

This lack of assistance has caused you to make some mistakes. These have primarily been due to the change in procedures between the Personal and Commercial Loan departments. You had much more autonomy and authority over there, probably because the loans were much smaller. In addition, there are many more government regulations to worry about over here. Besides, you really miss the close contact with people that was built into your old job. That's why you took your first job in the bank. You have always been a very people-oriented person and received great satisfaction from helping them. Now, you just seem to be buried in paperwork and committee meetings. Some days, you regret accepting the offer to transfer. You're not sure this stepping-stone to advancement is worth the lost enjoyment you received in your former position.

Assignment for Chris Jakobsen

Your interview with Pat is scheduled for her office. In preparation for the interview, Pat has asked you to complete a copy of the performance-appraisal form as a self-evaluation. Prior to the interview, complete the form in Exhibit 1. Do not review the background information for Pat's role.

Exhibit 1 Interview with Chris Jakobsen

Employee Performance Appraisal

DATA COMPLETED

NAME   Chris Jakobsen
DATE OF BIRTH   6/22/65
YEARS OF EMPLOYMENT   3
OFFICE LOCATION BRANCH 4   DEPARTMENTAL 9
DEPARTMENT   Commercial

PRESENT JOB TITLE   Loan Officer
CONVERSION CODE   32
YEARS IN PRESENT POSITION   6 months
SOC. SEC. NO.   555–33–9999
EDUCATION   B.A.—Business

Select the statement under each of the following categories that best describes the individual.

Quality of Work

General excellence of output with consideration to accuracy—thoroughness—dependability—without close supervision.

_____ Exceptionally high quality. Consistently accurate, precise, quick to detect errors in own and others' work.

_____ Work sometimes superior and usually accurate. Negligible amount needs to be redone. Work regularly meets standards.

_____ A careful worker. A small amount of work needs to be redone. Corrections made in reasonable time. Usually meets normal standards.

_____ Work frequently below acceptable quality. Inclined to be careless. Moderate amount of work needs to be redone. Excessive time to correct.

_____ Work often almost worthless. Seldom meets normal standards. Excessive amount needs to be redone.

Quantity of Work

Consider the amount of useful work over the period of time since the last appraisal. Compare the output of work to the standard you have set for the job.

_____ Output consistently exceeds standards. Unusually fast worker. Exceptional amount of output.

_____ Maintains a high rate of production. Frequently exceeds standards. More than normal effort.

_____ Output is regular. Meets standards consistently. Works at steady average speed.

_____ Frequently turns out less-than-normal amount of work. A low producer.

_____ A consistently low producer. Excessively slow worker. Unacceptable output.

Cooperation

Consider the employee's attitude toward the work, the employee's coworkers, and supervisors. Does the employee appreciate the need to understand and help solve problems with others?

_____ Always congenial and cooperative. Enthusiastic and cheerfully helpful in emergencies. Well-liked by associates.

_____ Cooperates well. Understands and complies with all rules. Usually demonstrates a good attitude. Liked by associates.

_____ Usually courteous and cooperative. Follows orders but at times needs reminding. Gets along well with associates.

_____ Does only what is specifically requested. Sometimes complains about following instructions. Reluctant to help others.

_____ Unfriendly and uncooperative. Refuses to help others.

Knowledge of the Job

The degree to which the employee has learned and understands the various procedures of the job and their objectives.

_____ Exceptional understanding of all phases. Demonstrates unusual desire to acquire information.

_____ Thorough knowledge in most phases. Has interest and potential toward personal growth.

_____ Adequate knowledge for normal performance. Will not voluntarily seek development.

_____ Insufficient knowledge of job. Resists criticism and instruction.

_____ No comprehension of the requirements of job.

Dependability

The reliability of the employee in performing assigned tasks accurately and within the allotted time.

_____ Exceptional. Can be left on own and will establish priorities to meet deadlines.

_____ Very reliable. Minimal supervision required to complete assignments.

_____ Dependable in most assignments. Normal supervision required. A profitable worker.

_____ Needs frequent follow-up. Excessive prodding necessary.

_____ Chronic procrastinator. Control required is out of all proportion.

Attendance and Punctuality

Consider the employee's record, reliability, and ability to conduct the job within the unit's work rules.

_____ Unusual compliance and understanding of work discipline. Routine usually exceeds normal.

_____ Excellent. Complete conformity with rules but cheerfully volunteers time during peak loads.

_____ Normally dependable. Rarely needs reminding of accepted rules.

_____ Needs close supervision in this area. Inclined to backslide without strict discipline.

_____ Unreliable. Resists normal rules. Frequently wants special privileges.

Knowledge of Company Policy and Objectives

Acceptance, understanding, and promotion of company policies and objectives in the area of the employee's job responsibilities.

_____ Thorough appreciation and implementation of all policies. Extraordinary ability to express objectives and encourage others to meet them.

_____ Reflects knowledge of almost all policies related to this position.

_____ Acceptable but fairly superficial understanding of job objectives.

_____ Limited insight into job or company goals. Mentally restricted.

_____ Not enough information or understanding to permit minimum efficiency.

Initiative and Judgment

The ability and interest to suggest and develop new ideas and methods; the degree to which these suggestions and normal decisions and actions are sound.

_____ Ingenious self-starter. Superior ability to think intelligently.

_____ Very resourceful. Clear thinker—usually makes thoughtful decisions.

_____ Fairly progressive, with normal sense. Often needs to be motivated.

_____ Rarely makes suggestions. Decisions need to be checked before implementation.

_____ Needs detailed instructions and close supervision. Tendency to assume and misinterpret.

Supervisory or Technical Potential

Consider the employee's ability to teach and increase skills of others, to motivate and lead, to organize and assign work, and to communicate ideas.

_____ An accomplished leader who can earn respect and inspire others to perform. An articulate and artful communicator, planner, and organizer.

_____ Has the ability to reach and will lead by example rather than technique. Speaks and writes well and can organize and plan with help.

_____ Fairly well informed on job-related subjects but has some difficulty communicating with others. Nothing distinctive about spoken or written word.

_____ Little ability to implement. Seems uninterested in teaching or helping others. Careless speech and writing habits.

_____ Unable to be objective or reason logically. Inarticulate and stilted in expression.

Overall Rating

There are five alternatives in each category. The first alternative is worth 5 points, the last alternative is worth 1 point. Place a number from 1–5 by each of the selected alternatives and total the score for all nine categories. Then select the appropriate overall rating.

_____ Outstanding (45–39)

_____ Above Expected (38–32)

_____ Expected (31–23)

_____ Below Expected (22–16)

_____ Unsatisfactory (15–9)

Observer's Feedback Form

RATING

1 = Low

5 = High

Introduction

1. Did interviewer

_____ use appropriate greeting?

_____ build rapport?

_____ orient interviewee to the interview?

_____ refer to taking notes?

Body

2. Did interviewer

_____ praise individual's strengths?

_____ focus on specific concerns?

_____ compare perceptions of the problems?

_____ probe for underlying causes?

_____ reach agreement on performance expectations and goals?

_____ discuss specific plans of action for improving deficiencies?

_____ make specific references to the appraisal form?

Conclusion

3. Did interviewer

_____ provide opportunity for interviewee to make suggestions and ask questions?

_____ summarize interview?

_____ specify when next appraisal interview will be held?

Nonverbals

4. Did interviewer

_____ use nonverbal behaviors to maintain open climate and good rapport?

_____ avoid use of uhs and uhms?

_____ maintain good posture?

_____ maintain eye contact?

Comments:

PRACTICE

Employment-Selection Interview at Smith Farley Insurance

Smith Farley is a rapidly growing insurance firm located in Peoria, Illinois. It offers general lines of insurance, including auto, fire, life, and health. It prides itself on its competitive rates, excellent agent relations, and fast claim service. Employees of the firm appreciate its no-layoff policy, generous pay and benefits, and family-oriented culture. Next to Caterpillar, it is the largest employer in the community, a source of employee pride.

Smith Farley has taken the lead in computerizing the insurance business. Agents and claim handlers conduct much of their business using laptop computers in their offices and in the field. Furthermore, the agents' and claim handlers' offices are all networked with one another as well as with the regional offices. This permits rapid transfer of information, including rate changes, new applications, and claims.

To support this massive computer system, the firm has installed state-of-the-art computer hardware in its 10 regional office centers. In addition, the company has a large software development and maintenance department, which has doubled in size in the past five years and now employs 800 programmers. These programmers are generally recruited directly from college. Although they need no previous experience, any relevant experience can help new programmers move quickly into management or senior technical positions.

Programmer/analysts use typical programming languages to develop computer applications for the insurance business (e.g., new claim-handler and customer application forms), for the corporate headquarters staff (e.g., accounting and personnel records), and the computer system itself (internal procedures and controls). Data processing positions range from extremely technical design of complex computer networks to routine maintenance of existing programs.

All new programmers are put through a 16-week school in which they are oriented to the company and the data processing department, brought up to speed on the relevant programming languages and tools, and socialized into the corporate culture. To meet the heavy demand for computer applications, the data processing department has been authorized to hire two cohorts of 60 programmers a year.

To attract programmers to the firm, Smith Farley offers above-average starting salaries and rapid promotions during the first five years. After that, individuals can continue to pursue the technical career option, which leads to a senior analyst's position that pays about $10,000 above industry average, or they can move into management. The consistently high performance of the firm and its ongoing expansion of data processing afford ample opportunity for promotion into senior positions.

You are J. R. Henderson, a 20-year employee of Smith Farley. For the past 10 years you have been working in the personnel department, primarily interviewing job candidates for the data processing department. You enjoy your work—the constant contact with young, enthusiastic college graduates is invigorating—but sometimes you find the heavy travel schedule taxing.

For example, during the next week you will be traveling to three cities: first to nearby Bloomington, then to New Orleans and Atlanta. In addition to the regular campus interviews you have scheduled in these areas, you have received several résumés in response to local newspaper ads. In sifting through these inquiries, three résumés caught your interest. You have made arrangements to interview all three applicants during this trip.

Assignment

Review Exhibits 1 through 5 and prepare a list of questions you would ask these three job candidates. Using the Interview Guide planning form at the end of the chapter, review the general questions you should ask all three. In addition, identify several specific questions you would like to ask the candidate(s) you are assigned, based on their résumés and cover letters.

Review your proposed questions in small groups. What points did you overlook? What questions need to be reworded or discarded?

Using the questions you think are most appropriate, be prepared to conduct selection interviews with these job candidates in class. Prior to each interview, think about the questions each candidate is likely to ask you about the company, the community of Peoria, and the specific jobs available. In addition, identify your "selling points"—the specific features of the company, the community, and the jobs you think each candidate would find most attractive. Also review the general behavioral guidelines and the six-step PEOPLE approach to selection interviews (Table B.8). Remember: The interviewing process influences the content of the information exchanged.

Following the interview, take a few minutes and grade the interviewee on each of the seven criteria on the Interview Guide (5 = high, 1 = low). Justify your grades with specific comments. Then make an oral report to the observer assigned to your interview; include a recommendation. (Assume the observer is the director of recruiting for your firm.) After your report, for those criteria related to the interview itself (as compared with the background of the assigned role), discuss your observations with the interviewee. Following this discussion, an observer will give you feedback on your performance as an interviewer using the Observer's Feedback Form as a guide.

Exhibit 1 Smith Farley Insurance Job Posting

A. POSITIONS OPEN

1. *Programmer/Analyst*—Auto & Life Company Data Processing Trainee openings leading to Programmer/Analyst positions at the conclusion of *16-week* training program. The DP Trainee is trained in the programming skills necessary to either develop new or to revise data-processing programs that help administer over 10 million auto, life, fire, and health insurance policies.

2. *Analyst*—Computer Operations Support Trainee opening leading to *Analyst* positions at conclusion of a *nine-month* training program. Computer Operations Support is responsible for technical operations support for the Regional Data Processing Offices, including: developing operator procedures, developing and administering training, problem resolution, and coordinating implementation of new systems and major changes for Regional Data Processing Offices.

B. MAJORS CONSIDERED

We are recruiting for three Data Processing Departments (Auto Data Processing, Life Data Processing, and Computer Operations Support), each having different requirements, which are as follows:

1. *Auto Data Processing:* Strongly prefer applied computer science, computer technology, and MIS majors, but will consider other majors with 12–15 hours of computer science academic background. Strongly prefer *3.0 overall GPA*.

   Logical analysis, problem-solving skills, and communication skills are important for expected job performance. Candidates should possess course work in *COBOL, C, C++,* and/or *Java*.

2. *Life Data Processing:* Most college majors are acceptable (i.e., mathematics, business or related majors, English, music, and science).

   Student must have a sincere interest in and aptitude for data processing. Only students with a *3.5 overall GPA* will be considered.

3. *Computer Operations Support:* Most business majors are acceptable (i.e., business, business administration, finance, economics, accounting, etc., with 6–10 hours of computer science academic background). Prefer a *3.0 overall GPA*.

   Student must have a sincere interest in and aptitude for data processing.

C. CITIZENSHIP REQUIREMENTS

Must be citizens or permanent residents.

D. LOCATION

These positions will be located at the corporate headquarters in Peoria, Illinois.

Exhibit 2 Interview Guide for Data Processing (DP)

APPLICANT'S NAME _____   SCHOOL _____

INTERVIEW DATE _____   GPA _____

LOCATION _____ TIME _____   MAJOR _____

CRITERION	FOCUS	GENERAL QUESTIONS	APPLICANT-SPECIFIC QUESTIONS
Aptitude/ Knowledge	Determine if exposure to and retention of a high-level computer language and development methods are adequate.	Of the DP courses you have had, which was the most beneficial and why? Explain in detail the most difficult DP assignment you have had. How do you rate yourself as a programmer? Why?	
Interest/ Experience	Determine if interest and record of success in DP studies or work has been sustained (2+ years).	How did you first get interested in DP? What about it do you like the most? The least? Can you give me an example of a DP-related experience you have had that was satisfying? Not satisfying? What is your professional goal?	
Ability to work with others	Determine success of achieving results in team effort.	Do you feel you work more effectively on a one-to-one basis or in a group? Describe a situation in which you worked as a member of a team. What approach did you take to get people together and establish a common approach to the task?	

CRITERION	FOCUS	GENERAL QUESTIONS	APPLICANT-SPECIFIC QUESTIONS
Commitment/ Initiative	Determine level of success in achieving task completion in light of task complexity, adversity, load, level of knowledge, and so forth.	What approaches do you use to get people to accept your ideas or goals? What is a big obstacle you had to overcome to get where you are today? Do you consider yourself a self-starter or are you better at implementing the plans of others?	
Communi-cation	Determine quality of written/spoken word.	Would you rather write a report or give a verbal report? Why? Do you think you are a good listener? What qualities do you need to be a good listener? How do you handle a situation when you are explaining something and the other person doesn't understand?	
Problem solving/ Decision making	Determine if applicant has a record of addressing relatively complex projects.	In your opinion, what are the most difficult problems with which a programmer/analyst must deal? What particular strengths do you have that allow you to deal with these problems? What design methods do you use to create a program? Describe how to use them. Describe the most complex program you have ever written.	
Other:	Stability Maturity Leadership Personal appearance		

PRACTICE

Exhibit 3 Résumé

William L. Henderson II

Campus
700 North Camden #107
Normal, IL 61761
(309) 454–6178

Home
1915 Western Hills
Arlington Heights, IL 60004
(312) 255–5738

OBJECTIVE	*Analyst/Data Processing*
EDUCATION	Illinois Wesleyan University, Bloomington, Illinois
	Expected Degree 2007

OBJECTIVE   *Analyst/Data Processing*

EDUCATION   Illinois Wesleyan University, Bloomington, Illinois
Expected Degree 2007
Major: Computer Science   Major GPA: 3.75
Business Administration   GPA: 3.03

EDUCATIONAL   Dean's List Spring Semester 2007
HIGHLIGHTS   ACM Award Spring Semester 2007

STUDENT   *ILLINOIS WESLEYAN UNIVERSITY*
ACTIVITIES   Member of Gamma Ray Social Fraternity (3 years)
                Pledge Class President; In-House Activities; Intramurals; Offset
                Chairman; Social Committee.
            Member of Varsity Football Team (2 years)

WORK   CENTRAL STATES INSURANCE, Bloomington, IL
SUMMARY   Auto/Divisional Programming—Corporate
(Part time   *Position:* DP—Intern
during college)

                ILLINOIS WESLEYAN UNIVERSITY, Bloomington, IL
                Office of Admissions
                Position: Admissions Counselor Aid
                Computer Lab
                Position: Lab Assistant

(Summers)   PREMIER CHECK PRINTERS, INC., Des Plaines, IL
                Printing presses (2 years)
                Position: Press Assistant/Operation
                SOFTWARE, ETC., Arlington Heights, IL
                Sales, Inventory, Shipping, Ordering, Partial Management

                Position: Salesman

AVAILABILITY June 2008
REFERENCES   References available upon request

Exhibit 4 Résumé

Bryan E. Jensen
4364 Peachtree Place
Lilburn, Georgia 30247
Home (404) 381-8909

OBJECTIVE   *Project Leader/Systems Analyst* with supervision potential
BACKGROUND Anticipated the decline in manufacturing jobs and retrained in
computer science. Presently have two associate degrees and
four years of in-depth experience. Accepted temporary position
at Caterpillar to gain experience. The economic recession in
the Midwest prompted my relocation to Atlanta. Accepted my
present position to broaden my experience. I am now seeking
a permanent career position with a midwest employer located
in a "smaller" city. I will be an asset to a progressive company.
I am well motivated, resourceful, versatile, work well with others, and accept responsibility readily.

HARDWARE	IBM 370—Models 3090E, 3083, 3084, 4341; IBM PC/XT; 486, Power PC
SOFTWARE	Case Tools: Knowledgeware GAMMA
	Databases: IMS-DL/I, DBII—SQL, Access, Oracle
	Communications: IMS—MFS, TSO—ISPF
	Languages: C, C++, Java
	Related: BTS, DDLTO, Fileaid-IMS, Datavatage, IMS-Online, SPUFI, QMF, OS/MVS-XA, JES2, Fileaid, Panvalet, Infopac, SDSF, JES-Master, Design/I, All-In-One, Diagram Master, Excel, Word PowerPoint, Dreamweaver

EXPERIENCE
03/07–

Continental Service Corporation, Macon, Georgia (Corporate)
Senior Systems Analyst/Team Leader

Guided planning, estimating, analysis, and development of major areas of IMB DB/DC Billing System. It has a 2.5 million customer base and is located in 42 states. Use Method/I life cycle/ methodology. Utilized Pacdesign (Yourdon) for system design and Pacbase for completion of deliverables and code generation.

01/04–03/07

Federal Reserve Bank, Savannah, Georgia (Corporate)
Project Leader (10/06–03/07)

Supervised eight analysts and programmers through the implementation of a billing system for Federal Reserve Districts throughout the United States. Presented written and verbal status reports, employee-performance reviews, and time-planning estimates/schedules to upper management.
(09/05–10/06)

Led development of IMS DB/DC billing system. Analyzed requirements to produce data-flow diagrams and logical data model. Participated in team presentation of system. Created program specifications. Investigated and resolved code-generation problems. Provided support to other team members.
(01/05–08/05)

Received Merit Award for outstanding performance. Designed, programmed, and tested accounting interface to all corporate IBM and branch Unisys applications. Provided training and support during parallel test and acceptance of accounting system. Redirected installation efforts for an accounting deposit module that had fallen behind. Provided production support of newly implemented accounting system.
(04/04–12/04)

Installed accounting software from tape. Modified all JCL to district standards. Installed and modified job-submission system. Documented and instructed the users on the system and the results of each job.
(01/04–03/04)

Designed, wrote, tested, and documented IMB DB/DC programs for system used to report the dollar amount of checks as they clear the Reserve.

03/03–12/03

Caterpillar Tractor Company, Chicago, Illinois (Corp.)
Programmer

Programmed, tested, and documented IMS DB/DC programs from specifications for Man and Material Management System. (Due to be laid off 01/04)

04/97–06/01   Skilled Trades Machinist (last position held—layoff)

EDUCATION   Illinois Central College; East Peoria, Illinois—2001, Associate in Applied Science, Data Processing Technology Bradley University; Peoria, Illinois (1998–1999) Fifteen hours past Associate toward Manufacturing B.S. Illinois Central College; East Peoria, Illinois—1995, Associates in Applied Science, Manufacturing Technology.

PERSONAL   Married, one child. Enjoy outdoor activities. Well motivated. References available upon request.

Exhibit 5 Résumé

Mary Lynn Smith
3922 North Blair Street
New Orleans, Louisiana 70117
(504) 945–6077

CAREER OBJECTIVES

Entry-level position in artificial intelligence research with an industrial firm and eventual managerial capacity in such a firm.

EDUCATION

Dillard University, Division of Natural Sciences, New Orleans, LA.
B.S. degree, Mathematics major with Computer Science minor, May 1999,
G.P.A.: 3.58/4.0 (overall), 3.82/4.0 (major)

Courses in Mathematics:

Calculus I, II, III	Complex Variables	
Modern Algebra I & II	Real Algebra	Differential Equations
Advanced Calculus	Linear Algebra	Engineering Statistics

Courses in Computer Science:

Computer Fundamentals	BASIC	Advanced BASIC
Systems Analysis	Pascal	FORTRAN

HONORS AND ACTIVITIES

University academic scholarship, University and National Dean's Lists, Kappa Beta Alpha and Beta Kappa Tau Honor Societies, Kappa Delta Pi Mathematics Society, and Dillard University Concert Choir.

WORK EXPERIENCE

Computer Services, Inc., Systems Operator/Payroll Processor, Summer, 2007.
—Performed system backups, file verification, programming, and payroll processing.
—Verified payroll figures and prepared tax reports.

Black Computer Operators Association, Teacher, 8/06.
—Prepared the South New Orleans Computer Science Team for a national competition.

The South New Orleans Team placed first in the national competition.

Washington Elementary School, Summer Mini Camp, Teacher, 7/06–8/06.
—Taught children how to use computers and educational software.

Observer's Feedback Form

RATING

1 = Low

5 = High

Opening

1. Did interviewer

_____   use appropriate greeting?

_____   build rapport?

_____   orient interviewee to the interview?

_____   use appropriate transition to body of interview?

Body

2. Did interviewer

_____   clearly define structure of the interview?

_____   use transitions between topics?

_____   ask questions based on available information and needs?

_____   probe when necessary?

_____   solicit behavioral examples?

Closing

3. Did interviewer

_____   offer organizational or job information?

_____   invite questions?

_____   answer interviewee's questions appropriately and specifically?

_____   state when and how interviewee will be contacted?

Nonverbal

4. Did interviewer

_____   act poised?

_____   dress appropriately?

_____   speak articulately?

_____   act enthusiastically?

_____   use appropriate language style?

_____   maintain eye contact?

_____   use purposeful gestures?

Comments:

PRACTICE

SKILL *LEARNING*

- Conducting Effective Meetings: A Short Guide for Meeting Managers and Meeting Participants
- The Five Ps of Effective Meetings
- Suggestions for Group Members
- Summary and Behavioral Guidelines

SKILL *PRACTICE* ▽

- Preparing and Conducting a Team Meeting at SSS Software
- Role Diagnosis
- Meeting Evaluation Worksheet

C

Conducting Meetings

SKILL DEVELOPMENT OBJECTIVES

- IMPLEMENT GUIDELINES FOR PLANNING AND CONDUCTING EFFECTIVE MEETINGS
- ENHANCE THE VALUE OF MEETINGS ATTENDED

Conducting Effective Meetings: A Short Guide for Meeting Managers and Meeting Participants

Becoming a skillful planner and conductor of meetings—a meeting manager—is a prerequisite for managerial and organizational effectiveness. There are several reasons this skill is a crucial one. One reason is because so much of a manager's time is spent in meetings. A 3M Company study, done in the late 1980s, found meetings occupy a large percentage of a manager's workweek. These researchers found the number of meetings had doubled over the last decade. As you move up the hierarchy, meeting demands increase substantially. The more senior the manager is, the more meetings he or she attends (3M, 1994).

A second reason is meetings are a significant cost. This research found the compensation for managers "just being there" had nearly tripled. About 15 percent of most companies' personnel budget was spent on meeting matters. And in the last decade these demands have increased substantially. With flatter organizations and an emphasis on teams and teamwork, the number of meetings has grown exponentially.

A third reason becoming a skillful meeting manager is crucial is meetings are the place where most corporate decisions are actually made, or reviewed. Hence, the matter of decision quality—the amount of useful results from the meeting—becomes crucial for the health of the organization. The skilled meeting master can "produce" a meeting that results in high-quality decisions—not her or his decisions, but decisions that truly reflect the group's.

A fourth reason relates to the concept of whole life, as opposed to work life. In these days of the boundaryless organization, skills that are useful at work are also useful and important away from work. Many people spend a substantial portion of their time in non-work-oriented meetings. For example, any community volunteer work; church activity; or participation in art councils, youth programs, and civic associations

---

We are grateful to John Tropman, who prepared this section based on the material the authors had in the previous editions.

requires a lot of meetings. Failure here can have a great impact on our social fabric. Robert Putnam of Harvard University has developed a thesis about the decline in "social capital" in American society (Putnam, 2000). Collective activities seem to be on the decline across a wide range of organizations. One of the reasons for this decline is unorganized meetings that frustrate participants rather than help them contribute to the organization's goals. Folks may figure they just do not want to waste their time.

Because meetings are such a pervasive activity both in and out of work settings, being a skillful meeting manager has important rewards beyond those associated with team building. Meeting groups, if properly managed, can make higher-quality decisions than individuals. The phrase "if properly managed" is the key. If not properly managed, meetings become the supreme organizational and civic time waster. They can actually set the organization back by making rotten decisions when problematic processes such as folly (Tuchman, 1984), groupthink (Janis, 1983), the Abilene paradox (Harvey, 1974), the garbage can model of organizational choice (Cohen, March, & Olsen, 1972), or the "boiled frog syndrome" (Tichy & Devanna, 1986) come into play.

The Five *P*s of Effective Meetings

Effective meeting managers know the five steps in preparing for and conducting meetings: (1) purpose, (2) participants, (3) plan, (4) participation, and (5) perspective.

1. Purpose

Purpose refers to the reason for which a meeting is held. There are three functions a meeting performs—to make announcements, to make decisions, and to brainstorm. Of these three, only the second two count as reasons for actually holding a meeting. When information can be conveyed by a memo or phone call, when people are not prepared, when key people cannot attend, when the cost of a meeting is higher than the potential payoff, and when there is no advantage to holding a meeting, no meeting should be called (3M, 1994). In short, if there are no decisions to be made, nor any brainstorming to do, cancel the meeting.

Productive meetings *result* from good decision making and brainstorming. A meeting should be called when one or more of the following conditions applies:

❏ *Information sharing.* When all needed information is not held by any single person, when ideas will be stimulated by getting people together, and when it is not clear what information is needed or available.

❏ *Commitment building.* When individuals need to become committed to a course of action and when they are involved in its planning and implementation.

❏ *Information disseminating and feedback.* When many people must receive the same message in the same way, e-mail is good. However, when the real issue is not the dissemination, but gauging the reaction and allowing for "ventilation," then a meeting is very helpful.

❏ *Problem solving.* Groups outperform the best individuals in accomplishing complex tasks and making high-quality decisions where various policies or information are needed. Therefore, meetings should be called to manage complex problems and outline the options for decisions through brainstorming.

2. Participants

The second *P*, **participants**, refers to the individuals invited to attend a meeting. In conducting an effective meeting, it is important to determine the *size, composition*, and *skills* of the participants. Meetings can fail because too many or too few participants attend or because the wrong mix of people is present. If a meeting is too large, discussion may be superficial and diffuse; few people will be able to participate. If a meeting is too small, not enough information will be shared and problems will not be adequately solved. Odd numbers of participants work best because even numbers have a higher propensity of causing the group to polarize.

Meeting composition refers to three main dualistic dimensions:

❏ Homogeneity–Heterogeneity
❏ Competition–Cooperation
❏ Task–Process

A homogeneous group is composed of members with similar backgrounds, personalities, knowledge, or values. Homogeneous groups produce less conflict and disagreement, but their outcomes may be mundane and unimaginative. On the other hand, heterogeneous groups produce more differences among individuals, which leads to criticisms and disputes, but potentially to more novel, complex solutions to problems as well.

With regard to the competition–cooperation dimension, research on its effect in problem-solving meetings is compelling. Groups whose members are working toward a common goal and who adopt a cooperative stance toward one another perform more effectively and produce higher levels of member satisfaction than groups whose members are striving to fulfill individual needs or are pursuing competing goals. Cooperative groups also demonstrate more effective interpersonal communication, more complete divisions of labor, higher levels of involvement, and better task performance.

On the task–process dimension, meetings are more effective if they have participants who generate a balance of both task and process. Task-oriented participants are "all business." They have little tolerance for joking or for discussions of feelings and friendships. The task is accomplished efficiently, but satisfaction may be low. Process-oriented participants emphasize esprit de corps and participation. They are sensitive to participants' feelings and satisfaction. They may sacrifice accomplishment in favor of members' enjoyment. (This usually turns out to be a bad choice; the greatest enjoyment comes from accomplishment.) For meeting participants, one tip is not to refrain from using your default (or usual) style (task or process) but, rather, "Do what is not being done." If there is a lot of process going on, you can emphasize task. If there is an "all task" mind-set, then add a bit of process.

Skills address the competencies participants bring to the meeting. We can think of *general* and *specific* skill sets. In general, the four generic skill sets Cohen, March, and Olsen (1972) identify should be present in the meeting *at the same time*. First are the problem knowers—participants who have some sense of the problem under discussion. Second are the solution providers—participants who are creative and imaginative, but may not know the problems. Third are the resource controllers—participants who sign off on money, people, and resources needed for most decisions; therefore, they need to be in the loop. Finally, there are people called "decision-makers-looking-for-work"—the "organizational archbishops" who "bless" or affirm decisions. If all these skill sets are in the same room at the same time, and the process is a good one, the likelihood of a high-quality decision (timely, creative, participative) is great. In terms of specific skills, the particular knowledge that might be needed in a particular situation can be ascertained as one plans for the meeting, using the rule of halves, which will be mentioned later in this chapter. It is true individuals may double up—and fit more than one of these categories. That is fine. Just be sure you have them all.

3. Planning

The third *P*, **planning**, refers to preparation of the meeting agenda. Often, the justification for a meeting is clear (e.g., we need to determine how to get fuel to troops at the front), and the appropriate individuals are in attendance, but the meeting still seems to flounder, wander aimlessly, or is unable to produce a final decision. Such meetings often begin with the leader saying, "We have a problem I think we all need to sit down and discuss." The leader's erroneous assumption is because a problem exists and all participants understand it, the meeting will be successful. Unfortunately, participants may come to the meeting unprepared, may be unaware of critical information, may be unclear about their specific roles, and may be confused about how to achieve the objective. Conversely, the meeting planner may try to cram too much into a single meeting, schedule too many presentations, handle too many documents, or cover too much business. Research suggests there are a number of rules for planning meetings effectively (Tropman, 1996). The following is a list of the most important:

The Rule of Halves All agenda items for an upcoming meeting must be in the hands of the agenda scheduler no later than one-half of the time interval between the last meeting and the upcoming meeting. If meetings are held weekly, the person constructing the agenda should gather agenda items for the next meeting by the halfway mark in the week. This allows time to sort and cluster items, handle some items one-on-one outside the meeting, and produce and distribute an agenda in advance of the meeting. It also allows for the assembling of special skills, as driven by the developing agenda.

The Rule of Sixths Approximately two-thirds of the agenda should be focused on current agenda items. The remaining third should be subdivided into two-sixths. One of those sixths of meeting time should be spent on past agenda items and follow-up. The remaining sixth of the meeting should be spent on brainstorming for the future. Continuity is thus maintained and agenda items don't slip through the cracks.

The Reports Rule Meetings go better if the usual round of "reports" does *not* occur. Rather, the information that is contained in the "reports" is reorganized into specific items—announcement, decision, brainstorming.

The Rule of Three-Fourths Packets of information, including minutes from the past meeting and an agenda, should be sent to meeting participants at the three-quarter point between meetings. For example, if a weekly meeting is scheduled, the packet should be sent out approximately two days before the next meeting.

The Agenda Rule Agendas for meetings should be written with action verbs or sentence summaries, not with single words. Rather than saying "Minutes," for example, use "Approve Minutes." Rather than "Production Report," use "Determine Production Schedule." This provides clarity and impetus for what the meeting should accomplish. Figure C.1 illustrates this process.

The Rule of Thirds All meetings are divided into three parts: (1) a start-up period in which less difficult items are covered, latecomers arrive, and people get on board; (2) a heavy work period in which the most difficult items are considered; and (3) a decompression period in which the meeting begins to wind down. *Instructional items* should be handled in the first period, *items for decision* should be handled in

Figure C.1	The Weekly Meeting	
1. Approve Minutes		2:00–2:05
2. Announcements		2:05–2:10
	New desks ordered	
	$1,000 each to your account	
3. Retreat Location (Action)		2:10–2:15
	Key West seems best	
4a. Vendor Selection (Action)		2:15–2:25
	A new vendor for gaskets	
	would like some business	
4b. Disposal of Broken Gaskets (Action)		2:25–2:35
	Trash? Sell abroad/fix?	
5. Permission to Ship (Action)		2:35–3:00
	Ship part with scratch?	
	Give discount?	
6. Improving Quality (Brains)		3:00–3:38
7. Adjourn		3:38–3:40

SOURCE: *John Tropman.*

the second period, and *items for discussion* should be handled in the third period.

Executive Summary Rule   Reports circulated to meeting participants should always contain executive summaries or options memos. An executive summary highlights key points and conclusions of the report. An options memo summarizes alternatives to be discussed and decided on. This eliminates the need to sift through many pages to find relevant information and to spend meeting time shuffling through the report.

The Agenda Bell Rule   This rule is a more specific rule about when certain types of agenda items should be covered. Agenda items should be considered in order of ascending controversiality, then attention should be turned to discussion and decompression items. Figure C.2 shows a typical agenda bell for a meeting.

The Agenda Integrity Rule   All items on the agenda should be discussed, and items not on the agenda should not be discussed. This rule helps ensure meeting participants do not sidetrack the meeting with items that are tangential, for which no one has prepared, or for which insufficient information is available.

The Temporal Integrity Rule   This rule is simple: Start on time and end on time. Follow a time schedule in the meeting itself. This ensures all agenda items are given adequate time, latecomers are not rewarded by having the meeting wait for them, and people can count on finishing at a certain point.

The Minutes Rule   Minutes of meetings should have three characteristics: agenda relevance (information recorded is related to an agenda item), content relevance (minutes should be written in a form that follows the agenda so it is easy to find pertinent material with a quick review), and decision focus (minutes should reflect decisions, conclusions, and actions agreed upon, rather than the processes by which the decisions are reached). After a brief summary of each item, skip a line and place the action or result in a box. Here is where names are named, times are timed, and so on. The key item is easy for everyone to see.

These 10 rules of meeting preparation help to ensure that when individuals arrive for a meeting and the meeting begins, a structure and plan will be in place to make the meeting productive and efficient.

LEARNING ⓘ

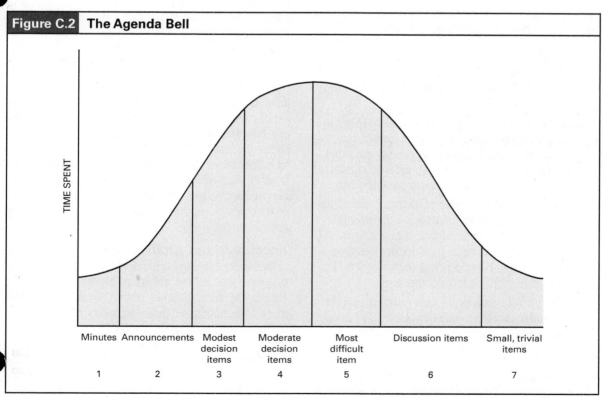

Figure C.2   The Agenda Bell

TIME SPENT

| Minutes | Announcements | Modest decision items | Moderate decision items | Most difficult item | Discussion items | Small, trivial items |
| 1 | 2 | 3 | 4 | 5 | 6 | 7 |

SOURCE: *John Tropman.*

4. Participation

The fourth *P*, **participation**, refers to the actual process of meetings and the methods used to ensure meetings involve everyone present.

Provide Introductions Meeting participants should be introduced to each other and helped to feel comfortable together, especially if controversial issues are to be considered.

Establish Ground Rules It should be made clear what amount of participation is expected, what variations from the agenda will be tolerated, and what the time frame will be. Establishing a structure for the meeting at the outset helps keep the meeting on track.

Establish Decision Rules Decision rules are norms that make participants comfortable. Establish them at the beginning of the meeting. Because there are no neutral decision rules, meeting managers usually have to use several at once—a complex intellectual task. The most common are the extensive rule, the intensive rule, the involvement rule, the expert rule, and the power rule.

The *extensive rule* is majority rule. Each meeting participant votes on alternatives, and the alternatives with a majority of the votes wins. However, there are variations of this rule, which should be noted:

❑ *Highest total.* When more than two alternatives are being considered, none may get a majority of the votes. The alternative with the highest number of votes is adopted.

❑ *Straw vote.* A nonbinding vote is taken to get a sense of the participants' feelings toward various alternatives. This may happen several times before a decision is reached in order to eliminate nonsupported alternatives from consideration.

❑ *Weighted rating.* Meeting participants can divide 100 points among alternatives, so the strength of their support can be tallied. If four alternatives exist, for example, a participant can give 90 points to one and 5 points to two others. The alternative with the most points wins.

❑ *Ranking.* Alternatives are rank ordered, and the alternative receiving the highest average ranking is adopted.

If the *intensive rule* is used, those who care most win. Through discussion, rather than voting, individuals who feel deeply can share that feeling with the group. Groups will try to be as accommodating

as possible. However, problems occur if the majority cares a lot, but not "most," or if there are two groups that care deeply but differently. It requires a lot of imagination and attempts to come up with a solution that pleases the "shallow feelers" and the "deep feelers."

In the *involvement rule*, the person or subgroup that has to carry out any action gets to pick, or has it their way. Their downstream involvement gives them a particular view, which may not always be for the overall best. Using the *expert rule*, the participant with the law or science on his or her side wins. But neither law nor science is infallible by any means. Using the *power rule* means the boss wins.

Any one of these rules can work, but quality decisions with the greatest buy-in (and hence, sticking power) usually come from consensus. Consensus, in this case, means a decision is taken that meets, and can be shown to meet, each of the rules—it satisfied the greatest number of those who feel strongly, those who must carry it out, the experts, and the boss.

Sometimes it is necessary to proceed "in principle." Although agreement cannot be reached on all specific details, certain general principles can be agreed upon. The priniciples, rather than the entire proposal, are accepted. For example, you and your partner may decide in principle to have Italian food Friday night. Details (such as if you will go out, and if not, who will do the cooking) might remain unresolved for the moment while a range of details is explored.

Use a Variety of Media To maintain the interest of meeting participants, use various media to present information. Handouts, overhead transparencies, slides, flip charts, videos, and blackboard diagrams are all helpful in maintaining interest and increasing the efficiency with which information is presented and processed. Participants should be able to use at least two of their senses during a meeting (for example, seeing and hearing).

Encourage and Establish Participation Participation in a meeting should be equitable among participants, which does not mean everyone must make exactly the same number of comments. Those with more information or those with vested interests in the topic will participate more. However, it is important to control the overparticipator or the person who dominates the discussion, as well as encourage those who may have something to contribute but may not be inclined to share it. Equity should also be maintained among different points of view, so representatives of one side of an argument don't dominate the discussion. Ways to promote discussion among meeting participants include the following:

- Ask open-ended questions rather than questions that can be answered with a "yes" or a "no."
- Ask questions using the language of the participants rather than using jargon or recondite terminology.
- Encourage participants to share personal experiences that relate to the topic being considered.
- Use examples from your own experience to clarify points.
- Make eye contact with those to whom you are talking and summarize their points when they finish their statements.
- Ask group members for their reactions to points made by other meeting participants.
- When appropriate, involve others in answering a question asked of you.
- Remember communication comes in a strand of two parts—the report part (information) and the rapport part (connection and feeling). Be sure to attend to both parts.
- As the leader, make certain you facilitate the discussion rather than dominate it.

Summarize

Close the meeting by summarizing the decisions reached, tasks assigned, progress accomplished, key points discussed, and what was learned in the meeting. Review action items that will be reported on at the next meeting. Help meeting participants feel a sense of accomplishment for having spent their time in the meeting. This may be a good time to anticipate the next meeting by identifying when minutes and the next meeting's agenda will be distributed and what preparation will be required.

5. Perspective

The last *P* is **perspective**. Perspective directs us to view the meetings from a distance. It means evaluating each meeting and, every so often, the decisions of and process of the meeting series. At the end of each meeting, for example, you can use KSS methodology to do a quick and simple assessment. Pass out a piece of paper to each participant. Ask each participant to respond under each of the three letters—*K*, *S*, and *S*. *K* means "keep"—What went well about this meeting that we

should keep or expand. *S* means "stop"—What about this meeting is nonproductive and should be stopped or phased out. *S* means "start"—What about this meeting is not happening and should be started. You may get the usual irreverent responses (for example, "better doughnuts"), but if you look for serious patterns of feedback, you can constantly improve the meeting series. The next week, give the participants the results (in summary form) and let them know how you are using their feedback to improve the meeting.

Suggestions for Group Members

So far in this discussion of effective meeting management, we have focused on the role of the meeting manager—the person who calls, plans, and serves as the meeting's "conductor." This role is key to the success of any group activity. However, meeting participants also bear responsibility for the meeting's effectiveness. It is important for each participant to appreciate the impact of her or his contribution, both in shaping the short-term outcomes of meetings and affecting long-term career opportunities. The success of the meeting is the responsibility of everyone present, and even those not present, in the sense that these latter folks have the responsibility to let their views be known in advance. The best meetings are those in which meeting managers and other participants each take some responsibility for meeting leadership.

Following are several pointers for contributing to the effectiveness of meeting from a non-manager's perspective.

1. *Determine if you need to attend the meeting.* Don't attend merely because you have been invited. If you have doubts about whether the meeting's agenda applies to you, discuss with the meeting manager why he or she believes your presence is important. Under the rule of three-fourths, you will know what is coming up in fairly specific detail. This information should help.
2. *Prepare.* Acquaint yourself with the agenda, and prepare any reports or information that will facilitate *others'* understanding of the issues. Come prepared with questions that will help you understand the issues.
3. *Be on time.* Stragglers not only waste the time of other participants by delaying the meeting or by requiring summaries of what has happened, but they also hinder effective team building and hurt morale.

4. *Ask for clarification on points that are unclear or ambiguous.* Often, you will find others in this room have the same questions but were too timid to speak out.

5. *When giving information, be precise and to the point.* Don't bore everyone with anecdotes and details that add little to your point.

6. *Listen.* Keep eye contact with whomever is speaking, and try to ascertain the underlying ideas behind the comments. Be sensitive to the effects of your nonverbal behavior on speakers, such as slouching, doodling, or reading.

7. *Be supportive of other group members.* Following the guidelines on supportive communication, acknowledge and build on the comments of others. ("As Jane was saying...")

8. *Assure equitable participation.* Take the lead in involving others so everyone's talents are used. This is especially important if you know that critical information from particular points of view are not being included in the discussion. This can be rectified by encouraging those who rarely participate. ("Jim, your unit worked on something like this last year. What was your experience like?")

9. *Make disagreements principle-based.* If it is necessary to disagree with, or challenge, the comments of others, follow the guidelines for collaborative conflict management in the text. For example, base your comments on commonly held principles or values. ("That's an interesting idea, Bill, but how does it compare with the president's emphasis on cost cutting?")

10. *Act and react in a way that will enhance the group performance.* Leave your personal agendas at the door and work toward the goals of the group.

Summary and Behavioral Guidelines

Meetings are a pervasive part of organizational life, especially for managers. Few important initiatives are forged without extensive and intensive group efforts. However, meetings are one of the most maligned aspects of organizational membership. To avoid poorly managed meetings, a Five-Ps approach was presented.

1. **Purpose** Use meetings to accomplish the following purposes:
   - ❑ Decisions
     - ❑ A complex problem needs to be resolved using the expertise of several people.
     - ❑ Group members' commitment to a decision, or to each other, needs to be enhanced.
   - ❑ Brainstorming
   - ❑ Ideas about a problem need to be explored, such as:
     - ❑ Precipitating and predisposing causes
     - ❑ What is the root cause?
     - ❑ Are there more effective and efficient ways we could approach this problem?
     - ❑ What is the evidence?
     - ❑ What does the evidence prove?
   - ❑ Announcements
     - ❑ Information needs to be shared simultaneously among several people.

2. **Participants** Make decisions regarding who and how many to invite based on the following:
   - ❑ The size of the group should be comparable with the task. (For interactive groups, five to seven participants tend to work best.)
   - ❑ A balance between individuals with strong task orientations and others with strong group-process orientations should be sought.
   - ❑ Individuals should share some common goals or values.
   - ❑ All relevant experience and knowledge need to be represented.

❑ The group's composition should reflect the goals of the meeting. (Homogeneity encourages solidarity and commitment; heterogeneity fosters creativity and innovation.)

❑ Be sure the general skills of problem knowing, problem solving, resource controlling, and key decision makers are on board.

3. **Plan** In preparing for the meeting, be sure to do the following:
   ❑ Provide for adequate physical space, audiovisual equipment, and so on.
   ❑ Establish priorities by sequencing agenda items and allotting time to each item.
   ❑ Prepare and distribute an agenda before, or at the beginning of, the meeting.
   ❑ Choose the most appropriate decision-making format structure for each item (for example, ordinary group discussion, brainstorming, or one of several consensus-building techniques).

4. **Process** In managing the group dynamics, specify the target time length, and highlight specific tasks by doing the following:
   ❑ Establish process ground rules, such as how decisions will be made.
   ❑ Allow members to become acquainted (if necessary) and make them feel comfortable.
   ❑ When critical thinking is important, refrain from expressing strong personal opinions. Also, assign the role of critical evaluator to a group member.
   ❑ Sustain the flow of the meeting by using informational displays.
   ❑ Encourage the group not to stray from assigned tasks.
   ❑ Manage the discussion to achieve equitable participation.
   ❑ Discourage the premature evaluation of ideas.
   ❑ Prevent "social loafing" by assigning specific responsibilities and stressing the importance of group tasks.
   ❑ Discourage "conceptual misers"—those who opt for the "quick fix."
   ❑ Counteract the natural tendency for groups to make risky decisions by touching base with participants prior to the meeting so discussion-induced trends can be detected. (The rule of halves helps with getting this information.)
   ❑ Deal with disruptive members by using supportive communication and collaborative conflict management skills.
   ❑ Conclude the meeting by summarizing what was accomplished, reviewing assignments, and making preparations for subsequent meetings, if necessary.

5. **Perspective** Evaluate each meeting using the KSS (Keep, Stop, Start) methodology by asking the following:
   ❑ What went well in this meeting that we should keep?
   ❑ What was nonproductive that we should stop or phase out?
   ❑ What didn't happen in this meeting that we want to start in the future?

6. **Group Members** Foster constructive group dynamics as a participant by doing the following:
   ❑ Take time to prepare for the meeting, and gain a clear understanding of the purposes of the meeting.
   ❑ Respect other group members by arriving on time and leaving personal agendas at the door.
   ❑ Listen to other group members, be supportive of them, and clarify and build upon points made by others.
   ❑ Encourage participation by all members.

EXERCISES FOR CONDUCTING MEETINGS

Preparing and Conducting a Team Meeting at SSS Software

Part 1

Refer to the SSS Software In-Basket exercise at the end of this section. Assume the role of Chris Perillo. Since you are new to your position, you decide to hold a meeting with some or all of your direct reports tomorrow afternoon (Tuesday). You want to be brought up to date as well as to handle the items of business introduced in your e-mail, phone messages, and memos.

1. Review each of the 16 items in the SSS Software In-Basket exercise. This is the "business" to be covered in this meeting.

2. Determine the *purpose* of the meeting, the *participants* (who should attend), the *plan* (write an agenda; establish a time limit for the meeting) as well as the meeting *process* you will use, using the appropriate Behavioral Guidelines.

Part 2

3. Now select the nine other individuals who will be attending the meeting and assign them their roles in the Health and Financial Services Group. Each team member should realistically play the role assigned to him or her, even if not much specific information exists for the role in the memos. Each team member should play the role as though he or she were attending the first team meeting with a new leader. Each person should be prepared to make recommendations for each in-basket item pertaining to their role. The team should consist of:

   Chris Perillo, Vice President
   Bob Miller, Group 1 Manager
   Wanda Manners, Group 2 Manager
   William Chen, Group 3 Manager
   Leo Jones, Group 4 Manager
   Mark McIntyre, Group 5 Manager
   John Small, Group 6 Manager
   Marcus Harper, Group 8 Manager
   Armand Marke, Customer Service Manager
   Michelle Harrison, Office Administrator

4. At the conclusion of the meeting, assigned observers will provide feedback, using the Meeting Evaluation Worksheet as a guide.

Role Diagnosis

This exercise is intended to help you identify and practice effective role performance in meetings.

Listed on the next page are a set of roles organized into three categories. As you are observing a team meeting, put check marks by the roles performed by the team members you are observing each time they make a comment or display behaviors that match one of the roles listed on the next page. If you are analyzing your own team after it has completed its meeting, put names of team members next to the roles they played. (See the chapters on Building Effective Teams and Teamwork for more information about these roles.)

Task-Facilitating Roles
Direction-giving
Information-seeking
Information-giving
Elaborating
Coordinating
Monitoring
Process-analyzing
Reality-testing
Enforcing
Summarizing

Process (Relationship-Building) Roles
Supporting
Harmonizing
Tension-relieving
Energizing
Developing
Facilitating
Processing

Blocking Roles
Overanalyzing
Overgeneralizing
Fault finding
Premature decision making
Presenting opinions as facts
Rejecting
Pulling rank
Dominating
Stalling

What suggestions do you have for improvement in the team members' performance? Identify some specific suggestions for more effective role performance in the meeting. Who could have done more and who could have done less? Why?

Meeting Evaluation Worksheet

It is important individuals planning, conducting, and participating in meetings are asked periodically to evaluate the effectiveness of the time spent meeting together. The following worksheet can be used for this purpose.

PRACTICE

To gain experience evaluating meetings, use the following questions to assess the effectiveness of a class or work-related project or staff meeting:

1. What is the specific purpose of the meeting?
2. Who was invited to attend? How were they contacted? Was the way in which the meeting announced appropriate (e.g., face-to-face, e-mail, secretary phone call)?
3. Was the agenda that was constructed consistent with the following rules?
   - ❏ The Agenda Rule (use action words)
   - ❏ The Rule of Sixths (two-thirds current items, one-third past and future items)
   - ❏ The Rule of Thirds (one-third warm up, one-third work, one-third wind down)
   - ❏ The Reports Rule (reports nonexistent; content reordered into specific items—announcements, decision, and brainstorm issues)
   - ❏ The Agenda Bell Rule (agenda ordered according to a bell-shaped "level of difficulty" process)
   - ❏ The Temporal Integrity Rule (start and stop on time)
   - ❏ The Minutes Rule (someone assigned to keep minutes)
4. What was done especially well in preparing for this meeting?
5. To what extent were the rules of effective meeting process followed in the meeting? Rate each step in terms of its effectiveness in the team meeting:

	Ineffective	Effective
1. Review purpose	_____	_____
2. Make introductions	_____	_____
3. Establish ground rules	_____	_____
4. Use informational displays	_____	_____
5. Ensure participation	_____	_____
6. Summarize conclusions	_____	_____

6. What could have been improved upon? What was omitted?

SSS Software In-Basket Memos, E-Mails, Faxes, and Voice Mails

ITEM 1 – E-MAIL

TO: All Employees
FROM: Roger Steiner, Chief Executive Officer
DATE: October 15

I am pleased to announce that Chris Perillo has been appointed as Vice President of Operations for Health and Financial Services. Chris will immediately assume responsibility for all operations previously managed by Michael Grant. Chris will have end-to-end responsibility for the design, development, integration, and maintenance of custom software for the health and finance/banking industries. This responsibility includes all technical, financial, and staffing issues. Chris will also manage our program of software support and integration for the recently announced merger of three large health maintenance organizations (HMOs). Chris will be responsible for our recently announced project with a consortium of banks and financial firms operating in Tanzania. This project represents an exciting opportunity for us, and Chris's background seems ideally suited to the task.

Chris comes to this position with an undergraduate degree in Computer Science from the California Institute of Technology and an MBA from the University of Virginia. Chris began as a member of our technical/professional staff six years ago and has most recently served for three years as a group manager supporting domestic and international projects for our airlines industry group, including our recent work for the European Airbus consortium.

I am sure you all join me in offering congratulations to Chris for this promotion.

ITEM 2 – E-MAIL

TO: All Managers
FROM: Hal Harris, Vice President, Community and Public Relations
DATE: October 15

For your information, the following article appeared on the front page of the business section of Thursday's *Los Angeles Times*.

> *In a move that may create problems for SSS Software, Michael Grant and Janice Ramos have left SSS Software and moved to Universal Business Solutions Inc. Industry analysts see the move as another victory for Universal Business Solutions Inc. in their battle with SSS Software for share of the growing software development and integration business. Both Grant and Ramos had been with SSS Software for over seven years. Grant was most recently Vice President of Operations for all SSS Software's work in two industries: health and hospitals, and finance and banking. Ramos brings to Universal Business Solutions Inc. her special expertise in the growing area of international software development and integration.*

Hillary Collins, an industry analyst with Merrill Lynch, said "the loss of key staff to a competitor can often create serious problems for a firm such as SSS Software. Grant and Ramos have an insider's understanding of SSS Software's strategic and technical limitations. It will be interesting to see if they can exploit this knowledge to the advantage of Universal Business Solutions Inc."

ITEM 3 – E-MAIL

TO: Chris Perillo
FROM: Paula Sprague, Executive Assistant to Roger Steiner
DATE: October 15

Chris, I know in your former position as a group manager in the Airline Services Division, you probably have met most of the group managers in the Health and Financial Services Division, but I thought you might like some more personal information about them. These people will be your direct reports on the management team.

Group #1: Bob Miller, 55-year-old white male, married (Anna) with two children and three grandchildren. Active in local Republican politics. Well regarded as a "hands-off" manager heading a high-performing team. Plays golf regularly with Mark McIntyre, John Small, and a couple of VPs from other divisions.

Group #2: Wanda Manners, 38-year-old white female, single with one school-age child. A fitness "nut" has run in several marathons. Some experience in Germany and Japan. Considered a hard-driving manager with a constant focus on the task at hand. Will be the first person to show up every morning.

Group #3: William Chen, 31-year-old male of Chinese descent, married (Harriet), two young children from his first marriage. Enjoys tennis and is quite good at it. A rising star in the company, he is highly respected by his peers as a "man of action" and a good friend.

Group #4: Leo Jones, 36-year-old white male, married (Janet) with an infant daughter. Recently returned from paternity leave. Has traveled extensively on projects, since he speaks three languages. Has liked hockey ever since the time he spent in Montreal. Considered a strong manager who gets the most out of his people.

Group #5: Mark McIntyre, 45-year-old white male, married (Mary Theresa) to an executive in the banking industry. No children. A lot of experience in Germany and Eastern Europe. Has been writing a mystery novel. Has always been a good "team player," but several members of his technical staff are not well respected and he hasn't addressed the problem.

Group #6: John Small, 38-year-old white male, recently divorced. Three children living with his wife. A gregarious individual who likes sports. He spent a lot of time in Mexico and Central America before he came to SSS Software. Recently has been doing mostly contract work with the federal government. An average manager, has had some trouble keeping his people on schedule.

Group #7: This position vacant since Janice Ramos left. Roger thinks we ought to fill this position quickly. Get in touch with me if you want information on any in-house candidates for any position.

Group #8: Marcus Harper, 42-year-old African American male, married (Tamara) with two teenage children. Recently won an award in a local photography contest. Considered a strong manager who gets along with peers and works long hours.

Customer Services: Armand Marke, 38-year-old male, divorced. A basketball fan. Originally from Armenia. Previously a group manager. Worked hard to establish the Technical Services Phone Line, but now has pretty much left it alone.

Office Administrator: Michelle Harrison, 41-year-old white female, single. Grew up on a ranch and still rides horses whenever she can. A strict administrator.

There are a number of good folks here, but they don't function well as a management team. I think Michael played favorites, especially with Janice and Leo. There are a few cliques in this group, and I'm not sure how effectively Michael dealt with them. I expect you will find it a challenge to build a cohesive team.

ITEM 4 – E-MAIL

TO: Chris Perillo
FROM: Wanda Manners, Group 2 Manager
DATE: October 15

CONFIDENTIAL AND RESTRICTED

Although I know you are new to your job, I feel it is important I let you know about some information I just obtained concerning the development work we recently completed for First National Investment. Our project involved the development of asset management software for managing their international funds. This was a very complex project due to the volatile exchange rates and the forecasting tools we needed to develop.

As part of this project, we had to integrate the software and reports with all their existing systems and reporting mechanisms. To do this, we were given access to all of their existing software (much of which was developed by Universal Business Solutions Inc.). Of course, we signed an agreement acknowledging the software to which we were given access was proprietary and our access was solely for the purpose of our system integration work associated with the project.

Unfortunately, I have learned some parts of the software we developed actually "borrow" heavily from complex application programs developed for First National Investment by Universal Business Solutions Inc. It seems obvious to me one or more of the software developers from Group 5 (that is, Mark McIntyre's group) inappropriately "borrowed" algorithms developed by Universal Business Solutions Inc. I am sure that doing so saved us significant development time on some aspects of the project. It seems very unlikely First National Investment or Universal Business Solutions Inc. will ever become aware of this issue.

Finally, First National Investment is successfully using the software we developed and is thrilled with the work we did. We brought the project in on time and under budget. You probably know they have invited us to bid on several other substantial projects.

I'm sorry to bring this delicate matter to your attention, but I thought you should know about it.

ITEM 5A – E-MAIL

TO: Chris Perillo
FROM: Paula Sprague, Executive Assistant to Roger Steiner
DATE: October 15
RE: Letter from C.A.R.E. Services (copies attached)

Roger asked me to work on this C.A.R.E. project and obviously wants some fast action. A lot of the staff are already booked solid for the next couple of weeks. I knew Elise Soto and Chu Hung Woo have the expertise to do this system and when I checked with them, they were relatively free. I had them pencil in the next two weeks and wanted to let you know. Hopefully, it will take a "hot potato" out of your hands.

ITEM 5B – COPY OF FAX

C.A.R.E.
Child and Adolescent Rehabilitative and Educational Services
A United Way Member Agency
200 Main Street
Los Angeles, California 90230

DATE: October 11

Roger Steiner, CEO
SSS Software
13 Miller Way
Los Angeles, California 90224

Dear Roger,

This letter is a follow-up to our conversation after last night's board meeting. I appreciated your comments during the board meeting about the need for sophisticated computer systems in nonprofit organizations and I especially appreciate your generous offer of assistance to have SSS Software provide assistance to deal with the immediate problem with our accounting system. Since the board voted to fire the computer consultant, I am very worried about getting our reports done in time to meet the state funding cycle.

Thanks again for your offer of help during this crisis.

Sincerely yours,

Janice Polocizwic

Janice Polocizwic
Executive Director

ITEM 5C – COPY OF A LETTER

SSS SOFTWARE
13 Miller Way
Los Angeles, CA 90224

DATE: October 12

Janice Polocizwic
Executive Director, C.A.R.E. Services
200 Main Street
Los Angeles, California 90230

Dear Janice,

I received your fax of October 11. I have asked Paula Sprague, my executive assistant, to line up people to work on your accounting system as soon as possible. You can expect to hear from her shortly.

Sincerely,

Roger Steiner

Roger Steiner
cc: Paula Sprague, Executive Assistant

ITEM 6 – E-MAIL

TO: Michael Grant
FROM: Harry Withers, Group 6 Technical Staff
DATE: October 12

PERSONAL AND CONFIDENTIAL

Our team is having difficulty meeting the submission deadline of November 5 for the Halstrom project. Kim, Fred, Peter, Kyoto, Susan, Mala, and I have been working on the project for several weeks, but we are experiencing some problems and may need additional time. I hesitate to write this letter, but the main problem is our group manager, John Small, is involved in a relationship with Mala. Mala gets John's support for her ideas and brings them to the team as required components of the project. Needless to say, this has posed some problems for the group. Mala's background is especially valuable for this project, but Kim and Fred, who have both worked very hard on the project, do not want to work with her. In addition, one member of the team has been unavailable recently because of child-care needs. Commitment to the project and team morale have plummeted. However, we'll do our best to get the project finished as soon as possible. Mala will be on vacation the next two weeks, so I'm expecting some of us can complete it in her absence.

ITEM 7 – VOICE MAIL MESSAGE

Hello, Michael. This is Jim Bishop of United Hospitals. I wanted to talk with you about the quality assurance project you are working on for us. When Jose Martinez first started talking with us, I was impressed with his friendliness and expertise. But recently, he doesn't seem to be getting much accomplished and has seemed distant and on edge in conversations. Today, I asked him about the schedule and he seemed very defensive and not entirely in control of his emotions. I am quite concerned about our project. Please give me a call.

ITEM 8 – VOICE MAIL MESSAGE

Hi, Michael. This is Armand. I wanted to talk with you about some issues with the Technical Services Phone Line. I've recently received some complaint letters from Phone Line customers whose complaints have included long delays while waiting for a technician to answer the phone, technicians who are not knowledgeable enough to solve problems, and, on occasion, rude service. Needless to say, I'm quite concerned about these complaints.

I believe the overall quality of the Phone Line staff is very good, but we continue to be understaffed, even with the recent hires. The new technicians look strong, but are working on the help-line before being fully trained. Antolina, our best tech, often brings her child to work, which is adding to the craziness around here.

I think you should know we're feeling a lot of stress here. I'll talk with you soon.

ITEM 9 – VOICE MAIL MESSAGE

Hi, Chris, it's Pat. Congratulations on your promotion. They definitely picked the right person. It's great news—for me, too. You've been a terrific mentor so far, so I'm expecting to learn a lot from you in your new position. How about lunch next week?

ITEM 10 – VOICE MAIL MESSAGE

Chris, this is Bob Miller. Just thought you'd like to know John's joke during our planning meeting has disturbed a few of the women in my group. Frankly, I think the thing's being blown out of proportion, especially since we all know this is a good place for both men and women to work. Give me a call if you want to chat about this.

ITEM 11 – VOICE MAIL MESSAGE

Hello. This is Lorraine Adams from Westside Hospital. I read in today's *Los Angeles Times* you will be taking over for Michael Grant. We haven't met yet, but your division has recently finished two large million-dollar projects for Westside. Michael Grant and

I had some discussion about a small conversion of a piece of existing software to be compatible with the new systems. The original vendor had said they would do the work, but they have been stalling, and I need to move quickly. Can you see if Harris Wilson, Chu Hung Woo, and Elise Soto are available to do this work as soon as possible? They were on the original project and work well with our people.

Um…(long pause) I guess I should tell you I got a call from Michael offering to do this work. But I think I should stick with SSS Software. Give me a call.

ITEM 12 – VOICE MAIL MESSAGE

Hi, Chris, this is Roosevelt Moore calling. I'm a member of your technical/professional staff. I used to report to Janice Ramos, but since she left the firm, I thought I'd bring my concerns directly to you. I'd like to arrange some time to talk with you about my experiences since returning from six weeks of paternity leave. Some of my major responsibilities have been turned over to others. I seem to be out of the loop and wonder if my career is at risk. Also, I am afraid I won't be supported or seriously considered for the opening created by Janice's departure. Frankly, I feel like I'm being screwed for taking my leave. I'd like to talk with you this week.

ITEM 13 – E-MAIL

TO: Michael Grant
FROM: Jose Martinez, Group 1 Technical Staff
DATE: October 12

I would like to set up a meeting with you as soon as possible. I suspect you will get a call from Jim Bishop of United Hospitals and want to be sure you hear my side of the story first. I have been working on a customized system design for quality assurance for them using a variation of the J–3 product we developed several years ago. They had a number of special requirements and some quirks in their accounting systems, so I have had to put in especially long hours. I've worked hard to meet their demands, but they keep changing the ground rules. I keep thinking, this is just another J–3 I'm working on, but they have been interfering with an elegant design I have developed. It seems I'm not getting anywhere on this project. Earlier today, I had a difficult discussion with their controller. He asked for another major change. I've been fighting their deadline and think I am just stretched too thin on this project. Then Jim Bishop asked me if the system was running yet. I was worn out from dealing with the controller, and I made a sarcastic comment to Jim Bishop. He gave me a funny look and just walked out of the room.

I would like to talk with you about this situation at your earliest convenience.

ITEM 14 – E-MAIL

TO: Chris Perillo
FROM: John Small, Group 6 Manager
DATE: October 15

Welcome aboard, Chris. I look forward to meeting with you. I just wanted to put a bug in your ear about finding a replacement for Janice Ramos. One of my technical staff, Mala Abendano, has the ability and drive to make an excellent group manager. I have encouraged her to apply for the position. I'd be happy to talk with you further about this, at your convenience.

ITEM 15 – E-MAIL

TO: Chris Perillo
FROM: Paula Sprague, Executive Assistant to Roger Steiner
DATE: October 15

Roger asked me to let you know about the large contract we have gotten in Tanzania. It means a team of four managers will be making a short trip to determine current needs. They will assign their technical staff the tasks of developing a system and software here over the next six months, and then the managers and possibly some team members will be spending about 10 months on site in Tanzania to handle the implementation. Roger thought you might want to hold an initial meeting with some of your managers to check on their interest and willingness to take this sort of assignment. Roger would appreciate an e-mail of your thoughts about the issues to be discussed at this meeting, additional considerations about sending people to Tanzania, and about how you will put together an effective team to work on this project. The October 15 memo I sent to you will provide you with some information you'll need to start making these decisions.

ITEM 16 – E-MAIL

TO: Chris Perillo
FROM: Sharon Shapiro, VP of Human Resources
DATE: October 15
RE: Upcoming meeting

I want to update you on the rippling effect of John Small's sexual joke at last week's planning meeting. Quite a few women have been very upset and have met informally to talk about it. They have decided to call a meeting of all people concerned about this kind of behavior throughout the firm. I plan to attend, so I'll keep you posted.

ITEM 17 – E-MAIL

TO: All SSS Software Managers
FROM: Sharon Shapiro, VP of Human Resources
DATE: October 15
RE: Promotions and External Hires

YEAR-to-DATE (JANUARY THROUGH SEPTEMBER) PROMOTIONS AND EXTERNAL HIRES

Level	Race					Sex		
	White	African American	Asian	Hispanic	Native American	M	F	Total
Hires into Executive Level	0	0	0	0	0	0	0	0
	(0%)	(0%)	(0%)	(0%)	(0%)	(0%)	(0%)	
Promotions to Executive Level	0	0	0	0	0	0	0	0
	(0%)	(0%)	(0%)	(0%)	(0%)	(0%)	(0%)	

(continued)

PRACTICE

Level	White	African American	Asian	Hispanic	Native American	M	F	Total
Hires into Management Level	2	1	0	0	0	2	1	3
	(67%)	(33%)	(0%)	(0%)	(0%)	(67%)	(33%)	
Promotions to Management Level	7	0	1	0	0	7	1	8
	(88%)	(0%)	(12%)	(0%)	(0%)	(88%)	(12%)	
Hires into Technical/ Professional Level	10	6	10	2	0	14	14	28
	(36%)	(21%)	(36%)	(7%)	(0%)	(50%)	(50%)	
Promotions to Technical/ Professional Level	0	0	0	0	0	0	0	0
	(0%)	(0%)	(0%)	(0%)	(0%)	(0%)	(0%)	
Hires into Non-management Level	4	10	2	4	0	6	14	20
	(20%)	(50%)	(10%)	(20%)	(0%)	(30%)	(70%)	
Promotions to Nonmanagement Level	NA	NA	NA	NA	NA	NA	NA	NA

SSS SOFTWARE EMPLOYEE (EEO) CLASSIFICATION REPORT AS OF JUNE 30

	Race					Sex		
Level	White	African American	Asian	Hispanic	Native American	M	F	Total
Executive Level	11	0	1	0	0	11	1	12
	(92%)	(0%)	(8%)	(0%)	(0%)	(92%)	(8%)	
Management Level	43	2	2	1	0	38	10	48
	(90%)	(4%)	(4%)	(2%)	(0%)	(79%)	(21%)	
Technical/ Professional Level	58	20	37	14	1	80	50	130
	(45%)	(15%)	(28%)	(11%)	(1%)	(62%)	(38%)	
Nonmanagement Level	29	22	4	4	1	12	48	60
	(48%)	(37%)	(7%)	(7%)	(2%)	(20%)	(80%)	
Total	141	44	44	19	2	141	109	250
	(56%)	(18%)	(18%)	(8%)	(1%)	(56%)	(44%)	

NOTE: The SSS Software exercise is used with permission. Copyright © 1995 by Susan Schor, Joseph Seltzer, and James Smither. All rights reserved.

A

ability: the product of aptitude multiplied by training and opportunity. p. 265

abundance approach: the right side of the performance continuum, characterized by concepts such as striving for excellence and being ethically virtuous, which are especially relevant to the skill of leading positive change. p. 449

accommodating approach: a response to conflict that tries to preserve a friendly interpersonal relationship by satisfying the other party's concerns while ignoring one's own. It generally ends with both parties losing. p. 313

achievement orientation: an emphasis on personal accomplishment and merit as the basis for getting ahead, used in contrast to an ascription orientation. One of the key dimensions that identifies international culture differences. p. 53

advising response: a response that provides direction, evaluation, personal opinion, or instructions. p. 208

affective orientation: an emphasis on open displays of emotion and feeling as being acceptable, used in contrast to a neutral orientation. One of the key dimensions that identifies international culture differences. p. 52

ambidextrous thinking: the use of both the left and right sides of the brain, indicative of the most creative problem solvers. p. 156

analytical problem solving: a method of solving problems that involves four steps: (1) defining the problem; (2) generating alternative solutions; (3) evaluating and selecting an alternative; and (4) implementing and following up on the solution. p. 150

anticipatory stressor: the anxious expectation of unfamiliar, uncertain, or disagreeable events. p. 95

appropriately challenging goals: one of the factors affecting the motivating potential of stated goals—hard goals tend to be more motivating than easy goals. p. 271

ascription orientation: an emphasis on attributes such as age, gender, or family background as the basis for getting ahead, used in contrast to achievement orientation. One of the key dimensions that identifies international culture differences. p. 53

attraction: also referred to as personal attraction, "likability" stemming from agreeable behavior and attractive physical appearance; a combination of behaviors normally associated with friendships that has been shown to contribute to managerial success. p. 233

autonomy: the freedom to choose how and when to do a particular task; one of the characteristics of an intrinsically satisfying job. p. 103

avoiding response: an unassertive, uncooperative reaction to conflict that neglects the interests of both parties by side-stepping the issue. The resulting frustration may engender power struggles as others rush to fill the leadership vacuum. p. 313

B

benchmarking: comparing current levels of performance to the highest standards available, by finding best practice, studying it in detail, and planning to exceed it. p. 457

bias against thinking: the inclination to avoid mental work, one indication of the conceptual block, complacency. p. 156

blocking roles: behaviors that stand in the way of or inhibit the effective performance of a team, or that subvert team member effectiveness. p. 425

brainstorming: a technique designed to help people solve problems by generating alternative solutions without prematurely evaluating and rejecting them. p. 162

C

centrality: the attribute of a position in which the occupant is a key member of informal networks of task-related and interpersonal relationships. The resulting access to information, resources, and the personal commitment of others is an important source of power. p. 237

clarification probe: question(s) designed to clarify information given by the interviewee. p. 209

closed questions: interview questions designed to elicit specific information from interviewees by restricting the possible answers the interviewee can give. Useful when time is limited and/or when answers to open questions need clarifying. p. 519

coaching: interpersonal communication used by managers to pass along advice and information or to set standards for subordinates. p. 196

cognitive style: the manner in which an individual gathers and evaluates information he/she receives. p. 48

collaborating approach: the cooperative, assertive, problem-solving mode of responding to conflict. It focuses on finding solutions to the basic problems and issues that are acceptable to both parties rather than on finding fault and assigning blame. Of the conflict management approaches, this is the only win-win strategy. p. 314

collective feeling: a feature of compassionate organizations, in which managers plan events where people can share feelings such as grief, support, or love. p. 453

collective noticing: a feature of compassionate organizations, in which managers notice or simply become aware when employees suffer or experience difficulty. p. 453

collective responding: a feature of compassionate organizations, in which managers ensure an appropriate response is made when healing or restoration is needed. p. 453

collectivism orientation: an emphasis on the predominance of groups, families, or collectives over individuals, used in contrast to individualism orientation. One of the key dimensions that identifies international culture differences. Also referred to as communitarianism. p. 52

commitment: the conceptual block that results when an individual endorses a particular point of view, definition, or solution. p. 152

comparative standards: standards that compare current performance to similar individuals or organizations, one of several different kinds of best practice standards. p. 457

compassion: in an organization, the capacity to foster collective noticing, feeling, and responding. p. 453

competence: areas in which a person performs fine—not stellar, but good enough. p. 456

complacency: the conceptual block that occurs not because of poor thinking habits or inappropriate assumptions but because of fear, ignorance, self-satisfaction, or mental laziness. p. 155

compression: the conceptual block that results from an individual's looking at a problem too narrowly, screening out too much relevant data, or making assumptions that inhibit solving the problem. p. 153

compromising response: a reaction to conflict that attempts to find satisfaction for both parties by "splitting the difference." If overused, it sends the message that settling disputes is more important than solving problems. p. 314

conceptual blocks: mental obstacles that restrict the way a problem is defined and limit the number of alternative solutions that might otherwise be considered. p. 148

conformity level: the second level of values maturity, at which moral reasoning is based on agreement with and support of society's conventions and expectations. p. 55

congruence: exactly matching the communication, verbally and nonverbally, to what an individual is thinking and feeling. p. 197

conjunctive communication: connection of responses to previous messages in such a way that conversation flows smoothly. p. 205

consistent goals: one of the factors affecting the motivating potential of stated goals—it is difficult to pursue goals that are inconsistent or incompatible. p. 271

constancy: the conceptual block that results from using only one way to look at a problem—to approach, define, describe, or solve it. p. 150

continuous improvement: small, incremental changes team members initiate. p. 415

core competence: an aggregation of individual team member skills, including knowledge, styles, communication patterns, and ways of behaving. p. 415

core self-evaluation: a concept that captures the essential aspects of personality; it accounts for the five personality dimensions (neuroticism, extroversion, conscientiousness, agreeableness, and openness). p. 48

counseling: interpersonal communication used to help subordinates recognize their own problems rather than offering advice, direction, or a right answer. p. 196

creating irreversible momentum: ensuring positive change gains such momentum that it becomes institutionalized and cannot be thwarted. p. 466

creative problem solving: a method of solving problems that involves four stages: preparation, incubation, illumination, and verification. p. 157

D

deep breathing: relaxation technique of taking several successive, slow deep breaths, then exhaling completely. p. 112

defensiveness: focusing on self-defense rather than listening; occurs when an individual feels threatened or punished by the communication. p. 197

deficit approach: the left side of the performance continuum, characterized by concepts such as solving problems and making a profit, which has garnered much more attention than the abundance approach but is less relevant to the skill of leading positive change. p. 449

deflecting response: a response that switches the focus from the communicator's subject to one selected by the listener; or simply the change of subject by the listener. p. 208

delegation: assignment of responsibility for tasks to subordinates. p. 386

descriptive communication: objective description of the event or behavior that needs modification; description of the reaction to the behavior or its consequences; and suggestion of a more acceptable alternative. p. 199

diffuseness orientation: an emphasis on integrating work, family, and personal roles in a society, used in contrast to specificity orientation. One of the key dimensions that identifies international culture differences. p. 387

dignity (and liberty): the ethical decision principle that a decision is right and proper if it preserves the basic humanity of individuals and provides the opportunity for them to have greater freedom. p. 59

direct analogies: a Synectic problem-solving technique in which individuals apply facts, technology, and previous experience to solving a problem. p. 159

disciplining: a motivational strategy by which a manager reacts negatively to an employee's undesirable behavior in order to discourage further occurrences. Disciplining may be useful up to a point but does not encourage exceptional performance. p. 276

disconfirmation: a "put-down"; or the feeling resulting from communication that demeans or belittles the recipient and threatens his or her sense of self-worth. p. 197

disjunctive communication: responses that are disconnected from what was stated before. It can result from (1) a lack of equal opportunity to speak; (2) long pauses in a speech or before a response; or (3) when one person decides the topic of conversation. p. 205

disowned communication: attribution to an unknown person, group, or some external source; allows the communicator to avoid responsibility for the message and therefore avoid investing in the interaction. p. 205

distributive bargaining perspective: negotiation tactic that requires both parties to sacrifice something to resolve the conflict—to divide up a "fixed pie." (Contrast with the integrative approach.) p. 314

double-barreled question: a problematic question that actually consists of two questions that should be asked separately in order to avoid confusing the interviewee. p. 520

E

effort: an important source of power suggesting personal commitment. p. 235

elaboration probe: question(s) designed to pursue a topic further when an interviewee has responded with superficial or inadequate information. p. 209

emotional intelligence: the ability to manage oneself emotionally and to manage relationships with others. p. 48

empowerment: the use of acquired power to give others power in order to accomplish objectives; it strikes a balance between lack of power and abuse of power. p. 366

enactive strategy: a method of managing stress that creates a new environment by eliminating the stressors. p. 92

encounter stressor: the type of stressor that results from interpersonal conflict. p. 94

environmentally induced stress: conflict-fostering tension induced by such organizational factors as budget tightening or uncertainty caused by rapid, repeated change. p. 312

equity: workers' perceptions of the fairness of rewards based on the comparison of what they are getting out of the work relationship (outcomes) to what they are putting into it (input). p. 284

ethical decision making: a well-developed set of moral principles used when making decisions. p. 57

evaluative communication: a statement that makes a judgment about or places a label on other individuals or on their behavior. p. 198

Everest goals: goals that represent an ultimate achievement, an extraordinary accomplishment, or a beyond-the-norm outcome. p. 419

expertise: cognitive ability resulting from formal training and education or from on-the-job experience; an important source of power in a technological society. p. 233

external locus of control: the viewpoint of an individual who attributes the success or failure of particular behavior to outside forces. p. 62

extrinsic outcomes: rewards for performances that are controlled by someone other than the employee—usually the supervisor—such as appreciation, job security, or good working conditions. (Compare with internal motivators.) p. 278

F

false bipolar question: a poorly worded interview question, implying the choices are mutually exclusive, when in fact, the respondents are more likely to have mixed feelings (e.g., do you approve or disapprove of overtime work?). p. 520

fantasy analogies: a synetic problem-solving technique in which individuals ask, "In my wildest dreams, how would I wish the problem to be resolved?" p. 159

feedback: information regularly received by individuals from superiors about their performance on a job. Knowledge of results permits workers to understand how their efforts have contributed to organizational goals. p. 103, 272

flexibility: the freedom to exercise one's judgment—an important prerequisite for gaining power in a position—particularly in tasks that are high in variety and novelty. p. 239

flexibility of thought: the diversity of ideas or concepts generated. p. 162

flexible communication: the result of the willingness of the coach or counselor to accept the existence of additional data or other alternatives and to acknowledge that other individuals may be able to make significant contributions both to the problem solution and to the relationship. p. 203

fluency of thought: the number of ideas or concepts produced in a given length of time. p. 162

forcing response: an assertive, uncooperative response to conflict that uses the exercise of authority to satisfy one's own needs at the expense of another's. p. 312

forgiveness: in an organization, the capacity to abandon justified resentment, bitterness, and blame, and instead, to adopt positive, forward-looking approaches in response to harm or damage. p. 453

forming stage: first stage of team development in which the team is oriented to each other and establishes clarity of purpose. p. 408

frameworks: familiar patterns that managers can use to clarify complex or ambiguous situations. p. 447

funnel sequence: a sequence of interview questions that begins with general questions and moves toward more and more specific questions. p. 521

G

goal characteristics: effective goals are specific, consistent, and appropriately challenging. p. 271

goal setting: the foundation of an effective motivational program, which consists of (1) including employees in the goal-setting process; (2) setting specific, consistent, and challenging goals; and (3) providing feedback. p. 271

goal-setting process: the critical consideration is that goals must be understood and accepted if they are to be effective. p. 271

goal standards: standards that compare current performance to publicly stated goals, one of several different kinds of best practice standards. p. 457

gratitude: in an organization, the frequent expression of thankfulness that leads to reciprocal behavior, equity, and justice. p. 454

groupthink: one of the pitfalls in group decision making that occurs when the pressure to reach consensus interferes with critical thinking. When the leader or the majority appear to prefer a particular solution, holders of dissenting views are reluctant to speak out. p. 168

H

hardiness: a combination of the three characteristics of a highly stress-resistant personality—control, commitment, and challenge. p. 113

hierarchical needs model: a general theory of motivation, positing that behavior is oriented toward need fulfillment, and that human needs tend to be arranged hierarchically (i.e., lower-level needs must be fulfilled before higher-order needs become salient). p. 281

human capital: a person's abilities and competencies ("I know the answer to the question"). Compare with social capital. p. 467

I

idea champion: person who comes up with the innovative solutions to problems. p. 169

ideal standards: standards that compare current performance to an ideal or perfect standard, one of several different kinds of best practice standards. p. 457

ignoring: a manager's neglect of both the performance and the satisfaction of employees. Such a lack of effective leadership can paralyze a work unit. p. 268

ignoring commonalities: a manifestation of the commitment block—the failure to identify similarities among seemingly disparate situations or data. p. 152

illumination stage: in creative thought, the third stage, which occurs when an insight is recognized and a creative solution is articulated. p. 157

imagery and fantasy: a relaxation technique using visualization to change the focus of one's thoughts. p. 112

imagination creativity: the pursuit of new ideas, breakthroughs, and radical approaches to problem solving. p. 143

imperviousness in communication: the failure of the communicator to acknowledge the feelings or opinions of the listener. p. 203

imposing: a manager's exploitation of employees by assigning tasks with the sole emphasis on performance and without regard to their job satisfaction—usually disastrous in the long term. p. 268

improvement creativity: the pursuit of incremental improvements on existing ideas. p. 145

improvement standards: standards that compare current performance to improvements made in the past, one of several different kinds of best practice standards. p. 457

incongruence: a mismatch between what one is experiencing and what one is aware of, or a mismatch between what one feels and what one communicates. p. 197

incubation creativity: the pursuit of creativity through teamwork, involvement, and coordination among individuals. p. 146

incubation stage: an early stage in creative thought in which mostly unconscious mental activity combines unrelated thoughts in pursuit of a solution to a problem. p. 157

indifference: a type of communication in which the other person's existence or importance is not acknowledged. p. 202

individualism orientation: an emphasis on the self, uniqueness, and individuality, used in contrast to collectivism orientation.

One of the key dimensions that identifies international cultural differences. p. 52

indulging: a manager's emphasis on employee satisfaction to the exclusion of employee performance; the resulting country club atmosphere hinders productivity. p. 268

informational deficiencies: breakdowns in organizational communication. Conflicts based on the resulting misunderstandings tend to be common but easy to resolve. p. 311

initiator role: the part played in a conflict management model by the individual who first registers a complaint with another person who is the "responder." p. 320

innovation: large, visible, discontinuous changes; breakthroughs. p. 139

innovativeness: fostering new ideas among individuals by methods such as placing them in teams and separating them at least temporarily from the normal pressures of organizational life. p. 7

instrumental values: those values that prescribe desirable standards of conduct or methods to reach a goal. p. 54

integrating: a motivation strategy that emphasizes job performance and job satisfaction equally—a challenging strategy for a manager to implement, but one that can result in both high productivity and high morale of employees. p. 269

integrative perspective: negotiation tactic in which the focus is on collaborative ways of "expanding the pie" by avoiding fixed, incompatible positions. (Contrast with distributive approach.) p. 314

internal locus of control: the viewpoint of an individual who attributes the success or failure of particular behavior to his/her own actions. p. 62

interpersonal competence: the ability to manage conflict, to build and manage high-performance teams, to conduct efficient meetings, to coach and counsel employees, to provide negative feedback in constructive ways, to influence others' opinions, and to motivate and energize employees. p. 46

interview: a specialized form of communication conducted for a specific, task-related purpose. p. 518

intrinsic outcomes: job characteristics inherent in the job itself, over which the manager has no control, and that determine whether or not a particular employee will find that job interesting and satisfying. (Compare with external motivators.) p. 278

invalidating communication: that which denies the other person the possibility of contributing to the communication. p. 202

inverted funnel sequence: a sequence of interview questions that begins with specific questions and moves toward more and more general questions. p. 521

investment creativity: the pursuit of rapid goal achievement and competitiveness. p. 145

issue-focused conflict: interpersonal conflicts that are substantive, or content, oriented. See people-focused conflict. p. 309

issue selling: influence strategy characterized by being the champion or representative of an issue. p. 246

J

Janusian thinking: thinking contradictory thoughts at the same time; conceiving two opposing ideas to be true concurrently. p. 161

L

leadership: a temporary, dynamic condition that can be developed and demonstrated by any person willing to choose to adopt a certain mind-set and implement certain key skills and competencies. p. 446

leading positive change: a management skill that focuses on unlocking positive human potential, creating abundance and human well-being, and acknowledging that positive change engages the heart as well as the mind. p. 449

leading question: a tricky interview question that includes the desired answer in the question itself. While useful in a sales interview, it can lead to biased answers in other types of interviews. p. 520

learning stair: a model, developed by researchers at the National Training Laboratories in Bethel, Maine, that grades learning retention; at the lowest level, people remember only 5 percent of what they hear in a lecture, while at the highest level, people remember 90 percent of what they teach to others. p. 466

learning style: the way in which individuals perceive, interpret, and respond to information. Four main learning styles exist. p. 48

left-hemisphere thinking: brain activity concerned with logical, analytic, linear, or sequential tasks. p. 156

legitimacy: conformity with an organization's value system and practices, which increases one's acceptance and thus one's influence in that organization. p. 235

life balance: the development of resiliency in all areas of one's life in order to handle stress that cannot be eliminated. p. 106

locus of control: the second dimension of orientation toward change; the viewpoint from which an individual judges the extent to which he/she controls his/her own destiny. p. 62

M

manifest needs model: a general theory of motivation, positing that individuals can be classified according to the strengths of their various needs, which are often divergent and conflicting. p. 281

measures: methods for assessing levels of success. p. 468

mediator role: the conflict management role played by the third party who intervenes in a dispute between an "initiator" and a "responder." p. 320

metrics: specific indicators of success. p. 468

milestones: benchmarks to determine when detectable progress will have occurred. p. 468

morphological synthesis: a four-step process intended to expand the number of creative alternatives available for solving a problem. It involves combining the different attributes of a problem together in unique ways. p. 164

motivation: a combination of desire and commitment demonstrated by effort. p. 265

muscle relaxation: technique of relaxation by easing the tension in successive muscle groups. p. 112

N

need for achievement: an expressed desire for accomplishment and recognition. p. 281

need for affiliation: an expressed desire for social relations. p. 282

need for control: the desire to maintain for oneself a satisfactory balance of power and influence in relationships. p. 380

need for power: an expressed desire for control, or influence, over others. p. 282

negative deviance: change toward illness, error, conflict, and the like, usually depicted as a shift to the left along the continuum that shows normal, healthy performance in the middle. p. 449

negative energizers: people who deplete the good feelings and enthusiasm in others and make them feel diminished, devalued, or criticized. p. 452

negotiation strategies: two broad approaches or perspectives used for resolving differences or allocating scarce resources— integrative and distributive. p. 314

neutral orientation: an emphasis on rational and stoic approaches to problem solving, used in contrast to an affective orientation. One of the key dimensions that identifies international cultural differences. p. 52

noninquisitiveness: the failure to ask questions, obtain information or search for data; an example of the complacency block. p. 155

norming stage: the second stage of a team's development in which expectations become clear, a group identity is formed, and the norms become clear and accepted. p. 408

O

open questions: interview questions designed to elicit general information from interviewees—how they feel, what their priorities are, and how much they know about a topic. Useful for establishing rapport, they can be time-consuming. p. 519

orchestrator: person who brings together cross-functional groups and necessary political support to facilitate implementation of a creative idea. p. 169

organizational culture: the values and basic assumptions that typify an organization. It refers to the most basic elements of an organization, or "just the way things are around here." p. 54

orientation toward change: an individual's adaptability to ever-increasing levels of ambiguity and turbulence. p. 48

owned communication: statements for which a person takes responsibility, acknowledging that he or she is the source of the message; an indication of supportive communication. p. 205

P

participants: individuals invited to attend a meeting. p. 553

participation: the actual process of meetings and the methods used to ensure that meetings involve everyone present. The involvement of individuals—in addition to a single leader—in an activity. p. 556

particularism: an emphasis on relationships and close personal connections to govern behavior, used in contrast to universalism orientation. One of the key dimensions that identifies international cultural differences. p. 52

"path goal" theory of leadership: The theory focuses on managers clearing a path toward their employees' goals. It proposes that a manager's involvement should vary according to what subordinates need, how much they expect, and how much support is available to them from other organizational sources. p. 272

people-focused conflict: interpersonal conflict that is personal (e.g., a clash between different personalities or interpersonal styles). See issue-focused conflict. p. 309

perceptual stereotyping: defining a problem by using preconceptions based on past experience, thus preventing the problem from being viewed in novel ways. p. 152

performance: the product of ability multiplied by motivation. p. 249

performing stage: stage of a team when it is able to function as a highly effective and efficient unit. p. 409

personal analogies: recommended as part of Synectics, whereby individuals try to identify themselves as the problem, asking the question, "If I were the problem, what would I like? What would satisfy me?" p. 159

personal differences: variations among individuals' values and needs that have been shaped by different socialization processes. Interpersonal conflicts stemming from such incompatibilities are the most difficult for a manager to resolve. p. 310

personal management interview program (PMI): a regularly scheduled, one-on-one meeting between a manager and his or her subordinates. p. 211

personal values: an individual's standards that define what is good/bad, worthwhile/worthless, desirable/undesirable, true/false, moral/immoral. p. 48

perspective: the evaluation of a meeting from a distance. p. 557

planning: preparation for the meeting agenda. p. 554

positive deviance: change toward excellence, perfection, psychological "flow," and the like, usually depicted as a shift to the light along the continuum that shows normal, healthy performance in the middle. p. 416

positive energizers: people who strengthen and create vitality and liveliness in others. p. 452

positive energy networks: interconnected groups of vitality and liveliness creators, being a member of which has been shown to be more predictive of success than being at the center of an information network or influence network. p. 452

positive interpersonal relationships: relationships that create positive energy and physiological, emotional, intellectual, and social consequences. p. 190

preparation stage: a stage in creative thought that includes gathering data, defining the problem, generating alternatives, and consciously examining all available information. p. 157

principled level: the third and highest level of values maturity in which an individual judges right from wrong by following internalized principles developed from personal experience. p. 55

proactive personality: a dispositional tendency to effect change in one's environment. p. 239

proactive strategy: a method of managing stress that initiates action in order to resist the negative effects of stress. p. 92

probing response: a response that asks a question about what the communicator just said or about a topic selected by the listener. p. 209

problem-solving process: an approach to conflict resolution that focuses on identifying underlying problems, or issues, and brainstorming solutions. p. 320

process: a sequential set of activities designed to lead to a specific outcome. p. 47

process improvement: stage in process management where process itself is changed so as to foster advancement. p. 408

purpose: the reason a meeting is held, including information sharing, commitment building, information disseminating, and problem solving and decision making. p. 552

Q

quality circles: A problem-solving process originating in Japan in which teams who meet to discuss issues and make recommendations to upper management. p. 404

R

reactive strategy: a method for managing stress that copes with the stressors immediately, temporarily reducing their effects. p. 92

reason: the influence strategy that relies on persuasion and appeals to rational consideration of the inherent merits of the request in order to gain compliance. It is explicit and direct, not manipulative. p. 243

reassigning: moving the poor performer to a position more consonant with his or her skill level and aptitude. p. 267

reciprocity: an influence strategy through which a manager uses bargaining as a tool for exacting a subordinate's compliance. This approach operates on the principle of self-interest and respect for the value of the interpersonal relationship. p. 243

recreational work: work that people willingly engage in due to characteristics such as clearly defined goals, objective evaluations, frequent feedback, the presence of personal choice, consistent rules, and a competitive environment. p. 464

redirection: a behavior-shaping process that follows a reprimand and gives the offender the opportunity to receive a future reward by modifying his or her behavior. p. 277

refitting: adapting the requirements of a job to an employee's abilities in order to improve poor performance. p. 267

reflected best-self feedback: a technique that managers can use to enhance positivity and focus on strengths, by providing people with feedback on their strengths and unique capabilities rather than their weaknesses. p. 456

reflecting response: a response that serves two purposes: (1) to confirm a message that was heard and (2) to communicate understanding and acceptance of the other person. p. 210

reflection probe: nondirective question(s) used for either elaboration or clarification of information; it generally mirrors or repeats some aspect of the interviewee's last answer. p. 209

reflective probe: a response to a communicator by reflecting back in one's own words what the communicator said. The purpose is to clarify the message and help the communicator feel open and safe in sharing more messages. p. 524

reframing: stress-reduction technique of redefining a situation as manageable. p. 109

rehearsal: relaxation technique of trying out stressful scenarios and alternative reactions. p. 113

reinforce: when rewards are linked to desired behaviors they are said to reinforce those behaviors (i.e., increase their frequency). p. 277

relational algorithm: a blockbusting technique for combining unrelated attributes in problem solving by connecting words to force a relationship between two elements in a problem. p. 164

relationship-building roles: those that emphasize the interpersonal aspects of the team. p. 422

release: dismissing an employee from the organization after all other tools for improving performance have failed. p. 267

relevance: the characteristic of a position whose tasks relate most closely to the dominant competitive goals of an organization and therefore enhance the power of the occupant. p. 240

repetition probe: a repeated or paraphrased question used if the interviewee has not directly answered a question the first time. p. 209

reprimand: a behavior-shaping approach used to transform unacceptable behaviors into acceptable ones; the discipline should be prompt and it should focus on the specific behavior. p. 277

resiliency: one's capacity to cope with stress. p. 106

respectful, egalitarian communication: treating subordinates as worth-while, competent, and insightful by emphasizing joint problem solving rather than projecting a superior position. p. 203

responder role: the part played in a conflict management model by the person who is supposedly the source of the "initiator's" problem. p. 323

resupplying: managerial option for overcoming an employee's lack-of-ability problem that focuses on supplying the support needed to do the job. p. 267

retraining: a management tool for overcoming the problem of an employee's poor performance, especially needed in rapidly changing technical work environments. p. 267

retribution: an influence strategy that involves a threat—the denial of expected rewards or the imposition of punishment. It usually triggers an aversive response in the subordinate and the breakdown of the interpersonal relationship. p. 243

reverse the definition: a tool for improving and expanding problem definition by reversing the way you think of the problem. p. 160

rewarding: the motivational strategy that links desired behaviors with employee-valued outcomes. Such positive reinforcement gives an employee more incentive for exceptional accomplishment than does disciplining. p. 276

right-hemisphere thinking: mental activity concerned with intuition, synthesis, playfulness, and qualitative judgment. p. 156

rigidity in communication: a type of message that portrays the communication as absolute, unequivocal, or unquestionable. p. 202

role incompatibility: the conflict-producing difference between workers whose tasks are interdependent but whose priorities differ because their responsibilities within the organization differ. The mediation of a common superior is usually the best solution. p. 311

rule breaker: the person who goes beyond organizational boundaries and barriers to ensure success of the creative solution. p. 169

S

self-awareness: a knowledge of one's own personality and individuality. p. 44

self-centered level: the first level of values maturity. It contains two stages of values development, moral reasoning and instrumental values, which are based on personal needs or wants and the consequences of an act. p. 55

self-determination: feelings of having a choice. p. 369

self-disclosure: revealing to others ambiguous or inconsistent aspects of oneself, a process necessary for growth. p. 46

self-efficacy: empowered feeling of possessing the capability and competence to perform a task successfully. p. 368

sensitive line: an invisible boundary around one's self-image, which, if threatened, will evoke a strong defensive reaction. p. 45

separating figure from ground: the ability to filter out inaccurate, misleading, or irrelevant information so the problem can be defined accurately and alternative solutions can be generated. p. 154

situational stressor: the type of stressor that arises from an individual's environment or circumstances, such as unfavorable working conditions. p. 94

skill variety: an attribute of a job that uses an individual's talents and abilities to the maximum and thus makes the job seem worth-while and important. p. 103

small wins strategy: a strategy for individuals to use for coping with stress; it involves celebrating each small successful step, especially changes that are easy to implement and that build momentum, in the attack on a large project. p. 374

SMART goals: goals that are specific, measurable, aligned, realistic, and time-bound. p. 373

social capital: a person's social connections ("I know someone who knows the answer to the question"). Compare with human capital. p. 552

source credibility: a judgment about the extent to which information can be believed, three attributes of which are trustworthiness, expertise, and dynamism. p. 470

specific goals: goals that are measurable, unambiguous, and behavioral. p. 271

specificity orientation: an emphasis on separating work, family, and personal roles in a society, used in contrast to diffusion orientation. One of the key dimensions that identifies international cultural differences. p. 53

sponsor: person who helps provide the resources, environment, and encouragement that the idea champion needs in order to work. p. 169

stakeholder expectations: a best-practice standard in which current performance is compared with the expectations of customers, employers, or other stakeholders. p. 457

storming stage: team development stage in which members question the team's direction, the leader, roles of other members, and task objectives. p. 408

strength: areas in which a person is an outstanding performer, has special capabilities or talents, and does better than most people. p. 456

stressors: stimuli that cause physiological and psychological reactions in individuals. p. 92

structural holes: a gap in your personal network such that two people to whom you are connected are not connected to each other. p. 238

subdivision: the breaking apart of a problem into smaller parts. p. 163

superiority-oriented communication: a message that gives the impression that the communicator is informed while others are ignorant, adequate while others are inadequate, competent while others are incompetent, or powerful while others are impotent. p. 202

supportive communication: communication that helps managers share information accurately and honestly without jeopardizing interpersonal relationships. p. 193

symbolic analogies: symbols or images that are imposed on the problem; recommended as part of Synectics. p. 159

synectics: a technique for improving creative problem solving by putting something you don't know in terms of something you do know. p. 158

T

task-facilitating roles: those that help the team accomplish its outcome objectives. p. 422

task identity: an attribute of a job that enables an individual to perform a complete job from beginning to end. pp. 103, 376

task significance: the degree to which the performance of a task affects the work or lives of other people. The greater its significance, the more meaningful the job is to the worker. p. 103

terminal values: those values that designate desirable ends or goals for an individual. p. 54

thinking languages: the various ways in which a problem can be considered, from verbal to nonverbal or symbolic languages as well as through sensory and visual imagery. Using only one thinking language is one indication of the constancy block. p. 150

threat-rigidity response: the tendency of almost all individuals, groups, and organizations to become rigid, meaning conservative and self-protective, when faced with a threat. p. 46

time stressor: the type of stressor generally caused by having too much to do in too little time. p. 94

tolerance of ambiguity: an individual's ability to cope with ambiguous, fast-changing, or unpredictable situations in which information is incomplete, unclear, or complex. p. 61

two-way communication: the result of respectfulness and flexibility. p. 203

U

uniquenesses: areas in which a person has special capacities, gifts, talents, or skills. p. 456

universalism: the ethical decision principle that a decision is right and proper if everyone would be expected to behave in the same way under the same circumstances. p. 51

V

validating communication: a message that helps people feel recognized, understood, accepted, and valued. It is respectful, flexible, two-way, and based on agreement. p. 202

values maturity: the level of moral development displayed by individuals. p. 54

verification stage: the final stage in creative thought in which the creative solution is evaluated relative to some standard of acceptability. p. 157

vertical thinking: defining a problem in a single way and then pursuing that definition without deviation until a solution is reached. p. 150

visibility: the power-enhancing attribute of a position that can usually be measured by the number of influential people one interacts with in the organization. p. 239

vision of abundance: an image of a positive future, a flourishing condition, and a legacy about which people care passionately, which a leader articulates in order to promote positive change. p. 460

vision statement: a leadership document that outlines an organization's guiding values and principles, provides a sense of direction and possibilities, and inspires optimism and hope for a better future. p. 460

W

weaknesses: areas in which a person is underdeveloped, un informed, or has little skill. p. 456

work design: the process of matching job characteristics and workers' skills and interests. p. 278

INTRODUCTION REFERENCES

American Management Association. (2000). Managerial skills and competence. National survey by AMA, March–April 2000. (N = 921)

Andersen Consulting Company. (2000). *Skills needed for the e-business environment.* Chicago: Author.

Bandura, A. (1977). *A social learning theory.* Englewood Cliffs, NJ: Prentice Hall.

Bass, B. (1990). *Handbook of leadership: Theory, research, and managerial applications,* 3rd ed. New York: Macmillan.

Blimes, L., K. Wetzker, and P. Xhonneux. (1997 February 10). Value in human resources. *Financial Times.*

Boyatzis, R. E. (1996). Consequences and rejuvenation of competency-based human resource and organization development. In Richard Woodman and William A. Pasmore (Eds.), *Research in organizational change and development,* Vol. 9. Greenwich, CT: JAI Press.

Boyatzis, R. E. (2000). Developing emotional intelligence. In C. Cherniss and D. Goleman (Eds.), *Development in emotional intelligence.* New York: Bantam.

Boyatzis, R. E. (2005). Self-directed change and learning as a necessary meta-competency for success and effectiveness in the 21st century. In R. Sims and J. G. Veres (Eds.), *Keys to employee success in the coming decades.* Westport, CT: Greenwood Publishing.

Boyatzis, R. E., D. Leonard, K. Rhee, and J. V. Wheeler. (1996). Competencies can be developed, but not in the way we thought. *Capability, 2:* 25–41.

Boyatzis, R. E., S. S. Cowen, and D. A. Kolb. (1995). *Innovation in professional education: Steps on a journey from teaching to learning.* San Francisco: Jossey-Bass.

Brodbeck, F., et al. (2000). Cultural variation of leadership prototypes across 22 countries. *Journal of Occupational and Organizational Psychology, 73:* 1–50.

Burnaska, R. F. (1976). The effects of behavioral modeling training upon managers' behavior and employees' perceptions. *Personnel Psychology, 29:* 329–335.

Cameron, K. S., R. E. Quinn, J. DeGraff, and A. V. Thakor. (2014). *Competing values leadership: Creating value in organizations.* New York: Edward Elgar.

Cameron, K. S., and D. A. Whetten. (1984). A model for teaching management skills. *Organizational Behavior Teaching Journal, 8:* 21–27.

Cameron, K. S., and D. O. Ulrich. (1986). Transformational leadership in colleges and universities. In J. Smart (Ed.), *Higher education: Handbook of theory and research* Vol. 2 (pp. 1–42). New York: Agathon.

Cameron, K., and M. Tschirhart. (1988). Managerial competencies and organizational effectiveness. Working paper, School of Business Administration, University of Michigan.

Cameron, Kim S., and Robert E. Quinn. (2011). *Diagnosing and changing organizational culture.* San Francisco: Jossey-Bass.

Cohen, P. A. (1984). College grades and adult achievement: A research synthesis. *Research in Higher Education, 20:* 281–291.

Cox, T. H. (1994). *Cultural diversity in organizations: Theory, research, and practice.* San Francisco: Barrett-Koehler.

Cox, T. H., and R. L. Beal. (1997). *Developing competency to manage diversity.* San Francisco: Barrett-Koehler.

Curtis, D. B., J. L. Winsor, and D. Stephens. (1989). National preferences in business and communication education. *Communication Education, 38:* 6–15.

Davis, T. W., and F. Luthans. (1980). A social learning approach to organizational behavior. *Academy of Management Review, 5:* 281–290.

Goleman, D. (1998). *Working with emotional intelligence.* New York: Bantam.

Greenberg, E. (1999). Broadcast Transcript, National Public Radio Morning Edition, October 26.

Hanson, G. (1986). *Determinants of firm performance: An integration of economic and organizational factors.* Unpublished doctoral dissertation, University of Michigan Business School.

Holt, J. (1964). *How children fail.* New York: Pitman.

Huselid, M. A. (1995). The impact of human resource management practices on turnover, productivity, and corporate financial performance. *Academy of Management Journal, 38:* 647.

Huselid, M. A., and B. E. Becker. (1997). The impact of high-performance work systems, implementing effectiveness, and alignment with strategy on shareholder wealth. *Academy of Management Best Papers Proceedings:* 144–148.

Katzenbach, J. R. (1995). *Real change leaders: How you can create growth and high performance in your company.* New York: New York Times Business, Random House.

Kolb, D. A. (1984). *Experiential learning: Experience as the source of learning and development.* Englewood Cliffs, NJ: Prentice Hall.

Latham, G. P., and L. P. Saari, (1979). Application of social learning theory to training supervisors through behavioral modeling. *Journal of Applied Psychology, 64:* 239–246.

Leonard, D. (1996). *The impact of learning goals on self-directed change in management development and education.* Unpublished doctoral dissertation, Weatherhead School of Management, Case Western Reserve University.

Luthans, F., S. A. Rosenkrantz, and H. W. Hennessey. (1985). What do successful managers really do? An observation study of managerial activities. *Journal of Applied Behavioral Science, 21:* 255–270.

Mintzberg, H. (1975). The manager's job: Folklore and fact. *Harvard Business Review, 53:* 49–71.

Moorehead, B. (n.d.). http://www.snopes.com/politics/soapbox/paradox.asp.

Moses, J. L., and R. J. Ritchie. (1976). Supervisory relationships training: A behavioral evaluation of a behavioral modeling program. *Personnel Psychology, 29:* 337–343.

Nair, K. (1994). *A higher standard of leadership.* San Francisco: Barrett-Koehler.

Pfeffer, J. (1998). *The human equation: Building profits by putting people first.* Boston Harvard Business School Press.

Pfeffer, J., and J. F. Veiga. (1999). Putting people first for organizational success. *Academy of Management Executive, 13:* 37–48.

Porras, J. I., and B. Anderson. (1991). Improving managerial effectiveness through modeling-based training. *Organizational Dynamics, 9:* 60–77.

Quinn, R. E. (2000). *Change the world.* San Francisco: Jossey-Bass.

Quinn, R. E., and J. Rohrbaugh. (1983). A special model of effectiveness criteria: Towards a competing values approach to organizational analysis. *Management Science, 29:* 363–377.

Rhee, K. (1997). *Journey of Discovery: A longitudinal study of learning during a graduate professional program.* Unpublished doctoral dissertation, Weatherhead School of Management, Case Western Reserve University.

Rigby, D. (1998). *Management tools and techniques.* Boston: Bain and Company.

Smith, P. E. (1976). Management modeling training to improve morale and customer satisfaction. *Personnel Psychology, 29:* 351–359.

Staw, B. M., L. Sandelands, and J. Dutton. (1981). Threat-rigidity effects in organizational behavior: A multi-level analysis. *Administrative Science Quarterly, 26:* 501–524.

Tichy, N. M. (1993). *Control your destiny or someone else will.* New York: Doubleday.

Tichy, N. M. (1999). *The leadership engine.* New York: Harper Business.

Trompenaars, F., and C. Hampden-Turner. (1998). *Riding the waves of culture.* Understanding diversity in global business. New York: McGraw-Hill.

U.S. Office of the Comptroller of the Currency. (1990). http://www.occ.treas.gov.

Van Velsor, E., and L. Jean Britain. (1995). Why executives derail: Perspectives across time and culture. *Academy of Management Executive, 9:* 62–72.

Vance, C. M. (1993). *Mastering management education.* Newbury Park, CA: Sage.

Weick, K. E. (1995). *Sensemaking in organizations.* Thousand Oaks, CA: Sage.

Welbourne, T., and A. Andrews. (1996). Predicting performance of initial public offering firms: Should HRM be in the equation? *Academy of Management Journal, 39:* 891–919.

Wheeler, J. V. (1999). *Organizational and environmental supports and opportunities for self-directed learning following graduate education.* Unpublished doctoral dissertation, Weatherhead School of Management, Case Western Reserve University.

Whetten, D. A., and K. S. Cameron. (1983). Management skill training: A needed addition to the management curriculum. *Organizational Behavior Teaching Journal, 8:* 10–15.

CHAPTER 1 REFERENCES

Agor, W. H. (1985). Intuition as a brain skill in management. *Public Personnel Management, 14:* 15–25.

Alexander, K. L. (2000, February 22). No Mr. Nice Guy for Disney. *USA Today:* B1–B2.

Allan, H., and J. Waclawski. (1999). Influence behaviors and managerial effectiveness in lateral relations. *Human Resource Development Quarterly, 10:* 3–34.

Allport, G., P. Vernon, and G. Lindzey. (1960). *Study of values.* Boston: Houghton Mifflin.

Allport, G., R. Gordon, and P. Vernon. (1931, 1960). *The study of values manual.* Boston: Houghton Mifflin.

Anderson, C., and C. E. Schneider. (1978). Locus of control, leader behavior, and leader performance among management students. *Academy of Management Journal, 21:* 690–698.

Andrews, K. (1989, September–October). Ethics in practice. *Harvard Business Review:* 99–104.

Armstrong, S. J. (2000). The influence of cognitive style on performance in management education. *Educational Psychology, 20:* 323–339.

Armstrong-Stassen, M. (1998). Downsizing the federal government: A longitudinal study of managers' reactions. *Revue Canadienne des Sciences de l'Administration, 15:* 310–321.

Atwater, L. E., & Yammarino, F. J. (1992). Does self-other agreement on leadership perceptions moderate the validity of leadership and performance predictions? *Personnel Psychology, 45*(1), 141–164.

Bar-On, R. (1997). *Bar-On emotional quotient inventory: Users manual.* Toronto: Multi-Health Systems.

Barnett, C. K., & Pratt, M. G. (2000). From threat-rigidity to flexibility-toward a learning model of autogenic crisis in organizations. *Journal of Organizational Change Management, 13*(1), 74–88.

Bernardi, R. (1997). The relationships among locus of control, perceptions of stress, and performance. *Journal of Applied Business Research, 13:* 108.

Bernardi, R. A. (2011). The relationships among locus of control, perceptions of stress and performance. *Journal of Applied Business Research (JABR), 13*(4), 1–8.

Berscheid, E., and E. H. Walster. (1978). *Interpersonal attraction.* Reading, MA: Addison-Wesley.

Bigoness, W., and G. Blakely. (1996). A cross-national study of managerial values. *Journal of International Business Studies, 27:* 739–752.

Bilsky, W., and S. H. Schwartz. (1994). Values and personality. *European Journal of Personality, 8:* 163–181.

Blau, G. (1993). Testing the relationship of locus of control to different performance dimensions. *Journal of Occupational and Organizational Psychology,* 66, 125–138.

Bonnett, C., and A. Furnham. (1991). Who wants to be an entrepreneur? *Journal of Economic Psychology, 66:* 125–138.

Bono, J. E., and T. A. Judge. (2003). Core self-evaluations: A review of the trait and its role in job satisfaction and job performance. *European Journal of Personality, 17:* 5–18.

Boone, C., Brabander, B., & Witteloostuijn, A. (1996). CEO locus of control and small firm performance: an integrative framework and empirical test*. *Journal of Management Studies, 33*(5), 667–700.

Boone, C., and B. de Brabander. (1997). Self-reports and CEO locus of control research: A note. *Organizational Studies, 18:* 949–971.

Boyatzis, R. E. (1982). *The competent manager: A model for effective performance.* New York: Wiley.

Boyatzis, R. E. (1998). Self-directed change and learning as a necessary meta-competency for success and effectiveness in the 21st century. In R. Sims and J. G. Veres (Eds.), *Keys to employee success in the coming decade.* Westport, CT: Greenwood.

Boyatzis, R. E. (2008). Competencies in the 21st century. *Journal of Management Development, 27*(1), 5–12.

Boyatzis, R. E., D. Goleman, and K. Rhee. (2000). Clustering competence in emotional intelligence: Insights from the Emotional Intelligence Inventory. In R. Bar-On and J. D. A. Parker (Eds.), *Handbook of emotional intelligence* (pp. 343–352). San Francisco: Jossey-Bass.

Brouwer, P. J. (1964). The power to see ourselves. *Harvard Business Review,* 42, 156–165.

Brown, N. W. (1997). Description of personality similarities and differences of a sample of black and white female engineering students. *Psychological Reports, 81:* 603–610.

Budner, S. (1962). Intolerance of ambiguity as a personality variable. *Journal of Personality, 30:* 29–50.

Cable, D., and T. A. Judge. (1996). Person-organization fit, job choice decisions, and organizational entry. *Organizational Behavior and Human Decision Processes, 67:* 294–311.

Cameron, K. S. (1994). Strategies for successful organizational downsizing. *Human Resource Management Journal,* 33: 89–112.

Cameron, K. S., and R. E. Quinn. (2011). *Diagnosing and changing organizational culture.* San Francisco: Jossey-Bass.

Cameron, K. S. (2011). Responsible leadership as virtuous leadership. *Journal of Business Ethics.* 98: 25–35.

Cassidy, S. (2004). Learning styles: An overview of theories, models, and measures. *Educational Psychology, 24:* 419–444.

Cavanaugh, G. F. (1980). *American business values in transition.* Englewood Cliffs, NJ: Prentice-Hall.

Cervone, D. (1997). Social-cognitive mechanisms and personality coherence: Self-knowledge, situational beliefs, and cross-situational coherence in perceived self-efficacy. *Psychological Science, 8:* 156–165.

Cervone, D. (1997). Social-cognitive mechanisms and personality coherence: Self-knowledge, situational beliefs, and cross-situational coherence in perceived self-efficacy. *Psychological Science, 8*(1), 43–50.

Chan, D. (1966). Cognitive misfit of problem-solving style at work: A facet of person-organization fit. *Organizational Behavior and Human Decision Processes, 68:* 194–207.

Chenhall, R., and D. Morris. (1991). The effect of cognitive style and sponsorship bias on the treatment of opportunity costs in resource allocation decisions. *Accounting, Organizations, and Society, 16:* 27–46.

Church, A. H., & Waclawski, J. (1999). Influence behaviors and managerial effectiveness in lateral relations. *Human Resource Development Quarterly, 10*(1), 3–34.

Clare, D. A., and D. G. Sanford. (1979). Mapping personal value space: A study of managers in four organizations. *Human Relations, 32:* 659–666.

Coleman, D., G. Irving, and C. Cooper. (1999). Another look at the locus of control-organizational commitment relationship: It depends on the form of commitment. *Journal of Organizational Behavior, 20:* 995–1001.

Cools, E., & Van den Broeck, H. (2007). Development and validation of the Cognitive Style Indicator. *The Journal of psychology, 141*(4), 359–387.

Cools, E., and H. Van den Broeck. (2007). Development and validation of the Cognitive Style Indicator. *Journal of Psychology, 14:* 359–387.

Covey, S. R. (1989). *The seven habits of highly effective people.* New York: Simon & Schuster.

Cox, T. H. (1994). *Cultural diversity in organizations.* San Francisco: Barrett-Koehler.

Cromie, S., I. Callaghan, and M. Jansen. (1992). The entrepreneurial tendencies of managers. *British Journal of Management, 3:* 1–5.

Darrow, B. (1998, November 16). Michael Dell. *Computer Reseller News:* 124–125.

Dollinger, S. J., F. T. L. Leong, and S. K. Ulicni. (1996). On traits and values: With special reference to openness to experience. *Journal of Research in Personality, 30:* 23–41.

Duval, T. S., Silvia, P. J., & Lalwani, N. (2001) Self-Awareness & Causal Attribution: A Dual Systems Theory. Boston: Springer.

Eckstrom, R. B., J. W. French, and H. H. Harmon. (1979). Cognitive factors: Their identification and replication. *Multivariate Behavioral Research Monographs, 72:* 3–84.

Elliott, A. L., and R. J. Schroth. (2002). *How companies lie: Why Enron is just the tip of the iceberg.* New York: Crown Business.

Elsayed-Elkhouly, S. M., and R. Buda. (1997). A cross–cultural comparison of value systems of Egyptians, Americans, Africans, and Arab executives. *International Journal of Commerce and Management, 7:* 102–119.

Erez, A., and T. A. Judge. (2001). Relationship of core self–evaluations to goal setting, motivation, and performance. *Journal of Applied Psychology, 86:* 1270–1279.

Feist, G. J., and F. Barron. (1996). Emotional intelligence and academic intelligence in career and life success. Presented at the American Psychological Association Meeting, San Francisco.

Fisher, S. G., W. D. K. Macrosson, and C. A. Walker. (1995). FIRO-B: The power of love and the love of power. *Psychological Reports, 76:* 195–206.

Fisher, S. G., W. D. K. Macrosson, and M. R. Yusuff. (1996). Team performance and human values. *Psychological Reports, 79:* 1019–1024.

Freud, S. (1956). *Collected papers* (Vols. 3 and 4). London: Hogarth.

Fromm, E. (1939). *Selfishness and self-love.* William Alanson White Psychiatric Foundation.

Furnham, A., Crump, J., Batey, M., & Chamorro-Premuzic, T. (2009). Personality and ability predictors of the "consequences" test of divergent thinking in a large non-student sample. *Personality and Individual Differences, 46*(4), 536–540.

Gibbs, J. C., & Schnell, S. V. (1985). Moral development "versus" socialization: A critique. *American Psychologist, 40*(10), 1071.

Gilligan, C. (1979). Women's place in man's lifecycle. *Harvard Educational Review, 49:* 431–446.

Gilligan, C. (1980). Moral development in late adolescence: A critique and reconstruction of Kohlberg's theory. *Human Development, 23:* 77–104.

Gilligan, C. (1982). In a different voice: Women's conceptions of self and morality. *Harvard Educational Review, 47:* 481–517.

Gilligan, C. (1988). Two moral orientations: Gender differences and similarities. *Merrill-Palmer Quarterly, 34:* 223–237.

Glew, D. J. (2009). Personal values and performance in teams: An individual and team-level analysis. *Small Group Research, 40*(6), 670–693.

Goleman, D. (1995). *Emotional intelligence.* New York: Bantam.

Goleman, D. (1998). *Working with emotional intelligence.* New York: Bantam.

Goleman, D. (1998). What makes a leader? *Harvard Business Review, 76:* 92–102.

Grant, A. M. (2013). Rocking the boat but keeping it steady: The role of emotion regulation in employee voice. *Academy of Management Journal, 56:*1703–1723.

Haase, R. F., D. Yul Lee, and D. L. Banks. (1979). Cognitive correlates of polychronicity. *Perceptual and Motor Skills, 49:* 271–282.

Hammer, T. H., and Y. Vardi. (1981). Locus of control and career self-management among nonsupervisory employees in industrial settings. *Journal of Vocational Behavior, 18:* 13–29.

Harris, J. R., & Sutton, C. D. (1995). Unravelling the ethical decision-making process: Clues from an empirical study comparing *Fortune* 1,000 executives and MBA students. *Journal of Business Ethics, 14*(10), 805–817.

Harris, S. (1981, October 6). Know yourself? It's a paradox. *Associated Press.*

Harter, S. (1990). Causes, correlates, and the functional role of global self-worth. In R. J. Sternberg and J. Kolligan (Eds.),

Competence reconsidered. (pp. 67–97). New Haven: Yale University Press.

Hayes, J., and C. W. Allinson. (1994). Cognitive style and its relevance for management practice. *British Journal of Management, 5:* 53–71.

Hemingway, C. A. (2005). Personal values as a catalyst for corporate social entrepreneurship. *Journal of business ethics, 60*(3), 233–249.

Henderson, J. C., and Paul C. Nutt. (1980). The influence of decision style on decision making behavior. *Management Science, 26:* 371–386.

Hendricks, J. A. (1985, May–June). Locus of control: Implications for managers and accountants. *Cost and Management:* 25–29.

Hewett, T. T., G. E. O'Brien, and J. Hornik. (1974). The effects of work organization, leadership style, and member compatibility upon the productivity of small groups working on a manipulative task. *Organizational Behavior and Human Performance, 11:* 283–301.

Hough, J. R., & Ogilvie, D. T. (2005). An empirical test of cognitive style and strategic decision outcomes*. *Journal of Management Studies, 42*(2), 417–448.

Jacobson, C. M. (1993). Cognitive styles of creativity: Relations of scores on the Kirton Adaptation-Innovation Inventory and the Myers-Briggs Type Indicator among managers in the USA. *Psychological Reports, 72:* 1131–1138.

Johnson, R. E., Rosen, C. C., & Levy, P. E. (2008). Getting to the core of core self-evaluation: a review and recommendations. *Journal of Organizational Behavior, 29*(3), 391–413.

Johnston, C. S. (1995). The Rokeach Value Survey: Underlying structure and multidimensional scaling. *Journal of Psychology, 129:* 583–597.

Jones, S. H., & Wright, M. (2010). Effect of cognitive style on performance in introductory financial accounting and the decision to major in accounting. *Global Perspectives on Accounting Education, 7.*

Jordan, J., Brown, M. E., Treviño, L. K., & Finkelstein, S. (2013). Someone to look up to executive–follower ethical reasoning and perceptions of ethical leadership. *Journal of Management, 39*(3), 660–683.

Judge, T. A., A. Erez, J. E. Bono, and C. J. Thoreson. (2002). Are measures of self-esteem, neuroticism, locus of control, and generalized self-efficacy indicators of a common core construct? *Journal of Personality and Social Psychology, 83:* 693–710.

Judge, T. A., A. Erez, J. E. Bono, and C. J. Thoreson. (2003). The core self-evaluation scale: Development of a measure. *Personnel Psychology, 56:* 303–331.

Judge, T. A., Bono, J. E., Erez, A., & Locke, E. A. (2005). Core self-evaluations and job and life satisfaction: The role of self-concordance and goal attainment. *Journal of Applied Psychology, 90*(2), 257–268.

Judge, T. A., Bono, J. E., Erez, A., & Locke, E. A. (2005). Core self-evaluations and job and life satisfaction: The role of self-concordance and goal attainment. *Journal of Applied Psychology, 90*(2), 257–268.

Judge, T. A., and J. E. Bono. (2001). Relationship of core self-evaluations traits—self-esteem, generalized self-efficacy, locus of control, and emotional stability—with job satisfaction and job performance: A meta-analysis. *Journal of Applied Psychology, 86:* 80–92.

Kirton, M. J. (2003). *Adaptation–innovation in the context of diversity and change.* London: Routledge.

Kohlberg, L. (1969). The cognitive-developmental approach to socialization. In D. A. Goslin (Ed.), *Handbook of socialization theory and research.* Chicago: Rand McNally.

Kohlberg, L. (1976). Moral stages and moralization, the cognitive-developmental approach. In T. Lickona (Ed.), *Moral development and behavior.* New York: Holt, Rinehart & Winston.

Kohlberg, L. (1981). *Essays in moral development,* Vol. 1. New York: Harper & Row, pp. 409–412.

Kohlberg, L., and R. A. Ryncarz. (1990). Beyond justice reasoning: Moral development and consideration of a seventh stage. In C. Alexander and E. J. Langer (Eds.), *Higher stages of human development.* New York: Oxford University Press.

Kolb, D. A., R. E. Boyatzis, and C. Mainemelis. (2000). Experiential learning theory: Previous research and new directions. In R. J. Sternberg and L. F. Zhang (Eds.), *Perspectives on cognitive, learning, and thinking styles.* Mahwah, NJ: Lawrence Erlbaum.

Kren, L. (1992). The moderating effects of locus of control on performance incentives and participation. *Human Relations, 45:* 991–1012.

Lickona, T. (1976). Critical issues in the study of moral development and behavior. In T. Lickona (Ed.), *Moral development and behavior: Theory, research, and social issues.* New York: Holt, Rinehart & Winston.

Liddel, W. W., and John W. Slocum Jr. (1976). The effects of individual-role compatibility upon group performance: An extension of Schutz's FIRO theory. *Academy of Management Journal, 19:* 413–426.

Locke, E. A., K. McClear, and D. Knight. (1996). Self-esteem at work. *International Review of Industrial/Organizational Psychology, 11:* 1–32.

Lozano, J. M. (1996). Ethics and management: a controversial issue. *Journal of Business Ethics, 15*(2), 227–236.

Martin, R., Thomas, G., Charles, K., Epitropaki, O., & McNamara, R. (2005). The role of leader-member exchanges in mediating the relationship between locus of control and work reactions. *Journal of Occupational and Organizational Psychology, 78*(1), 141–147.

Maslow, A. H. (1962). *Toward a psychology of being.* Princeton, NJ: D. Von Nostrand.

Milgram, S. (1963). Behavioral study of obedience. *Journal of Abnormal and Social Psychology, 67:* 371–378.

Miller, D., M. F. R. Kets de Vries, and J. M. Toulouse. (1982). Top executive locus of control and its relationship to strategy-making, structure, and environment. *Academy of Management Journal, 25:* 237–253.

Mitchell, L. E. (2002). *Corporate irresponsibility: America's newest export.* New Haven: Yale University Press.

Moore, T. (1987, March 30). Personality tests are back. *Fortune:* 74–82.

Newton, T., and A. Keenan. (1990). The moderating effect of Type A behavior pattern and locus of control upon the relationship between change in job demands and change in psychological strain. *Human Relations, 43:* 1229–1255.

Nwachukwu, S. L. S., and S. J. Vitell. (1997). The influence of corporate culture on managerial ethical judgments. *Journal of Business Ethics, 16:* 757–776.

O'Reilly, B. (1999). The mechanic who fixed Continental. *Fortune, 140:* 176–186.

Oginska-Bulik, N. (2005). Emotional intelligence in the workplace: Exploring its effects on occupational stress and health outcomes in human service workers. *International Journal of Occupational Medicine and Environmental Health, 18*(2), 167–175.

Parker, V., and K. Kram. (1993). Women mentoring women. *Business Horizons, 36:* 101–102.

Phillips, J., and S. Gully. (1997). Role of goal orientation, ability, need for achievement, and locus of control in self-efficacy and goal-setting processes. *Journal of Applied Psychology, 82:* 792–802.

Plaue, n. (2012) A quarter of wall street executives say you have to be unethical to succeed. www.businessinsider.com. July 10th.

Posner, B., and J. Kouzes. (1993). Values congruence and differences between the interplay of personal and organizational values. *Journal of Business Ethics, 12:* 341–347.

Posner, B. Z. and Schmidt, W. H. (1982). *Managerial Values and Expectations.* New York: AMACOM.

Posner, B. Z. and Schmidt, W. H. (1992). Values and the American manager. A update updated. *California Management Review, (34)* 80–94.

Rest, J. R. (1979). *Revised manual for the Defining Issues Test: An objective test of moral judgment development.* Minneapolis: Minnesota Moral Research Projects.

Rest, J. R., Narvaez, D., Thoma, S. J., & Bebeau, M. J. (1999). DIT2: Devising and testing a revised instrument of moral judgment. *Journal of Educational Psychology, 91*(4), 644–659.

Rice, Michelle. (1999). Rugged mountains and lifelong connections: Adrian Manger. *Australian CPA, 69:* 36–37.

Rogers, C. R. (1961). *On becoming a person.* Boston: Houghton Mifflin.

Rokeach, M. (1973). *The nature of human values.* New York: Free Press.

Rosenthal, R. (1977). The PONS Test: Measuring sensitivity to nonverbal cues. In P. McReynolds (Ed.), *Advancement on psychological assessment.* San Francisco: Jossey-Bass.

Rotter, J. B. (1966). Generalized expectancies for internal versus external control of reinforcement. *Psychological Monographs, 80:* 1–28.

Rozell, E. J., Pettijohn, C. E., & Parker, R. S. (2002). An empirical evaluation of emotional intelligence: The impact on management development. *Journal of Management Development, 21*(4), 272–289.

Ryan, L. R. (1970). *Clinical interpretation of the FIRO-B.* Palo Alto, CA: Consulting Psychologists Press.

Salovey, P., & Grewal, D. (2005). The science of emotional intelligence. *Current directions in psychological science, 14*(6), 281–285.

Salovey, P., and J. Mayer. (1990). Emotional intelligence. *Imagination, Cognition, and Personality, 9:* 185–211.

Schein, E. H. (1960). Interpersonal communication, group solidarity, and social influence. *Sociometry, 23:* 148–161.

Seeman, M. (1982). On the personal consequences of alienation in work. *American Sociological Review, 32:* 273–285.

Slaski, M., & Cartwright, S. (2003). Emotional intelligence training and its implications for stress, health and performance. *Stress and Health, 19*(4), 233–239.

Snarey, J. R., and G. E. Vaillant. (1985). How lower- and working-class youth become middle-class adults: The association between ego defense mechanisms and upward social mobility. *Child Development, 56:* 899–910.

Sosik, J. J., & Megerian, L. E. (1999). Understanding leader emotional intelligence and performance the role of self-other agreement on transformational leadership perceptions. *Group & Organization Management, 24*(3), 367–390.

Sosik, J., and L. E. Megerian. (1999). Understanding leader emotional intelligence and performance: The role of self-other agreement on transformational leadership perceptions. *Group and Organization Management, 24:* 367–390.

Spector, P. E. (1982). Behavior in organizations as a function of employee's locus of control. *Psychological Bulletin, 47:* 487–489.

Spencer, L. M., & Spencer, P. S. M. (2008). *Competence at work models for superior performance.* John Wiley & Sons.

Spencer, L. M., and S. M. Spencer. (1993). *Competence at work: Models for superior performance.* New York: Wiley.

Stackman, R. W., Connor, P. E., & Becker, B. W. (2006). Sectoral ethos: an investigation of the personal values systems of female and male managers in the public and private sectors. *Journal of Public Administration Research And Theory, 16*(4), 577–597.

Sternberg, R. J. (1996). *Successful intelligence.* New York: Simon & Schuster.

Sternberg, R. J., and L. F. Zhang (Eds.). (2000). *Perspectives on cognitive, learning, and thinking styles.* Mahwah, NJ: Lawrence Erlbaum.

Stevens, B. (2012). How ethical are U.S. business executives? A study of perceptions. *Journal of Business Ethics,* 1–9.

Sweeney, P., D. McFarlin, and J. Cotton. (1991). Locus of control as a moderator of the relationship between perceived influence and procedural justice. *Human Relations, 44:* 333–342.

Teoh, H. Y., and S. L. Foo. (1997). Moderating effects of tolerance for ambiguity and risk–taking propensity on the role conflict–perceived performance relationship: Evidence from Singaporean entrepreneurs. *Journal of Business Venturing, 12:* 67–81.

Timothy, A., C. Thoresen, V. Pucik, and T. Welbourne. (1999). Managerial coping with organizational change: A dispositional perspective. *Journal of Applied Psychology, 84:* 107–122.

Trompenaars F. & Hampden-Turner, C. (2004). *Managing People Across Cultures.* Mankato, MN: Capstone Publishers.

Trompenaars, F. (1996). Resolving international conflict: Culture and business strategy. *Business Strategy Review, 7:* 51–68.

Trompenaars, F., and C. Hampton-Turner. (1998, 2011). *Riding the waves of culture.* New York: McGraw-Hill.

Tubbs, W. (1994). The roots of stress-death and juvenile delinquency in Japan: Disciplinary ambivalence and perceived locus of control. *Journal of Business Ethics, 13:* 507–522.

Valentine, S. R., Godkin, J., & Doughty, G. P. (2008). Hispanics' locus of control, acculturation, and wellness attitudes. *Social work in public health, 23*(5), 73–92.

Vance, C. M., K. S. Groves, Y. Paik, and H. Kindler. (2007). Understanding and measuring linear–nonlinear thinking style for enhanced management education and professional practice. *Academy of Management Learning and Education Journal, 6:* 167–185.

Watson, D. (2000). *Mood and temperament.* New York: Guilford.

Weick, K. E. (1993). The collapse of sensemaking in organizations. *Administrative Science Quarterly, 38:* 628–652.

Weick, K. E., and K. Sutcliffe. (2000). High reliability: The power of mindfulness. *Leader to Leader, 17:* 33–38.

Wheeler, R. W., and J. M. Davis. (1979). Decision making as a function of locus of control and cognitive dissonance. *Psychological Reports, 44:* 499–502.

Whetten, D. A., & Cameron, K. S. (1994). "Organizational effectiveness: Old models and new constructs." In Gerald Greenberg (Ed.) Organizational Behavior: The State of the Science. New York: Lawrence Erlbaum Associates.

CHAPTER 2 REFERENCES

Adler, C. M., and J. J. Hillhouse (1996). Stress, health, and immunity: A review of the literature. In Thomas W. Miller (Ed.), *Theory and assessment of stressful life events.* Madison, CT: International University Press.

Adler, J. (1999, June 14). Stress, *Newsweek,* 56–61.

Adler, J. (2005). *My prescription for anti-depressive living.* New York: Regan.

Adler, V. (1989). Little control equals lots of stress. *Psychology Today, 23:* 18–19.

American Institute of Stress. (2000). www.stress.org/problem. htm.

American Psychological Association. (2009). *Stress in America.* Washington DC: APA.

Andersen, M. B., & Williams, J. M. (1999). Athletic injury, psychosocial factors and perceptual changes during stress. *Journal of Sports Sciences, 17*(9), 735–741.

Anderson, C. R. (1977). Locus of control, coping behaviors and performance in a stress setting: A longitudinal study. *Journal of Applied Psychology, 62:* 446–451.

Auerbach, S. M. (1998). *Stress management: Psychological foundations.* Upper Saddle River, NJ: Prentice Hall.

Baker, W. (2012). "A dual model of reciprocity in organizations." In Cameron, K. S. and Spreitzer, G. M. (Eds.). *Oxford Handbook of Positive Organizational Scholarship.* New York: Oxford University Press.

Baker, W. (2013). "Making Pipes, Using Pipes: How Tie Initiation, Reciprocity, and Positive Emotions Create New Organizational Social Capital." In Borgatti, S. P., Brass, D. J., Halgin, D. S., Labianca, G., and Mehra A. (Eds.). *Research in the Sociology* of Organizations, Volume on Contemporary Perspectives on Organizational Social Network Analysis (in press).

Balzer, W. K., M. E. Doherty, and R. O'Connor. (1989). Effects of cognitive feedback on performance. *Psychological Bulletin, 106:* 410–433.

Bandura, A. (1997). *Self-efficacy: The exercise of control.* New York: W. H. Freeman.

Bandura, A. (2012). On the functional properties of perceived self-efficacy revisited. *Journal of Management, 38*(1), 9–44.

Beary, J. F., and H. Benson. (1977). A simple psychophysiologic technique which elicits the hypometabolic changes in the relaxation response. *Psychosomatic Medicine, 36:* 115–120.

Bell, C. R. (1998). *Managers as mentors.* San Francisco: Barrett-Koehler.

Benson, H. (1975). *The relaxation response.* New York: William Morrow.

Bramwell, S. T., M. Masuda, N. N. Wagner, and T. H. Holmes. (1975). Psychosocial factors in athletic injuries. *Journal of Human Stress, 1:* 6.

Brockner, J., and B. M. Weisenfeld. (1993). Living on the edge: The effects of layoffs on those who remain. In J. Keith Murnighan (Ed.), *Social psychology in organizations: Advances in theory and research.* Englewood Cliffs, NJ: Prentice Hall.

Cameron, K. S. (1994). Strategies for successful organizational downsizing. *Human Resource Management Journal, 33:* 189–212.

Cameron, K. S. (1998). Strategic organizational downsizing: An extreme case. *Research in Organizational Behavior, 20:* 185–229.

Cameron, K. S., D. A. Whetten, and M. U. Kim. (1987). Organizational dysfunctions of decline. *Academy of Management Journal, 30:* 126–138.

Cameron, K. S., M. U. Kim, and D. A. Whetten. (1987). Organizational effects of decline and turbulence. *Administrative Science Quarterly, 32:* 222–240.

Cameron, K. S., S. J. Freeman, and A. K. Mishra. (1991). Best practices in white-collar downsizing: Managing contradictions. *Academy of Management Executive, 5:* 57–73.

Cantor, N., and J. F. Kihlstrom. (1987). *Personality and social intelligence.* Englewood Cliffs, NJ: Prentice Hall.

Chen, G. (2007). *Subject-object meaningfulness in knowledge work.* Unpublished honors thesis, Organizational Studies Program, University of Michigan.

Coddington, R. D., and J. R. Troxell. (1980). The effect of emotional factors on football injury rates: A pilot study. *Journal of Human Stress, 6:* 3–5.

Contrada, R. J., & Baum, A. (Eds.). (2011). *The handbook of stress science: Biology, psychology, and health.* Springer Publishing Company.

Cooper, C. L. (1998). *Theories of organizational stress.* New York: Oxford University Press.

Cooper, C. L., and M. J. Davidson. (1982). The high cost of stress on women managers. *Organizational Dynamics, 11:* 44–53.

Cooper, M. J., and M. M. Aygen. (1979). A relaxation technique in the management of hypocholesterolemia. *Journal of Human Stress, 5:* 24–27.

Cordes, C. L., and T. W. Dougherty. (1993). Review and an integration of research on job burnout. *Academy of Management Review, 18:* 621–656.

Covey, S. (1989). *Seven habits of highly effective people.* New York: Wiley.

Cowley, C. (2000, June 14). Stress-busters: What works. *Newsweek:* 60.

Curtis, J. D., and R. A. Detert. (1981). *How to relax: A holistic approach to stress management.* Palo Alto: Mayfield Publishing Co.

Davidson, J. (1995). *Managing your time.* Indianapolis: Alpha Books.

Davis, M., E. Eshelman, and M. McKay. (1980). *The relaxation and stress reduction workbook.* Richmond, CA: New Harbinger Publications.

Deepak, M. D. (1995). *Creating health: How to wake up the body's intelligence.* New York: Houghton Mifflin.

Dellbeck, M., and S. Shatkin. (1991). *Scientific research on the transcendental meditation process.* Fairfield, IA: Maharishi International University of Management Press.

Dyer, W. G. (1987). *Teambuilding.* Reading, MA: Addison-Wesley.

Eliot, R. S. (2010). *Is It Worth Dying For? How To Make Stress Work For You–Not Against You.* Random House Digital, Inc.

Eliot, R. S., and D. L. Breo. (1984). *Is it worth dying for?* New York: Bantam Books.

Emmons, R. (2008). *Thanks: How the New Science of Gratitude Can Make You Happier.* Boston: Houghton Mifflin Harcourt.

Farnham, A. (1991, October 7). Who beats stress and how? *Fortune:* 71–86.

Fisher, C., and R. Gitelson. (1983). A meta-analysis of the correlates of role conflict and role ambiguity. *Journal of Applied Psychology, 68:* 320–333.

Fredrickson, B. L., Cohn, M. A., Coffey, K. A., Pek, J., Finkel, S. M. (2008). "Open hearts build lives: Positive emotions, induced through loving kindness meditation, build consequential personal resources." *Journal of Personality and Social Psychology, 95:* 1045–1062.

French, J. R. R., and R. D. Caplan. (1972). Organizational stress and individual strain. In A. J. Marrow (Ed.), *The failure of success.* New York: AMACOM.

Friedman, M. (1996). *Type A behavior: Its diagnosis and treatment.* New York: Kluwer Academic Publishers.

Friedman, M., and D. Ulmer. (1984). *Treating type A behavior and your heart.* New York: Alfred A. Knopf, 84–85.

Friedman, M., and R. H. Rosenman. (1974). *Type A behavior and your heart.* New York: Knopf.

Gardner, H. (1993). *Multiple intelligences: The theory in practice.* New York: Basic Books.

Gittell, J., K. Cameron, and S. Lim. (2006). Relationships, layoffs, and organizational resilience. *Journal of Applied Behavioral Science.*

Goldberg, H. (1976). *The hazards of being male.* New York: Nash.

Goldberger, L., & Breznitz, S. (Eds.). (2010). *Handbook of stress.* New York: Simon and Schuster.

Goleman, D. (1998). *Working with emotional intelligence.* New York: Bantam Books.

Gordon, A. (1959). *A day at the beach*. Copyright © 1959 by Arthur Gordon. All rights reserved. Reprinted by permission of the author. First published in the *Reader's Digest*.

Greenberg, J. (1987). *Comprehensive stress management*, 2nd ed. Dubuque, IA: William C. Brown Publishers.

Greenberger, D. B., and S. Stasser. (1991). The role of situational and dispositional factors in the enhancement of personal control in organizations. *Research in Organizational Behavior, 13:* 111–145.

Griest, J. H., et al. (1979). Running as treatment for depression. *Comparative Psychology, 20:* 41–56.

Hackman, J. R., G. R. Oldham, R. Janson, and K. Purdy. (1975). A new strategy for job enrichment. *California Management Review, 17:* 57–71.

Hackman, R. J., and G. R. Oldham. (1980). *Work redesign*. Reading, MA: Addison-Wesley.

Halberstadt, A. G., Denham, S. A., & Dunsmore, J. C. (2001). Affective social competence. *Social development, 10*(1), 79–119.

Hall, D. T. (1976). *Careers in organizations*. Santa Monica, CA: Goodyear.

Hendricks, W. (1996). *Coaching, mentoring, and managing*. Franklin Lakes, NJ: Career Press.

Hepburn, G. C., C. A. McLoughlin, and J. Barling. (1997). Coping with chronic work stress. In B. H. Gottlieb (Ed.), *Coping with chronic stress*. (pp. 343–366). New York: Plenum.

Hill, E. J., Hawkins, A. J., Ferris, M., & Weitzman, M. (2001). "Finding an Extra Day a Week: The Positive Influence of Perceived Job Flexibility on Work and Family Life Balance." *Family Relations, 50*(1), 49–58.

Hobson, C. J., J. Kamen, J. Szostek, C. M. Nethercutt, J. W. Tiedmann, and S. Wojnarowicz. (1998). Stressful life events: A revision and update of the Social Readjustment Rating Scale. *International Journal of Stress Management, 5:* 1–23.

Holmes, T. H., and R. H. Rahe. (1967). The social readjustment rating scale. *Journal of Psychosomatic Research, 11:* 213–218.

Holmes, T. H., and R. H. Rahe. (1970). The social readjustment rating scale. *Journal of Psychosomatic Research, 14:* 121–132.

Holt-Lunstad, J., Smith, T. B., and Layton, J. B. (2010). "Social relationships and mortality risk: A meta-analytic review." *PLoS Med, 7:* e1000316.

Holzel, B. K., Carmody, J., Vangel, M., Congeton, C., Yerrametti, S. M., Gard, T., and Lazar, S. W. (2010). "Mindfulness practice leads to increases in regional brain gray matter density." *Psychiatry Research: Neuroimaging, 191:* 36–43.

Hubbard, J. R., and E. A. Workman. (1998). *Handbook of stress medicine: An organ system approach*. Boca Raton, FL: CRC Press.

Ivancevich, J. M., and M. T. Matteson. (1980). *Stress & work: A managerial perspective*. Glenview, IL: Scott Foresman.

Ivancevich, J., and D. Ganster. (1987). *Job stress: From theory to suggestions*. New York: Haworth.

Jourard, S. M. (1964). *The transparent self*. Princeton, NJ: Von Nostrand.

Judge, T. A., and J. E. Bono. (2001). Relationship of core self-evaluations traits—self-esteem, generalized self-efficacy, locus of control, and emotional stability—with job satisfaction and job performance: A meta-analysis. *Journal of Applied Psychology, 86:* 80–92.

Kahn, R. L., and P. Byosiere. (1992). Stress in organizations. In Marvin Dunnette and L. M. Hough (Eds.), *Handbook of industrial and organizational psychology* (pp. 571–650). Palo Alto: Consulting Psychologists.

Kahn, R. L., et al. (1964). *Organizational stress: Studies in role conflict and ambiguity*. New York: Wiley.

Karasek, R. A., T. Theorell, J. E. Schwartz, P. L. Schnall, C. F. Pieper, and J. L. Michela. (1988). Job characteristics in relation to the prevalence of myocardial infarction in the U.S. Health Examination Survey and the Health and Nutrition Examination Survey. *American Journal of Public Health, 78:* 910–918.

Katzenbach, J. R., and D. K. Smith. (1993). *The wisdom of teams*. Boston: Harvard Business School Press.

Kobasa, S. (1982). Commitment and coping in stress resistance among lawyers. *Journal of Personality and Social Psychology, 42:* 707–717.

Kobasa, S. C. (1979). Stressful life events, personality, and health: An inquiry into hardiness. *Journal of Personality and Social Psychology, 37:* 1–12.

Kok, B. E., Coffey, K. A., Cohn, M. A., Catalino, L. I., Vacharkulksemsuk, T., Algoe, S. B., Brantley, M., Fredrickson, B. L. (2012). "How positive emotions build Physical health: Perceived positive social connections account for upward spirals between positive emotions and vagal tone." (Working paper, University of North Carolina, Chapel Hill.)

Kram, K. (1985). *Mentoring at work*. Glenview, IL: Scott Foresman.

Kuhn, A., and R. D. Beam. (1982). *The logic of organizations*. San Francisco: Jossey-Bass.

Lakein, D. (1989). *How to get control of your time and your life*. New York: McKay.

Latack, J., A. J. Kinicki, and G. Prussia. (1995). An integrative process model of coping with job loss. *Academy of Management Review, 20:* 311–342.

Lawler, E. E., S. A. Mohrman, and G. E. Ledford. (1992). *Employee involvement and total quality management*. San Francisco: Jossey-Bass.

Lehrer, P. M. (1996). *The Hatherleigh guide to issues in modern therapy*. New York: Hatherleigh Press.

Levinson, J. D. (1978). *Seasons of a man's life*. New York: Knopf.

Lewin, K. (1951). *Field theory in social science*. New York: Harper & Row.

Likert, R. (1967). *The human organization*. New York: McGraw-Hill.

Locke, E., and G. Latham. (1990). *A theory of goal setting and task performance*. Englewood Cliffs, NJ: Prentice Hall.

Lusch, R. F., and R. R. Serpkenci. (1990). Personal differences, job tension, job outcomes, and store performance: A study of retail managers. *Journal of Marketing, 54:* 85–101.

Maddi, S. (2013). Thirty Years of Hardiness Validational Research and Practice. *Hardiness*, 19–28. Springer Netherlands.

Maddi, S., and S. C. Kobasa. (1984). *The hardy executive: Health under stress*. Homewood, IL: Dow Jones-Irwin.

Masten, A. S., and M. J. Reed. (2002). Resilience in development. In C. R. Snyder, and S. J. Lopez (Eds.), *Handbook of positive psychology* (pp. 74–88). New York: Oxford University Press.

Masten, A. S.; Obradovic, J. (2006). "Competence and resilience in development." *Annals of the New York Academy of Sciences* 1094: 13–27.

Mayer, J. D., Roberts, R. D., & Barsade, S. G. (2008). Human abilities: Emotional intelligence. *Annu. Rev. Psychol., 59,* 507–536.

McNichols, T. J. (1973). *The case of the missing time.* Evanston, IL: Northwestern University Kellogg School of Business.

Mednick, M. T. (1982). Woman and the psychology of achievement: Implications for personal and social change. In H. J. Bernardin (Ed.), *Women in the workforce.* New York: Praeger.

Milgram, S. (1963). Behavioral study of obedience. *Journal of Abnormal and Social Psychology, 63:* 371–378.

Miller, K. E., & Rasmussen, A. (2010). War exposure, daily stressors, and mental health in conflict and post-conflict settings: bridging the divide between trauma-focused and psychosocial frameworks. *Social Science & Medicine,70*(1), 7–16.

Mintzberg, H. (1973). *The nature of managerial work.* New York: Harper & Row.

Mishra, A. K. (1992). *Organizational responses to crisis.* Unpublished doctoral dissertation, University of Michigan School of Business Administration.

Murphy, L. R. (1996). Stress management in work settings: A critical review of health effects. *American Journal of Health Promotion, 11:* 112–135.

Northwestern National Life Insurance Company (NNL). (1992). *Employee burnout: Causes and cures.* Minneapolis, MN: Author.

Oldham, G. R. (2012). "The design of jobs: A strategy for enhancing the positive outcomes of individuals at work." In Cameron, K. S. and Spreitzer, G. M. (Eds.). *Oxford Handbook of Positive Organizational Scholarship,* 651–663. New York: Oxford University Press.

Orme-Johnson, D. W. (1973). Autonomic stability and transcendental meditation. *Psychosomatic Medicine, 35:* 341–349.

Panko, R. R. (1992). Managerial communication patterns. *Journal of Organizational Computing and Electronic Commerce, 2*(1), 95–122.

Peters, T. (1988). *Thriving on chaos.* New York: Knopf.

Pfeffer, J. (1998). *The human equation: Building profits by putting people first.* Boston: Harvard Business School Press.

Pilling, B. K., and S. Eroglu. (1994). An empirical examination of the impact of salesperson empathy and professionalism and merchandise salability on retail buyer's evaluations. *Journal of Personal Selling and Sales Management, 14:* 55–58.

Porath, C., Spreitzer, G. M., Gibson, C., and Garnett, F. G. (2011). "Thriving at work: Toward itys measurement, construct validation, and theoretical refinement." *Journal of Organizational Behavior.*

Putnam, R. (2013). *Bowling Alone.* New York: Simon & Schuster.

Rahe, R. H., D. H. Ryman, and H. W. Ward. (1980). Simplified scaling for life change events. *Journal of Human Stress, 6:* 22–27.

J. W. Reich, A. J. Zautra & J. S. Hall (2010). *Handbook of adult resilience.* New York: Guilford Press.

Rosenthal, R. (1977). The PONS Test: Measuring sensitivity to nonverbal cues. In P. McReynolds (Ed.), *Advances in psychological measurement.* San Francisco: Jossey-Bass.

Rostad, F. G., and B. C. Long. (1996). Exercise as a coping strategy for stress: A review. *International Journal of Sport Psychology, 27:* 197–222.

Saarni, C. (1997). Emotional competence and self-regulation in childhood. In P. Savoey and D. J. Sluyter (Eds.), *Emotional development and emotional intelligence.* New York: Basic Books.

Schein, E. H. (1960). Interpersonal communication, group solidarity, and social influence. *Sociometry, 23:* 148–161.

Selye, H. (1976). *The stress of life,* 2nd ed. New York: McGraw-Hill.

Shoda, Y., W. Mischel, and P. K. Peake. (1990). Predicting adolescent cognitive and self-regulatory competencies from preschool delay of gratification: Identifying diagnostic conditions. *Developmental Psychology, 26:* 978–986.

Siegman, A. W., and T. W. Smith (Eds.). (1994). *Anger, hostility, and the heart.* Mahwah, NJ: Lawrence Erlbaum and Associates.

Singh, J. (1993). Boundary role ambiguity: Facts, determinants, and impacts. *Journal of Marketing, 57:* 11–30.

Singh, J. (1998). Striking balance in boundary-spanning positions: An investigation of some unconventional influences of role stressors and job characteristics on job outcomes or sales-people. *Journal of Marketing, 62:* 69–86.

Sorenson, M. J. (1998). *Breaking the chain of low self-esteem.* Stone Mountain, GA: Wolf Publications.

Spencer, L. M., and S. M. Spencer. (1993). *Competence at work: Models for superior performance.* New York: Wiley.

Spreitzer, G. M., Sutcliffe, K. Dutton, J. E., Sonenshein, S., and Grant, A.M. (2005). "A socially embedded model of thriving at work." *Organizational Science,* 16: 537–549.

Stalk, G., and T. M. Hout. (1990). *Competing against time.* New York: Free Press.

Staw, B. M., L. Sandelands, and J. Dutton. (1981). Threat-rigidity effects in organizational behavior. *Administrative Science Quarterly, 26:* 501–524.

Sternberg, R. (1997). *Successful intelligence.* New York: Simon & Schuster.

Stone, R. A., and J. Deleo. (1976). Psychotherapeutic control of hypertension. *New England Journal of Medicine, 294:* 80–84.

Stranks, J. (2013). *Stress at work.* Routledge.

Sutcliffe, K., and T. Vogus. (2003). Organizing for resilience. In K. S. Cameron, J. E. Dutton, and R. E. Quinn (Eds.), Positive organizational scholarship. San Francisco: Barrett-Koehler.

Thoits, P. A. (1995). Stress, coping, and social support processes: Where are we? What next? *Journal of Health and Social Behavior, 36:* 53–79.

Trompenaars, F. (1996). Resolving international conflict: Culture and business strategy. *Business Strategy Review, 7:* 51–68.

Trompenaars, F., and C. Hampden-Turner. (1998). *Riding the waves of culture.* New York: McGraw-Hill.

Turkington, C. (1998). *Stress management for busy people.* New York: McGraw-Hill.

Ungar, M. (2008). "Resilience across cultures". *British Journal of Social Work* 38 (2): 218–235.

Vinton, D. E. (1992). A new look at time, speed, and the manager. *Academy of Management Executive, 6:* 1–16.

Wadey, R., Evans, L., Hanton, S., & Neil, R. (2012). An examination of hardiness throughout the sport injury process. *British journal of health psychology, 17*(1), 103–128.

Weick, K. (1984). Small wins. *American Psychologist, 39:* 40–49.

Weick, K. E. (1993a). The collapse of sensemaking in organizations. *Administrative Science Quarterly, 38:* 628–652.

Weick, K. E. (1993b). The KOR experiment. Working paper, University of Michigan School of Business Administration.

Weick, K. E. (1995). *Sensemaking in organizations.* Beverly Hills, CA: Sage.

White, M., Hill, S., McGovern, P., Mills, C., & Smeaton, D. (2003). "High-performance Management Practices, Working Hours and Work–Life Balance." *British Journal of Industrial Relations, 41*(2), 175–195.

William, R., and V. Williams. (1998). *Anger kills: 17 strategies to control the hostility that can harm your health.* New York: Harper Collins.

Wolff, H. G., S. G. Wolf, and C. C. Hare (Eds.). (1950). *Life stress and bodily disease.* Baltimore: Williams and Wilkins.

Wright, M. O. D., Masten, A. S., & Narayan, A. J. (2013). Resilience processes in development: Four waves of research on positive adaptation in the context of adversity. In *Handbook of Resilience in Children,* 15–37. Springer.

Wrzesniewski, A. (2012). "Callings." In Cameron, K. S. and Spreitzer, G. M. *Oxford Handbook of Positive Organizational Scholarship.* New York: Oxford University Press.

Yogi, M. (1994). *Science of being and art of living: Transcendental meditation.* New Haven, CT: Meridian Books.

CHAPTER 3 REFERENCES

Adams, J. L. (2001). *Conceptual blockbusting: A guide to better ideas.* Cambridge, MA: Perseus Publishing.

Albert, R. S., and M. A. Runco. (1999). A history of research on creativity. In R. J. Sternberg (Ed.), *Handbook of creativity.* Cambridge: Cambridge University Press.

Amabile, T. M. (1988). A model of creativity and innovation in organizations. In L. L. Cummings and B. M. Staw (Eds.), *Research in Organizational Behavior, 10:* 123–167.

Basadur, M. S. (1979). *Training in creative problem solving: Effects of deferred judgment and problem finding and solving in an industrial research organization.* Unpublished doctoral dissertation, University of Cincinnati.

Ben-Amos, P. (1986). Artistic creativity in Benin Kingdom. *African Arts, 19:* 60–63.

Black, J. S., and H. B. Gregersen. (1997). Participative decision making: An integration of multiple dimensions. *Human Relations, 50:* 859–878.

Blasko, V. J., and M. P. Mokwa. (1986). Creativity in advertising: A Janusian perspective. *Journal of Advertising, 15:* 43–50.

Bodycombe, D. J. (1977). *The mammoth puzzle carnival.* New York: Carroll & Graf.

Cameron, K. S., R. E. Quinn, J. DeGraff, and A. V. Thakor. (2014). *Competing values leadership: Creating values in organizations.* New York: Edward Elgar.

Chu, Y-K. (1970). Oriented views of creativity. In A. Angloff and B. Shapiro (Eds.), *Psi factors in creativity* (pp. 35–50). New York: Parapsychology Foundation.

Cialdini, R. B. (2001). *Influence: Science and practice.* Needham Heights, MA: Allyn and Bacon.

Collins, M. A., and T. M. Amabile. (1999). Motivation and creativity. In R. J. Sternberg (Ed.), *Handbook of creativity.* Cambridge, UK: Cambridge University Press.

Covey, S. R. (1998) "Creative orientation." *Executive Excellence, 1:* 13–14.

Crovitz, H. F. (1970). *Galton's walk.* New York: Harper & Row.

Csikszentmihalyi, M. (1996). *Creativity: Flow and the psychology of discovery and invention.* New York: Harper Collins.

Csikszentmihalyi, M. (2013). *Creativity: The Psychology of Discovery and Invention.* New York: Harper Perennial.

de Bono, E. (1968). *New think.* New York: Basic Books.

de Bono, E. (1973). *CoRT thinking.* Blanford, England: Direct Educational Services.

de Bono, E. (1992). *Serious creativity.* New York: Harper Collins.

de Bono, E. (2000). *New thinking for the new millennium.* New York: New Millennium Press.

De Bono, E. (2010). *Lateral thinking: Creativity step by step.* HarperCollins e-books.

DeGraff, J., and K. A. Lawrence. (2002). *Creativity at work: Developing the right practices to make innovation happen.* San Francisco: Jossey-Bass.

Dutton, J. E., and S. J. Ashford. (1993). Selling issues to top management. *Academy of Management Review, 18:* 397–421.

Einstein, A. (1919). Fundamental ideas and methods of relativity theory, presented in their development. (© 1919, G. Holton). Unpublished manuscript.

Ettlie, J. E., and R. D. O'Keefe. (1982). Innovative attitudes, values, and intentions in organizations. *Journal of Management Studies, 19:* 163–182.

Feldman, D. H. (1999). The development of creativity. In R. J. Sternberg (Ed.), *Handbook of creativity.* Cambridge, UK: Cambridge University Press.

Festinger, L. (1957). *A theory of cognitive dissonance.* Stanford: Stanford University Press.

Finke, R. A., T. B. Ward, and S. M. Smith. (1992). *Creative cognition: Theory, research, and applications.* Cambridge, MA: MIT Press.

Getzels, J. W., and M. Csikszentmihalyi. (1976). *The creative vision: A longitudinal study of problem finding.* New York: Wiley.

Gigerenzer, G., & Gaissmaier, W. (2011). Heuristic decision making. *Annual review of psychology, 62,* 451–482.

Gladwell, M. (2005). *Blink.* Boston: Little, Brown.

Goll, I., and A. M. A. Rasheed. (1997). Rational decision making and firm performance: The moderating role of environment. *Strategic Management Journal, 18:* 583–591.

Gordon, W. J. J. (1961). *Synectics: The development of creative capacity*. New York: Collier.

Hawn, C. (2004, January). If he's so smart... *Fast Company*: 68–74.

Heider, F. (1946). Attitudes and cognitive organization. *Journal of Psychology, 21:* 107–112.

Hermann, N. (1981). The creative brain. *Training and Development Journal, 35:* 11–16.

Hudspith, S. (1985). *The neurological correlates of creative thought*. Unpublished PhD Dissertation, University of Southern California.

Hyatt, J. (1989, February). The odyssey of an excellent man. *Inc.:* 63–68. Copyright © 1989 by Goldhirsch Group, Inc. Reprinted with permission of the publishers, 38 Commercial Wharf, Boston, MA 02110.

Interaction Associates. (1971). *Tools for change*. San Francisco: Author.

Janis, I. L. (1971). *Groupthink*. New York: Free Press.

Janis, I. L., and L. Mann. (1977). *Decision making: A psychological analysis of conflict, choice, and commitment*. New York: Free Press. Copyright © 1977 by the Free Press. Reprinted with the permission of the Free Press, an imprint of Simon & Schuster.

Juran, J. (1988). *Juran on planning management*. New York: Free Press.

Koberg, D., and J. Bagnall. (2003). *The universal traveler: A soft system guidebook to creativity, problem solving, and the process of design*. Los Altos, CA: William Kaufmann.

Koestler, A. (1964). *The act of creation*. New York: Dell.

Koopman, P. L., J. W. Broekhuijsen, and A. F. M. Wierdsma. (1998). Complex decision making in organizations. In P. J. D. Drenth and H. Thierry (Eds.), *Handbook of work and organizational psychology*, Vol. 4 (pp. 357–386). Hove, England: Psychology Press/Erlbaum.

Kuo, Y-Y. (1996). Toaistic psychology of creativity. *Journal of Creative Behavior, 30:* 197–212.

Lockwood, T. (2009). *Corporate Creativity: Developing an Innovative Organization*. NY: Allworth Press.

Maduro, R. (1976). *Artistic creativity in a Brahmin painter community* (Monograph 14). Berkeley: University of California Center for South and Southeast Asia Cultures.

March, J. G. (1994). *A primer on decision making: How decisions happen*. New York: Free Press.

March, J. G. (2006). Rationality, foolishness, and adaptive intelligence. *Strategic Management Journal, 27*(3), 201–214.

March, J. G. (Ed.). (1999). *The pursuit of organizational intelligence*. New York: Blackwell.

March, J. G., and H. A. Simon. (1958). *Organizations*. New York: Wiley.

Markoff, J. (1988, November 2). For scientists using supercomputers, visual imagery speeds discoveries. New York Times News Service, *Ann Arbor News*, D3.

Martindale, C. (1999). Biological bases of creativity. In R. J. Sternberg (Ed.), *Handbook of creativity*. Cambridge, UK: Cambridge University Press.

McKim, R. H. (1997). *Thinking visually: A strategy manual for problem solving*. Parsippany, NJ: Dale Seymour Publications.

McMillan, I. (1985). Progress in research on corporate venturing. Working paper, Center for Entrepreneurial Studies, New York University.

Medawar, P. B. (1967). *The art of the soluble*. London: Methuen.

Miller, S. J., D. J. Hickson, and D. C. Wilson. (1996). Decision making in organizations. In S. R. Clegg and C. Hardy (Eds.), *Handbook of organizational studies* (pp. 293–312). London: Sage.

Mitroff, I. I. (1998). *Smart thinking for crazy times: The art of solving the right problems*. San Francisco: Barrett-Koehler.

Mumford, M. D. (Ed.). (2011). *Handbook of organizational creativity*. Academic Press.

Mumford, M. D., W. A. Baughman, M. A. Maher, D. P. Costanza, and E. P. Supinski. (1997). Process-based measures of creative problem solving skills. *Creativity Research Journal, 10:* 59–71.

Nayak, P. R., and J. M. Ketteringham. (1986). *Breakthroughs!* New York: Rawson Associates.

Nemeth, C. J. (1986). Differential contributions of majority and minority influence. *Psychological Review, 93:* 23–32.

Newcomb, T. (1954). An approach to the study of communicative acts. *Psychological Review, 60:* 393–404.

Nickerson, R. S. (1999). Enhancing creativity. In R. J. Sternberg (Ed.), *Handbook of creativity*. Cambridge: Cambridge University Press.

Osborn, A. (1953). *Applied imagination*. New York: Scribner.

Poincare, H. (1921). *The foundation of science*. New York: Science Press.

Raudsepp, E. (1981). *How creative are you?* New York: Perigee Books/G.P. Putnam's Sons. Copyright © 1981 by Eugene Raudsepp. Reprinted with the permission of the author, c/o Dominick Abel Literary Agency, Inc.

Raudsepp, E., and G. P. Hough. (1977). *Creative growth games*. New York: Putnam.

Ribot, T. A. (1906). *Essay on the creative imagination*. Chicago: Open Court.

Riley, S. (1998). *Critical thinking and problem solving*. Upper Saddle River, NJ: Simon & Schuster.

Rothenberg, A. (1979). *The emerging goddess*. Chicago: University of Chicago Press.

Rothenberg, A. (1991). Creativity, health, and alcoholism. *Creativity Research Journal, 3*: 179–202.

Rothenberg, A., and C. Hausman. (2000). Metaphor and creativity. In M. A. Runco (Ed.), *Creativity research handbook*, Vol. 2. Cresskill, NJ: Hampton.

Roukes, N. (1988). *Design synectics: Stimulating creativity in design*. Berkeley, CA: Davis Publications.

Scope, E. E. (1999). *A meta-analysis of research on creativity: The effects of instructional variables*. Ann Arbor, MI: Dissertation Abstracts International, Section A: Humanities and Social Sciences.

Scott, O. J. (1974). *The creative ordeal: The story of Raytheon*. New York: Atheneum.

Siau, K. L. (1995). Group creativity and technology. *Journal of Creative Behavior, 29:* 201–216.

Smith, G. F. (1998). Idea-generation techniques: A formulary ofactive ingredients. *Journal of Creative Behavior, 32:* 107–133.

Starko, A. J. (2001). *Creativity in the classroom: Schools of curious delight*. Mahwah, NJ: Lawrence Erlbaum.

Sternberg, R. J. (Ed.). (1999). *Handbook of creativity.* Cambridge: Cambridge University Press.

TAN, S. N., & Parnell, G. S. (2013). Design Creative Alternatives. *Handbook of Decision Analysis*, 149.

Tichy, N. (1983). *Strategic human resource management.* New York: Wiley.

Trompenaars, F., and C. Hampden-Turner. (1987). *Riding the waves of culture: Understanding cultural diversity in business.* Yarmouth, ME: Nicholas Brealey Publishing.

Trompenaars, F., and C. Hampden-Turner. (2004). *Managing people across cultures.* Mankato, MN: Capstone Publishing.

Tushman, M. L., and P. Anderson. (1997). *Managing strategic innovation and change.* New York: Oxford University Press.

Van de Ven, A. (1997). Technological innovation, learning, and leadership. In R. Garud, P. Rattan Nayyar, and Z. Baruch Shapira (Eds.), *Technological innovation: Oversights and foresights.* Cambridge: Cambridge University Press.

von Oech, R. (1986). *A kick in the seat of the pants.* New York: Harper & Row.

Vroom, V. H., and P. W. Yetton. (1973). *Leadership and decision making.* Pittsburgh: University of Pittsburgh Press.

Vygotsky, L. (1962). *Thought and language.* Cambridge, MA: MIT Press.

Vygotsky, L., Hanfmann, E., & Vakar, G. (2012). *Thought and language.* MIT press.

Wallas, G. (1926). *The art of thought.* London: C. A. Watts.

Ward, T. B., S. M. Smith, and R. A. Finke. (1999). Creative cognition. In R. J. Sternberg (Ed.), *Handbook of creativity.* Cambridge: Cambridge University Press.

Weick, K. E. (1979). *The social psychology of organizing.* Reading, MA: Addison-Wesley.

Weick, K. E. (1984). Small wins. *American Psychologist, 39*: 40–49.

Weick, K. E. (1995). *Sensemaking in organizations.* Beverly Hills, CA: Sage.

Williams, S. W. (2001). *Making better business decisions: Understanding and improving critical thinking and problem solving skills.* SAGE Publications, Incorporated.

Williams, W. M., and L. T. Yang. (1999). Organizational creativity. In R. J. Sternberg (Ed.), *Handbook of creativity.* Cambridge, UK: Cambridge University Press.

Wonder, J., and J. Blake. (1992). Creativity East and West: Intuition versus logic. *Journal of Creative Behavior, 26*: 172–185.

Zeitz, P. (1999). *The art and craft of problem solving.* New York: Wiley.

Zhou, J., & Shalley, C. (Eds.). (2008). *Handbook of organizational creativity.* Lawrence Erlbaum Associates.

Zhou, J., and C. E. Shalley. (2003). Research on employee creativity: A critical review and directions or future research. *Research in Personnel and Human Resources Management, 22:* 165–217.

CHAPTER 4 REFERENCES

Argyris, C. (1991). Teaching smart people how to learn. *Harvard Business Review, 63:* 99–109.

Athos, A. and J. Gabarro. (1978). *Interpersonal behavior.* Englewood Cliffs, NJ: Prentice Hall.

Baker, W. (2000). *Achieving success through social capital.* San Francisco: Jossey-Bass.

Barnlund, D. C. (1968). *Interpersonal communication: Survey and studies.* Boston: Houghton Mifflin.

Beebe, S. A., S. J. Beebe, and M. V. Redmond. (1996). *Interpersonal communication.* Boston: Allyn & Bacon.

Bodie, G. D., St. Cyr, K., Pence, M., Rold, M., & Honeycutt, J. (2012). Listening competence in initial interactions I: Distinguishing between what listening is and what listeners do. *International Journal of Listening, 26*(1), 1–28.

Boss, W. L. (1983). Team building and the problem of regression: The personal management interview as an intervention. *Journal of Applied Behavioral Science, 19:* 67–83.

Bostrom, R. N. (1997). The process of listening. In O. D. W. Hargie (Ed.), *The handbook of communication skills.* London: Routledge.

Bowman, G. W. (1964). What helps or harms promotability? *Harvard Business Review, 42:* 14.

Brownell, J. (1986). *Building active listening skills.* Englewood Cliffs, NJ: Prentice Hall.

Brownell, J. (1990). Perceptions of effective listeners. *Journal of Business Communication, 27:* 401–415.

Burleson, B. R. (2009). Understanding the outcomes of supportive communication: A dual-process approach. *Journal of Social and Personal Relationships, 26*(1), 21–38.

Cameron, K. S. (1994). Strategies for successful organizational downsizing. *Human Resource Management Journal, 33:* 89–122.

Kim Cameron, K. S., Mora, C., Leutscher, T., and Calarco, M. (2011). Effects of positive practices on organizational effectiveness. *Journal of Applied Behavioral Science, 47:* 266–308.

Carmeli, A., Brueller, D., & Dutton, J. E. (2009). Learning behaviours in the workplace: The role of high-quality interpersonal relationships and psychological safety. *Systems Research and Behavioral Science, 26*(1), 81–98.

Carrell, L. J., and S. C. Willmington. (1996). A comparison of self-report and performance data in assessing speaking and listening competence. *Communication Reports, 9:* 185–191.

Council of Communication Management. (1996). Electronic communication is important, but face-to-face communication is still rated high. *Communication World, 13:* 12–13.

Covey, S. R. (1989). *The seven habits of highly effective people.* New York: Simon & Schuster.

Crocker, J. (1978). Speech communication instruction based on employers' perceptions of the importance of selected communication skills for employees on the job. Paper presented at the Speech Communication Association meeting, Minneapolis, Minn.

Cupach, W. R., & Spitzberg, B. H. (Eds.). (2007). *The dark side of interpersonal communication.* Psychology Press.

Cupach, W. R., and B. H. Spitzberg. (1994). *The dark side of interpersonal communication.* Hillsdale, NJ: Lawrence Erlbaum.

Czech, K., & Forward, G. L. (2010). Leader communication: Faculty perceptions of the department chair. *Communication Quarterly, 58*(4), 431–457.

Czech, K., & Forward, G. L. (2013). Communication, Leadership, and Job Satisfaction: Perspectives on Supervisor-Subordinate Relationships. *Studies in Media and Communication, 1*(2), 11–24.

Dutton, J. E. (2003). *Energize your workplace: How to create and sustain high quality relationships at work.* San Francisco: Jossey-Bass.

Dutton, J. E. and Ragins, B. R. 2007). *Exploring Positive Relationships at Work.* Mahaw, NJ: Lawrence Erlbaum.

Dyer, W. G. (1972). Congruence. In *The sensitive manipulator.* Provo, UT: Brigham Young University Press.

Ellis, K. (2004). The impact of perceived teacher confirmation on receiver apprehension, motivation, and learning. *Communication Education, 53*(1).

Fredrickson, B. L. (2001). The role of positive emotions in positive psychology: The broaden-and-build theory of positive emotions. *American Psychologist, 56:* 218–226.

Fredrickson, B. R. (2009) *Positivity.* New York: Crown Books.

Furnham, A. (2008). *Personality and intelligence at work: Exploring and explaining individual differences at work.* Routledge.

Gackenbach, J. (1998). *Psychology and the Internet: Intrapersonal, interpersonal, and transpersonal implications.* New York: Academic Press.

Geddie, T. (1999). Moving communication across cultures. *Communication World, 16:* 37–40.

Gibb, J. R. (1961). Defensive communication. *Journal of Communication, 11:* 141–148.

Gittell, J. H. (2003). A theory of relational coordination. In K. S. Cameron, J. E. Dutton, and R. E. Quinn (Eds.), *Positive organizational scholarship.* San Francisco: Barrett-Koehler.

Gittell, J. H., K. S. Cameron, and S. Lim. (2006). Relationships, layoffs, and organizational resilience: Airline industry responses to September 11th. *Journal of Applied Behavioral* Science, *42:* 300–329.

Glasser, W. (1965). *Reality therapy: A new approach to psychiatry.* New York: Harper & Row.

Glasser, W. (2000). *Reality therapy in action.* New York: Harper Collins.

Golen, S. (1990). A factor analysis of barriers to effective listening. *Journal of Business Communication, 27:* 25–35.

Gordon, R. D. (1988). The difference between feeling defensive and feeling understood. *Journal of Business Communication, 25:* 53–64.

Gudykunst, W. B., S. Ting-Toomey, and T. Nishida. (1996). *Communication in personal relationships across cultures.* Thousand Oaks, CA: Sage.

Gudykunst, W. B., and S. Ting-Toomey. (1988). *Culture and interpersonal communication.* Newbury Park, CA: Sage.

Haas, J. W., and C. L. Arnold. (1995). An examination of the role of listening in judgments of communication competence in coworkers. *Journal of Business Communication, 32:* 123–139.

Haney, W. V. (1992). *Communication and interpersonal relations.* Homewood, IL: Irwin.

Hansen, G. S., & Wernerfelt, B. (1989). Determinants of firm performance: The relative importance of economic and organizational factors. *Strategic management journal, 10*(5), 399–411.

Hanson, G. (1986). *Determinants of firm performance: An integration of economic and organizational factors.*

Unpub-lished doctoral dissertation, University of Michigan Business School.

Hargie, O. D. W. (1997). Communication as skilled performance. In O. D. W. Hargie (Ed.), *The handbook of communication skills.* London: Routledge.

Harvey, P., & Harris, K. J. (2010). Frustration-based outcomes of entitlement and the influence of supervisor communication. *Human Relations, 63*(11), 1639–1660.

Heaphy, E. D., & Dutton, J. E. (2008). Positive social interactions and the human body at work: Linking organizations and physiology. *Academy of Management Review, 33*(1), 137–162.

Heaphy, E. D., and J. E. Dutton. (2006). Embodying social interactions: Integrating physiology into the study of positive connections and relationships at work. *Academy of Management Review* (in press).

Huselid, M. A. (1995). The impact of human resource management practices on turnover, productivity, and corporate financial performance. *Academy of Management Journal,* 38, 635–672.

Huseman, R. C., J. M. Lahiff, and J. D. Hatfield. (1976). *Interpersonal communication in organizations.* Boston: Holbrook Press.

Hyman, R. (1989). The psychology of deception. *Annual Review of Psychology, 40:* 133–154.

Imhof, M., & Janusik, L. A. (2006). Development and validation of the Imhof-Janusik Listening Concepts Inventory to measure listening conceptualization differences between cultures. *Journal of Intercultural Communication Research, 35*(2), 79–98.

James, W., cited in D. R. Laing (1965). Mystification, confusion, and conflict. In I. Boszormenya-Nagy and J. L. Franco (Eds.), *Intensive family therapy.* New York: Harper & Row.

Johnston, M. K., Reed, K., & Lawrence, K. (2011). Team Listening Environment (TLE) Scale Development and Validation. *Journal of Business Communication, 48*(1), 3–26.

Knapp, M. L., and A. L. Vangelisti. (1996). *Interpersonal communication and human relationships.* Boston: Allyn & Bacon.

Kramer, D. A. (2000). Wisdom as a classical source of human strength: Conceptualization and empirical inquiry. *Journal of Social and Clinical Psychology, 19:* 83–101.

Kramer, R. (1997). *Leading by listening: An empirical test of Carl Rogers' theory of human relationship using interpersonal assessments of leaders by followers.* Ann Arbor, MI: Dissertation Abstracts International Section A: Humanities and Social Sciences, Volume 58.

Loomis, F. (1939). *The consultation room.* New York: Knopf.

Losada, M., and E. Heaphy. (2004). The role of positivity and connectivity in the performance of business teams. *American Behavioral Scientist, 47:* 740–765.

Madlock, P. E. (2008). The link between leadership style, communicator competence, and employee satisfaction. *Journal of Business Communication, 45*(1), 61–78.

Maier, N. R. F., A. R. Solem, and A. A. Maier. (1973). Counseling, interviewing, and job contacts. In N. R. F. Maier (Ed.), *Psychology of industrial organizations.* Boston: Houghton Mifflin.

McGregor, D. (1960). *The human side of enterprise.* New York: McGraw-Hill.

McNaughtan, E. D. (2012). *Muted Motherhood: A Standpoint Analysis of Stay-at-home Mothers* (Master's Thesis, Southern Utah University).

Nichols, M. P. (2009) *The Lost Art of Listening: How Learning to Listen Can Improve Relationships.* Boston: Guilford Press.

Nie, N. H. (2001). Sociability, interpersonal relations, and the internet reconciling conflicting findings. *American behavioral scientist, 45*(3), 420–435.

Ouchi, W. (1981). *Theory Z.* Reading, MA: Addison-Wesley.

Peters, T. (1988). *Thriving on chaos.* New York: Knopf.

Pfeffer, J. (1998). *The human equation: Building profits by putting people first.* Boston: Harvard Business School Press.

Randle, C. W. (1956). How to identify promotable executives. *Harvard Business Review, 34:* 122.

Reis, H., and S. L. Gable. (2003). Toward a positive psychology of relationships. In C. L. M. Keyes and J. Haidt. *Flourishing: Positive psychology and the life well-lived* (pp. 129–160). Washington, DC: American Psychological Association.

Rogers, C. W. (1961). *On becoming a person.* Boston: Houghton Mifflin.

Rogers, C., and R. Farson. (1976). *Active listening.* Chicago: Industrial Relations Center.

Rosen, S. (1998). A lump of clay. *Communication World, 15:* 58–59.

Schnake, M. E., M. P. Dumler, D. S. Cochran, and T. R. Barnett. (1990). Effects of differences in superior and subordinate perceptions of superiors' communication practices. *Journal of Business Communication, 27:* 37–50.

Sieburg, E. (1969). *Dysfunctional communication and interpersonal responsiveness in small groups.* Unpublished doctoral dissertation, University of Denver.

Sieburg, E. (1978). *Confirming and disconfirming organizational communication.* Working paper, University of Denver.

Spitzberg, B. H. (1994). The dark side of (in)competence. In William R. Cupach and Brian H. Spitzberg (Eds.), *The dark side of interpersonal communication.* Hillsdale, NJ: Lawrence Erlbaum.

Steil, L. K. (1980). *Your listening profile.* Minneapolis: Sperry Corporation.

Steil, L., L. Barker, and K. Watson. (1983). *Effective listening: Key to your success.* New York: Addison-Wesley.

Stephens, J. P., Heaphy, E., and Dutton, J. E. (2012) "High quality connections." In Cameron, K. S. and Spreitzer, G. M. (Eds.) *Oxford Handbook of Positive Organizational Scholarship,* 385–399, New York: Oxford University Press.

Sternberg, R. J. (1990). *Wisdom: Its nature, origins, and development.* Cambridge: Cambridge University Press.

Synopsis Communication Consulting of London. (1998). *The human factor: New rules for the digital workplace.* London: Author.

Szligyi, A. D., and M. J. Wallace. (1983). *Organizational behavior and human performance.* Glenview, IL: Scott Foresman.

Thorton, B. B. (1966). As you were saying: The number one problem. *Personnel Journal, 45:* 237–238.

Time. (2000, June 19). Embarrassing miscue: 31.

Triandis, H. C. (1994). *Culture and social behavior.* New York: McGraw-Hill.

Trompenaars, F. (1996). Resolving international conflict: Culture and business strategy. *Business Strategy Review, 7:* 51–68.

Trompenaars, F., and C. Hampden-Turner. (1998). *Riding the waves of culture.* New York: McGraw-Hill.

Waller, G., Corstorphine, E., & Mountford, V. (2007). The role of emotional abuse in the eating disorders: Implications for treatment. *Eating disorders, 15*(4), 317–331.

Walters, J. (2005). Fostering a culture of deep inquiry and listening. *Journal for Quality and Participation,* 28(2), 4–7.

Wiemann, J. M. (1977). Explanation and test of a model of communication competence. *Human Communication Research, 3:* 145–213.

Wolvin, A., and C. Coakley. (1988). *Listening.* Dubuque, IA: W. C. Brown.

Yrle, A. C., Hartman, S., Galle, W. P. (2002). "An investigation of relationships between communication style and leader-member exchange." *Journal of Communication Management,* 6(3), 257–268.

CHAPTER 5 REFERENCES

Adler, P. S., and S. Kwon. (2002). Social capital: Prospects for a new concept. *Academy of Management Review, 27:* 17–40.

Agle, B. R., N. J. Nagarajan, J. A. Sonnenfeld, and D. Srinivasan. (2006). Does CEO charisma matter? An empirical analysis of the relationships among organizational performance, environmental uncertainty, and top management team perceptions of CEO charisma. *Academy of Management Journal, 49:* 161–174.

Allen, R. W., D. L. Madison, L. W. Porter, P. A. Renwick, and B. T. Mayer. (1979). Organizational politics: Tactics and characteristics of actors. *California Management Review, 22:* 77–83.

Allinson, C. W., S. J. Armstrong, and J. Hayes. (2001). The effects of cognitive style on leader-member exchange: A study of manager-subordinate dyads. *Journal of Occupational and Organizational Psychology, 74:* 201–220.

Anderson, C., O. P. John, D. Keltner, and A. M. Kring. (2001). Who attains social status? Effects of personality and physical attractiveness in social groups. *Journal of Personality and Social Psychology, 81:* 116–132.

Bacharach, S. B. (2005, May). Making things happen by mastering the game of day-to-day politics. *Fast Company:* 93.

Baum, L., and J. A. Byre. (1986, April). Executive secretary: A new rung on the corporate ladder; but hitching her star to the boss can work both ways. *BusinessWeek:* 74.

Bennis, W., and B. Nanus. (2003). *Leaders: Strategies for taking charge,* 2nd ed. New York: Harper Collins.

Bies, R. J., and T. M. Tripp. (1998). Two faces of the powerless: Coping with tyranny in organizations. In R. M. Kramer, and M. A. Neale (Eds.), *Power and influence in organizations.* Thousand Oaks, CA: Sage.

Bolman, L. G., and T. E. Deal. (1997). *Reframing organizations: Artistry, choice, and leadership.* San Francisco: Jossey-Bass.

Breen, B. (2001, November). Trickle-up leadership. *Fast Company:* 70.

Buell, B., and A. L. Cowan. (1985, August). Learning how to play the corporate power game. *BusinessWeek:* 54–55.

Bunderson, J. S. (2002). Team member functional background and involvement in management teams. *Academy of Management Proceedings, OB:* 11–16.

Bunderson, J. S. (2003). Team member functional background and involvement in management teams: Direct effects and the moderating role of power centralization. *Academy of Management Journal, 46:* 458–474.

Bunker, K. A., K. E. Kram, and S. Ting. (2002). The young and the clueless. *Harvard Business Review, 80:* 80–87.

Burt, R. S. (1997). The contingent value of social capital. *Administrative Science Quarterly, 42:* 339–365.

Canfield, F. E., and J. J. LaGaipa. (1970). Friendship expectations at different stages in the development of friendship. Paper read at the annual meeting of the Southeastern Psychological Association, Louisville.

Chiu, L. (2001). Locus of control differences between American and Chinese adolescents. *Journal of Social Psychology, 128:* 411–413.

Chiu, L. H. (1972). A cross-cultural comparison of cognitive styles in Chinese and American children. *International Journal of Psychology, 8:* 235–242.

Choi, I., R. E. Nisbett, and A. Norenzayan. (1999). Causal attribution across cultures: Variation and universality. *Psychological Bulletin, 125:* 47–63.

Cialdini, R. B. (2001). *Influence: Science and practice,* 4th ed. Boston: Allyn & Bacon.

Cohen, A. R., and D. L. Bradford. (2003). Influence without authority: The use of alliances, reciprocity, and exchange to accomplish work. In B. M. Staw (Ed.), *Psychological dimensions of organizational behavior,* 3rd ed. (pp. 359–367). Englewood Cliffs, NJ: Prentice Hall.

Conger, J. A., and R. N. Kanungo. (1998). *Charismatic leadership in organizations.* Thousand Oaks, CA: Sage.

Conner, J., and D. Ulrich. (1996). Human resource roles: Creating value, not rhetoric. *Human Resource Planning, 19:* 38–49.

Cuming, P. (1984). *The power handbook.* Boston: CBI Publishing Co.

Daly, J. P. (1995). Explaining changes to employees: The influence of justifications and change outcomes on employees' fairness judgments. *Journal of Applied Behavioral Science, 31:* 415–428.

DeGeorge, R. T. (1999). *Business ethics.* Upper Saddle River, NJ: Prentice Hall.

Deal, T. E., and A. A. Kennedy. (1982). *Corporate cultures: The rites and rituals of corporate life.* Reading, MA: Addison-Wesley.

Dilenschneider, R. (2007). *Power and influence: The rules have changed.* New York: McGraw-Hill.

Dilenschneider, R. L. (1990). *Power and influence: Mastering the art of persuasion.* New York: Prentice Hall.

Dirks, K. T., and D. L. Ferrin. (2001). The role of trust in organizational settings. *Organization Science, 12:* 450–467.

Dutton, J. E., and R. B. Duncan. (1987). The creation of momentum for change through the process of strategic issue diagnosis. *Strategic Management Journal, 83(3):* 279–295.

Dutton, J. E., and S. J. Ashford. (1993). Selling issues to top management. *Academy of Management Review, 18(3):* 397–428.

Dyer, W. G. (1972). Congruence. In *The sensitive manipulator.* Provo, UT: Brigham Young University Press.

Emerson, R. M. (1962). Power-dependence relations. *American Sociological Review, 27:* 31–40.

Erez, A., V. F. Misangyi, D. E. Johnson, M. A. LePine, and K. C. Halverson. (2008). Stirring the hearts of followers: Charismatic leadership as the transferal of affect. *Journal of Applied Psychology, 93:* 602–616.

Fisher, A. (2005, March 7). Starting a new job? Don't blow it. *Fortune:* 48.

Furman, W. (2001). Working models of friendship. *Journal of Social and Personal Relationships, 18:* 583–602.

Gabarro, J. J., and J. P. Kotter. (1980). Managing your boss. *Harvard Business Review, 58:* 92–100.

Gabarro, J. J., and J. P. Kotter. (2007). Managing your boss. In K. P. Coyne, E. J. Coyne, L. Bossidy, J. J. Gabarro, and J. P. Kotter (Eds.). *Managing UP,* 2nd ed. (HBR Article Collection). Boston: *Harvard Business Review.*

Gardner, J. (1990). *On leadership.* New York: Free Press.

Gelman, E. (1985, September). Playing office politics. *Newsweek:* 56.

Giamatti, A. B. (1981). *The university and public interest.* New York: Atheneum.

Grove, A. (1983). *High output management.* London: Souvenir Press.

Hinings, C. R., D. J. Hickson, J. M. Pennings, and R. E. Schneck. (1974). Structural conditions of intraorganizational power. *Administrative Science Quarterly, 21:* 22–44.

Hoerr, J. (1985, December). Human resource managers aren't corporate nobodies anymore. *BusinessWeek:* 58.

Hogg, M. A. (2001). A social identity theory of leadership. *Personality and Social Psychology Review, 5:* 184–200.

Hosmer, L. T. (1995). Trust: The connecting link between organizational theory and philosophical ethics. *Academy of Management Review, 20:* 379–403.

Hosoda, M., E. F. Stone-Romero, and G. Coats. (2003). The effects of physical attractiveness on job-related outcomes: A meta-analysis of experimental studies. *Personnel Psychology, 56:* 431–462.

Kanter, R. (1979). Power failures in management circuits. *Harvard Business Review, 57:* 65–75. Copyright © 1979 by The President and Fellows of Harvard College. Reprinted with the permission of *Harvard Business Review.* All rights reserved.

Kaplan, R. E., and M. Mazique. (1983). *Trade routes: The manager's network of relationships* (Technical Report #22). Greensboro, NC: Center for Creative Leadership.

Kipnis, D. (1987). Psychology and behavioral technology. *American Psychologist, 42:* 30–36.

Kipnis, D., S. M. Schmidt, and I. Wilkinson. (1980). Intraorganizational influence tactics: Explorations in getting one's way. *Journal of Applied Psychology, 65:* 440–452.

Kipnis, D., and S. M. Schmidt. (1988). Upward-influence styles: Relationship with performance evaluations, salary, and stress. *Administrative Science Quarterly, 33:* 528–542.

Korda, M. (1991). *Power: How to get it, how to use it.* New York: Warner Books.

Kotter, J. P. (1977). Power, dependence and effective management. *Harvard Business Review, 55:* 125–136.

Labich, K. (1995, February 20). Kissing off corporate America. *Fortune, 131:* 44–52.

Langlois, J. H., L. Kalakanis, A. J. Rubenstein, A. Larson, M. Hallam, and M. Smoot. (2000). Maxims of myths of beauty? A meta-analytic and theoretical review. *Psychological Bulletin 126:* 390–423.

Lawrence, R. R., and J. W. Lorsch. (1986). *Organization and environment: Managing differentiation and integration.* Boston: Harvard University Press.

Leger, D. M. (2000, May). Help! I'm the new boss. *Fortune:* 281–284.

Marwell, G., and D. R. Schmitt, (1967). Dimensions of compliance-gaining strategies: A dimensional analysis. *Sociometry, 30:* 350–364.

May, R. (1998). *Power and innocence: A search for the sources of violence.* New York: Norton.

McCall, M. M., Jr., and M. M. Lombardo. (1983). What makes a top executive? *Psychology Today, 26:* 28–31. Copyright © 1983 by Sussex Publishers Inc. Reprinted with the permission of *Psychology Today.*

McClelland, D. C., and D. H. Burnham. (2003). Power is the great motivator. *Motivating People, 81:* 117–126.

Mechanic, D. (1962). Sources of power of lower participants in complex organizations. *Administrative Science Quarterly, 7:* 349–364.

Miller, R. (1985). Three who made a difference. *Management Review, 74:* 16–19.

Morris, M. W., J. M. Podolny, and S. Ariel. (2000). Missing relations: Incorporating relational constructs into models of culture. In P. C. Earley and H. Singh (Eds.), *Innovation in international and cross-cultural management* (pp. 52–90). Thousand Oaks, CA: Sage.

Mulder, M., L. Koppelaar, R. V. de Jong, and J. Verhage. (1986). Organizational field study. *Journal of Applied Psychology, 7:* 566–570.

Mulgan, G. (1998). *Connexity: How to live in a connected world.* Boston: Harvard Business School Press.

Pascale, R. (1985). The paradox of "corporate culture": Reconciling ourselves to socialization. *California Management Review, 27:* 26–41.

Perrow, C. (1970). Departmental power and perspectives in industrial firms. In M. N. Zold, (Ed.), *Power in organizations.* Nashville, TN: Vanderbilt University Press.

Peters, T. (1978). Symbols, patterns, and settings: An optimistic case for getting things done. *Organizational Dynamics, 7:* 3–22.

Pfeffer, J. (1977). Power and resource allocation in organizations. In B. Staw and G. Salancik (Eds.), *New direction in organizational behavior.* Chicago: St. Clair Press.

Pfeffer, J. (1981). *Power in organizations.* Marshfield, MA: Pitman.

Pfeffer, J. (1994). *Power and influence in organizations.* Boston: Harvard Business School Press.

Pfeffer, J., and A. Konrad. (1991). The effects of individual power on earnings. *Work and Occupations, 18:* 385–414.

Schein, E. H. (1999). *The corporate culture survival guide: Sense and nonsense about culture change.* San Francisco: Jossey-Bass.

Schmidt, S., and D. Kipnis. (1987). The perils of persistence. *Psychology Today, 21:* 32–33.

Shipper, F., and J. E. Dillard. (2000). A study of impending derailment and recovery of middle managers across career stages. *Human Resource Management, 39:* 331–345.

Sparrowe, R. T., R. C. Liden, and M. L. Kraimer. (2001). Social networks and the performance of individuals and groups. *Academy of Management Journal, 44:* 316–325.

Stewart, T. A. (1992, May 18). The search for the organization of tomorrow. *Fortune:* 92–98.

Tedeschi, J. T. (1974). Attributions, liking and power. In T. L. Huston (Ed.), *Foundations of interpersonal attraction.* New York: Academic Press.

Thompson, L. (2001). *The mind and heart of the negotiator.* Upper Saddle River, NJ: Prentice Hall.

Triandis, H. (1994). *Culture and social behavior.* New York: McGraw-Hill.

Trompenaars, F. (1996). Resolving international conflict: Culture and business strategy. *Business Strategy Review, 7:* 51–68.

Tully, S. (1993, February 8). The modular corporation. *Fortune:* 106–114.

Yukl, G. (2002). *Leadership in organizations,* 5th ed. Upper Saddle River, NJ: Prentice Hall.

CHAPTER 6 REFERENCES

Abbott, R. K. (1997). Flexible compensation: Past, present, and future. *Compensation & Benefits Management, 13:* 18–24.

Adria, M. (2000). Making the most of e-mail. *Academy of Management Executive, 14:* 153–154.

Alderfer, C. P. (1977). A critique of Salancik and Pfeffer's examination of need-satisfaction theories. *Administrative Science Quarterly, 22:* 658–672.

Atkinson, J. W. (1992). Motivational determinants of thematic apperception? In C. P. Smith (Ed.), *Motivation and personality: Handbook of thematic content analysis.* New York: Cambridge University Press.

Bennis, W. (1984). The four competencies of leadership. *Training and Development Journal, 38:* 15–19.

Bennis, W. (2003). *On becoming a leader.* Cambridge, MA: Perseus Books Group.

Birch, D., and J. Veroff. (1966). *Motivation: A study of action.* Monterey, CA: Brooks-Cole.

Bitter, M. E., and W. L. Gardner. (1995). A mid-range theory of the leader/member attribution process in professional service organizations: The role of the organizational environment and impression management. In M. J. Martinko (Ed.), *Attribution theory: An organizational perspective*. Delray Beach, FL: St. Lucie Press.

Boehle, S., K. Dobbs, and D. Stamps. (2000). Two views of distance learning. *Training, 37:* 34.

The boss as referee. [Accountemps survey]. (1996, September). *CMA Management Accounting Magazine, 70(7):* 32.

Butler, T., and J. Waldroop. (1999, September–October). Job sculpting: The art of retaining your best people. *Harvard Business Review:* 144–152.

Choi, I., R. E. Nisbett, and A. Norenzayan. (1999). Causal attribution across cultures: Variation and universality. *Psychological Bulletin, 125:* 47–63.

Cook, A. (2005, May). Money's a sure-fire motivator—Isn't it? *Promotions and Incentives:* 56–59.

Cropanzano, R., and R. Folger. (1996). Procedural justice and worker motivation. In R. M. Steers, L. W. Porter, and G. A. Bigley (Eds.), *Motivation and leadership at work*. New York: McGraw-Hill.

Davidson, O. B., and D. Eden. (2000). Remedial self-fulfilling prophecy: Two field experiments to prevent golem effects among disadvantaged women. *Journal of Applied Psychology 85:* 386–398.

Fisher, A. (2005, March 7). Starting a new job? Don't blow it. *Fortune:* 5.

Ganzach, Y. (1998). Intelligence and job satisfaction. *Academy of Management Journal, 41:* 526–536.

Gerhart, B. A. (2003). *Compensation: Theory, evidence, and strategic implications*. Thousand Oaks, CA: Sage.

Graham, M. E., and C. O. Trevor. (2000). Managing new pay program introductions to enhance the competitiveness of multinational corporations (MNCS). *Competitiveness Review, 10:* 136–154.

Hackman, J. R., and G. R. Oldham. (1980). *Work redesign*. Reading, MA: Addison-Wesley.

Harter, J. K., F. L. Schmidt, and T. L. Hayes. (2002). Business-unit-level relationship between employee satisfaction, employee engagement, and business outcomes: A meta-analysis. *Journal of Applied Psychology, 87:* 268–279.

House, R. J., and T. R. Mitchell. (1974). Path-goal theory of leadership. *Journal of Contemporary Business, 3:* 81–97.

Jackson, P. (2000). Interview with Phil Jackson by Bob Costas. MSNBC.

Janssen, O. (2001). Fairness perceptions as a moderator in the curvilinear relationships between job demands, and job performance and job satisfaction. *Academy of Management Journal, 44:* 1039–1050.

Jay, A. (1967). *Management and Machiavelli, an inquiry into the politics of corporate life*. New York: Holt, Rinehart & Winston.

Kerr, S. (1995). On the folly of rewarding A, while hoping for B. *Academy of Management Executive, 9(1):* 7–14.

Kerr, S. (1996, July 22). Risky business: The new pay game. *Fortune:* 94–97.

Kleiman, C. (2005, June 14). Awards for workers get better as they get personal. *Chicago Tribune:* 2.

Knight, D., C. C. Durham, and E. A. Locke. (2001). The relationship of term goals, incentives, and efficacy to strategic risk, tactical implementation, and performance. *Academy of Management Journal, 44:* 326–338.

Komaki, J., T. Coombs, and S. Schepman. (1996). Motivational implications of reinforcement theory. In R. M. Steers, L. W. Porter, and G. A. Bigley (Eds.), *Motivation and leadership at work*. New York: McGraw-Hill.

Kopelman, R. E. (1985, Summer). Job redesign and productivity: A review of evidence. *National Productivity Review:* 237–255.

Kotter, J. (1996, August 5). Kill complacency. *Fortune:* 168–170.

Latham, G., M. Erez, and E. Locke. (1988). Resolving scientific disputes by the joint design of crucial experiments by the antagonists: Application to the Erez-Latham disputes regarding participation in goal setting. *Journal of Applied Psychology, 73:* 753–772.

Lawler, E. E. (1987). The design of effective reward systems. In J. Lorsch (Ed.), *Handbook of organizational behavior*. Englewood Cliffs, NJ: Prentice Hall.

Lawler, E. E. (1988). Gainsharing theory and research: Findings and future directions. In W. A. Pasmore and E. R. Woodman (Eds.), *Research in organizational change and development* (Vol. 2). Greenwich, CT: JAI Press.

Lawler, E. E. (2000a). *Strategic pay*. San Francisco: Jossey-Bass.

Lawler, E. E., III. (2000b). *Pay strategies for the new economy*. San Francisco: Jossey-Bass.

LeDue, A. I., Jr. (1980). Motivation of programmers. *Data Base, 3:* 5.

Levering, R., and M. Moskowitz. (2003, January 20). 100 best companies to work for. *Fortune, 147:* 127.

Locke, E. A., and G. P. Latham. (2002, September). Building a practically useful theory of goal setting and task motivation. *American Psychologist, 57:* 705–717.

Luthans, F., and A. D. Stajkovic. (1999). Reinforce for performance: The need to go beyond pay and even rewards. *Academy of Management Executive, 13(2):* 49–57.

Maslow, A. H. (1970). *Motivation and personality,* 2nd ed. New York: Harper & Row.

McCauley, L. (1999). Next stop—the 21st century. *Fast Company, 27:* 108–112.

McClelland, D. (1971). *Assessing human motivation*. New York: General Learning Press.

McClelland, D. C., J. W. Arkinson, R. A. Clark, and E. L. Lowell. (1953). *The achievement motive*. New York: Appleton-Century-Crofts.

McClelland, D. C., and D. H. Burnham. (2003). Power is the great motivator. *Harvard Business Review, 81:* 117–126.

McGregor, D. (1960). *The human side of enterprise*. New York: McGraw-Hill.

Michener, H. A., J. A. Fleishman, and J. J. Vaske. (1976). A test of the bargaining theory of coalition formulation in four-person groups. *Journal of Personality and Social Psychology, 34:* 1114–1126.

Moe, M. T., and H. Blodget. (2000, May 23). *The knowledge web. Part 4: corporate e-learning—feeding hungry minds.* Merrill Lynch & Co.

Murlis, H., and A. Wright. (1985). Rewarding the performance of the eager beaver. *Personnel Management, 17:* 28–31.

Murray, B., and B. Gerhart. (1998). An empirical analysis of a skill-based pay program and plant performance outcomes. *Academy of Management Journal, 41:* 68–78.

Nelson, B. (2000). Are performance appraisals obsolete? *Compensation and Benefits Review, 32:* 39–42.

Nelson, N. (2005). *The power of appreciation in business: How an obsession with value increases performance, productivity, and profits.* Malibu, CA: MindLab Publishing.

Nelton, S. (1988, March). Motivating for success. *Nation's Business:* 25.

News-Gazette. (1987, January): 6.

Parker, G. (2001). Establishing remuneration practices across culturally diverse environments. *Compensation & Benefits Management, 17:* 23–27.

Perry, M. (2000, January). Working in the dark. *Training Media Review:* 13–14.

Peters, T., and R. H. Waterman. (1982). *In search of excellence.* New York: Warner Books.

Pfeffer, J. (1995). Producing sustainable competitive advantage through the effective management of people. *Academy of Management Executive, 9:* 55–71.

Quick, T. L. (1977). *Person to person managing.* New York: St. Martin's Press.

Quick, T. L. (1991). Motivation: Help your star performers shine even brighter. *Sales and Marketing Management, 143:* 96.

Reese, S. (1999, July). Getting your money's worth from training. *Business and Health:* 26–29.

Schriesheim, C. A., and L. L. Neider. (1996). Path-goal leadership theory: The long and winding road. *Leadership Quarterly, 7:* 317–321.

Shamir, B., R. J. House, and M. B. Arthur. (1993). The motivational effects of charismatic leadership: A self-concept based theory. *Organization Science, 4 (4):* 577–594.

Stajkovic, A. D., and F. Luthans. (2001). Differential effects of incentive motivators on work performance. *Academy of Management Journal, 4:* 580–500.

Steers, R. M., L. W. Porter, and G. A. Bigley. (1996). *Motivation and leadership at work.* New York: McGraw-Hill.

Sue-Chan, C., and M. Ong. (2002). Goal assignment and performance: Assessing the mediating roles of goal commitment and self-efficacy and the moderating role of power distance. *Organizational Behavior and Human Decision Processes, 89:* 1140–1161.

Taylor, W. C. (1995). At Verifone it's a dog's life (and they love it?). *Fast Company, 1:* 115.

Thompson, D. W. (1978). *Managing people: Influencing behavior.* St. Louis, MO: C. V. Mosby Co.

Tichy, N. (1997, April). Bob Knowling's change manual. *Fast Company:* 76.

Tomlinson, A. (2002, March 25). T&D spending up in U.S. as Canada lags behind. *Canadian HR Reporter, 15:* 1–18.

Triandis, H. C. (1994). *Culture and social behavior.* New York: McGraw-Hill.

Vroom, V. (1964). *Work and motivation.* New York: Wiley.

Weiner, B. (2000). Intrapersonal and interpersonal theories of motivation from an attributional perspective. *Educational Psychology Review, 12:* 1–14.

Wood, R., and A. Bandura. (1989). Social cognitive theory of organizational management. *Academy of Management Review, 14(3):* 361–383.

Zingheim, P. K., and J. R. Schuster. (1995). Introduction: How are the new pay tools being deployed? *Compensation and Benefits Review* (July–August): 10–11.

CHAPTER 7 REFERENCES

Adler, N. J. (2002). *International dimensions of organizational behavior,* 4th ed. Cincinnati, OH: South-Western.

Adler, R. B. (1977). Satisfying personal needs: Managing conflicts, making requests, and saying no. In *Confidence in communication: A guide to assertive and social skills.* New York: Holt, Rinehart & Winston.

Adler, R. B., L. B. Rosenfeld, and R. F. Proctor. (2001). *Interplay: The process of interpersonal communication.* Fort Worth, TX: Harcourt, Inc.

Alder, R. B., and G. Rodman. (2003). *Understanding human communication,* 8th ed. New York: Oxford University Press.

Argenti, J. (1976). *Corporate collapse: The causes and symptoms.* New York: Wiley.

Bazerman, M. H., and M. A. Neale. (1992). *Negotiating rationally.* New York: Free Press.

Blackard, K., and J. Gibson. (2002). *Capitalizing on conflict: Strategies and practices for turning conflict into synergy in organizations: A manager's handbook.* Palo Alto, CA: Davis-Black Publishing.

The boss as referee. [Accountemps survey]. (1996, September). *CMA Management Accounting Magazine, 70(7):* 32.

Boulding, E. (1964). Further reflections on conflict management. In R. L. Kahn and E. Boulding (Eds.), *Power and conflict in organizations.* New York: Basic Books.

Brown, L. D. (1983). *Managing conflict at organizational interfaces.* Reading, MA: Addison-Wesley.

Cameron, K. S., M. U. Kim, and D. A. Whetten. (1987). Organizational effects of decline and turbulence. *Administrative Science Quarterly, 32:* 222–240.

Catch a falling star. (1988, April 23). *The Economist,* 88–90.

Caudron, S. (1992). Subculture strife hinders productivity. *Personnel Journal, 71(2):* 60–64.

Cox, T. H. (1994). *Cultural diversity in organizations: Theory, research, and practice.* San Francisco: Barrett-Koehler.

Cox, T. H., and Blake, S. (1991). Managing cultural diversity: Implications for organizational competitiveness. *Academy of Management Executive, 5(3):* 45–56.

Cummings, L. L., D. L. Harnett, and O. J. Stevens. (1971). Risk, fate, conciliation, and trust: An international study of attitudinal differences among executives. *Academy of Management Journal, 14:* 285–304.

de Dreu, C. K. W., S. L. Koole, and W. Steinel. (2000). Unfixing the fixed pie: A motivated information-processing approach to integrative negotiation. *Journal of Personality and Social Psychology, 79:* 975–987.

de Dreu, C. K. W., and L. R. Weingart. (2002). Task versus relationship conflict: A meta-analysis. *Academy of Management Proceedings, CM:* B1–B6.

Eisenhardt, K. M., J. L. Kahwajy, and L. J. Bourgeois III. (1997, July–August). How management teams can have a good fight. *Harvard Business Review:* 77–85.

Fisher, R., and S. Brown. (1988). *Getting together: Building a relationship that gets to yes.* Boston: Houghton Mifflin.

Gage, D. (1999, December). Is having partners a bad idea? *IndustryWeek,* Growing Companies Edition: 46–47.

Gendron, G., and B. O. Burlingham. (1989, April). The entrepreneur of the decade: An interview with Steve Jobs. *Inc.:* 123.

The GM system is like a blanket of fog. (1988, February 15). *Fortune:* 48–49.

Gordon, T. (2000). *Parent effectiveness training.* New York: Three Rivers Press.

Grove, A. (1984, July). How to make confrontation work for you. *Fortune:* 74.

Hines, J. S. (1980). *Conflict and conflict management.* Athens: University of Georgia Press.

Hofstede, G. (1980, Summer). Motivation, leadership, and organization: Do American theories apply abroad? *Organizational Dynamics:* 42–63.

Jehn, K. A. (1997). A qualitative analysis of conflict types and dimensions of organizational groups. *Administrative Science Quarterly, 41:* 530–557.

Jehn, K., and E. A. Mannix. (2001). The dynamic nature of conflict: A longitudinal study of intragroup conflict and group performance. *Academy of Management Journal, 44:* 238–251.

Karambayya, R., and J. M. Brett. (1989). Managers handling disputes: Third party roles and perceptions of fairness. *Academy of Management Journal, 32:* 687–704.

Keashly, L. (1994). Gender and conflict: What does psychological research tell us? In A. Taylor and J. B. Miller (Eds.), *Conflict and gender.* Cresskill, NJ: Hampton Press.

Kelly, J. (1970, July–August). Make conflict work for you. *Harvard Business Review, 48:* 103–113.

Kilmann, R. H., and K. W. Thomas. (1977). Developing a forced-choice measure of conflict-handling behavior: The MODE instrument. *Educational and Psychological Measurement, 37:* 309–325.

Kim, S. H., and R. H. Smith. (1993). Revenge and conflict escalation. *Negotiation Journal. 9:* 37–44.

Kipnis, D., and S. Schmidt. (1983). An influence perspective in bargaining within organizations. In M. H. Bazerman, and R. J. Lewicki (Eds.), *Bargaining inside organizations.* Beverly Hills, CA: Sage.

Korabik, D., G. L. Baril, and C. Watson. (1993). Managers' conflict management style and leadership effectiveness: The moderating effects of gender. *Sex Roles, 29(5/6):* 405–420.

Kressel, K., and D. G. Pruitt. (1989). *Mediation research: The process and effectiveness of third party intervention.* San Francisco: Jossey-Bass.

Latham, G., and K. Wexley. (1994). *Increasing productivity through performance appraisal.* Reading, MA: Addison-Wesley.

Lombardo, M. M., and R. W. Eichinger. (1996). *The Career ARCHITECT Development Planner.* Minneapolis: Lominger Ltd.

Maslow, A. (1965). *Eupsychian management.* Homewood, IL: Irwin.

Memeth, C. J., B. Personnaz, M. Personnaz, and J. A. Goucalo. (2004). The liberating role of conflict in group creativity: A study in two countries. *European Journal of Social Psychology, 34:* 365–374.

Morris, W., and M. Sashkin. (1976). *Organizational behavior in action.* St. Paul, MN: West Publishing.

Morrison, A. M. (1996). *The new leaders: Leadership diversity in America.* San Francisco: Jossey-Bass.

Murnighan, J. K. (1992). *Bargaining games: A new approach to strategic thinking in negotiations.* New York: William Morrow.

Murnighan, J. K. (1993). *The dynamics of bargaining games.* Upper Saddle River, NJ: Prentice Hall.

Pascale, R. (1990, February). Creating contention without causing conflict. *Business Month:* 69–71.

Pelled, L. H., K. M. Eisenhardt, and K. R. Xin. (1999). Exploring the black box: An analysis of work group diversity, conflict, and performance. *Administrative Science Quarterly, 44:* 1–28.

Perot, H. R. (1988, February). How I would turn around GM. *Fortune:* 48–49.

Phillips, E., and R. Cheston. (1979). Conflict resolution: What works. *California Management Review, 21:* 76–83.

Phillips, K. W., K. A. Liljenquist, and M. A. Neale. (2009). Is the pain worth the gain? The advantages and liabilities of agreeing with socially distinct newcomers. *Personality and Social Psychology Bulletin, 35:* 336–350.

Porter, E. H. (1973). *Manual of administration and interpretation for strength deployment inventory.* La Jolla, CA: Personal Strengths Assessment Service.

Rahim, M. A., and A. A. Blum. (1994). *Global perspectives on organizational conflict.* Westport, CT: Praeger.

Ruble, T., and J. A. Schneer. (1994). Gender differences in conflict-handling styles: Less than meets the eye? In A. Taylor, and J. B. Miller, (Eds.), *Conflict and gender.* Cresskill, NJ: Hampton Press.

Ruble, T., and K. Thomas. (1976). Support for a two-dimensional model of conflict behavior. *Organizational Behavior and Human Performance, 16:* 145.

Savage, G. T., J. D. Blair, and R. L. Sorenson. (1989). Consider both relationships and substance when negotiating strategically. *Academy of Management Executive, 3:* 37–48.

Schmidt, W. H., and R. Tannenbaum. (1965, November–December). Management of differences. *Harvard Business Review, 38:* 107–115.

Seybolt, P. M., C. B. Derr, and T. R. Nielson. (1996). Linkages between national culture, gender, and conflict management styles. Working paper, University of Utah.

Sillars, A., and J. Weisberg. (1987). Conflict as a social skill. In M. E. Roloff and G. R. Miller (Eds.), *Interpersonal processes: New directions in communication research*. Beverly Hills, CA: Sage.

Smith, W. P. (1987). Conflict and negotiation: Trends and emerging issues. *Journal of Applied Social Psychology, 17:* 631–677.

Stroh, L. K., G. Northcraft, and M. Neale. (2002). *Organizational behavior: A management challenge,* 3rd ed. Mahwah, NJ: Lawrence Erlbaum Associates.

Thomas, K. (1976). Conflict and conflict management. In M. D. Dunnette (Ed.), *Handbook of industrial and organizational psychology.* London: Routledge and Kegan Paul.

Thompson, L. (2001). *The mind and heart of the negotiator,* 2nd ed. Upper Saddle River, NJ: Prentice Hall.

Ting-Toomey, S., G. Gao, P. Trubisky, Z. Yang, H. S. Kim, S. L. Lin, and T. Nishida. (1991). Culture, face maintenance, and styles of handling interpersonal conflict: A study in five cultures. *International Journal of Conflict Management, 2:* 275–296.

Tjosvold, D. (1991). *The conflict positive organization.* Reading, MA: Addison-Wesley.

Trompenaars, F. (1994). *Riding the waves of culture: Understanding diversity in global business.* New York: Irwin.

Trompenaars, F. (1996). Resolving international conflict: Culture and business strategy. *Business Strategy Review, 7:* 51–68.

Volkema, R. J., and T. J. Bergmann. (2001). Conflict styles as indicators of behavioral patterns in interpersonal conflicts. *Journal of Social Psychology, 135:* 5–15.

Wanous, J. P., and A. Youtz. (1986). Solution diversity and the quality of group decisions. *Academy of Management Journal, 1:* 149–159.

Weldon, E., and K. A. Jehn. (1995). Examining crosscultural differences in conflict management behavior: Strategy for future research. *International Journal of Conflict Management, 6:* 387–403.

Wilmot, W. W., and J. L. Hocker. (2001). *Interpersonal conflict.* New York: McGraw-Hill.

Xie, J., X. M. Song, and A. Stringfellow. (1998). Interfunctional conflict, conflict resolution styles, and new product success: A four-culture comparison. *Management Science, 44:* S192–S206.

CHAPTER 8 REFERENCES

Abrahamson, E. (1996). Management fashion. *Academy of Management Review, 21:* 254–285.

Adler, A. (1927). *Understanding human nature.* Garden City, NY: Garden City Publishing.

Alinsky, S. D. (1971). *Rules for radicals: A pragmatic primer for realistic radicals.* New York: Vintage Books.

Alloy, L. B., C. Peterson, L. Y. Abrahamson, and M. E. P. Seligman. (1984). Attributional style and the generality of learned helplessness. *Journal of Personality and Social Psychology, 46:* 681–687.

Anderson, C., D. Hellriegel, and J. Slocum. (1977). Managerial response to environmentally induced stress. *Academy of Management Journal, 20:* 260–272.

Ashby, R. (1956). *Design for the brain.* London: Science Paperbacks.

Asplund, J. and Blacksmith, N. (2012). "Productivity through strengths." In Cameron, K. S. & Spreitzer, G. M. (Eds.). Oxford Handbook of Positive Organizational Scholarship, pages 353–365. New York: Oxford University Press.

Averill, J. R. (1973). Personal control over aversive stimuli and its relationships to stress. *Psychological Bulletin, 80:* 286–303.

Babakus, E., Yavas, U., Karatepe, O. & Avci, T. (2003), "The effect of management commitment to service quality on employees' affective and performance outcomes," *Journal of the Academy of Marketing Science 31*(3), 272–86.

Baker, W., R. Cross, and M. Wooten. (2003). Positive organizational network analysis and energizing relationships. In K. S. Cameron, J. E. Dutton, and R. E. Quinn (Eds.), *Positive Organizational Scholarship* (pp. 328–342). San Francisco: Barrett-Koehler.

Bandura, A. (1977). Self-efficacy: Toward a unifying theory of behavioral change. *Psychological Review, 84:* 191–215.

Bandura, A. (1986). *Social foundations of thought and action: A social cognitive theory.* Englewood Cliffs, NJ: Prentice Hall.

Bandura, A. (1989). Human agency in social cognition theory. *American Psychologist, 44:* 1175–1184.

Bandura, A. (2012). On the functional properties of perceived self-efficacy revisited. *Journal of Management, 38*(1), 9–44.

Barber, B. (1983). *The logic and limits of trust.* New Brunswick, NJ: Rutgers University Press.

Bennis, W., and B. Nanus. (1985). *Leaders: The strategies for taking charge.* New York: Harper & Row.

Bernard, C. I. (1938). *The functions of the executive.* Cambridge, MA: Harvard University Press.

Biron, M., & Bamberger, P. (2010). The impact of structural empowerment on individual well-being and performance: Taking agent preferences, self-efficacy and operational constraints into account. *Human Relations, 63*(2), 163–191.

Block, P. (1987). *The empowered manager: Positive political skills at work.* San Francisco: Jossey-Bass.

Bookman, A., and S. Morgan. (1988). *Women and the politics of empowerment.* Philadelphia: Temple University Press.

Bramucci, R. (1977). A factorial examination of the self-empowerment construct. Unpublished doctoral dissertation, University of Oregon.

Brehm, J. W. (1966). *Response to loss of freedom: A theory of psychological reactance.* New York: Academic Press.

Brief, A., and W. Nord. (1990). *Meanings of occupational work.* Lexington, MA: Lexington Books.

Brouwer, S., Reneman, M. F., Bültmann, U., van der Klink, J. J., & Groothoff, J. W. (2010). A prospective study of return to work across health conditions: perceived work attitude, self-efficacy and perceived social support. *Journal of occupational rehabilitation, 20*(1), 104–112.

Bunderson, J. S., & Thompson, J. A. (2009). The call of the wild: Zookeepers, callings, and the double-edged sword of deeply meaningful work. *Administrative Science Quarterly, 54*(1), 32–57.

Byham, W. C. (1988). *Zapp! The lightening of empowerment.* New York: Harmony Books.

Cameron, K. S. (1998). Strategic organizational downsizing: An extreme case. *Research in Organizational Behavior, 20:* 185–229.

Cameron, K. S., D. A. Whetten, and M. U. Kim. (1987). Organizational dysfunctions of decline. *Academy of Management Journal, 30:* 126–138.

Cameron, K. S., J. E. Dutton, and R. E. Quinn. (2003). *Positive organizational scholarship.* San Francisco: Barrett-Koehler.

Cameron, K. S., M. U. Kim, and D. A. Whetten. (1987). Organizational effects of decline and turbulence. *Administrative Science Quarterly, 32:* 222–240.

Cameron, K. S., S. J. Freeman, and A. K. Mishra. (1991). Best practices in white-collar downsizing: Managing contradictions. *Academy of Management Executive, 5:* 57–73.

Cameron, K. S., S. J. Freeman, and A. K. Mishra. (1993). Organization downsizing and redesign. In G. P. Huber, and W. Glick (Eds.), *Organizational change and design.* New York: Oxford University Press.

Cameron, K. S., and R. E. Quinn. (2011). *Diagnosing and changing organizational culture.* San Francisco: Jossey-Bass.

Caprara, G. V., Vecchione, M., Alessandri, G., Gerbino, M., & Barbaranelli, C. (2011). The contribution of personality traits and self-efficacy beliefs to academic achievement: A longitudinal study. *British Journal of Educational Psychology, 81*(1), 78–96.

Chan, Y. H., Taylor, R. R., & Markham, S. (2008). The Role of Subordinates' Trust in a Social Exchange driven Psychological Empowerment Process. *Journal of Managerial Issues,* 444–467.

Coch, L., and J. R. P. French. (1948). Overcoming resistance to change. *Human Relations, 11:* 512–532.

Conger, J. A. (1989). Leadership: The art of empowering others. *Academy of Management Executive, 3:* 17–24.

Conger, J. A., and R. N. Kanungo. (1988). The empowerment process. *Academy of Management Review, 13:* 471–482.

Coonradt, C. (2007) *The Game of Work.* Layton, UT: Gibbs Smith Press.

Coonradt, C. A. (1985). *The game of work.* Salt Lake City: Shadow Mountain Press.

DeCharms, R. (1979). Personal causation and perceived control. In L. C. Perlmuter and R. A. Monty (Eds.), *Choice and perceived control.* Hillsdale, NJ: Erlbaum.

DeGraff, J., and K. A. Lawrence. (2002). *Creativity at work: Developing the right practices to make innovation happen.* San Francisco: Jossey-Bass.

Deci, E. L., & Ryan, R. M. (2012). Overview of self-determination theory. *The Oxford Handbook of Human Motivation,* 85.

Deci, E. L., J. P. Connell, and R. M. Ryan. (1989). Self-determination in a work organization. *Journal of Applied Psychology, 74:* 580–590.

Deci, E. L., and R. M. Ryan. (1987). The support of autonomy and control of behavior. *Journal of Personality and Social Psychology, 53:* 1024–1037.

Deutsch, M. (1973). *The resolution of conflict: Constructive and destructive processes.* New Haven, CT: Yale University Press.

DiClemente, C. C. (1985). Perceived efficacy in smoking cessation. Paper presented at the Annual meeting of the American Association for the Advancement of Science, Los Angeles.

Dorio, M., & Shelly, S. (2011). *The Complete Idiot's Guide to Boosting Employee Performance.* Penguin.

Drucker, P. (1988, January–February). The coming of the new organization. *Harvard Business Review:* 45–53.

Durkheim, E. (1964). *The division of labor in society.* New York: Free Press.

Eisenhart, K. M., and D. Charlie Galunic. (1993). Renewing the strategy-structure-performance paradigm. *Research in organizational behavior.* Greenwich, CT: JAI Press.

Esmaeili, M. T., Karimi, M., Tabatabaie, K. R., Moradi, A., & Farahini, N. (2011). The effect of positive arousal on working memory. *Procedia-Social and Behavioral Sciences, 30,* 1457–1460.

Freire, P., and A. Faundez. (1989). *Learning to question: A pedagogy of liberation.* New York: Continuum Publishing.

French, J. P. R., Jr., and B. Raven. (1960). The bases of social power. In D. Cartwright and A. Zander (Eds.), *Group dynamics* (pp. 607–623). New York: Harper & Row.

Gagné, M., & Deci, E. L. (2005). Self-determination theory and work motivation. *Journal of Organizational behavior, 26*(4), 331–362.

Gambetta, D. (1988). *Trust: Making and breaking cooperative relations.* Cambridge, MA: Basil Blackwell.

Gecas, V. (1989). The social psychology of self-efficacy. *Annual Review of Sociology, 15:* 291–316.

Gecas, V., M. A. Seff, and M. P. Ray. (1988). Injury and depression: The mediating effects of self concept. Paper presented at the Pacific Sociological Association Meetings, Las Vegas.

Gemmill, G. R., and W. J. Heisler. (1972). Fatalism as a factor in managerial job satisfaction. *Personnel Psychology, 25:* 241–250.

Gibb, J. R., and L. M. Gibb. (1969). Role freedom in a TORI group. In A. Burton (Ed.), *Encounter theory and practice of encounter groups.* San Francisco: Jossey-Bass.

Gilbert, S., Laschinger, H. K., & Leiter, M. (2010). The mediating effect of burnout on the relationship between structural empowerment and organizational citizenship behaviours. *Journal of Nursing Management, 18*(3), 339–348.

Goddard, R. D., W. K. Hoy, and A. W. Hoy. (2003). Collective efficacy beliefs: Theoretical developments, empirical evidence, and future directions. *Educational Researcher, 33:* 3–13.

Golembiewski, R. T., and M. McConkie. (1975). The centrality of trust in group processes. In C. Cooper (Ed.), *Theories of group processes.* New York: Wiley.

Greenberger, D. B., S. Stasser, L. L. Cummings, and R. B. Dunham. (1989). The impact of personal control on performance and satisfaction. *Organizational Behavior and Human Decision Processes, 43:* 29–51.

Greenberger, D. B., and S. Stasser. (1991). The role of situational and dispositional factors in the enhancement of personal control in organizations. *Research in Organizational Behavior,* Vol. 13, (pp. 111–145). Greenwich, CT: JAI Press.

Greenleaf, R. K. (2002). *Servant Leadership.* Costa Mesa, CA: Paulist Press.

Hackman, J. R., G. R. Oldham, R. Janson, and K. Purdy. (1975). A new strategy for job enrichment. *California Management Review, 17:* 57–71.

Hackman, J. R., and G. R. Oldham. (1980). *Work design*. Reading, MA: Addison-Wesley.

Hammer, T. H., and Y. Vardi. (1981). Locus of control and career self-management among nonsupervisory employees in industrial settings. *Journal of Vocational Behavior, 18:* 13–29.

Harris, L. (2002). *Harris Poll #31*. New York: Harris Interactive.

Harter, S. (1978). Effectance motivation reconsidered: Toward a developmental model. *Human Development, 21:* 34–64.

Heath, C., & Heath, D. (2007). *Made to stick: Why some ideas survive and others die*. Random House Digital, Inc..

Helliwell, J. F., & Huang, H. (2011). Well-being and trust in the workplace. *Journal of Happiness Studies, 12*(5), 747–767.

Huber, G. P. (1980). *Managerial decision making*. Glenview, IL: Scott Foresman.

Kahn, W. A. (1990). Psychological conditions of personal engagement and disengagement at work. *Academy of Management Journal, 33:* 692–724.

Kanter, R. (1983). *The change masters*. New York: Simon & Schuster.

Kanter, R. M.: 2008, Transforming Giants, *Harvard Business Review* 86(1), 43–52.

Langer, E. J. (1983). *The psychology of control*. Beverly Hills, CA: Sage.

Langer, E. J., and J. Rodin. (1976). The effects of choice and enhanced personal responsibility. *Journal of Personality and Social Psychology, 34:* 191–198.

Lau, D. C., Lam, L. W., & Wen, S. S. (2013). Examining the effects of feeling trusted by supervisors in the workplace: A self-evaluative perspective. *Journal of Organizational Behavior*.

Lawler, E. E. (1992) *The ultimate advantage: Creating the high involvement organization*. San Francisco: Jossey-Bass.

Lawrence, P., and J. Lorsch. (1967). *Organizations and environments*. Homewood, IL: Irwin.

Leana, C. R. (1987). Power relinquishment versus power sharing: Theoretical clarification and empirical comparison on delegation and participation. *Journal of Applied Psychology, 72:* 228–233.

Locke, E. A., and D. M. Schweiger. (1979). Participation in decision making: One more look. In B. M. Staw and L. L. Cummings (Eds.), *Research in organizational behavior*, Vol. 1 (pp. 265–340). Greenwich, CT: JAI Press.

Locke, E.A. and Latham, G.P. (2006). "New directions in goal-setting theory," *Current Directions in Psychological Science, 15*(5): 265–268.

Lorinkova, N. M., Pearsall, M. J., & Sims, H. P. (2013). Examining the Differential Longitudinal Performance of Directive versus Empowering Leadership in Teams. *Academy of Management Journal, 56*(2), 573–596.

Luhmann, N. (1979). *Trust and power*. New York: Wiley.

Maddux, J. E. (2002). Self-efficacy. In C. R. Snyder and S. J. Lopez, *Handbook of positive psychology* (pp. 277–287). New York: Oxford.

Manz, C. C., and H. Sims. (1989). *Super-leadership: Teaching others to lead themselves*. Englewood Cliffs, NJ: Prentice Hall.

Martin, J., M. Feldman, M. J. Hatch, and S. Sitkin. (1983). The uniqueness paradox of organizational stories. *Administrative Science Quarterly, 28:* 438–452.

Marx, K. (1844). *Early writings*. Edited and translated by T. B. Bottomore. New York: McGraw-Hill.

Maynard, M. T., Gilson, L. L., & Mathieu, J. E. (2012). Empowerment—fad or fab? A multilevel review of the past two decades of research. *Journal of Management, 38*(4), 1231–1281.

McClellend, D. (1975). *Power: The inner experience*. New York: Irvington.

McGregor, D. (1960). The human side of enterprise. New York: McGraw Hill.

Mishra, A. K. (1992). Organizational response to crisis: The role of mutual trust and top management teams. Unpublished doctoral dissertation, University of Michigan.

Mishra, A. and Mishra, K. (2013). *Becoming a Trustworthy Leader*. NY: Routledge Press.

Neufeld, R. W. J., and P. Thomas. (1977) Effects of perceived efficacy of a prophylactic controlling mechanism on self-control under painful stimulation. *Canadian Journal of Behavioral Science, 9:* 224–232.

Newman, W. H., and K. Warren. (1977). *The process of management*. Englewood Cliffs, NJ: Prentice Hall.

Organ, D., and C. N. Greene. (1974). Role ambiguity, locus of control, and work satisfaction. *Journal of Applied Psychology, 59:* 101–112.

Ozer, E. M., and A. Bandura. (1990). Mechanisms governing empowerment effects: A self-efficacy analysis. *Journal of Personality and Social Psychology, 58:* 472–486.

Paglis, L. L. (2010). Leadership self-efficacy: research findings and practical applications. *Journal of Management Development, 29*(9), 771–782.

Pieterse, A. N., Van Knippenberg, D., Schippers, M., & Stam, D. (2010). Transformational and transactional leadership and innovative behavior: The moderating role of psychological empowerment. *Journal of Organizational Behavior, 31*(4), 609–623.

Pratt, M. G. and Ashforth, B. E. (2003). "Fostering meaningfulness in working and at work." In Cameron, K. S., Dutton, J. E. & Quinn, R. E. (Eds.). 309–327 San Francisco: Berrett Koehler Positive Organizational Scholarship.

Pratt, M. G., and B. E. Ashforth. (2003). Fostering meaningfulness in working and at work. In K. S. Cameron, J. E. Dutton, and R. E. Quinn (Eds.), *Positive organizational scholarship* (pp. 309–327). San Francisco: Barrett-Koehler.

Preston, P., and T. W. Zimmerer. (1978). *Management for supervisors*. Englewood Cliffs, NJ: Prentice Hall.

Quinn, R. E. (2005). *Building the bridge as you walk on it*. San Francisco: Jossey-Bass.

Quinn, R. E., and G. Spreitzer. (1997). The road to empowerment: Seven questions every leader should consider. *Organizational Dynamics, 25:* 37–49.

Rappoport, J., C. Swift, and R. Hess. (1984). *Studies in empowerment: Steps toward understanding and action*. New York: Haworth Press.

Rawsthorne, L. J. & A. J. Elliot (1999). "Achievement goals and intrinsic motivation: a meta-analytic review." *Personality and Social Psychological Review*, 3: 326–344

Rose, S. M., and B. L. Black. (1985). *Advocacy and empowerment: Mental health care in the community.* Boston: Routledge and Kegan Paul.

Rothbaum, F., J. R. Weisz, and S. S. Snyder. (1982). Changing the world and changing the self: A two-process model of perceived control. *Journal of Personality and Social Psychology, 42:* 5–37.

Runyon, K. E. (1973). Some interaction between personality variables and management style. *Journal of Applied Psychology, 57:* 288–294.

Ryan, R. M. and E. L. Deci (2000) "Self-determination theory and the facilitation of intrinsic motivation, social development, and well-being." *American Psychologist*, 55: 68–78.

Sashkin, M. (1982). *A manager's guide to participative management.* New York: American Management Association.

Sashkin, M. (1984). Participative management is an ethical imperative. *Organizational Dynamics, 12:* 4–22.

Schneider, J. A., and W. W. Agras. (1985). A cognitive behavioral treatment of bulimia. *British Journal of Psychiatry, 146:* 66–69.

Schwalbe, M. L., and V. Gecas. (1988). Social psychological consequences of job-related disabilities. In J. T. Mortimer and K. M. Borman (Eds.), *Work experience and psychological development through life span.* Boulder, CO: Westview.

Seeman, M., and C. S. Anderson. (1983). Alienation and alcohol. *American Sociological Review, 48:* 60–77.

Seibert, S. E., Wang, G., & Courtright, S. H. (2011). Antecedents and consequences of psychological and team empowerment in organizations: a meta-analytic review. *Journal of Applied Psychology*, 96(5), 981.

Seligman, M. E. P. (1975). *Helplessness: On depression, development, and death.* San Francisco: Freeman.

Sewell, Carl. (1990). *Customers for life.* New York: Pocket Books.

Solomon, B. B. (1976). *Black empowerment: Social work in oppressed communities.* New York: Columbia University Press.

Spreitzer, G. M. (1992). *When organizations dare: The dynamics of individual empowerment in the workplace.* Unpublished doctoral dissertation, University of Michigan.

Spreitzer, G. M. (2008). Taking stock: A review of more than twenty years of research on empowerment at work. *Handbook of organizational behavior*, 54–73.

Staples, L. H. (1990). Powerful ideas about empowerment. *Administration in Social Work, 14:* 29–42.

Staw, B., L. Sandelands, and J. Dutton. (1981). Threat-rigidity effects in organizational behavior: A multilevel analysis. *Administrative Science Quarterly, 26:* 501–524.

Thomas, K. W., and B. A. Velthouse. (1990). Cognitive elements of empowerment: An interpretive model of intrinsic task motivation. *Academy of Management Review, 15:* 666–681.

Thornton, B., & Tizard, H. J. (2010). Not in my back yard: Evidence for arousal moderating vested interest and oppositional behavior to proposed change. *Social psychology*, 41(4), 255.

Trompenaars, F. (1996). Resolving international conflict: Culture and business strategy. *Business Strategy Review*, 7: 51–68.

Trompenaars, F., and C. Hampden-Turner. (1998). *Riding the waves of culture.* New York: McGraw-Hill.

Urwick, L. (1944). *Elements of administration.* New York: Harper and Brothers.

Vogt, J. F., and K. L. Murrell. (1990). *Empowerment in organizations.* San Diego: University Associates.

Vroom, V. H., and A. G. Jago. (1974). Decision making as social process: Normative and descriptive models of leader behavior. *Decision Sciences, 5:* 743–769.

Vroom, V. H., and P. W. Yetton. (1973). *Leadership and decision making.* Pittsburgh: University of Pittsburgh Press.

Weick, K. E. (1979). *The social psychology of organizing.* Reading, MA: Addison-Wesley.

Weick, K. E. (1984). Small wins. *American Psychologist, 39:* 40–49.

Weick, K. E. (1993). Collapse of sense-making in organizations. *Administrative Science Quarterly, 38:* 628–652.

Weinstein, N., & Ryan, R. M. (2011). A self-determination theory approach to understanding stress incursion and responses. *Stress and Health, 27*(1), 4–17.

White, R. W. (1959). Motivation reconsidered: The concept of competence. *Psychological Review, 66:* 297–333.

Wrzesniewski, A. (2003) "Finding positive meaning in work." In Cameron, K. S., Dutton, J. E., and Quinn, R. E. (Eds.) (pp. 296–308) San Francisco: Berrett Koehler.

Wrzesniewski, A. (2003). Finding positive meaning in work. In K. S. Cameron, J. E. Dutton, and R. E. Quinn (Eds.), *Positive organizational scholarship* (pp. 296–308). San Francisco: Barrett-Koehler.

Wrzesniewski, A. (2012) Callings. In Cameron, K. S. and Spreitzer, G. M. (Eds.) Oxford Handbook of Positive Organizational Scholarship. (pp. 45–55) New York: Oxford University Press.

Xanthopoulou, D., Bakker, A. B., & Fischbach, A. (2013). Work engagement among employees facing emotional demands: The role of personal resources. *Journal of Personnel Psychology, 12*(2), 74.

Zand, D. E. (1972). Trust and managerial problem solving. *Administrative Science Quarterly, 17:* 229–239.

Zhang, X., & Bartol, K. M. (2010). Linking empowering leadership and employee creativity: The influence of psychological empowerment, intrinsic motivation, and creative process engagement. *Academy of Management Journal, 53*(1), 107–128.

Zimmerman, M. A. (1990). Taking aim on empowerment research: On the distinction between individual and psychological conceptions. *American Journal of Community Psychology, 18:* 169–177.

Zimmerman, M. A., and J. Rappaport. (1988). Citizen participation, perceived control, and psychological empowerment. *American Journal of Community Psychology, 16:* 725–750.

CHAPTER 9 REFERENCES

Ancona, D. G., and D. Caldwell. (1992). Bridging the boundary: External activity and performance in organizational teams. *Administrative Science Quarterly, 27:* 459–489.

Asch, S. E. (1951). Effects of group pressure upon the modification and distortion of judgments. In H. Guetzkow (Ed.), *Groups, leadership, and men.* Pittsburgh: Carnegie Press.

Belschak, F. D., & Den Hartog, D. N. (2009). Consequences of Positive and Negative Feedback: The Impact on Emotions and Extra-Role Behaviors. *Applied Psychology, 58*(2), 274–303.

Ben-Hur, S., Kinley, N., & Jonsen, K. (2012). Coaching executive teams to reach better decisions. *Journal of Management Development, 31*(7), 711–723.

Bonebright, D. A. (2010). 40 years of storming: a historical review of Tuckman's model of small group development. *Human Resource Development International, 13*(1), 111–120.

Cameron, K. S., and D. A. Whetten. (1981). Perceptions of organizational effectiveness in organizational life cycles. *Administrative Science Quarterly, 27:* 524–544.

Cameron, K. S., and D. A. Whetten. (1984). Organizational life cycle approaches: Overview and applications to higher education. *Review of Higher Education, 6:* 60–102.

Cameron, K. S. (2013) *Practicing Positive Leadership.* San Francisco: Berrett Koehler.

Campion, M. A., G. J. Medsker, and A. C. Higgs. (1993). Relations between work group characteristics and effectiveness: Implications for designing effective work groups. *Personnel Psychology, 46:* 823–850.

Cialdini, R. B. (1995). *Influence: Science and practice,* 3rd ed. Glenview, IL: Scott Foresman.

Clarke, J., and A. Hobson. (2005). *Above all else: The Everest dream.* Toronto: Stewart Publishing.

Cohen, S. G., and D. E. Bailey. (1997). What makes teams work: Group effectiveness research from the shop floor to the executive suite. *Journal of Management, 23:* 239–290.

Cox, T. H. (1994). *Cultural diversity in organizations: Theory, research, and practice.* San Francisco: Barrett-Koehler.

Dew, J. R. (1998). *Managing in a team environment.* Westport, CT: Quorum.

Dewey, J. (1933). *How we think.* Boston: Heath.

Dewey, J. (1933). How we think: A restatement of the relation of reflective thinking to the educational process. *Lexington, MA: Heath.*

Druskat, V., and J. Wheeler. (2000). Effective leadership of self-managing teams: Behaviors that make a difference. Working paper, Weatherhead School of Management, Case Western Reserve University.

Druskat, V., and S. Wolff. (1999). The link between emotions and team effectiveness: How teams engage members and build effective task processes. *Academy of Management Best Paper Proceedings,* Organizational Behavior Division.

Dyer, W. G. (1987). *Team building: Issues and alternatives.* Reading, MA: Addison-Wesley.

Edmonson, A. (1999). Psychological safety and learning behavior in work teams. *Administrative Science Quarterly, 44:* 350–383.

Freud, S. (1921). *Group psychology and the analysis of the ego.* London: Hogarth Press.

Gladstein, D. (1984). Group in context: A model of task group effectiveness. *Administrative Science Quarterly, 29:* 497–517.

Greiner, L. (1972, July–August). Evolution and revolution as organizations grow. *Harvard Business Review:* 37–46.

Gully, S. M., D. S. Divine, and D. J. Whitney. (1995). A meta-analysis of cohesion and performance: Effects of level of analysis and task interdependence. *Small Group Research, 26:* 497–520.

Guzzo, R. A., and M. W. Dickson. (1996). Teams in organizations: Recent research on performance and effectiveness. *Annual Review of Psychology, 47:* 307–338.

Hackman, J. R. (1987). The design of work teams. In J. W. Lorsch (Ed.), *Handbook of organizational behavior.* Englewood Cliffs, NJ: Prentice Hall.

Hackman, J. R. (1990). *Groups that work (and those that don't).* San Francisco: Jossey-Bass.

Hackman, J. R. (1993). Teams and group failure. Presentation at the Interdisciplinary College on Organization Studies, University of Michigan, October.

Hackman, J. R. (2003). *Leading teams.* Cambridge, MA: Harvard Business School Press.

Hamilton, B. H., J. A. Nickerson, and H. Owan. (2003). Team incentives and worker heterogeneity: An empirical analysis of the impact of teams on productivity and participation. *Journal of Political Economy, 111:* 465–497.

Hayes, N. (1997). *Successful team management.* Boston: International Thompson Business Press.

Helliwell, J. F., & Huang, H. (2011). Well-being and trust in the workplace. *Journal of Happiness Studies, 12*(5),

Janis, I. (1972). *Victims of groupthink.* Boston: Houghton Mifflin.

Katzenbach, J. R., and D. K. Smith. (1993). *The wisdom of teams.* Boston: Harvard Business School Press.

Kouzes, J. M., & Posner, B. Z. (2011). *Credibility: How leaders gain and lose it, why people demand it* (Vol. 244). Wiley.

Kouzes, J., and B. Posner. (1987). *The leadership challenge.* San Francisco: Jossey-Bass.

Kramer, R. M. (1999). Trust and distrust in organizations: Emerging perspectives, enduring questions. *Annual Review of Psychology, 50:* 569–598.

Lawler, E. E. (1998). *Strategies for high performance organizations.* San Francisco: Jossey-Bass.

Lawler, E. E. (2003). *Treat people right.* San Francisco: Jossey-Bass.

Lawler, E. E., S. A. Mohrman, and G. E. Ledford. (1995). *Creating high performance organizations: Practices and results of employee involvement and total quality management in Fortune 1000 companies.* San Francisco: Jossey-Bass.

Lidz, F. (2000). Up and down in Beverly Hills. *Sports Illustrated, 92*(16): 60–68.

Locke, E. (1990). *A theory of goal setting and task performance.* Upper Saddle River, NJ: Prentice Hall.

Manz, C., and H. Sims. (1987). Leading workers to lead themselves: The external leadership of self-managing work teams. *Administrative Science Quarterly, 32:* 106–128.

Mesmer-Magnus, J. R., & DeChurch, L. A. (2009). Information sharing and team performance: a meta-analysis. *Journal of Applied Psychology, 94*(2), 535.

Mitchell, S. M., & Prins, B. C. (2004). Rivalry and diversionary uses of force. *Journal of Conflict Resolution, 48*(6), 937–961.

Mullen, B., and C. Copper. (1994). The relation between group cohesiveness and performance: An integration. *Psychological Bulletin, 115:* 210–227.

Pagonis, W. G. (1993). *Moving mountains.* Cambridge, MA: Harvard Business School Press.

Parker, G. M. (1996). *Team players and teamwork: The new competitive business strategy.* San Francisco: Jossey-Bass.

Peters, T. (1987). *Thriving on chaos.* New York: Knopf.

Quinn, R. E. (2005). *Building the bridge as you walk on it.* San Francisco: Jossey-Bass.

Quinn, R. E., and K. S. Cameron. (1983). Organizational life cycles and shifting criteria of effectiveness: Some preliminary evidence. *Management Science, 29:* 33–51.

Schein, E. H. (1976). What to observe in a group. In C. R. Mill and L. C. Porter (Eds.), *Reading book for human relations training.* Bethel, ME: NTL Institute.

Senge, P. (1991). *The fifth discipline.* New York: Doubleday.

Shin, S. J., Kim, T. Y., Lee, J. Y., & Bian, L. (2012). Cognitive team diversity and individual team member creativity: A cross-level interaction. *Academy of Management Journal, 55*(1), 197–212.

Shuffler, M. L., Burke, C. S., Kramer, W. S., & Salas, E. (2012). Leading Teams: Past, Present, and Future. In Runsey (Eds.). *The Oxford Handbook of Leadership,* (144). Oxford University Press.

Srivastava, A., Bartol, K. M., & Locke, E. A. (2006). Empowering leadership in management teams: Effects on knowledge sharing, efficacy, and performance. *Academy of Management Journal, 49*(6), 1239–1251.

Trompenaars, F. (1996). Resolving international conflict: Culture and business strategy. *Business Strategy Review, 7:* 51–68.

Trompenaars, F., and C. Hampden-Turner. (1998). *Riding the waves of culture.* New York: McGraw-Hill.

Tuckman, B. W. (1965). Developmental sequence in small groups. *Psychological Bulletin, 63:* 384–399.

Turner, M. E. (Ed.). (2000). *Groups at work: Advances in theory and research.* New York: Lawrence Erlbaum.

Verespei, M. A. (1990, June 18). Yea, teams? Not always. *Industry Week:* 103–105.

Wellins, R. S., W. C. Byham, and J. M. Wilson. (1991). *Empowered teams.* San Francisco: Jossey-Bass.

Yeatts, D. E., and C. Hyten (1998). *High performing self-managing work teams: A comparison of theory to practice.* Thousand Oaks, CA: Sage.

CHAPTER 10 REFERENCES

Avey, J. B., Wernsing, T. S., & Luthans, F. (2008). Can positive employees help positive organizational change? Impact of psychological capital and emotions on relevant attitudes and behaviors. *The Journal of Applied Behavioral Science, 44*(1), 48–70.

Baker, W. (2001). *Achieving success through social capital.* San Francisco: Jossey-Bass.

Baker, W., R. Cross, and M. Wooten. (2003). Positive organizational network analysis and energizing relationships. In K. S. Cameron, J. E. Dutton, and R. E. Quinn (Eds.), *Positive organizational scholarship: Foundations of a new discipline* (pp. 328–342). San Francisco: Barrett-Koehler.

Bartunek, J. M., Rynes, S. L., & Ireland, R. D. (2006). What makes management research interesting, and why does it matter? *Academy of Management Journal, 49*(1), 9–15.

Baumeister, R. F., E. Bratslavsky, C. Finkenauer, and K. D. Vohs. (2001). Bad is stronger than good. *Review of General Psychology, 5:* 323–370.

Bennis, W., and B. Nanus. (1985). *Leaders: The strategies for taking charge.* New York: Harper & Row.

Biswas-Diener, R., Kashdan, T. B., & Minhas, G. (2011). A dynamic approach to psychological strength development and intervention. *The Journal of Positive Psychology, 6*(2), 106–118.

Bollier, D. (1996). *Aiming higher: Twenty-five stories of how companies prosper by combining sound management and social vision.* New York: Amacom.

Boyatzis, R. E., Smith, M. L., & Blaize, N. (2006). Developing sustainable leaders through coaching and compassion. *Academy of Management Learning & Education, 5*(1), 8–24.

Bright, D. S. and Exline, J. J. (2012). Forgiveness at four levels: Intrapersonal, relational, organizational, and collective-group. In Cameron, K. S. and Spreitzer, G. M., (Eds.)., Oxford Handbook of Positive Organizational Scholarship. New York: Oxford University Press.

Bright, D. S., K. S. Cameron, and A. Caza. (2006). The ethos of virtuousness in downsized organizations. *Journal of Business Ethics, 64:* 249–269.

Caldwell, C., & Dixon, R. D. (2010). Love, forgiveness, and trust: Critical values of the modern leader. *Journal of Business Ethics, 93*(1), 91–101.

Cameron, K. S. (1985). Iacocca's transformation of Chrysler; Excerpts from Lee Iacocca's speeches to his top management team, 1979–1984. (In possession of the author.)

Cameron, K. S. (2003a). Ethics, virtuousness, and constant change. In N. M. Tichy and A. R. McGill (Eds.), *The ethical challenge* (pp. 185–193). San Francisco: Jossey-Bass.

Cameron, K. S. (2003b). Organizational virtuousness and performance. In K. S. Cameron, J. E. Dutton, and R. E. Quinn (Eds.), *Positive organizational scholarship: Foundations of a new discipline* (pp. 48–65). San Francisco: Barrett-Koehler.

Cameron, K. S. (2008). Paradox in positive organizational change. *The Journal of Applied Behavioral Science, 44*(1), 7–24.

Cameron, K. S. (2012). *Positive Leadership.* San Francisco: Berrett Koehler.

Cameron, K. S. (2013) *Practicing Positive Leadership.* San Francisco: Berrett Koehler.

Cameron, K. S. (2014). "Advances in positive organizational scholarship." *Advances in Positive Organizational Psychology,* 1: 23–44.

Cameron, K. S. Mora, C., Leutscher, T., & Calarco, M. (2011). "Effects of positive practices on organizational effectiveness." *Journal of Applied Behavioral Science,* 47: 266–308.

Cameron, K. S., D. A. Whetten, and M. U. Kim. (1987). Organizational effects of decline and turbulence. *Administration Science Quarterly, 32:* 222–240.

Cameron, K. S., Quinn, R. E., DeGraff, J., & Thakor, A. (2014). *Competing Values Leadership: Creating Value in Organizations*. Revised Edition. Northampton, MA: Edward Elgar.

Cameron, K. S., and A. Caza. (2002). Organizational and leadership virtues and the role of forgiveness. *Journal of Leadership and Organizational Studies, 9:* 33–48.

Cameron, K. S., and D. O. Ulrich. (1986). Transformational leadership in colleges and universities. *Higher Education: Handbook of Theory and Research, 2:* 1–42.

Cameron, K. S., and M. Lavine. (2006). *Making the impossible possible: Leading extraordinary performance—The Rocky Flats story*. San Francisco: Barrett-Koehler.

Cameron, K. S., and R. E. Quinn. (2011). *Diagnosing and changing organizational culture*. Reading, MA: Addison-Wesley.

Carlzon, J. (1987). *Moments of truth*. Cambridge, MA: Ballinger.

Christie, R., and S. Lehman. (1970). The structure of Machiavellian orientations. In R. Christie and F. Geis (Eds.), *Studies in Machiavellianism* (pp. 359–387). New York: Academic Press.

Cialdini, R. B. (2000). *Influence: The science of persuasion*. New York: Allyn & Bacon.

Clifton, D. O., and J. K. Harter. (2003). Investing in strengths. In K. S. Cameron, J. E. Dutton, and R. E. Quinn (Eds.), *Positive organizational scholarship: Foundations of a new discipline* (pp. 111–121). San Francisco: Barrett-Koehler.

Coonradt, C. (1985). *The game of work*. Salt Lake City: Shadow Mountain Press.

Coonradt, C. (2007). *The Game of Work*. Layton, UT: Gibbs Smith Press.

Cooperrider, D. L. (1990). Appreciative management and leadership: The power of positive thought and action in organizations. San Francisco: Jossey-Bass.

Csikszentmihalyi, M. (1990). *Flow: The psychology of optimal experience*. New York: Harper Perennial.

Datta, D. K., Guthrie, J. P., Basuil, D., & Pandey, A. (2010). Causes and effects of employee downsizing: A review and synthesis. *Journal of Management, 36*(1), 281–348.

Davis, M. (1971). That's interesting! *Philosophy of the Social Sciences, 1:* 309–344.

Dutton, J. E., P. J. Frost, M. C. Worline, J. M. Lilius, and J. M. Kanov. (2002, *January*). Leading in times of trauma. *Harvard Business Review:* 54–61.

Emmons, R. A. (2003). Acts of gratitude in organizations. In K. S. Cameron, J. E. Dutton, and R. E. Quinn (Eds.), *Positive organizational scholarship: Foundations of a new discipline* (pp. 81–93). San Francisco: Barrett-Koehler.

Emmons, R. A. (2007). *Thanks!* New York: Houghton Mifflin.

Enright, R. D., and C. Coyle. (1998). Researching the process model of forgiveness within psychological interventions. In E. L. Worthington (Ed.), *Dimensions of forgiveness* (pp. 139–161). Philadelphia: Templeton Foundation Press.

Enrique, J. (2000). *As the future catches you*. New York: Crown Business.

Fredrickson, B. L. (2003). Positive emotions and upward spirals in organizations. In K. S. Cameron, J. E. Dutton, and R. E. Quinn (Eds.), *Positive organizational scholarship:* *Foundations of a new discipline* (pp. 163–175). San Francisco: Barrett-Koehler.

Fredrickson, B. L., & Branigan, C. (2005). Positive emotions broaden the scope of attention and thought-action repertoires. *Cognition & Emotion, 19*(3), 313–332.

Frost, P. J. (2003). *Toxic emotions at work: How compassionate managers handle pain and conflict*. Cambridge, MA: Harvard Business School Press.

Glynn, P. (1994). Toward a politics of forgiveness. *American Enterprise, 5:* 48–53.

Gold, T. (2002). *Open your mind, open your life*. Springfield, IL: Andrews McNeel Publishing.

Gottman, J. (1994). *Why marriages succeed and fail*. New York: Simon & Schuster.

Hazen, M. A. (2008). Grief and the workplace. *Academy of Management Perspectives, 22,* 78–86.

Helmick, R. G., and R. L. Petersen. (2001). *Forgiveness and reconciliation: Religion, public policy, and conflict*. Philadelphia: Templeton Foundation Press.

Kanov, J. M., S. Maitlis, M. C. Worline, J. E. Dutton, and P. J. Frost. (2003). Compassion in organizational life. *American Behavioral Scientist:* 1–54.

Kirschenbaum, D. (1984). Self-regulation and sport psychology: Nurturing and emerging symbiosis. *Journal of Sport Psychology, 8:* 26–34.

Kotter, J. (1999). *John Kotter on what leaders really do*. Cambridge, MA: Harvard Business School Press.

Lewin, K. (1951). *Field theory in social science*. New York: Harper & Row.

Losada, M., and E. Heaphy. (2003). The role of positivity and connectivity in the performance of business teams: A nonlinear dynamics model. *American Behavioral Scientist, 47:* 740–765.

McCraty, R., and Childre, D. (2004). The grateful heart. In R. A. Emmons and M. E. McCullough (Eds.), *The psychology of gratitude* (pp. 230–255). New York: Oxford University Press.

McCullough, M. E., R. A. Emmons, and J. Tsang. (2002). The grateful disposition: A conceptual and empirical topography. *Journal of Personality and Social Psychology, 82:* 112–127.

Meyerson, D. (2001). *Tempered radicals*. Cambridge, MA: Harvard Business School Press.

Nahrgang, J. D., DeRue, D. S., Hollenbeck, J. R., Spitzmuller, M., Jundt, D. K., & Ilgen, D. R. (2013). Goal setting in teams: The impact of learning and performance goals on process and performance. *Organizational Behavior and Human Decision Processes, 122*(1), 12–21.

Perot, H. R. (1988). A vision for General Motors. Internal company document. General Motors Corporation, Detroit, MI.

Pfeffer, J. (1998). *The human equation: Building profits by putting people first*. Boston: Harvard Business School Press.

Powley, E. H. (2009). Reclaiming resilience and safety: Resilience activation in the critical period of crisis. *Human Relations, 62*(9), 1289–1326.

Quinn, R. E. (2000). *Change the world.* San Francisco: Jossey-Bass.

Quinn, R. E. (2004). *Building the bridge as you walk on it.* San Francisco: Jossey-Bass.

Quinn, R. E., J. E. Dutton, and G. M. Spreitzer. (2003). Reflected best-self exercise: Assignment and instructions for participants. Center for Positive Organizational Scholarship, Ross School of Business, University of Michigan. Product #001B.

Ramlall, S. J. (2008). Enhancing employee performance through positive organizational behavior. *Journal of Applied Social Psychology, 38*(6), 1580–600.

Rath, T. (2001). *Now Discover Your Strengths.* New York: Gallup Press.

Rego, A., Ribeiro, N., & Cunha, M. P. (2010). Perceptions of organizational virtuousness and happiness as predictors of organizational citizenship behaviors. *Journal of Business Ethics, 93*(2), 215–235.

Roberts, L. M., G. Spreitzer, J. Dutton, R. Quinn, E. Heaphy, and B. Barker. (2005). How to play to your strengths. *Harvard Business Review, 83:* 75–80.

Salancik, G. R. (1977). Commitment of control of organizational behavior and belief. In B. M. Staw and G. R. Salancik (Eds.), *News directions in organizational behavior.* Chicago: St. Clair Press.

Sculley, J. (1987). Apple's identity and goals. Internal company document. Apple Computer, Inc., Cupertino, CA.

Seligman, M. E. P. (2002). *Authentic happiness.* New York: Free Press.

Selznick, P. (1949). *TVA and the grass roots.* Berkeley: University of California Press.

Simmel, G. (1950). *The sociology of Georg Simmel.* Glencoe, IL: Free Press.

Tichy, N. M. (1993). *Control your destiny or someone else will.* New York: Doubleday.

Tichy, N. M. (1997). *The leadership engine.* New York: Harper Collins.

Tutu, D. (1998). Without forgiveness there is no future. In R. D. Enright and J. North (Eds.), *Exploring forgiveness.* Madison: University of Wisconsin Press.

Tutu, D. (1999). *No future without forgiveness.* New York: Doubleday.

U. S. Army Strategic Leadership Program. (2003). Personal communication. Boston, MA.

Walsh, J. P. (1999). Business must talk about its social role. In T. Dickson (Ed.), *Mastering strategy* (pp. 289–294). London: Financial Times/Prentice Hall.

Weick, K. E. (1981). Small wins: Redefining the scale of social problems. *American Psychologist, 39:* 40–49.

Weick, K. E. (1993, Winter). Small wins in organizational life. *Dividend:* 20–24.

Zhang, X., & Bartol, K. M. (2010). Linking empowering leadership and employee creativity: The influence of psychological empowerment, intrinsic motivation, and creative process engagement. *Academy of Management Journal, 53*(1), 107–128.

SUPPLEMENT A REFERENCES

Barrett, H. (1977). *Practical uses of speech communication,* 4th ed. New York: Holt, Rinehart & Winston.

Collins, E., and M. Devanna. (1990). *The portable MBA.* New York: Wiley.

Dubrin, A. J. (1985). *Contemporary applied management.* Plano, TX: Business Publications, Inc.

Endicott Report. (1992). Baton Rouge: Louisiana State University Press.

Gelles-Cole, S. (1985). *The complete guide to executive manners.* New York: Rawson.

Gronbeck, B. E., et al. (1992). *Principles of speech communication,* 11th ed. New York: Harper Collins.

Lucas, S. (1989). *The art of public speaking,* 3rd ed. New York: Random House.

Mambert, W. A. (1976). *Effective presentation.* New York: Wiley.

Maruca, R. F. (1996). Looking for better productivity? *Harvard Business Review, 74:* 9–10.

Miller, G. A. (1967). *The psychology of communication.* Baltimore: Penguin.

Osborn, M., and S. Osborn. (1991). *Public speaking.* Boston: Houghton Mifflin.

Peoples, D. A. (1988). *Presentations plus.* New York: Wiley.

Poor, E. (1992). *The executive writer: A guide to managing words, ideas, and people.* New York: Grove Weidenfeld.

Reingold, J. (2004, October). The man behind the curtain. *Fast Company:* 100–104.

Sanford, W. P., and W. H. Yeager. (1963). *Principles of effective speaking,* 6th ed. New York: Ronald Press.

Seiler, W. J. (1971). The effects of visual materials on attitudes, credibility, and retention. *Speech Monographs, 38:* 331–334.

Sprague, J., and D. Stuart. (1996). *The speaker's handbook,* 4th ed. Fort Worth, TX: Harcourt Brace College Publishers.

Sproule, M. (1991). *Speechmaking: An introduction to rhetorical competence.* Dubuque, IA: William C. Brown.

Wells, W. (1989). *Communications in business,* 5th ed. Belmont, CA: Wadsworth.

Wilcox, R. P. (1967). *Oral reporting in business and industry.* Upper Saddle River, NJ: Prentice Hall.

SUPPLEMENT B REFERENCES

Beer, M. (1987). *Meetings: How to make them work for you.* New York: Van Nostrand Reinholdt.

Downs, C. W., G. P. Smeyak, and E. Martin. (1980). *Professional interviewing.* New York: Harper & Row.

DuBrin, A. J. (1981). *Human relations: A job-oriented approach,* 2nd ed. Reston, VA: Reston Publishing Company.

Lopez, R. M. (1975). *Personnel interviewing.* New York: McGraw-Hill.

Maier, N. R. F. (1958, March–April). Three types of appraisal interviews. *Personnel:* 27–40.

Sincoff, M. Z., and R. S. Goyer. (1984). *Interviewing.* New York: Macmillan.

Stano, M. E., and N. L. Reinsch, Jr. (1982). *Communication in interviews*. Upper Saddle River, NJ: Prentice Hall.

Stewart, C. J., and W. B. Cash, Jr. (1985). *Interviewing: Principles and practice,* 4th ed. Dubuque, IA: Brown.

SUPPLEMENT C REFERENCES

3M Meeting Management Team. (1994). *Mastering meetings*. New York: McGraw-Hill.

Cohen, M., J. March and J. Olsen. (1972). A garbage can model of organizational choice. *Administrative Science Quarterly, 17:* 1–15.

De Tocqueville, A. (1841). *Democracy in America*. New York: Langley.

DeBono, E. (1985). *The six thinking hats*. Boston: Little, Brown.

Harvey, J. (1974, Summer). The abilene paradox. *Organizational Dynamics:* 63–80.

Janis, I. (1972). *Victims of groupthink*. Boston: Houghton Mifflin.

Janis, I. (1983). *Groupthink: Psychological studies of policy decisions and fiascoes*. Boston: Houghton Mifflin.

Putnam, R. (2000). *Bowling alone*. New York: Simon & Schuster.

Rothman, J., J. Erlich, and J. Tropman. (2000). Strategies of community intervention, 6th ed. Itasca, IL: F. E. Peacock.

Tichy, N., and M. Devanna. (1986). *The transformational leader*. New York: Wiley.

Tropman, J. E. (1996). *Effective meetings,* 2nd ed. Thousand Oaks, CA: Sage.

Tropman, J., J. Erlich, and J. Rothman. (2000). *Tactics of community intervention,* 4th ed. Itasca, IL: F. E. Peacock.

Tuchman, B. (1984). *The march of folly: From Troy to Vietnam*. New York: Knopf.

INDEX

Page numbers followed by "f" indicate figures and those followed by "t" indicate tables.

A

A. H. Robins, 58
AAL, 405
Abbott, R., 283
Abilene paradox, 552
Ability, 265–266
About Google, 376
Abrahamson, L. Y., 381
Abuse of power, 230–231
Achievement culture, 53, 229, 421, 427
Achievement goals, 102
Active control, 370
Active listening exercises, 223
Acton, J. E. E., Baron, 230–231
Adams, J., 148, 152, 157
Adhocracy skills, 9
Adler, C. M., 103, 107, 311
Adler, R. B., 321, 322t, 325
Advising responses, 208
Affective orientation, 52, 214
Affectivity, 94
Agenda bell rule, 555, 555f
Agenda integrity rule, 555
Agenda rule, 554
Agle, B. R., 233
Agor, W. H., 61
Agras, W., 369
Agreeable behavior, 234
Agreeableness, 48, 64
Aguinis, H., 237
Albert, R., 157
Alcoholics Anonymous, 146
Alderfer, Clay, 281
Alessandri, G., 369
Alienation, 372
Allen, R., 241
Allinson, C., 48, 234
Alloy, L. B., 381
Allport, Gordon W., 48
Amabile, T. M., 157
Amana Refrigeration Co., 151
Amazon, 174
Ambidextrous thinking, 156
    exercise for, 156t
AMD, Inc., 149
American Can Co., 283
American Management Association, 58
American Men and Women of Science, 50
American Psychological Assoc., 90
American Society for Training and
    Development, 267
Analogies, 158–159
Analytical problem solving, 144t, 150,
    167f, 171
    behavioral guidelines, 171–172
    exercises, 175–176

limitations of, 143
steps in, 139–142
Ancona, D., 406
Andersen, M. B., 95, 112
Anderson, B., 9
Anderson, C., 63, 234, 369
Andrews, A. O., 5
Anteby, M., 274
Anticipatory stressors, 95, 103–106
Apex Communications Co., 490, 507
Apple Computer, 140, 143, 173–174,
    312, 421, 462
Apple II, 173–174, 312
Apple Newton, 174
Apple Store, 173
Application exercises, 8
Aptitude, 265
Argenti, J., 306
Ariel, Sheira, 239
Ariely, D., 276
Arkinson, J., 281
Armstrong, S. J., 61, 234
Armstrong-Stassen, M., 62
Arthur, M. B., 272
Artificial constraints, 154–155
Ascription culture, 53, 229, 388,
    421, 427
Ashford, S., 246, 279
Ashforth, B., 109, 371
Asplund, J., 367
Association for Fitness in Business, 107
Association to Advance Collegiate
    Schools of Business (AACSB), 177
AT&T, 107, 236, 405
Athos, A. G., 210
Atkinson, J., 271
Attraction, 233–234
Atwater, L. E., 48
Auerbach, S. M., 91
Autonomy, 103, 272, 279
Avci, T., 366
Averill, J., 381
Avey, J. B., 450
Avocado Computers exercise, 346

B

Babakus, E., 366
Baby Boomers, 280
Bacharach, Samuel, 228
Bagnall, J., 164
Bailey, D. E., 405–406, 414, 424
Baker, W., 110, 127, 190, 452, 465
Bakker, A. B., 369–370
Balkundi, P., 233
Bamberger, P., 368
Bandura, A., 7, 107, 368–369, 372–374
Bank of America, 58

Bank of Boston, 58
Banks, Donald L., 62
Bannister, Roger, 374
Barbaranelli, C., 369
Barber, B., 371
Bargaining, 243
Bargh, J. A., 231
Baril, G., 316
Barker, B., 445
Barker, L., 191, 210
Barling, J., 107
Barnett, C. K., 46
Barnett, T. R., 191
Barnlund, D., 202
Barrett, P., 490
Barrick Gold Corporation, 58
Barron, F., 50
Barsade, S. G., 102
Bartol, K. M., 376, 419, 452
Bartunek, J. M., 462
Basadur, M., 157
Bass, B., 9
Basuil, D., 450
Bateman, T. S., 239
Batey, M., 60
Batten, J., 429–430
Battle Creek Foods, 508–509
Baum, A., 91, 94
Baumeister, R., 452
Bazerman, M., 314
Beal, R. L., 13
Beane, Billy, 307–308
Becker, B. E., 4
Beer, M., 530
Behavior-shaping strategies, 275–276,
    276f, 277
    exercises, 299–304
    extrinsic outcomes, 278
    improving, 278t
    intrinsic outcomes, 278
    redirecting, 277
    reinforcement, 277
    reprimanding behaviors, 277
Bell, Alexander Graham, 150
Bellah, Robert, 109
Ben-Amos, P., 165
Benchmarking, 457–458
Ben-Hur, S., 411
Bennigan's, 178, 180
Bennis, Warren, 3, 229–230, 271, 368,
    370, 459
Bergmann, T. J., 312
Bernardi, R. A., 63
Berscheid, E., 47
Bethune, Gordon, 74
Bian, L., 412
Bias against thinking, 156

Bies, R., 247
"Big Five" personality dimensions, 48,
    63–64
Bigley, G., 265
Billingsley, Taylor, 490, 507
Bilsky, W., 54
Bingham, J. B., 235
Birch, D., 282
Biron, M., 368
Biswas-Diener, R., 90, 455
Bitter, M. E., 265
Black, B., 369
Blackard, K., 306
Blacksmith, N., 367
Blaize, N., 453
Blake, J., 311
Blanks, Maurice, 74
Blasko, V., 161
Blimes, L. K., 5
Blink (Gladwell), 139
Block, P., 370, 375, 380
Blocking roles, 425–426
Blodget, H., 267
Blu Dot, 74
Blum, A., 316
Bodenheimer, George, 235
Bodie, G., 206
Boeing Co., 421
Bogomolny, Richard, 460
Bohr, Niels, 159
Boiled frog syndrome, 552
Bollier, D., 460
Bonebright, D. A., 408
Bonnett, C., 63
Bono, J. E., 63–64
Boone, C., 63
Boss, W., 211, 213
Bosses
    abusive, 247–248, 248t
    influence, 246
Boss-subordinate relationships, 235
Bostrom, R., 207–208
Boulding, E., 308
Bourgeois, L. J., 306
Bowers, D. G., 108
Boyatzis, R. E., 7–9, 45, 48, 51, 60, 453
Brabander, B., 63
Bradley, B., 309
Bradley's Barn exercise, 345–346
Brainstorming, 162–163
Bramucci, R., 371
Bramwell, S. T., 95
Branigan, C., 452
Bratslavsky, E., 452
Breen, B., 246
Brett, J. M., 326
Breznitz, S., 94

Bright, D., 109, 451*f*, 454, 470
British Petroleum (BP), 479
Brouwer, P. J., 45, 369
Brown, M. E., 57
Brown, S., 102, 109, 307, 315
Brownell, J., 191–192, 197, 202, 210
Brueller, D., 190
Brunel, M. I., 159
Buddha, 56
Budget Rent-a-Car, 65
Budner, S., 62
Buffett, Warren, 446
Bunderson, J., 231, 233, 278, 370
Bunker, K., 230
Burke, C. S., 406
Burke, James, 475
Burleson, B. R., 197
Burlingham, B., 314
Burnaska, R. F., 9
Burnham, D., 231, 282
Burnout, 91
Burstiner, I., 275*t*
Burt, R., 232, 238
Business schools, 177–178
Business Week, 177–178, 230
Byham, W., 380, 404
Byosiere, P., 92, 94
Byrne, Patrick M., 74
Byron *vs.* Thomas, exercises, 221–223

C
Cable, D., 54, 234
Calarco, Margaret, 191
Caldwell, D., 406, 454
Callahan, I., 63
Cameron, K. S., 6–10, 46–47, 54, 94,
    109–110, 143, 191, 312, 375,
    377, 380, 408, 420, 446–450,
    451*f*, 452, 454, 456, 458,
    469–470, 478, 480
Campion, M., 412
Canfield, F., 234
Cantor, N., 102
Caplan, R. D., 103
Caprara, G. V., 369
Cardinal Health, 241
Career orientation, 108
Carlzon, Jan, 468–469
Carmeli, A., 190
Carnegie, Andrew, 403
Carrell, S. E., 191–192
Carrier, 405
Cartwright, S., 50
Casciaro, T., 234
Case of the Missing Time, 117–121
Case studies
    Case of the Missing Time, 117–121
    Cash Register Incident, 431–432
    Changing the Portfolio, 390–391
    Coke versus Pepsi, 172–173
    Communist prison camp case,
        67–68
    Computerized exam case, 69
    conflict management, 332–336
    Creativity at Apple, 173–174
    Dynica Technologies, 253
    Educational Pension Investments,
        332–336
    Electro Logic, 289–295
    empowerment, 389–391
    Find Somebody Else, 216–217
    Minding the Store, 389–390
    motivation, 289–295
    positive relationships, 216–219
    power, 253
    problem solving, 172–173
    Rejected Plans, 217–219
    stress management, 114–121

Tallahassee Democrat's ELITE team,
    428–430
    teamwork, 428–432
    Turn of the Tide, 114–117
    vision statements, 471–477
Cash, W., 524
Cash Register Incident case, 431–432
Cassidy, S., 59
Castro, Fidel, 410
Caterpillar, Inc., 280
Cavanaugh, G. F., 54
Caza, A., 109, 449, 451*f*, 454, 470
Center for Creative Leadership, 230
Center for Leadership and Change
    Management, 246
Centrality, 237–239
Cervone, D. P., 45
CH2MHill, 462
Chambers, John, 453
Chamorro-Premuzic, T., 60
Chan, C. K., 61
Chan, Y. H., 371
Change. *See also* Positive change
    escalation of, 447
    heliotropic effect, 469–470
    orientation towards, 47–48
Changing the Portfolio case, 390–391
Charismatic leadership, 233–234
Charles, K., 63
Chen, Chris, 293
Chen, G., 108
Chen, Serena, 231
Chenhall, Robert H., 61
Chesapeake Energy, 230
Cheston, R., 316
Childre, D., 455, 455*f*
Choi, I., 265
Chevron Corporation, 58
Christensen, Bob, 292
Chrysler, 458, 462
Chu, Y. K., 165
Church, A. H., 48
Churchill, Winston, 240
Cialdini, R., 150, 152, 241, 417–418,
    465
Cisco Systems, 453
Clan skills, 9
Clare, D. A., 54
Clarification probes, 209, 524
Clark, R., 281
Clarke, Jamie, 421
Client relationships, establishing, 280
Clifton, D., 455, 457
Closed questions, 519
Coaching, 195–196, 207
Coakley, Carolyn G., 210
Coats, D., 234
Coca-Cola Co., 172–173
Cochran, D. S., 191
Coddington, R. D., 95
Cognex Corporation, 274
Cognitive intelligence, 102
Cognitive Style Indicator, 38, 42, 80–81
Cognitive styles
    creating style, 60–61
    defined, 59
    knowing style, 60
    planning style, 60
    self-awareness and, 47–48, 59
    three dimensions of, 60*t*
Cohen, M. D., 552–553
Cohen, S., 109, 405–406, 414, 424
Coke versus Pepsi case, 172–173
Colbert, A. E., 271
Cole, Robert, 511
Coleman, Daniel F., 63
Collaborative problem solving, 319–321
Collective efficacy, 369

Collective emotion, 453
Collective feeling, 453
Collective noticing, 453
Collective responding, 453
Collectivism, 52, 229
Collins, E., 491
Collins, M. A., 157
Combining tasks, 279
Commitment (conceptual block),
    152–153
Commonalities, ignoring. *See* Ignoring
    commonalities
Communicating Supportively
    Assessment, 190
Communication
    accuracy, 192–193
    behavioral guidelines, 505–507
    congruence, 197–198
    conjunctive, 205
    cultural differences, 192, 214
    defensiveness, 197
    descriptive, 199–201
    disconfirmation, 197
    disjunctive, 205
    disowned, 205–206
    effective, 191–193
    egalitarian, 203
    either/or statements, 204
    electronic, 191
    evaluative, 199–201
    exercises, 219–223
    factual precision, 501–502
    flexibility, 203
    global, 204
    imperviousness, 203
    incongruence, 197–198
    indifference, 202
    ineffective, 192–193, 193*f*
    invalidating, 202
    listening, 206–208
    mechanical precision, 501
    obstacles to, 197, 197*t*
    one-way message delivery, 206
    oral, 490–494, 498, 499*t*, 500
    owned, 205–206
    person-oriented, 201
    presentations, 490–505
    problem-oriented, 201
    pronunciations, 192*t*
    responding, 207–210
    rigidity in, 202
    specific, 204
    superiority-oriented, 202
    supportive, 193–199, 202–208,
        214–215, 524
    supportive listening, 206
    tone, 502–503
    two-way, 203
    validating, 202
    verbal precision, 502
    written, 490–491, 493, 499*t*,
        501–503
Communication Styles Assessment, 190
Communist prison camp case, 67–68
Communitarianism, 388, 421
Community, 101
Companies. *See* Organizations
Compassion in organizations, 453
Competing values framework, 9–11, 143
    model of, 10*f*
Complacency, 155–156
Compression of ideas, 153–155
Computerized exam case, 69
Conceptual blocks
    artificial constraints, 154–155
    bias against thinking, 156
    commitment, 152–153
    complacency, 155–156

    compression, 153–155
    constancy, 150
    exercises, 175–176
    in problem solving, 143
    limitations of, 148
    noninquisitiveness, 155–156
    overcoming, 157, 171
    separating figure from ground,
        154–155
    single thinking language, 150–151
    types of, 149, 149*t*, 150
    vertical thinking, 150
Conflict
    advantages of, 306
    ambivalence towards, 307–308
    focus of, 309
    interpersonal, 306–329
    model of, 313*f*
    organizational success and, 306–307
    sources of, 309–310, 310*t*, 311
    types of, 308–309
Conflict management, 306
    accommodating approach, 313
    approaches to, 312–314, 315*t*,
        316–317, 317*f*, 318–319
    avoiding response, 313–314
    behavioral guidelines, 330–332
    clarifying questions, 324, 325*f*
    collaborating approach, 314, 319–329
    compromising response, 314
    conflict focus, 309–310
    conflict source, 310, 310*t*, 311
    cultural differences, 311–312
    diagnosing exercises, 336–337
    diagnosing types of conflict,
        308–309, 329
    distributive bargaining, 314–315
    environmentally induced stress, 312
    ethnic culture, 316
    facilitating, 328
    forcing response, 312–313
    gender differences, 316
    improving skills exercises, 358–362
    informational deficiencies, 311
    initiator-problem identification,
        321, 331
    initiator-solution generation,
        323, 331
    integrative perspective, 314–315
    interpersonal dispute exercises,
        347–358
    issue-focused conflict, 309
    mediator-problem identification,
        326–328, 332
    mediators, 320, 326–329
    mediator-solution generation,
        328–329, 332
    model of, 330
    negotiation strategies, 314–315, 315*t*
    people-focused conflict, 309
    personal differences, 310–311
    personal preferences, 316
    problem-solving approach, 314,
        319–323
    responder role, 323–324, 325*f*
    responder-problem identification,
        323–324, 331
    responder-solution generation,
        325–326, 331
    role incompatibility, 311–312
    rules of engagement, 308
    situational factors, 317
    SSS Software exercise, 336–345
    strategy selection, 315–319
    strategy selection exercises, 345–347
    types of conflict, 308
    uncertainty, 312
    XYZ approach, 321–322, 322*t*, 323

Conformity level of maturity, 55
Confrontations
    collaborating approach, 319–320
    initiators, 320–321
    initiator-problem identification, 321
    mediators, 320
    responder, 320
Conger, J., 233, 366, 368–370
Congruence, 197–198
Conjunctive communication, 205, 206*f*
Connell, J., 369
Conroy, Meg, 293–294
Conscientiousness, 48, 64
Constancy, 150
Continental Airlines, 74
Continuous reinforcement, 285–286
Contrada, R. J., 91, 94
Contribution goals, 102
Conventional level, 55
Cook, A., 108
Coolidge, Calvin, 142
Cools, E., 48, 59–61
Coombs, T., 275
Coonradt, Chuck, 375, 382, 463–464
Cooper, Christine L., 63, 100
Cooperrider, D. L., 470
Copper, C., 424
Cordes, C. L., 95
Core self-evaluation, 47
    effects of, 65*f*
    job performance and, 64–65
    job satisfaction and, 64
    locus of control, 64
    neuroticism, 64
    self-awareness and, 48
    self-efficacy, 64
    self-esteem, 64
Core Self-Evaluation Scale (CSES), 38,
    43–44, 82–83
Corning Inc., 405
Corstorphine, E., 202
Cosier, R. A., 61
Counseling, 195–196, 207
Courtney, Henry, 170
Courtright, G., 366
Covey, Stephen, 47, 96, 101, 110
Cowen, S. S., 7
Cox, T., 13
Cox, T. H., 311, 412
Coyle, C., 453
Crant, J. M., 239
Creating irreversible momentum, 466
Creative problem solving
    accountability, 168–169
    ambidextrous thinking, 156
    analogies, 158–159
    approaches to, 143–146, 166
    behavioral guidelines, 171–172
    brainstorming, 162–163
    business success and, 148–156,
        169–170
    commitment, 152–153
    conceptual blocks, 143, 148–157,
        163
    cultural differences, 165–166
    exercises, 176–177, 182–184
    flexibility of thought, 162
    fluency, 162–163
    fostering, 170, 170*f*, 171
    generating alternatives, 162, 162*t*,
        163–164
    idea champions, 169–170
    illumination, 157
    incubation stage, 157
    information gathering, 157
    innovation, 169
    Janusian thinking, 161–162
    management skills and, 166–169

    mentors, 169
    minority views in, 168
    model of, 167*f*
    morphological synthesis, 164
    multiple roles, 169–170
    orchestrators, 169
    preparation stage, 157–158
    problem definition, 157–162
    relational algorithm, 164–165
    rule breakers, 169
    subdivision, 163–164
    synectics, 158–159
    teamwork, 168
    techniques for improving, 162*t*
    verification, 157–158
Creative Style Assessment, 134,
    137–139, 186
Creativity
    approaches to, 143, 147*f*
    competitiveness, 145
    cultural differences, 165
    fostering, 166–168, 168*t*, 170,
        170*f*, 171
    imagination, 143, 147
    improvement, 144–145, 147
    incubation, 146–147
    investment, 145, 147
    types of, 146*f*, 147
Creativity at Apple case, 173–174
Credibility, 417–419
Crocker, J., 101–102, 109, 191, 207
Cromie, S., 63
Cropanzano, R., 284
Cross, R., 452
Crovitz, H., 164
Crucial Conversations (Patterson,
    et al.), 324
Crump, J., 60
Csikszentmihalyi, M., 139, 157–158
Cultural differences
    affective orientation, 52, 94, 214
    communication, 192, 214
    conflict management, 311, 316
    creativity, 165
    egalitarian cultures, 94
    empowerment, 386–388
    encounter stressors, 94
    engagement, 386–388
    organizational culture, 54
    rewards, 274
    situational stressors, 94
    teamwork, 421–422
    time management, 53
    time orientation, 388, 421, 427
    time stressors, 94
    uncertainty, 312
Cultural values
    achievement culture, 53, 229,
        421, 427
    affective values, 388, 421, 427
    ascription culture, 53, 229, 388,
        421, 427
    collectivism, 52, 229
    communitarianism, 388, 421
    diffuseness, 53, 165, 388, 421
    dimensions of, 52*t*
    external control, 53, 165, 388
    individualism, 52, 214, 229,
        387–388, 421
    influence strategies, 246
    internal control, 53, 165, 388
    neutral orientation, 52, 214
    neutral values, 388, 421, 427
    particularism, 52, 165–166, 214,
        388, 421
    specificity, 53, 165, 388, 421
    universalism, 51, 165–166, 214,
        387–388, 421

Cuming, P., 244
Cummings, L., 370
Cummings, R., 389–390
Cupach, W. R., 192–193, 197, 202
Customer service
    empowerment and, 376
    supportive communication and, 194
Czech, K., 197–198

D
Dairy Queen, 144
Daly, J., 246
Dana Corporation, 169, 405
Dane, E., 233
Darrow, B., 73
Darwin, Charles, 403
Datta, D. K., 450
Davidson, J., 95, 100
Davidson, O., 271
Davis, John, 63
Davis, M., 125
Davis, Murray, 461
Davis, Ron, 216–217
Davis, T., 7
Day, Charles, 501
"The Day at the Beach" (Gordon), 117
De Bono, Edward, 150
De Dreu, C., 309, 315
De Jong, R. D., 244
Deal, T., 236
DeButts, John, 236
DeChurch, L. A., 419
Deci, E., 369, 371–372
Decision dilemmas, 70–71
Decision making
    ethical, 57
    first impressions, 139
Deep breathing, 112
Deep relaxation exercise, 125–126
Deepak, M., 112
Defensiveness, 197
Defining Issues Test, 38, 79–80
"The Defining Issues Test," 38–39
Deflecting responses, 208–209
DeGraff, J., 7, 10, 139, 143, 447
Dell, Michael, 73
Dell Computer, 73, 174
Deming, Edward, 508
Denham, S. A., 102
Derr, C., 306
Descriptive communication, 199, 199*t*,
    200–201
Deutsch, M., 371
Devanna, M., 491, 552
Developing Self-Awareness Skill
    Assessment, 38–44
Diagnosing Poor Performance
    and Enhancing Motivation
    Assessment, 264, 304
Diagnosing the Need for Teambuilding
    Assessment, 402–403, 441
Dickson, M., 405–406, 414, 422
DiClemente, C. C., 369
Diener, E., 90, 106
Diffusion (cultural), 165
Dilenschneider, Robert, 229
Dillard, J., 230
Direct analogies, 159
Dirks, K., 236
Disciplining, 276–277
Disconfirmation, 197
Disjunctive communication, 205
Disney, Walt, 143, 147
Disney Corporation, 459
Disowned communication, 205–206
Divine, D., 424
Dixon, R. D., 454

"The Doctor's Dilemma," 40
Dominant competitive issues, 240–241
Dorio, M., 376
Double-barreled questions, 520
Dougherty, T. W., 95
Doughty, G. P., 63
Dow Chemical, 58
Dow Corning, 58
Downs, C., 518, 530
Druskat, V., 417, 424
DuBrin, A., 509, 518
Duckworth, A., 375
Dumler, M. P., 191
Duncan, R., 246
Dunham, R., 370
Dunn, Keith, 178–181
Dunsmore, J. C., 102
Durham, C., 271
Dutton, J., 46, 91, 108, 110, 190–191,
    194, 246, 380, 424, 445,
    453, 456
Duval, S., 45
Dyer, W., 197, 244, 403
Dynica Technologies case, 253

E
E. F. Hutton, 58
eBay, 174
Eckstrom, R., 59
Eden, D., 271
Edmonson, A., 417
Educational Pension Investments case,
    332–336
Effective Empowerment and
    Engagement Instrument, 366,
    399
Effort, 235
Egalitarian communication, 203
Egalitarian cultures, 94
Eichinger, R., 311
Einstein, Albert, 161
Eisenhardt, K., 306, 308–309
Elaboration probes, 209, 524
Electro Logic case, 289–295
Electronic brainstorming, 163
Electronic communication, 191
Eliot, R. S., 92, 94
Elliot, A. J., 372
Ellis, K., 202
Embedded pattern, 154*f*
Emmons, R., 111, 454–455, 455*f*
Emotional arousal, 374–375
Emotional bank accounts, 101
Emotional competence, 49–50
Emotional intelligence, 7
    defined, 48, 50
    management skills and, 51
    as a predictor of success, 50–51
    self-awareness and, 47–50
    stress and, 102–103
Emotional Intelligence Assessment
    instrument, 38, 51
Emotional Intelligence (Goleman), 49
Employees
    agreeable behavior, 233–234
    autonomy, 272, 279
    centrality, 237–239
    charisma, 233
    committed, 264
    disciplining, 275–276
    diversity, 311
    effort, 235
    equity, 284
    expertise, 232–233
    feedback, 279–280, 284, 286
    flexibility, 239
    goal setting, 271–272
    initiative, 275*t*

Employees (*continued*)
intrinsic outcomes, 278
leading positive change, 451
legitimacy, 235
management response to behavior, 275–276
meetings and, 557–558
motivation, 264–269, 274, 278–279, 279f, 280–286
negative energizers, 452–453
outcome preferences, 282–283, 283t, 284
performance, 265
physical appearance, 234
positive energizers, 452–453
public commitments, 464–465
reassigning, 267
recreational work, 464
refitting, 267
reinforcement, 273–274
relationship with boss, 235, 235t
releasing, 267–268
relevance, 240–241
resources, 267
resupplying, 267
retraining, 267
rewards, 273–276, 281–288
shift workers, 265
task difficulty, 272
task structure, 272
teamwork, 404
visibility, 240
work design, 278–279
Employment-selection interviews, 525t, 527–528, 528t
exercises, 542–549
PEOPLE-oriented process, 528, 529t
Empowerment, 366–368
active control, 370
activities for, 397–399
attitudes towards subordinates, 380
behavioral guidelines, 389
collective efficacy, 369
creating confidence, 377
cultural differences, 386–388
dimensions of, 368, 368t, 369–372, 373f
emotional arousal, 374–375
emotional support, 374
engagement, 381, 381t, 382–386, 388f
exercises, 391–397
fostering, 368, 371–377, 378t–379t, 381
goal setting, 372–373
information sharing, 375–376
inhibitors to, 380–381
meaning, 368, 370–372
modeling, 374
need for control, 380
outcomes and, 376
personal consequence, 368, 370, 372
personal insecurities, 380
personal mastery, 373–374
personal security, 371
power v., 367t
prescriptions for, 373f
principles of, 378
self-determination, 368–369, 372
self-efficacy, 368–369, 372
small-wins strategy, 374
SMART goals, 373
social support, 374
task identity, 376
trust, 368, 371–372
Encounter stressors, 94, 100–101, 103
Endicott Report, 490

Engagement, Empowered
activities for, 397–399
advantages of, 381t
cultural differences, 386–388
empowerment and, 381–386, 388f
fostering, 381–386
model of, 383f
principles of, 384–386, 387f
Enright, R., 453
Enron, 58, 174, 229
Epitropaki, O., 63
Equity, 284
Erez, A., 233
Ernst & Young, 280
Eroglu, S., 103
"The Escaped Prisoner," 39–40
Eshelman, E. R., 125
Esmaeili, M. T., 374
ESPN, 235
Ethernet, 174
Ethical decision making, 57–59
Ethiraj, S. K., 271
Ettlie, J. E., 137
European Economic Union, 454
Evaluative communication, 198–201
Evans, R., 107
Everest goals, 419–421
Excite (search engine), 238
Executive Development Associates exercise, 391–392
Executive summary rule, 555
Exline, J. J., 454
Expertise, 232–233
Expertise power, 367
Extensive rule, 556
External control, 53
External locus of control, 62–63, 165
External Locus of Control score, 63
Extrinsic outcomes, 278
Extroversion, 48, 64
Exxon Mobil Corp., 58

F
Facebook, 238
False bipolar questions, 520
Fantasy analogies, 159
Farh, C. I. C., 306
Farh, J., 306
Farnham, A., 101
Fast Company, 74–75
Fawkes, Brian, 73
Federal Express, 405
Feedback systems, 103, 279–280, 285–286
effective, 426t
forced-choice ratings, 528
graphic rating scales, 528
personal capabilities, 456, 456f, 457
reflected best-self feedback, 456–457
teamwork, 426–427
Feist, G. J., 50
Feldman, D., 150, 164
Ferrin, D., 236
Ferris, M., 106
Festinger, L., 150
Financial Times, 177
Finast Supermarkets, 460
Find Somebody Else case, 216–217
Finke, R. A., 157, 163–164
Finkelstein, S., 57
Finkenauer, C., 452
Fiol, C. M., 237
Firestone Tire & Rubber Co., 58
First Chicago, 97
First impressions, 139
Fischbach, A., 369–370

Fisher, C., 237, 270
Fisher, R., 315
Fisher, S. G., 54
Five-figure problem, 159f
Fleming, Alexander, 153
Flexibility, 239
in communication, 203
of thought, 158
Flourishing Scale, 90, 106, 131
Fluency, 162–163
Foerstner, George, 151, 155
Folger, R., 284
Folly, 552
Foo, Liang, 62
Force field analysis, 91–92, 92f
Forced-choice ratings, 528
Ford, Henry, 174, 403
Ford, William Clay, 462
Ford Motor Co., 58, 140, 421, 462
Forgiveness, 453–454
Forming identifiable work units, 279
Fortune 500, 174, 267
Fortune 1000, 404
Fortune magazine, 75, 173
Forward, G. L., 197–198
Fostering well being, 90–91
Foxboro Co., 285
Frameworks, 447–448, 470, 470f
positive change, 451f
Frankl, Victor, 367
Franklin, Benjamin, 403
Fredrickson, B., 113, 191, 452
Freeman, S. J., 375
French, J., 59, 103, 367
Freud, Sigmund, 45, 408
Fromm, Erich, 45
Frost, P. J., 453
Frustration, heart rhythms, 455f
Fry, Art, 151, 153, 155, 170
Funnel interview sequence, 521, 522t
Furman, W., 234
Furnham, A., 60, 63, 191

G
Gabarro, J. J., 210, 235t
Gable, S. L., 190
Gagne, M., 369
Gaining Power and Influence Assessment, 228, 261
Gaissmaier, W., 140
Galle, William P., 191
Gallup Organization, 264, 276
Gandhi, Mahatma, 56, 98, 146, 367, 371, 446, 452
Ganzach, Y., 278
Garbage can model, 552
Gardner, Howard, 102
Gardner, John, 229
Gardner, W. L., 265
Gates, Bill, 476
Gecas, V., 366, 368–369
Geddie, T., 207
Gehry, Frank O., 178
Gelles-Cole, S., 491
Gemmill, G., 369
Gender differences, conflict management, 316
Gendron, G., 314
Geneen, Harold, 236
General Dynamics, 58
General Electric, 58, 140, 280, 405
General Mills, 405
General Motors, 58
Generalized reciprocity, 110–111
Generalized reciprocity exercise, 127–128
Generation Y, 280

George Mason University, 283t
Gerbino, M., 369
Gerhart, B., 265
Getting, Ivan, 151
Giamatti, A. Bartlett, 250
Gibb, J. R., 197, 371
Gibb, L., 371
Gibbs, J. C., 57
Gibson, J., 306
Gigerenzer, G., 140
Gilbert, S., 375
Gilligan, Carol, 57
Gilson, L. L., 367–368
Ginelli, P. J., 294
Gittell, J., 191
Give and Take (Grant), 278
Gladstein, D., 406
Gladwell, Malcolm, 139
Glasser, William, 205
Glew, D. J., 54
Global communication, 204
Global Crossing, 58
Gloucer, Tom, 462
Glynn, P., 454
Goal setting, 271
achievement and, 102
anticipatory stressors and, 104
challenging, 271
characteristics of, 271
consistency, 271
contribution, 102
empowerment and, 372–373
Everest goals, 419–421
feedback, 272
model for, 104f
performance and, 419f
process of, 105, 271
SMART goals, 105, 127, 419–421
specific goals, 271
Goddard, Roger, 369
Goddard Space Flight Center, 103
Godkin, J., 63
Goizueta, Roberto C., 173
Goldberger, L., 94
Goleman, Daniel, 7, 47–51, 102, 191
Golembiewski, R. T., 371
Golen, S., 192–193
Goodfellow, Matthew, 511
Goodson, Gene, 169
Google, 109, 471–474
Gordon, Arthur, 117
Gordon, E., 321
Gordon, R. D., 197
Gordon, William, 158
Goyer, R., 518
Graham, M., 274
Grant, A. M., 48, 50, 108–109, 238
Grant, Adam, 278
Graphic rating scales, 528
Gratitude, 111–112, 454–455
heart rhythms, 111f, 455f
Gratitude journals, 111
Green Day (band), 238
Greenberger, D. B., 103, 366, 370, 381
Greene, C., 369
Greenleaf, R. K., 381
Greenpeace, 502
Greiner, L. E., 408
Grewal, D., 50
Groupthink, 168, 410–411, 552
Grove, A., 233
Grove, Andrew, 306–307
Gudykunst, W. B., 214
Gully, S., 424
Guthrie, J. P., 450
Guzzo, R., 405–406, 414, 422

H

Haas, J., 279
Haase, Richard F., 62
Hackman, J. R., 103–104, 279f, 302, 372, 376, 405–406, 408, 412, 414, 417
Hackman-Oldham Job Diagnostic Survey, 509
Halberstadt, A. G., 102
Hall, John, 107
Halliburton Co., 58
Hamilton, B. H., 405
Hammer, T. H., 63, 369
Hampden-Turner, C., 51, 94, 165, 422, 427
Hanfmann, E., 150
Hansen, G. S., 195
Hanson, G., 5
Hanton, S., 107
Hare, C. C., 94
Hargie, O., 191
Harmon, H., 59
Harris, J. R., 57–58
Harris, K. J., 198
Harris, M., 46, 65
Harter, J. K., 64, 268, 455, 457
Hartman, Sandra, 191
Harvard Business Review, 308
Harvey, J. B., 552
Harvey, P., 198
Harvey, William, 159
Hatfield, J. D., 207
Hausman, C., 161
Hawkins, A. J., 106
Hayes, J., 48, 234, 268
Heaphy, E., 110, 190, 194, 209, 445, 455
Heider, F., 150
Heisler, W., 369
Heliotropic effect, 469–470
Helliwell, J. F., 371, 417
Hellriegel, C., 369
Helmick, R., 454
Helplessness, 372
Hemingway, C. A., 48
Henderson, J., 61
Hepburn, C. G., 107
Hermann, N., 156
Hess, R., 369
Hewlett-Packard, 140, 195
Hickson, D. J., 143
Hierarchical needs theories, 281, 281t
Hierarchy skills, 9
Higgs, A., 412
Hill, E. J., 106
Hill, J., 161
Hill, S., 106–107
Hillhouse, J. J., 107
Hill-Popper, M., 110
Hilton Hotels, 65
Hite, B., 280
Hitler, Adolf, 148, 204
Hobson, Alan, 421
Hobson, C. J., 94
Hocker, J., 311
Hoffman, Ken, 389–390
Hofstede, Geert, 312
Hogg, M., 234
Holmes, Thomas, 94–95
Holt, John, 14
Holt-Lunstad, J., 110
Honda Motor Co., 145, 147
Honda-Yamaha Motorcycle War, 145
Honeycutt, J., 206
Honeywell International Inc., 509
Hosmer, L. T., 58, 236
Hosoda, M., 234

House, R., 272
Hout, T. M., 94
How Creative Are You? Assessment, 134–136, 147, 184–185
Hoy, A., 369
Hoy, W., 369
Hozel, B. K., 113
Huang, H., 371, 417
Hubbard, R., 91
Huber, G., 384
Hudspith, S., 156
Huffy Bicycle Co., 109
Human capital, 467–468
Hurst, C., 234
Huselid, Mark, 4, 194
Huseman, R. C., 207
Hyatt, J., 181
Hyman, R., 197
Hyten, C., 414

I

Iacocca, Lee, 458
iCars, 174
iCloud, 174
Idea champions, 169–170
Ignoring commonalities, 152–153
Imagery and fantasy, 112
Imagination, 143, 147
Imberman, Woodruff, 511
Imhof, M., 206
Imperviousness in communication, 203
Implementation, 142
Imposing management style, 268
Improvement (creativity), 144–145, 147
In Search of Excellence (Peters and Waterman), 285
Inc. magazine, 314
Incongruence, 197–198
Incubation (creativity), 146–147
Indifference in communication, 202
Individual differences, 13–14
  self-awareness and, 47
Individualism, 52, 214, 229, 387–388, 421
Indulging management style, 268
Influence. *See also* Power
  activities for, 259–261
  agreeable behavior, 234
  bargaining, 243
  behavioral guidelines, 251–252
  comparison of strategies, 244–245, 245t
  cultural differences, 246
  effective use of, 229
  exercises, 255–256
  ingratiation, 243
  intimidation, 243
  manipulation, 244
  model of, 250f
  neutralizing influence attempts, 247–249
  persuasion, 243–244
  power and, 241–244, 249–250
  reason, 241, 243–244, 249
  reciprocity, 241, 243–244, 248–249
  retribution, 241, 243–244, 248
  strategies for, 241, 242t, 243–246
  upward, 246
Influencer (Patterson), 229
Information-gathering interviews, 527
Ingratiation, 243
Innovation, 139, 169, 174
Innovative Attitude Scale, 134, 136–137, 185
Institutional power, 282
Instrumental values, 48, 54

Integrating motivation strategy, 269, 270t, 271, 287f
Intel, 306–307
Intensive rule, 556
Interaction Associates, 158
Interaction management, 205
Intermountain Healthcare, 264
Internal control, 53
Internal locus of control, 62–63, 165
Interpersonal attraction, 234
  agreeable behavior, 234
  charisma, 233
  physical appearance, 234
Interpersonal competence, 46–47
Interpersonal relationships
  abuse of power, 230–231
  agreeable behavior, 234
  benefits of, 190–191
  boss-subordinate, 235
  communication, 191–193, 193f, 194–215
  conflict, 306–329
  congruence, 198
  performance-appraisal, 529
  personal differences, 310–311
  positive, 191
Interviews
  behavioral guidelines, 531–532
  clarification probes, 524
  climate of, 523–524
  closed questions, 519, 520t
  concluding, 525
  conducting, 523–524, 531–532
  double-barreled questions, 520
  effective, 518–519
  elaboration probes, 524
  employment-selection, 527–528
  exercises, 532–549
  false bipolar questions, 520
  funnel sequence, 521–522
  guidelines for, 519f
  guides, 524
  information-gathering, 527
  inverted funnel sequence, 521–522
  leading questions, 520
  mixed-model, 530
  open questions, 519, 520t
  performance-appraisal, 528, 530, 530t
  planning, 519, 531
  preparation for, 522–523, 523t
  probes and, 524–525, 526t
  problem solving, 530
  question types, 519–520, 521t
  recording, 526–527
  reflective probes, 524–525
  repetition probes, 525
  sample questions, 525t
  setting of, 522
  structuring, 521–522
  supportive communication and, 524
  tell-and-listen, 530
  tell-and-sell, 530
  transitions, 522
Intimidation, 243
Intolerance of ambiguity, 48
Intrinsic outcomes, 278
Inverted funnel interview sequence, 521, 522t
Investment (creativity), 145, 147
Involvement rule, 556
iPads, 174
iPhones, 143, 174
iPods, 174
IQ (intelligence quotient) scores, 7, 50, 102
Ireland, R. D., 462
Iron Law of Power, 316

Irving, Gregory P., 63
Isenbarger, K., 518
Issue selling, 246, 247t
Issue-focused conflict, 309
ITT Corp., 236
iTunes Store, 173–174
ITV, 174

J

J. P. Morgan, 58
Jackson, Phil, 264
Jago, A., 382, 384
James, William, 203
Janis, I., 168, 410–411, 552
Jansen, M., 63
Jansky, Karl, 150
Janson, R., 103, 376
Janssen, O., 284
Janusian thinking, 161–162
Janusik, L. A., 206
Jay, Anthony, 266
Jehn, K., 309, 311, 316
Job dimensions
  autonomy, 279
  feedback, 279
  skill variety, 279
  task identity, 279–280
  task significance, 279–280
Job performance, 64–65
  ability, 265
  abundance approach, 449
  aptitude, 265
  benchmarking, 457–458
  continuum of, 448f, 449
  deficit approach, 449
  deficit gaps, 449
  exercises, 295–298
  feedback, 285–286
  formula for, 265
  leader involvement in, 272f
  morale, 268
  motivation, 265–287
  reinforcement, 273–275, 284–287
  resources, 265–266
  rewards, 273–276, 281–288
  satisfaction and, 268f
Job redesign, 103–104, 280
Job satisfaction, 64, 108
Jobs, Steve, 143, 173, 314, 403, 446, 462
John, Oliver P., 234
Johnson, R. E., 48
Johnson & Johnson, 471, 475
Johnson Controls, 169
Johnston, M. K., 54, 206
Jones, S. H., 61
Jones, Tom, 236
Jonsen, K., 411
Jordan, J., 57
Jordan, Michael, 403
Judge, Tim A., 48, 54, 62–64, 234

K

Kahn, R. L., 92, 94
Kahwajy, J. L., 306
Kaifeng, J., 268
Kamenica, E., 276
Kanov, J. M., 453
Kanter, Rosabeth, 230, 237, 246, 254, 375, 380
Kanungo, R., 233, 366, 368–370
Kaplan, R., 237, 240
Karambayya, R., 326
Karatepe, O. M., 366
Kashdan, T. B., 455
Katzenbach, J., 9, 405, 414, 417, 428, 430

Kawashima, Kihachiro, 145, 147
Keashly, L., 316
Kekule, Friedrich, 153
Kelleher, Herb, 74
Keller, Helen, 204
Kellogg, M .S., 275*t*
Kelly, D. R., 375
Keltner, D., 234
Kennedy, A., 236
Kennedy, John F., 410
Kentucky Fried Chicken, 150
Kern, Rex, 467
Kerr, S., 274
Kerr, William Rolfe, 98
Kettering, Charles, 141
Ketteringham, J. M., 149, 151–153, 155–156
Khurana, R., 110
Kihlstrom, J. F., 102
Kilmann, R., 316
Kim, M. U., 46–47, 94, 312, 450
Kim, S., 322
Kim, T. Y., 412
Kinley, N., 411
Kipnis, D., 241, 316, 319
Kirton, M. J., 48, 61
Klausen, Pat, 291
Kleinbaum, R., 238
Kleindienst, G., 161
Knapp, M., 197
Knight, D., 64, 271
Knight-Ridder, 429–430
Kobasa, Suzanne, 95
Koberg, D., 164
Koestler, A., 153
Kohlberg, L., 54–58
Koike, Hisao, 145
Kok, C., 113
Kolb, D. A., 7–9, 60
Komaki, J. L., 275
Konrad, A., 237
Koole, S., 315
Kopelman, P., 280
Koppelaar, L., 244
Korabik, D., 316
Kotter, J. P., 235*t*
Kotter, John, 269, 446
Kouzes, J., 54, 417
Krackhardt, D., 238
Kraimer, M., 237
Kram, K., 48, 230
Kramer, R., 207
Kramer, W. S., 406, 417
Kreiner, G. E., 109
Krenl, L., 63
Kressel, K., 326
Kring, A. M., 234
Kroc, Ray, 144, 147
Kuo, Y. Y., 165

L

LaGaipa, J., 234
Lahiff, J. M., 207
Laibson, Richard, 178–179, 181
Lalwani, N., 45
Lam, L. W., 371
Landman, J., 108
Langer, E., 370, 381
Langlois, J., 234
Language
    alternative, 459
    feelings and emotions, 151
    multiple thinking, 150–151
    nonverbal, 151
    presentations and, 493
    pronunciations, 192*t*
    sensory, 151
    single thinking, 150–151

types of, 150–151
    visual imagery, 151
Lao Tsu, 44
Laschinger, H. K., 375
Lateral thinking, 150
Latham, G. P., 9, 104*f*, 271, 372
Lau, D. C., 371
Lavelle, Louis, 230
Lavine, M., 109–110, 446, 449, 470
Lawerence, K. A., 139
Lawler, Ed, 273–274, 283, 404–405, 414
Lawrence, K., 206
Lawrence, P. R., 110, 143, 240
Layton, J. B., 110
Leadership Roles in Teams, 441
Leadership skills, 9
    benchmarking, 457–458
    charisma, 233–234
    competing values framework, 9–11
    credibility, 417–418, 418, 419
    Everest goals, 419–421
    identifying strengths, 455–456
    leading positive change, 446–470
    management skills and, 10–11, 447
    organizational values, 236
    servant leadership, 381
    small-wins strategy, 465
    SMART goals, 419–421
    teachable points of view, 466–467
    teamwork, 417–419
    trickle-up, 246
Leading Positive Change Assessment, 444, 485
Leading questions, 520
Leading Up (Useem), 246
Learning stairs, 466, 467*f*
Learning style, 48
Ledford, G. E., 404–405
LeDue, A. L., 282
Lee, C., 306
Lee, Dong Yul, 62
Lee, J. Y., 412
Lee-Chai, A. Y., 231
Left-brain thinking, 156, 461
Leger, D., 228
Legitimacy, 235–236
Lehrer, P. M., 92, 100, 106
Leiter, M., 375
Leonard, D., 7
Leonard, Mike, 216–217
Leutscher, Trevor, 191
Levinthal, D. A., 271
Levy, P. E., 48
Lewin, Kurt, 91, 465
Lewis, Michael, 307–308
Liden, R., 237
Lidz, F., 405
Life balance, 106–107, 107*f*, 124*f*
Life-balance analysis exercise, 123–124
Likable people, characteristics of, 234*t*
Likert, R., 94
Lilius, J. M., 453
Liljenquist, K. A., 311
Lim, S., 191
Listening skills
    active listening exercise, 223
    effective, 207
    responding, 207–208
    supportive listening, 206–208
Lobo, M. S., 234
Locke, E. A., 64, 104*f*, 271, 372, 419
Lockheed Martin, 58, 511
Locus of control, 48, 64
    external locus of control, 62–63
    internal locus of control, 62–63
Locus of Control Scale, 38
Lombardo, M., 230, 311

Long, B., 106
Lopez, R., 518
Lorinkova, N.M., 382
Lorsch, Jay, 240
Los Angeles Clippers, 405
Losada, M., 209, 455
Lowell, E., 281
Lublin, J., 274
Luhmann, N., 371
Lusch, R. F., 103
Luthans, F., 7, 273, 450
Lynn, David, 179

M

Macintosh computer, 143, 167, 174, 312
Mackey, Alison, 264
Macrosson, W. D. K., 54
Maddi, S., 107
Maddux, J., 369
Madison, D. L., 241
Madlock, P. E., 191
Madoff, Bernie, 229
Maduro, R., 165
Magnetrons, 148, 150–151, 153, 155, 167
Maier, A. A., 206
Maier, N., 206, 530
Mainemelis, C., 60
Major League Baseball, 250, 307–308
Malden Mills, 462
Mallozzi, Jim, 110, 477–480
Mambert, W. A., 490
Management and Machiavelli (Jay), 266
Management skills
    abundance approach, 449
    attraction, 233–234
    behavior shaping strategies, 277–278
    centrality, 237–239
    charisma, 233–234
    combining tasks, 279
    communication, 191–215, 490–505
    competing values framework, 9–11
    conducting meetings, 552–559
    conflict management, 306–329
    cultural differences, 51–54, 239
    deficit approach, 449
    defining, 6–7
    develop model, 8*t*
    developing, 7–8, 13
    disciplining, 275–277
    effective, 5–6, 6*t*
    effort, 235
    emotional intelligence and, 51
    empowerment, 366–381, 388
    engagement, 381–386, 388
    expectations of subordinates, 272
    expertise, 232–233
    extrinsic outcomes, 280
    feedback, 280, 285–286, 288
    financial performance and, 5
    flexibility, 239
    forming identifiable work units, 279
    fostering creative problem solving, 166–170, 170*f*
    fostering initiative, 275*t*
    frameworks, 448
    goal setting, 271–272
    influence, 241–250
    interviews, 518–532
    intrinsic outcomes, 278, 280
    issue selling, 246, 247*t*
    job performance and, 272
    leadership skills and, 10–11, 447
    leading positive change, 448–470
    legitimacy, 235–236
    listening, 206–208
    locus of control, 63
    model of, 12*f*

motivation, 264–265, 268–275, 279–280, 280*t*, 281–288
    need theory, 282
    neutralizing influence attempts, 247–249
    path goal of leadership, 272–273
    performance expectations, 270, 449
    political competence, 228–229
    power, 230–239, 249–250
    presentations, 490–505
    proactive personalities, 239
    problem-solving, 139
    quality circles, 508–510, 510*f*, 511–515
    reinforcement, 285–286
    relevance, 240–241
    rewards, 276–277, 280–286
    self-awareness, 44–62
    social networks, 238–239
    speaking skills, 490
    status quo and, 446
    time management, 96–100
    visibility, 239–240
    written communication, 501–503
Managers
    ability deterioration, 266–268
    characteristics of, 73–75
    cognitive style, 60–61
    competent, 4–5
    diagnosing exercises, 73–75
    establishing client relationships, 280
    ethical decision making, 57–59
    expertise, 232–233
    ignoring, 268
    imposing, 268
    increasing authority, 280
    individual differences, 13–14, 47
    indulging, 268
    integrating, 268
    interactions with subordinates, 274–275
    involvement, 272, 272*f*, 273, 273*t*
    managing down, 228
    managing up, 228
    manipulative, 244
    meetings with subordinates, 211–214
    overspecialization, 233
    personal inadequacies, 230, 231*t*
    powerful, 229–230
    proactive personalities, 239
    reassigning, 267
    refitting, 267
    relationship with employees, 235*t*, 275–276
    releasing, 267–268
    resupplying, 267
    retraining, 267
    self-interested, 231
    skills performance, 6–7
    subordinate feedback, 211–214
    values conflicts, 58
Managing down, 228
Managing Interpersonal Conflict Assessment, 306, 362
Managing up, 228
Mandela, Nelson, 367
Manifest needs model, 281–282
Manipulation, 244
Mannix, E., 309
Manz, C., 370, 417
March, J., 141, 143, 152, 162–163, 552–553
Market skills, 9
Markham, S., 371
Markkula, Mike, 173
Marlowe, David, 101
Marriott, Bill, 376

Marriott Corporation, 376
Martin, E., 518
Martin, R., 63
Martin Marietta, 58
Martindale, C., 156
Maruca, R. F., 490
Marwell, G., 241
Maslow, Abraham, 45, 281, 307
Massinger, Philip, 44
Masten, A. S., 106–107
Masuda, M., 95
Matchstick configuration, 152*f*
Mathieu, J. E., 367–368
Matsushita Electric, 514
Matthews, M. D., 375
Mayer, J., 49, 102, 241
Maynard, M., 367–368
Mazique, M., 237, 240
McCall, M., 230
McCauley, C. R., 108
McClear, K., 64
McClelland, David, 231, 281–282, 366
McClendon, Aubrey, 230
McConkie, M., 371
McCraty, R., 455, 455*f*
McCullough, M., 111, 455, 455*f*
McDonald's, 144, 147
McFarland, Robert, 73
McGovern, P., 106–107
McGregor, Douglas, 268
McGuffey's Restaurant, 178–181
McKay, M., 125
McKee, Annie, 51
McLoughlin, C. A., 107
McNamara, R., 63
McNaughtan, E. D., 192
Meaningful work, 108–109, 109*t*,
    110–111, 279, 368, 370–372
Measures, 468–469
Mechanic, D., 234–235
Medawar, P., 158
Mediation, 326, 326*t*, 327, 327*t*,
    328–329
Medsker, G., 412
Medtronic, 109
Meetings
    agenda bell rule, 555, 555*f*
    agenda integrity rule, 555
    agenda rule, 554
    behavioral guidelines, 558
    competition-cooperation, 553
    conducting, 552
    effective, 552–558
    evaluation exercise, 561–562
    executive summary rule, 555
    exercises, 560–570
    extensive rule, 556
    ground rules, 556
    group members, 557–559
    homogeneity–heterogeneity, 553
    intensive rule, 556
    involvement rule, 556
    media use, 556
    minutes rule, 555
    one-on-one, 212
    participants, 553–554, 558–559
    participation, 556–558
    personal management interviews,
        211–214
    perspective, 557, 559
    planning, 554, 559
    power rule, 556
    process of, 559
    productive, 553
    purpose of, 552–553, 558
    reports rule, 554
    rule of halves, 554
    rule of sixths, 554

rule of thirds, 554
rule of three-fourths, 554
summarizing, 557
task-process, 553
temporal integrity rule, 555
weekly, 554*f*
Megerian, L. E., 48
Memeth, C. J., 306
Mentors, 169
Merrill, Roger, 170
Mesmer-Magnus, J. R., 419
Messmer, M., 309
Metrics, 468–469
Meyerson, D., 451
Microsoft, 140, 471, 476
Microwave ovens, 148–150, 153, 155
Milestones, 468–469
Milgram, Stanley, 57, 95
Milgram's obedience study, 57
Millennial generation, 228–229, 278
Miller, G. A., 494
Miller, K. E., 95
Miller, L., 267
Miller, S. J., 143
Mills, C., 106–107
Minding the Store case, 389–390
Minhas, G., 455
Mintzberg, Henry, 100
Minutes rule, 555
Mischel, W., 103
Mishra, A., 368, 371, 375, 377, 381
Mishra, K., 381
Mitchell, R. K., 57
Mitchell, T., 272, 413
Mitroff, Ian, 143
Mixed-model interviews, 530
Modern Healthcare, 264
Moe, M., 267
Mohrman, S. A., 404–405
Mokwa, M., 161
Moneyball (film), 307
Monitoring and managing time exercise,
    126–127
Monsanto Co., 58
Montgomery, Chalida, 295
Moore, T., 65
Mora, Carlos, 191
Moral judgment, stages of
    development, 55*t*
Moral Research Center (Univ. of
    Minnesota), 57
Morale, 268
Morcott, Woody, 169
Morgan, S., 289
Morgan Stanley, 283
Morphological synthesis, 164, 164*t*
Morris, Deigan, 61
Morris, M., 239
Morrison, A., 311
Moses, 56
Moses, J. L., 9
Motivating Potential Score (MPS),
    509, 511
Motivation
    behavioral guidelines, 288–289
    diagnosing exercises, 295–298
    exercises, 301–304
    goal setting, 271–272
    hierarchical needs theories, 281
    integrating strategy, 287*f*
    intrinsic outcomes, 278
    job performance and, 265–266
    manager interactions, 274
    manifest needs model, 281–282
    need theory, 282
    performance expectations, 270
    program of, 269–276
    reinforcement, 273–275, 284–287

rewards, 273–275, 281–287
    work design, 278–280
    work environments and, 264–265
Motorola Mobility Inc., 429
Mott, F., 429–430
Mountford, V., 202
Moving Mountains (Pagonis), 407
Mowday, R. T., 108
Mulder, M., 244
Mulgan, G., 229
Mullen, B., 424
Multiple thinking languages, 150–151
Mumford, M. D., 143
Murnighan, J., 314, 320
Murphy, L. R., 106
Murray, H., 281–282
Murrell, K., 369, 371
Muscle relaxation, 112
Myers-Brigg Type Inventory (MBTI), 59
MyManagementLab, 38, 134, 190, 226,
    228, 264, 281, 306, 366, 368,
    399, 402, 407, 444
MySpace, 238

N
Nahrgang, J. D., 461, 464
Nair, K., 9
Name recognition, 240
Nanobombs, 3
Nanus, Bert, 230, 368, 370, 459
Narayan, A. J., 106
National Training Laboratories, 466, 467*f*
Nayak, P. R., 149, 151–153, 155–156
Neale, M., 311, 314, 319
Need for achievement, 281–282
Need for affiliation, 282
Need for power, 282
Need theory, 282
Negative energizers, 452–453
Negotiation strategies, 314–315, 315*t*
Neider, L., 272
Neil, R., 107
Nelson, Noelle, 276
Nelson, W. H., 268
Nemeth, C., 168
Network centrality, 237–238
Neufeld, R., 369
Neuroticism, 48, 64
Neutral orientation, 52, 214
Neutralizing unwanted influence
    attempts, 247–249
    exercises, 256–259
Newcomb, T., 150
Newman, W., 380
"The Newspaper," 41
Newton, T. J., 63
NeXT, 314
Ng, T. W. H., 63
Nichols, M. P., 207
Nicholson, Geoffrey, 170
Nickerson, J. A., 405
Nickerson, R., 157, 160
Nie, N. H., 191
Nielson, T., 306
Nike, 462
Nine-dot problem, 154*f*
Nisbett, R. E., 265
Nishida, T., 214
Nohria, N., 110
Nonempowerment, 380
Noninquisitiveness, 155–156
Nonverbal language, 151
Norenzayan, A., 265
Northcraft, G., 279, 319
Northrop, 236
Nuer, N., 109
Nutt, P., 61
Nwachukwu, Saviour, 54

O
Obedience study, 57
Obradovic, J., 107
O'Connor, E. J., 237
Oginska-Bulik, N., 48
O'Keefe, R. D., 137
Oldham, G. R., 103–104, 279*f*, 302,
    372, 376
Olivier, M., 109
Olsen, J. P., 552–553
Omnicom Group, 173
One-sided messages, 492*t*
One-way message delivery, 206
Ong, M., 271
Open questions, 519
Openness, 48, 64
Oral presentations, 490–494, 498,
    499*t*, 500
Orchestrators, 169
O'Reilly, B., 75
Organ, D. W., 369
Organizational cultures, 54, 236
Organizations
    Abilene paradox, 552
    alternative language, 459
    boiled frog syndrome, 552
    collective emotions, 453
    communication, 192
    compassionate, 453
    conflict in, 306, 307*f*
    deficit gaps, 449
    dominant competitive issues,
        240–241
    folly, 552
    forgiveness, 453–454
    garbage can model, 552
    gratitude, 454–455
    groupthink, 552
    hierarchies in, 228–229
    human capital, 467–468
    informal network, 238
    positive relationships, 191
    power, 232
    public commitments, 464–465
    recreational work, 464
    support, 273
    symbolic events, 458–459
    symbols, 462
    teachable points of view, 466–467
    unethical behavior, 57–58
    values, 236
    vision of abundance, 460–464, 463*t*
    vision statements, 460–462
Orientation towards change
    internal locus of control, 63
    intolerance of ambiguity, 48
    locus of control, 48, 62
    self-awareness and, 47–48, 61
    tolerance of ambiguity, 61–63
OS operating system, 174
Osborn, A., 162
Outcome preferences, 282–283
Overstock.com, 74
Owan, H., 405
Owned communication, 205–206

P
Paglis, L. L., 373
Pagonis, Gus, 407, 409, 412–417,
    419–420, 422
Palo Alto Research Center, 174
PAMS. *See* Personal Assessment of
    Management Skills (PAMS)
PandaWhale, 238
Pandey, A., 450
Panko, Raymond, 100
Papa Johns, 58

Park, C., 243
Park, L. E., 101
Park, N., 112
Parker, R. S., 48, 51, 422, 424
Parker, V., 274
Parker Manufacturing, 216–217
Parnell, G. S., 148
Parsons, Wendell, 267–268
Particularism, 52, 165–166, 214, 388, 421
Pascale, R., 236, 306
Passive control, 370
Path goal of leadership, 272–273
Patterson, Kerry, 229, 324
Pauling, Linus, 155
Peake, P. K., 103
Pearsall, M. J., 382
Pelled, L., 311
Pence, M., 206
Penicillin, 153
Pennebaker, J. W., 102
People-focused conflict, 309
PEOPLE-oriented process of interviewing, 528, 529t
Peoples, D. A., 490, 499
PepsiCo., 51, 172–173
Perceptual stereotyping, 152
Performance. See also Job performance
    continuum of, 448f, 449
    diagnosis, 295–298
    negative deviance, 449
    positive deviance, 449
problems, 265–268, 449
Performance-appraisal interviews, 528–530, 530t
    exercises, 535–541
Persian Gulf War (Desert Storm), 407–409, 412–416, 422
Personal analogies, 159
Personal Assessment of Management Skills (PAMS), 15–33
Personal change, 45
Personal consequence, 368, 370, 372
Personal culture, identifying exercise, 75–77
Personal Empowerment Assessment, 366, 399
Personal Inventory Assessment (PIA)
    Cognitive Style Indicator, 38
    Communicating Supportively Assessment, 190
    Communication Styles Assessment, 190
    Core Self-Evaluation Scale, 38
    Creative Style Assessment, 134
    Defining Issues Test, 38
    Diagnosing Poor Performance and Enhancing Motivation assessment, 264
    Diagnosing the Need for Teambuilding Assessment, 402–403
    Effective Empowerment and Engagement Instrument, 366, 399
    Emotional Intelligence Assessment instrument, 38
    How Creative Are You? assessment, 134
    Innovative Attitude Scale, 134
    Leading Positive Change Assessment, 444
    Locus of Control Scale, 38
    Managing Interpersonal Conflict assessment, 306, 362
    Personal Empowerment Assessment, 366, 399
    Positive Practices Survey, 444
    Problem Solving, Creativity, and Innovation Assessment, 134

Reflected Best-Self Feedback Exercise, 444–446
Self-Awareness Assessment Instrument, 38
Strategies for Handling Conflict assessment, 306, 362
Team Development Behaviors Assessment, 402
Tolerance of Ambiguity Scale, 38
Work Performance Assessment, 264
Personal management interview (PMI) program, 211
    benefits of, 213–214
    characteristics of, 213t
    effects of, 212f
    one-on-one meetings, 212–213
    role-negotiation session, 211–212
Personal mastery, 373–374
Personal power, 229–231, 231f, 232. See also Power
    agreeable behavior, 233–234
    charisma, 233
    determinants of, 232t
    effort, 235
    expertise, 232–233
    legitimacy, 235–236
    manifest needs model, 282
    physical appearance, 234
    sources of, 232–233, 237, 237t
    trustworthiness, 236
Personal security, 371
Personal values
    core values, 97, 98t
    cultural values, 51–54
    instrumental, 48, 54
    priorities, 97
    self-awareness and, 47–48, 51
    terminal, 48, 54
    values maturity, 54–57
Personality, 63
Person-oriented communication, 201
Persuasion, 243–244
Peter Principle, 266
Peters, D., 94
Peters, Tom, 143, 236, 285
Petersen, S., 454
Peterson, C., 112, 375, 381
Peterson, Ralph, 462
Pettijohn, C. E., 51
Pfeffer, Jeffrey, 4, 94, 233, 237, 274
Phelps, Inc. exercise, 346–347
Philip Morris International, 58
Philips Electronics, 97
Phillips, E., 316
Phillips, K. W., 311
Physical appearance, 234
Pieterse, N., 366
Pilling, B. K., 103
Plato, 44
Platte, E., 161
Plaue, N., 58
Plews, E., 480
PMI. See Personal management interview (PMI) program
Podolny, J., 110, 239
Poincare, H., 157
Polaroid, 174
Political competence, 228–229
Ponderosa, 178
Poor, E., 501
Porath, C., 106
Porras, J. R., 9
Porter, L. W., 108, 241, 265
Positional power
    centrality, 237–239
    determinants of, 237t
    flexibility, 239
    relevance, 240–241

sources of, 237
visibility, 239–240
Positive change
    activities for, 483–485
    alternative language, 459
    assessment, 444–446
    behavioral guidelines, 470–471
    benchmarking, 457–458
    climate of positivity, 452–457, 458t
    collective emotions, 453
    collective feeling, 453
    collective noticing, 453
    collective responding, 453
    commitment to the vision, 463–465, 466t
    compassion, 453
    creating, 452–453
    exercises, 481–483
    feedback, 444–446
    financial performance, 451f
    forgiveness, 453–454
    fostering sustainability, 466–470
    frameworks, 448–451, 470, 470f
    gratitude, 454–455
    heliotropic effect, 469–470
    human capital, 467–468
    identifying strengths, 455–456
    irreversible momentum, 466, 469t
    leadership skills and, 447–451
    learning stairs, 466–467, 467f
    metrics/milestones, 468–469
    overcoming resistance, 459
    positive energy networks, 452–453
    public commitments, 464–465
    readiness for change, 457–459, 460t
    recreational work, 464
    reflected best-self feedback, 456–457
    small-wins strategy, 465
    symbolic events, 458–459
    symbols, 462
    teachable points of view, 466–467
    teamwork, 455–456
    vision of abundance, 460–463, 463t, 466, 469t
    vision statements, 460–462
Positive deviance, 416
Positive emotions, 191
Positive energizers, 452–453
Positive Practices Survey, 444, 485
Positive relationships, case study, 216–219
Posner, B. Z., 54, 417
Post conventional level, 55
Post-it Notes, 149–153, 155, 169
Power. See also Influence
    abuse of, 230–231, 250
    activities for, 259–261
    behavioral guidelines, 251–252
    distaste for, 229
    effective use of, 229–231, 231f, 232
    empowerment v., 367t
    exercises, 254–255
    expertise, 367
    indicators of, 230t
    influence and, 241–244, 249–250
    informal network, 238
    institutional, 282
    model of, 250f
    motives behind, 231
    network centrality, 237–238
    organizational, 232
    personal, 229–231, 231f, 232–237, 282
    positional, 237–240
    referent, 367
    reward, 367
    sanctioning, 367

social network, 238
structural holes, 238
traditional, 367
Power rule, 556
Powerlessness, 230, 369, 372
Powley, E. H., 452
Prahalad, C. K., 421
Pratt, M. G., 46, 109, 371
Preconventional level, 55
Prelec, D., 276
Presentations
    audience-appropriate, 492
    behavioral guidelines, 505–507
    delivery of, 500
    effective, 491, 491f, 499
    enthusiasm, 499–500
    exercises, 507–516
    formal, 493
    introductions/conclusions, 495t
    listeners, 495
    objections, 504–505
    one-sided messages, 492t
    oral, 490–494, 498, 498t, 499, 499t, 500
    organization of, 493, 494t
    practicing, 498–499
    preparation stage, 491
    primacy, 494–495
    purpose of, 491–492, 492f, 493
    questions, 503–504
    recency, 494–495
    road map, 494
    sandwiching, 493
    speaking notes, 498
    strategies, 491
    structure, 491, 493
    styles, 491, 497–498
    supplements, 491
    supporting materials, 491, 495–496, 496t
    two-sided messages, 492t
    visual aids, 494, 496–497, 497t, 499
    written, 490–491, 493, 499, 499t, 501–503
Preston, P., 380
Primacy, 494–495
Principled level of maturity, 55
Prins, H. A., 413
Priorities, 97
Proactive personalities, 239
Probing responses, 209
Problem definition
    analogies, 159
    elaborating on, 159–160
    reversing, 160–162
    synectics, 158–159
    techniques for improving, 162t
Problem solving
    analogies, 158–159
    analytical, 139–143, 144t
    artificial constraints, 154
    behavioral guidelines, 171–172
    collaborative, 319–329
    conceptual blocks, 143
    conflict in, 308
    creative, 143–171
    defining the problem, 140–141
    evaluating alternatives, 141–142
    generating alternatives, 141
    implementation of the solution, 142
    improvement of, 166
    interviews, 530
    model of, 140t
    problem definition, 158–162
    process of, 320
    separating figure from ground, 154
    teamwork, 406

Problem Solving, Creativity, and Innovation Assessment, 134
Problem-oriented communication, 201
Proctor, R., 321
Productivity, 108, 109f
Professional burnout, 91
Prudential, 110
Prudential Real Estate and Relocation Co., 477–480
Pruitt, D., 326
Psychological resiliency, 107
Public speaking, 498t. See also Oral presentations
Pucik, V., 62
Purdy, K., 103, 376
Putnam, Robert, 111, 552
Pythagoras, 44

Q

Quality circles, 404, 508–510, 510f, 511–515
Quick, T., 266
Quinn, Bob, 416
Quinn, R. E., 7, 9–10, 54, 143, 372, 380, 408, 445–447, 451, 456

R

Radio astronomy, 150
Ragins, B., 191
Rahe, Richard, 94–95
Rahim, M., 316
Rainbow, Jacob, 157
Ramlall, S., 452
Ramsey, Joseph, 170
Randle, C., 191
Rappoport, J., 369–370
Rasmussen, A., 95
Rath, T., 455, 457
Raudsepp, E., 136
Raven, B., 367
Rawsthorne, L. J., 372
Ray, M., 369
Raytheon Company, 148, 151, 153, 167
RCA, 58
Reagans, R. E., 231
Reality therapy, 205
Reason, 243–244, 249
Recency, 494–495
Reciprocity, 110–111, 243–244, 248–249
Reciprocity networks, 110
Recreational work, 464
Red Frog Events, 450
Reed, M. G., 106, 206
Referent power, 367
Reflected best-self feedback, 456–457
Reflected Best-Self Feedback Exercise, 444–446, 481–482
Reflecting response, 210–211
Reflection probes, 209
Reflective probes, 524
Rehearsal, 113
Reich, John, 107
Reingold, J., 491
Reinsch, N. L., 527
Reis, H. T., 190
Rejected Plans case, 217–219
Relational algorithm, 164–165
Relationship-building roles, 422, 424, 424t, 425
Relationships, 101
Relevance, 240–241
Rendon, J., 241
Renkoo, 238
Renwick, P. A., 241
Repetition probes, 209, 525
Reports rule, 554
Resiliency, 106–113

Responses, 207–208
advising, 208
deflecting, 208–209
probing, 209
reflecting, 210–211
Rest, James, 57, 79
Retribution, 243–244, 248
Reuters, 462
Reward power, 367
Reward systems, 273–277, 280–285
Rhee, K., 7, 48
Ribot, T., 157
Rifkin, Adam, 238
Right Management Consultants, 270
Right-brain thinking, 156, 461
Rigidity in communication, 202
Ringer, Robert, 229
Riordan, Joseph, 509
Ritchie, R. J., 9
Rittie, R. J., 9
Roberts, L. M., 445
Roberts, R. D., 102
Rockwell, 58
Rocky Flats Nuclear Arsenal, 110
Rodin, J., 381
Rodman, G., 321
Rogers, Carl, 45, 197–198, 208
Rohrbaugh, J., 9
Rokeach, M., 48, 54
Rold, M., 206
Role-negotiation sessions, 211–212
Rose, S., 369
Rosen, C. C., 48
Rosenfeld, L., 321
Rosenthal, R., 103
Ross, L., 265
Ross, T., 161
Rostad, F., 106
Rothbaum, F., 370
Rothenberg, A., 161
Roukes, N., 158
Rozell, E. J., 51
Rozin, P., 108
Ruble, T., 61, 312, 313f, 316
Rucci, Tony, 241
Rule breakers, 169
Rule of halves, 554
Rule of sixths, 554
Rule of thirds, 554
Rule of three-fourths, 554
Runco, M., 157
Runyon, K., 369
Rust, Ed, 236
Rutherford, Ernest, 159
Ryan, R., 369, 371–372
Ryncarz, R. A., 54
Rynes, S. L., 462

S

Saari, L. M., 9
Saarni, C., 102
Saks Fifth Avenue, 389–390
Salancik, G., 464
Salas, E., 406
Salovey, P., 49–50
Sanctioning power, 367
Sandelands, L., 46, 91
Sanders, Harland, 150
Sandwiching, 493
Sanford, W., 54, 490
Sauer, S., 232
Savage, G., 316
SCAMPER, 160
Scandinavian Airlines, 468–469
Schein, E. H., 236, 422
Schembechler, Bo, 403
Schepman, S., 275
Schippers, D., 366
Schmidt, A. M., 279

Schmidt, F. L., 268
Schmidt, W. H., 241, 244, 316, 319
Schmitt, D., 241
Schnake, M. E., 191–192, 197
Schneer, J., 316
Schneider, C., 63, 369
Schnell, S. V., 57
Schor, S., 21
Schriesheim, C., 272
Schroth, R. J., 57
Schwalbe, M., 369
Schwartz, B., 108
Schwartz, Jeff, 109, 462
Schwartz, S. H., 54
Scott, O. J., 151
Sculley, John, 462
Seeman, N. C., 63, 369
Seff, M., 369
Seibert, S. E., 239, 366
Seiler, W., 496
Self-awareness, 44–47, 65
activities for, 77–78
behavioral guidelines, 66–67
case studies, 67–69
cognitive style, 47–48, 59, 60t, 61–62
core aspects of, 49f, 66f
core self-evaluation, 47–48
cultural values, 51–54
emotional intelligence, 47–51
ethical decision making, 57
individual differences, 47, 65
orientation towards change, 47–48, 61–62
personal change and, 45
personal values, 47–48, 51, 54–57
satisfaction with, 76f
self-disclosure and, 46–47
self-disclosure exercises, 72–73
sensitive line, 45–46
Self-Awareness Assessment Instrument, 38
Self-centered level of maturity, 55
Self-determination, 368–369, 372
Self-disclosure, 46–47, 72–73
Self-efficacy, 64, 368–369, 372
Self-esteem, 64
Self-knowledge, 45–46
Self-managing work teams, 404, 406
Seligman, M., 112, 369, 381
Seltzer, J., 21
Selznick, P., 465
Senge, Peter, 405–406
Sensitive line, 45–46
Sensory imagery, 151
Separating figure from ground, 154f, 155
Serpkenci, R. R., 103
Servant leadership, 381
Seybolt, P., 306, 316
Shakespeare riddle, 153f
Shalley, C., 143
Shamir, B., 272
Shawbel, Dan, 228
Sheehan, Michael, 491
Shelly, S., 376
Shenandoah Life Insurance Co., 405
Shift workers, 265
Shillman, Robert J., 274
Shin, S. J., 412
Shipper, E., 230
Shoda, Y., 103
Shuffler, M. L., 406
Siau, K., 163
Sibley, W. A., 161
Sieburg, E., 202, 205
Siemens, 58
Sillars, A., 311

Silva, P. J., 45
Silver, Spence, 149–152, 155–156, 166–170
Simmel, G., 454
Simon, H., 141
Simon, H. A., 162–163, 447
Simon, L. S., 234
Sims, H., 370, 382, 417
Sincoff, M., 518
Singh, J., 104
Single thinking language, 150–151
Situational stressors, 94
Skill Assessment, Developing Self-Awareness, 38–44
Skill competency, 8
Skill variety, 103, 279
Skilling, Jeff, 229
Slaski, J. J., 50
Slocum, J., 369
Small-wins strategy, 105–106, 374, 465
Small-wins strategy exercise, 121–123
SMART goals, 105, 127, 373, 419–421
Smeaton, D., 106–107
Smeyak, G., 518
Smith, D., 405, 414, 417, 428, 430
Smith, M. L., 453
Smith, P. E., 9
Smith, R., 322
Smith, S. M., 157, 163–164
Smith, T. B., 110
Smither, J., 21
Snarey, J. R., 50
Snyder, S., 370
Social capital, 552
Social intelligence, 102
stress and, 102–103
Social media, 238
Social networks, 238–239
cultural differences, 239
Social Readjustment Rating Scale (SRRS), 86–89, 94–95, 130
Social Security Administration, 280
Socrates, 44
Solem, A. R., 206
Song, X. M., 316
Sony Corp., 421
Sophocles, 230–231
Sosa, M., 238
Sosik, J. J., 48
Sources of Personal Stress, 89
Southwest Airlines, 74, 174
Sparrowe, R., 237
Speaking notes, 498
Specificity (communication), 204
Specificity (cultural), 53, 165
Spencer, Graham, 238
Spencer, L. M., 45, 102
Spencer, Percy, 148, 150–151, 153, 166–168
Spencer, S. M., 45, 102
Spitzberg, B. H., 192–193, 197, 202
Sponsors, 169
Sports Illustrated, 405
Sprague, J., 492
Spreitzer, G. M., 106, 366, 368, 370–372, 376, 445, 456
Srivastava, A., 419
SSS Software exercise, 21–31, 336–345, 560–570
St. Cyr, K., 206
Stajkovic, A., 273
Stalk, G., 94
Stam, M. C., 366
Stamp-Rite, 267
Stano, M. E., 527
Staples, L., 369
Stasser, S., 103, 366, 370
State Farm, 236

Staw, B., 46, 91
Steen, T. A., 112
Steers, R. M., 108, 265
Steil, L., 191, 202, 210
Steinel, W., 315
Stephens, J. P., 194
Stereotyping based on past experiences, 152
Stern, I., 243
Sternberg, R., 50, 59, 102, 139, 153, 157, 162, 207
Stewart, C., 524
Stewart, Martha, 58
Stone-Romero, E., 234
Stranks, J., 93
Strategies for Handling Conflict Assessment, 306, 362
Stress
    assessment of, 89
    coping with, 92
    driving forces, 92
    effect on economy, 91
    effects of, 91
    job-related, 103–104
    model of, 93f
    restraining forces, 92
    sources of, 94t
    stressors, 92–93
Stress management, 90
    anticipatory stressors, 95, 103–106
    autonomy, 103
    behavioral guidelines, 113–114
    case study, 114–121
    community, 101
    contribution goals, 102
    cultural differences, 94
    decision-making, 104
    eliminating stressors, 95, 95t, 96
    emotional intelligence, 102–103
    enactive strategies, 92–93
    encounter stressors, 94, 100–101, 103
    environmentally induced stress, 312
    exercises, 121–131
    feedback, 103–104
    generalized reciprocity, 110–111
    goal setting, 104–105
    gratitude, 111–112
    job redesign, 103–104
    life balance, 106–107
    meaningful work, 108–111
    proactive strategies, 92–93
    psychological resiliency, 107
    reactive strategies, 92–93
    relationships, 101
    resiliency, 93, 106–113
    short-term strategies, 112–113
    situational stressors, 94, 103–104
    skill variety, 103
    small-wins strategy, 105–106
    social intelligence, 102–103
    task identity, 103
    task significance, 103
    time management, 95–100
    time stressors, 94, 96, 103
    well-being, 93, 106–112
    wellness programs, 107
Stress Management Assessment, 86
Stress reduction techniques
    deep breathing, 112
    imagery and fantasy, 112
    muscle relaxation, 112
    rehearsal, 113
    visualization, 112
Stringfellow, A., 316
Stroh, L., 319, 326
Structural holes, 238
Stuart, D., 492

Students
    collective efficacy, 369
    self-efficacy, 369
Subdivision (problem solving), 163–164
Success, 63
Sue-Chan, C., 271
Sullivan, Barry, 97
Superiority-oriented communication, 202
Supportive communication, 193
    attributes of, 194t
    behavioral guidelines, 215
    coaching/counseling, 195–196, 207
    congruence, 197–198
    conjunctive, 205
    cultural differences, 214
    customer service and, 194
    descriptive, 198, 200–201
    disjunctive, 205
    disowned, 205–206
    evaluative, 198–201
    exercises, 224–226
    goal of, 194
    incongruence, 197–198
    interviews, 524
    invalidating, 202
    owned, 205–206
    personal management interviews, 214
    person-oriented, 201
    principles of, 197
    problem-oriented, 201
    responding, 207–211
    specific, 204
    supportive listening, 206–207
    two-way, 203
    validating, 202–203
Supportive listening, 206–207
    responding, 208
    response types, 207f
Sutcliffe, K. M., 46, 107
Sutton, C., 58
Swift, C., 369
Symbolic analogies, 159
Symbolic events, 458–459
Symbolic language, 151
Symbols, 462
Synectics, 158–159
Szilagyi, A. D., 221

T

Tallahassee Democrat's ELITE team case, 428–430
Tan, S. N., 148
Task identity, 103, 279–280, 376
Task significance, 103, 279–280
Task-facilitating roles, 422–423, 423t, 424
Taylor, J. C., 108
Taylor, R. R., 371
Team Development Behaviors Assessment, 402
Teams/teamwork, 402
    activities for, 439–440
    advantages of, 403–405, 427
    advertisements, 404f
    behavioral guidelines, 427–428
    blocking roles, 425–426
    composition, 405
    consensus building role, 425
    creative problem solving in, 168
    credibility, 417–419
    cultural differences, 421–422, 427
    desirability of, 404–405
    effective, 407
    elaborating role, 425
    enforcing role, 425

Everest goals, 419–421
    exercises, 432–439
    feedback, 426, 426t, 427
    forming stage, 408–409
    groupthink, 168, 410–411
    high-performing, 415, 415t, 416, 424, 428f
    impact of, 406t
    inhibitors to, 405
    leadership of, 417–419
    membership in, 422–425
    motivation, 405
    norming stage, 408–410
    performing stage, 408, 414–416
    positive communications, 455–456
    positive deviance, 416
    productivity and, 168
    quality circles, 404
    relationship-building roles, 422–424, 424t, 425
    skill development, 404, 406–407
    SMART goals, 419–421
    stages of development, 408, 408t, 409–416
    storming stage, 408, 411–414
    structure, 405
    task-facilitating roles, 422–423, 423t, 424
    tension relieving role, 425
    types of, 405–406
    unproductive roles, 425
    work teams, 404–405
Tebbe, Mark, 73
Technological innovation, 174
Tedeschi, J., 234
Telephones, 150
Tell-and-listen interviews, 530
Tell-and-sell interviews, 530
Temporal integrity rule, 555
Tennessee Valley Authority (TVA), 465
Teoh, H. Y., 62
Terminal values, 48, 54
Texting, 191
TGI Friday's, 179–180
Thakor, A. J., 7, 10, 143, 447
Thales, 44
Theory X, 268
Theory Y, 268
Thinking
    ambidextrous, 156, 156t
    bias against, 156
    flexibility in, 158, 162
    left-hemisphere, 156, 461
    multiple thought languages, 150–151
    right-hemisphere, 156, 461
    single thinking language, 150–151
Thoits, Peggy A., 94
Thomas, G., 63
Thomas, K., 312, 313f, 316, 369–370
Thompson, D., 274
Thompson, J. A., 370
Thompson, L., 234, 239, 246, 278, 309, 314, 320
Thoresen, C. J., 62
Thornton, T., 370
Thorton, D., 191
Threat-rigidity response, 46
3M Company, 149–152, 155–156, 167–170, 552
Tichy, N., 9–10, 446, 466, 552
Timberland Company, 109, 462
Time management, 53, 95–96
    activities matrix, 96, 96f, 97
    core principles, 97, 98t
    strategies, 98–100
    time use, 99t
Time Management Assessment, 86

Time stressors, 94, 96, 103
Time use, 99t
Timmer, Jan, 97
Ting, S., 230
Ting-Toomey, S., 214, 316
Tizard, H. J., 370
Tjosvold, D., 306
Tolerance of ambiguity, 61–62
Tolerance of Ambiguity Scale, 38, 42–43, 62, 81–82
Tone, 502–503
Toyota, 58, 471, 474
Traditional power, 367
Training programs, 265, 267
Travelers Insurance, 280
Trevi'o, L. K., 57
Trevor, C., 274
Triandis, H., 214, 229, 274
Trickle-up leadership, 246
Tripp, T., 247
Trompenaars, Frans, 13, 51, 62, 94, 165, 214, 229, 311, 388, 421–422, 427
Tropman, John, 552, 554, 554f
Troxell, J. R., 95
Trust, 368, 371–372
Trustworthiness, 236
Tsang, J., 111, 455
Tschirhart, M., 6
Tuchman, B., 552
Tuckman, B., 408
Turkington, C., 100
Turn of the Tide case, 114–117
Turner, M., 417
Tutu, Desmond, 454
Twitter, 191
Two-sided messages, 492t
Two-way communication, 203
Tyco International, 58

U

U. S. Army, 466
U. S. Department of Labor, 276
U. S. Marine Corps., 246
U. S. News and World Report, 177
U. S. Patent Office, 157
Ulrich, D., 450
The Unconscious Conspiracy (Bennis), 271
Unethical companies, 57–58
Ungar, M., 107
Union Carbide, 58
United Chemical Co., exercises, 219–221
Universalism, 51, 165–166, 214, 387–388, 421
University of Chicago, 281
University of Michigan, 421, 456, 464
Useem, Michael, 246
Using Influence Strategies Assessment, 228, 261

V

Vaillant, G. E., 50
Vakar, G., 150
Valdez, Tom, 180
Valentine, S. R., 63
Validating communication, 203
Values conflicts, 58
Values, cultural. *See* Cultural values
Values maturity, 54–55, 58–59
    gender bias, 57
    stages of development, 55–57
Van den Broeck, H., 48, 59–61
Van Knippenberg, A., 366
Van Orden, J., 518
Vance, C. M., 8–9, 59

Vangelisti, A., 197
Vardi, P., 63, 369
Vecchione, M., 369
Veiga, John F., 4
Velthouse, B., 369–370
Verespei, M., 405
Verhage, J., 244
Vernon, Philip E., 48
Veroff, J., 282
Vertical thinking, 150
Very Fast, Very Accurate (VFVA), 289
Vinton, L., 94
Virgin Atlantic Airlines, 182
Visibility, 239–240
Vision of abundance, 460–463, 463t,
    464–466
    commitment to, 463–465, 466t
    institutionalizing, 469t
Vision statements, 460–462
    case study, 471–477
Visual aids, 494, 496–497, 497t, 499
Visual imagery, 151
Visualization, 112
Vitell, Scott, 54
Vogt, J., 369, 371
Vogus, T. J., 107
Vohs, K. D., 452
Volkema, R. J., 312
Volvo, 405
Von Oech, Roger, 159, 169
Von Treitschke, Heinrich, 229
Vroom, V., 265, 382, 384
Vygotsky, L., 150

W

Waclawski, J., 48
Wadey, Ross, 107
Wagner, N. N., 95
Wall, T., 108
Wall Street Journal, 75, 241
Wallace, M. J., 221
Wallas, G., 157
Waller, G., 202

Wal-Mart Co., 58, 174
Walsh, Jim, 449
Walster, E., 47
Walter Reed Army Institute of
    Research, 101
Wang, G., 366
Wanous, J. P., 306
Ward, T. B., 157, 163–164
Warren, K., 380
Waterman, Robert, 285
Watson, C., 316
Watson, K. W., 210
Weber, Max, 109
Weick, K. E., 46, 91, 374, 465
Weiner, B., 271
Weingart, L., 309
Weinstein, N., 369
Weisberg, J., 311
Weisz, J., 370
Weitzman, M., 106
Welbourne, T. M., 5, 62
Welch, Jack, 446
Weldon, E., 311, 316
Well-being
    developing, 106–112
    exercises, 121–128
    fostering, 90
Wellins, R. S., 404, 406
Wellness programs, 107
Wells, L., 491
Wen, S. S., 371
Wernerfelt, B., 195
Wernsing, T. S., 450
Westinghouse Furniture Systems, 405
Westphal, J. D., 243
Wetzker, K., 5
Wheeler, J. V., 7
Wheeler, R. W., 63, 417
Whetten, David A., 8, 46–47, 94, 312,
    408, 450
White, M., 106–107
White, R., 370
White Castle, 144

Whitney, D., 424
Who's Who, 50
Wiemann, J., 205
Wilcox, R. J., 490
Wilkinson, I., 241
Williams, J. M., 95, 112, 143
Williams, W. M., 157
Willmington, D. E., 191–192
Wilmot, W., 311
Wilson, Bill, 146
Wilson, D. C., 143
Wilson, J. M., 404
Windows (software), 174
Winning Through Intimidation
    (Ringer), 229
Witt, L. A., 271
Witteloostuijn, A., 63
Wolf, S. G., 94
Wolf, Stewart, 101
Wolff, H. G., 94, 424
Wolvin, Andrew D., 210
Wooden, John, 403
Wooten, M., 452
Work environment
    employee performance, 265
    increasing authority, 280
    job redesign, 280
    meaningful work, 109–110, 279
    motivating, 264–265, 268, 279–280
    productivity and, 108, 109f
    reframing, 109
    satisfaction with, 108–109
    shift workers, 265
    supportive, 272
    work design, 278–279
Work Performance Assessment, 264,
    298–299, 304
Work teams, 404–405
Workers. *See* Employees
Workman, E. A., 91
World Trade Center, 462
Worline, M. C., 453
Wozniak, Steve, 173

Wright, M., 61
Wright, M. O. D., 106
Written communication, 490–491, 493,
    499t, 501
    factual precision, 501–502
    mechanical precision, 501
    proper format, 503
    tone, 502–503
    verbal precision, 502
Wrzesniewski, A., 108–109, 371–372

X

Xanthopoulou, D., 369–370
Xerox Corporation, 174, 413, 467
Xerox dissemination process, 413f
Xhonneux, P., 5
Xie, J., 316
Xin, K., 311

Y

Yale University, 250
Yamaha Motor Co., 145
Yammarino, F. J., 48
Yang, L., 157
Yavas, U., 366
Yeager, W., 490
Yeatts, D., 414
Yetton, P., 382
Youtz, A., 306
Yrle, Augusta C., 191
Yukl, G., 233
Yusuff, M. R., 54

Z

Zand, D., 371
Zappos, 368, 376
Zautra, Alex, 107
Zeitz, Paul, 143
Zhang, Li-fang, 59
Zhang, X., 376, 452
Zhou, J., 143
Zimmerer, T., 380
Zimmerman, M., 368–370